THE CAMBRIDGE HISTORY OF THE NATIVE PEOPLES OF THE AMERICAS

VOLUME III:

South America

THE CAMBRIDGE HISTORY OF THE NATIVE PEOPLES OF THE AMERICAS

VOLUME I: NORTH AMERICA
Edited by Bruce G. Trigger and Wilcomb E. Washburn

VOLUME II: MESOAMERICA
Edited by R. E. W. Adams and Murdo MacLeod

VOLUME III: SOUTH AMERICA
Edited by Frank Salomon and Stuart B. Schwartz

THE CAMBRIDGE HISTORY OF THE NATIVE PEOPLES OF THE AMERICAS

VOLUME III

SOUTH AMERICA

PART 2

Edited by

Frank Salomon
University of Wisconsin-Madison

Stuart B. Schwartz
Yale University

CAMBRIDGE
UNIVERSITY PRESS

PUBLISHED BY THE PRESS SYNDICATE OF THE UNIVERSITY OF CAMBRIDGE
The Pitt Building, Trumpington Street, Cambridge, United Kingdom

CAMBRIDGE UNIVERSITY PRESS
The Edinburgh Building, Cambridge CB2 2RU, United Kingdom http://www.cup.cam.ac.uk
40 West 20th Street, New York, NY 10011-4211, USA http://www.cup.org
10 Stamford Road, Oakleigh, Melbourne 3166, Australia
Ruiz de Alarcón 13, 28014 Madrid, Spain

First published 1999

Printed in the United States of America

Typeface Adobe Garamond 11/13 pt. *System* DeskTopPro$_{/UX}$® [RF]

Library of Congress Cataloging in Publication data
South America / edited by Frank Salomon, Stuart B. Schwartz
p. cm. – (Cambridge history of the Native peoples of the Americas)
Includes bibliographical references and index.
ISBN 0–521–33393–8
1. Indians of South America–History.
I. Salomon, Frank. II. Schwartz, Stuart B. III. Series.
E77.N62 1999
970.004'97–dc20 95-46096
CIP

A catalog record for this book is available from the British Library.

Volume I: North America ISBN 0 521 34440 9 hardback complete set
Volume I: North America, Part 1 ISBN 0 521 57392 0
Volume I: North America, Part 2 ISBN 0 521 57393 9
Volume II: Mesoamerica ISBN 0 521 65205 7 hardback complete set
Volume II: Mesoamerica, Part 1 ISBN 0 521 35165 0
Volume II: Mesoamerica, Part 2 ISBN 0 521 65204 9
Volume III: South America, Part 1 ISBN 0 521 63075 4
Volume III: South America, Part 2 ISBN 0 521 63076 2
Volume III: South America ISBN 0 521 33393 8 hardback complete set

CONTENTS

Part 2

ILLUSTRATIONS

MAPS TO PART I

FIGURES TO PART I

MAPS TO PART 2

FIGURES TO PART 2

14

THE CRISES AND TRANSFORMATIONS OF INVADED SOCIETIES: THE LA PLATA BASIN (1535–1650)

JUAN CARLOS GARAVAGLIA

This chapter concerns the early years of invasion in the southeastern part of South America, specifically the vast basin of the Río de la Plata (sometimes called River Plate). Its scope includes all of Paraguay, as well as Tucumán and Cuyo in modern Argentina. How can we capture the essential characteristics common to the histories of these three areas?

Here, as in most other areas of America, indigenous societies that did not build strong centralized power structures, and that consequently lacked tributary or semitributary systems for the production and circulation of surpluses, faced Europeans for whom such systems were the essence of politics. In these cases European conquest did not mean a state takeover of an existing state, as in the Andes or central Mexico, but rather a long and arduous campaign to "pacify the territory" and build a labor-exploiting system amid native societies of drastically unfamiliar constitution. It was the difficulty of this process, from the European viewpoint, which attached the label "marginal" to such areas. (To some degree the formerly Inka-ruled areas of Andean Argentina, with their more complex native polities, formed exceptions.)

In broad strokes these commonalities create a common history. First, the Spanish found it necessary to overcome nearly every group through armed struggle. Although the presence of a few "allies" made part of the job easier, military conquest was still a difficult road for the Europeans to travel.

Second, the colonists devised numerous ways to extract surplus by controlling indigenous peoples' labor. All of these systems were variations on obligatory "personal service" – that is, labor levies which crown officials could assign to favored Spaniards or to local industries and other applications. Theoretically the crown tried to hedge personal service with rules distinguishing "tributary Indians" and "tributary age," but regulation did not work as planned; for example, forced labor obligations fell on multiple members of the same family. In Paraguay and Tucumán, this system survived until the end of the colonial era.

A third common element among these colonizations is that *mestizaje*, or miscegenation, began quite early. "Racial" mixing pervaded the entire area covered in this study. The reasons were numerous and complex. Political reasons included the fact that some of the conquerors felt obliged to join the family networks of ethnic leaders. In Paraguay an additional motive was to accumulate a labor force based on women. Along all the frontiers, the scarcity of European women inclined men to seek out native mates. Finally, general poverty made it necessary for many of the newly arrived or their children to become small producers and peasants right away, thus sharing the life, hardships, and even the language of indigenous peasants, especially in Paraguay.

One of the most noticeable cultural outcomes of *mestizaje* was the peculiar case of bilingualism in Paraguay. This was one of only two American societies (the other being Haiti) where bilingualism was not exclusively the consequence of discrimination forcing subordinates to learn a European tongue. Only a little more than a century after the arrival of the Europeans, poor peasants, powerful "feudal" *encomenderos* and artisan townsmen – all regarded as Spaniards by their contemporaries – spoke Guaraní as readily as Spanish. Nevertheless we must not forget that this was a colonial situation. Without a doubt Guaraní was used only in certain spheres of social life, while other spheres, considered more important, were reserved for Castilian.

Finally, a general observation about sources and the indigenous "word": Only rarely do we hear the direct voice of the natives. Usually native voices are heard through many filters, so that the original is almost completely muffled by a complicated series of transcription and translations. For example, in Córdoba one interpreter translated from Castilian into Quechua and another from Quechua into Sanavirón. Thus we can get some idea of the hazards that await us in the few documents that purport to give a "true" image of indigenous opinion. The rarity of words written directly by natives has to do with the low level of stratification in the indigenous society the Europeans found. The state's agents rarely found native elites who could be readily trained as agents of indirect rule, and they did not create an intra-indigenous civil apparatus that generated its own papers. Even the missionaries made little effort to foster bicultural elites of the sort that elsewhere produced literate spokesmen. The picture was somewhat different in Jesuit missions, where missionaries formed councils that did write letters and petitions (see Chap. 1).

THE EUROPEAN INVASION OF THE RÍO DE LA PLATA REGION AND PARAGUAY

The Guaraní were part of the large group of peoples who spoke languages of the Tupí-Guaraní linguistic family, which, before the European invasion, stretched from Amazonia to the delta of the Río de la Plata. There were differences among the many groups, but the lack of serious archaeological studies makes it difficult for us to evaluate and compare these differences today. The Tupí inhabited the lower middle part of the Amazon Basin and much of the Atlantic coastal area from the Amazon to Cananea. From there to the present boundary of the Brazilian state of Rio Grande do Sul, we find the Guaraní, who also occupied the great rivers of the inland plateau. The southern limit of Guaraní settlement was just below the Río de la Plata delta. Those groups who occupied this territory were called the "island Guaraní," and their remains have been found as far south as present-day San Isidro, on the outskirts of the city of Buenos Aires.

The Prehispanic Guaraní

Thanks to their skill as canoe navigators, different Guaraní groups fanned out along the great waterways that wind through the tropical and subtropical forests of South America. Of special interest is the huge basin of the Paraná, which covers thousands of kilometers from the Chapadão dos Veadeiros to the Atlantic. The tributaries that create this giant river system run eastward from the flanks of the Andes; as we see later, these valleys formed important corridors for both native mobility and Spanish incursion. The semisedentary slash-and-burn type of agriculture, which allows cultivation to combine with travel, and the prophetically motivated quests influential in Guaraní indigenous culture, accentuated native movements across this landscape. The Chiriguanos, closely related to the Guaraní, went as far as the spurs of the Andes in the course of their westward migrations.

The Guaraní lived in the multifamily houses (*malocas*, actually *ocas*) typical of the Amazon, each housing several domestic units under the leadership of a chief. Several of these *malocas* constituted a "village" (*taba*) led by a higher-ranking chief. These groups cemented their alliances through the marriages of their ethnic leaders (*mburuvichá*), thus knitting a network of political alliances that could become quite extensive.

As in many stateless South American societies, the leader was usually polygamous. This reinforced his capacity to establish political alliances and gain access to the labor force of his *tovajá* (brothers-in-law). During peacetime he was an arbitrator within his community. His power increased enormously during wartime and tended also to acquire a markedly religious or prophetic character. As among other peoples of the tropical forest, one of the central sources of leaders' control lay in their generosity, which was based in turn on their ability to operate at the center of various circles of reciprocity and on their ability as public speakers.

We also frequently encounter shamans (*pajé*) – men knowledgeable about illness, medicine, and weather forecasting. A gifted *pajé* could rise to the status of *karaí* – that is, a "great shaman" known beyond his community and licensed to lead major feasts. A *karaí* could attract a political following and even threaten the political control that the ethnic leaders had over the village. Warfare and an elaborate ritual complex of revenge on captives, including cannibalism, were the essence of political conduct.

Subsistence was based on several varieties of corn (*Zea mays*), manioc (*Manihot utilissima*), beans (*Phaseolus vulgaris*), and squash (*Lagenaria vulgaris*). Villagers also grew cotton, peanuts (*Arachis hypogea*), and *yerba mate (Ilex paraquariensis). Mate*, drunk as an infusion, was gathered during the prehispanic era and probably was a ritual item, as was one kind of tobacco. People domesticated the muscovy duck (*Cairina moschata*); early references to "chickens" (1519) probably refer to chickens introduced by the Europeans, even when they seem to refer to the "Araucanian hen" (*Gallus inauris*), but there are not many detailed studies.

Spaniards called the cultivation system *roza*. The men slashed and burned a section of forest, which women then planted. This system required settlements to move about in order to accommodate the long fallow periods needed for vegetation to regenerate. Hunting and fishing were complementary activities of primary importance. Agricultural productivity was fairly high; in Paraguay two annual crops of corn were the norm. Spaniards preferred to settle near Guaraní territory to take advantage of this abundance.

The European Invasion

Senior captain Juan Díaz de Solis was the first Spanish navigator to reach the banks of the Río de la Plata, and he gave it its misleading name 'Silver River'. Díaz' expedition sailed up the river to the mouth of the Uruguay and was defeated by natives in 1516. Among the survivors was Alejo García, who, pressing on inland with a Guaraní band of migrants, became the first European to see the Andes. Another, Francisco del Puerto, proved very useful to the next European navigator, the Venetian Sebastian Cabot. Cabot reached the Río de la Plata in 1527 and went as far as the Carcarañá River (now Santa Fe), where he established Fort Sancti Spiritus. Two years later the natives attacked and burned down the fort. The survivors immediately returned to Spain.

Fired up by fantasies aroused by Pizarro's arrival in Seville in 1534, Don Pedro de Mendoza signed a crown pact to make a new attempt to conquer the Río de la Plata. His extravagant and motley expedition (apparently he had more than 1,200 men) included a man we may justly consider the first authentic chronicler of La Plata, the Bavarian Ulrich Schmidl (or Schmidel), author of a celebrated *Chronicle* that was published in German in 1567. Pedro Hernández, the chronicler of Alvar Núñez Cabeza de Vaca, also sailed in Pedro de Mendoza's fleet.

The first attempt to found Buenos Aires took place in 1536. A native siege forced some of the expeditioners to flee up the Paraná to the site of Cabot's fort, where they set up camp. Juan de Ayolas and Domingo Martínez de Irala were in this party. This was the starting point for those who founded the city of Asunción del Paraguay, next to the hamlet of Lambaré, in the land of the Carios – a Guaraní group. Asunción was the first stable Spanish city in the region and the "mother of cities" from which all later expeditions would depart, both up the Paraná River and downstream, or south, to the point where it empties into the Río de la Plata (see Map 14.1).

Asunción spearheaded a quick growth of "cities" – actually small outposts – through the Guaranían lands. Early ones were Ciudad Real del Guayrá (today the site of the Itaipú Dam in Brazil) in 1557, and Villa Rica del Espiritu Santo, first founded in 1577 and again in 1589, at the confluence of the Ivai and Corumbati rivers, which cut through the

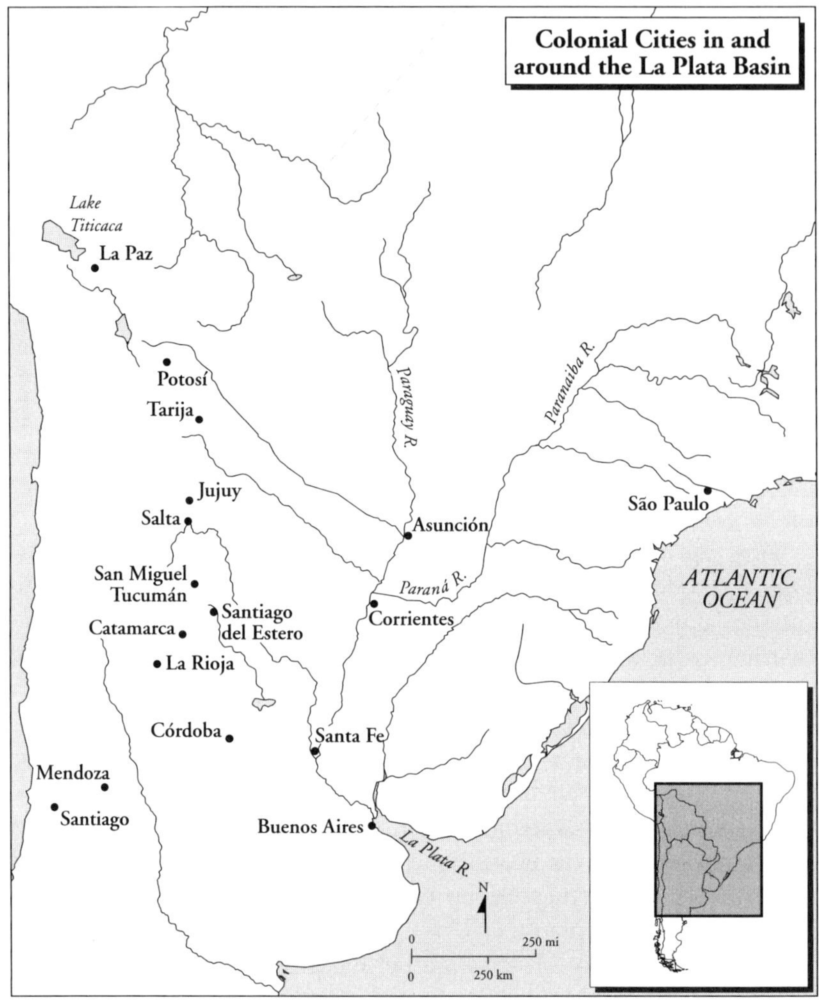

Map 14.1

Paraná plateau. Finally in 1593 Rui Díaz de Guzmán established the city of Santiago de Xerez on the Mbotetey River near Paraguay. About 80 leagues away lay Santa Cruz de la Sierra, founded in 1558 by Nufrio (or Ñuflo) de Chávez in the foothills of the Andes. This was part of an attempt, which failed, to find a direct route to the silver-mining hub of Potosí and thus end the isolation of the Spaniards in Asunción.

Bandeirante activities destroyed and depopulated most of these cities.

Bandeirantes were Portuguese adventurers who led expeditions of mestizos and Tupí Indians looking for other Indians to capture and enslave. They were active from the beginning of the seventeenth century to the fall of the so-called province of Mbaracayú on the River Jejuy in 1676.

Downstream along the Paraná, or south of Asunción, Santa Fe de la Vera Cruz was established by Juan de Garay in 1573 near the remains of the old Cabot fort. Buenos Aires was founded again in 1580, Concepción del Bermejo in 1585 (in an effort to establish easier communication with the Peruvian Tucumán road), and San Juan de Vera de las Siete Corrientes in 1588. All these Spanish towns were creations of the restless "young men of the land," the mestizos of Asunción, who were born of Cario-Spanish unions in the early years of colonization.

Early Interethnic Relationships (1537–1555)

A traditional theme of studies of Paraguay – which led to a triumphalist historical literature of dubious value – is the so-called alliance between the Spanish invaders and the Carios of Lambaré after a Spanish victory. This alliance undeniably existed, but it must be viewed in the light of the considerations outlined later in the chapter.

The Carios, accepting defeat at the hands of the Europeans, were obliged to ally themselves with the victors against the Guaycurú, a warring group of Chaqueño indigenes. It appeared at first that the Guaraní of Lambaré had gained a powerful ally, with whose help they defeated their Chaqueño enemies several times and took large numbers of prisoners. But, of course, they did not know that their new allies had come to stay and would keep on increasing their demands.

The local people handed over women as a sign of recognition of the alliance (as they had among themselves) and in exchange received Spanish gifts – mainly iron hatchets and fish hooks, extremely valuable tools in that setting. Some individuals came to possess more than seventy women, and the average number, so we read, was ten women per Spanish man. Women in fact constituted an accumulation of labor power. First, the woman worked for the Europeans – as they had for their Indian husbands, or so Spaniards reported – weaving, carrying burdens, or tilling the soil. In addition women also gave Spaniards access to the labor of their male relatives, as women's fathers and brothers were traditionally obligated to "help" their sons-in-law and brothers-in-law. The Spanish claimed these women as theirs to profit by, as well as for sexual relations.

This resulted in the early, intense process of ethnic mixing that produced the mestizo "young men of the land."

Europeans, aspiring to be "big men," renowned for ability to collect and redistribute wealth, rapidly became involved in concentric webs of reciprocity with the Indians; but the difference from tradition lay in the attitude of these new and powerful relatives if an Indian should fail to fulfill his part of the bargain. The so-called Aracaré rebellion is the event that best illustrates the different expectations that the Spaniards and the Carios brought to the alliance. In 1542, a few years after the founding of Asunción, Spaniards went north in search of a direct route to Peru, which they were obsessed with finding. Aracaré was the chief of a group from the Jejuy River, north of Asunción. When Aracaré suddenly refused to continue serving the expedition and retreated without violence, the Spaniards had to return to Asunción. The governor, Alvar Núñez Cabeza de Vaca, ordered his second in command, Domingo Martínez de Irala, to bring the Guaraní leader to justice for his "rebellion." Martínez de Irala ordered him hanged, and this was soon done. The outcome was predictable: two "brothers" of the dead chief, Tabaré and Guacaní, led an attack against the Spaniards to avenge him and square accounts. Once defeated in battle, they made peace and Tabaré was pardoned.

What is the most plausible interpretation of these events, and what do they tell us about the Spanish-Guaraní "alliance"? First, one fact must be stressed: Aracaré did not rebel against the Spaniards; he simply refused to serve them. Why did he refuse? Because the Spaniards, bypassing the accepted practices of the indigenous people, were abusing their allies. They required men to serve during expeditions inland in jobs reserved for women, and they made them hand over provisions without giving them anything in return, sometimes acting forcibly. The Guaraní allies had ceased to be warriors and had become "slaves" or "women." One Guaraní "brother-in-law" of a Spaniard, refusing to carry a burden for the Europeans, said on that occasion "that they shouldn't give him that load because he did not use them so, and that if he had to carry something, then they should give him arms since he was going to war, and not clothes or things like that."[1] Tabaré himself said, according to a witness, "you can see that we are already women of the Christians since

[1] This quotation and the one that follows are both taken from document number 49/945, fols. 245 and 248, from the Colección Gaspar García Viñas (copies of the Archivo General de Indias), located in the Biblioteca Nacional of Buenos Aires, Manuscript section.

we carry burdens like women do." That is, the Spaniards were no longer acting like allies but like "masters" of the Guaraní. Cabeza de Vaca's violent response in sentencing the Guaraní leader for the "crime" of not wanting to help the invaders during an invasion had a clear objective: to put things in their "right" place, forcing the Indians to serve the Spaniards, one way or another. Thus it was no alliance, at least not a reciprocal or symmetrical one. Scarcely 3 years after these events, most of the Guaraní groups in the region were in open rebellion against the Spanish, and the latter managed to end the revolt only after considerable fighting.

In a word, there was in fact an "alliance" between the Carios of Asunción and the Europeans, but the new arrivals quickly violated the terms of alliance. Given the context we have just described, it could not have been otherwise. Spaniards converted the early reciprocal arrangement of gifts and countergifts into a sharply asymmetrical relationship. Indians slowly came to realize that the Spaniards did not share their ideas about the "alliance." When this discrepancy produced reactions, even nonviolent ones, the Spanish response was brute force, thus opening the way to a more open, undisguised domination.

Toward the end of 1555, Governor Martínez de Irala put aside political fictions about alliance and decided to "share out the land," giving the first *encomiendas* to "well-deserving" colonists in Paraguay.

The Era of the Encomiendas

Encomienda was a far-flung colonial institution under which whole native populations or villages were granted in trust to chosen colonists, along with the privileges of taxing and governing them, and the responsibility to defend and Christianize them. It took a royal decree to grant an *encomienda*, and it constituted the highest form of crown patronage. The first round of *encomiendas*, granted to 320 individual colonists, affected somewhere between 20,000 and 27,000 Indians, according to various documents. These Indians were forced to pay tribute to their new Spanish lords, and in May 1556 Martínez de Irala issued the first ordinances on the actual tribute administration of *encomiendas.*

Encomienda was a trusteeship over people rather than an entitlement to land. Paraguayan *encomiendas*, like those of Tucumán and Cuyo, were based exclusively on personal service – that is, they extracted rent in the form of labor, not in kind. In fact the crucial element that distinguishes this marginal region from the nuclear areas of central Mexico and the Andean empire (where tribute came to include payment in goods) was the dominance of personal service within the framework of the *encomienda.* It was a tax payable in sweat. This feature was also characteristic of nearly all the other marginal areas, from the Yucatán to Paraguay.

Right from the beginning of the institution we can distinguish two different types of *encomienda: encomiendas mitayas* (from the Quechua word *mit'a*, literally 'turn') and the *encomienda* with *yanaconas* or *originarios. Encomienda mitaya* entitled a Spanish colonist to "his" Indians' personal service by turns. The word *mitayo* mean 'a person subject to, or carrying out, a *mita* obligation.' *Mitayos* were to keep living in their own villages while serving in rotation on the Spaniard's lands or doing other tasks. Sometimes the products of their service were also called *mita.*

The terms *yanacona* and *originario* applied to Indians who lived and worked on the lands of their Spanish lords, with or without their families. *Encomienda* uprooted them from their native communities, as in the *naborías* of the Antilles. The word *yanacona* also comes from Quechua; in Inka-era usage it applied to all servitors separated from their communities, including high-status specialists, but in the colony it acquired a connotation not far from bondage.[2] The Paraguayan usage of the word *originario* differs sharply from its Andean homonym, which referred not to *encomienda* status but to standing within indigenous polities. The term *originario* was more common in Paraguay, while *yanacona* was more often used in Tucumán and Cuyo.

Chronologically it seems likely that the use of *yanaconas* or *originarios* existed even before Martínez de Irala legalized the sharing-out of native labor (*repartimiento*) in 1555. Let us look at the sources of this special social condition.

One factor that led to the *originario* system arose as a consequence of the Spanish-Guaraní alliance. Relatives of the Spaniards' Guaraní women came, as was customary, to "help" their brothers- and fathers-in-law. They were often forced to stay on the Spanish farms and to live away from their native villages from then on. Another more obvious origin lay in raids. The Spanish were in the habit of going out to raid Indian

[2] *Yanacona,* though a plural form in Quechua, was often treated as singular in Spanish. When the word is used in its colonial Spanish sense, we allow the Spanish plural *yanaconas.*

villages for provisions, which often included the open taking of human booty (especially men and young women). This practice was quite frequent, as evidenced in documents from the earliest periods, starting in 1543.

Besides these two likely origins, reinforcing factors seem to have arisen after the organization of the *encomiendas* in 1555–1556. One was "yanaconization" of the *mitayos*, a process by which people legally entitled to stay in their home villages were taken under so-called protection by Spaniards when they went to Asunción to "pay" *mita*, and in time were enslaved by out-and-out purchase. The 1651–1652 *visita* (judicial tour of inspection) by Garabito de León shows that 12 percent of all the *yanaconas* in Asunción were born elsewhere than on their patron's property; most of these (72%) were ex-*mitayos* converted, for better or for worse, into *originarios*.

The origins of "protection" lie in the climate of violence. Open violence followed some of the Guaraní rebellions; for example, after the Spanish defeated the Indian leader Tabaré, thousands of Indians were distributed as "prizes" to the soldiers. Faced with such danger many Indians decided to seek the protection of a powerful Spaniard and in this way shield themselves from worse fates, much as European serfs had done during the European high Middle Ages. The purchase of Indian "hands" also was frequently coerced. Often an indigenous leader or the father of a family would as a last resort sell a youth in order to avoid the total destruction of his village or his house.

What was the ratio of *originarios* to the total number of *encomendados*? The figures we have are from later periods. At the time of Garabito de León's inspection (1651–1652), about one-fourth of the total number of *encomendados* were *originarios* who lived on Spanish farms and *estancias* (ranches). Social conditions for the *originario* Indians were atrocious even by colonial standards. The *originario* worked all his life starting at a very early age – the notion of "tributary age" did not effectively exist for these Indians during the sixteenth and seventeenth centuries. Nor did there seem to be any weekly schedule. Although ordinances and regulations applicable to *originarios* did go into effect in Paraguay (Ramírez de Velazco, 1597; Hernandarias, 1603; Alfaro, 1611 and 1618), Andrés Garabito de León's tour of inspection did not confirm the effectiveness of such laws. The Indians and their families worked on the farm or plantation all week including Sunday. Wives and daughters had to fulfill their obligation by spinning thread for the Spanish lords.[3] On holidays, which were fairly frequent, they were allowed to work on their own land. As the colonial era advanced, *originarios* became a diminishing fraction of the total *encomienda* population. Nevertheless at the end of the eighteenth century, the personal service *encomienda* still existed, and more than 6 percent of the Indians in service were *originarios*.

We turn now to the *mitayos*, the tribute-paying Indians who dwelled in native settlements. The first Indian villages (in the Spanish meaning of the term) were established a little after the *encomiendas* of 1555, beginning with the reorganization of pre-*encomienda* but already European-generated settlements. As early as the 1540s, documents repeatedly spoke of a need to "create" villages in order to rationalize the process of exploitation of the natives and to ensure more efficiently the reproduction of the labor force, which was threatened by the continuing practice of "yanaconization" and the appropriation of women. There was a flagrant contradiction between the Spanish attempt to fix the *originario* Guaraní villages in one place and the Indian need for mobility connected to shifting swidden agriculture. This problem remains unstudied for this period.

In the Asunción region, these primitive villages were replaced – after a period of severe rebellions – by the *reducciones*, or settlements of Christian Indians created by the Franciscan fathers in the 1580s. (The early concept of "reduction" differed from the North American idea of "reservation" insofar as the former aimed chiefly at concentrating natives in church-controlled model villages. The role of the state in bounding politico-legal native territory was weak.) But in other areas, like Mbaracayú, Guayrá, Villa Rica, and the Xerez region, *encomenderos* kept living in "their" villages until well into the seventeenth century. In some cases, especially Xerez and Guayrá and to some extent Mbaracayú and Villa Rica, the villages were destroyed by the *bandeirantes*. In any case the process of reorganizing the Guaraní villages must have taken quite a long time, because even the first Río de la Plata Council, which met in Asunción in 1603, repeatedly insisted that there was a need "to get the Indians to settle down."

How did compliance with the *mita* differ in these villages and in the

[3] The Indians of Juan de Osorio's *encomienda* answered, "They usually worked spinning cotton for their mistress . . . but if they did not start spinning early that day they were scolded and beaten with a stick and sometimes hurt. (*Visita* of Garabito, Asunción 1651, in the Archivo Nacional de Bolivia, EC.1651.29, fol. 74 vta; see also fols. 5 vta, 58 vta, 85, 85 vta, 144 vta, 310 vta, etc.).

Indian mission villages later created by the Franciscans? The first ordinances about *encomiendas*, issued by Martínez de Irala in 1556, did not set any scheduling limits for the fulfillment of the *mitas*. They determined that during each turn the *encomendero* could use the service of one-fourth of his tributaries, but "when clearly necessary," he could use up to half of them. The fact that there was no time limit on the exploitation of the labor force might seem to indicate that the *encomendero* was free to decide the term. But in fact it was actually the result of hard negotiations between the ethnic leaders of the villagers and the stewards or administrators whom the *encomendero* appointed to govern in the villages. In the new regulations that went into effect after 1597, the time factor makes its first appearance. Governor Ramírez de Velazco issued new directives and established three different types of *mitas*, depending on the distance from the villages to the place of work. The draft lasted from 2 to 6 months, and the *encomendero* could use only a maximum of half his tributaries in each turn. This directive indicates that from 1555 to 1597 the distinction between *originario* and *mitayo* was very vague, because the *mitayo* had to serve almost without time limit as well. One can well imagine that this stage intensified the process of "yanaconization" of the *mitayos* coming in from native villages.

A few years later, in 1603, Governor Hernandarias issued new ordinances. The repeated proclamation of this legislation reflects awareness of a catastrophic situation in the villages. Problems were arising due to the excessive demands made by the Spanish *encomenderos* and owners of other industries, once the exportation of *yerba mate* had begun. The new rules reiterated the differential arrangements according to distance, but they shortened the length of the turns and established that only one-third of the tributaries should serve these turns, except during harvests of "bread and wine." These new regulations give some indication of distress in the indigenous labor force, but we strongly doubt their efficacy. In remote areas like Mbaracayú and Guayrá, it was extremely difficult to enforce compliance, and the productive demands of *yerba mate* made it exempt from these time limits.

Thus we come to the 1611 tour of inspection, carried out by Don Francisco de Alfaro, an *oidor* of the *Audiencia* of los Charcas. (Each *audiencia* was a panel of justices called *oidores*, collectively responsible for governing the largest territorial divisions under the viceroyalty.) Alfaro had also passed through Tucumán, as discussed later. With his commission as *visitador*, or traveling judge, he had a clear charge: to eliminate the system of servitude that had grown at the margin of legality, and to place the local natives under the law of the Indies. The visiting judge himself pointed out in his correspondence that this matter was "so confusing that it is hard to know where to begin." Let us look at Alfaro's plan.

The *oidor* Alfaro first of all proposed the elimination of personal service, but for any natives who wanted to continue in service, he established a very sensible reduction in the amount of work required. First, the time that each *mitayo* was required to work was reduced from 4 months to 1 month; second, the staffing of each turn was reduced to one-sixth of the total number of tributaries subject to the turn. Influenced by the Jesuits, he also decided to prohibit forced labor absolutely in the gathering of *yerba mate.*

A near-revolt on the part of injured colonists followed Alfaro's inspection. The net result here, as had happened in Tucumán, was that most of the dispositions became dead letters. The most important reforms were deleted by the time the ordinances were confirmed in 1618. Neither was personal service eliminated, nor was length of service limited. Personal service was finally accepted by the court in the face of persistent economic realities that made it unthinkable to convert rents paid in the form of labor to rents in money. Length of service, rather than being radically limited, increased again from 1 to 2 months; even longer periods were common practice in some areas, like the Mbaracayú region, a *yerba mate* production area where forced labor remained legal.

The Assignments of Forced Labor

In Paraguay, as in most of Spanish America, the assignment of workers by the state apparatus to non-*encomendero* entrepreneurs was common from very early times and lasted in some form until the end of the colonial period. Just as Indians from the valley of Mexico had to go to the "bread corvée" and those from Alto Peru (now Bolivia) to the Potosí mines, the Indians of the Paraguayan communities were obliged to fulfill two kinds of non-*encomienda* service: the *mandamientos* ('mandates') and the *beneficio yerbatero* ('yerba mate exploitation').

The mandates lasted until the end of the colonial period. Through a *mandamiento* from the governor or his lieutenant, a group of Indians from each village was assigned to an entrepreneur – whether or not he was an *encomendero* – for a specific job or period of time. In this way the problems arising from the lack of a free labor market were solved ad hoc. For most of the colonial period, the whole transportation system, both by land and river, depended on government mandates. River transportation was especially crucial in moving Paraguayan products – wine, *mate*, tobacco, and others – to centers of redistribution and consumption.

The *beneficio yerbatero* was a grant of forced labor under which Spaniards could require natives to work for months gathering wild *yerba mate*. It was subject to state scheduling guidelines meant to facilitate the seasonal harvesting and processing of this highly saleable product. In 1629, during the government of Céspedes Xeria, an ordinance was issued in Mbaracayú; this document is one of the oldest testimonies we have about the early period of the *beneficios yerbateros* in this key area – before the first great wave of *bandeirantes*, which ended in 1632 with the fall of Guayrá. An Indian's term of service lasted 6 months, divided into 4 months working in the *yerba mate* fields and 2 months hauling the product to the river ports. Some *mitayos encomendados* worked *mate* alongside others who worked for non-*encomendero* enterprises. There might even have been some Indians who were *enganchados* – that is, "hooked" by offers of credit and then semisalaried. The governor's lieutenant had the power to open and close the period of the *beneficio* and to arrange the distribution of the labor force among the *encomenderos* and the non-*encomendero* enterprises. Until the Paraguayan rebellions of the *comuneros* during 1720–1730, the *beneficios yerbateros*, structured more or less as we have described, were the most important mechanism for recruiting an indigenous labor force to produce the most important trade commodity connecting Paraguay and the Andean market (and one of the most widely traded commodities in the whole Peruvian territory).

The Indigenous Reaction: Prophecy and Reducciones

From the very beginning Guaraní actions challenge the traditional historical view that presents them as meek allies of the Spaniards. In fact resistance movements began with the founding of Asunción in 1537. Resistance increased after Domingo Martínez de Irala instituted the first grants of *encomienda* in 1555, which provoked uprisings and rebellions. Some of these movements, such as the uprisings of 1556 and 1575–1579, seriously jeopardized European colonization of Paraguay. Resistance showed a clear religious component, discussed later on.

In 1556, the year of the first ordinances of *encomiendas*, several documents mention that the Indians of Asunción would not sow seed or go to work for the Spaniards. Instead they spent all day singing and dancing "like madmen . . . until they were dying of hunger and exhaustion." The Spaniards violently repressed this commotion and used brute force to break refusal to work for the newly appointed *encomenderos*. This behavior bears a family resemblance to anticolonial religious movements in many parts of South America before 1575.

In 1575–1579, another movement swept the area. The leader was a renowned shaman (*karaí*) called Overa "the resplendent." The first wave swept the whole northern region of Asunción, essentially the Jejuy River area. Later it encompassed nearly all the Indians who lived in the *encomienda* villages, except the most remote villages around Villa Rica.[4] After two or three confrontations, Overa defected, and the Guaraní were defeated and harshly repressed.

This movement seems to have been characterized by strong intertribal conflict as well as by resistance against the European invaders. Intranative issues complicate any interpretation of the events as having been exclusively a "messianic" movement, as Alfred Métraux understood it to be. More recently Hélène Clastres advocates a complex interpretation, seeing in this episode a movement of internal political struggle between ethnic leaders and *karaís*, as was the later rebellion led by another *karaí*, Guariverá.

Religious phenomena among the Tupí must be distinguished from those among the Guaraní, Clastres holds. In the former group the prophetic phenomenon is one of protest against the social order, a protest that led to the quest for the "Land without Evil." In the case of Overa and Guariverá, the phenomenon entailed a much more politicized power struggle within the group. It must be stressed, however, that most information about Overa comes from Father Lozano's chronicle, written two centuries later, in the mid–eighteenth century, rather than from contemporaneous documents. By contrast the earlier sources on the Tupí are much richer, especially the chronicles of André Thevet (1557), Jean de Léry (1578), and even a few later ones, such as those of Claude d'Abbeville and Yves d'Évreux from the early seventeenth century. We cannot ignore the fact that some of the apparent differences have to do with the different types of information available.

[4] Martín Barco de Centenera, in the 20th canto of his *Argentina*, writes at length of this event and transcribes some of the rebels' Guaraní "chants."

A few Europeans actually met believers making their arduous way through unknown territory in search of the "Land without Evil." In 1609 La Ravardière, a Huguenot captain with a French royal concession, met a group of Potiguara believers who had wandered from Pernambuco. He took them to the island of São Luiz de Maranhão, where Father Yves d'Évreux found them 3 years later. Clastres relates the story the *cacique* Jacoupen told D'Évreux:

I remember Yurupari's [a malign spirit's] cruelty toward our nation; he made us all die, and persuaded our Barbers[5] to bring us into the middle of a strange forest, where we danced endlessly, having nothing else to eat than hearts of palm and game, with the result that several died of weakness and exhaustion. Having come out of there and having sailed on the ships of the Mburubicha[6] La Ravardière to this island of Maragnan, Yurupari laid another ambush for us, inciting Tupinambá [a rival coastal people] through a Frenchman to massacre several of our people and to eat them.[7]

Prophetically led migrations brought many believing groups to disastrous ends. But they undeniably show that by the end of the 1570s, Spanish control over the *encomienda* villages was shaky, and that resistance had acquired a marked religious and prophetic accent. At this crucial moment the Franciscan fathers intervened, creating the first resettlement villages of "converted" Indians.

Although the Franciscans had participated in the first Spanish expeditions to the region, it was only after 1574 that Franciscan work became closely connected to indigenous life. In that year the first convents were established. Among the Franciscans who went to Paraguay were Fray Luis de Bolaños, Fray Juan de Rivadeneyra, and Martín Ignacio de Loyola, the last a close relative of the founder of the Society of Jesus. All of them played central roles in the creation of the Catholic "reductions." "Reduction" in eastern South America had a different meaning than in the Andes (see Chap. 15). In the Andes it meant reorganizing an already agrarian population into nucleated diocesan parishes. In the east it entailed the even more drastic scheme of forcing a complete social transfor-

[5] The Jesuit missionary Martin Dobrizhoffer mentions that barbering was a religious duty among Guaraníans, both cropping men's hair to make a larger forehead, and shaving the heads of the bereaved. See his 1784 *Account of the Abipones* in its 1822 translation (New York, 1970), vol. 2, 16–18.

[6] The term *mburuvichá* variously spelled, means 'ethnic leader' – in this case, of the French.

[7] Hélène Clastres, *The Land-Without-Evil. Tupí-Guaraní Prophetism* [1974] (Urbana and Chicago, 1995), 51–52.

mation, from shifting horticultural and/or hunter-gatherer ways of life to a would-be utopian village theocracy under the rule of the orders. Franciscans and Jesuits would take different approaches to the venture.

In 1580 the first Franciscan *reducción*, Los Altos, was founded about 40 kilometers east of Asunción; this enclave was created with a little more than a thousand Indians who formerly had lived in five separate villages. There ensued a complex process of reorganizing the original territory of the Guaranís, now serving in *encomienda* to the Spaniards. Los Altos was soon followed by two other *reducciones*, Itá and Yaguarón, also near Asunción. In a little less than a decade, the Guaranís around Asunción were relocated onto *reducciones. Encomienda* service became normalized, in keeping with the general policy promoted by the viceroys of New Spain and Peru, especially Viceroy Toledo of Peru.

Right away the Franciscans began the same experiment with several indigenous groups to the north and east of the city, but much farther away. In the north there were three Guaraní groups, the Tobatines, the Guarambarenses and the Itatines. We know them by the names of their most powerful ethnic leaders, although we know little about their ethnic identities. Between 1580 and the end of the sixteenth century, a series of *reducciones* was founded: Tobatí, Jejuy, Atirá, Itapané, Perico, and Guarambaré. This contributed enormously to reinforcing Spanish control over the area north of Asunción.

How can we explain the Franciscan friars' success? On what did they base these Guaraní *reducciones* and those of other ethnic groups like the Ñuaras in the village of Perico? These *reducciones* antedate by 30 years the famous ones that the Jesuits established in the 1610s in Guayrá. Is it possible to establish some connecting link between the Franciscan experience and the later Jesuit one?

One comparison can be developed around the clash between two "Messianisms," the Guaraní and the Christian, as does Louis Necker (whose [1979] book is based in part on the ideas in an article by Maxime Haubert [1969]). There is no doubt that conversion struggles occurred, in both Franciscan and Jesuit missions; one has only to read the documents in José María Blanco's (1929) book on the martyrdom of Father Roque González Santa Cruz and his colleagues in Guayrá. This death was undoubtedly a result of struggle for control of the village between the priests and a powerful *karaí* named Nezú, whom Gonzáles had accused of sorcery. If the documents are correct, Nezú went so far as to reverse the ritual of baptism, summoning "some baptized children and with water that he brought out from underneath himself, saying it was sweat or liquor that he had distilled from his body, he washed their heads, chests and backs and scrubbed their tongues, saying that thus the baptism was removed . . . and he baptized the children and gave them heathen names."[8] A document from Blanco's book shows how Potirava, a Guaraní "apostate," understood quite well the relation between the *reducciones*, the loss of a specific kind of control over the environment, and the colonial experience. Potirava's purported words were:

> Have we not until now had a common living in the mountains around us, without possessing the valley any more than the forest? Then why do you consent to let our Indians, and what is worse, our successors, be subjected to this hypocritical captivity on *reducciones* that alienates us from nature? Perhaps there are not enough examples in Paraguay of what kind of men the Spaniards are, of the damage they have done to us, of how they fatten themselves by using us?[9]

One reason Franciscans sometimes won such struggles was that they were the first to understand that a thorough knowledge of Guaraní language and customs was indispensable. Early *mestizaje* aided their project. Some of Bolaños' fellow friars were Guayrá mestizos, and they wrote the first catechism in the Guaraní language (c. 1586, published in Europe in 1607). We have seen that the ethnic leaders, called *mburuvichá* were distinguished, among other things, by their skill with words. Some of the younger friars, Fray Luis de Bolaños especially, seem to have been particularly expert in this area.

Another factor that played a key role in the Franciscans' success was the example they set in their personal lives. They tried to be living antitheses to the greedy and often impious European colonists whom Indians knew so well. This same phenomenon had occurred 50 years earlier in New Spain, among the celebrated twelve monks led by Motolinía. Genuinely poor and without material possessions – as were the ethnic leaders, let us not forget – the Franciscans sought to represent themselves as Christian people of dignity, worthy of native respect. They

[8] Document quoted in J. M. Blanco, *Historia documentada de la vida y gloriosa muerte de los Padres Roque González de Santa Cruz, Alonso Rodríguez y Juan del Castillo de la Compañía de Jesús, mártires del Caaró e Yjuhí* (Amorrortu, Buenos Aires, 1929), p. 473.

[9] Blanco, J. M., op. cit., p. 525. (Of course, Potirava's discourse is highly polemical, but no doubt there is truth in the underlying ideas.)

promised a better world (a peculiar kind of "Land without Evil") in the hereafter, a concept that was not alien to some central aspects of the Guaraní worldview.

Although the Franciscans' success was based on all these elements, as discussed by Necker, that success (like the subsequent success of the Jesuits) can only be understood in the context of contemporary interethnic relations. First, the colonists' repeated and violent demands gave rise to rebellions and uprisings, which the Spaniards used a posteriori to justify their own acts of warfare. Second, the Indians were seriously affected by a demographic crisis (discussed later). Given these conditions the Franciscans seemed to be the most credible interlocutors to help them out of an endless circle of violence. The contrast between their benevolent paternalism and secular strong-arm tactics echoes Aesop's fable, as retold by La Fontaine, about the struggle between the wind and the sun: The gently warming sun will make a stubborn man remove his cloak, but the violent wind only makes him clutch it harder. The Jesuits, already present in the region on exploratory missions, learned this lesson from the Franciscan experience.

The Jesuit Reducciones

The Society of Jesus established *reducciones* in Paraguay from 1610 (see Map 14.2) to 1768 (see Map 14.3). To speak of this experience is to take on an ideologically charged topic. Even before the Enlightenment, Western historiography privileged this particular missionary experience, exempting it from basic critiques of domination. Among the reasons for this fascination is its widespread influence among enlightened Europeans, who thought they saw in it a practical utopia.

It is true that the Jesuits created a totalizing social regimen, but the *reducciones* should not be taken as expressions of a full-blown utopian "model." The Jesuit "model" was in reality the result of slow evolution over time amid a set of complex and contradictory factors.

The most important factor is that the Franciscan experiment, which had already developed new ways to firm up colonial control, preceded Jesuit experience by a margin of nearly 30 years. This meant political control, but above all it meant ideological control, and here the Christian religion played a crucial role as an element of "Westernization." Still, putting cultural control into practice has to do with control *tout court*. In the case of the Guaraní, the colonists felt that their domination of the villages was in serious danger as a result of indigenous resistance. Control

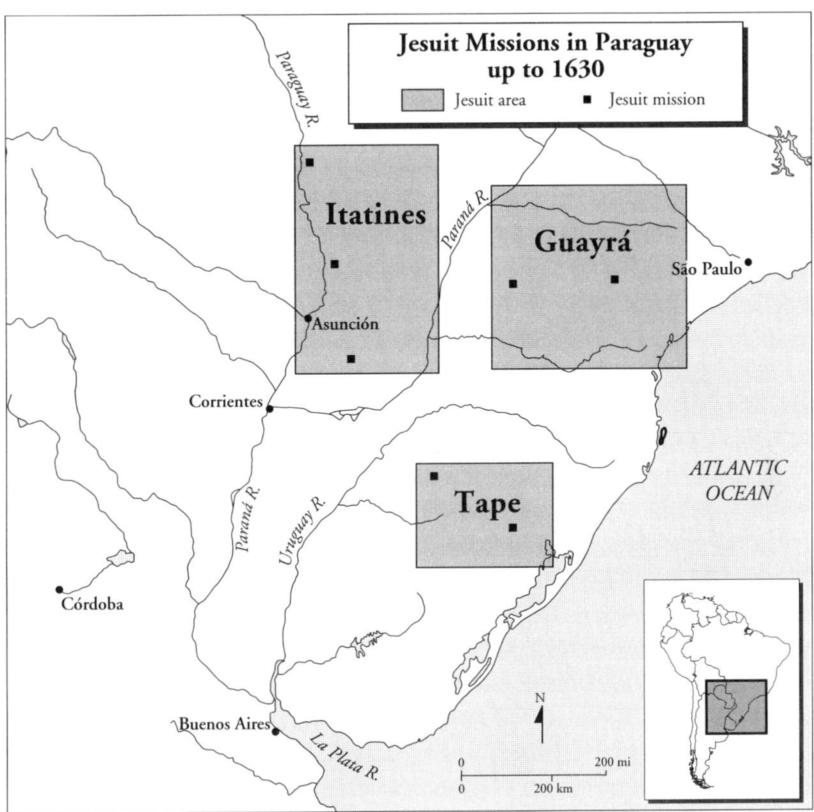

Map 14.2

over the labor force was the next element in the causal chain: The *encomenderos* wanted "their" Indians to fulfil their *mitas.* Furthermore the assignment of workers by representatives of the state could be effective only within the framework of consolidated villages. In some places the most important issue was territorial reorganization and the concomitant release of indigenous lands for appropriation and exploitation by the colonists. This seems to have been the case with the first three Franciscan *reducciones* near Asunción, where grazing livestock was a goal.

Judging by these factors, it is hard to distinguish the Jesuits' initial experience in creating *reducciones* from the general colonial policy of the period. The differences become apparent, however, when we observe the later, more complex, and progressive evolution of the *reducciones* in Paraguay starting around 1610. The Jesuits began the task of establishing

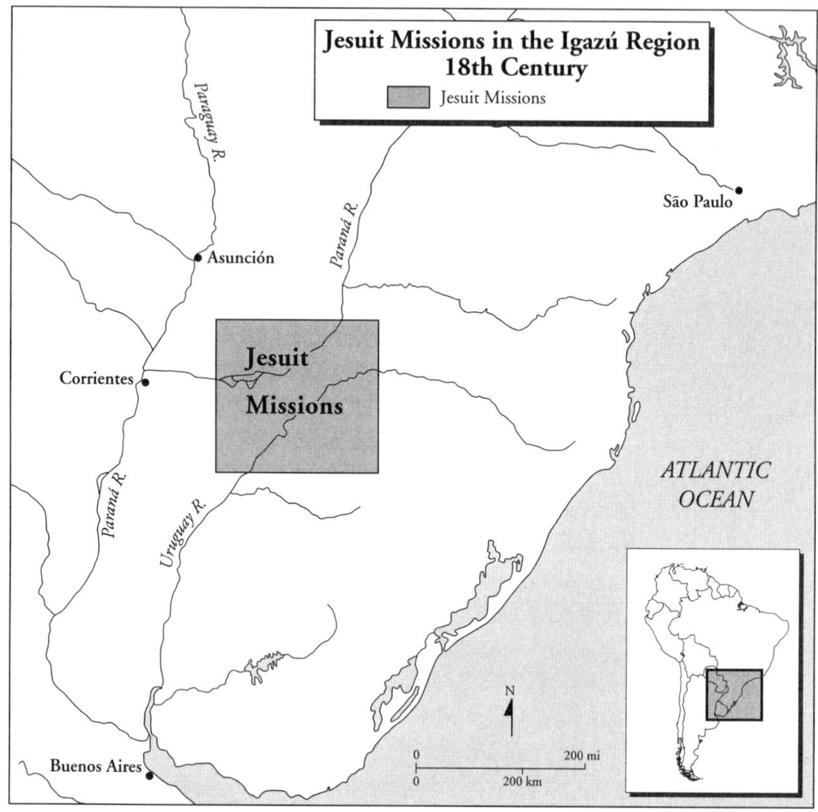

Map 14.3

reducciones with the aid of then-governor Hernandarias. The venture coincided with two other influential events: Francisco de Alfaro's tour of inspection to study the *encomenderos*, and the *bandeirante* raids, which were intensifying during this period. These two factors highlight the dangers and traps that the Indians confronted. On one hand there were the *encomenderos* and the governors, whose demands for fulfillment of the *mitas* and mandates became more and more burdensome in parallel with the recent expansion of *yerba mate* into various markets. On the other hand there were Portuguese adventurers who sacked villages and enslaved Indians. Those taken would end their days in the sugar mills of Brazil. Jesuits captured a strategic position by wedging themselves between these two forces.

The Jesuits were obliged to tolerate the existence of *encomiendas* on some of their oldest missions. San Ignacio Guazú, for example, kept *encomiendas* going well into the eighteenth century. Yet Jesuits were thoroughly successful in exempting the Indians in their other *reducciones* from all personal service to the Spaniards and from all orders by the governors. As for the *bandeirantes*, there was obvious collusion on more than one occasion between Portuguese and Spanish colonists, but the Jesuits always organized the defense of their villagers – with varying degrees of success – against these merciless raiders. The Jesuits quickly realized that only by making their *reducciones* autonomous from the colonists' demands could their missionary movement have any future. Thus along this frontier between the two Iberian empires, the *reducciones* played a fundamental defensive role. (They served a similar role in several internal conflicts between the crown and the colonists.) In this way the Jesuits established their own niche and transformed what they saw as the traditional warlike impulses of the Guaraní.

Let us take a brief look at the internal workings of the *reducción*. Relations between the missionaries and the ethnic leaders were based on two systems, used alternately or jointly, depending on the circumstances. The first was based on the powers of persuasion, gifts, and the eloquence of the missionary. The second method came into play to back up this "benevolent" approach: force against overly recalcitrant leaders or *karaí* (whom the missionaries called sorcerers).

When we look to the Jesuit missionary literature of the period, detailing the day-to-day functioning of *reducciones* after the initial act of religious conversion, one regularity stands out: the emphasis on paternalism. The relationship between the priest and the Indian is consistently presented as like that between father and child. This father–child model does not evolve over time but marks a historical constant. Hence the figure of the priest was made heroic and extrahistorical: the authentic founder who was responsible for everything, and around whom the whole economic life of the mission village revolved. Some Jesuit chroniclers even went so far as to credit the priests with introducing agriculture and weaving. Indeed Jesuit insistence that the Indians toil at agriculture whether or not it made ecological sense helps explain the repeated demographic catastrophes on *reducciones*; even the most intelligent of the Jesuits seemed unable or unwilling to understand that human beings could not be pushed into agrarian toil beyond their limits, or that farming might run counter to indigenous self-interest. Agriculture seemed to Jesuits as necessary as Christianity, and in this regard they behaved more like colonists than like ethnologists.

The use of force as well as persuasion in daily *reducción* life is documented in many sources. One famous chronicler spoke of "invisible chains," such as music, festivals, and fancy clothes. When these failed to achieve the ideological control the Jesuits required, force was used widely and repeatedly as a last resort. Even the internal documents of the Society of Jesus call attention to this on more than one occasion, warning the missionaries about the dangers of "abuse" in the use of force.

As for the economic functions of the *reducciones*, their internal structure is by now well known. During part of the week, the Indians worked to sustain their family groups; this work was called *abambaé*. During the rest of the week, they labored in the interest of the *reducción* and the Indians who had no family to support them, such as widows, the infirm, and orphans; this work was called *tupambaé*. This obviously served to recreate, within a new framework, the two patterns of reciprocity and redistribution that had existed in the prehispanic societies. Priests simply "inflated" the *tupambaé*, or redistribution, by substituting themselves – imperfectly – for the ethnic leaders, who were the former centers of circles of reciprocity and redistribution.

Despite the power of the missionaries, ethnic leaders maintained an active presence. In fact throughout the century and a half of the Jesuit *reducciones*, these ethnic leaders played definite roles in the political, social, and economic life of the *reducción*. There were ongoing changes in this situation – for example, in terms of individual control of the *yerba mate* trade. At least for a time, the ethnic leaders and some prestigious family heads enjoyed fairly free trade relations with Spanish merchants. But this situation changed slowly until the priests assumed total control over the Indians' property and economic rights. In any case the chiefs' political and economic importance within the *reducción* lasted well into the eighteenth century. Of course some ethnic leaders were completely coopted by the missionaries.

Guaraní Demography in the Paraguayan Region

The nature and the fate of missionized society were deeply conditioned by demographic facts: Both the baseline fact of a dispersed population, and the historic decline of numbers as epidemics, famine, and raiding devoured the artificially concentrated population.

Some time ago the late Pierre Clastres estimated for the prehispanic Guaraní a density of four inhabitants per square kilometer. William Denevan, however, arrived at a much lower density, suggesting an average of one inhabitant per square kilometer. A recent work by Warren Dean estimates – for the only partly comparable Tupí of the Brazilian coast – a density even higher than Clastres' figure, or more than four inhabitants per square kilometer. Probably, as we shall see, the average density lies somewhere between Clastres' high estimate and Denevan's low one.

The first serious statistics we have about the region controlled by Asunción come from Martínez de Irala's census. They indicate a maximum of 27,000 "warriors" among the Indians of the *reparto.* (*Reparto* was the "sharing-out" of Indian service.) Susnik calculates a total of 100,000 *encomienda* Indians. Since the original family structures had been destroyed, this evaluation seems about right. We do not know exactly how far this first assignment of native labor extended, but Villa Rica and Guayrá are excluded from this calculation. The significant point is that even before the great invasion of *bandeirantes* in 1632, half of the 100,000 Indians alive in 1555 had died. The regions of Guayrá and the so-called del Tape (that is, between the Uruguay River and the Serra do Mar), had sheltered about 260,000 Indians at the beginning of contact with the colonists but suffered a demographic decline even greater than in the Asunción area. This was especially pronounced in Guayrá because of the *bandeirante* invasions and their consequences.

Adding the various figures together yields a rough estimate of half a million Guaraní at the moment of European invasion, with a density halfway between those estimated by Clastres and Denevan, or around two inhabitants per square kilometer. This half million was reduced to one third or one quarter of a million during the first 50 years of contact. The first serious demographic inspection carried out in the region was done by Andrés Garabito de León in 1651–1652. His report gives us the dramatically lower figure of 14,360 tributary Indians – and we know nothing about the Guaraní groups who were still outside the direct control of colonists. Adding to this approximately 15,000 Indians controlled by the Jesuits on their *reducciones,* the total number of Indians under Spanish domination would be about 30,000 maximum. In sum, in a little over a century, assuming that there were still groups of Guaraní who had escaped direct control by the Spanish, the population had fallen to less than one tenth of the preinvasion number.

Except for one factor, the causes of this population decline differ little from those in other areas. The invaders brought diseases that erupted as epidemics with grim regularity every 10 years. The Guaraní were in epidemiological contact with the Europeans from the first voyages in the early sixteenth century. Along with this went famines, loss of access to many food resources, war and repression, and increase in the burden of work along with the new economic activities.

The unique factor is that life in Guaraní villages was made more difficult during the contact era after the foundation of Asunción because many Indian women were "handed over" to the Spaniards. This had a disastrous effect on indigenous demography. In addition, during the first 50 years, the original territory was reorganized and the *reducciones* were established in policy and practice. These factors greatly worsened the situation by concentrating people at risk of illness. If we add to this the repeated expeditions of the *bandeirantes* to capture Indian slaves, we have a fairly complete picture of the causes of this region's especially severe demographic catastrophe.

INDIANS AND SPANIARDS IN COLONIAL TUCUMÁN

Northwestern Argentina, unlike the Tupí-Guaraní heartlands, formed for a short time part of the Inka domains, and is in some respects a part of the Andean cultural orbit. For the archaeological Late Period, C.E. 850 to the arrival of the Inka around 1480 (see Chap. 9), northwestern Argentina is commonly divided into the valleys, the *puna* or high plains, the subandean ranges, Santiago del Estero, and the central mountain ranges of Córdoba.

Tucumán and Northwest Argentina to the Mountain Ranges of Córdoba: An Ethnic Panorama at the Moment of Contact

In following this scheme it pays to remember Fredrik Barth's warning about the confusion that may ensue when archaeologists identify "ethnic groups by the characteristics of the cultures they carry."[10] Unfortunately, this happens fairly often even in the most serious and best documented studies on the area. Furthermore, a superficial reading of written sources and chronicles often yields errors like calling an ethnic group by

[10] Barth, Fredrik (ed.), *Ethnic Groups and Boundaries. The Social Organization of Culture Difference*, Boston, 1969.

the name of its leader, naming a "region" after a leader who happened to be reported in it, or giving ethnic status to a linguistic category. A lot of dead wood must be cleared from this road and we are only at its beginning.

We first consider a valley region making up part of what was formerly known in the literature as the "Diaguita region." In Chapter 9 Rivera treats it prehistorically as part of the South Andean region. This was where most of the population was concentrated and the most important cultural centers were located.

It consists of broad valleys of uneven terrain lying between 1,500 and 3,000 meters above sea level. Average precipitation was low (250 mm) but with wide variations throughout the region. The vegetation cover was scrub and cactus. Two uncultivated plants that were very important food sources for humans throughout Tucumán, as well as in Cuyo, were *chañar* and carob. *Chañar (Geoffrea decorticans* or *Gourliea decorticans*) is a shrub of the legume family whose hard wood had many uses and whose fruit was used in the preparation of *arrope*, a kind of vegetable honey. Carob is a tree with very hard wood, also useful for many purposes. Its fruit was used in several ways: as a sweet, *patay*, and in various beverages, including *añapa*, a nonalcoholic drink, and *aloja*, which is fermented. The Quechua name for the carob tree, *taku*, has survived in many of the Tucumán region's toponyms to the present day (Taco Ralo, Taco Pozo, Tacoyoj, etc.).

The climate is dry and warm with a median temperature of 20° Celsius, and winters are mild with many sunny days. Irrigation agriculture was widespread, primarily on the slopes of volcanoes and on valley floors. Camelids were well adapted to the environment, especially the llama (*Lama glama*) and probably the alpaca (*L. pacos*). The other two, the vicuña (*L. vicugna*) and the guanaco (*L. guanacoe*), were hunted. Archaeological remains show that a great deal of human traffic passed through this area. Access was possible from the north, through the high plains or *puna*, from the east via the rivers that link the area with the subtropical forests, and from the west via passes through the Andes.

In using this valley landscape, prehispanic people chose a different settlement pattern from the one adopted later by the Europeans. The largest agropastoral areas – by archaeological evidence – covered hillsides and *punas* or high plateaus, with villages located below in the intermediate zones. The valuable valley bottoms were zones of confrontation and conflict.

The four most important cultures of this period were Sanagasta or Angualasto in the south, Belén, Santamaría, and the Quebrada de Humahuaca. Probably Sanagasta, Belén, and Santamaría formed part of the same set of communities that were called Diaguitas, with certain features in common, among which was language. Let us look briefly at what we know today about these four cultures.

Sanagasta or Angualasto occupied the south, in what is today La Rioja and San Juan. The people practiced a horticultural economy based on corn (*Zea mays L.*), squash (*Lagenaria vulgaris*), and beans (*Phaseolus vulgaris L.*). They also bred llamas and gathered various fruits (such as the carob). The population pattern was one of small communities and dispersed small polities affiliated in larger but not centralized groups. There is no evidence of the large defense constructions that characterized the rest of this region during the Late Period.

In the Belén Valley and the Aubacán Valley, a characteristic culture called Belén extended from the location of the present city of La Rioja to the Santa María Valley; its most important center was in the Hualfin Valley. Before the Inka arrived, the population was concentrated in semiurban centers at strategic locations. Large land areas were covered with agricultural terraces several hectares in size. The people of Belén also tended flocks of llamas and used their wool. Everything indicates that this culture was one of the nerve centers of the so-called Diaguitas, being specifically the domain of the Hualfín.

Santamaría culture was localized in the Yocavil and Calchaquí valleys as far as the Quebrada de Humahuaca. This culture was characteristic of the center of the Calchaquí valleys. Here we find intensive agriculture based on irrigation with many terraces and dams. The people also tended flocks of llamas and other camelids. In the last prehispanic stage, we find a population pattern of villages protected with defensive walls, located at high altitude on hillsides. Some villages housed more than 1,500 inhabitants. The inhabitants eventually united into federated groups, among whom links of language and culture imparted a sense of unity and sociopolitical integration.

The people of these three cultures and their kin spoke Cacan or Diaguita. This language had three divisions: in the north, Calchaquí, in the center Cacan proper, and in the south Capayan.

The culture of the Quebrada de Humahuaca is somewhat different. The Quebrada is a valley more than 170 kilometers long by 3 kilometers wide, through which runs the Grande or Humahuaca River. The valley runs north–south, encompassing climatic variations and therefore markedly varied phytogeography. From earliest times it was a route connecting the low area of the subtropical forests with the *puna* region. The Quebrada de Humahuaca can be divided into three climatically distinct sections. In the first, which reaches from the site of the present-day city of Jujuy (1,258 m) to Volcán (1,700 m), the Quebrada is oriented to the southeast, allowing humid winds from the east to penetrate and produce high humidity and annual precipitation of 900 millimeters. The vegetation is subtropical. From Volcán northward the Quebrada climbs steeply to Uquía (2,800 m), where annual precipitation declines to 200 millimeters. The third sector extends from Uquía to Tres Cruces (3,300 m), with precipitation about the same as the previous sector.

By linguistic criteria the valleys can be considered as a border area with respect to the rest of northwest Argentina. Their economy was fundamentally agricultural and rested on the cultivation of corn. In this transition zone between the subtropical forest and the high plains, there were many maize varieties. Terracing and great stone silos give clear evidence of the importance of agriculture. Most of the villages stood at high altitudes and were fortified. Post-Tiwanaku cultural influences, coming from Chile, are apparent. The people were very warlike. Several different ethnic groups from this period are known collectively as the Omaguacas. This was a region of permanent interaction between the Chichas of the region south of present-day Bolivia and the Atacamas, who lived in the Chilean desert of the same name. Some groups of Omaguacas seem to have controlled small agricultural fields in the eastern region, specifically in the valley of Zenta, and this may have given rise to a possible confusion between this ethnic group and the Ocloyas (p. 1053).

The second region we consider comprises the *puna*, or high plateaus. The Argentinian *puna* encompassed what is today the west of Jujuy and Salta and the western part of Catamarca as far as the district of Belén. It is a cold high plain 3,300 to 3,400 meters above sea level, with several ranges that form closed basins where the rivers end in small lakes and salt deposits. The vegetation is sparse and rain does not exceed 100 millimeters annually. The climate is harsh. In the oases the products cultivated were various Andean tubers: oca (*Oxalis tuberosa*), ulluco (*Ullucus t.*), and potato (*Solanum t.*), as well as quinoa (*Chenopodium quinoa*), an herbaceous annual used for its grain, and – very rarely – several varieties of corn. The major *puna* economic activity was grazing because its grasses were ideal pasture for native camelids. The llama herders were the lords of the *puna*. In the Late Period this region was an area of intense trading of livestock and other products; in addition, herders controlled the trade in salt, taken from immense salt deposits. The ethnic identity of the groups who inhabited this area is not known.

The third region we study comprises the sub-Andean ranges. In this zone the transitional nexus between the Andean massif and the Chaco plains was even more pronounced. Depending on altitude we find four natural formations. The transitional jungle extends from an altitude of 500 meters to 1,200 meters, with very tall trees, lianas, and a dense undergrowth of grasses and bushes. Above this, more mountainous jungle extends up to 1,500 meters. Even higher the forests climb the mountain slopes, from 1,500 to 2,500 meters, with pines and alders predominating. Above this is the sub-*puna* region, with its warm dry climate and scrubby vegetation. Here we find a range of ethnic groups (Ocloyas, Paypayas, Churumatas, Osas and Chuis) which apparently were not originally from this zone and functioned – in a multiethnic settlement – as intermediate groups between Andean and Chaco-dwelling peoples.

Through the Zenta Valley run the Zenta, San Andrés, and Santa Cruz rivers, joining with the Bermejo. This valley was largely settled by the Ocloyas and the Churumatas, who were possibly related to the Chichas, according to some sources. They were not of local origin and were probably brought there as *mitmaq* ('political transplants', an Inka term) to function as an ethnic buffer vis-à-vis the Chaco groups, as happened in Yamparáes. But this connection is debatable. In addition to the obvious objective of defense, another purpose of installing *mitmaq* (often called *mitimaes* in the colonial period) was to facilitate exchange. Chaco forest products (lumber, feathers, leather, honey, etc.) were traded for products from the high regions, such as metals, salt, and clothing.

As a fourth region we consider Santiago del Estero. This region, with its plains and low hills, presents special characteristics. From the phytogeographic point of view it belongs to the Chaco area, with more than 500 millimeters of annual precipitation and a warm median temperature of 20° Celsius. It is crossed by two great rivers, the Salado ('salty') and the Dulce ('sweet'), whose annual floods are used to advantage in the region's agriculture. Santiago del Estero was in reality another transition zone between northwest Argentina, the Chaco hunting and gathering groups, and the relatively nearby cultures of the coastal tropical forest.

Formerly it was believed that three distinct cultures occupied the area successively: the Mercedes, Sunchituyoj, and Averías. This image was based on limited archaeological data, and lack of radiocarbon studies renders the chronology dubious. Recently new interpretations have been proposed, especially by Ana María Lorandi and her associates.

According to these researchers there were two cultural traditions: Mercedes and Chaco/Santiago. One of them, the Mercedes, was a cultural extension from the nearby mountain ranges toward the Santiago plains. The other, Chaco/Santiago, arose partially within this area, and followed another sequence, in which Sunchityoj was the local culture and Averías was more closely related to the high plains. In the Late Period we find three successive patterns of subsistence: Las Lomas (C.E. 800–1200), characterized by villages bordering waterways where inhabitants hunted, fished, and gathered; Quimili (1200–1350), with more densely populated villages where agriculture appears, at least on the Dulce River; and Icaño-Olama (1350–1600), featuring large, powerful communities where agriculture surpassed its subsidiary role and replaced other productive activities.

The early Spanish chroniclers' descriptions of this area are clear enough to require little additional comment:

> [T]hey have built villages all along a very large dale, a long stone's throw in width and 30 leagues long, so that when the river rises, it empties into this dale and in summer it dries up and then the Indians of all the villages take many fish and when it dries up they sow corn.[11]

Textile production was a significant activity as evidenced by countless spindle whorls or *muyunas*. These are pieces of fired clay used as counterweights to make the spindle rotate and roll up thread during spinning. The latest research by Lorandi and her associates proposes the plausible hypothesis that the Inkas recruited *mitmaq* in this area without actually occupying the territory. Archaeological remains and other cultural elements, including the diffusion and establishment of Quechua and textile technology, seem to corroborate this hypothesis.

We take as the fifth region the central Ranges of Córdoba. This region of Argentina encompasses the mountain ranges of the present provinces of Córdoba and part of San Luis, as far as the Conlara River, the frontier of the Cuyan group called Huarpes. Probably inhabited since before

[11] Diego Fernández de Palencia, "Historia del Perú," in *Crónicas del Perú*, edited by Juan Pérez de Tudela, Madrid, 1963/1965.

6000 B.C.E., its first agricultural settlements arose around C.E. 500. These settlements formed the nucleus of the prehispanic peoples known to the Spanish conquerors as Comechingones and Sanavirones.

Settlements consisted of the typical half-buried houses so widely diffused in other parts of America, according to the chroniclers in the *Relación Anónima* (c. 1573) and Sotelo de Narváez (1582). They may have been based on exogamous patrilineal lines, as they were dispersed and located at medium distances from each other. The agricultural subsistence pattern was based on corn, squash, and beans. There was some irrigation from mountain lakes and gullied streams – one can still see some rudimentary forms of water control of the kind called *"jagüeyes"* ('artificial seeps'). Flocks of camelids also seem to have been abundant, and carob and *chañar* trees provided an important complementary source of food (especially in years of low rainfall). Of course, the abundance of deer, guanacos, hares (*Dolicotis australis*), and the ostrich-like *ñandú (Rhea americana)* provided abundant reserves of animal protein. Their natural setting at that time was densely forested. Everything seems to indicate that the mountains were densely populated at the time of the Spanish invasion.

The people knew how to weave and to cure leather for clothing. As for language, the Sanavirones apparently spoke a language related to that of the Santiago area. This might explain the name "road of the Sanavirones" given to the path that connected the Córdoba ranges with Sumampa and Ojo de Agua, in Santiago del Estero. The Comechingones, who lived in the central area of the mountains, spoke two related dialects. Recent research shows that different dialects of the same language linked the Sanavirones and the Comechingones.

Inka Expansion

Apparently it was during the reign of Tupaq Inka, the next-to-last prehispanic sovereign, that northwestern Argentina was partially annexed to the imperial lands. Inka influence was more visible in some places than others, being stronger in communication corridors such as the valleys. The Inka presence was short, perhaps less than a century.

Imperial administrative establishments overlooked access roads to the valleys, such as Potrero de Payogasta and Tambo de la Ciénaga. There are also several *pukarás* or fortresses such as Andalgalá, in what is now the Argentine province of Catamarca. There too, *tambos*, or waystations, accommodated Inka caravans and messengers. Scattered across a large part of northwest Argentina, these sites provide archaeological testimony of Inka domination. The Inka also occupied areas near mineral deposits, such as Famatina (present day La Rioja), Aconquija (Tucumán), and El Arenal (Catamarca).

Inka domination brought important technical changes in pottery and metallurgy; these tend to be associated with urban centers. In addition, reinforcement of Quechua as the *lingua franca* was one of the most noticeable results. Another important element was the diffusion of the system of *mitmaq*, as discussed for in the sub-Andean ranges and in Santiago del Estero. It is possible that this was only an acceleration of an earlier process. In any case, the most relevant factor was the Inka use of these "marginal" areas as buffer zones for the empire against the aggressive ethnic groups of the lowlands.

Apparently the Inka did not find it any easier to penetrate the valleys than the subsequent European invaders did. While the Inka installed fortifications in a few strategic places and used the *mitmaq* system, relations were always tense, as was usual in Tawantinsuyu's frontier zones.

In areas where Spanish invasions were weak, what Crosby called the "Columbian exchange" of flora and fauna was often well underway before political confrontations began. Interior Argentina of the late-Inka and post-Inka era was a case in point. Two European legumes were apparently among the first plants that the Indians adopted: green peas (*Pisum sativum*) and broad beans (*Vicia fava*), which were planted in addition to (and sometimes replaced) native beans (*Phaseolus vulgaris L.*). Sources also indicate that two imported grains diffused rapidly: wheat (*Triticum aestivum*) and barley (*Hordeum* spp.). The advantage of these was that they could be intercropped with maize (which in turn was planted with the legumes) because they had complementary growing cycles, thus permitting maximum utilization of arable land.

Indians also adapted rapidly to the large domestic animals introduced by Europeans. This is probably due to long experience with the American camelids llama and alpaca. The horse was introduced in the region at least by 1535; in 1566 we have the first mention of horse theft by Indians. By the 1570s there is clear evidence that some groups had adopted the horse in Tucumán.

Sheep may have been the first large European animals adopted to good effect by the Indians. Their diffusion probably began in the Cuyo region. Even before the city of Mendoza was founded in 1561, the Huarpes of Cuyo seem to have had sheep. Sheep appear to have spread rapidly throughout Tucumán, and by the end of the century Indian herds appeared in various places (e.g., Santiago del Estero, Córdoba). Perhaps by mere oversight, there is no mention in the sources of pigs or goats, which diffused quickly among Indians in other regions. Cattle, on the other hand, seem to have spread less quickly. Recent research places them in indigenous hands in Tucumán no earlier than the seventeenth century.

Among small domestic animals, the chicken (*Gallus gallus*) seems to have spread the quickest and soonest; most probably it came from Paraguay, where it had been introduced in the 1530s, or from Chile, where Almagro's followers brought it in 1535. The probable existence of a local fowl, the "Araucanian hen" (*G. inauris*), complicates this issue. The so-called American mountain turkey (*Penelope obscura*) also existed in this area, further confusing the identification of poultry.

But diffusion was hardly a one-way street. Spaniards, often forced by circumstance, rarely hesitated to eat indigenous products. Corn and some byproducts of carob and *chañar* (such as the beverages *aloja* and *patay*) were among the first such foods. Many of the early Tucumán colonists had previous experience in Peru and so were already familiar with Andean tubers and quinoa.

The Spanish Conquest of Tucumán

The first Spanish conqueror to pass fleetingly through the region was Diego de Almagro in 1545, on his way to Chile from Peru. The first incursion with real objectives of conquest was organized by Captain Diego de Rojas in 1552 and was undertaken the following year.

The Spanish invasion of Argentina's northwest was conditioned by previous events in Peru. During the time of Pizarro, the Peruvian colonies had lived in a constant state of turmoil. Unclaimed and unassigned land in Peru quickly became too scarce to absorb the numerous would-be conquistadores. The resulting commotion made colonial rulers eager to unburden the colony of its politically uncontrollable elements. In effect, they sent the most boisterous adventurers to claim the hinterlands, including the far inland Andes. Because of this "spillover" pattern, northwest Argentinian conquest chronology lags 15 to 20 years behind the early or Pizarran history of Spaniards in the Andes. Until the definitive founding of the city of Santiago del Estero in 1553, Spanish settlement had not really begun in any permanent way anywhere in the area.

Early, more-or-less adventurist, military incursions included that of Diego de Rojas. Rojas' companions included Felipe Gutiérrez and Nicolás de Heredia. This party traversed the Quebrada de Humahuaca and the valleys of Calchaquí (separating in Chicoana into two groups). Rojas met his death in Santiago del Estero during combat with the natives. Subsequent political discord in the expedition led to a retreat back to Peru.

Heredia and Mendoza managed to reach the remains of the fort founded by Cabot in 1527 on the Carcarañá River. But because it seemed useless to continue toward the already established city of Asunción del Paraguay (1537), they decided to go back to Peru. They finally arrived in 1546, nearly 3 years after they had left. This first expedition, though a political failure, afforded Spaniards a better knowledge of the terrain and the difficulties that would confront them later.

The "Pacifier" Pedro de La Gasca first consolidated crown power by pounding down the Pizarros' and other would-be feudal leaders' factional armies, then found himself facing the same problem that Vaca de Castro had confronted a decade earlier: How to get rid of all those restless soldiers? This led to a new expedition to Tucumán. Juan Núñez de Prado had charge, starting out in 1549 with 200 men, many of them veterans of Rojas' expedition versed in knowledge of the route to Tucumán. This expedition produced the first Spanish settlements in the Tucumán territory. Jurisdictional conflicts with the governor of Chile, Pedro de Valdivia, lasted for nearly 15 years, until a royal decree of 1563 definitively established the region as independent from Chile.

Only the towns that were being established in the part of Cuyo east of the Andean range remained within Chilean jurisdiction: Mendoza in 1561, San Juan de la Frontera in 1562, and later, probably in 1594, San Luis de la Punta, in the central mountain ranges. Until the eighteenth century the Cuyo region, in spite of its intense economic contacts with the Tucumán area and the Río de la Plata, was formally a dependency of Santiago de Chile.

Santiago del Estero was founded in 1553 as one of several Spanish "cities," but it was the only one to survive a series of attacks then sweeping Tucumán. Santiago del Estero played a role in Tucumán similar to that of Asunción in Paraguay and upper and lower Paraná: It was the "mother city" from whence the Spaniards ventured out to found other towns in the succeeding decades.

Colonial Tucumán: The Potosí Road and the "Frontier"

Beyond Santiago del Estero a series of very humble Spanish settlements survived because of their relations with the mining areas of upper Peru, and especially with the silver-mining dynamo, Potosí. Connections between the Tucumán frontier and the mining center intensified after the 1570s, fanned by a silver production boom. Technological advances – namely, the amalgam process introduced in Potosí during Viceroy Toledo's term – led to a substantial increase in silver production, and thus both increased Potosí's attractiveness and polarized the mining industry in the whole Alto Peru region. This had repercussions that reached as far as Tucumán and the Río de La Plata.

Besides primary orientation toward the mines in what would later be Bolivia, two other elements contributed to the economic rhythm of the initial colonial period in Tucumán: relations with Chile, and connection to the Río de La Plata river system and from there to the Atlantic. These early Spanish nuclei molded Tucumán's character by organizing a corridor for many different mercantile currents. Human bearers, mule trains, and oxcarts moved the goods between these distant sites. Transportation thus became one of the main activities in which the first colonists employed Indians under the *encomienda*, as explained later.

In 1565 about fifty Spaniards left Santiago del Estero and founded San Miguel del Tucumán. In 1567 Esteco (also known as Talavera de Madrid) was established; it was moved and then abandoned a little more than a century later, in 1692, after an earthquake. These first three "cities" – really just villages – contained no more than 350 inhabitants at the end of the 1560s, according to the official "cosmographer" López de Velazco. Even these modest figures were certainly too high.

These three towns were located outside the most densely populated area of the valleys because of the Indian presence. Indigenous resistance was total and completely successful, and, as we see later, it was not quelled until the middle of the next century. Spaniards attacked the valley groups from a base in the plains of Santiago. This pattern of conquest, by now well established, heightened conflicts between the inhabitants of the lowlands and the high valleys.

In 1573 a group of Spaniards led by Jerónimo Luis de Cabrera, governor of Tucumán, built the city of Córdoba de la Nueva Andalucía in the central mountainous area. In time it replaced Santiago del Estero as the most important trade town in Tucumán. In the center of the Río de la

Plata territory, the city was a true crossroads between the Atlantic, Cuyo, and northern Tucumán. Flanked on the west by an area of fertile valleys and on the south by grazing land, the city's setting virtually guaranteed its future prosperity. The expedition that met the hosts of Juan de Garay from Asunción at the Carcarañá River started out from Córdoba. This, then, was the frontier between two colonizing currents, one from Tucumán and another from Paraguay.

Indigenous peoples fiercely resisted Spanish attempts to colonize Salta. In 1582, after several failed attempts to quell this resistance, the Spanish finally established a base in the Salta Valley. There they founded the town of Lerma (later called Salta), near the Calchaquí area. Calchaquí became an important center of indigenous resistance. About 10 years later, in 1591, Todos los Santos de la Nueva Rioja was established, and the year after that, Madrid de las Juntas – which did not last long. One more city was founded during the sixteenth century on the Potosí road: The city of San Salvador was founded in 1593 in the Jujuy Valley, right at the entrance to the Quebrada de Humahuaca.

At the end of the sixteenth century, Santiago del Estero and Córdoba were the largest Spanish villages. No more than 250 "Spanish" settlers (not all of them hailed from Spain) made up the nucleated population of all these small villages; 150 of them were *encomenderos* who ruled the lives of tens of thousands of tributary Indians. The total population was somewhere between 150,000 and 270,000, depending on which of the frankly unreliable sources one accepts.

Indigenous population declined during the early colonial period. Numerous testimonies provide extensive qualitative data about demographic collapse, but as yet there are no serious quantitative studies allowing accurate estimates. One sounding, however, gives us an idea of the general population trend. According to some sources, there must have been between 80,000 and 86,000 tributary Indians in Santiago del Estero at the time of the first *reparto* or labor distribution in 1553. There were only 18,000 in 1586 and 3,358 in 1673–1674. That is, the aftermath of the *reparto* was death or flight for almost 60,000 people in only 30 years. This is a strikingly steep depletion even for the generally disastrous period of the early colony.

What do we know about white–Indian relations in the earliest period in the areas controlled by the inhabitants of the Tucumán cities? The answer is, very little. There was almost no research on this topic until about a dozen years ago, and we have had to rely in part on studies of uneven quality done more than 50 years ago. The few recent works reveal a varied and complex picture, sketched in the pages that follow.

In the previous section we noted that the *encomiendas* were based on personal service, as in Paraguay. In the Tucumán area as in Paraguay, there were two basic ways in which personal service was rendered: *mita* and *yanaconazgo. Mita* was obligatory labor served by turns. *Yanaconazgo* or bondage was more common in this region due to its proximity to Peru, where the term (often in the variant *yanaconaje*) and the practice originated.

Unlike the other regions, however, Tucumán does not seem to have suffered the system of *repartimiento de trabajo* (state-assigned compulsory labor), which was so widely applied in early colonial New Spain, Peru and, closer to Tucumán, Paraguay. Although the so-called *mita de plaza* was somewhat similar to the *repartimiento*, its impact on indigenous society was much weaker, because the former almost always consisted only of sending a few Indians each week to work at urban tasks for the colonists. It is obvious that, as in Paraguay, these systems of labor control generated considerable tensions. In addition, there was a strong tendency for some *mitayos* to become *yanaconas*, mimicking the "yanaconization" of the *mitayo* labor force in Paraguay. The effects extended beyond the *encomienda* proper, because *yanaconas* were also assigned to work for individuals other than their *encomenderos*. In this way other Spaniards gained the "right" to perpetual service from any Indian who was uprooted from his native village. This abuse violated original *encomienda* "rights."

Obviously, also as in Paraguay, war dragged people into *yanaconazgo*. Indians captured as spoils of war were assigned to perpetual servitude to their captors. This practice encouraged the raiding of indigenous villages. Simply by treating one's victims as prisoners of war one could turn them into one's own bondsmen and women. Thus non-*encomenderos* – colonists who were not granted personal service by Spanish law – had every reason to indulge in raiding indigenous villages. Moreover native "war" in reaction to the theft of people justified "reprisals." The longer indigenous resistance persisted in colonial Tucumán, the longer the raids continued in the area. This was the case even after the legal suppression of the *yanacona* system by Alfaro in 1611. As late as the middle of the eighteenth century, there was evidence that hunting expeditions for human prey continued, organized by Tucumán colonists. By this time the victims were Chaco Indians.

One of the peculiarities of Tucumán *yanaconazgo* was that in de facto practice convents and religious orders owned tributary Indians. This was prohibited by Spanish law, but rulers turned a blind eye. As for the duration of this condition, we know that there were "perpetual" *yanaconas* as in Peru, but there were also grants of *encomiendas* of *yanaconas* limited to "two lives"; that is, after a grantee's immediate heir enjoyed the grant it expired.

Little attention has been paid to one very important function of the Tucumán *yanaconas*: their role as culture brokers. As interpreters or *pobleros* (bosses resident among native households), *mita* crew chiefs, and even as unofficial catechists, bicultural natives (*ladinos*) mediated between Spaniards and Indians. While these particular *yanaconas* were often outsiders – sometimes from Peru – they might also come from within the jurisdiction. Their roles, as one might well imagine, carried a set of conflicting obligations. Many *yanaconas* readily abused their intermediary position, and often Indian rage was unleashed against them. Yet they were also potential resistance leaders. As Juan de Matienzo reminds us, *yanaconas* could "go to the Indians of the *repartimientos* and lead them in uprisings and take away their fear of the Spaniards."[12] Mediation was not an easily governed process. It became more important and also more unpredictable where *kurakas* had only weak control over the population. This was the case where *kurakazgo* itself was a colonially implanted institution.

Many Indians did become a permanent labor force for *encomiendas* and this influenced their organization into villages. In the area of Santiago del Estero, several important *encomienda*-era settlements have recently been studied. We address in some detail those of Soconcho and Manogasta, studied by Judith Farberman, and the *encomienda* of Maquijata, investigated by Juan Pablo Ferreiro. Moving on to Córdoba, our discussion centers on Quilpo, studied by Gaston Doucet.

Soconcho and Manogasta were two indigenous settlements near the Río Dulce floodplain, in the Santiago del Estero region (a few leagues south of the city). Since the early 1550s – the era of Núñez de Prado, one of the first conquerors to enter Tucumán – these two towns were the economic mainstays of their jurisdictions, and beginning with Pérez de Zurita (1558–1560), they were placed "under his majesty's crown." (That is, the expired *encomienda* was not reassigned but reverted to the crown

[12] Juan de Matienzo, *Gobierno del Perú* [1567], (Paris-Lima, 1967).

treasury.) These two communities were clearly the result of the early colonial consolidation of several hamlets of different ethnic groups who spoke a variety of languages (Tonocoté, Lule, Sanavirón, and Cacán).

These villages, from their earliest Spanish domination, were devoted to textile production based on a rich prehispanic tradition. They made coverlets, hosiery, and cotton textiles to be sold in Potosí and Chile, the two dominant markets until the beginning of the next century. Cotton was harvested in the same small villages or brought from other villages. In addition to these textiles, villages paid a variety of food products as tribute.

Strictly speaking, only males between the ages of fifteen and fifty were tributary Indians according to the 1576 *ordenanzas* of Gonzalo de Abreu. In fact, in Soconcho and Manogasta, the tributary Indians were from that bracket but the textile tribute also exploited the labor of women as spinners. Also, boys from the age of ten to fifteen were obliged to make stockings, boil resin and cotton, and do other "light work" all year long.

One interesting aspect of these villages relates to *kurakas*. Although the presence of these ethnic leaders is documented, their role was apparently considerably weaker than in the Andes. Abreu's *ordenanzas* calls the local Indians "people of little reason and obedience to their chiefs." In Soconcho and Manogasta in 1584, there were eleven "*parcialidades*" ('sectors') with their respective *kurakas*, probably a heritage from the consolidation of the different prehispanic groups. At that time the two villages had just over 800 inhabitants, and 15 percent of the tributary Indians were "absent." This is because in the first years, before the villages came under crown control, they had also paid tribute in men; that is, Indians were sent to Potosí. This tribute was one of the first elements that seriously undermined the structure of the communities. Although the villagers were theoretically direct subjects of the royal crown, local Spaniards forced them to do *mita* service anyway, on top of the spinning, weaving, and other routine productive tasks mentioned above.

Maquijata presents a different case. Located on two sites, it had one center 80 kilometers west of Santiago del Estero on the flanks of a low mountain range and another center in Alto Ancasti (today Catamarca). A multiethnic community, it straddled a typical transition zone, with intense contacts among the Chaco groups, the people of Santiago, and the farmers and herders of the mountain valleys. In 1580 the *encomendero* of Maquijata, Antonio de Mirabal, lived in far-off Mizque in upper Peru and the *encomienda* was run by a Spanish administrator. Of course, many *pobleros* lived in the village proper.

Tribute was paid mainly in textiles (sandals and stockings) and several other products gathered in the nearby hills. These local products included honey, *cebil* (*Anadenanthera macrocarpa* or *Piptadenia m.*, used to cure hides and as a hallucinogen), hemp (*Bromelia hyeronimi*, used for the soles of the sandals), a resin called "*pez*" in the sources (a byproduct of *Cercidium australe*, a leguminous plant), and a kind of *peten* (that is, tobacco, extracted from a plant known as *coro*, probably *Nicotiana alata*).

Women spun cotton used by the sandal makers and stocking makers, who were men of tributary age. Cotton had to be brought from other villages because it was not produced in the area. The market for these textile products was, of course, Potosí, and the textiles woven in Maquijata were sent there. As in Soconcho and Manogasta, Indians were sent to Potosí and Chile to work as bearers.

Quilpo, a village in Córdoba, is undoubtedly the best-known Tucumán case. Probably located in the present department of Cruz del Eje, a province of Córdoba, where its toponym is preserved, this village (the result of the relocation of several original indigenous communities) was granted in encomienda to the Soria family, one of the first colonial families of Córdoba. A detailed set of accounts from 1595–1598 provides an in-depth look at this village.

The Indians, under the *poblero*'s surveillance, had to work first and foremost producing textiles, mostly cotton, linens, and woolen cloth, which were the main elements of tribute. The quantities were small – 400 *varas* of woolen cloth and a little more than 560 *varas* of linen was the annual average (one *vara* equals 0.84 m, or 27 in.). However, by sending cloth to the markets in Potosí or Chile the *encomendero* could make a substantial profit thanks to the high demand for these products (see figures provided by Doucet and the documentary sources cited by Assadourian).

Furthermore, the Indians were also obliged to serve the *encomendero*, whether in his city house or on his nearby ranch. In addition, some of the *encomendero*'s livestock and crops were produced on land occupied by the community of Quilpo, with labor provided by his Indians. Finally, as in the other cases, the Indians worked as bearers and mule-drivers on trips to Chile and other places.

These three studies of *encomiendas* in the early period are the only ones based on continuous documentation. In all three, certain features stand out. First of all, in all these places the "villages" of the *encomienda* were regroupings of earlier indigenous communities. Here, then, the process is similar to that of establishing *reducciones* in other areas, but here it was accomplished solely through the actions of the *encomenderos* – that is, without the organized religious or governmental intervention that characterized the Andes, New Spain, and even Paraguay. The first item in Gonzalo de Abreu's ordinances (1576) strictly mandated that the *encomenderos* make their *encomendados* "settle down and build their houses together in one or two villages."

In their reorganization of the original territory, the Spanish colonists, as one might imagine, seldom attended to indigenous needs. In the case of Santiago, by hindering but not completely cutting off the Indians' access to necessary forest products and resources, they accelerated the indigenous food crisis. Carob, *chañar*, honey, "pez," *chaguar* (maguey), and other products were affected, in addition to fishing and hunting. Such resources were indispensable as foods that complemented their crops (which were always at the mercy of drought). Spanish extraction had destroyed – or at the very least, broken – down the original subsistence pattern.

For example, the case of carob points up differences between indigenous use and Spanish demands. Abreu's ordinances required that the season for harvesting carob be respected. The Indians apparently retained exclusive usufruct rights to carob trees. The carob harvest was intended to be consumed by the indigenous peoples themselves. However, carob had multiple uses, which figured prominently in the colonists' enterprises: food for the Indians while serving the *mita*, and food for domestic animals. Thus Spaniards seem to have understood early on that they could "reserve" the carob trees to feed the Indians and, at the same time, they could exchange this food for labor in their agrarian and textile operations.

Second, the three cases in question show that attrition among males was always very high. Whether we are speaking of the labor draft that sent Indians to the mining centers in what is now Bolivia, as in the first period of Soconcho and Manogasta, or of the utilization of men as bearers to Potosí and Chile, many never returned.

All three cases have a third feature in common: the function of administrators as organizers and mediators. The administrators and *pobleros (sayapayas*, according to the terminology of Abreu's ordinances) were indispensable in organizing the exploitation of the indigenous labor force, and they functioned as mediators between *encomenderos* and *enco-*

mendados. Sayapaya comes from a Quechua verb meaning 'to stand and stay'.

On the other hand a few details differentiate the three cases analyzed. In spite of the weak power of the ethnic leaders compared to the power of their counterparts in the Andes, at least in Santiago del Estero there seems to have been a denser substratum of relations within the framework of the indigenous community. This may help explain why the indigenous communities of Santiago endured so long. They were almost unique in this regard in Tucumán and in some cases survived until the end of the colonial period. These villages were constantly replenished, too, with Indians brought from other areas. Newcomers included the "denaturalized" Indians of the Calchaquí valleys. Chaco natives entered at the end of the seventeenth century and during part of the eighteenth. The Chaco immigration occurred later in Matará, one of the longest-lived Santiago communities, which endured until the nineteenth century.

By contrast in Córdoba it is evident that the old reorganized Indian settlements quickly fused with the Spanish ranches and small farms. Fusion occurred because, among other reasons, the Spanish colonists invariably located part of their agricultural operations near indigenous villages, in order to get an easy grip on the labor force assigned them. Another factor is that the prehispanic substratum seemed less consolidated in community structures and finally offered less resistance against the Spanish onslaught. In any case, these Córdoban Indian "villages" were really just tiny hamlets; one individual who visited the city of Córdoba in 1598 reported that the 476 Indians "in service" who were counted in the census belonged to eighty-two communities. Everything indicates that we are dealing here with politically formed tribes (see Chap. 21) and not cultural-linguistic ethnic groups.

In addition, many of the colonists who settled in the Córdoban valleys and mountains, as well as the San Luis mountains, were themselves quite poor. Their descendants were soon obliged to work with their own hands. The shortening of social distances created a more open environment for intense and relatively early racial mixing between Indians and colonists. Some important *encomenderos*, such as Tristán de Tejeda, did not shy away from marrying well-known mestizas.

As we have seen, the *encomienda* and *mita* systems were subject to widespread abuses. How did the crown respond to this situation? Some inspections resulted in reforms. We have already mentioned that in 1611 the *oidor* Francisco de Alfaro, sent by the Audiencia of Charcas, traveled through Tucumán to inspect the Indians in that jurisdiction. His report provides an excellent opportunity for understanding the state of interethnic relations as the seventeenth century was getting underway. Among other things the *oidor* prohibited personal service and the servitude of *yanaconas* and wrote a set of administrative guidelines to standardize the situation of the Tucumán *encomiendas* with regard to the laws of the Indies. From 1613 on *encomenderos* in most of the cities concerned, as well as their municipal councils and some Tucumán governors, presented the crown with a series of documents strongly protesting the visiting judge's actions.

Among these documents, one outstanding item written in 1613 refers to the town of Esteco/Talavera.[13] It provides an in-depth look at the situation of the subjected Indians of Tucumán. These papers document many of the procedures referred to earlier: the dispatching of Indians as bearers to Potosí, their labor on farms and agro-pastoral *estancias*, the weak presence of the *kurakas*, the persistence of dependence on carob and *chañar*, the extremely weak structure of the Indian communities (except Santiago), and the widespread use of *yanaconas* for personal service in Spanish homes and enterprises. The continued mention of all these practices shows that Alfaro's 1611 ordinances probably were not even officially implemented in Tucumán. Scarcely 2 years after his tour of inspection, the proposed reforms were already a dead issue.

Indigenous Resistance in the Calchaquí Valleys

Indigenous resistance was very strong throughout the area, as mentioned previously, which obliged the Spaniards to situate their first settlements on the low plains. It proved impossible to establish lasting settlements in the high valleys. The Spanish actions replicated the Inka conquerors' behavior a century earlier, for the Inka lords too had only partially dominated the ethnic groups of the mountain valleys. We will now examine this resistance more closely.

The valleys we refer to in particular as the Calchaquí valleys are formed by two rivers, the Calchaquí and the Santa María. Both meet in Cafayate (modern Salta). Subregions of note include the Pulares, Calchaquí, and Yocavil valleys.

[13] "Información levantada en Talavera de Madrid . . ." [1613], *Revista de la Biblioteca Nacional de Buenos Aires* 3: 11 (1939), 411–511.

These three valleys were occupied by different ethnic groups whose identification is extremely difficult and raises many doubts even today, in spite of the more detailed and careful recent studies by Ana María Lorandi and other investigators. The complex aboriginal mosaic is further complicated by later migrations, some of which resulted from the Inka conquest, especially including the presence of *mitmaq*s.

Settlements also varied widely in their relations with the European invaders: At one extreme we have the Pulares, whose behavior tended toward silent acceptance and mute reticence, and who even complied with some service to their *encomenderos*. At the other we note the resistance and open fighting of the Quilmes and Tolombones. In between we find almost every gradation. Spanish attempts to dominate all these ethnic groups were often thwarted by lack of centralized native leadership, and thus of leaders, with whom to negotiate. Whereas some ethnic groups fought one another, others maintained friendly ties sealed by marital alliances among ethnic leaders.

Post-Inka as well as prehispanic *kuraka* positions were probably transmitted through patrilineages. The *kurakas* generally associated with one another, and they deeply believed themselves to be the social superiors of "common" Indians. In this situation confederations formed sporadically among various groups as circumstances demanded, such as to quell uprisings, but leadership was generally quite dispersed.

Within a framework of general resistance, there were repeated waves of open warfare against Spain. The first great uprising took place in 1560–1563, led by Juan Calchaquí. This *kuraka* from Tolombón effectively deterred further Spanish settlement in the valleys until 1585. From then until 1630, some of the valley groups fulfilled their "obligations" to the *encomenderos* – albeit reluctantly, as we have seen.

In 1630 the "great rebellion" of the Calchaquí broke out, mobilizing most of the indigenous groups of the valleys, and it lasted until 1643. Although the Spaniards finally suppressed it and removed some groups to become *yanaconas*, they left the region as soon as the repressive campaign was over. Clearly they had realized that short of uprooting the whole population there was no prospect of controlling this region. After their withdrawal, an Andalusian adventurer named Pedro Chamijo, also called Bohórquez, appointed himself the Calchaquí "Inka" and led the last major Calchaquí attack from 1656 to 1664. Once again the indigenous people suffered defeat. They were uprooted by order of the governor, Mercado y Villacorta, and divided up among the *encomenderos* of

Salta, San Miguel del Tucumán, and La Rioja. Considerably more than a century after the promulgation of the New Laws they were finally converted into *encomendados* and forced to provide personal service.

The most warlike group, the Quilmes, was disbanded. Several hundred Quilmes had already been divided up as human chattel among élite Córdoba families, and others had fled to escape this fate. The rest were obliged to rebuild their settlement 1,200 kilometers lower, only a few leagues from the city of Buenos Aires, in the middle of the *pampa*. There they were forced into a *reducción* of less than 800 individuals, and by 1680 there were only 455 persons living in the community. The resistance had been overcome. But it had endured over 130 years since the beginning of the conquest, and it was stamped out only at the cost of practically depopulating the valleys.

THE INDIGENOUS PEOPLE OF CUYO UP TO THE ERA OF THE "WAR FRONTIER"

The Cuyo region comprises the Argentinian provinces of San Juan, Mendoza, and part of San Luis. In the prehispanic era the region was occupied by three different ethnic groups. The north-central area, extending to approximately the Diamante River, was occupied by the Huarpes. This group, in turn, was divided into three families: the northern Huarpes, or Allenticac (in present San Juan), the Millcayac Huarpes (Mendoza), and the Puntanos Huarpes (San Luis), as far as the Conlara Valley. There, as we have seen, the ethnic picture shifts to groups related to those of the central range south of the Diamante River – that is, the Puelches and the Pehuenche, who were related to the cordilleran and Patagonian peoples.

Peoples of Cuyo in the Prehispanic Era

The Huarpes, present in the area from C.E. 500, lived in hamlets of 50 to 100 inhabitants and developed fairly advanced irrigation systems – indispensable in this truly arid ecosystem. In addition to practicing agriculture based on corn, beans, quinoa, and squash, they herded llamas, hunted guanacos, and gathered carob. The Inka presence began a little more than half a century before the European invasion. It seems to have been important throughout the area; it is manifest in the diffusion of llama herding, as well as the adoption of the Quechua language by some Huarpes groups.

Our discussion of relations between the Huarpes and Spaniards centers in the Mendoza area, about which we know the most, thanks to María Rosario Prieto's excellent studies. In the modern Mendoza area, there are three morphologically contrasting regions: in the west, mountains; in the south, the wedge-shaped volcanic region called Payunia; and in the center and east, the plains. Lakes exist in the northeast border San Juan province.

In the mountain region we find the principal mountain range, the frontal range, and the foothills range. The first two areas were uninhabited and only considered suitable for foraging. The main types of vegetation are different species of *Stipa, Festuca* and *Poa*, all tough high-altitude grasses. The foothills, in contrast, consist of valleys, ravines and small plains. With maximum altitudes of 3,000 meters and vegetation consisting of *Stipa tenuissima* and *Adesmia* spp., they were home to a sizable animal population of guanacos, rheas, and a variety of rodents and birds. The rivers flowing from the high peaks provided generous irrigation water for the valleys. This region was first occupied by hunting and gathering groups around 2000 B.C.E.

The piedmont valleys, the habitable region par excellence, descend from the frontal mountains. The most important prehispanic settlement nuclei were located there in tectonic depressions (the Huentata Valley, the depression of the Huarpes, and the depression of the Salinas del Diamante). The alluvial cones of the rivers (from north to south: Mendoza, Tunuyán, Diamante, Atuel, and Grande) were ideal places for the development of irrigation systems and they supported moderately dense populations.

The plains area, which extends from the piedmont and the volcanic region of Payunia, supported dense growths of carob trees (*Proposis alba, P. nigra), caldenes (P. caldenia), chañares (Geoffrea decorticans*), and grasses in the sixteenth century. The carob tree was an important source of nutrition and wood in this area, just as it was for the Tucumán indigenous groups discussed previously.

Finally, the Payunia volcanic region, covered with shrubby vegetation (*solupe*, or Ephedra ochreata), offered a landscape similar to the Patagonian plateau, suitable only for pastureland. The abundance of guanaco suggests that this region was utilized intensively by the hunting groups mentioned earlier.

The Huarpes, as we have seen, preferred to live in the piedmont valleys. A few years after the Spanish arrived, most of the population appears to have been concentrated in the three valleys at the foot of the mountains, particularly in Huentata and Uco. The Huarpes of Huentata achieved a rather high degree of control over water resources. Following a dispersed settlement pattern, each hamlet had its own small irrigation canal. The Spaniards later named these canals after the chieftain of each group. Agriculture was complemented by llama herding, river and lake fishing, and guanaco hunting. Finally, the exploitation of carob, with its gamut of byproducts, completed the Huarpes' available resources.

The European Invasion

For about 10 years the Spanish unsuccessfully tried to establish a foothold in Huarpes territory. Expanding mining and agricultural activities in Chile required additional indigenous laborers, and the Spanish sought them in Cuyo. Gradually Cuyo itself took on economic importance, and laborers were put to work closer to home. The first Spaniard to pass through the region was Francisco de Villagra in 1551. Spaniards immediately began to establish *encomiendas*. In this early period, however, the *encomenderos* lived in Chile, and the Cuyo Indians were obliged to cross the Andes and travel a great distance to serve their overlords there. As we see later, this arrangement was long-lived. No stable settlement was formed until the city of Mendoza was founded 10 years later, in 1561. The following year, a new Chilean expedition founded San Juan de la Frontera, and, probably in 1594, a contingent from Cuyo established San Luis de la Punta.

Once Mendoza was founded *encomenderos* began to live on the eastern side of the mountains in future Argentina, but only until 1570. From then until 1610 the Cuyo *encomenderos* returned to the practice of living in Chile. The *encomienda* was organized, as in Paraguay and Tucumán, around personal service and the distinction between *mita* and *yanaconazgo*.

The Cuyo *mita* had however a particular regional characteristic: Tributary Indians had to perform their service on the Chilean side of the mountains, regardless of the place of residence of the *encomendero*. Generally each turn was composed of one-third of the tributaries. This led to the establishment of a complementary system between the two sides of the Andes, which lasted a century. Until the 1580s the *mitayos'* destination in Chile was the royal mines, and after the 1580s, the fields where wheat for the Lima market was raised.

How did the Spaniards secure the services of the Huarpes on the other side of the mountains? In most cases, "rental contracts" were applied, through which the *encomenderos* openly rented the indigenous laborers they controlled out to non-*encomendero* entrepreneurs. In theory the *encomenderos* divided the money they received with the Indians, in a 3:1 ratio, but they rarely adhered to this in practice.

In addition to the *mita* system there was, as in the other areas we have studied, a *yanacona* system. Indians who fell under this system lived in the Cuyo *encomenderos'* city houses or on their farms and ranches. Incipient regional agricultural production of wine, distilled liquor, and nuts linked Cuyo to the urban markets of Tucumán and the Río de la Plata delta. The growth of agriculture and trade depended on *yanaconas'* labor in the irrigated fields that the Spaniards began to build in the valleys. This was especially important after the mid–seventeenth century. Previously there seem to have been few modifications to the prehispanic irrigation systems in the Huentata Valley.

The data on the indigenous population of this region is as scanty and unreliable as that for Tucumán. In 1586 Canelas Albarrán wrote a *Descripción* of the kingdoms of Peru (in Rosenblat 1954). In it he mentions about 4,000 "subject" Indians in Mendoza and San Juan. This would give a total of 20,000 Indians by his estimates (probably including, besides Huarpes, several *encomiendas* of Puelches and Pehuenches south of Mendoza). The indigenous population declined for several reasons. Among them were the effects of the *mita* and flight from service. There was a net drain of Indians to other areas, particularly those sent to Chile who, once they arrived, stayed there. Although Albarrán discusses this phenomenon, no known statistics enable us to evaluate these population losses.

Especially from the end of the sixteenth century onward, the phenomenon of Indian flight is reported in the same sources. The tributary Huarpes fled to the southern frontier, in Puelche territory. From prehistoric times, the Huarpes, Puelches, and Pehuenches had established exchange relations in the south of Mendoza. Now these contacts were revived, through the two Spanish frontier zones – one up to the Diamante River and the other from the Diamante to Atuel, in the Spanish cattle-grazing lands. Until the widespread outbreak of war in southern Mendoza, these contacts familiarized the southern ethnic groups with European customs and livestock. The outbreak of open war on this southern frontier in 1660, converting it into a battle zone or "war frontier" for nearly a century, marks the end of our study of the Cuyo area.

CONCLUSIONS

Is it possible to draw any conclusions from such diverse experiences? In principle, some of the traits we have observed, both in the Paraguayan area and in Tucumán and Cuyo, parallel the overall process of European invasion in America. These widespread regularities included violent social disruption, rapid demographic fall, loss of resources, resistance movements, and a slow process of mutual adaptation between the indigenous peoples and the newcomers.

But as pointed out in the Introduction, the existence of systems that extracted surpluses through personal service rather than through tributes – given the lack of any such tradition in the native societies – gave a distinctive regional character to relations between the world of the invaders (whether these were European or mestizo) and the world of the area's indigenous peoples. Domination through personal service made it necessary for the *encomenderos* and/or their emissaries – administrators, stewards, strawbosses – to be present constantly in Indian villages. It is also a significant regularity that these villages were themselves results of a deep reorganization of the original habitat. Amid this wholesale alteration of both prehispanic native patterns and ideal Spanish ones, Indians entrusted in *encomienda* and their families very commonly ended up living in their colonial overlord's house or on his ranch. This factor accentuated a practical closeness between statuses which in theoretical hierarchy stood far apart. Closeness imposed by circumstance brought about an early speedup in the what was already a very early process of miscegenation. Other social factors, including exploitation of native norms of marriage, and demographic imbalances conspired to widen the spread of *mestizaje*.

Another especially important trait of regional history is rebellion. Whether we consider the northwestern area of Argentina, where armed resistance dragged on in the Calchaquí valleys until the end of the era under study, or whether we consider Paraguay, whose last indigenous rebellion took place at Arecayá in 1660, it is easy to show that some indigenous groups' attitudes were anything but submissive.

In the end the combination of early miscegenation with resistance and an intense exchange of cultural traits from natives to Spaniards and vice versa, left indelible traces. From music to dress, from diet to language, *mestizaje* is a reality with roots of unsuspected depth. If this seems obvious in a bilingual country like modern Paraguay, it is less easy to detect as one strolls through the streets of Buenos Aires. But studies of folk culture show that it is still there, a presence in material life and in the collective imagination – for example, in the persistence of Quechua as a vernacular in the country's northwestern provinces, and the presence of Quechua terminology and concepts in both rural folklore and social organization. Even now the traces of the early cultural exchange are more evident in Argentina than is commonly supposed, and certainly the indigenous struggle for survival had been successful enough to form a strategic factor in the makeup of the country through the Independence Era.[14]

BIBLIOGRAPHIC ESSAY

No contemporary text affords an overview of historic processes for the whole region because historians have specialized in northwestern Argentina or Paraguay but not both. The headings that follow are intended to help the reader through their respective literatures.

Paraguay and the Río de la Plata

On the pre- and posthispanic Guaraní, despite the years elapsed, the books of Alfred Métraux still provide an essential introduction: *La civilisation matérielle des Tribus Tupi-Guarani* (Paris, 1928); "The Guarani," in *Handbook of South American Indians*, II (Washington, 1948); and *Religion et magies indiennes d' Amérique du Sud* (Paris, 1967). The only well known English-language monograph is *Spanish-Guaraní Relations in Early Colonist Paraguay* by Elman Service (Westport, 1971). Some of Branislava Susnik's studies are also required, although sometimes difficult, reading: *El indio colonial del Paraguay. El Guarani Colonial*, I

[14] Quechua is still the usual rural language in the province of Santiago del Estero. Even a casual look at such regional lexicons as the *Diccionario de regionalismos de la Provincia de La Rioja*, published in 1961 by Julián Cáceres Freyre, shows the persistence of innumerable indigenous words in peasant vernacular – and this in La Rioja, a province that has not had any "official Indians" (i.e., government-recognized ones) for a very long time. In Susana Chertudi's 1960 collection of narratives *Cuentos folklóricos de la Argentina*, the version of the far-flung "Three Brothers" story, which is told in the old province of Tucumán, gives the youngest and smartest brother a Quechua name, the *shulca* (i.e., 'the lastborn'). And *minga*, from the Quechua term for a communal work party, remained the name of the wheat-harvesting festival in the countryside of mid–nineteenth-century Buenos Aires, a long way from the northwest Argentinian reaches of the former Inka state.

(Asunción, 1965) and *Apuntes de Etnografía Paraguaya* (Asunción, 1971). On the indigenous people of the tropical forest in general, the collected studies of Pierre Clastres are very useful: *La Société contre l'État* (Paris, 1974), also available in English as *Society Against the State* (New York, 1987), and *Récherches d'anthropologie politique* (Paris, 1980). On religious topics specifically the reader should consult Hélène Clastres, *La Terre Sans Mal. Le prophétisme tupi-guarani* (Paris, 1974), recently translated as *The Land-Without-Evil. Tupí-Guaraní Prophetism* (Urbana and Chicago, 1995), and Judith Shapiro, "From Tupá to the land without evil: The Christianization of Tupi-Guarani cosmology," *American Ethnologist* 14 (1987), 126–139.

The best current study on the dispersion of plant and animal species, for Paraguay as well as for Tucumán and Cuyo, is that of Angel Palermo, *Innovación agropecuaria en el mundo indígena colonial de la Argentina* (Buenos Aires, in press).

The early periods of colonial Paraguay have received considerable attention. On the subject of interethnic relations, see Maxime Haubert, "Indiens et Jesuites au Paraguay, rencontre de deux messianismes," *Archives de Sociologie des Religions* 27 (1969), 119–133. There are two important studies by Louis Necker, "La réaction des Indiens Guarani à la Conquête espagnole du Paraguay, un des facteurs de la colonisation de l'Argentine à la fin du XVIe. siècle," *Bulletin de la Société Suisse des Américanistes* 38 (1974), and *Indiens Guarani et chamanes franciscains. Les premières réductions du Paraguay (1580–1800)* (Paris, 1979). Also on this topic see Juan Carlos Garavaglia, *Mercado interno y economía colonial* (México DF, 1983), and Florencia Roulet, "Dos episodios tempranos de resistencia guaraní al orden colonial: los levantamientos de Aracaré y Tabaré (1542–1543)," *Cuadernos Americanos* 20 (1990), 205–228. The foundation for our analysis of the Jesuit *reducciones* is Juan Carlos Garavaglia's "I Gesuiti del Paraguay: utopia e realtà," *Rivista Storica Italiana* 93 (1981), 269–314. The Spanish version is in *Economía, sociedad y regiones* (Buenos Aires, 1987). On indigenous leadership, see *Ava y Karai: Ensayos sobre la frontera Chiriguana, siglos XVI–XX* by Thierry Saignes (La Paz, 1990).

The section on the pre- and posthispanic demography of Paraguay was adapted from William Denevan, "The aboriginal population of Amazonia," in W. Denevan (ed.), *The Native Population of the Americas in 1492* (Madison, Wisconsin, 1976); Pierre Clastres, *La Société contre l'État* (also available in English as *Society Against the State*); Juan Carlos

Garavaglia, *Mercado interno y economía colonial*; and Warren Dean, "Las poblaciones indígenas del litoral brasileño de São Paulo y Río de Janeiro. Comercio, esclavitud, reducción y extinción," in Nicolás Sánchez Albornoz (ed.), *Población y mano de obra en América Latina* (Madrid, 1985).

Primary sources on Paraguay quoted in the text are Domingo Martínez de Irala's "Relación" [1556] in Enrique de Gandía, *Historia de la conquista del Río de la Plata y del Paraguay, 1535–1556* (Buenos Aires, 1932), and Martínez de Irala's "Ordenanzas" [1556], in R. de la Fuente Machain, *El gobernador Domingo Martínez de Irala* (Buenos Aires, 1939). The original 1567 German of Ulrich Schmidl (spelled Schmidel in some editions) is *Warhafftige und liebliche Beschreibung etlicher fürnemen Indianischen Ladtschafften un Insulen* . . . , and the best Spanish version is E. Wernicke's *Crónica del viaje a las regiones de la Plata, Paraguay y Brasil* (Buenos Aires, 1948). Martín Barco de Centenera's book, *Argentina Y Conquista Del Rio De la Plata, Con Otros Acaecimientos de los Reynos del Peru, Tucumán y estado del Brasil*, was first published in Lisbon in 1602. (It must not be confused with the similarly titled work of Rui Díaz de Guzman, *Historia Argentina del descubrimiento, población y conquista de las provincia del Rio de la Plata*, cited in the text; the latter was compiled in 1612 and first published in Buenos Aires in 1835). The *Ordenanzas* of Ramírez de Velazco [1597] and of Hernandarias [1603] were published by J. C. García Santillán in *Legislación sobre indios del Río de la Plata en el siglo XVI* (Buenos Aires, 1928). The Ordenanzas of Céspedes Xeria [1629] were published by Jaime Cortesão in the *Annaes do Museu Paulista*, II (São Paulo, 1926), 208–214. An excellent collection of chronicles and documents of the earliest period covering the whole Río de la Plata area (including Tucumán) is that of José Torre Revello in *Documentos históricos y geográficos relativos a la conquista y colonización rioplatense*, I, *Memorias y relaciones históricas y geográficas* (Buenos Aires, 1941).

The following classic authors who were also cited can be considered primary sources: André Thevet, *Singularités de la France Antarctique* [1557] (Paris, 1878); Jean de Léry, *Histoire d'un voyage faict en la terre du Brésil* (La Rochelle, 1578), ably translated as *History of a Voyage to the Land of Brazil. Otherwise called America* (Berkeley, 1990); Claude d'Abbeville, *Histoire de la mission des Péres Capucins en l'isle de Maragnan et terres circonvoisines* (Paris, 1614); Yves d'Evreux, *Voyage dans le Nord du Brésil, fait durant les années 1613 et 1614* [1615] (Leipzig/Paris, 1864); Antonio Ruiz de Montoya, *Conquista espiritual hecha por los religiosos de la Compañía de Iesus en las Provincias del Paraguay, Uruguay y Tape*

(Madrid, 1639); Francisco Xarque, *Insignes missioneros de la Compañía de Jesús en la provincia del Paraguay* (Pamplona, 1687); and Lodovico Antonio Muratori, *Il cristianesimo felice nelle missioni de'padri della Compagnia di Gesú nel Paraguai* (Venice, 1743).

The monumental work by Father Pedro Lozano, *Historia de la conquista del Paraguay, Río de la Plata y Tucumán*, in five volumes, was written at the end of the first half of the eighteenth century; published in Buenos Aires between 1873 and 1875, it is one of the most valuable sources for any analysis of the period for both Paraguay and Tucumán. Father Antonius Sepp's important writings were originally published in German in 1696 – his chronicle of journeys – and in Latin in 1709. Spanish versions of his works are published in *Relación de viaje a las misiones jesuíticas* (Buenos Aires, 1971), and *Continuación de las labores apostólicas* (Buenos Aires, 1973); some unpublished work appears in *Jardín de flores paracuario* (Buenos Aires, 1974). José María Blanco included numerous documents of particular relevance to the first phase of the *reducciones* in his *Historia documentada de la vida y gloriosa muerte de los Padres Roque González de Santa Cruz, Alonso Rodríguez y Juan del Castillo de la Compañía de Jesús, mártires del Caaró e Yjuhí* (Buenos Aires, 1929). The documentation in the Archivo General de Indias on this topic is enormous. The best guide remains the work begun by Pablo Pastells, S. J., *Historia de la compañía de Jesús en la Provincia del Paraguay (Argentina, Paraguay, Uruguay, Perú, Bolivia y Brasil)* (Madrid, 1912/1948).

Prehispanic and Colonial Tucumán

A valuable general reference is the work of Alberto Rex González and José A. Pérez, *Historia Argentina, Argentina indígena, vísperas de la conquista* (Buenos Aires, 1976). For a more recent treatment, the reader may consult the manual by Marta Ottonello and Ana María Lorandi: *Introducción a la arqueología y etnología. Diez mil años de Historia Argentina* (Buenos Aires, 1987), and the work of R. Raffino, *Poblaciones indígenas en Argentina. Urbanismo y proceso social precolombino* (Buenos Aires, 1988). A useful, brief synthesis is Alberto Rex González' article, "Cincuenta años de arqueología del noroeste argentino (1930–1980): apuntes de un casi testigo y algo de protagonista," *American Antiquity* 50:3 (1985), 505–517.

On colonial Tucumán there are a few specific studies. On the *puna* area, see G. Madrazo, *Hacienda y encomienda en los Andes. La Puna argentina bajo el Marquesado de Tojo, siglos XVII–XVIII* (Buenos Aires, 1982), and S. Sánchez and G. Sica, "La frontera oriental de Humahuaca y sus relaciones con el Chaco," *Bulletin de l'Institut Français d'Études Andines* 19:2 (1990), 469–497. On this same theme, see Gastón Doucet, "Acerca de los churumatas con particular referencia al antiguo Tucumán," *Revista Histórica* 17: 1 (993), 21–91; see also Juan Pablo Ferreiro, "El Chaco en los Andes. Churumatas, Paypayas, Yalas y Ocloyas en la etnografía del Oriente jujeño," *Población y Sociedad* (Tucumán) 2 (1994), 3–23, and Daniel Santamaría, "El campesinado indígena de Jujuy en el siglo XVII. Un estudio sobre las formas de integración étnica en situación colonial," *Proyecto NOA* 3 (Seville, 1992).

On Santiago del Estero, a valuable study by Juan Pablo Ferreiro is "Encomienda, tributos y sociedad. El caso de Maquijata, 1600–1603," in Ana María Lorandi (ed.), *Charcas y el Tucumán. La colonia en los siglos XVI al XVIII* (Buenos Aires, 1997). Two articles by Judith Farberman are useful: "Indígenas, encomenderos y mercaderes: los pueblos de indios santiagueños durante la Visita de Luján de Vargas (1693),"*Anuario* del Instituto de Estudios Histórico-Sociales (IEHS), 6 (Tandil, 1991), and "Migrantes y soldados. Los pueblos de indios de Santiago del Estero en 1786 y 1813," *Cuadernos del Instituto Ravignani* 4 (Buenos Aires, 1992), as well as her doctoral dissertation, *Famiglia ed emigrazione: Santiago del Estero, 1730–1820*, Scuola Superiore di Studi Storici, Università degli Studi, Repubblica di San Marino (1995). These last two works, although focused on a later period, trace the history of Santiago communities back to the conquest.

On the area in general and the region that is now the province of Córdoba, there are several articles by Gaston Doucet in advance of his forthcoming thesis: "Notas sobre el yanaconazgo en el Tucumán," *Revista de Investigaciones Jurídicas* 6:6 (Mexico, 1982); "Los réditos de Quilpo. Funcionamiento de una encomienda cordobesa a fines del siglo XVI (1595–1598)" *Jahrbuch für Geschichte von Staat, Wirtschaft und Gesellschaft Lateinamerikas* 23 (Cologne, 1986), 63–119. I especially recommend "En torno a la población aborigen y a las encomiendas de indios del antiguo Tucumán. Acotaciones a un libro laureado," *Revista de Indias* 47:179 (1987), 253–313. This critical essay on A. L. González's book, *La encomienda en Tucumán* (Seville, 1984), examines in great detail the various population statistics in the text and includes an exhaustive review of the traditional bibliography. The question of population has been also analyzed by Janet Pyle in "A reexamination of aboriginal population estimates for Argentina," in Denevan's edited volume, *The Native Population of the Americas in 1492*. Josefina Piana de Cuestas, in *Los indígenas de Córdoba bajo el régimen colonial, 1570–1620* (Córdoba, 1992), offers a complete picture of this crucial period in Córdoba.

The Calchaquí valleys and their rebellions have been studied mainly by Ana María Lorandi and her associates. See Ana María Lorandi and Roxana Boixadós, "Etnohistoria de los valles calchaquíes en los siglos XVI y XVII," in *Runa* 17/18 (1987/1988), 263–419; and Ana María Lorandi and Cora Virginia Bunster, "Reflexiones sobre las categoriás semánticas en las fuentes del Tucumán colonial. Los valles calchaquíes," in the same issue of *Runa* on pages 221–263. Boixadós other works include: Roxana Boixadós and Miguel Angel Palermo, "Transformaciones en una comunidad desnaturalizada: los quilmes, del valle Calchaquí a Buenos Aires," *Anuario* of the IEHS, 6 (Tandil, 1992), and Roxana Boixadós, "Indios rebeldes – indios amigos. Los famatinas en la sociedad colonial riojana," in Ana María Lorandi (ed.), *Charcas y el Tucumán. La colonia en los siglos XVI al XVIII* (Buenos Aires, in press). See also Ana E. Schaposchnik, "Aliados y parientes. Los diaguitas rebeldes de Catamarca durante el gran alzamiento," mimeograph (Buenos Aires, 1994). On the Tucumán-area uprisings, see R. Cruz "La construcción de identidades étnicas en el Tucumán colonial: Los amaichas y los tafíes en el debate sobre su 'verdadera estructuración étnica'," in *Relaciones* [journal of the Sociedad Argentina de Antropología, Buenos Aires] 18 (1995), 65–92.

Of course, the pioneering studies of Carlos Sempat Assadourian are indispensable for any analysis of relations between this area and the mining centers of Alto Perú. See his *El sistema de la economía colonial. Mercado interno, regiones y espacio económico* (Lima, 1982). Some interesting aspects of the relation between *encomendero* elites and the Tucumán church are covered in J. Marchena Fernández, "Señores de indios y pastores de almas: encomenderos y frailes en el Tucumán del siglo XVII," in *Proyecto NOA* 1 (Seville, 1992).

Cuyo

On the prehispanic period in Cuyo, see Ottonello and Lorandi's *Introducción a la arqueología y etnología . . .*, 136–138, and Catalina Michelli,

"Los huarpes protohistóricos," Instituto de Investigaciones Arqueológicas y Museo, Universidad Nacional de San Juan (1983).

The later period, especially for Mendoza, has been studied by María del Rosario Prieto and her associates in the following works: "Enfoque diacrónico de los cambios ecológicos y de las adaptaciones humanas en el NE árido mendocino," in collaboration with Elena M. Abraham de Vázquez, in *Cuadernos del CEIFAR* 8 (1981) 109–139; "Relación entre clima, condiciones ambientales y asentamientos humanos en la provincia de Mendoza en los siglos XVI, XVII y XVIII," in *Revista de Historia de América* 100 (1985), 79–118; "Consecuencias ambientales derivadas de la instalación de los españoles en Mendoza en 1561," in collaboration with Carlos F. Wuillod, *Cuadernos de Historia Regional*, Universidad Nacional de Luján, Argentina, 2:6 (1986), 3–35; and "La frontera meridional mendocina durante los siglos XVI y XVII," *Xama* 2 (Mendoza, 1989), 117–131.

The primary sources relating to Tucumán and Cuyo quoted in the text are "Relación anónima de una expedición a la comarca de Córdoba,"[c. 1573], in Ricardo Jaimes Freyre, *El Tucumán colonial (Documentos y mapas del Archivo de Indias)*, I (Buenos Aires, 1915), 79–82; "Ordenanzas" of Gonzalo de Abreu (1576), in Roberto Levillier, *Gobernación del Tucumán: Papeles de gobernadores en el siglo XVI. Documentos del Archivo de Indias*, II (Madrid, 1920), 32–45; "Relación" of Pedro Sotelo de Narváez (1582), in R. Jaimes Freyre, *El Tucumán colonial . . .*, 85–100; and "Discripción de todos los reinos del Perú . . ." by Juan Canelas Albarrán (1586), in Angel Rosenblat, *La población indígena y el mestizaje en América*, I (Buenos Aires, 1954), 260–262 – this is not a complete transcription, as the document is still unpublished; the original is in the Biblioteca Nacional in Madrid [Ms. 3178].

Among the many collections of documents on Tucumán, only a few are important for the early period. Roberto Levillier edited several works on the governance of Tucumán – namely, *Gobernación del Tucumán: Probanzas de méritos y servicios de los conquistadores*, 2 vols. (Madrid, 1919/1920); *Gobernación del Tucumán: Papeles de los gobernadores en el siglo XVI*, as before; and *Papeles eclesiásticos del Tucumán*, 2 vols. (Madrid, 1926). Father Antonio Larrouy also edited a variety of documents: *Documentos del Archivo de Indias para la historia del Tucumán*, 2 vols. (Buenos Aires and Tolosa, 1923–1927); see also Manuel Lizondo Borda, *Documentos coloniales relativos a San Miguel de Tucumán y a la gobernación del*

Tucumán, 6 vols. (Tucumán, 1935–1949). Numbers 11 and 12 of Volume 3 of the *Revista de la Biblioteca Nacional de Buenos Aires*, 1939, contain many of the Tucumán documents relating to Alfaro's tour of inspection and to the reactions of the colonists, as well as documents relating to the Jesuit *reducciones* in Paraguay.

15

THE COLONIAL CONDITION IN THE QUECHUA-AYMARA HEARTLAND (1570–1780)

THIERRY SAIGNES[1]

In the early years of the twentieth century, scientists in the Tarapacá desert of Chile's Pacific shore found the mummified corpse of a colonial native nobleman, a *cacique.* They were able to date the mummy precisely because he carried in a pouch a 1680 document certifying that the deceased had paid "the papal bull for the holy crusade." This tax entitled those who paid it to indulgences that would shorten their stay in Purgatory. To be buried in an ancestor cave according to the ancient rites, it seems, colonial Andeans felt one also had to obtain the promise of Christian salvation. This idea marks one of the stages in the long process of integration that took place in the course of hispano–Andean colonial coexistence. The same cultural complexities that the dead man's family apparently envisioned in terms of an Andean-Christian afterlife, make it hazardous to analyze the colonial experience of daily life. This chapter concerns the transformations experienced by the indigenous Andean populations from Pasto (in southern Colombia) to Tucumán (in northwestern Argentina), from the reforms of Viceroy Francisco de Toledo (1569–1581) to the Túpac Amaru II wars of 1780 (see Map 15.1). Toward the end of this era, most of these peoples were still Aymara, Quechua, and Pukina speakers, and they still lived in recognized native polities – about 1.5 million persons, 400,000 of whom paid tribute in 1750 – but they had become bearers of a culture and social organization so transformed that the depths of change still resist historiographic conceptualization.

A thorough bibliographical survey shows that despite innovative recent work we still know very little about most of the stages in this long-term

[1] The late Thierry Saignes provided a draft manuscript of this chapter. Translation and editing were carried out posthumously. The translation, by Elborg Forster, was edited by Frank Salomon. The draft had only minimal indications of footnoting, which have been followed out as much as possible.

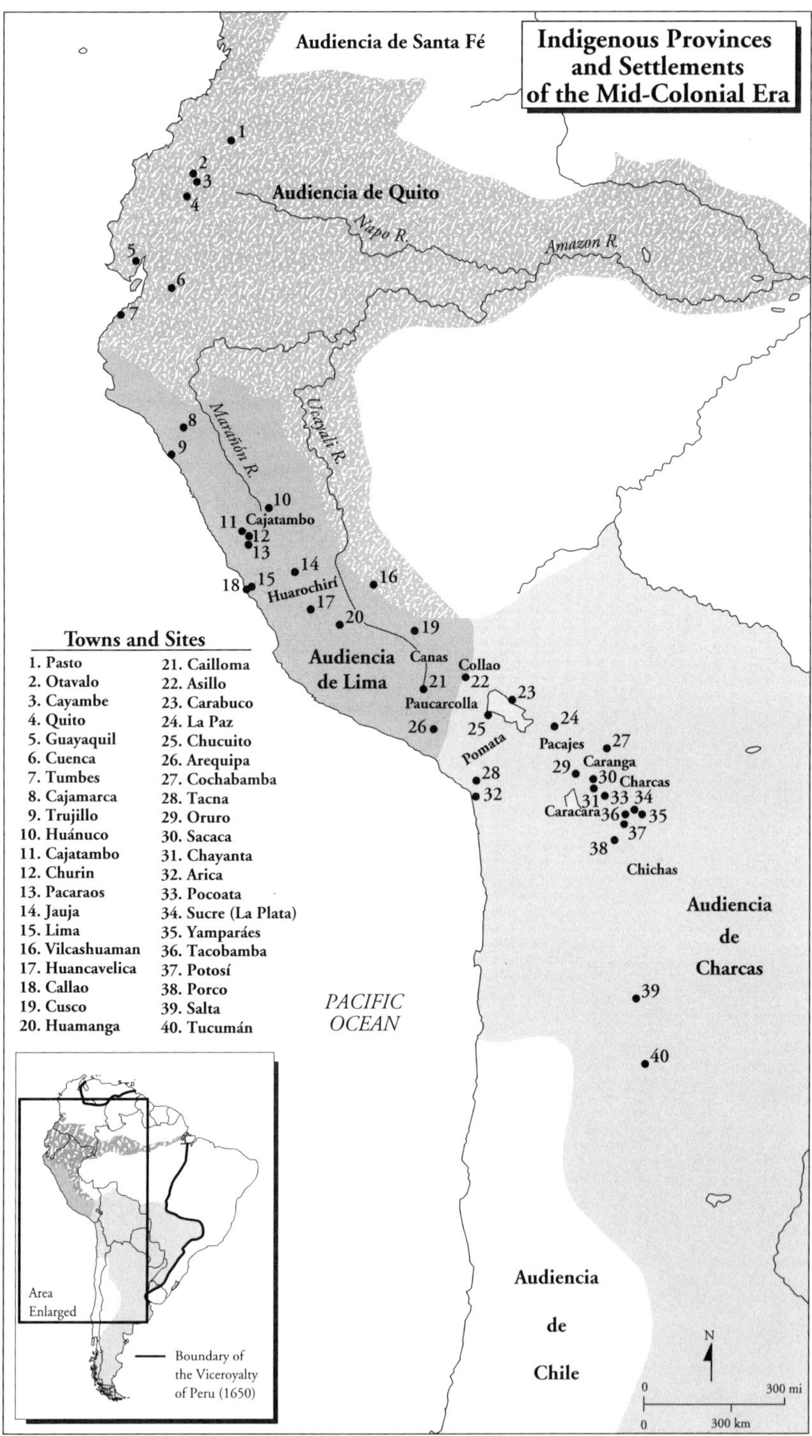
Indigenous Provinces and Settlements of the Mid-Colonial Era
Audiencia de Santa Fé
Audiencia de Quito
Napo R.
Amazon R.
Marañón R.
Ucayali R.
Cajatambo
Huarochirí
Audiencia de Lima
Canas
Collao
Paucarcolla
Pomata
Pacajes
Caranga
Charcas
Caracara
Chichas
Audiencia de Charcas
PACIFIC OCEAN
Audiencia de Chile
Towns and Sites
1. Pasto
2. Otavalo
3. Cayambe
4. Quito
5. Guayaquil
6. Cuenca
7. Tumbes
8. Cajamarca
9. Trujillo
10. Huánuco
11. Cajatambo
12. Churin
13. Pacaraos
14. Jauja
15. Lima
16. Vilcashuaman
17. Huancavelica
18. Callao
19. Cusco
20. Huamanga
21. Cailloma
22. Asillo
23. Carabuco
24. La Paz
25. Chucuito
26. Arequipa
27. Cochabamba
28. Tacna
29. Oruro
30. Sacaca
31. Chayanta
32. Arica
33. Pocoata
34. Sucre (La Plata)
35. Yamparáes
36. Tacobamba
37. Potosí
38. Porco
39. Salta
40. Tucumán
Area Enlarged
Boundary of the Viceroyalty of Peru (1650)
N
0
300 mi
0
300 km

Map 15.1

development, from the thematic, as from the regional point of view. Hence any synthesis of the colonial history of the Andean world is bound to be premature. The outline formulated here is provisional and attempts to trace only those few trends that appear to be most significant. It proposes a global explanatory framework at some expense of nuance and caution.

The central thesis can be stated in a few words. Once the overarching integrity of Andean hierarchical control had been destroyed (especially upper-level organizations like the Inka and macroregional states and cults), domestic units took over many control functions. Domestic economy came to ensure economic coherence by handling mercantile and nonmercantile exchanges and by sustaining social cohesion. Household and small groupings achieved this by imposing their own logic upon colonial institutions via a double strategy. On one hand, they reconstituted larger kinship networks through baptismal sponsorship and the solidarity of coresidence, reinforced by municipal offices and religious confraternities. On the other, domestic units also ensured cultural cohesion by bringing colonial Christianity into line with prehispanic cults, an amalgamation they judged necessary to maintain general fertility and cosmic order. In the pages that follow, the term "household" is used interchangeably with "domestic unit." But it pays to remember that Andean domestic units often exceeded the usual range of the modern word "household," either by being multigenerational, or collaterally extended, or by keeping more than one home.

Over the two post-Toledan centuries, three areas of action manifest these processes: the crisis of ethnic mediation marked by the early ascendancy and gradual failure of the *caciques*; the restoration of social cohesion through markets and migrations; and the creation of a colonial Andean culture with specific material, artistic, and religious aspects. The apparent clarity of this schema cannot, however, mask the fact that colonial native culture was cobbled together out of Andean and European elements with unending dissensus and ambiguity. It lacks the attributes traditionally associated with the phrase "a culture": internal consistency and outer boundedness. The result was an "Indianness" that over time hardly conformed to the conceptions of those who had initiated it.

THE CRISES OF ETHNIC MEDIATION

In the prehispanic Andes, the chiefs of politically structured ethnic units were called *qhápaq* in Pukina, *mallku* in Aymara, and *kuraka* in

Quechua (colonial spellings vary). They had the power to mediate between their peoples and the exterior world, both in religious and sociopolitical matters. Their powers were analogous to those of the "sacred kings" of Africa. Inka domination reinforced their political function, which the imperial state used for its own purposes, but it played down their magical responsibilities for collective health and prosperity. These the Inka entrusted to a state-run or subsidized clergy.

Perceived by the Spanish as "native lords," and soon designated by the Taïno name *caciques*, early colonial chiefs suffered the effects of ancient tensions among social segments (e.g., descent groups) that Spaniards had reactivated by civil wars and the division of the territory into *encomiendas*. From the start the leaders called *caciques* sought to make use of the new imperial structure Spain instituted. The Spanish ideas of *fuero* (distinctive legal rights proper to corporative social groups), and of inheritable rank linked to ancient local dominion, gave toeholds for relegalizing the power that native lords had at first defended by creating ad hoc military alliances with Europeans (see Chap. 12). Indigenous authorities headed hierarchically structured local collectivities that Spaniards saw as small sovereignties ("Inkas, all of them"). At the same time, for their subjects, local lords functioned as mediators before external powers such as the colonial state and the forces of nature. As Spanish dominion solidified, especially by the 1560s, leaders faced opposing demands: on the one hand, they were called upon to ensure the reproduction of the community. On the other, they had to fulfill Spaniards' increasingly pressing demands for native workers and for the Christianization of "the people called Indians." The period of civil war among Spaniards, ending in 1548, and the subsequent years of administrative indecision, had afforded a respite. But half a lifetime after the Spanish invasion, new forces appeared on the scene: fast-growing cities full of Spaniards and Africans, Christian (especially Jesuit) missions of unprecedented militancy and ambition, and soon afterward, a viceroy arriving with a mandate to hammer down the unstandardized arrangements built up during the unstable era of invasion.

The Toledan Reforms and the Andean Peoples

In 1569 Philip II sent to Peru a new viceroy no less determined than himself to rid the crown of dependency on preexisting polities, including Inka and even local ethnic ones. Much more than earlier viceroys, Viceroy Francisco de Toledo, a scion of the great nobility, meant to be literally the king's alter ego. He meant to rein in the world-be feudal Spanish elites that battened on *encomienda* grants. Neither would sovereignty be shared in any measure with Indians. Toledo cut off the long-standing parleys with the Inka resistance, which had fought on since 1532 from its redoubt at Vilcambamba. In 1572 Toledo's armies captured and executed the last sovereign Inka, Túpac Amaru I. But how could he wring from Indians the wealth that Spain desperately needed for its wars against Islam and Protestantism? How could he insert "Indians" irreversibly into the orthodoxy of a church and a state they would never even see? From the viceroy's viewpoint, three issues were crucial: setting up a tribute apparatus that would extract wealth from native societies without at the same time wrecking their ability to feed themselves and Spaniards; mobilizing the huge labor force needed to mine the Andes' silver; and implanting among barely Catholicized people a rigorous, self-reproducing system of parish governance such as the Council of Trent had mandated.

No bureaucrat was ever more intensely research-minded than Toledo, who spent 1570–1575 in a massive tour of inspection and commissioned lawyers and churchmen to compile a history of Inka "tyranny." The native dynasties reclaimed from Inka usurpation were to be recognized as dependents of the crown and, through the "royal patronage," the Church. "In Vilcashuaman Toledo symbolically sat himself in the throne atop the magnificent sun temple built after the Inka conquest of Huamanga"[2] not to symbolize continuity, but to demonstrate the irreversible replacement of society's Inka apex. Influenced by plans of Juan de Matienzo, Toledo implemented a vast program of "reduction." Regrouping about 1.5 million "Indians" into 600 *reducciones* during the 1570s and 1580s, the Toledan regime required each community to install novel governmental institutions (especially the *cabildo* or town council) under the supervision of *corregidores* or district governors of natives. The creation of a non-kin based and nontraditional authority to rival ethnic lordship was intentional. "Reduction" also involved proposals, sometimes carried out, to uproot pre-Inka and Inka *mitmaq* (extraterritorial) colonies and to dismantle the "vertical" production outliers that supplied goods of diverse ecological origin. At the same time – a time when the

[2] Steve J. Stern, *Peru's Indian Peoples and the Challenge of Conquest: Huamanga to 1640* (Madison, 1982), 77.

native labor force was shrinking and the Spanish population rocketing upward – these forced resettlements

> established the levies that either channeled goods and labor directly to members of European society or else forced the Indians to offer their goods and their labor time on the European market in order to meet the demands imposed upon them. The latter tactic provided a general subsidy to the members of European society who were unable to obtain a direct subsidy from the royal authorities.[3]

Native lord would become responsible, too, for supplying regularized rotating quotas of forced laborers to serve the huge mines at Potosí (Bolivia), Huancavelica (Peru), and many lesser ones. Enforcing the sacraments and helping uproot the ancient deities called *huacas* were also responsibilities of local rulers. They were encouraged to adopt Spanish mores (except for arming themselves with steel and gunpowder) but charged at the same time to enforce sumptuary laws against mass hispanization. Along with these burdens, the Toledan regime would bring tempting commercial opportunities both legal and illegal; but at first, when the program was still malleable, it most of all brought discord about how to implement absolutism in America, and what native political authority could mean under it.

Structural Ambivalence: Old and New Forms of Legitimacy

Assembling *ayllus*, the ancient corporate kin groups that shared landholdings and putative ancestry, into "Indian towns," was at first largely a brute-force operation involving gross distortion of political traditions. Old-style *caciques* (called *kuraka* in Quechua) had typically been spokesmen of the highest-ranked *ayllu*, authorized to speak for the community as a whole. The Spanish project involved modifying the kin-based model of politics toward one in which state interests could override, or at least counterbalance, local dynastic process. One part of this revision was the heightening of a concentrated territorial center (where a small number of Spaniards such as priests and visiting judges could oversee a large number of natives). Apart from the descent matrix, control of the spatial center would be the future crux of social control. (Older Andean schemes had possessed ceremonial centers, but the *ayllus*

[3] Karen Spalding, *Huarochirí, an Andean Society Under Inca and Spanish Rule* (Stanford, 1984), 159.

tended to reside dispersed over far-flung landholdings.) Organized on a drastically simplified and uniformized Castilian-style grid pattern, the new settlements were to look inward onto the parish church, council house, and the local lord's residence. Authority was to be visibly divided at its center, with *cacicazgo* and council working side by side. Toledo also decreed that the authority of the *caciques* was to be restricted to rural settlements and that they should be allotted fixed salaries and a limited number of subordinates but never allowed to develop their regimes idiosyncratically.

As the Toledan regime took shape, the crown was for a time unsure about what place to assign the ethnic chiefs in the tributary system. The core issue was whether the *ayllu* should remain an impenetrable social unit, owing its tribute collectively to the *cacique* and obedient to his decisions about implementing it within Andean rules of political economy, or whether the *cacique* was merely to be the crown's agent in enforcing a tribute assigned per capita by crown judges to household heads. In a memorandum sent to Viceroy Francisco de Toledo, the *racionero* (prebendiary) Villareal like many Spaniards echoed the opinion that *caciques*' power should be minimized, because they would only use it to rob Indians, enrich themselves, support concubines, and take over natives' properties when they died. As a remedy he proposed to place control in the hands of the rural clergy. On the other hand, there were strong arguments for letting the traditional lords run tribute administration according to Andean norms. Juan Polo de Ondegardo, an ethnographically minded lawyer specializing in "Indian" matters, warned Viceroy Toledo of the danger of "liberating" the Indians from community control as represented by the ethnic authorities. "The day we decide to count and tax all Indians individually, so that if they have paid they are no longer under the domination and authority of the caciques and under their orders, being free to go wherever they want, we will have taken away the restraint that holds them together in an orderly manner, for this is the way in which they survive and have survived before the Christians obtained these realms: if one could put this fact to the test for only one year, one would clearly see their destruction."[4]

The problem that was to haunt those who governed the viceroyalty for the next two centuries could not have been stated more succinctly.

[4] Juan Polo de Ondegardo "Relación de los fundamentos" [1571], in Carlos A. Romero (ed.), *Colección de libros y documentos referentes a la historia del Perú*, Ser. 1, vol. 3 (Lima, 1916), 180–181.

Should ethnic authorities mediate colonial power? Or should the indigenous society be administered directly?

For their own part the *caciques* made an eloquent and enticing case for the former option. At summit meetings they sought to persuade the viceroyalty that Spain would profit more by a permanent system of indirect rule. They offered a settlement of 800,000 pesos to abandon the idea of hispanicizing tribute. Although they did not win full autonomy, they convinced the touring viceroy that their support was indispensable to the fresh start he was planning. Together with the responsibility for collecting a per capita tribute and recruiting the rotating mining crews (*mita* in hispano-Quechua jargon), they obtained legitimation of considerable inheritable powers. They were to set up colonial towns but do it in part according to the pattern of the ancient ethnic jurisdictions. In addition they were given guaranteed access to lands situated in remote valleys.

In the southern Andes it was decided to create eleven "*mita* captaincies" patterned upon the pre-Inka chiefdoms or "kingdoms" of the South-Central Andes in order to mobilize the requisite number of Potosí miners from the vast area stretching from the Canas to the Chichas. The holders of these prestigious posts – who were in principle appointed for 1 year, but usually stayed on for several years – were recruited from the regional dynasties. This allowed them to reestablish a high-powered magistracy over their scattered subjects, who had been moved to different reductions and sometimes even provinces. The link between mining, with its insatiable demand for far-traveling labor, and the need for macroregional political authority to organize it, may have to do with the long survival of macroscale native polities in what is now Bolivia as compared to the more fragmented patterns of native authority emerging in the north. Over the long haul – throughout most of the period we study in this chapter – the *caciques* generally maintained their ascendancy over rival civic forms within each Andean group, albeit with declining legitimacy.

It was thus in context of an ambiguous modernization, arising out of a compromise between the crown and the Andean chiefdoms, that old ethnic and dynastic rivalries were activated in the competition for regional offices, like the *mita* captaincies or the paramount native magistracies called *alcaldías mayores de naturales*. This last office, created in 1560 to administer royal justice in minor cases, allowed the great *caciques* to circumvent the provisions by which Toledo intended to keep them out of the administration of indigenous villages. In the central Sierra and in the "kingdom of Quito," this office was highly desirable to old ruling families such as the Puentos of Cayambe (Ecuador), a lineage that owed part of its prestige to long and ferocious anti-Inka resistance near the northern Inka frontier, or the Hachos and the Hatis who built rich chiefdoms a little farther south. Some of these "social climbers" (as Spalding calls them) also wangled appointments and commercial opportunities in Spanish cities. Don Pedro de Zámbiza, a non-Inka politician who sided with Spanish invaders of Quito, made his career this way. The native elites' offensive also underlay the famous "Memorandum of Charcas" (1582), which exalted the grandeur of the confederation of Aymara-speaking warriors that ruled an enclave deep in the Bolivian highlands. In this memorandum the Ayaviri lineage of Sacaca recalls its loyal service to the Inkas and to the conquistadors, at the same time claiming a number of fiscal exemptions and honors that would place it on an equal footing with the Spanish nobility. In 1587 Fernando Ayaviri Cuisara was the first to obtain the post of *alcalde mayor de los naturales* of Potosí and Charcas. The office passed to his son Juan 10 years later.

With support from officials of the *audiencia* of Charcas, Cuisara not only prevailed over the claims of another regional leader, Juan Colque Guarachi, who had the backing of Viceroy Toledo, but also regained the preeminence that Toledo had denied him in assigning salaries and staff. (*Audiencias* were panels of governing judges appointed from Spain to rule large regions. The term was also applied to the region so ruled.) This case testifies to some noble families' emerging attachment to the new foci of regional power, the *audiencias*, in opposition to the centralizing aspirations of the court at Lima. *Caciques* learned to build power through a whole network of political support within the colonial system. Those who had strong allies could afford to oppose even *audiencias* and viceroys.

Economic initiative was another course of action. Early on the *caciques* took the lead in innovation by adopting Old World crops and techniques apt to increase productivity, diversification, and specialization. They took advantage of their pivotal position between, on one hand, the community sector, which was governed by the principles of reciprocity and redistribution, and, on the other, the Spanish market sector, where both labor and "gifts" were measured as commodities. They used the former to steer a labor force into the latter – for example, by selling the labor duty their subjects owed them to Spanish employers. Their personal gains in this domain were remarkable. The testament of 1588 of Diego Caqui, *cacique* of Tacna, reveals that in addition to arable land and shellfish gathering or fishing sites, he owned "four vineyards and a cellar to produce and store 2,000 jars of wine a year, a drove of llamas, two galleys and one barge to trade along the coast."[5] In 1598 the *caciques* of the Quirúa valleys near La Paz cultivated vast stretches of wheat, which they ground in their own mills before selling it to the corregidor. The correspondence conducted in the 1620s between Don Diego de Chambilla, the upper moiety lord of Pomatas (Lupaqa), and his attorney Pedro Mateos, a Peru-born Spaniard, allows us to see how the circulation of Andean products (camelids, hot peppers, cloth) was connected with trade and mining. "All were exchanged for cash most of which went to help Chambilla 'fulfill' his *mita*."[6]

These economic achievements needed further validation in the social and cultural sphere. *Caciques* increasingly adopted Spanish material trappings. More and more of them moved to the urban centers of the viceroyalty – Quito, Lima, Huamanga, Cusco, La Paz, Potosí, and Chuquisaca, among others – where they lived in lavish style in every respect, from housing to clothing. Plainly they meant to rival the wealthiest Spaniards. Juan Ayaviri wore "showy and costly Spanish costumes, riding on horseback escorted by slaves and servants in the town of Potosí" (1598). To be seen on horseback was a matter of asserting the quality and the merits of the indigenous nobility. The Aymoros, a family of Yampara seigneurs, lived in a "towered palace" on the main square of La Plata (Sucre). Other nobles had the coat-of-arms granted by the king of Spain chiseled above their main entrance, ate from gold or silver dishes engraved with their blazon, and had their portraits painted. One of these noblemen, Don Fernando Ayra Chinchi of Pocoata, "goes to sleep with music and ostentatiously tastes all the soups and desserts" and had his luxuries painted in gold by a painter.[7] In Quito some native noblewomen born around the time of Spanish invasion (whether of aboriginal or Inka parents) became spectacular fashion plates, working the silks of Asia and the baubles of Italy into new costumes of Andean splendor.

5 John V. Murra "Aymara Lords and Their European Agents at Potosí," *Nova Americana* 1 (1978), 233.

6 John V. Murra, "Aymara Lords and Their European Agents at Potosí," *Nova Americana* 1 (1978), 275.

7 Pedro Ramírez del Aguila, in Jaime Arana (ed.), *Noticias politicas de Indias y relacion descriptiba de la Ciudad de La Plata . . . 1639* (Sucre, 1978).

What are we to make of the sumptuous *mise en scène* of the *caciques* amid their colonial decor? Certainly they saw their sumptuary rivalry with Spanish elites as a way to uphold Andean political prestige. By no means did they mean to loosen their grip on traditional Andean symbolic and cultural instruments of domination. However, beyond sumptuary choices, combining Andean with Spanish rules of the game proved problematic. Native nobles' quest for recognition through high office opened a breach in solidarity. Heirs of the oldest dynasties found themselves challenged by new candidates who used discrepancies between Spanish and Andean rules of kinship as a margin for maneuver. In cases of accidental interruption of the customary order of succession (usually from father to son or from elder to younger brother), unconventional contenders sometimes won the highest offices. The great lords' increasing distance from local roots allowed cadet lineages, aggressive despite their "secondary" genealogical claims, to advance because they remained closer to subjects' ways of life.

And succession was not the only line of fracture native politicians could exploit in building power. They also innovated in using the Andean schemata that organized power in space. Andean schemata were typically dualistic; they conceived of each political space as composed of halves or moieties – *saya* being the most common term – which were symmetrical in form and complementary in function but of unequal rank. (Regions embroidered variations on dualism: In the Collao and Charcas, modern Bolivia, nested dualisms extended from village to macroregional scale; in Peru, dualisms were sometimes oriented to upstream and downstream or left- and right-bank "halves" of river basins.) In the new conjuncture, lineages from "lower moieties" could sometimes invert or overthrow the old dominion of "upper moieties" or even promote new structures at all levels of social and spatial organization.

Consider the case of the multiethnic collectivity to which the already-mentioned Charcas gave their name. The Spanish gave the name Charcas to the *audiencia* founded in 1561 at Chuquisaca (Sucre, Bolivia). But Charcas actually constituted only the "inferior" moiety of the old Charcas "confederation." This new and reduced Charcas was in turn formed by two territorial groups whose hierarchy also got inverted. The *audiencia* rejected the former ethnic capital, Sacaca, where the Ayaviri family ruled, as provincial capital (*cabecera*) and chose a second town, Chayanta. One finds the same inversion of hierarchy among the Caracara "nation." It was also constituted by two territorial subentities (Macha, the ethnic capital, and Chaqui). During the Toledan regime, the *cacique* of Chaqui and the Visisa, Alonso Choquevilca, wangled preferential treatment in terms of salary and personnel. These reversals continued in a haphazard fashion – at Choquevilca's death the *cacique* "from below" (*urinsaya*), Carlos Seco, became the upper authority. Similarly, at Macha the lineage of a secondary *ayllu*, the Ayra Chinchi of Ayriutu, acceded to all the prestigious regional offices. Such reversals of rank also happened in the important Lake Titicaca "kingdom" of Chucuito between the Lupaqa (Lupaca) dynasties of Cari and Poma Catari.

At Machaca, the smallest market town of lakeside Pacajes, a parvenu lineage known as the Fernández Guarachis won a fantastic ascendancy. Incumbents of the "lower moiety," they came to occupy the highest provincial offices. With the 1720 appointment of Joseph Fernández Guarachi as *"Alcalde Mayor de los Quatro Suyos,"* an honorific office symbolically re-creating the wholeness of the Inka empire, the political ascent of *caciques* issued from "inferior" polities reached its zenith. But lesser cases were common far and wide; the same thing occurred even in the former core of Inka power, at Asillo, where in 1668 Bartolomé Tupa Hallicalla, the *urinsaya cacique*, gained appointment as a land use constable (*maestre de campo*) of the eight parishes of Cusco.

A suit brought against one of these brilliant opportunist *caciques* by his subjects shows that success depended on practicing a number of economic "abuses." Don Fernando Ayra Chinchi was accused of appropriating communal flocks and land for his own use. On the land he settled wandering strangers (*forasteros*) whom he charged rent, and from whom he extracted arbitrary tributes and labor services.[8] At the other extreme of the viceroyalty, in the Ecuadorian north, the Hati *caciques* of Latacunga followed the same road to wealth. At the death of the head of the clan in 1579, the office went to his "brother," who much later turned out to be an impostor. Economic success came quickly to this man, Don Francisco Hati: His flock of sheep increased from 500 head in 1582 to 12,000 in 1605. A 1614 inspection record shows that his profits rested on four types of activity: the privatization of communal land (especially remote coca plantations and salt deposits); profitable long-distance commerce; income from public offices such as the "governorship" of natives (his son became *alcalde mayor* of Quito); and especially the incorporation

[8] Pedro Ramírez del Aguila, in Jaime Arana (ed.), *Noticias politicas de Indias y relacion descriptiba de la Ciudad de La Plata . . . 1639* (Sucre, 1978).

of "vagabonds" or "outsiders" (*forasteros*, also translatable as 'strangers') not only into the mass of tribute payers but into the work force of his private estate. By this means he created the largest private workforce in the region. His great fortune assured his legitimacy as well as the support of regional authorities all the way up to the *audiencia*. But the Hatis' prosperity was challenged anew at the end of the seventeenth century, when family disputes forced them to sell off much of the patrimony they had so skillfully accumulated.

The year 1690 brought Potosí an investigation of fraudulent practices by *caciques*. It showed that one-third of them, among them the Ayra Canchi family, laid heavy economic burdens on their subjects not just to satisfy legal colonial levies but also to enrich themselves. By that time some of the prestigious dynasties, like the Ayaviri, the Cari, or the Colque Guarachi, had long ceased to play a major role. Perhaps the losers lost out because of excessive respect for "moral economy" and the duty to redistribute wealth among their subjects. As for the success of the new contenders, it was due above all to their expertise in commercial accumulation. The mercantile reorientation of the *ayllus*, in a setting of endemic fiscal corruption, afforded brilliant opportunities for "social climbing." When the "new men" of the seventeenth century took over from the old lineages, they knew more than their predecessors about strategies of financial and judicial manipulation and about forming alliances with local and regional government agencies.

Yet in the long run, and especially in the eighteenth century, their houses too suffered an all but inexorable erosion of power. Once-powerful lineages suffered economic impoverishment, arbitrary dismissal, or replacement at the hands of *corregidores* (crown-appointed district governors) and parish priests. And this erosion was much more than locally south Andean. After 1680 the native dynasties of what had once been the northernmost Inka domains deteriorated into more or less predatory arms of Spanish commerce and taxation. "Intruder *caciques*" (as Karen Powers names them) took over one *cacicazgo* after another, bringing low the legitimacy of their titles. When native groups retained integrity of internal process, they did so through nondynastic ritual and civil leadership, often within emerging latifundia.

What was the cause of this decline? Had native dynasties lost the serious political support of the viceroyalty and the *audiencias* as they deteriorated into routine tribute-collecting agencies? Or perhaps by placing the main emphasis on using the cultural tools of the hispanic sphere, *caciques* forgot how to handle those of their subjects? On the other hand, one can also wonder whether the *caciques* did not succeed in elaborating a synthesis between the two traditions and whether, once this synthesis had been internalized by both the *ayllus* and the Spanish authorities, they simply became obsolete.

The Struggle for Memory and Citizenship: Inventing Tradition

In the early seventeenth century *caciques* were often held responsible for "perpetuating idolatry among the Indians," because it was known that they wielded great power over their subjects. Arriaga warned that *caciques* would go to great lengths to support and shelter "wizards," hide the *huacas* (non-Christian superhuman beings), sponsor non-Christian celebrations, and teach the traditions and fables of their ancestors.

What became of legitimating links to the old gods when the old dynastic lineages were broken or displaced by "new men?" Even the native foes of "idolatry" worried about loss of legitimacy. Early in the seventeenth century, the bicultural writer Felipe Guaman Poma de Ayala (himself an unsuccessful contender for the powers of a deep-rooted *cacique* family) deplored the rupture: "Already the caciques by caste and the natural lords are gone!" When Indians moved away and abandoned villages, how could collective memory of land inheritance, the mainstay of resource claims, be maintained? And how could the great governing *caciques* of the *reducciones*, ever more assimilated to the Spanish elite, remain the repository of legitimate claims? The most powerful natives were moving farther and farther from the lesser notables (*principales*), who actually kept close contact with the *ayllus*. Who would preserve collective knowledge of origins and holdings?

The memory of the group was inscribed in the very landscape: Mountaintops, rocks, and cliffs permanently testified to the final transformation each *ayllu*'s founders had undergone – the change into immortal rocks or crags. The landfeatures – mountainsides, ledges, and river plains, and even the crests of cordilleras – were crisscrossed by innumerable paths that attested to the presence of the ancestors and to the power of the sacred. Time, too, was punctuated by celebrations, banquets, and funeral rites in which songs with dances (*taqui*) and sacrifices revived these fabled moments. At the end of the sixteenth century, according to some few informants, these assemblies or "solemn drinking bouts" still commemorated the heroic times of the interethnic wars fought under the Inka, as well as the more recent struggle against the Spanish rulers. Thus the post-Toledan "geographical reports" quote a man as saying: "It is important to them to be considered brave for having been brave in war." Each dance or song had as correlate an exact claim over the land or water whose conquest it celebrated. But what was to become of that mythical and historical memory in the long term? In the first half of the seventeenth century, Father Cobo already noted that Indians of different groups were beginning to mix their dances, which came to lose ethnic specificity.

Because of the mnemonic techniques peculiar to Andean culture, close ties to a very long past required the recourse to several nonwritten media: sculpture, painting, textiles, music, *khipus* (or knotted-cord records), and songs. Sumptuary gifts received from the Inka (for example, diadems, or tunics of fine cloth woven in a checkerboard pattern and adorned with feathers) still figured in the wills of such sixteenth-century *caciques* as Garcia Mamani de Tapicari, Diego Collín of Panzaleo, and Alonso Maldonado of Otavalo. Wills of the seventeenth century, like that of the great *cacique* Fernández Guarachi in 1637, no longer mention these relics of past times. Father Cobo claimed that almost nothing was left, except for a few plates of precious metal that were used in secret ceremonies and sacked in the campaigns to eradicate the old religion.

The *caciques* had a very different public in mind when they appealed to the long-term collective memory, and this explains neglect of some traditional vehicles. Whatever the origin of their lineage, whether it dated back to pre-Inka times, or owed its power to Inka intervention, or even rested on Spanish favor, colonial lords always felt they had to invoke a double credential: that of genealogy and that of empire. In this manner they sought to recall the grandeur of the past and to renew the feudal contract between the "lords of the earth" and the universal monarch. Guaman Poma made this explicit when he said: "Who is the Inka? The Catholic King." This appeal to the past was often brought to bear in polemical circumstances, usually when it became necessary to choose one dynastic branch from among several collaterals, or one particular ethnic dynasty that would be able to establish regional hegemony, or even the indigenous nobility as opposed to colonial élites. In all these circumstances the power of the *caciques* derived its legitimacy from heavily reconstituted collective memory.

Memory, then, was a strategic resource. At Potosí one room in the house of Juan Colque Guarachi, "lord of the Quillacas," sheltered a family archive of manuscripts and *khipus*. At the end of the sixteenth century, these two systems of memory keeping – Spanish and Andean – still existed side by side. But one may wonder whether the *khipus* were not becoming subordinate to the written form. In noting the change of media it is important to keep in mind that written memory-keeping causes profound distortions. Oral memory, which is a creative reconstruction rather than a passive repetition, operates by a different logic than the written word, which allows for accumulation of data over time and for manipulations of all kinds.

In a universe where specific codes – that of colors, for instance, which functioned according to a system of oppositions and transitions – structured genealogical and mythical, foundations, writing or knotting acquired a logic of its own apart from context. Because of the autonomy of the written word, paper embodied legitimation by its very existence. This accounts for the Indians' love of lawsuits, which astounded the colonial observers: Regardless of whether one lost or won the case, the very fact of bringing home a set of duly signed and certified documents already meant victory. Yet by the same token, privileging the written word amounted to choosing and organizing only that which should be preserved and forgetting everything else.

Schooling was a priority for the *caciques*. They saw in schooling a way to grip intellectual tools that would help them deal with colonial domination and at the same time assert their own preeminence. At first they sent their sons to live with families of royal administrators connected with the *audiencias* or even to the viceregal court. Thus young Hernando Ayaviri, the principal author of the "Charcas memorandum," recalled that he was "educated among Spaniards and priests" of Chuquisaca. The effect of education was clearly demonstrated at Potosí in 1606, where the corregidor demanded that each *ayllu* furnish two workers (*tributarios*) for the compulsory labor service (*mita*) "free of charge." He obtained such workers from groups "whose captains are not educated (*ladinos*)" but not from "*ladino* captains who knew how to defend themselves." Archives contain many complaints that "by communicating regularly with the Spanish authorities, the *caciques* have become experts and commit a thousand acts of deceit, among them that of hiding their Indians." As the *corregidor* of Pacajes put it in 1608: If the "caciques send their sons to work for court reporters, writers, scribes, and attorneys, it is because they want them to learn to write complaints."

Spanish ambivalence about educational policy in the colonial period stands out clearly in debates about the social impact of "colleges and seminaries for the sons of *caciques*," most of which were entrusted to the Jesuits. Two colleges founded in the 1620s under royal sponsorship, one at Lima (in the designated native ghetto of El Cercado) and the other at Cusco, were severely criticized in 1635, both for the financial burden they imposed on the indigenous sector (payment for them involved a lien on communal resources) and for their effect on the students: "They do not learn [Christian] doctrine but the malice and sins that come from their nature, and they become so biculturally adroit (*ladinos*) that when they return to their towns they are true demons. They dress like very rich Spaniards and start court cases against *corregidores* and parish priests." (Of course, the bishops of Cusco and Huamanga were also voicing fear of Jesuit power when they criticized Jesuit colleges.) Another critique came from Chuquisaca, where the episcopal college-seminary, like those of La Paz, Huamanga, and Quito, admitted sons of *caciques*: "Good caciques, but also had bad ones, have come out of the seminaries, for once Spanish training enters their minds alongside their natural inclinations, they are harmful." Yet the same document concedes that "all the caciques give their children to the Spanish so that they will serve them and learn the language, reading and writing, which they prize very highly."[9]

Caciques put writing to use building their families' corporate privileges. Innumerable times, they orchestrated local memory by using questionnaires and, with lawyers' help, setting down the results in *probanzas* (evidential briefs) to obtain honors, exemptions, or pensions. A *probanza* was organized around a list of questions about the lineage's memory of its ancestors' exploits as transmitted orally and by *khipus*. *Probanzas* were highly selective samplings of memory, because they concentrated on the pre-Inka glory of the lineage concerned, its services to the Inka or Spanish empire, and favors received in exchange. In other words they explained only the public side of a lineage's relationship with state power. Nonetheless such papers could successfully congeal memories into canonical versions. Thus the *caciques* of the seven "nations" allied to the Charcas all claimed to have had alliances with the Inka and with the Pizarros; all of them blamed the initial resistance on the Pacajes; and all of them boasted that they had offered the silver mine of Porco to the

[9] Pedro Ramírez del Aguila, in Jaime Arana (ed.), *Noticias politicas de Indias y relacion descriptiba de la Ciudad de La Plata . . . 1639* (Sucre, 1978).

Pizarros. Litigants wrote claims of a pro-Spanish economic role when it came to tribute collection and furnishing of labor crews for the mines, and they remembered political credentials such as support when Spanish authorities needed armed help during emergencies like the Quijos uprising in western Amazonia, or English corsair raids on the coast, or the campaign against the chronically resistant Chiriguano of the viceroyalty's southeastern hinterland. Likewise descendants of the Inka princes, now dispersed throughout the vast area between Quito and Potosí, preserved stereotyped memories of an alliance with the Spanish crown, and of pensions and coats of arms that Emperor Charles V bestowed on the grandsons of Wayna Qhapaq Inka.

By the eighteenth century this pro-Spanish reading and writing of the Inka past converged with visual spectacles. Inka portraits were carried in religious and civic processions. Paintings depicting such subjects as the (imaginary) marriage of Ignatius de Loyola's nephew to a woman of royal Inka blood were understood to signify the allegiance of the indigenous community. The Inka as an emblematic figure strengthened any native appeal to a holistic and hierarchical order.

The deployment of memory was thus threefold. Memory was written (in the *probanzas*). It was made visible and audible in civic/hurban spectacles (for example, in processions on the occasions of Spanish royal births and deaths). And it was choreographed as sacred rite or as folk art. The choreographic tradition enjoyed a long life; dances of the conquest, such as "Moors and Christians" and shows as didactic celebrations of the sacraments (*autos sacramentales*) were the forerunners of such historical dramas as *Ollantay* and the *Tragedy of Atahuallpa*. These dramatic representations spread from the towns to the countryside, where they became parts of Carnival and Corpus Christi festivals. What they transmit, even in our day, is not so much a "vision of the vanquished" as a "version for the vanquished" designed to remind them periodically that their legitimacy as Christians was inseparable from their historic defeat.

It was in order to short-circuit the exclusionary and marginalizing measures of the local colonists (estate owners, parish priests, etc.) that the native authorities and the leaders of the *ayllus* appealed directly to the king of Spain. Meeting at Potosí in 1608, the leaders of three great Charcas confederations wrote to him:

> All things well considered, Your Majesty does not have in his kingdoms more humble nor more useful vassals than us, as can be seen by the riches sent to Spain and those enjoyed by the Spaniards living in this land, where the bread they eat is kneaded by the natives and produced by their sweat and their labor.

It is only fair that orders be given to examine this situation so that we will be spared and able to preserve ourselves . . . , for even though we are Indians, we are necessarily subject to death, illness, poverty and the other accidents of nature that no one has ever taken into consideration. . . . What we demand is just, and we hope to serve our king, lord, and father with loyalty and humility even to the point of expending our fortunes as we are doing.[10]

Many Spaniards, such as the mine administrator Felipe de Godoy or the researchers Juan and Ulloa in the Quito region between 1735 and 1744, agreed that the *caciques* and the Indians felt strong loyalty to the person of the king, and that all desired to renew their direct contract of alliance with him. Such a contract implied protection and guaranteed ownership of their land in exchange for their consent to the extraction of colonial wealth. Indeed by the end of the colonial era, Andean popular thought tended to equate the political contract with recognition of humanness (*runa, jaque*) itself. To be recognized as subjects of His Majesty and as communicants of the Church separated people from archetypes of the not-really-human: *gentiles* or prehistoric cannibals, who continued to exist in the form of prechristian mummies in ruins, or barbarians at the edges of Amazonia (the Yumbos, Chunchos, and Chiriguanos). In myth, though, the breakthrough into civilization once marked by the advent of the god Wira Qucha had shifted to the advent of another solar figure, represented first by the Inka and later by Christ. All non-Christian life had been cast back into the primal darkness by the conquering Christ. In the prevailing ideology the colonial *ayllus* would gradually and inexorably cut themselves off from the non-Christian other.

The Struggle for Local Social Control

In the wake of Toledo's reforms, the economic and political hegemony of the *caciques* came into danger, first at the hands of crown agents charged with intermediary government functions, and then because their own subjects tended to flee the "reductions" and settle elsewhere. Power relations between the *caciques* and the representatives of the colonial order were played out through collaboration and rivalry in varying proportions. Until the end of the sixteenth century, local *corregidores* and parish priests needed the *caciques'* cooperation to get access to indigenous labor. Such de facto understandings often turned out harmful to crown revenues. Local officials were liable to make themselves useful to *caciques*

[10] Saignnes' note on the source of this passage says only "ADI."

by taking tribute payers off the officials lists, or diverting tribute money to commercial operations in which *caciques* could also invest. In exchange for silent connivance, the *caciques* enjoyed a relative cultural autonomy. These practical arrangements flourished especially in the regions most actively involved in the internal market spawned by mines and towns.

A report to the viceroy by Father Lorenzo Valvi, an excellent connoisseur of local conditions between Cusco and Potosí, provides very clear evidence of the tacit nonaggression pact – a caricature on the local level of the alliance between the *ayllus* and the crown – among the three intermediate-level authorities. In order to obtain Indians, he reported, the corregidor "does not want to interfere in their affairs, all he wants is to please the Indians and let them live as they wish." The priest, for his part, let them have "idolatrous ceremonies in exchange for their money" and their silence about his own corrupt practices. And in return the offenses of the *caciques* are "covered up because they [caciques] are needed." Should an administrative inspection arrive, woe to the Indian who would dare demand justice against this triad![11]

Father José de Arriaga produced a fine example of collusion when he copied an intercepted "note" sent by a lieutenant corregidor to a *cacique*. "Brother X, I am sending you today a certain number of bottles of wine. See to it that they are sold in so many days and at such and such a price. Since I look after your business, look after mine."[12] Guaman Poma's famous drawing of a *cacique* getting drunk at the *corregidor*'s table also illustrates this kind of complicity.

The modus vivendi founded on assigning different spheres of influence to the three principal wielders of authority remained in effect as long as all parties profited from the general growth in wealth created by the size of the population (or increasing squeezes on lesser population) and the expansion of mercantile relations. As we see later, in the earliest phase even desertion of the reductions could be a source of new profits, especially for the *caciques*. But when the ratio of resources to exactions became too unbalanced, de facto collaboration gave way to bitter rivalry that very soon went beyond purely economic matters and upset local balances of power.

Here are three examples illustrating how success and failure depended

[11] Saignes' notes on the source of this passage says only "1609, ADI."

[12] Pablo José de Arriaga, *The Extirpation of Idolatry in Perú* [1621], L. Clark Keating, trans. (Lexington, Kentucky, 1968) p. 71.

above all on the *caciques'* ability to enlist the support of the networked interests crisscrossing colonial society. In the first case a seventeenth-century parish priest of Pachas, in central Peru, felt himself secure enough to go on the offensive because he had the support of the area's former *corregidor*, now administrator of local *obrajes* (textile mills). The priest tried to eliminate the *cacique* Leandro Pomachagua by accusing him of misusing Church property, sheltering "idolatrous outsiders" in his textile mills and pastures, and also of covering up the doings of the shaman Luis Guanco Yachac. These charges boomeranged against the priest. The *cacique*, having proven that he spent the money he had earned to decorate the church, feed the poor at the hospital, and pay the tribute of "deceased or absent" Indians, proceeded to accuse the priest of having misused the "properties, dues, and livestock" of the Church. Backed by the new *corregidor* and the local Spanish élites, this *cacique* was able to make witnesses for the prosecution admit that the priest had forced them to lie. A popular uprising soon freed him from prison and forced the authorities to expel the priest.[13]

The second case occurred much farther south, in the eastern valleys of the Collao in what is now Bolivia. Francisco Casasaca, *cacique* of the reduction of Hilabaya, ruled a mixed population of *yunkas* (lowlanders) and *mitimaes* (transplanted groups, in this case of Pukina and Aymara origin). Casasaca, a descendant of the governor of the *mitimaes* named by the Inka, had obtained his office in 1650 and held it despite the tensions caused by multiethnic coexistence. He set about to get rid of the local priest. In August 1667 he asked the bishop of La Paz to transfer Father Fernando del Castillo and his friends, including his nephew, Captain Juan de Segura, alleging that they were troublemakers. Three months later, a judge came to investigate the situation, and in particular to examine land records. The *ayllus* availed themselves of this opportunity to claim and obtain lands "taken from them" by the *cacique* Casasaca. Thereupon the priest took the offensive. It was said that he and his nephew were seen "at the judge's door offering money and wine to the *ayllu* chiefs (*hilacatas*) in order to persuade them to denounce the *cacique*." The charges against the latter included extreme harshness in collecting the tribute and meting out punishments, forcing his subjects to buy hats and wine, seizing thirty-six *forasteros* living as

[13] Luis Millones, "Religión y poder en los Andes: los curacas idólatras de la sierra central," *Cuadernos del Consejo Nacional de la Universidad Peruana* 24–25 (1977), 79–81.

yanacona (servitors detached from communities) on communal land set aside for raising the tribute of "absent inhabitants," and renting out a group of other *forasteros* to mine owners at Puno. All of these expedients were normal means of meeting the demands of colonial exactions; the only novelty was the opportunity to expose them. The Spanish people living in the these valleys and the corregidor testified in Casasaca's favor, stating that they considered him "the best *cacique* of the province." But to no avail. He sent to La Paz and then to the *audiencia* of Charcas, where he was condemned in 1669 to a 2,000-peso fine and a 10-year exile.

As soon as the sentence was published, the *ayllu* chiefs called for the return of their "good, prudent, and generous governor, in order to see once again a large population and good order in the reduction." But all they obtained was the shortening of the exile term by 4 years.[14] Neither the support of the *corregidor*, nor that of his ally the *encomendero*, could protect this *cacique* against the priest's maneuvers, which undoubtedly had an economic background.

A third example occurred on the neighboring high plateau, north of Lake Titicaca. The great *cacique* of Asillo, Bartolomé Tupa Hallicalla, had been appointed in 1648. His career was impressive. In 1661 Tupa Hallicalla received the title of "infantry captain," and in 1667 Viceroy Conde de Lemos appointed him "brigadier general of the eight parishes of Cusco." In 1673, married to a Spanish woman from a patrician family of Cusco, he applied to the Council of the Indies for an *encomienda* or a high office and was engaged in combating corruption in the mita (compulsory labor) system at Potosí. By 1675 he owned 22,000 llamas.

In that year the local priest, allied with the bishop of Cusco, began his offensive against Tupa Hallicalla and succeeded in having all of his holdings impounded. Despite his appeals to superior courts at Charcas, Lima, and Madrid, the *cacique* was unable to procure decisions in his favor, for the priest had the new *corregidor* on his side. Old and ruined, Hallicalla died shortly after 1678 at Chuquisaca. In the struggle for regional hegemony between the Church and a great *cacique*, the latter succumbed to stronger political forces.[15]

These village-level struggles demonstrate a tangled web of material as well as symbolic power running through daily life. Struggles tended not

[14] Saignes' note on the source says "ANB [Archivo Nacional/Bolivia?] E 1669–33."
[15] Luis Miguel Glave, *Trajinantes* (Lima, 1989), 279–304.

to polarize in simple oppositions between social strata but rather between opposing networks of clientage that each involved *both* Indians and Spanish settlers. Reversals of alliances, which were frequent in this situation, show that in the last analysis the fundamental question always was: Who has power *here and now?*

Besides the three parties struggling visibly in these cases, a hidden fourth was also felt to have power in the here and now: the shaman, or Andean religious practitioner. In the last two conflicts just described, Casasaca and Tupa Hallicalla held office in local Catholic brotherhoods and officiated at celebrations in the regional sanctuary of Copacabana. That shielded them from charges of sorcery. However, in the first case, the fact that the *cacique* covered up the activities of the shaman was at the core of the dispute, for this shaman was accused of having caused the death of a woman, and it was said that one of his "helpers" possessed the "god of fortune who would make him rich." This fourth contender could sometimes tilt a struggle for local power among the *caciques*, the priests, and the *corregidors*. And the shaman sometimes competed with the *cacique* for the right to mediate with the autochthonous powers, what could still be seen as the source of true legitimacy.

Many Andean peoples believed it was in exchange for offerings and sacrifices that *caciques* received the life force contained in the mummies of their ancestors. In the second section of the third part of this essay (under the heading "The Genesis of an Andean Christianity," p. 1134), we see changes made in the cult of the dead and the ancestors, but it can already be stated that in remote areas – particularly in backlands of the archbishopric of Lima – the *ayllus* continued to worship the mummies of their founding parents as the guarantors of collective health and prosperity. In such areas representatives of the ancestors derived added legitimacy from this cult. It was useful to them in their economic activities, which involved the collection of the tribute. Rivalry over religiously based ability to levy contributions seems to figure in the background of a court action against the priest of the church of San Damián, Francisco de Avila. This dispute led to Avila's investigation of "idolatrous practices" in 1608. Its results were secretly compiled to become the famous Quechua "Manuscript of Huarochiri"[16] (see Chap. 9) and publicized

[16] Two recent editions are Gerald Taylor (ed. and trans.), *Ritos y tradiciones de Huarochirí del siglo XVII* (Lima, 1987), and Frank Salomon and George Urioste (eds. and trans.), *The Huarochirí Manuscript* (Austin, 1991).

through persecutions and through Avila's sermons. But here, too, alliances spanned ethnic lines: Pro-Jesuit extirpators allied with ambitious local native politicians would face the combined opposition of diocesan local priests and humbler parishioners. The ordinary parish priest benefited by a monetary modus vivendi, the ordinary villager by a tacit tolerance of religious pluralism.

Astute *caciques* used this situation to dodge persecution. Although well informed on the cult of the mummies, extirpation campaigns rarely attacked the great native leaders of local towns. In the seventeenth century, the great regional *cacique* of Huarochiri, Sebastián Quispe Ninavilca, a good Christian and an effective collaborator of the Spanish authorities, covered up the practices of local shamans, so that no trace of a cult of mummies was to be found. In sheltering native religiosity, they also made room for less governable shifts in non-Christian belief. We see later that as the Indians were Christianized, many came to feel that the energy contained in the bodies of the mummies migrated toward the mountains and into amulets (*illa, conopa*) owned and handed down within domestic units.

The *caciques* therefore had to reckon with the man who tended to monopolize the use of magic, the shaman. Called "sorcerer," "master," or "minister" in Spanish documents, he had a great variety of titles in the native languages. Sometimes the *caciques* sought the support of the shaman in order to shore up disputed power. Such was the case of Don Francisco Gamarra, "second person" (i.e., lower-moiety counterpart) of the *cacique* at Santiago de Iguari in mid–seventeenth-century central Peru, twice imprisoned for "idolatry" because he kept going around "accompanied by his sorcerer Pedro Pisco."[17] Sometimes politicians needed the shaman to ensure the success of an undertaking: Thus Don Juan de Mendoza, the governor of Lampas, traveled to Hacas to consult the shaman Hernando Hacaspoma so that his son Don Alonso would do well at the school for natives in el Cercado and eventually succeed him. And sometimes they sought the shaman's help to get rid of an adversary in a court case, as did Don Salvador Ango, the governor of Otavalo in 1703, who asked a shaman of mixed ancestry to cast a disease-causing spell on a Spanish general.

These few cases of collaboration represent only a very thin layer – the layer that reached the written surface of judicial investigations – of the

[17] Ana Sánchez, *Amancebados, hechiceros y rebeldes: Chancay, siglo XVII* (Cusco, 1991), 169–188.

murky and ambiguous relations between *caciques* and the shamans. These two powers were now forced to share the sacred and the profane aspects of a power once united in the "sorcerer king." Together they faced a new and alien contender for exclusive spiritual and temporal power, the parish priest. Backed by a whole chain of village church functionaries (wardens, sacristans, cantors, sponsors of saints, etc.) as well as by the Spanish hierarchy, the priest enjoyed many advantages. Many priests used their leverage on primary production to set up both legal and illegal businesses ranging from embroidery to gunpowder manufacture. Depending on the state of economic power relations, Spaniards who gradually, illegally, but permanently moved into the reductions – the *corregidor* or his representative, the owners of estates or textile mills (*obrajes*), tradespeople, and *mestizos* – would side with one or the other party.

With so many alliances and investments tied into local micropolitics, the general state of the economy cut deep into the innermost local affairs. Beginning in the 1680s a law of "saleable offices" required *corregidores* to buy their posts. Of course they responded by increasing their exactions on Indians, and they did so with relative impunity because they could shift the onus of collection onto the *caciques*. In 1690 at Potosí, investigators questioned native leaders about abuses perpetrated by the *caciques* of the "sixteen provinces subject to the *mita*." This investigation shows how the expedients leaders adopted in order to meet colonial exactions (such falsifying numbers of tribute payers and *forasteros* or faking land records) themselves eroded the old dynasties and caused some to disappear or merge with no less-abusive families of *mestizo caciques*. This decline became even more pronounced in the eighteenth century. In the South-Central Andes, the apparent prestige of the Guarachi dynasty of Pacajes or the Sinani dynasty of Carabuco masked their growing alienation from the *ayllus*. Aligning themselves more and more closely with the Creole elites, to whom they were bound by ties of marriage and baptismal sponsorship, the *cacique* class fell into all but irreparable discredit. By the mid – eighteenth century, Indians mounted increasingly frequent lawsuits against their own *caciques* and even assassinated some of them. These tensions eventually fueled the great wars of liberation of 1780.

Not all the changes were so evidently revolutionary. The old dynasties' decline was connected also to the rise of new indigenous élites who claimed, as *caciques* had of old, the ability to mediate between the forces of the earth and those of heaven. Christianity excluded Indians from priesthood, but ambitious parishioners found room for leadership in the interstices between clergy and laity. They did so particularly in the proliferating devotional groups (confraternities or brotherhoods) that interceded before heaven, cared for the dead, sponsored festivals, and sometimes also provided credit. Parish clergy, who often spearheaded open opposition to the *caciques*, unintentionally fostered rival leadership by encouraging lay elites. Working together these two groups consciously agreed to establish new forms of religious validation within the framework of the Christian liturgy. It was a costly initiative. In the eighteenth century observers blamed confraternity ceremonialism for taking too much money out of local economies. Yet confraternities enjoyed firm support from both the clergy and municipal authorities. Coordination between these two power centers may have built up the "fiesta cargo system" formerly widespread in the Andes, under which each adult had to pass through an interlaced series of onerous civil and ceremonial offices. Confraternities proved the key to a gradually unifying system of local civil and ecclesiastical officeholding. As they accrued religious as well as civic prestige, non-noble leaders were able to break *caciques'* monopoly over rituals in village centers. This power shift, which is very evident in the Collao and Charcas regions in the second half of the eighteenth century, may have occurred in the Andean world as a whole but its chronology and spread have yet to be clarified.

To sum up, the two centuries that followed Polo de Ondegardo's warning that the Spanish crown needed the *caciques* but at the same time should suspect and control them, proved him justified. While building up their position as privileged interlocutors of the imperial crown, the *caciques* strove to perpetuate, even exalt, their symbolic and material power. They drew on the reservoir of tradition (especially the practice of ancestor worship) but at the same time exploited hispanization (and especially mercantile opportunity). They succeeded in integrating the "Indian republic" into the colonial system without in the process watering down its distinctive ethnic standing. They attained the pinnacle of their splendor in the decades after Toledo, when this process was still highly dynamic. But their very success proved fatal to them in the long run.

After the 1630s growing economic pressures and severe population decline gradually undercut native authorities' power bases. *Caciques* reacted in different ways depending on their degree of legitimacy and their ability to tap new resources. Fraudulent schemes to avoid taxes, such as the nonreporting of native tribute payers and "outsiders" living on communal land, became less effective as ever-larger numbers of people were removed, not just from the tax rolls but from their *caciques'* physical reach. Under these circumstances the personal enrichment of the *caciques* decreased because they increasingly had to use the money they collected to cover municipal expenses. It cost a lot simply to continue the collectivity: When mine labor levies were not fulfilled, cash had to cover the shortfall. Then there were tribute deficits, forceable sale of goods shared out by the state, and tithes.

What determined the fate of most dynasties of *caciques* in the Central Andes in the long run (i.e., in the two centuries from Toledo to Túpac Amaru II [1580–1780] was their ability to meet all the financial demands of colonial power – in the end simply to put the squeeze on their subjects. Their ability to do so depended on local factors, varying as widely as the regional geography from Pasto (Colombia) to Tucumán (Argentina). One important variable was the ecology and the economic specialization of each region in relation to the internal market created by mining. Another was the historical solidity of the dominant lineages, and the marriage strategies by which they built patrimony and linked themselves to the Spanish, Creole, and mestizo segments of the new regional and imperial oligarchies.

By the early 1700s the failure of the *caciques*' strategy for remaining at the top of the hierarchy became obvious. Serious friction developed between local dynasties and households unwilling to tolerate abuses. *Caciques* could not keep the discontented away from autochthonous cults and emerging non-noble elites. Nor did external structures consistently support *caciques*. The colonial state, which had vacillated between indirect rule and direct intervention, gave freer rein to the hegemonic claims of parish priests and *corregidores*. Up to a point midcolonial Spaniards were willing to afford the *caciques* a symbolic compensation for the loss of their political, social, and economic preeminence, by letting them claim homology with the figure of the Inka. But these ploys were no match for the new forms of legitimacy and social control emerging amid conflict everywhere from agropastoral hamlets to mining towns and markets.

Little by little, myriad small struggles between old and new native elites were profoundly restructuring the Quechua, Aymara, and Pukina language communities and indeed colonial society as a whole. The old hierarchies of status and blood had been replaced by new ones based on economic effectiveness and the ability to evolve new forms of mediation between the autochthonous and the Christian sources of power. The next section of this chapter sketches these new departures.

REBUILDING SOCIAL BONDS

In laying down the basic regimen of Indian taxation, Viceroy Toledo fatefully decided to combine two kinds of levies: those on individuals and those on collectivities. Writing from Potosí, the mining entrepreneur Luis Capoche best summarized the outcome: "The tribute was determined on the basis of the amount each *repartimiento* (fiscal district) had to pay . . . and then it was determined what each individual Indian had to pay according to his name and his *ayllu* . . . , and he was taxed in the form of labor services in order to oblige him to work and to give him a sense of his affairs." This system immediately raised the problem of tribute payers who died or did not return to their homes and yet continued to be carried on the census. Another question was how to calculate the tribute: Should it be the same for everyone? Capoche also recalled the criticism voiced by the officers of the *audiencia*: "The tribute should be levied either on the collectivity, or on the actual number of taxable Indians, *but not under a rule that includes both these criteria*; for if this is done, it is collected as a lump sum and the living are made to pay for the dead."[18] Others, including the learned Jesuit José de Acosta, focused on the consequences of forcing the Indians to sell their labor for taxes in cash: "The Indians are obliged to earn money by their labor and to forsake their towns in order to find someone who will hire them."[19] Against its authors' intentions, this tax policy permanently sabotaged all efforts at separating the Indian and Spanish "republics."

The dangerous ambiguity of Toledo's formula became manifest when, beginning in 1587, a decade of epidemics and climatic disasters (severe freezes and droughts) forced many households to abandon their regular surroundings. As a result the *ayllus* fell below the level of population that had permitted them to meet their fiscal and labor service obligations. Levies stayed unadjusted. Faced with the prospect of paying more than their shares, those who at first stayed put increasingly gave up and left,

[18] Luis Capoche, *Relación general de la villa imperial de Potosí* (Madrid, 1969), 180–189 (italics added by Saignes).

[19] Lima, 2 March 1577, AGI/S [Archivo General de Indias/Sevilla], Lima 314.

thereby further aggravating both the deficit and the disaggregation of communities.

Debates about taxing natives continued for two centuries. From varied positions all sectors of society aimed to reconstitute the Toledan order, even though it had contained the seeds of its own destruction. The solution came from indigenous actors themselves, in particular women, who forged new ties on a more voluntary basis by arranging exchanges among domestic units and with the outside world. Their activities wrought profound changes in the human landscape of the central Andes.

The Struggle for Social and Demographic Recovery: Mobility and Reproduction

The early colonial "demographic collapse" of the Andean peoples forced native politicians to invent new ways of capturing labor, and these inventions would later affect the shape society took as native population recovered. The terrifying mortality of Andean peoples in the early decades of Spanish rule has preoccupied historians ever since Las Casas proclaimed the "destruction of the Indies." Modern Andean researchers, following the lead set by Borah's Mexican studies, confirmed startling initial depopulation rates throughout the ex-Inka domains as influenza, measles, smallpox, and other newly imported diseases ravaged an immunologically defenseless population. Cook's 1981 synthesis reveals an overall pattern so destructive that it helps one understand early Andean authors' preoccupations with apocalypse. From 1520, the last prehispanic decade, to 1630, the total Indian population of Peru as estimated by Cook fell from 3,300,574 to 601,645. By 1600 the once-opulent peoples of coastal Peru had already all but disappeared. Highland depopulation was more gradual and, in the end, less catastrophic but still severe. "The Indian population of the highland region fell from 1.045 million to 585,000 in the half-century following 1570. In the same period the coastal population collapsed from 250,000 to 87,000."[20] What growth of Indian population did occur, happened in new urban "Sowetos" like Lima's El Cercado and Arequipa's Yanahuara or at crossroad and port settlements attracting traders and artisans.

The Indian population of the viceroyalty as a whole bottomed out around 1730. The lands of what is now Ecuador followed an atypical

[20] Noble David Cook, *Demographic Collapse: Indian Peru, 1520–1620* (New York, 1981), 253.

curve; though no less damaged by the post-1532 disasters, its censuses show a dramatic recovery – one historian speaks of a "population explosion" in 1590–1660 – more than a century before the rest of the viceroyalty began to recover.

As Sánchez-Albornoz and others delved into the shrinking demographic universe, it became clear that our impressions of both depletion and recovery are affected by population flows as much as by population sizes. Death shrank communities but so did migration. Indeed, early colonial Peru was a society taking to the roads. Massive numbers of individuals and households "disappeared" from administrative view as they sought opportunity, or simply a way to dodge levies, in far-off cities, estates, mines, textile mills, and villages. Early colonial native lords replenished their disease-depleted political bases by taking in "outsiders" (*forasteros*) as resident aliens, hiding them as much as possible from Spanish officials. The results amounted to a massive replacement; at the end of the seventeenth century, "outsiders" made up 80 percent of some Andean towns. Powers thinks the apparent early recovery in Ecuador is largely an artifact of "invisible" migrants' resettlement in areas where they became administratively visible again.

Colonial bureaucrats worked incessantly on statistical measurement of the native labor force (particularly its male component). Inspection and calculation was an indispensable first step toward assigning levies. Higher levels of government needed to find out whether global population shifts were positive or negative – the steep decline of the coastal populations, for instance, was known beyond doubt, but the growth of population in the sierras was disputed. Above all it was necessary to find out about the causes of population changes, such as epidemics, flight, migrations, abuse by Spanish colonists, and so on.

However, the intermediary government agents who, like *caciques*, parish priests, and *corregidores*, were supposed to produce periodic or long-term lists – censuses or parish registers – were not only careless but had a personal interest in underrepresenting the number of tribute payers, the better to divert local surplus or labor to their own use. Domestic units in their own right resisted pressures and frauds by evading inscription on the registers – especially because they had to pay for it – and often by moving to other villages, towns, mines, or estates where they could adopt new identities.

Thus there are no "unweighted" or "raw" statistical data to provide us with objective information on the demography of the Aymara-,

Quechua-, Pukina-, or "Yunga"-speaking populations. All data are likely to be distorted, either because they were manipulated by the local authorities or because households responding to climatic, biological, and economic factors might not be where they were supposed to be. Another source of distortion was the miscegenation of different ethnic groups: Real demography sometimes escaped the categories provided by questionnaires.

Nevertheless it is possible to reconstruct an overview of the gross changes in population and its disposition over the landscape. In the Central Andes, in Inka times and probably long before, the obligation to produce and pay tribute dictated a strict timetable for migrations. This timetable was based on the dates of the crucial agricultural and pastoral operations in the different vertically tiered production zones that ranged from the high steppes to the *yunkas* (hot lands) of the Pacific coast and the Amazonian piedmont. Most of the chiefdoms or kingdoms, depending on their size, controlled pieces of some or all of these zones. Within the endogamous and strongly hierarchical kinship groups (*ayllus*), an individual's stage in the life cycle – that is, his age and position in the kin group – determined his access to the income from fields and flocks. As individuals aged and rose in hierarchy, they gradually spent more and more time close to the village center and held larger roles there. Depending on its wealth and prestige, a domestic unit could have access to one or several levels of the ethnic territory and thus have one or several dwellings ("double domicile").

In 1565 a new division of the regional space into provinces (or *corregimientos*) altered this arrangement. Then in 1575 rearrangement into forced resettlement villages (*reducciones*) changed it again – especially by amputating some villages' "archipelagos" of outlying fields and pastures – without, however, abolishing ecological diversity altogether. The reductions where several *ayllus* (sometimes coming from different ethnic groups) were gathered together constituted the new framework for enforcing the tribute quota (*tasa*), the rotating labor service (*mita*), and later the forced purchase of merchandise (*repartos de mercancías*). There was to be only one local category, that of the "native" (*natural*), later changed to *originario*. (In towns and on latifundia, Andean persons were inscribed as *yanacona*, 'servitors'.) With tributary and villager status largely fused, the simple step of moving to a neighboring village, or to a city, afforded at least partial escape. Soon the traditional absenteeism caused by the production-related and fiscal constraints of communal organization was aggravated by temporary and then permanent waves of flight. The greatest problem for the native authorities charged with updating population records was to check on the reality of deaths and absences. That was not easy, because priests failed to register some deaths, and fugitives, as well as being hard to find, changed their names and their declared status.

A concrete case is that of the Lupaqa chiefdom on the western shore of Lake Titicaca. The summary of the famous *Visita de la provincia de Chucuito* of 1567 illustrates the hazards of demographic surveys. The total figure is 15,404 tribute payers. Seven years later, the census ordered by Toledo shows alongside the 15,032 tribute payers residing in the seven administrative towns (*cabeceras*) 2,748 other tribute payers living in neighboring or more remote regions. Of this group 2,200 men were at Potosí as rotating mine workers (*mitayos*). In other words, 28 percent of the tribute payers were not present in the province. It should be pointed out here that the figure for 1573, a total of 17,779 adult males, is higher than that yielded by the earlier fiscal survey. Does this indicate a spurt of population growth, or more efficient record keeping that included "absentees" traced to the south central areas of the Andes?

Almost a half-century later, the bishop of La Paz in 1618 was equally stunned to find that although everyone agreed that the province was devastated, the new census count of 15,859 heads of families was more, not less, than the 13,364 tribute payers recorded at the end of the sixteenth century. In both cases one would like to know the reasons for these variations: Did they reflect the return of the "absentees," changed criteria for registration, or more meticulous investigation? Which statistical basis can we trust enough to analyze the changes in Lupaqa demography?

Farther north, in the *audiencia* of Quito (Ecuador), we find the same irregularities and contradictions. The total tribute-paying population of the *audiencia*, for instance, was listed as 30,000 in 1600, yet in the years 1620–1630, the authorities estimated it at 80,000. At Riobamba estimates declined from 6,800 tribute payers in 1580 to some 4,000 in 1590, only to rise to 8,181 in 1605. Such estimates make any demographic study extremely uncertain. Local samplings as well reveal major fluctuations, which were in fact related to migratory movements and to the creation of "*parcialidades de la Corona*" ('crown sectors') that served to shelter and tax "outsiders" living far from their villages. In the 1620s a regulatory change allowed the more enterprising *caciques* to integrate many "outsiders" and "vagabonds" into their estates or into the local *ayllus*.

In sum, attempts to measure the indigenous population ran into a threefold set of obstacles. One was the cyclical mobility of the population due to ecological and economic causes; another was the search for means of escaping taxation and labor services; and the third was finagling by government agents. Every colonially established village was the scene of constant comings and goings, in which the *ayllus* lost "native born members" and gained migrants or "outsider" newcomers. Thus, to return to the case of Chucuito, it should be noted that in 1645 the number of "natives" had fallen to 3,194, while the number of "outsiders" listed was 1,290. Forty years later, these figures were respectively 4,378 and 2,874 tribute payers. In the South-Central Andes, from the Canas to the Chichas, the census of 1683–1684 makes it possible to compare the evolution of numbers since 1575 and 1645. The findings confirm at the aggregate level the conclusions advanced by Viceroy La Palata and cited in the studies of Sánchez-Albornoz, Assadourian, and Evans: For the most part, the "absentees" from certain areas can be found in other areas that received migrants, so that global figures do have an indicative value concerning the most significant population trends.

After the decimation of the indigenous population along the coast, and after the great waves of epidemics around the turn of the seventeenth century, the tribute-paying population of the South-Central Andes fell to its lowest level so far in the middle of the seventeenth century. A slight recovery that became visible by 1683 was subsequently canceled by the epidemics of 1687, 1707, and especially by the catastrophic epidemics of 1719–1720, which killed almost a third of the rural Andean population. It was not until the middle of the eighteenth century that one finds a recovery. Significant growth continued until the end of the century.

This numerical overview does not say anything about the profound internal transformations experienced by the indigenous population, particularly where spatial and social mobility was concerned. Approximately half of the domestic units left their *ayllus* and original reductions to live elsewhere and find niches less vulnerable to exploitation. In most villages the back-and-forth shifting between departures and new arrivals was very intense and frequent. It was interspersed with periods of "root taking" (for "outsiders" could legally "naturalize themselves"). Seeming stabilization could gave way to new forms of instability, sometimes created by transfers between categories: Thus the son of a "native" (*originario*), pinched for land and money, might adopt the status of an "outsider."

Wide differences occurred among regions. On the high plain, for example, in the province of Paucarcolla (north of Lake Titicaca), the number of tribute payers fell to only half of what it had been two centuries earlier, and moreover 60 percent of the population consisted of "outsiders." The province of Carangas (south of Oruro) lost three-fourths of a population that included only 15 percent "outsiders." By contrast the valleys of Cochabamba doubled their population, with an 83 percent immigrant boom.

In reconstructing the microlevel processes that generated these numbers, one must stress the fact that these displacements, often sanctioned by marriages away from home, signaled a break with *ayllu* endogamy. Locally rooted kindreds increasingly accepted recently arrived in-laws and gave them greater ritual importance. Under the impact of flight, epidemics, and Christian norms, the Andean kinship system was forced to adopt a more flexible structure. But we do not know much about adjustments in practices of marriage, succession, postmarital residence, or size of households, because crown inspectors recognized only the model of the nuclear family. Domestic units certainly varied with social status: Houses of *caciques* contained many "adopted" orphans, especially in times of epidemics, as well as "serving women" who may have been concubines. At the lowest end of the social scale, there were many "widows" with or without children. Their lack of coresident adult kin suggests utter poverty.

The greatest unknowns are the natural trends of natality, mortality, and fertility, which are extremely difficult to calculate precisely because of the mobility of the population and the tendency of parish registers to underregister women and children. Some samplings – those undertaken at Aymaya (Charcas) by B. Evans, at Yanque (Collaguas) by N. D. Cook, and at Machaca (Pacajes) by N. Wachtel – show the following traits: high levels of natality and mortality, strong annual fluctuations in the numbers of births and deaths, and crises of unusually high infant mortality (for the most part due to smallpox). One can assume that the stress of the murderous epidemics that, accompanied by severe food shortages, occurred in 1580–1620 and again in 1719–1721, caused villages to be first temporarily and then permanently abandoned. Epidemic illness or famine associated with epidemics also caused temporary sterility in many women. Some epidemics were followed by rapid local recoveries, visible in the very young median age of these populations (for example at Otavalo in 1582 or at Sipe-Sipe in 1645). This recovery may have had to do with a relative immunization of the population (only half of a population needs to have acquired immunity to a given germ to slow down and even block an epidemic) as well as with improved nutrition in the form of animal and plant proteins.

This matter of female fertility takes us to the enigmatic core of indigenous demography and social change. Beyond famine amenorrhea and the possible stress of the conquest, the Jesuit missionary José Gumilla saw "voluntary sterility and flight to other provinces" as the main causes of population decline. He found sterility among women "married to Indians," while those married to "non-Indians" were among the most fertile, "because their children were no longer Indians, the [children] no longer get counted among tribute-payers, they have a better color and a better fortune, and count for more than Indians do." As a counterexample, he cited the Jesuit reduction of Juli on the shores of Lake Titicaca, which sheltered a large, prosperous, and constantly growing indigenous population.[21] Other observers felt that these two attitudes coexisted. Thus, according to the Franciscan Monsalve, women were the first to abandon their native communities, thereby forcing the men to flee as well.[22] Guaman Poma, for his part, constantly reproached Indian women for letting themselves be seduced by Spaniards and mestizos, and even by blacks and mulattoes, "thus bringing forth an infinity of halfbreed brats, denatured Indians, mulattoes, and African-native mixed bloods".[23] Churchmen of the 1630s echoed his indignation, writing that the highland bishoprics of Quito, Huamanga, Cusco, La Paz, and Chuquisaca contained so many mestizos that in the long run, they feared, "the Indian nation would disappear." Besides actual miscegenation natives found other ways to save their children from labor service and tribute. One was to claim that their progenitor belonged to a tax-exempt category, such as the mule-drivers or legalized "outsiders." Another was to move to a town and to place them into a convent or entrust them to a confraternity that would train them to become specialized *yanaconas* (servitors) or artisans.

[21] Saignes' attribution, "Gumilla 1747, part II, chapters 26–27" may refer to Joseph Gumilla's *Historia natural civil y geográfica de las naciones situadas en las riveras del río Orinoco* (Barcelona, 1741, and other editions).

[22] Saignes: "Monsalve, *Reduccion universal de todo el Peru*, 1650."

[23] Felipe Guaman Poma de Ayala, in John V. Murra, Rolena Adorno, and Jorge Urioste (eds.), *Nueva cronica y buen gobierno* [1615] (Madrid, 1987), folios 395, 981.

These maneuvers, like miscegenation, cut *caciques'* political access to labor power. Throughout the seventeenth century the *caciques* of the high plain complained about such stratagems when they assembled at Potosí.

How should one interpret the conduct of the women, which in the long run compromised the survival of the *ayllus*? Was it resignation to the law of the victor, a sign of that "disillusionment with life" detected by N. Sánchez-Albornoz, or, on the contrary, a new thrust within a radical movement of defiance and female-led self-help? To be sure, these testimonies refer to the period after the great epidemics, which may have given rise to a true crisis of confidence in the future of the *ayllus* and their ability to withstand the colonial system. But one should also keep in mind that these same movements of "flight" to the towns, and indeed all other forms of migration, established new ties between the countryside and urban markets. These ties were what created the conditions for the material survival of the *ayllus*.

Participation in the Market, Access to Land, and Internal Differentiation

Studies on the circulation of goods have often found a contrast between the prehispanic system, based on reciprocity and redistribution, and the colonial system of commercial exchange. Local investigations of the indigenous concepts of exchange and money show, however, that the forms of a monetary economy introduced by the Spanish were not completely alien to the Andean world. One can gain some sense of how money appeared to Andean people by tracing clues in ritual. In northern Potosí libations (*ch'allas*) were poured out to the three central forms of fertility: to the prototype of the plants (*llallagua*), the flocks (*pacara*), and money (*paxsima*). In this belief sacrificial exchange does not create money, but it does increase its fertilizing power; money fed by sacrifice reproduces itself. There may not have been any basic categorical difference between market activities and reciprocity. Around 1610 the Aymara language, according to Bertonio, had only one verb, *thaata*, signifying "to buy," "to sell," and "to exchange." Money was neutral in itself, but its good use – that is, its circulation, which spreads new life through society – made it a moral good. A debt is today called *wanu* in Quechua ('manure') because it fertilizes interpersonal relationships.

One segment of indigenous society thus very quickly understood, accepted, and applied the mechanisms of generalized exchange and the large-scale circulation of goods and money. Potosí became a spectacular demonstration of this development. By the middle of the sixteenth century, its daily market, where rows upon rows of metalware, coca, fine cloth, and foodstuffs were displayed, had already become, as the well-traveled Pedro Cieza de León judged, "the greatest fair in the world." Because of its role in generating colonial wealth, Potosí symbolized the pact between the metal producer and the new Emperor, successor to the Inka and hence guarantor of universal fertility. And if the emperor's American vassals came to the *chacra del rey* ("the king's field," as the mine was called) in warlike attire in fulfillment of their *mita* obligation, it was in order to "do battle" with the obscure forces that held the metal in thrall and to exploit the riches that were destined to fertilize the Andean space before being sent on to the metropolis. Moreover, this society of former warriors did not find it difficult to launch itself into commercial ventures, which it considered a new form of contest. This indigenous vision of wider exchanges and of the tribute obligation as a matter of reciprocity in the pact between the *ayllus* and the universal monarch thus converged with the goal that Toledo intended to achieve by his reforms (i.e., the insertion of the Indians into the colonial market).

In principle the indigenous vision did not challenge the tributes, the mining *corvée*, the forced sale of merchandise, or even the ecclesiastical tithe, only the manner in which they were applied. Objections arose when local authorities, taking advantage of their position as exclusive intermediaries of power, arbitrarily decided who had to pay tribute or serve as a *mitayo*, or when they altered the price of the foodstuffs the Indians had to sell by way of tribute or on the urban market. Authorities courted resistance when exercising their power to set prices for compulsory purchases of foodstuffs, or when deciding which products could be used to pay tithes and the commercial taxes called *alcabalas* and *sisas*. In short, anger and revolt were aroused not by monetization as such but by injustices born of fraud and illicit profit making on the part of "bad stewards." Crooked *caciques* were felt to violate the pact under which the sovereign owed the subjects protection.

The mercantilist state saw nothing wrong with forcing monetization or extracting levies in cash. One can distinguish three channels of forced commerce: transactions that went to the state, those that went to the market, and those that went to the Church. When it came to collections, all three channels entailed the thorny problem of how to establish fiscal and social control over the indigenous population. First of all, there was competition among the beneficiaries of these exactions, as we have seen in connection with local conflicts. Secondly, new methods of collection that would cover the entire Andean space had to be developed to cope with the abandonment of resettlement villages. Where onerous labor services had become unbearable – like services to mines of Potosí and Huancavelica, or to the waystations on the busiest highways – migrations toward areas where control was less strict, such as the piedmonts of the central highlands and the towns, became unstoppable. In their early phase, these migrations took place with the consent of the *caciques* as part of a redeployment of *ayllus'* economic strategies, but in the long run home ties became weaker, and the migrants, especially in subsequent generations, gave up their rights in their communities of origin. This was the justification for the reforms of the Viceroy Duque de La Palata, who in the late seventeenth century "reduced" the "outsiders" to the places where they had settled. The measure was systematically implemented beginning in 1730.

These reforms placed "outsiders" who owned land into the same tribute category as "natives" of the community. Implicitly, tribute paying was now decided by land access and political inclusion in the community, which meant that the ancient criteria of birth or membership in a kinship group had at last been abrogated. This reversal was related to the desperation of *caciques* who did not hesitate to rent *ayllu* fields to "outsiders" and *mestizos*, or even to Spanish settlers. In pursuing rental revenues they sometimes used force to evict tribute payers returning from their tours of labor service. Such rental agreements were more or less regularly converted into legalized ownership on the occasion of the "land inspections" (*composiciones de tierras*). At the end of the sixteenth century, the middle of the seventeenth, and the beginning of the eighteenth, bouts of *composición* greatly shrunk enclaves of nontaxable land.

The changing possession of land within the *ayllus*, and alienation of land to the hands of non-Indian buyers, presuppose the existence of a land market. Not much is known about this market. It apparently operated at three levels: in the allocation and succession of family plots within the *ayllus*, in the allocation of community property, and in the leasing and taxation of lands by means of annuities (*censos*). In the second half of the eighteenth century, when the demographic recovery was no longer in question, market pressures aggravated conflicts over land within communities, between communities, and between communities and estates.

Access to the market also varied with the social status of the Indians. In the sixteenth century, *caciques* used their position of power to steer the communities' relation to the market. They would try to impose the highest prices for their farm produce in order to raise the sums needed for the tribute. But as a result of migrations, many more households gained direct access to the market. Domestic units living on land belonging to an *ayllu* or an estate (in both cases the renters were "outsiders" called *arrendires*) had sufficient freedom of movement to market any agricultural surpluses they might produce. And even during this period, the servitors referred to as *yanacona* could also sell their harvest directly in the nearest market town.

As for transactions between domestic units, recent studies seem to indicate that barter was carried out on the basis of a "counting currency" or imaginary unit of value, which formed the intellectual link between the commercial and the intraethnic circuits of reciprocity. Two different methods of pricing coexisted, one fluctuating with the market and one steadied by "permanent" customary barter equivalences. Households could choose depending on their estimate of current advantage. But it is possible that the peasant economies of the seventeenth and eighteenth centuries were more integrated in the internal market than we know, unable as we are to unravel the relation between monetary and nonmonetary practice. In any event Larson's studies of the Cochabamba Valley show that in the seventeenth and eighteenth centuries local communities competed successfully with the estates as suppliers of grain to the urban markets.

Some commandeering of peasant surpluses took place via preemption while produce was being conveyed to urban markets, mining towns, or fairs. When peasants arrived at these places with their merchandise, they were assailed by middlemen called *arquiris*, many of them of *mestizo* origin, who bought cheap by intercepting suppliers on behalf of retailers (often women vendors called *gateras, cancheras,* or *regatonas*). There was often an element of duress. In the eighteenth century municipal governments of the South-Central Andes complained in vain about this operation, which provided the middleman with an opportunity for speculation but thrived because it met a perceived need on the part of peasants who wanted to acquire cash quickly without having to deal with the urban market. More scandalous in the eyes of the producers and middlemen was the multiplication of "customs" taxes on supposedly tax-exempt indigenous products such as coca, maize, llamas, and textiles. "Customs" levies were to give rise to protests and disturbances in the eighteenth century.

One other set of burdensome and constantly increasing exactions were the various species of "God's rent." These included the share of the parish priest's salary to be paid by the "outsiders," the fees for sacraments (*obenciones*), the gifts (*ricuchicu*) given on feast days, and the money donated by honorary officials (*alfereces, mayordomos*) on festive occasions. Parishioners were also expected to subsidize their priests with ordinary supplies like firewood, fodder, and meals. Most galling, however, were the Church tithes and twentieth-taxes extended to indigenous products and *arrendires* in the 1650s. Tithes provoked numerous conflicts in which local communities were the losers.

By devising an adjustable scale of measurements, it is possible to arrive at a region-by-region profile of the indigenous economies. From the ecological and biological point of view, the Andean slope is divided into three major levels: the foothill piedmont, the temperate valleys, and the inter-Andean high plateaus. The highlands played a dominant role, thanks to the silver mines (located along the axis Caylloma-Puno-Oruro-Potosí-Chichas, which roughly follows the spine of the Andes), the great herds of camelids (providers of wool, meat, and transportation), and a large population. But within the highland corridor itself, there was a contrast between the drier western section, with its orientation toward the coastal desert and its river-valley oases, an area that was more highly appreciated among the Aymara, and the more humid eastern section, which looked out on the Amazonian forests and was considered inferior. The westward-looking, seaward perspective connoted mines, overseas exports, and a wide-ranging mercantile capitalism. The eastward-looking, Amazonian perspective connoted the production of crops, and dense virgin forests reachable by a network of middle-sized towns that were strongly integrated with their hinterland (Quito, Cuenca, Huamanga, Cusco, La Paz, Cochabamba, La Plata, and Salta). Urban zones divided the Andean space differently, the network of each making a distinctive transverse cut through orographic, economic, and political units. These determined productive specialties (for example, Cochabamba was the cereal producer for Potosí and Oruro, and the Mantaro Valley became

Lima's granary) and manufacturing activities (such as the textile mills of Quito and Cusco). Trade between production zones and areas of export or consumption secondarily promoted a series of circuits moving money, coca, and wine. Some commercial axes (Potosí-Arica, Lima-Cusco-Potosí) benefited ethnic groups living along the traffic paths, but living near major roads also brought burdens like compulsory service to travelers. Other regions, like the valleys of Larecaja and Arequipa and those near the Pacific coast, experienced the ruination of the *ayllus* together with market integration. In these areas natives gradually had to cede their lands to the Spanish. Sales were not solely a matter of economics. They were facilitated by a greater fragility of ethnic and political structures due to more heterogeneous settlement.

In the aggregate Andean integration into the market, with its successes and failures, raises the problem of the accumulation of wealth as a source of internal differentiation. In the early phase the groups that played a mediating role with the outside world, like the *caciques* and individuals connected with the Church or with tax collection, benefited materially from their differentiated roles. However, they also redistributed their profits in the form of ceremonial or sumptuary outlays, such as the building of churches and the purchase of sacred objects and paintings. In later phases it is not clear whether religious festivities and votive donations served to level fortunes or on the contrary to create deep inequalities of wealth.

Each mechanism of accumulation and internal differentiation became effective only in the context of precise economic and demographic conditions. In the seventeenth century, which was characterized by a shortage of labor power and by a great expansion of the internal market, highly effective integrative mechanisms connected town with country, and natives with "outsiders" who gradually became naturalized. Starting in the middle of the eighteenth century, against a background of economic and biological recovery as well as of greater fiscal pressure and a sharpening shortage of land, exclusionary mechanisms began to prevail.

In short, participation in market relations did not automatically lead to the disintegration of the community. In areas characterized by weak ethnic structures, it may have contributed to this outcome, but in other cases it actually reinforced the existing integrative structures. Each outcome makes sense only its own framework of ethnic and social organization.

Patterns of Ethnic Fragmentation and Community Restructuring

On the eve of the Túpac Amaru II wars (1780–1783), the political and ethnic map of the Andes looked very different from what it had been when Toledo reorganized the viceroyalty. Not only had the beheading of the first colonial Inka Túpac Amaru in 1572 put an end to expectations of Inka dynastic continuity, but large multicommunity chiefdoms and kingdoms had largely disappeared. In most areas they were replaced by a raft of local communities, each internally heterogeneous insofar as it contained both "natives" and "outsiders." But there were countertendencies. Throughout these two centuries some episodes of regional restructuring brought forth forms of social consolidation and articulation as solid as those they replaced.

As we have seen, some ancient political jurisdictions, where *caciques* used the law to have their rights recognized and resisted economic pressures, did succeed in attaching old supralocal powers to new colonial offices such as that of *alcalde mayor de naturales* or *capitán de mita.* At the macroregional level, the most striking example of this was the geographical coincidence of the new mita area of Potosí with the Inka *Qullasuyo* (one of the four world-quarters composing the ideal geography of the Inka state). The *caciques* of the former southern quarter reconstituted a kind of neo-imperial court at Potosí. On the whole in the course of the seventeenth century, demographic changes and increasingly harsh taxation led to the breakup of these major jurisdictions and caused native society to reconstitute itself around smaller poles of regional and local integration.

The main foci of integration were the reduction villages, formed in the 1570s and 1580s by forced settlement. Although they had enjoyed little legitimacy at first, some eventually became centers of social, political, and cultural (especially religious) control. These new administrative units were not always arbitrary, for their borders often coincided with those of previous territorial units (*llacta* in Quechua, *marka* in Aymara), and some of them had in fact been founded by the Inkas. Sometimes resettlement helped emancipate the lower-ranking segments of society (that is, lower "moieties" and *ayllus*) from centers of power where they lived at a disadvantage. In other cases the reduction plan itself was Andeanized: an Iberian-style village could become an autonomous Andean microcosm by dividing it into two opposing yet complementary halves, which, cutting through both the town and the territory, were comprehensive enough to organize all material and symbolic relations. Under the protection of the church's patron saint, who represented the power of heaven or the conquering state, these towns functioned in their residents' eyes as poles of civilization and legitimacy. *Ayllus* lived in "neighborhoods" spatially arranged around the central square according to dualist and hierarchical logic.

At the opposite pole from this center of civility extended "savage" outlying areas of collectively held but uncultivated territory: the high grasslands, the desert slopes, the rugged canyons. Many groups had members both in town (*pueblo*) and in remote hamlets (*estancias*) closer to herding or agricultural areas. So individual households could have a share in both central and remote domains and might move between them with the rhythm of the ritual calendar.

In actual historical process, however, it was difficult to complement an Andean model with a really Andean-controlled social practice. For one thing many domestic units only partially occupied the reduction settlements. Some groups had abandoned "reductions" during the waves of epidemics of the late sixteenth century. Others, especially in the most remote regions like the eastern Andes, had never finished their construction. Most commonly, domestic units tended to abandon places where colonial exactions were heavy because of closeness to the main routes.[24] By the same token, such reductions were also the first to be invaded by the Spanish and the mestizos, even though they were officially off limits. In the valleys communal land very soon began to pass to private buyers who built estates, often close to the reduction. These estates, illegal but hard to fight off, sought to monopolize the collectively held factors of production: water, pastures, and firewood. In the valleys along the Pacific coast and in the border regions of the eastern Andes, Andean towns usually bordered plantations that raised sugar cane or livestock.

It is thus hard to say whether the reductions came to be occupied by "non-Indians" because they were abandoned by the indigenous domestic units, or because they were taken over by Spanish and mestizo intruders. These two processes probably occurred together and hastened native retreat into the peripheral hamlets. Hamlets that built a chapel could raise their status to that of "annex" (*anejo*), and some were soon promoted to the rank of secondary parish. They became scenes of real,

[24] Saignes: "See the observations of the Jesuit priest Ayanz on the 'Royal Road between Cusco and Potosí in 1596'."

though often exogenous, change. If most of the "natives" left for faraway places, the "annex" hamlets took in other migrants from different places. This phenomenon is well documented for the South-Central Andes, where the polemic over the flight of the natives – a serious threat to the Potosí mines' labor supply – has provided us with a great deal of information. The ecclesiastical chronicler of Charcas, Ramírez de Aguilar, summarized the situation of the "native towns" (*pueblos de indios*) in 1639: "Even though there are no more than 130 *doctrinas* (missionary parishes), every parish has outside the main town many other hamlets with 50 to 100 heads of families, which they call 'annexes,' each with its chapel and confraternities. All of this comes to some 600 towns in the *puna* [high-altitude grassland] and valley, where there are many Indians, both native-born and newcomers, whom they call *mitimaes*."

"Annexes" could come to outweigh their "centers." This development took place in a context of labor shortage. In the next century, with population rebounding, a certain number of annexes became veritable "new towns." The 1770s brought a reorganization of the parishes, and in some cases recognition of annexes' achievement. Some of the newly recognized communities embarked upon reconquest of abandoned territory, both in the high pastures and in the inhospitable foothills (*montaña*). The proliferation of new communities invariably created new rivalries with the authorities of the original reduction towns, because, whether Andean or Spanish, they all meant to preserve their control over the hinterland.

One major problem for understanding how rural communities evolved is to find out how the indigenous inhabitants managed relations with migrants. Dictionaries of the native languages of the early seventeenth century distinguish among "settled outsider" (*mitmaq* in Quechua, *maluri* in Aymara), unstable or passing stranger (*caruruna, sariri jaqe*), and stranger without *cacique* or obligations (*qquitayacuk, huayqui*). All these terms are evidently spoken from the viewpoint of the receiving village. In the face of the intense waves of population exchange, the labels attached to the newcomers were eventually modified in such a way that they matched the vocabulary of marriage alliances. By the middle of the seventeenth century, some of the "outsiders" – those who had married into their receiving village – were referred to as "sons-in-law and nephews." (Of course this terminology did not prevent them – any more than it did the original inhabitants – from starting new cycles of migration.) The vocabulary of marriage alliance also served to symbolize the relation of genealogical subordination that came to characterize the relations between "annexes" and official centers: The crosses and statues that decorated the village chapels were considered the "sons-in-law" of those belonging to the church in town. On high religious holidays, such as the patron saint's day, the feast of the True Cross, or Corpus Christi Day, the images of the chapels went down to town to pay homage to those of the church and to partake of their sacredness. These patterns endure to the present in some places.

In addition to kinship built up by marital alliance, migrants and domestic units also built another relationship which, though more artificial, proved an equally effective means of integrating newcomers into wider and more open networks of exchange. This was baptismal sponsorship (*compadrazgo*), under which a baby's parents and godparents became bound by a consecrated alliance. Brought over from the Iberian peninsula, this form of ritual kinship caught on widely. It offered a double advantage. On one hand it compensated to some extent for the loss of relationships formed earlier within the framework of the endogamous *ayllus*. On the other, this elective, flexible, and far-reaching relationship was well adapted to the new kinds of dependency that ran through colonial society. *Compadrazgo* worked both horizontally, among domestic units living in widely dispersed places, and vertically, connecting rich patrons with poor clients. Everybody from viceroy to orphans needed *compadres*. Examination of parish registers reveals that the choice of godparents for baptism and marriage was sometimes governed by an egalitarian logic of alliance involving spatial complementarity (parents might seek *compadres* of their own rank who had access to advantageous ecological levels, or townfolk might ally with country couples who could supplement their diet). Other times humble households sought protection, credit, or prestige by inviting as godparents richer, more powerful, or ethnically advantaged families. The richer party gained allies who could be called on for help ranging from musclepower to political support; the poorer, protection.

Given these two modalities of alliance, exogamous marriage and baptismal sponsorship, one is led to wonder about possible transformations of the *ayllu* itself. If new kinds of linkage actually did the job of organizing society, was the nominal continuity of each *ayllu* any more than a verbal residue? Andean kinship centered on the household. In reckoning kinship anyone speaking for a house could, depending on the circumstances, emphasize either its bloodlines or its alliances, so *ayllus* and their members hardly lacked flexibility to define their rights opportunely in litigation (etc.). But the fact that legal actions about lands and waters tended to become a major forum for *ayllu* mobilization may have bent the social form toward a more territorial definition than Andean tradition required. (For example, Spanish courts tended to doubt claims, quite valid in Andean terms, that *ayllu* land control had nothing to do with contiguous territoriality.) It is possible that under pressure of resettlement and litigation, as well as of epidemics and migration, the *ayllu* gradually became a more territorial group. The main sources, such as censuses, do not reveal how much human, material, and ritual wealth the *ayllus* were able to transmit. We do know that *ayllus* defended hereditary collective land titles far into the eighteenth century. Had they not found a function within the colonial struggle for resources, the *ayllus* might have become empty shells maintained for simple reasons of administrative convenience (e.g., as census and tax categories), but they seem to have done more.

Alongside the *ayllu* the colony introduced crosscutting organizations that may have rivaled or even undercut the refurbished Andean organizations. One of the most dynamic was a new and highly successful religious unit we have already mentioned – namely, the voluntary *cofradía*, or confraternity. Members, sharing devotion to a saint, were bound to help each other and see to each member's burial. Indigenous parishes within Spanish towns were the first to set up confraternities, but they began to proliferate rapidly throughout the countryside in the first third of the seventeenth century. In 1609 a parish priest serving near Cusco remarked that "there is no end to the novelties and bribery added every day to the confraternities' costly festivities, nor to the new flags, and the solicitation of funds." The Franciscan Bernardino de Cárdenas thought Peru was producing too many brotherhoods: "There is no small town or village without four or five Indian confraternities, and in the largest ones there are ten, twelve, and twenty: every confraternity has its own flag, which is brought out on the feast day, and to this end, each year, they elect one Indian as their patron (*alférez*)."[25] At Potosí in 1654 the *corregidor* deplored this custom because it put a heavy financial burden on the "principal Indians who are already in charge of collecting the *mita*."

This situation has led some to see in the "cargo system" (that is, the requirement of increasingly costly festival sponsorships as the gateway to

[25] Saignes indicates the source only as "Cochabamba, 1632."

full civic status) a form of "ritual theft or impoverishment." At first the *caciques* and well-to-do families seem to have borne all these charges, which were bound to increase their prestige. But in a context of economic stringency and in conjunction with other exactions, expensive celebrations seemed to function as a mechanism for economic leveling and redistribution. We do not know exactly when these annual obligations began to rotate within the *ayllus*. We do see that in the long run sponsorship made the individual dependent on the community, because potential sponsors had to call on a large network of mutual help (i.e., to rely on those who had obligations to him, and also to incur new debts). Sponsoring festivals did force households into self-exploitation, but it was not an unproductive use of labor, savings, or credit. A "career of prestige" rewarded it. To support a festival sponsor was to invest in his or her future, guaranteeing reciprocal support when one needed it. And the debtor was not necessarily the loser, because every creditor now acquired a vested interest in his or her future solvency.

We also do not know just how, in the early colony, these ritual roles fitted in with the civil offices making up the town councils. We have already seen that in the period of their ascendancy, the immediate post-Toledan decades, indigenous nobilities often reduced the councils to formal functions. It is quite possible that religious validation was what made individuals believable as municipal officers, a development that favored gradual integration of the ritual and the council hierarchies into a single civic-religious "cargo system." Perhaps the cumulative sacred legitimation of councilmen, who were otherwise temporary (usually annual) functionaries, contributed to the shift of power away from the ancient local and regional dynasties as the great age of the *caciques* waned later in the seventeenth century. By the eve of the Túpac Amaru II revolt, hereditary lords were already suffering margination at the hands of a hierarchy of rotating communal authorities called *warayuqkuna* ('holders of staffs of office') in the region of Cusco, or *kuraqkuna* ('elders') in southern Bolivia. Where political units had become highly fragmented, these completely local officeholding systems could influence people powerfully.

To what extent should the confraternity be seen as an alternative to the *ayllu*? In central Peru, the superposition was perfect – at Pacaraos, for example, each of the four *ayllus* had its own confraternity – and the confraternity often inherited land consecrated to prehispanic *ayllu* divinities, which gave it an important economic role. The general success of the two non-*ayllu* forms of collective organization – namely, confraternities and municipal councils – probably had nothing to do with hostility to old forms. It had much to do with being locally controlled and with ability to manage new categories of population created by migration. Apparently these institutions were flexible and contractual enough to let natives and newcomers coexist and indeed to legitimate the newcomers' insertion into the community, including their access to land, by assigning them responsibilities in the round of cargos.

To summarize, gradual insertion into the market economy and growing emancipation from the tutelage of the ethnic lords did not automatically dissolve ties based on membership in an ethnic group. Ancestor worship, the cult of sacred places, and ritual or marital exchanges respecting old lines of consanguineal kinship all persisted. *Ayllus* often succeeded, through the ministrations of their *caciques* or of new elites, in creating marketable surpluses and at the same time sustaining relations of reciprocity within their own orbits. The mechanisms included a double circuit of exchanges based, respectively, on a selective use of money and a non- or quasi-monetary barter system. With these props to internal solidarity, *ayllus* were able to defend their territorial integrity and protect the reproduction of their community. Of course this was not achieved everywhere. In many places the weakness of ethnic political structures, and disadvantages vis-à-vis the market economy – for example, the absence of livestock in certain valleys – made it easy for Spanish settlers to intrude and shatter ties founded on lineal descent.

Endogenous change was only part of the picture. Colonial observers noticed that "only the most docile and least spirited [Indians] stayed at home." Internal migrations promoted a new social web founded on market relations. Ritual validation also occurred within institutions borrowed from the Iberian world, such as baptismal sponsorship, the confraternity, and the town council. As these imported sources of power were accepted, hierarchies founded on blood and age gave way to others that had to do with the acquisition of commercial wealth and with technical competence. In big areas of colonial native life, status was not so much inherited as achieved. All the same as new elites made their way upward through the costly "cargo system," their ascent itself depended enough on community solidarity to re-create and not replace local roots and identities.

TOWARD A COLONIAL ANDEAN CULTURE

Andean natives' attachment to their dogs seemed "extraordinary" to Lope de Atienza, who observed the Audiencia of Quito in the late sixteenth century, and also to the Jesuit Cobo who studied Lima and Charcas in the first half of the seventeenth. Spanish dogs were especially popular, so much so that the autochthonous breed seemed about to disappear in favor of the imported breed or its mixed offspring. Why were Andean people ready to adopt the "other" dog of Spanish or mixed race, bring it up "like a son," and leave the American breed to extinction? Could it be that the dog, which in South Andean folk belief mediates between the living and the dead, symbolized in its incarnation as a European or mixed-blood animal, the power of mediation with the conquering Wira Quchas (as Spaniards were called) or with the Christian Beyond? At one great *cacique's* funeral, the corpse was replaced "in the coffin by a large dog wrapped in a shroud, with its face covered by a piece of cloth." When the dog went to a church burial, the *cacique's* corpse was placed in a *chullpa* (prehispanic-style burial tower).

Atienza also reported that when night fell, Indians moved in the dark, seeing at best by the weak gleam of glowing embers. Hence Father Cobo said: "I once asked an Indian of great intelligence which of the things the Spanish had brought was most useful to human life, and he replied: 'the candle, because by converting night into day it prolongs human life.' So the Indians became great consumers of tallow candles."[26] Tantalizing clues to the subjective value of transatlantic novelties appear in testimonies about, for example, the dreams of accused "idolators." But the transformation of daily life in the Andes still largely eludes us.

At the level of basic ideological tenets, the opposition between the two cultural systems that were forced to cohabit was not as total as it would appear. The basic differences are obvious: While the Christian West lived by an ontological dualism in which Christ represented the exclusive model of mediation between this world and the next, the Andean universe rested on a unitary view of the visible and the invisible, held together by the figure of the Inka. It was in theology above all, particularly in the central notion of divinity, that disagreement stood out so fatefully. Andean–European likenesses are less obvious (to the European view) than are differences, but are just as important. The Iberian world

[26] Bernabé Cobo, *History of the Inca Empire* [1653] (Madrid 1964), Book 10, chapter 3.

view, tinged with mercantile-era humanism, carried within it large fragments of a pre-Christian traditional worldview that postulated the shared presence of the living and the dead and the continuity of inanimate and animate phenomena. Even in the dogmatic world of the counterreformation, points of convergence between these two cultural universes existed in the unspoken assumptions of folk practice. Among these were the belief in the equivalence of microcosm and macrocosm based on analogies and homologies, a model of origins explaining the growth and decline of the stars, minerals, plants, and animals, and some medical models and classifications involving the powers of plants. Simultaneous processes of cultural conflict, assimilation, and displacement, operating differently around different symbolic clusters, gave rise to a hybrid or syncretic culture. This was what Kubler and later Stern have characterized as the "colonial Andean" culture.

Material Culture and the Visual Arts

European dominion swiftly transformed material life, starting with diet. Some European cultigens spread rapidly – notably, wheat, grapes, and sugar cane. Chickens became common in the Andes with amazing speed, followed swiftly by sheep and goats, and then large beasts: cattle, donkeys, horses, and mules. It is true that tribute demands (mostly for wheat and chickens) stimulated adoption, but the main reason was local demand for novel products: bread, mutton, sheep's wool, wine (later, distilled liquor), and byproducts like tallow candles or the strong leather of European animals. At the mine metropolis of Potosí, observers writing in the early seventeenth century noted a shift away from freeze-dried potatoes and maize beer toward bread and wine, which had come to connote social distinction. New consumer habits had some harmful effects, among them the slow crowding out of vigorous native plants like *quinua* (*Chenopodium* spp., a freeze-resistant, protein-rich high altitude grain) and *tarwi* (the tasty "bean" of lupine). Invasive plants like clover, wild mustard, and wild turnip harmed Andean cultigens. In some areas sheep ranching displaced llamas and alpacas into higher, usually poorer, pasturage or even eliminated them.

Andean products also shifted in usage. Coca consumption, though important for millennia in ritual context, was secularized by new commercial sources and its consumption massified. Maize, formerly often distributed as hospitality food or beer by the nobility, the bureaucracy, and the Inka army, also became commoditized. Andean people ripped away from older kinship and political channels of distribution (*yanaconas*, and then laborers taken to the silver mines of Collao and Charcas) exerted demand for commercial coca and maize beer. This demand was met by a combined communal and mercantile circuit.

Western technology was seen not just as productive but as meaningful. Its meanings included a novel ideal of material and intellectual power capable of mastering and transforming – rather than interpreting and exchanging with – the nonhuman world. Andeans saw the achievement of this ideal in the conquest of night with artificial lights, or the mastery of animal strength through horse and cattle technology. (The New World had no native domesticates larger than llamas, which are not large enough to carry an adult.) They also saw mastery in the harnessing of air and water to drive mills that produced large amounts of cornmeal for brewing. Andean people saw moral costs as well as advantages in material advances. Garcilaso reported Indians' critical astonishment at the "laziness of the Spaniards" who relied on oxen to till the earth, and their more admiring surprise at the use of falcons for hunting. Andeans were glad enough to ease demands on musclepower by adopting the plough, the wheelbarrow, and the cart wherever they could (although none of these could replace local technology on steep fields, which Europeans never learned to cultivate or terrace). And they invested in commercially valuable animals when they could. By the first third of the seventeenth century, mules with their impressive loadbearing capacity were displacing llamas on major trade routes connecting Tucumán, Potosí, Lima, and Quito.

Clothing, the "social skin" that makes the man or woman, had traditionally indicated membership in a group and rank within it. The Inka regime forbade changing insignia without permission. In colonial society it still signaled ethnicity and other social variables and remained subject to sumptuary laws. Within this regimen clothing could carry traditional meanings too risky to express elsewhere: Andean textiles, an art form charged from remote prehistory with signifying the invisible, evoked the alliance between the living and the dead, including the ancients. Viceroy Toledo's prohibition of picturing divinities was not strictly obeyed in textile art. Cobo saw cloths depicting animals and plants of religious significance. Geometric motifs expressed fundamental Andean concepts of space and time in a visual language whose regional grammars are just beginning to be decoded. Cloth that covered stones or statues of saints absorbed the power of a lineage's ancestors or recharged them with celestial power.

Andean weavers' skill and productivity deeply impressed Spaniards. Textile tribute soon became a massive levy on domestic labor. This posed intercultural problems for all sides. If woven clothing bore ethnic marks, to whom could it be sold? Standard pieces were produced for the market of rural and urban servitors, who had to be clothed by their masters at a rate of two pieces per year (following a norm carried over from Inka military provisioning). But what of the clothing distributed to the *ayllus* as part of the forced sales imposed by later colonial *corregidores*? Some of that clothing came from textile tribute, and some was made in mills (*obrajes*). Who bought it? Did buyers wear it, and if so in home settings or when traveling to town? Or did they resell it to migrants? Perhaps clothing made to circulate in commerce was an early realization of generic, rather than specifically ethnic, Indianness.

"Geographical reports" of the 1580s emphasize that two categories set apart from the community, the *caciques* and the *yanacona*, tended to adopt Spanish dress. Markers of social prestige could also cross boundaries inside the hierarchies of the Andean world. Thus Atienza reported from the *audiencia* of Quito toward the end of the sixteenth century that "the equality and the liberty of all the Indians are such that *chipana* (bracelets) which formerly only seigneurs and nobles were permitted to wear, are today worn by everyone who can afford them." Similarly the *caciques* and "*mita* captains" who met at Potosí in 1608 denounced the many servant girls who abandoned the "native dress of their generation for the attire usually worn by the *palla* (Inka princesses) of Cuzco." They therefore called, as Guaman Poma de Ayala had done, for regulations forbidding servant girls to wear "shirts, skirts, and espadrilles, for this is how they become corrupt and leave their families. The *hatunruna* (adult plebeian men) should also be forbidden to dress like *yanacona* in wool cloth and silk and to wear *abadejos*, shirts, and shoes." The same request was repeated a half-century later.

Sumptuary laws about clothing expressed municipal authorities' readiness to join *caciques* in trying to suppress counterfeit signs of rank, and to slow down the de-Indianizing of vassal Indians. They threatened to take away people's capes and wigs and to put the wearers back into their "tunics and native attire." The repeated promulgation of this legislation shows that it had little effect. By the eighteenth century, sumptuary violations no longer caused much concern. Alonso Carrió de la Bandera explained how an Indian could "pass for a cholo" by washing, combing his hair, and putting a clean shirt on; and dressing [in European clothes] and shoes could make him into a "nominal mestizo." Contemporary drawings show that mixed clothing with borrowings and adaptations from both models became the rule and also created new regional variations.

When did costumes characterizing the inhabitants of a specific ecological level (the coastal plain, the highlands, and the rain forest) or a specific occupation (muleteer, herdsman, artisan) come into being? In certain regions such clothing replaced ethnic costume. The tilt toward occupational dress may have to do with migrants' preference for occupations themselves connected with clothing, adornment, and bodily decorum. Weaving, leatherworking, hosiery, embroidering, dyeing, tailoring, shoemaking, and hatmaking were trades open to nonpeasant Indians.

The covering of the highest and lowest parts of the human body, the head and the feet, mattered most for signaling group membership. Headdress design and color had long indicated regional or ethnic identity. Did the quick success of the felt (or animal skin) hat betray a desire to escape pigeonholing? Wearing a European-style hat may have been a sign of social and geographical mobility; hats could be combined with communal headdresses (*chucu*) and other Andean insignia such as fringes, turbans, headcloths, or headbands. The appropriateness of Andean or Spanish headgear and footwear depended on context. When Indians went, for example, to worship at an ancient Andean shrine, they were not to wear Spanish clothing, "not even a hat or shoes" according to Arriaga. But for the migrant, hats and shoes, even without stockings, represented the surest means of avoiding getting spotted as absentees from an identifiable area.

The colonial architecture of churches and public buildings followed Spanish structural plans, but here too, Indians could fashion a "social skin": painting, reliefs, and all the artisanry of surfaces. Even though the churches rebuilt in the eighteenth century between Arequipa and Potosí preserved a formal structure borrowed from the European baroque, their decor was directly inspired by the Andean flora and fauna, including such superhuman presences as the sun or the siren mermaids. Historians of architecture write of the "mestizo style." Similar motifs adorned certain textiles, like the so-called transitional women's *lliclla*s, rugs, and hangings. This Andean decor – which even shows Amazonian features such as monkeys, parrots, palm trees, and manioc, and sometimes also represents historical clichés such as the Inka conquest of the *chunchos*, or Amazonian "savages" – occurred in multiple media. It commonly appeared on *queros* (painted or enameled wooden beakers), *mates* (gourd vessels), and receptacles for everyday use.

For a time pre-hispanic pieces circulated as "antiquities" – that is, valued vestiges of a desecrated past. It appears that they continued to be used in clandestine rituals into the seventeenth century. During that century they gradually ceased to figure in *caciques'* wills, and in the mid-colonial era, their prestige declined. Cobo reported that valuable heirloom antiques were already hard to find before 1650. (Of course looting of pre-Christian tombs, which was legal, continued apace.) One therefore wonders whether they still meant anything to people, aside from the value of their weight in precious metal.

The Genesis of an Andean Christianity

Spanish colonial intellectuals furiously debated the impact of evangelization on indigenous consciousness and the people's attitudes toward philosophical issues: life and death, time and space, the mediating role of Christ and the Catholic Church in preparing for the future salvation of the soul. Radically divergent answers were proposed. Some thought the Indians a flock of sincere and devout believers. Others felt sure their practice of Christianity was superficial and barely concealed fierce attachment to prehispanic beliefs. Present-day historians and ethnographers are equally divided. In 1946 Kubler paraphrased with approval the bishop of Quito, de la Peña y Montenegro, who attested in 1668 that by 1660 the conversion of the Quechua Indians to Catholicism was an accomplished fact. Duviols, the pioneer modern historian of Andean missionization and persecution, holds this view on the whole while also seeing conversion as compatible with certain Andean beliefs, especially in the area of healing.

Father M. Marzal proposes three stages for the process of Christianization: "intensive Christianization" from 1551 to 1608; the great campaigns to extirpate "idolatry" from 1608 to 1660; and the "crystallization of an Andean religious system" after 1660. N. Wachtel agrees with this schema. But historians such as C. D. Valcárcel or P. Borges and especially anthropologists and missionaries, such as S. Monast in Carangas, emphasize the survival of "purely" Andean beliefs and rites to this very day. They hold that one can at best speak of religions in coexistence. Any attempt to make sense of colonial culture forces one to state how the indigenous population was able, over two centuries, to juxtapose or integrate into a single entity the two complexes of meaning – autochthonous and Christian – that formed the core of religious practice.

In analyzing the process of religious accommodation, one must above all face up to its chronological and geographical unevenness. Religious change was related to integration with colonial markets and to cohabitation with the Spanish settlers. Here one reencounters divergences between regions that were more open to such modernizing influences – Quito or Collao, for example – and those that were more isolated or less affected by the Spanish intrusion, such as the outlying high hinterlands of Lima, Huamanga, or Arequipa.

The most difficult task of evangelization was rendering the main tenets of the Christian religious system into Andean language. Founded on the ontological duality between heaven and earth, or spirit and matter, Christianity centered on a remote, all-powerful God whose otherness separated life on earth from contact with the invisible. Andean religion, by contrast, was founded on the unity of the cosmos. It catalogued "the tangible world in all its singularity," according to Andean "orders of things" – taxonomies and genealogies that placed beings into homological relations aligning the high and holy with the mundane. For example, a llama constellation and an amulet of llama fertility belonged in the same category with llama pastures and the animals themselves; all partook of a common species energy (*camay*) and were not to be merged with other homological clusters. Andean thinking detected in the dogmatic proposal of conversion a merging of such essential (in the strict sense of the word) categories, and explained Europe itself within them. The Dominican Francisco de la Cruz reported that in native eyes, "The Indians are not descended from Adam like the Spanish, for they have a different origin . . . an Indian always begets an Indian, and a Spaniard a Spaniard, just as a black begets a black." Hence "the law of the Christian is good for the Spanish and necessary, since they are descended from Adam, but not for them [the Indians], for they do not need it."[27]

Depending on the greater or lesser permissiveness of the religious orders, some practical accommodations were made. Some clergy allowed diffusion of a popular Mediterranean Christianity, imbued with what

[27] Letter to the King, 1657. AGI [Archivo General de Indias/Sevilla], Lima 57; cited in Manuel Marzal, *La transformación religiosa peruana* (Lima, 1983), 133–137.

others saw as undesirable "superstitions" and Greco-Latin references. These bits of pre-Christian iconography, particularly representations of animals, appealed to Indians for whom animals were invested with the full force of the sacred. A sort of semiological blind man's buff ensued, in which churchmen tried, very fallibly, to predict the reception and interpretation of symbols. In order to represent the Trinity – and particularly to avoid showing the Holy Ghost in the form of a dove – Christian artists preferred to paint three Christs, and sometimes three-headed Christs. In doing so they unintentionally recalled threefold prehispanic divinities. The Trinity was also interpreted as the fruit of the Sun-God and the Virgin-Moon, who procreated a Christ-Son; Christ himself could even be perceived as the younger or older brother of the devil.

The failure of evangelization was also blamed on linguistic misunderstandings. Many priests did not know the indigenous languages, and the Indians did not know Spanish, or refused to speak it even if they did. Spaniards tried to palliate this situation in two ways, by extending the use of Quechua and Aymara as "general languages," and at the same time by teaching Spanish to the Indians. This resulted in the creation of an artificial Quechua, a compromise between the dialect associated with Chinchay Suyu and that of Cusco, and the extension of Aymara at the expense of Pukina and Uruquilla, which became extinct in the course of the eighteenth century. At similar dates the northern parts of the ex-Inka domains lost most ethnic languages such as Puruhá and Cañari.

It also resulted in many mistranslations and errors in rendering Christian concepts. Thus the concept of "communion of saints" became *hucllachacuininta* in Quechua, a word that the young villagers in charge of teaching dogma transformed into "game of saints" (*pucllachacuininta*). This mistake was enough to bring down the condemnation of the extirpation judges. But how can they be blamed? The root *huc* ("one") – the Cusco form of the numeral – and the entire composite word derived from it, were practically incomprehensible in context, unlike the word formed with the root *puklla-* ('to play'). Likewise Guaman Poma, a fervent Catholic, spontaneously transformed many of the Christian prayers in his Quechua versions. He had no choice, because a literalistic translation thrown across the doctrinal and linguistic gulf would have arrived as gibberish.

The linguistic obstacle compounded the insufficient intellectual and theological training of many parish priests. Incompetent in the first place, many were also frequently absent from the countryside and shouldered their parishes onto more or less temporary replacements. Pastoral visitations and investigations for the extirpation campaign repeatedly noted these shortcomings, without managing to do much about them. Admittedly the large size and the difficult terrain of the parishes, along with the Indians' tendency to leave the central villages and migrate, or to settle in outlying hamlets, made the task almost impossible.

The relative shortage of priests heightened the importance of the numerous locals attached to the Church (sacristans, administrators of church property, cantors, and sponsors of saint festivals). This privileged group, which in certain reductions did not have to pay the tribute, occasionally included almost the entire adult male population. These intermediaries were not without ambivalence about the Andean cults. Father Avila of Huarochirí Province denounced apparently church-oriented people as backsliders if not apostate traitors: "Many Indians who speak our language (*ladinos*), who know how to read and write and have been educated with priests and Spanish teachers, and others who are cantors and music masters of their church, teach their children as soon as they reach the age of reason to be idolators and take them to sacrifices as Christians take their children to church."[28] Left to their own devices, these mediators elaborated an extremely heterodox syncretism.

The most serious obstacle to an effective Christianization, however, was the perception that evangelization and the Church were deeply involved in the system of colonial exploitation. "The priests and preachers exercise their functions in such a way that the Indians believe them to be more interested in the profits they can make than in teaching them the faith" was a 1657 judgment.[29] Because a large part of the clergy did indeed think first about acquiring wealth, they not only lost sight of their spiritual tasks but also forgot (though seminaries had insisted) the Indians had to be prepared to receive sacraments and major doctrinal truths. It was not just a matter of low priorities. Some clergymen explicitly refused to provide their flocks with primary and religious education, because education might reveal unfairness in the Indians' condition and cause them to turn against their clergy. Indians were well aware of their exclusion from certain sacraments such as communion and ordination, as well as of the priests' neglect of any spiritual dimension. In other words, Indians' demand for a true Christianization was not met.

[28] 1611, AGI [Archivo General de Indias/Sevilla], Lima, 301.

[29] Saignes' note indicates only "F. de la Cruz, 1657."

This threefold limitation – doctrinal ambiguity, linguistic slippage, and sociological neglect – explains why contemporaries wrote very pessimistic diagnoses. Arriaga already felt in 1621 that the Indians spoke their devotions "like parrots." A century later, in the *audiencia* of Quito, the Spanish travelers Juan and Ulloa delivered a bitter dose of realism:

> Each priest chooses a blind Indian to say catechism to the others. Standing in the middle of the group, the blind man intones prayers word for word, not singing them properly or reciting them well. The audience repeats after him. Sometimes the blind Indian does it in the Inka or Indian language common to the area, at other times in Spanish, which is not intelligible to anyone. Lasting a half hour or more, this instruction is not fruitful . . . they know only how to sing and to repeat verbatim certain fragments of the catechism. . . . Of the little they do know, their comprehension is so small that if one asks the identity of the Holy Trinity, sometimes they reply it is the Father and at other times they reply that it is the Blessed Virgin.[30]

In 1782 a seasoned expert on Peru, the postal inspector Alonso Carrió de la Bandera, thought much the same: "The priests do not properly explain the Gospel to the Indians, for they do not understand their language. Their assistants do not do it because they do not understand the Gospel or the letter of the Latin language." As a result, "through their chanted or spoken poems the Indians preserve many of their idolatries and tales of their ancestors' grandeur."[31] The practices outlined later suggest that these gloomy estimates of Church performance were not unfounded.

The cult of the dead and ancestor worship occupied a central position in ancient Andean religion. Mummified corpses, especially those of founders of *ayllus* or kingdoms, were thought to contain a sacred energy, a life-giving force (*"camaquen", "enqa", "illa"*) that could give riches and health or their opposites. Colonial leaders descended from these ancestors, the *kuraka* and *mallku* called *caciques* by Spaniards, inherited this power. The Andean moral economy assumed that it formed the foundation of leaders' legitimacy, always on the condition that they use it for their subjects' good. In this hierarchical world, everyone received power according to the qualities of his or her ascendants, just as one's fortune and position after death were similar to those one enjoyed among the living. Although the concept of death was basically unitary, the cult of

[30] Jorge Juan y Santacilia and Antonio de Ulloa, in John Jay TePaske (ed.), *Discourse and Political Reflections on the Kingdoms of Peru* (Norman, Oklahoma, 1979), 116–117.

[31] Alonso Carrió de la Bandera, in Pablo Macer (ed.), *Reforma del Perú* [1782] (Lima, 1966).

the dead in general should be distinguished from ancestor worship, which mainly concerned *caciques.*

We know almost nothing about prehispanic understandings of what happened to deceased individuals after death. What left the body but endured elsewhere was an individual essence imagined as "soul," "breath," "shadow," or "spirit": It was a rarified presence that could be called back to the mummified body in ritual. It is difficult to trace how theories of death changed under the pressure of evangelization and coalesced into colonial-era beliefs about the role of the dead in the renewal of fertility. The objective of funeral rites apparently remained unchanged. It was a matter of sending the deceased person away without offending him, and without losing his benefactions on the living. This implied a relationship with the past and the future founded on debt and reciprocity. The cosmos was perceived as a finite and stable entity that included animate and inanimate beings, the living and the dead. Thus it was said at the time of an epidemic: "So many Indians have died that all they can get in Upaymarca is a tiny piece of land, no bigger than your fingernail." Upaymarca was the high place where the dead dwelled; it was imagined as a field or farm.[32]

Christianity, which is founded on the central mystery of the incarnation of a God, his crucifixion, entombment, and resurrection, could look from Andean perspective like a funerary religion related to notions of transgression and expiation. This made sense in the indigenous framework, but there was room for doubt about practice. One of the central signs of Christianization was the shift from exposing dried or embalmed corpses in ancestor caves (*machay*) or funerary towers, to burying them, which the Indians at first perceived as suffocating them. The struggle over the resting place of the dead – church and cemetery versus grotto and tower – continued until at least the end of the seventeenth century. Villagers did not hesitate to rescue corpses from burial vaults in churches and place them into caves. Corpse rescues tended to take place where surveillance was light and visits by clergymen rare, especially in towns whose populations had moved to outlying annexes.

It is possible that concentrating most funerary ceremonies in the month of November, between All Saints (November 1) and Saint An-

[32] Hernando Hacas Poma, in Pierre Duviols' *Cultura andina y represión: procesos y visitas de idolatrías y hechicerías, Cajatambo, siglo XVII* (Cusco, 1986). The citation, from Cajatambo (1657), is on p. 171.

drew's Day (November 30), served to ensure continuity of the cult, which now took place in cemeteries. Surely having the dead present in the heart of the "civilized" space of the village, where the villagers met every Sunday for the festive celebrations of the Catholic liturgy, would keep the dead close to the living. Ritual drinking bouts and annual offerings of maize beer and food on the graves perpetuated these ties. Moreover burying the dead must have reinforced belief in the direct role of the dead in the cyclical renewal of nature, particularly that of plants and minerals.

Rituals that substituted for older Andean forms were celebrated even in cities. Every year on the eve of Saint Andrew's Day, the Indians and *mestizos* of Cochabamba (modern Bolivia) disinterred dead bodies and exposed them in their church, where they drank all night with their ancestors. They then took the heads to their homes in order to honor them before reinterring them. The honors included a series of masses, responses, vigils, and novenas "with the body present," culminating in the request that the dead help in appealing for life-giving rains.

As for the cult of the mummies in prehispanic holy sites, it did continue in isolated areas such as Andagua (near Arequipa, Peru) until the middle of the eighteenth century. Annual rituals provided the mummies with changes of clothing and food offerings. Political leaders in Andagua claimed access to the "first and true owners" of the community's wealth – namely, mummies – and this claim occasioned conflict and tension by challenging colonially authorized officers. Later modifications of cult may have been affected by the need to reduce such conflict, which attracted repression. The power incarnated in mummies of founding ancestors was gradually transferred to three new locations: mountain tops, the bell-tower (*torre mallku*), and bundles of sacred textiles belonging to ancestors.

Colonial Christianity conflated the enduring dead with devils, and by doing this, it also gave the devil a positive or at least tractable aspect. This is most visible in the miners' carnival practiced in the southern Andes. In missionary lexicon the devil was called *supay*, a colonial Quechua gloss using an older word for 'shade', which also referred to the soul of the dead. At carnival time, this ambiguous class of beings was (and still is) honored for its mastery of untapped wealth. In theatrical representation the Virgin Mary and Saint Michael Archangel domesticated the devil(s). Demons incarnating the "spirits" of the dead hastily retreated into the earth. There they were made to do the work of germination – plant fertility, but also the "growth" of metals underground – with the moon's help. Carnival marked the conclusion of the local cycle of the dead which, connected with the season of rain and sowing, had begun at All Saints.

Just like the *wakas* or holy objects, the statues of Christian saints were endowed with sacral power and thought to be *camaquen*, repositories of species energy or *camay*. However, according to early colonial preachers of Andean cults, saints' power was not available to Indians because saints belonged in a different order. Ynes Upiay confessed in 1657 that she had helped persuade natives "not to worship God our lord because that was for Spaniards and that they [Indians] had another god namely the *malquis* [mummies] who gave them food, wealth, life, and health, fields and everything they needed, and the God of the Spanish gave them nothing."[33] During the colony – we do not know when – the antithesis between saints and "idols" yielded to an integrated hierarchical arrangement, whose relations of subordination could at times be reversed. At Hacas (Peru), for instance, the votive celebration of San Pedro did not start until offerings had been presented to the *waka*. On the other hand, the *wakas*, now seen as powers (or "spirits") of the landscape, were governed by heavenly powers of Christendom.

This rearrangement was related to the spectacular rise in the number of confraternities responsible for votive celebrations and funerals. We have already seen the sociological implications of this proliferating form of solidarity. The confraternity boom was also related to the desire to partake of the power of the "Spanish *waka*," according to an anecdote conveyed by Arriaga, who tells of a small town where the four confraternities already had four very handsome statues of their respective saints but some people had stopped invoking them because they felt a need to visit stronger and newer saints that they had not yet "bought." The continual founding of new confraternities made for more and more masses and celebrations, a fine source of profit for the local clergy. By 1630 the civil and upper ecclesiastical authorities were trying in vain to slow the trend down and even to stop it. But they failed completely. These local brotherhoods had irresistible appeal; banding together in confraternities, with their hierarchy of offices grouped about their flag, amounted to setting up a strategy for material and ritual self-

[33] Pierre Duviols, *Cultura andina y represión: procesos y visitas de idolatrías y hechicerías, Cajatambo, siglo XVII* (Cusco, 1986), 297.

organization, in which Indians could at last take charge of their own cultic needs.

It was within this new framework that an indigenous cosmology evolved over the next two centuries. This new synthesis grouped together on one side Christ, the Virgin, and the saints, perceived as splinters of the sun, and on the other the spirits of the mountains, seen as cthonic divinities. The help of both these powers *in equal proportion* was necessary for the reproduction of the local community. Every year at the festival of the patron saint, the holders of the celebratory offices (*alférez, mayordomos*) therefore had to identify themselves with the hierarchy of celestial powers charged with taming the "savage" powers embedded in the animate landscape of the countryside. Only then could the cyclical renewal of the cosmos take place. For this purpose every annex carried out rituals involving its chapel, the statue of its saint, and its cross. Addressed *both* to the "pagan" and the "Christian" powers, these rituals were designed to strengthen local autonomy.

We know much less about the readjustments connected with the Christianization of sacred places (crosses, oratories, statues) or with the redefinition of the often prehispanic objects containing mediators of fertility (amulets and statuettes called *illa* or *conopa*). These sacred things were seen as miniature domestic instantiations of the prototypic life force(s), *camay*, which fostered each kind of good: llamas, tubers, and so forth. Similarly much work remains to be done on the proliferation of images of the Virgin and of Marian sanctuaries in the seventeenth and eighteenth centuries. Related to an increase in local and regional pilgrimages throughout the Andean area, Quechua Marianism apparently responded to the Marian fervor exploding throughout the Catholic world by rooting it in landscape features seen as both sacred and female. In the northern Andes, pilgrimage shrines known as "virgin mothers" were usually built over already-sacred canyons and springs where holy waters and curative minerals come out of the rock.

Shamanism, Stimulants, and Subversive Dreams

In imperial Inka religion, priests regulated relations among the living, the dead, and the gods according to a system of structured and codified knowledge. Their monopoly of relations with the invisible and a hierarchical cosmos did not leave much room for shamanic practices founded on direct access to the "spirits." After the fall of the empire, however,

Inka priests were among the first to be persecuted. Some of them continued their ministrations, particularly old men who lived in remote areas, because they were charged with serving an ancient sacred place or the mummies of a chiefdom or an *ayllu*. But many of these establishments were abandoned (or taken over). Colonial pressures selected in favor of new specialists who, less attached to particular places, could move about throughout the Andes. These were apparently the persons referred to as "sorcerers" by their enemies. At the same time the use of stimulants such as coca, alcoholic beverages, and hallucinogens was spreading.

These changes in the early colonial era raise questions about the degree of entrenchment and acceptance of the colonial system. The changes conquest had brought, particularly the forcible melding of sometimes hostile *ayllus*, and migrations that created tensions on a more individual level, had generated conflicts about whole new ways of life as well as anxieties about the demise of old traditions. The apparent flourishing of shamanism and other innovative forms may relate to a set of underlying expectations about some kind of "cosmic revolution" proper to an early colonial moment of uncertainty and danger.

As early as the middle of the sixteenth century, the lawyer and Inka expert Polo de Ondegardo reported changes in shamanic practices. Young men and women were practicing and getting payment in offerings rather than in live sacrifices. Specialization seemed to ramify: Healers and diviners worked with hallucinogens, and other individuals claimed ability to predict the future from observation of coca leaves, spiders, snakes, or beans. Most tellingly, straightforward sorcerers now coexisted with healers who, claiming to have received their "power from God, from the Fathers, or from the Apostles," carried out their "ceremonies" after Catholic confession.[34] Somewhat later, Murúa wrote of "wandering Indian medical men who call themselves licenciates" (using a term referring to a professional credential of Spanish lawyers) and claimed to have received the Church's approval.[35]

Calling on the shaman was a way to fortify connection with the cosmos and to stimulate the circulation of cosmic energy. People manipulated sacred objects in combinations that included both amulets and

[34] Juan Polo de Ondegardo, "De los errores y supersticiones de los Indios" [1584], in Carlos A. Romero (ed.), *Colección de libros y documentos referentes a la historia del Perú*, Ser. 1, vol. 3 (Lima, 1916) pp. 1–44. See especially Chs. X–XIV.

[35] Martín de Murúa, in Manuel Ballesteros Gaibrois (ed.), *Historia general del Perú* [1611?] (Madrid, 1986), book 2, Chs. 26 and 27.

small statues of saints, showing that they felt the need of a twofold consecration within the Andean–Christian context. But integrating Christianity was a job to be done under conditions that also put new constraints on relations with other sacred forces. Andean shamanic power was founded above all on access to the powers transmitted from origin times to living people through the chain of superhuman-to-human genealogy: *waka*, ancestor mummy, *cacique*. These hierarchical structures had long held the *ayllu* together, but with the Christian assault on the mummies and the old shrines, they now had to be vested exclusively in the mountain divinities, called *mallku* in Aymara. Only the mountain lords and their actions in the form of climatic forces were beyond the power of the Spanish to desecrate. The power (*camac*) contained in mummies, also called *illa*, was therefore transferred into the lightning bolt (*illapa*; on the Andean heights lightning strikes are common and often fatal). Lightning could be seen as a mountain's awesome response to a consultation. The condor, sometimes imagined as the reincarnation of a great shaman, became the messenger flying between the snowy crags and humanly inhabited lands.

During these two centuries, the Kallawaya (also written Callahuaya) of the eastern valleys of the Collao – the keepers of the Qulla/Pukina heritage, in which meteorological divinities like lightning played a major role – became itinerant specialists in a therapeutic shamanism that was both sought after and feared. Confession lay close to the core of healing because illness was perceived as the consequence of a disorder, a perturbation of the cosmos. This implies notions of transgression, guilt, and punishment, which were central to prehispanic beliefs. Polo notes that the idea of sin came to be applied not just to actions but to thoughts (or intentions) as well, implying a process of internalization and individuation under the influence of Christianity.

All this is poorly known, given the clandestine nature of magic curing, but it matters greatly for appreciating the anxiety that gripped early colonial people. The need for the traveling shaman-healer had much to do with the dangerous disruptions that shook indigenous society. Some of these dangers came from perturbation in relations with land. Migrations separated people from their places of origin, and thus from their ancestors. This problem could be palliated by bringing along stones and bones that symbolized them. Other dangers were economic and had to do with the accumulation of wealth; celebratory spending associated with officeholding in a market-driven system may have served to soften immoral inequalities. Psychic stresses multiplied as the *ayllus* took to the roads. Emigration implied treason toward the kin group and the dissolution of ethnic identities.

Born of the fragmentation of the *ayllus*, proliferating conflicts among communities pitted the traditionalists – who recruited their followers among poor, deprived, and marginalized strata, often including the "sorcerers" and shamans – against the new notables advancing in the market economy and espousing then-modern Catholicism. Andean therapies that violated Lima's laws and challenged colonial authority were thus implicit appeals to restore social cohesion. Healers were known to the community and licensed to deal with its secrets. In the colonial setting, accusations of sorcery and recourse to shamanism revealed a state of internal tension and violence to the shrewd gaze of other candidates for the monopoly of village power: priests, *caciques*, and *corregidores*.

The colonial era brought an increasingly widespread and casual consumption of coca, alcohol, and, to a lesser extent, hallucinogens. This was related to the abolition of ceremonialisms and sumptuary privileges associating coca with ritualized authority, from the Inka downward. Spanish times brought commercial pressure to permit the highly profitable mass sale of stimulants to Indians. Andean commoners' eagerness to consume reflected above all the search for greater energy and for restored communication with the sacred.

The coca leaf contains vitamins and alkaloids that modify or pace the transformation of staple dietary carbohydrates into glucose. At high altitude it therefore appeared to be a power concentrate. At the same time it was also a vehicle of reciprocity among people and between humans and the gods, because it was used in the main rites of offerings, sacrifices, and divinations. The massification of the coca market is associated with the ascendancy of mining, and its production curves match those of silver production at Potosí. But we know nothing at all about the leaves produced and exchanged within individual communities. Complaints about taxes and tolls levied on coca became increasingly frequent in the eighteenth century.

Information about the social use of hallucinogens, such as achuma (*Trichocereus pachanoi*, the San Pedro cactus), espingo (*Ocotea* sp.) and *chamico* (*Datura stramonium*, a source of atropine) is rare, simply because drug-visionary practices were seen as highly transgressive. Spanish chroniclers agreed that their consciousness-altering effects were "marvelous" and tend to confirm their widespread use. The conviction that hallucinations contain truths was evident in shamanic practices as well as in some popular subversive movements.

Drinking alcohol was a way to acquire the power of fertility. Viceroy Toledo himself acknowledged that "all idolatry comes with drinking bouts" and that "no drinking bout comes without superstition or idolatry." Alongside fermented drinks, distilled alcohol seems to have taken the place of the less easily available hallucinogens. Both were used with the same intention, that of rapidly achieving a state of altered consciousness.

As with coca a spectacular rise in alcohol use after the conquest reflects the break with the strict social norms of the Inka era. It probably also had to do with processes of psychic adaptation to the new colonial realities. From the authorities' constant complaints about drunkenness, one can ascertain that social drunkenness (as opposed to individual alcoholism) had several different meanings. At the cosmic level, on occasions of agrarian and funeral ritual, it was to stimulate the circulation of fertilizing energy and at the same time to reactivate the group's relations with the past, with the ancestors, and with the land. At the social level, drinking renewed ties among the drinkers by multiplying acts of resiprocity – Andean drinking is always reciprocal – and infusing feelings of heightened energy into the social bond. Drunkenness also had specific cultural correlates. When drunk, Andean people who did not freely speak Spanish would often use Spanish words, as if showing off ability to manipulate the conqueror's cultural register while refusing to be merged in Spanish identity.

Rounds of social drunkenness paralleled the increasingly influential Catholic liturgical calendar. And if drinking parties often took place in the cemetery around the church, it was no doubt because this was the place where the dead were closest to the living. Pervasive drinking, as it came to mark not only communal rituals but also the more individual and secular stages of the life cycle, dramatized profound changes in indigenous behavior. The new social cohesion built around specifically colonial complexes like confraternities and baptismal relationships was particularly associated with drinking. It conferred upon these relationships a halo of ritual validation in their own right, leaving them independent from the tutelage of the old authorities such as the *caciques* and the Inka.

These tendencies sometimes fostered popular fantasies of subversion, hidden under apparent complaisance. "They used to send bars of Potosí silver by llama, entrusting all the riches going to Spain to Indians who slept outside every night, with only six or eight Indian shepherds guarding 500 bars." Thus the chronicler Ramírez del Aguila described the situation in 1639, before the shipping of silver was entrusted to Spanish mule trains. More than a century later, a Jesuit chronicler still spoke of the remarkable internal security commercial transport enjoyed in the viceroyalty of Peru. This tranquility can largely be explained by Indians' loyalty to the crown and to the colonial order. Yet loyalty coexisted and contrasted with a latent expectation of a "reversal" (*pachacuti*) of the existing power relation. *Pachacuti* would include the expulsion of the Spanish. This expectation came out in the extravagant speech of drunkenness, as reported by an estate owner from the valleys around Potosí. "The Indians" he wrote, "have very firm hopes that the Spanish will have to give up their lands and leave them [the Indians] behind as free people."[36] Just as the first Spaniards, called Wira Quchas after the god who had marked a new era, had arrived when the twelfth Inka announced the end of an age, so new signs presaging the Spaniards' impending departure would appear. And who would replace the Spanish?

The reversal or *pachacuti* could be imagined as a "natural" catastrophe, such as the explosion of the volcano Omate (Huayna Putina) near Arequipa in February 1600, which was interpreted as a blow aimed at destroying the Spanish. Other earthquakes, like the one that struck Cusco in 1646, and tidal waves, like the one that wrecked the port of Callao in 1746, were also perceived as forerunners of a universal upheaval. At times this somewhat passive expectancy combined with more active conspiracies, which usually counted on the intervention of powerful outside allies. In the 1580s the *caciques* of the Collao and of Charcas appealed to British pirates, but their letters to "our Lutheran brethren" were intercepted. In 1613 Indians of the Central Andes hoped to enlist the help of "savages" in the Amazonian foothills. Significantly both these uprisings were to erupt on Easter Sunday and then were postponed until Corpus Christi. That is, the original scheduling was to coincide with the period during which the Spanish God, Christ, was dead, and the rescheduling with the winter solstice, when the sun, having reached its lowest position on the horizon, seems to hesitate before resuming its ascendant course and thus favors the outbreak of chaos. Other plots as well were to be carried out on exceptional dates hospitable to occult forces – for

[36] Saignes' note on the source reads only "ANB [Archivo Nacional de Bolivia?] Cartas 877."

example, in years formed by three identical numbers such as 1666 and 1777. Unusual moments in time opened the way for insurrection to usher in a new time.

But the very fact that these subversive macro-Andean plots were aborted before they could be carried out – either betrayed or abandoned – indicates that they probably did not go beyond the stage of vague hopes and feverish talk. Ineffectual talk of transformation might flare up when *caciques* were involved in legal initiatives on vital issues such as the abolition of the *mita* or personal service. What really did take place were local *jacqueries* or peasant revolts in response to specific abuses, like those that broke out in the Bolivian tropics of Sonqo (then written Zongo) in 1624, 1644, and 1664 or at Churin (Cajatambo, Peru) in 1663. The next century saw a multitude of local or regional conflicts, in many of which rebel Indians found allies among other social strata. Rebellion usually had economic motives, and in fact many *caciques* were complicit in the abuses rebels fought. But not all were. Well before the general conflagration of 1780, certain *caciques* made strenuous efforts to rally discontent around the emblematic figure of the Inka and call for reforms before it was too late.

Neither the conspiracies plotted in Charcas in 1580 and 1613 nor the Zongo uprisings appealed to Inka symbolism. But by the first half of the seventeenth century, the famous jurist Solórzano had heard from central Peru news about beliefs associating the Inka with the coming reversal: "There are Indians who superstitiously believe that the Inka will rise again and therefore preserve for him all the rich mines known to them."[37] This is confirmed by the men who attacked the *obraje* of Churin in 1663, claiming that "this land belongs to our Inka king." The theme resounded again and again, in more and more radical terms, during the recurrent protests of the following century.

There was, however, another path to insurrection, one that borrowed the forms of the Christian message, and that had a long though hidden history in heterodox ideas about sainthood and incarnation. Already in 1560 the preachers of the *taqui oncoy (taki unquy)* had announced that in "the resurrection of the *waka*" that would "destroy the Spanish and their god," the bodies of living Indians would become superhuman by incarnation: "The said *waka* were no longer incorporated in stones, nor in trees or springs as at the time of the Inkas, but lodged in the bodies of

[37] [1648] in M. Marzal, *La transformación religiosa peruana* (Lima, 1983), 85.

Indians, where it made them speak, so that they began to tremble when they said that they had the *waka* in their body." Some leaders of this early resistance seem to have taken the names of Christian saints. Much later, in 1777, Spaniards again heard that "Indian women were becoming saints and called themselves Saint Mary or Magdalene and other names of saints." By internalizing in their bodies the power of the sacred, in the form of a sainthood that also subsumed pre-Christian sacra, Indian protagonists revealed the profound transformation of their religiosity. Documents fleetingly evoke the Messianic movements that accompanied flare-ups of sanctification. Native messiahs were eminently subversive figures. One of them was the Christ of Tacobamba near Potosí, who in the 1580s went about with apostles and female saints, telling his followers to drink maize beer as Christ's blood and eat *achuma* (the hallucinogenic San Pedro cactus). Another was Paucarcolla, who "with the cross upon his shoulders and wearing the crown of thorns, the rope around his neck and barefoot, was venerated by the Indians" in the 1720s. Countless shamans proclaimed themselves *Santiago* (Saint James the Apostle, who figures in Iberian tradition as a warrior saint), or the Virgin, or the "brother" of Christ, or of the devil.

These movements of Christian heterodoxy imply the internalization of the imported religious message, but they also voice the discontents of conversion: especially, the Indians' deep frustration at being excluded from the priesthood and from all ecclesiastic dignities. By 1750 the viceroy himself had noted as much and pointed it out in a letter.

Indeed, from one point of view, it was not the failure but the success of conversion that threatened Spain; compared to native rebels, the Spanish looked like rather lukewarm Christians. A seventeenth-century *cacique* of the region around Huamanga dared tell the Jesuit father Francisco Patiño that "his priest was also an idolator," explaining that "by day and by night he adores his idols, which are his silver coins (*patacones*)." The true Christians were now the Indians. They were ready for the revolutionary proclamation of a truth they had long suspected – namely, that their Spanish oppressors were demons, heretics, and excommunicated sinners. The *correigdores* had proven apostates and traitors to the crown. Two centuries after the unrest of *Taki Unquy*, the issue was no longer the return of the *waka*; it was the restoration of "the kingdom of His Divine Majesty" on earth. It is hard to tell which fact better commemorates the vast scope of the changes that had occurred in the two centuries after the Toledan reforms: the fact that by 1780 the rebel

Inka Túpac Amaru II could build a vast challenge to Spanish rule on the memory of the Inka age, or the fact that in doing so he and thousands of rebels felt sure they were preparing a return to Christianity.

BIBLIOGRAPHIC ESSAY

Note to the reader: The draft that Thierry Saignes left at his untimely death contained only sketchy bibliographic information. The essay included here is an attempt to follow his notes and allusions in their original order (that is, the order of topics in the chapter), supplementing them with other sources and especially with those available in English.

Several outstanding treatments of Andean society from Toledan times to the "Age of Rebellion" are available in English. Among the classic syntheses predating Saignes' research are George Kubler, "The Quechua in the Colonial World," in Julian H. Steward (ed.), *Handbook of South American Indians*, Vol. 2 (Washington, 1946), 331–410; John H. Rowe, "The Incas under Spanish colonial institutions," *Hispanic American Historical Review* 37 (1957), 155–199; and Charles C. Gibson, *The Inca Concept of Sovereignty and the Spanish Administration in Peru* (Austin, 1948). Kenneth Andrien contributes to his own volume *Transatlantic Encounters* (edited with Rolena Adorno; Berkeley, 1991) a useful essay "Spaniards, Andeans, and the early colonial state in Peru" (see pp. 121–148). The most notable advances since the *Handbook of South American Indians* are regional case studies. Peruvian examples are Karen Spalding, *Huarochirí, an Andean Society Under Inca and Spanish Rule* (Stanford, 1984) and Steve J. Stern, *Peru's Indian Peoples and the Challenge of Conquest: Huamanga to 1640* (Madison, 1982). Karen Vieira Powers, *Andean Journeys: Migration, Ethnogenesis, and the State in Colonial Quito* (Albuquerque, 1995) studies what is now Ecuador in demographic perspective. Josep M. Barnadas, *Charcas: orígenes históricos de una sociedad colonial* (La Paz, 1973) covers what is now Bolivia. Nathan Wachtel's *Le Rétour des ancêtres: les Indiens Urus de Bolivie, XXe-XVIe siècle. Essai d'histoire regressive* (Paris, 1990) recovers the story of a distinctive people now enclaved among Aymara-speakers. Also worth study is Thérèse Bouysse-Cassagne, *La identidad aymara. Aproximación historica, siglo XV, siglo XVI* (La Paz, 1987).

For an Andean viewpoint on Toledan times, see Felipe Guaman Poma de Ayala, in John V. Murra, Rolena Adorno, and Jorge Urioste (eds.),

Neuva cronica y buen gobierno [1615] (Madrid, 1987). Rolena Adorno, *Guaman Poma: Writing and Resistance in Colonial Peru* (Austin, 1986) offers a guide to the "author and prince's" European learning. A telling contrast arises from reading primary sources about native formations prior to Toledan times – for example, Garci Díez de San Miguel, in John V. Murra (ed.), *Visita hecha a la Provincia de Chucuito* [1567] (Lima, 1964) – and records of post-Toledan times – for example, Noble David Cook (ed.), *Padrón de los indios de Lima en 1613* (Lima, 1968).

For Spanish viewpoints, see the Peruvian *Relaciones geográficas de Indias*, edited by Marcos Jiménez de la Espada and republished in three volumes (Madrid, 1965); these have recently been augmented by Pilar Ponce Leiva (ed.), in *Relaciones histórico-geográficas de la Audiencia de Quito (siglos XVI–XIX)* (Quito, 1992), which includes later and less-known "geographical reports" about Ecuador. A rich travel narrative is Diego de Ocaña, in Arturo Alvarez (ed.), *A través de la América del Sur (1599–1605)* (Madrid, 1987). The last part of the period yielded extraordinary reports, including notably Jorge Juan y Santacilia and Antonio de Ulloa's two major accounts of their 1735–1744 travels: John Jay TePaske (ed.), *Discourse and political reflections on the kingdoms of Peru*, (Norman, Oklahoma, 1979), and *A Voyage to South America* (the English version being an abridgment; Boston, 1978). Hundreds of pictures, many ethnographic, illustrate Baltasar Jaime Martínez Compañón y Bujanda, *Trujillo del Peru* [c. 1782–1788] (Madrid, 1978).

Regarding Saignes' "domestic unit of production", recent literature emphasizes gender roles. See Luis Miguel Glave, "Mujer indígena, trabajo doméstico y cambio social en el virreinato peruano del siglo XVII . . . 1684," *Bulletin de l'Institut Français d'Études Andines* 16:3/4 (1987), 39–69. Elinor C. Burkett's "Indian women and white society: The case of sixteenth-century Peru," in Asunción Lavrin (ed.), *Latin American Women: Historical Perspectives* (Westport, Connecticut, 1978), pp. 101–128, concentrates on the early colonial period.

The largest bloc of literature on crises of ethnic mediation consists of Toledan studies proper. Spalding's *Huarochirí* (as before), 156–169 and 209–227, contains a searching native-oriented analysis of the Toledan regime. Saignes' quote from Villareal appears in Guillermo Lohmann Villena, "El memorial del racionero Villarreal al Virrey Toledo," *Histórica* 5:1 (Lima, 1981), 33–36. Juan Polo de Ondegardo presented his brilliant argument for permanent indirect rule as "Relación de los fundamentos [1571]," published in Carlos A. Romero (ed.), *Colección de libros y documentos referentes a la historia del Perú*, Ser. 1, vol. 3 (Lima, 1916), 45–188. A 1990 Madrid edition of Polo by Laura González Pujana and Alicia Alonso carries the title *El mundo de los Incas*. Juan de Matienzo expounded his scheme of government in Guillermo Lohmann Villena (ed.), *Gobierno del Peru (1567)* (Lima and Paris, 1967). Ricardo Levillier's biography *Don Francisco de Toledo, supremo organizador del Perú, 1515–1582* (Buenos Aires, 1940) contains in its second volume *Sus informaciones sobre los Incas (1570–1572)*. See also John Hemming's *The Conquest of the Incas* (New York, 1970), 392–456. Robert S. Chamberlain, "The concept of the 'Señor Natural' as revealed by Castilian law and administrative documents," *Hispanic American Historical Review* 19:2 (1930), 130–137, gives important background. Guillermo Lohmann Villena, *El Corregidor de indios en el Perú bajo los austrias* (Madrid, 1957), is a classic study of the official supervisors with whom Toledan and post-Toledan ethnic lords had to contend constantly. On forced resettlement, Alejandro Málaga Medina, "Las reducciones en el Perú," *Historia y Cultura* 8 (1974), 141–172, and Daniel Gade and Mario Escobar, "Village settlement and the colonial legacy in southern Peru," *Geographical Review* 72:4 (1982), 430–449, are still helpful.

Old and new forms of legitimacy, and Andean articulation with Spanish commerce and politics, come into focus via studies based on administrative papers: Waldemar Espinoza Soriano, "El alcalde mayor indígena en el virreinato del Perú," *Anuario de Estudios Americanos* 17 (1960), 183–300; John V. Murra, "Aymara lords and their European agents at Potosí," *Nova Americana* 1 (1978), 231–243; Thierry Saignes, "De la borrachera al retrato. Los caciques andinos entre dos legitimidades – Charcas," *Revista Andina* 5:1 (1987), 139–170; and, with particularly telling ethnographic detail, María Rostworowski de Díez Canseco, *Conflicts over Coca Fields in XVIth-Century Peru* (Ann Arbor, 1988). Saignes makes substantial use of Pedro Ramírez del Aguila, in Jaime Arana (ed.), *Noticias politicas de Indias y relacion descriptiba de la Ciudad de La Plata . . . 1639* (Sucre, 1978).

The struggle for memory and citizenship and the invention of traditions are demonstrated both ethnographically and historically in Gary Urton, *The History of a Myth. Pacaritambo and the Origin of the Incas* (Austin, 1990). Chantal Caillavet's "Rituel espagnol, pratique indienne: L'occidentalisation du monde andin par le spectacle des institutions coloniales," in *Structures et Cultures des Sociétés Ibéro-Américaines au-delà du modèle socio-économique* (Paris, 1990), 25–41, emphasizes ceremonial processes. Luis Capoche, *Relación general de la villa imperial de Potosí* (Madrid, 1969), records a seventeenth-century view of the mining heartland. For the dramas of Ollantay and Atahuallpa, a convenient edition is Teodoro L. Meneses (ed.), *Teatro quechua colonial. Antología* (Lima, 1983).

The unequal struggle to defend native holy places against Catholic "extirpation" has a particularly rich literature. The seminal work is Pierre Duviols, *La lutte contre les réligiones autochtones dans le Pérou colonial. "L'extirpation de l'idolatrie," entre 1532 et 1660* (Lima and Paris, 1971); many of its primary sources are reproduced in Duviols (ed.), *Cultura andina y represión: procesos y visitas de idolatrías y hechicerías, Cajatambo, siglo XVII* (Cusco, 1986). A different view than Duviols' is expressed in Antonio Acosta, "La extirpación de idolatrías en el Perú. Origen y desarollo de las campañas. A propósito de *Cultura andina y represión," Revista Andina* 5:1 (1987), 171–195. Two recent monographs in English narrate this controversial era: Nicholas Griffths' *The Cross and the Serpent* (Norman, Oklahoma, 1996) and Kenneth Mills' *Idolatry and Its Enemies* (Princeton, 1997).

A compilation of "extirpation" trials heavily overlapping Duviols' is Juan Carlos García Cabrera (ed.), *Ofensas a dios, pleitos e injurias: causas de idolatrías y hechicerías: Cajatambo siglos XVII–XIX* (Cusco, 1994). The "how-to" literature for persecutors included Cristóbal de Albornoz, *Instrucción para descubrir todas las guacas del Perú y sus camayos y haziendas* [1581/1585], reproduced in C. de Molina and C. de Albornoz, *Fábulas y mitos de los Incas,* Henrique Urbano and Pierre Duviols, eds. (Madrid, 1989). (The same volume contains an important Toledan text by Cristóbal de Molina "Cuzqueño," the *Relación de las fábulas y ritos de los Incas* [1573]. See also Pierre Duviols, "Un inédit de Cristóbal de Albornoz," *Journal de la Société des Américanistes* 56 [1967], 7–39. An important translated source is Pablo José de Arriaga's merciless manual for persecutors, *The Extirpation of Idolatry in Perú* [1621], L. Clark Keating, trans. (Lexington, Kentucky, 1968). A related later work is by Pedro de Villagómez, *Exhortaciones e instrucciones acerca de los indios del Arzobispado de Lima* [1649], published as Vol. 12 of Carlos A. Romero (ed.), *Colección de libros y documentos referentes ala historia del Perú* (Lima, 1919). *Catolicismo y extirpacion de idolatrias, siglos XVI–XVII: Charcas, Chile, Mexico, Peru,* edited by Gabriela Ramos and Henrique Urbano (Cusco, 1993), offers comparative studies on the matrix of persecution.

Two recent editions of the most important colonial Quechua-language source, an anonymous 1608 manuscript containing lore about the non-Christian deities of a Peruvian district, are Gerald Taylor (ed. and trans.), *Ritos y tradiciones de Huarochirí del siglo XVII* (Lima, 1987), and Frank Salomon and George Urioste (eds. and trans.), *The Huarochirí Manuscript* (Austin, 1991). Jesuit documents adding context to this source appear as appendices to José María Arguedas (trans.), and Pierre Duviols (ed.), *Dioses y hombres de Huarochirí* (Lima, 1966). Case studies of social conflicts in which non-Christian or heterodox leaders figured as contenders for social control include Luis Millones, "Religión y poder en los Andes: los curacas idólatras de la sierra central," *Cuadernos del Consejo Nacional de la Universidad Peruana* 24–25 (1977), 73–87; Ana Sánchez, *Amancebados, hechiceros y rebeldes: Chancay, siglo XVII* (Cusco, 1991); and Frank Salomon, "Shamanism and politics in late colonial Ecuador," *American Ethnologist* 10:3 (1983), 413–428.

Control of labor was often contested over mining issues. Potosí, the giant silver mine that financed Spanish imperialism, has a giant literature: Jeffrey A. Cole, *The Potosi mita, 1573–1700: Compulsory Indian Labor in the Andes* (Stanford, 1985); Peter Bakewell, *Miners of the Red Mountain: Indian Labor in Potosí, 1545–1650* (Albuquerque, 1984); and, from the pioneer generation of researchers, Lewis Hanke, *The Imperial City of Potosi: An Unwritten Chapter in the History of Spanish America* (The Hague, 1956).

Among the main advances since the *Handbook of South American Indians* is a profusion of regional and local studies about *cacicazgo* and internal social control at the community level. Udo Oberem "Über den Indianischen Adel im kolonialzeitlichen Ecuador," *Lateinamerika Studien* 7 (1980), 31–41, synthesizes pre-1980 knowledge of North Andean nobles. Since then Chantal Caillavet has produced meritorious case studies including, for example, "Caciques de Otavalo en el siglo XVI. Don Alonso Maldonado y su esposa," *Miscelánea Antropológica Ecuatoriana* 2 (1982), 38–55. For later colonial times in the Quito jurisdiction, see Segundo E. Moreno Yánez, "Don Leandro Sepla y Oro, un cacique andino de finales de la colonia: estudio biográfico," in Sophia Thyssen and Segundo E. Moreno Yánez (eds.), *Memorias del primer simposio europeo sobre antropología del Ecuador* (Quito, 1985), 223–244. María Rostworowski de Diez Canseco, "Testamento de don Luis de Colán, curaca en 1622," *Revista del Museo Nacional* (Peru) 46 (1982), 507–543, gives a Central Andean case. Waldemar Espinoza Soriano has discovered and excerpted numerous new sources on Peruvian ethnic nobles – for example, "Los señoríos de Yaucha y Picoy en el abra del medio y alto Rímac (siglos XV y XVI)," *Revista Historica* (Lima) 34 (1983/1984), 157–279. Olinda Celestino, "La religiosidad de un noble cañare en el valle del Mantaro, siglo XVII, a través de su testamento," *Revista de Indias* 44:174 (1984), 547–557, emphasizes a *cacique's* relations with religious confraternities. Silvia Rivera, "El Malku y la sociedad colonial en el siglo XVII: el caso de Jesús de Machaca," *Avances* (La Paz) 1 (1978), 7–27, delivers data from Charcas, in the South. Robert D. Wood, *Teach Them Good Customs: Colonial Indian Education and Acculturation in the Andes* (Culver City, California, 1986), describes the schooling of bicultural *caciques*.

The rebuilding of social cohesion after conquest is a main theme of the monographs mentioned in the opening paragraph. More specialized literature on the struggle for social and demographic recovery has grown around attempts to measure the post-Pizarran demographic disaster. Woodrow Borah, "The historical demography of aboriginal and colonial America: An attempt at perspective," in William M. Denevan (ed.), *The Native Population of the Americas in 1492* (Madison, 1976), 13–34, is a retrospective by a main innovator in Latin American demographic history. Another, Nicolás Sánchez-Albornoz, offers his synthesis in *The Population of Latin America: A History* (Berkeley, 1974). The Andes proper yielded widely discrepant estimates; see, for example, C. T. Smith, "Depopulation of the Central Andes in the 16th century," *Current Anthropology* 11 (1970), 453–464, and Daniel E. Shea, "A defense of small population estimates for the Central Andes in 1520," in William M. Denevan's volume (cited earlier), 157–180. Understanding of population change has been greatly clarified by the history of epidemics. Henry F. Dobyns, "An outline of Andean epidemic history to 1720," *Bulletin of the History of Medicine* 37 (1963), 493–515, synthesizes handily, and Linda A. Newson, "Old World epidemics in early colonial Ecuador," in Noble David Cook and W. George Lovell (eds.), *"Secret Judgments of God": Old World Disease in Colonial Spanish America* (Norman, Oklahoma, 1992), 84–112, and Suzanne Austin Alchon's monograph, *Native Society and Disease in Colonial Ecuador* (New York, 1991) expand on the anomalous North Andean case. Javier Ortiz de la Tabla Ducasse offers methodological cautions in "La población ecuatoriana en la época colonial: cuestiones y cálculos," *Anuario de Estudios Americanos* 37 (1980), 235–277. Following Sánchez-Albornoz' counsel some recent efforts concentrate on distinguishing migration from mortality. See Brian Evans, "Migration processes in upper Peru in the seventeenth century," in David M. Robinson (ed.), *Migration in Colonial Spanish America* (New York, 1990), pp. 62–85, and Ann M. Wightman, *Indigenous Migration and Social Change: The Forasteros of Cuzco, 1570–1720* (Durham, 1990). Noble David Cook has provided the major synthesis: *Demographic Collapse: Indian Peru, 1520–1620* (New York, 1981).

Native participation in the market was the object of an ethnographic-historical collaboration published in Olivia Harris, Brooke Larson, and Enrique Tandeter (eds.), *La Participación indígena en los mercados surandinos: estrategias y reproducción social, siglos XVI a XX* (La Paz, 1987) available in English as *Ethnicity, Markets and Migration in the Andes* (Durham, North Carolina, 1995). Its context is a greatly expanded literature on economic history; see, for example, Carlos Sempat Assadourian, *El sistema de la economia colonial: mercado interno, regiones y espacio económico* (Lima, 1982), or Enrique Tandeter and Nathan Wachtel (eds.), *Precios y producción agraria. Potosí y Charcas en el siglo XVIII* (Buenos Aires, 1983). Luis Miguel Glave, *Trajinantes* (Lima, 1989), focuses on the social history of the native long-distance transport industry. Change in land tenure forms a core concern of Brooke Larson's *Colonialism and Agrarian Transformation in Bolivia: Cochabamba, 1550–1900* (Princeton, 1988). The commoditization of land was a fateful change for Andean communities, now documented in many good regional studies. See Christiane Borchart de Moreno, "La transferencia de la propiedad agraria indígena en el corregimiento de Quito hasta finales del siglo XVII," *Caravelle* 34 (1980), 5–19, and, also from Ecuador, Nicholas P. Cushner's study of emerging latifundism, *Farm and Factory: The Jesuits and the Development of Agrarian Capitalism, 1600–1767* (Albany, 1982). For the Peruvian oasis valleys, see Robert G. Keith, *Conquest and Agrarian Change: The Emergence of the Hacienda System on the Peruvian Coast* (Cambridge, Massachusetts, 1976), and a later, more native-oriented study by Susan E. Ramírez, *Provincial Patriarchs: Land Tenure and the Economics of Power in Colonial Peru* (Albuquerque, 1986).

The commoditization of labor had particularly dramatic effects in the textile economy because both *caciques* and Spaniards harnessed Andean textile expertise to primitive industrialism. See Mary Money de Alvarez, *Los obrajes, el traje y el comercio de ropa en la Audiencia de Charcas* (La Paz, 1983); "The sweatshop of South America" in John Leddy Phelan, *The Kingdom of Quito in the Seventeenth Century* (Madison, 1967), pp. 66–86; and Fernando Silva Santisteban, *Los obrajes en el virreinato del Perú* (Lima, 1964).

On patterns of community restructuring amid the transformed economy, see Olinda Celestino and Albert Meyers' pioneering study of the religious brotherhoods, *Las cofradías en el Perú, región central* (Frankfurt am Main, 1981), and Roger N. Rasnake's historically informed ethnography, *Domination and Cultural Resistance: Authority and Power among an Andean People* (Durham, North Carolina, 1988).

The colonial Andean culture of which Saignes takes Lope de Atienza's observations as emblematic – see his *Compendio historial del estado de los indios del Peru* [1575?], Jacinto Jijón y Caamaño, ed. (Quito, 1931) – is also visible in many other primary sources. Bernabé Cobo's 1653 *History of the Inca Empire* contains much, but the colonial-oriented parts are not in Roland Hamilton's 1979 and 1990 translated excerpts. A convenient full Spanish edition is that prepared by Fernando Mateos (Madrid, 1964). For late-colonial Charcas (Bolivia), Saignes favors Alonso Carrió de la Bandera, *Reforma del Perú* [1782], with transcription and prologue by Pablo Macera (Lima, 1966).

On colonial material culture and the visual arts, two leading monographs are Teresa Gisbert, *Iconografía y mitos indígenas en el arte* (La Paz, 1980), on plastic arts, and Valerie Fraser, *The Architecture of Conquest: Building in the Viceroyalty of Peru, 1535–1635* (New York, 1989), which concentrates on Dominican monumental church building. *Guaman Poma de Ayala: the Colonial Art of an Andean Author*, edited by Mercedes López-Baralt (New York, 1992), contains important visual complements to Adorno's literary studies; see especially the chapters by Maarten Van der Guchte and Tom Cummins. *Converging Cultures, Art and Identity in Spanish America*, edited by Diana Fane, is the richly illustrated catalogue of a museum exhibit including colonial Andean textiles (New York, 1996). Comparable material appears in *Andean Esthetics*, edited by Blenda Femenias (Madison, Wisconsin, 1987).

The genesis of a distinctive Andean folk Christianity becomes partly visible in a literature overlapping the literature of persecution. A particularly rich monograph is Sabine MacCormack, *Religion in the Andes: Vision and Imagination in Early Colonial Peru* (Princeton, 1991). Manuel M. Marzal, *La transformación religiosa peruana* (Lima, 1983), offers a stagewise model of processes beyond the clergy's control. Regarding degrees of acculturation, see Carlos Daniel Valcárcel *Historia del Perú colonial* (Lima, 1982–1986), or Pedro Borges, *Métodos misionales en la cristianización de América, siglo XVI* (Madrid, 1960). For the institutional constraints, see Rubén Vargas Ugarte, *Historia de la iglesia en el Perú*, 5 vols. (Burgos, 1960–1965); or the more compact treatment by Fernando de Armas Medina, *La cristianización del Perú (1532–1600)* (Sevilla, 1953). Regarding involvement of the Church in economic exploitation of natives, see Bernard Lavallé, "Las doctrinas de indígenas como núcleos de explotación colonial; siglos XVI–XVII," *Allpanchis* 19 (1982), 151–171. Nathan Wachtel, *The Vision of the Vanquished: The Spanish Conquest of Peru through Indian Eyes, 1530–1570* (New York, 1977) pioneered the interpretation of folk Christianity as a reworking of Andean schemata.

An important part of the theoretical and practical agenda of evangelization was linguistic work, especially circa 1600. Bruce Mannheim, *The Language of the Inka Since the European Invasion* (Austin, 1991), analyzes the transformation of Quechua into a Church-promulgated *lingua franca*. *Concilios limenses 1551–1772*, Rubén Vargas Ugarte, ed. (Lima, 1951–1954), displays the institutional reasoning behind it. The first book printed in Peru was a Quechua-Aymara-Spanish catechism, whose facsimile is *Tercero cathecismo y exposición de la doctrina christiana por sermones* [1585], in *Doctrina christiana y catecismo para instrucción de indios. Facsímil del texto trilingüe* (Madrid, 1985), 333–777. Diego Gonçález Holguín's *Gramática y arte nueva de la lengua general de todo el Perú llamada lengua Qquichua o lengua del Inca [1607]* (Genoa, 1842), and his 1608 *Vocabulario de la lengua general de todo el Peru llamada lengua Qquichua o del Inca* (reedited Lima, 1952, and Lima, 1989), illustrate the impressive level of Jesuit linguistic work and also its theological biases.

To explore the background of Saignes' argument about the cult of the dead and ancestor worship as colonially refashioned, see Lorenzo Huertas Vallejos, *La religión en una sociedad rural andina (siglo XVII)* (Ayacucho, 1981), and Tom Dillehay (ed.), *Tombs for the Living* (Washington, D.C., 1994). Gerald Taylor, "*Supay,*" *Amerindia* 5 (1980), 47–63, explains how an Andean image of the shade of the dead became demonized in Christendom.

Regarding the cults of saints among Andean Catholics, an important early source is Alonso Ramos Gavilán's *Historia del santuario de Nuestra Señora de Copacabana* [1621], edited by Ignacio Prado Pastor (Lima, 1988). Mary Dillon and Thomas Abercrombie argue that European deities were radically transfigured; see "The destroying Christ: An Aymara myth of conquest," in Jonathan Hill (ed.), *Rethinking History and Myth:*

Indigenous South American Perspectives on the Past (Urbana, 1988), 50–77. For the folk genesis of two still-vigorous Peruvian saint cults, see Luis Millones, "Los sueños de Santa Rosa de Lima," *Historia* (Chile) 24 (1989), 253–266, and María Rostworowski de Diez Canseco, *Pachacámac y el Señor de los Milagros. una trayectoria milenaria* (Lima, 1992).

For the colonial popularity of therapeutic shamanism, see Juan Polo de Ondegardo, "De los errores y supersticiones de los Indios" [1584], Carlos A. Romero (ed.), in *Colección de libros y documentos referentes a la historia del Perú,* Ser. 1, vol. 3 (Lima, 1916), 1–44, and Martín de Murúa, *Historia general del Perú* [1611?], Manuel Ballesteros Gaibrois (ed.) (Madrid, 1986), especially Book 2, Chs. 26 and 27.

The democratization of access to stimulants, especially coca, was linked to mining and the mine *mita*; see Thierry Saignes, "Potosí y la coca. el consumo popular de estimulantes en el siglo XVII," *Revista de Indias* 48:182/183 (1988), 207–235. John V. Murra (ed.), *Visita de los valles de Sonqo en los yunka de coca de la Paz: 1568–1570* (Madrid, 1991), documents a booming production area. On alcoholic drinks, see Lorenzo Huertas Vallejos, "Producción de vinos y aguardientes en Ica, siglos XVI al XVII," *Historia y Cultura* (Lima) 21 (1991–1992), 161–218.

Popular fantasies of subversion became prominent research topics in the wake of Alberto Flores Galindo, *Buscando un inca* (Lima, 1988), and Manuel Burga, *Nacimiento de una utopia: muerte y resurrección de los incas* (Lima, 1988). John H. Rowe's earlier and still interesting "El movimiento nacional incac del siglo XVIII" appeared in *Revista Universitaria* (Cusco) 43 (1954), 17–47. Regarding the linked ideas of cataclysm and social justice, see Thérèse Bouysse-Cassagne and Phillippe Bouysse, "Volcan indien, volcan chrétien. Á propos de l'éruption du Huaynaputina en l'an 1600, Pérou Méridional," *Journal de la Société des Américanistes* 70 (1984), 43–68. Saignes cites Francisco Javier Eder in Josep M. Barnadas (ed.) *Breve descripción de las reducciones de Mojos* [1772] (Cochabamba, 1985).

16

WARFARE, REORGANIZATION, AND READAPTATION AT THE MARGINS OF SPANISH RULE: THE SOUTHERN MARGIN (1573–1882)

KRISTINE L. JONES

The effective southern border of Spanish control emerged early in the sixteenth century with the creations of a series of small scattered *postas* (forts) linking the early colonial settlements of Buenos Aires, San Luis, Mendoza, Santiago, and Concepción. This frontier changed very little in the sixteenth, seventeenth, eighteenth, and early nineteenth centuries. The relative autonomy of native societies south of this frontier was assured over the centuries in part because apart from small outposts that served the needs of passing ships, like Puerto Deseado (Carmen de Patagones) on the Atlantic coast and Valdivia and Chiloé on the Pacific coast, the Spanish presence in the Southern Cone was minimal after 1600 until the nineteenth century. Most of the Spanish activities and resources were oriented to the north to support the mining industry. However, the initial negotiations over this frontier between Spanish conquistadors and the native people they encountered in the early colonial period resulted in reorganization and adaptations among Indian societies that allowed them to maintain political sovereignty well into the late 1800s. That native peoples numbering at least between 100,000 to 300,000 individuals were able to resist conquest and colonization for nearly four centuries deserves our attention when considering the history of South America.[1]

[1] A careful demographic study of the Southern Cone is yet to be carried out. By the end of the nineteenth century, there were roughly 150,000 Indians "conquered" and "pacified" in the final Indian wars in Argentina (around 30,000) and Chile (100,000) – at least according to turn-of-the-century censuses in each country. Documents from the eighteenth century, when more intensive European reconnaisance of southern territories began, suggest the existence of many more – perhaps as many as 500,000 or more, though this estimate can only be approximated through a general familiarity with the wide variety of military records, travel accounts, and archaeological records of both Chile and Argentina, and should by no means be considered definitive. Considering the careful and extensive ethnohistorical research of demographic trends among untaxed and

We are accustomed to imagining the political boundaries of the Spanish empire in the southern cone of South America as following the north–south axis of the Andes, extending to the tip of Tierra del Fuego. We can see this north–south orientation projected in the historical mapping of colonial and national political boundaries as they were increasingly subdivided and defined over the centuries. By the twentieth century this political process ultimately resulted in the (still disputed) establishment of the national border of over 2,000 miles dividing the countries of Chile and Argentina.

The first task inherent in understanding interethnic reorganization and readaptation at the margins of Spanish rule is to challenge that north –south perspective and to imagine instead an east–west (or west–east) boundary. Nearly all of the territory south of this boundary – roughly defined by the military outposts linking the colonial settlements of Buenos Aires, San Luis, Mendoza, Santiago, and Concepcion – remained free of Spanish colonial rule. With the exception of a few heavily defended Spanish outposts along the Atlantic and Pacific coasts, native peoples claimed and enjoyed sovereignty in this vast region known as Patagonia by the Europeans. It was not until the late nineteenth century that the *pampas* grasslands, the Patagonian steppes, and the southern cordilleran highlands of the Andes (called Araucania) fell under the political dominion of the Argentine and Chilean states.

The region south of this boundary contains a wide continuum of environmental zones. Fertile grassy *pampas* extend from the Atlantic coast to the more arid *pampas* and foothills of the eastern Andean cordillera. The eastward flowing Río Colorado and Río Negro emerge from the more densely forested southern cordillera to carve out a natural boundary separating the *pampas* and the arid Patagonian steppes to the south. The precipitous inclines of the Andes, which contain a variety of microclimatic regions and numerous mountain passes, give way in the west to a

unbaptised indigenous peoples in other areas of the Americas, it is likely that the important pandemics of measles and smallpox (especially in the sixteenth and seventeenth centuries) and cholera, as well as smallpox (in the eighteenth and nineteenth centuries), which swept through the Americas, had the same decimating consequences within Araucania. There is ample anecdotal evidence to suggest significant depopulation due to introduced diseases, but then at the same time the native population was integrating captive Spanish women and children by the tens of thousands. Until a systematic demographic study is conducted, any population estimate of these people prior to their military conquest can only be a rough estimate – most likely an underestimate.

relatively narrow but rich coastal region traversed by numerous river valleys. Further south, the spine of the southern cordillera breaks down into volcanic peaks carved out by a series of glacial lakes that empty into dozens of rivers and streams. These rivers plunge into the Pacific Ocean through a narrow strip of coastline punctuated by countless inlets and islands. In the extreme south, the east and west coasts of the continent merge into the separate land mass of Tierra del Fuego and the treacherous Straits of Magellan.

FIRST ENCOUNTERS, FIRST INVASIONS

The range of harsh climates and geographic extremes in the Southern Cone of South America did not necessarily limit the range of different native groups to specific environmental zones. Instead we know from the scant archaeological record that interethnic relations linked several groups in this southern sphere, and that trade goods moved along a roughly east – west axis that cut across the Andes. In fact the east–west orientation of interethnic relations in the Southern Cone may actually have countered the southward trend of imperial expansion from the Central Andean highlands.

The prehistory of indigenous peoples in the south remains sketchy, and even the nature of early encounters with Spanish colonists has yet to be explored fully. Early Spanish colonial efforts focused on the fabulous riches of the Inka empire to the exclusion of the less material attributes of native people at the margins of Spanish rule. The complex systems of agriculture, settlement, and governments (not to mention mines) of the Inka and other civilizations represented potential sources of wealth and civilization to the Spanish. In contrast attributes such as mobility and social fluidity, consensus decision making, and individual autonomy, more characteristic of the so-called nomadic tribes, represented a threat to the social order to the Spanish, particularly for fragile frontier colonies. This dialectic, then, contributed directly to the formation of a colonial frontier bounded by marginal societies.

ARAUCANIA: PREHISTORY AND ENCOUNTER

Archaeological and ethnohistorical research has mirrored the tendency to focus on the Central Andean civilizations, and so what we know about the early history of the people in the Southern Cone likewise tends to be defined in terms of their relation to the more populated centers. As archaeologists continue to examine the traces of Andean civilizations and ethnohistorians fill in the records of the Inka empire, it has become increasingly believable that the southern margins of Inka influence extended as far south as the Maipo River and as far east as present-day Salta, Jujuy, and San Juan. Interethnic relations at the southern margins of Inka rule were complicated by the conflicting interests of local settlements and populations. On the one hand, the attractions of trade with the Inka drew the natives of the coastal valleys of central Chile into the redistributive Inca sphere of influence. On the other hand, existence in the deserts and mountain forests fostered a more autonomous and free-ranging approach toward life, and it militated against more developed agricultural settlement patterns that formed the base of the Inka administrative *mit'a* system. The Diaguita, who occupied the coastal region north of the Aconcagua River, mediated a buffer zone between the Inka stronghold among the Aymara-speaking Atacama region and the people the early chroniclers called the Promaucaes (probably Quechua *purum awka*, 'wilderness enemies') south of the Maipo River. Although the Promaucaes fell within the influence of the Inka, they shared a common language (Mapundungun), social organization, and religious beliefs with all the people living to south of the Mapocho River. Beyond that southern boundary – that is, beyond the dominion of the Inka state – lay the region called Araucania by the Spanish (see Map 16.1).

The assumption of cultural homogeneity among the Araucanians (also called Mapuche) would be a mistake. The majority of the Mapuche-speaking people along the southern Pacific coast and in the forested regions of the cordillera maintained political and cultural autonomy vis-à-vis the Inka. Although they retained their cultural traditions of individuality and consensus decision making at the level of the basic kinship unit, and although these tendencies conflicted with the centralizing tendencies of the Inka state, some groups did opt for, or were coerced into, collaboration with the Inka (or, later, the Spanish, and in the nineteenth century, the Chileans or Argentines). In fact a tradition of internecine warfare, usually stemming from charges of witchcraft, characterized intra-Mapuche relations as well as interethnic relations at the southern margins of the Inka empire.

Although a common language (albeit with many dialects) and belief system and a relatively permanent settlement pattern was shared within Araucania, different emphases in subsistence activities and relations to

Sixteenth Century: First Encounters
Pampas
Tehuelche (Southern)
Huilliche
Mapuche/Araucanos
Pehuenche
Missions defeated in 1598
BOLIVIA
AYMARA
ATACAMEÑOS
DIAGUITA
MOCOVÍ
ABIPON
DIAGUITA
PICUNCHE
PACIFIC OCEAN
Paraná R.
Uruguay R.
BRAZIL
GUARANIES
HUARPE
Córdoba
COMECHINGONES
CHILE
Mendoza
URUGUAY
Santiago de Chile
San Luis
CHARRUA
HUARPE
PROMOCAES
ARGENTINA
Buenos Aires
PEHUENCHE
QUERENDIE
PAMPAS
Concepcíon
Colorado R.
SERRANOS
TEHUELCHE (NORTHERN)
"MAPUCHE"
Valdivia
Negro R.
HUILLICHE
Carmen de Patagones
ATLANTIC OCEAN
Chiloé I.
TEHUELCHE (SOUTHERN)
N
0
300 mi
0
300 km
ALACALUF
ONAS
SELKNAM
YAMANES

Map 16.1

the land led to regional differences, and these differences were reflected in the ways the people called themselves.[2] In the region north of the Nuble River lived the Picunche (*picu*, 'north'; *che*, 'people'). Between the Nuble River and the Imperial River lived the Mapuche (*mapu*, 'land'; *che*, 'people'), who made a living by planting and harvesting crops grown in the rich volcanic soil. Further south lived the Huilliche (*Huilli*, 'south'), who harvested fruits and berries found in the lush forest and lake region of the southern cordillera and on the Island of Chiloé. Other groups, including those who fished along the coast and those who farmed the coastal plains (*lafkenche*, 'people of the coast'), likewise identified themselves according to their relationship to the land.

The people who lived in the western inclines of the cordillera and harvested the pine nuts of the *araucaria* tree called themselves Pehuenche (*Pehuen*, 'pine'; *che*, 'people'). Archaeologists speculate that the people who inhabited the eastern side of the cordillera and the surrounding foothills, also called Pehuenche, originally were both culturally and linguistically autonomous but were pulled into the Araucanian sphere of influence in the sixteenth and seventeenth centuries. The Pehuenche maintained a buffer position between the Huilliche to their south and the Huarpe to their north, who negotiated relations with the Inka. The arid *pampas* grasslands to the east and south remained an arena open for hunting and gathering, in usufruct with the Pampas groups.[3]

Not long after the Spanish arrived at Cuzco, they followed Inka pathways south into established settlements in the central river valleys along the Pacific coast. The experience of those Araucanians who had resisted the expansion of Tihuantinsuyo had served them well. Early

[2] This chapter follows Cestmir Laukotka's *Classification of South American Indian Languages*, Vol. 7, Johannes Wilbert (ed.) (Los Angeles: 1968), which classifies these languages as part of the Mapuche stock, including "Mapuche or Araucano or Auca, Picunche, Pehuenche, Moluche or Nguluche, Huiliche or Veliche, Chilote or Chauquéz, and Ranquelche," 273–274. Contemporary speakers call the language *Mapundungun*. See also Harriet E. Manelis Klein and Louisa R. Stark (eds.), *South American Indian Languages: Retrospect and Prospect* (Austin, 1985).

[3] In the absence of more precise nomenclature, we use the term Pampas groups/peoples/bands to refer to the Indians who shared a common language and were variously called Querandie, Puelche, and Serrano by contemporary Spanish observers. These would be the speakers of Gennaken and Chechehet, in Loukotka's language classification, although Casamiquela includes both in what he calls Gününa-küne. I am following Rodolfo Casamiquela, *Un nuevo panorama etnológico del area pan-pampeana y patagonica adyacente* (Santiago: Ediciones del Museo Nacional de Historia Natural, 1969). A contradictory interpretation placing the Querandie – and even the Araucanians in the XII and XIII centuries, in the cultural sphere of the Guaraní – can be found in P. Sabastian Englert, "Lengua y Literatura Araucanas," *Anales de la Facultad de Filosofía y Educación, Universidad de Chile* I:2–3 (1936), 80–81.

Spanish armies, accustomed to warfare organized by the state, were unprepared for the guerilla resistance tactics of the kin-organized armies, and the costs of continuing such losses soon put the brakes on the Spanish advance.[4] Of course not all of the Araucanians opted to resist, and many fell under the jurisdiction of Spanish *repartimiento* (labor drafts) and outright enslavement. The Picunche in the central valley, most of whom sought friendship with the Spanish, were soon weakened by small pox and typhus epidemics, and they fell under Spanish domination through forced labor in mining and agriculture in the encomienda system. As in other regions colonized by the Spanish, the encounter in the central valley led to depopulation through disease and epidemics, land expropriation, and harsh labor systems, as well as the creation of a rural mestizo society with its own unique contributions in the Spanish colonial system.

Spanish colonization in the sixteenth century disrupted traditional indigenous interactions in the central valley and with neighboring groups toward the north and provoked a reorientation of intercultural relations within Araucania to favor trading relations and other types of alliances with people in the east. Sometime in this period the Pehuenche, the people inhabiting the region north of Lake Nahuel Huapi on the eastern slopes, were pulled into greater Araucania. The Huilliche in the southern cordillera were attracted to the new Spanish maritime outpost on the island of Chiloé, where they traded coarse, warm, and waterproof Mapuche textiles woven from sheep wool in exchange for iron tools. Indeed the Huilliche contributed directly to the sixteenth- and seventeenth-century textile market that linked Chiloé by sea with Lima. These ponchos were also prized by the Pampas groups in the east (who the Mapuche called Puelche, or people of the east). The Pampas peoples traded salt and sometimes captives in exchange for the textiles.

In the first decades of Spanish exploration and attempts to colonize Araucania, starting with the founding of Concepción by Pedro de Valdivia in 1550, relations between different Araucanian clans and the Span-

[4] The first recorded European to explore the southern Pacific coast was Hernando de Magellanes, who briefly stopped along the coast before rounding the straits bearing his name. In 1536 Diego de Almagro began his reconnaissance south from Peru, arriving into the valley of Copiao, and his Captain, Juan de Saavedra, explored the Valparaiso Bay before they returned to Peru. Ultimately it was Pedro de Valdivia who became identified as the definitive conquerer of Chile, in part because his was the expedition that resulted in the foundation of Santiago in the Mapocho Valley in 1540. Sergio Villalobos, Osvaldo Silva, Fernando Siva, Patricio Estelle (eds.), *Historia de Chile* (Santiago: Editorial Universitaria, 1974), 96.

iards were uneasy but not openly hostile. However, a particularly cruel campaign in 1556 to impose the *encomienda* system in the imperial region by burning homes, crops, and seeds (to weaken native resistance) resulted in widespsread famine and epidemics, including typhus. General discontent soon consolidated into active resistance in a general uprising in 1554–1557. Gerónimo de Vivar, in *Crónica y relación copiosa y verdadera de los reinos de Chile*, described the resistance strategies of this uprising, and we can see the beginnings of a hierarchical military structure among the Indians as a result of their conflicts with the Spaniards.

> Seeing themselves so victorious over the Spaniards, having killed fifty-one of them, the Indians were more than a little exhilarated, believing that now no Christians could resist them. They created a large gathering, and called together all the principals from the entire territory. They held this gathering in Tocape. And there they celebrated large ceremonies, and it seemed to them necessary to name one leader whom to obey and to communicate about the war with the Spanish.
>
> They called up Colocolo, leader of 6,000 men, Paylaguala, leader of 5,000, Paycavi, leader of 3,000, Yllecura, leader of 3,000, Tocapel, leader of 3,500, Teopolican, leader of 4,000, and Ayllacura, leader of 5,000. Among all of these men there were great differences, because each of them was a leader of himself, and there had been great rivalries between them.
>
> Mallarupue, a leader of 6,000, seeing the discord among them, being old and therefore not a part of the rivalries, arrived and told them to be quiet, and begged them to listen. And he spoke to them in this way: "How is it, brothers and friends, seeing how we are gaining victory over our enemies, and that those who stay are little able to resist our forces, how is it that you permit discord among yourselves? I want to do my part, because I am no longer good for anything else, if you want to take advantage of my experience."

Mallarupe suggested a competition of strength to determine the strongest of the assembled war leaders. He located a massive tree trunk to be lifted by each of the leaders present, and Teopolicán emerged as the strongest.

> Witnessed by all those men present, they were astonished and amazed by the strength of Teopolican, with the ease with which he lifted that heavy trunk. He was then received by all the Indian leaders around, and he made them his captains. He made Lautaro his general, . . . and he gave him three thousand Indians, no less warlike than the Spanish soldiers themselves.[5]

[5] Gerónimo de Vivar, *Crónica y relación copiosa y verdadera de los reinos de Chile* (Chile, Colección Escritores Coloniales, Editorial Universitaria, 1987), 242.

The Spaniards temporarily gained the upper hand, and the wars were temporarily put down in 1557 with the defeat of Lautaro, but localized resistance to colonization continued for the next four decades, and Spanish settlement proceeded slowly at best.

Within larger Araucania the indirect consequences of the first half-century of the encounter were absorbed within an astonishingly resilient social milieu. The basic organizational unit, the kin unit called *lef*, belonged to a community structure (*rewe*, literally 'willow altar') informally headed by leaders called *lonkos*. Contemporary Spanish chronicles by missionaries, such as Diego Rosales, and military men, such as Pedro de Valdivia and Francisco Bascuñán, reveal the existence of totemic clans and complex kin terminology for systems of clans, moieties, and tribes. Not all anthropologists agree whether the kinship system was patrilineal or matrilineal, but most have come to accept the assessment of George Peter Murdock and Louis C. Faron that the Mapuche system was mostly characterized by the patrilineal "Omaha" kinship system.[6] Part of the confusion may be due to sometimes uncritical ethnohistorical assessment of contemporary sources without close attention to specific historical contexts. In recent years scholars have turned again to closer reading of colonial documents, and a systematic review of colonial dictionaries in historical context may reveal shifts in vocabulary for kinship that record the historical changes and regroupings within Araucania; however, such analysis remains to be carried out.

The Mapuche lived in sturdy wooden structures (called *rukas*) with multiple doors (from two to eight, according to Pedro de Valdivia), one for each wife. Sororal polygamy was preferred, and the richer men had up to ten to twenty wives, according to the Spanish missionary Diego de Rosales (in the 1630s). In Araucania young men captured their wives in surprise raids against neighboring communities and were then required to compensate the "bride's" family and to normalize relations, usually with a ceremonial sacrifice around the ceremonial *rewe* (altar). If unhappy wives returned to their parents, the parents were obligated to reimburse the groom. Captured Spanish women and children, on the other hand, were considered spoils of war.

In the division of labor, men tended the fields and livestock, and women "were made to work at grinding grain, and carrying water,

[6] Horacio Zapater, *Aborigenes chilenos a través de cronistas y viajeros* (Santiago: Andrés Bello, 1978), 66.

chicha, wood, the harvests, without end," as Padre Rosales observed.[7] Another missionary observed that each wife had to make her husband one poncho or blanket each month, indicating that textiles were being produced not only for their own use but also for trade. Meanwhile, men tended fields of corn, beans, potatoes, quinoa, pumpkins, and lima beans. Coastal people fished for large sea bass and other rich marine resources. Spanish livestock, particularly goats and sheep, became "an important and new source of sustenance for them," according to Alonso González de Najera.[8]

On the western cordillera and coastal plains, the localized subsistence activities of the different communities formed a pattern in which the intercultural frontiers between the Picunche, Promaucaes, and Diaguita were blurred in a kind of continuum. The Spanish settlement of Santiago and the central valley tended to pull the Picunche within the colonial sphere, while Mapuche activities south of the Nuble and Bío Bío rivers centered on agricultural endeavors in the rich volcanic plains and the pasturage and *auracaria* forests on both sides of the cordillera. The Mapuche intensified their activities and relations with people in the eastern slopes of the cordillera. It was sometime in this period that the Pehuenche were pulled into greater Araucania. The Pehuenche controlled the cordillera, from which they raided the settlements of both Creoles and the so-called friendly Indians for livestock and for captives on both sides of the Andes, including Mendoza.

A cultural openness and adaptability facilitated the ready acceptance of new goods and technology, and the Mapuche and their neighbors within Araucania adopted new technology to their own use almost at once. By the end of the sixteenth century, missionaries observed that European crops like wheat and peas could be found in Mapuche fields in the Nahual Huapi area. Sheep grazed along with llama in the mountain meadows. Horses extended the range of travel and communication among friendly communities and added to the range of hunting parties, not to mention war parties. The spread of wild apple trees throughout

[7] Horacio Zapater, citing the Jesuit missionary Rosales, 63. In his book *Aborígenes chilenos a través de cronistas y viajeros* (Santiago: Editorial Andres Bello, 1978), 15, the Chilean anthropologist tells us: "The seventeenth century provides us important chronicles [of the interior frontier]. These were written by Jesuits [Valdivia, Rosales, Ovalles] and by military [Gonzales de Najera y Bascuñan]. Their experience living with the Indians, their capacity for observation, and their knowledge of the native language by two of the Jesuits [Valdivia and Rosales] validates these sources for the researcher."

[8] As cited in Zapater, *Aborigenes Chilenos a traves de cronistas y viajeros*, 161.

the southern forests added a staple to the Mapuche diet; the Huilliche (sometimes called Manzaneros by the Spanish) were famed for their production of apple *muday* (hard cider). In fact, the material basis of Mapuche society appears to have improved as an indirect result of the encounter.

The temporary frontier peace came to a dramatic end in 1598, when Araucania again erupted in a spontaneous revolt. Discontent centered on the decision of the newly appointed governor Martín García Onez de Loyola to establish a military fort in Mapuche territory south of the Bío Bío River in support of new Jesuit missionizing efforts. Widespread and bloody campaigns followed this Spanish betrayal of Mapuche territorial claims, and every Spanish settlement between the Maule River and Osorno in the south was wiped out. Thousands of Spanish women and children were taken captive in 1598, and they were soon integrated into the household economy of their Mapuche captors. Loyola was captured and decapitated, and his defeat was celebrated in ceremonial form by exhibiting his skull throughout Araucania in subsequent years, perhaps as proof of the mortality of the Spaniards.[9]

In this general uprising Spanish settlers were expelled from Araucania south of the Bío Bío River, and the river defined the boundaries of Spanish colonial rule that remained more or less the same for the next two centuries. The southern outposts of Spanish colonization were bounded by the Maule and Bío Bío rivers, south of which lived the Mapuche.

In this frontier zone Spanish missionaries, having begun with the Franciscans in 1553 and followed by the Jesuits in 1593, continued to carry out conversion attempts. After the 1598 uprising Jesuit missionizing activities were protected by defensive forts, and they continued until the expulsion of the Jesuits from the Americas in 1767. However, after the general uprising of 1598, it was clear that the Mapuche were resistant to colonial rule, and in 1622, a royal cédula finally declared that these "royal patrimonial Indians" in the southern frontier were not "*encomendable*," and could not be called into *mitas* and personal service. In contrast the Picunche who opted to live around the colonial outposts of Concepción and Chillan were obliged to participate in the *mit'a* system throughout the sixteenth century.

[9] Jeronimo de Quiroga, *Memorias de los sucesos de la guerra de Chile* (Santiago, Editorial Andres Bello, 1979) 274.

PAMPAS PREHISTORY AND ENCOUNTER

When the Araucanian, Pehuenche, and other groups of the southern cordillera foraged east into the arid *pampas*, they occasionally encountered hunters moving west from the humid *pampas* south of the Río de la Plata. The Araucanians called these people the "Puelche," which means "People of the East" in their language.

The first Spanish attempt under the leadership of Pedro de Mendoza to settle at the mouth of the Paraná River in 1536 was fiercely resisted by people who called themselves the *Querandie*, described by Ulrich Schmidel, a German missionary who traveled with Mendoza.

> These Querandies do not have fixed residences, they roam through the territory like gypsies. When they travel in summer (usually over distances of 30 leagues), if they don't find water or thistles, they find and kill deer or wild beasts and drink the blood; if they didn't, they would die of thirst.[10]

Mendoza tried to subjugate the Querandi, who resisted with

> arrows, and darts, and a kind of lance, or half-lance, with a sharp stone point. . . . They have stone balls . . . and they throw them around the feet of the horses [or deer – guanaco – when they hunt] until they fall, and with these stones they killed our captain and hidalgos.

Although the Spanish lost their captain and two officers in this 1536 battle, they managed to take the village, which the Querandi had abandoned, leaving behind stores of fish, grains, and furs. However, the Querandi returned within a month, and with the assistance of allied Timbue and Charrua allies from the north, they routed the Spaniards.

While anthropologists, linguists, and ethnohistorians continue to piece together the ethnohistorical picture of the inhabitants of the Río de la Plata at the time of these first encounters, it is generally accepted that the majority of the people living in the *pampas* south of the Río de la Plata and the Río Negro shared a common language (Gennaken) and general cultural attributes.

Archaeological research indicates that in the delta region small bands of people lived in small horticultural settlements, supplementing their crops with a mix of fishing, hunting, and gathering. Trade and warfare characterized their relations with Guaraní neighbors upriver. In the lush

[10] Ulderico Schmidel, "Viaje al Rio de la Plata y Paraguay," in Pedro de Angelis (ed.), *Colección de obras y documentos*, Vol. VI (Buenos Aires: Plus Ultra, 1970), 269.

grasslands that stretched south to the Río Negro, other Pampas groups relied more heavily on the hunt for guanaco and the seasonal gathering of tuberous plants.

The few documents extant suggest the possibility that the Querandie enjoyed a relatively advantageous position as mediators in informal trading systems that linked them between the Guaraní to the north as well as to the more mobile Pampas groups who hunted in the *pampas* grasslands to their south. Their hostile reception of the Spanish may have been motivated by a desire to protect their positions as intermediaries in the flow of trade goods along the river and into the *pampas*, where furs, feathers, and salt from the salt flats in the interior *pampas* were exchanged for *yerba mate* from the north.

However, when Juan de Garay returned in 1580 to reestablish the settlement, he discovered that the majority of the Querandie had disappeared, and the territory had been claimed by people speaking the language common to all the *pampas* groups to the south. A document dating to the foundation of Buenos Aires in 1580 recorded the following:

> Of the Querandi nation, and those who belonged to it, it has been erased even to its name, and the few who survived the extinction of their race moved to the Río Negro, where they became confused with, or at best founded, the Teguelchos.[11]

In the following century the small settlement of Buenos Aires developed slowly and more or less undisturbed by Indian hostilities. Occasionally Pampas hunting and raiding parties would raid outlying farms for livestock, but more often Indian relations with the colonists were peaceful trading encounters.

Part of the reason for the dramatic change of social conditions in less than half a century can be found in profound transformations in the environment. These changes had completely changed interethnic dynamics in the four intervening decades. The stray cattle and horses left behind by various expeditions wending their way up the Paraná River had found a perfect ecological niche in the *pampas*. Stray horses and cattle proliferated rapidly into herds numbering into the thousands. At the same time, Old World diseases had spread through direct and indirect contact, and Spanish documents suggest significant disease and depopulation among the native groups living along the river. Sixteenth-century Spanish de-

[11] Juan de Garay, "Fundación de Buenos Aires," in de Angelis (ed.), *Colección*, III, 433.

scriptions of travel on the Paraná River routinely speak of pock-marked bodies floating in the river, and references to abandoned native settlements also point to significant depopulation of the Pampas peoples.

The displacement of native populations in the Río de la Plata in the first half of the sixteenth century as a result of disease and warfare also resulted in the breakdown of precontact trade systems, which allowed Spanish settlers to step into place as the new intermediaries in the native flow of goods. Occasional exchanges for tobacco and *mate* had traditionally linked Pampas groups into a north–south trade route along the Paraná River, but Spanish colonization began to disrupt this pattern. The small settlement of Buenos Aires was little more than an afterthought established to protect and ensure the flow of Spanish production from Jujuy, Tucuman, and Misiones in the northwest toward the mining centers in Bolivia and Peru. Even so, some of that production destined for the mining centers, especially sugar and *aguardiente*, informally circulated back into the traditional interband trading networks in the southern *pampas*. Creole merchants in the colonial outpost of Buenos Aires traded these new stimulants, as well as the traditional tobacco and *mate*, in exchange primarily for salt, as well as worked leather goods, furs, and rhea feathers. Soon even more Pampas bands joined into the informal exchange networks.

Another trade route with an east–west orientation linked the peoples of the *pampas* to the peoples of the cordillera. A series of water holes (called *salados* because of their saltiness) provided a route through the arid *pampas* south to the Río Negro. The enormous herds of horses and cattle that flourished in the *pampas* grasslands in the sixteenth century were easily available to native groups even prior to any direct encounters with the Spanish. *Pampas* groups north of the Salado quickly adapted horses for hunting and trading purposes.

Tehuelche Prehistory and Encounter

South of the Río Negro there lived scattered bands of people who hunted and foraged the vast Patagonian steppes on foot. They also spoke a language related to that of the Pampas Indians.[12] The Araucanians called

[12] Casamiquela refers to a *Günüken-küna septentrional* in *Un nuevo panorama*, 58. Loukotka' classification separates these languages from *Genneken* into the *Patagon* or *Tshon* stock, including the Téuesh or Chewache from the Cordillera Central, the Poya in the vicinity of Lake Nahuel

these people the Tehuelche ('people of the south'), a name that the Spanish adopted. First-hand archival accounts of the Tehuelche do not appear until the late seventeenth century, when colonial administrative reforms prompted exploration of its territorial claims in Patagonia, but the work of archaeologists suggest that the Tehuelche maintained a lifestyle that had changed little over millenia. The Tehuelche traveled by foot in small family bands, following seasonal movements of the guanaco and the rhea (Argentine ostrich). Their seasonal hunting and gathering pattern was punctuated by trading fairs with Pampas groups to the east (just north of the Rio Negro) and with expeditions to Araucanian settlements in the southern cordillera.

Like the Pampas groups with whom they shared a language, the Tehuelche lived a precarious and simple life in material terms, keeping warm against the cruel Patagonian winds with skin capes and makeshift skin lean-tos. Early European expeditioners making their way around the straits occasionally encountered bands of these people along the coast, and the hardiness of these people in the harsh Patagonian environment astonished the Europeans, and stories of the Patagonian giants, sometimes embellished with the myth of the antipodes, colored early accounts of voyages along the Patagonian coast and around the straits (and to some extent continue today).

As was common in the age of exploration, Europeans carried trinkets for barter, and their encounters may have established a pattern of ritual exchange that lasted well into the mid–nineteenth century. Although a thorough review of the records of maritime travel along the Patagonian coast in the sixteenth and seventeenth century is far from complete, the occasional hint of European encounters with the native peoples along the east coast describe exchanges similar in form to those described by North American whalers in the nineteenth century. In fact, we know very little of the history of Patagonia from the written record until the mid–eighteenth and nineteenth centuries, when the Europeans began to turn their attentions to the exploration of the southern cone.

Huapi, the Péeneken or Tehuelche between the Cordillera Central and Atlantic Ocean, and the Aoniken or Tsoneca, in southern Patagonia (contemporary Chubut and Santa Cruz). Apart from the Tsoneca, I find Casamiquela's evidence for the similarities between the northern and southern languages more convincing for the Patagonian peoples.

Seventeenth and Eighteenth Centuries

In the seventeenth century, south of the Bío Bío River, greater Araucania enjoyed a florescence of stable life based on horticulture in small settlements scattered throughout the cordilleran slopes and coastal plains. This is not to suggest that pestilence, epidemic disease, or natural catastrophes from earthquakes and volcanic eruptions did not occur; indeed there is relatively little research from which to draw many generalities. What is clear, however, is that a cultural openness and acceptance of new ideas and beliefs, and a willingness to incorporate western crops and technology, facilitated and strengthened the dynamism of a separate and autonomous Araucanian social context.

One direct account of life within Araucania can be found in the memoirs of the Spanish military chief Francisco Nuñez de Pineda y Bascuñán, who spent 7 months in captivity among the Mapuche in 1629 and became their defender as a result of his experience. In *Cautiverio Feliz*, his descriptions of curing ceremonies (which he calls witchcraft) carried out by a *machis* (curer, shaman), of *parlamentos* (gatherings to ceremonialize ties between political allies), and of ceremonial sacrifices reveal a rich and complex ceremonial life.[13]

Ritual sacrifice was central to ceremonial life within Araucania, and these sacrifices took place around a central altar called *rewe* (also the word for the core social unit). To the Spaniards, the beheading of Loyola and ceremonial exchange of the skull throughout Araucania had provided the first example of this practice, and the image of the bloodthirsty Araucanians persisted throughout the following centuries, embellished by many accounts of a sacrificial ceremony that included the removal and exchange of a still palpitating heart from the sacrificial victim – which in at least one case was a captured Spanish soldier. Looking behind this frightening image, we can see that ritual sacrifice, usually of animals, functioned for the Mapuche as a way of stabilizing and mediating the balance between the temporal and cosmic and between the living and their totemic ancestors. Although a symbolic exegesis of this ceremonial language is far beyond the scope of this essay, it is clear that the Mapuche worldview tended toward inclusivity and adaptability of the new and

[13] Francisco Nuñez de Pineda y Bascuñán, *Cautiverio Feliz* (Santiago: Editorial Universitaria, 1989), and José Anadon, *Pineda y Bascuñan: Defensor del Araucano* (Santiago: Editorial Universitaria, 1977).

unfamiliar to their own ends, rather than a closed and exclusive system, (such as the Inka worldview, for example). Perhaps the most telling symbol of this openness is the historical change in the choice of the ceremonial animal, which in the sixteenth century was usually a guanaco, but by the seventeenth century was more often a white sheep – that new creature that appeared with the Spanish.

ARAUCANIANS AND THE "PERMANENT WAR"

By the mid–seventeenth century, Indian–white relations in Chile had settled into a state of permanent war. Mapuche forces defended a fortified military frontier along the course of the Bío Bío River, maintaining the southern coast and both faces of the cordilleran highlands as their effective domain. Several well-watered mountain passes at low elevations allowed the easy travel and movement of livestock through the southern Andes and provided easy access to the *pampas* and Patagonia for the Araucanians.

In contrast the only route available to the Spaniards between Santiago and Mendoza required travel over a precipitous and dangerous pass through the highest part of the Andes. A series of *postas*, or waystations, linked Mendoza, San Luis Río Quarto, and Buenos Aires, providing resting places for travelers on the overland journey, as Concolorcorvo, the mule-driver–satirist and others observed.[14] This line of *postas* also defined the effective southern frontier of Spanish settlement and influence; it was a boundary that scarcely changed in the next two centuries (see Map 16.2).

Araucanian influence began to dominate frontier relations in the vast grasslands south of this east–west frontier by the end of the seventeenth century. Spanish and Creole settlers and Jesuit missionaries living in the zone defined and defended by the *postas* on the west side of the cordillera were always alert to the possibility of raids by Araucanian warrior parties. On the other hand, a social fluidity in this frontier zone also operated to permit the easy exchange of ideas and goods. East of the cordillera, Araucanian quasi-military hunting parties (sometimes called Aucas, from the Quechua, meaning 'enemy') originating in settlements around Lake

[14] Concolorcorvo (Calixto Bustamante Carlos Inca), *El Lazarillo de ciegos caminantes desde Buenos Aires hasta Lima* (1773); Introduction by Ventura García Calderón, Biblioteca de cultura peruana, Vol. 6 (Paris: Desclee, de Brouwer, 1938).

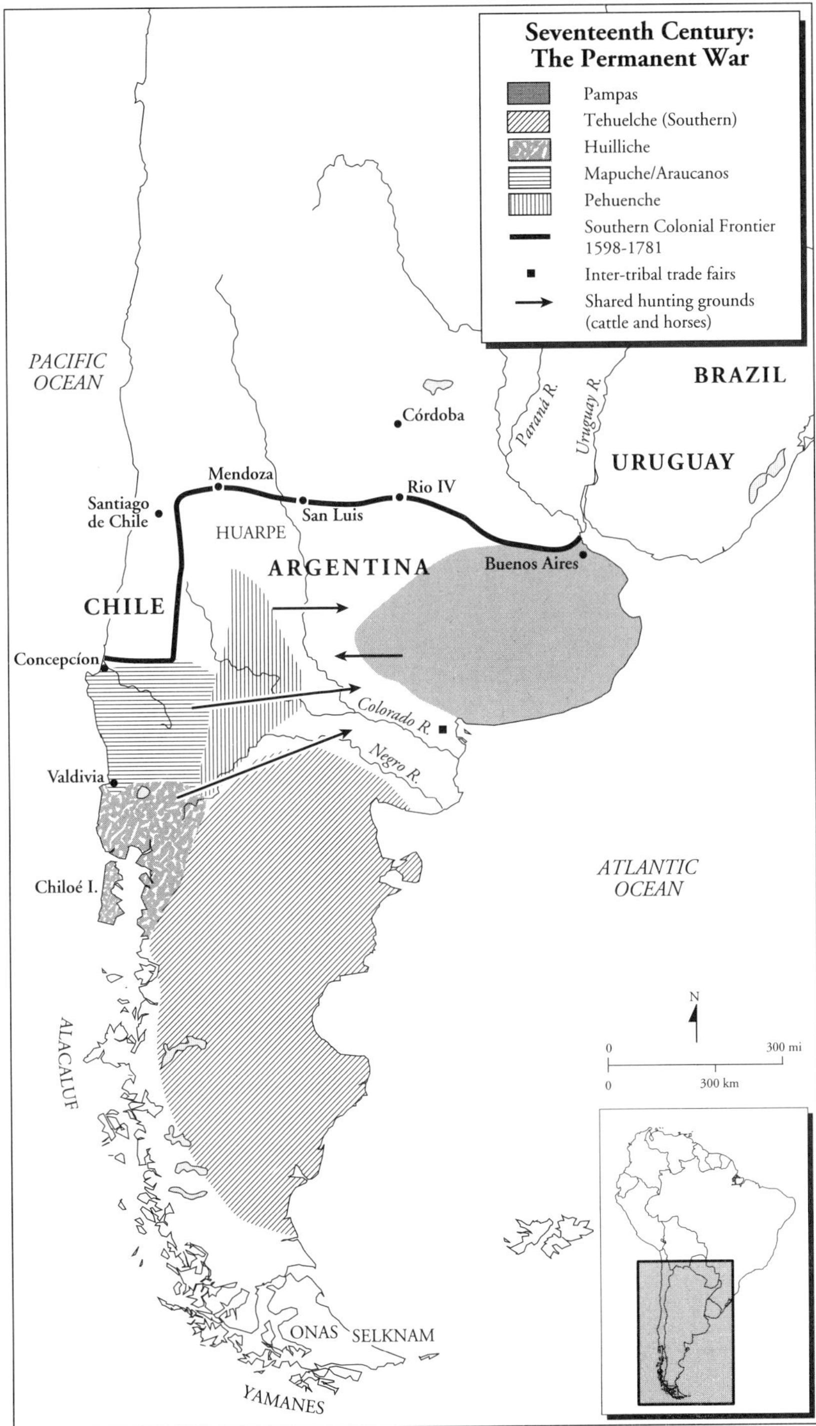

Seventeenth Century:
The Permanent War
Pampas
Tehuelche (Southern)
Huilliche
Mapuche/Araucanos
Pehuenche
Southern Colonial Frontier
1598-1781
Inter-tribal trade fairs
Shared hunting grounds
(cattle and horses)
PACIFIC
OCEAN
BRAZIL
Córdoba
Paraná R.
Uruguay R.
URUGUAY
Mendoza
Rio IV
Santiago
de Chile
San Luis
HUARPE
ARGENTINA
Buenos Aires
CHILE
Concepcíon
Colorado R.
Negro R.
Valdivia
ATLANTIC
OCEAN
Chiloé I.
N
0
300 mi
0
300 km
ALACALUF
ONAS
SELKNAM
YAMANES

Map 16.2

Nahuel Huapi (the headwaters of the Neuquen River) pushed east and north into the *pampas*, following the established trade routes along the *salados* (salt flats). Araucanian sorties harassed some Pampas groups as well as Spanish colonists as far east as Río Quarto (south of Córdoba).

On the Atlantic coast, following the initially bellicose relations with the Spanish, Pampas groups in the littoral arrived at a point of truce with Creole settlers, and they regularly participated in Buenos Aires markets. By the seventeenth century, Buenos Aires was well established as a frontier outpost in the littoral, and Pampas traders were frequently seen in the market place dealing in rhea feathers, textiles, and other items.

When the Pampas bands adopted the horse and introduced European goods into traditional interband trading networks, opportunities for trade increased. Occasional Tehuelche bands were attracted north of the Río Negro to take part in an annual trade fair traditionally located in the well-watered *pampas* near present-day Tandil, which, according to some interpretations, produced a revitalization among all of the Gennakan-speaking bands, Pampas and Tehuelche alike.

PEACE TALKS AND WAR PARTIES IN ARAUCANIA

Between 1723 and 1725 general uprisings throughout western Araucania in response to frontier conflicts over commerce resulted in the Spanish implementation of a policy of *parlamentos* (negotiations and peace treaties) in Chile. Spanish officials first tried this tactic in Tapihue in 1716 and, following a general uprising in 1723, instituted a general policy of formal treaty making. Chilean historian Luz María Méndez has documented and described this institution.

> An emissary called the commissioner of the nations goes to the four *butalmapus* [four "corners" of Araucania; this term for the organization of Araucania may be more of a Spanish imposition than reflective of indigenous structure] with a message from the new president to the *toquis* and other *úlmenes* to gather to meet reciprocally in order to better consolidate the peace established by his predecessors. The same ceremonies that were carried during peace treaties are repeated in this conventional congress. The great majority of *úlmenes* attend this meeting, not only to personally meet the new chief of the Spanish, but also to deduce by his physiognomy the peacefulness or warlike tendencies of his nature.[15]

[15] Juan Ignacio Molina, *Compendio de la Historia Civil* (Colección de historiadores de Chlie y documentos relativos a la historia nacional, tomo XXVI, cap. IV, 1618), quoted by Luz Maria

These *parlamentos* involved significant expense to the government – ranging from 2,000 to 10,000 pesos – to cover costs of feeding up to 4,000 participants and providing iron implements and other trade items to ensure peaceful relations. Rich archival evidence of just one *parlamento* reveals what must have been a colorful and thrilling spectacle.

Spanish authorities looked carefully for the site to hold the *parlamento*, one that was strategically safe and provided adequate water, firewood, and pasture for livestock. The movement of troops to the site also attracted Creole traders and producers to sell their goods. Fresh beef and mutton was prepared in great quantities for consumption, as well as wheat grain and, of course, great quantities of cane alcohol and wine. A large ceremonial ground was divided into two large rectangles united in the center by a palisaded passageway. In one rectangle a ramada was constructed to shade the participants during days of speeches and ceremonies; the other remained open for the gathering of troops and artillery and displays of horsemanship. Spanish military erected temporary ramadas for lodging outside the area, and Mapuche set up teepee-like *toldos* two or three kilometers distant. Over a period of several days, many speeches were accompanied by displays of horsemanship, races, and great gift exchanges of colorful clothing, hats, belts, ribbons, and decorative household objects, metal tools, tobacco, and livestock. Between 1726 and 1803 – that is, until the end of colonial rule – the *parlamentos* regulated an uneasy truce in the frontier on the western side of the cordillera (see Map 16.3).

On the eastern side of the cordillera south of Mendoza, however, a very different dynamic was in operation. Between 1711 and 1744 a series of *malones* (raids) plagued the frontier outposts that linked Mendoza to Buenos Aires. Most of these actions were organized by Pehuenche hunting parties operating out of their cordillera strongholds. In some cases Pampas groups or Tehuelche, allied through kin ties, joined in these actions. What accounts for the difference in frontier relations on the western and eastern slopes of the cordillera?

Throughout Araucania the prior century of political and military frontier negotiations with the Spanish had ultimately contributed to a militarization and political stratification within Araucanian society. The basic community social units were much more organized and stratified into a hierarchical social system, in which regional *toquis* ranked over

Mendez in Sergio Villalobos et al. (eds.), *Relaciones Fronterizas en La Araucanía* (Santiago: Ediciones Universidad Católica de Chile, 1982), 117–118.

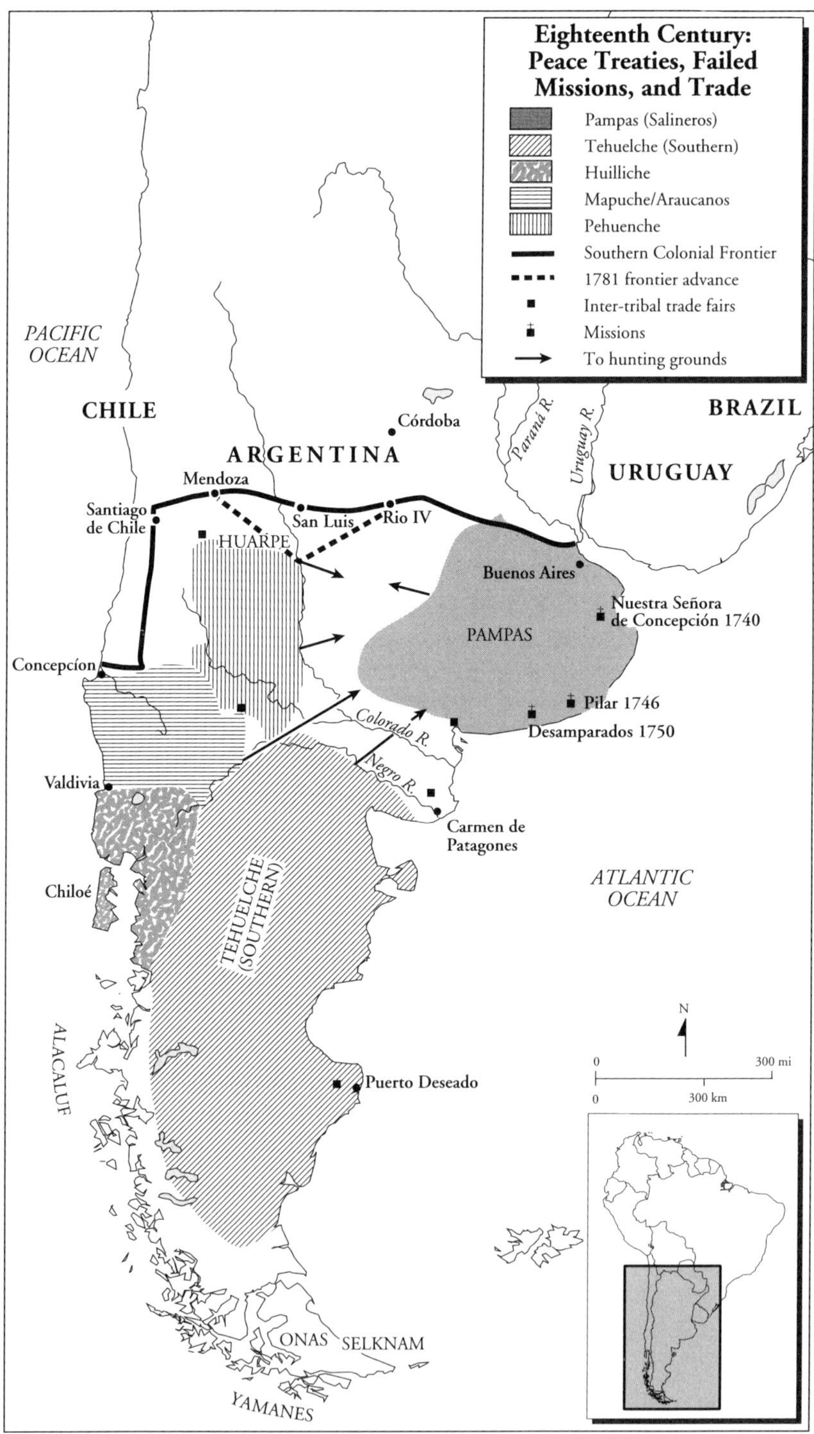

Eighteenth Century: Peace Treaties, Failed Missions, and Trade
Pampas (Salineros)
Tehuelche (Southern)
Huilliche
Mapuche/Araucanos
Pehuenche
Southern Colonial Frontier
1781 frontier advance
Inter-tribal trade fairs
Missions
To hunting grounds
PACIFIC OCEAN
CHILE
ARGENTINA
BRAZIL
URUGUAY
Córdoba
Paraná R.
Uruguay R.
Mendoza
Santiago de Chile
San Luis
Rio IV
HUARPE
Buenos Aires
Nuestra Señora de Concepción 1740
PAMPAS
Concepcíon
Pilar 1746
Desamparados 1750
Colorado R.
Negro R.
Valdivia
Carmen de Patagones
Chiloé
TEHUELCHE (SOUTHERN)
ATLANTIC OCEAN
ALACALUF
N
0
300 mi
0
300 km
Puerto Deseado
ONAS
SELKNAM
YAMANES

Map 16.3

local *úlmenes*, mirroring Spanish military structures. Diplomatic interactions with the Spanish in the *parlamentos* in Chile formalized mutually understood ceremonies by which both the Spanish and the Araucanians came to common agreement. In this way, Araucanian ceremonial forms (such as ceremonial sacrifices around the community *rewe*) were transformed into more formal *parlamento* with the Spanish to incorporate changing historical conditions.

Relatively peaceful frontier relations on the west side of the cordillera negotiated through the *parlamentos* allowed the Araucanians to direct their energies to the east side of the Andes, where they carried out militaristically organized hunting parties. The largesse of the *cimarrones* (herds of wild cattle and horses) and greater opportunities for intertribal trade attracted more and more Araucanian hunting parties into the grasslands east of the cordillera.

By the eighteenth century a preference for horse meat over beef was established in Araucania. As consumption of cured, salted meat (*charqui*) within Araucania increased, so too did the numbers of mounted hunting parties sweeping into the *pampas*. Creole settlers and ranchers along the frontier feared the *maloqueros* coming from Chile, who, unbound by treaty agreements on the eastern side of the cordillera, were as apt to raid the livestock and property of a frontier ranch as to hunt the *cimarrones*. Within Araucania the exchange of livestock, captives, and goods obtained in these raids (called *malocas* in Chile, and *malones* in Argentina) was often mediated by the relatively free movement of Creole traders who traveled throughout Araucania, offering iron implements, trinkets, silver spurs and bridle bits, and stimulants in exchange.

REJECTION OF THE MISSIONARIES

The wild herds of *cimarrones* in the *pampas* south of Buenos Aires that attracted the Araucanian hunters east from the cordillera also prompted greater numbers of Pampas (Puelche) bands to pitch their camps in the arroyos and watering holes in the region. The small frontier settlements of Lujan, Areco, Matanza, and Magdalena emerged as satellite suppliers for the emerging city of Buenos Aires. Gaucho hunting expeditions had shifted from the Entre Ríos grasslands to the southern *pampas*. The mobility offered by the horse had also allowed the Indians a wider range for hunting, gathering, and trading, and intercultural competition over resources in the *pampas* intensified.

In this arena of competition, hostilities between settlers and different Pampas (Puelche) bands increased in the early 1700s, and between 1737 and 1739, after the allied Pampas chief Cacapol died, his son Cangapol (Bravo) headed a series of *malones* against the Magdalena frontier south of Buenos Aires, where ranching activities were beginning to intensify. A series of locally negotiated peace treaties negotiated in 1739 between individual Creole settlements and local Pampas bands lasted only briefly. In 1740 Cangapol led a *malon* against the partido (county) of Magdalena, the southernmost ranching region where Creole (descendants of Spanish colonists) activities were most intense. In this one raid over 200 colonists were killed, captives taken, and over 20,000 livestock carried off. The governor of Buenos Aires, Ortíz de Rozas, moved to negotiate a peace treaty with Cangapol and other local Pampas bands, in which the Pampas ceded the territory north of the Río Salado in exchange for trading rights and sovereignty south of the river. In a series of measures proclaimed in the 1740s, the *cabildo* of Buenos Aires took measures to control that trade. While "authorizing" Indian entrance into the city "so that they could sell their ponchos" (ponchos made in Araucania and traded in the *pampas*), the *cabildo* explicitly prohibited in 1742, 1744, 1745, and 1747 "the sale or exchange of wine and aguardiente, in the city or in the country, with the Pampas Indians."[16]

Another article of the peace treaty with Cangapol permitted the establishment of Jesuit missions south of the Salado River. The Jesuit Matías Strobel founded the first settlement, Nuestra Señora de la Concepción, on the banks of the Salado River in 1740; another Jesuit, Thomas Falkner, explored the hostile Indian territory south of the river 4 years later, and in 1747 he founded the Reducción de Nuestra Señora del Pilar in the vicinity of present-day Mar del Plata. The Pampas bands rejected Jesuit attempts to missionize them outright, and the missions were abandoned within 3 years. The Jesuits blamed their failure to settle the Pampas bands on the bad faith of Creole *pulperos* (traders), who encouraged clandestine trade in alcohol and other stimulants in exchange for cured hides, rhea feathers, boleadores, and ponchos.

At the same time, the Pampas Indians blamed the Creole settlers and traders robbing them of their goods, to which they responded by organizing *malones* to recuperate their goods from the Spanish. These intensified intercultural conflicts in the *pampas* in the eighteenth century re-

[16] AGN (Archivo General de la Nación, Argentina): Bandos, Libro 1, Folios 132 y 133, See also Bandos, Libro 1, Folios 14–15, 1742, Folios 39–40, 1744, folios 7, 1745.

quired adaptive strategies among all the parties involved; as Creole gauchos adopted more and more of the indigenous technology, like boleadores and ponchos, the Pampas Indians likewise incorporated new concepts of social forms.

One particularly significant development was the shift from consensus making at the level of the band to more concerted joint efforts under the leadership of war chiefs like Cangapol. This change tended to reinforce the status of successful warriors and a somewhat more hierarchical social organization, a prototype of a patriarchal tribe, though not as complex as the system among the Mapuche.[17] At the same time, however, individual bands negotiated all kinds of temporary alliances; it was not uncommon that two or more Pampas bands might join together to retaliate against liberties (spying, kidnapping) taken by another; in other instances Pampas bands might ally themselves with Tehuelche and Araucanian hunting parties. This fluidity in political alliances bewildered and frustrated the Creoles, who were unable to distinguish between "friendly" and "enemy" Indians.

Such confusion was understandable, because by this time Araucanian hunting and war parties penetrated deep into the *pampas*. The English Jesuit Thomas Falkner's *Description of Patagonia and the Adjoining Parts of South America* provides a snapshot of the complex intertribal relations in the *pampas* and Patagonia, in which description of the groups from Araucania of the Mapuche linguistic groups (Moluches [probably Mapuche], Picunche, Pehuenche, Huilliche, and Puelche) is contrasted to that of the Pampas Indians, of the Gennaken linguistic family (Taluhets, Diuihets, Chechehets, Tehuelhets), while the Leuvuches (the followers of Cangapol) appear to have been in a state of linguistic and cultural transition, having acquired a great many Araucanian terms through trade. Of the former group, Falkner's descriptions are second hand. Falkner suggests that the Taluhets and Diuihets (Tehuelche) originally lived in the environs of Buenos Aires but were pushed out by the 1740s and operated often in concert with the Araucanians.

They (Diuihets) are of the same wandering disposition with the Tahuhets, and are not much more numerous, having been greatly destroyed in their attempts to plunder the Spaniards, sometimes taking part with the Taluhets, at other

[17] In fact, Cangapol's son, Cacique Bravo, assumed the leadership role in negotiating territorial rights and rights of access to the salt flats with the new viceregal government in the 1780s and 1790s. Cacique Bravo dealt directly with León Rosas, the father of the future governor of Buenos Aires and president, Juan Manuel de Rosas. (Archivo General de la Nación, Sala 9, 24–26, Leg. 14, Exp. 26, 179.)

times with the Pehuenches, and frequently making their excursions alone, on the frontiers of the mountains of Cordova and Buenos-Ayres, from the Arrecife to Lujan; killing the men, taking the women and children for slaves, and driving away the cattle.

The Chechehet lived to the south and east around the Río Colorado and appear to have been least influenced by either the Spanish or Araucanian interlopers.

They are perpetually wandering about, and move their habitations, and separate, for the most trifling motives, and oftentimes from no other reason, but their natural propensity to roving. Their country abounds only in the lesser kinds of game, as hares, armadilloes, ostriches, etc. producing few or no guanocoes. When they go up to the mountains of Tandil and the Casuhati, on account of the scarcity of horses, they are so very unskillful in hunting, etc., that they never bring back any on their return, unless their neighbors the Tehuelhets give them some.

In contrast the Leuvuches, the followers of Cangapol, held a critical intermediary role between all the groups.

This people seem to be composed of the Tehuelhets and Chechehets, but speak the language of the latter, with a small mixture of the Tehuel tongue. On the eastern side they reach to the Chechehets; on the western, they join to the Pehuenches and Huilliches; on the north, they border on the Diuihets; and to the south, on the other Tehuelhets. . . . This nation seems to be the head of the Chechehets and Tehuelhets, and their Caciques, Cacapol and his son Cangapol, are a kind of petty monarch over all the rest. When they declare war, they are immediately joined by the Chechehets, Tehuelhets, and Huilliches, and by those Pehuenches who live most to the south, a little lower than Valdivia."[18]

THE NORTHERN TEHUELCHE AS INTERETHNIC TRADERS

The Tehuelche bands ranging in the desert south of the Río Negro continued to maintain their hunting and gathering existence on foot. Only the northern bands made use of horses, which required steady and reliable sources of water. These northern bands, ranging near the headwaters of the Río Neuquen and the Río Negro, joined with Cangapol to take advantage of their intermediary position between the southern Araucanians (Huilliche) and the Pampas bands to the north.

Sporadic encounters between the Tehuelche and European sailing

[18] Thomas Falkner, *A Description of Patagonia and the Adjoining Parts of South America,* Arthur E. S. Neumann (ed.) (Chicago: Armann & Armann, 1935), 101–103.

vessels seem to have had little impact on native social and political organization. The Tehuelche continued to hunt the guanaco in the seasonal pattern they had followed for millenia. Falkner commented on what he called the Tehuelhets:

Of all nations upon earth, there is no account of any so restless, and who have such a disposition to roving as these people: for neither extreme old-age, blindness, nor any other distemper, prevents them from indulging this inclination to wander.[19]

Unlike their neighbors to the north and west, the Tehuelche did not adopt the horse for travel, probably because of the scarcity of adequate water, but they did eat them when available. The introduction of durable European trade goods (like iron) through trade with European vessels into the trading networks in Patagonia also created demand for these items.

Even so it is clear that the European arrival in Patagonia did have indirect consequences for the Tehuelche. The log from a 1770 expedition into Patagonia noted abandoned Indian settlements, observing:

Smallpox was always one of the scourges that decimated the Indian population after the arrival of the Spanish. When smallpox resulted in death, the Indians abandoned the cadavers and all their belongings, for fear of contagion. They rarely returned to erect their tents in places where there had been deaths due to this cause.[20]

The appearance of herds of horses had also attracted mounted Araucanian forays deeper into Tehuelche country along the river systems of Río Colorado and Río Chobut, and began to impact on Tehuelche intercultural relations. An excerpt from the Spanish exploration of Bahía sin Fondo on the Patagonian coast in 1773 reveals that intertribal interactions in the Patagonian interior were by no means simple. A captive Pampas woman who spoke Spanish accompanied a small band of Tehuelche who boarded the ship, and she described life with the Tehuelche for the expeditioners.

These Indians don't worship, apart from some veneration for the sun, they eat guanaco, rheas, and horse meat; they dig small sweet potatos to eat raw and cooked, and other roots which they toast to make a flour to make their *poleadas*

[19] Ibid., 109.
[20] "Diario de capitán D. Juan Antonio Hernández," in de Angelis, *Colección de Obras y Documentos*, vol. IV, 110.

(gruel), and also a small mustard-like seed which they grind. [She also said] that upriver there are many tehuelche and auca (Araucanian) Indians, but they are far; that the tehuelches are poor and the aucas are rich, they even have domestic cattle, horses, and sheep in abundance, that they make textile blankets and ponchos, and that they also plant crops.[21]

RAIDERS AND TRADERS

By the middle of the eighteenth century, the shape of intercultural relations in the Southern Cone had been radically transformed. The *cimarrones*, tremendous herds of wild horse and cattle that flourished in the grasslands, attracted Araucanian hunting and raiding parties and Chilean *conchavadores* (traders) east from the cordillera, salt caravans, gauchos, and *pulperos* south from the littoral, and Tehuelche trading delegations north from Patagonia, all of whom competed for this rich resource in the traditional homelands of the Pampas Indians. Although livestock for consumption and for sale was the primary goal for these hunting parties, the increased intercultural encounters prompted a secondary market for ponchos woven in the heart of Araucania, for furs, ostrich feathers, and salt obtained by Pampas and Tehuelche bands deep in the *pampas* and Patagonia, and for tobacco, arms, and *aguardiente* offered by the *pulperos* (itinerant Creole traders) in the frontier regions south and west of Buenos Aires and the *conchavadores* (traders) moving into Araucania in Chile. Itinerant traders were so commonly seen within Araucania that when missionary Fray Pedro Angel de Espineira traveled across the cordillera in 1758 to visit the Pehuenche, he had to stress the spiritual rather than commercial nature of his visits to the *tolderias* (tent encampments) by saying that "we had not come to look for their ponchos, land, sheep, or cattle, but their souls."[22]

In this dynamic, new interethnic arena, linguistic terms were traded freely, political alliances emerged and disappeared in a pattern of localized raiding and warfare, and marriages linked bands with tribes with municipalities, and all this in an arena completely outside colonial or indigenous dynastic control. This situation was not destined to last. What had begun as simple hunting of a natural resource – the *cimarrones* – was

[21] "Extracto resumido de . . . la expedición del descubrimientos de la Bahia sin Fondo," in de Angelis, *Colección,* IV, 169.

[22] From *Relación del viaje y mision a los pehuenches, 1758*, reprinted in Jorge Pinto R. et al. (eds.), *Misioneros en la Araucanía: 1600–1900* (Temuco: Ediciones Universidad de la Frontera, 1988), 240.

now viewed by colonial authorities as a regulated activity subject to government license. By the mid–eighteenth century, the *cimarron* herds were mostly decimated as a result of intensified and wanton hunting, and local colonial authorities stepped in to ban the slaughter of calves and to issue monopoly licenses for the hunt. In both Buenos Aires and in Chile, authorities attempted to control the trade carried on beyond the limits of the *postas*, to little avail.

Colonial settlements to the east and south of Mendoza and Buenos Aires continued to be plagued by a series of *malones* in the second half of the eighteenth century. During this period countless locally negotiated temporary agreements between and among Araucanían, Pehuenche, Pampas and Tehuelche bands and individual frontier settlements created a mosaic of interethnic relations in which could be found variously hostile and friendly Indian bands (see Map 16.4).

As trading and raiding in the Argentine *pampas* increased in the seventeenth century, a process of intertribal acculturation changed the face of intertribal as well as interethnic relations. The militarized and hierarchically organized Araucanian warrior societies that expanded their hunting and raiding activities east of the Andes deep into the *pampas* grasslands forged alliances through trade and warfare with the *pampas* and Tehuelche bands they encountered. This "Araucanization of the desert" included the expansion of Mapundungun – the common language of Araucania – as a kind of *lingua franca* adopted by the Pampas and even Tehuelche groups for trading purposes. The bilateral kinship systems of the Pampas and Tehuelche melded well with cross-cousin preferential marriage customs (the "Omaha" system) of the Araucanians, and political marriages resulted in an incipient patrilineal – and ultimately militaristic and hierarchical – kinship network that linked Pampas and Tehuelche bands into an increasingly complex intertribal puzzle.

Decisions about raiding or trading were made at the level of individual lineage leaders or bands rather than along uniform ethnic lines. Colonial authorities grew worried about the uncontrolled activities of Creole traders, who were not even deterred from their commerce with bands known to have raided for Creole captives and livestock.

By 1788 the *cabildo* of Buenos Aires called for extreme measures against "those who treat, or serve as a spy for the Indians" and insisted "that all inhabitants of the country who are in the most risk be gathered in the forts." The *cabildo* of Buenos Aires also sponsored enormous expeditions to the salt flats controlled by *cacique* Cangapol's (sometimes also called

Araucanian Diaspora
1779–1828
Pampas
Tehuelche (Southern)
Huilliche
Mapuche/Araucanos
Pehuenche
Military Frontier 1779
Rosa's campaign 1833
Principal cattle trails
PACIFIC OCEAN
CHILE
BRAZIL
Paraná R.
Uruguay R.
Córdoba
ARGENTINA
URUGUAY
Santiago de Chile
Mendoza
San Luis
Rio IV
Junín
Luján
Buenos Aires
Tandil
Concepcíon
Calfucurá
Colorado R.
Negro R.
Laja
Valdivia
Llaima
TEHUELCHE (SOUTHERN)
Chiloé I.
ATLANTIC OCEAN
N
0
300 mi
0
300 km

Map 16.4

Bravo) followers in an attempt to assume a monopoly over salt sources. In 1796 the Navy captain Félix de Azara carried out a careful reconnaissance of the guard posts and forts of the southern boundary of the viceroyalty of Buenos Aires and reported the following to the viceroy:

> The Indians from the cordilleran foothills took notice of the wild livestock and began to drive great herds to Chile, whose presidents had contract for livestock with these Indians. They [Indians] could not survive in their own land without some work, and they moved into the country of the wild herds, and some intermixed with the Pampas [Indians]. . . . By the middle of this [eighteenth] century the herds and this precious resource of hides was exhausted.[23]

From this point the accusations of the Argentines against the Chileans intensified and would continue to color border negotiations during the national period.

THE BOURBON REFORMS AND INDEPENDENCE

In this climate of increased competition for resources in these rich *pampas* grasslands, notions of territoriality and property began to shift. As a part of the Bourbon Reforms in the late 1700s, the Spaniards had stepped in to consolidate the frontier outpost system and to begin regulating trade. Efforts to control an incipient frontier market by regulating exchanges and claiming herds as property was a common, though differentially interpreted, goal not only of the Spanish but also of all other parties involved. Where once the riches of the *pampas* had been free to all, the decimation of the *cimarrones* by Creole, Araucanian, Pampas, and Tehuelche hunters created a situation of scarcity in the face of rising demand. Territorial rights were fiercely contested, and peace treaties specified those rights in terms that detailed intimate knowledge of the land. On the west side of the Andes in Chile, in the threat of a general uprising in Araucania because of land usurpations following the expulsion of the Jesuits in 1767, the Spanish had ceded all the territory between the Canoas and Damas rivers to the Mapuche by prohibiting the formation of "ranches or raising cattle south of the Río Bueno."[24] According to Chilean historian Leonardo León Solis, "with the consolidation of the frontiers in the Bío Bío region and the province of Cuyo, and in the

[23] Félix de Azara, "Reconocimiento de la frontera," in de Angelis, *Colección*, VIIIA, 149.

[24] Raul Molina O., *Territorio Mapuche Huilliche de Osorno y Legislación* (Santiago: Programa Juridico Popular Centro el Canolo de Nos Sociedad Mapuche-Huilliche Monku Kusobkien Freder, 1991).

context of territorial restructuring that affected the different Araucanian groups during the first half of the eighteenth century, the movement across the cordillera began to lose its purely military character and was converted into traffic in goods and livestock."[25] The southern colonial frontier linking Mendoza, San Luis, and Río Cuarto east of the cordillera remained the same, but south of Buenos Aires the newly reauthorized Spanish militia negotiated peace treaties with Pampas bands that allowed Spanish settlement of lands north of the Salado River in exchange for a one-time presentation of "gifts" and access to local trade in frontier *pulperías* (trading posts), monitored by the *guardias* (colonial forts).[26]

There is little question, then, why Araucanians in Chile and Pampas bands in Argentina took the royalist side in the independence struggles at the turn of the century. When the British blockaded the port of Buenos Aires in 1806, *Cacique* Chocorí and his Pampas forces presented themselves to the Buenos Aires *cabildo* to offer their support.[27] Mapuche and Huilliche warriors in Chile joined royalist armies to protect their hard-fought territorial rights in the struggle against Creole liberals rising up against the crown.

NINETEENTH CENTURY

The "permanent war" that had characterized southern frontier relations in the Southern Cone for nearly three centuries had allowed the autonomy and political sovereignty of the Araucanian, Pampas, and Tehuelche people. Over the years a tremendous restructuring of political organization, social forms of kinship and ceremonial life, language, worldview, and subsistence activities had strikingly transformed the face of the non-Spanish world in the southern cone.

Araucanian Expansion and Permanent Settlement in the Pampas

Following the independence of Chile in 1818, the new government incorporated the southern territories of Valdivia, Osorno, and Chiloé and

[25] Leonardo Leon Solis, *Maloqueros y Conchavadores*, 61.

[26] AGN, Sala 9, 24-3-6, Leg. 14, Exp. 26, 179. This treaty was negotiated by León Rosas, who served as interpreter and agent of the viceroyal government. His son, Juan Manuel de Rosas, was later to build on the diplomacy of his father after his military campaign in 1833.

[27] *Acuerdos del extinguido cabildo*, Serie IV, Tomo II, Libros LIX, L, LXII, 1805–1807 (Buenos Aires: Fraft, 1924).

sponsored reconnaissance expeditions into central Araucania, which stimulated mild pressure for Araucanian territory. Shortly thereafter an Araucanian diaspora from the cordillera began, in part pushed by this pressure on their lands, but also pulled by the riches to be found in the Argentine "desert." Hundreds of families following different *lonkos* moved permanently into the *pampas* and established permanent tribal encampments, complete with hide *toldos* (tents) and horse corrals, all protected by graded military societies. Different lineage leaders, through diplomacy, treachery, intermarriage, trade, or warfare, forged complex political alliances that linked them to native Pampas and Tehuelche bands (see Map 16.5).

The Vorogano followers of Calfucurá settled on the shores of the Salinas Grandes, quickly usurping authority over the resident Pampas followers of Mariano Rondeau and establishing control of the critical salt sources. Calfucurá, who had been born near Llaima in Chile, had followed his family to settle with the Ranqueles before leading his followers to the Salinas Grandes.

> By taking control of the Salinas Grandes, Calfucurá consolidated his position as a major player in the rapidly growing market linking livestock production in Argentina and sales in Chile. At the same time, Calfucurá consolidated the political sovereignty of his people and used this position to build an effective intertribal confederation that not only resisted subjugation but also improved temporarily the living standards of his people. . . . In [a] transformation of traditional government, Calfucurá inculcated in his followers the idea that his leadership was of divine origin. This explanation established legitimacy for his lineage and created a dynastic rule over the pampas in the following decades. As in the past, cultural adaptability and receptivity to change resulted in societal transformation that protected and enhanced political sovereignty.[28]

The Ranquel settlements were located south of San Luis between the Río Quinto and the Río Colorado at the headwaters of the Río Chalileo in an area of thick reeds (*ranquel* in Mapundungun) (see Map 16.6). During subsequent years the Ranqueles themselves emerged as a powerful force under the leadership of Llanquetruz (a Tehuelche leader who had married into Ranquel society). The Ranqueles offered sanctuary for Creole *vagos* and *malentrenidos* (vagabonds) fleeing both conscription and the increasing stranglehold of caudillo ranchers during the first half of the century.

[28] Kristine L. Jones, "Calfucurá and Namuncurá: Nation builders of the pampas," in Judith Ewell and William Beezeley (eds.), *The Human Tradition in Latin America: The Nineteenth Century* (Wilmington: Scholarly Resources, 1989), 180.

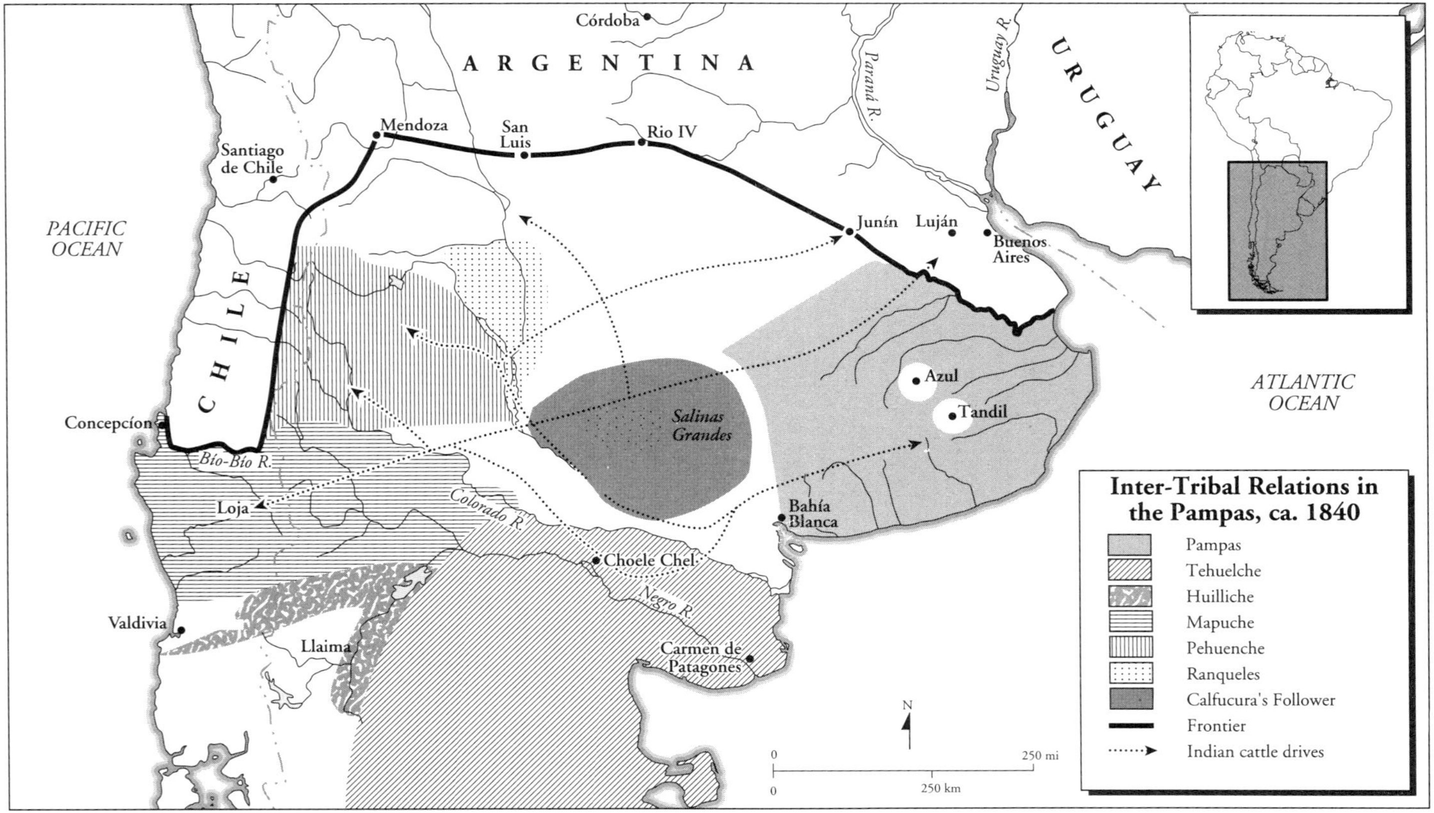

Inter-Tribal Relations in the Pampas, ca. 1840
Pampas
Tehuelche
Huilliche
Mapuche
Pehuenche
Ranqueles
Calfucura's Follower
Frontier
Indian cattle drives
ARGENTINA
URUGUAY
CHILE
PACIFIC OCEAN
ATLANTIC OCEAN
Córdoba
Mendoza
San Luis
Rio IV
Junín
Luján
Buenos Aires
Santiago de Chile
Concepcíon
Bío-Bío R.
Loja
Valdivia
Llaima
Salinas Grandes
Azul
Tandil
Bahía Blanca
Colorado R.
Choele Chel
Negro R.
Carmen de Patagones
Paraná R.
Uruguay R.
N
0
250 mi
0
250 km

Map 16.5

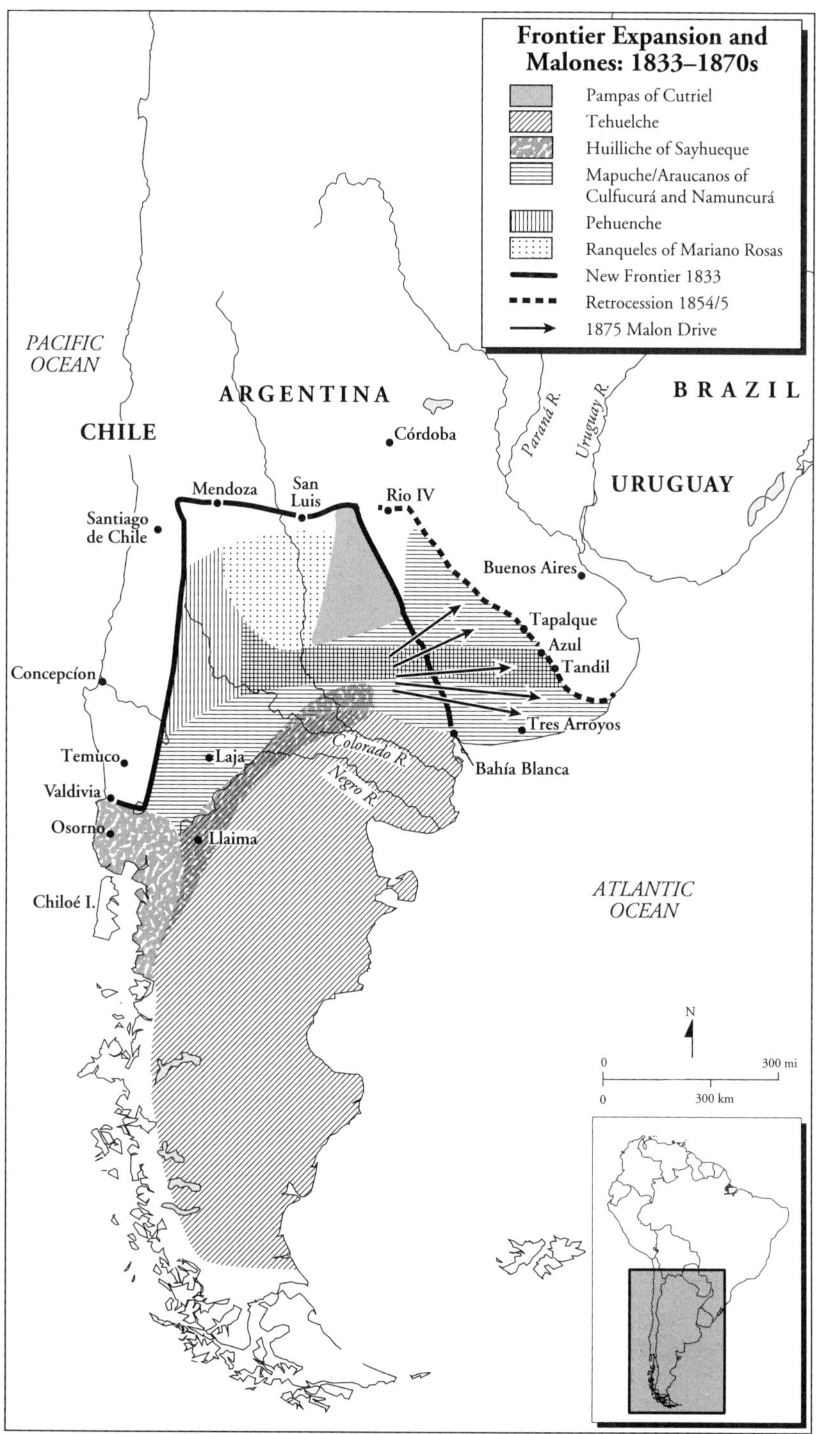

Frontier Expansion and Malones: 1833–1870s
Pampas of Cutriel
Tehuelche
Huilliche of Sayhueque
Mapuche/Araucanos of Culfucurá and Namuncurá
Pehuenche
Ranqueles of Mariano Rosas
New Frontier 1833
Retrocession 1854/5
1875 Malon Drive
PACIFIC OCEAN
ARGENTINA
BRAZIL
CHILE
Córdoba
Paraná R.
Uruguay R.
URUGUAY
Mendoza
San Luis
Rio IV
Santiago de Chile
Buenos Aires
Tapalque
Azul
Tandil
Concepcíon
Tres Arroyos
Colorado R.
Temuco
Laja
Negro R.
Bahía Blanca
Valdivia
Osorno
Llaima
Chiloé I.
ATLANTIC OCEAN
N
0
300 mi
0
300 km

Map 16.6

By mid-century, the integration of Creoles into Ranquel society resulted in a kind of mestizo society (like the metís society of Canada), but their allegiances tended more to their Mapuche and Huilliche neighbors to the west and south rather than their Creole neighbors. South of the Ranqueles, the Huilliche continued to live the traditional horticultural life in the eastern slopes and mountain passes of the cordillera around Nahuel Huapi and near the headwaters of the Neuquen River.

A combination of factors encouraged the permanent settlement of the Araucanians in the *pampas*, the region into which they had previously sent hunting and raiding parties. Increased opportunities for trade with Chilean *conchavadores* in the west and Argentine *pulperos* in the east now favored a substantial exchange of goods and livestock along an east–west axis. Control of the salt sources allowed the Voroganos of Calfucurá a competitive edge in the production of salted hides and *charqui*. The Huilliche stronghold in the Nahuel Huapi region and their control of the mountain passes allowed them to play a neutral role as intermediaries in the exchange of horses and cattle that were herded from the *pampas* along trails following water holes and the banks of the Río Colorado and sold in the Bío Bío region. Indeed expansion of some lineages through political marriage with Tehuelche bands in the late eighteenth century had strengthened and fortified the Huilliche presence west of the cordillera. Likewise the Ranqueles enjoyed a considerable trade with the Pehuenche and the Chilean *conchavadores* who came over the mountain passes at the headwaters of the Laja River.

In the early nineteenth century, links to the market economy were tenuous; most of the production, circulation, and consumption of the goods in this informal economy remained within Araucania. Within two decades, however, the transformation of an indigenous trading system and its incorporation into the market economy was complete. The relatively uncontrolled trading system, fueled by habit-forming merchandise like cane liquor (*aguardiente*), tobacco, sugar, and *yerba mate*, stimulated the flow of hides and cattle to the port city of Buenos Aires as well as west of the cordillera deep into Mapuche territory. The *cimarrones* were gone, and most of the remaining livestock had been branded and claimed as personal property. The hunting economies of gauchos and Indians alike shifted to horse and cattle trading. Dependence on Creole markets became inescapable for the Indians.[29]

[29] This process mirrors in many ways the consequences of the fur trade in Canada in the eighteenth century, as Eric Wolf describes in *Europe and the People Without History*. The alcohol component

Indian society grew increasingly militarized and hierarchical as the rhythm of raiding and trading picked up. The *malones* permitted greater opportunities for increased status, wealth, and power. In this system, status for men could be achieved by valor in battle, and material wealth increased not only by the spoils of the hunt or raiding but also by the labor of women and captives. Increased integration into a market economy had tremendous consequences for the sexual division of labor, and captive Creole women and children, as well as livestock, were the material basis for production. Increased intertribal trading in textiles meant more work for Mapuche wives. Increased reliance on fresh and cured meat versus traditional food crops meant more time caring for herds and butchering and curing the meat for *charqui*. In the early nineteenth century, the Englishwoman Maria Calcott Graham observed the conditions for women in the *pampas*:

> Their flocks are entirely managed by their women and slaves [Christian women], who watch alternately during the night, mounted on horseback, and going the rounds among the cattle: if a sheep or any animal should be missing the unfortunate woman is stripped and flogged in a most barbarous manner. The occupation of the women during the day is to catch and saddle the horses of the Indians, and cook their food.[30]

In Argentina, the few locally negotiated peace treaties of the 1790s fell apart after 1812. There followed nearly two decades of relatively uncontrolled trade in the frontier south of Buenos Aires. *Pulperías*, the distributive institutions of this frontier trade, grew over sixfold between 1781 and 1816.[31] Enormous quantities of *aguardiente*, tobacco, and *yerba mate* moved into the southern regions of Buenos Aires in exchange for hundreds of thousands of cow and horse hides.

Argentine ranchers took steps to control frontier commerce in the 1820s, shutting Indian traders and gauchos out of the market. Local landholding ranchers joined forces to create a frontier militia to replace

in the Canadian fur trade, or the trade in furs and buffalo hides with Plains tribes along the Missouri River, or the trade in hides throughout Apachería and Comanchería, is well known in a popular sense, but the economic consequences have yet to be studied. Apart from works such as Arthur J. Ray and Donald B. Freeman's study of the fur trade economy, *Give Us Good Measure: An Economic Analysis of the Relations between the Indians and the Hudson Bay Company before 1763* (Toronto: University of Toronto Press, 1978), few economic historians have really focused on the specific mechanisms by which native peoples in the Americas were integrated into the market economy, much less the scope and measure of the trade. Is it enough to say that they were simply conquered through addiction?

30 Maria Calcott Graham, *Journal of a Voyage to Brazil and Residence There During Part of the Years 1821, 1822, 1823* (London: Longman, Hurst, Roes, Orme, Brown and Gren, 1824), 427.

31 AGN, Sala XIII, 14-3-6 (1781 & 1786), 14-4-1 (1791), 14-4-2 (1796), 14-4-1 (1801), 15-1-5 (1816).

the royalist forces following independence. In the process gauchos were coerced into service as ranch hands for the ranchers, leaving Indian traders little option but to accept allotments of *aguardiente*, sugar, tobacco, and flour in exchange for their "pacification." In 1825 the provincial government took over the costs of what they named "peaceful trade with the Indians," and by 1828 a treaty network administered through seventeen new guard posts ensured the dependency of scores of Pampas, Araucanian, and Tehuelche bands.[32] In the next two decades, the provincial government moved to consolidate and control the rural ranching economy by excluding license to commerce in livestock to all but titled landholders. When markets closed to Indian traders, more and more *caciques* opted for allotments. Between 1835 and continuing annually until 1851, quarterly rations, including horses, subsistence, and what the government called "vices," the habit-forming *aguardiente*, tobacco, and *yerba mate*, were distributed among the followers of allied *caciques*.[33]

The Indians who remained outside the treaty system responded with intensified raiding for the livestock upon which they depended to obtain those "vices" of tobacco, sugar, and *aguardiente* to which they had grown accustomed. Negotiation over the exchange and redistribution of material wealth profoundly shaped the complex web of exchange relationships within Araucania itself.

As demand for livestock increased within Araucania, so too did the demand for labor to watch the herds, cure the hides, and perform other tasks necessary to support the needs of the mobile encampments. In raids against Creole properties, Araucanian and Pampas militia usually killed the men, but they abducted women and children. By the mid–nineteenth century, captive women and children in Araucanian camps numbered in the hundreds. When Pampas Indians took captives, it was most often to trade them with Araucanians for manufactured goods, *aguardiente*, or food. In contrast the Araucanians integrated captives into their economic activities and within their more hierarchical social structure. Offspring of captured women and their captors were claimed by their fathers and fully integrated into Mapuche society according to patrilineal kinship rules, ensuring the continuation and strength of their respective lineages.

[32] La Plata, Archivo historico de la Provincia de Buenos Aires, "Negocio pacifico con el indio 1825–28."

[33] "Negocio Pacifico con los indios, rendiciones de cuentas," AGN Sala 3, 17-8-5 (1835–39), and 17-8-6 (1840–58).

If the spoils of the *malones* in the late eighteenth century were intended for domestic consumption within Araucania, by the mid–nineteenth century the demand for the livestock was clearly market driven. However, caudillo politics in Argentina had effectively closed commercial markets in the southern frontier to gauchos and Indians alike. A system of *compadgrazgo* (fictive kinship) and coercion bound the gauchos and "pacified" Indian bands to the increasingly powerful landholding caudillos. Under the vice of military defeat and dependency on the "vicios," now only available through the allotment system, "conquered" Indians had little option but to acquiesce in the face of expanding ranching activities in Buenos Aires province. In contrast the relative autonomy of nonallied bands/tribes located in the great salt flats, in Patagonia, and in the southern cordilleran heartlands permitted continued access to trade, an option not available to Creole gauchos and allied Indian bands along the frontier. Even so, the consolidation of property, now defined as land as well as livestock, into the hands of relatively few Argentine landholders, narrowed the opportunities for commerce.

EXPORT ECONOMIES AND THE IDEOLOGIES OF CIVILIZATION AND OCCUPATION

The demand for livestock and captives grew as a result of market demands *within* Araucania as well as for the opportunities for exchange along the southern Creole frontier in Argentina and Chile. The transition to a more mobile lifestyle and the dependence on horses and cattle completely transformed Araucanian labor systems. Subsistence efforts shifted from simple agricultural activities organized at the community level to a gender-biased and hierarchical tribal system to husband large herds of livestock and to produce the hides, salt, and dried meat for a growing market. The sexual division of labor shifted to favor a system that recruited warriors to join in armies of thousands, and that tied women down to preparing hides and *charqui*, not to mention caring for livestock and producing woven textiles. In this way indigenous labor systems adapted to the changing demands of the same market system that stimulated Argentine expansion into the *pampas* south of Buenos Aires and prompted Chilean penetration south of the Bío Bío River in the second half of the nineteenth century.

In Chile a *Comisario de Naciones* in Osorno between 1822 and 1848 undertook a paper process of delimiting Mapuche and Huilliche community lands, a process in which the remaining or "surplus" (often the best for farming) fell to the state. The development of a new export sector began to stimulate new pressures for Mapuche territory along the southern coast. When new markets suddenly opened for Chilean wheat as a result of the California gold boom in 1850, demand for the rich farming land in southern Chile suddenly soared. After the expulsion of the Jesuits, the few remaining Creole and Araucanian priests were unable to counter Creole penetration into Araucania. The Chilean state took over the Araucanian mission in 1837 and invited twenty-four Italian Franciscans to the college of Chillan. Shortly thereafter, the Italian Capuchino order took over the mission but never achieved much success because of the difficult political struggles in mid–nineteenth-century Chile.

In 1852 the Chilean government moved to claim all "surplus" lands not legally recognized as Indian lands in the earlier incomplete and vague reconnaissance efforts – in deed if not in fact. In 1858 the first German colonists arrived to settle and farm in the untilled lands. The liberal project to colonize the south with immigrant Europeans proceeded despite the fury of the resident Mapuches. When the bottom fell out of the export market in California and Australia, the crisis stimulated further pressure to occupy the southern frontier (as the region was now called) to increase production and generate alternative markets in Argentina for the Chilean export economy. An ideology for occupying the land found a voice in the discourse over national sovereignty, in which the theories of "superior" and "inferior" races informed the discussion.

The Mapuche responded to the Chilean penetration into their territory variously. According to local needs and perceptions, some Araucanian communities responded with violence, others opted to seek redress working within the governmental system, and others migrated east over the cordillera to join the growing encampments in the *pampas*. Some communities decided to join forces with the liberals in the civil wars between 1851 and 1859, a move that prompted the conservative government in 1866 to impose the *Ley de Radicación Indígena*, a reservation policy modeled after the U.S. example.

In Argentina the intertribal alliance system, established to protect the Buenos Aires frontier under the leadership of Juan Manuel de Rosas, broke down after his defeat in 1852. Rebellion and uprising spread among the allied tribes. This uneasy peace that had protected Buenos Aires province broke down the frontier, which was pushed back to colonial boundaries. However, where once this frontier had been the focus of a flourishing commerce open to Creoles and Indians alike, it was now blockaded and fortified by a highly trained national army.

In the 1860s and 1870s, nonallied bands responded to what was in effect a trade embargo, an indisputable act of war. Where limited skirmishes had characterized frontier relations in the first half of the century, and social fluidity and mobility had contributed to the formation of Creole and Araucanian society alike, by 1860 the problem was distinctly polarized into an Indian–white enmity. Several tribes and bands joined together to carry out a series of crippling *malones* under the leadership of Calfucurá. Paradoxically the allotment system established in the first half of the century in Argentina had directly contributed to the organization and militarization of Calfucurá's, and other tribes. Indeed it even contributed to a kind of political primogeniture! The names of most of the most-feared Araucanian leaders of this decade, including Calfucurá and his son Namuncurá, and Llanquetruz and his son Baigorrito, had first appeared on the allotment records of the 1840s and 1850s.[34]

As a historical footnote, in tune with the spirit of the times, a French explorer named Aurelio Antonio de Touonens in 1860 arrived at the Chilean port of Valdivia with the intention of establishing himself as a monarch among the Araucanians. The self-proclaimed "Rey Orllie" saw the struggles of nation building in the Southern Cone as an opportunity, much as did other nineteenth-century adventurers (most notably William Walker in Nicaragua). This man who would be king, having received some success among some of the tribes of Araucania who sought to build their defensive alliances, extended his invitation to the Tehuelches to join his kingdom, but by 1874 his reign came to an end as his "subjects" turned their efforts to defending their northern borders.

In the 1870s major *malones* led by confederated tribes virtually depopulated the southern frontier of Buenos Aires. The population of one frontier town, 25 de Mayo, dropped from 5,000 to 600 after thousands of head of livestock and several hundred women and children were

[34] The records of "Negocio Pacífico con los indios, rendiciones de cuentas," AGN Sala 3, provide detailed information about the amounts remitted from the Comisaria General to provide specific goods ("yeguas, alimentos, vicios") to specifically named *caciques*.

carried off in one *malon*. To the Argentines these attacks against the properties that formed the very basis for the Argentine export economy and national sovereignty could no longer be tolerated.

THE CONQUEST AND PACIFICATION OF ARAUCANIA

Much as the discourse in Chile about occupying "the frontier" was couched in the ideology of "superior" and "inferior" races, so too was the emerging national goal of "civilization" in Argentina based on ideas of race. Following the end of the Paraguayan War, and with the era of caudillo politics over, the Argentine government was able to turn its attentions and resources to resolving the "Indian problem" in a series of military campaigns known as the "Conquest of the Desert." The picture of horsebound forces carrying Remington rifles as well as traditional lances and bearing the feathers and painted banners of graded military societies sweeping in to carry off the noble frontier women is as familiar as the images of the Plains Indians in North America, and a similar ideology motivated national policies of both the Argentine and Chilean governments. In all three cases the theory of "the inferior race" justified conquest dressed in the moral cloak of "civilizing" and thereby settling the Indians (see Map 16.7).

In 1872 Argentine General Ignacio Rivas, backed by the (mostly Pampas) forces of Catriel, defeated Calfucurá in a battle and recovered 70,000 head of cattle, 16,000 horses, and many sheep. The continued danger of Indian attack prompted the Minister of War Adolfo Alsina to construct a defensive line of frontier outposts connected by telegraph lines, and provisioned Indians who sought refuge north of this boundary. In 1873 Alsina even constructed a ditch (popularly referred to as Alsina's Folly), 610 kilometers long, 3 varas deep, and 2 varas wide, to prevent the loss of Argentine livestock.

The Araucanians, now being pressured by Chilean settlement in the coastal agricultural regions west of the cordillera and by Argentine expansion into the *pampas* grasslands, had little choice but to respond to military invasion with warfare. First, however, they had to resolve intertribal enmities that worked against them and to raise armies capable of resisting the Argentine army.

A French visitor traveling through the *pampas* between 1869 and 1874 summarized the situation of Catriel's followers situated near the frontier town of Azul:

Republican Military Expansion, Conquest, and "Pacification" 1870s–80s
Frontier of 1869
New border of 1876
Alsina's ditch 1876
Roca's military operations 1879–80
Chilean-German Colonization and Mapuche Reduction 1866–83
Frontier 1883
PACIFIC OCEAN
BRAZIL
Paraná R.
Uruguay R.
ARGENTINA
URUGUAY
Mendoza
San Luis
Rio IV
Santiago de Chile
Buenos Aires
CHILE
Azul
Tandil
Salinas Grandes
Concepcíon
Colorado R.
Negro R.
Temuco
Laja
Bahia Blanca
Valdivia
Choele Chel
Osorno
Carmen de Patagones
ATLANTIC OCEAN
N
0
300 mi
0
300 km

Map 16.7

Catriel's tribe lived before deep in the desert; but once peace was made with the government of Buenos Aires, they came to establish themselves a few leagues from Azul and consented in not molesting the Christians further, in exchange for an annual subvention of money, cattle, mares, tobacco, yerba, and clothes from the State. The cacique was named general, and his subalterns or *capitanejos* received as well different grades of allotments in accordance with their anterior hierarchical position. This tribe in those times was composed of some four thousand people, including one thousand five hundred lances [warriors]. After having been maintained and submissive, during which years they had offered the government their active participation in various invasions [against enemy tribes], they had just tired of the restrictions on their liberty. . . . About four or five years ago, they rebelled, and, accompanied by their chief, they fled into the desert with their families and livestock.[35]

In 1875 Argentine President Adolfo Alsina tried to effect peace with Calfucurá's descendant, Namuncurá, through peace treaties and diplomatic endeavors, as well as his defensive ditch. Namuncurá carried out a voluminous diplomatic and public relations campaign, at times with the press, at other times with the Church, in an attempt to present the arguments and complaints of his followers. In a letter to the Archbishop of Buenos Aires in 1875, he wrote:

As minister and representative of God I hope you will help me in my affairs to be in good favor with the Superior Government and that the Superior Government respect me and that it not take away from me the lands it wants to take in Carhué (on the island of Choele Chel on the Río Negro) and to stop the hordes that are following the railroad as far as Chilio Chel (Río Negro); this form of disposition is not for the good of the country for the other caciques; we are owners of these lands and we don't want the lands around Carhué taken away; they are the only ones we can work and that God has shown us how to hunt [with boleadores], where there are herds [we need] to cover our bodies and to satisfy our needs and where we keep the majority of our horses which we have always wintered there in the service of our work.[36]

Negotiation broke down, however, and in a major offensive in 1875, a confederation of armies under the leadership of Namuncurá raided five southern *partidos* (counties) in Buenos Aires province, killing over 300 people, taking another 500 captive, and carrying off over 300,000 head of livestock. Namuncurá counted among his supporters the Ranqueles troops and, in a surprise turnabout, Catriel's forces.

[35] H. Armaignac, *Viajes pos las pampas argentinas* (Buenos Aires: EUDEBA, 1974), 119.

[36] Reprinted in Adalberto A. Clifton Goldney, *El Cacique Namuncurá: el Ultimo Soberano de la Pampa*, 2nd ed. (Buenos Aires: Editorial Huemul, 1963), 234.

Further south, well-financed exploratory expeditions began the process of mapping and claiming the Patagonian territories south of the Rio Negro for the Argentine government. Description of Tehuelche lifeways is recorded in one of the most famous accounts, *At Home with the Patagonians*,[37] by Englishman George Chaworth Musters, in which we see how little had changed for these people. This is not to say that they did not consider themselves sovereign peoples, as Argentine geographer Francisco P. Moreno discovered when he met with them in his reconnaisance of Patagonia in 1876–1877.

> The grand war gatherings [parlamentos], in which the explorer must present the reasons that bring him into the regions where the Pehuelche or the Mapuche is king, have no meaning for the hospitable Patagonian who receives the explorer. He does not find here the powerful character of the warrior so notable in the Limay region. However, the Patagonian is no less brave a defender of his sovereignty, as stories of their combat testify.[38]

Nonetheless the appearance of these friendly explorers heralded the beginning of the end for the Tehuelche.

The influential *Sociedad Rural Argentina* voiced bitter complaints against the ineffective defensive tactics of Alsina and supported the aggressive ideas of General Roca, who wanted the *malones* stopped. When Argentine President Domingo Sarmiento assumed office, he appointed Roca to lead what turned out to be the final Argentine offensive in 1878–1879. Namuncurá, hearing of the preparations, took pains to build up defensive forces and sent for help from the Mapuche along the Pacific coast. Pascual Coña, a Chilean Mapuche *cacique*, recalled the incident in his memoirs as dictated to Padre Ernesto Wilhelm de Moesbach in the 1920s.

> Upon arriving, the messenger, coming from the Argentine Indians, said: "Chiefs Chaihueque [Huilliche], Namuncurá (Vorogano), Foyel and Ancatrir [Ranquel] sent me, they charged me, "Go see the nobles [*caciques*] in Chile." This is the reason for my arrival here. By order of my chief I tell you, the Chilean chiefs, the following. "There are, then, the huincas [whites], and we are going to rise up against them we Argentine Indians have had enough of them . . . we are going to join together to fight against them.[39]

[37] (London, 1871 and 1873).

[38] Francisco P. Moreno, *Viaje a la Patagonia Austral: 1876–1877* (Buenos Aires, Ediciones Solar, 1969), 217.

[39] Wilhelm de Moesbach, 1st ed. 1930 (Santiago: Imprenta Pucará, 3rd ed., 1984), 271.

In this final war, however, the Argentine forces prevailed, and the offensive resulted in the rescue of 150 captives and the return of over 15,000 head of cattle to Creole ranchers. The defeated forces of Namuncurá were settled in small reserves situated at the headwaters of the Neuquen River and along the banks of Lake Nahuel Huapi.[40] Most, however, ended up working as peasants (called *paisanos* in Argentina) on the cattle and sheep ranches that proliferated after the *Conquista del Desierto*.

State policies for the "Conquest of the Desert" in Argentina and the "Pacification of the Frontier" in Chile ultimately ended the political sovereignty and autonomy of the Indian world in the Southern Cone in the 1880s, and Araucania was for the first time separated by the north – south political boundary between Argentina and Chile. In fact control of national boundaries had not been possible until the late nineteenth-century consolidation of the Argentine and Chilean states, and the Indian world had maintained a strategic advantage by negotiating the fluidities of the entire frontier region.

Their defeat was final and demoralizing. Pascaul Coña reported: "The fate of the disgraced Mapuches went from bad to worse. They [Mapuche] had not captured much from the Chileans in the final *malon*, but the Chileans grew rich, thanks to the herds stolen from the Mapuches."[41]

The separation by force of Araucania into *reducciones* in Chile and *reservas* in Argentina contributed to the contemporary cultural and political separation of the "Argentine" and "Chilean" Mapuche. Even though the national frontiers are relatively fluid, and the Mapuche do tend to move back and forth over the mountain passes, in over a century since then distinctive cultural differences have emerged. Twentieth-century ethnographies describe and even tend to reinforce the perception of separate Mapuche worlds.[42] Administrative policies of different national governments have tended to further separate and differentiate the Chilean Mapuche from the Argentine Araucanians. Even so, historic ties continue to bind Araucania. In 1992, the "quincentennial year," dozens

[40] See another Argentine literary classic, *Viaje al pais de los araucanos*, by Estanislao S. Zeballos (Buenos Aires: Hachette, 1960), for a view of Araucanian society in Argentina immediately after the 1880 "Conquest of the Desert."

[41] Pascual Coña, *Testimonio de un Cacique mapuche*, 287.

[42] Mischia Titiev, *Araucanian Culture in Transition*, Occasional Contributions from the Museum of Anthropology of the University of Michigan No. 15 (Ann Arbor: University of Michigan Press, 1951); Inez Hilger, *Araucanian Child Life and its Cultural Background (Chile Argentina*, Misc. Collection, V. 133, No. 42 (Washington: Smithsonian, 1957); Louis C. Faron, *The Mapuche Indians of Chile*, (New York: Holt Rinehart and Winston, 1968).

of *caciques* from both sides of the national borders met in Chile for the first time in over a century to claim their continued cultural sovereignty after 500 years of invasion.

BIBLIOGRAPHIC ESSAY

Understanding interethnic relations in the Southern Cone requires a basic familiarity with not only the political and administrative developments of the colonial era but also the national histories of both Argentina and Chile. Because national historiographic interpretations from each nation have at different times directly contradicted the other, and because those historiographic traditions have been put to different nationalistic ends in each country, it is important for the ethnohistorian to screen for these tendencies to understand indigenous and interethnic historical movements not necessarily limited by national boundaries. Given that caveat, this bibliography mentions some of the more useful sources from both countries, as well as from other sources.

Beginning with bibliographic sources, consult the *AHA Guide to Historical Literature*, Mary Beth Norton and Pamela Gerardi, eds., 2 vols., Section 36, "Native Peoples of the Americas" II, (New York, 1995), 1159–1161. An OAS publication complied by T. Welch, *The Indians of South America: A Bibliography* (Washington, 1987) categorizes mostly ethnographic sources by country (Indians of Argentina, Indians of Chile). Other useful bibliographic surveys of otherwise obscure sources include Susana Santos Gomez's *Bibliografía de viajeros a la Araucanía*, 2 vols. (Buenos Aires, 1983), and P. Meinrado Hux, *El Indio en la Llanura del Plata: Guía Bibliográfica* (Provincia de Buenos Aires, 1984) for Argentina. Kris Jones, "Nineteenth-century travel accounts of Argentina," *Ethnohistory* 33 (2) (1986), 195–211, is an example of how textual analysis of travel literature can lead to deeper understandings of Indian participation in frontier development.

General sources for understanding the precontact situation include J. Roberto Bárcenas, ed., *Culturas indígenas de la Patagonia* (Spain, 1992), Tom D. Dillehay, *Araucanía: presente y pasado* (Santiago, 1990), and Jorge L. Hidalgo et al., *Culturas de Chile: prehistoria, desde sus orígenes hasta los albores de la conquista* (Santiago, 1989).

Important published collections of documents include Pedro de Angelis, ed., *Colección de obras y documentos relativos a la historia antigua y moderna de las provincias del Rio de la Plata*, 8 vols. (1st ed., 1836) (Buenos

Aires, 1969). The published work of British Jesuit Thomas Falkner, *A description of Patagonia and the adjoining parts of South America* (1st ed., 1744) (New York, 1976) provides one of the very first glimpses into interethnic relations east of the Andes in the eighteenth century. There are many sources for Chile; one could start with J. T. Medina's *Colección de documentos inéditos para la historia de Chile* Primera Serie, 30 vols. (Santiago, 1888–1902). The scholar should also relish the countless traveler accounts of the frontier region; Spanish, French, and, later, English and Americans alike published their impressions of life at the margins of Spanish colonial rule (see Gomez, op. cit.). There are numerous published captivity accounts (the majority by men, though most captives were women) that begin in the sixteenth century with Francisco Nuñez de Pineda's *Cautiverio feliz y razón de las guerras dilatadas de Chile* (Santiago, 1989).

There are several classic national histories of Indian–white relations in the Southern Cone. For Argentina, Juan Carlos Walther's *La Conquista del Desierto* (Buenos Aires, 1970), a survey of Argentine relations with the politically autonomous indigenous peoples in the southern frontier, is still considered the standard. The very title of the book ("the conquest of the desert") sums up an Argentine perception of the resolution of conflicts that had lasted for centuries but intensified in the nineteenth century. For Chile, Ricardo Ferrando Keun, in *Y Así Nació la Frontera: Conquista, Guerra, Ocupación, Pacificación 1550–1900* (Santiago, 1986), provides a chronology of Chilean relations with Mapuche people that led to what came to be called the "pacification of the frontier." Another classic is T. Guevara Silva, *Historia de la civilización de Araucanía*, 3 vols. (Santiago, 1898–1912).

British-trained Chilean historian Leonardo Leon Solís is one of the first scholars to detail the trans-Andean patterns of Araucanian (Mapuche) raiding and trading that began as early as the sixteenth century and coalesced into a highly developed and ritualized phenomenon by the eighteenth century; see his important work, *Maloqueros y conchavadores en Araucanía y las pampas, 1700–1800* (Temuco, 1990). American historian Richard Slatta has published considerable material on the gaucho side of nineteenth-century conflicts with the Indians, including his popular monograph on *Gauchos and the Vanishing Frontier* (Nebraska, 1983). Kris Jones' work on interethnic commercial relations in the nineteenth century in these regions of conflict provides a perspective somewhat more from the Indian side, see "Indian – Creole negotiations in the southern frontier," in M. Szuchman and J. Brown, eds., *Revolution and Restoration* (Nebraska, 1994), "Calfucurá and Namuncurá: Nation builders of the Pampas," in J. Ewell and W. Beezley, eds., *The Human Tradition in Latin America: The Nineteenth Century* (Wilmington, 1984), and "Civilization and barbarism and Sarmiento's Indian policy," in J. Criscenti, ed., *Sarmiento and His Argentina* (Boulder, 1993).

In "Comparative ethnohistory and the Southern Cone" (*LARR* 33 (1) [1994], 107–115), I reviewed other ethnohistorical publications from both Argentina and Chile in a larger comparative context to raise questions about further research directions, and I paraphrase that work again here. Chilean sociologist José Bengoa's *Historia del pueblo Mapuche: Siglos XIX Y XX* (Santiago, 1985) offers a valuable sociocultural survey of Mapuche history, although it can be criticized for occasional indiscriminate or anachronistic use of historical evidence, such as citing observations from nineteenth-century chronicles as descriptive of sixteenth-century society. Leonardo Solis's detailed and carefully researched work (op. cit.) challenges the idea of an unchanging or "ahistorical" Mapuche culture and reveals the Mapuche as actors affecting their own destiny. Other Chilean historians have recently provided studies of frontier relations with the Mapuche west of the cordillera, including Sergio Villalobos, *Los Pehuenches en las vida fronteriza* (Santiago, 1989), S. Villalobos, et al., eds., *Relaciones fronterizas en la Araucanía* (Santiago, 1982) and S. Villalobos et al., eds., *Araucanía: temas de historia fronteriza* (Temuco, 1988). Jorge Pinto has carried out historical investigations of social relations "within" the frontier in *Misioneros en la Araucanía* (Temuco, 1988) and in other work forthcoming. French historian Jean-Pierre Blancpain's recent monograph, *Les Araucans et la frontiére dans l'historie du chile au XIX siecle* (Frankfurt, 1990), provides an overview of the conquest and colonization of Araucania in Chile, locating the discussion within larger questions about European colonization in the Americas.

Anthropologists in both Argentina and Chile continue to contribute to our knowledge of Mapuche social and political organization. For Chilean work, see Rolf Foerster and Sonia Montecino, *Organizaciones, líderes y contiendas Mapuches 1900–1970* (Santiago, 1988), Osvaldo Silva et al., *Encuentro de etnohistoriadores* (Santiago, 1988). For an Argentine perspective, read Raúl Mandrini, "Desarollo de una sociedad indígena pastoril en el área interserrana bonarense," *Anuario IEHS* 2 (1987), 71–95; Miguel Angel Palermo, "Reflexiones sobre el llamado 'complejo ecuestre' en la Argentina," *Runa* 16 (1986), 157–178; and "La innovación agropecuario entre los indígenas pampeano-patagónicos: génesis y procesos," *IEHS* 3 (1988), 43–90. Rodolfo Casamiquela, in *Un nuevo panorama etnológico del área panpampeana y patagónica adyacente* (Santiago, 1969), was one of the first Argentine scholars to attempt an ethnohistorical synthesis of the Southern Cone. Although his text is daunting, his use of linguistic, archaeological, and archival sources persuasively documents the growing influence of the Araucanians among native Pampas peoples west of the Andes prior to the arrival of European observers.

Two important autobiographical sources of the Araucanian perspective of history can be found in Pascual Coña's *Vida y costumbres de los indígenas araucanos en la segunda mitad del siglo XIX*, 3rd ed. (Santiago, 1984), and in M. Inez Hilger's *Huenu Namku: An Araucanian Indian of the Andes Remembers the Past* (Oklahoma, 1966).

There is relatively little literature published in English about Indians in the Southern Cone, and those unable to read Spanish will have to rely on standard and somewhat dated anthropological and encyclopedic sources. (Part of the reason for lack of more recent research by North American scholars is of course the dominance of military governments in the 1970s and 1980s, during which time native peoples in both Argentina and Chile suffered, and anthropological field work was discouraged.) Important ethnographic monographs published in English include the classics of Louis C. Faron's *Mapuche Social Structure* (Urbana, 1961), and his *The Hawks of the Sun: Mapuche Morality and Its Ritual Attributes* (Pittsburgh, 1964), and Mischa Titiev's *Araucanian Culture in Transition* (Ann Arbor, 1951). Students continue to enjoy Robert C. Padden's "Cultural adaptation and militant autonomy among the Araucanians of Chile, 1550–1730," most recently reprinted in John Kicza, ed., *The Indian in Latin American History* (Wilmington, 1993). Susan Socolow's study of released Creole captives, "Spanish captives in Indian societies: Cultural contact along the Argentine frontier, 1600–1835," *HAHR* 72.1 (1992), 73–99 is another popular source. Ann Chapman's *Drama and Power in a Hunting Society: The Selk'nam of Tierra del Fuego* (Cambridge, 1982) is also important.

Of course the classic source remains Julian H. Steward, ed., *Handbook of South American Indians* (New York, 1963), especially vols. 1 "The Marginal Tribes", 2 "The Andean civilizations, and 5, "The Comparative Ethnology of South American Indians." See also Samuel K. Lathrop, "Indians of the Paraná Delta, Argentina," *Annals of the New York Academy of Sciences* 33 (1932), and *The Indians of Tierra del Fuego* (New York,

1928 and 1978). Chilean anthropologist Bernardo Berdichewsky wrote entries on the "Abipon," "Ashlushlay," and "Araucanians" in the *Encyclopedia of Indians of the Americas*, Keith Irvine, ed. (St. Clair Shores, Michigan: Scholarly Press, 1974). In the *Encyclopedia of Latin American History and Culture*, Barbara A. Tenenbaum, ed. (New York, 1996) see my entries on Alakaluf, Araucanians, Calfucurá, Huincas, Malones, Mapuches, Namuncurá, Patagones, Pehuenches, Querandí, Ranqueles, Selk'nam, Tehuelches, and Yamaná.

Historians are beginning to address issues about the participation of people like the Mapuche – and the Pampas and the Tehuelche and Selk'nam and Ona – in regard to the development of the modern nation-states of Chile and Argentina. Twenty years ago scholars of Latin America tended to treat Argentina as the "exceptional" case of a Latin American country *without* an Indian presence. In a similar case of historical presentism, the Indians of southern Chile became transformed by historians into the "peasants" of the twentieth century. Both approaches suffer from a historical blindness in which the "Indian" does not figure. Unfortunately, the lack of attention to the very real presence of the Mapuche, Tehuelche, and Puelche Indians in the history of Argentina and Chile during the colonial period, through independence, and into the twentieth century leaves us with many questions, not just about these peoples but about Latin American history in general. This chapter is just a beginning in the search to understand how the conflict between indigenous understandings of territoriality and Western notions of private property was resolved in the context of European immigration, colonization, and settlement, and how these policies shaped the development of the modern nations of Chile and Argentina.

17

THE WESTERN MARGINS OF AMAZONIA FROM THE EARLY SIXTEENTH TO THE EARLY NINETEENTH CENTURY

ANNE CHRISTINE TAYLOR

GEOGRAPHICAL AND CULTURAL SETTINGS

The aboriginal populations of the western fringe of the Amazon Basin live in close proximity to one of the most spectacular breaks in natural features in the continent.[1] For centuries they also lived on the edges of two great hegemonic empires, first that of the Inka and then that of the Spanish crown. Until recently the combination of these two factors seemed sufficient reason to justify including all such groups in a single "*montaña* society" category exemplifying a distinctive "cultural zone." The postulate of a homogeneous region inhabited by homogeneous societies is, however, largely fallacious. It arises from a perspective based on the high cultures of the Andes that long determined a biased view of the lowlands. Geographically, ethnographically, and even historically, the western sub-Andean fringe is by no means a uniform whole.

Landscape

Nowadays the term *montaña* refers in a general way to the eastern slopes and foothills of the Andes. It thus encompasses several clearly differentiated ecological zones, stretching from the so-called *ceja de montaña* ('brow of the mountain'), a fringe of dense, mist-cladden, low-growing forest ranging in altitude from 3,500 to 2,800 meters, down through the cloud forest to the high tropical rainforest of the Amazonian plains. The cultural and geographical area loosely designated by the term *montaña* extends from the headwaters of the Caquetá, in southern Colombia, to the headwaters of the Mamore (one of the major tributaries of the Madeira) in southern Bolivia.

[1] This chapter was translated by Elborg Forster and edited by Frank Solomon.

From the sources of the Caquetá to the upper Napo, the standout features of the *montaña* are its breadth and relatively gentle relief. The undulating plateau, with its southwesterly inclination, is broken up by U-shaped valleys such as the Sibundoy, San Miguel (formerly Sucumbíos), and Baeza valleys. These cut so far back into the cordillera (which is very narrow in the area) that their headwaters lie hardly more than 60 kilometers from the Pacific coast. Farther south the slopes of the western cordillera become steeper, dropping into sunken but fairly wide and fertile valleys such as those of the Zamora and the Upano rivers, running from north to south and cut off from the Amazon plain by bleak secondary chains like the Cutucù and the Cordillera del Condor. At latitude 4° South, there is a further transition. The Andes suddenly lose altitude and subside into a tangle of hills and valleys running in varied directions. This ecologically diverse zone is both the main natural corridor between the Amazon Basin and the Pacific coast, and a climatic and topographical boundary between the northern Andes, which lie packed around a central corridor sharply divided by volcanic "knots," and the Central Andes which are dry, of vastly greater width, and threaded with very deep valleys. Below latitude 8° South, the outer flanks of the massif become increasingly vertiginous. Densely wooded and mist-shrouded canyons create an almost impassable barrier between the mountains and the great lateral valleys of the Huallaga and the Ucayali, which are themselves divided by a range of hills whose forest cover is occasionally broken by areas of savannah known as *pajonales* ('strawlands'). The upper valley of the Huallaga, which slopes gently down to the Tingo Maria Basin, is one of the very few eastern regions where the transition between the two types of geographical environment becomes less marked. The headwaters of the Madeira River form yet a different zone, which is topographically exceedingly complex around the sources of the Madre de Dios and simpler and more regular around the tributaries of the upper Beni; these form a series of warm, dry inland fjords, the *yungas*, separated from the piedmont proper by a further mountainous barrier dominating the easily flooded savannahs of the *llaños*.

The Montaña *at the Present Time*

In part because of their harsh climate and exceptionally heavy rainfall, the eastern flanks of the cordillera north of the Napo, though nominally colonized since the sixteenth century, have remained to this day sparsely inhabited by nonindigenous populations; hence the continued presence in the region of such Indian groups as the Sibundoy Inga and Khamsa, the Cofán (Kofanes) and the Siona-Secoya. Combined, the two huge southeastern districts of Colombia, Caquetá, and Putumayo, barely have 340,000 inhabitants. On the other hand the more easterly Ecuadorian plains are now dotted with homesteads and small towns connected with the exploitation of the chief oil resources of the country; over 200,000 people are concentrated in an area of less than 52,000 square kilometers. South of the Pastaza, colonization is still largely confined to the sub-Andean fringe, and the pioneer front practically disappears between the confluence of the Zamora and the Upano and the eastward bend in the Marañon. In all, the population of this vast region is probably no more than 300,000, and the two chief towns of the south Ecuadorian Oriente, Macas and Puyo, both have fewer than 15,000 inhabitants, though the latter is growing fast.

The Amazon region of Peru presents an entirely different scale of phenomena. Several towns along the major rivers have populations of hundreds of thousands, and an almost unbroken string of hamlets line the main watercourses. The many roads and other lines of communication up to the *sierra* are jammed with thick traffic and a steady flow of settlers seeking to escape the economic, social, and political disasters besetting the country; in many areas deforestation is now causing major ecological and climatic changes. A few figures suffice to indicate the scale of the process: the population of the *Oriente* of Peru has increased from around 160,000 in 1890 (barely 4% of the total population of the country) to over 2 million at the present time (over 10%), and according to the census of 1981, its annual rate of growth in some provinces (e.g., Rioja and Manu) exceeds 15 percent. The most intensively settled areas are obviously those nearest the *sierra*, where migrants automatically follow the roads opened up at times of booms in quinine and rubber production in Jaen-Bagua, the high central *montaña*, and the Iñambari Valley in Madre de Dios.

In Bolivia the northern *montaña* is much less "developed" and urbanized than it is in Peru, though it has been quite heavily settled since the beginning of the century. A total lack of interest on the part of the central government in that part of its territory has in fact stimulated massive local investment by the cocaine industry over the past 15 years. The dry *yungas* are occupied by Quechua- or Aymara-speaking Indians, whereas the piedmont itself has been largely taken over by Spanish-speaking, small-scale homesteaders. Nevertheless there are still few towns in the Amazon region of northern Bolivia – in fact Santa Cruz is the only important urban center in the whole of the lowlands – and the local economy, when it is not connected with coca, is little more than an extension of that of the *sierra*.

The marked differences between Peru, its neighbors, and Colombia are ultimately due to the active part played by the Peruvian state in the process of integrating the Amazon territory and to the nature of the local population, which is now for the most part urban, whereas in Colombia, Ecuador and Bolivia it is still predominantly rural (see Map 17.1).

Current Ethnographic Patterns

The populations of this western fringe of the Amazon Basin are just as varied linguistically and ethnically as the environments in which they have developed. While the Quichua-speaking Inga and the Khamsa (a much smaller group, of unknown linguistic affiliation) occupy the low-lying Andean valley of Sibundoy, the northern valleys where the cordillera opens out are the habitat of the remnants of the western Tukanoan family, such as the Coreguaje and Macaguaje, which once occupied a large part of the region between the Caquetá and the upper Napo. They dwell alongside one or two small groups of uncertain origin, like the Cofán and the presumed extinct Andakis. The middle course of the Caquetá and Putumayo is the territory of the Witoto and Bora-Miraña groups, both nearly wiped out during the rubber boom of the late nineteenth century. Further east and south other western Tukanoan cultures such as the Siona-Secoya and the Mai Huna of Peru (rarely consisting of more than a few hundred individuals, with the whole western Tukanoan group not exceeding 3,000 persons) mingle with a Quichua-speaking native population spread over the whole area between the upper Pastaza and the Aguarico and along the Napo. These Indians, known as Quijos or Napo Runa, and known in the Bobonaza-Curaray as Canelos Quichua, form a 40,000-strong population surrounding the Waorani, a linguistically isolated group of about 1,200 people.

The great Jívaro block, now numbering at least 70,000 individuals, is divided into several major dialect groups (Aguaruna, Shuar, Huambisa, Achuar, and "Main Shuar," or Shiwiar of the Tigre-Corrientes) spread over an immense territory bounded on the north by the Bobonaza, on the east by the valley of the Pastaza, on the west by the Andes, and on the south by the Río Mayo. It is bordered all along its frontiers by

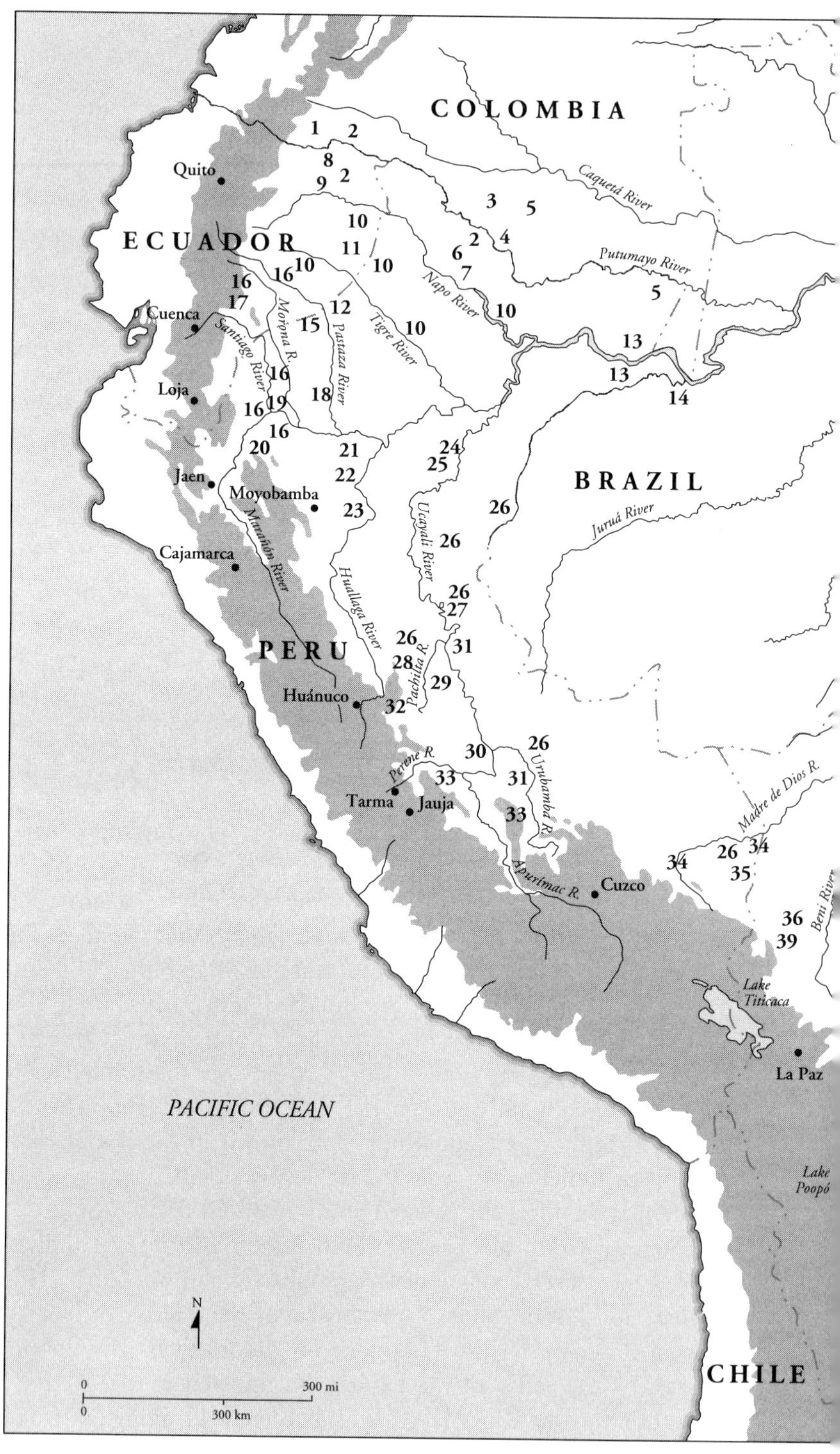
COLOMBIA
Caquetá River
Putumayo River
Quito
ECUADOR
Napo River
Cuenca
Santiago River
Morona R.
Pastaza River
Tigre River
Loja
Jaen
Moyobamba
BRAZIL
Juruá River
Ucayali River
Cajamarca
Marañón River
Huallaga River
PERU
Pachitea R.
Huánuco
Perené R.
Tarma
Jauja
Urubamba R.
Madre de Dios R.
Apurímac R.
Cuzco
Beni River
Lake Titicaca
La Paz
PACIFIC OCEAN
Lake Poopó
N
0
300 mi
0
300 km
CHILE

Map 17.1

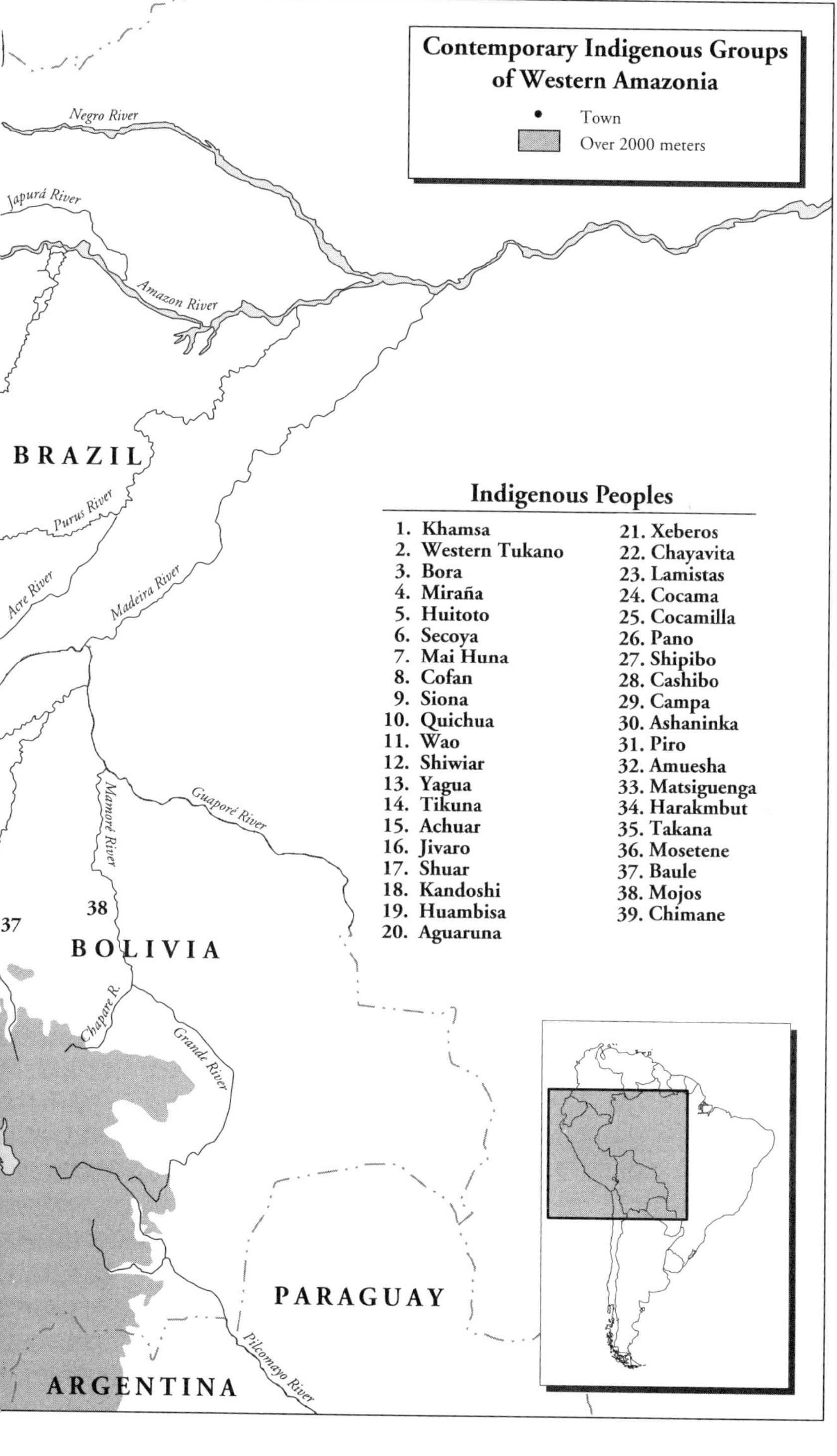

Contemporary Indigenous Groups of Western Amazonia
Town
Over 2000 meters
Negro River
Japurá River
Amazon River
BRAZIL
Purus River
Acre River
Madeira River
Guaporé River
Mamoré River
38
37
BOLIVIA
Chapare R.
Grande River
PARAGUAY
Pilcomayo River
ARGENTINA
Indigenous Peoples
1. Khamsa
2. Western Tukano
3. Bora
4. Miraña
5. Huitoto
6. Secoya
7. Mai Huna
8. Cofan
9. Siona
10. Quichua
11. Wao
12. Shiwiar
13. Yagua
14. Tikuna
15. Achuar
16. Jivaro
17. Shuar
18. Kandoshi
19. Huambisa
20. Aguaruna
21. Xeberos
22. Chayavita
23. Lamistas
24. Cocama
25. Cocamilla
26. Pano
27. Shipibo
28. Cashibo
29. Campa
30. Ashaninka
31. Piro
32. Amuesha
33. Matsiguenga
34. Harakmbut
35. Takana
36. Mosetene
37. Baule
38. Mojos
39. Chimane

apparently "assimilated" Quichua-speaking groups such as the Lamista, the Andoas, the Napo Runa, and by the Tupian Cocama and Cocamilla, as well as by the Cahuapanan-speaking Xebero and Chayavita.

The Huallaga and Ucayali valleys, to a point some way upstream from Pucallpa, are occupied by *ribereños*, some half-caste and others considered *nativos*. The latter are chiefly remnants of the riparian Pano populations such as the Shipibo, Setebo, and Conibo. Further upstream, on the Urubamba, the Piro, another seemingly "detribalized" population, form the easternmost component of the pre-Andean Arawak family, a large group of populations generically known as Campa, which also includes the Amuesha, Ashaninka, No-Matsiguenga, and Matsiguenga and numbers some 80,000 individuals. To what extent these cultures form a sufficiently coherent linguistic, historical, and sociological whole to be seen as a single category is still a matter of debate. The country to the east of the Ucayali is host to small groups of interfluvial Pano, such as the Cashinahua, Yaminahua, Nahua, and Amahuaca. The sources of the Madre de Dios are inhabited by a sprinkling of small groups whose numbers fell drastically during the rubber boom; some of them – the Amarakaeri, Wachipaeri, Sipiteri, and Toyoeri – are Harakmbet-speaking, others are Panoan, and yet others speak Takana, presumably a linguistic subfamily of Arawak. These groups extend into Bolivia even though most of the *montaña* is now occupied by highland settlers, whereas the eastern lowlands are still inhabited by indigenous groups such as the Mosetene, Chimane, and Baure, the latter remnants of the formerly large Arawak Mojos population. Further south two Tupian groups, the Sirionó and the far more numerous (and largely assimilated) Chiriguano, share their territory with the many colonists settled in that area.

The population of the eastern Andean piedmont is socially divided into three main categories. First, the mestizo or half-caste settlers (it should be noted that sierra Indians migrating permanently into forest areas abandon their indigenous identity), often labeled as *racionales*, meaning rational or civilized people. Second, the so-called *nativos*, a large body of detribalized and seemingly acculturated indigenous groups, some of which, like the Cocama or the Shipibo, are mostly Spanish-speaking riverside peasants distinguishable only by virtue of their self identification as *nativos* from the nonindigenous rural half-castes. Others, such as the Lamista, Napo Runa, and Chayavita, still form discrete "ethnic" groups, though their lifestyle and culture is close to that of the generic *nativos*.

They are generally Quichua-speaking and locally are often called "mission" or *manso* (i.e., 'domesticated') Indians. Third, the societies labeled "traditional" by ethnologists and *aucas* by their fellow dwellers in the Amazon Basin. This category includes either small, recently contacted "primitive" groups inhabiting remote areas, such as the Waorani, the interfluvial Pano or the Záparo Arabella, or large groups of "fierce Indians" like the Campa and the Jívaro, whose vitality is generally attributed to their warlike nature and militant resistance to Spanish domination.

In terms of the cultural features usually employed in ethnological typologies, both the "tame" and the "wild" societies of the upper Amazon have a uniform profile. Until recently both were characterized by a pattern of dispersed settlement, by an economy combining hunting, gathering, and slash-and-burn horticulture with sweet manioc as a staple, by a frugal but technically refined material culture, and by an acephalous political organization or, more specifically, a high degree of local autonomy in the management by households or small communities of economic resources, political power, and contacts with the supernatural. Religious systems were marked by a relatively low degree of exteriorization or formalization, few large-scale collective rituals, and a highly developed shamanistic system with ramifications spreading between ethnic groups; with the notable exception of some Arawak and eastern Tukano groups, few of these cultures had ritual specialists and an explicit cosmological canon.

Beyond this, however, two clearly differentiated sets of political institutions and kinship systems should be recognized. The first is that of the Christianized Indians, whose political and ritual organization has been greatly influenced by civil or ecclesiastical colonial models. Their kinship is characterized by a hybrid nomenclature which is largely Andean but retains some features typical of elementary two-section terminologies. Pseudo-kinship ties (*compadrazgo* and *compadrinazgo*) and genealogically distant marriage play an important structural role in such systems. The second set is that of the "traditional" groups such as the Jívaro, Waorani, Campa, and Záparo, virtually all of which have Dravidian-type kinship systems with two-section terminologies and repetitive, symmetrical marriage between more or less closely related bilateral cross-cousins, as well as real or imaginary (i.e., shamanic) shifting and ephemeral war chieftaincies.

The distinction must not be too hard and fast, however, because the group identities concerned are not strictly exclusive. Indeed they are closely interwoven. The Quichua-speaking Christianized groups act as a transculturation frontier for the "wilder" tribes, while fostering their own ethnogenesis (and the shamanic ability on which it is partly based) by means of their relations with the apparently less "acculturated" *Indios bravos*. Even the *mestizo* groups are far from being irreversibly and completely "de-Indianized."

The Andes/Amazon Split: Nature or Culture?

Most of the inhabitants of the coastal and Andean regions see the lowland Indian populations – in contrast to the highland ones – as entirely extraneous to the historical traditions that have shaped their countries, and as a blot on their national identity rather than a positive contribution to it. In their view the Amazon region and its inhabitants are a different world, historically and sociologically as well as geographically; at best a promising though rowdy frontier, at worst a dumping ground for vague utopian ideas, rebels, and down-and-outs. In short, for all the nationalist rhetoric and bellicist posturing they have expended over their eastern lowlands, the Andean countries have experienced great difficulty in fitting the Amazon inhabitants into their economic and civil life. This sharp division has of course permeated the intellectual traditions underlying Americanist studies, so much so that for a long time highland and lowland specialists were content to remain totally ignorant of each others' terrain and work. Specialists in the Amazon area themselves so fully absorbed the prejudices linked to an implicitly evolutionist perspective that they long followed the example of their Andean-oriented colleagues and saw the *montaña* as a milieu irredeemably hostile to civilization. The "tropical forest cultures" of the region were therefore taken to be the involuted product of societies doomed to a Malthusian and atomistic fate by the harshness of their environment. They were belittled as incapable of drawing inspiration from the example of their highland neighbors and at the same time lacking the ritual and social-organizational complexity of the "true" Amazonian groups. The frontier separating them from the highlands and civilization was thus seen as an entirely "natural" one. Their past was reduced to a sequence of blind ethological grouping, with one wave of migrants ousting another in an attempt to take over a coveted piece of *várzea* or alluvial valley, only to be displaced in its turn by the pressure of the next.

And yet between 1538 and 1560, the Spaniards traveling through those same lowlands for the first time had no notion of such a harsh and summary duality. Indeed at the time, the western Amazon was far from being a marginal zone; up to 1570 the southern part of the equatorial piedmont of the Andes was in fact inhabited, urbanized, and administered to a greater degree than the corresponding Andean and coastal zones. Moreover the *montaña* as a social and geographical category had yet to be invented. At first the word simply designated the "cloud forest" regions to the east of Cuzco inhabited by the Antis Indians. There was no term to indicate the eastern piedmont of the Andes or its inhabitants generically. In addition the milieu was not always judged to be displeasing and hostile. Some of the first Spanish captains tended to praise its temperate climate, its pleasant horizons, and the fertility they saw in the exuberant *selva* vegetation. Nor were the lowland societies perceived as being essentially inferior to, or different from, those of the highlands. They were *behetrías*, of course, autonomous small sovereignties, but then so too were many of the Andean communities, particularly the Chibchan groups in the south and center of present-day Colombia. In fact at that time the term was applied to any culture escaping the direct control of the Inka state, whatever its habitat. Furthermore a number of the *montaña* societies had large, village-dwelling, culturally homogeneous populations, with complex, highly stratified social systems and ostentatious political or religious institutions, and were thus often wrongly perceived as extensive, centralized polities. In short, the inhabitants of the Amazon region initially were not considered to be all savages or their milieu an overgrown hell unworthy to be inhabited by Spaniards.

THE *MONTAÑA* IN PRE-COLUMBIAN TIMES

Pre-Inka Data

We still have only a very limited knowledge of the ways in which the *montaña* societies evolved in the transitional zone between the Andes and the Amazon Basin. It has long been recognized that the Andeans developed ingenious ways and means of access to forest resources and borrowed cultural features from the forest dwellers themselves, but it was taken for granted that such initiatives came from the highland populations. However, archaeological research over the last 20 years, in the wake of the pioneering work of D. Lathrap, has shown that in certain places the high *ceja* had been inhabited by populations originating in the

Amazon region since very early times and that sometimes these had even extended their habitat up into the highlands. The processes described clearly indicate cultural and ethnic, if not political, continuities between Andean and Amazon peoples. The links were interactive, not simply a migratory movement followed by separation and differentiation of the original stocks. The intrusion of groups from the Amazon tropical forest into the mountains south of Loja provides a relatively well-documented example of the phenomenon. That portion of the sierra had in fact been occupied since around the seventh century C.E. by a people of probably Jívaro origin known as the Palta, which before the Inka conquest seems to have been socioculturally very close to its Bracomoro neighbors of the Zamora and Chinchipe, Jívaro groups themselves very similar to the *montaña* Shuar of the early twentieth century. Other parts of the Andes offer traces of similar phenomena: The Khamsa of the Sibundoy Valley are thought to be of Amazon origin, and the upper Huallaga, for example, was inhabited by Arawak groups related to the contemporary Amuesha. It is even likely that the Chupacho of Ortiz de Zuñiga's famous *Visita* were closely akin to these communities. Elsewhere relatively homogeneous cultural or linguistic groups spread across both the sierra and the foot of the mountains. Such groups tended to be divided into distinct but allied districts. For example, the Quijo chiefdoms of the upper Napo are described by Cieza de León as being very close to those of the Panzaleo around highland Latacunga; in fact it is through the mediation of a highland *cacique*, and thanks to his kin-ties with a Quijos chieftain, that the Spaniards first gained a foothold in the upper Napo Valley. The (probably) Cañar inhabitants of the high grasslands around Lake Ozogochi, southeast of Riobamba, and those of the valley of the upper Upano were also organized, it appears, in independent chiefdoms closely linked by trade and marriage relations. In yet other areas, purely political rather than ethnic or linguistic continuities brought together groups occupying very different environments. The so-called Quillacinga federation included, for instance, Indians who may have been Amazonians from Sibundoy, Pasto Andeans, and coastal groups of the Chibcha-Barbacoa family.

Even when Andeans and Amazonians were clearly separated spatially and socially, they were still closely associated through complex and diversified systems of relations. In certain high *selva* regions, for example, there were multiethnic villages and *cocales* where Andeans and families from the Amazon area lived side by side. The latter were delegated by downstream groups for purposes of trading, surveillance, and containment of highlanders' attempts to colonize or conquer. Specific locations, often described as "markets" by the Spaniards, were also places for meetings and regular or seasonal trade between mountain and valley groups sharing a common "no man's land." Amazonian political and trade delegations also frequently went to Andean towns – Huánuco and Cochabamba in particular – to negotiate exchange relations and alliances.

All these piedmont cultures, of course, were closely tied to societies localized further downstream or to the east. Thus the Kallawaya chiefdoms on the outer slopes of the Bolivian cordillera acted as intermediaries between Aymara or Quechua highland *cacicazgos* and the lowland Mojo, Takana, and lesser Arawak groups. The Campa Antis were one of the poles of a vast trade network linking the great chiefdoms of the Ucayali, the Pano interfluve groups, and the Urubamba Piro. Similar relations tied the Sibundoy Indians and the Chibcha to the western Tukano groups of the Colombian piedmont and tied the Quijos of the upper Napo to the Tupian Omagua.

Such linkages clearly played a key role in the great trans-Amazon trade circuits brought to light by recent archaeological and ethnohistorical research. Locally these circuits articulated two kinds of networks. One involved a chain of riverside groups specializing in long-distance trade, like the Piro, Conibo, or Omagua, carrying goods to and from the Colombian piedmont and the Cuzco region, and through the upper Amazon area down to the central Amazonian Solimões (Tápajos-Madeira). This latter area was itself the terminus of extensive trade networks crisscrossing over Guyana and northern Amazonia. The second network associated the riverine groups and the societies of the interfluve and high forest by means of a diffuse range of dyadic ritual trade partnerships, such as the Jívaro *amigri* or the Campa *yompar* relations, thereby complementing and extending the river-based long-distance circuits.

Both sets of links certainly had a political dimension. Just as the *señores* of the northern Andes established, manifested, and reproduced their authority by managing certain types of trading relations and monopolizing the distribution of certain "exotic" effects, the power of the Conibo and Ucayali Cocama chiefs was partly based on privileged access to goods of great value like silver and gold ornaments from Cuzco brought in by the Piro, long specialized in the trade between Andean Quechua and riverside Amazonian peoples. In sum, "vertical control" was not a one-way mechanism, and it is clear that the *montaña* societies developed strategies just as varied and complex – in order to secure access to highland populations and resources – as those that the Andeans created in order to benefit from the products of the eastern forests.

The Inka Period

Although the cultures of the western fringe of the Amazon Basin were closely linked with, and in many ways comparable to, the neighboring Andean societies, they nevertheless appear to have remained outside every major political formation that grew on the coast or in the Central Andes, including that of the Inka. Why despite its expansionist policy did the Tahuantinsuyu fail to conquer these groups, and why did they come to be painted as barbarians unworthy of assimilation in the traditions of the Inka "fourfold domain"?

In this connection one should allow for a considerable gap between actual historical events and processes (insofar as they can be reconstructed) and Inkaic as well as early colonial historiographic stereotypes. To begin with, on quite a few occasions the Inka did in fact conquer and incorporate various piedmont populations, particularly those of the upper Marañón and to some degree those of the region between the Marañón and the lower Huallaga. They also managed to dominate people of the upper Huallaga, and above all those of the piedmont areas of the north of Bolivia. In all those regions the Inka installed *mitimaes* and deported part of the local people. They imposed tribute, created alliance and affinity relations between the Cuzco aristocracy and local leaders, and exploited the resources of the area according to the models developed by the imperial administration. However, it is also clear that relations between the Inka and the *montaña* societies cannot be reduced to a stark alternative between conquest and assimilation, on one hand, or unremitting hostility and the sealing off of all relations, on the other.

In their drive to incorporate neighboring polities, the Inka usually sought gradually to undermine chiefdoms' independent systems of external relations, and to assume for themselves the control of external factors that underpinned local forms of authority and sometimes collective identities. Initially they used a strategy of gifts rather than resort to arms. The aim was to redirect trade and marriage links underlying local power relations toward Cuzco, thus making sure that the empire's vassal authorities would remain dependent. The assimilation of the Kallawaya lords, whose power was based on mediating relations between highland Quechua and Aymara groups and the Arawak chiefdoms of the *llaños*, closely follows this model: The Inka set up a line of *mitimaes* in the upper foothills to channel and oversee links among political formations in the various ecological zones. In the same way, they cut through the web of relations between the Chupacho and their Moco and Panatagua neighbors of the upper Huallaga with a line of fortified garrisons. But these practices should be seen as attempts to strip intertribal links of their political content rather than as ways of interrupting relationships, particularly trade ones. Indeed the interzonal exchange the Spaniards called *rescate* (that is, barter between domestic units outside a marketplace, as opposed to exchanges of a diplomatic or sumptuary nature led by specialized corps) seems to have been encouraged all along the boundaries of the empire. Furthermore in a fair number of cases, the Inka had neither the time, the capability, nor the will to apply their ideal strategy of assimilation. As a result other types of relations between the Andeans and their piedmont neighbors were tolerated, ignored, or even actively fostered.

In the Campa-Antis region, for instance, part of which had been conquered and assimilated into the empire, the eastern frontier remained open and ill-defined; unlike that in the upper Huallaga, it fluctuated around a no-man's-land dotted with multiethnic villages to which the lowland Antis sent relays of small groups of settlers, ostensibly in tribute. Their vassalage seems to have been largely nominal, however, because the Andeans never managed to penetrate beyond the edges of the cloud forest. The Inka desire to preserve certain kinds of ties with lowland groups is also clear from the fact that in some zones depopulated by the flight of the previous inhabitants, they installed, in a departure from their usual practice, *mitimaes* linguistically and socially akin to the local population so as to restore the links the piedmont people had broken. A phenomenon of this nature seems to have occurred in the upper valley of the Chinchipe, where Palta colonies that had adopted Inka ways lived alongside "wild" Jivaroan Bracamoro, the very people who had, according to tradition, inflicted a bitter defeat on the soldiers of Huayna Capac.

As for the Amazonian peoples, they applied or developed a variety of strategems in their dealings with the empire, some of which were later redeployed against the Spanish. The tactics worked out by the Antis in their confrontation with highland societies provide a good illustration of the margin of maneuver that Inka frontier policy offered the lowland groups. One such tactic consisted in dispatching toward the imperial limits groups of temporary settlers, whose task was to mediate trade and alliance relations between uplands and lowlands, and to act as a defensive buffer between the two population blocs. In a sense such colonies had the same role as that given by Cuzco to frontier *mitimaes*. Sometimes they were sacrificed in order to avoid greater losses, as seems to have happened with the Moco, who were neighbors of the Chupacho. A second ploy was simply to ensnare the Inka (and later the Spaniards) by manipulating the asymmetrical relations that the empires were trying to impose on the piedmont societies; by offering repeated gifts, lowlanders forced would-be rulers or allies to make increasingly frequent return gifts in keeping with their status. Finally in some cases groups classed as outgoing military *mitimaes* were in fact more in the line of permanent delegations sent on missions into Inka territory by the Amazonian chiefdoms: A Cashinahua group, perhaps contacted during one of the expeditions that the Inka sent to the Mojo via the Madre de Dios, is recorded as living at Opatari, in Antis territory, alongside a group of settlers of various origins. In the same way, there are traces of a nucleus of Arawak Mojo settlers apparently removed from the savannahs to the Bolivian piedmont by their own free will.

It should be stressed that military operations against lowland groups seem at times to resemble forms of ritual antagonism, in the manner of a *tinku* (Quechua 'ritual battle'), far more than wars of conquest or enslavement. When viewed in this light, some of these expeditions may simply have been a concrete expression of the generalized dualist scheme underlying a repeated series of dichotomies (Colla/Chuncho, Palta-Chachapoya/Bracamoro, possibly Huanca/Chiriguano) rather than a manifestation of straitforward expansionism. Many aspects of Inka mythology and iconography suggest that the eastern *selva* figured as a complementary and hierarchically ordered element of identity, within an encompassing model postulating opposition between a superior, male, Andean half and a feminine, inferior, and threatening lowland half. It is then reasonable to ask whether the image of absolute barbarity that the Inka are supposed to have projected onto the Amazonian peoples might not have arisen as a result of a Spanish confusion. For the Spanish it was no doubt hard to distinguish highland Andean models of antagonistic complementarity (moieties in ritual combat, for example) from Inka prejudice and hostility to groups with diverging political ideologies and purposes, such as the Campa or Jivaroan Bracamoro. It is likely that the two forms of opposition between *serranos* and Amazonians – one inclusive, complementary, linking hierarchically ordered and ritually antagonistic halves; the other exclusive, more selective, rooted in a perception of irreconcilable sociopolitical formulas – became hybridized when the Inka empire fell. As a result the lowland peoples en bloc were depicted in the earliest chronicles with a much more markedly and negatively alien otherness than was really the case within the relationships prevailing during the Inka period.

In sum, the ties between the Inka and the Amazonian peoples were in fact much more flexible, ambiguous, and unstable than the imperial tradition, as transmitted by the colonial chroniclers, would have us believe. There were many gradations between complete incorporation and permanent hostility, and it is clear that rather than being imposed, such relations were often negotiated with Amazonian groups, sometimes to their advantage. Thus even in areas bordering on tribes noted for their hostility toward the Inka, the spread of the empire did not entail a physical break between Andeans and Amazonians. However, major changes in their relationship did occur in the wake of Inka expansion. The empire's conquest and assimilation strategies certainly involved a profound reorganization of systems of vertical control along the whole length of the cordillera. Their first effect was a gradual closure of the upland chiefdoms and a consequent severance of the political links between populations in distinct ecological levels. This entailed the disappearance of some of the institutional mechanisms that such alliances had previously fostered or employed. Alongside this, in the central *selva* at least, Inka pressures seem to have triggered an intensification or extension of the simultaneously military and trading networks of the lowlands, notably the one underlying the Arawak confederations. Finally, Cuzco ideology firmly relegated *selva* populations to a status of antagonistic inferiority, a polarization inevitably entailing new definitions of tribal identities. Inka policy thus preconditioned the processes of transculturation and the shifts of identity so common in the societies of the eastern piedmont from the second half of the sixteenth century onward. Even if highland and lowland peoples still remained physically, economically, and sociologically very close, a conceptual, political, and cultural boundary between them thus gradually evolved and took force during the Inka period.

THE HISPANIZATION OF THE WESTERN AMAZONIAN REGION

Ethnographic Aspects of the Upper Amazonian Region in the Sixteenth Century

The ethnographic landscape of the western margins of the Amazon region at the dawn of the Spanish conquest was very different from that of today. The difference, however, does not lie primarily in the geographical distribution of the tribal blocs. Although there have been overall migrations and indeed drastic reductions in the territories occupied in precolumbian times, the locations of the surviving ethnic groups have not varied a great deal since the sixteenth century (see Map 17.2).

Although a substantial group of Tupi Omagua occupied the area around the junction of the Aguarico and Napo, most of the northern zone was inhabited by Tukano groups, the most important being the riparian Napo Encabellados and the Icaguates ("Orejones"), mixed with one or two groups of unknown origin, such as the Abijiras or Aushiris, a formerly opulent riverside society whose all but dispossessed descendants at the present are probably the Waorani. The piedmont properly speaking, from the upper Caquetá to the upper Napo, seems to have been the habitat of both Tukano and Chibcha groups such as the Cofanes and perhaps the Khamsa and Quijos. The immense area between the middle valleys of the Napo and the Pastaza was almost exclusively occupied by the Záparo, a large linguistic family subdivided into a multitude of tribes such as the Gaes, the Shimigaes, the Záparo proper, and the Iquitos, all of whom except the latter were apparently associated with an interfluve habitat.

The Candoa bloc, which was culturally very close to that of the Jívaro, extended from the lower valley of the Río Tigre to the lower Morona; it also included several dialect groups such as the Maynas, Kandoshi or Muratos, Roamainas, Tocureos or Guallpayos, and others. The Jívaro tribes themselves occupied the higher hilly land between the Pastaza and the Huasaga, west of the Morona, the Marañón Valley from the left bank of the Chinchipe as far as the junction of the Santiago, and the whole region to the south between the Nieva and Mayo rivers. The upland Jívaro, or Paltas, had already undergone a transculturation process that had led them to adopt a highly Inkaized "Andean" identity. In the south they adjoined a series of tribes of uncertain origin mostly – like the Chachapoyas, of whom some were certainly *mitimaes* – already Quichuicized when the Spaniards arrived.

These Inkaized tribes extended from the higher reaches of the Huallaga as far as the territories of the Hibitos and Cholones, whose linguistic affiliation has never been determined, and who separated them from the nearest members of the great pre-Andean Arawak bloc, in this case the Pantagua and Amuesha. The lower Huallagua was occupied by an indeterminate set of groups generically known as the Motilones, the survivors of whom were to constitute the nucleus of the colonial Lamistas. The Cahuapanans, a small linguistic family including the Xébero, the Chayavita, and the Cahuapano, fit in between the Jívaro and the Motilones.

The great Tupí groups (Cocama and Omagua) extended along the banks of the Marañón and the lower Ucayali, below the Pano tribes of the middle Ucayali and its major tributaries (Conibo, Setebo, Shipibo, and Amahuaca, collectively known as the Chamas). More scattered and "primitive" populations from the same linguistic stock (e.g., the Mayoruna, Remo, Cashinahua, Yaminahua, Sharanahua) occupied the whole eastern hinterland of the Ucayali.

The various Arawak groups extended in an almost unbroken fringe from the Sacramento *pampas* to the Bolivian *llanos* but were highly diversified linguistically (Campa, Piro, and Mojo are all distinct languages, as are the tongues of the Takana subfamily spoken by the Apolobamba, Leco, Araona, and Toromona tribes). The Arawak orbit was also diversified culturally, because it included riverside dwellers like the Piro and mountain people such as the Pantagua, powerful chiefdoms like those of the Mojos or the Araona, and much more egalitarian and atomized groups like the Matsiguenga or the "Chunchos" of the eastern foot of the Cordillera Real. The Arawak belt was, however, broken in the Madre de Dios, the habitat of the enigmatic "Mashcos" and other Harakmbet tribes localized in the cold valleys of the upper *montaña*; some small Pano groups affiliated with the Yaminahua and Amahuaca occupied the lower areas.

The most striking contrasts between the upper Amazon in the sixteenth century and the same zone today involve differences in scale and sociological style. Their chief feature now is a high degree of apparent uniformity, but the range of socio political configurations at the end of the precolumbian period ran from relatively small and "simple" societies, like those of the Záparo or the interfluve Pano, to large riverside tribes like the Conibo or the Omagua, with elaborate material cultures, exten-

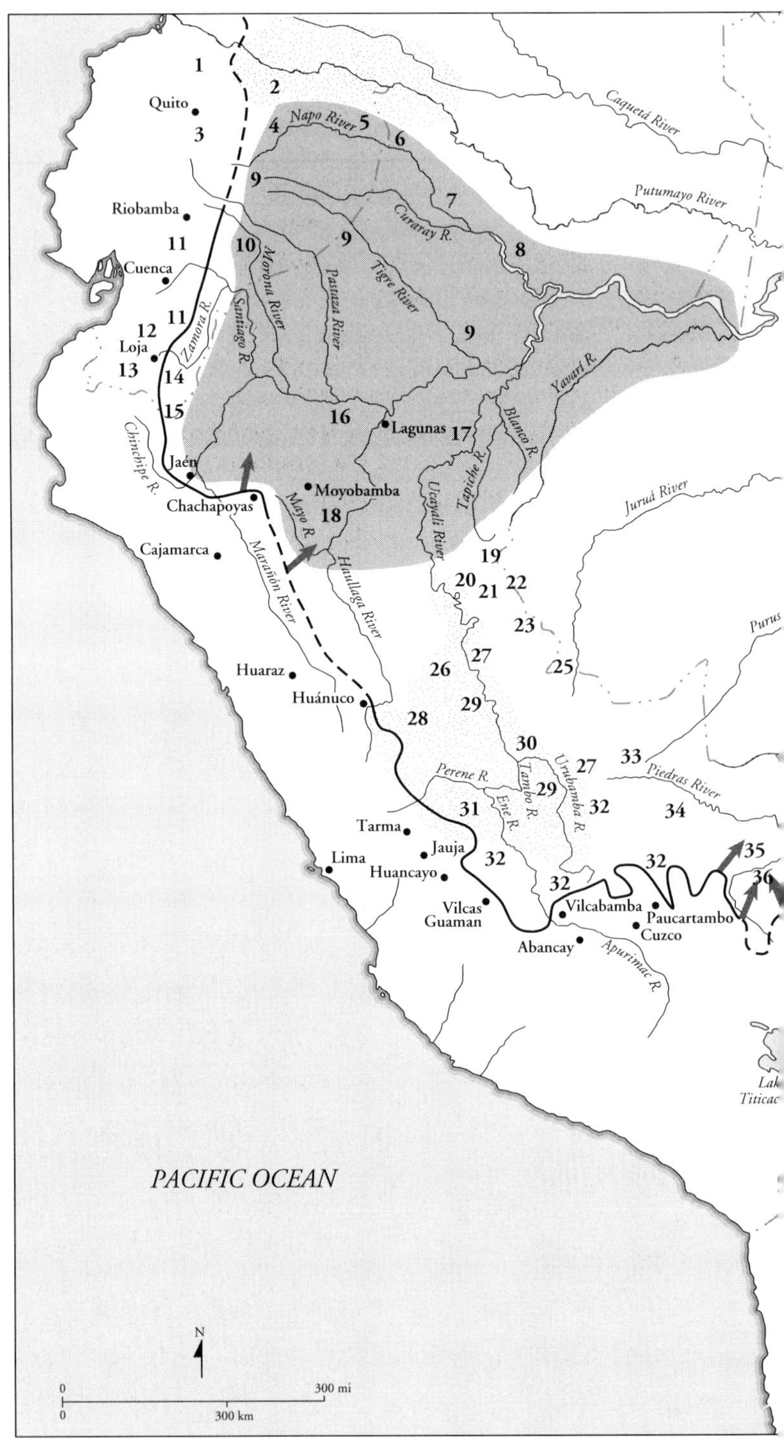

Quito
Riobamba
Cuenca
Loja
Jaén
Chachapoyas
Cajamarca
Moyobamba
Lagunas
Huaraz
Huánuco
Tarma
Jauja
Lima
Huancayo
Vilcas Guaman
Vilcabamba
Abancay
Paucartambo
Cuzco
Napo River
Caquetá River
Putumayo River
Curaray R.
Tigre River
Pastaza River
Morona River
Santiago R.
Zamora R.
Chinchipe R.
Marañon River
Mayo R.
Haullaga River
Ucayali River
Tapiche R.
Blanco R.
Yavari R.
Juruá River
Purus
Perene R.
Tambo R.
Ene R.
Urubamba R.
Piedras River
Apurimac R.
PACIFIC OCEAN
N
0
300 mi
300 km

Map 17.2

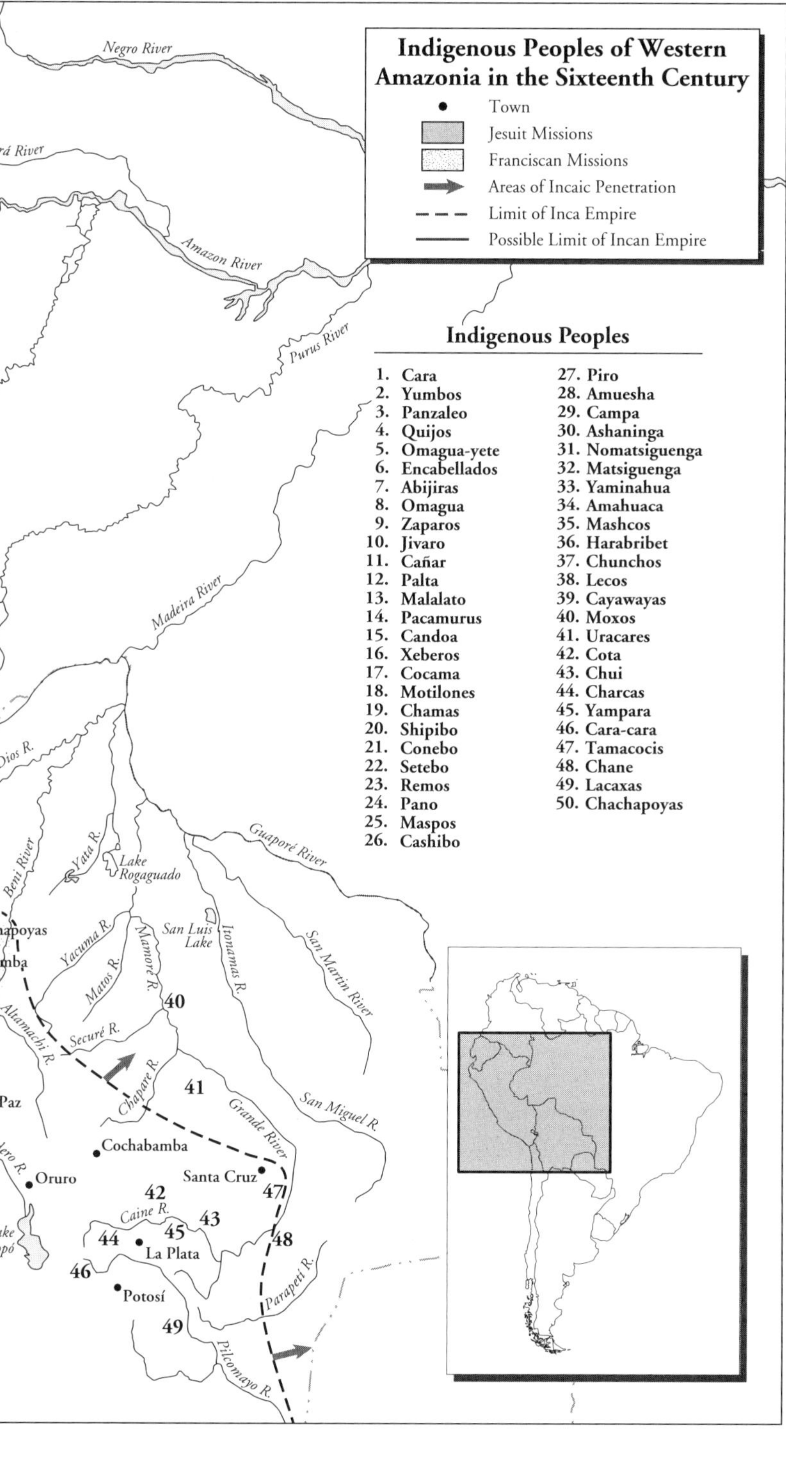
Indigenous Peoples of Western Amazonia in the Sixteenth Century
Town
Jesuit Missions
Franciscan Missions
Areas of Incaic Penetration
Limit of Inca Empire
Possible Limit of Incan Empire
Indigenous Peoples
1. Cara
2. Yumbos
3. Panzaleo
4. Quijos
5. Omagua-yete
6. Encabellados
7. Abijiras
8. Omagua
9. Zaparos
10. Jivaro
11. Cañar
12. Palta
13. Malalato
14. Pacamurus
15. Candoa
16. Xeberos
17. Cocama
18. Motilones
19. Chamas
20. Shipibo
21. Conebo
22. Setebo
23. Remos
24. Pano
25. Maspos
26. Cashibo
27. Piro
28. Amuesha
29. Campa
30. Ashaninga
31. Nomatsiguenga
32. Matsiguenga
33. Yaminahua
34. Amahuaca
35. Mashcos
36. Harabribet
37. Chunchos
38. Lecos
39. Cayawayas
40. Moxos
41. Uracares
42. Cota
43. Chui
44. Charcas
45. Yampara
46. Cara-cara
47. Tamacocis
48. Chane
49. Lacaxas
50. Chachapoyas
Negro River
Amazon River
Purus River
Madeira River
Dios R.
Beni River
Yata R.
Lake Rogaguado
Yacuma R.
Matos R.
Mamoré R.
San Luis Lake
Itonamas R.
Guaporé River
San Martín River
Altamachi R.
Securé R.
Chapare R.
Grande River
San Miguel R.
Paz
Cochabamba
Oruro
Santa Cruz
Caine R.
La Plata
Potosí
Parapetí R.
Pilcomayo R.
40
41
42
43
44
45
46
47
48
49

sive village habitats, intricate political and religious institutions, and a marked social hierarchy. Furthermore tribes belonging to the same ethnic group and even the same political entities often occupied very different environments, as is still the case with the Jívaro; and even when populations stuck rigidly to either a riverside or an interfluvial territory, varied types of trade relations linking them to groups from other milieux gave them stable and regular access to the resources of other areas. This means that the ecological specialization associated with the *montaña* groups, and the sharp distinction between riverside and interfluve cultures so often used in models of historical development, was in fact much less evident then than it is now. A further striking diachronic contrast lies in the demographic and territorial scale of the ethnic and linguistic blocs, as opposed to that of tribal or dialect groups. In the past the former were a great deal less fragmented than they are now. Far from being the mosaic of culturally and linguistically composite groups depicted in such canonical work as that of Steward and Metraux or Lathrap, the upper Amazon area in the late precolumbian age seems to have been divided into relatively homogeneous ethnic and linguistic zones, even though each might house highly varied political formations. Finally, the cultures at the foot of the mountains were still closely joined to the upland world, in terms of both physical proximity and exchange relations. The Amazonian peoples still regularly sent delegations and migrants to the high towns, while the Andeans came down into the forests as temporary or permanent settlers within Amazonian groups, seasonal workers in the lowland archipelagos, trading delegations, occasionally as fugitives, and finally as refugees as the Inka empire collapsed.

The colonial history of the western Amazon thus implied an overall trend toward increased cultural homogeneity, a breakdown of macrosystems and regional networks to the benefit of intermediate or purely local levels of organization, and a growing spatial, sociological, and symbolic distancing between upland and lowland societies. The details and causes of this process form the subject of the following pages.

Iberian Penetration, Expansion, and Retreat: The Birth of a Frontier

Most of the exploration, conquest, and occupation in colonial times of the eastern Andean foothills took place between 1538 and 1580, except in the upper Marañón area, where two major pacification expeditions were sent in 1616 and 1635; both of these later *entradas* were attempts to reestablish Spanish control over regions that had been nominally conquered and colonized. The history of the conquest is part of the Hispano-Creole historiographical canon and has been abundantly though unevenly documented, so there is no need to detail it here.

The first attempts to colonize the Amazonian region were fueled by gold prospecting, first by panning alone and later by mining, especially in the Zamora Valley and the Condor massif. However, Spanish penetration took very different forms in the northern *montaña* and in the region beyond latitude 8° South.

In the latter area, none of the innumerable eastward *entradas* yielded durable colonial foundations. The great majority of them ended in disaster, and their only lasting effect was to compound the geographical and ethnographic ignorance shrouding the southern *montaña* until the middle of the nineteenth century. Indeed the frontier that emerged at the end of this early phase of exploration and conquest was much more shallow than that of the Inka empire. In certain cases *montaña* groups even succeeded in extending their territory upward as a result of Inka resistance around Vilcabamba. In the same era a westward Chiriguano surge threw the limits of the Andean and Spanish presence in the southern cordillera back at least a hundred kilometers into the mountains. Although colonial settlers replaced the Inka *mitimaes* formerly sent to separate the piedmont districts from those of the *llanos* and the *montaña* in the upper Beni area, their attempts to gain territory to the east by overcoming the defensive alliances between Andeans and "Chunchos" were never successful. All along the southern frontier, the Indians tolerated new settlements in the hope of forcing the Spaniards into unequal trading relations, as they had done with the Inka, and thereby obtaining iron tools. But as soon as the whites tried to enslave the natives or push them back toward the interior, they were immediately expelled and frontier trade turned to pillage. The piedmont peoples also managed to hide from the Spaniards the location of the gold mines worked in Inka times, and they successfully closed the region to any attempts at evangelization until the end of the seventeenth century. As a consequence the old Inka *limes* turned into a sort of no-man's-land patroled by mixed groups of former *mitimaes*, Andean refugees, and lowland "Chunchos," which evolved in the context of a parasitic frontier economy oscillating between peaceful trade and mutual plundering.

In the Madre de Dios and the central *selva*, the Campa Antis and their allies adapted the tactics they had used against the Inka to meet the Spanish offensive, first by supporting the Vilcabamba resistance in the hope of creating a buffer region between themselves and the Spaniards, and later by fomenting, with the same objective, a rebellion of black slaves brought in to work the sugar-cane and coca plantations that the local natives had abandoned. In addition a ceaseless flow of Pantagua delegates and Anti "captains" (who were really no more than heads of households) streamed to Huánuco or other sierra settlements, taking advantage of the Spaniards' ignorance of the real nature of their political institutions to obtain western goods in exchange for ostensible submission. As soon as the whites tried to use these alliances to penetrate the *montaña*, however, all the piedmont groups immediately joined forces in a remarkable display of cohesion, discipline, and tactical awareness to push them back to where they came from. Once again trade rapidly turned into plunder, particularly among the Panatagua, who took to stealing and slaughtering cattle on a large scale. Like the Bolivian piedmont the central *montaña* was thus effectively closed to Spanish penetration. The Indians were quite prepared to welcome small-scale trading expeditions and, later on, missionaries in small groups, but throughout the sixteenth and seventeenth centuries they gave up very little of their land to the colonists, and the only colonial settlement in the whole of the southern *montaña* that eventually took root – after a series of displacements – was Santa Cruz; significantly this town was founded by colonists immigrating from the Chaco and Río de la Plata rather than by settlers from the Andean pioneer fringe.

The situation in the north offers a complete contrast. The Marañón Valley, the area between the Marañón and the lower Huallaga and the whole of the northern *montaña* as far as the sources of the Caquetá and the Putumayo were traversed by an uninterrupted series of *entradas* from 1538 onward, a number of which repeated conquests that others had already made or claimed to have made. Later secondary expeditions radiated outward from the original colonized areas, notably in the Napo Valley and in the upper Marañón. Hundreds of *encomiendas* were distributed by the *capitanes* in charge of the various *entradas*, though many of these, particularly in the Jivaroan area, were of little profit to their beneficiaries because of native resistance or flight; elsewhere, however, notably in the Marañon, the upper Napo and upper Caquetá and Putumayo, the Spaniards achieved a degree of control over the native population sufficient to exploit it ruthlessly. The Spanish occupation thus brought in its wake a massive influx of immigrants (Spaniards or half-castes, foreign soldiers of fortune, and sierra Indians sent to the mining gangs as *oyaricos*) and the consolidation of a relatively dense network of towns; indeed between 1540 and 1580 more towns were founded in what later became Ecuadorian Amazonia than in the equatorial *sierra* or coast. The careful administrative division applied to the region testifies to its importance for the Spaniards: Around 1560, no fewer than five *gobiernos* (Mocoa, Quijos, Macas, Yaguarzongo, and Jaen) shared the (largely unmapped) territory at the foot of the mountains, whereas the single *gobierno* of Quito covered the Andean massif and the coast over some 5 degrees of latitude (see Map 17.3). The degree of administrative interest, the density of *encomiendas*, and the high level of colonization in the region, however, was by no means paralleled by an increase in state control or order, and the material importance of the first settlements should not be overestimated. The honored title of "cities" given to these foundations may accurately reflect the importance of the urban model in Hispanic representations of social life and its spatial arrangement, but it hardly expresses the reality of these squalid and ephemeral boom towns, which probably resembled the *garimpos* of present-day Brazil more than the medieval villages of the Iberian peninsula. Nor should the chroniclers' image of a heroic process of urbanization and taming of the wilds obscure the colonists' extraordinary mobility and piratical life-style; these men frequently disobeyed or rebelled against the authorities mandated by the highland centers, and they routinely launched plundering, slaving, or prospecting expeditions very distant from their settled bases (in 1629, for example, barely 10 years after the town was founded, the inhabitants of Borja on the Marañon had already scoured the banks of the Pastaza up to the point where it leaves the cordillera). This, alongside with their role in the spreading of lethal epidemics, explains why the towns and their inhabitants had an effect out of proportion to their demographic scale and economic importance on the populations of the upper Amazon region.

Relevant to this context is the still little explored issue of slavery and its effects on the native groups the *montaña*. Although slaving in this area never reached the scale it had in the Guianas and throughout the Portuguese lowlands, the practice of hunting down and capturing Indians for labor (*sacar piezas*, as the colonists baldly called it) is amply attested in the colonial sources. Forbidden by the crown in principle, slaving developed under cover of colonial institutions such as the *encomienda*, or

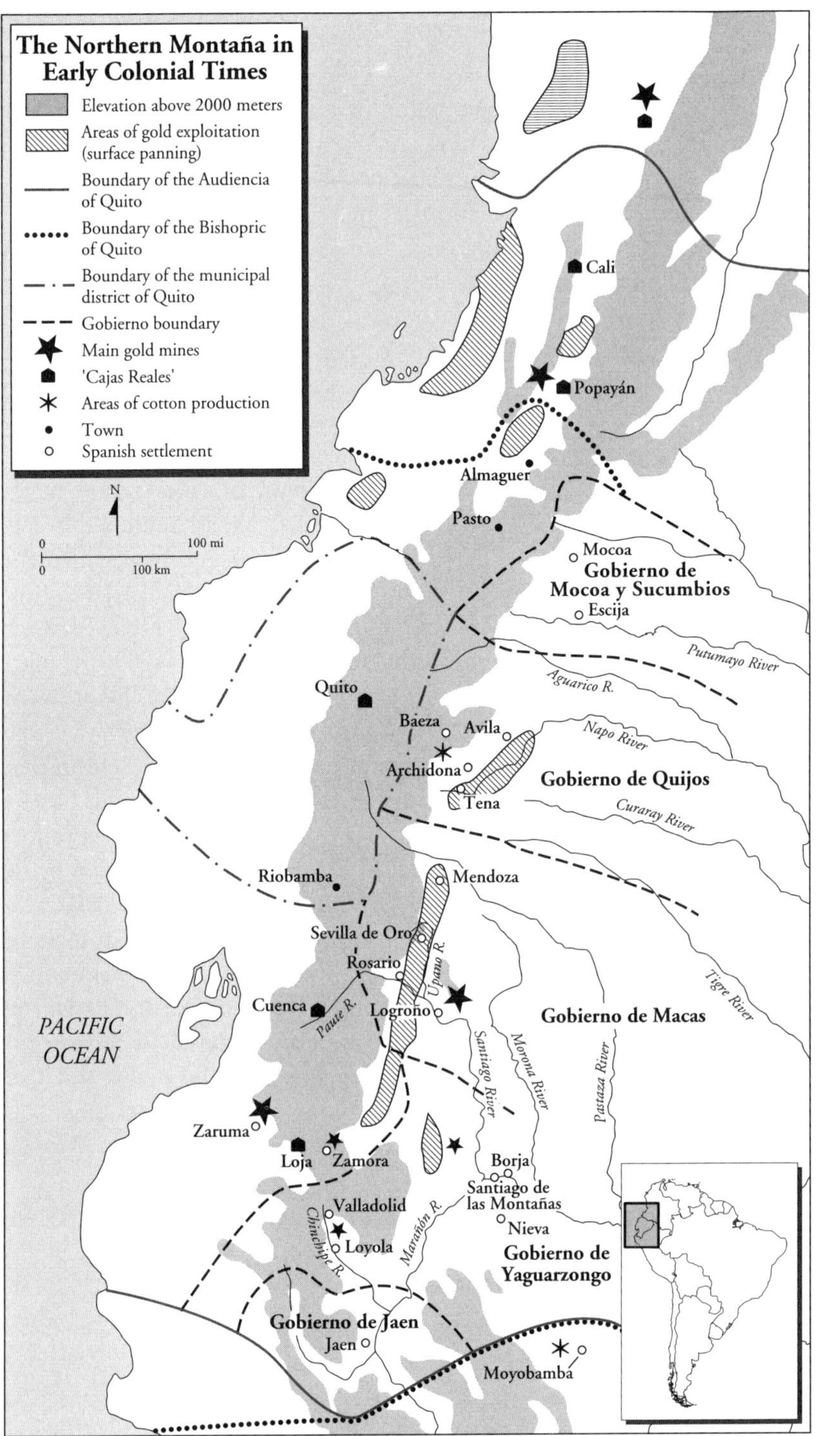
The Northern Montaña in Early Colonial Times
Elevation above 2000 meters
Areas of gold exploitation (surface panning)
Boundary of the Audiencia of Quito
Boundary of the Bishopric of Quito
Boundary of the municipal district of Quito
Gobierno boundary
Main gold mines
'Cajas Reales'
Areas of cotton production
Town
Spanish settlement
N
0
100 mi
0
100 km
Cali
Popayán
Almaguer
Pasto
Mocoa
Gobierno de Mocoa y Sucumbios
Escija
Putumayo River
Aguarico R.
Quito
Baeza
Avila
Napo River
Archidona
Tena
Gobierno de Quijos
Curaray River
Riobamba
Mendoza
Sevilla de Oro
Upano R.
Rosario
Cuenca
Paute R.
Logroño
Tigre River
Gobierno de Macas
PACIFIC OCEAN
Santiago River
Morona River
Pastaza River
Zaruma
Loja
Zamora
Borja
Santiago de las Montañas
Valladolid
Chinchipe R.
Marañón R.
Nieva
Loyola
Gobierno de Yaguarzongo
Gobierno de Jaen
Jaen
Moyobamba

Map 17.3

legal provisions governing the treatment of certain categories of Indians. In the Marañon Valley, for example, until the middle of the seventeenth century, it was enough to claim that a given Indian group consisted of *cimarrones* (escaped *encomienda* Indians), or simply harbored fugitives, to justify launching a slave raid against it. During the mission era merciless wars *a fuego y sangre* were unleashed against "apostate" or obstinately rebellious groups such as the Gaes or Jívaro; captives taken in the course of such expeditions were sold into slavery or distributed to the participating *encomenderos*. The Mainas Jesuits themselves were not entirely innocent in this respect; thus "free" or mission Indians could be farmed out to neighboring colonists on the excuse that the reduction could no longer afford their upkeep, or even sold to Portuguese slavers if the latter agreed to spare a valued mission post. Finally, outside areas controlled by the missions or colonists in the far north and far south, the real or purported cannibalism of groups such as the Witoto, Bora-Miraña or Tupian Sirionó, and Chiriguano was often invoked as a pretext for buying and enslaving Indian war captives.

Practices of this sort raise the question of the existence of indigenous forms of slavery in preconquest times, and that of the extent of voluntary Indian participation in the colonial slave trade. Some scholars point to the radical differences in the moral and symbolic value placed on captives to emphasize the incommensurability of European slavery and native ways of using prisoners or dependents. Others have argued that insofar as indigenous captives were used for their labor and were alienable, they can legitimately be considered as slaves, even if they were never subjected to the objectification and inhuman treatment meted out by the Europeans. However, the "alienability" of war prisoners in precolonial contexts is not well established, and the indigenous trading of captives may have been no different from the various forms of adoption, or the offering of children to kin and even outsiders, common even today in many Amazonian cultures. Still, there is no question that, here as elsewhere in the lowlands, Indian groups did reorient some of their practices to cater to the Spanish or Portuguese demand in slave labor. Cases in point are the sale by tribes of the Caquetá-Putumayo area of the wives and children of sacrificed captive warriors to the colonists of the upper Magdalena, or, later on, the trade of "orphans" for steel axes with the Portuguese established on the Rio Negro. In the central Andean *montaña*, the Piro obtained, and sold to the Spaniards, children suspected of sorcery by the Campa (raiding or trading for captives seems in fact to have been a common practice among the pre-Andean Arawak, but very little is known of the uses they served in precolonial times). Likewise the Tupi Omagua and Cocama for a while both intensified and redirected their war patterns to escape enslavement by supplying prisoners to the Spaniards and later to the insatiable Portuguese. So far, however, no attempt has been made to quantify the western Amazonian slave trade, and it is still impossible to estimate even approximately the number of Indians taken into captivity.

The link between the slave trade and the *encomienda* as it developed in the lowlands needs emphasizing, because it is one of the factors that account for the peculiar nature and the remarkable persistence of this institution in the *montaña*. Although the *encomienda* was officially suppressed in 1721 – in fact well after it had ceased to be relevant in the highlands – titles and the privileges that went with them were still recognized in the lowlands as late as 1730. Local governors also retained the right to create and distribute *encomiendas* insofar as they undertook to establish new colonist settlements; throughout the seventeenth century this measure served both as a cover and as an incentive for launching slave and conquest raids (one of the most notorious of these expeditions was the ultimately unsuccessful attempt by Martín de la Riva Herrera to establish the settlement of Santander at the mouth of the Pastaza in 1660). Whereas in the highlands the *encomienda* was primarily a means of extracting tribute from sedentarized and well-controlled Indian populations, in the lowlands it long retained many of the features it had acquired during the earliest phases of the Spanish colonization of the Antilles. In the first place it served essentially as a legal framework for the capture and control of native labor rather than as a fiscal device, simply because native production was usually too meager, too costly to transport, or too cheap in market terms to be worth obtaining. Second, it often came to have a territorial – rather than a sociopolitical – base, because many Indian societies of the area lacked clear-cut and hereditary positions of power. Further, the relative nomadism of groups accustomed to shift their habitat periodically because of soil impoverishment and game scarcity forced the colonists either to follow their Indians or to delimit an area in which they must remain; thus lowland *encomiendas* in fact became privately appropriated territories, the object of endless squabbling and litigation between colonists. At the same time, Spanish control was too weak and the colonists too poor, particularly after the collapse of the frontier, to turn these proto-*haciendas* into profitable establishments;

encomienda Indians served mostly to collect produce such as panned gold, fibers (*pita*), false cinnamon (*canela*), wild cacao, or resins (what the Portuguese called *drogas do sertao*) and to provide domestic service (i.e., feed, clothe, and transport their masters). For many Spaniards the only way of not going completely native was to own natives. This paltry slave economy generated very little wealth, but its effects on the indigenous societies of the *montaña* were nonetheless devastating. By contemporary accounts, only one in ten captives remained at a year's end; the rest fled or died of epidemic disease, ill treatment, and despair. Demand for slave labor thus remained consistently high, and captives were relatively easy to procure by backwoodsmen used to roaming the jungle. Moreover by the early seventeenth century, many Amazonian groups had adopted a pattern of scattered habitat, and such dispersed groups were highly vulnerable to raiding parties often consisting of a mere handful of colonists and a few native mercenaries. The basis of interaction between *encomenderos* and *encomendados* was therefore quite distinct from that in the highlands. Lowland *encomiendas* were geared to the extraction of labor – the value of which was mainly symbolic – and the institution combined extreme devaluation of Indian work or production with a degree of negotiation, though brute force was immediately resorted to whenever the colonists were in a position of strength – not that frequent an occurrence. The *encomienda* thus turned into a highly flexible, and hence durable, cover institution for the control of native labor, and many of the forms of exploitation developed in the late eighteenth and nineteenth centuries – the *reparto* system, the *hacienda*, and the outright or barely disguised slavery that resurfaced during the rubber boom – were in fact initially experimented with in the framework of the Amazonian *encomienda*.

Around the turn of the century (between 1580 and 1624, depending on the region), the northern *montaña* frontier began to collapse. The failure of the Spanish to consolidate the colonization of this area is due to several factors: the disappearance of the local indigenous population as a result of flight, massacre, or epidemic disease; hasty and anarchical settlement owing to the rivalry between highland *cabildos* – and the prominent Spanish families that controlled them – over the possession of their eastern hinterlands and their resources; inadequate control of native labor; and above all the discovery of more profitable mining areas in the uplands of southern Colombia, in Peru, and in Bolivia. For a time the Spanish colonists tried to reorient the local economy toward cotton growing (at first cotton was the main wealth demanded of the Indians in *encomienda*), particularly in Quijos, Macas, and Moyobamba. But because of insufficient production and difficulties of transport, local cotton never became an export produce. Textiles, however, did come to play an important role in the upper Amazonian region, insofar as the yard of rough cotton material became the standard unit of payment to the worker Indians of the lowlands and remained so until the early twentieth century.

From 1580, then, most of the immigrants moved back to the sierra or abandoned their *encomiendas*. As had happened in the corresponding area in Bolivia, the frontier shriveled and fossilized. Uprisings broke out in all the towns along the foot of the mountains (a number of them being fomented by renegade half-castes rather than by Indians). The two most famous were the ill-fated insurrection headed by Quijos *pendays* (shamans) in 1579, who managed briefly to unite the Omagua and the majority of the Quijos and destroyed the towns of Avila and Archidona, and the legendary revolt of the Jívaro in 1590 – in fact a coalition of lowland Cañar and Shuar – which destroyed Logroño and so frightened the colonists that many of them fled to the highlands. By the end of the century, outside Moyobamba there remained only a handful of settlers in the so-called cities: Some, like Logroño and Sevilla de Oro, had simply disappeared; others had shrunk to hamlet size; and some, like Zamora, were only seasonally inhabited. The access routes into the Amazon region fell into disrepair and disuse. In 1600 there remained only three correctly marked and properly maintained tracks along the whole length of the northern *montaña:* a southern one via Chachapoyas and Moyobamba, a second one starting from Loja through Valladolid and the Chinchipe Valley, and a third route from Quito via Baeza and the Napo, long considered the easiest route to the upper Amazon region. The track from Macas to Riobamba seems to have been little used, and the one through the upper Pastaza Valley was only opened in the eighteenth century. Elsewhere the Indians managed to regain control of some key passages between the highlands and the lowlands, particularly in Jivaroan territory.

Within a few decades Spanish occupation successfully dismantled what remained of the physical continuities and economic links fostered or tolerated by the Inka state. Unlike Inka expansion Spanish colonization brought about a decisive change in the human geography of the *montaña*. At first, so many settlers and deported *serraños* swarmed into the lower regions that for a time those harsh areas were more densely populated than the fertile southern valleys around Loja. Precisely because of the devastation wrought by the first wave of colonization, however, natives gradually abandoned the slopes and eastern valleys closest to the Andean towns. The widening gap between the highlands and lowlands, and the expansion of the no-man's-land between them, induced communities that had formerly acted as links between the two populations either to move back into the *sierra* villages or to seek refuge in the lowlands further east. Many highland Indians forced to work the eastern gold mines and placers completely abandoned their original identity and merged into the forest populations. Others, like the Cañar Indians of the Upano Valley, drifted away from the Andean communities to which they had previously been linked and developed a hybrid forest society akin in many ways to that of the contemporary Canelos Quichua. It was closely associated to the nuclei of Spanish population subsisting in the region and formed for two centuries a transculturation front for the northern Jívaro. Yet other piedmont groups established small, isolated colonies in areas inaccessible to slave hunters, particularly on the upper Pastaza and the eastern flanks of Sangay Volcano, at Huamboyas.

The spatial, social, and economic split between highland and lowland peoples exacerbated an ethnic and cultural polarization that had already began in the Inka period. Ultimately it imprisoned both Andeans and the Amazonian peoples in exclusive and antithetical identities. Paradoxically the Spaniards themselves became trapped in the antinomy they had done so much to create. As the gulf between the "civilized" highlands and the "wild" forests widened, the colonists who had stayed in the lowlands became increasingly marginalized and ultimately more isolated than the Indian societies whose habitat they shared. In many respects they became assimilated to the deculturated Indians they lived with, even to the extent of dressing, eating, and sheltering themselves in the same way and adopting a pidgin version of their language. Such were the Jivaroized Macabeos described by nineteenth-century travelers.

The same process of polarization also occurred at the base of the South and Central Andes, but this area, unlike the northern *montaña*, did not become depopulated until much later. Some groups of the upper *montaña*, like the Panatagua or the Hibitos and Cholones of the mid-Huallaga, maintained their traditional role of intermediaries between the peoples of the Andes and those of the *selva* well into the eighteenth century. Elsewhere the frontier was pushed so far up the mountains that the lowland groups kept control of the eastern flanks of the cordillera all the way to the "cloud forest." Nevertheless here too colonial reorganization and shaping of the bordering Andean communities led to a partial dismantling of highland–lowland relations, fostering the imposition of ethnic categories as rigidly dichotomous as those in the northern *montaña*.

Native response to Spanish occupation or attempted penetration of the lowlands bears little resemblance to the stereotypes transmitted by the epic tradition typical of frontier regions. Contrary to the stock notion received from Creole historiography, the *conquistadores* were more often than not received peacefully, though warily, by Amazonian peoples; in some cases they were in fact invited to settle in Indian territory. At first the Indians were eager to establish stable trading relations with the whites, in order to ensure regular access to the material and nonmaterial goods the Europeans brought with them, while at the same time striving to avoid enslavement and disease. At that stage the Indians probably did not have a unitary view of the whites, just as it took the Spaniards a decade or two to forge the notion of *indio* and the attitudes that went with it. The internal violence of the colonists' world, its factionalism, and the complexity of its social structures, led the Indians to hope that they might still find their own equivalent of El Dorado – to wit, a type of white man finally willing to establish profitable, symmetrical, and intelligible relations with them.

These dispositions soon collapsed when faced with the Spaniards' greed and their determination to enslave and disempower the Indians. Rebellion broke out everywhere after a few decades, increasingly massive flight followed attempts to create alliances, and the colonization frontier shrunk drastically as a consequence. Yet even then the links with the colonists were, from the Indians' point of view, not entirely broken. The frenzied plundering and pillage by many piedmont groups – highly unusual in the context of traditional lowland patterns of warfare – may have been a negative relation to the colonists, but it remained a relation: Forced exchange is not at all the same thing as the absence of exchange. Nor did the consolidation of the frontier, and the widening gulf between the Amazon and the Andes that it fostered, prevent lowland delegations from continuing to travel as far as Huánuco, Cuzco, or La Paz in hope of saving a relationship that probably meant far more to them than to the Spaniards. The symptoms of real despair – collective abandonment of lands, the collapse of birth rates, messianist movements reversing the agenda of normal life, and resignation to a radical impoverishment that masqueraded as archaic tradition – were not to appear until much later, toward the end of the seventeenth or in the eighteenth century. Before reaching that stage the Indians of the *montaña* tried to play their one remaining card, that of the missionaries. As long as they seemed guided by interests different from those of the *capitanes,* and offered the possibility of another kind of relationship than that imposed by the colonists, the religious would be allowed or even encouraged to settle among the forest populations, provided they brought metal tools and came unaccompanied by nonreligious intruders.

The Age of the Missions

The establishment of missions in the upper Amazon region was directly linked to the rise of the frontier as a line demarcating the areas subject to central power and those that were nominally owned but not controlled, and separating the territory of "civilized" populations from that of the savage infidels. Delegating the management of the empire's marches to the religious orders seemed the only way of affirming the crown presence. In effect the role of the missions was to pave the way for the spread of colonial institutions through cultural means, essentially by indoctrinating the Indians in the pedagogic virtues of work and ridding them of their habits of "laziness," the root of their condition as savages. This solution, however, accurately reflected the ambiguous status of the Amazonian reaches and of their relationship to central authority, insofar as missions both represented the state and could not help but perpetuate the very marginality that lay at the root of their intervention. Missions were also highly ambivalent institutions from the viewpoint of the Indians, because they were clearly agents of oppression (and the harbingers of a terrifying mortality), even if they sometimes offered indigenous societies their only chance of survival. Colonists and the religious themselves suffered conflicts of interests too. Both competed in capturing the Indians, either for *encomiendas* or reductions as well as for the meager wealth they could provide; yet the two sectors depended on each other for their own survival. Indeed it was the rapacity and the ongoing pressure of the settlers that helped to drive otherwise reluctant Indians into the mission reductions; without the missionaries and the native levies recruited in the reductions, however, the colonists would scarcely have had the means of extracting from the "free" or *encomienda* Indians the work they needed for their livelihood.

Throughout the colonial era the Jesuits and Franciscans shared the evangelization and administration of the *montaña* almost to the exclusion of other religious orders. The Franciscans, particularly from the end of the seventeenth to the end of the eighteenth centuries, established large missions in the upper Beni (the Apolobamba missions, in present-day Bolivia), the central *selva* (Peru), and the upper Caquetá-Putumayo (Colombia). The Jesuits founded, somewhat earlier, two extensive missions, one in the upper Marañon (Mainas) and the other in Mojo territory, in the Bolivian *llanos*; both of these were taken over by the Franciscans after the Jesuits' expulsion in 1768. Dominicans and Augustinians worked more sporadically and controlled only one or two enclaves in any sustained way.

The Franciscans settled in Huánuco as soon as it was founded in 1542 but did not succeed in breaking through into Pantagua territory, on the upper Huallaga, until 1631. By that time the frontier had been established, and the Indians could no longer obtain western goods by means of the plunder or trading typical of the preceding decades. The Cerro de la Sal Mission was opened up slightly later. Neither this nor the Panatagua foundations lasted more than a few years; the Indians would repeatedly drive the religious out by force, almost always as a result of an influx of colonists attracted by the Cerro's reputation (especially c. 1640) as a gold bonanza. Nonetheless the Pantagua mission eventually did take hold, and by 1670 the great majority of these Indians had already been "converted." Meanwhile the Franciscans also pushed on through Huánuco and the Tingo María depression toward the Ucayali, where for the first time they encountered the Shipibo (known at the time as Callisecas), and then toward the Madre de Dios. Almost all of them were killed in the process, and the Ucayali was abandoned in 1671. A further attempt was then made to break through into Campa and Amuesha territory; during this campaign the route from the Perené to the upper Ucayali was opened up. The Conibo contacted on that occasion proved to be more receptive than the Shipibo to the apostolic efforts of the Franciscans, and a mission to them was established near the mouth of the Pachitea in 1685. The Franciscans then clashed with the Jesuits of Mainas, however, who were seeking to extend their hold on the valley from their bases among the Cocama, at the mouth of the river. After vicious legal disputes, the boundary between the two missions was fixed by the Spanish crown at the level of the Conibo reduction, which the Jesuits had taken over in the meantime, which meant that the Franciscans lost their main levies against the Urubamba Campa and Piro. Their efforts on the Ucayali were thus doomed to failure; in addition the Pantagua mission was virtually wiped out by a terrible epidemic in 1670. They decided therefore to try once more to gain a foothold in the Cerro de la Sal. This region, as they clearly perceived, played a strategic role in maintaining the interethnic network of alliances and trade standing so effectively in the way of mission penetration. Initially this campaign was quite successful; between 1709 and 1726 the Franciscans established five mission villages in the area, opened up the route from Huánuco to Pozuzo, and managed to enter the Sacramento *pampas*. In short, the immense Campa territory was finally opened up to them, and they lost no time in setting up a missionary college in Ocopa, near Jauja, in 1724, to train their men for their work.

The revolt of Juan Santos Atahuallpa in 1742 and the messianic movement he unleashed along the whole of the central *selva* (except among the Panoan populations in the Ucayali Valley) brought the expansion of the Franciscan mission to an abrupt end. For over 50 years the region remained closed to them and indeed to all whites. Juan Santos was a half-caste from the Andes, associated for a time with a Jesuit priest with whom he probably traveled to Spain. For largely unknown reasons he sought refuge among the Campa and rapidly fanned the flames of messianic sentiments already latent among the Arawak. He led them into a war lasting over 10 years, routed two generals sent from Lima, captured all the forts overlooking the *montaña*, caused the death of over 600 Spaniards and 50 missionaries, and ruined several important towns, including Moyobamba, Tarma, and Andamarca. In 1752, however, the rebels inexplicably withdrew from their advance positions in the highlands to the lowland forests; what eventually became of their leader is still unknown. This episode from the colonial past still holds an important place in Andean and piedmont peoples' historical imagination. The period of isolation that followed the rising also played a crucial part in the development of sociological and political institutions characteristic of the piedmont groups of the central *selva*. In particular it is likely that the Amuesha priesthood complex associated with temple forges owes a great deal to this enigmatic formative experience.

Thus it was the Ucayali that the Franciscans chose as the theater of their campaign to restore control from 1771 onward. In 1791 they did manage to bring together two Pano riverside societies, the Setebo and the Conibo, in a mission at Sarayacu. The upper Ucayali yielded to their pressure 20 years later, and they finally managed to bring the Urubamba Piro into a reduction. In the hope of regaining their hold over the *montaña* Arawak groups, they also launched a series of exploratory expeditions in an attempt to improve communications between their bases and their Urubamba and Ucayali missions. They also sought reconnection with the old Jesuit reductions in Mainas, on the Marañón, which they inherited for a time after the 1768 expulsion of the Jesuits.

From a very early date the Franciscans also tried to establish missions in Quito's jurisdiction, on the upper Napo and the upper Putumayo, in western Tukano territory (the Mocoa and Sucumbios mission). These Indians invariably rebelled and took flight after a few years, almost as soon as the flow of iron tools dried up. The religious then attempted an entry by way of the Napo and the Aguarico in 1632. These new missions, which affected large riverside populations, also collapsed some 15 years later. From 1686 on, therefore, the Franciscans concentrated on the upper Putumayo and the Caquetá. Meanwhile, the Mainas mission began to expand, and the Jesuits gradually took over the Napo Valley, with the result that in 1694 the Franciscans lost their last remaining reductions on the upper Napo and the Curaray. From then on they labored almost exclusively on the Putumayo and the Caquetá. Work on the former was interrupted by a first series of rebellions in 1711; they returned to the Caguan and the Caquetá in 1726, working outward again to the Putamayo, where they succeeded in founding fourteen missions in about 10 years. Toward the middle of the century, however, they had already lost five of them, and despite repeated attempts to evangelize and stabilize the Tukano groups, they did not manage to make the mission prosper. A widespread rebellion swept away the Caquetá missions in 1790.

The Apolobamba mission was less extensive and more short lived. Although Franciscan missionaries, as well as Augustinians, began exploring the upper reaches of the Beni Valley in 1622, they were expelled by the Arawak and Tacana populations as soon as they attempted to settle and control the Indians. The first stable mission was established among the Leko in the late seventeenth century, and eventually eight reductions, situated along the effluents of the Beni, came to regroup the Araona, Eparamona, Aguachile, and Leko inhabiting this area; they subsisted nominally until 1808. The establishment of these missions coincides with the breakdown of the trade and alliance circuits uniting highland and lowland peoples, as epidemic diseases, colonist intrusion, and military harassment decimated or chased away the piedmont groups.

Allowing the missionaries in thus came to be seen as the least onerous way of obtaining goods of western or highland origin. Moreover the population of these missions always remained very small, and there is good evidence that the Indians here followed the well-established Arawak custom of "sacrificing" a few local groups or families by sending them to trade with the whites and act as a shield for the bulk of the population scattered throughout the more inaccessible parts of the *montaña*.

Of all the western Amazonian mission establishments, that of the Jesuits of Mainas was by far the most important, both because of its size (at its height, it counted some forty reductions and stretched from the Andes to the Rio Negro and from the upper Napo to the middle Ucayali) and the cultural influence exerted by the models of training and supervision developed there.

There are three discernible phases in Mainas Mission history. The first, from the 1634 arrival of the Jesuits in Borja, on the Marañon, up to 1660, was a period of intensive exploration, close collaboration with the local settlers (who had campaigned for their presence, in hopes that missionaries would help them control and stabilize a dangerously rebellious Indian population), and development of techniques of reduction. During this phase the Jesuits pacified and regrouped what was left of the Mayna population, the Xeberos and the groups of the lower Pastaza and Huallaga, including many Cocama; these Tupian people and the Xeberos came to be the Jesuits' (and often the colonists') main levies. The second, from 1660 to 1700, was marked by a great wave of expansion in the Curaray-Tigre sector, accompanied by the foundation of scores of reductions; the bulk of the Zaparaon and Candoan tribes were contacted at this time, as well as some of the riverine and interfluvial Pano south of the Marañón. The third, from 1720, featured a second wave of *entradas* and foundations much further east, toward the Napo Basin and the middle Amazon, in the so-called *mision baja*; at this time the earlier mission front (the *mision alta*) had shriveled as a result of rebellions, desertion, and high mortality in the reductions. This eastward expansion, which mainly affected riverine Tupian societies, was slowed down by Portuguese pressure and finally stopped in its tracks in 1768 by the expulsion of the order (see Map 17.4).

To all outward appearances the development of the Jesuit mission was spectacular. Within 100 years the company managed to establish over seventy-four reductions, bringing together over the years several tens of thousands of Indians (nominally 160,000 in 1700).

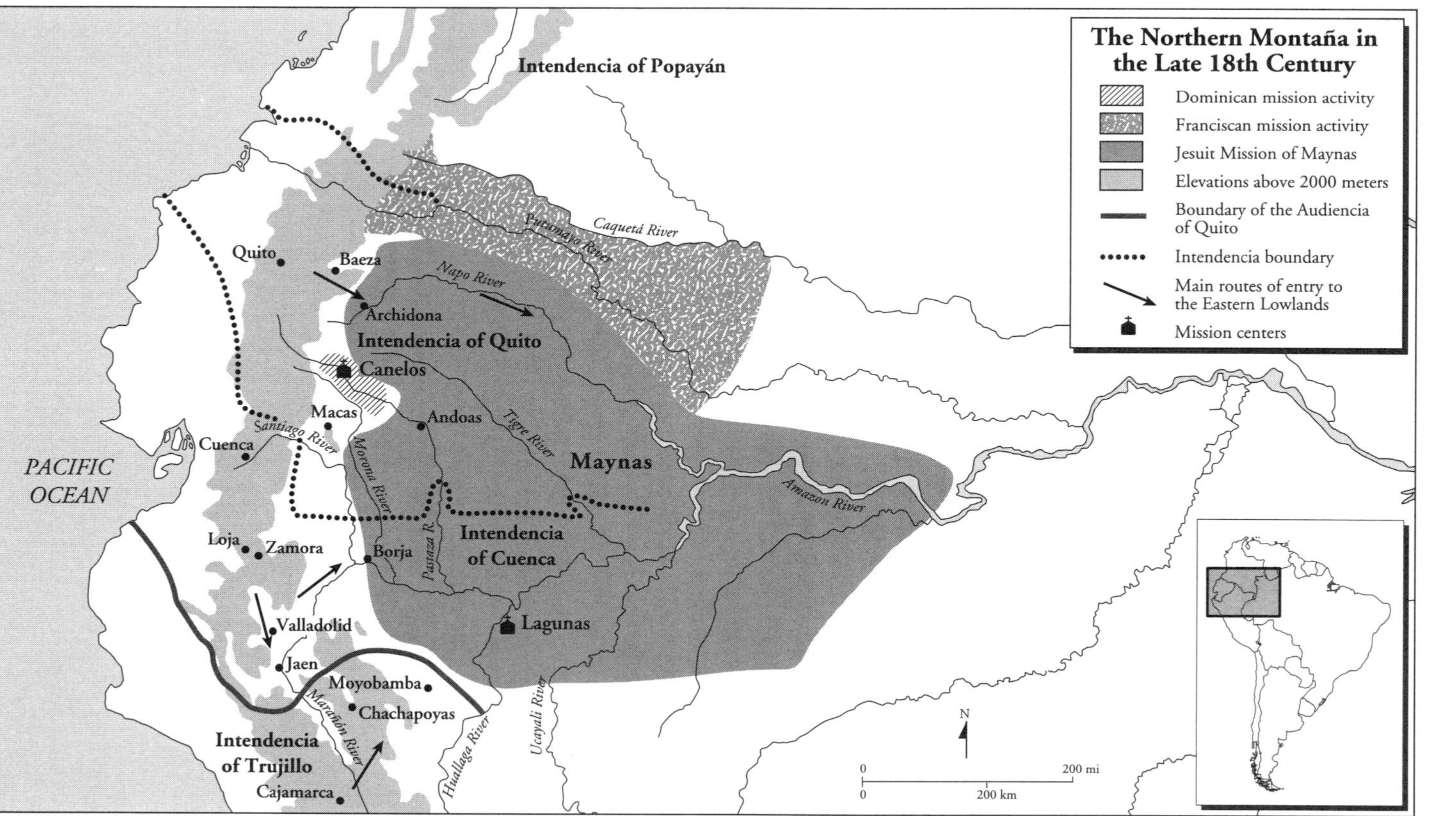
The Northern Montaña in the Late 18th Century
Dominican mission activity
Franciscan mission activity
Jesuit Mission of Maynas
Elevations above 2000 meters
Boundary of the Audiencia of Quito
Intendencia boundary
Main routes of entry to the Eastern Lowlands
Mission centers
Intendencia of Popayán
Caquetá River
Putumayo River
Napo River
Quito
Baeza
Archidona
Intendencia of Quito
Canelos
Macas
Andoas
Tigre River
Maynas
Santiago River
Cuenca
PACIFIC OCEAN
Morona River
Pastaza R.
Intendencia of Cuenca
Amazon River
Loja
Zamora
Borja
Valladolid
Lagunas
Jaen
Moyobamba
Chachapoyas
Marañón River
Huallaga River
Ucayali River
Intendencia of Trujillo
Cajamarca
N
0
200 mi
0
200 km

Map 17.4

In reality, the edifice was vulnerable, and most of the reductions lasted only a short while. Such fragility was due to several factors – first, the small number of missionaries, of whom there were never more than a score or so at a time to train and supervise in theory almost 200,000 people (the estimated population of the mission territory at its height), and to protect them from increasingly frequent and violent Portuguese slave raids. Second, the Indians suffered terrible mortality in the reductions and hated the discipline enforced by the missionaries; as a consequence they fled continually and almost invariably rebelled after a few years of Jesuit regime. More importantly the mission lacked a coherent and organized administrative and military infrastructure; in other words the colonization front was sufficiently rooted to provide the Jesuits with a permanent "clientele" fleeing from the exactions of *encomenderos* or slavers but not sufficiently developed to make it possible for the religious to strengthen their control over the Indian population of so vast a territory. Finally, the relative poverty of the Mainas mission meant that the Jesuits simply did not have enough goods to make it worthwhile for the Indians to accept sustained contact with them, or successfully to keep out traders from the colonist settlements, as they were able to do in their wealthy Paraguay and Mojos missions, where cattle, cash crops, and highly marketable craft industries flourished.

Despite its tenuous hold and its many failures, the Mainas mission left lasting traces among the indigenous populations of the upper Amazon. One is an appalling demographic scar. The grim hunts for new converts organized several times a year with the help of tens if not hundreds of armed native recruits, the Jesuits' determination to make their victims live in villages on the banks of great rivers, thereby exposing them to the full fury of the epidemics that hit the mission at least once a generation, as well as a very low birth rate and high endemic mortality rate linked to psychological stress, unhealthy living conditions, and malaria, all help to explain why the population in the mission region fell from some 200,000 in 1550 to 20,000 or 30,000 in 1730.

In the surviving groups numerous cultural features began as adaptations to the Jesuit presence, beginning with the adoption of Quichua by groups all along the Napo, the Marañón, the lower Huallaga, and Ucayali. In many societies spatial and residential organization clearly reflects such adaptation: for example, the regular alternation between a nucleated habitat and dispersion in family hunting lodges in outlying territory known as Purina among the Quichua-speaking Indians, or the arrangement of villages in *barrios*, as at Andoas or among the Lamistas. Mission-related kinship and demographic structures include the abandonment of polygyny and the early male marriage typical of the Quichua-speaking *selva* societies, and in some cases the adoption of genealogically distant marriage patterns, as opposed to the ideal of close cross-cousin marriage favored by many groups. Some politico-ritual institutions (variable hybrids of a simplified Andean *cargo* system and of para-ecclesiastical European village organizations) are directly inherited from the mission. Modifications in dress are also traceable to mission influence: By the end of the eighteenth century, there were almost no longer any naked Indians in the upper Amazon region. New crops (rice and bitter manioc), certain kinds of specialized production, such as the manufacture of curare for trade or sale by the Tikuna and the Lamista, and the convoying of salt from the Huallaga by the Napo and Bobonaza Quichua, all are Jesuit legacies.

The Jesuit missions in the eastern Bolivian lowlands also left a deep mark on the local indigenous cultures, although Jesuits remained less than 80 years in this region (they entered Mojo territory in 1675 and founded the first of their fifteen missions in this area in 1684). The Indians' acceptance of missionary presence in this area was due to much the same combination of circumstances as in the upper Marañón: The formerly powerful Mojo chieftaincies had lost their ties to the westward piedmont groups (including the Chiriguano) and hence to western and Andean goods; they had come under increasingly frequent attack from Santa Cruz slave raiders (soon to be succeeded by the Paulista *bandeirantes*); and they were deeply demoralized by epidemic mortality. The Jesuits spread the use of the Arawak Mojo language as "standard Indian" throughout the northern *llanos* (as they had imposed Quichua in the upper Marañón) and introduced the Indians to horses, cattle raising on a large scale, and highly specialized craft production. They also replaced the elaborate religious, social, and territorial organization of the Mojo and Baure with Christian beliefs, a European type village-based habitat, and a political structure combining ecclesiastical and civil Spanish statuses.

At first sight the methods used by the Jesuits and Franciscans to evangelize, train, and supervise the Indians seem very similar. Both orders shared the same obsession with concentrating and settling populations in one spot, rooted in the same adhesion to a village model of social organization, and the same determination to unify or do away with the "babel" of Indian languages. Both used iron as a means of attracting and converting the natives; they had an identical desire to impose a totally alien way of life; and finally both orders accepted the terrible mortality in their reductions with the same resignation and often indifference.

Nevertheless major differences separated the two orders. The Jesuits generally operated in the upper Amazon with a large escort of soldiers and native recruits, and they tried to persuade, or if that were impossible, to compel, a local group or set of groups to move to the banks of a large river, where they could be resettled either on a completely new site or in an already established reduction. To this end they provided supplies of food, salt, clothing, and housing as well as Christianized Indians to teach the neophytes the behavior expected of them. Traditional political and social structures were thus of very little consequence within the Jesuit approach and were rapidly dismantled to make way for the hierarchical, highly normative system imposed by the mission.

For their part the Franciscans, who before the eighteenth century could never have approached the central *selva* groups accompanied by soldiers, and who were too weak politically to obtain military support in the Mocoa-Sucumbíos area, had evolved out of necessity a means of contact less blunt and more respectful toward Indian figures of authority and forms of sociability. They tried to establish alliances with a local chief by means of gifts of iron tools – the forges they immediately set up in their missions played a major part in this respect – without at first attempting to persuade him to leave his territory, only asking him several years later to bring his people to the mission station. There in theory he would still be leader of his group. In many cases the presence of Franciscans thus led to a considerable increase in the power of traditional Indian authorities, whether they were war chiefs, as was the case among the Campa, or priestly leaders, as with the Amuesha.

The two orders also diverged markedly in the views of society underlying their missionary enterprises. The Jesuit reductions were rooted in the idea of a completely autonomous "republic of Indians," nominally subject to the power of the crown, but in fact independent of the local administration. The Company of Jesus always saw the presence of settlers, particularly *encomenderos*, as a threat and a hindrance to its efforts. Jesuits were in no way "assimilationists." Indeed, in elaborating a syncretic native culture transmitted by the Quichua spoken in the mission and inculcated by the education and discipline of the reductions, they explicitly aimed at preserving the Indians' "difference." In fact the widespread use of Quichua (or of standardized Mojo in the *llanos*) met the Jesuits' need for a language that was "indigenous" and yet not specific to any particular culture. Nevertheless, with relatively important groups long settled in the reductions, catechesis (which in principle was to be long and detailed) actually took place in the vernacular. Other aspects of indigenous culture – ornamentation, the use of plumage for art and decoration, and certain ritual choreographies – were, in the context of the baroque esthetic typical of the Jesuits, retained for their decorative or dramatic value. On the other hand, indigenous sociopolitical organization was ruthlessly dismembered in favor of a model of marriage, kinship, and sociability developed by the Jesuits; they also imposed a proliferating system of often derisive liturgical or community *cargos*.

The diaries and correspondence of M. Uriarte ([1774] 1986), a Jesuit operating in Mainas between 1750 and 1768, paint a grim and detailed picture of life in the reductions. The daily cycle in the Omagua reduction he was in charge of (San Joaquin, population 600) was as follows: reveille at 5, obligatory mass, formal salute to the resident missionary, a quick meal before setting off for work at 7 according to the tasks assigned to each sex and age group, return to the family house and a meal at 3 PM, mass, and a stringent curfew after dark. As for the political and ecclesiastical structure of the settlement, it was organized as follows. An overall governor, named for life, ruled the Indian population, while each *parcialidad* (ethnic quarter) had its own theoretically hereditary *capitan*; these were seconded by an *alferez* (submayor) and a "sargent of the militia" in charge of setting up the *entradas*. Every year each quarter (divided into *barrio alto* and *barrio bajo*) would also elect *varayos*, subject to the Omagua *alcalde mayor's* authority. Their duties were to report to the missionary morning and evening, to make sure that nobody would fall back into "antique ways" during Sunday and feast-day celebrations, to provide manioc beer in moderate quantities to visiting Indians; to keep the communal canoes, missionary's residence, and church in a proper state of repair; to designate the weekly round of *mitayos* (two from each *barrio*) in charge of feeding the missionary and his *muchachos* (presumably servants); to get the women to clean the village every Saturday; and finally to select the men for the annual salt convoys and turtle-egg collecting, as well as for the *despacho general* to Quito. Ecclesiastical charges included six *fiscales* (three from each quarter), named in the missionary's presence, each with small and large *varas*, subject to an

Omagua *fiscal mayor*. These officials' duties were to set a good example and keep the church clean, to designate the weekly round of church-bell ringers (one set for the morning, one for the evening), and to make sure the bell was rung for the numerous special masses, to recite prayers in clear and slow voices, to verify that nobody crept out of the church during sermons or catechesis, to keep track of births and illness and inform the missionary, to check that nobody drank at night or invited others without due permission, to prepare and organize the three main annual processions (Corpus Christi, Holy Virgin, and Patron Saint) as well as the Cross for Holy Week, and finally to make sure everyone had confessed at the proper moments.

The economic life of the institution was based on the principle that overall the mission was to be autonomous, though linked to the network of *haciendas* managed by the order elsewhere in the administrative district. The reductions themselves, however, were not to be independent. To the contrary they were part of an elaborate system of specialized local production, generally imposed or at least developed by the mission, so that each one, although self-sufficient regarding daily food requirement, produced a specific trading commodity distributed under monopoly conditions by the Jesuits. This was how they managed to harness for their own benefit, and in fact greatly expand, the indigenous trade in salt and curare.

As opposed to the conventual utopia of the Jesuits, the ideal of the generic agrarian village community was the driving force behind the Franciscan missions. If the aim of the former was to produce decoratively exotic counter-Reformation Catholics, the latter sought rather to recreate early Christian peasants. Ideologically the Franciscans were openly "integrationist." They used Quichua explicitly to that end on the assumption that the Indians were still too primitive to learn Spanish directly. They objected to the presence of settlers only if colonists failed to respect their way of life or, most importantly, hindered their work of conversion. In this system there was little local specialization but rather a range of artisans within each community, following the model of a rural community in Europe. In principle Franciscans had no objection to their missions forming part of the local colonial economy. Indeed each mission village was expected to become self-sufficient by selling its products in the *sierra*. These products were the result of native *mita* work probably more onerous than that demanded in the Jesuit reductions; in fact there is good evidence that by the eighteenth century the Franciscan missions of the central *selva* were exporting large amounts of sugar-cane alcohol for sale to the sierra Indians.

One of the great paradoxes of the history of the upper Amazon area is that each of the two orders found itself in circumstances far better suited to the aims of the other. The Jesuits invaded a region where their numerical weakness compelled them to downplay their ideal of political autonomy and come to terms with the settlers and the Spanish authorities; morever they had to introduce an elaborate system of specialized production with little basis in the traditional context. By contrast the area the Franciscans occupied was a zone void of colonists, strictly out of bounds until the early eighteenth century to the colonial authorities (which was itself the reason for both their being there and their repeated failures). Furthermore it lay within an area notable for its traditional system of specialized production, in particular the manufacture of bars of salt by the Campa and Amuesha, who jointly managed the resources of the Cerro de la Sal, thereby governing a web of trade interdependencies that played a vital part in inter- and intraethnic relations, whereas the Franciscans would have been far more at home with the relatively more self-contained and isolated societies of the north. Traces of this historical role reversal or miscasting surface even in the messianism of Juan Santos Atahuallpa, whose anti-Franciscan and anticolonial utopia looks disturbingly like a "Republic of Indians" on the Jesuit model, but without Jesuits.

The Birth of the Modern Amazon Region

The main effects of the upheavals accompanying Spanish settlement – expeditions for conquest, epidemics, incursions by slavers and missionaries – on the territoriality, habitat, and culture of the upper Amazon groups must now be assessed.

Alongside the desertion of large portions of the eastern side of the cordillera, one of their earliest consequences was the gradual abandonment of the riverside zones by the Indians as the Europeans began to occupy them. In the process many of the groups of the area eventually adopted a pattern of dispersed habitat. This form of settlement had existed in the western Amazon Basin long before the Spanish conquest, but only as an alternative alongside village-type habitats or big multifamily longhouses. These generally disappeared during the seventeenth century, giving way to Jívaroan-style settlements in isolated domestic units. Residential and social atomization in turn led to a growing autonomy of local groups with respect to material and symbolic reproduction, as well as to a greater mobility of domestic units as a result of the new pedological, cynergetic, and epidemic constraints. New types of collective behavior also arose in response to the threats posed by an altered environment. The chief of these was the adoption of a crisis tactic characterized by the suspension of trade, dispersion and flight to areas of refuge, and a maximum level of social atomization. These crisis behaviors often surfaced again during the rubber boom.

In terms of social formations as such, rather than their underlying settlement patterns, structures particularly vulnerable to atomization and to the breakdown or restriction of intertribal exchange networks were radically transformed or simply eliminated. The economically and politically stratified settled riverine village societies of the Napo and the Ucayali were the chief victims of this process, as were the highly integrated multitribal polities now typical only of the Vaupés area of Colombia, though they were once perhaps a feature of the piedmont in the south of that country as well. More generally the marked stratification characteristic of some western Amazonian societies – the Tupians, the Arawak Mojo, and Baure – gave way either to purely ritual hierarchies or to far more informal, unstable, and egalitarian political systems, as the traditional figures of power were devalued by their connivance with colonial authorities or by loss of wealth and control over their groups' destinies. Modifications of kinship structures in the wake of demographic collapse, shifts in forms of habitat, and loss of social stratification, all are difficult to document for groups that remained outside the mission network, and in any case are hard to evaluate because the link between demographics and forms of kinship – particularly of marriage – is still very obscure. It has been suggested, however, that the elementary, Dravidian-type systems common to many groups of the area and the complex patterns found among contemporary riverside groups such as the Piro and Shipibo may both be postconquest avatars of an earlier common model or family of models.

The disappearance of sociological configurations and indeed of whole societies was not the only characteristic feature of the period. New social forms also emerged from the clash of Indian and colonial institutions. In very schematic terms the processes of change undergone by the cultures of the upper Amazon region reflect three types of strategies used temporarily or durably, successively or simultaneously.

The first was that of absolute isolation and independence from colonial control at all costs, even if it meant drastic cultural impoverishment and a deliberately assumed process of involution. The present-day Waorani, who are probably the descendants of the complex Abijira riverside society, are a remarkable but by no means unique example of this option. The Cashinahua, and no doubt other interfluve Pano groups, oscillated every half-century or so between total withdrawal, implying rejection of any contact with the world of the whites or anything to do with it, and a cautious opening up to the sources of supply of metal.

The second was that of ethnic dissolution by means of flight and individual or collective transculturation. The rapid disappearance of the Candoa groups (Maynas, Roamainas, Guallpayos, Andoas, "Muratos," and the like), and the ceaseless confusion regarding the cultural affiliation of such societies, which are sometimes classified as Jívaro, sometimes as Záparo, and sometimes as "unidentified," is partly explained by factors of that type. Given its dramatic history and the many displacements endured by some of its dialect groups, the Candoa linguistic family, which was originally homogeneous, probably underwent a process of ethnic or cultural transformation from around 1600 as a result of which it gradually combined with and subsequently became identified with Záparo populations. During the latter half of the seventeenth century, certain Záparo tribes enjoyed a privileged status with the missionaries because of their apparent docility – the San Javier de los Gayes reduction was for a time the showpiece of the Mainas mission – and their willingness to act as intermediaries in "domesticating" other more recalcitrant ethnic groups. Candoan identity, on the other hand, carried an in-built risk of enslavement because Candoans had been subjugated by the colonists and shared out among *encomenderos* before the arrival of the Jesuits. They were hence at great risk from the incursions of slavers, unlike the Záparo, who had been Christianized by the Jesuits and were thus "free." In short, for the indigenous populations temporarily or permanently opting for "collaboration," the Záparo groups provided a model of adaptation enabling them to come to terms with the dominant society as painlessly as possible. This explains the phenomenon of Zaparoization, which seems to have been a feature of a range of societies of very diverse cultural origin throughout the second half of the seventeenth century. A comparable process of Jesuit-induced Mojoization has been posited for various groups of the eastern Bolivian lowlands, confronted with the choice of remaining true to their cultural choices but highly exposed to slave raids and killing expeditions, or of adopting an alien dialect, identity, and lifestyle under the protection of the wealthy Jesuit mission.

The southern piedmont of present-day Colombia provides a related example of the creation of a composite fugitives' society, though in this case an independent and indeed aggressively anti-Spanish one. J. Friede has convincingly argued that the Andaki, a group notorious throughout the seventeenth and eighteenth centuries for its constant attacks on colonial settlements in the area between the upper Caquetá-Putumayo and the headwaters of the Magdalena, are in fact a postconquest conglomerate of Pijao, Cofan, and western Tukano Indians, many of them escapees from the *encomiendas* of the upper Magdalena Valley. According to recent hypotheses advanced by G. Reichel-Dolmatoff and R. Wright, the Tukano themselves present another instance of such a hybrid culture. It has been mentioned earlier that these groups followed a common pattern in dealing with the missionaries: They would accept reduction for a few years and then abscond and let others take their places as neophytes. It is suggested that some of these ex-converts (it is hard to know whether the "nations," or *parcialidades*, that the missionaries listed were clans, local groups, or larger bodies) gradually migrated northeastward in the direction of the region between the lower Caquetá and the middle Negro, an area virtually void of white presence throughout the seventeenth century. Subsequently it is likely that they moved on up the Vaupés and its tributaries where, under growing pressure from Portuguese slaving raids from 1730 on, they seem to have developed, along with the local Arawak groups (of northern Maipuran stock) and the autochtonous "Maku," the singular multitribal and multilinguistic syncretic Vaupés culture we know today. Ultimately the distinctive features of the eastern Tukanoan world – linguistic exogamy, male initiation rites, the Yurupary complex, and the political and ritual ranking of clans and sibs – may thus be attributable as much to the Arawak societies formerly settled in the region, and to the epidemics and incursions of slavers and missionaries in the colonial environment, as to the aboriginal Tukano culture as it developed in its northern *montaña* hearth.

Purely individual flight and transculturation clearly went on constantly during the era of the reductions. Sometimes fugitives would assimilate into groups who were still independent, or regroup to form small, short-lived cells in unsettled areas, a process that eventually generated social aggregates with no well-defined tribal identity, particularly in the region between the Tigre and the Napo. These did not make up a population of generic Indians properly speaking, because the essential element needed to establish such social categories was missing – namely, a permanent white presence. The Indians were not economically, socially, or politically organized by a shared relationship of exploitation at the hand of colonists, as was to be the case later during the rubber boom and beyond. What happened rather was a growth of formations characterized by a suspension or freezing of specific tribal membership, which was replaced or superseded by a blurred, shifting identity based on inclusion in loose sociological networks (in which a common shamanistic system probably played a central part) and a shared syncretic culture transmitted in mission Quichua. Under cover of or alongside the shared language, however, the vernaculars were often kept alive, in that new refugees were constantly arriving, and this phenomenon of multilinguism – which persisted until recent times in the Tigre Valley – is perhaps the key to the continued transmission of submerged identities within these aggregates. What distinguished this type of formation from the half-caste *ribereño* populations encountered along the Amazon and its major tributaries was thus the persistence of a specific if rather overshadowed tribal identity.

The most original social forms evolving at this time, and certainly the most important ones in terms of interethnic dynamics, were the colonial "tribes" created in the reductions or around Spanish settlements. These cultures – such as the Lamista, Canelos, Andoas, "Quijos" from the eighteenth century onward, and Xebero – had certain affinities with the groups just mentioned (multitribal origins, the development of a syncretic culture, and the use of Quichua), but from the very start a combination of factors endowed them with a clearer social structure and gave them a cohesion and homogeneity lacking in the Tigre-Napo aggregates. They hence possessed a specific "tribal" identity clearly perceived both from within and without. However diverse the frameworks in which such social formations arose – Jesuit reductions, small colonial towns, or zones of refuge under distant supervision from the Dominicans – they present enough common features to justify their inclusion in a single category. All were based on a grouping of culturally disparate societies: *Motilones* in the case of the Lamistas; Záparo and Candoa in that of the Andoas; highland, and Napo Quichua, and Jívaro/Záparo in that of the

Canelos; and so on. Within them the specific characteristics of each tribe are sometimes hidden or completely submerged and sometimes ritually emphasized, but they are always subordinated to an externally created collective identity. Furthermore there is a fundamental Indian–white split in these overall identities themselves that makes the original tribal affiliations largely irrelevant. This is because they are all based on a structural duality between, on the one hand, the behavior and institutions visible to (and imposed by) the colonists, and the open sphere in which the *alli runa*, the Christianized *mansos*, live and move alongside whites or half-castes, and, on the other hand, the closed sphere of the nonvisible aspects of their culture, the world of the *sacha runa* ('forest' or 'wild people'), masters of a natural and symbolic environment that the whites could not penetrate but which, in the forest space of the *purina*, is closely tied to the *auca* societies surrounding it.

This explains, of course, the role of brokers played by such tribes between the still autonomous *selva* population and the dominant colonial society. The former were provided the manufactured goods to which the "brokers" had special access, as well as models of manipulative behavior toward whites; the "brokers" were also, and still are, a formidable source of shamanistic power, feeding on their close proximity to the white world. To the latter, the "brokers" meekly offered their labor and its fruits, which constituted a means of regulating difficult relationships with the *aucas* and the resources they might control, and, particularly in the nineteenth century, a mechanism for territorial and economic expansion via the *purina-caserío*-half-caste village-*purina* cycle. In this pattern the presence of the mestizo retailers that invariably came to settle at the core of native villages gradually drove the Indians to search for new areas of settlement in which to establish first individual hunting lodges and later small hamlets as new members joined the household of the original *purina* group. These growing settlements eventually attracted the mestizo dealers to whom their inhabitants became, and the whole process then started all over again.

As for the "infidels," herded back into the interfluvial areas of refuge, their contacts with the colonization front in the northern *montaña* were to be filtered until well into the twentieth century through these buffer tribes living near colonial settlements and along major communication routes. The Napo Runa, for example, were linked in this way to the western Tukanoan populations and the Huaorani, the Canelos to the Záparo and the northern Jívaro, the Andoas to the Jívaro-Candoa and the eastern Záparo (the Shimigaes and the Záparo proper), the Lamistas and the Chayavitas to the Aguaruna, and so on. The triadic configuration typical of the northern upper Amazon region – linking whites and "tame" and "wild" Indians – did not begin to crumble until the *aucas* were gradually brought into the sphere of patron–client bonds as it spread through the area in the wake of the rubber boom. Even then the patterns of social and linguistic behavior grounded in the colonial interethnic system continued to shape relations between *manso* and *auca* Indians until the latter began creating their own political organizations.

Because of their high degree of assimilation, these postconquest indigenous formations were long neglected by social scientists. Within the last two decades, however, a growing body of research has revealed the complexity of these societies and has highlighted the difficulties posed by their study. Anthropologists have underlined the strong and ongoing ethnicity of these cultures and have consequently elected to treat them as self-contained societies no different in essence from the "traditional" groups dealt with in terms of the classical monographical approach. There is good reason for this; Canelos Quichua or Xebero individuals are themselves quick to underline the specificity of their rituals, kinship and family structures, territoriality, oral traditions, and history to justify the tribal or "traditional" nature of their society. Yet it can equally be argued that these hybrid colonial groups should be viewed as forming a generalized transformational culture rather than as distinct societies in the usual anthropological sense of the term. Their mode of reproduction offers evidence of this: Groups such as the Canelos persist in terms of identity thanks to the small but steady inflow of "wild" Indians just as much as by autonomous demographic reproduction. Furthermore cultural transmission depends as much on processes of deliberate "deculturation" – the playing down of psychologically salient aspects of "wild" cultures – as on the development of specific traditions, because these mostly originate in a stock of representations common to the "traditional" cultures. This is in fact why individuals from *auca* groups can so easily move in and out of these *manso* societies without having to acquire a whole new register of cultural knowledge. It is true that full-scale bilinguism is far from widespread in the upper Amazon, insofar as people who, through temporary transculturation have become proficient in another language (e.g., Quichua), do not attempt to transmit this mastery to their offspring. Yet both the linguistic and the social skills necessary to function as a recognized member of a *nativo* society seem to be acquired easily and speedily. It is therefore likely that, for all their empirical divergence, *auca* and *manso* cultures share a great deal of common ground and that the differences between them are rooted in contrasting forms of contextualization of cultural knowledge operating in a few restricted, culturally stressed domains of social life, rather than in the building up of entirely distinct registers of tradition.

There is one area, however, in the which the Quichua and *nativo* groups have elaborated a specific set of notions: that of history. All the cultures involved seem to share linear and periodized historical ideologies very different from those of the "traditional" groups of the region. In general terms the latter do not have any specific genre of historical discourse; in fact history as we understand it, and in particular the history of relations with whites, is surprisingly absent from indigenous discursive forms, scarcely mentioned in myths (and then only in highly oblique ways), and rarely reenacted as such in ritual. There are of course many exceptions to this generalization. The pre-Andean Arawak cultures have several genres – some epic, some autobiographical – concerning the history of their relations with encroaching outsiders, and they share with the Cashinanahua and riverine Pano (Shipibo and Conibo) a mythic or legendary corpus centered on the figure of the Inka; in this tradition the Inka acts as a metaphor for any kind of powerful, threatening foreigners, and he is portrayed alternately as a benevolent culture hero or as a stingy and sometimes cannibalistic partner. Nonetheless throughout most of the upper Amazon, reference to the past and present of interethnic relations is concentrated in shamanic practice and discourse, which manipulates a wealth of symbols and icons culled from the world of whites and *manso* groups. The connection between curing chants and indigenous styles of historicity lies in the fact that both illness and history are viewed as processual phenomena rather than as a sequence of structured states linked by a chronological narrative. Hence sickness functions as the major metaphor for the painful and unaccountable change that is the essence of postconquest history for most Amazonian cultures.

The hybrid colonial tribes and the *nativos* undoubtedly share this shamanic conception of historicity, but they also have a periodized historical discourse, according to a threefold scheme dividing their past into ancient "times of wildness," "times of slavery" (among the *nativos*) or "times of grandparents" (among the Canelos), and present-day "times of civilization." Yet this linear, historical structure reflects a static view of states of social organization, each characterized by a certain relation of identity to "otherness" and hybridization, just as much as actual phases of the past. Thus "Times of wildness" refers to a stereotyped vision of *auca* culture as marked by "ignorance" (i.e., of the outside world), bellicism and linguistic and social self-containment. "Times of slavery" evokes the forced apprenticeship, under the rule of patrones (rubber bosses, or *hacendados*), of "proper" ethnic mixing and of "proper" systems of production and consumption (e.g., the exchange of forest products for manufactured goods and the right combination of imported and "wild" food). "Times of civilization" denotes the living out, in conditions of individual freedom and political autonomy, of this henceforth internalized knowledge concerning the processes of interethnic and intercultural *mestizaje*.

The historical narrative of the *nativo* groups aptly illustrates the complex nature of these social formations, because it is both a local tradition underpinning a particular tribal identity, through shared reference, and a generalized discourse about processes of cultural hybridization common to many entirely unrelated *manso* groups. In this respect it clearly reveals their dual character as specific tribes and, simultaneously, as templates of change and transculturation. In short, the "assimilated" *manso* groups are in some sense an organic extension of the *auca* societies, and their identity and physical persistence depend on the ongoing existence of "traditional" hinterland tribes. At the same time, the latter have remained "wild" only because of the development of these hybrid buffer groups, and their "traditionality" is therefore a product of the selfsame history that has shaped the acculturated, "domestic" indigenous societies of the upper Amazon.

Overall the picture that emerges from the missionary and administrative chronicles of the second half of the eighteenth century is particularly bleak as far as the northern *montaña* is concerned. From the demographic point of view, the decrease in the population of the area between 1550 and 1780 is estimated to be 80 percent or, taking into account the total disappearance of many tribes, a fall of at least 50 percent in those groups that were most isolated and least directly affected by the colonial presence. The terrible mortality and the consequent disintegration of the social fabric in that part of the Amazon Basin was largely due to the presence of numerous and relatively concentrated centers – either reductions or colonial establishments – for the propagation of infectious diseases, connected by the dense communications network linking the Jesuit missions to each other and to Spanish–*mestizo* poles of settlement. Epidemics thus spread very rapidly and over great distances. Throughout the seventeenth century they surged across the region roughly every 20 years, or every generation. Then, after a relative lull between 1690 and 1750, the process accelerated once again as the number of reductions in the "lower region" and Portuguese settlements on the middle Amazon grew. The decade 1750–1760 probably marked the absolute demographic nadir in the central and northern upper Amazon region.

The Záparo were among the chief victims of the disaster, disappearing almost completely, with scarcely more than a few hundred survivors left on the plateau between the Pastaza and the Tigre. Of the great Candoa bloc, there remained only a small group of "Muratos" (i.e., Kandoshi and Shapra) along the tributaries of the lower Pastaza. The Tukano were scattered in isolated pockets throughout a huge area, all their major riparian tribes such as the Encabellados having long vanished. The remaining Aushiri disappeared deep into the forests of the upper Curaray, where they were not heard of again, under the name of Aucas, until the end of the nineteenth century. As for the Napo, by 1750 it became virtually devoid of human life throughout the upper half of its course.

The Jivaroan tribes, however, managed to preserve their autonomy and most of their territory throughout the colonial period without having to suffer the disadvantages of a "pseudo-archaic" condition. The exceptional resilience of this ethnic group was due to a set of very particular circumstances. On the one hand, it had an in-built advantage for adapting to the upheavals in its environment because its social and territorial organization already had all the requisite features to resist colonial aggression in the most favorable conditions: a widely scattered habitat, movable scales of internal tribal differentiation, highly atomized and economically, symbolically, and ritually autonomous local groups. On the other, the Jívaro tribes commonly used or secreted, probably since Inka times, buffer groups to form a transculturation area round the perimeter of their ethnic territory (as they did with the Canelos) and to broker their relations to nonindigenous populations. They had alternative means of access to manufactured goods through networks connecting the Shuar groups of the upper foothills and certain very isolated Andean populations, notably those of the higher Paute Valley in Azuay-Cañar. Nevertheless the Jívaro were a unique case in the northern part of the upper Amazon area, and although they forfeited neither their traditional culture nor their independence, they did lose a great part of their population in the mid-colonial period.

The situation in the central *selva* and further south was far less disheartening. The Indian societies of that region were in fact infinitely better able to resist the colonist-missionary onslaught, even to the point of being able, between 1742 and 1770, to clear the region of all nonnatives. In 1780 almost all the precolumbian populations were still in place, clearly smaller in number but less depleted than those of the northern *montaña*. Neither their traditional habitat nor their social organization had been fundamentally changed. They did not experience until much later, in the nineteenth and twentieth centuries, processes of ethnogenesis comparable to those that took place in the northern *montaña* in the seventeenth and eighteenth centuries and that gave birth to new tribal societies. There were two local exceptions to this relatively positive state of affairs: the Panatagua, and more generally the populations of the upper and middle Huallaga, who were annihilated by epidemics and their consequences by the end of the seventeenth century; and, subsequently, the riverside Pano under Jesuit tutelage, such as the Conibo, who were greatly reduced in numbers and disintegrated in the mid–eighteenth century.

The marked differences between the two sectors of the western Amazon region with regard to their colonial history are attributable to a number of factors. First and foremost was the absence of colonial settlements on the eastern side of the central cordillera: Until the nineteenth century, the huge tract of lowland between Moyobamba, in northern Peru, and Santa Cruz, in southern Bolivia, remained void of significant colonist settlements. This meant that the seats of infection from which pathological conditions of European origin spread were fewer than in the Pastaza-Marañón region, as were incursions by whites for slaving, trade, or land occupation. Also, in the early stages at least, Franciscan missionary strategies weakened indigenous societies less than those of the Jesuits because they tended to isolate the groups contacted (and subsequently contaminated) instead of integrating them into vast networks of communications; moreover Franciscan tactics initially entailed lesser physical and psychological upheavals than the Jesuits' policy of reduction. A further factor was the sheer expanse and ruggedness of the areas where fugitives could take refuge, as well as the Spaniards' lack of geographical knowledge. Whereas the Marañón Valley and its major tributaries were thoroughly mapped by 1680 and crisscrossed by slaving expeditions or missionary *correrias*, large portions of southeast Peru were still in fact, if not in name, terra incognita until the middle of the nineteenth century.

It must also be borne in mind that the pre-Andean Arawak of the central *selva*, like the Jívaro, enjoyed alternative sources of supply for metal tools, because by the late sixteenth century the Campa and Amuesha had developed native forges using the abundant ores of the Cerro de la Sal region. In terms of trade goods of Andean origin, they were less dependent on the missionaries than the northern *montaña* Indians, because while the latter were cut off almost everywhere from the highland populations by the desertion of the eastern slopes, the peoples of the central *montaña* exercised enough control over the *selva* up to the high *ceja* to deal directly with the Quichua at certain key points, notably on the Ene and the Apurimac.

The essential difference between the two regions and the two sets of populations, however, arises from their respective systems of ethnic and tribal interactions. The central *selva* groups were closely integrated by a macronetwork of exchange of goods and persons centered on the Campa communities of the Cerro de la Sal, and they were grounded in a system of managed complementarity in the production of luxury craft goods. The network was built up by contextually extending the Campa prohibition on intratribal violence to other ethnic groups. Nevertheless the system also had an openly military dimension. The multicommunity trading expeditions it entailed afforded an opportunity to organize raids on groups excluded from this political structure, primarily the interfluve Panoans. It therefore offered an ideal support for the defensive confederations initially developed in Inka times and gradually spread to include the riverside Pano groups, to such an extent that in the eighteenth century it could unite all the Campa (including the Amuesha), the Piro, the riverside Pano, and even the Tupi of the lower Ucayali. Such massive military alliances were short-lived, but their occurrence points to a model of multiethnic political organization clearly present in the minds of those participating – the Campa historical tradition attached to military exploits bears witness to this – and suggests a very inclusive overall identity linked to the idea of a shared territory. The cultural infrastructure of confederative defensive warfare also included extraordinarily detailed linguistic, geographical, and ethnographic knowledge of the central *selva* as a whole.

The extreme north of the *montaña* also offers traces of a confederative defensive strategy akin to that adopted by the societies of the central *selva*, insofar as it seems to have been based on a highly integrated preexisting trade system linking the Sibundoy Kamsa, the western Tukano, and possibly the Paez and Cofan of the Sucumbios area. However, in this area armed resistance to the Spaniards implied the dissolution of prior ethnic identities within the context of entirely new tribal formations, such as the Andaki, dedicated to traditional style warfare against the colonists. Such aggressive hybrid groups of colonial origin are reminiscent of the notorious pirates of the central Amazon, the composite and nomadic Mura of the Madeira who terrorized Portuguese colonists of the middle Amazon Valley throughout the eighteenth century.

In the rest of the northern *montaña*, the mode of intertribal and interethnic relations underlying the Arawak confederation was unknown and even unthinkable. In the first place exchange networks were much more diffuse in that area, loosely linked to specialized production, and based on dyadic individual relations rather than on political units acting collectively. In fact such systems were not perceived as collective institutions at all. They did not, therefore, foster the emergence of encompassing collective identities, even under political stress. In addition, institutionalized forms of homicide – feuding or intertribal war – were a permanent and basic feature of social structures in almost all the cultures of the area. Symbolic predatory wars, either internal to the ethnic unit, as with the Jívaro, or against other ethnic groups, as with the Cocama and possibly the Záparo, played an essential part in interethnic relations and even intragroup social-ritual reproduction. Such forms of warfare offered no sociological basis for concerted defensive groupings like those existing at the foot of the East Andes. On the contrary they encouraged the Spaniards to manipulate hostilities and furthered the ethnogenesis of groups specialized in "ethnic soldiering," like the Cocama and the Xebero, around the missions and towns. The frequent but short-lived and localized rebellions that broke out all along the northern piedmont in the late sixteenth century thus present a marked contrast to the large-scale, concerted military action of the pre-Andean Arawak coalitions. The rapid collapse of the only two known attempts at intertribal military operations against the Spaniards in the north – the revolt spearheaded by the Quijos shamans in 1576 and the lowland Cañar-Jivaroan attack on Logroño and Sevilla de Oro in 1590 – testifies to the difficulty of translating guerilla-type tactics adapted to internecine feuding into strategically planned operations involving larger social units. In short, the societies of the northern upper Amazon region right from the start were more "atomized" and less closely interconnected than those of the central *montaña*. Jesuit attempts to integrate them into wider networks that were centered on the missions paradoxically only increased their growing disintegration and isolationism.

THE END OF THE COLONIAL ERA AND THE BEGINNING OF THE REPUBLICAN PERIOD IN THE UPPER AMAZON REGION

The characteristic feature of the end of the colonial era was a marked shrinkage of the colonization front. The central *selva*, united by the Juan Santos uprising, remained solidly closed to non-Amazonians. Between 1760 and 1840 the towns of the northern piedmont and those lying in the Marañón Valley lost on the average two-thirds of their population. The Bourbon reforms and then the wars of independence captured the attention of Creole political elites, who were either totally uninterested in such marginal and unproductive areas or at best given to ill-informed utopian dreams about them. In short, the emerging nations were too busy re-creating their centers to bother about reconquering peripheral areas. Consequently the few missionaries still around rapidly deserted them. After a few years of disastrous mismanagement, the Mainas reductions were taken away from the Franciscans and handed over to the secular clergy, whose incompetence finally ruined what was left of the Jesuit edifice. The Ocopa college was abandoned in 1823, as were all the Ucayali missions save one.

As the nonindigenous inhabitants left the forests and the hold of the settlers and missionaries weakened, the Indian populations went through a period of renaissance. The increase in the number of local groups and the growth of new villages around the turn of the century clearly shows an inversion of their hitherto downward trend, particularly among the Quichua-speaking societies to the north of the Marañón. These groups were probably among the earliest Amazon populations to adopt a pattern of steady demogaphic expansion, as opposed to the steady-state regime typical of the more traditional societies. The partial return of Indians toward the banks of the great rivers – the Marañón upstream from Barrancas, the Pastaza, the Morona, and the Santiago – and the arrival in the one or two surviving *mestizo* villages of delegations of *Indios bravos* looking for western goods that their traditional go-betweens could no longer provide, were further symptoms of white withdrawal. In many cases these incursions generated panic among the whites unused to dealing with *aucas* face to face, and they fed both the rumors of increased

Indian insolence and the beleaguered colonists's sense of isolation and insecurity. Of course the disintegration of colonial structures in the *Oriente* did not work to the advantage of all the Indians. People on the missions nearest to mestizo towns, particularly the Lamista, Cocamilla, and Chayavita, were even more grievously exploited than in the past, because the civil authorities took over for their own benefit the system of compulsory labor introduced by the missionaries and made it if even more onerous. The lengthy and periodic *mita* imposed on Indians, first for defense against the Portuguese and later for boat building, was in fact to ignite local rebellions on more than one occasion.

Nevertheless the configuration typical of the upper Amazon region in the seventeenth and eighteenth centuries – namely, a demographically prostrate, devastated, and recomposed northwest, in contrast to a strong central *selva* still virtually free of intruders – was to be reversed abruptly during the nineteenth century. Whereas the northern piedmont remained economically stagnant and its *mestizo* population sparse practically up to, and even beyond, the beginning of the twentieth century, the region south of the Marañón, the lowlands east of the Pastaza, and the central *selva* were to experience during the second half of the nineteenth century an explosive period of development.

The early 1800s were marked by a decisive change in the axes of control over the upper Amazon region. The swing from north to south first took shape in political decisions turning the administration of a greatly enlarged Mainas province over to the civil and ecclesiastical authorities at Lima. More importantly from 1820 onward, an eastward economic thrust spread from the northern Peruvian Amazon. Improving communications and swelling local trade between the sierra and the *selva* paved the way for the expansion of the whole region from 1850 on, and Peruvian military, administrative, and political presence consequently gained solidity.

At first the economic awakening that began to spread to the whole of the Peruvian piedmont in those years merely implied intensified forest resource exploitation and a corresponding growth in the volume of trade between Indians and outsiders. Thus, in the first decades of the century, there was a marked increase in small-scale trading based on the gathering of gums and resins, *pita* fiber, cacao and vanilla production, and tobacco growing; panning for gold was also on the upsurge. Market growth fostered booms in extractive industry from 1850 on, particularly sarsaparilla, but also *cascarilla* (quinine) and *tagua* (vegetable ivory). Irresistibly the half-caste population of the upper Amazon region swelled. The Marañón Valley rapidly began to become urbanized. Iquitos grew from 277 inhabitants in 1850 to 15,000 in 1876 at the beginning of the rubber boom. Unlike its neighbors Ecuador and Bolivia, the Peruvian state from 1850 on took an active role in the reconquest of its eastern hinterlands: Peruvian troops marched against the Campas, supporting the colonization of the Chanchamayo Valley, from which the Indians were finally expelled around 1860. Lima then opened up the central *selva* to immigrant Europeans.

The profound and accelerated transformations that swept the region from 1820 clearly prefigured the upheaval of the coming rubber-tapping invasion. These forerunning changes also affected the area north of the Marañón, but only relatively marginally or indirectly; the sub-Andean fringe in particular remained sluggish until the early decades of the twentieth century. In 1900 Puyo was still a tiny Canelos hamlet, for example, and the mestizo population south of the Pastaza down to Gualaquiza did not exceed 400 people; what little economic development took place in this zone was fostered either by powerful *serrano* landowners or by emerging municipal or regional authorities, notably in Cañar-Azuay. Meanwhile the Marañón, Ucayali, and Huallaga valleys were caught up in a storm of commercial activities fostering an accelerated growth of cities amid the forest. The army, rubber bosses, and finally immigrants massively and increasingly violently besieged the jungle. The two great blocs of indigenous society – that of the upper Amazon and that of the central *selva* – now stood in an opposite situation to that of the preceding century. In the north the Indians once again left the riverside areas most accessible to river traffic, but large portions of the interfluve remained relatively unaffected. Even "tame" northern Indians such as the Napo and Canelos Quichua managed both to increase their numbers and to develop strongly explicit "tribal" ethnicities. In the south, on the other hand, riverside mission Indians became entirely dependent on their trade *patrones* and were so ruthlessly exploited by them that they sometimes sank into a state of anonymous and deculturated peonage. As for the "infidels," or free-dwelling unconverted groups, everything was now against them. Deprived of refuge areas, and tracked down by the rubber bosses and their native militia, groups such as the Harakmbet and the hinterland Panoans lost most of their people as well as control over their land. As for the Campa, who were caught between the army, the *patrones*, and impinging colonizers, they were impelled to relinquish their hold on the cloud forest and to give up large areas of lower forest to immigrants from the Andes. Cut off from both its vital termini – the highland Quechua and the riverside societies – the great regional trade network that had for so long underlain central *selva* Indians' resistance to foreign encroachment thus gradually broke up. Each ethnic group, and then each tribe, and finally each increasingly isolated community now stood alone to face the violent history of the Amazon region in modern times.

BIBLIOGRAPHIC ESSAY

To this day the only synthetic work covering the precolumbian, colonial and republican history of the native populations of the *montaña* is J. E. Steward's brief introduction to Part 3 of Vol. III of the *Handbook of South American Indians* (J. E. Steward, ed., 1948). This should cause no surprise. Although Steward is largely responsible for having canonized the notion of a *montaña* culture area, his view of the societies of this area as merely reacting to outside historical influences rather than as actors in their own right helped to entrench the idea that historical research was not essential in reaching an understanding of their cultures. Consequently ethnohistorical approaches began to develop only in the last 15 years. Still this monumental work remains an indispensable starting point for ethnohistorians and anthropologists alike, although the theoretical premises underlying the organization of the *HSAI* are now largely outdated. Steward's definition of the *montaña* is somewhat more restrictive than that adopted here, because it stretches only from the north of present-day Ecuador to the headwaters of the Madre de Dios. The upper Caquetá-Putumayo area is treated by Steward in Part 4 of the same volume, and the north of present-day Bolivia is dealt with by A. Metraux in Part 2. More recent synoptic works are less extensive in their coverage but also far more detailed. D. Sweet's pioneering "A rich realm destroyed the middle Amazon Valley, 1640–1750," 2 vols. (Ph.D. thesis, University of Wisconsin, 1974), although concentrating on the middle Amazon, has much to offer to students of the upper Amazon; F. Santos Granero's excellent *Etnohistoria de la Alta Amazonia, siglos XV-XVIII*, Colección 500 años, n° 46, (Quito, 1992), a synthesis of the many historical articles he has written, focuses on the upper Marañón area and the central *selva*, as does A. Chirif and C. Mora's lengthy essay, *Atlas de la comunidades nativas* (Lima, 1978), and A. M. D'Ans' useful introductory study

L'Amazonie Péruvienne (Paris, 1982). Both these works also cover republican and modern history. A special issue of the *Bulletin de l'Institut Français d'Etudes Andines* (X, 1981) offers a wealth of material on the Inka and early colonial periods in the upper Marañón, lower Huallaga and Ucayali, central *selva* of Peru, and northern Bolivia. The massive work by F. M. Casevitz Renard, T. Saignes, and A. C. Taylor, *L'Inca, l'espagnol et les sauvages. Rapports entre les sociétés amazoniennes et andines du XV° au XVII siècle* (Paris, 1989), translated to Spanish as *Al este de los Andes. Ensayo sobre las relaciones entre sociedades andinas y amazónicas, siglos XIV–XVIII* (Quito, 1986), a comparative study of highland–lowland relations in the northern *montaña*, the central *selva*, and the Bolivian piedmont from preinkaic times to the end of the sixteenth century, extends this latter publication, both in analytic scope and in detail. Other wide-ranging contributions on the ethnohistory of the upper Amazon or the central *selva* are those of A. C. Taylor, "Historia pos-colombiana da Alta Amazonia," in M. Carneiro da Cunha (ed.), *Historia dos Indios no Brasil* (São Paulo, 1992), 213–238, and "El otro litoral. El Oriente ecuatoriano en el siglo XIX," in J. Maiguashca (ed.), *Historia y región en el Ecuador, 1830–1930* (Quito, 1994), 17–67; F. M. Renard-Casevitz, "Guerre, violence et identité à partir de sociétés du piémont amazonien des Andes centrales," *Cahiers ORSTOM*, série Sciences de l'Homme et de la Société, Cahier Anthropologie et Histoire, 21:1 (Paris, 1985), 81–98; *Le Banquet Masqué. Une mythologie de l'Etranger* (Paris, 1991); "Guerriers du sel, sauniers de la paix," *L'Homme*, 33:2–4 (1993), 126–128, 25–44; and A. and P. Costales, "La familia ethnolinguistica Zapara," *Ethos* (Quito) 1 (1975), 3–33; and their series of six volumes, *La Nación Shuar. Documentación etno-historica* (Sucua, Mundo Shuar, 1977–1978). H. Llanos Vargas and R. Pineda Camacho's book, *Ethnohistoria del Gran Caquetá. Siglos XVI–XVIII* (Bogota, 1982), is an essential reference for the far northern *montaña*, and T. Saignes' *Los Andes Orientales; Historia de un Olivido* (Cochabamba, 1985) is an imaginative and erudite treatise on the ethnohistory of the Bolivian *Oriente*. Two very useful works on the modern history of the central *selva* of Peru are F. Barclay, M. Rodríguez et al.'s *Amazonia 1940–1990: el extravío de una ilusión* (Lima, 1991), and F. Santos Granero and F. Barclay's *Ordenes y Desordenes en, la Selva Central. Historia y economía de un espacio regional* (Lima, 1995). Since the 1980s, ethnohistory has become a booming field of research throughout Amazonia, as witnessed by the proliferation of scientific meetings devoted to this subject, notably in the International Congress of Americanists. Many of the papers presented at these symposia, relevant to the history of the western Amazon, have been published in Spanish by the amazingly productive Abya Yala editions of Quito. Two of these collections are particularly worth mentioning here: *Los Meandros de la Historia en la Amazonia* (R. Pineda Camacho and B. Alzate Angel, eds., 1990) and *La construcción de la Amazonia andina* (P. Garcia Jordán, ed., 1995).

Literature on the archaeology of the *montaña* is relatively scant, as it is for the lowlands in general, and much of it is highly specialized. Readers looking for a brief overview of the subject may turn to Donald Lathrap's much used, and much contested, *The Upper Amazon: Ancient Peoples and Places* (New York, 1970), and to the recent synoptic works of Luis Lumbreras, *Arqueología de la América Andina* (Lima, 1981); R. Ravines, *Panorama de la Arqueología andina* (Lima, 1982); and D. Lavalée, *Promesse d'Amérique. La préhistoire de l'Amérique du Sud* (Paris, 1995). The Ecuadorian scholar and disciple of B. Meggers, P. Porras Garces, was one of the first archaeologists to concentrate on the lowlands; his main fields of research were the Napo and Upano valleys. See *Contribución al estudio de la arqueología e historia de los valles de Quijos y Misagualli (Alto Napo)* (Quito, 1961); *Historia y arqueología de la ciudad española Baeza de los Quijos. Estudios científicos sobre el Oriente ecuatoriano*, I (Quito, 1974); and *Investigaciones Arqueológicas en las faldas del Sangay* (Quito, 1987), 15–34. His analytic perspective, however, is considered somewhat eccentric. T. Myers, following in the steps of Lathrap, conducted archaeological investigations at Yarinacocha ("The late prehistoric period at Yarinacocha, Peru," Ph.D. thesis, 1970). He has written a useful review essay on archaeological research in the eastern Andean piedmont, "Vision de la prehistoria de la Amazonia Superior" in F. Santos Granero (ed.), *1° Seminario de Investigaciones sociales en la Amazonia* (Iquitos, 1988), 37–87, as well as many stimulating and accessible papers on the precolumbian and colonial history of the upper Amazon. His account of Sarayacu, *Archeology and Ethnohistory of Sarayacu: A nineteenth century mission in the Peruvian montaña* (Lincoln, Neb., 1989) is also a fine illustration of the value of adopting a deep chronological perspective and combining archaeological and detailed ethnohistorical research. The same holds true of Roe's work, *Cumancaya: Archeological excavations and ethnographic analogy in the Peruvian montaña* (Ann Arbor, Michigan, 1973) because of the light it throws on the premises and methods underlying historical work on the *montaña* area. Mention should be made of the lively debate that arose following Lathrap, Gebhart-Sayer, and Mester's interpretation of the ceramic tradition associated with this site (1985) as testifying to the existence of a pluriethnic chiefdom of eastern Ecuadorian Quichua origin. See their "Further discussion of the roots of the Shipibo art style: A rejoinder to Dehoer and Raymond," *Journal of Latin American Lore* 13:2 (1987), 225–273. Other specialists, J. S. Raymond, W. Deboer, and P. G. Roe in *Cumancaya: A Peruvian Ceramic Tradition*, Occasional Papers, 2, Dept. of Archaeology, University of Calgary (Calgary, 1975), and Roe again in "The Josho Nahuanbo are all wet and undercooked: Shipibo views of the whiteman and the Incas in myth, legend and history," in J. D. Hill (ed.), *Rethinking History – Indigenous South American Perspectives on the Past* (Urbana, Ill., 1988), 106–135, hotly contested the reading of mythical and linguistic data made by these authors, and it firmly maintained the Panoan origin of the Cumancaya pottery tradition.

The issue of transregional trade circuits in precolumbian and early colonial times has received considerable attention during the last two decades. Following the seminal articles by U. Oberem, "Handel und Handelsgutter in der Montaña Ecuadors," *Folk* [Copenhagen] 8–9, (1966–67), 243–258; and and D. Lathrap, "The antiquity and importance of long distance trade relationships in the moist tropics of precolumbian South America," *World Archaeology* 5 170–186, Myers has taken up the subject in "Redes tempranas de intercambio en la Hoya amazónica," *Amazonia Peruana* IV:8 61–76. L. Román and A. Zarzar, *Relaciones intertribales en el Bajo Urubamba y Alto Ucayali* (Lima, Peru, 1983) have treated the networks of the Ucayali and Urubamba. See A. Porro, "Os Solimões ou Jurimaguas: território, migrações e comércio intertribal," *Revista do Museu Paulista* 29 (1983–84), 23–38, and "Mercaderia e rotas de comércio intertribal na Amazonia," *Revista do Museu Paulista* 30 (1985), 7–12, for documented trade routes and relations in the middle Amazon Valley. E. Reeve, "Regional interaction in the western Amazon: The early colonial encounter and the Jesuit years: 1538–1767," *Ethnohistory* 41:1 (1994), 106–138, has dealt with the transformation of trade circuits in the upper Amazon in the colonial period. Neil Whitehead's works, "The Mazaruni pectoral: A golden artifact discovered in Guyana and the historical sources concerning native metallurgy in the Caribbean, Orinoco and Northern Amazonia," *Archaeology and Anthropology* 7 (1990), 19–38, and "The ancient Amerindian polities of the Amazon, the Orinoco, and the Atlantic coast," in A. Roosevelt (ed.), *Amazonia Indians, from Prehistory to the Present* (Tucson and London, 1994), 33–53, though focusing on the Guyana-Orinoco region, are wide-ranging and rich in theoretical insight.

The question of demographic patterns in the western Amazon is approached at a general level by Sweet (1974); M. Denevan, "The aboriginal population of Amazonia," in M. Denevan (ed.), *The Native Population of the Americas in 1942* (Madison, Wis., 1976), 205–234; W. Grohs, *Los Indios del Alto Amazonas del siglo XVI a XVIII* (Bonn, 1974); and T. Myers, "El efecto de las pestes sobre las poblaciones de la Amazonia Alta," *Amazonia Peruana* 15 (1988), 61–81. Also very useful for comparative purposes are J. Ortiz de la Tabla, "La población ecuatoriana en el siglo XVI: fuentes y calculos," in S. Moreno Yañez (ed.), *Memorias del primer simposio europeo sobre antropología del Ecuador* (Quito, 1985), and L. Newson's studies, "Old World epidemics in early colonial Ecuador," in N. D. Cook and W. G. Lovell (eds.), *Secret Judgments of God: Old World Disease in Colonial Spanish America* (Norman, Ok., 1992), and *Life and Death in Early Colonial Ecuador* (Norman, Ok., 1995). U. Oberem, *Los Quijos: Historia de la transculturación de un grupo indígena en el Oriente Ecuatoriano, 1538–1956*, 2 vols. (Madrid, 1971) presents a detailed study of the Quijos-Napo area. Taylor's "L'évolution démographique des populations indigènes du haut Amazone depuis la Conquête," in Actes du symposium "Transformacion de la Sociedad," Colloque international, *Ecuador 86* two (Paris, 1989), 267–279, presents a more synthetic one of the northern Upper Amazon, while F. Santos Granero "Epidemias y sublevaciones en el desarollo demografico de las misiones amuesha del Cerro de la Sal, siglo XVIII," *Historica*, vol. XI:1 (1987), pp. 25–53; *Etnohistoria de la Alta Amazonia. Siglos XV–XVIII* (Quito, 1992), offers a meticulously researched essay on demographic trends in the central *selva* during the seventeenth and eighteenth centuries.

The history of the Spanish conquest of the eastern lowlands is, not unexpectedly, divided along national lines. Classic modern references for southern Colombia are E. Restrepo Tirado's *Descubrimiento y Conquista de la Colombia* (Bogota, 1919); for Ecuador, see J. Rumazo González's invaluable *La región amazónica del Ecuador en el siglo XVI* (Seville, 1946); for Peru, see J. San Román's *Perfiles históricos de la Amazonia peruana* (Lima, 1975), and D. Werlich's doctoral dissertation "The conquest and settlement of the Peruvian *montaña*," University of Minnesota, 1968. For Bolivia, the standard work is still E. Finot's *Historia de la conquista del Oriente boliviano* (Buenos Aires, 1939). J. M. Cuesta's three-volume study of the upper Marañón Valley in early colonial times, *Jaen de Bracamoros,*

3 vols. (Lima, 1984), though erratic and anything but synthetic, is very rich in detail, as are Alvarado Jaramillo, *Historia de Loja y de su provincia* (Quito, 1955); *Las provincias orientales de Ecuador* (Quito, 1964); and A. Anda Aguirre, *El Adelantado Juan de Salinas Loyola y su gobernación de Yaguarongo y Bracamoros* (Quito, 1980), on the south Ecuadorian *Oriente*. Many reports and chronicles by the *conquistadores* mentioned in these works have been published. The most famous and often quoted of these are G. de Carvajal's account of his journey down the Napo and Amazon in *Relación del Nuevo Descubrimiento del Famoso Rio Grande que descubrió . . . el Capitán F. de Orellana* (Quito, 1942 [1542]), and J. de Salinas Loyola's reports of his explorations of the upper Marañón Valley in Descubrimientos, Conquistas y Poblaciones de J. de Salinas Loyola," in M. Jiménez de la Espada (ed.), *Relaciones Geográficas de Indias – Perú*, Tomo IV (1965 [1571]), 197–232. Many more have been published in Jiménez de la Espada's edition of the *Relaciones Geográficas de Indias* (1965 [1881–1897]), probably the most widely used source in ethnohistorical writing about Spanish South America. It should be stressed that, due to longstanding frontier conflicts between Colombia, Peru, Ecuador, and Bolivia, a great deal of vital archival material concerning the history of the *montaña* has been gathered and published in support of national claims. The most important of these compendiums are those of E. Vacas Galindo, *Colección de documentos sobre limítes ecuatoriano-peruanos*, 3 vols. (Quito, 1902–1903); C. Larrabure i Correa, *Colección de leyes, decretos, resoluciones y otros documentos oficiales referentes al departamento de Loreto* (Lima, 1905); Rumazo-González, *Documentos para la historia de la Audiencia de Quito*, 9 vols. (Madrid, 1948); M. Cornejo and F. Osma, *Arbitraje de limítes entre el Perú y el Ecuador*, vols. 1–4, (Madrid, 1905), and vols. 5–7 (1906); and V. M. Maurtua, *Juicio de limítes entre el Perú y Bolivia*, 12 vols. (Buenos Aires, 1906). More recently several important collections of source material have been published with the general aim of "returning their history" to the indigenous inhabitants of South America; the volumes edited by the Centro de Estudios Teológicos de la Amazonia (CETA) and the Instituto de Investigación de la Amazonia Peruana (IIAP) in the *Monumenta Amazónica* series are a case in point, as are those published in the wake of the 500th anniversary of the "encounter," by P. Ponce Leiva (*Relaciones histórico-geográficas de la Audiencia de Quito, siglos XVI–XIX*, Quito, 1992) and by A. C. Taylor and C. Landazuri, *La Conquista de la región Jívaro (1550–1650). Relación documental, estudios y compilación*, Fuentes para la historia andina (Quito, 1994).

The published literature concerning the mission era in western Amazonia is discouragingly vast; judging by output mission history is the most intensively studied field of research in the lowlands. Much of it is done by religious authors who, during the late nineteenth or early twentieth century, collated and ordered archival material left by their missionary forbears. It is accordingly apologetic in tone and must be used with due critical caution, though it is nonetheless useful for that. Concerning the Jesuit mission of Mainas, the essential sources are J. Jouanen's massive two-volume *Historia de la Compañía de Jesús en la antigua provincia de Quito, 1570–1773* (Quito, 1941–1943); and J. Chantre y Herrera, *Historia de las misiones de la Compañía de Jesús en el Marañón español (1637–1767)* (Madrid, 1901). Both authors made extensive use of P. Maroni's history, written in 1738 and first published in 1889; a careful modern edition of this work appeared in the *Monumenta Amazónica* series (1988), along with the reports of A. de Zarate (1739) and J. Magnin (1740), as did other highly important sources, notably Cristobal de Acuña's classic *Nuevo Descubrimiento del Gran Río de las Amazonas* (1641), R. Barnuevo's *Relación Apologética* (1643), and F. de Figueroa account of the beginnings of the Mainas mission (1661), under the title *Informes de Jesuitas en el Amazonas.* The *Monumenta* also includes a reissue of Father M. Uriarte's fascinating *Diario de un Misionero de Maynas* (1986 [1774]). Two indispensable ethnohistorical studies of Mainas have been published: W. Grohs, *Los Indios del Alto Amazonas del siglo XVI al XVIII* (Bonn, 1974), and A. Golob's "The upper Amazon in historical perspective," Ph.D. thesis, City University of New York, 1984. Apart from their intrinsic interest, both of these scholarly works offer an excellent guide to the many archival sources not mentioned here. The Mojos Jesuit missions have received much less attention. The main sources are D. F. Altamirano, *Historia de la misión de los Mojos* (La Paz, 1979 [1891]), and F. Eder, *Breve descripción de las reducciones de Mojos [1722]* (Cochabamba, 1985). More recent works that may be consulted are J. Chávez Suárez, *Historia de Moxos* (La Paz, 1944); A. Parejas Moreno's *Historia de Moxos y Chiquitos a fines del siglo XVIII* (La Paz, 1976), as well as his *Historia del Oriente Boliviano, siglo xvi y xvii* (Santa Cruz, 1979); W. H. Virreira's *Tribus selvícolas y misiones jesuitas y franciscanas en Bolivia* (La Paz, 1986), and Z. Lehm Ardaya's brief but interesting comparison of the Mainas and Mojos missions, "Efectos de las reduccciones jesuiticas en las poblaciones indígenas de Maynas y Mojos" in F. Santos Granero (org.), *Opresión colonial y resistencia indigena en la alta Amazonia* (Quito,

1992), pp. 135–164. This is an area much in need of further investigation, both in terms of fieldwork and of archival research; so far, the abundant source material concerning the Mojos missions has been largely neglected.

The Franciscan missions of the central *selva* of Peru are also the object of massive works; chief among these are B. Izagguirre, *Historia de las misiones franciscanas y narración de los progresos de la geografía en el Oriente del Perú, 1619–1921*, 14 vols. (Lima, 1922–1926); and J. Amich's huge *Historia de las Misiones del Convento de Santa Rosa de Ocopa* [1854] Monumenta Amazónica, (Iquitos, 1988); M. Biedma, *La Conquista Franciscana del alto Ucayali* [1685], Monumenta Amazónica (Iquitos, 1989), is another essential source. Among modern historians, R. Alvarez Lobo, *TSLA – Estudio etnohistórico del Urubamba y Alto Ucayali* (Salamanca, 1984) is valuable, as are J. F. Lehnertz, "Land of the infidels. The Franciscans in the central *selva* of Peru," Ph.D. thesis, University of Wisconsin, 1974, and A. Craig, "Franciscan exploration in the central *Montaña* of Peru," *Actas del XXXIX Congreso Internacional de los Americanistas* Four (Lima, 1972), 127–144. Main sources on the Apolobamba missions are N. Armentia, *Relación historica de las misiones franciscanas de Apolobamba, por otro nombre, Frontera de Caupolican* (La Paz, 1903–1905) and R. Cardus, *Las Misiones Franciscanas entre los Infieles de Bolivia. Descripción de su estado en 1883 y 1884* (Barcelona, 1896); Virreira, *Tribus selvícola* (1986); and Metraux "The tribes of Mato Grosso and eastern Bolivia," *Handbook of South American Indians*, vol. 3, part 2 (1948), 349–454; "Tribes of the eastern slopes of the Bolivian Andes," *ibid.* 465–506, can be consulted for a short history of these Franciscan reductions. Sources on the northern Franciscan mission (Sucumbios-Caquetá) are more plentiful: Classic works are those of G. A. Robledo, *Las misiones franciscanas en Colombia* (Bogota, 1950), and *Apuntes historicos de la provincia franciscana de Colombia* (Bogota, 1953); F. M. Compte, *Varones Ilustres de la Orden Seráfica en el Ecuador* (Quito, 1885); Fr. Monclar and B. Carnet del Mar, *Relaciones interesantes y datos historicos sobre las misiones católicas del Caquetá y del Putamayo desde el año 1632 hasta el presente* (Bogota, 1924); and A. Vivanco, "Informe de los padres franciscanos de la región del Oriente," *Boletín de la Academia Nacional de la Historia* (Quito, 1941), 78–105. More recent studies dealing partially with this mission area are I. Bellier, *Los Mai Huna Tukano occidentales. Guia etnográfica de la Alta Amazonia* vol. 1 (Quito, 1994), 1–179; H. Llanos Vargas and R. Pineda Camacho, *Etnohistoria del Gran Caquetá: siglos XVI–XVIII* (Bogota, 1982); and R. Pineda Camacho and B. Alzate Angel (eds.), *Los meandros de la historia en Amazonia* (Quito, 1990).

Most of the ethnohistorical research on specific groups of the *montaña* has until very recently been conducted by anthropologists, sometimes with scant training in critical source reading. Monographical works on these cultures usually include a more or less detailed historical chapter, though often "history" in this context means postcontact history exclusively, particularly so when dealing with "traditional" cultures. Thus readers interested in the past of any given indigenous society or tribal set should turn to the standard ethnographies devoted to them. These are too numerous to list here, but it is perhaps useful to signal a few recent books that sucessfully combine an informed historical and ethnographic approach. M. Brown and E. Fernández present a riveting study of the "war of shadows" between guerilla movements, government forces, and indigenous societies in Campa territory in *War of Shadows: The Struggle for Utopia in the Peruvian Amazon* (Berkeley, 1992). P. Gow's subtle study of the *nativos* of the Urubamba, *Of Mixed Blood: Kinship and History in the Peruvian Amazon* (Oxford, 1991); N. Whitten's classic *Sacha Runa* (Urbana, Ill., 1976); B. Muratorio's *The Life and Times of Grandfather Alonso: Culture and History on the Upper Amazon* (New Brunswick, 1991), a vivid and highly readable account of historical memory among the Napo Quichua; F. Santos Granero's study of Amuesha ethics and theories of knowledge in *The Power of Love: The Moral Use of Knowledge Amongst the Amuesha of Central Peru*, London School of Economics, Monographs on Social Anthropology (London, 1991); and O. A. Aguëro, *El milenio en la amazonia. Mito-utopia tupi-cocama, o la subversión del orden simbólico* (Quito, 1994), a description of a millenarist cult among contemporary Tupi-Cocama groups are all obvious choices. Mention should also be made of the *Guia Etnografica de la Alta Amazonia* series. This ambitious editorial project, directed by F. Barclay and the indefatigable F. Santos Granero, aims at producing standardized, high-quality monographs on Indian groups of the *montaña* as defined here, as well as some synoptic regional or "ethnic" ones. So far two volumes have appeared: one on the societies of the lower Napo and middle Amazon (Mai Huna, Tikuna, Yagua) (1994), the other on the interfluve Pano (Matses, Uni, Yaminahua) (1994). A dozen more are in preparation. All these studies offer short but reliable historical synopses.

Readers particularly interested in the postcolonial tribal formations or *manso* category of Indians may turn to the already cited books on the

Urubamba Piro by P. Gow and on the Canelos Quichua by N. Whitten; other useful studies are those of Oberem on the "Quijos" (1971); F. Scazzochio's dissertation on the Lamistas, "Ethnicity and boundary maintenance among Peruvian forest Quichua," Ph.D. thesis, Cambridge University, 1979; M. E. Reeve on the Curaray Quichua, "Identity as process: The meaning of Runapura for Quichua speakers of the Curaray River, Eastern Ecuador," Ph.D. thesis, University of Illinois, 1985; and J. W. Hudelson, *La cultura quichua de transición. Su expansión y desarrollo en el Alto Amazonas* (Quito, 1988) on the Loreto Quichua. A. Fuentes, *Porque las piedras no mueren. Historia, sociedad y ritos de los Chayahuita del Alto Amazonas* (Lima, 1988) on the Chayavita, and A. Stocks, *Los Nativos invisibles. Notas sobre la historia y realidad actual de los Cocamilla del río Huallaga* (Lima, 1981) on the "invisible" Cocamilla of the lower Ucayali are equally interesting.

The issue of styles of historicity and forms of historical consciousness in these cultures is dealt with more particularly in the writings of P. Gow, *Of Mixed Blood* (1991), and his "Gringos and wild Indians. Images of history in western Amazonian cultures," *L'Homme* 33:126–128 (1993), 327–348; and "River people: Shamanism and history in western Amazonia," in C. Humphrey and N. Thomas (eds.,) *Shamanism, History and the State* (Ann Arbor, Mich., 1993). Also important are N. Whitten, *Sicuanga Runa* (Urbana, Ill., 1988); "Commentary: Historical and mythic evocations of chthonic power in South America," in J. Hill (ed.), *Rethinking History* (Urbana: University of Illinois Press, 1988), 282–306; and the aforementioned work of E. Reeve, B. Muratorio, and J. M. Mercier, *Nosotros los Napo Runas. Mitos e Historia* (Iquitos, 1979). Concerning the more "traditional" cultures, this topic is still little explored. The so-called "Inka stories" of the Shipibo-Conibo have been analyzed by Roe (1988) and in Lathrap, Gebhart-Sayer, and Mester (1985). Campa narratives have been studied by E. Fernández in *Para que nuestra historia no se pierda: testimonio de los Asháninca y Nomatsiguenga sobre la colonización* (Lima, 1986); M. Brown and E. Fernández in *The War of Shadows* (1992); and F. M. Renard-Casevitz, "Historia Kampa, memoria ashaninka," in M. Carneiro da Cunha (ed.), *Historia dos Indios no Brasil* (São Paulo, 1992), 197–212, who has also written a subtle interpretation of Matsiguenga myths dealing with relations to foreigners in *Le Banquet Masqué. Une mythologie de l'Etranger* (Paris, 1991). Jívaroan ways of conceptualizing history have been studied in terms of discourse analysis by J. Hendricks, "Manipulating time in an Amazonian society: Genre and event among the Shuar," in E. Basso (ed.), *Native Latin American Cultures Through Their Discourse* (Bloomington, In., 1990), 11–28; and *To Drink of Death. The Narrative of a Shuar Warrior* (Tucson, 1993), while A. C. Taylor has focused on the relation between techniques of forgetting the past and the production of autobiographical narrative in "Remembering to forget: Mourning, memory and identity among the Jívaro," *Man* 28:4 (1993), 1–26. There is a surge of interest currently in this field of study, and more detailed works on native styles of historicity – ethnohistory proper – will undoubtedly begin to appear in the near future.

18

WARFARE, REORGANIZATION, AND READAPTATION AT THE MARGINS OF SPANISH RULE – THE CHACO AND PARAGUAY (1573–1882)

JAMES SCHOFIELD SAEGER

The people of the Gran Chaco and those of the Paraná Plateau were culturally very different but for most of three centuries were tied together by the mutual hostility of the dominant peoples of each area. These Native American groups and their native and European allies and dependents fought with each other periodically, and warfare was the normal relationship between these two culture regions in the late sixteenth century. This chapter looks at the people of the Chaco in their aboriginal cultural state, as they got the artifacts that enabled them to make the changes that revolutionized their lives, as they chose missions when the culture of the mounted warrior no longer served their needs, and as they returned to the Chaco when the mission system fell into ruins. It also looks at the culture of the Guaraní as they adapted to the early Spanish settlers' demands for labor and women, as they moved into nucleated settlements that Europeans helped them to build – including Franciscan reductions, *encomienda* towns, and the Jesuit missions. It finally traces developments after the departure of the Jesuits and after independence.

THE PEOPLES OF THE CHACO

A flat alluvial plain sloping from west to east, the Chaco lies north of the Río Salado between the Río Paraná-Río Paraguay system to the east, the foothills of the Andes to the west, and the current Paraguayan-Bolivian border. In the 1500s nonsedentary, band-level peoples speaking Guaycuruan languages dominated much of the Chaco. The peoples whose descendants would later be known as the Abipon, Mocoví, Toba, and Pilagás inhabited the plains and scrub forests of the southern Chaco, while the ancestors of the Mbayá toured the northern Chaco above the

Río Pilcomayo. They were first known to their Spanish and Guaraní enemies by a variety of names such as Mepenes or Frentones and Guaycurú, which often reflected their appearance or style of dwelling. In the southeastern Chaco, Abipon peoples developed three major subdivisions by the 1700s that corresponded to bands: plains dwellers, forest dwellers, and a riverain people, once separate, who identified themselves as the Abipon after conquest. The Mocoví at contact lived along the western Río Bermejo, although some bands migrated eastward toward Santa Fe (Argentina) in the early 1700s. The Toba, often allied with the Mocoví, recognized three major subdivisions in the seventeenth century. The western Toba lived near the present border between eastern Paraguay and Bolivia; central Toba peoples circulated between the central Río Bermejo and the Pilcomayo near the Río Paraguay, where the Toba and Abipon, customary enemies, fought over eastern lands.

North of the Pilcomayo, the Mbayá lived adjacent to the civil province of Paraguay from about C.E. 1500 to the 1670s, when many bands spread across the Río Paraguay into northern Paraguay and the southern Mato Grosso, taking over an area in which they had conducted profitable raids when Jesuits and Guaraní founded missions in Itatín (see Map 18.1). By the 1760s they lived in bands that dominated, fought, and cooperated with each other; they conducted periodic raids on neighbors, including the Guaná (Chané) and the Guaraní. Guaycuruan peoples in the post-contact period organized their societies into three social classes: chiefs, commoners, and servants and slaves.

Another important Chaco group were the sedentary Guaná (Chané) of the northern Chaco. They were superior agriculturalists, the only Arawakian group in the Chaco; Andean influence on their culture was pronounced. In the southwestern Chaco lived the semisedentary Vilelas, subdivided into bands that Spaniards called Chunupíes, Pasaínes, Uacas, and Atalalas. Nearby lived the Tonocoté-speaking Lules, labeled Isistines, Toquistines, Oristines, and Tonocotés, and Matarás by Spaniards. Geographically Chaco peoples, they were culturally closer to Andean ways than to Chaco traditions, which resembled those of *pampas* groups. The Maskoy (Machicui) lived in the northeastern Chaco near the Río Confuso and the Rio Negro and were primarily cultivators, but they also hunted. After the European invasion and unlike the Guaycuruans, they rejected the horse culture, and they changed their lifeways less than the Guaycuruans. Along the Río Pilcomayo lived a number of Mataco-speaking groups, including the Chulupí, Chorotis, and Chorotismanjui.

Also scattered about the Chaco were the Mascoian Lengua-Enimagás

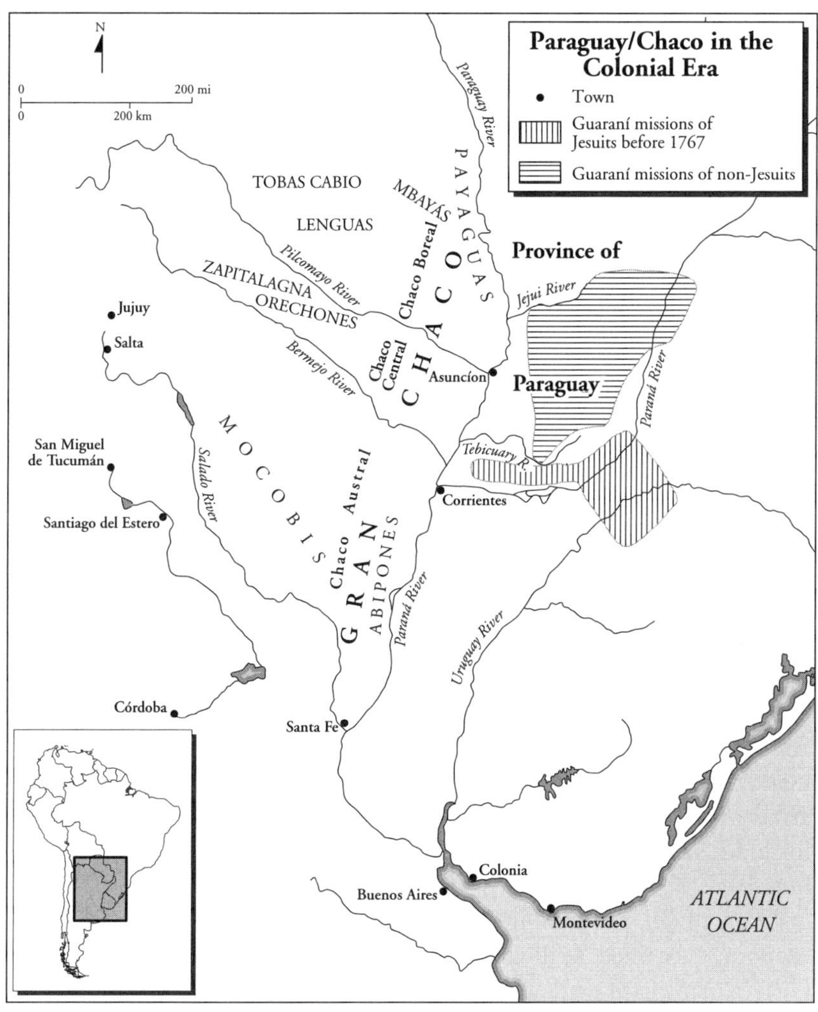

Map 18.1

and Mataco-Mataguayo peoples, often victims of Guaycuruan hostilities. Lenguas, who developed the horse culture, were Mascoians of the eastern Chaco who often fought the Guaycuruans. Most of the non-Guaycurú Chaco peoples were semisedentary horticulturalists who lived beyond Spanish authority but not beyond Spanish influence. After the punitive expedition in 1710 of the governor of Tucumán, Estebán Urizar y Arespacochaga, some sedentary groups accepted Spanish missions. The first reduction, San Esteban de Miraflores for Lules, was established in Tucumán in 1711.

The dominant groups in the Chaco were Guaycuruans, who acquired iron weapons and tools and horses in the late 1500s by barter and raids. "The adoption of the horse meant a profound sociocultural change, but was closely tied to the way of life of the colonial creole environment."[1] Men's work before and after horses revolved around hunting. Practiced individually and collectively with bows and arrows, garrotes, lances, and clubs, the search for game was the most honored calling in Guaycuruan society. It bestowed prestige and fed families. Men hunted deer, nutria, wild cats, and other large animals. After consuming these beasts, the conquerors won their personality traits. Raids, war, and hunting connected the Guaycuruans to the supernatural world, especially to those spirits who owned animals. Fishing was usually a supplemental activity. Warfare supported the economy, as Guaycuruan bands raided each other, the Guaraní, and later Spaniards for goods and captives for barter and service. Guaycuruan religion sanctioned the complementary skills of warfare and hunting. It glorified predatory military behavior, violent economic acquisition, and extreme ethnocentrism.

The horse revolutionized Guaycuruan lives after 1600. Horses extended their military reach, made their escape following a raid more secure, and broadened the area through which they could hunt. The Guaycuruans increasingly sought European artifacts, raided Spaniards, and traded with them for iron. The Guaycuruans began to hunt for a market. New technologies of European origin, including iron knives and arrow and lance points, allowed mounted Chaco peoples to harvest game for hides and skins in larger quantities. Most Guaycuruans hunted from horseback, although the Tobas dismounted to stalk animals.

From about 1600 to the 1740s, the now barter-based Guaycuruan economy sustained itself increasingly by the capture of livestock. The Guaycuruans used cattle and horses to eat, ride, and sell to Spaniards on the Chaco periphery, from Asunción and Santa Fe in the east to Salta in the west. In the seventeenth century vast herds of unattended cattle roamed the southern Chaco and adjacent Spanish areas like Santa Fe, Corrientes, and Santiago del Estero; but Spaniards increasingly protected livestock after 1700. Private hereditary property accompanied cattle to the Guaycuruan world. Some groups, like the Mbayá, began to raise sheep for wool. Most of the Guaycuruans rejected domesticating cattle

[1] Branislava Susnik, *Los aborígenes del Paraguay*, III/1: *Etnohistoria de los chaqueños, 1650–1910* (Asunción, 1981), p. 9.

but pursued them as large game, selling most, however, to Spaniards. In contrast to their use of cattle, all Chaco Guaycuruans practiced horse husbandry and often exchanged horses for Spanish goods. Guaycuruan commerce with Spaniards included captives, skins, and honey brought from the Chaco to pay for knives, hatchets, raw iron, points, fishhooks, and clothing.

Guaycuruan weapons and tools after 1600 became more formidable with iron points and edges. Because iron was scarce and because it rusted, however, most weapons were still of wood and bone, supplemented by stone weapons acquired by trade from beyond the stoneless Chaco. The Guaycuruans adapted European technologies to exploit horses and cattle; they copied Spanish saddles, bridles, ropes, and hobbles using local materials.

Despite the towering social prestige of the male-dominated activity of hunting large game, Guaycuruan women provided much food. They located, harvested, and prepared plant foods, especially the palm and the *algarroba* (carob tree); both yielded meat and flour. Women manufactured household utensils from gourds and other plants, creating pots, net bags, and clothing. Like hunting, gleaning plant foods had religious significance; it reflected the activities of supernatural powers. Women customarily cooked vegetable foods, rabbits, and other small game taken by themselves and children, and the large animals and – after 1600 – the beef that men provided. Women also wove rush reed mats for the portable houses in which they slept. After acquiring sheep in the 1600s, Mbayá women spun and wove wool on looms.

Postcontact warfare grew more lethal as the Guaycuruans fought each other for economic, personal, and religious reasons. They attacked sedentary Native American groups like the Guaraní and Spanish cities bordering the Chaco periphery, including Asunción, Santa Fe, Salta, and the Guaraní-Jesuit missions. The full force of Guaycuruan military resistance fell on Spanish and hispanized Native American communities between 1630 and 1730. Toba and Mocoví attacks pushed Spaniards from the city of Concepción del Bermejo, founded by Spanish settlers and local Matará in 1585. The Mbayá in the 1680s pushed the Paraguayan frontier to the south, causing the province to contract.

Guaycuruan–Spanish hostilities increased steadily into the 1730s when the Toba, Mocoví, and Abipon threatened Santa Fe, Salta, and Córdoba. Then, because of Spanish counterattacks and internal Guaycuruan conflicts, the intensity of warfare declined; but old animosities remained. With the development of missions after the 1740s, Guaycuruan violence took new forms, as the participation of Toba from the mission of San Ignacio de Ledesma in the anti-Spanish uprising of castes in Jujuy in 1781 demonstrated. The mission Guaycuruans fought rivals from other missions and often dominated enemies not supported by a mission culture and the subsidies that accompanied it.

Postcontact ecological changes ultimately impoverished Chaco peoples, as their use of knives and hatchets between 1541 and the 1740s changed the face of the land. Now more productive workers with iron implements devastated palm groves and stands of *algarroba*, which was also exploited by Spaniards because it yielded wood for Spanish furniture.

A distinctive feature of Chaco life was Mbayá subjugation of their neighbors, the Guaná (Chané). By the 1500s the interdependency between the sedentary Guaná and the nonsedentary Mbayá flourished. Originating in Mbayá conquest, marriages of Mbayá males and Guaná females of the *cacique* classes cemented the connection. The Guaná grew enough corn, beans, manioc, and sweet potatoes for themselves and for tribute to the Mbayá. They also cultivated cotton and tobacco for use and barter. The Guaná, who outnumbered the Mbayá, failed to copy rigorously Guaycuruan practices of abortion and infanticide; but Guaná couples customarily aimed for two sons and a daughter, producing a scarcity of Guaná females. Although the Guaná acquired horses, most rejected the move from cultivation to an equestrian society. Some bands, though, after 1800, when pressure from two European empires intensified other stresses, borrowed aggressive ways from the Mbayá. The Guaná joined missions in the 1760s and later for food and security. After the Jesuits left in 1767, the church and governments at all levels withheld funds necessary to sustain reductions for those Guaná in missions. By the 1790s Guaná peoples worked for Paraguayans as cowboys, laborers, and drovers but independently competed, often hostilely, with Creole and mestizo Paraguayans for land. In the nineteenth century many Guaná individually joined the Guaraní-speaking rural population of Paraguay.

When Europeans invaded the Plata region, the banks of the Río Paraguay were dominated by the Payaguá (or Evueví), Guaycuruan peoples whose habitat and economic patterns differed from the Chaco Guaycuruans. In the colonial period the Payaguá, who were divided into northern and southern bands, lived on islands in the Río Paraguay and along the west bank of the river between Cuiabá, Brazil and Corrientes,

Argentina. They traveled great distances by canoe. Living from fishing and gathering wild vegetable foods along the river, they also raided Guaraní settlements for harvested crop foods. Paddling swift large and small canoes, the Payaguá struck the Guaraní with lightning rapidity, taking food and women valued for their labor and to ransom. In the early 1500s the Payaguá were so powerful that Guaraní fear of them caused the Guaraní alliance with Spaniards in the 1540s. Until the 1750s Payaguá bands conducted waterborne guerilla warfare against shipping from Paraguay and the Jesuit missions. The Payaguá suffered when Spaniards massacred or captured them for the *encomiendas*, missions, or, occasionally, illegal but officially ignored chattel slavery. Intermittently trading with Spaniards and raiding Spanish shipping, the Payaguá, who numbered about 6,000 in 1600, secured knives, fishhooks, and needles but mostly remained traditional. The Payaguá supplied Spaniards with fish and often acted as brokers between hispanic communities and Chaco peoples, transmitting European artifacts beyond European settlement. In the eighteenth century Payaguá bands interdicted communication between Cuiabá and the Brazilian coastal towns. Payaguá forces won stunning victories in 1725, 1730, and 1739, when they annihilated large expeditions heading for the mines. They bartered profits to Paraguayans for tools, because gold, a "dirty metal," was scorned.

After the 1730s the Payaguá began moving to the hispanic world but rejected its ideological rationales, especially Christianity. Payaguá men of the settlement living at Asunción in the 1790s furnished the provincial capital with fish and worked for wages. Until the 1840s they also policed the river and guided travelers for cash, as Payaguá women sold pottery manufactures to Paraguayans. Other Payaguá in these years, though, toured the northern Río Paraguay and tributaries beyond the reach of Paraguayan influence and continued hostilities against Paraguayans into the 1850s.

In the first two centuries after contact, the Payaguá became more dependent on Europeans even when remaining hostile. Later the Payaguá in Asunción rejected Catholicism, although a few tolerated baptisms for children. Males in the 1800s often succumbed to alcohol and impotence; females whom they thus cut adrift then bore mestizo children of Paraguayan fathers. One obstacle to Payaguá survival was continued family limitation by abortion. Although epidemic diseases also took their toll, the visitations of the 1700s were not virgin soil epidemics and thus had limited lethality. In 1865 Payaguá society could still muster 500 soldiers for the War of the Triple Alliance, but most succumbed in the conflict. The last Payaguá, a woman, died in Asunción in 1942; but in the 1960s descendants of the Payaguá lived in the Chacarita riverbank slum of Asunción, where the name "Payaguá" was still an insult.

As the Payaguá threat to Spanish society declined, so did hostility from the mounted Guaycuruans. Guaycuruan aggression peaked in the 1730s, when southern Guaycuruans drained the Córdoba region of cattle, took captives, and executed hispanized persons. The Abipon and Mocoví halted the commerce of Santa Fe in 1732 and threatened the city's existence. The Mocoví, probably allied with Tobas, laid siege to Salta in January 1735, killing 100 people, capturing 200 more, and disrupting the city's public life for the next year. But these were the last great military triumphs of the southern Guaycuruans and the power of their Guaycuruan arms receded.

Several factors eroded Guaycuru strength and tempted culturally innovative bands to ask Spaniards for missions. One was the loss of females to Spanish raiders in the years of attrition warfare with Spanish society. Another was the increasing penetration of the Chaco by Spanish ranchers, lumber interests, and the missions of Lules and Vilelas. These incursions restricted Guaycuruan autonomy and intensified competition for resources and conflict among bands. The establishment of Spanish ranches with cowboys to guard livestock made the Guaycuruan cattle hunt more dangerous. In the 1730s serious epidemics spread from white to native societies, unbalancing further native life, and intensifying the harmful effects of iron tools, the grazing of domestic animals, and overhunting on the Chaco environment.

In the 1740s Mocoví and Abipon bands accepted offers of missions from Jesuits and civil officials in Santa Fe. The Mocoví, led by Ariacaiquin, Citaalin, and Aletin, and the Abipon, whose chief was Ychamenraiquin, moved into the San Javier and San Jerónimo reductions. By 1800 other Guaycuruans had settled at least seventeen more missions in Santa Fe, Corrientes, Paraguay, and Tucumán. The Guaycuruans were following the Lules, Vilelas, Lengua-Cochaboth, and Machikuy, who had earlier accepted missions. Most Chaco missions lasted until 1810, although a number disappeared a few years after their establishment. Missions in the Chaco needed subventions of cattle and tools, Spanish forbearance, and favorable locations. Guaycuruan missions like San Jéronimo, San Javier, and San Ignacio de Tobas, connected to Santa Fe and Jujuy, with generous endowments usually survived and grew. Other missions, like Timbó for the Abipon, whose people Paraguayans asked to acculturate immediately after the Jesuits departed and to forego further subventions, were short-lived; the people simply withdrew from Spanish influence. Those missions that got funds, food, a little peace, and time enough to develop lasted to the end of the colonial period, although finite Spanish resources constrained even the most stable missions in the Chaco. Spanish society could neither grant all Guaycuruan requests for missions nor even fund adequately each reduction established.

In missions, changes in Guaycuruan life, underway since contact, quickened. Old skills enabled men to become cowboys, artisans, and military auxiliaries. New skills sustained missions and then enabled men to drift into the Spanish economy. Women also used old economic skills in new ways, now spinning and weaving blankets and ponchos for the Spanish market. Women and later even men in missions practiced sedentary agriculture, growing corn, beans, and other crops. Mission Guaycuruans got surer access to food and to the European tools on which they now depended. All missions needed cattle for subsistence and trade. Mission residents, however, continued to gather *algarroba* and palm and to hunt wild and branded animals. Men in missions retained a military capability, which they employed against enemies from other missions and other adversaries in the Chaco.

After 1810 the collapse of colonial institutions interrupted the mission experiment. Some Guaycuruans drifted to the hispanic world in individual and small groups, a process that first began in the seventeenth century. The Abipon from Santa Fe joined the armies of Artigas, just as the Abipon from Santiago del Estero had fought against the English in 1806. Families of Guaycuruan soldiers away at war often dispersed to grow crops and raise cattle in family units. Some went to Argentine ranches and farms and stayed. Many surviving Abipon and Mocoví regrouped and joined missions established in Santa Fe by Italian Franciscans in the 1850s.

In northern Paraguay and the Mato Grosso after independence, the Mbayá split between Portuguese and Spanish jurisdictions. Their fathers and grandfathers had retained an offensive capability for a generation or two longer than the southern Guaycuruans. "They became a major peril to the settlers and travellers in Cuiabá and Mato Grosso during the 1730's."[2] Bands from Brazil raided Paraguay and suffered bloody reprisals by the Francia government, which destroyed palm groves on which many

[2] C. R. Boxer, *The Golden Age of Brazil, 1695–1750: Growing Pains of a Colonial Society* (Berkeley and Los Angeles, 1962 [paperback ed. 1975]), p. 266.

Mbayá still depended for food. The Mbayá within the Spanish orbit, living on the outskirts of Concepción, merged with the Guaraní-speaking proletariat of northern Paraguay. A few Mbayá in Brazil, called Caduveos, retained their identity into the twentieth century, when they were contacted by anthropologists D'Arcy Ribeiro, Kalervo Oberg, and Claude Levi-Strauss. Most Toba retreated even farther from Spanish power, remaining politically independent until the Argentine conquest of the Chaco in the 1870s and 1880s. These expeditions subdued, incorporated, unhorsed, and subjugated the resisting Toba and Mocoví, many of whom were living in bands of 50 to 60 families. By now many were biological mestizos, and most were significantly hispanized, the outcome of centuries of contact.

GUARANÍ SOCIETY

At contact with Europeans, the Guaraní culture was centered on the Paraná Plateau, rising from 1,000 to 2,000 feet above sea level and running from eastern Paraguay into the Brazilian states of Río Grande do Sul and Mato Grosso and into the mission province of Argentina. Some Guaraní also lived in the islands of the delta of the Río de la Plata. Most of the terrain on the Paraná Plateau is of alternating plains and hills. It is land of fertile soils, grasslands, and both evergreen and deciduous forests of such trees as pines, cedars, and palms.

Estimates of the preinvasion Guaraní population vary widely. Julian H. Steward estimates, for example, that in the 1520s, 200,000 Avá-Guaraní lived in modern Paraguay, Argentina, and Brazil.[3] At the other extreme, Branislava Susnik concludes that by 1640, 400,000 Guaraní still lived in the region of the civil province of Paraguay,[4] implying a precontact figure of 2 million or more of these horticulturalists who lived in the upper Plata region and southern Brazil. Some Guaraní traveled to the foothills of the Andes; a portion, whom Spaniards called Chiriguano, stayed, as the Guaraní migration to eastern Bolivia in search of a promised land lasted from the 1400s into the 1550s.

Within the northern Plata region itself, Guaraní moved to new lands

[3] Julian H. Steward, "The native population of South America," *Handbook of South American Indians*, 7 vols., ed. by Julian H. Steward (Washington, D.C., 1946–1959), V, p. 662.

[4] *El Rol de los indígenas en la formacíon y en la vivencia del Paraguay*, 2 vols. (Asunción, 1982–1983), I, p. 181.

frequently because of swidden agriculture. To sustain their garden plots of maize, bitter manioc, squashes, and sweet potatoes, they found new locations every 2 or 3 years. All Guaraní supplemented cultivation with hunting, and where Payaguá allowed them access to rivers, as with the Carios of central Paraguay, fishing.

Guaraní lived communally in large, thatched dwellings of about 300 people, and villages contained from one to eight such units. The basic social unit was the patrilineal extended family, the *tey'ĩ*, about 600 persons, headed by a chief whose noncoercive influence depended on oratory and prestige. Networks of these extended families determined the fourteen geographically defined Guaraní political units at contact. Some chiefs led several villages, but ethnocentric ideologies made such alliances difficult. Chiefs often had fifteen to thirty wives, whose male relatives then supported him politically. Religion was vital to the Guaraní. Endowed with magical powers, their shamans guided people toward a brilliant paradise, a "land without evil," and they controlled rain and illness.

Relations between Spanish males, whom the Guaraní first saw in the 1520s, and Guaraní females set the pattern for a permanent foundation. About 400 male Spaniards came to Paraguay in 1537, bringing iron tools – especially hatchets and knives, firearms, and horses. The Guaraní initially saw these European introductions as magical, but the political role they assigned Spaniards was practical. The Guaraní living near Asunción, first Carios then Tobatines, established a reciprocal relationship with Spaniards because of mutual need. Spaniards desired food and women and wanted Guaraní military auxiliaries and porters for the trans-Chaco journey to the Andes, where they hoped to find silver. Continuing the migration that transformed the Guaraní into Chiriguano, thousands of Guaraní joined Spanish expeditions to the Andes in the 1540s, and many refused to return afterward to their villages, causing a crisis in Guaraní life. The Guaraní employed Spanish allies against such traditional enemies as the Payaguá along the Río Paraguay and the pedestrian Guaycuruan in the Chaco. Guaraní enemies quickly became Spanish enemies, and allied forces like the expedition of several thousand Guaraní and two hundred Spaniards under Cabeza de Vaca in 1542 aimed to annihilate the southern Mbayá.

After the military alliance, the Guaraní next wanted iron tools to replace stone and bone implements. Hand-held iron hatchets revolutionized Guaraní work habits, reducing the time needed to clear trees for garden plots and rendering obsolete old cooperative work habits. Males could now fell giant trees individually or in small groups.

Spanish–Guaraní exchanges were built on Guaraní matrilocality, reciprocal favors, and marriage patterns. Matrilocality had caused families to value daughters, who attracted sons-in-law over sons, who left home to join distant wives. "Polygamy was the constitutional law of early Paraguay, which soon deserved the title of Mohammed's Paradise," writes a Paraguayan historian,[5] reflecting a sixteenth-century cleric's criticism of the first settlers. This characterizes an erroneous consensus about the abundance of women available to the Spanish founders of the Paraguayan colony. In the 1530s and 1540s, about six Guaraní women clustered about each Spaniard, not the mythical hundreds of female attendants. As wives, concubines, mothers, and domestics, Guaraní women were also conduits for exchanges between the two cultures of early Paraguay.

The Guaraní labored with their Spanish kin as new iron tools improved productivity and Spanish power overawed enemies. After a few years, however, the Guaraní discovered that Spaniards no longer reciprocated, as aboriginal traditions required. The Guaraní were considered not equal but inferior to Europeans. So the Guaraní stopped working. Their resistance escalated into uncoordinated, abortive rebellions in 1539, 1542 or 1543, 1546, and several between 1556 and 1580. In 1546 Guaraní males protested their loss of women to the Spaniards and revealed their dislike of infant mestizos, later the basis of ethnic Paraguayans. The mestizo preference for the world of their Spanish fathers was an unforgivable insult. The absence of children in Guaraní villages had disrupted normal patterns. Insufficient children remained to work, support the kinship system, and carry on traditional life. "The uprising of Oberá in the Guarambaré region in 1579 . . . can be considered as a paradigm of the many Guaraní liberation movements."[6] Known mainly through the poem of Archdeacon Martín Barco de Centenera,'[7] who served on the punitive expedition to suppress Guayracá, heir to the legacy of resistance, Oberá (also written as Overa) was a baptized Guaraní. He had experienced the oppression of the *encomienda*, and he resisted. Pulling Christian doctrine into the framework of Guaraní oratory, Oberá became a leader of Guaraní liberation. "He called himself a true son of God, born

[5] Efraím Cardozo, *El Paraguay colonial: las raíces de la nacionalidad* (Buenos Aires-Asunción, 1959), p. 64.

[6] Bartomeu Melià, *El Guarani conquistado y reducido: ensayos de etnohistoria* (Asunción, 1986), p, 35.

[7] *Argentina y conquista del Río de la Plata* (Lisbon, 1602); see especially Canto XX.

of a virgin, incarnated for the liberation of his people."[8] He named his son Guyraro as his pope, but his movement failed.

To overcome Guaraní protests, Spaniards in the 1540s at random took the laborers that they needed from nearby villages, an unpredictable demand that further devastated Guaraní communities. Thus Domingo Martínez de Irala designed the Paraguayan *encomienda* in 1556 to regulate the labor supply for conquerors and to lighten the oppression of the Guaraní. He awarded Guaraní and chiefs (now *caciques*), joined together by extended family (*tey'i*) or village (*teko'a*), to 300 Spaniards. These *encomiendas* firmly established the master–servant relationship characteristic of later Spanish–Guaraní relations. It coincided with the demographic decline of the Guaraní and their replacement by mestizos. Guaraní hostility to *encomiendas* caused some to flee from areas under Spanish control to peripheral regions.

Two substantially different versions of the Paraguayan *encomienda* emerged, the *encomienda mitaria* and the *encomienda originaria*. For the *mitaria* about 27,000 Guaraní families (between 116,000 and 162,000 persons) in central Paraguay were awarded initially in unequal lots to some 300 Spaniards. In Guairá, now in the Brazilian state of Paraná, *mitarios* in *encomiendas* larger than those of the cordillera around Asunción worked mostly in the dangerous *yerbales*, exploiting the shrub *Ilex Paraguayensis* for its leaves to make tea. They also grew sugar and cotton. In the absence of profitable Paraguayan commodities to pay tribute, the key to the *mitario* system in Paraguay and Guairá was the agricultural labor on estates and in *yerbales* that adult Guaraní males provided to their *encomendero*. Regulations theoretically limited this obligation to 2–3 months a year but also required the Guaranís to perform communal labor for their villages. They supported themselves and provided a surplus to feed and clothe the political and religious leaders appointed by the Spaniards. First the *caciques*, as the chiefs became known, received batons and the title "Don" to symbolize their elevated status, as Spanish authority imposed a hierarchy among the heretofore relatively egalitarian Guaraní. *Caciques*, Guaraní *corregidores*, and municipal officials were exempt from manual labor in *encomienda* and communal chores, although managerial skills and prestige coordinated the work.

Males exempt from *mita* and community obligations included *caciques*, artisans, *cabildo* officials, and males over fifty, although few lived

[8] Melià, *El Guaraní*, p. 37.

much beyond that age. Many females, also theoretically exempt from *mita* obligations, nevertheless worked on *encomenderos*' estates as spinners and domestic servants.

Francisco de Alfaro of the *audiencia* of Charcas came to Paraguay in 1610–1612 to reform *encomendero* abuses. He ordered the abolition of the *encomienda originaria*, separation of *originarios* from their *encomenderos*, and the Indians' relocation into segregated Indian towns. He also reduced the amount of *mita* labor that the Guaranís owed *encomenderos*, and he insisted on cash payment for labor instead of what he called "this tyrannical personal service."[9] Paraguayan *encomenderos* protested his labor policy, and surprisingly the Guaraní too opposed Alfaro's reform measures. Guaraní spokesmen still could think of the *encomienda* as reciprocity, an acceptable institution. *Mitarios* refused to work for wages, because such employment was servitude, not reciprocal exchange. In any event wages were impractical in a region without a money economy. Periodic revolts, such as that of the *encomienda* town of Arecayá in 1660, though, showed that many Guaraní wished to end Spanish exploitation, although Guaraní officials found ways to profit from the system. Other Guaraní became accustomed to colonial life and favored increasing hispanization.

Like *mitarios, originarios* also protested Alfaro's design. The *originaria* was similar to slavery, except for a prohibition against sale. *Originarios* included rebel Guaraní and non-Guaraní peoples captured in war; unlike *mitarios*, they lived permanently with their masters who held them for two or three lifetimes, that of the first master and one or two of his heirs. *Originarios* numbered about 10,000 in the early 1600s, and men and women labored continuously for their *encomendero*. By the later seventeenth century, *originarias* began to marry newly introduced African slaves, adding a new dimension to the servile population. The *originario* population continued to decline until the end of the colonial period. In 1726 and 1774, *originarios* in Asunción and Villa Rica numbered 1,010 and 941, a large fraction of whom were *zambos*, of mixed African and indigenous origin. They had no desire to exchange their current residences with *encomenderos* to start life anew in their own villages. *Originarios* might well be non-Guaraní taken in war and were usually women.

[9] Francisco de Alfaro, "Carta general de Relaçión de la visita de Tucumán y Paraguay," la Plata, February 15, 1613, in Enrique de Gandia, *Francisco de Alfaro y la condición social de los indios: Río de la Plata, Paraguay, Tucumán y Perú, Siglos XVI y XVII* (Buenos Aires, 1939), pp. 480–490.

Their children, fathered by *encomenderos*, were not subject to the same controls as their mothers.

Thus Guaraní and *encomenderos* together resisted the ordinances of Alfaro, and both versions of *encomiendas* continued to the end of the colonial period. When not serving *encomenderos*, *mitario* families lived in Altos, Atyrá, Tobatí, Guarambaré, Yaguarón, and other exclusively Guaraní pueblos, whose inhabitants around 1650 comprised about a third of Paraguay's 65,000 people. Aiming at self-sufficiency in cotton clothing and foodstuffs and at surpluses of sugar and beef to barter in the local economy, these towns acquired extensive lands in the early colonial period when land was plentiful, and they managed to hold them until the late 1700s. Many pueblos had large cattle herds, and some specialized in artisan ware. When Mbayá attacks in the later seventeenth century made the locations of six of these towns in the north of Paraguay untenable, the provincial government relocated the settlements nearer Asunción.

Guaraní towns constantly leaked inhabitants into Paraguay, as Guaraní escaped the status of "Indian." They became mestizos or simply "people," although they lived and spoke much as they had before. Outwardly mobile Guaraní sought to live first on the outskirts of their *encomienda* towns, permanently as dependent peons at the estates of their *encomenderos*, and then as farmers dispersed among the valleys of Paraguay. By such means they demonstrated that they were not "Indians," who had to live in pueblos. By the end of the colonial period, visitors to Paraguay had difficulty distinguishing among the Guaraní, acculturated Guaycuruan, and Paraguayan mestizos, all of whom spoke Guaraní. The *encomienda mitaria* and the communal system of the pueblos were exploitative institutions, but they integrated the Guaraní into colonial Paraguay and provided a vehicle for continued ethnogenesis.

The *mitario* population of Paraguay also declined into the 1720s, when it slowly began again to increase. In 1688 *mitarios* of Paraguay numbered 9,196, and 6,329 in 1726. Between the 1720s and 1793, however, the *mitario* population of the civil province increased by about 20 percent, while ethnogenesis also contributed to general population growth. Mestizo children of Guaraní mothers were exempt from *encomienda* and communal obligations and could choose where to live, causing Guaraní women to prefer Creole mates.

Colonial Guaraní resisted Spanish domination. In localized rebellions in the 1500s, men protested that cattle destroyed crops and that *mita* service was ignoble. These movements were often supported by self-interested mestizos and shamans seeking renewed influence. In later rebellions, like that of the people of the *encomienda* town of Arecayá in 1660, the Guaranís protested lack of economic freedom and mobility. Because merchants after 1650 preferred to employ mestizos for the hazardous work of *yerba* gathering, this declined as a Guaraní grievance.

Lay and clerical Spaniards denied that Indians were capable of producing without compulsion. Thus in the Paraguayan pueblos and in the later Jesuit missions as well, Spanish and Guaraní officials organized nonprivileged families communally for economic purposes. All healthy male and female Guaraní over seven or eight in Indian towns worked daily for the community. Men owed a further public service obligation, the *leva*, which obliged them to build and maintain forts; during this service they got meals but nothing more. The pueblos' fields and pastures remained safe from Creole and mestizo encroachment until the late eighteenth century, when *hacendados* and landless mestizo peasants began to take them. At about this time, however, the introduction of a money economy and wage labor also attracted significant numbers of Guaraní from the pueblos to Spanish estates, factories, and farms.

Although Guaraní in the civil province of Paraguay and those in the Jesuit missions disliked each other, both hated coercive labor, especially communal work. Many in the civil provinces even preferred *encomienda* service to communal chores, because the former removed them from village routine and offered a chance to escape. When in the villages, as they were most of the time, they preferred working at their own garden plots to communal duties. Speaking through *caciques*, they often denounced their own *cabildantes* and *fiscales*, and they uniformly resisted *leva* duties.

By 1600 Guaraní masses had lost their former lands. After the establishment of the *encomienda*, "Guaranís began to abandon the lands on their ancient, traditional, *tey'i*."[10] Now they had the communal properties of their new villages, which they worked under the supervision of Spanish priests, administrators, and Guaraní *cabildantes*. They also exchanged Guaraní modes of production for Spanish and mixed forms, as aboriginal culture disintegrated. Although cultural demoralization once caused the Guaraní to abandon cultivation, they eventually took up agriculture

[10] Susnik, *El Rol de los Indígenas*, I, p. 136.

again, grew vegetables for their own consumption, and raised such market crops as sugar and tobacco by new, intensive methods.

In the 1600s and 1700s, the most effective mode of resistance to communal labor, *leva*, or other hated obligations, became flight, not revolt, and 5 to 9 percent of the population, mostly adult males, was fugitive at any time. In the late colony some men and women elected to work for wages for creole and mestizo Paraguayans, preferring such labor to *encomienda* and communal chores, while *mitarios* who remained with the *encomendero* often squatted on his estate. Others fled south to Corrientes and Santa Fe, where they could escape being "Indians." Wives left behind by fugitives could work for Paraguayans as spinners but were often destitute and dependent on the community for charity. In smaller numbers women fled the villages to work for Paraguayans, but they more often returned. Despite popular legends, few Guaraní from the civil province or Jesuit missions fled to "the woods" after 1600.

When Guaraní men worked elsewhere for wages in the 1700s, their pueblos hired Creole and mestizo workers to harvest crops. In the late 1700s the Bourbon tobacco monopoly made burdensome demands on Guaraní who cultivated tobacco fields and labored in crown factories. Guaraní worked in the growing lumber industry and in Asunción shipyards. Some Guaraní became debt peons who could not do communal work obligations because of obligations to Paraguayan employers.

Although Paraguay in the 1500s received a less active missionary effort than Mexico or Central America, there too Catholicism had notable missionaries. In the late 1570s Fray Luis de Bolaños, O.F.M., preached in the Guaraní language near Asunción, and Guaranís and Franciscans founded the first Paraguayan mission, Altos, in 1580. Franciscans favored flexible missions, more open to outside influences than the later rigidly segregated Jesuit establishments, but Paraguayan missions of both orders followed Franciscan examples of postconquest Mexico. The Franciscans responded to the challenge of Guaraní shaman Oberá in 1579 and other similar movements; these were heavily influenced by Christian ideals. Like Oberá, "Indian messiahs . . . announced the arrival of golden ages in which the Indians would see themselves liberated from the Spaniards, and they preached holy wars against the latter."[11] Bolaños and his companion Alonso de San Buenaventura organized the reductions of Ypané

[11] Louis Necker, *Indios Guaraníes y chamanes franciscanos: las primeras reducciones del Paraguay (1580–1800)*, con prefacio de Magnus Mörner (Asunción, 1990), p. 86.

and Guarambaré, and with Guaraní cooperation Bolaños founded eighteen towns in Guairá (now Paraná, Brazil) in the 1580s and 1590s. Because they were also *encomienda* towns, many Guaraní–Franciscan missions were sources of labor for Creole and mestizo employers in Paraguay. The positive response to Franciscan overtures shows how the Guaraní welcomed the social and economic accommodations to Spanish ways available in Catholic missions. In central Paraguay Guaraní clustered in other towns with Bolaños's help. That Guaraní called Bolaños *Pa'i*, meaning shaman and culture hero, signifies the fusion of aboriginal and Catholic belief that occurred first in Franciscan pueblos and later in Jesuit missions.

JESUIT MISSIONS

Although Jesuits were relative latecomers to Paraguay, the Guaraní welcomed the social and economic benefits of their missions. The Jesuit reductions, developed almost a century after Europeans first touched the Río de la Plata, gathered in people whose contact with Europeans was already of two or three generations' duration. From the Indian perspective Jesuit foundations resembled Franciscan establishments in postconquest Mexico and conformed to Spanish legal norms. The Guaraní accepted Catholic missions initially for the material benefits, especially plentiful iron tools and food, and for security, but aboriginal religious traditions prevented their accepting Catholic beliefs in the first mission generations. Jesuit proselytizing included force. When some groups resisted Jesuit overtures, the fathers encouraged clients to attack the recalcitrant peoples. In theory advocating "natural liberty" for the Guaraní, Jesuits nevertheless severely regulated work and play, and Guaraní freedom of action in missions was as limited as it was in the *encomienda* towns of Paraguay.

In 1610 Jesuit fathers Marciel de Lorenzana and Francisco de San Martín founded San Ignacio Guazú near the confluence of the Río Paraná and Río Paraguay, which initiated a reduction complex that ran from east of the Río Uruguay to north of the Tebicuary. Also in Guairá (now Paraná, Brazil) in 1610, where 60 years earlier Spaniards had rounded up Guaraní like cattle to work the groves of *yerba*, Jesuit-favored *caciques* led the Guaraní into Loreto along the Pirapó, the other San Ignacio on the Paranapanemá, and then into eleven more missions in the 1620s. The existence of these missions infuriated *encomenderos* of old

Villa Rica, whose labor demands the Guaraní resisted. Simultaneously Jesuits also founded reductions in northern Paraguay between the Ypané and Apá rivers among the Itatín, but they moved this ethnic-regional Guaraní subdivision in 1659 to the Parána and Paraguay region because of hostilities from the Chaco and Brazil. From the mission center between Parána and Uruguay, reductions spread east and south in the 1600s along the Río Uruguay and into the present Brazilian state of Río Grande do Sul and north across the Paraná.

Brazilian slave raids caused Jesuits and Guaraní to move the northern missions to the south. In the late 1620s *paulista* marauders struck in Guairá and then raided Itatín missions. Thousands of Guaraní fell victim to these *mameluco* attacks. The Brazilians hunted Guaraní like beasts. When Jesuits tried to dissuade the pillagers, Brazilians denied that Jesuits were truly priests and called them "demons, heretics, [and] enemies of God." In the missions of San Antonio and San Miguel, "the poor Indians ran to take refuge in the church, where they [the Brazilians] killed them like cattle in a slaughter-house."[12] After the devastating raid of 1631, the Guaranís fled reductions to the safety of the forests, and, heeding shamans, some lost faith in Jesuits. Twelve thousand Guaranís, however, left Guairá in 1631 and made the arduous journey to the south, led by Father Antonio Ruíz de Montoya, exposing Spaniards of Villa Rica to attack and causing them to evacuate, too.

In the fertile fields and pastures of Misiones, Argentina, Guaraní with Jesuit instructors organized an effective militia, with firearms, European weapons, and discipline. By 1646 the viceroy of Peru had given the king the necessary assurances that let the men of the missions carry firearms. The Guaraní received muskets, powder, and shot from the government. Organized mission militias, however, had already stopped the irregular forces of the Brazilian marauders at the battle of Mbororé on the Río Uruguay in 1641, although the Guaraní and Jesuits eventually surrendered the western area, called Tapé (now Río Grande do Sul), to Brazil. Military successes nevertheless reinforced Jesuit prestige among the Guaraní and helped priests combat opposition from native religious practitioners.

Security allowed prosperity and population growth. Partial militariza-

[12] P. Antonio Ruíz de Montoya, *Conquista espiritual hecha por los religiosos de la Compañía de Jesús en las provincias del Paraguay, Paraná, Uruguay y Tapé* (2nd ed. Bilbao, 1892 [Madrid, 1639]), pp. 143–144.

tion meant, though, that the Guaraní provided the crown a force with which to counter insurrection and invasion, the largest in the region. Mission armies suppressed rebellions in Asunción in the 1640s, 1720s, and 1730s, exacerbating settler hostility to Jesuits. Guaraní forces also fought Spain's Portuguese enemies in the Banda Oriental and helped found Montevideo there in 1726. Military organization also gave prestige to native leaders and helped Guaraní captains direct public affairs. As early as 1649, when the mission population was 29,000, the Peruvian viceroy praised Guaraní defenses, set tribute at a lowly 1 silver peso a year, and exempted mission residents from labor service to lay Spaniards.

By the 1700s thirty Guaraní missions, whose population fluctuated from 80,000 to 120,000, were clustered in three places: east of the Río Uruguay in present-day Río Grande do Sul; between the Uruguay and the Río Paraná in Misiones, Argentina; and in southern Paraguay between the Paraná and the Río Tebicuary. In the 1740s independent Guaraní whom Spaniards called *monteses*, who lived near *yerbales* and clashed with Paraguayan gatherers, finally accepted Jesuit overtures. They established the final two Guaraní missions in Taruma, now west central Paraguay, for protection from Mbayá to the north.

Jesuits and the Guaraní built mission towns on the characteristic Spanish grid, although local conditions might alter the plan. Jesuit-designed Guaraní huts, which most residents disliked, were single-room stone or adobe structures lacking furniture. Residents sought to live on the outskirts of the mission near family plots and freedom from supervision. A fortunate few succeeded. Although some males fled missions to live in Spanish settlements, close supervision by Guaraní officials and priests made escaping missions more difficult than in Paraguayan *encomienda* towns. Nevertheless Guaraní sailors at downriver ports and militiamen on expeditions seized opportunities to liberate themselves.

Decisions of mission government were largely achieved as a result of a consensus among priests and Guaraní elites. Officeholders included members of municipal governments, militia captains, and artisans. Hereditary *caciques*, who often supported followers against other native officials, acted as brokers between elites and the people. Mission Guaraní depended on *caciques*, whose oratory once helped persuade them to accept reductions, to speak for them. The prestige of mission *caciques* initially reinforced Jesuit influence. Jesuits reinforced *caciques*' authority by granting them such perquisites as labor exemptions and respect, especially the title "don." Jesuits also created the *cabildos*, with temporary officeholders who more often spoke for Jesuits than did *caciques*.

Mission government resembled that of other native communities in Spanish America. Except for *caciques* and their firstborn sons, exempt by rank, all other adult men paid tribute to the crown, a peso a year. At the head of the native hierarchy of a mission was a Guaraní *corregidor*. A lieutenant, two *alcaldes*, four *regidores*, two *algualciles*, an *alcalde de la hermandad*, and a Guaraní *procurador* assisted him. As a badge of office, the *corregidor* carried a silver-tipped cane, while the others carried staffs to distinguish themselves. These officers directed the civil affairs of the mission in consultation with the priest. In military affairs the captains, lieutenants, and ensigns wore insignias to designate their ranks.

Like other indigenous communities in the Spanish empire, Guaraní missions accepted clerical tutelage, although they were more prosperous and efficient than most counterparts elsewhere. In each mission innovative Guaraní comprised a numerous artisan class, including "blacksmiths, carpenters, statue makers, gilders, silversmiths, weavers, hat makers, rosary makers, makers of organs, bells, and things of bronze, of spinets, harps, flageolets, bugles and other musical instruments, in addition to shoemakers, tailors, embroiderers, etc. . . . [They] worked in the priests' house."[13] In addition, each artisan worked the land, plowing the fields behind a pair of oxen and performing other farm tasks. They alternated their responsibilities. One week they saw to mission government or practiced trades, and the next week they worked in the fields. In the 6 months' dead time of the agricultural year, men constructed boats, built bridges and roads, and repaired houses and churches, in somewhat the manner of the *leva* duties of the *encomendados* of the civil province.

Each family head tilled his own private plot 4 days a week and the common fields on Mondays and Saturdays. Each mission also had its own cattle ranch and pastures for sheep, which might be as far as 50 leagues from the village center of the mission. Some twenty to thirty men and their families were stationed at these outposts as cowherds and shepherds. They drove twenty to forty head of cattle a week to the mission town for slaughter to feed the mission, depending on its size.

[13] José Cardiel, "Carta y relación de las misiones de la provincia del Paraguay (1747)," pp. 115–213 of Guillermo Furlong [Cardiff], S.J., *José Cardiel y su Carta-Relación (1747)* (Buenos Aires, 1953), p. 143.

The Guaraní relished veal, especially from heifers, and their inclination to kill young females angered the priests, because it retarded the increase of the herds, a matter of profit and mission economic growth of greater concern to Jesuits than to the Guaraní. Occasionally priests hired Spanish overseers to tend herds and to keep them from the Guaraní, and these employees directed Indian foremen and hands. From these ranches came high-quality hides for export to Europe.

Compulsion was a part of life in Jesuit missions. Before the coming of missions, agricultural labor was voluntary. In missions the Guaraní élite might labor of their own volition, "but for the rest," Jesuits thought, "it was necessary to beat them one or more times so that they sow and reap the necessary amount."[14] The Guaraní responded to Jesuit coercion by refusing to work in the manner prescribed by Jesuits. The Indians, for example, resisted preparing the soil for planting in the European fashion. They also preferred to work for their own immediate needs and put less emphasis on the market-oriented goals of the Jesuits than the priests did.

Women prepared and cooked meals, sewed, carried water, and gathered firewood. Guarded by elderly, respected *alcaldes*, presumably beyond sexual desire, women also spun cotton into yarn for the community on Wednesdays and Saturdays, although men were weavers. Women were prohibited from dancing in public festivals. Single adult women, women whose conduct offended the priests and the Guaraní élite, and those whose husbands were fugitives, all were cloistered in a house of retirement and correction. There they labored at the same tasks as women in families, although they were more closely guarded.

In matters of ritual the Guaraní publicly behaved in ways that Jesuits approved, accepting baptism and patron saints, but in the first generations they privately rejected much of Christianity. They merged Christian tenets with their own beliefs and clung to such cherished customs as plural marriages for *caciques* and child marriages. Chunks of aboriginal religion, ritual, and shamanic practices went underground, but long exposure to European religion contributed to the creation of a folk Christianity.

The Guaraní and Jesuits developed the mission complex into a thriving business enterprise, a mixture of communal and private form of production under the coercive paternalism of Jesuits. Priests allotted garden plots to families for their use but supervised communal holdings,

[14] Cardiel, "Carta y relación," p. 140.

while blocking Guaraní access to markets and communication with Spaniards unless Jesuits were intermediaries. Families worked their own plots and the common fields. They grew wheat, maize, manioc, and oranges for subsistence and raised cotton, sugar, and tobacco for sale. Jesuits guarded surplus produce in a mission warehouse, to which the Guaraní sought access.

Cattle herds helped support all missions, and the Guaraní demanded regular beef. Mission Guaraní also raised horses and sheep. The province exported hides, but the sale of high-quality *yerba maté (caamini)* from mission plantations brought the most profit, surpassing the inferior grade (*yerba de palos*) of lay Paraguayan exploiters. Women spun wool and cotton and made clothing and blankets for local use and sale by Jesuit middlemen; mission rafts and ships transported these goods to markets to the south.

As actors and as objects, mission Guaraní were crucial to the region's politics. In the 1640s they threatened the anti-Jesuit, Franciscan bishop of Paraguay, Bernardino de Cárdenas. In the 1720s they opposed the Paraguayans who rallied around Governor José de Antequera y Castro, an adversary of Jesuits, and Paraguayan rebels of the 1730s, who sought the labor of mission Guaraní. A militia force from the civil province thrashed an army from the missions sent by the viceroy to remove the serving governor, Antequera, in 1724; but a mission army of Guaraní troops oversaw the final defeat of the Paraguayan *comuneros* in 1735, intensifying the hostility between the civil and mission provinces of Paraguay. The Guaraní of the civil province had no military capacity and were interested witnesses to the uprising.

In 1754, when the thirty southern missions had 101,752 residents, seven reductions rebelled. In the Treaty of Madrid of 1750, Spain and Portugal agreed to exchange territory east of the Río Uruguay for land in the Banda Oriental. East of the Uruguay, seven missions, San Nicolás (population: 4,863), Santo Angel (5,421), San Luis (3,967), San Lorenzo (2,117), San Borja (2,841), San Juan Bautista (3,977), and San Miguel (6,450) had prospered for two generations. Guaraní residents there were ordered to abandon homes, fields, pastures, and livestock and move west. Ceding their homes to Brazilians enraged the Guaraní of these missions, whose mortal enemies they had been for a century, and they rebelled. Sepé, *corregidor* of San Miguel, whose people believed that their patron St. Michael had ordered them not to move, first led the resistance. Known by priests and other Spaniards as José Tiarayú, Sepé was also *alférez real* of the mission. Sepé conducted an effective Guaraní guerrilla effort, taking a Portuguese fort and spreading terror among the Portuguese invaders. He was killed in one of several skirmishes between the Guaraní resistance and the European allies. After he died Nicolás Ñeengirú (later referred to as King Nicolás I of Paraguay by enemies of the Society of Jesus), *corregidor* of Concepción, took over briefly, but he defected to the governor of Buenos Aires. To fight the Spanish and Portuguese allies, the Guaraní burned villages and staged productive raids. Soon, however, their forces began to suffer grievous losses while inflicting few casualties on their foes, because they lacked a unified command and lacked a coherent strategy. Especially disastrous was the battle of Caaibaté in February 1756, where the Guaraní suffered 1,400 deaths, the European allies but 3, and the war was over. The Guaraní followed Jesuits west for a time but returned to their homes in 1761, after the Portuguese and Spanish crowns nullified the treaty. An inquiry by Governor Ceballos of Buenos Aires cleared Jesuits of complicity.

In 1767, however, Spanish Jesuits fell victims to longstanding opposition, especially in Madrid. Among the anti-Jesuit winds then blowing were the regalism of the Spanish crown, nationalistic responses to Jesuit ultramontanism, the earlier French and Portuguese expulsions of Jesuits, and the royal desire to acquire Jesuit wealth. In 1767 Charles III expelled Jesuits from his dominions, and colonial officials obeyed the order in the Río de la Plata.

The missions slowly deteriorated after the Jesuits left. Replacement priests frequently knew no Guaraní. Spanish administrators, who found no great treasures, selectively abolished Jesuit controls essential to the enterprise. Mission prosperity vanished. New administrators were thieves, and the now poorly functioning system failed to produce sufficient wealth to sustain itself. Bureaucrats removed the legal safeguards preventing the sale of Guaraní property, and Spanish merchants, employers, and land-hungry settlers moved in. Officials sought abolition of Jesuit-sanctioned segregation of the Guaraní and their integration into colonial society and colluded with *hacendados* to usurp mission lands.

Mission society became increasingly dissonant after 1768. The Guaraní slowly drifted from missions. Skilled artisans, farmers, and herdsmen found employment in Spanish areas of the Río de la Plata, but they failed to "return to the forest," as many ill-informed works allege. Although Guaraní in central Paraguayan towns were often hostile to mission residents, *encomienda visitas* of the late 1700s reveal that fugitives from missions found refuge and wives in Paraguayan towns.

In the 1780s Guaraní of the *encomienda* towns and the thirteen missions under the *intendant* of Paraguay represented a quarter of the province's 100,000 people. Yet Indian rights dwindled. Land-hungry Paraguayan peasants, whose physical and cultural similarities to the Guaraní were striking, married Guaraní women and established title to formerly protected lands, joining the efforts of *hacendados* and speculators.

The communal system disintegrated in the late 1700s, and internal disputes racked Guaraní towns. Mission Guaraní, like those in former *encomienda* towns, slowly evaded legal obligations to the community, and some acquired substantial autonomy. Male Guaraní moved to Spanish haciendas and cities, and females sought "Creoles"(mestizos) to marry. Many moved to Brazil and Uruguay.

One other aspect of the Guaraní past, the language of the people, had a lasting influence. In the two provinces of Paraguay, the Guaraní language was subordinate to the Castilian language, as the Guaraní were dominated by Spaniards. Several factors, however, prevented Castilian from overwhelming Guaraní, and most conquerors adopted the language of the vanquished in Paraguay, rather than the other way around. Few immigrants from Spain followed the early conquerors, and few arrivals were female. In the upper Plata region, therefore, "the mestizo women, whose mothers had been Indians and whose husbands had learned Guaraní from their own mothers, continued to teach their children Guaraní."[15] The handful of Spanish-speaking administrators or clerics there had little opportunity to spread their language, because a Guaraní ethnic majority survived for years. Thus independent Paraguay evolved as a truly bilingual nation. In the mid–twentieth century, Guaraní-speaking Paraguayans outnumbered those who spoke Spanish by 92 to 52 percent.

In the Spanish era in both the civil province and the later Jesuit missions, "a colonial society spoke an indigenous language, but one that was not the language of the Indians."[16] Indians and mestizos had little opportunity to learn Spanish. Instead they spoke a changing Guaraní, which kept much indigenous vocabulary but incorporated numerous

[15] Joan Rubin, *National Bilingualism in Paraguay* (The Hague–Paris, 1968), p. 24.

[16] Bartomeu Melià, *El Guaraní conquistado y reducido: ensayos de etnohistoria* (Asunción, 1986), p. 236.

hispanisms. By 1800 the Guaraní of the civil province was a new language, different from its aboriginal ancestor. The alterations it had undergone resembled those in the Jesuit missions, where Guaraní was the only language spoken or written by Indians. It appeared in dictionaries, sermons, and other works, whose grammatical categories were increasingly hispanized. As with the speech of the Asunción region to the north, the colonial dependency of the mission culture robbed the language of its autonomy, to which such indigenous traditions as political and religious oratory had once given life. After 1768 the Creole and reduction models of the Guaraní language converged, and a generalized Paraguayan Guaraní emerged. In the nineteenth century, Guaraní was generally spoken during the regime of José Gaspar Rodríguez de Francia (1814–1840), but President Carlos Antonio López in the 1840s and 1850s encouraged the use of Spanish, as he abolished the Indian pueblos and ordered the people to renounce their Guaraní surnames. The War of the Triple Alliance (1864–1870), however, reinforced the use of Guaraní. Nevertheless Spanish power and the Spanish language were dominant influences. They separated the Guaraní language from Guaraní society and created the modern language from the indigenous one. A general rule today is that the more rural a person is, the more likely it is that he or she will speak Guaraní.

During the Wars of Independence, the Guaraní left missions south of the Paraná and joined *porteño* armies to fight Paraguayans. Manuel Belgrano's army in 1810 caused another exodus from missions. Although José Gervasio Artigas in the 1810s ravaged the mission country south of the Paraná, several thousand Guaraní men led by Captain Andresito Guacarari nevertheless joined the Artigas forces. Later many Guaraní soldiers died in the Argentine civil wars. In 1817 the Portuguese retook the area of the formerly rebellious seven mission towns east of the Río Uruguay. Residents of missions just south of the Paraná suffered again when Paraguayan Dictator Francia in the 1820s destroyed Candelaria, Loreto, Santa Ana, San Ignacio-miri, and Corpus to create a buffer to cordon Paraguay against the political violence to the south. Many Guaraní disobeyed Francia's order to move to Paraguay; instead they dispersed in northeastern Argentina and Uruguay. Under Francia the Guaraní who could not escape "Indian" status reluctantly maintained the communal system, although individuals could obtain exemptions. As the nineteenth century progressed, the government granted limited Guaraní mobility.

The processes of population dispersal and cultural adaptation that began soon after conquest culminated in the 1800s. Finally in 1848 Paraguayan President Carlos Antonio López, coveting those still-protected Guaraní lands of the former *encomienda* towns and missions and needing the military service of exempt Guaraní, then about 10 percent of the 400,000 Paraguayans, decreed the incorporation of the remaining Indians into the population as citizens of Paraguay. Legal segregation was over. The Guaraní got the legal rights of other Paraguayans, but they lost their protected status. In the process they yielded communal cattle and common lands. Remaining Guaraní, like the M'bya and Chorotis, continued to live in small bands in fringe areas far from hispanic influences and kept some ancient traditions like large, thatched, multifamily dwelling places into the twentieth century.

The history of the Native American peoples of the Gran Chaco and Paraguay is often described as exotic or unique. In fact, however, it was a region no more exotic than any other and was unique only in the sense that every place is unique. As we understand more about the history of the upper Plata region, we find that the descendants of the original Native American inhabitants make up the overwhelming majority of the Paraguayan nation and are a major component of the societies of northeastern Argentina. Over three centuries the native inhabitants experienced most of the same dislocations as other original Americans. Conquest, epidemic disease, armed resistance by native groups, messianic movements, and the creation and decay of mission systems disturbed their lives, and they were forced into accommodation with the European invader. Yet native peoples contributed a lasting vitality to the area that is obvious in the late twentieth century.

BIBLIOGRAPHIC ESSAY

An investigation of the history of native peoples of the Chaco and Paraguay must begin with three multivolume works by the Paraguayan anthropologist Branislava Susnik. The most thorough is *Los aborígenes del Paraguay*, 7 vols. (Asunción, 1978–1985); *El rol de los indígenas en la formación y en la vivencia del Paraguay*, 2 vols. (Asunción, 1982–1983) is a useful synthesis of the longer work; and *El indio colonial del Paraguay*, 3 vols. (Asunción, 1965–1971) still contains useful information, although it is largely superseded by the other two works.

An English reader might wish to begin an investigation of the Chaco peoples with Alfred Mètraux, "Ethnography of the Chaco," *Handbook of*

South American Indians, 7 vols., ed. by Julian H. Steward (Washington, D. C., 1946–1959), I, pp. 197–370. An important work that concentrates on the seventeenth and early eighteenth centuries is Pedro Lozano, S.J., *Descripción corográfica del Gran Chaco Gualamba* (Tucumán, Arg., 1941), and other Jesuit chronicles that deal with events of the eighteenth century are Martin Dobrizhoffer, *An Account of the Abipones: An Equestrian People of Paraguay*, 3 vols. (London, 1822; repr. New York, 1970); Florian Paucke, *Hacia allá y para acá (una estada entre los indios Mocobíes, 1749–1767)*, 4 vols. (Tucumán-Buenos Aires, 1942–1944); José Sánchez Labrador, El Paraguay *Católico*, 3 vols. (Buenos Aires, 1910–1917); José Cardiel, S.J., *Declaración de la verdad* (Buenos Aires, 1900); and "Carta y relación de las misiones la provincia del Paraguay (1747)," pp. 115–213 of Guillermo Furlong, S.J., *José Cardiel y su Carta-relación (1747)* (Buenos Aires, 1953). Works of lesser but not insignificant value are Salvador Canals Frau, *Las poblaciones indígenas de la Argentina: Su origen-su pasado-su presente* (Buenos Aires, 1953); Ludwig Kersten, *Las tribus indígenas del Gran Chaco hasta fines del siglo xviii* (Resistencia, Arg., 1968); Branislava Susnik, "Dimensiones migratorias y pautas culturales de los pueblos del Gran Chaco (enfoque etnológico)," *Suplemento antopológico: Universidad Católica* (Asunción, Paraguay), 1972, pp. 85–101; Antonio Serrano, *Los pueblos y culturas indígenas del litoral* (Santa Fe, Arg., 1955); Alberto Rex González and José A. Pérez, *Argentina indígena: Vísperas de la conquista* (Buenos Aires, 1972); and Enrique Palavecino, "Las culturas aborígenes del Chaco," *Historia de la nación argentina (Desde los orígenes hasta la organización definitiva en 1862)*, 10 vols., ed. by Ricardo Levene (Buenos Aires, 1936–1950), I, pp. 429–472. Works on eighteenth-century missions include James Schofield Saeger's "Another view of the mission as a frontier institution: The Guaycuruan reductions of Santa Fe," *HAHR* 65: 3 (1985), pp. 493–517, and "Eighteenth-century Guaycuruan missions in Paraguay," in *Indian-Religious Relations in Colonial Spanish America*, ed. by Susan E. Ramírez (Syracuse, N.Y., 1989), pp. 55–86.

Besides the previously cited works by Susnik, Cardiel, and Dobrizhoffer, which deal with the Guaranís as well as peoples of the Chaco, important works are Silvio Zavala, *Orígenes de la colonización en el Río de la Plata* (Mexico, 1977); and Louis Necker, *Indios Guaraníes Y chamanes franciscanos: las primeras reducciones del Paraguay* (Asunción, 1990). Useful essays are found in Bartomeu Meliá, *El Guaraní conquistado y reducido: ensayos de entohistoria* (Asunción, 1986). Still-valuable works that treat the Guaraní include Elman R. Service, *Spanish–Guaraní Relations in Early Colonial Paraguay* (Ann Arbor, Mich., 1954 [repr. 1971]); Enrique de Gandía, *Francisco de Alfaro y la condición social de los indios: Río de la Plata, Paraguay, Tucumán y Perú, siglos XVI y XVII* (Buenos Aires, 1939); and his *Indios y conquistadores en el Paraguay* (Buenos Aires, 1932); Ricardo Lafuente Machain, *El Gobernador Domingo Martínez de Irala* (Buenos Aires, 1939); Ramón I. Cardozo, *La antigua provincia del Guayrá y la Villa Rica del Espíritu Santo* (Buenos Aires, 1938); J. Natalicio González, *Proceso y formación de la cultura paraguaya* (Buenos Aires – Asunción, 1938); Alfred Mètraux, "The Guaraní," *Handbook of South American Indians*, III, pp. 69–94; and José L. Mora Mérida, *Historia social de Paraguay, 1600–1650* (Seville, 1973). A survey of the late *encomienda* based on analysis of *visitas* of the *encomienda* towns is James Schofield Saeger, "Survival and abolition: The eighteeenth century Paraguayan *encomienda*," *TAM*, Vol. XXXVII (July, 1981), pp. 59–85. Eighteenth-century observers' accounts include several works by Félix de Azara, including *Geografía física y esférica de Paraguay* (Montevideo, 1904); *Viajes por la América Meridional* (Madrid, 1934); and *Descripción e historia del Paraguay y Río de la Plata* (Asunción, 1896). Another visitor to the region, Juan Francisco Aguirre, also left a valuable record, "Diario del Capitán de Fragata de la Real Armada," *Anales de la Biblioteca* 1 (Buenos Aires, 1905), pp. 1–271, and 7 (1911), pp. 1–490.

A useful guide to the literature of the Guaraní missions of the Jesuits is "Las fuentes de información sobre las misiones jesuíticas de Guaraníes," *Teología* T. XXIV, No. 50 (1987), pp. 143–163. Although English-language introductions include Philip Caraman, *The Jesuit Republic in South America* (New York, 1975); and R. B. Cunninghame Graham, *A Vanished Arcadia, being some account of the Jesuits in South America* (London, 1901); the best traditional survey of the Jesuit missions is still Guillermo Furlong [Cardiff], *Misiones y sus pueblos de Guaraníes* (Buenos Aires, 1962); also significant is an economic history of the missions by Rafael Carbonell de Masy, S.J., *Estrategías de desarollo rural en los pueblos guaraníes (1609–1767)* (Barcelona, 1992). These can be supplemented with Alberto Armani, *Ciudad de Dios y ciudad del sol: El estado jesuíta de los Guaraníes (1609–1768)* (Mexico, 1982 [Italian ed., 1977]). Father Guillermo Furlong also collected and published the works of numerous missionaries, including *José Cardiel y su Carta-Relación (1747)* (Buenos Aires, 1953); *Antonio Sepp, S.J. y su "Gobierno Temporal" (1732)*; and a host of others. A basic documentary collection is *Cartas Anuas de la Provincia del Paraguay, Chile y Tucumán de la Compañía de Jesús (1609–*

1637) (Buenos Aires, 1927–1929), which should be supplemented by Ernest J. A. Maeder, *Cartas Anuas de la Provincia del Paraguay, 1637–1639* (Buenos Aires, 1984). Another source is Pablo Pastells and Francisco Mateos, *Historia de la Compañía de Jesús en la Provincia del Paraguay* (Madrid, 1912–1949), 9 vols., a collection of summaries of documents, mostly from the Archivo General de Indias. Such essential sources as Cardiel's "Breve Relación de las Misiones de Paraguay," are found in P. Pablo Hernández (ed.), *Organización social de las doctrinas Guaraníes de la Compañía de Jesús* (Barcelona, 1913), 2 vols. An essential participant account of the Guaraní exodus to the south is P. Antonio Ruíz de Montoya, *Conquista espiritual hecha por los religiosos de la Compañía de Jesús en las provincias del Paraguay, Paraná, Uruguay y Tapé* (2nd ed., Bilbao, 1892 [Madrid, 1639]); other basic Jesuit accounts include Pierre F. J. Charlevoix, *Histoire du Paraguay* (Paris, 1756), 3 vols., which has also been published in Spanish and English; Domingo Muriel, *Historia del Paraguay desde 1747 hasta 1767* (Madrid, 1918); and José M. Peramás, *La República del Platón y los Guaraníes* (Buenos Aires, 1947). For useful information about the Brazilian conflict with the missions and Portuguese–Guaraní relations, see John Hemming, *Red Gold: The Conquest of the Brazilian Indians, 1500–1760* (Cambridge, Mass., 1978).

19

DESTRUCTION, RESISTANCE, AND TRANSFORMATION – SOUTHERN, COASTAL, AND NORTHERN BRAZIL (1580–1890)

ROBIN M. WRIGHT
WITH THE COLLABORATION OF MANUELA CARNEIRO DA CUNHA AND THE NÚCLEO DE HISTÓRIA INDÍGENA E DO INDIGENISMO[1]

The indigenous peoples of Brazil responded to the European invasions in a variety of ways that drew on aboriginal social and cultural patterns but also transformed these in response to particular historical circumstances and opportunities. Through a series of case studies, this chapter offers a broad synthesis of the history of indigenous societies in Brazil from the colonial period to the beginning of the republic. Although vast areas have been left out of the discussion, the chapter, by concentrating primarily on the south, the central coast and northeast, and the Amazon Valley, traces the main themes and processes that characterized indigenous contact with Europeans. Within each area attention focuses on the dynamics of pre- and postcontact history of specific peoples and regions: the Guaraní, Kaingang, and Xokleng of the modern-day states of São Paulo, Paraná, Santa Catarina, and Rio Grande do Sul; the Payaguá and Guaykuru (also written as Guaycurú) of the Paraguay River drainage; the Kariri of the northeastern interior and Botocudo of the states of Espirito Santo, Minas Gerais, and Bahia; and for the Amazon Valley, the peoples of the *várzea* from the mid-to-upper Amazon and several of its main tributaries (the Tapajós, Madeira, and Negro; see Map 19.1). These cases are illustrative of processes that characterize much of lowland South America. Together they demonstrate that by the beginning of the twentieth century, the dynamics of change in indigenous societies were based

[1] The following members of the Núcleo and researchers from other institutions have contributed to this chapter: Beatriz Perrone-Moisés, John M. Monteiro, Sylvia Carvalho, Jaime Siqueira, Maria Hilda B. Paraíso, Beatriz G. Dantas, José Augusto L. Sampaio, Maria Rosário G. de Carvalho, Antonio Porro, Miguel Menendez, and Marta Rosa Amoroso.

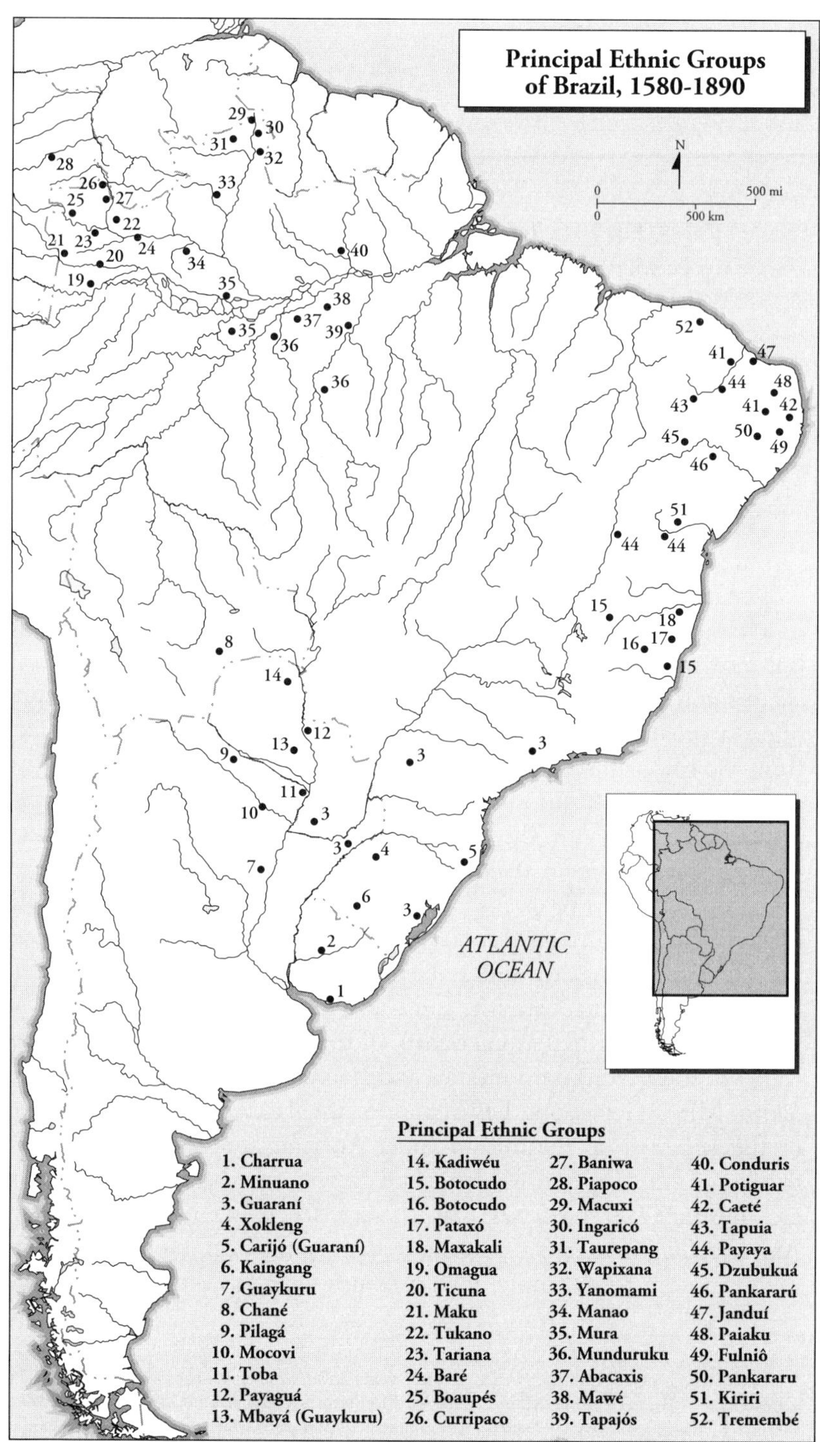

Principal Ethnic Groups of Brazil, 1580-1890
N
0 500 mi
0 500 km
ATLANTIC OCEAN
Principal Ethnic Groups
1. Charrua
2. Minuano
3. Guaraní
4. Xokleng
5. Carijó (Guaraní)
6. Kaingang
7. Guaykuru
8. Chané
9. Pilagá
10. Mocovi
11. Toba
12. Payaguá
13. Mbayá (Guaykuru)
14. Kadiwéu
15. Botocudo
16. Botocudo
17. Pataxó
18. Maxakali
19. Omagua
20. Ticuna
21. Maku
22. Tukano
23. Tariana
24. Baré
25. Boaupés
26. Curripaco
27. Baniwa
28. Piapoco
29. Macuxi
30. Ingaricó
31. Taurepang
32. Wapixana
33. Yanomami
34. Manao
35. Mura
36. Munduruku
37. Abacaxis
38. Mawé
39. Tapajós
40. Conduris
41. Potiguar
42. Caeté
43. Tapuia
44. Payaya
45. Dzubukuá
46. Pankararú
47. Janduí
48. Paiaku
49. Fulniô
50. Pankararu
51. Kiriri
52. Tremembé

Map 19.1

on an entirely different set of factors than those that had been their principal determinants in the colonial and imperial periods.

THEMATIC OVERVIEW

The cases selected for presentation illustrate one or more of the following themes, which have guided the construction of this chapter: (1) diversity of aboriginal sociocultural patterns; (2) patterns of penetration and conquest; (3) directions in Indian policy; (4) transformations in interethnic relations; and (5) forms of adaptation and strategies of resistance.

Diversity of Aboriginal Sociocultural Patterns

In all areas of Brazil, early explorers were astonished at the density and diversity of native populations. Such diversity represented complex and varied forms of spatial organization and settlement patterns reflecting different cultural orientations and adaptations to specific ecological circumstances. Thus the south had an altogether distinct human landscape in terms of spatial organization and group mobility from the Amazon floodplains and the eastern and northeastern interior.

The Guarani of southern Brazil and Paraguay were swidden agriculturalists, cultivating primarily maize, periodically moving their multifamily villages throughout a large region of the tropical and subtropical forests along the coastal floodplains and escarpment and along the major rivers of the Paraná-Paraguay system. Most of the interior to the west was the preferred habitat of nomadic hunting and foraging peoples, such as the Guaykuru (Guaycurú) and Gê-speaking peoples who characteristically were organized in highly mobile, small bands ranging, by land and water, over vast areas of the interior to hunt, forage, trade, and make war on enemy groups.

Similarly the greater part of the eastern and northeastern interior was occupied by hunting and gathering societies of the Macro-Gê linguistic stock, the Kariri language family, and numerous other unidentified language groups. The great diversity of peoples in the northeastern interior was nevertheless offset by a certain unity in adaptation to a specific kind of environment: the scrub-brush *caatinga*, the characteristics of which supported seasonal concentrations of people in a few, favorable niches.

By contrast societies of the densely settled Amazon floodplain were sedentary horticulturalists. Sixteenth-century chroniclers moreover left abundant evidence of stratified political and economic organization, complex territorial arrangements of chiefly and "vassal" settlements, intensive cultivation, surplus economies, and some animal domestication. Although their descriptions are suspiciously similar to Andean and Caribbean chiefdoms, nevertheless there are sufficient indications that the patterns found in the Amazon floodplains differed considerably from those encountered in other tropical forest societies known to the Portuguese.

Patterns of warfare and alliance, trade and commerce created the conditions of intergroup relations. Tupi warfare was deeply connected to fundamental social values and the practice of ritual sacrifice of prisoners. Among the Guarani the dynamics of local groups represented ever-shifting alliances and animosities, but with no indications of stratification among groups. In the Chaco the Guaykuru had developed a distinctive form of stratified social and political organization; sources typically characterize them as a "seignorial society," comprised of "noble, warrior, and captive castes," the last referring to prisoners captured in war. Preconquest hostilities between the Guaykuru and peoples of other linguistic groups formed an integral part of a complex mechanism of territorial control. Guaykuru raids were made apparently both for the purpose of dominating other peoples (such as the Guarani) and of creating symbiotic relations (as with the Arawakans). In the east, Botocudo bands were characterized by constant internal divisions, or fissioning, with each group defending hunting and gathering territories against the incursions of other groups.

In the Amazon Valley sixteenth-century explorers reported large, dense, and continuously settled areas of the floodplains divided into numerous, well-defined "provinces" separated by unoccupied zones, a sort of "no-man's-land," the transgression of which implied war. Although early reports of great "warlike nations" should be evaluated in terms of the military interests of the explorers, the situation in the mid–sixteenth century indicated a balance of power and territorial control among neighboring provinces and with peoples of the interior. Such relations of dominance were most clearly evident in the cases of Tupian societies. Besides producing intense politics they served to integrate local settlements into larger political units, with indications of centralized power, consistent with the European notion of "provinces."

Trade and commerce formed an integral complement to patterns of warfare and alliance. Throughout the Amazon, for example, early chroniclers reported vast networks of commercial and trade relations connecting peoples of the valley with the Andes and the north of the continent. One such long-distance network involved trade in gold artifacts, extending from the northern Andean chiefdoms to the peoples of the Solimões and to the Guyana chiefdoms via the Rupununi savannahs. From the sources it is evident that the Manao people of the Middle Rio Negro were key factors in several interlocking systems of gold production and exchange, and that there were several key locations, such as on the Solimões and the Rupununi savannah where trade took place. The famed "village of gold" and "Golden City of Manoa," which fueled the European imagination (and conquest) in the sixteenth century, were two such places of trade.

Early sources, particularly Jesuit ones, in both the south and Amazon Valley document widespread traditions that were fundamental to native spiritual organization and that would come to have enormous importance in the colonial context: for the Guarani, the prophet-inspired "Land without Evil" migrations; and for the peoples of the Amazon Valley, the complex of rituals and beliefs related to the ancestors, shamanism, sacred flutes and trumpets, and powerful spirits of the waters.

The "Land without Evil" movements of the Guarani have been interpreted in various ways by ethnologists and historians. For Pierre Clastres the development of strong chiefdoms among Tupi-Guarani groups prior to the arrival of the Europeans threatened the traditional order and provoked a reaction on the part of society to impede the appropriation of power by the chiefs. In this context prophets arose who directly contested chiefly authority and who, by invoking myths of the civilizing heroes through dance, song, and migrations, persuaded the Indians to abandon their villages in search of an earthly paradise. According to Hélène Clastres, Tupi-Guarani prophetism was exactly the inverse of a messianic movement because it derived from the conflicts and crises internal to native society and not external factors, such as crises provoked by the conquest.

These interpretations have been challenged by Bartomeu Melià in a stimulating essay on the Guarani "way of being." Supported by the earliest Jesuit sources, Melià suggests that the "Land without Evil" notion in fact refers to "intact soil, where nothing has been built." Melià suggests an important link between the constant search for new lands for villages and gardens and migrations due to prophetic inspiration. Both types of movements would have been inspired by the search for a geographical and spiritual space propitious to the renewal of an authentically Guarani way of being. Colonial penetration would have conferred great credibility to prophetic discourse and cataclysmology by provoking the development of migratory strategies and by threatening the physical and cultural survival of the Guarani.

A survey of the earliest historical sources throughout the northwest Amazon (from the mid-to-upper Amazon to the upper Orinoco) reveals the widespread distribution of a system of beliefs and rituals involving the use of sacred flutes and trumpets, masked dances, and the practice of ritual whipping, associated with a mythology the central themes of which include initiation, the ancestors, gender relations, warfare, and seasonal cycles. Early missionaries associated these rituals and the mythological heroes represented in them with the devil, or "Jurupary" (a Tupian thunder spirit).

Contemporary ethnological sources, however, have revealed that the myth/ritual complex represents a complex philosophy of social and cosmological reproduction. Some early observers noted the political importance of the rituals as a link between neighboring peoples, and the central role of the shamans and priestly ritual specialists as guardians of the traditions. In many cases powerful shamans (or chiefs, in the case of Tupian peoples) were attributed the extraordinary powers of the mythological heroes. Given the central importance of these traditions, it is to be expected that they would serve as key points of reference by which native peoples would understand and shape the impact of external pressures.

Patterns of Penetration and Conquest

The areas discussed in this chapter correspond to the most important areas of Luso-Brazilian expansion during the centuries considered. In the late sixteenth century, colonization was limited to plantation areas of the eastern coast, with concentrations in the northeast and southeast. In the seventeenth century – despite some French, Dutch, and to a lesser extent, British and even Irish attempts to secure small colonies in Brazil and the Amazon – Portugal was ultimately able to secure control over the country and expand its zone of influence westward and northward. Until well into the eighteenth century, however, actual occupation of the interior was limited; rather expansion meant explorations in the interior and contacts with native societies who, by force or persuasion, would be relocated from their territories to agricultural and commercial centers of the coast, or strategic locations on an ever-expanding frontier.

In the south the principal agents of such expansion were the *bandeirantes* (backwoodsmen, frontiersmen) whose constant expeditions served to supply an ever-growing demand for Indian labor. Coupled with the Jesuit system of mission "reductions" introduced in the early seventeenth century, the southern borderlands soon became a field of intense competition for Indian labor, leading to a virtual depopulation of the interior by the eighteenth century, forcing the *bandeirantes* to venture ever-greater distances in their search for slaves among numerous different peoples.

Similarly in the Amazon Valley, official and private slave troops operated from the early seventeenth century until the middle of the eighteenth. Various religious orders (Franciscan, Mercedarian, Jesuit) collaborated with the official troops in the search for slaves. At times official and private slavers worked together; at times in competition. Besides relocating incalculable numbers of native peoples (at least 1,000 slaves per year at the height of official slaving in the eighteenth century) to work in settlements and plantation areas of the coast, colonists used Indian labor for extractive activities – principally cacao and the so-called forest spices. As in the south the systematic depopulation of the principal rivers forced slave troops to venture ever-greater distances into the interior; by the end of the slaving period, the main banks of the Amazon and its principal tributaries had been desolated, crippling future attempts at economic development of the colony.

In the central coast captaincies, virtually all efforts to colonize the interior and to exploit its economic resources failed until the late eighteenth and beginning of the nineteenth centuries – in large part due to the militant resistance of the Aimoré and Botocudo. Consequently the crown abandoned the region, and it thus became a refuge for many Indian groups.

In the northeastern interior, however, following the defeat of the Dutch, the Portuguese crown specifically encouraged the region's colonization and enslavement of its indigenous population. Prolonged wars against indigenous resistance movements ultimately opened the way to expansion. By the late seventeenth century, cattle ranching had been introduced, which, together with the extensive settlement of the native population in mission villages, transformed the social landscape of the region.

Cattle raising and ranching were introduced in nearly all areas over the eighteenth and nineteenth centuries. In the Amazon Valley these had limited success in the upper Rio Branco region, but in the south, northeast, and central coast, ranching, coupled with plantation agriculture, assumed major importance. In the south the expanding cattle industry complemented a flourishing mining economy, particularly gold mines around Cuiabá to the west. In the Amazon, despite numerous experiments in commercial agriculture, the economy stagnated until the mid–nineteenth century when rubber extraction and exportation began. From then until the beginning of the twentieth century, the predominant form of labor in the Amazon was extractive, and with the severe droughts in the northeast at the end of the nineteenth century, the two regions became inextricably linked through the massive influx of northeastern migrants. The increasing navigation of the main rivers, the construction of the Madeira-Mamoré and other railways, and the building of a system of telegraph lines, from the latter half of the nineteenth to the beginning of the twentieth century, integrated the south, north, and coastal regions in unprecedented ways. In the northeast cacao plantations complemented cattle ranching; in the south there were coffee plantations and new migrations of European colonists. Yet indigenous lands continued to be invaded and reduced or threatened by ever-increasing pressures on all fronts of expansion.

Directions in Indian Policy

The cases also illustrate some of the critical questions that shaped Indian policy from the colonial period to the early republic. In numerous instances peoples served as examples or "models" for the implementation of specific policies consonant with, or in contradiction to, existing legislation.

The initial period of trade with the Indians, which lasted until roughly the middle of the sixteenth century, had by the seventeenth century been superseded by a colonization agenda. This entailed two basic policies toward the Indians. First of all, taking possession of the land implied direct exploitation of its resources as opposed to the previous century's system of barter. Direct exploitation, however, meant direct control of labor. Where capital was lacking and African slaves could not be obtained, the course of action was to look for local supply – that is, Indian labor, whether slave or nominally free. Second, basic policy sought to secure ever-expanding boundaries through the formation of alliances with or, if possible, total political control over strategically chosen Indian groups.

In many cases the two issues of labor and territorial disputes were interrelated; in others they operated independently. Portuguese disputes with the Dutch in the northern and northeastern territories directly involved the Manao and the Kariri. Portuguese disputes with the Spaniards on the upper Solimões and in the south involved the Omagua, Guaykuru, Payaguá, and Guarani. In all cases the question revolved around control over Indian labor and was characterized by Portuguese policies that were warlike and aggressive and often led to subsequent enslavement.

Despite the Indian Freedom Law instituted in the mid–eighteenth century, illegal slaving continued well into the nineteenth century, and even the unrestricted freedom supposedly guaranteed by the law was limited by cases of "exceptions" – peoples considered enemies of the crown, who presented impediments to colonial expansion, settlement, and development. Such was the case of the Mura of the Tapajós and Madeira rivers in the late eighteenth century. Their assaults on settlements were met with an elaborate military response and an equally elaborate ideological justification for their enslavement. In this and numerous other cases, the very images created by the Portuguese of warlike or "cannibal" peoples shaped Indian policy, fueling conquest or campaigns of extermination. In the first decades of the nineteenth century, the Botocudo were considered par excellence as Indians against whom war had to be waged and whose reputed "anthropophagy" justified the reinstitution of legalized slaving.

In the nineteenth century the dominant question revolved around the issue of land. Two cases presented here – the Botocudo and the Indians of the northeast – illustrate the kinds of artifices and subterfuges used to expropriate indigenous lands. In the northeast a policy of auctioning off indigenous lands went hand-in-hand with a veritable rush by local interests to occupy them, and with a long dispute that dragged on until the end of the Imperial period between municipalities, provinces, and the central government for possession of the spoils.

Various other issues appear in the cases: the use of Indian allies as frontline militia in conflicts over international boundaries, in provincial disputes with central government, and even in struggles between local interest groups. Evidently their long experiences in such disputes enabled native peoples to eventually bargain in favor of their own interests, especially to achieve some guarantee of their lands.

Finally, the cases of the Kaingang and Xokleng of southern Brazil illustrate some of the dominant conflicts in policy at the end of the nineteenth and beginning of the twentieth century. National debate was bitterly divided between the demands of a mentality dominated by notions of "progress" and racial superiority with its conviction that indigenous peoples were beyond the "social contract" and hence subject to conquest, and those who defended indigenous rights to territory. The debate came to a head as processes of colonization intensified and as atrocities committed against the Kaingang and Xokleng received public attention. As a result the tide turned in favor of the institutionalization of the protection of the Indian through the Indian Protection Service in 1910.

Transformations in Interethnic Relations

The consequences of Luso-Brazilian expansion were quite similar in two respects: first, a massive depopulation of the interior resulted from resettlement, enslavement, and disease, this last a factor for the three centuries under consideration; second, the assimilation of this ethnically diverse population into colonial society by transforming it into a homogeneous mass of either nominally free or slave laborers.

Among its other effects colonial penetration destabilized the balance of intergroup relations of alliance and warfare while introducing new elements to the internal political dynamics of native societies. Traditional enmities between Tupi and Guarani peoples were readily exploited in Portuguese slaving campaigns against the Guarani in the early seventeenth century. In the Chaco both the Spaniards and Portuguese used frontier hostilities between the Guarani and Guaykuru to their advantage. By the same token indigenous groups skillfully used alliances with foreign powers to further their own hostilities against their enemies. Each of the cases discussed in this chapter illustrates how native peoples wrestled with questions of survival and the advantages and disadvantages of allying with different powers.

As the Portuguese search for slaves increased, intertribal conflicts intensified, becoming more destructive and exploitative. In the Amazon Valley various cases demonstrate that, with the virtual elimination of once numerous and powerful peoples from the main banks of the rivers, their enemies of the interior occupied the spaces left open, creating an altogether new dynamic in intergroup relations.

European trade goods were rapidly assimilated into aboriginal networks of trade and commerce, and Europeans themselves were often seen as trade partners with whom social and political alliances could be made. With the continuing demand for labor in the colonies, however, the Portuguese sought to gain control over the networks themselves by eliminating groups who stood in the way, by exploiting trade relations to the point of disorganizing the logic and system of values governing production for trade, and by stimulating the emergence of native brokers who served colonial interests in obtaining products desired in European markets.

The massive truncation of aboriginal exchange networks made native societies vulnerable to incorporation into the processes of capitalist expansion. If the slaving economy of the seventeenth and eighteenth centuries transformed the social landscape of Brazil through resettlement and the creation of a homogeneous labor population on plantations linked to urban centers, the rubber boom, ranching, and coffee production of the nineteenth and early twentieth centuries transformed indigenous socioeconomic organization by linking local communities into a web of dependency through local, regional, and international networks of production and circulation.

Throughout the colonial period, with the constant "descents" (relocations) of peoples of diverse cultural origins from the backlands to colonial settlements, the emergent slave economies and societies inevitably became amalgamation of indigenous peoples whose distinct tribal identities were submerged into the single social status as slaves. Known as the "Carijó" in São Paulo (a term that had once referred exclusively to the Guarani), and "Tapuya" in the north and northeast, this neo-indigenous stratum had to be constantly replenished by new replacements due to high mortality, labor demands, and missionary activities. In the numerous cases of traditionally semisedentary, or nomadic hunting and gathering peoples, settlement meant radical transformations that many peoples in fact refused to accept until, unable to survive in increasingly hostile circumstances, they were forced to accommodate.

The process of forming a homogeneous generic Indian intensified from the mid–eighteenth century on, with the policy reforms of the Pombal regime. Indigenous resistance to resettlement, in the form of uprisings, or evasion and flight from colonial settlements, were often followed by efforts to regroup and reorganize, often within new territories and based on new forms of social and political organization. Settlement Indians, for their part, frequently sought to reconstruct a common identity, independent of their specific cultural origins, based on their common historical experiences in the settlements and a creative interweaving of diverse cultural traditions. Such a process of ethnogenesis, particularly clear in the case of settlement Indians of the northeast, eventually gained political meaning – to affirm Indian-ness, independent of specific tribal names or traditions, against the threat of forced extinction imposed by government policies.

Forms of Adaptation and Strategies of Resistance

Historical understanding of native survival strategies and social movements has often been limited by the erroneous presupposition found in much writing that the more dramatic – and hence better-documented – instances of collective resistance (such as armed rebellion, messianic movements, and uprisings) were the predominant native "responses" to conquest. It must be recognized that survival strategies were a constant feature of native life after contact and that native peoples were constantly engaged in the search for ways to incorporate, reject, modify, or work within the foreigners' systems as they understood them. As yet we are only beginning to understand the range of such possible options. Individual acts of defiance were certainly as common, if not more so, than collective resistance. Nonviolent means of subverting political and economic domination in many cases proved as effective a strategy as armed rebellion. Litigation through the courts was also a recourse available throughout the colonial period. The cases discussed essentially illustrate a series of long-term indigenous strategies to resist, subvert, or reverse domination through military, religious, and economic means.

Indians everywhere used armed resistance in a variety of forms. Mobility and mastery of the terrain advantaged nomadic peoples. Their guerilla-like attacks, raids on colonial settlements and expeditions, and pillaging of plantations deterred colonization and development. Colonists responded with brutal campaigns of extermination, "offensive wars," enslavement, and the infamous Indian hunters, forcing groups to accept settlement or suffer extinction. Mobility, coupled with intergroup alliances, proved to be an extremely effective strategy in the Chaco, where the allied forces of the riverine Payaguá and the horseback-riding Guaykuru were more than sufficient to hold off Spanish and Portuguese incursions until the second half of the eighteenth century.

The capacity of indigenous political structures to mobilize allies from among the same people or from other peoples was a critical factor and, in several cases, depended on the recognition of war leaders. The ad hoc confederation of Arawak-speaking peoples of the middle Rio Negro, under the leadership of the Manao chief Ajuricaba, against Portuguese expansion in the 1720s is a frequently cited example. Yet it should be remembered that the Manao confederation arose at a time of critical change on the Rio Negro and that, while Arawak political dynamics allowed for the emergence of war leaders in such times, the recognition of Ajuricaba was not unanimous. Pro-Portuguese factions existed among the Manao undermining a more effective and long-term resistance. Nevertheless Ajuricaba's defeat and suicide in 1727 became an important rallying point for indigenous resistance on the Rio Negro for generations afterward.

Rebellions, the armed uprising of peoples under colonial domination, were characteristic of Guarani and Gê-speaking peoples of the south during the period of Jesuit settlements and captivity from the late sixteenth to the latter half of the seventeenth century. Instances of rebellion are recorded in the Amazon and northeast throughout the colonial period. With the increasing transformation of the indigenous population into a neo-indigenous stratum of society, resistance merged with class consciousness in the Imperial period to produce the Cabanagem Revolt of the 1830s, in which significant numbers of Indians sided with peasant rebels against the dominant landholding class and sources of political power. Government forces, on the other hand, exploited traditional enmities between tribal peoples in the repression of the movement.

Indigenous peoples also relied on retreat and refuge in all periods. Several forms may be distinguished. There were flights en masse of whole peoples who, following military defeat or population loss from disease, migrated in several cases over extraordinary distances to reconstruct their societies in a new environment. The best known case is the series of Tupian prophetic movements in the first half of the sixteenth century from the coast of Pernambuco across the continent and eventually into the Amazon Valley. On a smaller scale were the Arawakan and Cariban prophet movements on the Rio Negro and Branco in the mid–to late nineteenth century, and the numerous Guarani movements in search of the "Land without Evil," which likewise were motivated in part by refuge from external pressures.

Mass dislocations of peoples were not always linked to religious motives, however, for there are countless cases of peoples who abandoned their homelands and fled to other territories to escape enslavement and disease. Sometimes retreat became a permanent strategy of survival involving the abandonment of sedentary, agricultural ways and the adoption of more mobile, nomadic patterns (for example, the Guajá of Maranhão and several Gê-speaking peoples of central Brazil).

Throughout the slavery and resettlement periods, individual and collective flight was a constantly used strategy to escape the often violent and degrading work conditions in the settlements. Yet when compared with the dim prospects of returning to a homeland already devastated by slave troops and disease, the protection offered by mission settlements may have seemed relatively more secure. The decision whether to attempt escape depended on a variety of local circumstances and individual considerations. For their part, colonial officials were constantly concerned with the problem of truancy and desertions and made every effort possible to resettle people far from their places of origin. During the nineteenth century, colonization and expansion had advanced to the point where retreat and flight seemed to present greater difficulties in all but the most remote areas of the frontier.

The large literature on messianic movements in lowland South America devotes substantial attention to Tupi-Guarani prophetism, "holiness movements," and the "Land without Evil" migrations. These and other movements are discussed in the course of this chapter, highlighting three major points. First, as a long-term strategy of resistance, messianism has been flexible and changeable in its ideology and practice. Among the same peoples we find ideologies of world destruction based in preexisting religious belief, followed by ideologies of transformation in Indian–white relations, or the assimilation of the white man's culture. Depending on the historical circumstances, messianism has been associated with militant resistance, flight and refuge, or the incorporation of elements of white culture. Evidently the nature of messianic ideology and its relation to political action have had important consequences for the directions of change a society adopts. By the same token preexisting patterns of religious belief have shaped the direction messianism has taken in the long run.

Second, the ties between messianism and Christianity are subtle and complex. Although the millenarian foundations of Christianity and its scenario of the return of the dead surely resonated in indigenous cultures and provoked a reawakening of traditional eschatologies, many messianic movements were outright and bitter rejections of Christianity, even where prophets took on biblical or saintly names, or the name of Christ. Finally, indigenous messianism and millenarianism are fundamentally spiritual and religious movements that cannot be understood solely through the political, economic, or social realities of contact, although such realities framed some of the main concerns of messianic ideologies. Guarani prophetism, as stated previously, predated first contact and was related to fundamental values contained in the Guarani "way of being." Even in the first century of contact, however, characteristics of the movements put in doubt the "Land without Evil" theme as their principal objective: Colonial prophets demonstrated their ability to unleash armed rebellions against the oppressors. Thus Guarani prophetism was rooted in both traditional and transformative kinds of action: traditional in the sense of preserving those elements fundamental to the Guarani – their identity and freedom – and transformative because it preached the destruction of the existing order precisely to achieve the first objective.

Similarly the so-called Jurupary cults of the northwest Amazon formed the basis of late seventeenth-century messianic movements on the Solimões whose leaders associated influential Jesuit missionaries with returning divine heroes, and nineteenth-century millenarian movements whose leaders – powerful shamans – improvised on the symbolism of the myths and rituals related to the complex to formulate a strategy of resistance to colonial domination. Traditional festivals of exchange and sacred music were also essential to the formation of a new pan-Indian religious identity in the colonial context.

Finally, there were a variety of ways native peoples were incorporated into, sought to use, or undermined colonial and imperial labor systems. Once powerful peoples such as the Manao and Tapajó sought to accommodate by becoming useful servants to the crown, acting as intermediaries or brokers in the slave trade and descents. The fate of slaves or "free" Indians was often a question of degree, depending on the conjuncture of state control, colonists' demands, and missionary policies. To many peoples there was no choice: With their numbers diminished and on the verge of extinction, they were forced to accept permanent incorporation as the only way to survive. Yet numerous instances of uprisings, evasions, and armed resistance to enslavement were constant impediments to the development of the slave economy. Where colonists used violence to corral labor, the Indians responded with violence, plundering, and stealing from plantations, villages, and expeditions. Furthermore, various peoples sought to maintain their relative autonomy through minimal participation in the colonial economy or through alternative economic activities. Indians in the south sold meat and animal hides in competition with colonial markets; the Mawé of the Madeira River commercialized *guaraná* and spices in competition with the Portuguese.

INDIAN POLICY AND LEGISLATION FROM THE COLONY TO THE REPUBLIC

To support its policies in relation to the Indian, the Portuguese crown followed two basic principles in legislation – one that applied to settled and allied Indians and which corresponded to the colonization agenda as such, and another that applied especially to war. Traditional analyses of colonial Indian legislation have tended to see it as "contradictory" and "wavering" between these two principles when, in fact, both served to guide emerging legislation in the same way as the law of peace and the law of war coexist in international law. In this sense the law of war and the subsequent possibility of enslavement should not be seen as "exceptions" to the rule or, as is often supposed, as concessions to political and economic pressures from the colonists on the crown. Within the legal system itself, war was as basic a principle as peace, and the enslavement of prisoners a natural legal consequence of the very judicial definition of war current at the time.

By the latter half of the sixteenth century, the principal actors in Portuguese expansion and policy relative to the Indians were already on the scene: the crown, the colonists, and the religious orders, especially the Jesuits. Religious orders had a strong claim to interfere in Indian affairs because the canonical reason for Portuguese and Spanish possession of the New World was evangelization of the "gentiles." On these grounds Alexander VI in 1493 had distributed the newly discovered continent among the two Iberian powers. All missionary orders readily cited these bases of the crown's title to the New World whenever their powers were challenged, but not all of them had the same degree of independence. The clergy was structurally tied to the state, and it was anything but monolithic. Through the system of *padroado*, which endured until the end of the nineteenth century, the papacy had delegated to the king of Portugal in his role as Grand Master of the Order of Christ, the right to control appointments of the secular clergy. As for religious orders (Franciscans, Carmelites, Benedictines, and Mercedarians), most were also financially dependent on crown support, and their numbers in the colony could easily be curtailed by financial pressure.

The Jesuits were probably the only exception. For one thing the Company of Jesus enjoyed strong support in Rome and did not solely depend on the crown's good will. For another, it succeeded in becoming to some extent financially independent of the crown, establishing its own plantations, relying on inheritances, and at times controlling an abundant Indian labor supply. But even the Jesuits could not prosper without state support, as their several expulsions from the colony demonstrate. Never did their affairs run so smoothly, on the other hand, than under Padre Antônio Vieira, a brilliant intellectual and probably the best writer in the Portuguese language, who was a favorite of King João IV; or during the long reigns of Pedro II and Dom João V (1680–1750), who favored the otherwise very powerful order. In 1655 Vieira was able to secure for the order a monopoly of temporal and religious rule over Indian villages in Maranhão and Pará, with the full support of the then Governor Vidal de Negreiros.

The Church, moreover, was not monolithic. Carmelites, Mercedarians, Franciscans, Benedictines, and Jesuits bitterly disputed their respective powers. The orders shared a reluctance to comply with the episcopal authority, and rivalry among them, or even among different provinces of the same religious order, made it all too easy for the crown to rule the Church.[2]

By the end of the seventeenth century, under the challenge of encroachments by foreign powers at its boundaries, Portugal launched an aggressive policy of occupation of the Amazon Valley. Missions were to be the instrument of this occupation, and a state policy of Portuguese presence, influence and trade in remote areas took precedence over colonists' private interests, which entailed a constant demand for Indian labor in the eastern settlements. As a result the Amazon was divided up among the Jesuits, the Franciscans of two Portuguese provinces, the Carmelites,

[2] In the seventeenth and eighteenth centuries, each regular order was meaningfully called a religion. It is noteworthy that the Mercedarians and Carmelites appear to have sided with settlers' demands on Indian labor. In the Overseas Council's consultation of 1672, for example, these two orders were strongly in support of the colonists' views. Mathias Kiemen, *The Indian Policy of Portugal in the Amazon Region, 1614–93* (Washington, 1954), 125.

and the Mercedarians. Missionaries were given carte blanche to establish Indian villages on the upper rivers, to remove foreign influence, and to secure Indian trade and war allies.[3]

The mid-eighteenth century was a period of extraordinary statesmanship and centralization of the Portuguese crown under the prime minister, the Marquês de Pombal. The emphasis of Pombal's Indian policy – so important to him that he sent his brother as governor of the captaincy of the Rio Negro on the upper Amazon – was the complete cultural assimilation of the Indians into colonial society. By expelling the Jesuits from the colony, Pombal also reduced the actors involved in shaping Indian policy to basically the state and the settlers.[4]

In colonial times law making on Indian affairs was distributed amongst several administrative levels. At the top of the hierarchy, the king would issue royal laws (*cartas régias*) and regulations (*regimentos alvarás, provisões*), mostly addressed to governors. The governors in turn, and at times town councils and local committees (*juntas*), could issue minor laws. From the early seventeenth century on, there were two separate governments in Brazil proper – Brazil and Maranhão e Pará. Thus legislation was not necessarily the same within the two colonies nor between Portugal and Brazil. Although royal laws could be general, most were surprisingly no less local in scope and ad hoc in spirit than their colony-issued counterparts.

In Indian matters the crown relied successively on two permanent advisory bodies and occasionally on special committees. The first was the Mesa da Consciência, created in 1532 by King João III to advise him on matters of conscience. The Mesa became very much involved with colonial affairs and greatly resented the later creation of the India Council (Conselho da India) and its successor, the Overseas Council (Conselho Ultramarino). The Mesa was able to retain its power to appoint secular clergy but, with time, seems to have lost its advisory role in theological matters. It was abolished in Brazil in 1828 and in Portugal in 1833.

Between 1580 and 1640 when Spanish kings also held the crown of Portugal, a short-lived India Council was created, although it never fully controlled colonial matters, which were handled by the Treasury Council (Conselho da Fazenda). Nevertheless the administration of Portuguese

[3] Ibid., 163.

[4] In 1798, the Pombaline Directorate was abolished, and the Indians were again declared free of administration. Yet administrators continued to exist until their formal reappearance in 1845.

colonies was kept separate from that of Spanish colonies. In 1643, shortly after the House of Bragança had restored Portugal's independence from Spain, the new king of Portugal created the Overseas Council, which could be consulted both by him and by private parties, and which was particularly active on Indian affairs during the seventeenth century.

When disputes over Brazilian Indian labor became too heated, the king would, in addition to these permanent bodies, also form ad hoc committees or *juntas* to examine particular legal issues. Thus a Junta das Missões, comprised of the most prominent theologians, three Portuguese bishops, and representatives of religious orders in Maranhão, was asked in 1655 to examine at length the legal foundations for Indian enslavement. Given the results and the ensuing protest from town councils in São Luis and Belém, another committee was formed 3 years later, but it only ratified the previous *junta*'s conclusions. Other *juntas* were formed in 1686 and 1693, but, as in 1672 and 1680, distressed by conflicting demands, the Overseas Council itself consulted all parties (except the Indians) concerning the best course of action.

As is well known, the conquest of America gave rise to intricate legal discussions and ultimately to the birth of international law. Two great problems divided the specialists, the issue of enslavement and titles to land in the New World. Francisco Vitoria, the great Spanish Dominican theologian and jurist, claimed that Indian chiefs had true dominion over the land and that only through "Just War" – that is, a war decided upon by legitimate authority, with a just cause, and a righteous intention – could Indians be enslaved. "Just War" was a concept forged during the Crusades against the Moors and had a very specific, though disputed, meaning. For Vitoria a "Just War" could not be the result of a mere difference in religion, nor the enhancement of the empire. Only the violation of one of the following rights would be sufficient: freedom of settlement, trade, and communication, and freedom to evangelize, which did not mean, however, that there was any obligation for the Indians to accept the Christian faith. In short, the principles defining war were extensively debated and grounded in legal arguments. Although hedged by restrictions, war was nevertheless often waged without legal justifications and often declared unjust and hence null. This sometimes resulted in the freeing of prisoners and their resettlement in villages.

"Indian nations," as they were called, could thus theoretically retain independence and be allies, enemies, or neutral. But they could allegedly also agree to become vassals of the king. This was done not only with the king of Portugal but also when the French began colonization projects in Maranhão in 1611, when they too claimed that local Indian chiefs had willingly given over their land to the queen regent and considered themselves her vassals. In 1660 Vieira could boast of having had fifty-three Indian chiefs of Marajó sign terms of fealty to the king of Portugal.

The principles on which the colonial project was based remained unchanged from the sixteenth through the eighteenth centuries (with some modifications in the Pombaline period). In essence the project was imagined as a peaceful process of relocation through persuasion in which Indians would be settled in villages where they would remain free, lords of their lands, converted and civilized. Ideally transformed into "useful vassals," these Indians would guarantee the sustenance of the colony through salaried work for the settlers, as well as its defense and occupation because they would comprise the bulk of the population of the colony. The importance of these Indians is unanimously recognized in all documents of the period, which state that colonization was impossible without them.

When colonial troops went to the hinterland in an *entrada*, they would normally do two things: ransom slaves (hence the name *resgate* given to such expeditions) – that is, acquire in exchange for goods, legal slaves from the Indians and those captives who were supposedly destined to be eaten. These were forced to pay for their rescue by a period of enslavement under the Portuguese. The *entradas* were also supposed to persuade Indian nations to become vassals of the king and "descend" (hence the term *descimentos* also used for such expeditions), or relocate from the backlands, to be settled in villages near colonial establishments. A successful peaceful *entrada* could therefore provide both Indian slaves and newly descended free Indians.

Although their status was different, slave and free Indians were part of a gradient of dependence. Slaves were full private property and were favored by the colonists. The state, for its part, tried to retain control over free Indian labor, which was only temporarily relinquished in favor of the missionaries when territorial expansion took precedence over private concerns in the Amazon. As soon as foreign boundaries were secured in the mid–eighteenth century, the state again took direct control over Indian villages.

Among lowland South American Indian peoples, full-fledged slavery, the use of people as an alienable commodity, seems not to have existed, and contrary to African societies where ready-made slaves could be acquired, in Brazil considerable legal ingenuity was needed to create them. Moreover the state needed both vassals to secure the country as well as workers to make it profitable. For revenues the colonists demanded labor, preferably in the form of slaves. Because vassals could not be enslaved, a compromise was made: Some Indians would be slaves, while others would be forced to work but be nominally free.

As a general rule and despite minor variations, an Indian could legally be a slave provided he or she had been captured in a "just war," either defensive or offensive. Theoretically at least, a decision had to be made on the justice of internecine wars. Indians who were "slaves" of a group against whom a "Just War" had been launched by the Portuguese were also, as enemy property, legal slaves. Indians who were held to be eaten by cannibals – a custom widespread among Tupi-speaking groups but widely imputed, for obvious reasons, to other groups as well – if ransomed by the expedition, would be legal slaves. This title was based on an erudite discussion of whether someone in peril of losing his life could relinquish his freedom or even his relative's freedom. The same reasoning was applied to the "voluntary enslavement" of hunger-stricken free Indians following the epidemics that devastated Bahian villages.

Indian peoples who traded with the Portuguese were thus implicitly, or explicitly, encouraged to wage wars on their neighbors and enemies to produce slaves. After Dom Pedro II, acting on Vieira's advice, promulgated the famous law of 1680 abolishing all Indian slavery, former Indian allies of the Portuguese traded their captives with the French. Alarmed at such an encroachment, the king decided in 1688 to revoke the law and reintroduce Indian slavery. Although the crown would probably have preferred at the outset to create a free labor market in the colony and secure a dependable Indian population, by then the system created by the slave trade had gained a dynamic of its own.

The crown tried to control the colonists' abuses by limiting the justifications of Indian enslavement: Thus from 1570 to 1609, a series of royal laws limited more narrowly the cases when Indians could be held. By 1595 only a "Just War" expressly launched by the king himself in a provision signed by his own royal hand could allow for it. The standard form of such laws was a declaration of the freedom of the Indians followed by an enumeration of the exceptions. Any exception was used by the colonists who evaded all control and, in 1609, an exasperated king declared that all Indians, Christian or gentile, should be set free. Two years later, under pressure from the colonists, the exceptions were reintroduced. The same occurred in the 1680s, but for different reasons. Over half a century later, Pombal once again declared full Indian freedom. Yet as late as 1808, Dom João VI, having fled the Napoleonic invasions and settled in Rio de Janeiro, waged an anachronistic war against the Botocudo in Minas Gerais, Espirito Santo, and present-day Paraná, in which slavery was once again introduced. It was finally abolished in 1833, but Indians were still sold as slaves until well into the middle of the nineteenth century.

The crown tried all along to retain control of slaving by monopolizing the conditions for sending expeditions. The crown appointed officials and also, at times, financed expeditions directly instead of permitting the colonists to organize them at their own expense so as to divide the spoils more easily amongst themselves. The crown, however, did not invest large amounts of capital in Maranhão and Pará, and sometimes it even used the expediency of paying officials and missionaries salaries in kind – that is, through Indian labor whether slave or free. Slaves were roughly distributed among those who had financed the expeditions, local and metropolitan officials, and clergy. In some periods from 1688 on, they were acquired from the crown who began financing expeditions.

Free Indians were brought into colonial villages called *aldeias*, separate from Portuguese settlements. The rationale for such descents was both the settling of the Indians – literally, their "domestication" – and convenience for evangelization. Colonists sought to have these villages close to their settlements, while the Jesuits preferred to have them located in more remote areas where colonists couldn't interfere as much.

Villages were more often than not multiethnic settlements where newly descended groups were brought in to replenish the decimated ranks of their predecessors. Epidemics, overwork, famine, desertion, and colonists' abuses regularly reduced the populations of *aldeias.* The documents nevertheless frequently state that it was necessary to punish the settlers who treated the free Indians as if they were their slaves, selling them and disposing of them in dowries or debt payments. Although such practices were common, the freedom of settled Indians remained a firm principle of the crown's policy. Even when descents were permitted to private parties, settlers were obliged to keep the Indians in the villages at their own expense, the only advantage being the exclusive redistribution of these Indians while they lived, although this did not exempt the settlers from paying salaries nor from respecting the stipulated time of service.[5]

A few *aldeias* could be designated to support religious orders or for some other special purpose, but more generally they were "distribution villages" (*aldeias de repartição*), providing labor to the royal administration and the colonists. Village Indians would at once reproduce themselves and the system, because they had a triple obligation: to sustain the villages, to take part as troops and rowers in further expeditions to bring more Indians down from the backlands, and to serve crown officials and private parties mostly in agricultural work, fishing, and gathering. It is small wonder that an important legal issue in the colony was concerned with the power to distribute Indians for work. Although village Indians were considered free, only for very short periods were they granted full independence from any administrator. The Pombaline Directory system was abolished in 1798, and Indians were declared free of administrators, but these continued to exist informally until their legal reappearance in 1845.

Controlling labor in the poorest regions of the colony, where land was plentiful but the labor force scarce, meant controlling the whole economy. Not surprisingly, administration of Indian villages was bitterly disputed throughout most of the seventeenth century among lay administrators and the clergy, with state officials, town councils, bishops, Franciscans, and Jesuits claiming either the office of administrator itself or the power to appoint incumbents. In times of compromise villages would be connected to all of these candidates. Otherwise, in Maranhão and Pará, the Franciscans in 1624 displaced lay administrators de jure, but not de facto, for less than ten years until lay captains took over again, while Jesuits achieved short-lived monopoly over all the villages from 1655–1661 and again from 1680–1688. In 1693 the regular orders were given full control of Indian villages, and the missions were distributed among them, an arrangement that lasted until the mid-eighteenth century.

Another important legal issue in this connection was the amount of work that could be extracted from free Indians. Free Indians had to

[5] All types of deception were used: One was to have free Indians marry slaves and thus retain them on these grounds. Whenever control could be evaded, any Indian obtained in the *entradas* would be registered as a slave, on the grounds that they were destined to be eaten.

maintain their own villages, and the more time they served the colonists or in expeditions, the less they could cultivate their own fields. Regulations of the value of Indian wages and the procedures for payment were other points of crown concern, as were the prices to be paid for Indian products. Indians were constantly cheated in every one of these stages.

Although the free Indians were seen as the backbone of the colonial system and their labor the sine qua non of the colony's sustenance, the project was severely undermined by day-to-day practices. Free Indians were frequently enslaved, and they abandoned villages en masse, depriving the colony of its indispensable labor force. Descents were made with violence, and there occurred all imaginable types of abuses and disrespect for labor legislation on the part of settlers. The crown nevertheless continued to believe in the viability of the project and constantly modified the manner of putting it into practice. At the level of application, then, and not of principle, one finds oscillations and contradictions. Even in the Pombaline period, the basic ideas did not change, and the great reform of Pombaline legislation was to wager on a radical transformation of the Indians into Portuguese subjects, based on the supposition that what had been responsible for the failure of the project until then was the Indians' natural "laziness" and their "odious" ethnic differences.

The end of the seventeenth century and the first half of the eighteenth witnessed the rapid territorial expansion that roughly accounts for present-day Brazil. This was largely secured by religious missions in the Amazon. When the Treaty of Madrid was signed in 1750, and the boundaries between Portuguese and Spanish colonies defined, the crown realized that internal control was, at least in the Amazon, largely in the hands of the clergy, above all the Jesuits. In fact the Jesuits controlled a continuous hinterland territory in the different parts of the Amazon, which included no less than all of its southern tributaries extending to Paraguay, through the provinces of Maynas and Mojos. Their control was symbolized linguistically. *Lingua geral,* a Tupian *lingua franca* invented by the Jesuits, predominated over Portuguese in the Amazon until the early twentieth century. Even though the crown favored the order in the early eighteenth century, it had to insist that the "Black Robes" teach *lingua geral* to the colonists' children.

Such an "empire-within-an-empire" was threatening. In the tide of anti-Jesuitism that resulted in the expulsion of the order from most European countries and even its extinction, Pombal did away with all administration of Indian villages by regular orders and ultimately expelled the Jesuits from Brazil in 1759. Once again Indian slavery was abolished. All segregation was to end; Pombal declared free Indian villages to be ordinary colonial settlements, open to everyone. New regulations called for Portuguese men to marry Indian women and established the use of the Portuguese language. The idea was to create an assimilated free population as the sole secure basis of the state. Slavery was to be restricted to Africans. As had been attempted in 1682, the crown launched a policy of introducing African slaves in Grão Pará, but pressure for labor once again grew from the colonists so that by the end of the 1750s, the directorate of the Indians was promulgated and lay administration was revived. Free Indians were once again forced to work.

Private greed of the new administrators, as opposed to the long-term political ambitions of religious orders, is often given as the reason for the decay of the village populations in the period of the directorate. The administrators were actually given 6 percent of the internal revenue of their villages for their fees, and this certainly encouraged exploitation. Indians deserted the old villages, and by 1798 the directorate was officially abolished.

Total secularization and the expulsion of the Jesuits changed the nature of Indian policy. No third party could interfere between the settlers and the crown. Although religious orders were reintroduced into Indian affairs in the 1840s, they never recovered their former importance.

When independence was proclaimed in 1822, a new period of statesmanship and modernization was launched by José Bonifácio de Andrada e Silva and the Emperor Pedro I. Not surprisingly, Andrada's Indian program was similar to Pombal's. He hoped to amalgamate a free assimilated population, which this time was to include emancipated African slaves and their descendants, to become the nation on which the new state would be formed. Consistently the constitutional draft of 1823 merely envisaged the evangelization and civilization of the Indians, while the constitution passed down by the emperor the next year did not mention Indians at all. When Dom Pedro's and Andrada's programs were defeated by local oligarchies, and the emperor forced to abdicate, the heirs of old-time settlers attained long-awaited power. Significantly, in 1834, the provinces were given the power to legislate on Indian issues, together with the central government.

By then the Indian question in central areas had changed. It was no longer primarily concerned with Indian labor and boundary expansion. The Indian issue was now dominated by land itself. It is true that, at the fringes of the empire, where capital was lacking, or on the economic frontiers, long-time problems were still of concern. Thus Indian labor in the Amazon was still at stake, while in Mato Grosso or Paraná, Indian groups were used in the opening up of new river routes. Official policy, however, was mainly concerned with land, and this had two complementary aspects which can be seen as two phases of a single process of expropriation. In the hinterland newly contacted groups in coveted areas would be concentrated in reduced portions of their former territories or, more rarely, settled in villages near neo-Brazilian establishments, as was done in previous centuries. The aim was to "clean" the land rather than to obtain labor. It is significant in this context that a debate over whether "savage Indians" should be exterminated or civilized took place for the first time in the early years of the empire. The discussion centered on the very humanity of the Indian and their ability to be "civilized."

In areas of early colonization, the land of former free Indian villages was coveted. By claiming that there were no more Indians in such villages, or that they had been assimilated, villages could be extinguished and their lands appropriated. From the 1860s on the imperial government, the provinces, and town councils disputed the land of these extinct villages.

Between 1798 and 1845 there is somewhat of a void in administrative rules. Indians could be directly obtained by private parties with little control. Paradoxically in some provinces the directorate, although officially abrogated, was still in force for lack of an alternative organization. In 1845 the *Regulation of the Missions* was passed in which, although lay administrators would govern the settlements, missionaries would serve as auxiliaries. In fact the Italian Franciscans held many of the administrators' posts for lack of alternative candidates.

In the upper Amazon, where the rubber boom was beginning, Indian labor was still all-important. Not until the 1870s, when Pará entrepreneurs replaced local rubber patrons in the very rich areas of the Juruá and Purús, did non-Indian labor – namely, the drought-stricken northeasterners – become important. Because the central government dealt mostly with Indian land, provinces like Amazonas, created in 1852, had a free hand in controlling Indian labor, which they did in ways in which the colonists had always dreamed.

The end of the nineteenth century and beginning of the twentieth were marked by an intensive process of economic penetration and conquest of unexplored territories. In the south the coffee economy of São

Paulo, European immigration in Santa Catarina, and the building of railroads and telegraph lines advanced throughout the interior. In the northeast and central Brazil, cattle ranching and colonization expanded deeper into hitherto isolated regions. In Amazonia rubber extraction reached a peak of intensity in the first two decades of the century, penetrating in its predatory and anarchic fashion into the most remote regions of the rainforest.

The consequences of this process were everywhere destructive for Indian peoples, as D. Ribeiro has documented in his *Os Indios e a Civilização.* Existing legislation, which tended to work against the protection of indigenous interests, aggravated this situation. "Evangelization and civilization" of the Indians were an attribute of the state governments; furthermore the constitution of 1891 gave the states the power to decide on lands in their respective territories.

National opinion was divided over the most effective policy to adopt in view of the chaotic situation of contact in the interior. Some argued that economic progress could not be impeded and advocated the extermination of groups who resisted; others believed that the Church had the exclusive right to civilize the Indians through the system of catechization; finally, an emerging lobby, supported by the political movement of Positivism, held that it was possible to incorporate the Indian into Brazilian society with the demarcation of indigenous territories and government protection.

The Positivists regarded indigenous peoples as "fetishists" living in the period of infancy in the evolution of the human spirit, and hence requiring protection so that they could evolve to a more advanced stage without the need for catechization by the Church. The fundamental objectives of the Positivists' program were to serve as the basis for the founding of the Indian Protection Service in 1910.

The critical testing ground for Positivist theory was developed in the field through the Rondon Mission. In the 1890s the imperial government initiated a program to put up telegraph lines connecting the political centers of the country to its frontiers. This project was to cut through thousands of kilometers of hitherto unexplored territory, which constituted the homelands of dozens of indigenous groups, many of whom were uncontacted and had the reputation of being hostile. For over 15 years the head of the mission, Candido Mariano da Silva Rondon, himself a militant Positivist, sought to establish a policy of peaceful contact with these groups. Nevertheless a careful reading of the expedition's reports reveals that the idealism of the project was backed by considerable demonstrations of military strength. Furthermore one of the mission's principal objectives of "attracting to pacify" – settling newly contacted groups at strategic locations along the route of the telegraph lines in order to form "agricultural colonies" and to train Indian laborers – in principle differed little from the eighteenth- and early nineteenth-century policies of settling and transforming frontier groups into loyal subjects of the crown.

When the Ministry of Agriculture was given control over the civilization and catechization of the Indians in 1906, thereby removing this power from the states, conditions were propitious for the implementation of the Positivists' program. In the midst of an intense national and international movement of public opinion, the government of President Nilo Peçanha created the SPILTN (*Serviço de Proteção aos Indios e Localização dos Trabalhadores Nacionais*, or Service for the Protection of the Indians and Settlement of National Laborers; more widely known as the S.P.I., Indian Protection Service) in 1910, under the direction of General Rondon, thus inaugurating a new phase in the history of the nation's relations to the indigenous peoples.

THE SOUTH

Southern Brazil presents a special challenge within the context of Brazilian Indian history. Certainly one of the most densely populated regions in precolonial times, the area now covered by the modern-day states of São Paulo, Paraná, Santa Catarina, Rio Grande do Sul, and Mato Grosso do Sul contains a sparse indigenous population today, with few exceptions limited to small and dispersed communities. At the same time, the regional historiographical traditions of these states have practically ignored the indigenous past. Notwithstanding this neglect the abundance of scarcely explored primary sources and the growing number of ethnographic and ethnohistorical investigations permit at least a preliminary synthesis, though marked primarily by uncertainties and discontinuities.

The Guarani, Guaykuru, and Kaingang were the principal indigenous groups of the region. Although other significant groups inhabited the area, these three stand out not only because of their numerical significance but also because it is possible to accompany the history of their relations with whites – and with each other – over a considerably long period. In addition it is worth noting that Guarani, Kaingang, and

Guaykuru groups have managed to preserve a great measure of autonomy, though facing constant threats to their cultural and even physical survival, including enslavement, confinement to missions, acute demographic decline, and deliberate policies of extermination over the course of nearly five centuries. Thus the indigenous history of southern Brazil allows for an examination of the complex relationship between the multiple forms of white penetration and the political strategies assumed by native peoples in adapting to a long series of ruptures and transformations.

Enslavement and Reconstitution of the Guarani

Around 1600 the vast southern borderlands between Portuguese and Spanish America were inhabited by numerous indigenous groups. Although in constant contact with Europeans since the first half of the sixteenth century, the Guarani – known to the Portuguese as Carijó (Cario in Spanish) – remained by far the most populous and widely distributed society of the region. Colonial travel accounts and Jesuit relations identified large concentrations of Guarani speakers covering an area as vast as 550,000 square kilometers, extending east–west from the Paraguay River to the Atlantic Ocean, and north–south from the captaincy of São Vicente to the modern border between Brazil and Uruguay. In spite of the first impression that these sources convey, the Guarani did not occupy the whole region homogeneously and exclusively. Most Guarani communities lived in the tropical and subtropical forests along the coastal floodplain and escarpment, as well as along the major rivers of the Paraná-Paraguay system. Much of the interior of the southern region, however, was covered by practically treeless plains or by tall pine forests, preferred habitats of the hunting and foraging peoples, especially the ancestors of the modern Kaingang and Xokleng, within Brazilian territory, and the Charrúa and Minuano to the far south, in what is now Uruguay. To the northwest, along the upper Paraguay, the Guarani disputed the regional space with the Guaykuru and Payaguá, foraging peoples whose subsequent adaptations to the horse and river transport, respectively, made them formidable adversaries not only for the Guarani but also for the competing Iberian powers.

Cultural and linguistic unity, as well as the structural similarities among Guarani political units, have contributed to a monolithic treatment of Guarani society. To be sure, Guarani speakers in areas as distant as the Andean foothills and the Atlantic coast shared many features in their social, political, and spiritual organization. All practiced swidden agriculture, producing the abundant maize crops observed by all early chroniclers, setting them clearly apart from their hunter-forager neighbors. Although occupation sites varied considerably in size – ranging from about a hundred to a few thousand inhabitants – the basic unit was the semisedentary agrarian village, composed of several multifamily residential lodges. Like the Tupinambá of coastal Brazil, the Guarani moved their villages periodically. These spatial movements, often associated with the will of local headmen but occasionally linked to broader, messianic-inspired migrations, constituted one of the central dynamics of Guarani society and history.

The question of Guarani political and spiritual leadership remains a controversial matter. The emergence of powerful leaders in the sixteenth century, many of whom led bitter and violent rebellions against Spanish rule, stands in sharp contrast to the prevailing historiography, which portrays the Guarani as passively inclined to colonial domination, especially with the penetration of articulate and persuasive outsiders, such as the Jesuits and even the *bandeirantes.* Far from the uniform portrait that emerges from the colonial sources, the political landscape was composed of complex configurations of alliance and animosity between local Guarani groups, and between Guarani and other indigenous societies, including the Guaykuru and Kaingang, among others.

A further problem lies in the tendency of Spanish and Portuguese observers to identify territories as controlled by pan-village *caciques*, raising the possibility of the existence of Guarani chiefdoms. Whether these *caciques* enjoyed the status of chiefs, or were projected into a regional leadership role by the circumstances of European conquest, when the presence of competing colonial interests restructured alliance formations, remains a question.

At the same time, modern scholarship has focused on the influential prophets, known to the Guarani as *karaí*, who spread a messianic message among villages, often convincing significant factions to embark upon long-distance journeys. The final destination of these journeys was the *yvy mara ey*, generally interpreted as the "Land without Evil." Firmly rooted in Guarani beliefs, migrations already had taken place long before the arrival of the Europeans. Through a careful reading of the prophets' discourse, which was diametrically opposed to the rigid, conservative codes of the shamans and headmen, Clastres considers the historical significance of the movements to be rooted in the inherent conflict between types of authority.[6]

This view has been challenged persuasively by Bartomeu Meliá and Noemia Díaz Martínez, based on a reading of Antonio Ruiz de Montoya's *Tesoro de la Lengua Guaraní*, where *yvy mara ey* is interpreted as "ground intact, where nothing has been built." According to these authors, both the term and the movement must not be removed from their historical context: After all, the concept of a "Land without Evil" fit rather comfortably with sixteenth-century Iberian images of an earthly paradise. The significance of moving to virgin lands, then, in part lay in the ecological necessity of constantly renewed land for swidden agriculture, while also reenacting a sort of spiritual renewal, through the symbolic encounter with their origins in the pure, unadulterated ancestral forest. This act of material and spiritual renewal gained new meanings in the colonial context, when Guarani identity was constantly under assault by competing European interests.[7]

This interpretation is consistent with another, fundamental aspect of indigenous culture, the notion of a specifically Guarani "way of being," which likewise has had an important role in the history of their relations to the whites. The Jesuit Ruiz de Montoya, for example, wrote in 1693 that when a Jesuit missionary attempted to establish a reduction at Itatín, "one of the main chiefs ordered him with much determination and severity to return to his land because they would not admit of another way of being than that which they had inherited from their ancestors."

Various passages of Ruiz de Montoya's *Conquista Espiritual* dramatically express the manner in which the Guarani – and in particular their shamans – defended their way of being in opposition to impositions by the foreigners. Referring to the Jesuits, one leader is reported to have said: "The demons have brought us these men, for with their new doctrines, they wish to rob us of the ancient and good way of being of our ancestors."[8]

The size, density, and spatial dimensions of the on-contact Guarani population has proved another source of controversy. Early demographic studies, predicated on the assumption of low densities and slow, insignificant growth among semisedentary populations in tropical environments,

[6] Hélène Clastres, *Terra Sem Mal* (São Paulo, 1978).

[7] Noemia Díaz Martínez, "La migración Mbya (Guaraní)," *Dédalo*, São Paulo, 24 (1985), 147–169; Bartomeu Melià, *El Guaraní conquistado y reducido* (Asunción, 1988), 17–29.

[8] Cited in Melià, op cit., 101.

ascribed exceedingly low estimates to the precolonial Guarani population. However, recent revisions of historical sources, the reevaluation of environmental limitation theories, and the growing archaeological evidence from large, complex occupation sites, all have opened the way for fresh estimates. Pierre Clastres, in a pioneer essay on Guarani historical demography, calculated the total precolumbian Guarani population at 1.5 million. More recently Bartomeu Melià has called attention to the methodological flaws in Clastres's estimates, which do not consider the regional specificity of native occupation and the historical dimension of Guarani dispersion. Nonetheless Melià himself comes up with surprising figures for both the Guairá and Tape regions during the first half of the seventeenth century, based on Jesuit and Spanish colonial reports: as many as 200,000 Guarani for Guairá and 60,000 for Tape.

Considering the extensive areas occupied by these peoples, Guarani populations and polities for the most part remained intact until the early seventeenth century, though facing increasingly frequent incursions by Portuguese and Spanish slave raiders, as well as the incipient missionary activities of the Franciscans. By 1600, however, the expansion of the peripheral Iberian economies, centered respectively in São Paulo and Asunción, began to exert new pressures on the Indians. Although at that point neither colonial power demonstrated any interest in occupying these territories effectively, both Spanish and Portuguese colonists coveted Guarani labor, upon which all of their agricultural and commercial activities rested. At the same time, the arrival of the Jesuits, who began to articulate their "reduction" system among the Guarani in 1609, also contributed to the rapid transformation of these southern borderlands into a field of intense competition between native populations and contending colonial actors.

Indeed by the 1620s the interests of Portuguese slavers and Spanish Jesuits clashed, resulting in far-reaching demographic and spatial changes throughout the whole region. During the previous century the settlers of Brazil's southernmost captaincy of São Vicente already had launched several expeditions seeking Guarani captives for the nascent sugar industry along the coast. However, judging from the influx of Tememinó and Tupinaé captives during this period, it would appear as though the expeditions did not strike any major blows against Guaraní populations.

During the early years of the seventeenth century, the coastal slave trade was the main source for Guarani captives taken to the southern Portuguese captaincies. As basically private enterprises, the slaving expeditions along the coast actually were composed of a mixture of private, royal, and missionary interests, not unlike the *tropas de resgate* (ransom expeditions) that emerged later in the century in the Amazon. Although the collusion of royal officials, many of whom had commercial or agricultural concerns based on Indian slavery, greatly facilitated the Indian traffic, the Jesuits were mainly interested in moving the Carijó of the Patos region, along the coast of modern Santa Catarina, to the mission villages near Portuguese settlements. Private interests most frequently prevailed, and in spite of Jesuit protests, authorities tacitly consented to the unjust enslavement of the Guarani.

The slave trade certainly intensified the inherent conflicts between contending colonial agents, but it also had a profound impact on internal Guarani relations. Besides exacerbating factional or ethnic divisions among Guarani groups, it facilitated the emergence of native slave brokers, usually headmen but also shamans, in effect providing a nontraditional means for the ascension of Guarani leaders.

Although the coastal trade flourished into the 1630s, the Portuguese colonists of São Paulo began to focus their attention on the Guairá region during the second decade of the seventeenth century. With the growth of an incipient commercial agricultural economy, the Paulistas (residents of São Paulo) tied their fortunes to the rapid expansion of the Guarani labor force. In order to meet their needs, the Portuguese slavers began to rely more on the paramilitary organization of raiding armies than on the Guarani intermediaries who had proved so important in the Patos trade. Bolstered by thousands of Tememinó warriors enslaved on earlier campaigns, the slaving expeditions soon produced a steady flow of Guarani captives from Guairá to São Paulo.

The Paulistas continued their raids on Guairá for several years without coming into frontal conflict with the Jesuits, though the Spanish Jesuits had begun to organize their mission system in 1609. After all, Guairá was a vast region, and the nonmission population continued to outnumber the reduction residents until the late 1620s. But the picture had begun to change by then, as the cumulative effects of intensified slaving, missionization, and epidemic disease tightened the availability of Guarani captives and gathered a greater proportion of the total Guarani population in the reductions. The Paulista assault on the missions, then, was not for geopolitical or moral reasons, as some have argued, but because it was there that appreciable numbers of Guarani were to be found.

Whether or not they set out to destroy the missions, the large-scale

Paulista expeditions that penetrated Guairá between 1628 and 1632 had a profound effect on the Guarani population. Several independent villages were attacked and burned, and their hapless residents were submitted to a grueling march to São Paulo. Thirteen missions were totally ruined, and many of the neophytes were enslaved. The Jesuits managed to preserve most of the residents of two missions, leading them on a long exodus to the Uruguay River. Other groups sought refuge in the dense forests, only to come into contact with whites over two centuries later. Within a few years Guairá became practically a vast wasteland, stripped of its once thriving Guarani population.

The Paulistas continued to raid Guarani populations throughout the 1630s, launching attacks on the independent villages and missions of the Tape province, near the Uruguay River. Although taking thousands of Guarani captives, these expeditions met increasing indigenous and Jesuit resistance. On the one hand, as the Jesuits began to seclude the missions from European settlement by setting up the focus of their work on the upper Paraguay and along the Uruguay, the slavers had to face greater distances, harsher terrain, and more challenging indigenous enemies in their pursuit of Guarani labor. On the other, the Jesuits began to arm and organize their wards to resist. Most resistance, however, seemed to depend on more traditional weaponry. This factor probably more than the others determined the end of the large-scale raids on Guarani territory. Unaccustomed to defeat, the Paulistas faced major setbacks in Uruguay province, especially at Mbororé in 1641. Although a few, scattered expeditions wandered back to Guarani territory, for all practical purposes, the Mbororé "disaster" marked the end of an era.

If one immediate consequence of the Paulista raids was the depopulation of Guairá, another more complex one was the transfer of thousands of Guarani captives to the Portuguese settlements and their integration into colonial society and economy. The prevailing historical literature, certainly more concerned with the *bandeirante*, or slave hunter, than with the slaves he hunted, contends that the Paulistas sold their captives to sugar planters on the coast. Yet evidence from São Paulo demonstrates that the massive influx of Guarani captives resulting from the slaving expeditions proved a decisive step in the formation of a slave society in the region.

Certainly more than 50,000 Guarani captives were introduced between about 1600 and 1640. The impact of this forced migration emerges clearly from local probate records in São Paulo during this period, when the concentration of Indians reported in inventories reached extremely high levels. Virtually every property holder left at least a few Indians to his heirs, while several wealthier Paulistas boasted hundreds of "native blacks" among their individual possessions. However, submitted to a harsh work regime and exposed to periodic epidemics and famines, this reconstituted indigenous population had a persistently high negative natural growth rate. As a result the Paulistas always remained heavily dependent on slaving expeditions for the reproduction of the local population, which meant the influx of captives of increasingly diverse ethnic origins, especially after 1640. Nonetheless, because of the elevated numbers introduced before the date, the Guarani remained the principal ethnic group within the captive population until the end of the century, which explains why the Paulistas adopted the term Carijó as a generic reference to all Indians under their control. Thus, even though captives from over 100 different ethnic origins were integrated into colonial Paulista society, Guarani patterns predominated.

As a historical process the reconstitution of the indigenous population in São Paulo involved adjustments on the part of both colonists and captives. Because of legal restrictions on Indian slavery, the Paulistas fought a lengthy ideological and institutional battle with the Jesuits and the crown, in defense of their perceived right to exploit native labor, which had been captured in the distant wilderness at great expense. Indeed Indian labor was so dear to the Paulistas that, according to an ironic Jesuit observer: "Even if the Eternal Father descended from Heaven with Christ crucified in his arms to tell them that the Indians were free, they would not believe it."[9] Over the course of the seventeenth century, the colonists succeeded in eliminating these opponents, through the institution of a system of "personal administration," which looked like freedom and functioned like slavery. Within this paradoxical institutional framework, the colonists faced greater difficulties in molding their Indian laborers into a single and consistent, colonial ethnic category. After all, the transformation of Indian to slave involved much more than the raw, economic exploitation of native labor at the crack of a whip: Religious conversion, fictive kinship through *compadrio* ties, and a strong paternalistic discourse also formed part of the colonists' arsenal.

For their part the captives themselves forged spaces of survival within the colonial context through several kinds of adaptive strategies, which

[9] *Visita* of Padre Antônio Rodrigues, January, 25 1700, Jesuit Archives, Rome, Brasilia 10, f. 2v.

ultimately reinforced the development of a collective identity. Although open rebellions did occur, especially in the 1650s and involving mainly Kaingang actors, the Indian captives of São Paulo defended their interests through a continual process of what Steve Stern has called "resistant adaptation." Throughout the century Indians challenged both their masters and colonial authorities with parallel economic activities, ranging from the maintenance of independent garden plots to the semiclandestine marketing of stolen cattle and pillaged crops. The frequent practices of truancy and running away, classic categories of slave resistance, also may be seen in this light, because almost all runaways circulated within the colonial labor force. Finally, once colonial justice was established in São Paulo on a permanent basis, Indians became frequent litigants, not only exploiting the contradictory legislation to guarantee their freedom but also manifesting a clear sense of identity as Carijós.

The historical experience of the Guarani who were taken to São Paulo may be reconstructed piecemeal from the surviving record, and it remains a story heavily marked by cultural transformation and demographic decline. Representing the vast majority of Paulista society in the seventeenth century, the population considered Indian in São Paulo had practically disappeared by 1750. To be sure, the Indians freed either by manumission or by the extinction of the personal service regime joined the legions of rural poor whites and *mestiços*. But they left their ethnic identity behind with captivity.

By the early eighteenth century, both colonists and royal authorities began to entertain genuine territorial designs. In response to the needs of a flourishing mining economy, the cattle industry began to spread to the south. After several years of mutually suspicious negotiations, the Portuguese and Spanish sought to settle the boundary issue with the ratification of the Treaty of Madrid (1750), which incorporated into Portuguese territory numerous Kaingang groups, as well as the seven Guarani missions (Seven Pueblos) of the east bank of the Uruguay River.

Although satisfactory from the Iberian standpoint, the Treaty of Madrid proved disastrous to the Guarani. The treaty stipulated that the Seven Pueblos were to move to Spanish territory within 4 years, taking with them their movable property (consisting mainly of cattle) and leaving behind their opulent buildings and prosperous plantations. The Guarani of these missions, approximately 30,000 strong, adamantly refused to move and began to organize their resistance as soon as the mixed boundary commissions established the first markers along the Uruguay.

Guarani leaders drafted petitions to the Spanish monarch, reminding him of their military services against the Portuguese and pleading that their traditional homelands be preserved. At the same time, they sought to negotiate a solution with the Portuguese, signing a treaty in 1754 that guaranteed land rights. In spite of this agreement, both Spanish and Portuguese were determined to carry out the terms of the Treaty of Madrid, and they organized a powerful military column to squash Guarani opposition. Setting out in late 1755 against the Seven Pueblos, the Iberian army began a merciless slaughter of Guarani troops: Following the single battle of Caibaté, in February 1756, over 1,400 Guarani lay dead while less than 200 were captured, all at the expense of a handful of European casualties. The so-called Guarani War soon came to an end, as the Seven Pueblos were surrendered to Portuguese control.

The Guarani movement of the 1750s almost immediately was blamed on the Jesuits. Pombal and his subordinates exploited the episode as a convenient argument in support of the final expulsion of the Jesuits from Portuguese territories in 1759. In truth the role of the Jesuits was minimal in the mobilization of Guarani resistance. The persistence of powerful native leadership, enhanced by the military organization developed during the colonial period, and the strong sense of Guarani ethnic identity certainly contributed to the articulation of the movement. More seriously, perhaps, the recognition of Guarani autonomy left the Iberian powers with little alternative, other than the diplomatically embarrassing decision to launch a brutal military campaign against Indians who were considered loyal, exemplary Christian subjects.

In the aftermath of the Guarani War, the expulsion of the Jesuits and the continued dispute between Iberian powers weakened the material and demographic base of the Seven Pueblos. The area was returned to the Spanish with the Treaty of San Ildefonso (1777) and was once again occupied by the Portuguese in the context of the 1801 war between Iberian states. What was left of the fabled wealth of the Seven Missions was destroyed rapidly by the Portuguese invaders, who ransacked crops, slaughtered cattle, occupied Indian lands, and sought to force the Guarani into the colonial labor force. Many Guarani sought refuge either in the Spanish colonies or in the isolated forests, while those who remained eked out a miserable existence, poignantly described by European observers to the region during the first quarter of the nineteenth century. According to Auguste de Saint-Hilaire, whereas 30,000 Guarani had populated the Seven Missions in Jesuit days, only 3,000 remained in

1821. Over the course of the nineteenth century, these Guarani remnants gradually became absorbed by the growing rural population of the region.

In spite of all these drastic setbacks, independent Guarani populations, though generally reduced to small groups, continued to flourish in southern Brazil after independence. In the nineteenth century, groups such as the Kaiowá, which had retreated previously either from slaving expeditions or the missions, began to resettle traditional Guarani territory. Other Guarani groups – the Ñandeva, Mbyá, and Apapokuva – undertook long-distance migrations in the nineteenth century. According to Curt Nimuendajú, who studied the Guarani in detail during the early years of this century, several "hordes" reached the Atlantic coast, apparently stimulated by the prophetic discourse of religious leaders.[10] Still others migrated during this century, establishing independent communities throughout the southern states of Brazil, many of which still exist today.

The Guaykuru and the Struggle for the Chaco Frontier

The Guaykuru language family included various groups, all of which contained warlike hunting and foraging peoples of the southern and central Chaco plains and the Paraguay River: Toba, Abipon, Mocoví, Pilagá, Payaguá, Guasarapo, and Egiyuayegi-Mbayá. Of these, the Kadiwéu, a subgroup of the Mbayá (the same as Lévi-Strauss' Kaduveo), are the only surviving members of this family in Brazil.

Since the sixteenth century, references to the Guaykuru are a major component in the literature on the south given the importance of their warlike posture in intertribal and interethnic relations. The name in fact was used less as an ethnic designation than as a term referring to all the aggressive hunting and foraging cultures of the Chaco west of the Paraguay River and between the Pilcomayo and Verde rivers. Sources of the sixteenth and seventeenth centuries refer to this area as the "Guaikuru Province," indicating a generalized ethnic/geographical designation in relation to hostile and warlike peoples.

With the exception of the Guasarapo, Abipon, and Payaguá, who were hunters and fishers, all other Guaykuru groups adopted the horse introduced to the Chaco by the Spaniards in the 1540s. The Guaykuru took

[10] Curt Nimuendajú, "Apontamentos sobre os Guaraní," *Revista do Museu Paulista*, n.s. 8 (1954), 9–57.

to horses with the skill and passion of North American Plains Indians or Chilean Araucanians. Besides becoming a central element of their culture, it gave them a wider range of action which, when faced by the advance of the European conquest, served as a tool of resistance that other groups could scarcely equal. *Bandeirantes* most feared an attack by mounted Guaykuru. Various horticultural peoples, less skilled in defense, came to accept the protection of the Guaykuru, whose greater mobility also facilitated their role in trading relations with Europeans.

The Payaguá (*Evuevi*, 'people of the river') were the most skillful canoe paddlers of the Chaco, dominating the Paraguay River from the Bermejo to the lands of the Guasarapos on the upper river. The Payaguá became specialized in river piracy and, in their assaults, took captives for ransom to trade with other peoples. Their traditional enemies, on the Paraná delta and east bank of the Paraguay, were the Guarani. From the beginning of the colonial period, this enmity between the Guaykuru and Guarani was a critical factor in relations with the Europeans.

The Guaykuru had developed a distinctive form of stratified social and political organization, perhaps more complex than that usually found among other indigenous societies of lowland South America. Sources typically characterize them as a "seignorial society" comprised of "noble, warrior, and captive castes," the last referring to prisoners captured in war. The more sedentary, horticultural peoples of the Chaco, especially the so-called "Guaná," Arawak groups of the upper Paraguay, were considered "vassals" of the Mbayá. Yet, in contrast to the relations of domination and subordination characterizing the Chiriguano (Guarani) and Chané (Arawak) to the northwest, relations among Guaykuru and Guaná were more symbiotic. The Xamacoco, Arawak "vassals" of the Mbayá, maintained their sociopolitical unity while periodically receiving visits from their horseback-riding "lords" who were obliged to present their hosts with what they asked of them. Such relations of symbiosis and domination between different linguistic groups were most likely part of a very generalized mechanism of territorial control. Indigenous reactions to conquest should be understood in terms of this dynamic, to the extent that both Europeans and Indians sought to use it to their own advantage.

The first expeditions to cross the Gran Chaco in the early sixteenth century, in search of a way to the legendary mountains of gold in Peru, met the Guaykuru and, from the first, the Indians engaged the Europeans in combat, invariably destroying or turning them back. Despite some attempts at peaceful settlement, the Indians consistently reaffirmed their militant resistance to contact whenever the Europeans failed to fulfill their promises or advanced into their territory. But by the second half of the sixteenth century, a slow process of colonization of the Chaco by the Spaniards was already in progress, which had caused the destruction of most peoples in the surrounding areas and dislocations of peoples within. After the Spaniards' subjection of the Guarani on the Prata, Guarani were utilized as guides, interpreters, and warriors in expeditions against the Guaykuru, fueling the traditional enmity between these two peoples. Various punitive expeditions were sent against the Payaguá and Mbayá, forcing them to retreat to the northern Paraguay River, where they established a powerful alliance against the invaders. Together the military prowess of the Guaykuru on land and the Payaguá on the rivers proved to be an invincible force for the next 150 years.

Hostilities between the Spaniards and the Guaykuru continued throughout the seventeenth century. In the first half of the century, Jesuit missions attempted but with little success to convert various Mbayá groups. Nor was it possible to contain the Mbayá in 1661 when they crossed the Paraguay River to attack the province of Itatín. The Indians destroyed the mission of Santa Maria de la Fe and looted the town of Xerez. Some remained in the conquered territory; others returned to the Chaco. As a result of these attacks, Spanish colonists lost control of the Paraguay north of Asunción.

In the latter half of the century, Paulista *bandeirantes* reached the *sertão* of Valarin and frequently engaged in battle with the Spaniards of Paraguay. In 1682 they established a base near the ruins of Xerez in Mboteteu, where they harassed the Payaguá and aroused their fury. Both the Payaguá and the Mbayá, however, continued their attacks throughout the early eighteenth century, now against Spanish missionaries and their Guarani neophytes, now against colonists' settlements. By mid-century the Payaguá advanced to the lands east of the Paraguay, assaulting Paulista expeditions who ventured into the area.

Around 1718 the Paulistas began mining in Mato Grosso after the discovery of gold at Cuiabá (Coxipó-mirim). Expeditions generally took 5 months from Porto Feliz to the Cuiabá rivers and faced attacks by the Kayapó on the Pardo and Itapiri rivers. Once on the Taquari River, expeditions entered Guaykuru land, where they faced the devastating combined attacks of the Mbayá and Payaguá. Year after year, and despite numerous attempts to subdue the Indians, expeditions to the gold mines were destroyed by these attacks. In the early 1730s a "Just War" was proclaimed against the Payaguá, and the resulting massive military expedition defeated the Indians.

This seemed to be a turning point because, although they and the Mbayá continued to attack the Portuguese until the 1750s and sixties, the attacks were less frequent, and as a result of punitive expeditions, diseases, and wars with their former allies the Guaykuru, Payaguá resistance began to diminish. In the 1750s both the Payaguá and the eastern and southern Mbayá signed peace accords with the Spaniards. In the 1760s the northern Payaguá sought asylum in the Spanish Jesuit missions and little by little settled in Asunción, where, by the end of the century, they promised to "live in peace." A century later there were reportedly no more than fifty Payaguá left.

Portuguese penetration of Mbayá territory had consolidated by the end of the eighteenth century. The foundations of the forts of Miranda, Coimbra, and Albuquerque – built in defense against Spanish threats – were located on Guaykuru lands on the upper Paraguay. Pressured by the advance of both the Spaniards and Portuguese, and conscious of the numerous acts of treachery by the Spaniards against them, the Mbayá sued for peace with the Portuguese. Two Mbayá chiefs signed a peace treaty in 1791 that, although vague and imprecise, defined the territory of the Mbayá and placed them under Portuguese protection. The Mbayá were declared subjects of the crown, demonstrating the intent of the colonizers to create a type of sovereignty over Guaykuru territory. A year later, and in a similar move, the governor of Paraguay sought peace with the Mbayá to the north of the Ipane.

The Mbayá were thus effectively divided between the Spanish and the Portuguese colonial spheres, and over the course of the early nineteenth century, Mbayá hostilities and alliances developed within this context. As the Paraguayan ranching front advanced, and military expeditions against the Mbayá continued, the Mbayá attacked Fort Coimbra. The Brazilians, for their part, spared no efforts to gain the trust of the Indians, gradually solidifying their alliance through presents and honors bestowed on Mbayá chiefs.

The Mbayá in several cases took advantage of Brazilian/Paraguayan rivalry to obtain favors from both sides. But despite occasional alliances with the Paraguayans, between 1814 and 1840 the Mbayá renewed their attacks on settlements to which the Paraguayans responded with the strengthening of their defense along the Paraguay River. In the war of

Brazil, Argentina, and Uruguay against Paraguay, the Kadiwéu (Mbayá who in the eighteenth century had been allies of the Payaguá), instigated and armed by the Brazilians, penetrated along the Apu and Miranda rivers attacking and destroying villages and the Paraguayan armed forces. The Kadiwéu suffered great losses, however, because they were given the most difficult missions to execute. In exchange for their participation in the war, they received what most interested them – an official document guaranteeing the right to their lands.

After the war, however, cattle ranchers began to establish themselves in the region, restricting the Indians to the territories they have inhabited until the present day. In 1872 a Brazilian military official named Malheiros set up a ranch on a stretch of the Paraguay called Barranco Branco, and for 20 years he assumed the post of Director of the Kadiwéu Indians. In this way he managed to take possession of a considerable part of indigenous territory. The picture left at the end of the nineteenth century is of a people numerically reduced, developing strategic alliances, and seeking to preserve the last refuge to which they had been pushed. As one Kadiwéu elder in 1989 remarked on the history of his people's land struggles: "For us to keep these lands cost the blood of our ancestors; this land no-one will take from us, the white man cannot take it, for this land cost us our blood, the blood of our ancestors."

The Kaingang and Imperial Expansion

Documentary evidence for the Kaingang is for the most part restricted to sporadic descriptions of Indian attacks and the corresponding organization of European repression. The ethnographic literature also presents limitations, because Kaingang society and culture has been reconstructed mainly from the shattered remnants of populations that suffered an exceedingly rapid process of disintegration.

Kaingang groups were basically hunting and foraging peoples, with relatively low population densities and high seasonal mobility. For most of the colonial period, Kaingang were present on the extensive plains of the interior plateau, establishing temporary camps alongside rivers and streams, which were soon abandoned and burned. They organized periodic foraging expeditions to the rich pine forests and even to the coast, where shellfish was collected. With the advance of colonial expansion, however, Kaingang mobility became increasingly restricted, as groups sought refuge in the subtropical and tropical forests throughout southern Brazil.

Early observers noted the relatively simple material culture of the Kaingang and were baffled by the complexity of Gê societies. Even small groups were divided in exogamic, patrilineal moieties, corresponding to the structure of Kaingang cosmology, and this division was present at all levels of social interaction. Although political authority was apparently diluted within the wider social structure, several sources indicate the presence of strong charismatic leaders, often wielding influence over several local groups or territories.

Known to the first Portuguese colonists and Jesuits as the Guaianá, the Kaingang developed a tradition of resistance to colonial domination over a considerably long period. Although some Kaingang were enslaved by the colonists and others placed in mission villages by the Jesuits already in the sixteenth century, for the most part the Portuguese showed little interest in the Guaianá. Always belittled when compared to the coveted Tupi and Guarani, the Kaingang fit the widely diffused Tapuia archetype as Indians considered of little use to the Portuguese. Despite these negative perceptions the Portuguese continued their slave raids, frequently enough to provoke a retreat from areas of European settlement by the end of the sixteenth century.

After 1640, however, when Portuguese slavers found it increasingly difficult to enslave the Guarani, they once again sought out the Guaianá. But the Kaingang proved less than satisfactory as slaves. Not only were they difficult to enslave, given their mobility and resistance to capture, but once submitted they continued to resist. Several major revolts rocked the São Paulo area in the 1650s, all associated with Guaianá captives. The increase in slave flight and truancy may also be related to the greater presence of these Indians in colonial slaveholdings. Not surprisingly the Paulistas began at that point to reorient their expeditions to new sources of Tupi, Guarani, and Arawak labor, to the distant north and northwest of São Paulo.

As a result colonial sources hardly mention the Kaingang during the late seventeenth and early eighteenth centuries. In the second half of the eighteenth century, though, the military and economic expansion of the Portuguese opened new fronts of conflict with the Kaingang. The growing cattle trade routes linking the far south to the mining zones became the frequent target of Indian raids, while the Portuguese occupation of the rich Guarapuava plains to the west of Curitiba brought on an increasingly aggressive posture by the Kaingang occupants of the region.

The official position was sealed with the severe Royal Order of November 5, 1808, which declared war on the Kaingang, permitting the legal enslavement of war captives for periods of up to 15 years. The same royal order recommended the partition of the land in *sesmarias* (land grants), demonstrating the intimate relation between economic expansion and official Indian policy. The following year a large expedition set out from the garrison at Santos, at the expense of royal coffers, to attempt the military conquest of Guarapuava, arriving on the plains in mid-1810. Initially the Kaingang met the Portuguese column with a concentrated attack, but they were soundly repelled by Portuguese artillery. Recognizing the strength of the invading forces as well as the fact that they were there to stay, the Kaingang fell back on more traditional tactics, such as repeated, small raids or retreat from the plains to the dense forests of adjacent regions. Even there they were not safe, however, because colonists bent the 1808 royal order to legitimize slave-raids against the Kaingang, often capturing women and children.

As the Portuguese began to establish a firm foothold in Guarapuava, Kaingang leaders faced a burning question: Should they continue to resist or make peace with the Portuguese? These alternatives divided Kaingang factions, which ultimately worked to the Europeans' advantage. In 1812 over 300 Kaingang agreed to live peacefully among the whites, forming a sort of mission village, which failed to prosper, however, because the Kaingang demonstrated little interest in adopting either Christian ways or settled agriculture. At the same time, factions of the same village had frequent conflicts with other subgroups, reflecting the political factionalism that marked internal Kaingang relations.

The conquest of Guarapuava set the tone for subsequent Indian–white relations in the context of cattle expansion, which extended southward to the rich plains of Palmas and Erexim by the mid–nineteenth century. Although the legal enslavement of Kaingang war captives was revoked in 1831, expanding imperial interests continued to exploit internal indigenous differences, throwing factions against one another and thus guaranteeing the permanence of violent conflict throughout the century. Kaingang resistance more and more assumed the character of raids, aimed either at striking glancing blows at the newcomers or to acquire foreign objects – above all, iron and iron tools.

Whatever their objectives, successive Indian raids brought on organized repression by public and private interests. Already in the 1830s, the province of Santa Catarina organized a regular pedestrian patrol to protect the cattle trail between Lajes and Curitiba. Cattle ranchers and military officials in the Palmas region recruited the services of Kaingang leader Vitorino Condá to pursue his "bitter rivalry" with the Indians of Paiquerê, offering guns, ammunition, and iron tools to Vitorino and his followers. These official and private incentives to attack Kaingang groups often resulted in bloody massacres, foreshadowing the emergence of professional *bugreiros*, or Indian bounty hunters, who served as important instruments in the extermination of whole peoples during the second half of the century.

Vitorino Condá's activities went far beyond these mercenary actions, however, which demonstrates that the simplified image of Kaingang attacks and subsequent white repression must be reviewed in terms of the intermediary roles played by Kaingang leaders. Native collaboration in the cattle regions was significant not only in clearing out hostile groups but also in offering labor services and in bolstering permanent settlements. Vitorino played an essential part in the opening of the road connecting Palmas to the old mission territory, acting as mediator between Brazilians and newly contacted Kaingang groups. He also served in the foundation of Nonoai, where he used a mixture of attraction and force to relocate dispersed Kaingang peoples at a single settlement. Apparently Vitorino's collaboration was not moved by self-interest alone; indeed his actions suggest the adoption of a strategy that sought to defend collective interests as well, in the face of a rapidly changing political scene. In the early 1850s, for example, he led a commission of leaders to Porto Alegre, where they solicited material aid from the president of Rio Grande do Sul Province, promising their loyalty to the emperor.

While this obedient and subservient posture reflected the formal relationship between many Indian groups and outside authority, relations with expanding settlers and local authorities often undermined any possibility for lasting conciliation. The occupation of the Erexim plains by ambitious cattle ranchers in the 1850s led to intense conflicts between settlers and the Indians of Nonoai, who were illegally dispossessed of their lands. As in the earlier expansion to Guarapuava and Palmas, settlers and authorities played off Kaingang internal dissent: Some sided with the whites; other dissident leaders, including the son-in-law of Vitorino, were persecuted and murdered in cold blood. Subsequently Vitorino and a considerable following abandoned Nonoai, establishing an independent settlement along the Uruguay River. After all, retreat proved the most effective means of preserving any measure of autonomy.

If the white settlers remained inclined to negotiate with the Kaingang, they adopted explicit policies of removal and extermination with the advance of the agricultural frontier during the second half of the century. Changing property relations, due to the Land Law of 1850, and the expansion of capitalist agriculture to the interior of the southern provinces opened new fronts of conflict with different Gê-speaking peoples. In Santa Catarina the mainly German immigrant communities launched brutal offensives against the Xokleng. In São Paulo and Paraná successive waves of land speculation, coffee expansion, and railroad construction pitted predominantly Brazilian settlers against the increasingly defensive Kaingang, who intensified their raids on isolated settlers, either to acquire much-coveted iron for their arrowheads or, as some authorities observed, to exact revenge on those who had dislodged them from their homelands.

In contrast to the Indian idealized by Romantic intellectuals in the major urban centers during the mid–nineteenth century, the Kaingang and Xokleng in effect occupied quite a different role within the ideological and economic contexts of the agricultural frontier: No longer a potential laborer or even an enemy, he became a definite obstacle to progress. In Santa Catarina any brief appearance by the Xokleng near the German settlements was sufficient to warrant the organization of violent repression. The settlers, through their own press as well as their influence among powerful Brazilian politicians, meticulously constructed a negative image of the Xokleng magnifying small, isolated raids into a permanent, terrifying threat to the lives, liberty, and property of these industrious European immigrants. In 1877 the president of Santa Catarina Province, Alfredo Taunay, recognized the glaring contradiction when he discouraged the director of Blumenau Colony from organizing a punitive raid, "since to me it seems that these expeditions always adopt the character of bloody reprisals, which does not correspond to our spirit of civilization."[11]

In short, while the settlers ultimately favored the use of terror to solve the "Indian question," and hired the services of the bloodthirsty *bugrei-*

[11] "Relatório do Presidente da Provincia," 1877, unpublished ms., in the Arquivo do Estado de Santa Catarina, Florianópolis.

ros, authorities wavered between pacification and extermination. Following the *Regimento das Missões* of 1845, the state stimulated the work of Italian Capuchins, though with limited success. In Santa Catarina they made a half-hearted attempt to pacify the Xokleng near the German communities of the Itajai Valley in the 1860s. However, frustrated by the sporadic contact and the continued retreat of the Xokleng, one friar dedicated himself to the white population of the Itajai colony, while the other delved into the wilderness in search of a more dense indigenous population – to no avail, however, because the Kaingang refused to convert.

For many authorities the refusal of the Xokleng and Kaingang to accept the pacific approach of the missionaries confirmed the negative image projected by the settlers, portraying the Indians as creatures without reason, to be hunted like wild beasts. In this view the only hope lay in the conversion and education of the children captured by the *bugreiros*. Squatters, land speculators, railroad companies and even the state placed *bugreiros* on their payrolls to clear out areas of their indigenous inhabitants. Indian hunters such as Martins of Santa Catarina or Joaquim Bueno earned wide reputations, the latter taking pride in the murder of over 2,000 Kaingang in western São Paulo by poisoning their drinking water.

The atrocities committed against the Kaingang and Xokleng were so shocking that the plight of these peoples became a cause célèbre in Brazil's urban centers and even in Europe. By the first decade of the twentieth century, civil societies aimed at protecting the Indians had emerged in Florianópolis, Rio de Janeiro, São Paulo, and Campinas, while the sharp accusations of Albert Fric and Hugo Gensch at the International Americanists' Congress in Vienna in 1908 stirred considerable controversy at the international level. But by then most of the damage had been done. When the final Kaingang holdouts of western São Paulo accepted their "pacification" in 1912, following the guidelines prescribed by the recently created Indian Protection Service, their numbers had been drastically reduced by the massacres. During the first years after pacification, over half of the remaining São Paulo Kaingang fell victim to measles. During the same period only three Kaingang children were born, all dying shortly afterward. The Xokleng of the Itajaí Valley, pacified in 1914, faced similar problems, as did the Kaingang of western Santa Catarina and Paraná.

After nearly four centuries of contact, the Kaingang had finally been dominated by the invading civilization. Over this long period they had adopted iron for weapons, they had persistently and often violently rejected missionary and settler advances, and they had retreated to increasingly inaccessible habitats. Faced with the rapid changes that occurred between about 1850 and 1920, however, the Gê peoples of southern Brazil found these strategies insufficient to turn back the inexorable tide of European expansion. The deliberate violence and the attendant population and territorial losses certainly fractured the identity and history of Kaingang and Xokleng peoples, but it did not destroy or even defeat them. Confined to miserable reservations or maintaining small *toldos* – independent villages with insecure land tenure – the Kaingang and Xokleng continue to struggle to preserve their ethnic identity and what remains of their land.

THE NORTHEAST AND THE CENTRAL COAST

In the case of the northeastern *sertão*, it is difficult to be precise about the nature of indigenous societies in view of the lack of early ethnographic information. Nevertheless it is evident that despite the enormous cultural diversity perceived by early chroniclers, these people were capable of forging a pan-Indian confederation to resist the Portuguese advance, following the expulsion of the Dutch, and to maintain it in operation for nearly a century. Furthermore, even after their systematic reduction in the mission settlements by the late eighteenth century, or because of it, the peoples of the northeast forged a new historical identity as settled Indians through which they were able to confront state policies of forced assimilation and sale of their lands in the mid–nineteenth century. The two cases presented in this section – the Kariri-speaking peoples and the Botocudo – illustrate diverse aspects of aboriginal politics, alliance formation in the face of colonial expansion, and transformations in ethnic identity.

The Botocudo, nomadic hunters and gatherers whose sociopolitical dynamic was characterized by constant group fissioning, were likewise capable of deterring colonial advance until the beginning of the nineteenth century. Like the Mura of the Madeira River and the Kaingang of the south, they came to symbolize for the colonists Indians against whom wars should be waged, "exceptions to freedom." Concerted, repressive action from the early nineteenth century on forced local groups, divided by internal politics and faced by increasingly hostile circumstances, to capitulate in order to survive.

Alliance and Identity in the Northeastern Sertão

In contrast to the relatively homogeneous Tupi and Guarani cultures of the coast, those of the vast regions of the northeastern interior presented to the early Portuguese chroniclers an enormous and bewildering diversity. This contrast formed the basis for the fundamental dichotomy between the Tupi and "Tapuya" (Tapuia in Spanish context) – a generic designation for "enemy others" originally used by the Tupi to refer to all peoples of the interior – that shaped conceptions about the Indians of Brazil and most especially the northeast throughout the colonial period.

At the end of the sixteenth century, Fernão Cardim wrote that "with most Tapuya, one cannot undertake conversion for they are very nomadic and have many different and difficult languages." The intense European curiosity about the Tupian peoples of the coast, whose relatively homogeneous cultures in one sense facilitated the imposition of direct and systematic contact, in no way extended to the peoples of the interior and *caatinga* regions whose enormous cultural diversity and spatial mobility baffled and dismayed even the most disciplined of European intellects. Conquest of these "Tapuya," proceeding from the advance of cattle ranching and missionary action, did not enhance an understanding of their societies, but it did result in the concentration of diverse groups in single settlements.

On the basis of various sources, Nimuendaju (1981) listed some eighty different ethnonyms in the area of the northeastern *sertão* and transition zones to the east and west, with a strong concentration of groups in the São Francisco Valley. Of these groups, those of the Kariri language family were predominant from Ceará and Paraíba to the northern part of the Bahian *sertão*.

Hypotheses on the precolonial period clearly suggest that various small groups had been forced away from the coast by the advance of the Tupi in their great migrations, which were still in process by the time of the European intrusion. Movements of groups to the west were limited by the presence of peoples of the Gê language family – Timbira and Akwé – also recognizably homogeneous as cultural and linguistic entities. Thus, despite the internal heterogeneity of groups of the *sertão*, one can identify a certain unity both in their contrast with neighboring groups of other linguistic families, and in their association with a specific environment, the *caatinga*, which supported the concentration of diverse groups in a few favorable niches. Such unity strengthened during the seventeenth and eighteenth centuries with the advance of the ranching frontier and missionary settlements.

By the end of the sixteenth century, the entire coast of the northeast had been conquered. The fact that Alagoas and Sergipe remained "untouched" for almost the whole century was possibly due to Bishop Sardinha's shipwreck in the region and subsequent reprisals against the Kaeté (Caeté). The war waged against the Indians of the Rio Real and Sergipe "for having killed many white people" led to the withdrawal of these populations to Bahia, where they fell victim to outbreaks of yellow fever and measles in the 1560s. The conquest of the region was undertaken only in the 1580s. Pernambuco, Paraíba, and Rio Grande, on the other hand, were first affected by the French who became allies of the Potiguar; the French were expelled in 1584, and the conquest of Paraíba was undertaken a year later.

The seventeenth century was notable for the Dutch invasions in Bahia and Pernambuco, for the indigenous revolts that took place during the Portuguese restoration, and for the occupation of the *sertão* by the cattle-ranching front, mainly after the withdrawal of the Dutch. In Pernambuco the Dutch West Indian Company developed its commercial project with the authorization and support of the United Provinces. Sugar and brazilwood constituted the company's principal exports. In this period (1630–1654) two distinct and opposed governments operated in Brazil, with Dutch control extending over Rio Grande, Paraíba, Itamaracá, and Pernambuco.

While the Indians of Bahia had been their most feared enemies during their short possession of Salvador (1624–1625), those of the *sertão* showed themselves to be Dutch sympathizers. They were often utilized in patrols against Portuguese raiders and were recruited for an expedition against a rebellion of black slaves at Palmares. One reason behind this alliance was certainly the religious freedom and tolerance prevalent during the governorship of Count Maurits of Nassau. Furthermore the Portuguese colonization of Ceará had extremely negative consequences for the Indians, creating a situation particularly favorable for the Dutch.

The Potiguar inhabited Paraíba, Pernambuco, and Rio Grande, and groups of the latter annually raided into Pernambuco particularly during the droughts. Conflicts between Indians (also Potiguar) and the Portuguese in Ceará reached a critical point in 1638 when the Indians pressured the Dutch to take the Portuguese fort. Shortly afterward the considerable increase in the indigenous population of Ceará led the Dutch council to establish a settlement there. Among those settled were two Potiguar leaders, Antônio Paraupaba from Rio Grande, and Pedro Potí from Paraíba, who had visited Holland in the 1630s to present formal protests against the miserable state of the Portuguese colony and to request assistance.

The so-called *Guerra dos Bárbaros* ('War of the Barbarians'), a general uprising of the Tapuya – or Confederation of the Kariri – began in 1687 as a reaction to the expansion of the Portuguese over indigenous lands following their victory over the Dutch, and it only came to an end at the beginning of the eighteenth century. The settlement of the region intensified after a royal order in 1654 in which Dom João VI conceded land grants to soldiers and officials who had fought in the War of Restoration. Little wonder that the Janduí initiated the revolt against such colonizers in Pernambuco and Piauí. Encouraged by Janduí victories, the Paiaku and later the Kratiú and Ikó in Ceará, and the Xukuru, Peja, Panati, and other natives of Ceará, Rio Grande do Norte, Piauí, Paraíba, and Pernambuco, all entered the struggle. The Portuguese retaliated with a large-scale expedition led by veterans of the Palmares wars and *bandeirantes*, attracted by the news that the war was declared "Just," and consequently captives could be enslaved.

In 1692 a major drought debilitated indigenous resistance, leading to the signing of a peace treaty between the king and the chief of the Janduí. In it the Indians promised 5,000 warriors to fight on the Portuguese side against foreign invaders in exchange for which they would receive guarantee of an area of 10 square leagues around their villages and would be considered free. Noncompliance with this treaty, however, prolonged the conflict. In 1715 a royal law renewed the crown's determination to either exterminate the rebels, remove them from the way of expansion, or intimidate them with such losses that they would submit to the Portuguese.

The progressive advance of colonization and the losses suffered by the rebels led to peace, first in the coastal regions and then the interior. After 1720 there are no more reports of the uprising. Scattered rebellions continued to take place, however, as in 1713, when settled and missionized Indians, including Tupi allies of the Portuguese, reacted to exploitation by the military at the forts.

The conquest of Piauí in the 1670s, the last to be done in the region, was followed by 50 years of cattle ranching and administration by the Jesuits. Control over the Indians who attacked the ranches was only considered complete in 1764 when João de Rego Castelo Branco waged a campaign against the Gueguê, who sued for peace and were later settled. A war against the Pimenteira, begun in 1776, ended only with their annihilation in 1809. The crown's determination in 1700 that the lands of mission settlements were inviolable at once sought to ensure the reproduction of these settlements and to put certain limits to the expansion of the ranches. It nevertheless left open the way for expansion on the remaining lands.

Having confronted the Portuguese colonizers in prolonged wars of resistance, the Indians of the northeast reached the nineteenth century in quite varied situations. While those in remote areas continued to resist contact, practically all others lived or had lived in settlements. Indians settled in Pernambuco at the beginning of the century were later found wandering throughout the *sertão*. In the 1850s Indians who had abandoned the settlements wandered along the frontier between Paraíba and Piauí, living by hunting and foraging, constantly moving their camps, having been nearly decimated by ranchers whose cattle herds they continued to attack.

The state continued to give special treatment to the settlements, as the crown had done before. Moreover the accumulation of experiences in the settlements and the merging of diverse cultural traditions gave rise to a distinct identity of the settled Indians that differentiated them from the regional population with whom they were in contact. Travelers in the mid–nineteenth century invariably noted the decadence and apathy of the settled populations, marked by conformity to and acceptance of an inevitable destiny of extinction. The image they left is of a population that had been so demoralized and disheartened by the extended missionary presence that nothing was left of their capacity to resist. Yet there is considerable evidence that conflicts, negotiations, accommodation, or cooptation formed part of a multifaceted modus vivendi in which old institutions, laws, or elements of material culture were utilized in diverse contexts, as the means by which the settled populations continued to maintain their ethnic identity over the generations.

In the first half of the nineteenth century, a series of revolts occurred in the northeast involving the indigenous population. In Alagoas and Pernambuco between 1832 and 1835, numbers of settled Indians participated in the "War of the Cabanos," a revolt in which plantation owners of the northeastern provinces sought to restore Dom Pedro I to the throne with the participation of judges, priests, and local authorities. It also mobilized large numbers of settled Indians, field laborers, and plantation dwellers. The movement spread throughout the northeast and Amazon Valley. It began as a conflict between the imperial government in Rio de Janeiro and the provincial élites who rebelled against central control of commerce and politics. Urban lower classes and peoples of the interior understood the struggle as one against political and economic domination, and the Cabanos Revolt became a popular struggle against all élites. The élites in effect had unleashed a powerful force that in the end they could not control. The revolt lasted until 1840, with its most violent period in 1835–1836.

Among the settled Indians of the northeast, the movement began in the north of Alagoas and quickly spread to other areas. The Kariri joined the rebels, but *lingua geral*–speaking Indians fought on the side of the government to suppress the movement. Alliances were formed and broken throughout the struggle, however. In 1835 the Indians of Alagoas surrendered and returned to their settlements, where they were utilized by the military and plantation owners to locate and destroy settlements of fugitive black slaves.

Other conflicts occurred in the nineteenth century; some involving Indians and regional populations against the ranchers, while in others Indians became involved in disputes between plantation owners. Such cases reflect a variety of situations in which settled Indians formed alliances with different actors and took to arms against the authorities and the existing order. The long history of mobilizing Indians as soldiers to suppress rebellions or to control the frontiers against foreign invasions was a critical factor in their participation in armed struggles. Their military function had served government interests, but it also made them a potential ally for discontented social sectors and a potential force in the struggle for the recognition of their rights. Furthermore it is evident that in various cases the Indians advanced their own cause by playing off powerful landowners against each other.

The transfer of the Portuguese crown to Brazil in 1808 and the subsequent acclamation of Dom Pedro I as emperor of Brazil in 1822 had a special significance for the Indians of the northeast, who saw in the emperor an all-powerful lord, a "Great White Father" to whom they owed obedience, and to whom they could plead for protection, especially of their lands, in return for their loyalty. Indigenous participation in the Cabanos revolt can be understood in part in these terms. During the long reign of Dom Pedro II (1840–1889), an almost messianic image of the emperor crystallized in the Indians' minds, as attested by present-day oral traditions that attribute land grants to the actions of the emperor. On numerous occasions Indians sought to personally contact the emperor in Rio de Janeiro to present their complaints and requests. At the same time, they sought out local and provincial authorities to defend their lands against those who attempted to take possession of them. In the nineteenth century the struggle for land became a critical question linked to the issue of racial mixture and acculturation.

From the mid–nineteenth century on, settlement Indians came to be referred to as "mixed" Indians, disqualifying and opposing them to the "pure" Indians of an idealized past. The idea of mixture implied assimilation, the transformation of the Indian into a non-Indian, which fit the emerging racial ideology of Brazil at the time. Indian policy held that Indians would abandon their identity and that settlements were a transition in this evolutionary process. "Mixed" Indians were easy targets for land expropriation. Numerous settlements were thus extinguished throughout the northeast during this time. The Indians, for their part, continued to appeal to the emperor and, on the local level, sought to reactivate elements of their traditional culture in order to emphasize their Indianness as a way of holding on to their lands.

In this complex play of forces and strategies throughout the nineteenth century, the Indians did not succeed in reverting the process of extinction of their settlements, through which the expropriation of their lands was legalized. At the end of the century, old collective properties were granted to municipal chambers, and others were parceled out to indigenous families or transformed into the private property of the ranchers. Nevertheless many Indians from the settlements that were legally extinguished have since then regained recognition of their titles to land and of their ethnic identity.

Resistance and Destruction of the Botocudo

During the colonial period, the Maxakali, Kamakã, Pataxó, and Botocudo (known as Aimoré throughout the colonial period) of southern

Bahia, Espirito Santo, and Minas Gerais, with their devastating incursions on colonial settlements, were responsible for the near complete economic collapse of the captaincies of Ilhéus, Porto Seguro, and Espirito Santo during the colonial period. These small forest-dwelling bands resisted the conquest of their territories until the beginning of the nineteenth century, when a bloody process of extermination began that lasted until the height of the cacao boom in southern Bahia in the early twentieth century.

The Botocudo belonged to the Macro-Gê linguistic stock and traditionally were seminomadic hunters and foragers. Their social organization was characterized by frequent internal divisions of groups (generally bands of 50 to 200 people organized in extended families) and a division of labor by sex and age. Their hunting and gathering territories were well defined and defended, this being the fundamental reason for conflicts among subgroups, with other neighboring groups, or with colonizers. Warfare and ritualized combat were constant features of political life due to such disputes over territory, which nearly always culminated in group fission.

Initial contacts occurred in the sixteenth century with the creation of the captaincies of Ilhéus and Porto Seguro. In Ilhéus violent contacts were the result of colonists' attempts to take Aimoré captives in order to replace the greatly diminished Tupinikin and Tupinambá labor force, following the revolt of 1550 and the smallpox epidemic of 1562–1563. In Porto Seguro initial conflicts were related to military expeditions promoted by the provincial lords of the captaincy in search of gold and precious stones in the region and in neighboring Espirito Santo. During the same period the Botocudo launched attacks on Jesuit settlements that were to last throughout the seventeenth century and against which Paulista *bandeirantes*, following the declaration of a "Just War" against the Guerén (Aimoré) in 1673, were sent in order to settle the conflicts.

The first attempts at settlements of the Botocudo in the early 1600s proved unsuccessful as the Indians continued to raid and attack settlements throughout the captaincies of Porto Seguro and Espirito Santo. As a strategy to defend Bahia in the seventeenth and eighteenth centuries, the Portuguese frequently used the Kariri and Payaya of Pernambuco as a buffer against the Aimoré. Yet this was insufficient to prevent the total economic collapse of these captaincies and their subsequent abandonment by the crown. The basis for this decision lay not so much in the crown's disinterest as its intent to transform the area into a buffer zone against uncontrolled access to the mines of Minas Gerais. Subsequently the region became a refuge area for the Indians who were able to sustain themselves in the forest interior, distant from the process of colonial expansion.

The collapse of mining brought profound transformations to the regional economy with dramatic effects on the indigenous peoples. The new economic options included cattle raising, commerce, and agriculture. The areas of production were the large rivers that flowed to ports in Espirito Santo and Bahia. Colonial settlement was initiated along these rivers as support for commerce, to combat the Botocudo, and to promote expansion. To overcome the difficulties of colonization, massive investments were made in road building and military posts.

Expansion coincided with a virtual lack of direction in Indian policy. Popular sentiment increasingly favored the use of violence to speed up the process of change, and Indian policy was expressed through a series of laws that attended to these needs. In Ilhéus, Porto Seguro, and Espirito Santo, expansion assumed its most aggressive form. The first military post was built on the Rio Doce, and by 1800 a pedestrian patrol was mobilized to combat the Botocudo. The Indians' attacks on the military post were the principal cause for the Royal Law of 1801, which declared an "offensive war against the anthropophagous Botocudo" and ordered the mobilization of troops throughout the territory "infested" by them. The same law established the conditions necessary for the allotment of lands along the rivers, thereby speeding up the process of domination. Both the reinstatement of "Just Wars" and the appearance of the "Indian hunters" accelerated the process of territorial expansion and the disorganization of indigenous societies that had survived in the areas marginal to mineral exploitation.

The hunting of the Botocudo forced numerous small bands to seek peaceful contact, submitting to settlement as a way of guaranteeing their survival. Several administrators attributed this change to hunger, which is confirmed by numerous reports that the Indians came to the posts in search of food or were raiding colonists' gardens.

The first area considered "pacified" was that of the Jequitinonha River Valley in Bahia. Nevertheless various groups continued to avoid contact by moving constantly through the forests and clashing with groups that had accepted contact with the military. In the early 1800s the Rio Doce region of Minas Gerais came under the control and administration of Guido Tomáz Marlière. Again various groups sought refuge in the forests of the Rio Doce and the Mucuri.

In the mid–nineteenth century the Mucuri Valley became the object of intensive penetration because of the actions of the Mucuri Company, which promoted European colonization in the region. The Jiporok, a Botocudo group of the Mucuri, led by Chief Poton, refused to establish contact. He was murdered because of this refusal, and the chiefs that had opposed him then negotiated for protection with the Ottoni family, administrators of the company. Resistance continued, however, with Jiporok attacks on ranchers and road builders. The Jiporok eventually accepted the building of a road through their territory, but they continued to seek refuge in the Mucuri forests.

By the mid–nineteenth century numerous settlements and military posts had been set up on the Pardo and Doce rivers. Various economic activities developed around the posts and settlements, which in most cases had emerged from towns and slave camps that were later transformed into prosperous municipalities in the three regions. Soldiers and their families as well as "tame" Indians, traditional enemies of the Botocudo, settled around these areas. The relations between the military and the Botocudo often became violent as a result of increases in effective military personnel, the building and supplying of new posts, and the continued emission of royal legislation.

The plan to "civilize" the Botocudo in this period was based on several key features: the use of warriors from enemy groups such as the Maxakali, or even "tame" Botocudo; the use of indigenous interpreters to attract them to contact; forced settlement and integration into the regional population; and intermarriage. Capuchin missionary activity among the Botocudo in the 1870s ultimately intensified the process of social disorganization.

Botocudo children (called *kurukas*) in particular were the object of a widespread commercial trade. It was a common practice for these children to be captured and sold to ranchers, authorities, and even to the emperor, Dom Pedro II. This inevitably escalated conflicts with the Botocudo, who attacked ranches to regain their children; in reprisal government administrators intensified their repression of the Botocudo along with continued occupation and development of the region. Meanwhile mixed marriages were stimulated in such a way as to complete the process of forced integration. In the settlements and military posts, the directors of the Indians and troop commanders assured the responsibility of arranging marriages. This practice effectively introduced monogamous marriage and accelerated the forced sedentarization of groups.

The exploitation of labor paralleled the process of sedentarization. From 1830 on Botocudo forced labor – especially in agriculture, road construction, military, and domestic services – intensified. The Botocudo held firm in their resistance, leading to further conflicts and refuge in unoccupied and unexplored areas.

Throughout this chronicle of violent repression of the Botocudo, the predominant patterns in their sociopolitical organization ultimately rendered them vulnerable to the concerted actions of the military and colonists. Botocudo nomadism and fragmentation could not stop the growing wave of colonization and its increasingly violent measures. Botocudo initiatives remained isolated – attacking ranches here and there, killing cattle, eliminating a colonist family – and were met by expeditions and campaigns to exterminate them. The dozens of small Botocudo bands relied mainly on the tactic of ambush, the hallmark of their resistance, spreading terror in the Mucuri and Doce river valleys. When Botocudo leadership was put to the test, as in the case of the warrior Vackman Pojixá in the early twentieth century, such leaders demonstrated their ability to foment resistance and cause problems for the colonists. In these cases the official strategy was either to eliminate the leaders or win them over.

Some of these leaders became extremely useful as agents of colonization and pacification. One of the better known examples of this pattern was Guido Pockrane, a Botocudo leader who became the right-hand man of Guido Marlière in his efforts to eliminate conflicts between Indians and colonists in the early nineteenth century. After assisting Marlière, Pockrane retired to the area of the Manhuaçu River, where he organized a settlement on the "civilized" model and attracted Botocudo to it. Loyal to the patterns he had been taught, Pockrane put the Botocudo to work in agriculture and subjected them to a severe disciplinary order. In recognition of his loyalty and work, administrators granted him special favors and awards.

In the late nineteenth century, some seven remaining Botocudo subgroups were located in a quadrangular area formed by the Doce, Mucuri, Suaçuí Grande, and São Mateus rivers. The existing settlements were extinguished and the lands auctioned off by the provincial government, leaving the indigenous groups to their fate. Due to the building of the Bahia-Minas and Vitoria-Minas railways, which penetrated the remaining territories of the Botocudo, the beginning of the twentieth century witnessed the transformation of southern Bahia, northern Espirito Santo, and the Rio Doce in Minas Gerais into the principal area of activities of the newly created Indian Protection Service. The *bugres*, a pejorative term by which the Botocudo were known around the Mucuri, represented a veritable nightmare for the railway engineers and construction workers; attacks and reprisals were common on both parts. The local newspaper, *O Mucuri*, suggested in 1905 that total annihilation of the Botocudo, killing them or taking them prisoner, was the only way to ensure public safety.

To facilitate railway construction, five "attraction posts" were created among the remaining groups. The tactic used by the SPI (Servico de Proteção ao Índio) was gradually to extinguish these posts, claiming a drastic reduction in population as a result of the agency's contacts. By 1918 one post was left on the Enim River, set aside for the Krenak and survivors of other settlements. In a little over a century, thousands of Botocudo had been virtually exterminated by colonists of Minas Gerais and southern Bahia, and the few survivors were practically eliminated from the historical memory of those regions. Even though their presence continues to be recorded, little is known of their culture and ways of life.

THE AMAZON VALLEY

The Amazon floodplain was a source of astonishment to the first European explorers in the mid–sixteenth century. Its population was dense, internally stratified, and settled in extensive villages, producing surpluses for a significant intertribal commerce of raw materials and manufactured products. The term *povoado* (settlement), used by the chroniclers to refer to indigenous demographic units, hardly merits the connotation of *aldeia* (village) that it has been given. A careful reading of the first sources suggests a continuous and probably quasi-linear settlement pattern along kilometers of riverbanks, which is consistent with an economy essentially connected to riverine resources and the annually flooded *várzea*. The sociopolitical organization of what the chroniclers called "provinces" was much more elaborate and internally differentiated than that of tropical forest societies. There are reports of local chiefs subordinate to regional chiefs with sacred qualities, hierarchically organized lineages, sacrifice of concubines at the death of chiefs, ancestor cults associated with preservation of the corpse through rudimentary techniques, and other evidence of social stratification.

None of this resisted the advance of the spice collectors, slave hunters, and missionaries who, coming from Belém do Pará, had reached the Tapajós in 1626, the Negro in 1656, and the upper Solimões in 1690. Their advance resulted in the dispersion and captivity of a majority of the riverine peoples. By the end of the seventeenth century, the Amazon *várzea* was practically depopulated and infested by the diseases brought by the whites. The mission industries – towns founded on the ruins of ancient indigenous settlements that functioned to corral a labor force to supply the plantations of the lower Amazon – likewise did not resist the bloodbath.

As this was taking place, the rounding-up or "descent" of Indians from the terra firme began. Indians were brought downriver at ever-greater distances from their homelands on the northern and southern tributaries of the Amazon. This process led to the formation of a neo-indigenous stratum of the riverine population constantly replenished by new descents due to the high mortality, the growing demand for labor, and the very philosophy of mission action. The first half of the eighteenth century was the golden age of the missionary economy based on Indian labor. It succeeded as a material and religious project to the extent that it was not undermined by competition with state and private initiatives and, consequently, was able to neutralize the cultural and linguistic differences of the indigenous nations, dissolving ethnic diversity into the homogeneity of the "Tapuya," generic Indians.

Certainly the Pombaline government and its system of Indian directorates hastened this process of amalgamation of indigenous identities. With the decline of the system's control by the end of the century, and even before, numerous peoples withdrew from colonial settlements to attempt to reorganize and reconstitute their societies, often in new territories and with new sociopolitical arrangements. Some kept a watchful distance from colonial settlements, superficially accepting "reduction" but actively maintaining their posture of nonparticipation in the construction of the colony.

The cases presented here illustrate, first of all, what would appear to be a paradox. The large-scale and complex societies of the *várzea* should have presented greater resistance to the Portuguese advance, yet by comparison with the Guarani of the south or the Kariri confederation of the northeast, there were no major, prolonged wars or interethnic alliances of significance on the Amazon and its main tributaries. Rather, in the course of a century and a half, this "rich realm of nature" was virtually destroyed principally by the devastating impacts of the slave trade and disease. Flight, retreat, and accommodation seem to have been the principal native strategies of survival.

Second, these cases illustrate extreme reactions on the part of colonial society to what was *perceived* as resistance. Genocidal campaigns were waged, for example, against the Manao and other Arawak-speaking peoples of the middle Rio Negro in their short-lived confederation to confront the Portuguese advance. On the Madeira relatively minor groups such as the Mura, who came to occupy the spaces left by their once powerful enemies, were likewise perceived as an obstacle to colonial expansion totally out of proportion to their real military strength.

Third, the cases focus on transformative, messianic movements. The earliest movements on record date from the late seventeenth century and appear to have been related to a widespread belief in the return of divine heroes, whose extraordinary powers were incorporated in powerful shamans or religious specialists. From early on such movements were also associated with native resistance to Portuguese expansion. By the nineteenth century it seems to have been the case that, with the decrease in importance of war leaders in northwest Amazon societies, shamans and prophets emerged as key figures in native resistance and in intermediating change. New religions were forged, grounded in aboriginal belief and practice and articulated through a selective use of Christian symbols, which in many cases strengthened the position of native societies vis-à-vis the whites.

Destruction and Retreat on the Solimões and Japurá

Between the mid–sixteenth century, when the first Iberian expeditions traveled along the Amazon, and the end of the century, changes had already taken place in the human geography of the upper and middle Amazon. Intertribal warfare and dislocations of peoples resulted from the introduction of European trade goods and the demand for slaves. Such changes multiplied in the first half of the seventeenth century with the combined effects of the slave trade and epidemics.

The region of the upper Solimões, inhabited in the sixteenth century by the Aparia and Aricana peoples, was in 1639 occupied by the Omagua who had lived some 300 kilometers upriver in a territory covering more than 700 kilometers along the Amazon (between roughly the Javari and Jutaí), "the largest and most extensive province of all," according to Acuña in 1561. Pedro Teixeira in 1639 spoke of some 400 villages of

Omagua, or one every 4 kilometers, but by the end of the seventeenth century, with their territory already devastated by at least 40 years of epidemics, the Jesuit Samuel Fritz listed thirty-eight villages and mapped twenty-two of them on islands. There were scores of others on the riverbanks. The Omagua had shifted their mode of settlement away from the riverbanks to the islands, most likely to defend themselves from their enemies.

Similarly the "province of Machiparo" to the west of the Omagua was in the seventeenth century occupied by the Aisuare, who had migrated upriver from their earlier location. This process, in which the Aisuare occupied a large part of the buffer zone that had once protected the Omagua from upriver enemies, was due both to the weakening of the Omagua and pressures exerted by Portuguese incursions from downriver. In the beginning of the eighteenth century, part of the Aisuare were attracted by the Jesuits to Spanish missions to the west, together with the Omagua and Yoriman, while the remaining numbers stayed in villages that the Portuguese Carmelites had inherited from the Spanish Jesuits.

The Yoriman (Culiman, Yurimagua, Solimões), a prosperous people famed for their ceramics, wide-ranging traders, and skill in warfare, were visited by the Portuguese in the second half of the seventeenth century in their search for the "River of Gold" and by slave hunters from whom they withdrew to the forest. At the end of the seventeenth century, they were living with the Aisuare on the periphery of Omagua territory and also spread out overland to the south. In the late seventeenth century, they were evangelized by the Jesuits and then the Carmelites.

The Paguana, whose large villages in the sixteenth century extended some 100 kilometers from the Purús to the Rio Negro, and who evidently maintained long-distance commerce with cultures of the Andes, were by the seventeenth century located 400 kilometers upriver, again as a result of Portuguese incursions.

Certainly the most dramatic of the migrations were undertaken by the Tupinambá of Tupinambarana Island around the mouth of the Madeira River. According to Acuña, Tupinambarana Island was "entirely settled by the valiant Tupinambás, people who were defeated in the conquest of Brazil, having left the lands of Pernambuco many years ago and set to flight as the Portuguese continued subjugating them . . . deserting eighty-four villages all at once." From the Brazilian northeast they then crossed over the plateau of southern Amazonia until at least some of them got to the first Spanish settlements in Bolivia. From there they would have gone down the Madeira finally to settle on the Island of Tupinambarana. Heriarte sets the beginning of the migration at 1600, "in three troops, in search of the earthly paradise." The date, however, is much too late because in 1538 Diogo Nunes had already met a fraction of them in Machiparo, the same group who reached Chachapoyas in Peru in 1549. More likely, from the second quarter of the sixteenth century and until the beginning of the seventeenth, not just three "troops" but a series of prophetic movements may have led many Tupi groups of the northeast in successive waves across Amazonia. In Acuña's time the Tupinambá of the middle Amazon were "children and grandchildren of the first settlers." They had dominated the inhabitants of the region "and with time married and established kinship amongst themselves, but the natives never forgot the superiority that the Tupinambá have over them. To those under their dominion, they give their daughters for wives."[12]

By the 1630s the supply of Indian labor was already running out in the region around Belém. The Indians who had survived the first incursions, having learned the bitter lessons of contact, fled the more frequently visited rivers seeking refuge in ever more distant regions of the interior. The more warlike groups offered fierce resistance in their territories. The Portuguese ended up avoiding them and struck instead at the as yet uncontacted groups, thus initiating ever longer voyages to the upper Amazon in search of new slaving grounds.

This voracity for servile labor is explained by the poverty of the inhabitants of Pará, who had no capital to pay the high prices for African slaves, by the limitations on labor control created by church and state, and by the low returns of the majority of slave-taking expeditions, which generally killed more Indians than they enslaved. Once they were brought to Belém and the farms of the region, the slave population had to be constantly replenished due its intractibility, truancy, sicknesses, and mortality.

Between 1640 and 1720 ransom troops (*tropas de resgate*) and punitive expeditions exhausted the entire middle and upper Amazon, as well as the lower courses of its principal tributaries. There is as yet no way to specify the number of expeditions and captives they took, much less the number of those who died in the conflicts or during transport under inhuman conditions, or in the epidemics resulting from first contacts and later in mission settlements, colonial towns, and villages.

[12] Maurício de Heriarte, *Descrição.*

To comprehend the massive depopulation of the *várzea*, one has to consider that the predatory actions of the slave troops struck populations already decimated by epidemics against which they had no resistance. These epidemics long preceded the arrival of the troops; for example, in 1648, years before the Portuguese began to frequent the territory of the Omagua, the Indians were affected by a smallpox epidemic lasting nearly 3 months that caused the deaths of perhaps a third of their population. Under these circumstances traditional cultural practices, such as infanticide (which seems to have had the function of maintaining demographic equilibrium), came to have perverse effects on the population balance.

In 1689 the Jesuit Samuel Fritz noted the combined effects of the ransom troops, epidemics, and flight on the Yurimagua population:

> The Yurimagua were once very warlike and the lords of almost the entire river. . . . Now however they are thoroughly despondent and consumed by the wars and slavery that the inhabitants of Pará have suffered and suffer. Their villages were once more than a league long, but after they saw themselves persecuted, many withdrew to other lands and rivers for their own safety.

In 1691, on returning to his missions, Fritz went up the Amazon recording the depopulation of a large part of the land. From the mouth of the Tapajós to the Urubu, nearly 600 kilometers of the once-populous provinces of the Tapajós, Conduris, Tupinambarana, and Aruaque, Fritz journeyed for 14 days seeing "neither villages nor people," except for the Jesuit village of Tupinambarana near Parintins. From the mouth of the Rio Negro to the Purús, more than 220 kilometers, which 50 years before had been populated by "infinite nations," Fritz went 9 days without seeing a village. The large settlement of Cuchiguara at the mouth of the Purús had been burned and abandoned for "everyone withdrew in fear." A short distance upriver Fritz passed through the old Yurimagua province of the Codajás-Coari region, and for 3 days saw no one, the new settlements of the Yurimagua, mixed with Aisuari, were also abandoned "because there was no more priests but rather the Portuguese burning, killing, and taking captives." Some 20 years later, after the Spanish Jesuits had withdrawn to the Marañon, Fritz was told by the Omagua that nearly all of the ancient Omagua province had been deserted.

As the banks of the Amazon lost their original inhabitants, new forces were at work tending to reestablish demographic equilibrium: on the one hand, spontaneous movements of accommodation, and on the other, the descents (*descimentos*). In the first case groups who before European occupation had pressured the riverine peoples, and for that reason were kept at a distance, now found the way open to the abundant resources of the *várzea*. With the progressive weakening of the Omagua, for example, inland peoples advanced to occupy the spaces left by their former enemies. Similar movements occurred on the middle Amazon where the Guayazis occupied Tupinambarana, and on the Madeira where the Torá in the early eighteenth century and the Mura later in the same century carried out similar occupations.

The descents of peoples from the interior to the banks of the Amazon also resulted from missionary action, at times in cooperation with, and at times competing with, the ransom troops. At the end of the seventeenth century, religious orders widened their sphere of influence throughout the region. The Jesuits held the territory south of the Amazon from the Tocantins to the Madeira; the Capuchins, the northern banks and its interior from Amapá to the Trombetas; the Mercedarians from the Trombetas to the Urubu; and the Carmelites, the enormous Solimões and Negro basins. Over time the missions and the population centers that grew along with them assembled highly diverse contingents of ethnic groups.

In practice missionary settlements depended for their success on the forces of individual missionaries, on native appraisal of missionaries to protect them from the destructive advance of the Europeans, and on their relative capacity to provide a constant supply of trade goods. Two examples illustrate this point: the Mercedarian mission on the Urubu, and the Jesuit and Carmelite missions on the Solimões from the late seventeenth to the early eighteenth centuries.

After an initial period of barter with Jesuit missionaries in the mid–seventeenth century, the Arawak peoples of the Urubu River and middle Amazon suffered increasing attacks by Portuguese slave hunters against which they reacted by destroying several expeditions in their territory. In 1664 Portuguese retaliation forced the Arawak to withdraw into the forests. Despite attempts to reestablish trade relations, conflicts continued until the late 1680s, when the Mercedarian Frei Theodósio da Veiga successfully persuaded the Arawak to descend the Urubu to mission settlements – the first and only missionary effort by the Mercedarians in Amazonia. The objective of the mission, however, was not strictly conversion, because the Indians were to serve as slave hunters themselves – that is, people who made war in the hinterlands to find slaves to sell to the Portuguese. Well into the early eighteenth century, the Arawaks made incursions on the upper Solimões to pay off debts to Portuguese traders. As long as the Urubu mission served this role as an institution for the mobilization of manpower, the Arawak were spared attacks from the Portuguese. With da Veiga's death around 1705, the mission work was carried on by less competent men, who managed to continue until the arrival of government and the settlement frontier in the mid–eighteenth century.

The early history of missions on the Solimões is likewise largely the history of the accomplishments of one individual, Father Samuel Fritz, described as a man of "extraordinary ability and tenacious temperament, whose single-handed undertakings over a period of two decades were to have a decisive impact on the history of the Solimões valley."[13]

Due to the attacks of the Portuguese slave hunters in the 1680s, the Omagua had requested the Jesuit mission at Maynas to send a priest to protect them. Fritz thus began his work at the mission of San Joaquín de Omaguas, which was to become his home-base, although he eventually visited all of the 38 Omagua settlements of the islands and banks of the Solimões. In 1689, three years after arriving from Europe, Fritz descended from the mission to the Yurimagua settlements of the middle Solimões, a region that the Portuguese were only beginning to frequent. There he founded the mission of Nuestra Señora de las Nieves de Jurimaguas, at the mouth of the Juruá River, the base for his evangelization of the Yurimagua, Aisuare, and Ibanoma.

The Indians viewed Fritz as a messianic figure, attributing to him the powers of certain deities, immortal godmen related to curing, rites of passage, and the powers of the rivers. In 1689 a chance event in Fritz's career seemed to confirm this image. Seriously ill and prevented by the floods from returning to the Spanish missions, Fritz went downriver to Belém to receive medical treatment. He wasn't allowed to return to the mission, however, because he was suspected of being a Spanish spy, and he was held in custody for 18 months. The news of his imprisonment reached the upper Amazon, where it was associated by the Indians with several natural disasters that occurred in his absence. Freed in 1691, he was escorted upriver, and on arriving at the missions, he learned of various movements organized around his person and supposed powers. Such manifestations continued until the beginning of the 1700s. Indians

[13] David Sweet, *A Rich Realm of Nature Destroyed* (Ann Arbor, University Microfilms, 1974), 409–413.

attributed various cataclysmic events (earthquakes) to Fritz' displeasure at their ignoring his instructions to descend the river to the missions.

The association between the Yurimagua belief in a powerful spirit of the rivers, Guaricaya, and the religious movement involving Fritz is found in the testimony of an anonymous Jesuit who organized Fritz' diary. He wrote that the Yurimagua began to attribute to Fritz supernatural powers analogous to those of Guaricaya:

> And as an evil spirit exercised such a despotic power over them, who from time to time suddenly appeared and cruelly beat them; and when he went, leaving in a canoe, and disappeared into the depths of the Rio Marañon; some feared that the Padre was a similar sort of spirit.[14]

In his absence many of the missionized Yurimagua and Omagua had withdrawn from the missions or reverted to their old ways. Thus Fritz dedicated the next 3 years after his return to renewing the work of "reduction." By 1695 the Portuguese had returned to patrolling the Solimões, and the Indians sought Fritz' protection, agreeing to follow him to the Spanish missions if the slave hunters became intolerable. Knowing of Fritz' success, and aware of his claims that the Solimões up to the mouth of the Negro was Spanish territory, the Portuguese military and Carmelite missionaries took action, forcing Fritz to leave all mission settlements as far up as the Omagua villages. Fritz' relations with the Omagua were by then beginning to deteriorate partly as a result of his failure to provide a constant supply of trade goods as the Carmelites later did, and partly due to his appeals to Spanish military force to control rebellious chiefs. Thus the chiefs of the region were faced with a strategic choice: either to follow Fritz to the Spanish reductions, or to cast their lot with the Portuguese. The Yurimagua, Aisuare, and Ibanoma followed Fritz, because the Carmelites and Portuguese colonists had enslaved them. Some of the Omagua abandoned the Spanish missions and in the following years cemented an alliance with the Portuguese, serving as brokers in obtaining slaves from enemy groups.

The story of the Omagua chief Payoreva illustrates the paradoxes in Omagua relations with the Spaniards and Portuguese. In 1701 Payoreva and his confederates organized an insurrection against the Jesuits at San Joaquín. The Spanish military arrested and imprisoned him and other

[14] Samuel Fritz, *Journal of the Travels and Labours of Father Samuel Fritz in the River of the Amazons between 1686 and 1723* (London, Hakluyt, 1922 [reprint, 1967]), 55.

rebellious chiefs and meted out exemplary punishment of their followers. Not long afterward Payoreva escaped from prison and returned to San Joaquín, where he persuaded the villagers to abandon the mission and withdraw to a place beyond the Jesuits' influence up the Juruá River. Fritz then sought to persuade the fugitives to return; most believed in him, but not Payoreva. Fritz counseled the Omagua of all settlements he later visited not to believe in the rebel chief who, for his part, had no further encounters with the missionary. Sources suggest that Payoreva may then have sought amicable relations with the Portuguese; around 1704, "either as a prisoner or by his own choice," Payoreva followed the great number of his fellow inhabitants of the Solimões who had been taken off to forced labor in Pará.

The Omagua were thereafter divided between being Portuguese or Spanish dependents. In 1711 and 1713, with the Portuguese threatening the Spanish missions on the Marañón, Fritz again transferred the settlements to the lower course of the Huallaga, where the mission of Nuestra Señora de las Nieves was rebuilt. Appointed Superior of the Jesuit missions in 1704, Fritz made occasional visits to the settlements of the Peruvian Amazon, but from then on he was largely concerned with the affairs of other areas and of the mission province as a whole.

Portuguese incursions on the Caquetá (Japurá) most likely date to the latter half of the seventeenth century, when the depletion of slaves on the Solimões led troops up the Rio Negro and Japurá. By the 1740s the lower Caquetá had become an important, permanent base for slave troops. The Miranha (Bora-Uitoto) of the middle Japurá in particular had an active role in the trade with the Portuguese, raiding the Juri and other groups from at least the mid–eighteenth century to the beginning of the twentieth. The Indians of the headwaters, such as the Cariban Umaua (not the same as the Tupian Omagua), on the other hand, were regular suppliers to the Spaniards. As everywhere in the Amazon Basin, from a large population of reportedly over fifty groups, by the late eighteenth century, the greater part had descended to important settlements on the Solimões (such as Ega, or Teffé) or relocated to the lower Rio Negro under the administration of the Indian directorates.

Following the Treaty of San Ildefonso (1777), Luso-Brazilian concerns to demarcate and colonize the Japurá opened the way to expansion. Attacks by the Mura, who had fled Portuguese incursions on the Madeira, impeded such expansion until their "voluntary reduction" in the 1780s.

All throughout the nineteenth century, the Japurá was unrelentingly raided by Portuguese slave hunters. Eyewitness reports by the scientific travelers Von Spix and Martius in the 1820s confirm that the military at Teffé negotiated slaves supplied by the Miranha and later sold them to élites at Barra (modern-day Manaus).

The Cabanagem Revolt of the 1830s had important effects on the Solimões and Japurá. In 1836 the town council of Ega joined the *cabanos* rebels, plantations were looted and burned, slave hunters were persecuted, and old accounts were settled with corrupt traders. The military of frontier towns suffered the reprisal of generations of oppression. During and following the revolt, there was a resurgence of ethnic identity among peoples such as the Omagua, also called Cambeba, who, since the eighteenth century, had been denied all traces of their culture. From their classification as "Tapuya," such peoples reasserted their specific identities, as evidenced in town registers beginning in the 1840s. This reaffirmation was cut short, however, with the reimposition of the Indian Directorate system in the 1850s, related forced labor programs, and the extractive and destructive regime of rubber gathering at the end of the nineteenth century.

Indigenous struggles to affirm identity reemerged in this century with the demarcation of lands and the recognition of economic autonomy. However divided and reconstituted as peoples, or reterritorialized on the Solimões, the descendants of the Omagua and other peoples of the Solimões and Japurá have never lost their sense of Indianness.

Indigenous and Colonial Dynamics on the Tapajós and Madeira

Until the mid–seventeenth century, the Tapajós and Tupinamba peoples of the Tapajós River region confronted a process of expansion the consequences of which were vassalage, slavery, and dislocation of the peoples of the interior. It is likely that the early historical relations that the Tupinamba had with other tribal groups led to a "Tupinization" of the Mundurukú and Mawé Indians. By the same token, the relations of domination exerted by the Tapajós over other groups like the Maraguá certainly had important consequences in terms of warfare and exchange.

As a result of intense contacts with the whites during the latter half of the seventeenth century, the Tapajós and Tupinamba rapidly withdrew. By 1690, only 30 years after the beginning of missionization in the region, little remained of the once populous Tapajós settlements situated at the mouth of the river, and by that time the Tupinamba were no longer referred to as a distinct group. Peoples that had been subjected or enslaved by the Tapajós quickly occupied the area left open by them, and the greater part of the information on the region in the following century refers to the new groups who emerged.

The large number of tribal designations found in the eighteenth-century sources (one Jesuit in 1714 listed eighty-five groups) suggests, if not the density of the region's indigenous population, its complexity and diversity. Of all these groups, the Mawé, Munduruku, Apiaká, and Kawahiwa on the Tapajós, and the Mura on the Madeira, are of greatest interest because of their lengthy influence on the history of the region.

Portuguese extractive activities in the area, begun in the early seventeenth century, initially had no fixed locations. Military colonization started with the construction of a fort at the mouth of the Tapajós and was later followed by reconnaissance expeditions up the Madeira and, by the mid–eighteenth century, by the establishment of cacao-producing farms. With the mining frontier that opened up the settlement of Mato Grosso in the eighteenth century, interest in a fluvial connection to Pará via the Tapajós-Madeira, which had formerly been prohibited (apparently to avoid a population exodus from Pará to the mines) now led to renewed navigation and penetration of the region. Various expeditions in the 1740s crossed through the Madeira River area, frequently encountering hostile Mura along the way. Based on the expeditions' reports, the crown developed a strategy for effective possession of the western frontier territory. Late in the same decade, official expeditions prepared the way for implanting Pombaline policies in the area.

In 1753 the crown lifted its prohibition of the Madeira route to Mato Grosso. In the following decades the Indians faced commercial fleets supplying the region of Mato Grosso with manufactured objects and black slaves. Despite the limited success of the Arinos mines, which had been exhausted by the late 1740s, the Tapajós River also gradually came to feel the permanent presence of the whites, and by 1816 the first measures were taken to regulate the navigation of the Tapajós-Madeira-Arinos fluvial system. On the Madeira hostile actions by the Arara, Mura, and Munducuru after the expulsion of the Jesuits led to an abandoning of settlements and decline in navigation. By the mid–nineteenth century, it was reported that few people ventured up the river in search of forest spices.

Under the new Brazilian nation, with the elevation of the captaincies to provinces and the creation of the province of Amazonas in 1852, the Tapajós-Madeira area was administratively divided among Amazonas, Pará, and Mato Grosso. The government of Amazonas gave special attention to the colonization and evangelization of the Madeira region. These activities and the beginning of the rubber boom led to a reactivation of navigation on the Madeira. Construction of the Madeira-Mamoré railway, extending to Bolivia, was initiated in 1878 but not completed until the beginning of the twentieth century.

Missionary activity accompanied governmental action. The Portuguese crown originally entrusted the mission field of the Tapajós-Madeira region to the Jesuits, who followed the well-known strategy of increasing the mission populations with Indians descended from upriver villages. This process produced a large-scale dislocation of village populations not only from the descents that concentrated people of different groups in the same settlements, but also because many Indians who abandoned the missions regrouped in places beyond their original homelands.

The Jesuits were intensely involved in the region from the second half of the seventeenth century to the beginning of the eighteenth. Contact with the missionaries and cacao traders frequently represented destruction for the Indians. The sad state of affairs in the Jesuit settlement of Abacaxis, a situation not unlike the rest of mission settlements in Grão Pará, serves as an example. Severely affected by smallpox epidemics at the end of the 1730s, this once populous village, first inhabited by the Abacaxi Indians and, after their decimation, by members of twenty-three other "nations," had been reduced at the end of the 1740s to less than 600 people.

With the Jesuits' departure all villages were raised to the level of boroughs or towns under secular administration. The Indian Directorate sought to maintain the settlements and administer Indian labor, policies that created considerable difficulties for missionary activities, which now continued under the Carmelites and Franciscans. Both orders worked intensively on the Madeira until roughly the mid–nineteenth century, often facing conflicts with slavers and traders, but with time their influence began to decline, becoming restricted to the Mawé and Mundurukú. By the end of the nineteenth century, Henri Coudreau, in his travels along the Tapajós, makes no reference to any mission settlements.

From the latter half of the seventeenth century, the more organized and effective presence of the whites destabilized Indian societies. One of the first consequences was population loss among the Tupinambá, Tapajós, and Iruri due to hostilities or epidemics. With the decrease in resistance of these groups, others of the interior came to occupy marginal territories, eventually suffering the same population losses.

With time, the increasing presence of the whites forced several groups into close contact. The Tapajós, for example, after initially bloody conflicts, were pressured by the Portuguese into supplying slaves they obtained through warfare with neighboring groups. This was followed by a period in which Indian–white relations developed on a more or less peaceful basis. With the exception of Mura resistance, there were few conflicts, and those that took place were mediated by the Jesuits.

Violent confrontations followed the expulsion of the Jesuits especially among groups like the Mawé and Mundurucu, where the "Black Robes" had been particularly active. This deterioration of relations occurred on the Mahués River, one of the places where the Jesuits had concentrated and where no confrontations were reported until the latter half of the century. The Mawé here conducted a brisk commerce of spices and *guaraná* with the Portuguese. In 1763, however, conflicts were reported between the Mawé and the whites, and in 1769 the government prohibited all commerce with the Mawé due to the Indians' killing of several traders. In the same period relations with the Mundurukú likewise deteriorated, beginning with the Indians' attack on the Fort of Tapajós, and lasting until a military force succeeded in imposing a peace settlement in 1795.

In the southern part of the Tapajós-Madeira area, peaceful contact was more common. No hostilities were recorded with the Pama and Karipuna until much later – with the expansion of rubber extraction and the construction of the Madeira-Mamoré railway. The whites utilized the Apiaká in navigation and extraction, rapidly incorporating them to the modus vivendi of the expanding frontier.

In large part, warfare structured the relations between indigenous groups and with the Europeans. The utilization of indigenous mercenary troops, especially the Mundurucu against other indigenous groups seems to have been a factor of major importance in population movements throughout much of the nineteenth century. The whites did not create hostilities between the Mundurucu and their neighbors but took advantage of those already existing. The conflicts between Mundurucu and

Mura warriors around 1786, which forced the Mura to leave the Madeira and head to the west, occurred prior to their alliance with the whites. Possibly Munducuru hostilities with neighbors like the Juma, Parintintin, and Apiaká, also began in this period.

By their very nature and purpose, the conflicts with Europeans were destructive, resulting in the enslavement of whole groups. Even in the case of the Tapajós, who were familiar with a form of servile labor in precolumbian times, exploitation was never as intense as under European domination. The mortality rate of Indians increased exponentially due to disease and violence. Finally, there were wars of intentional extermination such as that against the Mura.

Institutionalized contempt for the Mura originated with the Jesuits, who in 1738–1739 initiated a criminal process against them in the "Writ of Inquest against the Mura." According to this document, frequent attacks by a "nation of barbarous Indians called Muras" had been reported from the missions, where they were said to have killed many Indian rowers employed in cacao gathering on the Madeira. They had also killed a white man, commander of a canoe, and were stealing from gardens and attacking the Indian villages. These denunciations were used as justifications by colonists and missionaries who sought royal support for war against the Mura, thereby opening the Madeira region for the extraction of cacao. Through testimonies of people who had never been to the Madeira, and statements from merchants and military interested in commercial exploitation, the Jesuits mounted a legal campaign in which the missionaries' denunciations echoed in testimonies that repeated what they heard of the Mura. The inquest, however, was not considered sufficient to justify the crown's authorization of an offensive war. Because there was interest in opening the way to the mines of Mato Grosso, the crown decided that the Indians of the Tapajós-Madeira served a strategic function and thus the Madeira was spared from the actions of the ransom troops.

Accusations against the Mura, as "heathen pirates," were repeated in all documents on the Madeira during the 1740s. With the opening of the Madeira-Mamoré-Guaporé route, these accusations provided the basis for a series of measures ranging from standard warning signals used in navigation, to legalized capture of the Mura, despite the restrictive law protecting Indian freedom then in effect.

The war apparatus mounted against the Mura far surpassed their real threat, which consisted primarily of stealing from villages and boats. In the mid-1750s official correspondence actually declared that the Mura did not represent a substantial threat to Portuguese ships but were an imaginary danger, justifying the creation of military apparatus that the Portuguese needed to secure possession of the western frontier.[15]

In the decades following Jesuit expulsion, reports of attacks by the Mura spread from the Madeira to the Solimões and Rio Negro. Local authorities blamed the improductivity of villages in these regions on frequent Mura attacks, or even on the fear of these attacks. The superintendent and auditor Ribeiro de Sampaio, who traveled throughout Grão Pará in 1773–1774, viewed the Mura as a major impediment to the rational plans for agricultural development projected by the Pombaline government. When found or captured in the vicinities of towns, the Mura were killed, enslaved, or given as presents to the authorities.

By the end of the century, the technical experts of the first border commissions made Mura warfare a subject of literary and scientific descriptions. Alexandre Rodrigues Ferreira, for example, urged the governor to believe that no attempts at "reduction" of the Mura could succeed because they refused all contact, making them enemies of the crown and susceptible to punishment through offensive war. The profile of the Mura presented in his *Viagem Filosófica* (1788) essentially reiterates the view held by Ribeiro de Sampaio – that the Mura, whose terrible attacks or threats either immobilized the settler population or caused their flight to the cities, were an impediment to agricultural development. According to both accounts the Mura supposedly occupied an immense territory from the Tocantins to the Solimões and the interior of the Madeira, Negro, and Japurá river valleys.

A compilation of letters from authorities responsible for settling the Mura from 1784–1786 served as a source for a series of texts, such as the well-known poem *Muhuraida*, written in 1785 by H. J. Wilckens, an official of the Pombal administration. The poem reworks in extreme form all of the eighteenth-century images of the Mura and especially the notion of their immense territory. According to Wilckens the Mura had "expanded" from their original territory on the Madeira to occupy all

[15] At the same time, Governor Mendonça Furtado personally went to establish the new town of Borba, which would serve to control gold smuggling. There, he discovered two cannons that the Jesuits had received from previous administrators and which were used to frighten the Mura. The news of a "Jesuit artillery" reached the court, and the cannons were confiscated as evidence of the Jesuits' militarization against the colonial government. Rumors spread of an armed uprising of Indians and Jesuits, similar to that of the Guarani at the Seven Missions in 1753.

tributaries of the Amazon. Their nomadism, the generalized lack of knowledge about them, and the moving of colonial frontiers, which pushed the Mura population to the Japurá River, all are given as elements explaining their extraordinary "expansion."

The image of the "gigantic Mura" suggests that the real population size was considerably augmented by the inclusion of thousands of people occupying the forests thought to be Mura territory. These would have been "deserters" from colonial settlements who sought refuge among the Mura from the hard labor to which they were submitted in the villages. They included ex-rowers, "civilized and Christianized" Indians (or *ladinos*) who sought to escape the premature death that inevitably faced them.

In July 1784 Governor João Pereira Caldas received word from a military commander that five Mura had been in Ega looking for the priest and spoke of the end of killing and of their intent not to harbour any more *ladinos* from the villages. After 6 months another hundred men, women, and children returned, bringing turtles and sarsaparilla. Thus began the long process of the "reduction" of the Mura, which occupied the authorities of Grão Pará for 3 years, at the end of which, according to the documents, all the Mura were settled in villages.

A key figure in this process was the chief Ambrozio. Known as the "Murificado" (Mura-ified), who led the Mura to civilization, Ambrozio had been taken captive as a child with his mother from the village of Paraguari and brought up among the Mura. Married to a Mura woman, he barely spoke *lingua geral* and became in all respects like a Mura. He is described as a huge man, tall and muscular, with two wild boar bones perforating his upper and lower lips, following the Mura custom. He ultimately undertook the entire work of bringing the Mura as well as several Chumana and Iruri groups to the Negro, Japurá, and Madeira rivers. Between 1784 and 1787, seven Mura settlements had been established on the Solimões, Japurá, and Madeira. The last news of Ambrozio, in 1788, reports that he had been in Ega bringing presents of turtles for the chief and his group and trading for personal articles – a shirt, trousers, socks, hat, a pair of buckled shoes, and a walking stick. With the air of an official in the service of the crown, Ambrozio continued his mission to attract the Mura.

The relatively small number of Mura ascertained in the population surveys undertaken at the end of "reduction" (a total of 3,000) demonstrates that the eighteenth-century sources that claimed a population of

60,000 were greatly exaggerated, consistent with the image of the "gigantic Mura." Similarly the idea of their immense territory must be understood in the context of an expanding colonial frontier that dislocated the Mura from the Madeira to the Japurá. The efficiency of Mura "reduction" must also be evaluated in light of the evidence of a low and extremely fluctuating population in the settlements, which the Mura more often frequented in search of iron tools and supplies.

The institution of Murification, the assimilation of other Indians into Mura society, was another important process. It was at times defined as a voluntary action by Indians of different groups, settled or not, who joined the Mura; at other times it was seen as a practice derived from intertribal warfare in which prisoners of war would be integrated into the group. These two views are evidently not mutually exclusive. During the colonial period Murification fueled as much the fear of a supposed warlike expansion as the idea of an immense, unknown territory occupied by the Mura and those who had joined them.

Like other indigenous peoples, the Mura were swept into the political battles of the provincial governments in the nineteenth century. In Pará the adherence of indigenous communities to the Cabanagem Revolt did not occur in a cohesive way. Rather, it was formed by the large numbers of renegade Tapuya who lived in small groups with their chiefs, the descendants of runaways and deserters from the slavery and descent periods. Settled Indians responsible for the agricultural development of the colony were far more subject to the influence of lay and religious authorities and thus held contradictory positions in relation to the revolt. For example, in the time of Bararoá, one of the heroes of the *cabanos*, the Mundurucu chief Joaquim José Pereira and his followers sided with the legalists against the rebels.

From the minutes of municipal chambers of Amazonian towns, many of which came under the control of the *cabano* rebels for some time, it appears that the indigenous population was largely behind the rebellion. Defense plans against the *cabanos* included, for example, instructions to prevent the entrance of suspicious persons into the *malocas* (longhouses) of the Indians and to train people to be informants to infiltrate among the Indians. It is true that after their defeat in Belém, the rebels moved to the interior regions of the Tapajós and Madeira, where they recruited the Indians to continue their attacks on local towns. In the final phase of the revolt, Mundurucânia became the principal setting for the struggle, with the participation of the Mawé, Mundurucu, and Mura survivors of the massacre of 1838 in the region of the Autaz River. The final surrender of the *cabanos* took place in Lúsea in 1840.

Expansion on the Rio Negro and Messianic Resistance

As the largest of the western tributaries of the Amazon, the Rio Negro in precontact times served as a key channel for contact and communication between the native peoples of the northern part of the continent, including the sub-Andean regions, and the Amazon. The earliest records from the Orinoco floodplains to the Amazon Valley indicate that native societies were integrated into an extensive system of commerce, exchange, and interaction, the complexity of which can be determined only partially from the documents. Arawak peoples of the northern Maipure language family, by far the most important population from the middle Amazon to the Orinoco, played a key role in the functioning of this system, as evidenced by the wide-ranging commercial relations of the Manao of the middle Rio Negro and the Achagua of the Meta.

The ethnographic record of the early Rio Negro peoples is thin. The first chroniclers provided a fair description of the societies of the Amazon floodplain, but the majority of the Rio Negro societies, contacted only toward the end of the seventeenth and beginning of the eighteenth centuries when the driving forces behind expansion were intense, generated little ethnographic curiosity. Furthermore the Jesuits, who had left such detailed records on native peoples in other regions, here had a negligible or negative role. The few Jesuits on the Negro in the eighteenth century in fact facilitated the drastic depopulation through their participation in the slave trade. Thus the history of contact of unknown numbers of Rio Negro societies consists of a period of roughly 50 years of commercial relations, warfare, destruction, and accommodation to the European presence.

What happened on the Rio Negro in the first century of contact parallels the pattern of conquest and destruction on the middle and upper Amazon. Slavery, epidemics, descents, and forced labor left the region a virtual desert, crippling all later efforts to turn it into a productive colony. The nineteenth century proved little better because programs and policies to civilize the natives, and the rubber economy, served to perpetuate an exploitative system and to create dependence on external markets. It would be misleading, however, to represent the early contact history as one of simple conquest, because the record from the eighteenth through the twentieth centuries is replete with episodes of resistance and rebellion, many of which took the form of messianic and prophetic movements.

Well before the Portuguese entered the Rio Negro, the native peoples knew of their existence and had undoubtedly received trade goods from peoples of the Solimões already in contact. During the second half of the seventeenth century, slave troops accompanied by Jesuits periodically visited the lower Rio Negro, establishing commercial relations with the Tarumã. In 1694 the Portuguese constructed the Fort of Barra near the mouth of the river, partly in response to the "Dutch threat" and partly to prevent Spanish expansion down the Solimões, but principally to discourage the Tarumã from interfering with the slave trade and extraction of forest spices. By the end of the century, the Tarumã population had diminished to such an extent that the slave troops ranged further up the Rio Negro, reaching the territory of the Manao by the 1720s.

The most numerous and powerful peoples of the middle Rio Negro, the Manao, were also very enterprising traders, traveling and carrying goods from the Uaupés to the Solimões and to the Guyanas. By the late seventeenth century, they became involved in trading slaves to the Dutch, possibly replacing the role the Tarumã once had. At the same time, they were in contact with Portuguese slavers and Carmelite missionaries against whose advance they resisted. By the 1720s the Manao were engaged in the slave trade with both the Portuguese and the Dutch.

In 1723, with the intensification of slaving activities in Manao territory, and the division of Manao leaders over alliances with the Portuguese, various Manao began to attack a Portuguese ransom troop, then under the command of Manoel de Braga. The most famous of these leaders was Ajuricaba, who persuaded a number of other chiefs to form a confederation (here an ad hoc temporary association) in order to prevent the Portuguese from expanding their activities beyond the rapids of the middle Rio Negro.

A legend concerning Ajuricaba states that he was the son of the chief Huiuiebéue, one of the principal leaders of the Manao and grandson of Caboquena, known for his hatred of the Portuguese. As a young man he was unusually strong and desired by the daughters of the Baré and Tucano of the upper Rio Negro; yet he chose a Tariana maiden as his wife. Later he left his father's house in disagreement over an alliance that Huiuiebéue had made with the whites and later returned to avenge his father's assassination by them. It may be understood from this that

Ajuricaba's hostility to the Portuguese was related to previous violent encounters dating from the seventeenth century.[16]

The resistance of the Manao and their continuing attacks against the missions and ransom troops served as a pretext for a "Just War" led by Melchior Mendes de Moraes against the Manao in 1723. In fact the real reason for the war was based both on the chronic demand for slaves and the Manaos' preventing the Portuguese from gaining control of the trade. Ajuricaba was captured, but while facing certain execution he instigated a rebellion on board the ship that was to transport him and other Manao to Pará, and he died when he threw himself, still bound in chains, into the river. Traditional historiography has treated Ajuricaba as a "hero" and a "rebel" for his resistance to Portuguese "rule." A more critical interpretation, however, is offered by Sweet:

> In reality, Ajuricaba was never a Portuguese subject but the chieftain of an independent tribe in an area being infringed upon by Portuguese expeditions whose object was to transport its population into distant slavery. Regarding his "greatness" there is no evidence; having emerged as principal leader in a moment of crisis for his people, he was quickly and without great difficulty removed from the scene by the invaders – leaving the problem of leadership during that difficult period of transition to Portuguese rule to be solved by others, who struggled longer and achieved less fame.[17]

The resistance continued for several years after, as the Mayapena (possibly a Manao subgroup) repeatedly ambushed the troops on the Rio Negro. Consequently another "Just War" was launched against the Mayapena and their allies, as a result of which the middle Rio Negro by the 1730s was largely depopulated, leaving the passage for the slave troops to the upper Rio Negro unimpeded. In short, the wars against the Manao and Mayapena were waged against all Indians of the middle Rio Negro, who were consequently enslaved, forced to seek refuge, or forced to accommodate to the continuing demands of the slave troops and missionaries. For the next 20 years, slave troops were in operation at virtually all times on the middle and upper Rio Negro and Rio Branco. Records confirm that a minimum of 1,000 slaves a year were brought to Pará by official slave troops. Added to this were the equal numbers settled by means of Jesuit and Carmelite descents from upriver missions to the lower valley, and perhaps greater numbers of slaves taken by private slavers.

[16] Cited in Sweet, op cit., 534–536. [17] Ibid., 536–537.

In 1757 Manao survivors attempted a last effort to expel the Portuguese altogether from the Rio Negro. Even years after the suppression of that rebellion, visitors to the Rio Negro reported that the *caboclos* (of Indian–white descent) held a messianic belief that "Ajuricaba was still alive and would one day return to lead them against the European invaders."[18]

Evidently one of the keys to successful operation of the commerce was the formation of alliances with powerful chiefs of the upper Rio Negro and Orinoco, who served as guides and brokers of slaves. With each of these working for one or more of the troops, or involved in wars induced by the slavers, by the end of the 1740s, the region had suffered extensive population losses, leaving whole sections of the main rivers completely deserted.

Late in the 1740s official slaving on the Rio Negro began to decline – whether because of news about the atrocities regularly perpetrated under its aegis, or because it had proven unsuccessful as a means of raising revenue, is uncertain. In 1747 the crown ordered the withdrawal of the troops from the Rio Negro and 2 years later forbade its continuation. Yet the system died hard and continued unofficially well into the 1750s.

With the 1755 decree of Indian freedom, the system of descents intensified as new colonial settlements were established on the Rio Negro and lower courses of its main tributaries, under the control of military installed in newly built forts. In the late eighteenth century, cattle ranching was introduced to the Rio Branco, at first administered by the captaincy and later turned over to private individuals and the local Fort of São Joaquim.

The descents were implemented, however, at great cost, because they occasioned numerous desertions and rebellions of settled Indians and the consequent need to replenish the labor force needed for gathering cacao or to work in indigo and manioc plantations. The laborers were often acquired violently. Both on the upper Rio Negro and Rio Branco, aggrieved Indians abandoned settlements with frequency. Sources nevertheless confirm that the Rio Negro continued to be an important supplier of indigenous labor to Pará throughout the colonial period.

By the end of the eighteenth century, the Portuguese and Spanish colonies of the Rio Negro and upper Orinoco had fallen into a state of disorganization that enabled the surviving native peoples to recover in part from their losses. The Rio Negro had by then become a totally

[18] Ibid., 544.

different place, with vast sections transformed into "deserts." Except for the more inaccessible areas and a few relatively large colonial settlements, the indigenous population had been reduced to an impoverished fraction of its former size.

One of the effects of depopulation, here as elsewhere in the Amazon, was the disruption of intertribal relations controlling demographic and territorial expansion. Such was the case of the Yanomami, originally of the Parima mountain range northeast of the Rio Branco. In the early to mid–eighteenth century, contact had been established between Europeans and the Carib and Arawak groups that surrounded the Yanomami. These groups became the source of iron tools and new cultigens, such as the banana, for the Yanomami. With the decline in population of these groups due to slaving, epidemics, and descents, the Yanomami began to occupy territory to the south, a process that was to continue throughout the nineteenth century and first half of the twentieth.

Throughout much of the early nineteenth century, the Rio Negro remained a source of labor and products used in the sustenance of colonial settlements. In the early 1850s the provincial government in Barra launched a program for the "civilization and catechization" of the Indians of the interior. The government revived the Indian Directorate system, increased the number of missionaries, and instituted a program of "public service" in which government-sponsored chiefs were to send laborers and children to the capital. To accomplish these objectives directors relied on the support and alliance of traders and several powerful chiefs who acted as middlemen in negotiating resettlement, providing labor, and organizing punitive raids against peoples who resisted.

The increasingly arbitrary and abusive practices of this system in effect exacerbated an already tense situation on the upper Rio Negro, which was one of the principal causes of the messianic and millenarian revolts that erupted in the region from 1857 on. Two of the principal messiahs to emerge at this time were Venancio Kamiko, a Baniwa Indian of the Guainia in Venezuela, and Alexandre Christu, a Baniwa of the Orinoco. Numerous other messiahs appeared, but these were by far the best known.

Kamiko's prophecies of a world conflagration had a firm basis in the mythology, cosmology, shamanism, and ritual of the Baniwa; yet the new religion he preached also had definite political ends – the Indians would have their own priests and religious ceremonies, and through allegiance to the new religion, they would be freed from political and economic domination by the whites. Kamiko thus improvised on the symbolism of myth and ritual to formulate a millenarian strategy of resistance.

Alexandre sought to go a step further: According to the sources, hundreds of Indians participated in his ritual dances, and they were "disposed to resist" any interference by missionaries or military. Incidents of armed conflict led authorities to conclude that the movement represented "a kind of conspiracy against the civilized people," which could, if no action were taken, cause the expulsion of white authorities from the region. Alexandre preached that "gunpowder" would fall from heaven and that the existing relations between Indians and whites would be overturned such that the Indians would govern the whites in compensation for the time the whites had governed them.

With fears of an international conspiracy on the borders, the provincial government sent a commission with military forces to the region. No doubt due to their fear of reprisal and as a result of internal dissensions in Alexandre's movement, the followers dispersed. The messianic leaders fled with a number of their followers to the forests. While Kamiko continued to exercise a strong influence until his death in 1902, Alexandre abandoned his messianic quest, converting to Christianity in 1861. Those who chose not to follow Kamiko quickly sought to assure the authorities of their support, but on the condition that the military, traders, and missionaries who had contributed to their discontent be removed from the area. Shortly afterward the authorities complied with their demands and abolished the system of Indian Directorates. In effect the "civilization and catechization" program ceased altogether, and the region returned to the control of a few traders and military. The respite was brief because the rubber boom had reached the upper Rio Negro by the early 1870s.

The effects of the boom were critical because the indigenous population of the region became economically dependent on external markets mediated by the permanent presence of white traders. As in other areas of Amazonia, rubber exploitation was based on the control that rubber patrons exercised over the lands and resources of vast areas, which they exploited with their armies of rubber gatherers.

During the height of the boom, messianic movements led by powerful shamans and prophets continued on the upper Rio Negro. As a strategy of survival, messianism lasted as long as there were shamans whose own powers were seen as the key to controlling the violent and chaotic situation of the boom and its aftermath, or whose perceived access to the sources of the white man's power – Christian symbols or priests who had access to the mythological origins of the white man – was strong. To the extent it was the explicit policy of missionaries (Franciscans and Salesians on the upper Río Negro) to subvert the power of the shamans and to undermine the central importance of such institutions as ancestor rituals, the indigenous peoples became increasingly dependent on them for protection and a supply of trade goods. Indigenous messianic cults only survived in the more remote regions away from the missionaries, whereas indigenous strategies have more recently become concentrated in political movements.

On the Rio Branco forced recruitment of indigenous labor continued throughout the nineteenth century. This demand tended to increase with the exploitation of rubber from the 1850s on. In the last two decades of the century, the regional economy from domestic services to navigation, construction, and agriculture depended almost entirely on indigenous labor. Forced recruitment continued through expeditions undertaken by Indian intermediaries, causing the retreat of indigenous peoples from their territories in search of areas of refuge. Cattle ranching, undertaken by civilian colonists, began to fix indigenous labor in the region and to initiate a long period of land disputes that continue to the present day.

In this context prophetic movements also arose among Carib and Arawak peoples of the upper Branco. The first of these was probably the movement known as "Hallelujah" among Carib peoples around Mount Roraima in British Guiana. According to the tradition the Kapon and Pemon learned of Christianity from the missions, first from the Moravians on the British Guiana coast in the late eighteenth century and then from the Anglican missionaries among them in the nineteenth century.

From the beginning the Hallelujah religion was based on the idea that the acquisition of the white man's religious knowledge, codified in prayers and songs, would enable the Indians to transcend death and attain immortality. Hallelujah prophets, consistently preached that by constantly observing the new rituals, people would experience a change of skin, they would become "white," signifying not that they would become Europeans but that they would attain the brilliant, gleaming white of divine, celestial light. Jesus Christ, the Messiah, communicated to the people through the Hallelujah prophets, many of them shamans. Initially the prophets announced immediate access to a territorial utopia of abundance and immortality. With time this hope was deferred to the imminence of a heavenly utopia to be attained through ritual transformation, a celestial ascension of believers, and mystical union with the divine.

The Hallelujah movement spread rapidly among neighboring groups along the Venezuelan-Brazil border. In the early twentieth century, Adventist missionaries introduced new concepts that were assimilated and transformed by the prophets. In short, as on the upper Rio Negro, the Rio Branco movements were founded in ancient beliefs and practices related to shamanistic voyages and the promise, expressed in myth, of a utopia. Such beliefs and the historical migrations that they produced were given a strong legitimation through the acquisition of a knowledge and a language that were believed to have the power to effect the transformation the Pemon desired. Thus conversion to the new religions was not a rejection of traditional culture but rather an appropriation and reshaping of Christianity. Rather than fragmenting their societies, it helped to strengthen their position vis-à-vis the whites.

CONCLUSION

This survey of three centuries of contact has demonstrated that the correlations which can be drawn between underlying, aboriginal patterns and responses to the threats (and opportunities) of European contact with native peoples in Brazil have been complex and variable in each case. Although one would have expected a more organized resistance to expansion from the larger and more complex societies – such as those of the Amazon floodplains – in fact the opposite occurred. Such societies were the first to withdraw, seeking refuge in more distant areas and protection in mission settlements, and they were the first to experience catastrophic depopulation as a result of increasing intertribal warfare, slavery, and disease.

By contrast the more mobile hunting and foraging peoples were unquestionably those who presented the most consistent and long-lasting obstacles to colonial expansion, in most cases bringing colonists to their knees, and provoking crises in colonial projects and, in some cases, extreme reactions far beyond their real military threat.

At the same time, the very organization of hunting and foraging peoples into small groups, subject to fission and factionalism, rendered them vulnerable in terms of united strategies against continuing incursions and ever more violent assaults by colonists, military, and paramilitary organizations. Faced by hunger, disease, and military defeat, groups such as the Botocudo and Mura chose for settlement as some guarantee of survival, or they negotiated peace treaties and accords in return for guarantees of protection and land.

Traditional sociocultural patterns in some cases facilitated the emergence of pan-tribal political-military organizations in wars against the Portuguese. Indian participation in wide-ranging networks of trade and exchange, intertribal symbiosis between sedentary and mobile groups, the recognition of supralocal war leaders, and often alliances with other European powers who supplied munitions, all proved effective techniques of resistance. The long-term effectiveness of such confederations or alliances depended as much on historical circumstances as internal political dynamics. Europeans quickly perceived the strategy of playing off intergroup factions or traditional enmities – the familiar divide-and-conquer policy used everywhere in the Americas.

In no case did settlement prove to be a satisfactory solution or guarantee either from the Indians' or the administrators' points of view. Conflicts continued, "civilizational" programs produced negative results, and, more often than not, once people saw what settlement implied, they withdrew or maintained minimal relations with administrators.

Demographic decline and ethnic transformation were often the irreversible consequences of settlement. In areas where diverse peoples developed relatively long histories of settlement, they sought to conserve their ethnic distinctiveness by reconstituting aboriginal cultural patterns, which together with common historical experiences served as the parameters of a new sense of Indianness, maintained among some groups to the present day. The struggles of such peoples have been to affirm that identity and related rights to land against persistent efforts by the state to deny them.

There were numerous other ways that such forms of "resistant adaptation" – that is, where peoples under colonial domination have challenged or defied authorities by forging spaces of survival that ultimately reinforced collective identity – developed. Parallel economic activities, truancy and flight, litigation, and military training have been mentioned in this chapter.

One of the striking aspects in this history is the central importance of intermediaries who served as brokers or who in essence facilitated settlement and colonization. Such individuals sometimes emerged at times of critical transition; sometimes they acted in pursuit of personal or political ambitions; or they had the foresight to realize that the only way to confront the advance of colonization was through siding with the authorities. Such intermediaries often held the status of outsiders to the group, represented newly emergent and nontraditional forms of leadership, and in some cases were looked upon as quasi-messianic figures whose protection was the key to survival. Evidently, whole groups could also serve in the intermediary, broker role.

In the cases of messianic resistance movements, native leaders sought to forge new forms of religious organization, based largely on traditional beliefs, institutions, and practices, but clothed with the central symbols of Christianity. Far from being merely syncretistic or acculturational, such movements showed rather a continued belief in the efficacy of native power over the intrusive culture. Native prophets offered long-term strategies for relating to the whites, incorporating, rejecting, or modifying the symbols of the alien culture, which ultimately strengthened their own position.

Native perceptions of those in authority among the whites, such as the missionary or the king, likewise are critical to understanding why specific peoples appealed to such authorities during contact. As the sources of the white man's power and technical ability, these figures were associated often with returning godmen of native religion, the equivalent of powerful shamans.

Special problems were faced by peoples of the frontiers that, in the context of three centuries of expansion, involved a great many peoples discussed in this chapter. Caught between the competing advances of European powers, their options were to resist or seek alliances with whichever of the powers proved to be better trading partners, stronger militarily, or less of a threat. Clearly there were times when shifting alliances worked to the advantage of the peoples involved, but as the press for definition of international limits intensified, "nations" were often irremediably divided, seeking refuge or protection where they could reconstruct a mode of existence. The vulnerability of peoples on the frontier is exemplified by the Guaykuru, whose military prowess had deterred the advance of the Spaniards and Portuguese, but whose same skills were later exploited by the Brazilians in the war against Paraguay.

Three centuries of contact, in nearly every case discussed here, annihilated or reduced the once demographically strong and culturally rich populations of Brazil. By the beginning of the twentieth century, what remained were pockets of relatively isolated communities, living with insecure tenure on marginal lands. Yet conquest did not imply defeat, because in nearly all cases these communities – far from being mere survivors of a history marked by enslavement, forced relocations, wars of extermination, and acute population decline – represent long traditions of struggle to preserve and re-create their identity against overwhelming odds.

BIBLIOGRAPHIC ESSAY

For a general English-language introduction to the history of contact with native peoples in Brazil, the reader should consult John Hemming's two-volume work *Red Gold* (London, 1978), which covers the period from 1500 to 1760, and *Amazon Frontier* (London, 1987), from 1760 to 1910. At the time of their publication, both volumes were pioneering efforts to present a coherent and comprehensive history of the treatment of Brazilian Indians, but written from the perspective of "conquest history." The most important alternatives produced in recent years are the two volumes organized and edited by the Brazilian anthropologist Manuela Carneiro da Cunha: the first, a special issue of the *Revista de Antropologia*, 30/31/32 (1987/88/89), a collection of papers principally by Brazilian researchers on diverse aspects of indigenous history; the second, *História dos índios no Brasil* (São Paulo, 1993), a major collection of articles by more than two dozen specialists on archaeology, linguistics, physical anthropology, museum collections, Indian policy and legislation, and regional historical studies of upper Amazonia, southern Amazonia, the northeast, east, and south. Each of the articles contains excellent bibliographies for the topics and regions covered. As yet untranslated to English, the collection nevertheless offers the best of recent research on Brazilian Indian history. To be sure, it leaves large areas of the country out of its scope; yet one of its major repercussions is to have stimulated new and basic archival and fieldwork research. A *Guia de Fontes para a História Indígena no Brasil* (Guide to the Sources), organized by John Monteiro (Núcleo de História Indígena, São Paulo, 1993), currently in preparation, will be the first, comprehensive survey of archives in Brazil for sources relevant to indigenous history.

Indian Policy and Legislation.

The literature on the history of policy and legislation is complex but has been competently summarized by Perrone-Moisés and Carneiro da Cunha in *História dos Indios no Brasil*, 115–32, 155–74. Important works concentrating on colonial Indian policy are Mathias Kiemen's "The Indian policy of Portugal in Amazonia, with special reference to the old state of Maranhão," *The Americas* 5 (1948), 131–171; and *The Indian Policy of Portugal in the Amazon Region, 1614–1693* (Washington, 1954); Dauril Alden's "Black Robes vs. White Settlers . . ." in H. Peckham and C. Gibson (eds.), *Attitudes of Colonial Powers towards the American Indians* (Salt Lake City, 1969); Expedito Arnaud's "A legislação sobre os índios do Grão-Pará e Maranhão nos sécs. XVII e XVIII," *Boletim de Pesquisa do CEDEAM* 4 (1985), 34–72, for the Amazon region; and Georg Thomas' *Política Indigenista dos Portugueses no Brasil, 1500–1640* (São Paulo, 1982 [1968]) for the state of Brazil. Summaries of Indian legislation can be found in Hemming's two volumes. A comprehensive survey of nineteenth-century legislation has been undertaken by Carneiro da Cunha, *Legislação indigenista no século XIX* (São Paulo, 1993). Finally, Darcy Ribeiro's classic, *Os Indios e a Civilização* (Petrópolis, 1977), documents the effects of early twentieth-century policies and evaluates the work of Rondon and the SPI, but see the critical reevaluation by Souza Lima, in Carneiro da Cunha (1993), 155–174.

For an extensive bibliography on the Guarani, Bartomeu Melià et al., *O Guarani: Uma Bibliografia Etnológica* (Santo Angelo, 1987), provides an excellent starting point. Herbert Baldus' *Bibliografia Crítica da Etnologia Brasileira* (São Paulo, 1954, and Hannover, 1968), along with the third volume compiled by Thekla Hartmann (Munich, 1984), contain many commented references to relevant bibliographical matter.

As in the case of the related Tupinambá, Guarani studies raise the challenging question of the relationship between the "historical" and "ethnographic" Guarani. This problem receives novel treatment in Eduardo Viveiros de Castro, "Bibliografia Etnológica Tupi-Guarani," *Revista de Antropologia* 27/28 (1984–1985), 7–24. While superseded in part by later research on demography, leadership and shamanism, Alfred Métraux's solid article, "The Guarani," in J. H. Steward (ed.), *Handbook of South American Indians* (Washington, D.C., 1948), vol. 3, 69–94, remains the best available in English. The most complete ethnographic treatment of the Guarani within Brazilian territory is Egon Schaden, *Aspectos Fundamentais da Cultura Guaraní*, 3rd ed. (São Paulo, 1974). Bartomeu Melià, *El Guaraní conquistado y reducido* (Asunción, 1986), is a series of innovative ethnohistorical essays challenging many positions on demography, resistance, religion, and the missionary experience.

A valuable selection of documents from the Biblioteca Nacional of

Rio de Janeiro has been edited by Jaime Cortesão and Hélio Vianna in the seven volumes of *Manuscritos da Coleção de Angelis* (Rio de Janeiro, 1951–1970). Perhaps the most important single source on the Guarani of Guairá are the works of Antonio Ruiz de Montoya, S.J., *Conquista espiritual hecha por los religiosos de la Compañia de Jesus en las Provincias del Paraguay, Paraná, Uruguay y Tape* (Madrid, 1639) and *Tesoro de la lengua Guaraní* (Madrid, 1639).

On the size of the Guarani population at the time of contact, Pierre Clastres proposes new methods and estimates in *La société contre l'état; recherches d'antropologie politique* (Paris, 1974), which is systematically criticized by Melià in *El Guaraní*. Shamanism, religion, and prophetic movements have commanded considerable attention. Although treating the Tupi-Guarani peoples as a whole, Alfred Métraux's *La Religion des Tupinamba et ses rapports avec celle des autres tribus Tupi-Guarani* (Paris, 1928), contains valuable information on Guaraní religion. Hélène Clastres, *La Terre sans Mal: Le Prophetisme Tupi-Guarani* (Paris, 1975), is a detailed and innovative study of Guaraní shamanism and religious movements, though its conclusions have been challenged by Noemia Diaz Martinez, in "La migración Mbya (Guaraní)," *Dédalo* 24 (1985), 147–169.

On Guarani slavery in São Paulo, Edmundo Zenha, *Mamelucos* (São Paulo, 1970), focuses on the importance of Guarani labor, while John Monteiro's excellent *Negros da Terra. Indios e Bandeirantes nas orígens de São Paulo* (São Paulo, 1994), examines the formation of a slave society in São Paulo.

On the Seven Pueblos and the Guarani War, an important contemporary source is Jacinto Rodrigues da Cunha, "Diário da Expedição de Gomes Freire de Andrada às Missões do Uruguai," *Revista do Instituto Histórico e Geográfico Brasileiro* 16 (1853), 139–328. Demographic fluctuations among the mission populations are meticulously documented in Ernesto Maeder and Alfredo Bolsi, "La población de las misiones guaraníes entre 1702 y 1767," *Estudios Paraguayos* 2:1 (1974), 111–137.

On Kaiowá migrations and contact with the Brazilian population in the nineteenth century, the most important sources are the writings of the American adventurer John Henry Elliott, especially "A Emigração dos Cayuaz," *Revista do Instituto Histórico e Geográfico Brasileiro* 19 (1856), 434–448. Other Guarani migrations, supposedly attributable to prophetic impulses, are discussed in Curt Nimuendajú, "Apontamentos sobre os Guarani," trans. Egon Schaden, *Revista do Museu Paulista*, n.s., 8 (1954), 9–57.

Source material on the Kaingang is much more sparse than that available for the Guarani. The richly detailed account of Francisco das Chagas Lima, "Memória sobre o Descobrimento e Colônia de Guarapuava," *Revista do Instituto Histórico e Geográfico Brasileiro* 4 (1842), 43–64, remains the principal source for Kaingang history in the region of Guarapuava. Beginning in the 1830s, the published annual reports of provincial presidents from São Paulo, Paraná, Santa Catarina and Rio Grande do Sul include abundant information on Kaingang – white relations and conflicts. European travelers' accounts also provide important insights for both ethnographic and policy questions, among which Pierre F. A. Booth Mabilde, *Apontamentos sobre os indígenas selvagens da nação Coroados dos matos da Provincia do Rio Grande do Sul: 1836–1866* (São Paulo, 1983), and Franz Keller-Leuzinger, "Noções sobre os Indígenas da Provincia do Paraná," *Boletim do Museu do Indio* 1 (1974), 9–29, stand out.

Wilmar D'Angelis, *Toldo Chimbangue: História e Luta Kaingang em Santa Catarina* (Xanxerê, 1984), presents a detailed, politically engaged history of the Kaingang of Santa Catarina, while covering Paraná and Rio Grande do Sul as well. Silvia Helena Simoes Borelli, "Os Kaingang no Estado de São Paulo," in *Indios no Estado de São Paulo* (São Paulo, 1984), provides an ethnohistorical study for São Paulo. On Rio Grande do Sul, Dante Laytano, "Populações Indígenas: Estudo Histórico de Suas Condições Atuais no Rio Grande do Sul," *Revistas do Museu Júlio de Castilhos e Arquivo Histórico do Rio Grande do Sul* 7 (1957), seeks to place the Kaingang in historical perspective, while the Paraná Kaingang receive detailed treatment in J. Loureiro Fernandes, "Os Caingangues de Palmas," *Arquivo do Museu Paranaense* 1 (1941). On the relationship between Xokleng and Kaingang, see Francisco Schaden, "Xokleng e Kaingang," in Egon Schaden (ed.), *Homem, Cultura e Sociedade* (Petrópolis, 1972).

Late sixteenth-century sources on the Chaco include a letter written in 1594 by Barzana in *Monumenta Peruana* 5 (1970), 568–591, and Lizarraza's "Descripción breve de toda la tierra del Peru, Tucumán, Rio de la Plata y Chile," in *Coleção Biblioteca Argentina* 13 (1916), which reports on the author's travels in 1598. For the seventeenth century, sources are primarily Jesuit, such as Montoya's *Conquista* and Techo's *História de la Provincia del Paraguay de la Compañia de Jesús.* Eighteenth-century sources are still predominantly missionary, among which the more important are Dobrizhoffer's *An Account of the Abipones* (1822), Sánchez Labrador's *El Paraguay Católico*, written in 1770 (Buenos Aires,

1910), and Pastells' *Historia de la Compañia de Jesús en la Provincia del Paraguay* (Madrid, 1949). Also important are the travel diary of Juan Francisco Aguirre, written in 1793, which contains a wealth of information on the location of peoples of the Chaco; and an anonymous Spanish manuscript, written around 1767, published in Hoonder, "Die Volkergruppierung im Gran Chaco in 18 ten. Jahrhundert," *Globus* 83 (1903), 387–391. The most important of the chroniclers' reports for this century are Felix de Azara's *Voyages dans l'Amerique Meridionale* (Paris, 1809) and *Historia del Paraguay y del Río de la Plata* (Madrid, 1847).

In the nineteenth century, Francisco Rodrigues de Prado published a short study on the "Historia dos índios cavalleros ou da nação Guaycurú," *Revista do Instituto Histórico e Geográfico Brasileiro* 1 (1908), 21–44. For the eastern areas of the Chaco, sources include J. R. Rengger's *Reise nach Paraguay in den Jahren 1818 bis 1826* (Aarau, 1835); Alcides d'Orbigny's ten-volume *Voyage dans l'Amérique Meridionale* (Paris, 1835–1847); Hercules Florence's *Viagem Fluvial do Tietê ao Amazonas, de 1825 a 1829* (São Paulo, 1948); and Franz de Castelnau's *Expedition . . .* (Paris, 1850–1859). For Mato Grosso, besides several administrative documents, ethnographic reports by Guido Boggianni, *Os Caduveo* (São Paulo, 1945), and Émile Rivasseau, *A Vida dos Indios Guaycurús* (São Paulo, 1936), provide important information.

The most significant work of the twentieth century on the native peoples of Paraguay and the Chaco is that of Branislava Susnik – for example, *El indio colonial del Paraguay*, vol. III, pt. 1, "El Chaqueño: Guaycurúes, Payaguaés e Chané-Arawak" (Asunción, 1971); "Etnohistória de los puebles del Chaco," *América Indígena* 49 (1989), 431–490; and *Los Aborígenes del Paraguay*, vol. III, pt. 1, "Etnohistória de los Chaqueños (1650–1910)" (Asunción, 1981). Alfred Métraux's classic "Ethnography of the Chaco," in the *Handbook of South American Indians*, vol. 1 (Washington, 1948), 197–380, also stands out for its synthesis of ethnography.

For the northeast and central coast, various chapters of Hemming's *Red Gold* deal extensively with the early history of contact in the northeast. Primary sources for the seventeenth and eighteenth centuries include the Jesuit Padre Fernão de Cardim's *Tratado da Terra e Gente do Brasil* (São Paulo, 1978 [1625]), and Serafim Leite's collection of documents *História da Companhia de Jesus no Brasil* (Rio de Janeiro, 1938–1950). General surveys of the indigenous population include William Hohenthal's "As tribus indígenas do médio e baixo São Francisco," *Revista do Museu Paulista* 12 (1960), 37–71; Estevão Pinto's *Os Indígenas do Nordeste*

(São Paulo, 1935–1938); and the *Atlas das Terras Indígenas do Nordeste* (Rio de Janeiro, 1993).

Of the numerous studies on regional history, two are worth special mention: for Ceará, Carlos Studart Filho's *Páginas de História e Pré-história* (Fortaleza, 1966), and for Sergipe, Luiz Mott's *Sergipe del Rei: População, Economia e Sociedade* (Terenna, 1986). By far the most comprehensive studies of the Indian labor system in the northeast are by Stuart Schwartz, "Indian labor and New World plantations," *American Historical Review* 83 (1978), 43–79, and *Segredos internos: engenhos e escravos na sociedade colonial* (São Paulo, 1988). On the "Guerra dos Bárbaros," Maria Idalina de Cruz Pires' *Guerra dos Bárbaros: resistência indígena e conflitos no nordeste colonial* (Recife, 1990), provides an excellent treatment. Dirceu Lindoso's *A utopia armada: rebeliões de pobres nas matas do Tombo Real (1832–50)* (Rio de Janeiro, 1983), deals specifically with the Cabanagem revolt in the northeast.

On the Botocudo of the central coast, Maria Hilda Paraíso's essay in *História dos índios no Brasil* (op cit.), 413–430, contains an excellent discussion of primary and secondary sources. Important descriptions of Botocudo society were left by early nineteenth-century travelers, especially Prince Maximiliano Wied-Neuwied, *Viagem ao Brasil* (São Paulo, 1958 [1815–1817]); Auguste de Saint-Hilaire, *Aperçu d'un voyage dans l'intérieur du Brésil* (Paris, 1823); and J. B. von Spix and C. F. P. von Martius, *Reise in Brasilien in den Jahren 1817 bis 1820* (Munich, 1823–1831). These same authors also present material on the Maxakali and Pataxó. In this century three articles are worth mention: Guido Marliére's "Rio Doce," *Revista do Arquivo Público Mineiro* 11 (1906), 23–253, and 12 (1907), 497–668; Alfred Métraux's "The Botocudo," in the *Handbook of South American Indians*, vol. 1, 530–580; and Sonia Marcatto's "A repressão contra os Botocudo em Minas Gerais," *Boletim do Museu do índio* 1 (1970), 1–59.

The principal ethnographic descriptions for the seventeenth-century Amazon Valley, which also contain the history of European occupation, are the following: the *Compendio u Descripción de las Indias Occidentales*, by the historian Antonio Vásquez de Espinosa (Washington, 1948 [c. 1615]); the *Relación* of Pedro Teixeira (in *Anais do IV Congresso de História Nacional* 3 [1950], 173–204), based on his expedition in 1637–1638 from Gurupá to Quito; the classic *Nuevo descubrimiento* of Acuña in C. Mendes de Ameida (ed.), *Memórias para a história do extinto Estado do Maranhão*, vol. 2 (Rio de Janeiro, 1874 [1639]); the other *Nuevo descubri-*

miento by Laureano de la Cruz (2nd ed., Quito, 1885 [1653]), the first missionary to live for several years among the tribes of the upper Amazon, especially the Omagua; the *Descobrimento do Río das Amazonas e suas dilatadas provincias*, an anonymous work edited probably in Quito in early 1639 containing the narrative of the voyage of Domingos de Brieve and Andrés de Toledo, two lay Franciscans who had left the expedition of Juan de Palacio to the Encabellados and continued via the Amazon to Belém; the "Descrição do Estado de Maranhão, Pará, Corupá e Rio das Amazonas," by Maurício de Heriarte in Francisco Varnhagen (ed.), *História Geral do Brasil* (São Paulo, 1975 [1662]), 171–190; the "Chronica da Missão dos Padres da Companhia de Jesus no Estado do Maranhão," by the Jesuit João Felipe Bettendorf, *Revista do Instituto Histórico e Geográfico Brasileiro* 72 (1910), 1–697; and the *Diário* of Samuel Fritz, transcribed and summarized by Maroni in 1738, which contains the account of that missionary's work of nearly 40 years on the Peruvian and Brazilian upper Amazon, accompanied by a map locating the principal tribes known.

Of all these the "Chronica" by Bettendorf is by far the most important of the century for the middle Amazon and its southern tributaries, with extensive ethnographic information and an overall vision of Jesuit missionary work.

For the eighteenth century, important primary sources include: Carneiro de Mendonça's collection of correspondence of the Governor of Grão-Pará and Maranhão, Francisco Xavier de Mendonça Furtado, *A Amazônia na Era Pombalina* (Rio de Janeiro, 1963); the two historical and geographical surveys by Monteiro de Noronha, *Roteiro da Viagem da Cidade do Pará até as últimas colônias do sertã da província* (Belém, 1863 [1768]), and Francisco Xavier Ribeiro de Sampaio, *Diário de uma viagem que em visita e correição das povoações da Capitania de São José do Rio Negro fez o Ouvidor*. . . (Lisbon, 1825 [1775]); and the extensive reports produced by the naturalist Alexandre Rodrigues Ferreira, especially the *Viagem Filosófica pelas capitanias do Grãõ-Pará, Rio Negro, Mato Grosso, e Cuiabá, 1783–92* (Rio de Janeiro, 1971), and the *Viagem Filosófica ao Rio Negro* (Belém, 1983 [1787]). Padre João Daniel's "Parte Segunda do Thesouro descoberto no rio Amazonas," *Revista do Instituto Histórico e Geográfico Brasileiro* 2 (1916 [1840]), 291–314, provides a balance of the work of the Jesuit missions in Amazonia in the mid–eighteenth century and describes many of the customs of the indigenous "nations" to which he refers. Two sources provide critical information on the Mura: *Autos da Devassa contra os índios Mura do rio Madeira e nações do rio Tocantins*

(1738–39), facsimile and paleographic transcriptions (Manaus, 1986), and the "Notícias da voluntária redução de paz e amizade da feroz nação degentio Mura nos annos de 1784, 1785 e 1786," *Revista do Instituto Histórico e Geográfico Brasileiro* 36 (1873), 323–392.

The main ethnographic sources for the nineteenth century are scientific travelers' reports, among which the most significant are: Spix and Martius, op cit.; Henri Coudreau, *Viagem ao Tapajós* (São Paulo, 1977), *La France Équinoxiale* (Paris, 1887), *Voyage au Xingu* (Paris, 1896), *Voyage au Tocantins-Araguaia* (Paris, 1897), and *Voyage au Itaboca et a l'Itacayuns* (Paris, 1898); Henry Bates, *Um Naturalista no Rio Amazonas* (Belo Horizonte, 1979); Alfred Russell Wallace, *A Narrative of Travels on the Amazon and Rio Negro* (New York, 1890); Richard Spruce, *Notes of a Botanist on the Amazon and Andes* (London, 1908); and João Barbosa Rodrigues, *Exploração e estudo do valle do Amazonas – rio Tapajós* (Rio de Janeiro, 1875). The *Diccionário* compiled by Lourenço da Silva Araújo e Amazonas (Manaus, 1856) provides useful historical and geographical information, and the reports of the provincial presidents often contain extensive and detailed reports on the indigenous situation in various regions.

The vast corpus of secondary works on the history of Amazonia is too extensive to discuss in detail (see *História dos Indios no Brasil* for a more complete bibliography). David Sweet's doctoral thesis, "A rich realm of nature destroyed" (University of Wisconsin, 1974), although as yet unpublished, remains the classic work on the history of the middle Amazon from 1640–1750; and Carlos Moreira Neto's *Indios da Amazônia: de maioria a minoria* (Petrópolis, 1988), takes this history up to the mid–nineteenth century. Hector Vargas Llanos and Roberto Pinedo Camacho focus on the Japurá/Caquetá region from the sixteenth to the twentieth centuries in *Etnohistória del Gran Caquetá* (Bogotá, 1982). J. J. Chiavineto's *Cabanagem – o povo no poder* (São Paulo, 1984) is one of the few studies of this revolt in Amazonia.

The early history of Portuguese–Indian contact in the northwest Amazon is discussed extensively in Sweet's thesis. Useche Losada, *El proceso colonial en el Alto Orinoco-Río Negro (siglos xvi a xviii)* (Bogotá, 1987), undertakes a similar analysis for Spanish–Indian contact on the upper Orinoco/upper Rio Negro. Nadia Farage's *As Muralhas dos Sertões* (São Paulo, 1991), concentrates on early colonial history on the Rio Branco, important northern tributary of the Rio Negro. Two complementary works present compilations and analyses of mid–eighteenth century slaving documents: R. Wright's "Indian slavery in the northwest

Amazon," *Boletim do Museu Paraense Emílio Goeldi* 7 (1991), 149–179, and *O Livro das Canôas*, edited by Márcio Meira (São Paulo, 1994). Studies of the millenarian and messianic movements in the northwest Amazon include: R. Wright's doctoral thesis, "History and religion of the Baniwa peoples of the upper Rio Negro Valley," Stanford University, 1981; R. Wright and J. Hill, "History, ritual and myth: Nineteenth century millenarian movements in the northwest Amazon," *Ethnohistory* 33 (1986), 39–54; and Audrey Butt's "The birth of a religion," *Journal of the Royal Anthropological Institute* 90 (1960), 66–106.

Several other areas and peoples not discussed in this chapter have been the subject of historical studies: Gustav Verswijer's doctoral thesis on the Kayapó, *Considerations on Mekragnoti Warfare* (Ghent, 1985); Marivone Matos Chaim's study of eighteenth- and nineteenth-century indigenous settlements in Goiás, *Aldeamentos indígenas (Goiás 1749–1811)* (São Paulo, 1983); and the three volumes edited by the Centro Ecumênico de Documentação e Informação (CEDI) of the series *Povos Indígenas no Brasil* on the Javari, Amapá/North of Pará, and Southeast of Pará, each containing historical chapters (São Paulo, 1981, 1983, 1985).

20

NATIVE PEOPLES CONFRONT COLONIAL REGIMES IN NORTHEASTERN SOUTH AMERICA (c. 1500–1900)

NEIL L. WHITEHEAD

There already exist a number of basic chronological narratives of the course of the European occupation of northeastern South America from the Amazon to the Caribbean, but even where the fate of the native population is the focus of such accounts, little is said of changes occurring in the cultural and social practices of those indigenous populations themselves. It is the intention of this chapter to remedy that situation. Accordingly chronological narrative is balanced by extended analysis of the long-term historical processes that generated the major events, otherwise so ably captured in these narratives. In short, while rehearsing in outline the key moments of European colonial advance, beginning with the initial encounters between Europeans and Native Americans and the various attempts at colonial establishment, the main emphasis is on indigenous social process over the long term.

Until around the 1650s these attempts took place in two broad zones of colonial interest and activity: the lower Amazon River including the Maranhão captaincy on the one hand, and the lower Orinoco, coastal Guayana, and the Lesser Antilles on the other. A period of seemingly unstoppable colonial advance followed, up to the 1750s, at which point the tensions between the metropolitan regimes and the growing indigenous colonial élite found significant expression in changing policies toward missionary activity among native peoples. Finally, South American nationalism and neo-colonialism in the late eighteenth and nineteenth centuries provided the backdrop to the final phase in the incorporation of native peoples into the modern state.

An extended discussion of issues in current research and debate prefaces this analytical narrative. The historical anthropology of native South America stands at an important crossroads, requiring it to discard the outmoded conceptions and assumptions of earlier scholarship. The main results of this new scholarship are presented via a consideration of the political, economic, and cultural character of native society at the turn of the fifteenth century. This baseline provides a context for the examination of the change and innovation that occurred over the subsequent four centuries and permit, in conclusion, some assessment to be made of the genetic, social, and cultural continuities and disjunctures among native South Americans, then and now.

THE HISTORIOGRAPHY OF NATIVE SOUTH AMERICA

It is often thought that the peoples of northeastern South America were of marginal cultural and social significance when compared to the peoples of the Andean highlands or the Brazilian Atlantic littoral, because the initial progress and profitability of the colonial occupation centered on the latter regions. Native demographic presence away from these regions has been thought to have been minimal, their social systems simplistic, and their cultural repertoire either derivative from the Andes or inhibited by the rigors of material existence in a tropical "jungle" that supposedly blanketed much of the region. But just as there is a growing appreciation of the complexity, interdependency, and richness of the flora and fauna of the Amazon, so it is now realized that native society and culture also defies simplistic characterization. Indigenous sociocultural forms, as well as indigenous responses to the challenges of colonial occupation, were far more intricate, temporally extended, and historically various than had been thought. Peoples of this region had been schematically classified by previous scholars as displaying only a minimal regional organization, consisting of small-scale village settlements that experienced chronic instability due to a supposed lack of effective political authority within the native political tradition. In fact this image is an erroneous projection of current ethnographic representations into the past that has effectively masked the vast regional polities that once spanned this whole region, incorporating thousands of individuals into highly structured networks of alliance and exchange over which powerful élites held a dynastic dominance.

In effect there are really two epochs in the narrative of indigenous history from 1500 to 1900. The first epoch, extending until around the 1650s, is almost completely unknown to conventional ethnography and history but is now emerging from the latest research in archaeology and historical anthropology. This reveals the existence of both complex polities at the moment of contact with the Europeans. It also suggests that the Amazon Basin had been the site of some of the earliest settlement and ceramic production in the whole of the American continent.

As well as the historiographical issue of epoch, that of native agency has also been neglected and ethnohistorical writing on these regions of South America often implied that historical agency was essentially the preserve of the colonizers. As a result indigenous social and cultural change has been modeled as simply outgrowth of contacts with conquerors, traders, and missionaries.

Certainly the consequences of contact for native peoples were ultimately devastating, but it would be thoroughly misleading to assume simultaneously that this occurred in a uniform manner, either temporally or geographically. The many examples of continuity in native ethnic and cultural traditions, usually despite the best efforts of the colonizers, clearly illustrates that the native political economy could also be a determining factor in the history of colonial formation. In short the native contribution to colonial and national histories has been much more substantive than prevailing historical orthodoxy has allowed.

One glaring example of the consequences of these historiographical shortcomings has been a lack of appreciation of the importance of native military alliances and levies in the context of the establishment of European settlement. In conventional histories the "Indians" are seen as either inevitably bellicose or simply unable to resist the offer of European trade goods. But this representation of the colonial encounter ignores the critical political and military support that native leaders gave to the colonial enclaves at their inception, as well as the militarizing effects of colonial contacts themselves. Notwithstanding the hagiography of the Iberian chroniclers, in truth the political consent and active military assistance of some element of the indigenous population was a necessary stratagem of colonial occupation throughout this region, at least until the end of the eighteenth century. Accordingly the focus of analysis in this chapter is the cultural articulation and social interdependency that developed between the native peoples and their colonizers in the four centuries following the initial contacts of the 1530s in the Orinoco Basin and the 1540s in the Amazon.

It has become philosophically fashionable of late to doubt the possibilities for such an articulation, it being argued that "native" histories are inevitably enigmatic to the Western observer because they respond to a cultural logic that is impenetrable to Western modes of thought. This is but an inversion of the notion that the indigenes were irrelevant to the development of colonial systems, despite the importance of native alliances and information in overtly patterning European physical and cultural occupation. A very early, and still relevant, example of this process was the way in which Europeans used indigenous political categories, such as *caniba* ('enemy nation') garnered from the *caciques* ('élite leaders') of Hispaniola, or *faletti* ('barbarians') borrowed from the *adumasi* ('Arawak clan chiefs') of the Atlantic coast, to formulate colonial political strategy. In the region as a whole, where the vivacity of the indigenous political economy lasted into the eighteenth century, this cultural articulation between the invaders and the native population was a continuing process, especially in the sphere of botanical, geographical, zoological, and ethnological identification.

Military and ideological rivalries between the European colonial powers in northeastern South America themselves produced some especially favorable conditions for the persistence of native autonomy. Unlike other areas of South America, neither the Spanish nor the Portuguese achieved an effective occupation until the late seventeenth and early eighteenth centuries. In both the Amazon and Orinoco basins, as in coastal Brazil, the Iberians first had to expel other colonial interlopers, principally the Dutch, French, Irish, and English, and defeat their native allies. Non-Iberian European settlement in these regions underwrote the creation of new native élites rather than the ideological or military destruction of established leadership, which was a hallmark of Spanish and Portuguese conquest. In this sense the space for native agency was much greater in the sphere of the non-Iberian enclaves, and the historical analysis of this native agency and autonomy offers an object lesson in the possibilities for internally driven change among native peoples. Unfortunately modern anthropological theory has largely failed to recognize the historical dynamics of native agency when interpreting the archival and archaeological data. For example, the florescence of indigenous military chieftains along the Amazon in the sixteenth century has been related to an intractable and ancestral belligerency of the Amazonians. Such cultural attitudes supposedly reflected an underlying material imperative to occupy an ecologically desirable floodplain environment, rather than the obvious upheavals in economic and political circumstance that native peoples faced as an immediate consequence of colonial intrusion. Disease, warfare, slave raiding, and the influx of European manufactures, all combined to upset profoundly the stability of existing social and cultural forms.

A failure to appreciate how indigenous political and ideological forms were shaped by rapid reorientations, in the face of distant or even mediated contacts with the Europeans, thus undermines any claim by contemporary ethnography to be an implicit record of enduring aboriginal patterns, no matter how isolated the context in which such ethnography was recorded. The social and cultural systems recorded by modern ethnography are often taken to describe a state, or stage, of social evolution at which native groups have supposedly arrived by means of a continuous adaptation to the "rigors" of the "jungle" environment. This process of isolated adaptation is imagined to be uninterrupted by external intrusion, stretching back to the precolonial era. Socioeconomic organization, warfare, gender relations, and political culture all become frozen in historical time and so are best explained in terms of those ecological constraints that come to represent the only goad for social and cultural innovation. However, the colonial historical record repeatedly demonstrates that social and cultural survival usually entailed a loss rather than a growth of social and cultural repertoire, because strategies of mobility requiring occupation of less productive lands, or a forced retreat from zones of military conflict, set constraints more pressing and stringent than habitat. The societies and cultures that ethnographers describe thus represent the outcome of complex historical choices on the part of native peoples, and so the ethnological significance of given social and cultural patterns can only be assessed in this historical context.

Powerful chieftaincies of the sixteenth century, such as the Guayano, Tapajoso, or Manoa (see Map 20.1), were reduced in political organization to mere village associations by the eighteenth century. Equally the politically marginal ethnic formations of the sixteenth century, such as the Aruan, Mundurucú, or the Caribs, produced regionally dominant chieftaincies in the eighteenth and nineteenth centuries.

In a similar way our appreciation of the subtleties of colonial policy and the resulting complex consequences for native peoples has been rather simplistic. This is evident in the titles of many standard accounts of native Amazonia (see the Bibliographic Essay). These all stress the destructiveness of encounter but not the complexity of native responses, and this obviously distorts our understanding of the variety of transformations that were taking place amongst indigenous peoples. Likewise the

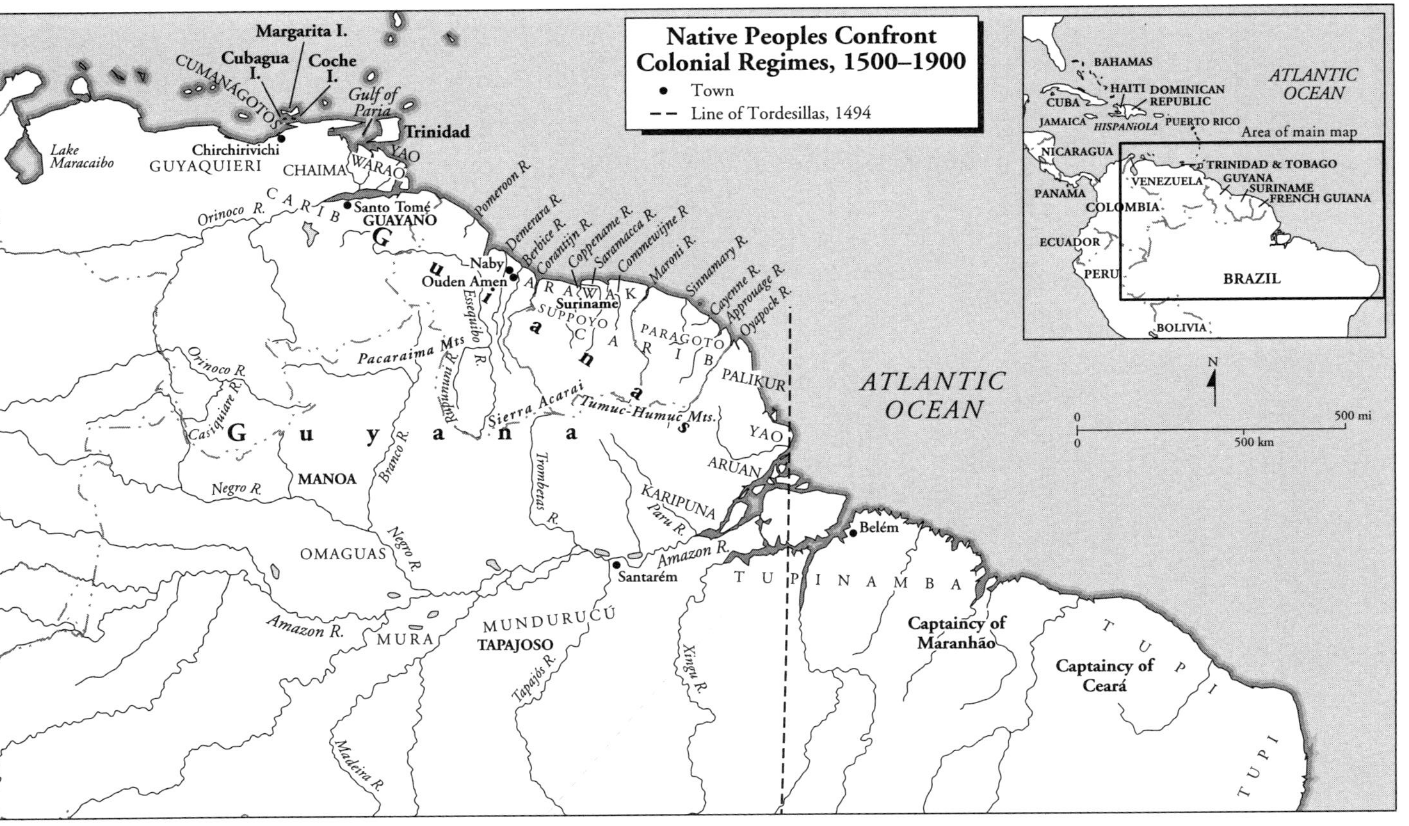
Native Peoples Confront Colonial Regimes, 1500–1900
Town
Line of Tordesillas, 1494
ATLANTIC OCEAN
BAHAMAS
CUBA
HAITI
DOMINICAN REPUBLIC
JAMAICA
HISPANIOLA
PUERTO RICO
Area of main map
NICARAGUA
TRINIDAD & TOBAGO
PANAMA
VENEZUELA
GUYANA
SURINAME
FRENCH GUIANA
COLOMBIA
ECUADOR
PERU
BRAZIL
BOLIVIA
N
0
500 mi
0
500 km
ATLANTIC OCEAN
Margarita I.
Cubagua I.
Coche I.
CUMANAGOTOS
Gulf of Paria
Trinidad
Lake Maracaibo
Chirchirivichi
GUYAQUIERI
CHAIMA
WARAO
YAO
CARIB
Orinoco R.
Santo Tomé
GUAYANO
Pomeroon R.
Demerara R.
Berbice R.
Corantijn R.
Coppename R.
Saramacca R.
Commewijne R.
Maroni R.
Sinnamary R.
Cayenne R.
Approuage R.
Oyapock R.
Naby
Ouden Amen
ARAWAK
Suriname
SUPPOYO
CARIB
PARAGOTO
PALIKUR
Essequibo R.
Pacaraima Mts
Rupununi R.
Sierra Acarai
Tumuc-Humuc Mts.
Orinoco R.
Casiquiare R.
Guiana
Guyana
YAO
ARUAN
MANOA
Branco R.
Negro R.
Trombetas R.
KARIPUNA
Paru R.
Negro R.
OMAGUAS
Amazon R.
Santarém
Belém
TUPINAMBA
Amazon R.
MURA
MUNDURUCÚ
TAPAJOSO
Tapajós R.
Xingu R.
Madeira R.
Captaincy of Maranhão
Captaincy of Ceará
TUPI
TUPI

Map 20.1

tendency to write history from monolingual records, or to write on narrow themes, such as the invention of the modern nation, means that native experience that transcends such limitations cannot be captured historiographically. For example, the standard representation of the European occupation of the lower and mid-Amazon River in the seventeenth and eighteenth centuries stresses the "Portuguese" picture, which actually only relates to certain later phases in that occupation. As such it is totally inadequate as a matrix for native history in the area as a whole. Comparison with other areas of Amazonia, particularly the Atlantic coast between the Orinoco and the Amazon, shows that, as in the pre-Portuguese occupation of the Amazon itself, neither slavery nor warfare were preponderant modes of interaction with the Europeans, while the missionaries were of negligible importance in most contexts. Moreover many native polities contained areas of multiple European occupations. Any formulation of regularities in historical process will have to be multilateral, considering the dynamics of native historical entities as much as the unfolding of colonial settlements and priorities.

The treatment of colonial histories as an extension of national historiographies has forestalled the integration of historical sources in European languages, because most historical writing still confines itself to the archives of one or another colonial power. As a result the native population appears as a backdrop or only an episodic element in these tales of national destiny. Native experience of European colonialism, on the contrary, was wider and more complex than this and cannot be adequately rendered by reference to a series of discrete encounters. As a result the development or decline of native polities remains enigmatic unless examined through the archives of more than one colonial power. Source criticism is thus vital to this integration, because the different colonial and modern records have very dissimilar historiographical qualities. For example, the non-Iberian material, generated as much by policies of cooperation as by strategies of military conquest, often permits a complexity of inference not available from Spanish or Portuguese writings.

A historiographical framework for the understanding of native Amazonia needs to distinguish the passage of time and the significance of events according to endogenous, or native, criteria as well as according to the timing and progress of European occupation. Although the lack of basic historiographical research on native Amazonia hampers this aim throughout the period under discussion, in the initial phases, the character of "first contact" and its political and demographic consequences provide a means for discriminating a number of historical trajectories, including extinction, among the then-extant native societies of Amazonia. With the progress of European occupation, the consequences of such initial encounters unfolded in a variety of ways, but because both colonial policy and native response showed consistency, meaningful generalization becomes possible.

Accordingly the general ethnological and ecological setting of native society at the point of contact with the Europeans is characterized, emphasizing factors driving native understanding of, and attitude to, European activities along the coasts and rivers. This context also clarifies constraints on native leaders that precluded certain kinds of action, such as large-scale military alliance, in response to these opportunities and threats. Following this comes a narrative of the key events in the European occupation, always partly structured by the disposition of the native population. This narrative falls into three phases: 1500 to 1650, 1650 to 1800, and 1800 to 1900. The periodization follows both European and native issues, but not by privileging events critical to non-native historiography. Using this methodology a particular event of great significance for the history of European colonialism, such as the emergence of financial institutions in the eighteenth century, may be tangential for understanding indigenous history, even though they are ultimately intertwined. By the same token, a minor policy decision on the part of a European colonial power could have a disproportionate effect on the intricate web of European and native alliances. For example, where alliances had been founded on the customary payment for certain kinds of services, such as occurred with slave-hunting service in the Dutch Guiana colonies at the end of the eighteenth century, a cessation or limitation of service payments undermined the military associations that native war-captains constructed. For these reasons this narrative also undertakes an analysis of the shifting strategies of native response and innovation.

The Ethnological and Ecological Setting

The region under discussion is bounded on the east by the Atlantic zone that extends from the mouth of the Orinoco to just south of the mouth of the Amazon. On the western limits the vast *llanos* (seasonally flooded savannahs) of Orinoco, which stretch to the foothills of the Colombian sierra, mark a geographical and ethnological discontinuity with the savannahs and upland forests of the Orinoco south bank. The Orinoco then is the northern limit of our region, which is bounded to the south by the Cassiquiare and Río Negro, which eventually flows into the Amazon and so to the Atlantic coast. Environed on all sides by immense bodies of water, the area became known to the Europeans as "the island of Guayana." Native place names often express in some form this aquatic nature of the region through toponyms that contain the root *para* or *parana* meaning, at one and the same time, both the "great water" of the rivers, and the Atlantic Ocean itself. In this environment it is dry land that exists contingently, constantly being reclaimed by the waters. In the cosmology of the Warao at the mouth of Orinoco, the delta floats on this great water, a leaky disk perilously sustained by appeasement of the Lords of Rain. To the south, for 90 miles from its mouth, the Amazon pushes back the great Atlantic swell. The first Europeans to coast through this outflow knew of the sweet water before ever sighting land, and so named it *Río de Mar Dulce* – 'the river of the sweetwater sea'.

This immense region of northeastern South America comprises around 3,240,000 square kilometers. It is ecologically very diverse, comprising localities of alternately parched and flooded upland savannah dotted with stands of forest: upland liana, bamboo, and palm forests, and a dense upland rainforest with unbroken canopy covering the valleys and hills. This forest climbs all the way to the foot of Mount Roraima, the highest peak in the region and the old, carbuncled heart of the granitic formations that once lay at the center of the ancient continent of Gondwanaland. Found at lower elevations are the floodplains and flooded forest with which this environment is popularly associated, as well as coastal savannahs, especially in the Guianas. More geographically restricted habitats, such as mangrove and palm swamps, occur at the mouth of the Orinoco and Amazon and along the intervening coast.

This ecological diversity carries over into the flora and fauna and, in part, has been actively sustained by native ecological practices. When the Europeans first arrived in these regions, they saw many evidences of large-scale irrigation works, ditching, draining, and mounding of the soil, as well as of forest clearance. However, as will become evident, the impact on native society of the European colonization was such as to render the region a wilderness in the eyes of the eighteenth- and nineteenth-century travelers whose descriptions formed modern attitudes to this region. As a result one of the key issues being debated among the anthropologists is whether this hot, wet, zoologically and botanically largely unknown environment is fundamentally inimical to human settlement; or whether, as the first chroniclers suggested, it was a terrestrial paradise. The weight of current scholarship tends toward the latter view, but the metaphor of "the jungle" is deeply embedded in non-native attitudes to this environment, and it is only through a better appreciation of past native Amazonian society and its interrelationships with the environment that we have come to understand something of the complexity and productivity of human adaptations.

This diversity of flora, fauna, and environment was matched by a florescence of human social and cultural forms that we can only dimly perceive through the lens of archaeology and history. Even that obscured view reveals a great variety of material and intellectual culture in the context of societies that organized many thousands of people, especially along the main river systems. Archaeology and linguistics summarize this variety in a way that also makes evident to us the important unities and continuities underlying variation. Three great language families inhabited this region – the Cariban, Arawakan, and Tupian. The Cariban and Arawakan linguistic groups dominated the region north of the Amazon but the Tupí to the south, who may have been migrating northward from the Atlantic littoral of Brazil during the fifteenth century, had notable cultural and social impacts on the island of Guayana. Their influence is evinced linguistically by the number of cognate words among these language groups, and socioculturally by shared ideological and political orientations. However, macrolinguistic categories are inadequate for the writing of a history of native peoples because the everyday structures of life, most particularly ethnic sentiment, did not simply follow these patterns of artifactual and cultural distribution. In any event, as historical agents in the face of an aggressive European colonialism, native people displayed no uniform response, either as cultural performers or as social actors. In consequence, and much to the chagrin of the colonizers, native response proved highly variable, often impervious to the practical reasoning of European policymakers and militarily resistant to the logic of warfare. Yet the project of conquest and colonization could not unfold without the active support of native people, as military levies, trade and business partners, translators, guides, lovers, and concubines. So the drama and histrionics of the moment of the very first contacts are soon replaced with mutually advantageous alliances, and the boundaries of ethnic identity are transgressed as the meaning of those ethnic identifications change or are replaced by new calls to solidarity with the French,

Dutch, or English against other native groups. In this process the categories of "native" and "non-native" became blurred, and so the need to redefine who is different and for what reasons became an obsession for the Europeans and natives alike. The Europeans encoded their prejudices in legal devices that criminalized certain ethnic formations, such as the *caribes*, but legitimated others, such as the *aruacas*. Anthropological identification and usage of such terms as "Cariban" and "Arawakan" are thus deeply marked by the colonial historical process, and are for this reason inadequate as historical or ethnological generalizations.

In native terms the significant unit of social and cultural identification and activity could be very fluid indeed, especially as the initial contact with the Europeans radically undermined a series of large-scale polities that had dominated this region. It should be emphasized, therefore, that there is a fundamental disjuncture between ancient and colonial Amazonia. Ancient polities were heterogenous in their ethnic and linguistic composition, operating regional economic networks through highly structured political relationships. Recent calculations of the aboriginal populations on the main rivers, and early European reports on the extent and nature of political allegiance to the native leaders, leave an overwhelming impression of complex and sophisticated human presence through time. The first chroniclers' comparisons within the Indus and Nile valleys were not merely geographical. The supposed poverty and marginality of what modern anthropologists have schematized as "Tropical Forest Society," especially away from the major floodplains, is simply not reflected in the historical materials. The problem is that these materials were underused. When they used histories at all, synthesizers often chose inaccurate secondary sources to make general assessments of the historical material. This faulty procedure led to disinterest in the systematic investigation of primary archive material.

NATIVE ECONOMY AND SOCIETY

Testimony from the early documents continually stresses the great abundance of both floral and faunal resources as well as the intensity with which they could be exploited. Evidence of this abundance, as well as the great productivity of native agricultural techniques, is clearly given by the chroniclers. Sometimes this can be directly quantified in detailed examination of the continuous exchange of foodstuffs for trade goods between native populations and Europeans. Later on this would ramify into a whole system of such exchanges, encompassing forest products (such as dyes, woods, animals), specially produced artifacts (such as ceramic wares, canoes, hammocks), and even persons in the form of slaves, concubines, and marriage partners. The Europeans offered metal tools, cloth, beads, mirrors, brass items, and, eventually, firearms and alcohol in return.

It is important to stress that the systems of production and exchange that serviced this burgeoning trade with the Europeans were not simply induced by the new economic and political opportunities. For example, native political economy was already geared to the production and exchange of food surpluses. This is demonstrated by the existence of indigenous markets and exchange systems in fish meal and manioc flour, as well as the large-scale ranching of turtles and iguanas, particularly along the main streams of the Amazon, Branco, Negro, Essequibo, and Orinoco. Moreover the use of seed and tuber crops, other than manioc, was far more common than modern ethnographic experience suggests. It even occurred in those regions that have been characterized as agriculturally unproductive, such as the Atlantic coast or the eastern highlands. Archaeological evidence also suggests that intensive cultivators once worked this region using mounding and irrigation techniques to control flooding, as on the Orinoco and the Amazon.

Anthropologists and human geographers unfamiliar with the historical and archaeological evidence tended to see "protein capture" through hunting as the critical aspect of ecological adaptation in Amazonia. This assumes both that the environment was agriculturally unproductive away from the immediate areas of the great floodplains of the Amazon and Orinoco, and that fishing was of marginal significance. It is therefore significant to note that, culturally, famine was a not a prevalent preoccupation. Although a specific "meat hunger" has been reported ethnographically, this is more productively understood in the context of the gendered division of labor throughout native society. As a result, the economic exchange of men's hunting returns for women's agricultural products is represented culturally by a sexual idiom, neatly captured in a modern Sharanahua woman's remark, "There is no meat, let's eat penises!"

Such cultural attitudes therefore have only a contingent relationship to actual levels of "protein availability" – the more so because differential access to dietary resources was a common feature of the social hierarchy in native social organization, before the conquest and colonization of this region.

Although the initial descriptions of this region repeatedly stress the ready availability of faunal resources and especially deer, poultry, and fish, any assessment of the original productivity of indigenous hunting and husbandry must also take account of the ecological impact of Old World species on New World flora and fauna. Wild cattle, pigs, and goats degraded portions of the grassland-savannahs, making them less favorable to the indigenous species, although this effect was more chronic than acute, as it had been in the Caribbean or on the Mexican plateau.

The organization of production within the native economies that the Europeans encountered was domestically based. That is, the household was the site of production, and the kinship relations of that household were at the same time the relations of production, as in the organization of agriculture and hunting discussed previously. At the same time, certain specialized craft products, such as ritual ceramic items, metalwork in gold and silver, lapidary, wood carving, weaving, and weaponry were sometimes specialties of particular ethnic castes. Key economic relationships were of necessity interethnic and intervillage, because this specialization of collective domestic production implied supporting economic relationships with producers of more mundane items. The distribution of the natural resources necessary for such products also influenced the local organization of production and was often directly related to the products groups produced, there being little trade in raw materials, except perhaps rough hewn stone for the manufacture of stone axes and certain minerals as pottery temper.

For these very reasons ethnic boundaries were not necessarily coextensive with particular economic, political, or linguistic systems. They might also be founded on a craft technique or specialization that was itself sustained by being part of a regional system of exchange. At a certain level of ethnic denomination, groups were known by reference to such an economic specialization in the production and exchange of particular items. The example of the *aruacas*, or Arawaks, of the Atlantic coast (*Lokono*), is often cited in this regard. They were the principal traders to the Spanish in the pearl-fishing colonies of the north Venezuelan coast of a flour known as *aru* or *yaruma* in the Lokono and Warao languages and were accordingly somewhat contemptuously referred to as *aru-ak*. So, too, the name *Warao* itself means 'canoe maker' or 'canoe owner' and reflects the antiquity of their proficiency in this art. These kinds of economically, rather than culturally, based ethnic designations are widely distributed, such as *panare* (traders), *naboresa* or *maku* ('laborers'), and *kaikussiana* ('dog breeders'). This also suggests that intergroup relations were far more intricately structured in the past than has been recorded in modern ethnography.

As a consequence of this great complexity and historical depth to such relationships, very widely dispersed groups were locked into patterns of mutually sustaining exchange at both a local and regional level. Of particular note in regional trade was the exchange of worked jade (*takua*) from the lower Amazon for goldwork (*calcuri*) from the lower Orinoco and circum-Roraima region. Another example was the use of specially manufactured shell disks and semiprecious stones as currency along the Guayana coast and Orinoco, well into historic times. However, these formal economic patterns cannot be simply assimilated to Western economic models. Terms of exchange were governed by aesthetic and ideological considerations rather than by a "purely" economic motive, such as commodity accumulation. This was very evident in the way in which the exchange of gold with the Europeans was managed and in the kinds of items for which it was traded. Native values emphasized the smell and brilliance of this metal, and its scarcity value was related to its cosmological significance in the ideologies of the native élites. Obviously Europeans saw in gold a financial value not relevant to the indigenous population, hence the apparent naiveté of native peoples in giving up rare metals for trinkets of brass and glass, which, however, possessed the critical properties of brilliance and smell (see also Chap. 11).

NATIVE POLITICAL ECONOMY

In a much broader sense economic exchange should be also understood to include warfare and raiding, as well as marriage, because it is with the political economy of native societies that we are concerned. Here the control of human labor, as well as its products, either through direct appropriation via indigenous servitude or indirect appropriation via marriage obligations, defined the native frameworks of political power. Moreover it is in this context, rather than by simplistic reference to native belligerency, that native warfare against both the Europeans and other native groups is to be understood. The apparently intractable regional feuding of the Arawak and Carib, for example, reflects their positioning vis-à-vis the colonial powers, as much as it does native cultural forms of warfare. Combat and the capture of enemies was already an idiom of political intercourse and economic exchange. As Europeans entered into these relationships, they disrupted native exchanges through the trading of native slaves, control of critical manufactured goods, and direct military conquest. In consequence the native political class that had grown up on the stability of these interactions lost influence. This allowed for the emergence of new political leaders with a very different material basis for their political influence – their connections to the invaders.

It is therefore worth emphasizing that complex indigenous economic systems were not necessarily coextensive with given agriculturally viable areas, such as a floodplain, but might unite fluvial and interfluvial areas. This gave economic access to the major waterways to those who lived in supposedly "marginal" environments, such as the Guayana highlands. Riverine people in turn gained access to highly valuable upland products, such as poisons, metal, and jewels.

For these reasons chieftaincy developed as much in the interfluvial as in the floodplain areas. Political power was exercised at a geographical distance via lines of economic interaction. These arteries of power, which generated variant forms of political complexity, have been recently redescribed in the modern era as the "routes of knowledge" for the spread of prophetic cults. The past political complexity of the uplands is therefore clearly illustrated by the history of the Lokono *adumasi* (chieftains) who, until the eighteenth century, constituted a powerful polity that straddled the Amazon and Orinoco drainage basins in the area of the Sierra Acarai and Tumuc Humuc, linking the Corentyn and Berbice with the Paru and Trombetas rivers.

Similarly the Manoan chieftains to the west and Karipuna to the southeast formed zones of political dominance based on their preeminence as regional traders. This Manoan polity (also discussed later) seems to have predated the colonial encounter. It was closely associated with the distribution of worked gold along the Negro, Branco, and lower Amazon. The Karipuna, traders of weapons, jewels, and esoteric carvings along the Amazon and Guayana coast, were related culturally to the Lokono and are sometimes not explicitly distinguished from Arawaks in the early sources. Indeed recent research has raised the possibility that this group was even more widely dispersed, possibly into the Caribbean islands, underlining the vast scale of indigenous networks of trade and war. They were encountered here by Columbus as the fearsome *caribe/caniba* ('cannibals').

Nonetheless the European usage of the terms *caniba/caribe* was highly political. In particular the contradictory and confusing way in which the term *caribe* and similar terms, such as *caniba, canima*, and *canibales*, are used in the early texts is thought to be a result of Columbus's own confusion and inability to understand what was being told to him – which of course it is. However, this uncertainty may also reflect a complex and even contradictory native sociopolitical reality. Its refraction through the lens of Columbus's observations and expectations is certainly challenging to reconstruct.

In some anthropological readings these confusions are assigned to the unreliability of the historical data in general, and the ethnological typology of "fierce Carib" and "timid Arawak" has been chosen from a number of possibilities that the ethnographic observations of Columbus actually permit. The reasons for this choice are many, but the prurient appeal of the image of a group of men advancing through the islands destroying and eating their enemies while copulating with their women is so powerful for Western culture that it may have overshadowed real behavior and belief circa 1492. Native testimony itself, and the writings of seventeenth-century missionaries in the field of ethnography and linguistics, seem to support this "conquest theory." But these are not independent evidence, because by this time the model itself had structured island Carib and European interactions for some 200 years.

This tendency to conflate ethnic groups in the writing of the conquest and colonization of the region is not just evidence of an ethnological ignorance on the part of the Europeans. It is also testimony to the rapid changes that occurred in indigenous society and political economy. Confronted either by direct conquest and occupation, epidemic diseases, or the many other kinds of disruption in existing social relationships that the Europeans induced, the reformulation of ethnic identity and political allegiances could be very widespread indeed. As a result the inconsistencies in the early documents, rather than suggesting that such materials are useless for the writing of native history, raise fundamental questions as to the validity of linguistically based schemes of historical and ethnological classification in both the Amazon and Caribbean regions. However, because the Europeans had the ability to affect native groups far beyond the immediate limits of their tiny colonial enclaves, their systematic and continuous involvement in the regional native political economy induced the development of European and native cooperation, despite the possibilities for extreme cultural misapprehension.

The polities that grew up around these networks of exchange and production could be of considerable demographic scale, integrating settlements spread over hundreds of square miles (see Map 20.1). The density of human settlement, as was indicated in the introduction, has been a key issue of anthropological and historical research. There is still little agreement over absolute numbers, but the clear tendency of research over the past two decades has been to revise steadily upward the very low estimates of earlier research. Precise demographic measurement clearly is hampered by the lack of precise records, our ignorance of the settlement patterns away from the major floodplains (from where most of the early observations are derived), a continuing uncertainty as to the potential of the Amazonian environment to support sustainable, intensive agriculture, and most significantly, the impact of European and African diseases on native populations. Thus it is not enough to note the apparent population decline of a given settlement or settlements, because even when epidemic disease can be shown to have been present, the overall decline in population may also be due to migration away from the disease centers. In fact, right across this region, the onset of pandemics seems to have been closely tied to the onset of missionary evangelization with its consequent relocation and concentration of the native population. This situation, entailing repeated exposure to Europeans and Africans, most certainly triggered the great pandemics of coastal Brazil and did likewise in Orinoco and along the Amazon. The important point is that the timing of these outbreaks of epidemic disease was not uniform, and not coeval with first contacts. In the Amazon it was not until the seventeenth century that sustained missionary evangelization, coupled with persistent lay economic exploration and exploitation of the interior populations, produced colonial records of epidemic disaster among the native population. In Orinoco this onset was even later, in the mid–eighteenth century. In the Guianas the mid–nineteenth century marks the bottoming-out of the native population.

The difference between native demographic trajectories in these regions is explained by the pattern of European occupation, the trajectories of native reaction, and the policies toward native populations that the various colonial powers pursued. Most importantly, it was the lack of any serious missionary effort by the French, Dutch, and English in the Guianas that most effectively delayed the onset of epidemics. There were some epidemics in this area before this date, but they did not recur frequently enough to drive population levels down to their minimum, or beyond to the point of extinction, as so often occurred in contexts where a newly reduced (and infected) population was continually augmented by the "salvation" of new converts brought in from outlying and previously uninfected villages. The history of missionary endeavor imparts a rhythm to the onset and decline of epidemic disease among the native population. For example, as the missionaries first moved into the Orinoco Basin in the late seventeenth century, the Caribs militarily expelled them, and the incursion left few demographic scars on the native population. However, when they returned some 40 years later, the greater permanence of their settlements produced epidemic disease among the converts. In the case of the Caribs themselves, their population fell some 80 percent, from around 120,000 persons to fewer than 20,000, in the period 1730–1780.

This pattern of demographic decline was repeated throughout this region, even if the timing varied widely. The fact that onset of epidemics was considerably later in the Guianas than in the Orinoco or Amazon meant this region also tended to function as a refuge area for groups avoiding the colonial waves of occupation and evangelization. It meant also that the population of this region underwent a number of changes in its ethnic structure. Immigrants were absorbed into, or disrupted, existing social and cultural practices. Paralleling, then, the "ethnocide" consequent on military conquest or missionary reduction was an "ethnogenesis" of new identities and social groupings formed from those that escaped the militant evangelism of the colonizers; as one missionary put it, "they do not hear the Voice of the Gospel, where they have not first heard the echo of gunfire."

Indigenous responses to this threat, as well as to the positive opportunities that European contacts could bring, were constrained by their own ideological practices. The critical decision to fight or flee in the face of invasion was the outcome of a series of decisions by both leaders and followers. The haphazard and unpredictable ways in which the Europeans acted often made consistent strategy toward them impossible. A native leader might have to deal with Spanish war captains, Dutch private traders, English slave hunters, and French pirates in rapid succession. The outcome of such encounters was then itself part of native calculation in subsequent dealings, and in this way the social and cultural disparities of the early contacts became overlaid with the intricate history of multiple relationships. In regions where the native population was faced with a more monolithic colonial presence, as in the mid-Amazon and Orinoco, the room for native agency in mediating the consequences of contact was less, and the outcome all too predictable – the destruction of society and culture or its incorporation into colonial state structures.

Whether the possibility existed for the evolution of more enduring strategies or whether preexisting sociocultural arrangements were maintained, the fundamental pattern of domestic production – that is, of households containing genealogically related kin – remained the bedrock of each political unit. The ideologies used to form political units may be broadly defined as trading-military or theocratic-genealogical. These ideological and cosmological frameworks generated significant political followings, able to exert effective force in extra-village political life. As already indicated, the intensity of this process of ethnogenesis was progressively increased by the European challenge to traditional political patterns. Indigenous political action was directed toward building personal followings through by manipulating genealogy, engineering martial enterprises, or displaying esoteric knowledge such as prophesy, the use of poisons, or the creation of sacred rattles.

The Caribs (Kariña) are a good example of the postcontact dominance of a trading-military polity that extended itself over the whole of this region. Previously of marginal significance to the extant chiefdoms, the manipulation of European alliances by a series of charismatic Carib leaders enabled them to exercise hegemony over many groups north of the Amazon Basin. Their rivals in this process were the Arawaks (Lokono), who stand as an example of the persistence of deeply reckoned genealogical power bases well into historic times. Because European contacts were in part productive of these political orientations, the dynamics of indigenous political culture are directly susceptible to study from the history of contact with the Europeans.

The Carib case has been intensely researched in the last decade. Their creative opportunism as long-distance traders and raiders is matched by the history of other groups in the southern zone of this region, particularly the Aruan, on the lower Amazon in the seventeenth century, and the Mundurucú in the nineteenth century. The term "colonial tribe" has sometimes been applied to such groups in order to communicate the way in which their rise to dominance is intimately connected to, without being solely dependent on, the advent of colonial occupation. The term also refers to the way in which such groups directly integrated ethnically diverse persons, either as slaves or wives, as well as bringing whole populations within their political control through dependency on the

European goods they could distribute. In such situations being *caribe* meant sharing the political and military orientations of Carib leaders but not necessarily their cultural proclivities as Kariña. This example of the divergence of a cultural heritage and an ethnic sentiment thoroughly confused the contemporary missionaries, as well as later anthropologists.

Nonetheless such groups, particularly the widely dispersed Caribs, could also face extremely divergent conditions in different segments of the population. In just this way the Caribs in the Dutch territories of Surinam bore the brunt of a Dutch military occupation of the previously English colonial enclave on the Surinam River, even as the Commander of the West Indian Company's post in Essequibo relied absolutely on Carib military levies.

By contrast some groups that were dominant at the moment of European arrival acted to preserve that position by defending lineage and matri-clan organization. This did not mean that other populations were not absorbed, but that absorption occurred through persisting genealogical principles. The structure of clans was preserved, but their number and ranking changed. For example, some of the Arawak clans can be shown to be quite recent in origin, representing post hoc rationalization of the wholesale incorporation of ethnically different persons. Combined with a principle of hereditary succession to leadership clan making in effect allowed Arawak leaders to augment their following without undermining the position of the élite leadership that still constituted a closely related genealogical unit. This process also occurred among the Palikur of the Oyapock River area.

Whatever the particular strategies that were used in this process of ethnic change and political realignment, the direct control of persons through genealogical manipulation, rather than claims on a portion of their labor or the juridical ownership and control of natural resources, was particularly critical to native leadership in this region. As was remarked of these ancient élites, "the Lords of [these] countries desire many children of their own bodies, for in those consist their greatest trust and strength."

The juridical prerogatives exercised by these élites is plain from their power to order executions or floggings for transgressions of customary practice. We cannot say with any certainty what the position of domestic servants was. Although they were called "slaves" by the Europeans, who certainly looked initially to justify their own practices by reference to native custom, the native terms that we know about, such as *macu* or *poito*, derive from wider usages that can also describe a specialized economic relationship entailing exchange of uncultivated forest products for cultivated garden ones (*macu*), or the labor obligations of a man to his father-in-law (*poito*). It was therefore most notable for the Spanish chroniclers that the Tapojoso chiefs of the mid-Amazon, at Santarém, refused to give up their slaves to appease the Portuguese, preferring military destruction to the implied dissolution of their house. It has often been remarked that Amazonian societies appear to have little interest in principles of descent and that the shallowness of genealogical reckoning is an important demonstration of the lack of historical or dynastic continuity. However, it is increasingly recognized that a number of modern groups employ a notion of descent, centered on the physical and cosmological notion of a dynastic "house" – that is, the survival of the "house" is given emphasis over the families that may at any one point occupy and constitute it. This ethnographic observation is important for allowing us to see how the absence of any readily recognizable juridical institutions of feudal control was no barrier to the formation and persistence of dynastic élites.

Special burial and marriage customs were claimed by the chiefs and shamans. The death of a chief or shaman would be the occasion for intense ritual activity, especially the feasting of allies and vassals, the sacrifice of servants and concubines, or the destruction of goods at the grave side. Elaborate rites of secondary burial included the preservation and manipulation of skeletal parts, as well as the manufacture of highly ornate burial urns. Polygamous marriage was the preference, if not the prerogative, of those in authority. There is some evidence that leaders also validated or prohibited the marriages of their followers.

In cultural terms élites were also marked off by body adornment, particularly the display of *guanin* ('goldwork') and *takua* ('greenstone pendants'), as well as bodily markings such as skull deformation and jeweled dental inlay. The body, of course, also displayed other indicators of social and cultural status, especially group categories. Painting with body dyes such as *roucou* or *genipapo* certainly expressed ethnic identification. More permanent face tattooing was used in a similar way, as well as to mark women as producers of *paiwari* or *cassiri* (manioc-based beer).

There are also indications that the chiefly élites were themselves integrated by certain kinds of cultural practice that supravened both ethnic and local political ties. This is suggested most strongly by the use of élite dialects and forms of diction, particularly by Arawakan speakers, such as the Lokono and Karipuna. The French used the term *carbeter* to refer to the oral performances that leaders of all kinds practiced and that ethnography has recorded up to the present day. Such performances simultaneously evince and establish an individual's authority. The continuity suggests a striking persistence in indigenous idioms of authority. Performance in a special speech register shades into the prophetic and oracular pronouncements of chiefs and shamans, some of which were directly recorded by the Europeans. Prophesy thus was a basis for unifying these roles in particularly eminent individuals. Strong evidence for the existence of supraethnic shamanic association – the *carai* – underlines the importance of cosmological idioms in political practice. Archaeological sites with megalithic structures also suggest that such shamanic élites may have achieved considerable transgenerational stability by the sixteenth century.

The political organizations that were generated by these sociopolitical dynamics are highly reminiscent of feudal formations. The control of people, rather than the redistribution or expropriation of specific economic resources, was the essence of political dominance. Indeed favorable analogies were often made between the political structures of Europe and those of native America. Although the desire to inflate the fruits of discovery or downplay the significance of native forms are always present in the European accounts, it is also the case that such analogies were understood and accepted by the natives and Europeans alike. As a result descriptive terms passed in both directions, most notably in the case of "captain" and *cacique*. Equally the use of terms like "king" or "lord" should not be lightly dismissed as fanciful embellishment when the contemporary readers of such accounts may be assumed to have been quite attuned to the implications of such usages – not least because the ascription of "polity" (i.e., political capacity) was such a critical issue in the ethnographic description of the early period.

Specific details about the regional political organization of these élites emerge from various early sources. For example, the *Acarawena* (king) of the Guayanos, Topiawari, described the regional political geography of the Orinoco and its left bank tributaries to Walter Ralegh in 1595. Ralegh's account strongly suggests that the political units of Topiawari's own domain were constituted through a three-tiered hierarchy of allegiances: first, by groups of villages each sharing a section of river and denoted through the linguistic element *cai* (island, landing place); second, by a number of such *cai* that went to form a province, denoted in

Spanish sources by the name of the principal *cacique*; and third, by a maximal unit (kingdom) comprising the contiguous reaches of a number of river systems, as with Topiawari's dominance of the Orinoco south bank. Another important example, because of the way it illustrates a quite conscious organization of such hierarchical units, is found in the sources pertaining to the flight of an *Acarawena* of the Yao, Anacajoury, from Trinidad south to the Oyapock River at the end of the sixteenth century. Anacajoury removed his extended family and an unknown number of their followers from Trinidad under threat of Spanish military invasion. However, the local groups in the vicinity of the Oyapock resisted Anacajoury's relocation, not least because he simply granted, through what political mechanisms is not known, rights of territorial usage to named *caciques*. These native colonial enclaves were defended militarily with support from the Europeans, who were also trying to colonize in this region. In both these contexts political authority was held at all levels by hereditary chieftains belonging to the *Acarawena*'s immediate family (i.e., a son or a nephew). Similar macropolitical structures may also be inferred from much later Lokono accounts given in the eighteenth century to the Moravian missionaries in Surinam.

The accuracy of such textual accounts is also supported by Spanish actions, because the Spanish explicitly followed such rules of succession when attempting to usurp Topiawari's accession to the kingship of the Guayanos. When the Spaniards executed the previous king Morequito, who had been Topiawari's nephew, they promoted the candidacy of the deceased king's nephew, having first baptized him "Don Juan."

An unequal distribution or access to all kinds of sociocultural and natural resources seems to have been the eventual consequence of the survival of these ruling families. It was therefore the management of this political inheritance of the past that persistently limited their leadership options in the face of the uncertainties of European contacts. In contrast the warrior and trading élites, such as the Caribs or Manoa, characterized by an aggressive exogamous polygamy that favored rapid and varied ethnic recruitment, were well poised to take advantage of the loss of political stability implied by the response of the *Acarawenas*, such as Anacajoury. In addition these élites actively extended the use of particular affinal categories, such as in the example of the Cariban term *poito* (see earlier), to give it meanings as various as 'son-in-law', 'partner', 'client', 'servant', or 'slave'. In this way they could achieve the political incorporation of politically and economically subject populations, through the manipulation of existing kinship idioms. Native categories notwithstanding, the political and economic dominance that these particular groups enjoyed in the colonial period was often a direct product of the European presence, because they based a large part of their political authority on the redistribution of European manufactures and on military specialization as "ethnic soldiers." It is therefore important to emphasize that it was because these new warring and trading élites, and their associated ethnic formations, challenged the influence of the established élites that the former have become represented to us in the European historical record as intractably rebellious and warlike. In short they appeared as *faletti* (barbarians) and as *caribe* (wild, fierce) to élites with precolonial native roots, as well as to the invading Europeans. For these reasons, among others, cultural and linguistic misapprehension was continuously mitigated by a congruence of political, military, or economic interest. It is to a narrative analysis of European interaction with these native polities, and their attendant reformulation, that we now turn.

Initial Encounters and Colonial Establishment to Circa 1650

Contacts between the Europeans and the indigenous population were uneven and sporadic throughout northeastern South America in this period. Moreover this region was largely unaffected by the great pandemics that hit coastal Brazil, the Caribbean, and Andean regions in the sixteenth century. As a result the relative autonomy of the native political economy persisted until the mid–seventeenth century. At that point Iberian missionary effort and the rapid development of Dutch and Portuguese plantations combined to dramatically alter native peoples' demographic and social position.

Despite this historic respite, the susceptibility of the native population to diseases introduced from both Africa and Europe proved an overriding factor in eventual European domination. As has already been indicated, the basic demographic trajectory of the native population for the next 400 years was downward, often catastrophically so. This occurred with accelerating frequency in the eighteenth century as direct European settlement, missionary resettlement of the native population, and African slave populations, previously negligible in number, expanded rapidly. This is not to suggest that contacts prior to this time had not resulted in localized epidemics. Indeed migration away from these epidemic episodes is a recurrent theme of native history in the sixteenth and seventeenth centuries. However, the Europeans still faced a relatively intact population, and certainly natives outnumbered intruders until the end of the seventeenth century. Moreover the institutions of colonialism so familiar from the Andean and Central American contexts, such as the *encomienda*, were all but absent in this region. Hence the need, even where the aboriginal population remained intact, to import slave labor; native labor power remained under the control of indigenous leaders. Although the Europeans had profound effects on the distribution and expression of political authority in all native societies, the native political economy remained dominant over the European one in this region. This is quite clearly demonstrated in European dependency on native goodwill, if not allegiance, for the regular supply of foods, raw and processed materials, labor power, geographical information, and political intelligence.

However, as will become apparent, the system of human and material exchanges that had sustained the regional native political economy eventually collapsed. It was interdicted piecemeal by the European occupations, which stabilized by around 1650. The disruption of regional relationships and the narrowing of native leaders' political autonomy in turn led to the disintegration, amalgamation, or extinction of many ethnic formations, as well as to a general deterioration in the productivity and scale of native economic practices. It is out of this process of the radical transformation of ethnic boundaries that the native groups of the eighteenth emerged, and it is largely from that period that most social continuities into the modern era can be traced.

The Lesser Antilles, Orinoco and Coastal Guayana. The Orinoco, Trinidad, and the north Venezuelan coast were first sighted by Europeans during Columbus's third voyage to the "New World" in 1498. On August 5th of that year, three vessels anchored in the Gulf of Paria. Although native canoes approached the vessels, orders given to the Spanish sailors to play their pipes and drums were understood by the natives as a call to combat. It is most likely that this reception was more perplexing for the Europeans than for the inhabitants of *Cairi* (Trinidad) and its environs because of complex connections between the peoples of the Lesser Antilles and those of the mainland. It seems unlikely that news of the prior encounters with Columbus would have failed to spread south along the arteries of trade and exchange – these linkages being evident in the flight of Anacajoury from Trinidad, as described earlier. Because of the pattern of prevailing winds and currents, most European shipping made initial landfall in the Lesser Antilles. This northerly fringe of the region under discussion was a zone of very intense contact and exchange between Europe and native America. However, these islands were not settled until the following century and then only partially until the eighteenth. As a result the native population of this area was utterly transfigured by such contacts. Yet it has retained cultural continuities that stretch all the way back to that fateful Columbian landfall in 1492. It is all too easy to fall into the narrative convention of European contact resulting in native destruction. It did, of course, but a more complex pattern of events produced the well-known moments of conflict and conquest. The still surviving native population of the Lesser Antilles therefore serves as an important reminder of the resilience and creativity of native responses to colonialism even as we must contemplate the brutal curtailment of response in so many other contexts.

The main source of European intrusion onto the South American mainland in the sixteenth century was the Spanish colony on Margarita Island, which served as an intermittent base for various *entradas* (armed incursions) made into the Orinoco *llanos* to the south in search of the land of *El Dorado* ('The Golden One'). The colony was not founded until the discovery of the pearlbeds in 1512, but within one year of Columbus's landfall in the Gulf of Paria, Alonso de Hojeda, the first of a series of Spanish adventurers, had already arrived. He was closely followed in 1501 by Pedro Niño and the Guerra brothers, Cristóbal and Luis. The Guerra's received licenses to hunt slaves from this region to supply the colony of Hispaniola, and Spanish merchants initiated a trade with the local Guayquieris for the native store of pearls. The best pearl-beds lay off the almost sterile islands of Cubagua and Coche; as a consequence, the colonists were completely dependent on access to the fresh water of the river Cumaná and the foodstuffs that the native Cumanagotos could supply. The tensions that grew from this alternating dependency and exploitation of the native population resulted in the first major confrontation between native forces and the Spanish. Although Bartolomé de Las Casas had personally been involved in establishing the first American monastery in the Cumaná region, at Chirichirivichi, this was destroyed and the colonists expelled by the repeated attacks on the pearl fishing colony by the Cumanagotos and their allies, principally the Chaima. By 1522 the region had been brutally reoccupied by the Spanish and had become a safe base for the exploration of the Orinoco, Trinidad, and the Atlantic coast.

The Spanish colonists, despite these conflicts, had developed significant trade links with some of the native groups of the Guayana coast, particularly the Lokono. The pearl fisheries at Margarita certainly required significant numbers of native slaves, and the population of the Caribbean shore of Venezuela suffered accordingly, but there is little evidence to suggest systematic slave raiding either along the Orinoco or along the Atlantic coast. However, the brief occupation of a site on Trinidad in 1531–1532 by Antonio de Sedeño, as well as the rival expeditions led by Diego de Ordás to the mid-Orinoco between 1531 and 1535, were accompanied by much bloodshed but did not result in permanent settlement.

Ordás was seeking access to the fabulous "land of Meta" where *El Dorado* was supposedly to be encountered. On his second attempt Ordás penetrated the Orinoco as far as the first major rapids some 600 miles upstream. On his first attempt he had become embroiled with the Warao at the mouth of the river. The third attempt ended with his death from poisoned arrows, and his nephew assumed command of the retreat to Margarita.

In 1536 Jeronimo Dortal made a new attempt to explore the Orinoco, but the sheer immensity of the *llanos*, and his failure to make native allies, provoked mutiny and the expedition's return to Margarita. Similar disasters overtook the Orinoquian expeditions of Gonzalo Jiménez de Quesada in 1536–1537 and Pedro Maraver de Silva in 1568.

Taken together, these expeditions on the mainland and the activities of Spanish slavers in the Caribbean islands caused a number of relocations by the native population. The Yao moved from Trinidad, and others escaped Spanish depredations on the Greater Antilles. However, there was no systematic Spanish establishment beyond the coastal strip of the Venezuelan shore. The first tentative Spanish incursions into the Orinoco Basin, like the first descent of the Amazon, were all carried out in pursuit of plunder, especially gold. It was not until the end of the sixteenth century that permanent occupation was envisaged, and then largely to forestall settlement by Spain's Protestant rivals, the English and Dutch. One might therefore say that whereas trade quickly led to simple plunder and conquest in the case of the Caribbean, the reverse was true to the north of the Amazon. There, relatively peaceful trade burgeoned despite a series of prior military adventures in search of the land of *El Dorado*. Furthermore, despite the early foundation of Chirichirivichi, there was no missionary activity similar to the Jesuit system of *aldeias* ("protected" villages) in coastal Brazil, in either the Orinoco or Amazon, until the late seventeenth century, and even later or not at all in the Guayana coastal zone.

Such circumstances combined to create a situation where native autonomy persisted far longer than elsewhere. Even during the rise of plantation economy in the late seventeenth century, the need for indigenous labor was limited because the African slave trade, already established to service the Brazilian and Caribbean markets, expanded to meet these new demands. Indeed it was the failure of the Dutch to situate themselves in Brazil that freed capital and resources for the development of their Guayana colonies. Likewise the French eventually turned to the Caribbean and Guayana after their earlier ejection from the province of Maranhão, south of the Amazon (discussed later) and from their establishments around Rio de Janeiro.

European settlement, and the fateful consequences for the native population that it would entail, commenced with the establishment of the Spanish fort of Santo Tomé, sometime in the late 1590s, under the auspices of the Berrio family. The Berrios were given the captaincy or governorship of "El Dorado." Antonio de Berrio's occupation of the lower Orinoco resulted in the total destruction of the extant ruling élites, which the Spanish then attempted to replace with a series of puppet rulers. However, just as the Portuguese and French in Brazil had found themselves dependent on the indigenous population for food and military support, so too in Orinoco and along the Guayana coast, where Dutch factories begun to spring up in the second decade of the seventeenth century, domination of, or alliance with, the indigenous population was critical.

For Antonio de Berrio, and subsequent Spanish governors, this was partly achieved through the Lokono, who had supplied the Margaritan colony with manioc flour since the 1530s and had extended their own settlements along the Guayana coast and into Orinoco with Spanish support. The local native population was also organized to service the fort and black slaves given to the Lokono for the production of the only cash crop – tobacco. However, the Spanish presence in the river was really only nominal, and any determined effort to dislodge them invariably succeeded, as the English and Dutch, in conjunction with their native allies, repeatedly found. The tenuous Spanish hold on their fort in Orinoco may be seen as a direct consequence of their earlier treatment of the native population because, although their connections with the Lokono had earlier ensured a supply of basic foodstuffs and valuable intelligence on the more hostile groups of the region, other native groups disadvantaged by this arrangement were eager for an active alliance with the Dutch and English.

Initial English interest in this area, stimulated by the expedition and writings of Walter Ralegh, centered on possible mineral wealth and, as such, was heavily influenced by the Spanish reports of goldworking cultures in the upland regions. Nonetheless, in the course of reconnaissances for an access route to these areas, much information was collected on the general trading potential of the coastal region. Principally this consisted of gold and silver work, specklewood, annatto dye, and oils. The region was also assessed as favorable for the plantation of sugar, rice, tobacco, and cotton.

The Dutch were the first actually to establish stable factories in the area; the English and French chose either to trade directly from their ships or attempt a number of abortive colonizing projects. By 1621, the date of the incorporation of the Dutch West India Company, there was a trading post on the Essequibo, followed by an establishment by the Van Peere family on the Berbice in the 1630s.

Vicente Yánez Pinzón, who had accompanied Columbus on his first voyage, made the first report on this coastal region, later known as the "Wild Coast," in 1499. Yánez Pinzón also recorded that the southern zone was known to the native inhabitants as *Paricora*, the domain of the Palikur, who still live there to this day. *Paricora* had been sighted earlier in the year by the flotillas of Alonso de Hojeda and Amerigo Vespucci as they descried the outflow of the Amazon for the first time. The long hiatus between these first sightings and actual settlement by the Dutch and English is partly due to the fact that the low-lying mangrove coast of this part of northern South America offered no immediate or obvious haven or entrepôt for interior exploration. Discoveries taking place in the Caribbean and around its littoral sufficiently preoccupied the Europeans over the succeeding decades to postpone settlement. Indeed the Amazon itself was virtually unknown until the 1540s. As mentioned, the Orinoco was not occupied until the 1590s despite its proximity to the prosperous colonies of the north Venezuelan coast and Antilles.

Nevertheless the native regional links that connected the Amazon and Orinoco basins, via the Rupununi savannahs in the east and the Cassiquiare watershed in the west, meant that at least diplomatic relations were necessary with the more eminent chiefs (*adumasi*) of the Lokono and Palikur, along the Wild Coast. Such relationships were critical to

Spanish efforts in settling the north coast of Venezuela because of the role of the *adumasi* in supplying foodstuffs to the booming pearl fisheries on Margarita. Traders also knew that native economic and political systems spread far into the interior.

It is probably because of its importance in these regional trade links that the river "Surinam" was so named by the indigenes. In the language of the *Karipuna* (Island Carib), who habitually raided the *aruacas* (Arawaks) for *caracoli* (golden artifacts), *sulinama* was the country and river that gave access to the Amazons, as it was also a manufacturing site for *takua* (greenstone amulets), known also as the "gifts of the Amazons." This upland link to the Amazon Basin was also well known to the first Dutch traders, such as Amos van Groenewegen and Hendrickson, who had traded for some 27 years with the upland Indians of Guiana. Dutch traders also participated in the exchange of steel tools for gold ornaments using Surinam as their entrepôt. This was probably managed with the Manoa of the Rio Negro acting as intermediaries for the sources of Amazon gold as far as the Rupununi savannahs, the trade then being taken up by the Arawaks (probably the Lokono) to the east and into Surinam proper. This strategic position in a regional network of élite exchange was an economic basis for the political power of the Lokono *adumasi* in the early colonial era. Such interconnections over the Guayana shield were quickly exploited by English, Irish, and Dutch traders from both the Guayana coast and the Amazon Basin.

For the Spanish the limited worth of this trade was outweighed by the search for military achievement and easy wealth in Peru and Colombia. Nonetheless it is from the Spanish sources that the first direct and substantive information concerning the indigenous population of the Surinam region comes.

Information was first collected in 1519–1520 for the Spanish crown by the *licenciado* Figueroa. His report vaguely indicated that *aruacas* were widely settled on the Wild Coast to the south of Orinoco. Some 30 years later Martín López more clearly described this region, and again in the period 1560–1575 Juan de Salas, Antonio Barbudo, and Rodrigo de Navarrete sent reports. These accounts relate that the Corentyn River formed the eastern limits of the *Provincia de los Aruacas*, and they describe a distinctly organized stratified group with a highly productive subsistence base. Rodrigo de Navarrete neatly summarized the political and economic position of the Lokono with regard to the Europeans when he wrote that "it is well known that in their country no want of provision is felt [and] at the end of [each] month . . . two thousand loads of *Cacabi* [cassava bread] can be supplied, each load being more than two *arrobas* [= 50 lb/23 kg]. Thus they have frequently assisted us, and even at the present day they relieve the hunger of the people of that island [Margarita]." It was also noted that they grew maize and sweet potatoes, highlighting this intensive agricultural system. It is reflected archaeologically in the form of various raised field and mound sites in ancestral Lokono territories.

The first non-Spanish traders and settlers along the Wild Coast thus entered a complex political situation governed by the persistence of powerful native political groupings. The French in their attempts to settle the Cayenne River region in the period 1620–1650 repeatedly ran afoul of these complexities. They were unable to maintain neutrality in conflicts between the Palikur and Caribs, which they themselves also fomented. Because this southern region of the Wild Coast was the destination of a number of groups and individuals fleeing the Spanish to the north, the impact of these native colonizers, as well as the European ones, rendered the situation very dynamic indeed. Ever-changing metropolitan political or military priorities repeatedly overrode local alliances with native leaders.

The conclusion of the Indian War of 1681 marked the definitive establishment of a Dutch Surinam and also marked a hiatus in the other colonial powers' struggle to occupy enclaves in the region. By this time the Dutch trading enclaves on Berbice and Essequibo had found a modus vivendi with both the Spanish to the north and the local native population, largely because of the emphasis on trading of the Essequibo enclave, which also secretly supplied the Spanish on the Orinoco.

Meanwhile Surinam became the scene of intense colonial rivalry among the French, English, and Dutch. A more detailed consideration of this episode serves as an exemplar of the kinds of problems and opportunities that native peoples faced along the whole coast. In these conflicts the indigenous population often played a critical role as auxiliary troops, as they did in consenting to settlement and trade in the first place. The Europeans soon realized that the most important Lokono (Arawak) and Kariña (Carib) leaders, who dominated the Wild Coast, were particularly receptive to these purposes, and so it was they who came to dominate relations with the colonial authorities. Later in the seventeenth century this was to lead to formal treaties of peace and a special exemption from slavery for some. Those native groups that were not part of this status quo, such as the Paragoto and Suppoyo, tended to retreat away from the coastal zone into the uplands. Their lack of a political connection to the European coastal zone made them the target of Arawak or Carib slavers supplying the burgeoning sugar plantations.

Until 1626 central Surinam was not a favored site for colonization. The Oyapock, Cayenne, Maroni, Berbice, and Essequibo rivers attracted the first Spanish, French, and English interlopers, with varying results. For example, in 1626 a colony of some 500 men and women from La Rochelle was established on the Saramacca River, but it was deserted by 1629 due to sickness and "the Indians being troublesome." In the manuscript of Colonel John Scott, *The Discription of Guiana* (British Library Sloane Collection 3662, fs. 37b–42b), we are told that 10 years later the French returned to the Saramacca with nearly four-hundred persons. Although they were tolerated until the year 1642, at that point "they grew careless, spread themselves to [the] Surinam [River] and Corentyn [River], had great differences with the Indians, and were all cut off in one day."

Hard on the heels of this disaster, the English brought out a further 300 families in 1643. These settled on the Surinam, Saramacca, and Corentyn rivers and "lived peaceably until the year 1645, at which time they espoused the quarrel of the French and were cut off by the natives." The French made one further attempt at settling the Saramacca, but they were expelled by the Caribs and Suppoyo in 1649. Contemporary with these efforts at the settlement of Surinam was the intermittent establishment of Dutch trading posts on the Surinam River, possibly entailing also some clearances for sugar plantations on the Maroni and Commewine rivers, as also occurred on the Berbice under the Van Pere family.

The disposition of the native population, as much physical as political, was a key element in the survival or destruction of these first colonies. By the middle of the seventeenth century, Caribs and Arawaks were clearly emerging as the dominant force, and although the Suppoyo and Paragoto were still of some significance in the calculations of the colonizers, it is more evident that by this time the political preeminence of the Arawak and Carib had become well established. Accordingly it is the development of adversarial identities between the Arawak and Carib that dominates native history in the latter part of the seventeenth century. Dutch–English rivalry over possession of the Surinam colony created the political and economic conditions for the emergence of relatively monolithic native power blocs, under the control of coastal Arawak and Carib leaders.

The Caribs were already established far more extensively in Surinam than the Arawaks. Yet it was the Arawaks who were eventually to win the favor of the colonial authorities. The hostility of the Carib to almost all European settlement in their territories is evident enough from the successive failure of the various colonies up to the 1650s, and in fact this hostility never really ceased. Colonists only achieved permanent settlement as a result of the direct military and economic domination of the Carib population, facilitated by the military support of the Arawaks from the Corentyn River.

In 1650 some 300 people were landed on the Surinam and Commewine rivers under the command of Anthony Rowse, "a gentleman of great gallantry and prudence, and of long experience in the West Indies. His making a firm peace with the Indians soon after his landing, and reviving the name of Sir Walter Ralegh, gave the English firm footing in those parts, and it soon became a hopeful colony." According to Francis Willoughby, who initiated this colonization, Rowse brought him two *adumasi* (native 'kings') who gave permission to settle among them. Still extant in 1660 the English colony then adopted the name "Willoughby Land" in recognition of Francis Willoughby's financial investment.

Despite this positive diplomatic beginning, contemporary descriptions of the English colony indicate that little cooperation came from either side. Unlike the Arawaks who supplied the Spanish, the Caribs appear to have given scant assistance in fishing or hunting, while the upland groups remained altogether hostile. The colony's exclusive economic orientation to sugar production meant that in contrast to Berbice or Essequibo, where direct trade with the native population supported a colonial economy, there was no real incentive to cultivate alliances with the Caribs.

In 1665 Lord Willoughby himself arrived in "Willoughby Land" and experienced the first recorded epidemic in the colony, which had originated in the jointly settled European and native town of Torarica. Notwithstanding this, various attacks were launched against the neighboring Dutch settlements on the Approuage, Pomeroon, and Essequibo in pursuance of the second Anglo-Dutch War of 1665–1667. Although a local neutrality was initially agreed between the French and English, eventually the English were also ordered to attack the French at the Sinnamary and

Cayenne rivers, following the entry of the French on the Dutch side in the war in Europe in January 1666.

The Caribs did not actively oppose the English, but the support of the Arawaks for the Dutch and French seems to have been far more important. In response to the threat of a joint raid by the Arawaks and Dutch from the Berbice River, the English attacked two Arawak "warehouses," probably the fortifications at Ouden-Amen and Naby villages between the Demerara and Berbice rivers. Altogether some thirty Arawaks were killed and seventy captured. As a result contingents of Arawaks assisted the French and Dutch in retaking the fort at Essequibo and a fortified position on the Pomeroon, which had been the subject of two earlier attempts at settlement, in 1639 and 1642. In Pomeroon the French "most inhumanely delivered them [English prisoners] to the cruelty of the Arawaks at the mouth of that river to be massacred."

Meanwhile the Surinamese colony fared worse; in the words of the Governor William Byam, "in August, God's Justice most sharply visited our transgressions, the sickness spreading throughout the colony." The indifference of the local Caribs to the fate of the English colony, enhanced by its fast deteriorating condition, stands in contrast to the persistent Arawak support for the Dutch in Berbice, Essequibo, and Pomeroon. Some of the local Caribs did serve as paddlers for the pirogues and even joined the English troops with "bundles of war-arrows," but for lack of provisions they retired to their villages within a few days.

Such was the scene when in February 1667 the Dutch admiral Abraham Crijnssen appeared with a fleet before the fort of Paramaribo and demanded English surrender. Byam refused, and the Dutch attacked the following morning. A sharp fight followed, but the English surrendered. Significantly the articles of capitulation recognized the role of the indigenous population in these rivalries and tried to ensure there would be no revenge taken against the Caribs by either the Dutch or Arawaks. However, it seems clear from subsequent events that the advent of Dutch rule in Surinam led to the promotion of Arawak political dominance over the local Caribs.

Although the English actually retook the colony 6 months later, Sir John Harman forced the surrender of the Dutch on October 7, 1667; but Articles III and VI of the Treaty of Breda, which ended the Anglo-Dutch War, required that the colony be handed back to the Dutch. The English gained New York (New Amsterdam) in return. The definitive establishment of the Dutch in Surinam over the next 20 years thus underwrote the process of ethnic transformation that the English had initiated. The Arawak clans moving into Surinam under Dutch protection, particularly the Schotje, effectively marginalized the powerful Carib chiefs of the Corentyn, Copename, Surinam, and Maroni rivers. The Dutch governor, Crijnssen, found he was unable to ignore past conflicts, and after further incidents, such as disputes between the Carib and Dutch traders on the Copename in 1675, open conflict with the Caribs followed in 1678. A new governor, Johannes Heinsius, arrived in December 1678. He acted quickly, reinforcing the fort at Paramaribo and sending small detachments to Para Creek and Torarica. He also forbade the planters to leave and tried to reassure them as to the stability of the Dutch government by requesting reinforcements from the Netherlands. Because these levies would take some time to arrive, he meanwhile tried to organize a *negercorp* from among the slaves. He also encouraged the Arawaks from Berbice, under the command of Lucas Caudri, to join him in a joint attack on the Carib in the Para Creek and along the Saramacca, with a second coordinate Arawak force, under their *adumasi* Warray, attacking the Caribs in the Copename River. Neither of these expeditions was militarily successful. In both cases the Arawaks eventually refused to fight, clearly suggesting that the hostility of Carib and Arawak was itself a product of such European conflicts, rather than their social or cultural distinctiveness. In any case these distinctive identities as *Arawak* and *Carib* were themselves relatively recent and so obscured the heterogeneity of the ethnic origins of their members.

Unable to simply play off Carib and Arawak, Heinsius pursued the policy of keeping up the military patrols of Dutch plantations, while trying by diplomatic means to divide the Caribs settled in the central regions from those to the east in the Corentyn region and to the west in the Maroni area. In this endeavor he was reasonably successful. The Carib chief Annassabo let him construct a fort on the Corentyn in early 1679 and, thanks to the personal intervention of Annassabo, Heinsius also received a contingent of 20 warriors from the formerly hostile chief Tonay for the fort at Paramaribo. Initially such overtures were less successful in the Maroni region because the activities of the *bokkenruylders* (Indian traders), always a difficult element for the colonial authorities to control, had alienated the Caribs. However, once agreement was reached that certain named traders would not be allowed into the Carib villages again, permission was given to construct a fort at the junction of the Cottica and Commewine. This site was chosen in order to inhibit communication between the Caribs of the central regions of Surinam and those of the Maroni River.

In April 1680 reinforcements of regular troops arrived from the Netherlands, effectively signaling an end to the need to cultivate further the outlying Carib communities. Although Heinsius died in July of the same year, his successors continued his strategy of attacking the Copename, Surinam, and Saramacca Caribs only after having first secured the neutrality of the eastern and western groups. The fact that they now had European troops at their disposal also meant that there was no need to rely exclusively on Arawak assistance.

Caribs who surrendered were well treated, not least because Carib aid to runaway slaves opened up the specter of a combined native and slave rebellion that could have overwhelmed the Dutch. It would nearly do so in Berbice some 90 years later. However, the further pacification of the Corentyn Caribs in 1684 and the resultant isolation of the Maroni chiefs meant that Dutch rule in Surinam never again suffered explicit challenge.

Here, then, in microcosm is the complex web of influences, impacts, and impositions that shaped relations between colonizers and indigenes. Comparable situations occurred throughout this region until the stabilization of the initial colonial enclaves by the turn of the eighteenth century. Although varied emphases in colonial policy, differing most strikingly between the Iberians and non-Iberians, obviously induced varied strategies and precluded others, the key point is that over time both European and native interactions were a product of those relationships and not some hypothetical and abstract cultural disposition, derived from the iconic moment of first contact.

Amazon River and Maranhão. First contacts were often much later along the Amazon, even at its mouth, because neither the Spanish nor Portuguese tried to settle the Maranhão region or the Amazon River shores until the seventeenth century. Before then other colonial powers limited their establishments to fortified trading posts. It is therefore significant that the early expeditions that first traveled the length of the Amazon, and the Orinoco, both departed from the Andean regions to the west. Francisco de Orellana left Quito for the "Land of Cinnamon" in the expedition of Gonzalo Pizarro in 1541, and Antonio de Berrio left Bogotá for the Orinoco in 1583. As in the case of the Orinoco, Orellana's expedition did not represent the first European intrusion into the Amazon Basin, but it did signal the start of a serious interest in its "discovery," a complex concept of the time that implied much more than a gathering of information. Up until this point these interior regions had been marginal to Spanish colonizing efforts.

The Portuguese first sighted Brazil from the fleet of Pedro Álvares Cabral in 1500, as it followed the southern part of the Atlantic coast. The first Spanish discovery of the Amazon had been made by Vincent Yánez Pinzón a few months earlier. Spaniards gave the name *Santa María de la Mar Dulce* to the outlet, which discharged so much fresh water into the ocean that it seemed a "sea" itself. As with the Wild Coast to the north, the region around the Amazon mouth was not particularly easy for sailing ships to navigate. The coastal environment of mangrove swamps made landings difficult, except at what was to become, partly for this very reason, São Luís de Maranhão. The captaincy of Maranhão, created by King João III in 1534, was the most northerly grant of land the Portuguese king made. The crowns of Portugal and Spain negotiated a treaty in 1494, which limited Portuguese possession in the New World to a region east of the "line of Tordesillas," variously calculated between 42° 30' and 50° West, during the subsequent 50 years. As a result almost all of the Amazon Basin lay outside Portuguese jurisdiction. Coupled with a lack of Spanish interest in the region, this created the conditions for the Dutch, English, French, and Irish trading ventures that represented the sole European occupations of the river until the 1630s. The Portuguese even desisted from their initial attempts to colonize Maranhã by 1554.

The first descent of the Amazon, by a party attached to the expedition of Gonzalo Pizarro, produced one of the most fascinating documents of this period. It contains sustained descriptions of the mighty native polities of this river, which had effectively disintegrated by the time of the actual colonization of the river almost 100 years later. Under the command of Francisco de Orellana, a small party, caught by the current, floated downstream the whole length of the river, battling the desultory attacks of the inhabitants, occasionally stopping to trade or to plunder. The disparity between the depiction of powerful overlords, vast populations, and near-urban scales of settlement, and the reports of decimated populations given by the missionaries a century later, have led some to doubt the probity of this early account. But much of the information given in Gaspar de Carvajal's account of the 1541 journey with Pizarro is confirmed by the only other contemporary journey down the Amazon, the expedition of Lope de Aguirre in 1560. Aguirre's notoriety as mutineer, traitor, and madman does little to lend credibility to the account. Recent archaeological and historical research nonetheless strongly suggests that many such accounts are far from fanciful, despite the unfamiliarity of the discursive practices of their authors.

The Amazon River was to remain marginal to Spanish colonial interest. Although parts of the upper Amazon were eventually integrated into the *audiencia* of Quito, it was the Portuguese, led by Pedro Texeira, who effectively occupied the Amazon Valley in the 1630s, in defiance of the Line of Tordesillas. This occupation also swept away the trading posts and forts that the Dutch, Irish, and English had established in the river as part of their effort to develop trade with the native groups of the Amazon and Guianas, following on the expeditions of Robert Dudley, Walter Ralegh, and Lawrence Keymis in the 1590s and the establishment of the Dutch West India Company in 1616.

The lower Amazon was extensively traded by the Dutch, Irish, and English who established a series of fortified factories in the lower reaches of the river during this period. They traded largely for hardwoods and dyes but also laid out profitable tobacco plantations. Unlike the Atlantic coastal zone along the lower Amazon, there was little in the way of intercolonial conflict, except with the nascent Portuguese settlements at the very mouth of the river. The vast reaches of the Amazon Basin and its numerous populations at first offered ample trading opportunities. European knowledge of the upland routes from the Atlantic coast, in the region of Surinam and Corentyn, to the Amazon Basin, also led to exploration of the northern tributaries by the Irish and English. In contrast the Dutch largely centered their efforts on the lower Xingu and Tapajos, with the English and Irish on the north bank at the mouth of the Amazon proper. This highland connection was to become significant again in the period when the Portuguese were assaying and occupying the Branco and Negro rivers. It was this traditional connection to the Atlantic Dutch colonies that provided a material base for native resistance to Portuguese *descimientos* (slave hunts) in the eighteenth century, as under the leadership of the Manoa chieftain, Ajuricaba.

As has been mentioned, the Portuguese rooted out these small settlements in the 1630s, although they had been so profitable to their owners that licenses to resurrect them were sought from both the Spanish and Portuguese crowns. Thereafter the Dutch and English concentrated their efforts on the rivers of the Wild Coast, particularly Surinam, Berbice, Essequibo, and Pomeroon, as well as the Caribbean islands. It was left to the French, who belatedly occupied the Cayenne and Oyapock rivers in the second half of the seventeenth century, to contest with the Portuguese for control of the Amazon mouth.

French interest in this region was driven both by their expulsion from the southern coastal colony at Rio de Janeiro in the 1560s and by their continued search for trade opportunities; although it was not until 1612 that La Ravadiére sailed with three ships to colonize the Maranhão region. Excellent contacts with the local Tupinamba, a testament to the long history of French trading along the whole Brazil shore, gave room for a broad complicity between the Tupinamba and the French, sealed by their mutual antagonism to the Portuguese and their native allies, the Potiguar. French plans to expand the colony through the conquest of the Camarapin and other native populations at the Amazon mouth appealed to the Tupinamba, and a joint expedition set out in 1613.

However, the Portuguese had already begun to occupy the area south of Maranhão, the captaincy of Ceará, and were constructing forts along the coast even as the French advanced into the Amazon with their native allies. In 1614 the Portuguese entered the Bay of Maranhão and inflicted heavy casualties on the French, though without taking the fort. At this point the Tupinamba began to desert the French cause. It was not until the end of 1615 that Portuguese reinforcements from Pernambuco finally expelled La Ravadière, thus ending forever the French occupation of Brazilian territories. Over the next two decades the Portuguese inexorably expanded their control over Maranhão and founded Belém do Pará right on the southern mouth of the Amazon. This involved an extended struggle with the Tupinamba over the next 3 years, until 1619. The Portuguese employed enemies of the Tupinamba, the Tapuias, as military auxiliaries. Despite a direct assault on the fortress of Belém in 1619, the Tupinamba were a spent force. The outbreak of smallpox in Maranhão in 1621 decimated even those Tupinamba who had been spared direct military conquest.

It is against this immediate background that Pedro Texeira led a series of expeditions designed similarly to win the upriver Amazon territories for the Portuguese and so integrate these northern regions of Brazil. However, compared to the southern captaincies, Maranhão was poor and undeveloped, and the "red gold" of the native inhabitants seemed a perfect resource for the development of the region. The legal fictions under which slaving of the native population was organized by the Portuguese were of two kinds. The first emphasized the "ransom" of captives who might otherwise have been put to death or even cannibalized. (The same legal formula was employed in Spanish territories.) The other was to justify the capture of natives as the pursuit of trade. The Capuchins, who had reached Pará with the first settlement, did little to oppose such slaving, although its brutal consequences soon became too much to ignore. The Jesuits, who replaced the Capuchins in the administration of the native population, documented them closely as part of their bid for control.

When Texeira led the first force into the Amazon in 1630, it comprised over 1,000 native levies and some 120 Portuguese. This force expelled the Irish, English, and Dutch settlements on the lower reaches of the Amazon. They were not reestablished, or only briefly. The next step was to push further up the river. Texeira led a second major force to this end in 1637. It reached the Spanish settlements by the end of the year and eventually the city of Quito, well within the viceroyalty of Peru, much to the consternation of Spanish authorities. Texeira began his return in early 1639, accompanied by the Spanish Jesuit, Cristóbal de Acuña. Acuña's account has become a key source on the native population along the river. As his crew passed the territory of the Tapajós, they encountered the son of the governor of Pará, named Bento Maciel like his father, and found him no more troubled by brutal exploitation of the native population than his father had been. Although Texeira forbade the "ransom" (i.e., kidnapping) of the Tapajoso and their personal servants, "scarcely had I turned my back when . . . [Maciel] fell upon the Indians with harsh war, although they desired peace." Such was the all too common experience of native leaders in the Amazon. Texeira's brother, the vicar-general of Maranhão, claimed that "almost 2 million" natives had been destroyed in the course of the Portuguese occupation of this region during the 1630s and 1640s, a pattern that was to continue unimpeded as Portuguese control was extended along the whole of the river and up its major tributaries over the next century.

The scale of both trade and planting in this region was initially far smaller than along the southern Atlantic shore of the South American continent or in the Greater Antilles. The Lesser Antilles and the Wild Coast, as well as the lower reaches of the Amazon and Orinoco, remained less desirable alternatives, as the primary efforts of the French and Dutch to hold colonies south of the Amazon shows. Nonetheless the impact of European activity on indigenous societies in the region was marked. It provoked a fundamental reorientation of native trade from an upland to a coastal focus. The demographic impact, as well as overt policy, forced a reorganization of political ties. Moreover knowledge of the Spanish and Portuguese occupation in the Orinoco, Amazon, and beyond, as well as the lessons of its local consequences, was thoroughly assimilated by native leaders. They learned actively to seek military alliance with Spain and Portugal's colonial rivals, understanding the need to impede Iberian attempts to control the region. Thus a reformed native leadership, utilizing new forms of ethnic consciousness, now faced the newly stabilized colonial regimes. As a consequence these new native identities expressed these new conditions. They show only problematical continuities with those that had preceded them. This social and cultural homogenization of the native population is reflected in the categories of colonial missionary ethnography. Missionaries employed linguistic categories to explain the distribution of native groups and to assess the best means for their conversion. No élite class of leaders any longer presented themselves as intermediaries, for they had been extinguished in the violence of colonial establishment. The vacuum that they left was either directly filled by the missionaries and slavers, or else their followers gravitated to emergent trading and warring chieftaincies, such as the Manoa, Arawak, Carib, Aruan, and in the nineteenth century, the Mura and the Munducucu. Such "colonial tribes" made up a complex historical inheritance from the ancient native polities. Some were amalgams of often highly divergent cultural traditions. Politically and economically their leaders premised themselves on situations of colonial conflict and rivalry. Accordingly, as the colonial economies of the region shifted from trade in forest products toward the laying out of plantations, so the importance of these groups declined commensurately. In any case the infrastructure by which Europe supported the American colonies was much more complete than in the sixteenth and early seventeenth century. Those colonies themselves also began to move toward forms of economic and political autonomy, foreshadowing the emergence of national states after 1800. Nonetheless our historical awareness of these outcomes should not be allowed to obscure the fact that new power groupings amongst the still autonomous native populations shaped colonial development for the next 100 years or so. It is that episode we next examine, beginning with an outline of the changing conditions of native autonomy in this period, and followed by an examination of the key colonial institutions that emerged to curtail this autonomy – the mission and the plantation.

Colonial Advance and Native Obedience (c. 1650 to 1800)

Commensurate with their newfound status such groups as the Carib, Manoa, or Arawak now used their preferential relations with the Europeans to consolidate and extend their political and economic influence through trade and raid. Moreover, against a background of severe demographic decline, the incorporation of remnant populations was more successfully managed by groups unencumbered by complex rules of marriage and descent. There is evidence that such kinship systems were abandoned in the light of changed conditions. It was therefore those groups who most actively sought contact with the Europeans, hoping thereby to alter their relations with other native groups, as well as those who had already suffered *reducción* or *descimiento* (i.e., political submission to the Spanish or a forced descent down river to Portuguese settlements), who were to face the brunt of the epidemics that swept this area in the eighteenth century. What the *conquistadores* had failed to achieve by force of arms against still independent tribes, the missionaries were to accomplish indirectly by the economic and political marginalization of regional leaders and traders. The demographic devastation of native populations facilitated this process; as a result the missions and their epidemics become the central native experience of this period. If they did not die of epidemic disease, then kin, clients, and enemies alike were still trapped in a state of isolated captivity, thereby undermining the economic and social exchanges that had once supported the autonomous political authority of the native leaders.

Similarly, as the range of Dutch, French, and English trade activities with the native population shrunk, due to the inception of sugar plantations along the Wild Coast, different native groups competed for the dwindling supply of European goods. Because the colonial authorities did all they could to defuse disruptive local conflicts, access to these European goods was heavily dependent on a willingness to conform to European expectations. An informal system of ethnic ranking emerged in regard to the distribution of these goods. Favored native leaders were also formally "conformed" in their authority by the colonial administration, who gave them special insignia of office it becomes increasingly evident that interior groups excluded from these arrangements were cynically targeted by native leaders. "Punitive" expeditions satisfied both European and native ambitions; significantly it was among such "punished" groups that millennial movements of native revival arose in the aftermath of the campaigns. By such means the dependency of "loyal" groups was also increased, because their willingness to act as European proxies ensured that any attempts to form pan-native alliances, such as had occurred during the initial resistance to European incursion, would fail.

Moreover native leaders were faced in this period with increasingly stable colonial enclaves. Thus by the end of the seventeenth century, the Spanish occupied the Pearl Coast, Trinidad, and the Orinoco. Their rivals, the English and French, held small sugar and tobacco plantations throughout the Lesser Antilles, as well as on the Atlantic coast of the Guianas. The Dutch in Surinam, Berbice, and Essequibo were undoubtedly the dominant force along the Guayana coast, as Spanish governors fruitlessly warned their monarchs. However, the French had stabilized a colony between the Maroni and Oyapock rivers and had garnered sufficient native alliances to dispute the intervening zone with the Portuguese at Belém.

The Mission Regime

Along the Amazon and Orinoco and their tributaries, the period from around 1650 to 1750 marks the zenith of the missionary *conquista de almas* ('conquest of souls'), which was at times scarcely less bloody than the *conquista a fuego y sangre* ('conquest by fire and blood') that had preceded it. As has already been indicated, the demographic consequences of evangelization were profound. This was largely because *reducción* or *descimiento* often involved the resettlement and concentration of native populations in close proximity to the Europeans and Africans, making them vulnerable to repeated epidemics. At the same time, missionaries were the last best hope of a native population that might otherwise be taken by slavers, particularly in the Portuguese territories. In contrast the Spanish crown's prohibition on native enslavement, dating from 1652, was largely observed. To stop slaving mattered because the anarchy of slaving undermined the relative stability of the *encomiendas*, which were the more prevalent colonial institutions for control of the native population in the Spanish regions.

Along the Amazon, however, all the easily accessible populations were progressively enslaved by 1700, despite efforts to outlaw the practice in 1680. The critical economic fact driving this policy was the high price of imported African slaves relative to the resources of the Portuguese colonists in Pará and Maranhão. Under pressure from the colonists the Portuguese king reintroduced slavery in 1688 and adjusted the terms of Jesuit control over the mission villages. In 1702 a new decree also extended slaving activities by allowing private colonists to go slaving by special royal license. In 1718 colonists were actively solicited to seek such licenses as labor needs became acute. The royal authorities themselves had the right simply to commandeer the mission populations for royal service, such as to build forts and roads or gather forest products. However, because such services could take months to complete, it could have a serious impact on the survival of that mission population. This was not just because of the contact with potential sources of diseases such as smallpox but also because such arbitrary demands upset the domestic economy by removing the adult males, who were mostly responsible for hunting, fishing, and the heavy work of clearing garden patches.

These usages by the authorities in turn restricted the supply of labor available to the private colonists. Pressures both to gain greater access to the mission *aldeias* and to continue the enslaving of autonomous native populations grew ever greater. Meanwhile the activities of Spanish missionaries in the upper Amazon toward the end of the seventeenth century, notably those of the Spanish-sponsored Jesuit Samuel Fritz, only reminded the Portuguese authorities of the absolute necessity to control the native population, either through their evangelization in situ or through their removal to the immediate proximity of colonial settlements, lest their political authority in the Amazon region be usurped by Spanish missionaries. It is therefore important to appreciate the mission was, apart from its evangelical purposes, a key institution of colonial expansion and was quite overtly used as such. In the absence of large military infrastructures, it was only through the direct control of people that a claim to territory could be made real.

Along the Amazon this situation became acute at the beginning of the eighteenth century. A series of disputes erupted over the control and return of "fugitives" from the missions of the Omaguas or *Cambebas* ('hammerheads'), as they were known due to their continuing practice of cranial deformation. By 1709 the situation had deteriorated to the point where a Portuguese force was dispatched to try and arrest Fritz and his companions. Spain and Portugal signed a treaty at Madrid in 1750, which fixed the boundary between the Spanish and Portuguese Amazon. But intense interest in control of the strategic Omagua territories had sealed the destruction of the native population, at least along the Amazon mainstream. By 1743, when the French expeditionary Charles de la Condamine traveled down the Amazon, he reported that all of the native population had "submitted or retreated far away."

All over this region the early eighteenth century brought increasingly frequent epidemics as a consequence of missionary activity and the burgeoning number of white colonists and black slaves amongst whom the newly "descended" indigenous groups were settled. These disasters, by draining away the already limited supply of labor, induced the colonists fiercely to oppose the missionaries over control of the dwindling native population. Their most effective advocate against the Jesuits was Paulo da Silva Nunes, an official of the authorities at Belém. His ferocious, if often unwarranted, accusations of Jesuit usurpation of royal prerogatives, of arming natives and dealing treasonably with the Dutch or Spanish, eventually moved the king to send an official to investigate. Although this report of 1734 was generally favorable to the Jesuits, ironically, by recognizing their achievements in creating a mission economy with native labor, it only served to accentuate those very aspects of their presence in the Amazon that were the source of the colonists' anxieties. In the context of the signing of the Treaty of Madrid, which adjudicated boundaries with the Spanish regions, the Jesuits and their upper Amazon missions were held to be an obstacle to the progress of demarcation. They were also accused of failure in their duties toward the native population. Coupled with a continual emphasis on the material wealth of some of the Jesuit *fazendas* (estates), the political climate was created for removing their control over the native population in 1754. Prominent in this development was the Governor of Maranhão and Pará, Mendonça Furtado, brother of the Marquis de Pombal, who had virtually supplanted royal power in Portugal. Indeed the Jesuits were to be expelled from Portugal itself in 1759 and from South America in 1760.

Similar tensions existed between the civil and ecclesiastical powers in the Spanish territories, but along the lower Orinoco it was the Capuchins and Franciscans who held the authority to evangelize the natives. In the late 1730s and early 1740s, the various missionary orders worked out a demarcation of their relative spheres of influence, which were largely respected. The Jesuits were assigned the western Orinoco *llanos* and the regions upriver from the Atures rapids. Downstream from this point the Franciscans were assigned the Orinoco north bank, and the Capuchins the south. Nonetheless the increasingly rapid decline of the native population from the 1730s onward, as the missionaries moved to occupy their concessions, brought to the surface the same kinds of conflict between colonist and missionary as to the control of their dwindling human resources. Nevertheless the Capuchins and Franciscans actually clung onto their estates and populations until the outbreak of the War of Independence, led by Simón Bolívar, from bases on the lower Orinoco. At this point many native groups sided with the forces of Bolívar.

In Orinoco, although the missionary occupation was sometimes violent, it was not associated with slave hunting in the same way it was along the Amazon. Rather it was the threat of Dutch influence over the native population, based on the long-distance trading activities of their Atlantic colonies, that largely determined the political attitudes of the Spanish toward the native population.

Central to these fears were the Caribs, who vied with the missionaries and civil authorities for control and influence over the Orinoco peoples. The seventeenth century saw little in the way of Spanish development of its outpost at Santo Tomé; indeed joint forces of Caribs, Dutch, and English raided and even on occasion expelled the Spanish garrisons there. In fact the Spanish largely maintained themselves through a local detente with the Dutch, and although this was sometimes upset by geopolitical considerations, the atrophy of Spanish colonization on the Orinoco can be directly related to the decline of the ruling house of Hapsburg in Europe. It was therefore not until the eventual succession of the new Bourbon dynasty that Spanish colonialism in this region was reinvigorated. A key tool in this revitalized colonialism was to be the advance of the missionaries. Nonetheless the normalization of relations with Spain's former Dutch colonies, expressed in the Treaty of Utrecht of 1713, left Spain's claim to trading monopolies in the Americas intact. So the issue of Dutch influence over the Orinoco populations through their association with the Caribs remained locally sensitive.

The first decades of the eighteenth century thus saw little in the way of renewed Spanish advance, but from the 1720s onward, both missionary settlement and direct Spanish colonization were augmented by the immigration of landless peasantry from both Andalucia and the Canaries. Until around 1740 the military challenge from Carib leaders was sufficient to put into question the eventual outcome of this struggle. It was really the steadily increasing impact of epidemics, as along the Amazon, that broke the back of the native population, setting the context for successful evangelization in the second half of the eighteenth century.

The prelude to colonial incorporation, from 1729 to 1740, was a period of fierce resistance by native leaders. At this moment we glimpse a final florescence of sustained and regionally organized opposition to European establishment. In Orinoco the war-chief Taricura dominated the decade as the opponent of the missionaries, while on the Rio Negro at this time the war-chief of the Manoa, Ajuricaba, similarly held Portuguese colonialism at bay. In both these cases, though to different degrees, trade with the Dutch colonies in the Guianas played an important role, because these native leaders' access to highly prized Dutch steel, cloth, and glass beads underwrote their political influence. Modern historiography has not always been careful to assess properly this generalized "Dutch connection" and its meaning for such leaders as Taricura and Ajuricaba. In fact the records of the Dutch administration suggest that Ajuricaba had only minimal and rather unsatisfactory direct dealings with the governor of Essequibo, largely because the Caribs interdicted his communication for fear of losing their own favorable position with the Dutch. Although contemporaries made much of Ajuricaba's "Dutch flag," whatever its significance, it was certainly not a token of allegiance to the Dutch. They were barely aware of the Manoas' existence, let alone complicit in face-to-face dealings with Ajuricaba.

In a similar way, Taricura, a Carib war-chief of the Barima River, emerges from a complex nexus of colonial propaganda and partial historiography. Implicated in the killing of an itinerant French cleric who was operating with the consent of the Spanish, Taricura, like Ajuricaba, seems to have quite suddenly opted for all-out warfare against the missionaries. This may well reflect the broad changes and transitions, described previously, that were occurring throughout the colonial world at this time. The advance of revitalized missionaries, the stabilizing diplomatic and political relations between previously antagonistic colonial powers, and new economic priorities that favored plantation over trade, all combined to create analogous problems for native leaders. They were solved in analogous ways across the region.

The Plantation Economy

In the Dutch enclaves of Essequibo, Demerara, Berbice, and Surinam, as well as the French enclaves at Korou, Cayenne, and the Oyapock River, the early part of the eighteenth century was a period of political consolidation and economic diversification. As has been indicated all these enclaves had their origins in trading with the local native population. However, over the last half of the seventeenth century, trade profits had become marginal to the profits from sugar planting.

Native leaders were therefore faced with a decline in their economic opportunities, even as their population base was also in decline and their political arrangements with the various colonial authorities rapidly shifting. The economic context of plantations meant that issues about the security and policing of colonial boundaries were becoming far more prominent. Some native leaders became even more important to the colonial authorities, but it also meant that groups deemed unimportant to the preservation of the capital investment involved in plantations were disadvantaged, if not actively exploited, as a source of slaves. For these colonial authorities the native population was viewed potentially as rebels or bush-police, slave-catchers, or military auxiliaries to defend the colony from attack. It is symptomatic of the increasingly marginal position of even the most powerful "colonial tribes," as in the case of the Caribs, that they were taken less and less into political account as administrators succeeded each other. Professional soldiery from Europe, or specially formed slave regiments, were now frequently used instead of native auxiliaries, especially against the maroon colonies of the interior of Surinam and Berbice.

Nevertheless within local spheres of influence the police role of certain native *caciques* was of vital importance, because the Dutch plantations experienced chronic problems in the day-to-day control of their black slave populations. Indeed, despite the military assistance of certain native leaders, Maroon enclaves sprang up throughout the region, particularly in Surinam, where the authorities eventually gave some Maroon communities formal recognition and diplomatic status. In the Spanish territories of Orinoco, even where the evangelization of native groups was nominally complete, pacification was unreliable. Sporadic rebellions against the mission regime occurred all over the Orinoco up to the War of Independence, and the cooperation of indigenous leaders remained vital to expansion of colonial authority.

Throughout this region conflicts among native groups were used to augment the effectiveness of evangelization, just as they were also used to secure colonial borders. As in earlier times the Europeans became the pretext for the settling of old scores, with the key difference that such conflicts now resulted also from a long history of interaction between native and colonizer. This long history of mutual interaction prepared the ground for both the growing independence of the colonial élite from its metropolitan origins, and the incorporation of the remnant native population into the nineteenth-century nations-state. At the end of the eighteenth century, colonial domination of the native population was effectively established. Native groups in the nineteenth century could maintain political independence only by deepening their retreat into the interior, or by choosing deliberate social isolation, even from others of the same tribe. It was in such a situation that the first modern ethnographers, such as Henri and Olga Coudreau, Robert and Richard Schomburgk, Carl Friedrich Martius and Johann Baptist von Spix, and Karl Von den Steinen, encountered the peoples of the interior. And it is also against this complex historical background that their ethnological inferences must be judged.

Nationalism and Neo-colonialism to 1900

Toward the end of the eighteenth century, the native peoples of the northeastern corner of South America still showed a considerable variety of society and culture, as well as significant autonomy from the colonial regimes that had implanted themselves throughout the region. In the northernmost area, the Lesser Antilles, Trinidad, and the *llanos* of the Orinoco, European dominance was unchallenged. The demographic preponderance of Europeans and Africans marginalized the native population. Indeed native society had come to include persons of African and European descent to such an extent that groups of "Black Caribs" or "Spanish Arawaks" had emerged. Ethnogenesis was a testament to the deep changes and dynamic responses with which native peoples had met colonialism.

Farther south, along the Atlantic coast, the Dutch and French had established stable, if not always profitable, plantation complexes. In these contexts native peoples were still valued as an informal militia that could be activated to control slave rebellions. Beyond that they were viewed with the nostalgic curiosity that set the tone of nineteenth-century ethnographic accounts and observations. The old colonial trope of the wild cannibal savage gave way to the image of the pathetic survivor of conquest eking out his last days in a mute rebuke to modernity. Of course this was more than a shift in literary tastes. It did reflect a rapidly changing conjuncture at the beginning of the nineteenth century in which native peoples had to endure further crushing epidemics, as well as the ferocity of unfettered capitalist exploitation. It had been a key complaint of the anticlericalism that produced both the Jesuit expulsions from Brazil, as well as the conflicts between civil governors and the Capuchin syndicalist mission system in Orinoco, that missionaries kept their neophytes in a state of "feudal" subjection. By this critics meant that their labor was not on the open market. This was a caricature; there is much evidence to show that both the Jesuits and Capuchins actually did try to accommodate demands for hired labor, but the point is that the demands of the spiritual economy could not be politically squared with those of the material economy, and it was the latter that excited the interest of the colonial and metropolitan élites. Amid such tensions the colonies and their metropolitan governments diverged and came into open conflict throughout the Americas.

In Brazil a number of complicating factors, such as the late date of the abolition of black slavery, the internal crises of the Portuguese state, and the sheer immensity of the Amazon region, attenuated these processes throughout the nineteenth century. As a result groups like the Kayapó, the Mundurucu and Xavante, inhabitants of the largely unknown southern tributaries of the Amazon, posed consistent military challenges to further Brazilian encroachments just as the Caribs, Manoas, and Aruan had in earlier times. However, these groups from the interior of Amazonia lacked the kinds of external European contacts that had been integral to sustained resistance and autonomy in Orinoco, on the Rio Negro, and along the Atlantic coast. Of necessity, relative isolation from, rather then engagement with, non-native society became a key strategy for survival. This contrasts with earlier times when contact, though always dangerous and sometimes disastrous, was necessary to sustain the scale of the native political economy. The negative consequence of strategies of retreat and isolation are retreat and isolation themselves. They entail a shrinking of the social sphere with a corresponding cultural conservatism. In turn ethnographers, taking these nineteenth-century contexts as historically given, molded their description to fit the prevalent image of soon-to-be-vanquished remnants of the aboriginal American idyll. However, as we have seen, ethnography thereby obscured the processes that gave rise to these sociocultural contexts. Moreover, driven by anxiety that continuities with the past were about to be swept away, ethnography also ignored more complex phenomena, such as the emergence of mixed groups like the Black Caribs or the *Cabanagem* of the Amazon (so-called from the *cabanos* or shacks in which the poor natives and mestizos lived). Until recently most observers pictured them as a testament to the dissolution of native society and culture, instead of its revitalization and persistence through new means.

The advent of this modern era was presaged in Amazonia by a 1755 royal edict, engineered by the Marquis de Pombal, which simultaneously declared "Indian liberty" and stripped the missionaries of all prerogatives over native labor. The latter was the more pressing motive for the colonial authorities. The governor of Pará, Mendonça Furtado, after he had made his inspection of the mission villages, and as the prelude to a publication of the 1755 edict, unilaterally decided to observe a transitional period during which the mission villages were put under the control of a civilian "director." This arrangement, known as the *Diretório* (Directorate), persisted for the next 40 years and was also extended to other regions of Brazil. A similar but more limited experiment was tried in the 1770s by the Spanish governor of the Orinoco, Manuel Centurión, but the local power of the Capuchins and the lack of consistent support from metropolitan Spain kept the system from growing beyond a few missions at the mouth of the Orinoco. The intent was the same in both cases: to integrate the native population into a "modern" society as quickly as possible, instead of allowing them to remain socially stagnant under the "feudal" control of the friars. So it was that the king of Spain, following the Portuguese lead, expelled the Jesuits from his empire in 1767, and Pope Clement XIV extinguished the order utterly in 1773. (It was revived at the end of the nineteenth century.) A similar fate befell the other missionary orders in South America, particularly where they sided with royalist factions in the emerging politics of independence.

Without the mediation of the missionaries, relationships between still autonomous native groups and the colonial authorities of necessity became militarized. Even where the missionaries' *tropas de resgate* (armed bands for the "rescue" of native souls) had used the persuasion of gunfire, their activities were premised on a very different set of ideas as to the purpose of such expeditions and the destiny of the natives captured by them. The Mura from the Madeira River and the Munducuru (Munduruku) from the Tapajos loom large in the conflicts of the last decades of the eighteenth century. Just as had the Arawaks and Caribs of earlier times, the Mura and Mundurucu expanded into an arena of contact, along the lower reaches of the Amazon, following Portuguese destruction and dispersion of the aboriginal native polities, especially the Tapajoso. As these emergent native forces clashed with each other and the first epidemics struck the Mura population, the Portuguese were able to negotiate a peace with the Mura. War against the Mundurucu continued into the 1790s until the reasonable treatment and release of two Munducucu captives led to a peace in 1795. Thereafter many Mundurucu were brought downstream to occupy the old mission villages of the Tapajoso.

To the north of the Amazon, and in the upper reaches of the Orinoco and Caroni, as well as in the Guayana Highlands, the boundaries of the colonial regimes were as yet not delineated. Just as had been the case in the demarcation of the Amazon River between Spain and Portugal, in the highlands of the Sierra Parima and Pacaraima, it remained unclear who controlled what. In this context the allegiances of the interior groups were important both for the legal establishment of a claim and for its practical defense. As a result boundary commissions for both the Portuguese and Spanish governments traveled into the interior in order to secure control of the headwaters of the Orinoco, Negro, and Branco and to assess the extent of Dutch and French influence inland from their coastal settlements.

This inquiry represented the zenith of external penetration into the interior for the next 100 years. The wars of independence against the Spanish obviated the rationale for imperial demarcation. Likewise, further east, and especially at the headwaters of the Branco, where the Pirara portage links the Amazon Basin to that of the Essequibo via the Rupununi tributary, the issue of Portuguese and Brazilian territorial claims remained unsettled until the end of the nineteenth century. Venezuelan claims against the late nineteenth-century demarcation with Guyana remain outstanding toward the end of the twentieth century. In all these situations, as in the era of the missions, the control or allegiance of the native population was critical, both practically and legally, to demonstrate rights of possession. As a result even very isolated groups found themselves confronted by a wave of exploratory expeditions, some with overt ethnographic purposes, in the wake of which new and virulent epidemics often broke out. Such activities eventually drove native populations down to their historic low-point in the early twentieth century.

The precise documentation of the overall effect of epidemics, in both this period and earlier, is fraught with uncertainty. At the moment it is broadly accepted that death rates in specific cases could have been as high as 80 percent of a given population, but it is not possible to judge if this was true in all situations. Moreover, given the continuing dispute as to the ecological bases of human settlement in Amazonia, it is also difficult to derive an estimate for populations at contact, though a total of 5 million is currently offered as a minimum for the whole of this region (including the Orinoco Basin and Guianas). The real point, however, is that there was a markedly different mortality among native and non-natives, that this was appreciated by all parties, and that it can be shown to have had concrete political and economic effects in determining the course of conquest and colonization. One has only to contemplate the terms of colonial endeavor elsewhere, as in Africa or Asia, to appreciate the enhancement this biological factor gave to the colonial and neo-colonial occupation and control of Native America.

The colonial regimes that had initiated that occupation now also faced a rising tide of dissent, as the colonists contemplated total independence from Europe. In 1822 Dom Pedro I proclaimed Brazil's independence, just as had Simón Bolívar in Venezuela, some 6 years earlier. The colonial regimes of the Dutch and French in the Guianas likewise underwent a reorientation to Europe, but for different reasons. The French colony in Cayenne, initially royalist, fell, as did the monarchy itself, to the forces of the new French Republic. In addition, as a consequence of the Napoleonic Wars in Europe, the British challenged both French and Dutch supremacy along the Wild Coast. Although the Dutch retained control of Surinam, the Essequibo, Demerara, and Berbice enclaves were relinquished to British control by the Treaty of London in 1814. Trinidad was unceremoniously seized from the Spanish in 1804. In 1808 a joint Anglo-Brazilian force seized the French colony of Cayenne, which the Brazilians occupied for the next 8 years until the Paris Convention of 1817.

In short, the effects of the changing conjuncture in Europe were felt right across the region and brought a series of consequences for native peoples. In some cases native levies were used to offset the navies and armies sent from Europe, as in Venezuela, where a special regiment of Caribs was formed to support Bolívar. On the other hand, in the revolt of the *Cabanagem*, which engulfed the whole of the lower Amazon from 1835 to 1836, the role of native people was diffused in a general social revolt against the old colonial élite and its inheritors in the newly independent Brazil. The revolt was brutally crushed in 1837–1838 and was followed by the outbreak of further epidemics. Smallpox and influenza, always the companions of war, also swept through the native populations of the Orinoco in the aftermath of the Venezuelan War of Independence. By the 1840s the native population was thus in very steep decline, reaching its nadir in Brazil at the turn of the twentieth century. In addition to the smallpox, influenza, and measles epidemics that were a constant factor since the time of first contacts, the endemic spread of malaria added another sharp downward twist to the spiral of native demographic decline.

In the Guianas a native population insulated from the main brunt of wars and revolutions faced an almost anachronistic wave of missionary work. The Moravians had been active among the black slave populations of Surinam since the mid–seventeenth century and had also briefly evangelized the Lokono (Arawak) of the Corentyn River, but there had been no comparable missionary effort to that in the Spanish and Portuguese territories. Similarly French Jesuits had attempted the evangelization of the Caribs in their territories on the Kourou River, but given the relatively late date of the inception of missionary work in the 1730s and its cessation at the start of the French Revolution in the 1770s, it had not had as profound an impact as elsewhere.

In British Guiana this final wave of colonial missionaries had the dubious distinction of eliminating the last vestiges of native autonomy, less through design than in consequence of the epidemiological differences between Europeans and natives. Coupled with this push into the interior was the manumission of slavery in both British Guiana and, somewhat later, Surinam. This meant not only that a more mobile black population acted as an additional disease vector but also that thousands of indentured laborers were shipped in from the Indian subcontinent, in order to undercut any market in free black labor. The native population therefore formed an ever-diminishing demographic element.

In this new context of national independence and remodeled colonialism, the native population seemed increasingly invisible, both as a separate genetic element and as autonomous society. Only a literal physical isolation preserved them. Across the whole now-empty region, outsiders found myriad opportunities for wildly profitable extraction of natural resources. In place of the "red gold" hunted in colonial times, rubber, timber, and minerals became the object of international capital investment. Both the Amazon and Orinoco were evaluated as commercial highways. Ambitious plans were drawn up to use Mississippi-style steamboats as vehicles of commerce between the Atlantic and Pacific. The ultimate expression of this neo-colonialism was undoubtedly the "rubber boom" in the upper Amazon and Negro at the end of the century, which has become an iconic moment in the historical representation of the native peoples of Amazonia. In the northeastern region there was no similar hunt for *balata* (raw rubber). Indeed it was British and Dutch plantations in Asia that effectively undercut the Amazon market and so burst the bubble of speculation and profit. However, there were a series of gold rushes in both the Guianas and Venezuela in the latter half of the nineteenth century, mirroring the better known Californian and Dakotan episodes in North America. This induced many hundreds of individual miners to invade the interior. All the ills of modernity, not just the infectious ones, went with them. Guns, alcohol, and wage labor, "civilized" nineteenth-century native groups, where spiritual appeal and armed capture could not.

In an apparent "last-gasp" response to this long history of destruction and retreat, messianic and apocalyptic movements sprang up. These occurred in the Rio Negro in the context of the rubber boom, and in upland Guyana and Venezuela in response to the invasion of miners, Protestant missionaries, and Portuguese boundary incursions over the Pirara portage. However, given the long history of prophetic leadership among native peoples, it is hard to judge whether this represented the last desperate expression of a vision of the vanquished, or the persistence of this grand tradition and its reaffirmation. Certainly in Rio Negro and in Guayana, the messiahs were sometimes *criollos*, or white men. One of these movements gave rise to the native religion of *Halleluia*, still practiced today by the Macuxi, Pemon, and Kapon (also called Akawaio) of the highlands, just as the Native American church (known as the Peyote religion) took root amid an analogous North American juncture.

For the most part native peoples across this region were no longer the subject of intense governmental interest, except where they related to issues of boundary demarcation. Demographically, surviving communities were of very small scale, perhaps no more than a few extended families even in the largest of villages. However, in the isolated upland regions, where the gold miners or rubber extractors were not always present, a more restricted native economy did persist into modern times. It is clear that contacts with the Venezuelans, Brazilians, and the still extant European colonies along the Atlantic coast were, and still are, important to these upland groups. Nonetheless they do maintain a measure of autonomy into the twentieth century as reflected in the spread of *Hallelujah*. Even along the larger waterways, the economic and political limitations of the new national governments of Venezuela and Brazil meant that the grandiose schemes for capital investment put forward in the early nineteenth century came to little. The gap between state designs to incorporate national territories fully, and the logistic and infrastructural realities, remains an important source of tension in current dealings with surviving native groups.

The rhetoric of difference, espoused by both native and national leaders, partly obscures the substantive contribution of the native population to the formation of modern nation-states. Equally it obscures the fact that the cultural and social character of native peoples today stems in part from their responses to the colonialism of the last 500 years. It has been the critical contribution of ethnographers to teach us the forms and content of native culture and society in the last 100 years or so, but it is only from a historical appreciation of the forces that shaped these formations that any useful understanding of their meaning and their persistence can be gained.

The rhetoric of difference is also involved in the writing of that history. However, the extension of that rhetoric beyond the brief moments of initial contacts is certainly questionable, because there were no indissoluble barriers between either native or European groupings, as we have seen. "White" Tupís and "Spanish" Arawaks, *Cabanos* as well as "Black," "Red," and "White" Caribs, are therefore all part of this story, even if they cannot be easily assigned to the rhetorical categories of vanquished and victor. Nor should the impacts of the American encounter on Europe be ignored. A cry went up among the poor of Andalucia in the sixteenth century that their land had become the "foreigners' Indies" and that they were treated as "Indians" were.

We may be suspicious, then, of a too-absolute antithesis between the European and the native. Such constructs may always be ignored or overcome in the mundane practice of everyday life. Undoubtedly the materials from which history is written will always supply the means to tell a story of European iniquity and native destruction, a story that has been told and retold since the sixteenth century. It has been the intent of this chapter to suggest that there are many other tales that need to be heard and that they may yet bring us to a new consciousness of the meaning of that long, and still unresolved, confrontation between native peoples and colonial regimes in northeastern South America.

BIBLIOGRAPHIC ESSAY

The potential sources for the understanding of the native history of this region are numerous, including not only scholarly studies but also the various writings of participants in that history – soldiers, missionaries, travelers, traders, and so forth. What follows, therefore, is a brief overview of the main printed and published book-length sources that relate to the issues raised in this chapter. Readers are encouraged to use the bibliographies of these works in turn to seek out further material, particularly those items in scholarly journals and reviews.

Very basic chronological narratives of the course of European occupation and its impact on the native peoples of Brazil can be found in John Hemming's works *Red Gold – The Conquest of the Brazilian Indians 1500–1760* (Cambridge, Mass., 1978) and *Amazon Frontier – The Defeat of the Brazilian Indians* (London, 1987), which takes the narrative up to the present day. These works also contain excellent bibliographies for further reading. The Dutch colonies are treated in C. Goslinga's *The Dutch in the Caribbean and on the Wild Coast, 1580–1680* (Assen, 1971), while the *Cambridge History of Latin America*, edited by Leslie Bethell (Cambridge, 1987) contains chapters by both John Hemming and Charles Gibson on the Spanish and Portuguese treatment of native populations. However, none of these works are concerned with a native perspective on the European occupation.

By contrast the more recent anthropological, as opposed to historical, studies are principally interested in this issue. Good introductory volumes to this current research are *Amazonian Indians – From Prehistory to the Present* (Tucson, 1995) a collection of the work of some twenty Amazonian specialists edited by Anna Roosevelt. A similar volume is the special English/French bilingual issue of the journal *L'Homme* (Paris, vols. 126–128). A general work on the changing views of contact between native South Americans and Europeans can be found in *The Meeting of Two Worlds: Europe and the Americas, 1492–1650* (London, 1995), edited by Warwick Bray. A detailed study of the confrontation of the Caribs and the colonial regimes can be found in N. L. Whitehead, *Lords of the Tiger-Spirit. A History of the Caribs in Colonial Venezuela and Guyana, 1498–1820* (Dordrecht, 1988). Finally, although it is now very much out of date, the *Handbook of South American Indians* (Washington, 1946–1950), edited by Julian Steward, still provides the most accessible compendium of ethnological descriptions of native peoples.

The significance of tropical ecology for human habitation has spawned a large, if specialized literature, that spans geography, botany, and environmental and regional studies. The most salient volumes for those interested in the historical-anthropological issues include *Resource Management in Amazonia: Indigenous and Folk Strategies* (New York, 1989), edited by Darrell Posey and William Balée, and *The Americas before and after 1492: Current Geographical Research* (Annals of the Association of American Geographers 82, #3), edited by Karl Butzer, and *Through Amazonian Eyes* (Iowa, 1993) by Emilio Moran. The issue of "ethnogenesis" has also loomed large of late because questions concerning the continuity between ancient and modern native society, and the meaning of ethnic affiliation, relate closely to the way in which ecological explanation has supplanted historical explanation in this region. The recent volume, *History, Power, and Identity: Ethnogenesis in the Americas, 1492–1992* (Iowa, 1995), edited by Jonathan Hill and Norman Whitten, provides an overview of current contributions on this topic.

The bedrock on which all these general and specialized volumes rests is, of course, the primary documentation itself. The vast majority of this is unpublished material in the national archives of France, the Netherlands, Portugal, Spain, Britain, and to a lesser extent other European countries such as Sweden, Ireland, and Denmark. The Vatican, as spiritual head of the Catholic missionary effort, also holds such materials, as do the individual archives of the various missionary orders. Generally such materials can only be consulted at these locales. However, a number of publication series have made some of the more important documents, or early printed sources, available to scholars in modern editions. These series include the *Colleción de Documentos Inéditos relativos al descubrimiento, conquista y colonización de las posesiones españolas en América y Oceanía*, 42 vols. (Madrid, 1864–1884) and J. K. J. de Jonge's thirteen-volume *De Opkomst van het Nederlandsch gezag in Oost-Indië* (Den Haag, 1862–1888). The *Calendar of State Papers, Colonial Series, America and West Indies.* (London, 1860, 1894). Generally the publications of the *Hakluyt Society* (London), the *Academia Nacional de la Historia* (Caracas), and the *Revista do Instituto Histórico e Geográfico Brasileiro* (São Paulo) offer a number of early titles, some in scholarly translation, as well as collections of primary documentation.

In particular the first chroniclers often record important information about native society before its conquest or collapse. Such is the case with the account of Gaspar de Carvajal, to be found in *The Discovery of the Amazon according to the account of Friar Gaspar de Carvajal and other documents*, edited by J. T. Medina and translated by B. T. Lee (New York, 1934). Also see the *Histoire de la mission des Pères Capucins en l'Isle de Maragnan et terres circinfines[. . .]* (Paris, 1614) by Claude d'Abbeville; Cristobal d'Acuña's "A New Discovery of the Great River of the Amazons," in *Expeditions into the Valley of the Amazons* (London, 1859), edited by C. R. Markham for the Hakluyt Society; Pedro de Aguado's *Recopilacion Historial de Venezuela* (Caracas, 1951); *Relaciónes Geograficas de Venezuela* (Caracas, 1964) edited by C. Arellano-Moreno; J. de Anchieta's *Cartas, informaçoes, fragmentos históricos e semoes* (São Paulo, 1988); Gonzalo Oviedo y Valdes' *Historia General y Natural de las Indias* (Madrid, 1959); and Padre Simon's *Sixth Historical Notice of the Conquest of Tierra Firme* (London, 1861), edited by C. R. Markham for the Hakluyt Society. Accounts of many of the early English expeditions and settlements are collected in Richard Hakluyt's *The Principal Navigations Voyages Traffiques & Discoveries of the English Nation* (Glasgow, 1903–1905) and Samuel Purchas's *Hakluytus Posthumus or Purchas His Pilgrimes* (Glasgow, 1905–1907).

Later works of importance include Samuel Fritz's *Journal of the Travels and Labours of Father Samuel Fritz in the River of the Amazons between 1686 and 1723* (London, 1922), edited by George Edmundson for the Hakluyt Society, as well as Walter Ralegh's *The Discoverie of the Large, Rich and Bewtiful Empire of Guiana* (London, 1596/1848), edited by Neil Whitehead, (Menchester and Norman, 1997), and his companion Lawrence Keymis's *A Relation of a Second Voyage to Guiana* (London, 1596). Robert Harcourt's *A Relation of a Voyage to Guiana* (London, 1613) completes this important English trilogy of exploration in the Guianas, which is supplemented by *Colonising Expeditions to the West Indies and Guiana, 1623–1667* (London, 1924), edited by V. T. Harlow, which brings together a number of such early English sources. Vásquez de Espinosa's *Compendio y Descripcion de las Indias Occidentales* (Madrid, 1969), which describes the first century of Spanish colonization in Venezuela, performs a similar task. An important account of Venezuela in the mid–seventeenth century is Jacinto de Carvajal's *Descubrimiento del Rio Apure* (Caracas, 1648/1956). The French enclave at the mouth of the Amazon is thoroughly described by Claude d' Abbeville in *Histoire de la mission des Pères Capucins en l'Isle de Maragnan et terres circinfines [. . .]* (Paris, 1614), and Yves d'Evreux, *Voyage dans le nord du Brésil, fait durant les années 1613 et 1614*, edited by F. Denis and A. L. Herold (Paris/Leipzig, 1864). The English, Dutch, and French enclaves of the mid–seventeenth century are described in Adriaan van Berkel's *Amerikaansche Voyagien* (Amsterdam, 1695), and Anthoine Biet's *Voyage de la France Equinoxiale en l'isle Cayenne* (Paris, 1664). The later progress of these colonies is covered by Storm van Gravesande's *The Rise of British Guiana – compiled from his despatches*, 2 vols. (London, 1911), edited by C. A. Harris and J. A. J. Villiers for the Hakluyt Society; Pierre Barrère's *Nouvelle Relation de la France Equinoxiale* (Paris, 1743); Jacques Bellin's *Description géographique de la Guiane* (Paris, 1763); Philippe Fermin's *Description générale, historique, geographique et physique de la colonie de Surinam* (Amsterdam, 1769); and Jan Hartsinck's *Beschryvinge van Guiana of de Wildekust in Zuid-Amerika* (Amsterdam, 1770).

The missionaries also left important records in the form of letters, some of which have been published as collections, as in the *Lettres Édifiantes et Curieuses VIII* (Paris 1781); Stæhelin's collection, *Die Mission der Brüdergemiene en Suriname und Berbice im achtzehnten Jahrhundert* (Paramaribo, 1913–1919), and Manuel da Nóbrega's *Cartas do Brasil, 1549–1560*, edited by S. S. Leite et al. (Rio de Janeiro, 1931). The missionaries also produced their own synthetic accounts from such sources, such as Pierre Pelleprat's *Relation des missions des peres Jesuites* in Venezuela (Paris, 1655), Felipe Gilij's *Ensayo de Historia Americana* (Caracas, 1965), Antonio Caulin's *História corográfica, natural y evangélica de Nueva Andalucia* (Caracas, 1966), and José Gumilla's *El Orinoco ilustrado y defendido* (Caracas, 1963).

These latter kinds of missionary sources also initiate systematic ethnological speculation about the indigenous population. But perhaps the first "scientific" approach is to be found in Edward Bancroft's *An Essay on the Natural History of Guiana* (London, 1769). More generally known is Alexander von Humboldt's *Personal Narrative of travels to the equinoctial regions of America* (London, 1852–1853), which covers this northeastern region of South America in some detail. In the nineteenth century such works of science cum travel literature multiply enormously, and only a few can be mentioned here. Henry Bates's *A Naturalist on the Amazon* (London, 1892), J. Chaffanon's *L'Orenoque et Caura* (Paris, 1889); Henri Coudreau's *La France équinoxiale* (Paris, 1887) and *Voyage a travers les Guyanes* (Paris, 1887); Jules Crevaux's *Voyages dans Amérique du Sud* (Paris, 1883); Theodor Koch-Gruneberg's *Zwei Jahre unter den Indianern* (Berlin, 1910); F. P. Penard and A. P. Penard's *De Menschetende Aanbidders der Zonneslang* (Paramaribo, 1907); Richard Schomburgk's *Reisen in Britisch Guiana* (Leipzig, 1841); Johann Spix and C. von Martius's *Travels in Brazil in the years 1817–1820* (London, 1824); Richard Spruce's *Notes of a Botanist on the Amazon* (London, 1908); Karl von den Steinen's *Unter den Naturvolken Zentral-Brasiliens* (Berlin, 1894); A. R. Wallace's *A narrative of travels on the Amazon and Rio Negro* (London,

1889); and Charles Waterton's *Wanderings in South America* (London, 1891).

The late advance of English missionaries in Guiana also saw the publication of important ethnological descriptions, including William Brett's *The Indian Tribes of Guiana* (London, 1868), Charles Barrington-Brown's *Canoe and Camp Life in British Guiana* (London, 1877), and Everard Im Thurn's *Among the Indians of Guiana* (London, 1883). The publication of these kinds of work signals the advent of modern anthropological literature, which can be sampled using the volumes indicated at the beginning of this essay.

21

NEW PEOPLES AND NEW KINDS OF PEOPLE: ADAPTATION, READJUSTMENT, AND ETHNOGENESIS IN SOUTH AMERICAN INDIGENOUS SOCIETIES (COLONIAL ERA)

STUART B. SCHWARTZ AND FRANK SALOMON

Peoples, tribes, and nations are not eternal entities. Of every named and believed-in society, one can ask not just where it came from but also who believed it to be real: its members, outsiders, or both? When, for how long, and why? In South America as elsewhere, colonial regimes, which so often sought to pigeonhole the groups they overpowered, at the same time unintentionally generated new social groups and sometimes whole new societies. These often escaped the ready categories of both American and European thought except under rubrics of social pathology, and yet many believed them to be real. Sometimes the newly generated categories became important to their members' sense of self, and, when mobilized, worked fateful changes on their surroundings. This chapter concerns the processes of ethnogenesis – the ways in which new human groupings came to be, and how they were categorized in colonial cultures. It emphasizes the search for factors contributing to their emergence, or non-emergence, as "new peoples" sharing belief in their own uniqueness, solidarity, and legitimacy. Each section focuses on a particular kind of encounter (rather than on a period or area) and highlights the characteristic ethnogenetic processes it generated.

Overall the chapter argues that while colonial society was prolific of new categories of people, not all new categories of people defined themselves as peoples. And for those that did, there were various choices for group definition besides internalizing the stigma of "mixed blood." Indeed groups that acquired a strong sense of corporate identity tended to define themselves in terms other than "mixture." In the pages that follow we have outlined the political and demographic reasons for these outcomes as well as for persistent "mixed" labeling where it occurred.

To understand the problem one must first of all accept the sheer unfamiliarity of colonial social categories. Colonial society used the language of "birth" (a semantic field including genealogy, supposedly inherited characteristics like color and moral disposition, and hereditary status) to discuss what would later be called "class" and "race." The unequal parts of society were often spoken of in terms of "blood"; people of similar "birth" or "blood" were suitable mates to each other. Bad or good sources and matches of "blood" in one's genealogy determined "purity," which had become an ideological obsession of Spanish Christians well before 1492. "Blood" and "purity" flourished as elements of ideology in Spain's wars against the Moors and Sephardim, and also in dealing with other kinds of Iberian diversity including the presence of enslaved Africans. In the Americas postulants to any high status had to undergo legal proceedings establishing genealogical "cleanness of blood" (i.e., freedom from any taint of non-Christian ancestry). The word "caste" (*casta*), which we now associate with Hinduism, arrived in South Asia as a ready-made Iberian concept referring to the sorts of people defined by "blood." Inequalities of power and class were reproduced through belief that any particular employment or status was appropriate to one *casta*, even diagnostic of it.

Thus people of mixed birth formed not so much a new category as a challenge to categorization itself. The caste idea, by making unequal wealth and power a matter of *qualitative* difference, repelled the idea of smooth gradients among kinds of humans. As a result *any* status claim by "mixed" individuals (and these claims were often quite explicit, taking the form of lawsuits) tended to sound illegitimate. The perception of *mestizaje* ('miscegenation') as a social evil reflects the poor fit between the colonial model, emphasizing bounded social corporations, and America's unprecedented social and class dynamic – a dynamic in which those born across categorical boundaries played increasingly innovative parts as the colonial era advanced and as "mixed" people filled social class roles vital to the colonial economy and state. Racism of the modern sort emerges relatively late in this story, but it does become visible before the dawn of independence.

Ethnogenetic processes run through the whole history of colonial societies and pervade indigenous societies' adaptation to European pressures. Not only at the margins of colonial domains, but even under the noses of urbanites and governors, new peoples kept arising from the interstices of empire. The scarce literature on mestizos and other new groups tends to focus on how colonial states and the Church dealt with these ex post facto. Our aim here is different; it is to clarify their emergence out of, and their impact on, Amerindian societies.

In one sense all the terms by which colonial American humanity typologized itself brought "new peoples" into at least classificatory being, because all reflected novel colonial relationships and distinctions. It is important never to assume that the persistence of a "native" or "prehispanic" label (or for that matter an old Iberian one) implies unchanging continuity. Even a seemingly transparent term like "Spaniard" (*español*) took on altered meanings as it was transformed from a term of birthplace affiliation (a Spaniard being, as was said, a *natural* of Spain) to one associated with the political power of the conqueror and with an exotic bodily type. Other colonial terms like "creole," "mestizo," and "*zambo*" ('Afro-Amerindian') labeled human categories that had not previously been named at all, at least not with the same level of reifying authority as after the conquest of the Americas. Sometimes, too, both Native American and Iberian terms persisted, lexically unchanged, while acquiring a different scope of reference. Modern ethnography clarifies the process; for example, in the 1980s northwest Amazonian peoples, under pressure to present themselves in categories amenable to Colombia's constitutional debate on "multiethnicity," redefined terms formerly referring to language-exogamous clans as names of "ethnic groups." Such reconceptualizations were endemic to colonial practice. Once they occur, and acquire behavioral force through political action, old terms never again refer precisely to their historical precedents.

The flux of colonial social categories often has been set in false antithesis to a firm and primordial indigenous world of permanent tribes and ethnic groups, purportedly existing before European contact or beyond the settlement frontier. It is a basic error to suppose prehispanic society was more stable than societies elsewhere. Native groupings no less than Euro-American ones were products of historical circumstance and definition. American peoples had their own self-and-other paradigms, their own ways of manipulating them, and ample experience of social anomaly and the unforeseen long before 1492. What occurred at the moment of contact was not so much a qualitative novelty as a vast upsurge in the complexity of social contacts among peoples, with drastically noncongruent schemes for describing the results. The upshot is a terminological puzzle woven deep into the fabric of colonial testimony.

CREATION OF NEW INDIGENOUS PEOPLES

The originally mistaken category "Indian" quickly evolved from a cursory overgeneralization to an innovative juridical category with real social consequences, and then, more slowly and ambivalently, to a sign by which peoples identified themselves. The process of making Tupinamba, Collagua, or Pecunche live out the "native" role as exemplars of the supercategories *indios* or *cabôclos*, simultaneously reducing intranative ethnic distinctions to a peculiar concern of subalterns, forms a consistent theme in colonial practice. To the degree that it succeeded, the consolidation of the colonial order during three centuries instilled in most Euro-Americans not growing but dimming consciousness of intra-"Indian" diversity. Nevertheless, long before this lumping term was introduced, and also long after, Amerindian societies had their own ways of making sense out of human diversity. What we know about their "ethno-ethnologies" – their local theories of diversity – indicates that many areas of the continent were already in effervescently ethnogenetic condition when the Spanish arrived. (See Map 21.1)

Archaeological clues and the testimony of native or half-native historians suggest that migration, fission, incorporation, and alliance were taking place among indigenous peoples in the prehispanic scene. Invasion and empire were not novel to western South Americans either. Among state-structured Andean societies, the longstanding practice of organizing production and governance by arranging specialist enclaves over the landscape had evolved into a practice of implanting politically sponsored colonies called *mitmaq*. These outliers remained bound to their home polities, but in their new niches they sometimes mutated into distinctive cultural groups. Along the Inka frontiers in Jujuy, Salta, and Tucumán (of modern Argentina), and on the eastern Andean piedmont among the Arawakans and Guaraní, *mitmaq* peoples would develop distinctive loyalties apart from their homelands. Stateless peoples were also moving and reforming before 1500. The Chiriguano of eastern Bolivia, formed out of Tupi-speaking migrants and Arawakan Guana, won a broad territorial dominance prior to Spanish occupation. Some archaeologists believe the crazy-quilt dispersion of Panoan and other dialectally fragmented language groups along the eastern wall of the Andes in Peru resulted from a long-term struggle for control of riverine bottomlands; less powerful groups may have retreated upstream through the Amazon River system

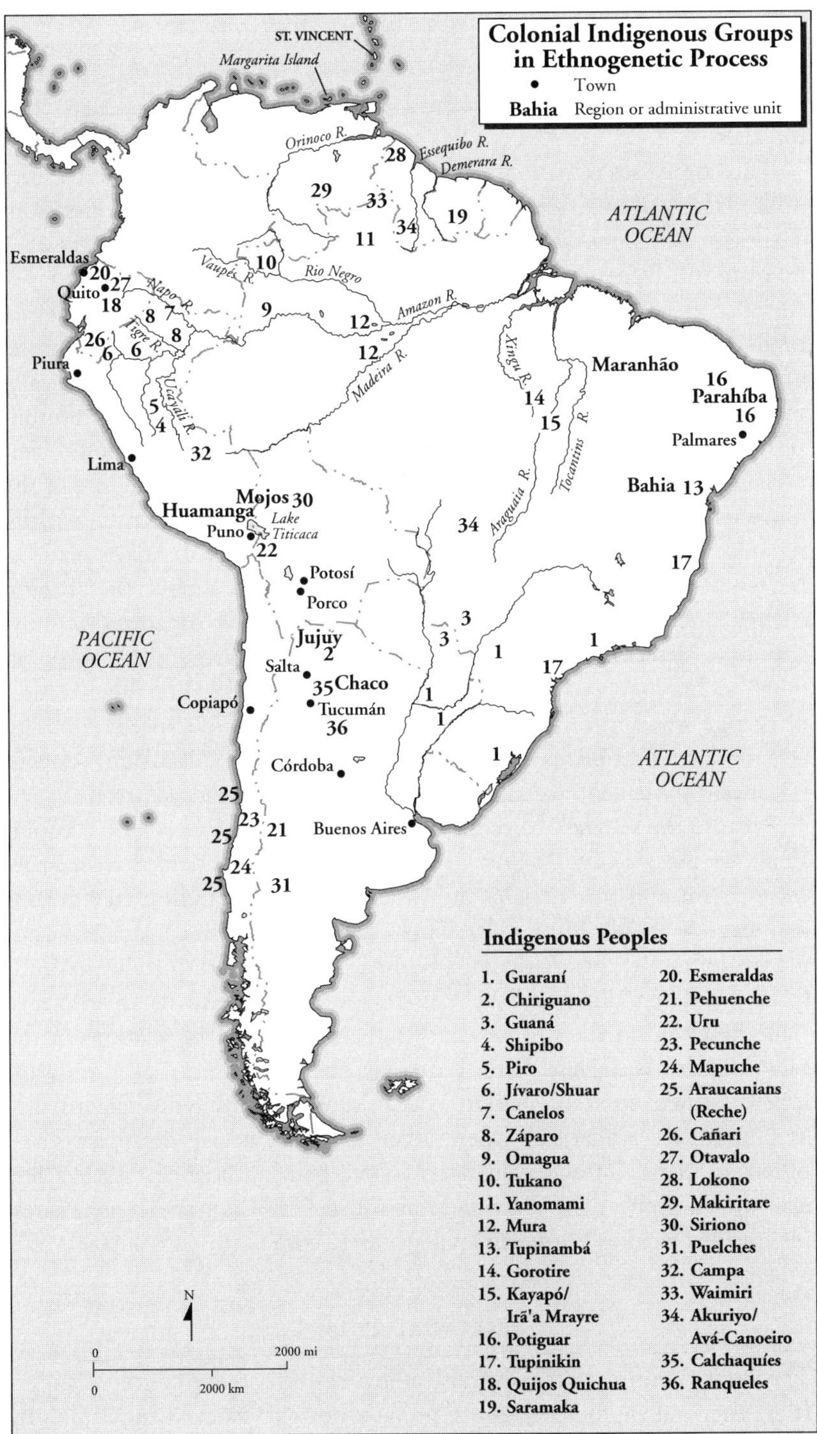
Colonial Indigenous Groups in Ethnogenetic Process
• Town
Bahia Region or administrative unit
ST. VINCENT
Margarita Island
Orinoco R.
Essequibo R.
Demerara R.
ATLANTIC OCEAN
Esmeraldas
Quito
Vaupés R.
Rio Negro
Napo R.
Amazon R.
Tigre R.
Piura
Madeira R.
Xingu R.
Maranhão
Parahíba
Palmares
Ucayali R.
Tocantins R.
Araguaia R.
Lima
Bahia
Mojos
Huamanga
Lake Titicaca
Puno
Potosí
Porco
PACIFIC OCEAN
Jujuy
Salta
Chaco
Copiapó
Tucumán
Córdoba
ATLANTIC OCEAN
Buenos Aires
Indigenous Peoples
1. Guaraní
2. Chiriguano
3. Guaná
4. Shipibo
5. Piro
6. Jívaro/Shuar
7. Canelos
8. Záparo
9. Omagua
10. Tukano
11. Yanomami
12. Mura
13. Tupinambá
14. Gorotire
15. Kayapó/ Irã'a Mrayre
16. Potiguar
17. Tupinikin
18. Quijos Quichua
19. Saramaka
20. Esmeraldas
21. Pehuenche
22. Uru
23. Pecunche
24. Mapuche
25. Araucanians (Reche)
26. Cañari
27. Otavalo
28. Lokono
29. Makiritare
30. Siriono
31. Puelches
32. Campa
33. Waimiri
34. Akuriyo/ Avá-Canoeiro
35. Calchaquíes
36. Ranqueles
N
0 2000 mi
0 2000 km

Map 21.1

until the cordillera, or perhaps Inka political constraints, dammed them together.

Thus processes of fission, readaptation, and recombination, sometimes under state pressure, were well underway before the European invasion. They certainly intensified afterward. Demographic change often triggered innovation. Demographic disasters reminiscent of the Caribbean occurred even in areas of little or no direct European presence, usually as a result of the wildfire Old World–pathogen epidemics or through the unequal spread of new military technology. Population collapse typically forced downward alterations in modular group size, rigidity of kinship arrangements, and sociopolitical centralization. The "Columbian exchange" of biota devastated complex societies and, as in the case of the Omagua of Ecuador and Brazil, led to the breakup of dense, wealthy riverine agricultural societies into separately recognized village peoples. Indeed South America's few hunter-gatherer groups, such as the Sirionó, though once taken to represent survivals of primitive organization, now appear to descend from groups that adapted to aggression by stripping down technology and organization for mobility's sake. But the direction of change was not uniform. Where horses made possible speedy mobility and communication, as among Chilean Mapuche, invasion fostered larger and more centralized federations than had existed before.

Because the stateless bases of precolumbian organization lacked equivalents in most *conquistadores'* experience, Europeans tended to misperceive them, and this remains an obstacle to understanding endogenous and reactive change historically. Thus when the Spanish chronicler Gumilla wrote in 1745 that Taricura, a Barima chieftain, had thirty wives, each from a different "nation," he was describing the basis of an extensive trade network on the Orinoco rather than international relations in the sense the words suggest. Early European observers often used European-style classifiers such as "nation" (inappropriately implying territoriality and linguistic affiliation) when other kinds of social organizations – phratries, clans, lineages, alliances – were being described. With a few exceptions, such as the matrilineal strain in Chibchan power structures, institutions lacking European analogs rarely come into clear focus.

COLONIAL TRIBES

The most common, but most misleading, classifier is the concept "tribe." It is often taken to represent a peculiar sort of stateless but militarily assertive society. Yet warlike stateless societies with multiple settlements and shared political identity seem not to be a spontaneous stage of evolution among stateless peoples. Rather they arise in areas where the outer fringes of state power pressed on peoples without states. Permanent outliers of states, such as extractive enclaves and trading ports, usually create demand for buffer zones patrolled by a militia. The most effective militias usually are recruited among natives of extant societies. By recognizing leaders and providing weapons, Europeans precipitated new and violent political dynamics, which they themselves then misperceived as primordial. Usually of heterogeneous origin, the resultant colonial tribes tended to pick up elements of European culture, such as insignia based on military uniforms, as emblems of emerging solidarity. Sometimes colonial tribes developed strong feelings of peoplehood and legitimacy, seeing themselves as potent possessors both of the universal truths revealed by Christianity, and of vitality rooted in local nature and supernature. The relation between "tribes" and states is pervasively paradoxical, because state governors tended to see in them the very opposite of governance, yet states – Spain, Portugal, France, Holland, and England conspicuously among them, and possibly the Inka state as well – regularly depended on "friendly tribes" in arms to buffer their own frontiers and capture runaways. When colonial tribal politics became an option for building indigenous identities, older elements of kinship and marriage, reciprocal political favor, trade, and common language acquired a potent new dimension: They could become sources for the power that grew from the barrel of a gun. In the long run, however, colonial tribes almost always proved highly vulnerable to dangerous political relations of dependency. Colonial tribes typically resided in the paths of infectious epidemics, and liquor traffic added epidemic addiction to their weaknesses. Women of colonial tribes lived at risk of sexual exploitation when European soldiers or traders demanded concubines. Many such groups fell into debt peonage as agriculture and extractive industry advanced, or suffered cannon-fodder mortality where frontiers met resistance.

Native American access to European trade goods and technology furthered the political rise of colonially aligned groups and élites at the expense of others. Colonial tribal warfare was a dangerous game for all players. It is still a contentious issue whether Amazonian and Orinoquian warfare complexes reflect "peripheral" peoples' never-ending struggle to gain access to European goods and alliances, or whether they reflect endogenous competition driven by tropical forest ecological and demographic stresses. For example, scholars debate whether modern warfare and violence among the Yanomami, a large forest-dwelling group on the Venezuelan-Brazilian frontier, grows endogenously from local culture and ecology or rather began with slaving, warfare, and disease in the seventeenth century. Needs for defense against Europeans, as in the case of the Chilean Reche (Araucanians) or needs to cooperate with them, as among the Spanish-assisted Carib Lokono, could both militarize indigenous society and transform its social organization and practice. Among the Yanomami, for example, warfare heightened the status of aggressive males, giving them an advantage in wife selection, and lowered the traditional status of women. Variations on this theme were played out across the hemisphere after contact.

During early wars of conquest, and in subsequent civil strife and imperial defense, Europeans' Indian allies like the Cañaris in Peru, or the Tupiniquim in Brazil, provided the colonial powers with indispensable military force. A good example is provided by the Tupi-speaking Potiguar in sixteenth-century Brazil. After a series of bitter wars against the French-allied Potiguar of Paraíba, the Portuguese concluded a peace and then moved a large contingent of them to Bahia to combat the Aimoré. The Portuguese reasoning was that the Aimoré could only be defeated by "forest creatures [*bicho do mato*] like themselves" and that the Potiguar taken from their homeland would not be able to rebel again. Later the Potiguar were deployed as shock troops against other Indian groups and against runaway black slaves. Their chief, Zorobabe, took advantage of his position to sell captives as slaves and purchase the accoutrements of European military status. Such power eventually made him dangerous to the colony, and he was eventually exiled to Portugal. The Portuguese colonial administrators generally remained ambivalent about the power of their indigenous allies, but some Portuguese who depended on them called *Brazis* (Brazilian Indians) the "walls and bulwarks" of the colony.

The categories "Carib" and "Arawak" are conspicuous examples of how new colonial relations altered the scope of old terms (Map 21.2). In Guiana and Venezuela the Karinya (also spelled Kariña) and other groups allied to the Dutch became known as Caribs, whereas the Lokono, in the service of the Spanish, were labeled Arawaks. The attributions were made without reference to language use. "Carib" identity – the word is cognate to 'cannibal' and connoted unreasoning bellicosity – was, in fact, formed and reinforced by hostilities with Spaniards rather than by the actual distribution of Cariban languages. The most famous colonially catego-

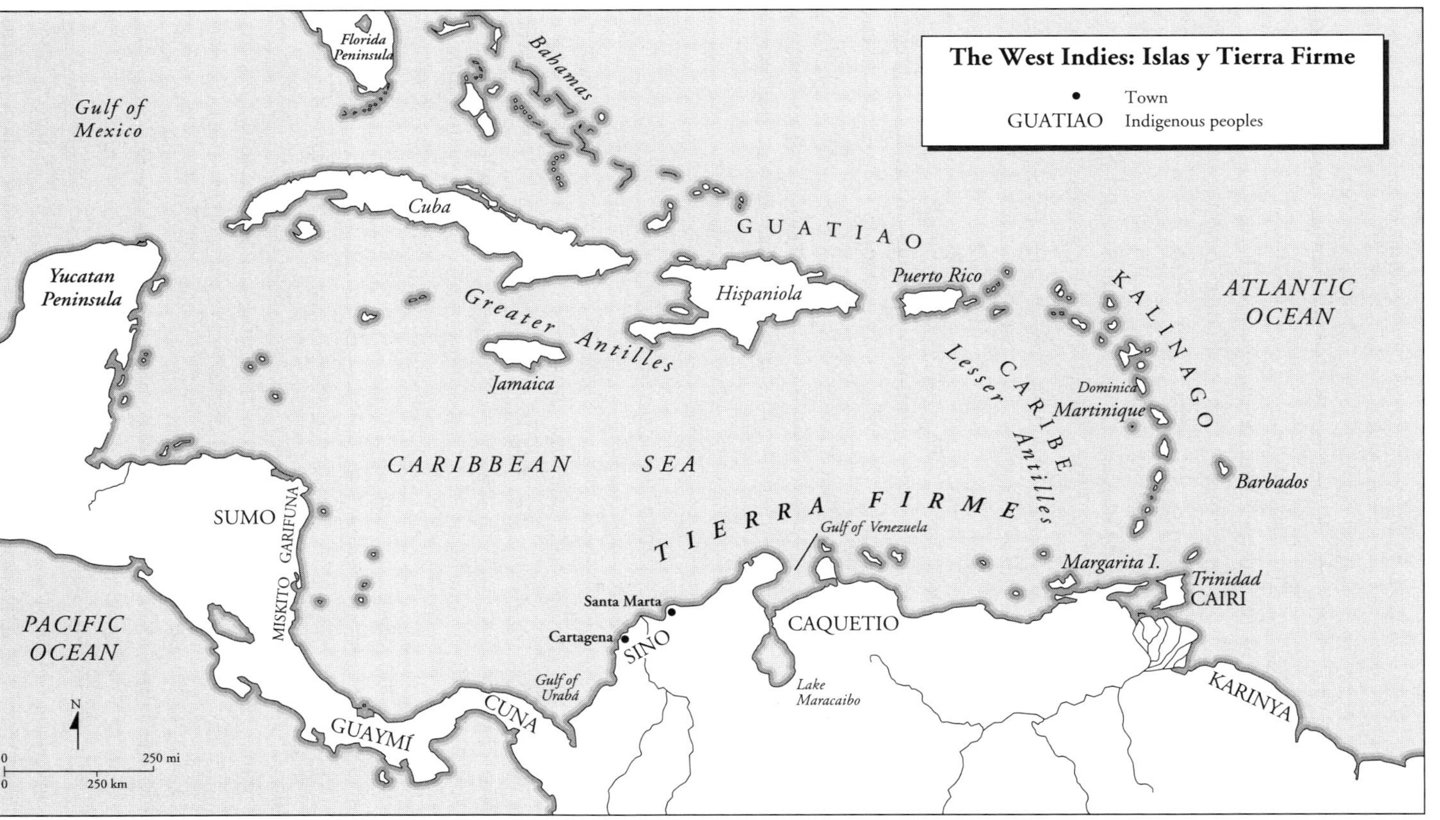
The West Indies: Islas y Tierra Firme
Town
GUATIAO Indigenous peoples
Gulf of Mexico
Florida Peninsula
Bahamas
Cuba
GUATIAO
Yucatan Peninsula
Greater Antilles
Hispaniola
Puerto Rico
KALINAGO
ATLANTIC OCEAN
Jamaica
Lesser Antilles
CARIBE
Dominica
Martinique
Barbados
CARIBBEAN SEA
TIERRA FIRME
Gulf of Venezuela
SUMO
GARIFUNA
MISKITO
Margarita I.
Trinidad
CAIRI
Santa Marta
Cartagena
SINO
CAQUETIO
PACIFIC OCEAN
Gulf of Urabá
Lake Maracaibo
KARINYA
N
0
250 mi
0
250 km
CUNA
GUAYMÍ

Map 21.2

rized "Caribs" were the Kalinago or "Island Caribs," who spoke an Arawakan language but had through trade and contact taken on Carib cultural elements including a warrior dialect with Karinya loan words.

Some colonial tribes formed not as auxiliaries to white frontier forces but as agglomerations of people displaced by them. A few of these also had their day as regional military powers. One, the Muras, coalesced in the Portuguese state of Maranhão along the Madeira and Rio Negro in the eighteenth century. The Mura were formed by groups who had fled missions, remnants of defeated villages, mestizos, deserters, and escaped black slaves. Their leader, Ambrosio, had been a mission Indian; he had a mestiza half-sister and a white captive brother-in-law. In 1785 a Portuguese officer recognized the Muras' composite makeup: "The empire of these miserable wretches is large, composed of many different languages and people kidnapped from the villages and people who have taken refuge among them, all going by the name of Mura." The Andoas, Quijos Quichua, and Xebero are peoples of the upper Amazon tributaries who also seem to have formed as gatherings of diverse ethnic fragments forged together under frontier pressures.

INDIANS: A NEW PEOPLE

For the Andean peoples, it was often direct coercion that forged new categories. As the Spanish state and church in the thickly peopled highlands acquired the ability not only to meddle among and then rule over native polities but even to enter and reorganize them from within, the category "Indian" gradually changed from a mere overgeneralization, in the service of political haste, to a consequential principle. As the crown sent more and more "laws of the Indies," legislators and administrators, missionaries and would-be feudal lords all strove to make American natives behave in practice as the various normative definitions of "Indians" dictated. Some Spaniards, those of Las Casian bent, saw the task as a matter of realizing the natives' naturally good inclinations under relative autonomy; others, like Viceroy Toledo (who ruled 1569–1581), understood Spanish sovereignty as a mandate to work the Andean "nations" into the fabric of empire as a closely supervised vassal peasantry. In the course of forcing natives into the new institutional forms that were to contain them, Spaniards imposed new and fateful constraints such as converting to Christianity, paying money tribute, working in forced labor detachments, and recognizing written records as supreme among forms of social knowledge. Each of these would become imperatives of behavior for millions of natives. The task of working within them (especially in the seventeenth century) would build a whole repertory of social habits around the originally vacuous word "Indian."

Because it was in the densely settled highlands of the old Inka domains that Phillip II and his successors most intensively enforced absolutist plans, these areas became the most revealing theater for studying how a galaxy of varied cultures became, as one anonymous Quechua writer put it in 1608, "the people called Indians."

The actual means of transformation are well documented, because the change that Spanish programs produced was as closely monitored as it was profound. In the 1570s Spain instituted a policy of *reducción*, or forced resettlement in nucleated parishes, in the face of population decline and colonial labor needs. This dislocated thousands of Indians and reshuffled peoples all over former Inka domains. The project to concentrate dispersed agropastoral settlements into uniform European-style towns rarely succeeded as planned, but its unintended results were somewhat regular if not uniform. They include the enduring antithesis between "native" outlands and high slopes, and "civilized" parish centers. In the face of population decline, tightening tribute and the regimen of forced labor quotas drove thousands from home and reshuffled whole populations. "Indian" villages continued to consist of named corporate parts called *ayllus*, defined on kinship criteria (usually as ancestor-focused kindreds) or "sectors" (*parcialidades*) on political ones. But intergroup relations were shifting from patterns that rested on ritualized reciprocity (or hostility) and Inka political distinctions to patterns based on relations of indirect rule, estate-like inequality, fortunes in the mercantile arena, and "foral" legalism. New forms of subordination replaced old and in doing so altered the implications of ethnicity even when terms stayed constant.

For example, the Uru of Bolivia were a farflung and anciently rooted group that had long been losing territory and some of its varied economic roles to the Aymara *curacazgos*. The Spanish regime tended to ratify Aymara lords' encroachments on Uru lands and their inclusion of Uru *ayllus* within Aymara polities. Over the long term the Uru were transformed into an ethnic underclass or pariah people. Driven down to, and literally into, Lake Titicaca, Urus became specialized in fishing and canoe hunting. The very term Uru acquired a stigma, representing the primitiveness and savagery that Andean natives associated with nonagricultural peoples. The diversity of their old territory and their former wealth was forgotten. Modern Aymara, paradoxically, regard the Uru as being a primordial people – the very example of timeless primitivity.

Colonial alterations in the schemata of social difference were occurring within the bosoms of most communities. New sectors and *ayllus* were recognized on the basis of residence, occupation, and circumstance. By the 1570s the distinction between *originarios*, or those born in a local community, and *forasteros*, or "outsiders" licensed as resident aliens, was well established all over the vast Peruvian viceroyalty. In time "outsider" *ayllus* became rooted and came to consist mostly of locally born people, without much connection to the *ayllu*'s village of origin. But as people took to the roads to avoid tribute levies in their homes, villages kept receiving "newcomer outsiders" (*forasteros advenedizos*), recent arrivals who belonged only conditionally to *ayllus* and might leave at will. Such people sometimes integrated into local populations by marrying in, by obtaining the local *kuraka*'s recognition, or by procuring the creation of whole new "outsider *ayllus*." Such units no longer claimed the common ancestor-focused descent central to older ideas of *ayllu*. The scale of this process of dislocation in the Andean world was enormous, involving hundreds of thousands of individuals. It has been suggested that the severe population drop among village "Indians" recorded in Alto Peru (now Bolivia) from 1573 to 1683 was as much due to the redefinition of "Indians" as "outsiders," vagrants, or *yanacona* (dependent servitors), and to migrations, as to actual deaths. By the mid–seventeenth century Peru had over 25,000 more or less uprooted servants. By the 1680s about half of the almost 65,000 workers subject to the mine labor draft of Potosí were "outsiders." In 1754 Alto Peru alone (roughly modern Bolivia) had 88,000 Indians listed as *originarios* and almost 55,000 "outsiders."

Did these changes result in the constitution of "new peoples" in the Andes? They probably did, but not by any such direct route as a coalescence of ethnic feeling bounded by categories like *yanacona* or "outsider." Rather state policies intended to drive the anomalous groups – unattached "outsiders," masterless servants, and "Indian vagrants" – into governable, taxable units, tended to foster the growth of populations with a very fluid, situationally manipulable sense of collective self. Although colonial bureaucrats, and perhaps some native lords, too, saw the spread of vagabondage and uncontrolled migration as a disruptive social pathology, at the same time all came to rely upon the existence of the very categories they deplored. For example, Spanish demand for literacy and bicultural competence in some native social roles (not only aristocratic roles but also humbler ones like village council scribe) produced thousands of people called *ladinos* (bicultural natives) all over the Andes. *Ladinos*, as cultural game players, incurred the distrust of both native peers and Spanish élites; in colonial usage the word connoted an ugly sort of cunning as well as a valuable competence. Similarly both Spaniards and native élites depended on a sector of mobile labor flowing among the ensconced blocs of village and city dwellers. To some extent the "shrinking net" of kin-structured relations that remained the core of Andean village organization succeeded in enduring the first two colonial centuries precisely because the unrecognized, uncategorized native people absorbed its have-nots and served its haves. The multiplication of people who were "Indians" in a situationally fluid sense has had a profound and enduring impact on Andean social relations. Even in the presence of highly corporate Indian villages, it helped prevent Andean "Indianness" from taking on the simple either–or quality that North American reservation systems have imparted.

Some of the most marked modern ethnic identities date not from remote prehispanic times but from the mid- or late colonial readjustments to the colonial situation. Certain groups seem to have built uniqueness on occupational roles: The identity of Bolivian Kallawayas, a people with prestige as healers, seems to have crystallized around the role of lowland–highland long-distance traders and consequently as connoisseurs of shamanic power. The obscure Ecuadorian Collaguazos (a minor group c. 1550), apparently parlayed itself into a position of prominence as it found urban niches and supplied proxy governors to the Spanish state.

Even when the colonial process preserved the peoplehood of Inka-era ethnic groups, this hardly occurred by the encystment and preservation of unchanging cultural essentials (as an older indigenism supposed). Rather a dual process of countervailing but inseparable tendencies shaped the Andean societies. On one hand, the legitimacy of local authorities rested on ability to maintain village control over resources (including cultural resources such as non-Christian shrines) and to uphold the moral economy of reciprocity. On the other hand, the continued existence of Andean collectivities as such in the larger setting required involvement in an unequal dialogue of power. Because by the late sixteenth century a working insertion of communities into the state apparatus had become unavoidable, every Andean community found ways to package its social organization within broadly "colonial Quechua" categories – that is, within a small inventory of simplified concepts such as *ayllu* and *cacicazgo* (colonial chieftainship) that the state employed as common denominators across ethnic differences. Recasting Andean organization in these terms involved a substantial amount of "invented tradition" (such as reinterpreting noble succession to make it resemble the patrilineal system of European dynasties). Much like the African rulers whom the British empire stamped into a mold of kingship, Andean authority structures were made over to square with a priori notions of the legitimate "native lord." The making of native lordship entailed canonizing certain versions of Andean mythohistory as truer than others; Urton shows how one village got its particular origin shrine ratified as the mythic place where the first Inka came out of the earth. Many versions of genealogy and hierarchy were generated as useful intercultural simplifications for such limited political contexts. But the resultant representations of collective selfhood gained immense importance in maintaining a strategy for survival. Like innumerable "cultural creolizations" throughout the colonial world, such representations eventually acquired apparent solidity, acceptance, and even the status of legitimate symbols of identity. In time colonial symbols, of Indianness, such as the staff of communal office, originally conferred as signs of a political authority countervailing *against* the "native lords," would be defended to the death as tokens of native legitimacy.

RELIGION AND THE INDIAN SENSE OF PEOPLEHOOD

Another realm in which the sense of collective self and other underwent drastic changes was that of cult and conversion. Ritual life welds a group together and perpetuates its hierarchies. Conversion and Christian missions disrupted "symbolic reproduction" everywhere. In the Andes Catholic clergy succeeded before 1570 in suppressing most of the great regional and interethnic ritual foci, such as the pilgimages in which people of varied ethnicity visited the sacred mountain Paria Caca, or the cult of Inka mummies. Local shrines and mummies did survive, and their cults fostered a long-lasting association between non-Christian worship and village localism.

In some areas, especially lowlands, missionaries did much more. Franciscans and Mercediarians, among others, physically relocated indigenous peoples at mission stations, creating economic dependencies, epidemics, and legal subordination as "neophytes." Missionary activity was especially vigorous along the margins of Iberian settlement, among semisedentary farmers like the Guaraní or the Tupi-speakers of coastal Brazil. Although missionaries and colonial governments were sometimes sensitive to ethnic and linguistic distinctions, fiscal and political pressures tended to drive a policy of mixing peoples together. In 1749 the Jesuit Father João Daniel reported missions along the Amazon in which thirty to forty different nations gathered together, many speaking mutually unintelligible languages. The thirteen missions of Mojos (Bolivia) in 1802 contained thirty distinct groups who spoke seven different languages. Missionaries sometimes used their neophytes to attract new groups to their tutelage, a tactic that resulted in further mixing of groups.

The promotion of particular indigenous languages as missionary *lingua franca* was a logical response to the ethnic situation in mixed missions. Today, speaking Quechua (in the Andean countries) or a Tupian language (in Amazonia) is considered a strong index of "Indian-ness." It has generally been forgotten that the vast spread of the two multiethnic American languages, Quechua and Nhengatu or Tupian *lingua geral*, were both eminently colonial processes. Before 1532 Quechua had spread repeatedly through the Andes, outward from a hearth somewhere in central Peru: first as a trading language, and again as the imperial tongue when Inka administrators seized on its wide usage to promote it as a language of state. But the language landscape that the Spaniards found remained one of immense heterogeneity, with Quechua sprinkled through it as a skill of élites, functionaries, and enclaves of people assimilated to Inka mores. Faced with unmanageable diversity, the Spanish state opted periodically for unrealistic plans to force learning of Spanish. The Church, however, devised, and efficiently practiced, a plan to seize on the extant "general language" – Quechua – and promote it as the language of Christianity. The first books published in South America were published as teaching materials for this effort (from 1584 onward). Within the old Inka domains it was the colonial officialization of Quechua which seems to have led to the extinction and near-extinction of numerous Andean ethnic tongues such as Cañari and Pukina (many of which lasted until the eighteenth century, and a few of which barely struggle on today). Of the non-Quechua languages only one, Aymara, remains in massive Andean use.

Meanwhile under Spanish and then Creole rule, Quechua surged forward to become by an immense margin the most spoken and the most far-flung of Native American languages. Not only did the padres succeed in making Quechua speech the hallmark of Indian legitimacy within the old Inka bounds; they promoted it in missions beyond them. Indeed the oldest extant grammar of the Quechua of the Ecuadorian-Colombian north, belonging to the late seventeenth century, seems to be a "how-to" book for getting natives along the old Inka frontier to behave as proper Indians, by speaking Quechua. Apparent traces of this late expansion are visible all around the fringes of Quechua's immense distribution: in southernmost Colombia; in the Ecuadorian and Peruvian Amazon headwaters, as for example among the Canelos, Andoas, and Quijos; in the northwestern marches of Argentina; and in the central Chilean lands where Spaniards continued an inconclusive Inka war against Araucania.

Missionization in many places produced synthetic, heterogenous societies in which former ethnic identities were overshadowed by a new collective identity originally imposed from outside. Prime examples of this process were the rise of Nhengatu or *lingua geral*, a homogenized form of Tupi, as the language of communication between the missionaries and their charges in Brazil.

As native peoples reacted to colonialism by forging local sacred ideologies, the decisive steps were often reconceptualizations of cultural "self" and "other." Mesoamericanists and Andeanists have both noted that in early colonial days, Amerindians tended to count Europeans as a foreign group of the same conceptual order as foreign Amerindians. Indeed the sense of "otherness" attached at first much more strongly to stereotyped native "others," such as Inka overlords and invaders, forest "savages," or hostile ethnic groups in adjacent valleys, than it did to the little-known and numerically insignificant Spanish seaborne raiders. Even after the Pizarran invasion, early political encounters in which Andean polities like the Cañari forged alliances on initially favorable terms, allowed hopes of autonomy among Europeans – or rather, the alternative to it had not been foreseen. Only after the collapse of negotiated relations, and the rapid rise of a steamrolling colonial power, did the realization dawn that Christians required not merely conversion but the destruction of the Andean deities. By the 1560s these factors combined to challenge the old concept of otherness: clearly Europe was a whole new kind of "other."

The cardinal events in realigning the peoples in Amerindian consciousness were the radical nativist movements that shook parts of South America within the first lifetime after invasion: the roughly contemporaneous Taki Unquy in Peru (1563) and *santidade* cults on the Brazilian coast (1559 to c. 1610). Nativism was significant not just in its radical refusal of the new power constellation; it also gathered the sacred symbols of many native peoples who had formerly considered each other foreign, on the same side of a great divide across which loomed the European power. In both movements the self-recognition of an overarching native category – "Indian" meaning authochtonous and legitimate, and not merely meaning tribute-bound – set the ideological framework for resistance that would flare at several later times.

Sometimes resistance movements expressed pointed historical ironies. The Inka, seen as oppressors and enemies by many groups prior to the European arrival, became the very embodiment of native legitimacy within only a half-century after it. The Ecuadorian Cañari, whose tombs and mummies their former Spanish allies had desecrated and looted in the 1560s, came to think of themselves as the progeny of the same Inka whom their great-grandparents had battled. As Inka political power ended, Inka identity, a symbol of supralocal civilization, took on special importance for disrupted ethnic groups or newly formed composites.

Inka-ism, or the "Andean Utopia," as Flores Galindo named it, developed repeatedly over the three colonial centuries into prophecies of an impending return of a divine "Inka king" who would vindicate all Indians and reverse the order of the world by granting America supremacy over Spain. In northern Ecuador nearly two centuries after the invasion, Otavalan Indians broke into festive neo-Inka enthusiasm on learning that a man of partly Inka ancestry had been appointed to a local government post. When the appointee, Don Alonso Arenas Florencia Inka, arrived on the scene, he showed his would-be-followers' charts thought to demonstrate genealogical links between local native notables and his own imperial Inka forebears. Spanish higher-ups perceived this as dangerously subversive, because they thought it implied the promotion of a rival monarchy to Spain's crown. A quick repressive prosecution snuffed out the excitement.

Most Indian revolts in the upper Amazon after 1570 – like that of the Pendes (1573; the term *pende* refered to shaman-preachers) or the Jívaro (i.e., Shuar, 1590) – were instigated and led by dissident mestizos who made it their mission to proclaim Indian-ness as a domain equal in worth and power to Spanish power. Some of the mestizo messiahs preached among Andean Indians sent to the lowland gold washings. Most had strong neo-Inka leanings. The memorable rebellion of Juan Santos, a highland Indian or mestizo who settled among the "Campa" (i.e., Asháninka), posed the most serious threat to Spanish authority in Peru up to the great rebellions of the 1780s. For a decade (1742–1752) Santos's bowmen included former mission Indians, some Asháninka *caciques*, Shipibo, and many highland deserters, as well escaped slaves and freedmen who combined to wage an effective guerilla war against the Spanish.

INTRA-INDIGENOUS *MESTIZAJE*?

By various routes colonialism brought together previously endogamous native groups and generated populations that, while clearly "Indian," escaped both native and Spanish ethnological pigeonholes. In Amazonia this process had a lot to do with clustering around poles of successful resistance; in the Andes it tended to follow urbanism and labor migration.

Although a few lowland South American groups managed to fight Spain off decisively, not even these were so disconnected from the rest of Native America as popular histories of hidden "tribes" suggest. The most astonishing of Amerindian victories over Europe was the "Jívaro" (Shuar) reconquest of several upper Amazon tributaries at the turn of the seventeenth century. They had a reputation for savagery, and perhaps cultivated it; whereas "pacified" Amazonians came under the disastrous *encomienda* regime, those classed as neophytes or infidels fell under the more manipulable regime regulating recent converts. As a result the "Jívaro" and the neighboring Záparo became magnets for a variety of groups in search of safety. People in their zone might escape colonization, or if it reached them, they would at least enter under relatively good conditions.

This process had ethnogenetic consequences. Areas where European colonization collapsed or was beaten back tended to attract individuals or multiple splinter groups fleeing missionary or slaving pressure elsewhere. How they related to each other varied widely. In the region of the Napo and Tigre rivers, now in Ecuador, a flux of individual fugitives gave rise to short-lived nontribal collectivities. Without a permanent European presence, these groups were not exactly colonial tribes, nor did they homogenize into generic "Indians"; vagueness of identity was itself an adaptive response because it afforded outsiders no handles on which to attach institutional links. In other places whole named groups, such as the Akuriyo and Waimiri of the Orinoco Basin, apparently retreated to safety. The Tupinambarana of the Amazon were reportedly a group that had migrated from the Brazilian coast in the sixteenth century to avoid contact.

Slaving was a powerful force in creating conglomerate "tribes," both from the flux of individuals and the movement of whole groups; slave raiders penetrating ever farther up the Amazon tributaries unintentionally crystallized a demographically unstable, floating neo-indigenous stratum known as Tapuias into what Portuguese observers took to be a tribe. The process of forced ethnogenesis through slaving bears a rough likeness to the forging of Afro-American culture, as Mintz and Price have delineated it, among the diverse Africans thrown together by servitude.

Once in a while the grouping of disparate clusters in safe areas gave rise to durable social constellations. The Canelos Quichua on the Ecuadorian headwaters of the Amazon arose as a multiethnic conglomerate of intermarrying Quijos, Achuar, and Zaparoans, all of whom adopted the Quichua language. In much of the western Amazon, the rubber boom of the nineteenth century seems to have been a catalyzing moment for such conglomerations. On the Lower Urubamba the Piro maintain a tradition that their ancient kin groups, or *neru*, did not marry each other but that during the rubber boom enslavement forced them to wed each other and also Matsiguenka and mestizos so that they are now "mixed people." Similarly on the Ucayali most of the present groups of Pano speakers are the result of historical fusions.

Partly because Amerindians tended to map organizational changes in kinship terms, fusions sometimes took place along prestructured lines. The Cubeo, a Tukanoan people of the northwest Amazon, apparently originated in a self-conscious attempt to reconstruct a damaged hierarchical set of descent groups. Along the Upper Rio Negro, Arawak-speaking peoples devastated by epidemics returned from headwater areas near the Spanish into lower waters in the hope of rebuilding ranked phratries.

In the Andes, too, native groups reassembled themselves into unprecedented combinations. Even in the countryside, prehispanic regional cultures passed to the hands of people rapidly absorbing newcomers who their ancestors would have considered foreign. Karen Powers argues that the seeming continuity of Ecuador's Quichua-speaking ethnic groups is actually the product of two ethnogenetic transformations. In the early colonial era, as Andean households fled labor levies and epidemics, native lords scooped up huge numbers of migrant families to build whole sectors of resident alien (*forastero*) tributaries. The strategy filled old political vessels, the *cacicazgos*, with a new human substance irreducible to inherited categories but capable of holding its own politically during the first colonial century. However, "demographic movements . . . accelerated the process of resource divestment and the decline of the colonial *cacique*." From 1680 on "intruder *caciques*" aligned with Spanish interests made native political units more harmful than helpful to the reproduction of households and *ayllus*. It was in other vessels that reconstituted ethnic groups took their now-recognizable forms: It was "the cultural predilection of ordinary Andeans to reconstruct the social organization of the *ayllu* inside the Spanish *obraje-hacienda* [textile mill-latifundium] complex that permitted ethnic and cultural survival."[1]

Meanwhile Spanish cities also collected large numbers of Indians more or less detached from their nominal homes. This process fostered Andean versions of intra-indigenous *mestizaje*. Lima's, Quito's, and Arequipa's city councils repeatedly set up designated satellite settlements to hold the labor force hired by Spanish urbanites. Like Johannesburg's Soweto four centuries later, they were designed for rigid segregation. The name of Lima's official Indian ghetto, El Cercado, means 'the enclosure', derived from a word meaning 'fence'. Founded in 1570 El Cercado was a separate parish with a different ritual calendar from the Spanish city. All the same El Cercado became a forcing house of acculturation. A mid–seventeenth century Spanish historian[2] wrote that "its residents . . . are so hispanicized that all of them, both men and women, understand and talk our language, and in their bodily grooming and the ornamentation of their houses, they seem Spanish. And to prove this, it suffices to say that they have over eighty black slaves." El Cercado also housed a school, where Jesuits taught young native nobles the norms of colonial *curacazgo*, and a walled "house of seclusion," where they brainwashed natives implicated in "idolatries." Less regulated native neighborhoods grew without permission in other parts of the city, especially near major markets, housing artisans, marketeers (often women, who appear early on as important retailers), sellers of coca and alcoholic drinks, craftsworkers, and temporary migrants. In other neighborhoods Indian servants lived in Spanish households, and some native families of Inka descent had servants of their own. Most cities designated certain parishes to give urban Indians

[1] Karen Vieira Powers, *Andean Journeys: Migration, Ethnogenesis, and the State in Colonial Quito* (Albuquerque, 1995), 173.

[2] Bernabé Cobo, *Historia del nuevo mundo* [1653] (Madrid: Biblioteca de Autores Españoles, 1964), vol. 2, 352–355.

the sacraments. Many communicants, however, were devoted to such churches as Quito's great Franciscan church, where Inka and aboriginal nobles patronized Indian sodalities that served the poor as credit unions and burial societies.

In the *cercado* of Lima, women played a disproportionate role as pioneers of urban Indian lifeways. They outnumbered men by about three to two in the Toledan census, accumulated more bicultural expertise because their work brought them inside Spanish families, and "dominated the marketplace."[3]

Amidst this dynamic and turbulent native urbanism, a great many Indians who had roots and rights in one of the sierra's pre-Inka ethnic chiefdoms married or just lived with mates from other groups. Early urban parish books like those of Quito's El Sagrario contain records of their marriages and baptisms, including the names of their home communities and godparents. In Quito godparents were often of African origin. The children of these unions were, in a sense, intra-indigenous mestizos: Fully Indian, they were nonetheless only equivocally members of any one Indian society. Not much is known about the life trajectories of those who first lived out the identity of generic "Indian." Most seem to have been poor, and many were active in the bustling market sector, where having numerous attenuated ties was perhaps worth more than having fewer and more englobing ones. The city also housed a privileged and indeed exclusivist "new people," the native high society comprised of colonially coopted Inka lineages and the aboriginal nobility married into them or connected by ritual kinship. Some early colonial Inka seem to have been glamorous people, patronized by Spanish élites and social climbers from both native and Spanish society.

INCORPORATING NON-INDIAN OTHERS

So far we have emphasized Amerindian ways of reorganizing or recombining Amerindian populations to deal with the European challenge. But at the physical and social margins of the colonial world, and also in cities, indigenous societies needed to incorporate people of European, African, or mixed birth.

Absorbing strangers was not of course an unprecedented issue. Indian

[3] Elinore C. Burkett, "Indian women and white society: The case of sixteenth-century Peru," in Asunción Lavrin (ed.), *Latin American Women: Historical Perspectives* (Westport, Conn., 1978), 111.

societies already deployed at least three (not necessarily exclusive) patterns for taking in "others." The first involved placing the alien individual by assigning him or her a slot in a kinship system. Most kin-structured societies highlight certain relations as prototypes of absorption problems. Often the treatment of in-laws – strangers whose integration holds the key to household reproduction – furnishes a matrix for conceptualizing the entry of stranger-allies. Thus in Paraguay the Guaraní called the Spanish who settled among them *tobaya*, or brother-in-law, the same term used for men of other peoples who had married into their group. Among them, as among the Chiriguano, a patrilineal social organization with matrilocal residence produced mestizos strongly allied to their maternal uncles. The latter often preferred to marry their cross-cousins, thus initiating a cycle of sustained alliance. The bond to the mother's patriline was strong enough to make a Spanish observer in 1575 fear a rising of the offspring, who might kill their Spanish fathers and join with their maternal uncles and cousins. On the Platine and Chilean frontiers, the integration of renegades, captives, and their mixed offspring into Araucanian societies created a complex web of lineage and ritual relations involving reciprocal obligations. When in 1774 the Pehuenche *cacique* Leviant appeared before the commander of the Santa Barbara fort and demanded the release from prison of a militia soldier, he was apparently fulfilling his obligations of kinship.

Another kinship model for incorporating strangers was captive adoption, which, a European traveler to northwestern Amazonia reported in 1915, was sometimes mistaken for slavery: "Slavery among the Indians themselves is hardly more than a word, since the slave belongs to the chief and soon is identified with his family. Although a slave often has the chance to escape, he rarely does so, because . . . he is usually as well off in his conqueror's house as his own." Adoptable "slaves" were typically orphans or widows of enemies killed in raiding. As in Africa, Europeans altered captivity into chattel slavery. In time whites mistook a northwest Amazonian word for "orphan captive" (*tama*) to be the name of the ethnic group from which Indians supplied commercial slaves.

Second, some American groups (typically politically structured ones) prefigured the problem of Old World peoples "ethno-ethnographically" much as Europeans did – that is, they modeled the alien by hypothetically extending preexistent maps of external relations to include them. They saw Europeans and Africans as new examples belonging to familiar classes of "otherness." In areas where European initiatives were too weak to overwhelm native polities rapidly, it seemed possible to control and eventually assimilate them by compromising them in ties of normal political reciprocity. This process gave rise to the "hispano-Andean alliances" worked out by the anti-Inka natives of Ayacucho, Peru. For the first 15 years of contact, they functioned with decisive efficiency as the political axis of post-Inka society.

However, the attempt to articulate Europeans through American-devised structures of interdependence was largely doomed by the fact that the militarily superior party – Europe – usually failed to understand and almost always failed to accept the potential complementarity implicit in native action. In the central Andes, for example, a far-flung pre-Inka folk model envisioned society as shaped by combats, but combat in a special sense: not merely grinding conflict but transition from strangeness and hostility to relations of complementary difference. Most of these societies understood society itself as a lasting system of interdependency between two irreducibly different kinds of people – namely, aboriginal groups associated with agriculture, wealth, rights of authochtony and the deities of the earth, and invaders associated with herding, military power, the heights, and the sky deities. Mythology and ritual tended to legitimate their political modus vivendi – which was in practice, of course, no less fragile and conflict-ridden than any other form of politics – as conflict transformed into complementarity through the union of invader and aboriginal deities in a joint ritual order. Had they wished to, Spaniards could have worked their way into such systems by the same means the Inka had already used – namely, state incursions packaged as reciprocal ritual transactions – to establish a new invader – aborigine complementarity. But the exclusivist strictures of Christianity closed off that option; acquiring ritual obligations within non-Christian contexts was beyond the pale of a post-tridentine Catholicism obsessed with doctrinal purity.

Third, American societies (especially village-level or confederated horticultural societies) sometimes conceptualized strangers mythically, likening the domain of the alien to the domain of the primordial. That is, faced with people who could not be explained in terms of the familiar "world as it is," they conceptualized the strangers by reference to a mythic time-before-time when the laws of the extant world had not yet taken effect. Barasana (northwest Amazonian) myth offers hypotheses of all-embracing explanatory power, which (like Newtonian science) explain imponderable change in terms of timeless categories and entities:

> [M]yths are made to keep pace with an ever-changing present in such a way as to convey the impression that nothing changes at all. Just as Whitepeople already had a virtual existence in the belly of the anaconda [which brought all Barasana clans into the world in their hierarchy, and also delivered whites] . . . so are all new things treated as if they had a potential existence somewhere in myth that experience merely makes manifest and actual.[4]

At first glance the mythopoeic response to invasion looks impractical, but recent anthropology argues that it can at least as well be envisioned as an enabling process: It locates the unforeseen within a world of known things, and it maps the ground for deciding paths of action. This is no less true of Europe (who needed to conceive of "Indians" as Ophirites, pre-Adamites, or the like before developing other models) than of Native America. In both cases the mythopoeic response was a factor in successes as well as failures. The Makiritare of the Orinoco appear to have interpreted the political problems posed by Spanish and Dutch strangers through the categories of sacred epic, and the resulting reorientation made possible renewed group commitments amid invasion. The result was a partially successful struggle for autonomy.

What makes the mythopoeic response look impractical today, is that it tends to treat invasion as susceptible to magico-religious procedures. But this is not inherently escapist either. It regularly fosters attempts to capture the powers of invaders via acts of sacred prowess and religious innovation. The Barasana

> apply to [Christianity] the same analogical matching that is applied to other aspects of White peoples' culture and which, by implication, suggests that their myths too were known all along. In this way, [the culture hero] Wãribi comes to be identified with God and Christ, his father the moon with the holy spirit, while he himself is the son of two virgin mothers. Similar treatment is given to elements of Christian ritual so that shamans are priests, dance songs are hymns, chants are prayers, ritual beeswax is incense, and hallucinogenic yage is communion wine.[5]

Because the powers of Christendom are thus "really" powers that the natives "already" possessed, shamans felt able to lead resistance by conducting Indianized masses or becoming Christ-like messiahs. This trajectory has repeated itself many times, especially in Amazonia, as shaman-

[4] Stephen Hugh-Jones, "Wãribi and the white men: History and myth in northwest Amazonia," in Elizabeth Tonkin, Maryon McDonald, and Malcolm Chapman (eds.), *History and Ethnicity* (London, 1989), 65.

[5] Ibid., 64–65.

politicians became leaders of rebellions with what (from the European viewpoint) sound like millenarian overtones. Because they involve heterodox baptism and prophecy, scholars often call them syncretic, but the term is misleading from the mythological point of view. Such movements occurred throughout western Amazonia in the later sixeenth century. Other outbreaks occurred in the Tukanoan lands in the late nineteenth century, and with varying degrees of vigor they periodically boil up in current society. Despite their superficially nativist aspect, mythopoeic responses can be highly inclusive of outsiders provided only that they are in some way recognizable as "lost" or exteriorized Indians. Mestizos or disaffected rural workers have joined and even led them.

AFRO-INDIAN PEOPLES

Indian societies showed considerable flexibility in the incorporation of African outsiders, and eventually of their offspring. Although slavery provides a common ground for all these encounters, regional disparities in Africans' and Indians' respective social position and power within colonial societies led to divergent histories of ethnogenesis.

Contact between diaspora Africans and Native Americans remains one of the least studied and least understood aspects of New World social history. Blacks seemed as strange as whites to Indians. Their appearance provoked some shock; the Chilean frontier produced a number of stories of captured blacks, who were washed and scraped to see if their color was inherent, and even of a black woman skinned alive so that other Indians could see something "so new and remarkable." Conflict began almost as early as contact. In newly founded Spanish cities, the city councils dealt over and over with brawls between slaves and Indian marketgoers.

There were good reasons for mutual hostility. Blacks and mulattoes served as auxiliaries of conquest and domination, using their fuller knowledge of Iberian culture to advantage in manipulating Indians. The Peruvian "Indian chronicler" Felipe Guaman Poma's bitter dislike of mulattoes reflects native élites' reaction. The viceregal government of Peru legislated repeatedly to rein in free blacks and mulattoes who exploited Indians. Early city council records in Quito record frequent brawls between Africans and Indians in the Indian marketplace.

The Europeans also gave Africans good reason to fear Indians. In areas where large-scale slave societies developed, Indians were often employed as slave hunters. In the Guianas, the Caribs tracked down black runaways on the Essequibo and the Demarara rivers. Traditions among the Saramaka maroons of Suriname evoke a history of hostility to Indian peoples, because colonial expeditions against self-emancipated blacks usually included Indian guides and auxiliaries. In Brazil in the sixteenth and seventeenth centuries, the great sugar plantation, Engenho Sergipe do Conde, paid Indians a per-head bounty for catching escapees. Planters and Jesuits argued that without "tame" Indians it would be impossible to control the black slaves. Virtually every runaway slave community or *quilombo* in Brazil, from the smallest Bahian hideouts to the great runaway kingdom of Palmares, were destroyed with the help of Indian guides or auxiliary forces.

But the Indian–black relationship was more ambiguous than these data suggest. Recent archaeological evidence from Palmares indicates the existence of indigenous pottery on the site and corroborates references to Indians in the runaway towns. Half a century after the destruction of Palmares, the Portuguese complained that black and mulatto slaves, men and women, were still fleeing to the old sites of Palmares and with Tapuia Indians (probably Gê-speakers) were forming into dangerous bands. Evidently strong tendencies countervailed black–Indian hostility, sometimes giving rise to "neoteric" societies on the margin of the colonial states.

Indeed Indian–black cooperation was the nightmare of colonial governments, and they took extreme measures to forestall it. After the 1647 earthquake that devastated Santiago de Chile, rumors of a rising of domestic Indians and blacks circulated as if by metaphoric association between the two kinds of disaster. In the district of Quito (modern Ecuador), Spaniards threatened with castration blacks who fled to Indian settlements. In 1706 the Portuguese crown ordered the governor of Bahía to prohibit masters from taking their slaves into the interior for fear that they might join in rebellion with Indians. Rewards and privileges were given to Indians who helped destroy maroon settlements or to black regiments that helped in defense against Indians. Nevertheless on plantations and farms Indians and blacks did work together and sometimes married. Beyond European control individual runaways joined Indian groups, sometimes as slaves, but sometimes also rising to positions of leadership. One Miguel, an escaped bicultural slave, in 1553 created a maroon community of blacks and hispanized Indians in Venezuela. He eventually led them in attacking the city of Bariquismeto, and this was not unique. Even after his defeat and recapture, the Spaniards suspected that free-ranging blacks were still stirring Tirajara Indian resistance. Less commonly Indians lead black rebellions. In 1603 Francisco Chichima, a Pilcozón Indian, led a general uprising in the sugar- and coca-producing areas of Acobamba-Apurimac in the eastern Andes. Withdrawing into the space between Spanish highland domains and the Amazon proper, he tried to establish a "land without whites." His leadership impressed Spaniards as a frightening exception to the rule that "generally the Indians are under the feet of the blacks who treat them badly in word and deed."[6] Chichima and ten black leaders were hung.

Escaped African or African-descended slaves, like mestizo and white renegades, sometimes coalesced with Indians to form mobile raiding or nomadic societies. In Venezuela's interior grasslands those natives who survived epidemics, cattle ranch expansion, and slaving became "hispanicized Indians" and intermarried with African escapees from the Caribbean coast. In 1789 some 24,000 hispanicized Indians and self-liberated Africans raided across the plains. Creole landowners and ranchers sought to settle these *zambo* bands in towns. Easily militarized they fought for the most part on the royalist side in the wars of independence.

At times blacks who integrated durably and autonomously into Indian groups, or Indians into maroon communities, formed new societies beyond Creole supervision. On the Pacific coast of sixteenth-century Ecuador, Africans accidentally freed by shipwreck joined with others who had escaped overland to build a sovereign society in the hinterland. The leaders Antonio de Illescas and Andrés Mangache mixed with Indians, adopted their customs and dress, and married daughters of *caciques*. For decades the "mulattos of Esmeraldas" formed an apparently immovable obstacle to Spanish rule over a zone strategic to the Pacific trade routes. By the turn of the seventeenth century, some fifty mixed-bloods governed the Indians, gathering a following of renegades and nonlocal Indians. Estimates placed their total number over 5,000. The crown government at Quito never managed to conquer them and finally appealed to negotiation. In 1599, when Francisco de Arrobe and his two sons appeared in Quito with golden earplugs and nose ornaments to conclude a treaty, they impressed onlookers as "astute and sagacious." A gala oil portrait of

[6] Cited in F. M. Rénard-Casevitz, Thierry Saignes, and Anne-Christine Taylor, *Al este de los Andes. Relaciones entre las sociedades amazónicas y andinas entre los siglos xvi y xvii*, 2 vols. (Lima, 1988), I, 225–26.

them in their brown and gold glory was painted to commemorate the occasion and sent to the king. Later Spanish attempts to establish control over Esmeraldas continued to depend on the cooperation of the "mulatto" descendants.

Indians who inhabited regions where maroon communities were forming needed either to defend themselves against maroon incursions or to integrate the newcomers through marriage and trade ties. The relative importance of African and Indian language and culture depended on a variety of political, demographic, and social factors. On the Caribbean coast of Honduras and Nicaragua, an exogamous group of Sumu Indians integrated numbers of black castaways from a slave ship and continued accepting later arrivals. Apparently first held as slaves or captives, these outsiders became so much a part of emerging fusion society that the society as a whole was eventually perceived as black. The Africans aided in getting firearms and other goods by dealing with buccaneers who frequented the poorly defended inlets of the coast. This population, known as the Miskito Indians, in time drove rival populations inland from the river mouths and developed a distinct cultural identity under British tutelage. Indeed in 1687 the British government in Jamaica recognized an indigenous "king of Mosquitia" as an ally against the Spanish. Miskitos used the connection to expand their political control and build an economic position as middlemen.

A similar fusion of escaped and castaway Africans with the island Carib population took place earlier in the lesser Antilles, especially on the island of St. Vincent, where a defined "Black Carib" group eventually emerged in distinction to the more Amerindian "Red Caribs." After defeat in the Carib War of 1795–1797, the British removed some 2,000 Black Caribs, or Garífuna, to the island of Roatán off the coast of Honduras. From there, after concluding a treaty with the Spanish, they migrated to the mainland. Phenotypically black but speaking the Arawak of the Island Caribs, the Black Caribs remained for the most part isolated from the other Indian and Afro-Indian populations of the Central American coast (although in Nicaragua they may have been partially absorbed by the Miskitos). Black Carib language, cassava-based horticulture, polygyny, and customs like the *couvade* all recall Caribbean Amerindian traditions, but Garífuna beliefs and ritual, especially those dedicated to ancestors, as well as music and dance, point to Africa.

Comparable fusion societies arose in South America wherever more or less independent native societies accepted many self-liberated Africans.

Few cases, however, are well researched. In the 1940s Brazil's Indian Protection Service made contact with groups of "Black Indians" – somatically African-like speakers of a Tupian language – on the upper Tocantins and the Araguaia rivers. Known as the Avá-Canoeiro, they seem to have been the progeny of Indian groups victimized and transplanted by *bandeirante* raiders in the eighteenth century but later reinforced by escaping blacks.

WHITE CAPTIVES AND RENEGADES

For "the people called Indians," assimilating Europeans posed a different set of problems from incorporating Africans or foreign natives, because colonial societies exerted weighty military and commercial pressures to "rescue" transfrontiersmen and especially women.

In a few cases European settlement frontiers failed and left pockets of colonists stranded. There ex-European transfrontier groups "Indianized" and turned into separate new Indian-like peoples. At the eastern foothills of the Ecuadorian Andes, the collapse of Spanish jungle "cities" left behind a population that Jívaroized and became known in the nineteenth century as the Macabeos.

More usually Europeans entered native communities as captives and lived under rules of captivity. To the degree that unique European pressures created unprecedented social dynamics, white captives became a different sort of social being from captives taken in prehispanic times.

Nonetheless prehispanic practice set a framework. For many peoples, to integrate captives into existing kin groups was the culmination of victory. Among the Caribs (Karinya) of the Orinoco and Guyana, the acquisition of young women and boys and the killing of adult men constituted the highest object of warfare.[7] The Brazilian Tupinambá celebrated the incorporation and then the destruction of captives with festive pomp. Captives could replace killed or captured relatives, or they could fill such roles temporarily until the time came to execute them in a collective vengeance for earlier war losses. The remarkable narratives of Hans Staden of Hesse, a captive among the Brazilian Tupiniquim (1557),

[7] That such raiding served pragmatic economic ends is suggested by the Suyá, a northern Gê group which in 1915 was raided by the Juruna or by rubber tappers, and who in response raided the Waurá to replace the women. The Waurá were chosen because Waurá women knew how to make pots, and this skill could liberate the Suyá from dependence on trade. See Anthony Seeger, *Nature and Society in Central Brazil* (Cambridge, Mass., 1981), 198.

and that of Piñeda de Bascuñán among the Chilean Araucanians (1603), give glimpses of aboriginal ideas about prisoners of war. Sometimes such systems went together with very sharp definitions of cultural self and other. In historic times, for example, the Shipibo-Conibo have seen themselves as full-humans and thus "civilized" while they considered neighboring indigenous peoples fit to be killed and their women "harvested" as captured wives. Indigenous kinship nonetheless used these distinctions to frame patterns for resolving otherness into subordinate membership, as among the Carib peoples of northern South America, where the category *poito* could mean son-in-law, ally, or trade partner, but under pressure from the Dutch, it increasingly came to mean captive – and, as European demand mounted, also prospective slave.

Given this sort of acquisitiveness toward people, it was not usually hard for Europeans at contact to find initial voluntary entrée, or even to become near-natives. The archetypal tale of Europeans gone "native" was the story of the two Spaniards who had been shipwrecked and captured in Yucatán before Cortez's arrival. One of them, Francisco de Aguilar, later joined Cortez and became his guide and interpreter; the other, Gonzalo Guerrero, having married a Maya woman, begun a family, and risen to prominence among his captors, chose to remain. He eventually led Maya resistance against the Spanish. Another once-notorious sixteenth-century case concerned four shipwrecked Spanish women who, when Tristán de Luna found them in Florida, refused to lea[illegible]heir children.

Right-thinking Europeans found it deeply disturbing that anyone would choose native "barbarism" and abandon the Church. Especially when men did so, "going native" primarily signified surrender to the "vice and idleness" that Europeans thought they saw in Indians. Where women captives are concerned the fascination of exotica shades into sheer romance. Both historical documentation and Argentinian fiction stereotype the image of the captive woman who falls in love with her Indian husband and refuses to return, or who runs away to rejoin her adoptive people.

Perhaps some people did refuse to return. It seems, however, that captives' reluctance to return was in fact related to Indian practices designed to destroy the captives' attachments to their original society. In the Southern Cone they were separated from other captives who were their kin and forbidden to speak Spanish. Wives of *caciques* humiliated female captives and sometimes shamed them by denying them proper clothing. Relief could be secured only by assimilation to Indian society. And the Spanish side also imposed disincentives to return. For young men captured in Chile, return would entail the constant danger of being pressed into the frontier army of the "American Flanders." The ironic case of a young Spaniard who returned to colonial society in Chile after 2 years of captivity, but who decided to remain disguised as an Indian to avoid military service, is instructive. He was eventually arrested as an escaped Indian tribute delinquent, and despite all the evidence he could muster, his only alternative was to flee back to his former captors.

Where male captives are concerned, South American versions of the "Pocahontas tale" are common. In them the explorer or soldier is saved by the love of the chief's daughter and then elevated by his father-in-law to mediate with the Europeans or lead his wife's people in war. Jerónimo de Albuquerque's rescue by the "Princess" Green Bow in the 1530s is the standard example. Francisco Martín, soldier of an ill-fated expedition in Venezuela, was captured by Indians, married a chief's daughter, and became a military leader. One chronicler reported that years later, long after being "rescued" by Spaniards, Martín so missed his wife and children that he went back to life as an Indian. A few versions bring us closer to the *realpolitik* of such cases. One enslaved *morisco* (an Iberian Muslim convert) who became a military leader among the Arawaks on the Uyapari River in 1544 led a flotilla of some fifty canoes to Margarita Island, where he reported that he had married seven or eight daughters of Indian leaders. In kin-structured societies marriage to daughters of leaders often signifies a political bond, where the wife taker becomes an indebted subordinate – in the case of Europeans, one obliged to reciprocate by procuring European technology. Success in this role might lead to power that no mere soldier could attain among Spaniards, and this seems sometimes to have been an appealing option. Juan Bautista Bernio in Tucumán won such power. So, for a time, did that strange "man who would be king," the Sevillian Pedro Chamijo (called Bohórquez) who lived among the Calchaquíes of Tucumán as a *cacique* in the 1650s and eventually styled himself "Inka," thereby courting the Spanish repression that destroyed him.

In only one area, however, does the historic record give a rounded account of Spanish captives as an institutionalized category with a distinctive role: the Araucanian societies of the Chilean and Platine frontiers. Colonial warfare in Chile yielded captives on both sides from the 1540s on. They became most numerous after the general uprising of 1598–

1603, and captive taking continued with sporadic intensity during other periods of increased fighting. In the La Plata River Basin, captive taking increased with the growth of the colony in the late eighteenth century, especially as mounted Araucanians began to raid across the Andes. In both areas the practice was widespread and prisoners numerous. Sometimes raiders seized whole families taking along their slaves, servants, and "friendly Indians." As early as the 1640s, a Spanish priest, himself captive for 15 years, reported that he knew of 200 men and 350 women held by the Araucanians. In Cuyo and Buenos Aires province, the increase in raiding in the eighteenth century led to an increase of captives, especially in the decade of the 1780s, and the raiding parties (*malones*) often sold the captive women and cattle to native Araucanian caravans returning across the Andes to Chile. The Chilean Coliqueo who migrated onto the Argentine *pampas* and raided in Buenos Aires were known as the "blonde Indians," so high was their reputed rate of miscegenation with Spanish women. Juan Manuel de Rosas, at war in Buenos Aires province, freed over 700 captives in 1834. Most of the men freed had been taken as children, and the women were typically about sixteen when captured. In 1869 Colonel Mansilla who visited the Ranqueles, an Araucanian composite group living on the *pampas* south of Córdoba, estimated that among the 8,000 to 10,000 Ranqueles, 600 to 800 had entered as captives. The acquisition of captives became, in fact, a constant element in the endemic warfare on the southern frontier. One nineteenth-century observer averred that "the honor of an Indian is computed by his train of captives and if any chief, however popular he might be, would undertake an expedition and deny that right to the Indians, he would not have one solitary follower."

Why did Spanish captives become so important to Araucanian society? Captive taking was one facet of a syndrome of changes transforming the Araucanian way of life after guns and horses came within easy reach. In the highly dynamic, warlike and competitive Araucania, which fought off Spain and then Chile and Argentina for some 380 years, captives played a number of roles. First, they were political pawns. Colonial-era changes aggrandized and centralized chiefly power, and leadership was hotly contested. Captives were war trophies constituting proof of valor. They were sometimes tortured and killed during ritual celebrations. Reports of mistreatment were common, but some Spaniards recognized that this was sometimes retribution for Spanish abuse of Indians. Perhaps chiefs thought, too, that hostages could serve as a disincentive to hurt natives on the far side of the frontier.

Second, captives were a productive resource. Some were incorporated in the group as laborers. Many were distributed and exchanged through Araucanian kinship networks. A number of Spanish captives referred to their captors as "masters" and saw themselves as enslaved. Francisco Núñez de Bascuñán, son of a Spanish commander, was captured in 1629 by the *cacique* Maulicán and well treated. His later account of captivity, sympathetic to his captors, became a classic frontier narrative. He reports the words of the *cacique* Quilalebo about the treatment of the Spanish captives:

> [T]hey eat with us, they drink with us and yes, they work in our company. Why do the Spaniards, I ask, consider us as bad as they say we are? In battle and in the treatment [of captives] one can see that they are worse and impose the cruelest conditions, for they treat their captives like dogs, holding them in stocks, with chains and manacles, confined in cells, and in continuous labor; poorly dressed, poorly fed, and branded like a horse, burned on their faces with fire.[8]

To this Thucydidian speech, Pineda y Bascuñán could only admit his embarrassment because "all he said, happens thus."

Third, captives offered a shortcut to technical parity. Blacksmiths, cooks, or folk healers might be particularly valued. Fourth, captured women were a supreme asset as political capital. A number of colonial observers such as Gonzalez de Nájera (1614) noted that as a rule captured men were killed but women were taken as sexual prizes and eventual wives. There is a historiographic problem here; emphasis on the capture and use of European women for pleasure is a suspectly obsessive theme in descriptions of the frontiers, perhaps reflecting sexual tensions in white society as well as militarist ideology. A modern accounting of Indian captives in colonial Chile identifies twice as many men as women, suggesting that in practice captivity followed the normal female-deficient demography of frontier society. Nonetheless, apart from questions about how many women the warriors took, warriors do seem to have valued women especially. Given Reche patrilineal and patrilocal traditions, female captives

[8] Francisco Núñez de Pineda y Bascuñán, *El cautiverio feliz* [1866], 309, cited in Juan Carlos Skews, "Twisted images of the encounter. The construction of the other in Nueva Extremadura," (unpublished paper, University of Minnesota, 1992).

may have been easier to integrate into lineages, and once having given birth less likely than men to flee. Their children were, as one observer put it, "so many ties and roots that bind them to their misfortune with a notable forgetfulness of God." Among the *ulmen* or top Araucanian leaders, polygyny was a sign of prestige. Wives increased a leader's capacity to wine, dine, and clothe his followers because women were the experts in farming, brewing, and weaving. In some respects the children of a foreign woman might be preferable heirs, because, in a patrilineal society, their mother's patrilateral kin were absent and therefore unable to press troublesome claims. The sixteenth-century case of Antonio Chicahuala, son of the *cacique* Gualacán and Doña Aldonsa Aguilera de Castro, who grew up an important *lonko*, or band chief, defines the pattern.

Fifth, captives were a commercial asset. The Chilean Reche, by the eighteenth century called Mapuche, sold them among themselves. One captive reported being sold seventy-three times in 12 years. In eighteenth-century Argentina, captives circulated widely. Commercialization facilitated rescue (*resgate*) by purchase in trade goods. Drawing on medieval Castilian precedents for ransoming captives from Muslims, colonial and later national governments sometimes bought captives using missionaries as agents and employing a "captives' fund" of charitable contributions.[9] In the nineteenth century many captives were recovered in this manner; especially for the Pampa groups, the captives' trade value may have mattered more than their social value.

Sixth and finally, in Araucania and elsewhere, Europeans themselves had varied motives for conniving with captivity and "going native." At early dates in Paraguay, Jesuit missionaries preferred to leave in place the many white captives of the Mbayá, the better to take advantage of their bilingualism and knowledge of Indian culture. Likewise the Portuguese in their African explorations had already developed the technique of leaving young men, often penal exiles, among newly encountered peoples to learn languages and serve as go-betweens. Cabral did this after his landfall in Brazil in 1500, even though the Tupi at first refused to accept the men. The first 50 years of contact on the Brazilian coast produced a

[9] In twelfth- and thirteenth-century Castile, some municipalities maintained *alfaqueques* or public ransomers, but unlike the practice in the Americas, ransoming captives from the Moors was usually done privately. See José Enrique López de Coca Castañer, "Institutions of the Castillian-Granadan frontier," in Robert Bartlett and Angus MacKay (eds.), *Medieval Frontier Societies* (Oxford, 1989), 127–149. This situation changed with the growth of the early modern state, as Philip II's actions after the Portuguese disaster at Alcacer Kebir in 1578 demonstrate.

number of castaways and renegades such as João Ramalho in São Vicente and Diogo Alvares, *Caramurú* in Bahía; these later served as important intermediaries between local indigenous groups and the Portuguese. For Europeans on the wrong side of the law, it was reassuring to have a native option. González Calvo de Barrientos, fleeing a crime scene in Peru, aided the *cacique* Michimalongo and turned up in 1542 in Copiapó among the Araucanians. Deserters and "renegades" became a fixture on the southern frontier. By 1600 there were over sixty Spanish, mestizo, and mulatto renegades among the Reche. One, Juan Barba, was a renegade priest who took to preaching against Christianity and praising the Araucanian way of life. In the war of the Pampa in the 1820s, the *cacique* Ancaleguen arrived for a parley accompanied by Creole outlaws dressed as Indians but equipped with silver spurs and saddles. When in 1752 three Puelche *caciques* and their 200 riders arrived for a parley, a number of Spaniards dressed like Puelches rode among them. Their interpreter was a Spaniard called Vauiu. By the nineteenth century even political "outs" could be found in the Indian camps. Men on the loose beyond the reach of the colonial or national states, and maybe also pushing the limits of traditional indigenous law, had little to gain from the conclusion of peace or the acceptance of Christianity. They were distrusted and hated by colonial authorities as long as they remained loyal to their Indian identity. At the same time, they often proved indispensable in negotiations. And they could become intelligence assets by returning to "civilization" as scouts and trailbreakers.

Even Spaniards sent to live among the Indians as representatives of colonial society stood in an ambiguous position. Beginning in 1647 Spanish "captains of friendlies" were appointed to live among the Chilean Araucanians, to hear their complaints, "cool their blood," and serve as go-betweens, spies, and brokers. Their success depended on their relationships to local *caciques*, reinforced by ritual and blood ties. Eventually certain Araucanian lineages ambitious to manipulate Spanish politics monopolized ties with the "captains." Never very numerous – there were sixty-six in 1774 – these Janus-faced operators were sometimes viewed as treasonous by Spanish authorities.

MESTIZAJE AND SOCIAL ANOMALY

The term "mestizo" is opposite to *castizo*, originally meaning categorically pure or of homogeneous origin and culture – a proper member of one's caste. To be *castizo* was an important component of legitimacy. Two points are commonly emphasized in historiography of "mixed people": first, that the mestizo sector grew rapidly almost from initial contact, and second, that despite the uncontrollability and obviousness of the process, Spaniards continued to regard it as anomalous and harmful. Spanish categorizations of social difference, Saignes and Bouysse-Cassagne have noted, depended not only on distinctions of estate but also on "blood," meaning inheritance or inborn quality, and on "milk," which would today be called nurture or socialization.[10] Toward 1600 Reginaldo de Lizárraga wrote that each person "will draw his inclinations from the milk he suckled. . . . He who sucked liar's milk, lies, and drunkard's milk, drinks." Persons whose standing by estate, blood, and milk all concorded were of unambiguous and acceptable identity; they might be low but also pure. The colonial situation, however, immediately fostered discords and anomalies in Spanish concepts of personal legitimacy. Even those of "pure Spanish blood" suffered some devaluation as Creoles, touched as virtually all Americans were by the milk (and, of course, the culture) of native or African wet nurses. No less a figure than the great Jesuit missionary Antônio Vieira made similar arguments about the Portuguese born in Brazil.

People of mixed birth, whose blood was "impure" and whose Spanish component was putatively polluted by "bad milk," constituted by their mere existence an insult to standing categories. In colonial usage "mestizo" was not so much the name of a firm social category as a term meaning a weakly defined person, one who might occupy varied social roles depending on demand and opportunity, but who was not really entitled by his or her "nature" to any of them. In other words, "mestizo" was not a stable member of the category set *español, indio, portugués*, or *inca*, but was a term of a different order, denoting nonplacement within the legitimate set. At first Spaniards tried to regularize the situation by treating mestizos as a separate hereditary category in its own right. Toledan-era parish books sometimes carried separate registers for mixed "castes." But the idea of a mixed-caste caste was a contradiction in terms, and the term "mestizo" tended always to lapse back into usages connoting degradation. So semantically potent was the taint of mixed blood,

[10] Thierry Saignes and Thérèse Bouysse-Cassagne, "Dos confundidas identidades: mestizos y criollos en el siglo xvii," *Senri Ethnological Studies* 33 (1992), 14–26.

that in time it tainted the word *casta* itself: By the middle to late colonial era, the phrase *las castas* ('the castes') did not refer to *castizo* people but rather the opposite; it was a shorthand term for "the mixed-blood population" (lumping together mestizos, mulattoes, and *zambos*, or Indian–African mixed-bloods). All these people were treated as impure, and they had to press any claim to legitimacy carefully. Juan and Ulloa wrote of "the mestizos, whose pride is regulated by prudence."[11]

This situation underlies both the protean action of mestizos in the shaping of native South America, and the transitoriness of cases in which "mestizo" became a collectively accepted self-identity. It is almost as if anomalous birth had forced forth a concept of the generic, uncategorized individual precociously, at a period when Iberian law and ideology had yet to find a social as opposed to pathological definition of the unmoored individual actor.

MESTIZOS AS INDIANS

It was Inka policy to offer gift brides, often daughters of the sovereign by secondary wives, as confirmations of political alliance. In the early days of Spanish Peru, *conquistadores* seized on Inka princesses and noblewomen, whether by gift or by less correct means, in the expectation of winning hereditary access to Inka wealth. In the early days they seem also to have thought Inka titles would find recognition in Spain as noble or even royal. The invasion had hardly begun when Atawallpa Inka gave Gonzalo Pizarro a girl named Quispe Sisa (Qispi Sisa, 'Crystal Flower', later known as Inés Yupanqui), born of his secondary royal wife, and Pizarro fathered her two children. The first, Doña Francisca Pizarro, was born in 1534 and became Pizarro's main heir. Pizarro did not marry Inés but did marry a different royal Inka and had a son by her in 1537. Lesser native families, for their part, lobbied for alliance with powerful invaders. Garcilaso de la Vega, a half-Inka intellectual of the first postinvasion generation, stated that when an Indian woman became pregnant by a Spaniard her whole family "came together to respect and serve him like an idol because he had become their relative." Garcilaso claimed he felt no stigma, writing that "I call myself a mestizo clear and plain, and feel honored by the name." But this was, by the time of writing (in the early

[11] Jorge Juan y Santacilia and Antonio de Ulloa, *A Voyage to South America* (New York, 1964), 136.

seventeenth century), a polemical position taken against a trend that had already made the word "mestizo" downright ugly.[12]

In fact royal Inka mestizos were viewed with intense suspicion by the Council of the Indies, and not without reason. They concentrated in their persons both the claims of an ungovernable *conquistador* élite and Inka aspirations to a continuing Peruvian sovereignty. Several of the most illustrious Inka mestizos, including Inés Huaylas Yupanqui's daughter Doña Francisco Pizarro, and Garcilaso Inca himself, were sent to Spain under political pressure and there lived comfortable but uprooted lives.

In less politically loaded cases, whether a child of mixed birth was to live among Indians or among Spaniards depended greatly on social position and on the fathers' decisions. Some fathers of mestizos neglected them; Felipe Guaman Poma drew a savagely satirical cartoon of a priest shipping away a whole mule load of his "bastard" mestizo babies in the saddlebags usually used for merchandise. But children of well-positioned Spanish fathers could, if the father chose, be taken up into Spanish society. They might do so (rarely) as legitimate offspring or (more usually) as recognized "natural" offspring. Fathers who hid their fatherhood sometimes gave informal parental support to an abandoned mistress' household. Diego Lobato de Sosa, a gifted priest in early colonial Quito who was himself the mestizo son of an Inka princess, provided a covert subsidy to an Indian woman who was almost surely his daughter's mother. (We know this because the mother dropped a broad hint about it in her will.) Although subject to stigma and challenge, people born of such unions could with luck and pluck make urban Iberian-style careers.

When fathers cast off their mestizo children, or when the fathers lived in native communities, or when the mothers chose to reside in them rather than keep to servile roles in Spanish society, the offspring would almost certainly live as Indians. The initial colonial period saw an almost immediate surge of such ill-regulated births. Early Brazil provides a case in point. Large numbers of young, single, and lightly supervised Portuguese and French men operating on the coast indulged in exploitative concubinage with Indian women. From their arrival in 1549, Jesuits sought unsuccessfully to rein in this practice. The permeability of the ethnic and cultural frontier shocked Jesuit observers. They saw mixed-

[12] Thérèse Bouysse-Cassagne, "Etre métis ou ne pas être: les symptômes d'un mal identitaire dans les Andes des XVIe et XVIIe siècles," *Cahiers des Amériques Latines* 12 (1991), 21.

blood *mamelucos* as souls lost to God. Father Leonardo Nunes thought it "a thing to make us weep continually."[13]

In the early, fluid days of the coastal colonies, Europe's social distinctions applied only loosely. Many mestizos and a few Portuguese felt native enough to adhere to the heavily native messianic cult called *santidade* that flourished in the 1560s in Jaguaripe (Bahía), Brazil. Eighteen of the thirty people charged with backing this revitalization movement were *mamelucos*, the most famous being Domingos Fernandes Nobre, or Tomacauna, who confessed to the Inquisition in 1591 that he had lived for 18 years among the Indians. He joined in their rites and tattooed his body, thereby making visible his participation in the ritual capture and killing of enemies. While claiming to have done these things to demonstrate his bravery, he admitted that he had never wanted to return from the backlands. There, he said, he could have plenty of women and eat meat on the prohibited days. European documents critical of miscegenation emphasized this freedom from restraint but usually overlooked the considerable ritual, social, kinship, and gender constraints that life among Indians entailed.

But the permeable social frontier, with casual sharing between Europeans and natives, could last only in those areas where European presence was thin. Where areas of dense and sedentary Indian populations came under full-blown Spanish governance, such as highland Peru and Ecuador, it was characteristic only of the first stages of conquest and settlement. Soon Spaniards sought to exclude mestizos from clerical and military careers and shunted most of them into ill-defined plebeian positions while accepting a few as conditional and vulnerable members of colonial élites. Although still able to move amidst the indigenous world, early Andean mestizos faced uncertain and marginal futures where local indigenous leaders ruled.

Mestizos retained full participation in native society longer on the frontiers and in the territories of horticultural and hunting peoples. In backlands like Chile, the Chaco, and Paraguay, mestizos enjoyed access to two radically different social universes, and they could choose between them. Mestizos were often thought to be effective warriors, having been raised in war. In both Chile and Paraguay, they were accused of introducing gunpowder and other European technologies to the Indians.

[13] Leandro Nunes to Jesuits of Coimbra (S. Vicente, 20 June 1551), *Monumenta Brasiliae. Monumenta Misionum Societatis Iesu* (Rome, 1956–1968), vol. I, 231–237.

Those who used their positions of confidence, leadership, or influence to serve as intermediaries with colonial societies became valued agents of empire. Examples include the children of Caramurú among the Tupinambá in Bahia of the 1530s; Pedro de Segura, mestizo *cacique* among the Chiriguanos (1590s); and Indian Warner (1657–1676), who lived among the Island Caribs on St. Vincent and whom the English commissioned as governor of Dominica. Those who used their linguistic, political, or technical knowledge to help indigenous resistance were called, like Bartolomé Sánchez Capillas in the Chaco, "mestizo dog" and "apostate tyrant."

Spanish higher-ups were never at ease with a policy that generated and even militarily relied on ill-controlled interstitial populations. A Spanish royal official in Chile in the 1770s thought that hanging a couple of dozen Indianized mestizos might go a long way to eliminating smuggling, vagabondage, and Indian rustling of livestock. But the threat was not so easily disposed of as a mere criminal matter. One Juan Muñoz, in Tucumán, was considered so dangerous that an expedition was mounted to bring him in. This was hardly idle paranoia. Union between mestizos and weakly governed natives really could forge powerful military forces. In the era of independence, on the Colombian side of the great interior grasslands, a large and lightly governed native (Guahibo and other) population absorbed and culturally assimilated a smaller body of mestizo free laborers. This free-ranging nomadic population, known as *llaneros* or "plainsmen," became after 1800 a ready-made and highly effective army against Spain.

MESTIZOS AS A NEW PEOPLE?

We suggested earlier that mestizos constituted not so much a new people as a new kind of people. Rarely did they band together to claim a corporate identity or foral rights as mestizos. Neither did they enjoy a normalized and legitimate cultural dual citizenship. On the whole those who made their lives among peasant Indians experienced their difference as an asset or as a stigma but rarely as an irrelevance. Those who entered Spanish society fared similarly.

But a great many mestizos, with increasingly many generations of "mixture" behind them, fitted into neither sociocultural set. In practice they were identified by economic class roles, such as retailer or artisan, whereas the cultural processes of social labeling tagged behind attaching ill-fitting typologies formulated on the rhetoric of *casta*.

The growth of a population of mixed origins presented colonial societies with endemic problems of definition, and individuals with questions of identity. The very inconstancy of such labels and terminology across regions and over time suggests the problem. Early Ibero-Americans turned first to Mediterranean cross-cultural experience, especially the Muslim frontiers. In Peru the first children born to Indian–white unions were called *genízaros* (Janissaries), a term referring to an élite unit of the fourteenth century Turkish military; it took hold only on peripheries like Chile.[14] The Portuguese also turned first to Turkish military terms, calling mestizos *mamelucos*. The word denoted a class of originally slave soldiers that seized the Egyptian sultanate and held it until 1517 – a telling clue to Iberian perceptions of the tension between degradation and potency that mixed blood was felt to entail. *Mameluco* also appeared in Spanish Paraguay and Laicacota (Peru). Illegitimate birth, too, was a major component of the semantic field "mestizo," because most mestizos were born of unsanctioned unions. *Cholo* had a reported Aymara etymology "bastard dog," and Portuguese simply used the term *bastardo*. As the term "mestizo" began to acquire a variety of pejorative connotations, it was sometimes replaced by milder labels. In Paraguay, eastern Upper Peru, and Ecuador, *montañés* – which suggests backlander or countryman, and which also may have been associated with an area of Spain that resisted Moorish rule – became the more polite term for people of mixed origin. It won some acceptance among the people it labeled.[15]

Although early colonial Iberians ideologically deplored miscegenation, they also connived at it in pursuit of tangible interest. One motive behind early Spanish attempts to foster marriages or unions with Indians was to acquire land and authority through inheritance. When Cardinal Cisneros wrote instructions (1516) to the Jeronymite fathers who went to prosely-

[14] The term *genízaro* was used in New Mexico to describe captive Indians and their children settled in communities under Spanish control.

[15] The term *montañés* supposedly was a translation from the Quechua *sacha runa* or "forest person," often applied to "savages" from the upper rain forests. Thierry Saignes and Thérèse Bouysse-Cassagne, "Dos confundidas identidades: mestizos y criollos en el siglo vii," *500 años de mestizaje en los Andes*, Senri Ethnological Studies 33 (1992), 14–26. An alternate etymology espoused by Caillavet and Minchom claims connection with the Spanish Cantabrian province (La Montaña), which, unconquered by the Moors, remained "pure." See "Les métis imaginaire: idéaux classificatoires et stratégies socio-raciales en Amérique Latine (xvi–xx siècle)," *L'Homme* 32:122–124 (1992), 115–132.

tize and settle Hispaniola, he suggested that they encourage marriages with the daughters of *caciques* so that in a short time all the *caciques* would be Spaniards (mestizos). Whether Taino social organization on Hispaniola was matrilineal (which would have fostered Cisneros's maneuver by giving male Spaniards' children clear title to their maternal families' privilege) is still uncertain, and whether the term *cacica* generally referred to women rulers or to the principal wives of Taino chiefs remains debatable. However, Las Casas and other earlier observers complained that Spaniards were marrying Indian women in order to acquire kinship rights that would allow their offspring to inherit leadership roles.

In Pizarran Peru some *conquistadores* hastened to wed Inka princesses, likewise assuming that their brides' noble standing would yield offspring with claims to the new kingdom's wealth. The crown frowned on opportunistic Inka–Spanish marriage, and children of these unions lived to see their nobility politically undercut. Their strenuous efforts to get themselves recognized as true nobles sometimes yielded crown consent to subsidize their privileges, but not much power. At lower levels of the ethnic power hierarchy, however, Spanish strategies of in-marriage did win important advantages – not nobility in the Iberian order but local dominance in the Indian order. In one of the few studies attentive to mestizos, a monograph on plebeian Quito, Minchom shows that in what is now Ecuador such maneuvers continued for a long time and had major consequences: "During the mid-colonial period, matrimonial alliances between Spaniards and cacicas [female inheritors of chiefdoms] permitted the white or Mestizo to integrate himself as an 'intruder' into positions of authority within the Indian communities, and was also a factor which was ultimately to play an important role in the transfer of land from Indian to Spanish hands."[16]

As the mestizo population began to grow from the second colonial generation onward, government policy became increasingly restrictive toward its full integration into colonial life. Mestizos and other new "castes" were painted as disruptive and politically unstable elements, not to be trusted. This was not pure delusion; in 1592–1593 the mestizos of a center-city parish spearheaded the antitaxation "Alcabala Rebellion" and mutinied again in the larger 1765 rebellion. Although at first mestizo bilinguals had been valued as agents for Indian conversion, whites hungry

[16] Martin Minchom, *The People of Quito, 1690–1810: Change and Unrest in the Underclass* (Boulder, 1994), 192–193.

for Church careers soon shouldered them out of the race for ordination. In 1568 Philip II ordered their exclusion from priesthood, and although this prohibition was overturned in 1588 on theological grounds, both the diocesan clergy and the orders severely restricted the entrance of mixed bloods into their ranks throughout the colonial era. In Peru mestizos were prohibited from inheriting *encomiendas* (grants of crown trusteeship over native polities) in 1549. *Encomenderos* were even restricted from marrying Indians to prevent them from engendering mestizos who might make politically dangerous inheritance claims. Mestizos were barred from public office in 1576, a royal decision that was repeated three times in the seventeenth century. As the repetition of this law suggests, the restrictions imposed or projected on peoples of mixed origin often conflicted with de facto American realities. The viceroy of Peru in 1573 countermanded a ban on mestizos in arms and authorized their participation in militias as long as they lived with "house and property in a Spanish settlement." Likewise Viceroy Salvatierra of Peru answered a 1653 royal policy letter prohibiting *castas* from wearing swords with an objection that it should not apply to mestizos "because they are very capable, wealthy, and friends of the Spaniards, and it will cause general resentment since they are free and in their own land." But this did not amount to a consensus of élites. In Chile mestizos, like mulattoes, were legally distinguished from Spaniards. Penal law singled out mestizos for "infamous" public whippings – infamy was considered a separate component of punishment, apart from the bodily suffering inflicted – when for the same crimes mulattoes received only fines or confiscations, which were not "infamous."

While facing colonial society's maze of opportunities and rebuffs, mestizos also had to define themselves vis-à-vis Indian society. In the Andean world mestizo *caciques* emerged, at first sponsored and later restricted by colonial policy. Peru had many antimestizo regulations after the mid–sixteenth century. In New Granada (Colombia), too, the *audiencia* issued a 1576 law prohibiting mestizos from acquiring chieftaincies in Indian villages. As with all restrictions on mestizos, local enforcement proved unsteady. Two cases are illustrative. In 1664 the heads of corporate sectors (*principales*) of Aracapi in Puna (Porco province) in the southern Andes denounced Francisco Castillo, their mestizo *cacique*. Castillo was married to an Indian woman and claimed that nobody else among the Indians could assume the obligations of fulfilling tribute quotas or supplying forced labor quotas for the mine draft. Yet in New Granada in the early eighteenth century, when two mestizos, Don Diego de Torres and Don Alonso de Silva, argued that they should be allowed to retain their positions as *caciques* of Turumequé and Tibasosa, it was their Indian subjects who took their side. Local *encomenderos* and the state-appointed attorney for Indians averred that mestizo rulers were detrimental to Indians. It seems that the slipperiness of mestizo rights allowed most groups to define their positions on such cases opportunistically.

In cities, too, the indefinition of mestizo social parameters was itself a key parameter. As Minchom writes: "Mestizos merged into either the creole elite, Indian society, or an indeterminate urban lower social stratum."[17] To some degree urban mestizos formed their own institutions. Seventeenth-century Quito saw the formation of a separate mestizo religious confraternity. But at the same time, explicit legal loci for mestizo identity blurred and faded; as early as 1600 the practice of maintaining separate baptismal books for mestizos was falling out of use. Later "mestizo" ceased even to be a census category.

On frontiers mestizos who took root in Indian societies filled a variety of roles. Among the Chilean Reche mestizos rose to the position of *cacique* and even organized raiding parties. "Almost all are leaders of the enemy's arms," complained one chronicler. With amazing regularity the leaders of messianic or millenarian frontier uprisings turned out to be mestizos who had opted for Indian lifeways or, in the Andes, bicultural Indians whose social circumstances resembled those of mestizos. In the eighteenth century, shamans accused of carrying out magical political assassinations of Spanish functionaries on behalf of Indian factions were typically mestizo or bicultural. One, the much-feared Juan Roza Pinto who terrorized a swath of western Ecuador by inflicting magical diseases, even bore the nickname "*El Mestizo*." The core of his mystique lay in his triple mastery of the occult – that is, the African lore he had learned from the descendants of Esmeraldas maroons, the European magic he learned from sailors, and the renowned shamanic arts of his Ecuadorian lowland home. When he was tried for sending illness to a Spanish official, prosecution and defense witnesses disputed his ethnicity. His clientele seems to have been mostly Indian.

Roza Pinto's arts symbolized magically what Iberians feared politically: mestizos' potential for leadership among Indians based on their unique multicultural competence, and their ability to relativize and manipulate

[17] Martin Minchom, *The People of Quito,* 62.

norms and beliefs from all sides. Mestizo leadership frightened many European observers, including the brilliant Jesuit Father José de Acosta, who warned in 1585 that "they are all of one breed (*casta*) and are relatives and they understand each others' thoughts, having been raised together." Acosta claimed that mestizos told the *caciques* the land was theirs and that native lordship was equivalent to Castilian titled nobility. In this sense they served both as translators and as subverters of Spanish custom and law. Their ability to bridge cultural differences made them potentially dangerous to the colonial societies. The aforementioned Indian Warner, supposedly the son of Sir Thomas Warner, governor of St. Kitts, lived with the Caribs on St. Vincent Island and was killed by his English half-brother, who perceived him as future trouble. In the viceroyalty of Peru, Indian–mestizo collaboration intensified through the mid–eighteenth century, as mestizos' position worsened. Excluded from religious orders and the university in Lima, they faced an intolerably low social ceiling. During the Huarochirí rebellion of 1750, Indians and mestizos presented a petition to the government specifically complaining of the discrimination against mixed bloods, "our relatives, children of caciques who suffer the same persecution as ourselves." Whites' fear of mestizos tended to drive mestizos into the arms of rebels. By 1780 mestizo participation in the massive Andean revolutions of Túpac Amaru II and the Bolivian Cataris had the flavor of a self-fulfilling prophecy.

NEW IDENTITIES AND NEW KINDS OF IDENTITIES

Mestizos retained for a long time their profile as a new kind of people – that is, people whose basic social locus depended on luck, strategy, and achievement at least as much as it depended on ascription. But the rules under which they approached the field of play changed over time. The line between mestizos and Indians remained permeable after the period of initial contact. In addition to the constraint that one's parentage and social class imposed, each person faced life choices increasingly influenced by state policies and demands. Over and over persons who sought to get out from under the forced labor service imposed on Indians living in traditional communities faced the choice of how to play their ethnic cards. Although some thought had been given to imposing tribute obligations on mestizos or creating mestizo villages, this proved impractical. The Spanish crown did impose tribute payments on mulattoes and *pardos* ('brownskins'), but outside of Lima and other cities, tribute proved difficult to collect because of these groups' mobility. In 1621 the viceroy of Peru referred to the tribute on the *pardos* as "of little substance and much noise." Eventually it was commuted to service in militia companies. Tribute and onerous neo-feudal obligations then became the lot, and even a diagnostic trait, of Indians.

The definition of who exactly was an Indian, however, remained malleable: "The Mestizo litigation of the 1770's [shows] the extreme socio-racial confusion of pre-Bourbon reform society. Many people in the lower strata did not belong definitively to Spanish or Indian society, and the official attempt to establish who the Indian population was for fiscal purposes underlined this previous lack of definitions."[18] Clever argumentation could make ethnic status depend on tributary, cultural, juridical, genealogical, linguistic, or (increasingly as time passed) body characteristics.

Because being a person of ambiguous standing improved one's chance of avoiding levies, or made it possible to maneuver among communal rights and outside opportunities, ambiguity became an asset as well as a stigma. The status of being mestizo acquired powerful attractions for "have-nots"; it brought tribute exemption and freedoms sometimes worth more than the poor safety of *ayllu* membership. By 1600 Indians already exploited a wide variety of strategies to evade state demands, including proof of noble descent or membership in exempted native categories such as Cañari allies. Natives could widen the cracks by exploiting the law's lack of clear genealogical definitions: How many degrees of noble or white blood-kin, and what kinds, made an exempt person? The derecognition of native nobility after the 1780 Túpac Amaru II rebellion closed one door to exemption but not what one anthropologist called "the mestizo escape-hatch."[19] In all periods suspicious Spanish thought Indian women married non-Indians just so that their children would be exempt from tribute and forced labor. By the mid–seventeenth century, at least one observer thought this tactic, along with disease and alcoholism, was helping to bring down the absolute numbers of the Indian population. Ramírez del Aguila in his *Noticias politicas de Indias* (1639) wrote: "The Indian race diminishes and the Spanish one increases as it thus attracts and consumes the Indians."[20]

[18] Martin Minchom, *The People of Quito,* 63.

[19] Marvin Harris, *Patterns of Race in the Americas* (New York, 1964).

[20] Cited by Thierry Saignes in *Caciques, Tribute and Migration in the Southern Andes* (London: Institute of Latin American Studies, 1985), 24–25.

Hispanizing one's language, dress, and lifestyle could help one along the escape route. How far one got was sometimes a matter of sumptuary daring – a lot depended on readiness to break ranks by putting on a Spanish-style cotton shirt and breeches. Indians who became mestizos not only dodged forced labor and tribute but also came under the usually negligent authority of the diocesan clergy rather than the stricter missionary clergy. "They change their clothes, putting on a cape, letting their hair grow and many putting on hose, and with this call themselves mestizos," wrote an irritated Spanish friar in 1713.[21] For the many children of Spanish–Indian or Spanish–mestizo unions who lived in Indian communities as Indians, even small amounts of Spanish "blood" offered hope of exemption through legal pleading. In Alto Peru, Antonio and Agustín Carillo won a suit in 1603 by showing that, although they lived in Potobamba, a village obligated to the *mita*, their mother was a mestiza and they were therefore exempt. The state's attorney in the *audiencia* of La Plata warned that this was a dangerous ruling that might flood the court with petitions by Indians claiming some Spanish background.[22]

That was not in fact what happened. Indians born of Church-sanctioned and recorded unions, living in Indian communities, and registered as tributaries found little opportunity to pass as non-Indians. Cases brought before the *audiencia* of Quito are illustrative of the process. In cases from circa 1680 to 1780, about 100 persons presumed to be Indians, usually men, tried to avoid tribute obligations by petitioning the court for recognition as mestizos. They usually provided testimony and witnesses about their genealogies. At the same time, local *caciques* and *cobradores* (tribute collectors) offered counterevidence. It was to both chiefs' and collectors' economic interest to increase the pool of tributaries, share the tax burden, and for these purposes challenge the petitioners. The would-be mestizos were usually poor people born of "illicit friendship" between Indian women and Spanish or mixed-breed men. A few of these underdogs won. One was Francisco Paz y Zambrano, from a town near Latacunga. He asked to be unlisted for tribute and forced labor on grounds of being a *montañés*: His father had been an Afro-Indian (*zambo*) and his mother a *montanés*. The local *cacique* Don

[21] Fray Manuel Pérez, cited by Magnus Mörner in *La corona española y los foráneos en los pueblos de Indios de América* (Stockholm, 1970), 145.

[22] Archivo Nacional de Bolivia, M 125, n. 2, cited in Jeffrey A. Cole, *The Potosí Mita 1573–1700* (Stanford, 1985), 35.

Lorenzo Hati argued that Paz y Zambrano's mother was an Indian, that her father's family really bore the conspicuously native surname Cayza, and that the family had been tributaries to the Hatis. Thus the father's racial designation should not remove Paz y Zambrano from the tribute rolls. The *audiencia* disagreed and made the petitioner a mestizo in 1731.

Arguments in these cases reveal that identity as Indian or mestizo was a contested matter involving economic interests. By putting mestizos outside both the Indian and the Spanish "republics," Spain had made the behavioral correlates of mestizo identity indefinite, and, once *mestizaje* became advantageous, this slipperiness came back to haunt the law: Varied behaviors could be adduced as proof of being mestizo. Up to a point mestizo was as mestizo did. Dress, association, custom, and appearance could make the difference. The result was a cycle of sumptuary tail chasing: Spaniards tried to distinguish themselves from Indians and mestizos by adopting ever-updated social markers like boots, swords, and wigs, while would-be mestizos followed behind seizing on the latest and most fashionable signs of being non-Indian. In 1703 the illegitimate mestizo Diego de Velasco, a merchant in Popayán, based his claim for exemption on his dress and occupation as much as his origin.[23] Wearing "Indian garb" (*traje de indio*) or "tunic and cloak" (*camiseta y manta*) was often used in the *audiencia* of Quito as an index of Indian status, or at least the *caciques* and tribute collectors tried to use it so. Would-be-mestizo petitioners countered that poverty alone made them dress as Indians.

However much custom, dress, language, and associations counted as markers of Indian or hispanic status when genealogy was unclear, Iberian elites never relinquished the conviction that in principle social identity was "really" a matter of blood. Even within the mestizo population, distinctions were made between "new" mestizos (born of white–Indian unions) and those whose mestizo ancestry occurred several generations back. Paradoxically mestizos themselves could appropriate the principle of castelike genealogical purity; in Quito persons whose parents were both mestizo called themselves "clean" or "pure" mestizos – on the grounds that they were not of mixed origin! That the genealogical principle was too indispensable to sacrifice becomes clear in the case of Ignacio de Aguilar, a putative mestizo from the highlands near Quito, who turned genealogy to his advantage in 1771:

[23] Archivo Nacional de Historia, Quito, Mestizos, caja 1, leg. 2.

> I agree that no *cholo* should be exempted by any corregidor from tribute obligations for being dressed in Spanish clothes or speaking Castilian, and although having the traits and customs of a Spaniard, he must be counted on the lists of tribute because none of these exterior things alter his Indian origins; in the same way, neither should our dress, language, nor customs be used to force us to pay tribute.[24]

This view was key to Spanish-speakers' implicit rules of social taxonomy. Although many Spaniards and Creoles felt that behaving in a Spanish rather than an Indian way was the very essence of rationality, they also believed that choosing such behavior for reasons of rationally calculated advantage, rather than inheriting it, was spurious and blameworthy.

With the decay of the society of juridical orders or estates, the ideology of hereditary inequality appears to have shifted gradually from group-oriented criteria (genealogy, surnames, fictive kinship) to purportedly inborn attributes of the individual, and especially to body type. In the late colonial era, foreshadowings of modern racism became evident. A number of authors have noted an increasing dependence on color and appearance in the determination of mestizo status after the mid–eighteenth century. Color was becoming more salient in all the racial categories, including that of *español.* Descriptive terms such as *blanco* ('white') and *rubio* ('blond') became common in suits, whereas previously simply the term "Spaniard" had sufficed. The increasing use of color and racial physiognomy was part of the "enlightenment" trend toward the rationalization and categorization of the physical world, which took on increasing importance in American social definitions.

The Túpac Amaru II and Catari rebellions of 1780 marked a massive failure of colonial systems of inequality. The trials that followed their repression underlined imperatives and strategies of caste identity as Spaniards sought to rebuild them. Many mestizos who had participated in the rebellion did so in reaction to Bourbon reforms, which sought to extend tribute and forced labor obligations to mestizos and mulattoes. Whites also joined the rebellion, but of the many accused who claimed to be "*españoles,*" almost none were born in Spain; their kinship ties, occupations, and lack of familiarity with Castillian Spanish indicated that they were, by common criteria, mestizos.[25] In the repression of the rebellion,

[24] Archivo Nacional de Historia, Quito, Mestizos, caja 1, leg. 23, 20–20v.

[25] Scarlett O'Phelan Godoy, *Un siglo de rebeliones anticoloniales: Peru y Bolivia 1700–1783* (Cusco, 1988), 248–249, 267–268. O'Phelan Godoy points out that of 102 individuals tried after the rebellion, 63 were classified as mestizos or peninsulares/criollos. See table 28, p. 268.

the Spanish government, always anxious to forestall cooperation across *casta* lines, treated the rebellious Creoles and to some extent the mestizos leniently, while inflicting the full weight of repression on Indians and especially the *cacique* class. The colonial state defined the rebellion as an essentially Indian movement because the implications of recognizing the general nature of complaint as colonial rather than racial, and the possibility of cross-caste alliance, were simply too dangerous.

The stratification of colonial society by body type was well entrenched by the eighteenth century. Late colonial *casta* typologies did not necessarily emerge as codified norms in the way later racial hierarchies did, but they tended to disguise and complicate the sometimes alternate and sometimes parallel hierarchies of social class, profession, juridical status (noble/commoner), and religious prestige. Mestizos and other people of mixed origins found it increasingly advantageous to associate with colonial institutions and thereby be defined as "people of reason" (*gente de razón*). At the same time, they suffered increasing restrictions and scrutiny of their "defects." They made their way by carrying on economic activities seen as typical of mixed-blood people: retailers of basic foodstuffs and beer, lower artisan work, and urban services above the menial bracket but below the professions, such as schoolteaching. Many sweated at urban wage labor in building trades, while others worked as millhands in the textile and wood industries. In the countryside the *castas* tended to fill important mediating roles between colonial élites and primary producers: They were strawbosses, slavedrivers, teamsters, petty merchants, middlemen trading in crops, and tax collectors over Indians. Many turned themselves into what indignant Indians called "false *caciques.*" In late colonial highland Bolivia, Indians working in towns at artisan trades tended to become parents of mestizos; "specialization and 'mestizaje' made up an indissoluble pair."[26] Toward the close of the colonial era in Colombia, "low" urban occupations including surgery and schoolteaching were so clearly associated with *mestizaje* that individuals suing to have their purity of blood or nobility ratified, "invariably argued as a proof of their social distinction that they ha[d] not done ignoble work" of these types.[27]

[26] Rossana Barragán, "Aproximaciones al mundo 'Chhulu' y 'Huayqui'," *Estado y Sociedad* (La Paz) 8 (1991), 77.

[27] Jaime Jaramillo Uribe, "Mestizaje y diferenciación social en el nuevo reino de Granada en la segunda mitad del siglo XVIII," in Darío Jaramillo Agudelo (ed.), *La Nueva historia de Colombia* (Bogotá, 1976), 207.

In this late colonial era, artists including popular writers and genre painters including a few well-known ones became interested in complex permutations of *casta*. Their works display in meticulously detailed gradations the differences among purported "kinds" of people according to racial nuance. The majority of the *casta* painting series were produced in New Spain, but some were done in Quito, Lima, and New Granada as well. The captions register what seems to have been a burgeoning slang lexicon of ethnic terms: "Spaniard and *china* beget quarterbreed *chino*. . . . Black man and Indian woman beget Sambo Indian."[28] The paintings seem to express a public consciousness that enjoyed playing with the piquant contrast between the categorical simplicity of an old Iberian model of caste and estate, and the ramifying complexity of social types known in America.

But what was the attraction of such paintings, and to whom? They form a highly repetitive genre, with the same stock figures, often in the same clothing, appearing from one set to the next. They are almost invariably secular-oriented. The scarcity of religious images weakens the hypothesis that parish priests used them to help sort people for registration of vital events in segregated records. The paintings were often done in sets of sixteen. Yet few in America could afford to commission so many or had the wall space to hang them. And why would they? What Lima merchant or Latacunga hacienda owner needed a scene of mulatto and mestizo domesticity on his drawing room walls when he might see it out the window? Surely many, if not most of the canvases, were painted for the export trade, souvenirs of America for returning Spaniards. Perhaps in the metropolitan market they served to display exotica of the colonies. This would explain the attention to detailing and labeling not only the racial categories but also the fruits and plants of America made so beautifully clear in the local types painted by the Quito artist Vicente Albán in 1783. They may also have enjoyed a half-scientific cachet. At a time when Linnaean taxonomy was a new and popular science, its application to the American peoples may have been fascinating. This combination of scientific curiosity with artfully tuned snobbism condensed a complex order of power in a period of transition. Elaborations of *casta* modeling were at the same time a final playing out of the colonial model of ascribed group identities, which soon would be put to corrosive tests as the Bolivarian generation and its heirs promoted ideas of liberal indi-

[28] Magnus Mörner, *Race Mixture in the History of Latin America* (Boston, 1967), 59.

vidualism, and a prologue to the nineteenth-century racism which would deeply compromise the liberal ideal of citizenship.

The divided and subdivided typology of mixed peoples as painted did not, of course, actually restructure the fluid practice of mixed people. Mestizos, mulattoes, *zambos,* and the rest continued to seek their life chances pragmatically. For them, and eventually for all of Latin America, it turned out to be a fateful fact that the protean individual, the person who makes or chooses a social role rather than inheriting one, first arose not among a rising and financially potent commercial bourgeoisie, as in Europe, but within a stigmatized and universally devalued sector existing mostly among the lower classes. To such people the promise of citizenship identity, as opposed to ascribed group identity, must have been an important one, and the finely tuned racism that vitiated it must have been a costly constraint. Racially compromised liberalism was to have a powerful effect on understandings of peoplehood in the emerging independent states. There is, therefore, much realism in the historic tendency of South America's millions of mixed-origin persons to identify themselves not as a new people called "the mestizos" but simply and decisively as "the people."

BIBLIOGRAPHIC ESSAY

On the issue of racial definitions and the process of *mestizaje*, there are a number of general works such as José Pérez Barradas, *Los Mestizos de América* (Madrid, 1948); Angel Rosenblat, *La población indígena y el mestizaje en América,* 2 vols. (Buenos Aires, 1954); Claudio Esteva Fábregat, *El mestizaje en Iberoamérica* (Madrid, 1982); and most importantly, Magnus Mörner, *Race Mixture in the History of Latin America* (Boston, 1967). Still-useful early treatments include Richard Konetzke, "El mestizaje y su importancia en el desarrollo de la población hispano-americana durante la época colonial," *Revista de Indias* 23–24 (1946); Gabriel Escobar M. "El mestizaje en la región en la región andina: el caso del Perú," *Revista de Indias* 24 (1964), 197–219; and Carlos Deustua Pimentel, "Algunos aspectos del mestizaje en el Perú durante el siglo XVIII," *Revista Histórica* 28 (Lima, 1965), 154–162. All of these studies essentially approach the process of *mestizaje* from the viewpoint of colonial society. A more innovative attempt is *Visions indiennes, visions baroques, les métissages de l'inconscient*, by Jean-Michel Sallmann, Serge Gruzinski, Annette Molinié Fioravanti, and Carmen Salazar (Paris, 1992). On the Afro-indigenous encounter, see Jack D. Forbes, *Africans and Native Americans: The Language of Race and the Evolution of Red–Black Peoples*, 2d ed. (Urbana, 1993). On the general issue of ethnogenesis, see *History, Power and Identity: Ethnogenesis in the Americas*, Jonathan D. Hilt, ed. (Iowa City, 1992).

More recent scholarship has emphasized problems of individual or collective identity and indigenous perceptions of the process. The works of Thierry Saignes are particularly important in this regard. See, for example, "Métis e sauvages: Les enjeux de métissage sur la frontière Chiriguano (1570–1620)," *Mélanges de la Casa de Velázquez* 18:1 (1982), 78–97; and, with Thérèse Bouysse-Cassagne, "Dos confundidas identidades: mestizos y criollos en el siglo xvii," in the special issue of *Senri Ethnological Studies* entitled *500 años de mestizaje* 33 (1992), 14–26. (See also Bouysse-Cassagne's "Etre métis ou ne pas être: les symptômes d'un mal identitaire dans les Andes des XVIe et XVIIe siècles," *Cahiers des Amériques Latines* 12 (1991), 7–27, which focuses on how the great mestizo historian Garcilaso Inca faced the dilemma.) Roswith Hartmann, "Un predicador quechua del siglo XVI," in Sophia Thyssen and Segundo E. Moreno Yánez (eds.), *Memorias del primer simposio europeo sobre antropologi'a del Ecuador* (Quito, 1985), 291–301, contains the biography of a half-Inka clergyman who attained prominence in early colonial Quito. Other attempts to construct identities within the colonial structure are examined in Chantal Caillavet and Martin Minchom, "Les métis imaginaire: ídeaux classificatoires et stratégies socio-raciales en Amérique latine (xvi–xxe siècle), *L'Homme* 32:122–124 (1992), 115–132; and also Nathan Wachtel, "Note sur le problème des identités collectives dans les Andes méridionales," *L'Homme* 32:122–124 (1992), 39–52. In *Andean Journeys: Migration, Ethnogenesis, and the State in Colonial Quito* (Albuquerque, 1995), Karen Vieira Powers sees the self-transformation of "Indian" societies as ethnogenetic, even when externally visible ethnic "tags" showed continuity.

The processes of fission, recombination, and readaptation among indigenous peoples before and after the conquest has generated extensive regional studies but has rarely been discussed as a general complex of features. Ethnic constructions in the Andes or on the Andean lowland frontiers have generated some of the best studies to date. See Nathan Wachtel, *La rétour des ancêtres. Les indiens Urus de Bolivie xx–xvi siècle* (Paris, 1990); Chantal Caillavet, "Entre sierra y selva: Las relaciones fronterizas y sus representaciones para las etnias de los Andes septentroniales," *Anuario de Estudios Americanos* 46 (1989), 71–91; F. M. Rénard-Casevitz, Thierry Saignes, and Anne Christine Taylor, *Al este de los Andes. Relaciones entre las sociedades amazónicas y andinas entre los siglos xv y xvii*, 2 vols. (Lima, 1988) I, 266–268; and Isabelle Combés and Thierry Saignes, *Alter Ego. Naissance de l'identité chiriguano* (Paris, 1991). A recent work on the cultural reevaluation of indigenous identity in national context is Cecilia Méndez G., *Incas sí, indios no. Apuntes para el estudio del nacionalismo criollo en el Peru* (Lima, 1993) An important work on the Chilean frontier is Guillaume Boccara, "Des Reche aux Mapuche: analyse d'un processus d'ethnogenèse," (Ph.d. thesis, École des Hautes Etudes en Sciences Soccales, Paris, 1997).

On the problematic use of the concept of "tribe," the work of Neil Whitehead on northwestern Amazonia and Guyana are suggestive. See his "Ethnic transformation and historical discontinuity in Native Amazonia and Guyana, 1500–1900," *L'Homme* 33 (2–4), 126–128 (1993), 285–305. The creation of the "Caribs" and "Arawaks" as tribes in the Caribbean is treated in Neil Whitehead, *Lords of the Tiger Spirit: A History of the Caribs in Colonial Venezuela and Guyana* (Amsterdam, 1989); and in the documents collected in Peter Hulme and Neil Whitehead (eds.), *Wild Majesty: Encounters with Caribs from Columbus to the Present Day* (Oxford, 1992). Much is owed to the earlier work of Jalil Sued Badillo, *Los Caribes: Realidad o fábula* (Río Piedras, 1978). John E. Hudelson, "The lowland Quichua as 'tribe'," in Jeffrey Ehrenreich (ed.), *Political Anthropology of Ecuador* (Albany, 1985), 59–79, deals with the issue in a culturally diverse zone. It can be compared with Mary Helms, "The cultural ecology of a colonial tribe," *Ethnology* 8:1 (1969), 76–84. For a general review of the problem of ethnic formation on the frontiers, see David A. Chappell, "Ethnogenesis and frontiers," *Journal of World History* 4:2 (1993), 267–275. The militarization that results from the formation of tribal categories is examined in Neil Whitehead and R. Brian Ferguson, *War in the Tribal Zone* (Santa Fe, 1992), especially its chapter "Tribes make states and states make tribes"; Jane Rausch's *A Tropical Plain Frontier: The Llanos of Colombia 1531–1831* (Albuquerque, 1984) illustrates militarization in the context of republican independence. A famous and widely debated case concerns the Yanomami in N. A. Chagnon, "Life histories, blood revenge, and warfare in a tribal population," *Science* 239 (1988), 985–992; R. Brian Ferguson, "A savage encounter: Western contact and the Yanomami war complex," in Whitehead and Ferguson (eds.), *War in the Tribal Zone* (Santa Fe, 1992), 199–229. How these processes occurred historically is examined by David Sweet in "Native resistance in eighteenth century Amazonia: The 'Abominable Muras' in war and peace," *Radical History* 53 (1992), 49–80.

The impact of migration, demographic decline, and population disruption on groupings and classifications within indigenous societies can be seen in Nicholas Sánchez-Albornoz, *Indios y tributos en el Alto Peru* (Lima: Instituto de Estudios Peruanos, 1978), 39–49; and Anne Wightman, *Indigenous Migration and Social Change: The Forasteros of Cuzco 1570–1720* (Durham, 1990), while Amalia Castelli, Marcia Koth de Paredes, and Mariana Mould de Pease (eds.), *Etnohistoria y antropología andina* (Lima, 1981), examine the meanings and uses of the concepts *ayllu* and *parcialidad.* Peter Gow's *Of Mixed Blood. Kinship and History in the Peruvian Amazon* (Oxford, 1991) is particularly suggestive of indigenous ways of viewing the creation of new ethnic categories, and Peter G. Roe provides a case study of such constructions in "The Josho Nahuanbo are all wet and undercooked: Shipibo views of the whiteman and the Incas in myth, legend, and history," in Jonathan Hill (ed.), *Rethinking Myth and History* (Urbana, 1988), 106–136. Among the fullest treatments of the theme is "Wāribi and the white men: History and myth in northwest Amazonia" by Stephen Hugh-Jones, in Elizabeth Tonkin, Maryon McDonald, and Malcolm Chapman (eds.), *History and Ethnicity* (London, 1989).

The colonial project of turning "Indians" from a misnomer into a meaningful juridical category and an ethnic reality underlies much scholarship on the colonial regimes. Notable modern studies that describe this process are Nathan Wachtel, *La vision des vaincus* (Paris, 1971); Karen Spalding, *Huarochirí: An Andean Society under Inca and Spanish Rule* (Stanford, 1984); and Steve J. Stern, *Peru's Indian Peoples and the Challenge of Spanish Conquest. Huamanga to 1640* (Madison, 1982), and, for comparative purposes, Serge Gruzinski "The net torn apart. Ethnic identities and Westernization in colonial Mexico, sixteenth to nineteenth centuries," in Remo Guidieri et al. (eds.), *Ethnicities and Nations* (Austin, 1988). See also Irene Silverblatt, "Becoming Indian in the Central Andes of seventeenth century Peru," in Gyan Prakash (ed.), *After Colonialism* (Princeton, 1995), 279–298. Regarding Quechua "general language" and "Indianness," see Bruce Mannheim, *The Language of the Inka Since the European Invasion* (Austin, 1991). The problems inherent in creating the colonial ethnic and social categories and then trying to keep them apart are detailed in Magnus Mörner, *La corona española y los foráneos en los pueblos de Indios de América* (Stockholm, 1970). The *Padrón de los indios de Lima en 1613*, edited by Noble David Cook (Lima, 1968), illustrates the urban intra-indigenous melting pot; on native women in cities, see Elinore C. Burkett, "Indian women and white society: The case of sixteenth-century Peru," in Asunción Lavrin (ed.), *Latin American Women: Historical Perspectives* (Westport, Conn., 1978), 101–128. Rolena Adorno's "Images of *Indios Ladinos* in early colonial Peru," in Kenneth J. Andrien and Rolena Adorno (eds.), *Transatlantic Encounters: Europeans and Andeans in the Sixteenth Century* (Berkeley, 1991), examines the slippery role of bicultural expertise. On the reconceptualization of Andean peoples as offspring of the Inka, see Alberto Flores Galindo's *Buscando un Inca* (Lima, 1988). On the attempt to create blacks and mulattoes as separate tax categories, see Ernesto Germán Peralta Rivera, "Informe preliminar al estudio de la tributación de negros libres, mulatos y zambahigos en el siglo xvii peruano," *Atti del xl congresso internazionale degli americanisti*, 4 vols. (Genoa, 1975), 3: 433–437. Jean Jackson offers a model of creolizing cultural process in the self-representation of "tribes" in "Is there a way to talk about making culture without making enemies?" *Dialectical Anthropology* 14 (1989), 127–143.

The role of missions in creating new affiliations and identities has not been studied in depth, but Marivone Matos Chaim presents evidence in *Aldeamentos indígenas (Goiás, 1749–1811)* (Brasília, 1983); as do James S. Saeger in "Eighteenth-century Guaycurúan missions in Paraguay," and Susan Ramírez (ed.), in *Indian-religious relations in colonial Spanish America* (Syracuse, 1989), 55–85. Various chapters in Manuela Carneiro da Cunha, *História dos índios do Brasil* (São Paulo, 1992) provide material on transformations in the missions; especially good in this regard is Anne Christine Taylor, "Historia pós-colombina da Alta Amazonia," 213–238; and Antônio Porro, "História indígena do alto e medio Amazonas. séculos xvi e xvii," 176–196. A suggestive article for comparative purposes is James Axtell, "Some thoughts on the ethnohistory of missions," *Ethnohistory* 29: 1 (1982), 35–41.

The case of Maroon–Indian cooperation in the attack on Barquismeto is found in José de Oviedo y Baños, *The Conquest and Settlement of Venezuela* [1723], edited and translated by Jeanette Johnson Varner (Berkeley, 1987), 98–99. Roger Bastide, *Les amériques noires* (Paris, 1967), provides a provocative chapter on the theme of black–Indian encounters. On these relations in Peru, there is material in Frederic Bowser, *The African Slave in Colonial Peru, 1524–1650* (Stanford, 1974), and in Jean-

Pierre Tardieu, *Noirs et indiens au Pérou* (Paris, 1990). On the creation of Afro–Indian populations, most attention has been focused on the Garífuna. See, for example, Nancie L. Gonzalez, *Sojourners of the Caribbean: Ethnogenesis and Ethnohistory of the Garifuna* (Urbana, 1988); and "New evidence on the origin of the black Carib," *Nieuwe West-Indische Gids* 57: 3–4 (1983), 143–172; on the maroon "kings" of Esmeraldas, see John Leddy Phelan's *The Kingdom of Quito in the Seventeenth Century* (Madison, 1967). Adam Szásdi discusses the history of this famous seventeenth-century portrait in "El trasfondo de un cuadro: 'Los mulatos de Esmeraldas' de Andrés Sánchez Galque," *Cuadernos Prehispánicos* 12 (1986–1987), 93–141; and N. E. Whitten, Jr., *Black Frontiersmen* (New York, 1974), provides a modern ethnography. The case of the Avá-Canoeiro is discussed in André A. de Toral, "Os índios negros ou os Carijó de Goiás: a história das Avá-Canoeiro," *Revista de Antropologia* (São Paulo) 27/28 (1984/1985), 287–325. Comparative perspectives are helpful; See Rebecca Bateman, "Africans and Indians: A comparative study of the black Carib and black Seminole," *Ethnohistory* 37:1 (Winter, 1990), 1–24; Kevin Mulroy, "Ethnogenesis and ethnohistory of the Seminole Maroons," *Journal of World History* 4: 2 (1993), 287–305; and Jack D. Forbes, *Africans and Native Americans*, 2nd ed. (Urbana, 1993).

There is nothing quite like the North American captivity narrative literature and analysis of it for South America, but for the Araucanian and Pampa frontiers, there are the classics Francisco Núñez de Pineda y Bascuñán, *El cautiverio feliz y razón de las guerras dilatadas de Chile* (Santiago, 1866), and Diego de Rosales, *Historia general del reyno de Chile. Flandes indiano*, 3 vols. (Valparaíso, 1877). Modern studies include Susan Socolow, "Spanish captives in Indian societies: Cultural contact along the Argentine frontier, 1600–1835," *Hispanic American Historical Review* 72:1 (1992), 73–100; Gabriel Guarda Geywitz, "Los cautivos en la guerra de Arauco," *Boletín de la Academia Chilena de la Historia* 54:98 (1988), 93–157; Osvaldo Silva Galdames, "El mestizaje en el reyno de Chile," *Senri Ethnological Studies* 33 (1992), 114–132; and Carlos Mayo, "El cautiverio y sus funciones en una sociedad de frontera," *Revista de Indias* 45:175 (1985), 235–243. Dealing more broadly with interethnic contacts in the region, the work of Leonardo León Solís, *Maloqueros y conchavadores en Araucania y las Pampas, 1700–1800* (Temuco, Chile, 1990); Sergio Villalobos and Carlos Aldunate's *Relaciones fronterizas en la Araucania* (Santiago, 1982); and Martha Betis Rosso, "Interethnic relations during the period of nation-state formation in Chile and Argentina," (Ph.d. thesis; New School for Social Research, 1983), all contain much information on the integration of Europeans and mestizos in Indian societies. Also still useful is Robert Charles Padden, "Cultural adaptation and military autonomy among the Araucanians of Chile," *Southwestern Journal of Anthropology* 13:1 (Spring, 1957), 103–121; and Mario Góngora, "Vagabundaje y sociedad fronteriza en Chile (siglos xvii a xix)," in *Estudios de la historia de las ideas y de historia social* (Valparaíso, 1980), 341–390. On European transformation of indigenous categories into ethnicities, see Roberto Pineda Camacho, "El rescate de los Tamas: análisis de un caso de desamparo en el siglo XVII," *Revista Colombiana de Antropología* 23 (1980–1981), 327–363.

On the ambivalent and changing position of mestizos in colonial and indigenous societies, see Stuart B. Schwartz, "Colonial identities: Race, class, and gender in the *Sociedad de Castas*," *Colonial Latin American Review* 4:1–2 (1995), 185–202. An important case study for early Peru is María Rostworowski de Diez Canseco, *Doña Francisca Pizarro, una ilustre mestiza 1534–1598* (Lima, 1989). Luis Miguel Glave and María Isabel Rémy have shown how formerly Indian "reductions" became mestizo towns in *Estructura Agraria y Vida Rural en Una Región Andina* (Cusco, 1983). The ways in which ethnic definitions could be affected by dress, language, and other social factors is mentioned specifically in Pedro Ramírez de Aguila, *Noticias políticas de Indias y relación descriptiva de la ciudad de La Paz* [1639] (Sucre, 1978), and is well illustrated in Martin Minchom, *The People of Quito, 1690–1810: Change and Unrest in the Underclass* (Boulder, 1994). Jaime Jaramillo Uribe deals in detail with matters of mixed blood, honor, and marriage in "Mestizaje y diferenciación social en el Nuevo Reino de Granada en la segunda mitad del siglo XVIII," in Darío Jaramillo Agudelo (ed.), *La Nueva historia de Colombia* (Bogotá, 1976), 173–216. For a partially parallel study from Bolivia, see Rossana Barragán, "Aproximaciones al mundo Chhulu'y 'Huayqui,' " *Estado y Sociedad* (La Paz) 8 (1991), 68–88. On mestizo participation in colonial indigenous rebellions, see Scarlett O'Phelan Godoy, *Un siglo de rebeliones anticoloniales: Peru y Bolivia 1700–1783* (Cusco, 1988), and Jay Lehnertz, "Juan Santos, primitive rebel on the Campa frontier (1742–1750)," *Actas y Memorias, XXXIX Congreso Internacional de Americanistas*, 5 vols. (Lima, 1972), 4: 111–127. Stern's "The age of Andean insurrection 1742–1782," in Steve J. Stern (ed.), *Resistance, Rebellion, and Consciousness in the Andean Peasant World, 18th to 20th Centuries* (Madison, 1987), 43–63, contains later researches on Juan Santos Atahualpa.

Although the era of independence and modern ethnography lie outside the scope of this chapter, readers may find useful Isabel Lausent's study of a Peruvian community in which, from 1870 on, the "mestizo" paradigm affected "mixed" Chinese: *Pequeña propiedad, poder y economía de mercado. Acos, Valle de Chancay* (Lima, 1983), and *The People of Aritama. The Cultural Personality of a Colombian Mestizo Village*, by Gerardo Reichel-Dolmatoff and Alicia Reichel-Dolmatoff (Chicago, 1961).

22

THE "REPUBLIC OF INDIANS" IN REVOLT (c. 1680–1790)

LUIS MIGUEL GLAVE[1]

There are moments when circumstances seem to pound away at existence itself: a lack of bread, or a feeling that everything is going badly. Native Andeans must have experienced many such moments during the various transformations in their way of life from the time of the conquest and colonial implantation onward. Nevertheless two centuries passed before conditions were ripe for indigenous people to rise up against the symbols of what oppressed them and against people for whom they had incubated a historic hatred. When they did they were influenced by explosive feelings, informed by new images of the world, and led by *caudillos* (charismatic strongmen) in whom they saw their own aspirations embodied.

Coexistence with the Euro-American "other" was a constant daily fact of life in the viceroyalty of Peru. It was never a simple one for anybody. The stratified and indeed estate-based social scheme recognized by officialdom and sometimes theorized as a set of paired "republics" – the "republic of Indians" and the "republic of Spaniards" – each with its own hierarchy, was crosscut by de facto differentiations of class, race, and access to power. The viceregal order that came under attack from Andean rebels and their allies was in some respects a typical European *ancien régime*, yet in others an unpredictably novel one shaped by peculiarly American forces including, as this chapter emphasizes, Inka and post-Inka institutions of leadership and ideologies of legitimacy. These pages synthesize the evidence concerning Andean rebellions and indigenous resistance from the end of the seventeenth century up to the penultimate colonial period, 1780–1800. It emphasizes forces within Indian society, forces traditionally neglected in favor of arguments about

[1] Translation from Spanish by Eileen Willingham, edited by Frank Salomon.

external factors, or macroscopic and "top–down" processes, which claim to explain revolt but usually explain only its context. The objective is to approach a political economy and an ethnology of mobilization, as well as to sound out Andean thinking and daily habits of resistance leading up to the late colonial explosions.

The "Republic of Indians" did not mount a single unitary assault on power but a number of qualitatively different struggles. These events included the wave of small movements throughout the *audiencia* of Quito (centered in what is now Ecuador) from 1680 on; the rebellion of Juan Santos Atahuallpa in the 1740s in Peru's central highland and central jungle regions; and the massive prerevolutionary insurrections led by Túpac Amaru II and Túpac Catari in the South Andean region starting in 1780 (see Map 22.1) The chapter ends with an account of post-revolutionary events and the effects of the conjuncture on local politics within indigenous communities circa 1790.

These conspicuous peaks of conflict were not the only events that merit attention. Less conspicuous events occurring in parallel are also ingredients of any explanation. Some key questions help bring the material into focus: What social, economic, and cultural attributes of indigenous society put peasants into play as rebel actors? How did the step from daily forms of resistance to social mobilization and violence come about? When and why did the indigenous population take up the cry for Inka-descended leadership? What factors explain the divided participation of the native noble lineages and the heterogeneity of the indigenous response? What cultural notions of legality and right informed rebel activism? And how did all of these respond to imperial frameworks of market and taxation?

We begin by studying the social and economic situation forming the background of rebel actions. This background includes the manner in which indigenous society was changing, and the corresponding change that took place in relations with the "Republic of Spaniards." These colonial "republics," though they represented a single colonial situation and a single macroscale economy, grew up as institutions of social segregation, meant to function as watertight compartments, each with its own set of laws. Some native leaders thought that ideal legality meant Indians and Spaniards in Peru should form distinct hierarchies side by side, each subordinate to the crown, but without one being subordinate to the other. The "Republic of Indians" in practice was not, however, an Inka residue but a specifically colonial order: Indians in towns, numbered and

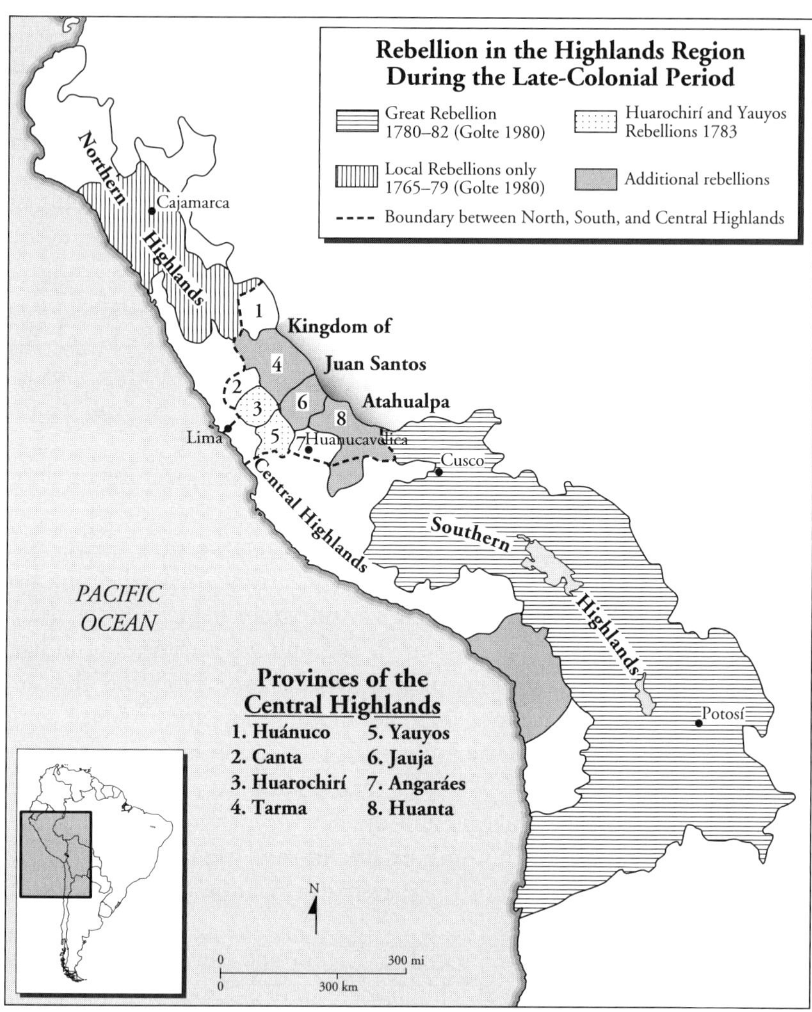

Map 22.1

controlled, subject to tribute payment, governed by their own authorities but ruled by Spaniards (the *corregidores de indios* or district governors of natives), who mediated between them and the state and who, in practice, proved to be their most tenacious exploiters. Indigenous people were protected by extremely complex laws, to which they knew how to appeal. At the same time, these same laws subjected them to subordinate status in colonial society and failed to protect them from predatory collusion between privileged Indians and Spanish clergy or bureaucrats (see

Chap. 15). Although the colonial Indian "republic" formed a social pyramid, and not just an ethnically labeled peasant class, the whole indigenous pyramid stood with increasing clarity under, rather than alongside, its Iberian counterpart. And its defensive value had been deeply compromised by economic penetration.

ECONOMIC CONSIDERATIONS

After the defeat of the initial resistance movements at the beginning of the colonial period (see Chap. 12), and the emergence of a short-lived nativism (the famous but still poorly understood sixteenth-century movement called Taki Unquy), the indigenous peoples faced colonial domination, by deploying a double practice.

The first practice was the legal strategy of adaptation.[2] It entailed visits to the viceregal courts, written petitions via the protectors and *procuradores* (legal representatives) of the indigenous population, as well as some more or less clandestine negotiating with *encomenderos* (Spanish overlords by crown grant) and *vecinos* (Spanish burghers). Vast sums of money were invested in such juridical maneuvers. Successful holders of native office used colonial legality itself to defend their interests and their subjects, or sometimes to sell those interests out cynically and thereby give a footing to rebellion against collaborationists within the hearth of indigenous society.

The second practice, also nonviolent, made up the "hidden face of the *reducción*" – that is, the unofficial internal dynamic of the resettlement towns (*reducciones*) into which Spaniards thought they had decisively placed the native majority. These parishes were indeed important but not in the way it appeared from the outside. They gave rise to a calculated and intense indigenous "diaspora": Indigenous people left their towns and "hid" themselves in other towns, the mining cities, valleys, or the nascent great estates or haciendas. Fugitive Indians in the diaspora became known as *forasteros* ('outsiders', or migrants separated from their kinship group and their descendants), and the art of controlling them was one that native lords or *kurakas* learned quickly (see Chap. 15). With migration and market involvement taken into account, no Andean group was any longer exhaustively definable as an ethnic group. Economic life,

[2] Steve J. Stern, *Peru's Indian Peoples and the Challenge of Spanish Conquest: Huamanga to 1640*, 2nd ed. (Madison, 1993).

forms of cooperation, and collective responses to the demands of the "others," all had given the indigenous way of life a permanently liminal nature. "Indian" lifeways consisted in good part of efforts to improvise novel tactics amid institutions hostile to innovation. Reproduction and daily life took place through stubborn maintenance of the ethnic economy (meaning that the factors of production and distribution were managed under a leadership with ethnic legitimacy and an extensive organization of feudal type), but at the same time, it occurred within full incorporation into the market, both in terms of goods and labor, and amid interpenetrating ethnic flows. The indigenous population displayed a delicate "plasticity" in its relations with the varied interests of economic and power groups.

What we observe, then, is "resistance through adaptation": legal and political initiatives combined with daily "tactics" of resistance to meet the long-term "strategy" of colonial domination.[3] Opportunities for daily resistance derived from shifting conditions within the ethnically categorized society. Members of Andean nations were differentiating into community Indians, estate-bound Indians, bearers and muleteers, miners, merchants, and so forth. The Andean ethnic groups (that is, the cultural-political blocs once recognized by Inka rule, e.g., Qulla or Qolla, Cañari or Yauyo) were becoming different peoples – peasant peoples. As they made innovative distinctions among themselves, they also related to each other – and to the non-Andean "others" – differently. This peasant transformation, which reinforced a more general Indian identity, would in time bring with it (in most regions) the end of the large territorialized ethnicities, as they had been reproduced during more than a century of daily colonial resistance.

This change, one of great magnitude for the ethnology of Andean indigenous society, sums up a long material and economic process. We know of it in part through colonial mine and agricultural accounts. In the state accountancy called *hacienda fiscal*, the registers dedicated to the Indians varied over time. Early on, payment of tributes was assigned in the form of a quota established according to native groups' resources, number of members, and skills. Assessments were often made in native products such as sandals, cloaks, or balls of alpaca-wool thread. This measurement of economic capacity was called the *tasa* – that is, the 'rate' that a community had to pay as a group. Within the assessed group,

[3] The model derives from Michel De Certeau, *The Practice of Everyday Life* (Berkeley, 1984).

Andean customary law acted as the "transformer" measuring out the group's debt in turns of household responsibilities. If the group came up short, it was its traditional ethnic leader (*kuraka*), not individual delinquents, who could be jailed. But in later colonial times, the *tasa* tributes little by little gave way to the first *padrones de tributarios*, or lists of tributary heads of households, divided according to their access to land. Under this system household heads who possessed land and family were called *originarios* ('natives'), and those who lacked full traditional rights (usually because they had migrated in while trying to avoid tribute payments elsewhere) were called *forasteros* ('outsiders'). Each tributary paid a tribute in money. Collective payments in kind gradually disappeared. The lists of tributaries were perfected over time yet never managed really to reflect the complex set of changes within Indian society. Inspectors and experts made untiring attempts to capture more accurately the daily process of cultural reproduction, and to identify changing social and economic categories within Indian society. For example, as village lords went on capturing and rooting 'outsiders' as subjects of their own, even forming "outsider *ayllus*" (using the Andean term for a corporate kin group), the 'native' and 'outsider' rubrics changed from categories of ethnic-territorial identification to tax categories registering economic variables (access to resources) and indices of social rank. These changes in tribute categories occurred within rural conglomerates that were themselves shifting in form from the *señorío* or ethnic lordship (post-Inka polity with kin-structured ruling lineages) to communities with multiple leadership structures re-created in the crucible of exploitation.[4]

This process, already notable in the post-Toledan order described by Saignes in Chapter 15 of this work, had gone far by the eighteenth century, when the Indians came up against new forms of organization imposed by Spain's new royal dynasty, the House of Bourbon (1700). The result of these changes may be called the end of the community-based tribute system. Because it was also the end of the era in which affiliations to old pre-Inka ethnic identities and ethnic lordship held in lineages with strong ethnic identities were the prevailing political facts, it

[4] For a historic model of the emergence of the peasant community as a product of colonial exploitation after several centuries of interaction, in the Mesoamerican case, see John Chance and William Taylor, "Cofradías and Cargos: An historical perspective on the Mesoamerican civil-religious hierarchy," *American Ethnologist* 12/1 (1985), 1–26. For a reformulation of the concept of closed corporation, which incorporates, at least in its conception, historical dynamics, see Eric Wolf, *Europe and the People Without History* (Berkeley, 1982).

could also be called the end of the "ethnic era" in politics and the beginning of the "peasant era."

The crucial time occurred between 1680 and 1730. The seventeenth century was an epoch of abundantly documented ups and downs in the area of fiscal reforms. After the great plague of 1720, the latifundist complex or hacienda, which would long dominate the Andes, took shape. The old system of *trajines*, under which long-haul transport was managed as a levy on ethnic groups, gave way to commercial muleteering, controlled by mixed-bloods. As the Bourbon regime embraced forced sale as a means to breathe life into Spain's export economy, governors of Indians were allowed and then required to make their subjects buy unwanted goods ranging from paper to hardware, called *repartos*. Together with the administrative signs that signaled a new conjuncture, there came changes within the indigenous sector itself: reorganization of the *ayllus* so as to remedy the disorders of migration, the redrawing of the ties of reciprocity, greater economic defenselessness, and tendency for indigenous élites to abandon collective ways of confronting colonial pressures and let each tributary face the system alone. The old community-based tribute system was exchanged for the more detailed and direct *padrones de tributarios* (lists of tributaries), which ended up being true fiscal censuses. In other words, during the Bourbon administrative transition, legislators and executives had to deal with a peasant society itself in transition.

The goal of this chapter, then, is to show how changes in indigenous society taking place on the slippery ground of Spanish administrative change gave rise to protest, new nativist mentalities, and Indianist affirmations. On the whole I argue that conditions for great social mobilization took shape only after the close of the ethnic era. The great Andean rebels were not engaged in reviving or continuing an Andean old regime. But this is not to imply that indigenous resistance in the age when ethnic affiliation and ethnic lordship still prevailed was only of the everyday variety, or that everything Indians did was part of the strategy of adaptation. Violent actions and conspiracies did surface well before 1700, but their nature differed from those of the eighteenth century, and we need to note them to observe how they differed from those of the major "age of rebellion."

Violent and determined as they were, early revolts had only inward-looking regional characters, without possibilities for taking root on a larger scale. It was in their geography that they etched the profile of what was to come later, in the eighteenth century.

For example, in a deep, coca-growing valley of the Eastern Andean *yunka* region (that is, the fringes of Amazonia), near La Paz, violent movements broke out several times from 1622 to 1626. Here, in Songo, the ethnic lords and the Indians, mostly migrants, or descendants of multiethnic *mitmaq* or Inka-era transplants, rose up against Spaniards. A later outbreak came in 1664. The boxed-in location of the towns where the indigenous population rebelled prevented the movement from spreading widely. However, in the nearby city of La Paz, the rumblings from the valley disturbed the authorities, who at the time were also confronting a situation rife with tension among the mestizo population. Fear of a possible alliance between mixed-blood people and indigenous people had always existed. The political situation of the entire La Paz area was very agitated at that time, and in 1661 the city's mestizos rioted violently. A confrontation with the non-"Spanish" population loomed as a truly dangerous and unknown possibility for the ruling colonial system.

Another local foretaste of what would someday become large-scale trouble occurred in 1632 on La Paz's high plains, where the stigmatized "Uros Uchusumas" lived on "floating islands" of reeds in the waters of Lake Titicaca. The Urus began to attack the most important transport routes for coca, wine, and people, assaulting passersby, and terrorizing the *corregidores* or governors of natives, who were the parties most interested in the smooth running of business. The Uru leader Pedro Laime guided his people in several victorious confrontations with the forces of one *corregidor*, who happened to be a close relative of the viceroy himself.

Chronic situations of insubmission meanwhile dogged the eastern Andean foothills. Far from La Paz the ever-resistant Chiriguanos had not yielded, despite several *entradas* ('forays') that soldiers and entrepreneurs undertook after drawing up agreements with the viceregal authorities and even with the Council of the Indies. Chiriguano zones were seen as ungovernable refuge and frontier areas, menacing the heart of the system at a time when it felt simultaneously threatened by internal tensions. Another troublesome periphery existed in the valleys of the far Andean southeast (today in Argentina), in the canyons inhabited by the Indians known as the Calchaquíes. There the romantic, at times grotesque, and finally tragic Andalusian Pedro Bohórquez, who had himself called "Inka," led a series of fights that Spain was able to suffocate only with great difficulty[5] (see Chap. 14). At the level of political legend and folk

[5] Teresa Piossek Prebich (ed.), *Relación histórica de Calchasquí*, written by the Jesuit Father Hernando de Torreblanca in 1696 (Buenos Aires, 1984).

ideology, his deeds reached far and wide, agitating colonial political society as a whole.

All of these events began to converge in the 1660s, and especially in the numerologically symbolic year of 1666 (the "three sixes" being identified with Satan), when a conspiracy was "discovered" among the *kurakas* of ethnic lords of Lima. It was a shadowy plot, in which many ethnic leaders seemed to be involved. The Indian conspiracy was quickly betrayed and aborted, but it had interesting ramifications: talk of insurrection was heard in Huarochirí near Lima, in the strategic Mantaro Valley, in Asillo in southern Qullasuyu (now the Bolivian frontier), in Cajamarca and in Tumbes in the northern sierra – in short, in all sorts of far-flung places and among ethnic groups that rarely interacted. How much was rumor, how much was the product of fear, and how much was born of an overly dramatic reading of unconnected events? Possibly a great deal, but the sheer contagion and staying power of rebellion as a theme suggested that new attitudes were being assimilated in the ill-controlled interstices of the colonial system, and in places where it was already slowly but surely changing.

Phantasms were feared along with real dangers: pirates, Indians in revolt, the devil, women, nature. The presence of God, the saints, and inspired mystics was felt to be quite evident at this time, expressing feelings about the unruliness and the increasing corruption of real-world experience. Actual mobilizations, actual economic protests, and actual threats to the viceroyalty did not form major parts of the history of the seventeenth century. Militias did not exist; they were not necessary. Yet even these vague foreshadowings form a kind of continuity.

What, then, happened to turn the last ruckuses and forebodings of the "ethnic era" into the real and deadly conflict loosed by eighteenth-century movements, particularly in 1780? The explanation for this historical change must be sought in the economic transformation – the mutation in the structures of society, of the market, and of the state – and its relation to the local powers of the heterogeneous Andean space. A model based on three institutions fundamental to the economic life of the indigenous population goes far toward interpreting it.

The first institution is the *reducción*, or Indian resettlement town – that is, the artificially nucleated parishes whose formation and early evolution are reviewed in Chapter 15. To understand the late colonial phases, one must take stock of the following factors: variations in strategies for managing resources inside 'reductions'; the quantity of resources in relation to the number of people; and linkages between all these and internal hierarchies with their mechanisms to reproduce power. From the few cases known in any detail, it seems that towns were internally transformed from ethnic formations into peasant ones. Fortunes of land tenure and market success came to differentiate sectors more than ranked lineage did, so the reproduction of outwardly "traditional" power would depend on harnessing the momentum of the new order to older symbologies with ethnic and "Inka" roots. This process would give rise to ceremonial forms that could be seen in Andean communities up to the current century.

Second, the tribute system must be examined. The "Republic of Spaniards" made several kinds of exactions on the "Republic of Indians," but however they are viewed, they all rested on the existence of the tribute. Economic histories have not emphasized this elemental fact enough. I do not mean to suggest that they have not taken into account the obvious existence of the tribute but rather that they have not placed it at the center of analysis. Researchers have been seduced by the spectacular complaints that other levies generated, while tribute has received only a few descriptive approximations or quantitative estimates. Thus protests against the abuses committed through the *mita* (or rotating forced labor levy), the *trajines* (or forced haulage system), the *corregidores'* forced distribution of commodities, along with their monopolistic schemes and abuse of personal service, all were the subjects that then and now have attracted analysts' attention. Tribute, on the other hand, was seen as something natural to that society – part of a great colonial pact, part of a deep feeling that combined personal relationships of dependency with a logic of exchanging reciprocal gifts, and with loyalties to the leadership of the *kurakas*. It is exactly the loss of this "naturalness" that we need to emphasize. As the market changed tribute became an economic imposition, pure and simple. Nonmonetary forms disappeared. Tribute collection was reduced to cash collection three times a year, with each tributary obliged to pay two of each three turns. The amount charged was calculated simply as what community resources could bear just short of provoking breakdown.

The turning point in the relation between tribute and resistance came about between 1690 and 1730. In this interval, for one, all indigenous people began to pay tribute, whether they were *originarios* or 'outsiders'. For another, in this period taxpaying ceased to be a community function as it had been under the old order; rather, as was noted previously, it became a matter of each household's individual responsibility to meet the quota corresponding to its entry on the registry. The peasant faced the state without a buffer. The end of the old collective quotas went together with internal social differentiation, the decline of ethnic lordships, and a more purely economic, less morally compelling political linkage to the colonial productive system through *kurakas* who were little more than bagmen.

The third institution we must consider is the market. The colonial market hardly resembled the "free market" later idealized by liberalism; it was a compulsory one, subject to open meddling by power groups, characterized by personal ties of dependence and at the same time by persisting bonds of ritualized reciprocity among the members of the "Republic of Indians." But all told it was indeed a market, with prices set in the plazas, with routes that constructed social space via supply and demand, and with sharp enough competition wherever political "fixes" did not obtain. This market also changed. From being a system that extracted goods generated, produced, and distributed inside ethnic circuits, and only turning into commodities as they left the bounds of peasant Indian society, the market became a system in which the colonial enterprises directly managed the work of production and sold the products within the bosom of indigenous society – or simply swallowed communities whole, creating latifundia.

Such was the upshot of the most important colonial transition, the one that began at the end of the seventeenth century and continued into the eighteenth. With regard to the internal market of the colony, this transition can be imagined by contrasting the two successive forms of market and control of resources.

The first form was one based on the extraction of surpluses from ethnic economies. The merchandise came from indigenous productive systems still controlled by native society. Workers made goods for the satisfaction of tributes without being salaried by any commercial investor, so the reproduction of the system was truly an internal matter. When commercial capital did extract indigenous resources and labor, it did so not by buying out grassroots productive systems but by leveraging political power so as to manipulate connections among local systems. The *corregidores*, functionaries who exercised political, military, and judicial power over the political parts into which indigenous society was divided, were the principal beneficiaries. They held the keys to articulating parts of the macrospatial system of control. No one could, for example, organize an enterprise to run a big mine – which required heavy transport across many jurisdictions and a supply of basic foodstuffs from a wide zone – without political entrée.

Much of this changed in the second form. In this latter-day Andean market, Indians as individuals or (mainly) as households were made into forced consumers of merchandise. That is, the market's function changed from extracting surplus without directly controlling production, to obligating the Indians to consume products for which they had to pay with their labor in spaces controlled by the new non-Indian proprietors. As forced consumers they could be made into forced producers who used not communal factors of production but factors (such as primitive manufacturing plants) under the control of commercially invested capital. As this cycle took hold, new reinforcing factors followed. The new proprietors bought up lands, which in many places meant expropriation at the expense of the Indians. Such was the emergence of what is known as the agropastoral great estate of colonial times, the *hacienda*. It became *the* enterprise par excellence and the hub of social relations in the rural world. Mercantile capitalism collaborated with these schemes. A state commercial monopoly marketed imports from Spain, but Lima merchants added imports entering legally and illegally from Asian markets by way of Pacific shipping.

As the agricultural estates expanded, those pockets of indigenous populations that avoided getting locked into the territory of the agrarian enterprises managed to regroup themselves in several ways. These free-standing indigenous towns and communities controlled scant resources and found themselves obliged to work on neighboring estates to procure the money needed both for monetary tribute (because the forms of tribute paid in species were disappearing) and for the debts with which the *corregidores'* forced sales saddled them. In this process the indigenous community, free-standing in its marginalization, emerges alongside the agropastoral estate as the other great product of late colonial rural Andean history.

These three elements combined with and played off one another, changing indigenous society from within. The transformation gave rise to conditions for the rebellions, and for a growing new sense of identity, which may be called generic Indianness. That is, a person's specific ethnic heritage (Qulla, Cañari, etc.) mattered less in accounting for her or his fortunes than the fact of belonging to that vast lumping category called "Indians," which imposed on all ethnic groups a common set of problems.

Where mentality and ideology are concerned, the era witnessed the birth of the "Andean utopia"[6] – that is, the hope of an Inka empire reborn to embody the wholeness of Indian society as such. It generated forms of messianism and idealized Indianism over and over. Utopianism posed a challenge to the native nobility. The *kurakas* could no longer be litigators and negotiators in the interests of ensconced ethnicity, as the old lords of the early colonial period and the seventeenth century had been. They needed to transcend their own cooptation and frequently bad repute, because many were themselves complicit in predatory businesses or at least protected by them. *Kurakas* were by no means unanimous in going along with such innovation. Rebel "kings" therefore had the appeal of internal reform as well as that of rebellion against outside abusers. Thus if the great neo-Inka would-be monarchs, soon to appear in the age that corresponds to Europe's and North America's bourgeois revolutions, did represent the extremes of general Indian identity building and even of mythological ideology, they nonetheless also represented an attempt at modernization within the Indian "republic" itself – albeit in a form Europe was ill equipped to recognize.

REGIONAL VARIANTS: UPRISINGS IN THE NORTH ANDES

Any model of social functioning must accept diversity and exceptions, the more so in an extremely heterogeneous universe such as the Andean world of the later colonial era. The area that most markedly took a distinctive path was the territory of the *audiencia* of Quito (now mostly in Ecuador), ruled with only nominal submission to the viceroy by a panel of judges in Quito. Far from the mines of the southern Andes and from the network of Peruvian forced haulage, this region built its own political and economic dynamic largely outside Lima's orbit. North Andean rural and indigenous society gave rise to several waves of mobilization and social protest different from the more famous Peruvian pattern.

Two witnesses' reports dating from the end of the seventeenth century give an idea of the process of late colonial change and of its Quito variant. One comes from the Augustinian friar Francisco Romero. Born

[6] Manuel Burga, *Nacimiento de una utopía. Muerte y resurrección de los incas* (Lima, 1988).

in America, probably in Peru around 1659, and a student at the Augustinian convent of Lima, Romero wrote a text expressing a nascent Creole critique toward the turn of the eighteenth century. His *Llanto sagrado de América* (*Sacred Lament of America*) denounced the abuse of the Indians' rights as an outrage to the reason and conscience of the king, who had putatively won American lands to show the path of goodness to the Indians. Romero traveled to Spain in 1690, and 4 years later he returned to preach in New Granada (now Colombia), where he confronted colonial burghers with an ardent defense of the Indians. This provocative position led to his transfer to a convent in Lima, where he died in 1705.

His text is a polemic in favor of the indigenous people, argued from the viewpoint of Christianity and the crown's political interests (as opposed to colonial élites'). It is partly a product of his own thinking but is also a product of mobilizations and complaints made by the indigenous population of the northern region.[7] Romero's *Sacred Lament* is not the only text that champions indigenous rights, but after a century of petitions and court cases, in which the discussion of indigenous society had diminished from energetic theological and legal questioning to a routine din of administrative hassles, the Augustinian's text sounded once again a note that had become muffled. Not for over a century had Spaniards really examined the Las Casian ideal: the ideal of an empire that would incorporate Indians as crown subjects with a full complement of rights – not as concessions but as recognitions of their society's own merits.

A second cleric whose protest reflected the degradation of colonial order as administered from Quito was Francisco Rodríguez Fernández. Rodríguez expressed Creole consciousness in a somewhat different idiom, deploying the arguments for the "primitive" – that is, ascetic and altruistic – Christianity which the Franciscans brought to America. He saw predatory Spaniards as the reasons why the American flock had strayed from Christianity. Rodríguez knew what he was talking about because he was parish priest of Ticsán [modern Tixán], in the central Ecuadorian highlands, where the economy of primitive textile industry and the spread of wool raising at indigenous expense had created a society full of corrupt *kurakas* as well as crooked governors and curates.[8] One of his polemical sermons was printed as "Original Sin. A Warning Exhortation

[7] Francisco Romero, *Llanto sagrado de la América meridional* (Lima, no date).

[8] Juan Pérez de Tudela, "Ideario de don Francisco Rodríguez Fernández, párroco criollo en los Andes (1696)," *Anuario de Estudios Americanos* 17 (1960). The document is located in the Biblioteca del Palacio, Madrid, ms. 1.466, f.282.

to the Kingdoms of the Indies, About the Deplorable State To Which Their Own Original Guilt, Together With The Enemy Serpent [i.e., Satan], Is Reducing Them." The Spaniards he knew so well were guilty of using fake legal arguments to make Indians work for them, while base Spanish migrants, of obscure origins, never took any tool into their hands, unless it were silverware – which, to top it all off, they did not know how to use properly.

Rodríguez's book, published at the end of the century, reproduces "Original Sin" (1679) and another sermon pronounced in Quito in 1684. Rodríguez Fernández sets forth a long denunciation of the *obrajes* (primitive textile mills) in a style that could be called baroque with rough edges. Like Romero he revived basically Las Casian theological and legal arguments, modernizing them to resonate with Creole opinion about royal privileges that corrupted relations between the republics.

The textile mills, the center of the northern economy, were a frequent object of denunciations and complaints. Whether or not they enjoyed official license, nearly all were run as sweatshops for native labor. Licensed ones drew a labor force provided under *mita* or rotating *corvée*, which took a fifth of the native towns' populations in each turn and worked them almost unlimited hours, sometimes shackled and sometimes half-starved, in dark, filthy sheds. Not all mills were Spanish enterprises. Some were community mills, in which local native lords yoked villagers to tribute and to mercantile enterprises from which they benefited little. In competition with community textile mills, private ones grew at a spectacular pace during the second half of the seventeenth century, unleashing competition for labor. Villagers, already exhausted from keeping their own plots and herds while also serving in community *obrajes*, faced the additional intolerable certainty of being dragged away by *corvée* to serve the business of entrepreneurs who sometimes had no link at all to their communities. Control of the *mita* became a key to business success, of course, and *corregidores* could parlay their administrative role into corrupt prosperity. Meanwhile mixed bloods and marginal operators set up unlicensed mills (called *chorrillos*) at the edges of towns and trapped, especially, the land-hungry, debt-burdened, or vagrant victims of the system.

Alchon's innovative thesis detects a relationship between demographic dynamics in the northern *audiencia* and the later disturbances.[9] The

[9] Suzanne Austin Alchon, *Native Society and Disease in Colonial Ecuador* (Cambridge, 1991), 151.

seventeenth century as a whole had presented a clear tendency toward demographic recuperation. The trend was so strong that, according to Alchon's calculations, the *audiencia*'s population, rebounding from the early colonial epidemics, doubled by around 1690. With this early demographic recuperation as the backdrop, the mill economy played on a boom in cheap labor and on tensions of a population that grew while its control of land shrank.

The breaking point came in 1690. The occasion was an administrative shift: The viceroy duke of Palata ordered a "general numeration" or detailed administrative census to serve as a data base for taxation and labor levies. It had the same destructive effects on northern indigenous people as on their southern counterparts. Changes in tribute amounts and the unmasking of migrants who had escaped tribute by avoiding their homes, caused the population to become volatile in many parts of the north. Nervous villagers experienced this reverse together with a series of other disasters: In 1691 a smallpox epidemic spread in from southern Peru; 1692 was a year of general famine because of poor harvests, and the same year brought measles and smallpox epidemics from New Granada (i.e., Colombia); in 1693 the epidemic continued, along with a wave of diphtheria that by itself caused 3,000 deaths. The overall loss surpassed 10,000. In 1698 an earthquake brought down the central-Ecuadorian cities of Latacunga, Ambato, and Riobamba.

Indians' chances of conventional legal redress were not good. Father Rodríguez, with his characteristic blackly satirical tone, knew exactly how royal tours of inspection could be prevented from exposing ills:

> If an Indian wants to complain, [local Spanish notables and conniving village chiefs] entomb him in the stocks. They post a servant youth as watchman at the inspector's door, to keep any memo from slipping under it. And for the inspector's amusement they'll get together a tableful of card players, and maybe win some graft. See how it's all done? Nighttime and games. And what comes of it? [. . .] That inspector, with his decrees and horrible, I mean honorable, reports poses for the admiration of the court, dispenses phony expertise, and puts himself up for another post.[10]

The northern picture shows a typical crisis of the *ancien régime*, marked by epidemics, catastrophes, famine, and general upheaval. After the textile boom came a long period of demographic stagnation and economic retraction during the course of the eighteenth century. Quito's

[10] In Pérez de Tudela (1960), 356. Translation by Frank Salomon.

early eighteenth-century experience generated the conditions for violent social protest earlier than that of the viceroyalty of Peru as a whole. Minchom notes an adverse situation from 1690 to 1720 compounded by 20 years of poor harvests.[11] The indigenous population nonetheless had to keep on paying tribute. Minchom sees in this epoch the beginnings of retreat and crisis in the textile mill system. More to the point it saw a breakdown in the established standards for interaction between "republics" and among social classes. What Platt has labeled the "colonial pact" – payment of burdensome tribute and labor in return for recognition of communities' corporate rights – had failed. At this point tumult and protests exploded.

North Andean social protest expressed itself in several waves of locally important violence, which have been well studied by Segundo Moreno.[12] Protest movements occurred in the context of colonial legislation trying to deal with the internal changes in rural society. These included norms that, by the end of the seventeenth century, banned community textile mills, and in 1705 even annulled the mill *mita*. But change in the system of production, and relation between the "Republic of Indians" and non-Indian economic agents, was not necessarily a liberating change. The replacement for *corvée* was often *concertaje* – that is, a supposedly voluntary form of labor contract that actually rested on politically reinforced debt peonage. All sorts of causes could trigger rebellions, especially from the beginning of the century to an intensified period of friction around 1740–1750. These revolts took fairly regular forms, characterized by the use of music to rally rebels, the taking of plazas and churches where officials and churchmen were imprisoned, the burning of buildings, and murders or lynchings of people accused of being *aduaneros* (agents of the tax policies). Sometimes rebels would crown their leader as a native king; a peculiar North Andean title was *guaminga*, but the pan-Andean terms and symbols of Inka sovereignty were also remembered. When put on trial rebels often said they understood the new taxation to be a policy of enslavement under which they would have to pay by giving their children into bondage. Perhaps this registers their indignation at having tribute transformed from a matter of communal responsibility to one in which the immediate family became liable. Women frequently egged men on

[11] Martin Minchom, *The People of Quito: Change and Unrest in the Underclass* (Boulder, 1994).

[12] Segundo E. Moreno, *Sublevaciones indígenas en la audiencia de Quito. Desde comienzos del siglo XVII hasta fines de la colonia* (Quito, 1985).

to increasingly daring violence and took part in violence by mutilating the bodies of lynched captives. These northern uprisings seem to have in common an emotional climate of fury, distress, and even despair among the rebels. In Quito the mobilizations, upheavals, and uprisings also had an urban component. An urban plebeian class that arose in the wake of the change in rural society added to *quiteño* political commotions, whose most important moment came in 1765.

This later stage of North Andean conflict corresponded to the same years when early episodes of what was to become a much greater combat were breaking out in the southern parts of the viceroyalty. Indeed the northern and southern histories may be connected along a continuum. Extensive information collected by Scarlett O'Phelan indicates that the northern extreme of present-day Peruvian territory was the area where outbursts registered with greatest frequency in the early part of the eighteenth century: in Cajamarca near the edge of the Quito jurisdiction, in the Andes east of Trujillo, and even in parts of Huaraz, not far from Lima, moving toward the central part of the country.[13] The Peruvian north had an economic and demographic profile much like that of Quito. The central zone and the southern core, however, would develop a different process, equally complex and much more far-reaching.

TOWARD EXTENDED REBELLION

Protests over tribute collection, forced labor quotas, forced sale or *reparto*, service in textile mills, and personal service to priests marked the eighteenth century. More and more these levies ceased to respect the institutional forms of the Indian "republic" but simply became levies on individuals undefended by communities. Many protests understandably targeted the immediate governors of Indians, the *corregidores*. The *corregidor* had by then become not just a despot-entrepreneur, bad enough in the seventeenth century, but a commercial monopolist with a political lock on alternative opportunities.

Viceroy José de Armendáriz, Marqués de Castelfuerte (1724–1735) reported "that from the imprudence of the *corregidores* and the insolence of the subjects have proceeded fatal events, including the death of some of the former, such as [the *corregidores*] of Azángaro, Carabaya, Cotabam-

[13] Scarlett O'Phelan, *Rebellions and Revolts in Eighteenth Century Peru and Upper Peru* (Cologne, 1985).

bas and Castrovirreyna." Murders of *corregidores* and plots against local authorities appeared in the north, center, and south of the viceroyalty. Although there had been rural riots since 1710, it was not until 1720–1725 that a rebel conjuncture spreading through the whole viceroyalty came about.

Three factors marked this conjuncture. First, a general epidemic decimated the population in 1720, leaving more than 200,000 dead. A series of catastrophic years befell the population, caused by the appearance of a "warm phenomenon" (that is, the El Niño or periodically warming climatic shift) off the Peruvian coasts. Clouds warmed by El Niño produced floods in the north. An uncontrollable yellow fever epidemic caused by the wet, mosquito-breeding heat ensued in coastal valleys. Then came droughts in the north and, by unlucky chance, two devastating earthquakes. Second, as the crown became more determined to make its empire solvent, new tax practices were instituted, and quotas for *mita* labor were increased. Third, Viceroy Castelfuerte wore out public patience with his authoritarian meddling. He won the nickname *Pepe Bandos* ('Joe Edicts'), because he made free with his power to change law by proclamation.

The beginning of Castelfuerte's rule coincided with the end of an actual civil war between the viceroyalty in Lima and the *audiencia* of Charcas (modern Bolivia) over Paraguayan jurisdiction. The Guaraní Indians rose up in arms against Governor Balmaceda, ready like others to fight economic abuses. Once the governor was removed from office, the *audiencia* of Charcas named José de Antequera as *visitador* or judge-inspector to investigate the abuses that the deposed governor had committed. But from Lima the viceroy ordered the restitution of the governor, unleashing a struggle known as the *rebelión de los comuneros* ('revolt of the communities' or 'commoners'), with the controversial governor himself as a leader. With the indigenous population's defeat, the Creole leader was executed in Lima. Far off in Asunción, Paraguay, protesters attacked Jesuit churches for their alleged support of the reinstated governor.

The viceroyalty went through several years of disturbances, manifested in local riots, one of which, in Cotabambas, Cusco, will do for an example. It occurred in 1730, when Juan Bautista Fandiño held the *corregimiento* of the province. Because he was a typical functionary-merchant among the indigenous population, because of his personality, or because of specific wrongs committed or rumored, the Indians rebelled against his authority. This outbreak like many others occurred during a festival. The concentrated *ayllus* of Cotabambas surrounded the authorities, trapped them in the church where they had sought refuge, freed indigenous leaders imprisoned for not paying *repartos* or tributes, and killed Fandiño. They may have expected neighboring provinces to follow their example, but this did not happen. Such attacks on the authorities occurred far and wide but without coordination. In the Cotabambas case troops arriving from Cusco crushed the rioters, and the viceroy ordered the execution of ten indigenous leaders.

But a spontaneous rebel convergence in the direction of the "Andean utopia" began to take shape, at least in the actors' ideas. In the 1737 Oruro uprising, a leader, the mestizo Juan Vélez de Córdova, had himself hailed as a descendant of the Inka. He sought to link himself to the prestige of a noble descendant of the Inka in Cusco, Juan Bustamante Carlos Inca. It is not known if the latter really did conspire with Vélez. What does become clear is that the invocation of a lost age, when indigenous culture was hegemonic, opened a new ideological horizon and became the common denominator of otherwise disconnected actions over diverse locales.

Along with the local movements (Cajamarca, Tarma, Arequipa, Paucartambo, Huanta, Potosí), other, less localistic movements emerged. In Azángaro in 1736 a chief called Cacma Condori tried to rally indigenous leaders in a confederated protest. None, however, as yet achieved a consistent orientation or a way to transcend each local or "racial" group's tendency to fight its separate battle.

"THE SPANIARDS' TIME IS UP": JUAN SANTOS ATAHUALLPA, A REBEL MESSIAH IN THE AMAZONIAN PIEDMONT

The first rebel to achieve a generalized insurgency was the man remembered by his nom de guerre, "The Inca Juan Santos Atahuallpa." Sometimes an additional unique epithet, "The Invincible," commemorates the fact that he alone among rebel leaders managed to defeat Spanish forces and build a stable rebel kingdom lasting a considerable time. It was he who sent a message containing the long-remembered sentence "The Spaniards' time is up" to the viceregal authorities.

The eastern piedmont, located in the geographic center of the viceroyal domain, but only poorly controlled, was experiencing an era of economic growth circa 1740. In the hot valleys near Jauja and Tarma, new products were being turned out in greater quantities. Missionaries with commercial ambitions were opening a path for Western civilization, and migrants from the highlands followed. Close to the so-called Cerro de la Sal ('Salt Mountain'), in a place called Quisopango, hidden amidst the jungle near the Ucayali River, an obscure highlander self-named Juan Santos Atahuallpa was establishing a headquarters with large numbers of armed indigenous followers.

It was said that Juan Santos had traveled the length and breadth of Peru spreading seditious ideas and passing himself off as a descendant of Inka sovereigns. He had forged an alliance with the "Campa" (Asháninka) via their chieftain Santabangori. The "Campa" were considered the most numerous "nation" of the Piedmont. Once mobilized they attracted allies from among the Piro, Mochohos, Siriminches, and Conibo.

Spanish troops waged four campaigns to capture the legendary rebel chief. The first, in 1742, penetrated the jungle in two columns. One column was defeated by Juan Santos, and the other took the general headquarters, stemming the resistance of the jungle dwellers who defended the leader's rear guard. Juan Santos got away. The next year the Spanish took the strategic settlement of Quimiri (present-day La Merced), in the Chanchamayo Valley, but the rebels besieged and regained it. When the royal militia tried to attack it and recover the dead, they found the roads and bridges destroyed. From Quimiri, Juan Santos communicated with Chanchamayo, where some Indians had joined the ranks of the royal troops against the rebels. Juan Santos sent them a message of unity, inviting highland migrants to join with the jungle residents (whom highlanders had usually treated as foreign, and whom they called by the disrespectful term '*chunchos*'). A scared witness, the Franciscan friar Amich, reported the appeal's success, telling how "the [immigrant highland] Indians of Chanchamayo that night held great festivities, dances, and drinking bouts, celebrating the coming of their Inka just as the *chunchos* did, singing in their [Quechua?] language that they would drink corn beer from the skulls of the priest and the magistrate." For a time Juan Santos circulated threatening messages and controlled the Chanchamayo region, but he returned to Quisopango because he preferred to keep his general headquarters in the jungle.

Until 1746 the rebel leader alone ruled the zone. After 3 years a new column of soldiers attempted to finish off the insurgent, who constantly made his presence known beyond the edges of his lowland stronghold.

Reportedly rebels and royalists clashed across the Chanchamayo without ever actually meeting frontally. At length the royalists retreated. From then on the authorities established negotiations with the rebel through missionaries. No agreement ensued. In 1750 a third military campaign was launched, but these legions met with the same fate as the first two expeditions. It was at this point that the "invincible" rebels began actions against towns in the highlands, especially Andamarca in 1752. The feared alliance between the jungle *chunchos* and highland peasants seemed a real possibility – which was what Juan Santos wanted. Juan Santos's seditious messages kept emanating from the *gran pajonal* (the great grassland, a stretch under Asháninka or "Campa" rule) until 1756.

This rebellion, alone since the "neo-Inka" state of 1535–1572, had military consequences all the way from Amazonia to the high Andes. It is also unique in its duration – over a decade. It is often characterized as mysterious; although it won not a single one of its objectives, it was never defeated and never even fully understood. Little is known about the individual who incarnated the movement charismatically and directed it strategically. The fleshing out of Juan Santos's biography remains a task that may never be realized. However, two things are known. First, the rebellion's real focal point was the low, hot valleys, where the population was a diverse amalgam of refugees and marginal migrants coexisting with the land's traditional Amazonian owners. The latter had not been subjugated and were barely catechized. Moreover this indigenous population had suffered decades of ethnocide and had strong motives to rebel. Second, Juan Santos did not manage to establish a full working alliance with the indigenous population of the sierra. Recent studies question this conclusion, emphasizing the indigenous band's triumph in Andamarca and the terror unleashed throughout the Central Sierra as the lowlanders' incursions stimulated popular attacks and riots.[14] Nevertheless the impenetrable rebel domain on the edge of the jungle was not duplicated anywhere in the highlands.

The most intriguing aspect is not the opacity of biographical and military facts; more important is the rebels' message. What has come down to us of the confused and messianic ideology that impregnated the leader's thinking reaches us in the form of statements made under pres-

[14] See the pioneering study by Stefano Varese, *La sal de los cerros* (Lima, 1973), for more on these populations and the rebellion. See also the essay by Steve J. Stern in his compilation, *Resistance, Rebellion and Consciousness in the Andean Peasant World. Eighteenth to Twentieth Centuries* (Madison, 1987).

sure, and from the writings of Franciscans and Jesuits. The image is frankly insufficient. But what does emerge clearly is the potent invocation of the image of the Inka. Juan Santos, *Apo-Inca* ('Lord Inka'), had appropriated an image *already* spread throughout the entire territory and made it the oppositional counterpoint to the socioeconomic process that we call "generic Indianization."

What differentiates Juan Santos as a messiah of the "Campa" and Amueshuas from the "Andalusian Inka," Pedro Bohórquez, who had acted analogously among the Calchaquíes a century earlier? A partially "Indian" birthright status, perhaps, but we really know nothing of his genealogy. Certainly Bohórquez exerted as much influence among the Calchaquíes as Juan Santos did among the indigenous of the central jungle region, even though Bohórquez must have seemed conspicuously foreign. The two hero-adventurers' fortunes were decided not so much by differences between their persons as between their eras. Bohórquez was a transfrontiersman living out a military fantasy beyond the bounds of his own system, marginal, a character out of the theater, almost baroque. Juan Santos was an effective politician working at a moment when his project was not quixotic or exotic but relevant to live issues throughout the Spanish system. That is why he became a spark in the blaze that would soon rock the Andean domains.

By the end of Juan Santos's career, 1756, the fear gripping the Andes was not the possibility of an uprising but rather the certainty that one could occur. We will see later that on the eve of the great rebellion of 1780, pent-up violence and fury was a constant in people's lives. Local disturbances, which had been spreading throughout the territory since the beginning of the century and which were becoming more numerous and closer together by mid-century, were a warning. Upheaval was seen where it existed – for many local and concrete reasons, not necessarily linked to Juan Santos's movement – and even where it did not. Creoles and mestizos hastened to uncover conspiracies, partly because rebel hunting might protect them from possible suspicions about their own equivocal commitment to the crown.

It was no coincidence that Jorge Juan and Antonio de Ulloa, authors of the famous *Noticias Secretas* (a remarkably intelligent intelligence report on colonial affairs, prepared for the Spanish crown) wrote the following about Juan Santos:

> This inconsiderate conduct that the *corregidores* show the Indians was the origin of the uprising of the *chunchos*, who recently withdrew their obedience and,

occupying sites neighboring Tarma and Jauja, in the eastern part of the Andes mountains, declared war on the Spaniards, in the middle of the year '42. . . . [A]nd these are some of the tyrannies that the *caudillo* told them he would try to reform, removing them from the government of the Spaniards; this was also the motive for fear that the entire province of Tarma would follow the rebel's band, fleeing the weight of tyranny, which seems to them to be ever increasing.

Fear was not a new sentiment. We have had many occasions to mention it in describing the crisis of the Andean baroque period. Terror, a mute feeling that informed beliefs, attitudes, and ways of living, was omnipresent. City-dwellers' fears, especially *limeños'*, fed by pirates, Englishmen, pagan gods and even rebel Indians, was at first of an extremely ethereal nature. It did not respond lucidly to the historical processes that were actually taking place. Early eighteenth-century anxiety was similar to the unease that middle-class inhabitants of Lima today feel in the face of the millions of poor migrants occupying the outskirts of the city. But the fear of 1742–1752 had a very real origin. The utopias of indigenous society had changed, and utopia became the banner of diverse social sectors that could not confront hunger or shortages in any way short of explosion. The coming of the Inka was no longer a utopia in the usual sense. It became an actual project in one region after another and was seen as an avenue of choice, not fantasy, in popular Andean sentiment almost everywhere. In 1780 it would have a name: Túpac Amaru II.

PRECURSORY REBELLIONS AND THE SLOW MILITARIZATION OF PERU

We know little about most of these local precursory rebellions. In 1750 in Huarochirí province, which contains the mountains overlooking Lima, collusion between mestizos and an indigenous group failed. The conspirators who allegedly sought to take Lima and restore the Inka empire were also supposedly involved in the jungle uprising, or at least trying to be. In Huarochirí, too, the leader had himself titled Inka, and although no march against the viceregal capital ever materialized, natives of some Huarochirí communities did attack Spaniards, killing more than a dozen in their vicinity. Beyond that the story recedes into colonial paranoia. How do we know that an urban–rural conspiracy existed? Through a confession to a friar, who denounced his penitent to the Viceroy Count of Superunda. What is clear is that in the Lima area and in Huarochirí, from 1660 on and again later in the epoch of Túpac Amaru II, in 1783, indigenous people were prone to "become stirred up," and that in such states the standing of the Inka grew along with discontent sparked by the conditions of economic reproduction.

The plan for the insurrection in Lima reveals that Indians now thought themselves capable of colossal deeds. The uprising was to take place in the heart of the city of Lima on a symbolic occasion: during the festivities of the Archangel Saint Michael, when indigenous nobles paraded with their arms, as they had been taught to do by the Jesuits in the seventeenth century. The plot as confessed shows signs of incorporating a symbolic numerology: 500 indigenous people were to attack the seat of government, and another 500, the citadel and fortress of Callao. On each corner of the city, fifty armed Indians would indiscriminately kill Spaniards, while another fifty would proceed to the houses of the *audiencia*'s principal ministers and exterminate them. The number five was, we know from an early Quechua source (see Chap. 1), the characteristic symbol of plenitude in Huarochirí's mythology, and the emphasis on multiples of ten suggests the Inka system of decimal management.

Conspirators were imprisoned on an informant's testimony, and after summary trial, executed in the central square. But the would-be leader, Francisco Inca, managed to flee. He reached Huarochirí and executed a *corregidor* along with other functionaries. The bodies were mutilated, like those of the rebels put to death in Lima. In the Huarochirí highlands a rebellion broke out, resounding with radical anti-Spanish rhetoric against the *mitas*, textile mills, tributes, and *corregidores*, and proclaiming the reestablishment of Inka government. The rebels sabotaged roads and bridges. Black slaves were called upon to rise up and tempted with the offer of freedom. But the rebellion was unable to expand far; combined forces from Lima and Tarma, returning from their defeats at the hands of Juan Santos, along with indigenous people from the nearby village of Langa, who opposed those from Huarochirí, quelled the rebels. The leaders were hung in Huarochirí, and others in Lima. Search operations mopped up by looking for insurgents in the province of Canta. Hamlets were burned, and all suspicious adult males were imprisoned. After the 1750 events, according to Spalding's detailed research, nothing changed in Huarochirí.[15]

But the multitude of local crises did work one major change on Spanish-Peruvian society by slowly, cumulatively militarizing it. Although military prowess in service to royal authority had long been a

[15] Karen Spalding, *Huarochirí: An Andean Society under Inca and Spanish Rule* (Stanford, 1984).

credential for power, the Peruvian military as a regular army with professional officers took shape only in the later eighteenth century. Before 1742 armies were created ad hoc by would-be seigneurs investing their money in armed bands to do the king's will, and by then reclaiming honors and payments after whatever victories they won. Formal garrisons in places of strategic importance were set up in response to naval harassment coming from British and other hostile ships. But the troops were marginal people from Spain, poorly paid and poorly equipped. Their effectiveness was low. By the later eighteenth century, successive defeats and the discredit of Spanish arms made room for change in the military sector.

Despite the fact that orders for formalizing and dignifying the military career arrived at about the time of the changeover from Hapsburg to Bourbon rule, no significant evidence exists for the actual functioning of regularly unified modern militias – as had begun to appear in Buenos Aires, Cartagena, Chile, and Central America, for example. In Peru they began to emerge late: in the period close to 1780 – the time of Túpac Amaru II – and, usually, only after the rebellion had already become a threat. The one major effort at formalizing the army before then – that of the military viceroy, Amat y Junient, who from 1736 on built up the famous Lima Dragoons and arranged to have militias prepared throughout the territory – yielded little result. Peruvian troops' effectiveness was poor when events put them to the test. But the presence of the officers in the countryside did prove a factor for change in the local power structure. A formal set of rules for the militias did not arrive until as late as 1793. The late chronology of Peruvian militarization suggests that Bourbon aspirations to an efficient state contributed to it, but that the project only became urgent after the cycle of great rebellions peaked during 1742–1782.

RESISTANCE AND REBELLION AMONG THE AFRICAN-ANDEAN POPULATION

African-born and African-descended slaves made up an important part of the viceroyalty's rural population, above all in the coastal valleys of central Peru. Their presence was significant, given constant racial and cultural mixing, but their influence on the indigenous population has not yet received much scholarly attention. It seems that a large portion of the rural Peruvian and Andean population experienced a process of colonial African-Andean ethnogenesis (see Chap. 21). North of present-day Ecuador, in the Chota Valley, modern villagers of partly African descent speak the indigenous language and dress like local peasants. Pockets of African-Americans also dwell in the present-day Bolivian valleys and in some valleys belonging to the eastern Peruvian Piedmont region. But above all the peasant inhabitants of Peru's seaward valleys along the central coast demonstrate a panorama of African-Amerindian-Iberian cultural and racial variety.

This came about because African slaves resisted Spain in their own way during what we call the "ethnic era." One arena was urban popular culture. In the cities "witchcraft" was practiced mostly by women, among whom Afro-Peruvians well-versed in the culture of their Andean clientele were prominent. Many African-Andean men found no such niche but rather made their way through the interstices of Lima social control as *cimarrones* (outlaw runaways). They took refuge in the *palenques* (a word of Antillean origin that means "inaccessible place"). *Palenques* functioned like whole fortified towns, dominated by self-emancipated African-Andean men. Along the Peruvian coast the most important *palenques* grew in the valleys near Lima and in the desert zones north and south of the city.

Self-liberated slaves in these ungoverned towns established links with indigenous people and with estate workers, both native and African. Pressing on urban society from the social margins, and sometimes involved in brigandage, they were nonetheless very well integrated in the economy and culture as a whole.

To the south of Lima, the *palenques* were located in the Mala Valley, particularly the hills known as Guarangal and Bujama. Testimonies report settlements of free blacks in places quite close to the viceregal capital, such as the arid hilly countryside of Chillón, Collique, Chuquititanta, and Carabaillo; Cajamarquilla in Huachipa; and the reed swamps of the Villa hacienda in the Surco and Chorrillos valleys. The *palenques* of the Garagay countryside were especially famous. The zone comprising Chancay and Supe was convulsed by revolts in the second half of the eighteenth century, with combats in Supe and Andahuasi. The radius of the Chancay mutiny extended as far as Cañete, Mala, and even Chincha and Ica. These toponyms add up to something like an atlas of circum-Lima villages, so it is easy to imagine nervousness about the black presence in the courts of the "City of Kings."

In Huachipa fascinating forms of religious syncretism surfaced. Along with Catholic rites, something like Voodoo was practiced. The leader,

General Francisco Congo – nicknamed Chavelilla – possessed special abilities; besides being a military and political boss (and builder of a fortress to protect his followers), he was reputed to be a sorcerer and shaman. His domain saw rivalries as a group called the Congos expelled those called Terranovas. Francisco Congo confronted the leader Martín Terranova, killing him in the end. But a tendency to break down intra-African and other barriers was already in evidence. On the economic side the *palenques* were linked to the urban market regardless of African-derived ethnicity. Women made baskets that they sold with the help of hacienda slaves. Their allies were the firewood vendors, freed blacks who brought wood to the city and returned guiding fugitive blacks and bringing news and goods. The link to the greater economy played a central role in the survival of the rural African-Andean communities.

In Carabaillo and Zambrano circa 1761, in the Chillón Valley, *palenques* took the form of long-term settlements, involved like other agrarian settlements in the rural crisis of the late eighteenth century. The area was characterized by dispersed black settlements, not militarized like Huachipa. In the Chillón Valley free villages, rivalries broke out between the African groups called Congos and Minas. Links with the market and with the haciendas were conspicuous.

Along with daily resistance at the social margins, we also find the first direct violent movements of the black slaves. Uprisings took place in San Nicolás de Supe, Andahuasi, and Villa. Between 1768 and 1779 revolts broke out on estates in the Nepeña Valley and in Supe and Andahuasi. Inhabitants of the *palenques* encouraged the rebels and ranged southward through affected territory as bandits. In these processes intra-African boundaries seem to have dissolved. The most important movement was a riot by the black slaves of the San José hacienda in Nepeña in 1779, just a year before the great indigenous rebellion. It began as a conflict between two men who each wanted to operate a confiscated estate held by the state after the expulsion of the Jesuits (in 1767). The first renter was succeeded, against his will, by the second. The dispossessed earlier renter allied himself with the estate's black slaves and incited them to revolt by spreading promises of liberty. The riot brought to light allegations of sexual promiscuity between the hacienda operator and a slave woman, and it exposed abuses in the issuing of rations.[16]

[16] On social movements among slaves and the black population, see Victoria Espinoza, "Cimarronaje y palenques en la costa central del Perú, 1700–1815," in *Actas del Primer Seminario sobre poblaciones inmigrantes*, II (Lima, 1988), 29–42. See also Javier Tord and Carlos Lazo, *Hacienda, comercio, fiscalidad y luchas sociales (Perú colonial)*, (Lima, 1981).

DISTURBANCES IN THE CITIES

The nature of the Andean city is still incompletely understood. There have been advances in the study of urbanistic ideas and the construction of urban political space, and certainly in urban economic history. Much less known is the history of indigenous urbanites, their cultural innovations, their interethnic contacts, and the way permanent urbanites connected with seasonal or involuntary migrants from Andean villages. Surely the "Spanish" city in America was not as strictly Iberian as its famous baroque facades suggest. Throughout the protests, the rebellions, and the urban uprisings, multiethnic traces emerged in urban riots and agitations. But at the same time in the great indigenous agrarian movements, the siege of the cities as such expressed the negative symbolic character that cities acquired in Andean peasant thought. Evidence of this exists for Quito, Cusco, Oruro, Cochabamba, Arequipa, and La Paz.

At Cochabamba in modern Bolivia in 1730, a mestizo member of the silversmiths' guild, Alejo Calatayud, led a violent popular uprising. Those were the years in which the new system of fiscal census was instated and higher tribute levels were posted, and some groups lost their exemptions from them. The city responded to Calatayud by exploding. Economic and class contradictions, combined with ethnic conflicts, inaugurated a new moment in the political struggle. Mestizos, Creoles, the city's indigenous population, muleteers, villagers from free-standing Indian communities, all attacked, surrounded, and seized the city. The protest in Cochabamba has been remembered as a movement to prevent the inclusion of mestizos in the tributary lists, but the conflict was actually much wider. If the fortunes of mixed bloods had been the only issue, why were artisan "mestizos" able to attract "Indian" allies? And if the protest was specifically urban, why did it end up involving peasants? Apparently the ethnic and social structure of the Cochabamba collectivity cannot be imagined apart from relationships between countryside and city, or apart from the unwanted effects of agrarian change within a colonial system trying to get in step with the times.[17] This mestizo mobilization demonstrates these first signs of spontaneous popular front formation, presaging the decline of the power and money blocs that *corregidores* and politically

[17] We know much about this regional process thanks to good studies, including the work of widest scope, by Brooke Larson, *Colonialism and Agrarian Transformation in Bolivia. Cochabamba, 1550–1900* (Princeton, 1988).

advantaged merchants were trying to shore up. The end of this local war was marked by fifty decapitations of alleged rebels.

Oruro was a different kind of South Andean city, built on silver-mining on the frozen heights, and housing a majority indigenous population. Soon after the Cochabamba events, the Oruro *corregidor* became the target of popular outrage. The protest leader was a mestizo called Juan Vélez de Córdoba. Proclaiming himself a descendant of the Inka, he claimed to be establishing links with prestigious Cusco nobles. Similar things occurred in Quito, in Arequipa, and even in Cusco not long before the eruption of the Túpac Amaru II uprising.

The most interesting case occurred in Arequipa, southern Peru, in January 1780. A violent outbreak focused popular wrath on the *aduanas* (customhouses) and *alcabalas* (tariffs), whose scope widened under the Bourbon policy of rationalization of the royal economy. In this region a new tax on alcohol proved especially inflammatory. The city rose up also against the forced sales of merchandise by *corregidores*, which affected mestizos and not just the indigenous population. Here as in Cochabamba, urban revolt crossed ethnic lines. Indeed, as David Cahill aptly points out,[18] the Arequipa event went well beyond antitax protest. It was a clear expression of class antagonisms: those without resources, the poor, attacked the "rich" as such. The alliance consisted of various groups, including a contingent of indigenous people from the parishes, who were clients of the muleteers and teamsters who had joined the revolt and who were these Indians' patrons and companions. Indigenous people and mestizos who frequented the *chicherías* (taverns serving corn beer) shared their feelings. Together they would discharge a fury that had been accumulating for decades. In what was historically a mere moment, the poor and people on the margins perceived the fragility of city defenses and rushed to the attack.

Detailed analysis of the so-called rebellion of the neighborhoods in Quito in 1765 leads to similar conclusions.[19] It too expressed class antagonisms compounded by the problems of Bourbon centralization and the discriminatory tensions specific to this compartmentalized society. Festival time turned from a playful inversion of identities into something

[18] David Cahill, "Taxonomy of a colonial riot: The Arequipa disturbances of 1780," in John Fisher and Allan Kuethe (eds.), *Reform and Insurrection in Bourbon New Granada and Perú* (Baton Rouge, 1988).

[19] Anthony Mcfarlane, "The 'Rebellion of the Barrios': Urban insurrection in Bourbon Quito," *Hispanic American Historical Review* 69/2 (1989).

more fateful. The symbolic peculiarities of festivals, such as alcoholic abandon and the license to speak the forbidden, undid normal social discipline and detonated plebeian action en masse, both in Arequipa and in Quito. Andean festivals often involve a "taking of the center," in which the *ayllus* or other celebrators temporarily invade spaces normally reserved for priests and governors; in moments of political tension, such invasions could easily take on a charge of real, even military, violence. As in Arequipa, Quito's rioters were not necessarily indigenous people. Mixed-bloods, and even Creoles harmed by the reforms, participated in the disturbances and tried to take over the city. The same occurred in 1781 in the highlands of Nueva Granada (Colombia), when the famous rebellion of the *comuneros* ('commoners') of Socorro in Tunja broke out. This event too was a movement against tax reforms, with the indigenous population allying themselves in demanding lands and better living conditions.[20]

Indigenous participation, so close to that of the urban plebs, highlighted the Andean face of "Spanish" cities. In Oruro and Arequipa, mixed urban crowds hailed the longed-for return of the Inka.[21] These were not indigenous movements as such, not even in Cusco, where several mestizo guild members joined in conspiracy to support Túpac Amaru II. They show that once the order of the "republics" was breached from above and questioned from within, it was by no means obvious or predictable what portions of each "republic" would follow what sort of leadership.

VIOLENCE AND DAILY CONTRADICTIONS IN A MICROCOSM: TÚPAC AMARU II'S HOME REGION

Over 100 case studies now document local protest actions, showing how an ascending spiral of violence toward the second half of the century, and the sporadic attempts at coordinating eruptions, such as those in the central highlands or Huarochirí, accurately presaged the revolutionary pinnacle of 1780. To understand this historic continuum, scholars of the rebellions have emphasized detailed microanalyses of districts located

[20] The most interesting comprehensive text on the process leading up to American independence curiously devotes much attention to this event. See Joseph Pérez, *La emancipación en Hispanoamérica* (Madrid, 1986). See also Anthony Mcfarlane, "Civil disorders and popular protests in late colonial New Granada," *Hispanic American Historical Review*, 64/1 (1984).

[21] Guillermo Galdós, *La rebelión de los pasquines* (Arequipa, 1967), 155.

within the insurrectionary provinces of 1780–1782. These studies helped clarify factors that led toward loyalty to the colonial order, or toward subversion. They also illuminate the key points of social tensions. Direct local resistance – no longer "adaptation" – is in evidence, but so are forms of cultural reproduction adhering to a larger social whole of state and economy. The overall logic must be viewed through a macrosocial model above and beyond case-study findings.[22] I provide, first, a microscale resumé of some events in the original hearth of the Túpac Amaru II revolt, and then go on to an overview of the major revolts (see Map 22.2).

Ward Stavig has explored attitudes, economic behaviors, daily life, family, and sexuality within the indigenous population of the rebellious provinces.[23] Túpac Amaru II's home is erroneously considered the unitary rebel zone par excellence in much of the literature. But after tracing the immediate antecedents of 1780 and the actions of key personages, it becomes possible to disaggregate the tangle of small conflicts historically misremembered as a single massive conflict.

The overall leader of the greatest rebellion, that of 1780 in Cusco and the southern Peruvian highlands, was the *kuraka* of Surimana, Pampamarca, and Tungasuca in Tinta, José Gabriel Condorcanqui, known as Túpac Amaru II. He was a prominent and successful man in the "republic of Indians," wealthy from his business in mule-train haulage, and attended by servants of his own. His dress (including the famous hat with a buckle, which has become a durable icon of Peruvian populism) and that of his wife Micaela Bastidas, seems to have been dignified in the style of well-to-do hispanized people. His nom de guerre, however, commemorates the last Inka ruler of an unconquered territory, the sovereign of the neo-Inka redoubt at Vilcabamba, whom Viceroy Toledo captured and killed 208 years before. He was not a backward-looking nativist but a leader interested in rehabilitating Peru under a distinctive form of polity informed by European ideas of modernity. He may have learned something about recent European political theory from members of Cusco's Creole élite, among whom works of "*philosophes*" circulated. He was inspired above all by the treasured memory of Tawantinsuyu, with whose sovereign lineage he apparently did have a genealogical link.

22 Jürgen Golte, *Repartos y rebeliones* (Lima, 1980). This valuable model is the most complete from the comprehensive, top–down viewpoint and has therefore been susceptible to criticism or has inspired other perspectives.

23 Ward Stavig, "Ethnic conflict, moral economy, and population in rural Cusco on the eve of the Thupa Amaro II Rebellion," *Hispanic American Historical Review* 68/4 (1988).

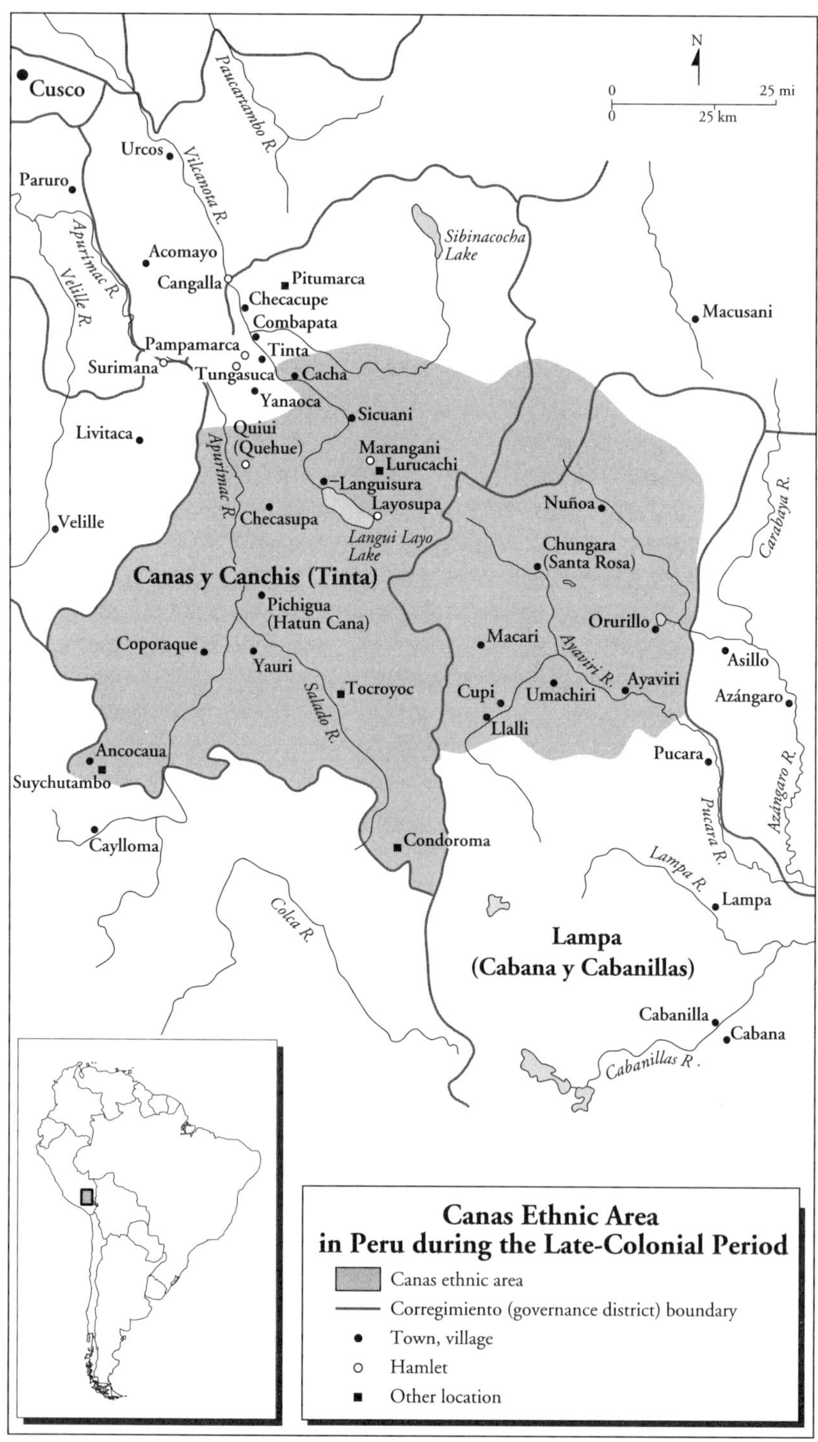

Cusco
Urcos
Paruro
Acomayo
Cangalla
Pitumarca
Checacupe
Combapata
Pampamarca
Tinta
Surimana
Tungasuca
Cacha
Yanaoca
Sicuani
Livitaca
Quiui
(Quehue)
Marangani
Lurucachi
Languisura
Layosupa
Velille
Checasupa
Langui Layo
Lake
Canas y Canchis (Tinta)
Pichigua
(Hatun Cana)
Coporaque
Yauri
Tocroyoc
Ancocaua
Suychutambo
Caylloma
Condoroma
Nuñoa
Chungara
(Santa Rosa)
Orurillo
Macari
Cupi
Umachiri
Ayaviri
Llalli
Macusani
Asillo
Azángaro
Pucara
Lampa
Lampa
(Cabana y Cabanillas)
Cabanilla
Cabana
Paucartambo R.
Vilcanota R.
Apurímac R.
Velille R.
Sibinacocha
Lake
Salado R.
Ayaviri R.
Carabaya R.
Azángaro R.
Pucara R.
Lampa R.
Colca R.
Cabanillas R.
N
0
25 mi
0
25 km
Canas Ethnic Area
in Peru during the Late-Colonial Period
Canas ethnic area
Corregimiento (governance district) boundary
Town, village
Hamlet
Other location

Map 22.2

Whether his was a secessionist cause is a debated matter; he sometimes gave signs of fealty to the Spanish crown yet also clearly sought sovereignty. Toward the Church he was not deeply hostile. Indeed considering the Church's part in village inequities, his followers behaved forgivingly toward the clergy.

On November 4, 1780, this man began to make his rebel aspirations real by capturing the *corregidor* of Canas and Canchis, Antonio de Arriaga. On November 10, he killed Arriaga. From that day to the moment when every subversive nucleus had been defeated, over approximately 2 years of civil war, some 100,000 lives were lost from an affected population of 1,200,000. A rate of war mortality in the neighborhood of 8 percent means that about one in every thirteen persons was killed. Obviously the killing must have left a trauma in the consciousness of both indigenous and white society. Although the number of deaths is disputed, it is substantial enough to underline the jump to a new order of magnitude in social conflict, one not seen in the Andes since the crisis of Spanish invasion.

What, exactly, happened on the local scene to unleash this firestorm? If viewed on the microscale, the causes turn out to appear quite different from the grand ideological crusade remembered in folk and popular history.

Túpac Amaru II's home was the province of Tinta near Cusco, and his immediate social universe was that of the Canas and Canchis ethnic groups, both Quechua-speaking, together with the clergymen, merchants, and petty officials gathered among them in parish centers. On January 6, 1780, the feast day of the Epiphany, in San Pablo de Cacha, the parish priest tried to relocate an image that was venerated by his indigenous parishioners. This led to a small riot. We know from the Quito case and other cases that scuffles about ritual and religious action were a constant feature of the conflictive rural scene, affording windows on the exact points where cultural dissensus generated anger. In this case the priest's African-Andean servant harassed the indignant peasants and mistreated them with the priest's consent. The priest's agent threatened the crowd that 400 soldiers would arrive "tonight, to run them through." As witnesses recalled, the crowd believed it, and many fled the towns.[24]

[24] Data from Ward Stavig, "Violencia cotidiana de los naturales de Quispicanchis, Canas y Canchis en el siglo XVIII," *Revista Andina* 6 (1985). Stavig draws on testimony registered in the Archivo Histórico del Cusco, Corregimiento Legajo 81.

This little fight formed part of a series of frictions caused by two factions: a faction headed by the *corregidor*, the very same Arriaga whom Túpac Amaru II would soon execute, and another led by churchmen under the direction of the bishop of Cusco, Juan Manuel Moscoso.[25] Several clerics of the bishop's party confronted the *corregidor's* party, which, to complicate matters, also counted a few priests in its ranks. The motive was a wrangle for control of goods and properties in the province's rural parishes and over ecclesiastical income. The renting of Church-owned land was actually a central economic and political issue, because Church-owned ranches and the landed endowments of the *cofradías* or religious brotherhoods (whose rise to rural power is discussed in Chap. 15) constituted the area's most important economic sector. Rural priests' income came directly from control of surpluses in the local sphere, and social acceptance of their political and moral influence varied along with tolerance of this power relationship. That is why details of priestly conduct like the relocation of an image could so easily come under angry scrutiny.

Population growth and pressure on resources had sharpened such contradictions. The pressure of scarcity was novel. Also at this time low prices and market saturation[26] complicated and strained the relationships among contenders for scarce resources. Reforms in viceregal economic policy added an increase in tribute pressure to the squeeze.

Hostilities between the factions had not fully erupted in February of 1780, but no doubt something was in the air. After he had expelled the priest's servant, *corregidor* Arriaga wrote: "When fires are not put out at once, their flames tend to consume even what is farthest away."

What kind of fire was he thinking about? Documents that came to light later convinced the foes of rebellion that Túpac Amaru II had been behind a conspiracy as early as 1776. Three dispatches found in Paucartambo, Cusco, and Arequipa revealed a wave of rumors circulating in Cusco that year. It was believed that in the year of the three sevens, an Inka would be crowned in Cusco. Probably no real conspiracy existed.

[25] Regarding Moscoso and his suspected connivance with the rebellion, see Rubén Vargas Ugarte, *Por el Rey y contra el Rey* (Lima, 1966).

[26] I have sustained this hypothesis in Luis Miguel Glave and María I. Remy, *Estructura agraria y vida rural en una región andina. Ollantaytambo entre los siglos XVI y XIX* (Cusco, 1983). The price curve on which the hypothesis is based is supported by the conclusions of Enrique Tandeter and Nathan Wachtel, *Precios y producción agraria. Potosí y Charcas en el siglo XVIII* (Buenos Aires, 1984).

John Rowe thinks it was a phantasm,[27] but a phantasm can be important insofar as it shows that circa 1776 the *corregidores* and functionaries paid insufficient attention to indicators of tension.

By February 1780 Arriaga did know that a maelstrom was brewing. He himself dared to encourage it, along with members of his band and those belonging to the bishop's band, both thinking that they could advantageously ride the storm. Two more actors in this case, Vicente de la Puente and Francisco Cisneros, left behind testimonies about the consequences.

Vicente de la Puente was an active player in Bishop Moscoso's faction. He was the priest in Coporaque in 1780, and testimonies describe him as a violent man. The *corregidor* Arriaga reported in July that de la Puente had been obliged to relinquish the priesthood of Accha in the neighboring province of Paruro "for harming the public tranquility." His imprudence and aggressiveness heightened tension in the towns of Canas, and at one point he had to win back his parish in Coporaque by outfacing public opinion.

His sworn enemy there was Francisco Cisneros, an Andalusian who had settled in the town of Sicuani (between Cusco and Lake Titicaca), married a local Creole woman, and had become one of Arriaga's factional right-hand men. Such "Spaniards among Indians" – a well-coined phrase of James Lockhart – used the power of violent coercion but succeeded only insofar as they retained public authority. Cisneros enjoyed the office of lieutenant *corregidor* – that is, executor of Arriaga's policies. In the proclamations that he signed in 1780, he also called himself "Captain of Infantry and Judge-Delegate." Cisneros seems successfully to have exercised the Arriaga faction's power throughout the province, and indeed functioned as interim *corregidor* when Arriaga was away.[28] Both the priest Puente and the lieutenant *corregidor* Cisneros were willing to push the factional fight as far as armed conflict.

Where were the native authorities in all this? Testifying in July, 4 months before the killing of Arriaga, the priest de la Puente laid accusations against the hereditary *kuraka* Eugenio Quispeaquino, also called *cacique* Sinanyuca, who held the office of native governor of Coporaque.

[27] John Rowe, "Las circunstancias de la rebelión de Thupa Amaro en 1780," *Revista Histórica* 34 (1984), 120. Rowe's study focuses on the concrete circumstances of the revolutionary setting, and I amplify his focus by considering what happened in other parts of the same region.

[28] Archivo Arzobispal del Cusco, XII.5.92.

In July de la Puente already knew the *kuraka* was presiding over instability: "It does not take much for [the Indians] to rise up." Later, on August 2, writing against Sinanyuca, he said that "the circumstances of the present time are critical. The Kingdom is stirred up; love of King and religion should compel us to strive for public tranquility."

A little while later, in Puente's parish of Coporaque, lieutenant *corregidor* Cisneros confronted the bishop's allies. He too alluded to the situation at hand: "I fear in all seriousness that we will all be lost because of the indignation with which they view us." Apparently the peasants' open readiness to react against outsiders was clear to all sides even as they wrestled over their respective economic interests and powers in ways likely to polarize politics.

The *cofradías* or religious brotherhoods had become the strongest institutions and the ones best placed to mediate between external social and cultural power and the community. The *ayllus* and *parcialidades* (that is, the corporate sectors making up the community) all gave devotion to a representative saint. All indigenous community members contributed labor, as a matter of reciprocity, to the production of goods that underwrote the saint's cult, and members also gave lands to the cult endowment as a matter of pious works. From the native point of view, the saint and his festivals formed the machinery for reproducing authority and solidarity, structure, and a firm boundary defining people who had village rights. From the outsiders' point of view, this structure formed a rich vein of social and physical resources.

Pastoral practice consisted in good part of ways to pull the surpluses of brotherhoods and endowments under the priests' control, and to manipulate the reproduction of power via brotherhood offices. Indigenous authorities who took on the rotating duty of *alférez* (organizer and financial underwriter of a religious festival) had to pay, among other costs, alms to the Church. The recent increase in numbers of parishioners, and the pressure of rival powers' claims on indigenous surpluses, made festival levies and alms ever more important to parish churches' incomes.

The hierarchy imposed a schedule of uniform rates, but it was not uniformly respected. Several provisions existed as to the quantity to be "donated" as alms and paid as fees for performing sacraments. These guidelines had been drawn up out of the need to replace the old pre-Bourbon personal services and priest-owned businesses with a more governable regimen. Nonetheless actual levels depended on many local factors. What determined the level was a subtle political relationship among parties, oscillating between contradiction and consensus: a moral economy. Legally a festival did not have to be paid for, but if one wanted to "come to an agreement" with Christendom's representative and enjoy a certain liberty of worship including leeway for non-European traditions, paying became worthwhile. Besides, in the Andes, worship had always been accompanied by gifts; the gift was a guarantee of fruitful reciprocity whether the relationship was human or superhuman. Peasants had Andean reasons for paying Spanish alms. In local everyday practice, priests who served indigenous parishes little by little felt their way to tacit agreements about the acceptable extraction of surplus in labor, goods, or money. Any change could instantly evoke accusations of excesses or abuses. In 1780, when changes were hard to avoid, all this hovered behind the details of priestly conduct.

Outside the ritual sphere another form of extraction had been developing: the ranches and properties of the Church. These afforded means for nonclerics to tap native surpluses, because they were often rented out to bidders who could themselves expect good profits. Moreover rentals interested Church officials far above the curates' level, because the rental income did not fill the immediate parish treasury but rather helped finance larger institutions including religious orders and convents. Such landed properties, most of which were endowed with considerable herds of cattle – the main wealth of the area – enjoyed the labor of *mitanis* or *séptimas* (that is, workers assigned to them by rotating communal labor). Church estates and landed endowments of religious brotherhoods were the only agrarian institutions that could viably rival private agropastoral estates.

Meanwhile, paralleling Church and estate sectors, the *corregidor*, with his monopoly business privilege via *reparto* or forced sale, controlled a third lever in the scramble for communal indigenous surplus. By 1780 this privilege of the *corregidores* had come under challenge for decades, sometimes by violent means.

The political conflicts of 1780 exploded amidst this framework of multilateral manipulation. In November 1779, in Sicuani, Bishop Moscoso had issued a long and fundamental *Auto de Visita* (*Act of Visitation*), prohibiting priests from managing or renting Church-owned ranches on their own, and ordering that any rental agreement (for example, of brotherhoods' land endowments) be stamped and approved by the diocese in Cusco. It was a proclamation of war on local power "fixes" involving persons hostile to the bishopric's faction, as one can see by tracing its consequences in a Canas ranching district close to the hub of the great rebellion.

At the time of the 1779 order, the two principal ranches of Yauri were put out to rent by the priest Justo Pastor Martínez. Both renters were indigenous notables. The renter of the one named Oquebamba was don Diego José de Meza and that of the one called Huine, don Francisco Guambo Tupa Ynga Roca. Both were about to become central actors in the rebel conjuncture. The renters were members of the political hierarchy of Yauri, a fast-growing village of indigenous herders on the high tundra. Meza, who later became the most noted *cacique* of the town, was the son of the head of the *ayllu* Huisa and scion to one of the richest and most influential families in one of the most important *ayllus* despite being a mestizo. Because of his Iberian surname, Meza occasionally appears in the record as a "Spaniard." His power base, nonetheless, was his indigenous *ayllu*. He worked as the *corregidor*'s collection agent and therefore formed part of the colonial state. His alliances extended to the most important local chiefs of Yauri and its environs.

The other main renter of the estates let by Yauri's priest was Francisco Guambo Tupa. He had similar social rank to Meza's, but his thoroughly Quechua surname suggests that he remained unambiguously tied to the old indigenous lineages. In contrast to Meza this *cacique* was indeed considered indigenous by the authorities, and he defined himself the same way. Indigenous standing favored his interests because he was also recognized as a native noble, an ethnic *kuraka* with a claim to ancient legitimacy and considerable wealth to back his status.

Father de la Puente, always a rugged factional fighter on Bishop Moscoso's side, now took on these Yauri men. The renters and their Indian hierarchy, conversely, were backed by the *corregidor* Arriaga through his delegated judge, don Antonio Cisneros. At least two of the disturbances breaking out in these months as a result are included in scholarly lists of "precursory" mobilizations heralding general rebellion. So they were, but not because of any conspiratorial link – rather because they embodied a general social tension in the area.

The most important confrontation occurred in Coporaque, between the *kuraka* Quispeaquino alias Sinanyuca, and Father de la Puente. Everything indicates that enmity between the priest and the *kuraka* had been smoldering for decades. The occasion was, once again, a festival – namely, Carnival time (February) of 1779. At Carnival priests displayed the sacred host to put a blessing on the Andean dances, in which hard-drinking indigenous people celebrated in the plazas the branding and shearing of their alpacas and sheep. Along with the Christian mass, celebrators carried out "payments" to Earth by giving her bleeding hearts of sacrificed animals and by sprinkling the walls of corrals and houses with a mixture of blood and red soil. In the ritual the indigenous population demonstrated its own reading of sacred time, while the priest made sure that the submission to the official God was respected. A delicate "moral economy" bargain allowed this tense cultural relationship and, through it, moral agreement with respect to resource use and levels of exploitation.

Had Father de la Puente been acting on his own behalf and that of his bishop, he would probably have respected the local modus vivendi. Unfortunately he also had the support of a high civil judge, the crown's agent *Visitador* Areche, and he owed this official a political favor. Areche was a Bourbon exponent of strong central control over ambitious bureaucrats like Arriaga and locally entrenched native politicians like Sinanyuca, Meza, and Guambo Tupa. He had advised de la Puente by letter on June 28 that he meant to combat the *corregidores* and execute an all-out attack on *caciques* who retained power in the towns. By May 1778 Areche had promulgated an "instruction . . . for the formation of new lists of tributaries" under whose terms the Andean leaders would lose control of tribute rolls, and collection would pass to crown-appointed mayors or governors. De la Puente therefore practically had a commission from the supreme government to act against Sinanyuca, who in turn recognized him as an enemy to the old modus vivendi.

Now came the moment of defiance. The indigenous population refused to pay the priest his expected *obvenciones* (extra payment for festival services). No concrete proof exists that *corregidor* Arriaga's lieutenant Francisco Cisneros was conspiring with Eugenio Sinanyuca in the refusal, but it does look that way. Cisneros carried out an order from the *corregidor* in backing the *kuraka*'s confrontation with the priest. The latter retaliated with a threat of excommunication. Agitation spread throughout the high tundras, the whole *puna* home of the Canas people. The *fiestas de tabla* (jousting games), for whose license the Church charged a jealously established tariff, were celebrated with indigenous rites only, and the indigenous leaders refused to pay the priestly fee.

Just as Arriaga had sent Cisneros into the center of the storm, Moscoso now dispatched a priest named Fuentes. On the basis of this priest's report and Father de la Puente's claims that he could not return to his parish, the diocese furnished an order against Sinanyuca, obliging him to report to Cusco under threat of excommunication. But the balance of forces was against the bishop's faction. Father Fuentes was harassed until he had to withdraw. The situation escalated into head-on violent confrontations, from which Sinanyuca emerged triumphant.

On first glance one would expect Sinanyuca to prove a "precursor" of Túpac Amaru II. Ensuing events, however, demonstrate an apparently contradictory alignment. Sinanyuca proved a defender of the crown in the midst of the territory where a blaze ignited that would, as Arriaga had predicted, consume the most far-reaching areas. *Corregidor* Arriaga committed himself to continuing his confrontation with the bishop's faction, but never got the chance, because not long after an imbroglio with de la Puente, he would be executed by Túpac Amaru II.

Thus when Túpac Amaru II seized the *corregidor* and killed him in November 1780, he set loose a conflagration that would enfold the Yauri fracas and thousands of other local fights that actually had no political or historical relation to his own project. From one point of view, the Yauri village appears part of a battlefront in which the rebel Inka opposed existing hierarchies wholesale. But this view-from-the-distance loses sight of what happened to real people. What did Sinanyuca and his peers actually do in the great rebellion?

They acted in a puzzlingly contradictory way, if one insists on looking at events from the viewpoint of macroscopic entities like the state. Former allies lined up on opposing sides. Those who should have supported Túpac Amaru II, because of his combative position vis-à-vis the established order, supported the king and the status quo. Some royal functionaries, putative defenders of the established order, threw their forces into the subversive struggle. Moreover no clear Indian versus non-Indian logic emerges: The indigenous leaders Sinanyuca and Guambo Tupa remained loyal to the colonial state, whereas the Spanish agents of the *corregidor*, including Cisneros, enlisted in the rebel indigenous forces. The major conclusion of our local history is that people acted in accordance with their immediate factional political needs amid local contradictions.

THE ANDEAN REVOLUTIONS

What then of the macroscale importance of Túpac Amaru II? The mobilization that Túpac Amaru II and his people initiated in November

1780 was at the beginning just one more in the series of violent actions over the decades. Nonetheless his movement quickly surpassed all others in extension, intensity, and political importance. As Flores Galindo has aptly put it, in his career several revolutions came up against one another and intermixed.[29] The cycle of revolt that José Gabriel Túpac Amaru II hegemonized had three foci or regional hearths, each with its own dynamic. Because they reached their respective peaks of rebelliousness at sequential times, they will for some purposes be treated as phases in the following discussions.

The first or Cusco revolt was the most symbolic and memorable, more because of the repressed forces it unleashed than because of any achievements it won. It began with the capture and death of the *corregidor* of Tinta, the ill-starred Arriaga, in November 1780. This was not simply another riot, like so many others in which the *corregidores* had been victims of "peasant furors." Arriaga's execution was a symbol, through which the rebel chief began to proclaim the return of the Inka. Túpac Amaru II's indigenous followers were organized hierarchically, like a feudal militia, with the Inka's whole family standing at the head of the troops. The early fighters were community Indians who joined spontaneously. Two weeks after killing Arriaga, they won an initial military victory against a royalist military column that left Cusco to crush them, and met them at Sangarará on November 18. The rebels then set out toward Cusco, ordering the *kurakas* to detain the *corregidores* of the provinces, promulgating decrees that announced deep reforms in indigenous work conditions, and assaulting and destroying the textile mills of Pomacanchis and Quispicanchis. Meanwhile an opposing war council was formed in the city, where *kurakas* who had not joined the rebels found refuge, and where *corregidores* and their allies fled to save their lives. The defenders sent their militia to repress the uprising. Insurgents killed over 500 people in the royalist band and set the town's church ablaze by firing a powder keg; flames could be seen from afar.

The upheaval was total. Rebels quickly dominated practically all the southern provinces between Cusco and Arequipa. Indigenous leaders lined up sometimes in the rebel camp and sometimes with the royalists. The crown force was greatly strengthened when another major chief and indigenous noble, Mateo Pumacahua – whose lineage had rivaled Con-

[29] Alberto Flores Galindo, "Las revoluciones tupamaristas: temas en debate," *Revista Andina* 13 (1989).

dorcanqui's since the time of the conquest – declared war on the rebel. For some 2 months both sides paused, searching for allies and taking reprisals against those who did not join up. Finally in January 1781 the rebels besieged Cusco. Battles ensued with thousands of deaths.

Many peasants in arms saw battle as an opportunity for ethnic revenge; generic Indianness often entailed generic rage against non-Indians. Yet in this period Túpac Amaru II steered his rebels away from nativism. He followed forms and styles of command that even a status-conscious Creole might consider politically dignified, issuing proclamations and orders close to Spanish style, acknowledging the crown. He meant to keep rebel rank open to mestizos and Creoles interested in forging a kingdom free of the outrageous advantages that the viceroyalty afforded peninsular Spaniards. The idea of an urban–rural multiethnic coalition, under Inka rule, was not so far-fetched as it sounds today, because Cusco's urban élites customarily paraded the mementos of Inka glory and the traces of Inka genealogy as blazons of their own superiority. They were proud that Cusco's great half-Inka chronicler Garcilaso Inca de la Vega had dazzled European readers (including Voltaire) for over a century. Pageantry used Inka imagery lavishly: paintings of the prehispanic dynasty, festival floats with Inka costuming, and other remembrances evoked a Tawantinsuyu now gilded by nostalgia. Túpac Amaru II's attitude toward the Church, including its vast properties, was lenient, even though the hierarchy had long excluded Indians from ordination. Bishop Moscoso of Cusco seems actually to have favored the rebel cause, so much so that he would not oppose rebel entry into the besieged city. (Recall the bishop's hostility to Sinanyuca of the Canas, whose tactical closeness to the *corregidor* had angered churchmen.)

The project of a broadly interethnic but ideologically Inka movement never really got a tryout, because the siege began to fail when a column advancing on the far side of the city under Túpac Amaru II's command failed to complete a pincer movement. Soon the city was beating back the rebels. This marked the waning of the Cusco hearth of revolt. In April 1781 Túpac Amaru II was taken prisoner, and he was executed in May.

The second hearth of revolt became paramount after that and remained so until to July 1781. It was concentrated farther south than Cusco, near Puno on Lake Titicaca. The struggle in this region and others still farther south had already been taking shape before the rebel king's death, and we can learn something about the contagion of disquiet and open agitation, at least from the Spanish point of view, by examining correspondence between La Paz authorities and the La Plata *audiencia* (concerned with securing the whole vast space of what is now Bolivia) at the beginning of 1781. The Spanish regime's spy network was truly impressive. Correspondence was always vital in those broad and complex spaces – vital but also unsure, because of local satraps' continual interference with the roads. The private messengers and the mails offered opportunities to tap and divert information. Letters were intercepted and used to ascertain the movements of factions.

When La Paz was under rebel siege, officials such as Lieutenant Colonel Sebastián de Segurola, an excellent chronicler as well as military man and politician, or functionaries such as Fernando Márquez de la Plata, charged with reporting to the *audiencia*, received reports, letters, edicts, and all types of documents swiped from rebel traffic. Márquez de la Plata, who was very close to the events, judged that Túpac Amaru II's strength was in decline from the Aymara domains of Titicaca to Cusco. He had lost force, he had been abandoned by some followers, and he had executed people for betraying him. Some town factions in rebel-held territory opposed or at least doubted the cause. Nonetheless Márquez de la Plata knew that Túpac Amaru II could return to La Paz, where rebellion was on the rise. He warned the *corregidor* of Puno that the whole *altiplano* was a cauldron of intrigues. Crown authorities had abandoned their public functions, discrediting themselves among the common people. Royalists were limiting their actions to the military side, and even then they acted only when it was impossible simply to hide out. Knowing this, La Paz residents feared a rebel onslaught.

Segurola himself wrote to Rueda on January 27, 1781, summarizing reports and correspondence intercepted from the Collao lakeside district: "The rebel [Túpac Amaru II] once again is trying to reach these places and I wish to inform you sincerely that the spirit of rebellion is general and common in all the provinces and in the city, and that it is not confined only to the number of Indians but overreaches these limits to touch many who do not hold themselves to be such."

The continued southward thrust of revolt after the killing of Túpac Amaru II was in some ways more significant than the rebel king's final offensive, because it shows that the movement had taken on a life beyond that of its leader. With Túpac Amaru II dead, leadership fell to his uncle, Diego Cristóbal. After a defeat at Layo, still within the nuclear zone of the Cusco revolt, rebel forces fell back on the zones they had consolidated in previous months, and from there they deployed military actions across the entire *altiplano*. These actions strengthened the rebels militarily. Indeed this period displays more militarization, less symbolic and ideological innovation, and few if any proclamations or political negotiations. It ended with a military victory by Diego Cristóbal Túpac Amaru II at Puno, overcoming resolute resistance by Pumacahua and his royalist Indian troops, and with the retreat of the royalist army. Choosing a locale at the border of the Aymara-speaking country, Diego Cristóbal turned toward his ally, the Aymara Apaza-dynasty indigenous chief of Azángaro (just north of Lake Titicaca) to create a political headquarters. Even though Azángaro fell short of offering a zone of perfect rebel solidarity, it had furnished the most important center for the continuity of the revolution whether seen in terms of social networks, political negotiation, or military strategy. The Quechua–Aymara base at Azángaro and the connection with this *kuraka*, Pedro Vilca Apaza, would prove a turning point in the character of the later rebellion: It would now become more deadly, more of a peasant war, and more hostile to cities as such.

Leadership at Azángaro was built around the late Inka's family: his uncle, two nephews, his son, all claiming the name of Túpac Amaru. But along with them the Diego Quispe family of Azángaro and above all, Pedro Vilca Apaza, were the main protagonists of the subsequent military actions.

The lakeside insurrection, and the fighting farther south, saw the local ascendancy of Pedro Vilca Apaza. Indeed Vilca Apaza was without a doubt the most singular figure of the revolution. Educated, literate, a rich property owner, linked to the mestizo-ized indigenous nobility – he was married to a daughter of the rival Chuquihuanca house – and well-versed in legal struggles, he threw himself fully into the rebellion and spread it throughout the *altiplano*.[30] When the Inka was captured, Vilca Apaza attempted to rescue him. Later he kept up the war in the high plains while Diego Cristóbal Túpac Amaru enjoyed his hospitality. When eventually the latter made an armistice with Spain, Vilca Apaza refused it and fought on alone, even after the Cusco and southern rebellions were defeated, to die a hero's death. This career of intransigence demonstrates the enormous difficulties that the revolution faced in combining a

[30] See Augusto Ramos Zambrano, *La gesta de Pedro Vilca Apaza* (Puno, 1971), and also his *Puno en la rebelión de Túpac Amaru* (Puno, 1982).

policy of negotiation and conciliation among classes, political interests, and lineages (the policy the Túpac Amarus favored) with the radical ethnic line of leaders like Vilca Apaza, who insisted on politically and culturally indigenous stances and messianic Andeanist ideology (albeit still admitting participation by mestizos, mestizo-ized chiefs, or even Creoles). The radical line was the stronger in rallying revolution, especially in the later phases, and generated the most active and numerous bases in the Aymara lakeside region and throughout the Cataris' southerly radius in La Paz and Chayanta.

The third and southernmost regional hearth saw a generalization of the violence and a convergence of several movements. Much of the conflict that flared late in the cycle of revolt had already undergone a longstanding local genesis, and it is important to recognize that these revolts were by no means only sequels to actions around Cusco. In general outline the later parts of the rebellion turned on repeated sieges of La Paz and the southward growth of a substantially Aymara-based rebellion around the persons of Julián Apaza and Tomás Catari, the native governor of Chayanta. Julián Apaza, a man of Aymara origin, "of uncertain family, a woman-chaser, illiterate and charismatic," as Germán Arciniegas has called him, launched the most violent revolutionary actions under his nom de guerre Túpac Catari. Although his example helped provoke outbreaks in Sica Sica, Chayanta and Oruro, he and Tomás Catari do not seem to have attempted systematic coordination with these movements. Neither were the Cataris, rebel Aymaras, close to the Túpac Amarus at the start. Julián Apaza Túpac Catari and Tomás Catari had ignited a series of Bolivian rebellions from 1776 on – that is, well before the events in Tinta. No evidence exists for preliminary contact between the two movements, even though it is clear that in 1780, while Túpac Amaru II laid siege to Cusco, Tomás Catari was already in the midst of a local conflagration with the miners and the *corregidores* of the Potosí region. It was the force of events only partly under their control that pushed the Cataris into political alliance with the Amarus – Túpac Catari styled himself "viceroy" of the Inka king – but even then their programmatic agreements seem imperfect.

With all these defects of unity, the southward transformation from "normal" local conflagrations to Great Rebellion spread like wildfire. The movement spoke to common experiences of frustration and exhaustion as colonial systems made greater demands but delivered declining security, and the idea of an Inka returning to set America to rights provided a resonant common language for expressing anger and hope. The southern movement was not completely bound by the old "Republic of Indians." It was able to spread beyond pigeonholed Indian polities into the spaces of social ambiguity, the domain of mixed bloods. Mestizos, Creoles, and castas of varied "race," all suffering economic problems and political exclusion, often fanned rebel flames. Many times they themselves incited indigenous people to rise up. But once Indians did rise up, they usually put their own stamp on the movement. Especially during the battles of southern Bolivia, they would turn against mixed-bloods as well as "Spaniards" and even attack them. As in Quito, Arequipa, and Cusco, the culture of colonial discontent had succeeded in rupturing boundaries but not in creating durable social alliances across them.

Although Túpac Catari in La Paz and Tomás Catari with his brothers in Chayanta effectively guided the southerly foci of revolt, which became salient toward the end of the insurrection, the Inka "royal family" called the Amarus retained wide legitimacy in the southern Andes. The original rebel's young nephew Andrés Túpac Amaru, who in Azángaro had been linked with a female relative of the high plains potentate Diego Chuquihuanca, now led the Cusqueño Inka colonels, and his symbolic and practical political prestige gave him supreme command in the La Paz region. Now he developed a romantic life to suit southern politics, a passion for Gregoria Apaza, who was a sister of Julián Apaza Túpac Catari.[31] Other Inka leaders in La Paz were Miguel Bastidas, a relative of the original rebel's widow Micaela Bastidas, and the rebel couple's young son Mariano Túpac Amaru.

But the rebel masses were probably not so unified as these alliances of command suggest. Reviewing the list of prisoners captured as the Catarista band fell near the end of the rebellion, one finds a high percentage of Umasuyo Qulla people from the Titicaca highlands. Although in gross outline the rebel forces from Cusco can be called Quechuas, and their allies from the high plains of present-day Bolivia Aymaras, this apical alliance perhaps marks less of an interethnic innovation than it seems at first glance, because some allying groups had historical overlap already:

[31] For the romantic life of the *caudillos* of the rebellion, see Teodosio Imaña, "De lo pasional en la vida de los caudillos indígenas de 1780," *Historia y cultura* 1 (1973). See also Zambrano, *Puno en la rebelión de Túpuc Amaru.*

The Canchis and Canas from Cusco, and some Qullas from the high plain, all derived from related Aymara ethnic groups.

Given the fault lines of region, ethnicity, dynasty, and class, what bridges (beyond the Inka ideology) made rebel coordination possible at all? It has been suggested that mercantile activity created common ground. Both Condorcanqui before he became Túpac Amaru II, and Apaza before he became Túpac Catari, were in the long-distance trade and transport business. Indeed many more or less bicultural Andean men were traveling vendors and mule-train drivers. They were the products of the market; their way of life had precedent in the *trajines*, the haulage system through which the native groups subsidized the colonial market during the "ethnic era." The muleteers, mule-traders, and travelers were the expression of material, cultural, and economic intermixing among peasant collectivities. That Túpac Amaru II called himself Inka does not remove him from the category of mestizo merchants. Perhaps such travelers used their movement among town peoples to establish subversive contacts; some respectable studies have suggested as much. But beyond conspiratorial suspicion, a more important question attaches to the mestizo style of those active in the market – a market that affected all aspects of social life. Not only mixed blood but mixed cultural choices figure prominently in the rebel way of life. Documents from the Aymara assault on Sorata describe thieving by both sides, mentioning that rebel fighters stole "Spanish" style garments and utensils. Given the strongly ethnic recruitment of the later rebellion, why did they not refuse and destroy the material culture of the enemy as Taki Unquy nativists had 220 years earlier? It seems rather that rebels sought to incorporate it – to become an active part of, or even to seize and master, what their ancestors and they themselves had contributed to creating.

From the very first, rebel actions on the Cusco front showed the same tendency. What, for example, happened to the Spanish goods that the *corregidor* Arriaga had been ready to sell when Túpac Amaru II killed him? Ward Stavig has found an invaluable document which reports that an indigenous man stole them.[32] The problem for the Canas, then, was not that Spanish goods were sold to Indians but how they were sold – in

[32] See Ward Stavig, "The Indian peoples of rural Cusco in the era of Thupa Amaro" (Ph.D. thesis, University of California – Davis, 1991), one of the best studies of daily life in the revolutionary era.

a manner generating conflicts of interest, damaging native commercial options, and aggravating poverty during cyclical economic crises.

The end of the rebel age was humiliating. Rebels kept seizing strategic towns and kept up the war from the May 1781 execution of Túpac Amaru II until November 1781. After several consecutive defeats, the execution of Túpac Catari, and the arrival of Spanish military reinforcements, the old leader Diego Cristóbal signed an armistice in Sicuani in 1782. After a year of tense waiting, he was taken prisoner and murdered in July 1783. A series of punitive military measures against the indigenous Túpac Amaru nobles followed, as well as a campaign to repopulate all of what is now Bolivia. Severe measures, described in the next section were designed to subdue the rebellious population and to make a future rebirth of Inka sentiment impossible by drastically depoliticizing the institutions of Andean community and culture.

CONSEQUENCES AND PROJECTION

It is a perennial task of Andean historiography to assess and reassess the meaning of the immense upheaval that crowned the cycle of rebellions begun in 1742 by Juan Santos Atahuallpa. Localized movements had been in the making for a long time, without attaining the scope of the events that occurred after 1780. These local struggles conventionally have been called "precursors" assuming they teleologically heralded a coming climax. But was the 1780–1782 outbreak ever a unitary phenomenon, beyond the tenuous articulation of alliances among its leaders? We have seen that events presented as parts of a single campaign often turn out on analysis to have been disconnected ground-level events, bridged at the summit by ideology, by exchange of strategic messages among rebel leaders trying to steer popular outbursts, by unsteady alliances, and to some degree by common understandings about economic and religious interests.

The more one widens scrutiny, the more one must appreciate the importance of grassroots idiosyncrasy, and the less real the image of a unified rebel state-in-process appears. In Oruro, and wherever rebels won local control, they awaited the arrival of their king, Túpac Amaru II, but they had usually fought things out on the basis of local forces already – they awaited the new Inka regime as something that might happen ex post facto.[33] Thus whether we consider insurrections previous to the Túpac Amaru II episodes, or those contemporaneous and posterior to it, we find an array of events partially synchronized by the great rebellion but not by that token distanced from peculiar local dynamics. In Cusco separate violent disturbances broke out in several provinces: Chumbivilcas, Paucartambo, Urubamba, Calca, the Inka capital itself, and even in the very same province of Tinta where Túpac Amaru II first launched his insurgency.

The many rebellions that add up to the Great Rebellion can also be conceived as political concomitants of an American crisis of the *ancien régime*. Rather than thinking of them only as Andean Indian rebellions in defense of a culture (though they were that, in a complex sense that also admitted the appropriation of non-native goods and symbols), or as peasant riots in defense of a "moral economy" (which they also were), it is helpful to compare them with the nearly simultaneous era of the great French Revolution of 1789. Both countries were experiencing general systemic crises closely related to an unsuccessful transition in systems of extraction from their peasantries. In both, production failed to diversify, division of labor failed to occur, markets became saturated, and prices fell precipitously to the detriment of the poorest. Paying daily living expenses became difficult and was made more so by rising exactions made on production. A crisis of saturation in a limited market could in either country reverse itself into a crisis of spiraling prices due to scarcity-generated famine. The state's capacity to confront such abrupt economic shifts was slight. Social discriminations and abuses became harder to bear, especially for those mixed bloods whose economic power had grown beyond the demeaning statuses that the ideologies of "pure Spanish blood" and ranked social estates assigned them. From the cities an intelligentsia enthusiastically discussing critiques of society could divide élite opinion and crystallize rival ideas of power. Images of redemption, the dream of ideal times, heated up the consciousness of a population frustrated by perennial crisis.

Yet Peru was to see no revolution of modernity. Perhaps if the colonial Andean state had not so firmly entrenched factors of ethnically defined estate – the "Republics" – or put such high social barriers among the

[33] Fernando Cajías, "Los objetivos de la revolución indígena de 1781: el caso de Oruro," *Revista Andina* 2 (1983).

varied sectors interested in a major restructuring, the rebellion would not have proven possible to defeat. In that subjunctive history Peru might not have diverged so far from the path of countries now seen as central to Western modernity.

But as it happened the diverse and discriminatory ethnic and cultural framework of the colony did have decisive effects of its own. If Bourbon statecraft and its crises formed one general antecedent, another specifically Andean one was the spontaneous and deep-rooted accord of popular ideas, images, and expectations about an Inkaic future. Utopia, messianism, prophecies, and the gradually built archetype of the Inka redeemer informed the action of the masses and even of the leaders.[34] If material culture is a guide, they may have been willing to incorporate much of the Spanish legacy but not to endure non-Indian rule any more.

Because it was in the end the victorious Bourbon regime that molded political institutions after the revolt, ethnic and cultural frameworks to which Spaniards felt bound also had decisive effects. In treating the rebellion as a disorder caused by peculiarly Indian errors and furies, and not primarily by the weaknesses and cruelties of imperial economy and policy, they constrained the reorganization of the viceroyalty to reproduce much of the old edifice of inequalities. This time, however, there was to be no more "illusory republic of Indians" (as the repressor Areche termed it) but rather a native domain defined mostly in negative terms: an arena of political subjection in which political process would have to be injected from without.

Having examined the Great Rebellion overall, one must ask about the consequences. The first point is simply that repression did not change the basic situation. Conditions for explosions of local contradictions, for violence and struggle among social sectors, continued. Although no generalized rebellion ensued until 1814, new studies show that the persisting basic tension generated tumults, mutinies, riots, and several small-scale conflicts.[35] On the other hand, the idea of Inka restoration and the return to an ideal past, converted into a half-Andean, half-Christian myth, remained a permanent legacy in popular thinking; myths of Inkarrí the

[34] Jorge Hidalgo, "Amarus y cataris: aspectos mesiánicos de la rebelión indígena de 1781 en Cusco, Chayanta, La Paz y Arica," *Chungara* 10 (1983). See especially Alberto Flores Galindo, *Buscando un inca. Identidad y utopía en los Andes* (Lima, 1988). See also John H. Rowe, "El movimiento nacional Inca del siglo XVIII," *Revista Universitaria del Cusco* 107 (1954).

[35] See Nuria Sala I Vila, "Revueltas indígenas en el Perú tardocolonial" (Ph.D. thesis, Universidad de Barcelona, 1989).

hidden redeemer (i.e., Inka Rey, 'Inka King') have been amply documented in many parts of the Andes by ethnographers, especially in the 1970s.

Rebellion did not lead in linear fashion to the questioning of the colonial link with Spain, nor was it a general revolutionary situation. It proved to be a violent moment in the slow expiration of a system that could finally be crushed by nothing less than its own weight, and dismembered by nothing less than its own insoluble contradictions.

The actual socioeconomic penalty of Andean defeat was a process of rearchaization in basic relations making up the social fabric. The indigenous communities closed in on themselves. With their avenues of "horizontal" unity draconically repressed, each village was left with the job of re-creating indigenous identities endogenously. This is not to say that they isolated themselves from society as a whole or became separate microsocieties. Instead internal hierarchies were partially redefined on the basis of individuals' or families' links to the outside, but not as political leaders – increasingly, rather, as clients. Fearing an ongoing threat from Inka utopias, the crown annulled those hereditary *kuraka* lineages that had demonstrated a lack of loyalty. In some cases substitute *caciques*, who not only lacked lineage legitimacy but often were not even members of the indigenous community, received appointments. Some were mestizo or Spanish outsiders. In effect what had been the mainstay role of Andean leadership for perhaps a millennium was degraded to the level of tax collector. With the depoliticization of properly indigenous roles, exogenous political and commercial leverage became even more decisive keys to power than they had been before. Kinship and symbols of local legitimacy were reconfigured into a new indigenous body, less tied to the specific ethnic roots that had informed peasant behavior in past centuries.

Meanwhile, in the sphere of the haciendas and the rural spaces under nonindigenous control, the amount of land renting increased. The most efficient conglomerates were destroyed, and the rural productive structure entered a sustained state of lethargy. The cities lost population to the countryside. The dream of colonial efficiency and increased rents, embraced by the enlightened officials with crown mandates, led to the exact opposite result.

On the level of the state, Bourbon reforms became the most conspicuous legacy of the rebellion (although, of course, they were an empire-wide phenomenon and not in any direct way caused by the revolt). The reform that weighed most heavily on the towns was the new web of state operations under the newly created system of *Intendencias*. ('Intendancies' replaced the old viceregal system with a less seigneurial, more managerial type of centralism.) The post–Túpac Amaru II period saw the creation of a new royal *audiencia* in Cusco, the disappearance of the *corregidores*, and the establishment of new hierarchies of authority in the countryside, completely disconnected from Andean organizational or agricultural systems.

Culturally speaking, fear of the Indianist ideology that had eventuated in war led to the persecution of Inka discourse. No more would the panoply of Inka family trees, enameled drinking goblets of Inka design, or Inka jewelry make visible the pride of native or urban-élite lineage. No more would Cusco house schools for sons of the indigenous élites, important though they had been for centuries in generating an Andean class able to rule in Spain's interest. On the contrary non-Andean Peru developed a near phobia about the educating of Indians, lest it again breed indigenous nationalism. Schools for Andean students did not completely disappear, but they took a low profile, and the use of the Quechua language was prohibited in them. Along with the legal annulment of the *kuraka* title in native towns, all inheritance of lineages as a matter of legal identity was also abolished. Performances of the Inka plays were prohibited throughout the viceregal territory. Even the classic book by the Inca Garcilaso de la Vega, the *Royal Commentaries of the Incas*, admired by readers throughout Europe for over a century, was proscribed.

Were the rebellions a precursor of national independence? The idea of a nationalism born within indigenous society and building upon the Inka inheritance as the core of an inclusive political culture was present. But in the heat of battle, Inka hopes proved inseparable from an Indianist messianism that made alliances with other *castas*, races, or classes unworkable, even when Túpac Amaru II tried to drive the revolution in an inclusivist direction. That, together with the ensuing repression, was the tragedy of the age. When South America did surge toward the expulsion of Spanish power, indigenous people did not start the anticolonial process or find a self-emancipatory role in it. Instead the complete opposite occurred. Indians emerged from the independence process more defeated than they had been in 1782, carrying only as memory what could have been the germ of a different society (see Chap. 23).

An economic and social cycle beginning between 1680 and 1730 was ending along with the century – violently. Another process unfolded in which many elements of the earlier situation persisted, while other new ones appeared very slowly. An increasingly Creole-influenced élite social structure, emerging from the ruins of the "two republics," would find ways to persist and put its mark on the scene for many decades to come, as independence brought about a long and lethargic search for nationhood on non-Andean terms.

BIBLIOGRAPHIC ESSAY

An abundant literature covers the indigenous rebellions and political disturbances of the eighteenth century, impossible to represent fully in an essay of this scope. We mention here only the items of broadest interest.

Steve J. Stern's compilation, *Resistance, Rebellion and Consciousness in the Andean Peasant World: Eighteenth to Twentieth Centuries* (Madison, 1987) offers a valuable conspectus. The first two parts of the book correspond to the eighteenth century. The book includes essays by the some of the most representative contemporary researchers on the topic. Stern himself, besides writing an introductory essay, collaborates with a paper that provides a new vision of the rebellion of 1742. Magnus Mörner's article in the Stern book, "Un intento de calibrar las actitudes hacia la rebelión en el Cusco durante la acción de Túpac Amaru II" develops a hypothesis sustained in his socioeconomic studies, such as *Perfil de la sociedad rural del Cusco a fines de la colonia* (Lima, 1978), and "Medidas como precios y como instrumentos para la explotación. Un expediente cusqueño del siglo XVIII," *Allpanchis* 15 (1980), which treats the official dispatches of 1780. Jan Szeminski collaborates in Stern's compilation with an essay compressing ideas he treated more fully in *La utopía tupamarista* (Lima, 1984). Alberto Flores Galindo's contribution sums up his *Buscando un Inca* (Lima, 1988). Flores Galindo was also the compiler of *Túpac Amaru II – 1780: Antología* (Lima, 1976), which includes his essay "Túpac Amaru y la sublevación de 1780." Some of his later articles are cited in the text of this chapter.

Stern's book also includes contributions by Leon Campbell and Frank Salomon, whose articles deal with ideology, religion, and resistance. Other fundamental authors central to the modern historiography of the rebellions do not appear in the compilation. A notable absence is Scarlett O'Phelan Godoy, among whose numerous works is the indispensable *Un siglo de rebeliones anticoloniales. Perú y Bolivia 1700–1783* (Cusco, 1988). Also missing is Jürgen Golte, author of *Repartos y rebeliones. Túpac*

Amaru y las contradicciones de la economía colonial (Lima, 1980). Golte's model has prompted criticism and new, different visions, such as that of Stern himself, and Ward Stavig in "Ethnic conflict, moral economy, and population in rural Cusco on the eve of the Thupa Amaro II rebellion," *Hispanic American Historical Review* 68/4 (1988), expanded in his soon-to-be published doctoral thesis. For moral economy in the Andean context, see Brooke Larson, "Explotación y economía moral en los Andes del sur andino: hacia una reconsideración crítica," in Frank Salomon and Segundo Moreno (eds.), *Reproducción y tranformación de las sociedades andinas, siglos XVI–XX* (Quito, 1991), 441–480, a collection that incorporates an excellent collection of studies, complementary to the vision of resistance developed by the collaborators in *Resistance, Rebellion, and Consciousness.*

For the concrete circumstances of the rebellious province in 1780, besides Stavig's studies, see John Rowe, "Las circunstancias de la rebelión de Thupa Amaro en 1780," *Revista Histórica* 34 (1984). See also Rowe's original article, "El movimiento nacional Inca del siglo XVIII," *Revista Universitaria del Cusco* 107 (1954), 17–47, and Luis Miguel Glave, *Vida, símbolos y batallas. Creación y recreación de la comunidad indígena* (Lima/Mexico, 1992).

The Peruvian *altiplano* zone in the present-day department of Puno, has been the subject of very interesting contributions by Augusto Ramos Zambrano, such as *Puno en la Rebelión de Túpac Amaru* (Puno, 1982). See also the collection edited by Samuel Frisancho, *Album de Oro del Departamento de Puno* (Puno, no date).

The leading scholar on the movements in what is now Bolivia is María Eugenia del Valle de Siles; see, for example, *Testimonios del cerco de La Paz* (La Paz, 1980), and her important *Historia de la rebelión de Túpac Catari* (La Paz, 1990). She has contributed to another important anthology, edited by Luis Durand: *La revolución de los Túpac Amaru. Antología* (Lima, 1981).

The period of Peruvian military nationalist rule, which led up to the bicentennial of the rebellion and the sesquicentennial of independence, provided impetus to publication of works such as Severo Aparicio's volume on behalf of the Comité Arquidiocesano para el bicentenario de Túpac Amaru, *Túpac Amaru y la iglesia. Antología* (Cusco, 1981). Above all the monumental *Colección documental de la Independencia del Perú* (Lima, 1973), in thirty volumes, is the essential vein of primary sources for the history of the late eighteenth century.

Many published documents appear in the thirteen volumes of the *Revista del Archivo Histórico del Cusco.* They include contributions of classic authors such as Jorge Cornejo Bouroncle, Horacio Villanueva Urteaga, and Manuel Jesús Aparicio. Aparicio later participated in the *Colección documental. . . .*

Books that treat the northern region include the indispensable *Sublevaciones indígenas en la Audiencia de Quito, desde comienzos del siglo XVIII hasta fines de la colonia* (Quito, 1985), by Segundo Moreno Yáñez. A new text in every way is that of Martin Minchom, *The People of Quito, 1690–1810* (Boulder, 1994).

References of all types may be found in the panoramic *Rebeliones indígenas en la América Española* (Madrid, 1992), by Angel Barral, with its useful annotated bibliography. This study follows the line of a classic Peruvian author, Carlos Daniel Valcárcel, who, after his *Rebelión de Túpac Amaru* (Lima, 1970) and others from the same period, published *Rebeliones coloniales sudamericanas* (Mexico, 1982).

Among the most useful, indispensable classic literature on rebellions is that by Boleslao Lewin: *La rebelión de Túpac Amaru y los orígenes de la emancipación americana* (Buenos Aires, 1957). In Peru in the 1940s, Francisco Loayza published various work about the rebellion of Juan Santos and about Tupac Amaru II – for example, *Genealogía de Tupac Amaru* (Lima, 1946). Other bibliography of interest is included in the footnotes.

23

ANDEAN HIGHLAND PEASANTS AND THE TRIALS OF NATION MAKING DURING THE NINETEENTH CENTURY

BROOKE LARSON

INTRODUCTION

The nineteenth century marks a critical turning point in the long, violent history of colonial encounters among economic élites, political authorities, and native Andean peasantries. Between the late eighteenth century and the early twentieth century, fledgling Andean republics emerged from the chaos of the independence era. Slowly, haltingly they began to dismantle the political and administrative apparatus of colonial rule. By 1825 they had broken the colonial bond, but the greatest challenges of nation building still lay ahead.

Deeply divided by ethnic, cultural, and class differences, yet born of Enlightenment principles of liberty, equality, and citizenship, the new republics of Colombia, Ecuador, Peru, and Bolivia were shaped by conflicts and contradictions inherent in postcolonial projects of modernity. For much of the nineteenth century, the defining political issue in these Andean republics was whether, and how, the republics should redefine and restructure the colonial relationship based on principles of caste and corporatism and codified in Hapsburg law as "dual republics." Indeed the very notions of *república*, nation, and race were semantic battlefields on which fractured élites and subject populations contentiously worked out meanings and legitimacies of political authority. They debated Indian[1] rights following the collapse of the Catholic monarchy and the

[1] The Cambridge Histories follow the English convention of capitalizing the word "Indian." But a good argument can be made for treating it throughout most of its history as a social descriptor without standing as a proper noun. As a generic category imposed by Europeans on all native peoples of the Americas in the sixteenth century, it was eventually inscribed with jural, political, social, cultural, and racial meanings. In this chapter I emphasize changing élite strategies of representation of indigenous Andean peoples, which transformed colonial-derived meanings and implications of "indian" (as a generic category of colonized natives, invested with a legal or

crisis of Bolivarian liberalism in the 1810s and 1820s. The postindependence years brought an avalanche of peasant claims and protests over the ambiguous and shifting terms of Indian integration into the new nations as war-weary republics withdrew ambitious liberal agendas thrust upon them by the liberators and instead looked for ways to restore a precarious *pax republicana*. But in the political-ideological void opened by independence, state power tended in turn to fragment and devolve to provincial élites and local authorities; liberal land reforms languished; tribute was restored; and Andean regional and export markets remained sluggish. This transitory political reprieve opened new spaces for Andean peoples to negotiate political pacts, recover lost lands, restore ethnic authorities, rearrange translocal networks of patronage, kinship, barter, and trade, and engage in ritual religious activities away from the watchful eye of modern nation builders. But if the postindependence decades of liberal retreat and agrarian decompression relaxed certain pressures on Andean lands, livelihoods, and corporate identities for several decades, they only heightened the political violence intrinsic to modern state making and incipient capitalist development in the Andes in the second half of the nineteenth century.

Indeed around the middle of the nineteenth century, global and national circumstances gradually began to transform ambivalent republics into aggressive, oligarchic states – the vanguards of capitalism and modernity. Andean republics began to break out of their economic and political isolation and move into global currents of trade, technology, and ideology. Coastal Peru led the way in the 1840s, when her islands of guano attracted European merchants and steamships to the Pacific waters. The export of nitrates, guano, wool, and minerals plugged the west coast of South America into the bustling Atlantic world. By the 1860s and 1870s, modernizing oases of sugar, wine, and cotton plantations flourished along the arid coastline of Peru. Cacao trees grew in the subtropical vicinity of Ecuador's main port city of Guayaquil. Nitrate mines pocked the coastal desert of Peru and Bolivia (the territory conquered by Chile in the War of the Pacific in the early 1880s). Tropical commodities like rubber and quinine also began to draw intrepid capitalists into the interior tropical frontiers.

Economic change came more slowly to the Andean highlands (see

customary corporate status) to an essentialized biocultural "Indian race," defined in opposition to "white" Spanish-speaking Creoles.

Map 23.1) widening the gulf between the modernizing, europeanizing coast and the "backward" Indian sierra. But by the 1870s tangible signs of economic change were everywhere. The first railroads lurched their way up over the Andean cordillera, connecting remote interior towns and regions of southern Peru to the coast. A steamship ferried across the deep blue waters of Lake Titicaca, in full view of llama caravans lumbering along ancient lakeshore trails en route to distant pastures and markets. Miners of southern Bolivia had pumped out the flooded shafts of old silver mines and were busily extracting ore again. About the same time, Colombian merchants discovered a rich source of quinine bark in the subtropical forests shading the eastern slopes of Páez territory in the southern department of Cauca. Along the northeastern slopes of Colombia, coffee plantations had taken root. Perhaps most dramatic of all was the violent enclosure movement that rapidly displaced Indian herding communities and traditional regional markets across the *altiplano* (high plateau) of southern Peru and northern Bolivia, as the world market began to absorb an increasing quantity of Peru's raw wool exports.

As elsewhere in Latin America, imperatives of export-driven modernization revived Creole interest in the doctrines of economic liberalism. Ascendant liberals pushed their pro–free-trade agendas: to dismantle protectionist barriers, develop their nation's infrastructure, promote export trade, encourage foreign investment, increase government revenue, and develop their domestic markets. Beyond these narrow economistic goals, however, economic liberalism projected a fundamental reordering of political, institutional, and discursive relations with the indigenous and mestizo peasants and laborers whose tribute and labor power had sustained the fledgling republics. Indian tribute, the symbolic and material mainstay of the dual-republic regime already partially restored after independence, had become but a minor source of state revenue by midcentury. For the first time since the 1820s, Ecuador, Peru, and Bolivia signaled their readiness to revoke Indian tribute. Peru led the way in 1854, followed by Ecuador in 1857 and Bolivia in 1874.

Creole entrepreneurs, driven by bourgeois or seigneurial values, now placed a premium on Indian land and labor. As capitalism entered a new territorial phase of expansion, Indian-held lands became a scarce, valuable, and conflict-ridden resource. Plunged into bitterly competitive regional and export markets, Andean communities of farmers, herders, artisans, traders, pack drivers, and seasonal laborers almost everywhere faced massive threats to their subsistence security, local autonomy, and

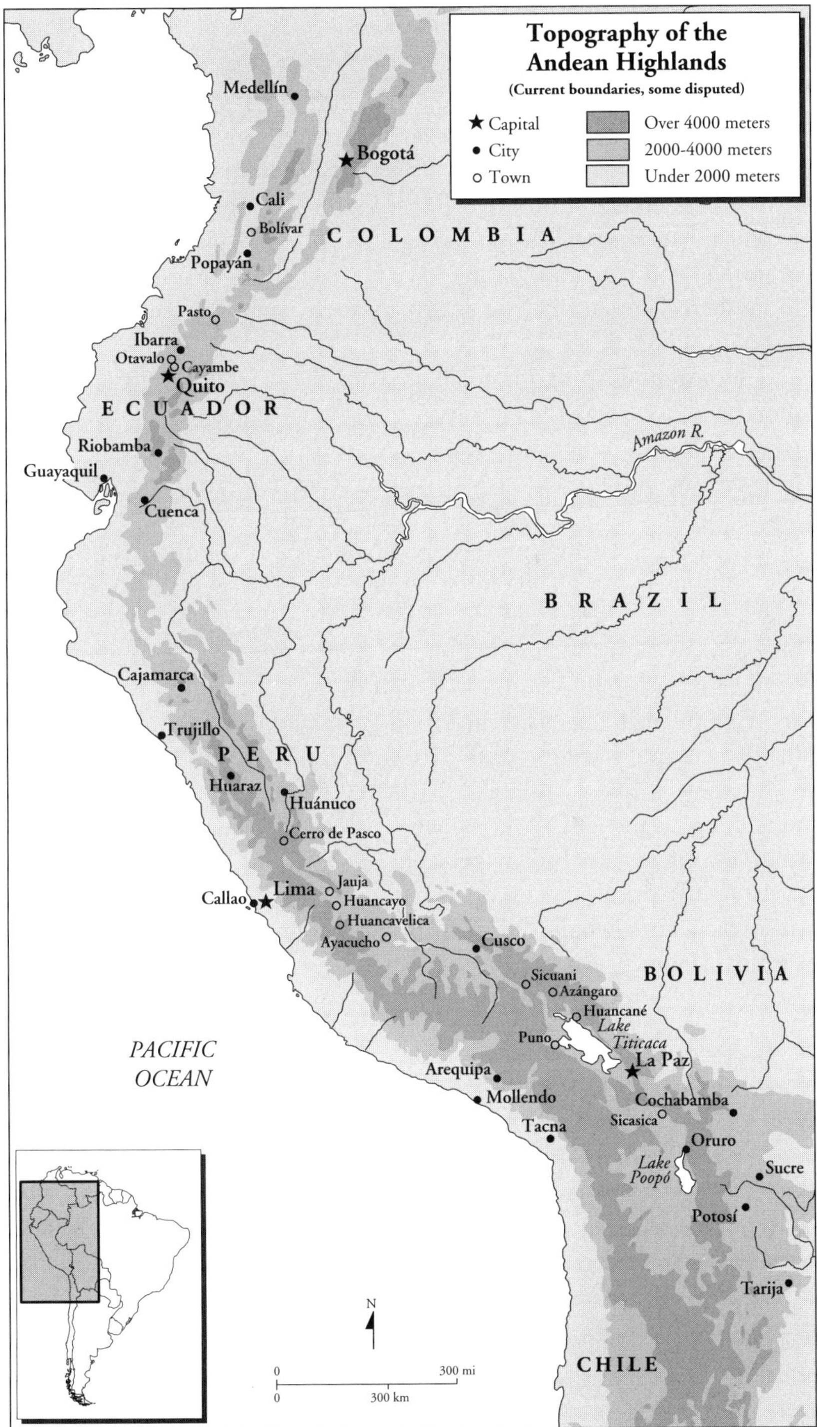

Topography of the Andean Highlands
(Current boundaries, some disputed)
Capital
City
Town
Over 4000 meters
2000-4000 meters
Under 2000 meters
COLOMBIA
ECUADOR
PERU
BRAZIL
BOLIVIA
CHILE
PACIFIC OCEAN
Amazon R.
Medellín
Bogotá
Cali
Bolívar
Popayán
Pasto
Ibarra
Otavalo
Cayambe
Quito
Riobamba
Guayaquil
Cuenca
Cajamarca
Trujillo
Huaraz
Huánuco
Cerro de Pasco
Lima
Callao
Jauja
Huancayo
Huancavelica
Ayacucho
Cusco
Sicuani
Azángaro
Huancané
Lake Titicaca
Puno
La Paz
Arequipa
Mollendo
Tacna
Cochabamba
Sicasica
Oruro
Lake Poopó
Sucre
Potosí
Tarija
N
0
300 mi
0
300 km

Map 23.1

symbolic space. No less important, they suffered a precipitous decline of their rights to collective existence and bargaining power as Indian citizen-subjects. In brief the uneasy *pax republicana* of postindependence rapidly gave way to an era of hostile nations, agrarian compression, and political violence. Late nineteenth-century agrarian violence, punctuated by bursts of warfare and rebellion, set the stage for new cycles of Indian insurgency in southern Peru and Bolivia during the early twentieth century high tide of political liberalism.

The economic progress so desired by the capitalist vanguard could only be as secure as their projects of national integration. State/society relations had to be radically altered if Creole nation builders were going to break the autonomies of native peasantries and reintegrate them into the emerging capitalist markets as peons on estates ("estate" in the sense of *hacienda*, i.e., latifundium), wage laborers, petty commodity producers and consumers, or smallholding farmers. Monied capitalism demanded new legal and judiciary systems, redefined property relations, elimination of corporate status (including rights of Indian propertied communalism), removal of indigenous authorities, and the moral regulation of its laborers. Enlightened liberalism and bourgeois authority mandated no less than a "cultural revolution" to be waged in the Andean heartlands.

But how would Creole élites, clinging to the europeanizing coast or inhabiting seigneurial enclaves, which were continually penetrated and undermined by the Indian peasants upon whom they depended, foist their own political and moral agendas on the rural Indian and mestizo majorities? How would they increase their control over Indian lands and surplus, channel peasant labor into the export economies, squeeze their landholdings onto the market, open up "unexplored" territories for colonization, and finally construct a unified national territory under Creole control?

More fundamentally, what would be the ideological mainstay of the imagined community (to use Benedict Anderson's famous phrase)? Creole nationhood was laying exclusive claim to civilization in countries where indigenous and other nonwhite subcultures remained stubbornly at the core of their social and economic geography, leaving the ideal and real nations profoundly mismatched. Indian removal, military extermination, or genetic assimilation were viable political options for those nations where nomadic or tribal "wild Indians" inhabited the nation's territorial, economic, and cultural frontiers. But such obvious (and brutal) solutions were not available to the Creole architects of the new

Peruvian, Bolivian, or Ecuadorian *patrias* (regional homelands), where highland Indians vastly outnumbered whites.

Furthermore the Andean republics never built strong, authoritarian states on a par with Argentina, Chile, or Mexico. There was no Andean analog to Mexico's *porfiriato*. When the Andean republics belatedly embarked on their journeys toward progress, they were thwarted by internecine strife, partisan warfare, civil wars, foreign invasions, and territorial loss. National sovereignty was more theory than reality, and as many dangers lurked within their national borders as without. It would be a long time before these republics possessed the capacity to discipline or "civilize" their Indian populations, or even protect their own national borders. Here, then, was the critical national question confronting the incipient Andean nation-states in the second half of the nineteenth century: how to resolve the "Indian problem" – interpreted by Creole discourses as the main impediment to order and progress – under deteriorating political conditions of unstable and despotic regimes, on the one hand, and escalating ethnic and peasant violence, on the other.

This chapter is not so interested in the answer to that question, because the so-called Indian problem as posed remains unresolved to this day. My aim instead is to explore the complex historical process by which the Andean republics constructed the "Indian problem" and turned it into the political and rhetorical centerpiece of their varied nation-building projects during the second half of the nineteenth century. It could be reasonably argued that Creole nation builders constructed their national narratives, by borrowing shamelessly from European notions of linguistic and ethnic nationalism, or from pseudo-scientific theories of social evolution and race. The "Indian race" was the necessary rhetorical "other" in their search for national identity, "whiteness," and civic society along European models. And, indeed, European theories of race and nation deeply penetrated Creole imaginings of nationhood, which increasingly became coterminous with white, Christian, Spanish-speaking, and capitalist standards. In the late nineteenth century, Creole national projects all set their sights on this ideal. The modern "Indian race" – the degenerate, impoverished, solemn descendants of the Inka, trapped as if in a time warp – stood as its stark antithesis.

But nation-building projects are not plucked from the heaven of pure ideas. They are rooted in the earth of social history. And never more so than in the Andes, where those projects came up against strong traditions of Andean agency, land-based *ayllus* (i.e., localized kindreds, and peasant communities), submerged and occasionally insurgent ethnic politics, and resilient popular cultures, memories, and discourses. It was not only the rugged hispanized *caudillos* (leaders of factional armies) riding across the nineteenth-century landscape who created endemic political instability and crises of authority, but also the more hidden counterforces of Andean peasant politics, militarized Indian movements, and cultural forms of resistance that went into the unmaking, and reordering, of postcolonial political formations. Once we emphasize the interactions, understandings, and practices of rural Andean peoples engaged in the conflictive processes of postcolonial transition, we begin to appreciate the powerful material and cultural counterforces that white nation builders came up against.

By inserting Andean peoples into the analysis of postcolonial transitions, we may also grasp the multiple, overlapping ways that the forces of capitalism and modernity insinuated themselves into the material and cultural lives of rural Indian peasants; how they coped with, adjusted to, and thought about the changing political order and their place in it; and how they shaped, or subverted, specific "civilizing" projects.

This chapter, then, is a cultural and political interpretation of Andean experiences and responses to nation-building projects in Colombia, Ecuador, Peru, and Bolivia. In each republic those projects involved a complex alchemy of political, economic, cultural, and discursive reforms. Reforms gradually paved the way toward exclusivist political systems, fragile civil societies, and incipient capitalist economies. Implicitly reforms were governed by a dual set of goals: to bring Indians into the economy as subsistence laborers, but to lock them out of the nation as citizens. How these four republics gradually came to define these goals, the means by which nation builders tried to realize them, and the social consequences of their efforts, all varied sharply. Each had its own unique combination of colonial, independence, and postindependence experiences, which acted upon distinctive regional, ethnic, and class configurations, as well as emerging national political cultures.

In broad terms Andean peasants throughout the North Highlands of Colombia and Ecuador were more fragmented, scattered, and assimilated into hispanized society than in the South Highlands of Peru and Bolivia. Colombia's Chibcha peoples retained *resguardos* (reservations), political and territorial units owned communally and guaranteed by the crown, but in many cases they saw them melt into amorphous smallholding and latifundist regimes. Highland ethnic enclaves – the Páez and Pasto Indians, for example – were by the nineteenth century confined to the isolated mountains of the southern Cauca department. And overall native peasantries composed a small minority of Colombia's heterogeneous communities of Creole, mestizo, mulatto, and African peoples. Ecuador's Indian peasantries constituted about half the republic's total population, although most lived outside of freeholding communities. Ecuador's unique colonial legacies of estates, textiles mills, debt, compulsory labor, and rural migration had taken their toll. There were ethnic exceptions, like the Otavalans, but they stood in stark contrast to deepening patterns of peasant immiseration. The territorial dimension of the "Indian problem" never loomed very large in these countries. And nineteenth-century processes of transculturation produced a growing mestizo population throughout much of the North Andes.

By contrast Indians composed large majorities in both Peru and Bolivia, and most were still attached in significant ways to freeholding communities or *ayllus* around the mid–nineteenth century. State and market expansion mandated the displacement of Indian farmers and herders from their lands, stocks, and market circuits, as well as their direct subordination to Creole political authorities or landlords. There Creole national projects would possess a particularly violent edge, as would Indian politics of defense and retribution. And during episodes of military invasion, civil war, and rebellion in the 1880s and 1890s, militarized peasants would force their way into the national theater of war, politics, and discourse to press their varied claims, concerns, and visions.

Against this backdrop it is reasonable to expect distinctive nation-building dynamics to develop in these four countries. Colombia's drive to modernize by absorbing Indians into a europeanizing majority had more affinity with Brazil's "whitening" project than with the semicolonial policies implemented by Ecuador, Peru, and Bolivia. But ethnic militarization and warfare in the southern mountains of Cauca ultimately forced Colombian élites to reinstate partial paternal protection of some Indian minorities. Conservative Ecuador delivered the task of "civilizing" Indians to the Church, and it used the state to coerce the flow of Indian labor into the nation's road-building program. But the state could not control the human hemorrhage of Indian communities, as many peasants moved into the orbit of cities, estates, and rural mestizo towns. In Peru and Bolivia the "Indian problem" proved potentially dangerous as war and rebellion escalated during and after the War of the Pacific. Peru's civilizing project rapidly collapsed into campaigns of military pacification of the Indian patriot-soldiers, rebels, and guerrillas, who would not lay down their arms or their ideals after war and betrayal. Peru's Indian policy became one of suppression, conquest, and demonization. Bolivia sustained colonial structures of tribute, corporate landholding, and caste longer than the other republics. Andean communities and *ayllus* continued to manipulate colonial-customary terms of the "tributary pact" until well into the nineteenth century. This situation put the Bolivian state on a direct collision course with Aymara- and Quechua-speaking communities across much of the northern *altiplano* and in the Southern Highlands of northern Potosí. Overall these projects and conflicts destroyed the basis of state legitimacy and instead prepared the ground for violent colonial reencounters in the early twentieth century. (For the geography of Aymara- and Quechua-speaking communities, see Map 25.1 on page 768.)

How is it possible to excavate native Andean social experiences, understandings, and actions through the multiple and distorting layers of Creole nation building? Certainly the intrinsic limitations of official colonial sources and eurocentric subjectivities plague historical research on the nineteenth-century Andes. There are perhaps fewer historical traces of Andean peoples in nineteenth-century government records than in any other period. For much of the century, Indians did not enter into republican sources or public conversations. This climate of administrative neglect was strongest in Colombia and Ecuador, which effaced Indians from their official census records following independence. And, in any event, statistical and narrative record keeping broke down all over the Andes during and after the wars. The great wealth of colonial judicial testimony dried up, royal inspections ceased, Indian policy debates subsided, and tribute records lapsed after the Bourbons went home. Neglect was compounded by racial scorn as learned authorities began to rediscover, typologize, and essentialize Indians in the emerging literary and scientific canon of the late nineteenth century. Some of the most acute social and natural histories and ethnographies of this era are found in the travel memoirs of European and North American visitors. They, too, cast an imperial eye over all they observed.

But until quite recently the virtual absence of rural Andean peasantries from nineteenth-century Andean historiography had more to do with implicit assumptions about native Andean societies and cultures than with the era's impoverished documentary base. Nineteenth- and early twentieth-century idioms and images of Indians as isolated, atomized, passive, parochial, and crushed under the forces of modernization still pervade much of the historical literature. Even among social and cultural historians of the rural Andean world, research on the great Andean rebellions of the late eighteenth century eclipsed historical interest in the complexly prosaic forms of Andean politics and popular culture in the postindependence period. Implicitly historians assumed that the submersion of the "Inka Utopia" and Indian political movements during the nineteenth century were legacies of Indian defeat and repression in the late eighteenth century (see Chap. 22). Thus this dark age slipped from historiographic view, wedged in between the late colonial age of Andean insurrection and the rise of modern *indigenismo*, peasant unionism, ethnology, oral testimony, and indigenous historiography in the twentieth century.

The materials and interpretations woven through this chapter suggest the limitations of such imageries and assumptions. I seek to understand the cultural continuities, changes, and legacies of Andean peoples in their continuous, interactive engagement with the cultural and political forms of nation making during this crucial period of postcolonial transition. Broadly there are three analytic areas in which to cultivate "interior historical perspectives" on nineteenth-century Andean experiences and actions.

First, struggles over land and its meaning intensified over the course of that century. In both material and symbolic ways, Indian land became the crucible within which Andean peoples confronted incipient capitalist culture. Andean communities throughout the entire region, from the shrunken Chibcha *resguardos* of northern Colombia to the resilient *ayllus* (kin-structured landholding corporations) of southern Bolivia, confronted a battery of anti-Andean laws, policies, and practices aimed at eliminating the legal basis of propertied communalism and removing hereditary ethnic authorities. These assaults on Andean territoriality – probably the most sustained and powerful territorial conquest since the late sixteenth and early seventeenth centuries – forced besieged Andean communities to tap deep cultural reservoirs of meaning, memory, and identity in contesting nascent bourgeois notions of property and rationality. The appropriation or seizure of Andean lands, pastures, and herds threatened more than their material means of survival; it threatened their whole claim to a collective existence, grounded in the shared symbolic and material space that formed their sacred-historic territorial domain.

Andean strategies of land defense took many different forms and unfolded in very different regional and national contexts. They also precipitated intense intra-Andean conflicts and readjustments that reflected the cultural interiorization of bourgeois forms of property holding and land use. But insofar as diverse communities of Andean peasants experienced assaults on their communal lifeways and legitimacies, these struggles often crystallized into collective counteroffenses and land recuperation campaigns. Most battles began over conflicting property claims: whether liberal divestiture laws could override Andeans' legal-customary rights to common lands and/or access to distant pastures, woodlands, coca fields, water, ice, salt, or other precious resources. Although Andean discursive strategies took diverse forms and bore different consequences, they invariably afford us insights into popular moral evaluations of the changing sociopolitical landscape, of their legitimate place in the cosmological order, and of the historical journeys they had traveled since precolonial times. That is, nineteenth-century Andean defenses of territoriality bear all the hallmarks of contests over essential meanings, histories, and identities embedded in everyday oral knowledges, ritual languages, and accumulated documentary evidences of *cacique* lineages, land titles, tributary payments, and other aspects of *ayllu* history.

The second interior pathway toward Andean cultural politics and perspectives is conjunctural: the record of popular actions and voices in moments of acute national or regional crisis – usually episodes of war, military repression, and cross-cultural diplomacy. Although the nineteenth-century Andes offers no match for the scope, intensity, or ideological coherence of Indian insurrection during the late colonial era, it was plagued by endemic regional violence, partisan warfare, *caudillo*-styled politics, occasional peasant uprisings, full-scale regional rebellions, and imperial invasion and warfare. The critical breakpoint in this roiling postcolonial landscape was the Chilean-Peruvian War of the Pacific (1879–1883) and its aftershocks. Big or small, these recurring occasions of violence, pillage, and rupture wreaked havoc on many Andean lives, forcing them to find new, often more precarious means of subsistence, security, and community. Militarism bred popular militias, bandits, guerrillas, and alternative networks of political patronage, and rivalry, which engulfed entire regions and pushed them to the margins of the republic. But these regions were also the breeding grounds of oppositional popular cultures and distinctive *patrias chicas* ('local homelands'), which Andean cadres participated in shaping. Poised on the interior frontiers, just beyond the reach of the state, these emergent nineteenth-century regional subcultures are still areas of historiographic obscurity.

Less so are those rare incandescent moments of popular Andean political participation in the interstices of empire and nation. By force or will, Indians were thrust into the political maelstroms of independence, successive partisan and civil wars, regional rebellions, and the great War of the Pacific. Where recorded, their mobilized actions, threats, and words often give insights into Andean peoples' lived experiences, as well as their real and imagined political communities. Contrary to much social-science wisdom about parochial peasant mentalities, Andeans had long traditions of engaging the state on material and moral questions. Indeed Indian judicial politics under colonial rule was one of the mainstays of Catholic monarchism. By the beginning of republican rule, Indians had already tasted the bitter fruits of a truncated, repressive regime of liberal reformism, first under Spanish constitutional liberalism in 1812 and later under Bolivarian liberalism in the mid-1820s. Indians subsidized and fought in the independence wars, joined partisan coalitions and regional strongmen, and spilled their blood in defense of the Peruvian *patria* during the War of the Pacific. They found themselves courted, or coerced, into partisan or national armies, and later marginalized, patronized or vilified by anti-Andean élite coalitions.

In these liminal moments Andean peasantries were compelled as never before to question and critique the morality of a political order, or party, that mobilized them as citizens or partisans only to denigrate them later as Indian barbarians or criminals. Poised briefly at the center of political chaos, Andeans entered into national polemics, evolving rhetorical and political strategies of self-representation and social critique. Andean popular discourses were polyvalent. They involved fragmented appropriations of hegemonic idioms and ideologies (monarchism, republicanism, federalism, nationalism, racism), often designed to contest, or dialogue with, hegemonic ideas, policies, and practices. But they were also transmuted and turned to autonomist ends. Usually Andean deployment of popular political "isms" merged with, or were infiltrated by, local cultural values and knowledges preserved in oral, written, pictographic, and ritual forms. It is in this protean intersection of popular political discourses and everyday cultural practices that we sometimes catch glimpses of nineteenth-century Andean social constructs of ethnic selfhood, otherness, and nation, and of the specific historical and cultural contingencies that shaped them.

Finally day-to-day intercultural engagements and negotiations of power, authority, and autonomy offer a third arena. Ultimately nationmaking "civilizers" sought to colonize Indian culture and consciousness in ways compatible with emerging bourgeois values of individualism, property, discipline, and conformity. Cultural redemption and reassimilation of Indians would be cajoled or coerced through mechanisms of social engineering and moral regulation and, where necessary, through cultural repression and reprisal. Once Creole discourses had reinvented Indians as the primordial "problem" of nation making, they assembled a discursive repertory from fragments of liberal-positivist and racist theories to legitimate this modern-aged "spiritual conquest" in the crusade for modernity. At the edge of the "civilizing" frontier, then, there raged ongoing micropolitical and semiotic battles over Andean rights to popular cultural practices, values, and identities.

Popular religion was a crucial site of cultural contestation and conflict, because nineteenth-century secular state builders sought to suppress or regulate religious festivities in Indian and mestizo towns. All across the Andes civilizing vanguards launched anti-Indian assaults. In the 1830s Bolivia got papal dispensation to reduce the number of religious feast days in order to limit the vice and laziness of Indians. In Peru during the early 1880s, while the War of the Pacific still raged, provincial town councils in the Central Sierra banned Indian fiestas out of fear of insurgent threats and uprisings. Both Colombia and Ecuador, in their separate ways, launched campaigns against the "barbarous" cultural practices of Indians. In the meantime the four republics invented civic traditions, replete with Bolivarian statues, patriotic processions and songs, bull runs, and the heraldry appropriate to newly liberated countries. In spite of the republics' repressive measures and invented traditions, however, popular religiosity flourished in Indian towns and *ayllus*. White civilizers condemned these cultural flashpoints as signs of their nation's backwardness and barbarity, an utter anathema to European norms of civil society. Republican Church hierarchies felt more ambivalence, depending on the political position and authority they held in their respective nations.

For Andean communities, on the other hand, the religious-ritual calendar organized the seasonal rhythms of communal life and provided micropolitical theaters for the expression of syncretic, alternative, and sometimes subversive cultural themes. For centuries Andean peoples had appropriated and transmuted Christian symbols and institutions. By the late colonial era Christian and indigenous deities commingled in dynamic cultural-religious syntheses. Andean interpretive uses of Christian deities and devils were as much a part of Andean religious repertories as were their specific local gods, sacred genealogies and landscapes, and pastoral-sacrificial rites that tapped ethnic memories and defined cosmographic territories. Religious fiestas were vital occasions drawing together people from the "halves" of dualistic societies to perform acts of ritualized solidarity and ritualized enmity. They were moments to release pressures, renew communal bonds and boundaries, trade, collect tribute and mobilize communal workforces, redistribute communal responsibilities and resources, install new officers of rotating civil-religious hierarchies, settle disputes, and reinvigorate communal efforts to recover stolen lands. In short these were the symbolically nodal points in the continuous reproduction and adaptation of ethnic community and identity. But popular cultures can also be read as social barometers of deteriorating ethnic, class, or communal relations; as counteroffenses against an increasingly hostile state; and as fluid arenas of conflict, adaptation, and change. Hegemonic myths to the contrary, Andean popular cultures were becoming more conflictive, textured, and diversified during the nineteenth century.

Here, then, we come to a central paradox in postcolonial highland Andean peasant history, one that has shaped historiographic approaches until quite recently. Nineteenth-century ideological constructs bifurcated Andean societies into whites and Indians. But in practice as opposed to ideology, diverse communities of Andean peasantries were pursuing everyday economic, political, and cultural strategies that undermined and challenged rigid Indian–white bipolarities.

To build exclusive white nations, predicated on false essentializing antinomies (white versus Indian; civilization versus barbarism), Creole élites developed ideological projects launching a new age of discovery, conquest, and colonization of the "Indian race." But these liberal-racial-evolutionary discourses that build rigid racial hierarchies, legitimated civilizing missions, and ultimately argued for the selective assimilation of Indians into the nation as its impoverished laboring class, were blind to (or suppressed) the significances of real, everyday social experiences and cultural changes occurring quietly but inexorably across the Andean highlands. They ignored or obscured, for example, the vigorous cultural innovations that produced distinctive social, regional, subcultures – such as the entrepreneurial Otavalan weavers of Ecuador or the *chola* communities of *chicha* manufacturers in Bolivia's Cochabamba valleys. They stigmatized ethnic political networks that emerged in wartime or in the escalating struggles over territorial rights, which stretched the horizons of Andean identity, memory, and cohesion. And, finally, hegemonic imaginings of the rural Indian hinterlands and the "Indian problem" could not recognize or acknowledge the multiple cultural and economic pathways that more and more Andean peoples were following out of an increasingly stigmatized Indianness. The nineteenth century was opening more interstitial spaces in regional economies, state bureaucracies, and on the edges of rural Indian society and white cities. The abolition of hereditary lordship, and the peasantization of Andean communities, created more need for transculturated Indians and mestizos, who could broker exchanges across ethnic, class, and language barriers. Rapidly centralizing and mercantilizing societies also collapsed sociocultural distances, creating new occupations in certain regions, and producing in turn a whole variety of culturally hybrid *castas* and mestizos that eroded and complicated rigid racial categories. One of the cultural legacies of nineteenth-century Andean history was the negotiation of diverse, ambiguous ethnic self-identities. These put the lie to racialized bipolarities, which became the public basis of Andean modernity.

THE PROJECT OF INDIAN INTEGRATION IN COLOMBIA: CULTURAL ASSIMILATION OR MARGINALIZATION?

On the northern periphery of the Andes, Colombia (known as New Granada until 1863) entered the mid–nineteenth century poised on the threshold of a liberal experiment in nation building. After two decades of halting reforms, tempered by protectionist measures, Colombian élites coalesced around the orthodoxies of economic liberalism. Where liberal economic ideas remained latent or embattled in the other Andean republics until the end of the century, they enjoyed virtual hegemony in Colombia from the late 1840s to 1880.[2] Thereafter the Conservatives seized presidential power, with an agenda not too different from that of their Liberal Party predecessors.

[2] In general terms economic liberalism refers to a corpus of ideology, theory, and policy that sought to relax institutional constraints on economic activity, allowing it to be governed by the free play of market forces. It also promoted the international division of labor through the alleged comparative advantages of each part of the world economy (given differing factor endowments). The precepts of economic liberalism underscore the strictures against governmental regulation of economic life and the international application of free trade policies. See Frank Safford, "The emergence of economic liberalism in Colombia," in Joseph L. Love and Nils Jacobsen, *Guiding the Invisible Hand: Economic Liberalism and the State in Latin American History* (New York, 1988), 35.

Having lived in economic isolation for decades, locked in the mountainous interior of the country, Colombian élites harbored hopes that tropical products (tobacco, quinine bark, coffee, sugar, and cotton) would find markets in Europe and the United States. A new generation of Liberals, bolder in their commitment to free-trade policies and anxious to test their ideas, swept into power in 1849. Within a decade the Liberals had put into place the cornerstones of their reform project. They fragmented and minimized the power of the national state between 1850 and 1880, while lifting restrictions on market activities. They tore down the tariff wall protecting Colombian artisans, legalized the immediate sale of reserved Indian lands (*resguardos*), and not least, abolished African slavery. Driven more by ideology than by real economic pressures, Colombia's nation builders embraced liberal prescriptions long before the country possessed an integrated national market or expanding export economy. Indeed free-trade liberalism sprouted in a comparatively hostile economic environment. Most export commodities were cut off from overseas markets by mountains and ravines, tropical climates, seasonal rainfalls, and enormous overland freight costs. Pack mules and human backs carried most cargo until the end of the nineteenth century, and transportation between the port of Cartagena and Europe was faster and cheaper than the overland route connecting the port to Bogotá. Indeed, North American and European traveler-writers who trekked into the interior of Colombia left discouraging impressions of exotic Indians and hostile landscapes, impeding scientific expeditions and economic progress (Fig. 23.1). But Colombian élites did not need the vicarious experiences of European travelers to appreciate the appalling state of their roads, the decadence of internal commerce, and growing regional economic autarchy. The yawning gap between utopian liberalism and stubborn social realities around 1850 disquieted many creole politicians and writers, who began the task of diagnosing the root causes of Colombia's economic backwardness. And they fixed their gaze on the inescapable presence of Indians and Africans in their midst.

Reinventing Indians as Economic Obstacles

Among the four Andean republics, Colombia's Creole élite was the first to produce a rhetorical argument that pinned the country's economic backwardness squarely on the concept of racial inferiority. Although the content of their racisms varied, most mid–century social theorists had

Figure 23.1. *Sillero* and *Cargueros* of the Quindio Pass in the Province of Popayán, ca. 1827. European travelers to Colombia following Independence were fixated on its mountains, rugged terrain, and impassable roads, widely considered to be the worst in South America. Unlike the southern Andes, where the upkeep of old Inka and colonial highways was sustained by corvée labor, Colombia's nineteenth-century roads deteriorated throughout the interior of the country. As mules became worthless transport animals, Indian backs became the preferred mode of transport and the most common visual symbol of South American barbarism and backwardness in early and mid-nineteenth-century European travel literature. In his survey of Colombia for the British government in 1824, for example, Colonel J. P. Hamilton wrote of the human beasts of burdens who carried cargo and people on their backs across the Quindio pass, the main east-west axis of the country. (From Col. J. P. Hamilton, *Travels Through the Interior Provinces of Columbia* [London: John Murray, 1827], 2 vols. 2: 211. See also, Taussig 1986: 296–305.)

not yet hardened into biological determinists.[3] Writers like José María Samper, Manuel Ancízar, and Augustín Codazzi explored the effects of climate, culture, and social institutions on the social characteristics of racial groups.[4] In particular, liberal writers were fond of invoking the Black Legend of Spanish colonial oppression to explain the degradation of Colombia's Indian and African races. Even Samper, the most rigorous racist of the group, did not wholly accept the premise of biological descent as destiny. As we shall see shortly, he firmly believed in the possibility of cultural redemption if certain measures were taken to instill in the inferior groups the values appropriate to a modern civil society. But however much they nuanced their studies of Colombia's "racial

3 Few ideas more firmly gripped the imagination of European social theorists than the idea that "races" that had achieved preeminence were superior, while those that occupied the lower tiers of the social order were inferior. Obviously racial doctrines had served as ideological props of European colonialism and slavery since at least the sixteenth century. But Latin America's europeanizing "white" minorities (as they increasingly thought of themselves) latched onto a new powerful set of pseudo-scientific arguments after the publication of Darwin's *Origins of Species* in 1859. In later decades Darwin's theory of evolution through natural selection was redeployed by social theorists to naturalize racial and class inequalities and rationalize the exercise of violence and domination in colonialist and capitalist ventures. They argued that individuals and races, like species, are engaged in a perpetual struggle for existence that leads inevitably toward the survival of the fittest. The font of late nineteenth-century scientific racism was fed by other intellectual streams as well: the writings of Herbert Spencer, Count Joseph Arthur Gobineau, and Auguste Comte, to mention a few of the most important. How Latin America's white ruling classes adapted and used these European theories, and to what effect, varied considerably, however.

What they shared was their own ambiguous "racial" status in the eyes of European and North American emissaries of civilization and progress in the nineteenth century. For Creoles who dared to peer into their own national "heart of darkness" and discover the "barbarian other" – those nonwhite inhabitants of coast, mountain, and jungle frontiers living in their midst – also rediscovered themselves as social inferiors of the "imperial other" – the European and North American travel writers and social theorists who held Spanish American élites in contempt. English writers, in particular, issued a blanket indictment of Spanish American society for its economic backwardness, indolence, and failure to exploit its resources. They assumed the inferior races to be indifferent to bourgeois virtues of enterprise, efficiency, comfort, and cleanliness. But they also cast Creole élites in the stereotype of retrograde colonials, still living off the servile labor of their African or Indian minions and, themselves, indifferent to the virtues of hard work, innovation, and enterprise. This essentialized landscape of Spanish American backwardness and neglect legitimated the new imperial thrust of capitalist bankers, merchants and entrepreneurs in the mid- and late nineteenth century. But the new rhetoric also proved useful to liberal élites in Spanish America, anxious to redeem their own images in European and North American eyes and to promote their national projects of modernity. For a pointed example of a North American traveler's view of "Caucasian debasement" among Spanish Americans, see H. Willis Baxley, *What I Saw on the West Coast of South and North America* (New York, 1865), 378–391; for a splendid interpretive approach, see Mary Louise Pratt, *Imperial Eyes. Travel Writing and Transculturation* (New York, 1992), 150–153.

4 José María Samper, *Ensayo sobre las revoluciones políticas y la condición social de las república colombianas* [1861] (Bogotá, 1984); Manuel Anzíbar, *Peregrinaciones de Alpha por las provincias del Norte de la Nueva Granada* (Bogotá, 1956); Augustín Codazzi, "Descripción jeneral de los indios del Caquetá," in Felipe Pérez, *Jeografía física i política de los Estados Unidos de Colombia*, 2 vols. (Bogotá, 1863), II.

types," they were beginning to produce a scientific and literary canon that associated "whiteness" with progress and civilization and its negative opposite, "nonwhiteness," with the obstacles that blocked the pathways to modernity.[5]

The social construction of race occurred in two types of "scientific" literature. The first type was the modern variant of discovery and exploration narratives. They were written by geographers, ethnographers, and essayists, and often illustrated by artists, all of whom sought to unlock the secrets of the nation's forgotten or forbidding frontiers. A spate of studies associated with the *Comisión Corográfica*, Colombia's first official geographic survey, focused attention on the country's demographic, economic, and sociocultural peculiarities (Fig. 23.2). More than a mere aggregation of facts, these studies provided a vision of a fragmented nation composed of distinctive regional and racial subcultures. Region and race served as the organizing principles of knowledge. Thus, for example, scientists depicted the innate characteristics of the "Harvesters of Aniseed: Mestizo and Indian Types, Province of Ocaña," and the "White Miners, Province of Soto" (Fig. 23.3). Of particular interest was the economic behavior of each racial group, implicitly measured against bourgeois virtues of thrift and hard work. Taken together these provincial surveys provided racial typologies, characterizations, and illustrations of Colombia's diverse regions and races.[6]

The new geography bipolarized Colombia into the civilized highlands populated by "white and mestizo types" and its savage hinterlands – the interior tropical forests of nomadic tribal peoples and the southern Pacific littoral and the Caribbean coastal region, where large concentrations of black people lived. Afro-Colombians, many recently emancipated, also inhabited inland pockets of rural and urban territory. But what they all putatively shared was their affinity for the torpor of the tropics, whether coastal or inland, and their "lamentable" indolence, superstition, and

[5] A cornerstone of the scientific canon was Colombia's first official geographic survey, known as the *Comisión Corográfica*, commissioned in 1849. Parts are published in Felipe Pérez, *Jeografía física i política de los Estados Unidos de Colombia*, 2 vols. (Bogotá, 1863). It authorized its investigators to produce detailed surveys of Colombia's topography, local populations, economies, and customs. This survey and related studies produced descriptive, statistical, and aesthetic profiles of Colombia's "racial types." It charted for the first time the "moral topography" of race, which located Colombia's diverse ethnic and racial groups both in geographic space and in the evolutionary time scale of human evolution. These excursions into Colombia's interior ethnic and racial frontiers were in quest of a sense of national self-identity.

[6] See Frank Safford's fascinating gloss on this set of surveys, "Race, integration, and progress: Elite attitudes and the Indian in Colombia," *Hispanic American Historical Review* 71:1 (1991), 20–27.

Figure 23.2. Camp Site of the *Comisión Corográfica*, in the Province of Soto, ca. 1850. The commission took the first official geographic survey of an Andean country. In contrast to late colonial expeditions focusing on flora and fauna, this new geography provided the first exploratory synthesis of regional and racial identities making up the interior landscapes of Colombia in the mid-nineteenth century. Source: *En busca de un país. La Comisión Corográfica.* (Bogotá: Carlos Valencia Ed., 1984).

Figure 23.3. Harvesters of aniseed: Mestizo and Indian "types," Province of Ocaña, ca. 1850. This watercolor painted by one of the artists of the Comisión Corográfica synthesizes region, socioeconomic occupation, and "racial type" (marked dramatically by clothing and by the positioning of the Indian engaged in work and the mestizo [overseer?] at rest). Source: *En busca de un país: la comisión corográfica. Selección de dibjujos* . . . (Bogotá: Carlos Valencia Editores, 1984).

volatility. Highland Indians occupied an ambiguous middle ground in this geocultural and racial order. Neither savage nor civilized, the highland Indians of the northeastern provinces near the city of Bogotá were the best candidates for cultural improvement and eventual assimilation, according to prevailing wisdom. Samper described the Chibcha of the eastern cordillera as "frugal but intemperate, patient but stupid," yet ultimately "civilizable." But if the northern Chibcha's failings were benign, his southern counterpart's was not. The Páez and Pasto Indians of the south were considered to be sedentary savages, not much farther up the evolutionary scale than the hunters and gatherers of the tropical forests. They were dangerous races: "resistant to civilization [and] unmoved by progress," according to Samper.[7] Indeed the Páez and Pastos had a long history of ethnic mobilization to defend or advance their collective interests. Samper was only codifying in racial terms the images, memories, and fears that white nation builders harbored toward the militant indigenous peoples of the far south.

As they peered into their nation's variegated "heart of darkness," the Liberal vanguard busily produced a corpus of prescriptive economic thought that aspired to a modernity in which a culturally homogeneous nation attended to the prosaic needs of commerce and industry. Borrowing precepts of political economy from Montesquieu and other Enlightenment thinkers, they associated the idea of civil society with commerce, money, and communication. The edges of market culture (ideally conceived) also divided civilization from barbarism. At best, Indians and Africans inhabited the frontiers of civilization, because they seemed to lack everything the Creole liberals identified as civilized: money, commerce, comfort, hygiene, Christianity, and the cultural values associated with such things. Indeed the new civilizing rhetoric defined the essence of Indianness and blackness as the antithesis of the *homo economicus*, the rational economic actor endowed with bourgeois cultural norms. Armed with their pseudo-scientific regional-racial typologies, Creole authorities manufactured images of lazy, antimarket Indians and Africans content to live in poverty and sloth. Liberal merchants were concerned with judging the lower orders by their potential as laborers and customers. By midcentury they had lost the earlier Bolivarian ideal of turning Indians into industrious yeoman farmers, simply by subdividing and privatizing *res-*

[7] Samper, *Ensayo sobre las revoluciones políticas*, 87–89; quoted in Safford, "Race, integration, and progress: Elite attitudes and the Indian in Colombia," 26.

guardo lands. Instead they saw the "darker races" as taking their "natural place" among the laboring poor who might, over time, form a mass domestic market for commodities. Thus there was much debate over the intrinsic worth of Colombia's African and Indian races as laborers and consumers, measured against the Caucasian ideal: "if we take a [black] Magdalena boatman or an Indian from Cundinamarca and compare him with an educated Bostonian, we will have before us both our starting point and our goal," wrote a leading Liberal reformer in 1896.[8] In the meantime Liberal intellectuals blamed Colombia's invertebrate national market on black and Indian indolence and indifference to material comfort. Ethnographers often pointed to the "typical" thatched-roof windowless huts of highland Indians as tangible evidence of their subsistent nature. Hence poverty and misery could be blamed on the victim and at the same time used to ascribe racial identity. Postcolonial categories of race and class converged.

Like other "civilizing" agents, Colombian liberals envisioned a culturally homogeneous, market-driven society moving rapidly into the company of cosmopolitan nations. Ideologically they shared more with the nation-building rhetoric and goals of their Brazilian, Argentine, and Chilean counterparts than with the postcolonial ambivalence of Creole élites in Ecuador, Peru, and Bolivia. Colombia's liberal counterparts in those countries continued to face powerful conservative forces still deeply wedded to colonial-paternalist traditions and vulnerable to tremors and eruptions from below. In contrast Colombian élites had inherited a strong Bolivarian tradition that laid the groundwork for the "civilizing" project of the 1850s, 1860s, and 1870s. Although Colombian reformers may have failed at realizing their utopian liberalism in the immediate postindependence period, they succeeded in breaking up *resguardo* lands and crushing Indian opposition throughout most of the northern provinces. Only in the southern provinces did they still confront militant indigenous communities. But in sharp contrast to Peru and Bolivia, Colombian Indians composed a small minority of the total population (perhaps as little as 16 percent in the late colonial period), and in the northeastern cordillera, most had mixed into the mestizo majority. Fewer still occupied *resguardo* lands, located in colder climates not suitable for

[8] Enrique Cortés, a leading Liberal educator published these words in his work, *Escritos varios* (Paris, 1896). Quoted in Marco Palacios, *Coffee in Colombia, 1850–1970: An Economic, Social and Political History* (New York, 1980), 72.

cultivating export crops (coffee, tobacco, etc.). Indian integration was deemed important for the purpose of expanding the consumer and labor markets, but not for the conquest of land. Furthermore tribute had long since withered away, removing any fiscal interest that the state might have had in preserving caste distinctions. Instead Colombia was lurching toward an idea of nation based on linguistic, cultural, and racial homogeneity. Liberal and conservative élites were united in a common concern: how to create out of ethnic and cultural diversity a new and purified white population on which "true nationhood" could be built. The goal was set. Only the means to reach it were in question.

Debates swirled around the potential for constructing a nation out of a patchwork of cultures and races. Most liberal thinkers imagined a nation emerging from several generations of biocultural regeneration, or in the parlance of the day, "whitening." Ultimately they sought to de-Indianize (and de-Africanize) Colombia over several generations through genetic assimilation into a vigorously expanding white population. New theories of evolution in the 1860s offered theoretical comfort to those who pushed the idea of genetic improvement through whitening. It was to be accomplished by both social and natural means. First, the state would import large numbers of European immigrants, attracted perhaps by a generous homesteading policy. Second, as European stock increased, the inferior races would disappear through high mortality rates and intermarriage. The liberals had high hopes for the genetic assimilation of highland Indians in particular. In fact this represented an urgent national priority in the second half of the nineteenth century, because it was believed that only through the intermarriage of Indians and mestizos, and mestizos and whites, would the nation accomplish its genetic integration and counteract the ominous sense that Colombia's black population was "naturally" more prolific and unruly.

Here, then, we begin to understand the peculiar ways in which Colombian nation builders "privileged" highland Indians as readily assimilable, and therefore civilizable. In Colombia the most intractable "problem of race" was attributed to blackness, not Indianness. The roots of this double standard of prejudice, of course, go back to the dawn of colonialism in the New World, when the crown and Church sanctified African, but not Indian, slavery. During the late colonial and independence periods, Enlightenment and Creole patriot discourses had disparaged and feared blacks, even as Bolivarian armies recruited and liberated Afro-Colombian slaves. Fears of black insurrection, banditry, endemic crime, and "natural fecundity" continued to preoccupy the dominant class throughout the nineteenth century. And as liberals consolidated their project of national integration, it was the highland Indian (particularly of the northern regions), not the black, whom they looked upon charitably as more likely to be absorbed by the superior races. Even the most racist of authors, José María Samper, was relatively optimistic about the natural processes of Indian atrophy. The new official surveys seemed to add scientific support to his projection. Manuel Ancívar, who surveyed Colombia's eastern and northeastern provinces in 1850–1851, proclaimed that Indians were rapidly disappearing into *mestizaje* and, by degrees, into whiteness. "Today one notes in the new generation the progressive improvement of the castes," he wrote about the province of Tunja. Although Indians are "still there . . . , you cannot see them."[9]

Thus Colombia's civilizing project charted the pathway toward nationhood through the process of cultural and biological *mestizaje* and, eventually, whiteness. This project would falter in the 1880s and 1890s, as the Conservative Party restored some traditions of the *sociedad de castas* (see Chap. 21). But Colombia's search for national identity through whitening would eventually excite the political imagination of liberals in the other Andean nations, although they reconstructed and applied this project of genetic improvement under very different national and historical circumstances. As we shall see, the mestizo often had powerful negative connotations in the dominant discourses on race and social evolution in the more deeply divided postcolonial societies of Ecuador, Peru, and Bolivia. But in Colombia the mestizo sector was valued for its power to move culture toward a homogeneous white, Christian, Spanish-speaking,

[9] Ancívar, *Peregrinación*, 214, 250; quoted in Safford, "Race, integration, and progress: Elite attitudes and the Indian in Colombia," 28. See also Peter Wade, *Blackness and Race Mixture. The Dynamics of Racial Identity* (Baltimore, 1993).

Chibcha descendants living in the departments of Cundinamarca, Boyacá, Santander, and Santander del Norte had all but disappeared by the mid–eighteenth century. Even in the "Indian province" of Tunja (where native peoples composed 40 percent of the total population in the mid–eighteenth century), whites and mestizos outnumbered Indians by more than ten to one in their own *resguardos*. Bourbon inspectors described a *ladino* countryside, where only a small percentage of the remaining Indians held legal rights to *resguardo* lands. As a result the republic's Bolívarian leaders inherited a land opening up to the possibilities of private colonization. They reached a consensus in the 1830s about the need to dismantle the *resguardos* and redistribute titled plots of land to Indians, before selling off the remaining tracts. The dilemma facing the land reformers was to distinguish between Indians and non-Indians in the highly integrated and densely populated *resguardos* in the Northeastern Highlands. Indeed the republic had officially expunged Indians from the national census and parish records following independence. Priests resorted to code words (such as *vecinos* and *feligreses*) to refer to non-Indians and Indians.

capitalist nationality. Although *mestizaje* represented a progressive force, it had not yet congealed into a symbol of racial synthesis or nonwhite national identity, as it would do in twentieth-century populist rhetoric. (In the 1920s and 1930s *mestizaje* would be reconfigured as a superior mix of races by Latin American nationalists eager to construct new legitimacies on more inclusive racial and class grounds.) Nineteenth-century meanings of *mestizaje* were embedded in the ideology and policies of whitening, which aimed to import massive amounts of European immigrants, eradicate racial-cultural diversity, and construct a monolingual nation and bourgeois market culture under a unitary rule of law. Such definitions of nationhood implicitly indicted the democratic or autonomist claims, and local cultural practices, of the diverse amalgams of mestizo, African, indigenous peoples.

This liberal vision of Indian integration propelled policymakers to hammer out the specifics of economic and cultural reform. One set of reforms was designed to redefine the relationship of Indians to the larger economy and polity. Anxious to stimulate commerce, the new Liberals wanted to hasten the subdivision and privatization of *resguardo* lands by removing the last restrictions on their sale. Yet they also sought to federalize land reform policies, allowing provincial governments to enact their own legislation. Thus the very federalist system that the Liberals put into place actually undermined their goals of agrarian integration and allowed extremely haphazard patterns of land reform. In the southern provinces of Popayán and Pasto, regional élites were more reluctant to break up *resguardos*, whereas Bogotá called for the immediate division of all remaining *resguardo* properties in its own province of Cundinamarca. In general, however, élite consensus turned against earlier protectionist policies and, in particular, removed the literacy clause that had forbidden illiterate Indians from selling their lands. After 1850 unlettered Indians were more vulnerable to litigants, merchants, and creditors who coveted their communal or family plots of land. Yet they also discovered how selective the application of civil equality could be. The Liberals imposed a literacy clause for the right to vote. Hurled into the market, but shut out of the political system, Colombia's indigenous poor were beginning to experience the double standards of citizenship.

The road to civilization and prosperity as mapped by nationalists also required the moral "redemption" of the "Indian race." We still have very little knowledge about nineteenth-century experiments in cultural suppression and reform, but the very idea of converting subsistent, antimarket Indians into disciplined workers and acquisitive materialists called for a massive "civilizing mission" and European immigration scheme beyond anything the federalist, laissez-faire government was capable of. "Liberal hegemony" had more vision than muscle in this regard. Even so, through its own rhetoric, the civilizing mission assumed a legitimacy of its own. Piecemeal measures were proposed and sometimes implemented. Moralizing the Indian character would require resocialization through education and religious indoctrination. Heathenism, drunkenness, fiestas, and other barbarian practices would have to be rooted out. Vagrancy and vagabondage needed to be controlled, the latter especially targeted to destitute Indian prostitutes who were seen as migrating to Bogotá in alarming numbers. In later years reformers would turn to problems of epidemic, disease, and hygiene. But for most of the nineteenth century, concern centered around moral discipline, crime, and punishment. The civilizing mission was to penetrate the intimate cultural spaces of local Indian lifeways.

Indian Dispossession, Defense or Defiance? North–South Contrasts

Beyond the cultural aggression that such projects sanctioned, the experiences and responses of Colombian indigenous groups varied sharply during the late nineteenth century. The weak, uneven, and contradictory application of liberalism, and after 1880 the counterreforms of the Conservatives, certainly contributed to patchwork patterns of social change. Moreover national land, labor, and export markets only began to expand in the 1870s. Thereafter the nature and intensity of commodity markets remained extremely uneven and acted unevenly on distinctive regional, class, and ethnic heritages. Without delving into specific regional variations, we can appreciate starkly different north–south highland patterns of social and cultural change under the converging pressures of market expansion and nation building. The official geography and ethnography of mid-century Colombia provides important clues about the nature of these regional contrasts: market pressures and Indian strategies of social reproduction were far more explosive in the south, among the Indians of Popayán and Pasto than elsewhere. Indian *caudillos* and *cabildos* in those provinces carried on militant traditions of *resguardo* land defense and recuperation, both inside and outside the bounds of civil law. Chibchan peoples farther north felt the pressures of poverty and dislocation no less intensely in the years after 1870, but their own long history of communal erosion, peasantization, and integration in local and regional markets (notwithstanding élite stereotypes to the contrary) foreclosed the possibility of insurgent ethnic responses to growing subsistence threats.

Late nineteenth-century expansion in commercial agriculture quickened the pace of change for most peasant communities in the highland areas of Cundinamarca, Boyacá, and Antioquia. Coffee spread rapidly along the western slopes of Cundinamarca and on the hills sloping down to the *llanos* in the east. Coffee flourished in warmer climates and was cultivated on private estates in pioneering zones. Established on foundations of the traditional latifundia, coffee cultivation often did not take place at the expense of communal lands or peasant smallholding, as it did in other parts of Latin America. Problems of peasant landlessness and dislocation in the eastern highlands did not stem directly from the rise of commercial coffee. In contrast the spread of cattle ranching across the grasslands surrounding the city of Bogotá gobbled up lands of the abolished *resguardos* and dislocated small-scale farmers and medium-sized landowners who had engaged in intensive cultivation of cereals, fruits, and vegetables. These ranches cleared the plains for extensive cattle grazing. But even in these hinterlands of Bogotá, where stock ranching had a potentially violent edge, there was no direct assault on *resguardo* lands. Communal lands had long since withered. And the territorial question, so explosive in other parts of the Andes in this period, no longer held primacy in this changing landscape of power.[10]

Consequently the roots of economic and cultural change must be sought in the subtle everyday forms of peasant initiative and survival, often under deteriorating circumstances. After 1870 the twin processes of estate growth and peasant dispossession gave rise to a floating labor force that eventually swelled the categories of tenant farmers, sharecroppers, and indentured servants (*concertados*). The convergence of overseas market incentives and liberal orthodoxies rapidly advanced the edge of coffee and cattle estates into highland areas of Cundinamarca, Boyacá, and Antioquia, zones already well connected to urban markets and overseas trade. But to explain the shift toward large landholding in Colombia simply in terms of external pressures is to overlook the complex internal dynamics of *minifundismo* (the tendency toward increasingly fragmented

[10] On Colombia's nineteenth-century political and economic history of coffee production, see Charles Bergquist, *Coffee and Conflict in Colombia, 1886–1910* (Durham, 1968); and Marcos Palacios, *Coffee in Colombia, 1850–1970: An Economic, Social and Political History* (New York, 1980).

smallholds). Partible inheritance, land disputes, and mounting population pressures on smallholding regimes did their part to prepare the way for estate expansion and peasant landlessness in many regions of Colombia. By the 1880s in parts of Cundinamarca and Boyacá, smallholding peasants were being transformed into servile laborers and sharecroppers living on estate lands that once belonged to the *resguardo* of their own grandparents. Within three generations small-scale farmers had seen the status of their lands change from *resguardo* into *minifundia* and eventually become swallowed up by a *latifundium.* As Orlando Fals Borda describes it, "white [land]owners simply watched over fences and boundary ditches with [the community of] Saucío, while the old *resguardo* started to look like a mouse-hole – hundreds of beings kept busy in Lilliputian pockets next to these estates."[11]

In more isolated eastern regions of Boyacá, land-starved peasants migrated into the lower temperate zones of coffee cultivation. Little is known about the process of labor expulsion from highland *minifundio* regions. To what extent did the grinding poverty of highland agriculture push surplus laborers into the expanding coffee zones? Did labor contractors (*enganchadores*) employ mechanisms of debt and coercion to draft seasonal pickers for the coffee plantations? Few clues are left to us by contemporary chroniclers, who generally described seasonal workers as drifting down from the mountains into the coffee zones and happily settling on the plantations with their families. These migratory workers were often categorized in regional-racial terms, which naturalized them as servile workers suited for the degradations of tropical field work. "The *indio* of Boyacá and Cundinamarca," wrote the Conservative intellectual, Vergara y Velasco, in 1901, "is a machine, for he serves all causes with equal passiveness and duty. . . . He obeys the bidding of the whites . . . whom he both fears and respects."[12] Many seasonal workers apparently did attach themselves to the new plantations. But popular stories and songs more often recount the injustices inflicted on migrants by infamous *enganchadores*, some of whom continued to operate well into the twentieth century.[13]

Communal disintegration and cultural *mestizaje* were already hall-

[11] Orlando Fals Borda, *Peasant Society in the Colombian Andes: A Sociological Study of Saucío* (Gainesville, 1955), 105.

[12] F. J. Vergara y Velasco, *Nueva geografía de Colombia* [1901], 3 vols. (Bogotá, 1974), 3:666; quoted in Palacios, *Coffee in Colombia*, 72–73.

[13] Palacios, *Coffee in Colombia,* 69–70.

marks of Colombia's northeastern highlands in the early nineteenth century. But after the 1870s further fragmentation of property, impoverishment, and transience eroded the bonds of traditional agricultural and artisanal communities. Population pressures, grinding poverty, and deteriorating market conditions were far more disruptive forces for traditional artisans and farmers than the grandiose civilizing missions, which were supposed to create industrious laborers and consumers out of slothful Indians. Yet even as the deepening subsistence crisis of the highlands created a casual labor force for the lowland coffee estates, some highland Indians found ways to prosper as small coffee producers, mule drivers, itinerant traders, labor contractors, and country lawyers. Indeed, in the north, where smallholding pressures were acute and where the structures of communal action and defense had crumbled, peasant family economies had to diversify into nonagricultural activities. And a small minority of peasant families were well positioned to prosper from the expanding market. For them the pathways out of poverty and Indianness often converged, as they slipped into the amorphous mestizo majority, which putatively shared with whites the positive attributes of acquisitiveness and enterprise.

The distinctive native groups of the southern provinces of Popayán and Pasto met the challenges of modernity under very different historical and regional circumstances. The south was a crucible of mercantile and political violence. *Resguardo* Indians clashed with hostile, then paternalist, republican policies, experienced successive civil wars, and saw the quinine industry ravage the forests, drain the villages of workers, and ultimately open up interior Indian frontiers to white colonization. Through years of endemic war and economic extraction, the southern ethnic groups were plunged into the vortex of state building and economic modernization. It was in the isolated mountains and leafy quinine forests of Páez and Pasto territories that liberal dreams of Indian assimilation died an early death.

Yet despite the violence of modernity, many indigenous communities could call upon their own ethnic traditions, memories, and identities to confront threats to their existence. At the core of ethnic politics lay the communal lands of the *resguardo*, now a smaller and weaker unit than in the eighteenth century but still the social and cultural basis of local community and identity. Although liberal legislation had abolished hereditary chiefdoms, some Páez communities had empowered their small, elected *cabildos* (councils) to litigate and negotiate deals to shield themselves against threatening land claims. The communities of Pitayó and Jambaló, for example, lived on the western slopes of the cordillera, where they were openly exposed to land-hungry hacendados who shared their borders. Their councils became the rallying points of defense against land encroachments. In the 1850s white entrepreneurs in search of quinine were astonished to meet "the Indian governor of Pitayó . . . [who] presented himself before us, armed and accompanied by many other Indians, in order to prevent us continuing our work and to embargo what quinine we had already harvested."[14] Other *cabildos*, especially those representing the remote interior hamlets of Tierradentro, had less experience dealing with republican policies, white land-grabbers, and the invasion of quinine entrepreneurs. As we shall see shortly, those Páez communities often fell victim to the forces of extractive agriculture. But whether strong or weak, the institution of Indian *cabildo* exercised limited power over municipal units. And as such it paled in comparison to the new breed of Páez political-military leader, who emerged from the din and dust of the independence struggle and successive civil wars to become self-styled, de facto *caciques* commanding loyalty from far-flung Páez communities and their local *cabildos*.

Páez territory became the hearth of Indian *caudillismo* in Colombia during the independence wars, when the Páez collaborated with patriotic armies as their porters, spies, messengers, and trailblazers. Later, during nine civil wars fought at various times throughout the century, the Indians were recruited to armies, often forcibly on festival days, to advance the causes of the Conservative or Liberal parties. Civilizing rhetoric aside, the white élites feared as much as they needed the "warrior tribes" of the Páez. Where liberal civilizers saw "sedentary savages," partisan military leaders saw "savage soldiers" who might be recruited to their cause, often under their own native commanders. A *caudillo* was not just an officer but a military chief with a following of his own. The rise of Páez military chiefs was not simply a function of military patronage. Most native *caudillos* rose to prominence among their own people in the heat of military action, and they used the battleground to acquire prestige and loyalty among widely dispersed communities.

These shadowy figures still elude the historian's eye, but the contemporary press provides glimpses of their contradictory influences and ac-

[14] *El Tiempo*, May 4, 1858; quoted in Joanne Rappaport, *The Politics of Memory: Native Historical Interpretation in the Colombian Andes* (Cambridge, 1990), 87.

tions. Some *caudillos* assimilated into Colombian society, wielding their influence on behalf of partisan politics, military recruitment, or land and mining investors. Others maintained their independence and used their guerrilla firepower to cement alliances among Páez communities, protect or reclaim *resguardo* lands, or retaliate against outside encroachers. Joanne Rappaport shows that Páez *caudillos* did not rely upon their military virtues alone to build their base of support but "cemented their dominion over broad expanses of territory, reproducing colonial *cacicazgos* by forging [strategic] marital ties."[15] Aspiring Páez chiefs consolidated their legitimacy across disparate communities by marrying the daughters of colonial *caciques* or by claiming noble descent. In this way the rise of guerrilla leaders among the Páez replicated the institution of hereditary *cacicazgo*, although the latter was abolished at the time of independence.

But postcolonial *cacicazgos* did not just signal symbolic defiance of republican law. They laid the groundwork for perpetual guerrilla warfare throughout the century, keeping the southern mountains of Cauca a dangerous place for white people. During the various civil wars, Páez forces were repeatedly used in military operations by Liberal and Conservative armies, and inevitably official news reports followed with stories of armed bands of Indians invading farm houses, stealing cattle, and terrorizing the white citizenry. Mobilized for military action, politicians and writers feared, Páez warriors quickly turned insurgent or criminal, more savage than soldier. They had long been associated with the most violent opposition to the liberal land reforms of mid-century, and they continued to be feared and hated. It is hardly surprising that the provincial élite of the Cauca Valley rejected the liberal ideal of Indian assimilation. Instead their Indian policies lurched between appeasement and repression.

That Páez *caudillismo* never escalated into a cohesive, militant ethnic movement had less to do with republican policies, however, than with the intrinsic weakness of nineteenth-century Páez politics. Native *caudillos* could wield their influence over dispersed Páez communities, but they also participated in the Colombian political party system. In Joanne Rappaport's words, "on the ground, a broad range of *caudillos* with conflicting party allegiances organized military units independently of one another."[16] Partisan divisions, as well as ethnic rivalries, ultimately

[15] Ibid., 90.

[16] Ibid., 93. See also María Teresa Findji and José María Rojas, *Territorio, economía, y sociedad páez* (Cali, 1985).

fragmented Páez warriors into competing bands. At times native *caudillos* used the pretext of war to launch raids on rival territories. In various military operations, Páez guerrilla bands waged war against each other from opposite sides of the partisan divide. During the War of the Thousand Days, which raged between 1899 and 1902, Páez soldiers from different regions fought pitched battles against each other, while autonomist guerrilla bands roamed the mountains in pursuit of their own ends. Páez practices of partisan politics and warfare probably served the interests of individual native *caudillos* and their communities in myriad ways. And they certainly revitalized translocal ethnic bonds and loyalties, which flew in the face of liberal laws abolishing colonial *resguardos* and *cacicazgos*. But ultimately the relentless cycles of warfare, pillage, rape, and dislocation that rode roughshod over Páez communities and often pitted Páez against Páez, left them more vulnerable than ever before to white invaders looking for easy conquests and quick profits.

Around mid-century a major source of quinine was discovered in the forests of the Cauca department, turning Páez territory into the newest economic frontier of the world market. Europe and North America demanded quinine to treat malaria, and Colombia became their major supplier. Quinine bark was collected in many interior regions, but the finest quality came from the area around Pitayó. As with rubber and other wild products available for the taking, this extractive industry catalyzed ecological and cultural changes, already set in motion by the militarization of Páez society. The collection of quinine was an intense, short-lived extractive industry that pillaged forests and villages alike. Rappaport writes that "the quinine boom moved like a wave across the [quinine-bearing] cinchona forests, leaving behind a wake of destroyed and dead plants."[17] It was Colombia's new gold rush, drawing thousands of white and mestizo merchants, entrepreneurs, and colonists to the region. The small town of Silvia exploded into a marketing center, populated by merchants, shopkeepers, muleteers, hacendados, and small farmers. They developed trading and credit relations with Páez bark collectors (*cascarilleros*), a new breed of Páez entrepreneur who sometimes earned good money in the bark trade. Because the boom coincided with the civil wars of 1854, 1859–1862, and 1876–1877, trading activities were risky, fluctuating, and frequently coercive. It was not unusual for bands of armed Indians to enter the town of Silvia and press their dried quinine

[17] Rappaport, *The Politics of Memory*, 97.

bark on unwilling merchants at a fixed price. Militarism, extraction, and trade combined to create a small élite of entrepreneurs among the Páez, who shattered entrenched stereotypes of slothful savages resistant to enterprise and hard work.

But it came at a terrible cost. There is no doubt that the quinine boom weakened the bonds of communal solidarity and territoriality. Like war the quinine industry drained off men and boys into the outer frontier of the industry. As the quinine frontier advanced into the interior, so did the *cascarilleros*, leaving behind their families, lands, and communal responsibilities for weeks or months at a time. Sometimes Páez households migrated and resettled in distant lowlands, closer to the quinine frontier. This pattern of dispersion and transience must have radically disrupted subsistence agriculture and eroded the institutions of communal life. Increasingly Páez traders and cutters negotiated their own mercantile deals with the monied world of the white export merchant. Not only were they vulnerable to raw commercial exploitation under radically unequal power relations, but such relationships chipped away at the Indian *cabildo* and *cacique* as the sources of communal authority and mediation with outsiders.

This situation proved devastating to the *resguardos*, suddenly under the twin threats of liberal land reforms and the invasion of entrepreneurs eager to annex lowland forests for their exportable treasures (quinine, and later sugarcane, coffee, and cattle). As noted earlier, land reforms had had an uneven impact on the southern *resguardos* over the first half of the nineteenth century. Indian protest, the noncompliance of Cauca élites, and the federalist political system itself had all undermined the Liberal Party's offensive against the *resguardo* in the Cauca provinces of Popayán and Pasto. But in the hands of the venturesome quinine capitalists, anti-*resguardo* legislation opened a new era of territorial conquest. Liberal laws dealt a double blow. On the one hand, the privatization of *resguardos* hastened the transfer of Indian lands to merchants, entrepreneurs, and foreign companies capitalizing on the quinine boom. On the other hand, Colombian policy aggressively promoted colonization of putatively "empty lands" (*los baldíos*) that supposedly composed Colombia's vast interior tropical forests.

After the 1860s the *baldío* ploy posed the worst threat to indigenous territorial and political autonomy. On ideological grounds it challenged *resguardo* rights and imposed borders where none had existed before. Where Páez territory ended and public land began was subject to conflicting, often violent, interpretation. The government acknowledged the problem in 1869: "Few *resguardos* have written title; instead actual possession gives indefinite extension to the imagined properties of Indians in the high regions of the cordillera."[18] In material terms procolonization schemes quickened the pace of land alienation, migration, and deforestation. These search-and-destroy operations continued until world demand for Colombian quinine subsided around the turn of the twentieth century. But massive internal colonization of Indian lands continued during the first three decades of the new century, as new commodities (sugar, coffee, and cattle) turned interior regions of Cauca into agroexport economies. By then, white encroachment on Indian land was preparing the groundwork for violent confrontation between dispossessed peasants and the Cauca Valley élite.[19]

Throughout the late nineteenth century, the threat to indigenous landholdings produced a counterforce of resistance and protest against the expansion of estates onto native communal properties. All during the republican period, the Indians of Popayán and Pasto were famous for the legal and military skills they deployed to preserve, recuperate, or reconstitute what remained of their patrimonies. As *baldío* claims and other threats of land loss grew more menacing, Indian communities intensified their search for colonial *resguardo* titles in local, provincial, and government archives. Indian *cabildos* schooled themselves in the fine points of the law to revalidate existing land titles or draft new ones. Through song, dance, verse, and stories, whole communities refreshed and reconstructed historical memories and topographical knowledge – reclaiming their historic and moral rights to *resguardo* land, including its sacred landmarks and inviolate boundaries. As happened in other native Andean societies, liberal policies of divestiture – ultimately designed to reinvent Indians as

[18] *Diario Oficial*, December 13, 1869; quoted in Rappaport, *The Politics of Memory*, 100–101. On Colombia's ambitious homesteading policy, internal colonization, *latifundismo*, and peasant protest, see the important study by Catherine Legrand, *Frontier Expansion and Peasant Protest, 1850–1936* (Albuquerque, 1986).

[19] The history of Páez communities does not end in the destruction wrought by the quinine trade in the late nineteenth century. Only three decades later Páez Indians mounted a militant ethnic campaign to recover lands and autonomy under a more protectionist state. Faced with new subsistence threats – as the regional Caucan élites expanded their coffee, sugar, and cattle estates onto the western slopes of the shrunken *resguardo* – the Páez reinvigorated and expanded their opposition to land grabbing under their leader, Quintín Lame. Joanne Rappaport documents this extraordinary pan-Indian movement in which literate, Spanish-speaking leaders, who came of age as Colombian soldiers and laborers in places far from their ancestral homelands, forged militant ethnic movements and inserted them into the national political of early twentieth-century Colombia (*The Politics of Memory*, chaps. 5 and 6).

individual laborers and consumers in an expanding capitalist, export-driven economy – provoked powerful backlash effects of ethnic and communal action and consciousness. They sparked Indian campaigns to defend or recover the rights to land and local self-government. The rise of latter-day Páez *caciques* – who positioned themselves as military chiefs of noble lineage and supralocal authority in spite of liberal laws liquidating hereditary *cacicazgos* – is the most dramatic instance of Páez resistance to civilizing projects. But it was the Indian town council, perhaps more than the military *cacique*, which continued to be a principal site of resistance to invasive land threats.

Curiously, in the last years of the nineteenth century, amidst the rush to colonize the interior tropical slopes of Cauca, the rise to power of the Conservative Party brought a small measure of hope to some Indian *cabildos* in the southern highlands. Although the Conservative Party shared the overarching goals of civilizing and modernizing Colombia through the process of whitening, it advocated a slower, more mediated route to modernity. First, the Conservative Party aimed to replace the federalist system with a more centralized state capable of correcting for the "excesses" of laissez-faire capitalism and secular liberalism. Second, the Conservatives favored a more gradualist approach to the civilizing project, and one that would give the Catholic Church a larger, multifaceted role to play. As regarded the southern highland tribes, the new Conservative regime wanted to bring a pragmatic balance to its Indian policies. So, for example, "to reduce savage Indians to civilized life," they were to be disciplined and socialized properly, and also set apart as legal minors in need of state protection and tutelage. Conservatives ostensibly granted legal protection to *resguardos* for a period of 50 years. Thereafter they could be subdivided and sold. Although provincial governments rarely had the means or will to enforce these paternal protections, the law galvanized Indian communities almost overnight. As rumors of Law 89 spread across the southern cordilleras, they unleashed a torrent of land claims, litigations, title searches, surveys, inspections, land invasions, and counterinvasions. In some areas legal claims escalated into long-term campaigns of "recuperation" aimed to recover stolen *resguardo* lands and forgotten communal histories. How many of these judicial battles were resolved in favor of Indian *cabildos* is not known. But the law emboldened landless and smallholding peasants, as well as shrunken *resguardo* communities, to advance their land claims on the basis of the new legal criteria of Indianness. The upshot was to catalyze a movement of legal "re-Indianization" as a necessary step toward land recovery. This in turn led to curious conflicts over the phenotypical, genetic, and cultural definitions of Indian identity in many local land struggles.[20]

Still, resurgent Indianness during the last years of the nineteenth century remained atomized at the local level and geographically confined to Colombia's southern highlands. It all happened a safe distance from the main urban centers of power and progress. Colombia's ruling oligarchs remained wedded to the project of modernity and civilization, but for the time being they could afford to pass paternalist laws patronizing (and hopefully pacifying) unruly Indians. Indeed, as they cast their eyes toward the "whitening" provinces surrounding the capital of Bogotá, they probably still felt somewhat optimistic. In the heartlands of coffee and commerce, the "Indian race" had all but vanished. And reducing the rest to civilization seemed to be a question of Indian regulation and discipline. Meanwhile the government would look to European immigration to hasten Colombia's march forward into the sunshine of modernity. Eventually Indians would disappear into cultural *mestizaje*, and mestizos in turn would absorb the superior traits of European immigrants, taking their place in history as the bearers of economic progress in the Colombian backlands. Even the bellicose Páez peoples had not managed to destroy those liberal illusions – not yet anyway.

ECUADOR: MODERNIZING INDIAN SERVITUDE AS THE ROAD TO PROGRESS

The breakup of Gran Colombia, a short-lived Bolivarian state covering most of northern South America, dissected the region along borders resembling old colonial viceroyalties. Across Colombia's southern border, Ecuadorian élites, heirs to the old *audiencia* of Quito, constructed a distinctly different nation-building project – one more deeply grounded in the country's colonial past, and responsive to the peculiar set of regional, ethnic, and partisan power balances that set Ecuador apart from its northern neighbor. Ecuador had emerged from the independence wars with a fairly cohesive aristocratic ruling class – badly damaged by the chaos of the wars, and regionally fragmented, but still largely intact and

[20] Not surprisingly white authorities anxious to deny the legitimacy of Indian land claims now began to narrow and stipulate carefully the racial parameters of Indianness! See Joanne Rappaport, *Cumbe Reborn: An Andean Ethnography of History* (Chicago, 1994), chap. 1.

deeply ambivalent toward Gran Colombian schemes of free trade, slave and tribute abolition, secular education, and even republicanism itself. Indeed monarchism continued to hold a powerful grip on the political imaginings of many an Ecuadorian politician well into the nineteenth century. Although Creoles never took the drastic step of inviting Napoleon III to send one of his nephews to rule its unruly lands (as did Mexican Conservatives in the 1860s), they found a strong, authoritarian leader in President Gabriel García Moreno, who quickly enlisted the Catholic hierarchy in his "civilizing mission." The capital city of Quito remained the site of Conservative rule, famous for its cacophony of Church bells and plethora of black-robed curates.[21] There, too, lived Creole landlords in close proximity to government ministries, military barracks, and a few literary salons, but convenient enough to their outlying estates and to densely populated Indian hamlets and mestizo towns throughout Ecuador's north-central highlands. After 1870 Liberal Party opposition grew more powerful, but it remained largely confined to the Guayaquil coast until the "Liberal Revolution" of 1895 catapulted a free-trade reformer into the presidency. In short the compass of political and ideological reform remained much narrower in nineteenth-century Ecuador than in Colombia. Rather than inventing a nation out of the liberal ideals of the Enlightenment, tempered by illiberal government schemes of cultural homogenization through whitening, Ecuadorian Creoles would fashion a conservative nationalism out of the shards of colonialism.

As everywhere in the Andes, Ecuador's nation-building experiments were conditioned and limited by the diverse interactions, experiences, and understandings of a cultural mosaic of peoples, of whom the overwhelming majority was poor, nonwhite, and illiterate. But ethnic balances and dynamics varied widely among the four Andean nations, as did the institutional and political legacies of specific colonial formations and the fallout from the independence wars. Even among the northern Andean nations of Colombia and Ecuador, ethnic balances were almost reversed at the end of the colonial era. In 1770 the *audiencia* of Quito

[21] This is not to deny the existence of Church–state tensions in republican Ecuador, however. Because the Church had such a powerful presence after independence, jurisdictional and power struggles raged. Some of those conflicts revolved around the Church's paternal control over Indians; for example, in the 1830s ecclesiastics protested republican decrees removing the right of priests to use corporal punishment to discipline Indians. But Church–state alliances were cemented by the papal Concordat of 1863.

(composed of what later became the republic of Ecuador and the southern provinces of Colombia) registered Indians as 50 percent of its population, while "*libres*" (free people of African or mixed descent) composed only 10 percent. In the *audiencia* of Santa Fé (the northern part of Colombia), Indians constituted 20 percent, and *libres* 50 percent.[22] A more rigorous census, compiled under the Bourbon reformers in 1785, estimated that Indians of colonial Ecuador composed 65 percent of the total population.[23] Long lapses in republican population counts defy attempts to trace Indian demographic change over the nineteenth century, although provincial censuses in the north-central provinces of the 1840s suggest that Indians still made up almost 50 percent of their total population.[24] But the predominance of highland Indians (as they were officially defined) created the social and demographic basis for adapting colonial practices and ideologies to the republican (dis)order.

Indian tribute, for example, made up one-third of tax revenues collected in the *audiencia* of Quito on the eve of independence. It was quickly restored once Bolivarian liberalism faded in the late 1820s. State finances continued to rely on Indian tribute until 1857 – not only for reasons of fiscal expedience but for fear of indigenous reprisals against more onerous schemes of taxation and military conscription.[25] In its thrust to restore elements of the colonial system of caste, symbolized by Indian tribute, the Ecuadorian élite shared much with their southern counterparts in Peru and Bolivia. And like Peru, Ecuador restored tribute without restoring to Indian communities the package of juridical rights and jurisdictions that had accompanied tribute obligations under the colonial system of dual republics. Indians owed tribute (now called the *contribución personal de indígenas*) but were denied legal rights to corporate landholding or hereditary chiefdoms. On tangible issues surrounding the ambiguous, fluid, and contested meanings of "*república*" – whether the new Ecuadorian republic should honor colonial legal codes or cus-

[22] Ward, *Blackness and Race Mixture: The Dynamics of Racial Identity in Colombia*, 54.

[23] Suzanne Austin Alchon, *Native Society and Disease in Colonial Ecuador* (Cambridge, 1991), 123.

[24] Galo Ramón Valarezo, "El Ecuador en el espacio andino: idea, proceso, e utopía," *Allpanchis* (Cusco) 35/36:2 (1991), 517–577; 548. On the absence of nineteenth-century demographic records on Ecuador's indigenous population, see Hernán Ibarra, "La identidad devaluada de los 'Modern Indians'," in I. Almeida et al. (eds.), *Indios. Una reflexión sobre la levantimiento indígena de 1990* (Quito, 1991), 319–349; 326–327. Twentieth-century census materials are nearly as impoverished as nineteenth-century records regarding ethnic and racial categories.

[25] Mark J. Van Aken, "The lingering death of Indian tribute in Ecuador," *Hispanic American Historical Review* 61:3 (1981), 429–459.

tomary rights claimed by disparate groups of Indian tributaries – Creole leaders maintained a calculated and prudent indifference. They were neither willing nor able to impose a uniform land reform policy or to flatten the traditional Indian hierarchy. And certain indigenous communities used the postindependence period of political fragmentation and uncertainty, as well as its judicial flux, to press their claims to territory, protection, and a certain measure of autonomy.

By mid-century, however, the signs of economic and ideological change were beginning to prod Ecuador's conservatives into a more aggressively reformist frame of mind. Regional balances between the sierra and coast were beginning to tip in favor of the latter, as overseas markets opened up to tropical agro-exports. Highland estates did not share in the growing prosperity of cacao plantations on the coast, for example, and this regional economic disparity only widened with time. Nonetheless the resurgent export economy permitted the government to shift its tax base from tribute to commercial and propertied wealth. Tribute revenues had already dwindled by the late 1840s, and by 1857 tribute was officially terminated. Ecuador's native highland peasants (still designated as "Indian") were redefined in civil law as *contribuyentes* – contributors to the nation, still, but putatively on the same legal footing as everyone else. They were now registered as propertyholders, taxpayers, and potential military recruits and subject to the same laws, obligations, and authorities as non-Indians. Official statistics effaced ethnic categories from the written record after 1857; Ecuador's first national census of 1876 cleansed "Indians" from the record. But in a revealing note to census takers, the government instructed them to collect information about Indians to facilitate tax collection and labor conscription.[26] This innocuous note in the margin, more than any ethnic-blind statistic, provides an important clue as to how Indians were going to fit into the posttributary republic bumping along the road to modernity and progress. As we shall see, state-run labor drafts – a colonial institution in modern guise – were to staff authoritarian projects of modernization in the 1850s, 1860s, and 1870s.

Coercing Indians into "Civilization" and Christianity

To mount such a project, Ecuador's reformers first had to overcome structural and demographic obstacles – partly of their own making.

[26] Ibarra, "La identidad devaluada de los 'Modern Indians'," 326–327.

Ecuador's strong latifundist estate tradition, the very font of Conservative ideology, stood fast against the currents of reform. For one thing the skewed ratio between communal and estate-bound Indians worked against Creole plans for state-controlled labor schemes. At the end of the colonial period, almost half of all registered Indians were landless laborers bound in one way or another to estates.[27] *Latifundismo* was more entrenched in the southern highlands around Cuenca. But even in Ecuador's north-central "Indian zone," economic and demographic forces since the seventeenth century had boosted Spanish–mestizo control over Indian land and labor, shrinking the legal pool of tributaries and labor drafts to a much smaller scale than that inherited by the republics of Peru and Bolivia. What distinguished patterns of Indian labor in colonial Ecuador was not the existence of servile relations in the private domain but their increasing importance in colonial agricultural and industrial production. Early waves of estate expansion, heavy taxation, and the pervasive practice of labor drafts for colonial enterprises and cities, all set in motion migratory streams that removed Indians from their kin groups and villages. By the mid–seventeenth century, evolving relations of dependence and retainership tied growing numbers of Indians into the dynamic and expanding production of food, textiles, and craft goods destined for cities, towns, and mines throughout the viceroyalty of Peru. Partly because of these severe social and demographic dislocations, seventeenth-century Ecuador emerged with considerable "comparative advantages" as the premier textile workshop of the Andean colonies. Its infamous textile sweatshops (*obrajes* or primitive mills) flourished mainly on the cheap, skilled labor of Indian retainers, supplemented by Indian labor drafts (Fig. 23.4).

Although the eighteenth century brought on a long period of economic contraction, demographic pressures, and ethnic revival and unrest, native peasant communities did not significantly reverse their long history of atrophy and decline. On the contrary, highland peasant economies, faced by the demographic and economic pressures inherent in smallholding regimes, diversified into trade, pack driving, craft production, and casual labor. And, as we shall see, growing numbers of Indian migrants melted into mestizo towns and cities across the northern highlands during the nineteenth century. Others set off for booming tropical plantations along the coast. Combined with the paternalist legacies of large estates that still controlled a massive sector of dependent peasants,

[27] Magnus Mörner, *The Andean Past: Lands, Society, and Conflict* (New York, 1985), 77.

Figure 23.4. *Obraje* workers, Province of Imbabura, ca. 1890. Although the heyday of Ecuadorian hacienda-*obraje* complexes was long past, primitive textile workshops like this one continued to thrive on the labor of contracted laborers (*conciertos*) and peons well into the twentieth century. This 1890 photograph offers a rare glimpse into indigenous working conditions in contrast to the prevailing aesthetic tendency to decontextualize and typologize Indians. Source: Lucía Chiriboga and Silvana Caparrini, eds., *Identidades desnudas. Ecuador, 1860–1920* (Quito: Abya-Yala, 1994), 53.

the expanding sector of Indian migrant and mestizo populations threatened to cripple state-sponsored projects of Indian exploitation and integration.

It is not surprising therefore that mid-century debates over the morality of Indian tribute also addressed the more fundamental question of Indian bondage on private estates. It was the beginning of a century-long exercise in ideological equivocation over the necessity and morality of indentured Indian labor. The debate subsided only when the agrarian reform law of 1964 officially terminated the institution of *huasipungaje* (resident peonage on estates).[28] Already by the mid-1850s parliamentary

[28] Conditions and terminologies of bondage varied considerably among regions, over time, and even within one enterprise. Very broadly, however, bondage normally implied that resident Indians owed certain labor services to their masters, who also expected Indians to demonstrate steadfast

debates indicted practices of labor recruitment and retention on highland estates. Inspired by the polemics surrounding slave and tribute abolition, Liberal and Conservative legislators clashed over the status of unfreedom that adhered to *conciertos* (Indians subject to long-term labor contracts). Whatever the specious conditions under which Indians were "hooked" into labor service, the lawmakers questioned the terms of indenture. Should Indians who redeemed their debt be "emancipated" and allowed to break bondage before their stipulated term of years was up? Or was indenture binding until the end of the contractual term? Should debt be inheritable generation after generation?

That the absolutism of landlord power, a fixture of rural Ecuador for centuries, became the subject of vigorous national debate, signaled the beginning of a subtle ideological shift in Creole thinking. These arguments not only tested the legitimate limits of power that Ecuador's powerful hacendados exercised over the nation's landless Indians. More profoundly they began to refocus national discourses on the "Indian problem." And once Creole élites began to nationalize the Indian problem, relocating it from the exclusive and narrow domain of private landlord concerns to the broad arena of public discourse, it would become the rhetorical centerpiece of an aggressive modernizing project under the "perpetual dictator" Gabriel García Moreno. It is perhaps ironic, then, that these muckraking debates of the 1850s also gave implicit confirmation to the practices of landlord paternalism and Indian servitude. Not only did legislators fail to enact laws limiting the power of labor contractors and landlords; the very language of parliamentary debate consolidated the image of the Ecuadorian highland Indian as a "poor, ignorant, and helpless" creature.[29] In the end this oratorical image of Indianness legitimated estate paternalism as benign and necessary,

loyalty and obedience to their personage. In return the master was to provide for the subsistence needs of dependent Indians, usually by granting them usufruct rights, access to woods and pastures, token wage payments, and occasional gifts and favors. In Ecuador nineteenth- and twentieth-century ideas and images of estate paternalism congealed under the label of *huasipungaje*. This static notion depicted peons as families of resident laborers who were permitted to have huts and garden plots, as well as pasture and water rights in return for their labor services and a small cash wage. Obviously the negotiation and contestation of paternal power relations was a constant dynamic – continually subject to everyday practices of sabotage, resistance, and neglect, and occasionally to insurgent actions from below. For a detailed, contemporary description of living and labor conditions on estates, see Friedrich Hassaurek, *Four Years among the Ecuadorians* [1867] (Carbondale, 1967), 169–172.

[29] Andrés Guerrero, "Una imágen ventrilocua: el discurso liberal de la 'desgraciada raza indígena' a fines del siglo XIX," in *Imágenes e imagineros. Representaciones ele los indígenas ecoatorianos, siglos XIX y XX* (Quito, 1994), edited by Blanca Muratorio, 197–252.

conveniently pegging liberal schemes of Indian integration as utopias to be postponed indefinitely.

Ecuador's peculiar conservative-authoritarian project of nation building crystallized under the repressive regime of Gabriel García Moreno, which lasted from his political ascendance in 1859 to his assassination in 1875. His iron-clad rule reversed decades of regional militarism, weak central governments, and innumerable constitutions. He sought inspiration for his own developmental model of state making not in Colombia's experiment in liberal federalism, but in French authoritarianism under Napoleon III. But García Moreno was pragmatic enough to realize that European models of militarist centralism had to be revamped to overcome the obstacles facing a republic as economically backward, impoverished, and undercapitalized as Ecuador. In its full scope his project rested on three main propositions: the need to modernize the bureaucratic and repressive apparatus of the state; the importance of bringing the Catholic Church back into the nation as the vanguard of "civilization" among the backward and heathen races; and, finally, the moral imperative of redeeming the "Indian race" and harnessing it to the engines of economic modernization.

From the vantage point of Indian peasants living outside the domain of paternal estates, perhaps the most visible sign of change was the thickening web of provincial bureaucracy that drew them more tightly into the state's net. With tributary protections gone, including the jurisdictional space granted (at least informally) to supralocal hereditary *caciques*, local ethnic authority devolved to Indian *cabildos*, whose members were elected to serve for only a year. At the micropolitical level, power was fragmented and distributed among a pool of small village headmen, councilmen, and strawbosses who answered not only to their own kinsmen and communities but also to municipal, parish, and provincial authorities. This localization of indigenous authority ran counter to the centralization of white–mestizo officialdom, as García Moreno worked to roll back decades of indigenous, provincial, and paternal autonomies. His army of bureaucrats began to infiltrate rural towns and villages, performing the routines and rituals of rule: collecting taxes, recruiting soldiers and laborers, adjudicating disputes, and disciplining vagrants, debtors, and other "criminal" sorts. Proliferating mestizo and white towns became links in a lengthening chain of command connecting Quito to dispersed Indian villages. As we shall see, new occupational and cultural spaces opened in the interstices of society for upwardly mobile, bilingual, and transculturated mestizos, called *indios ladinos* and *mistis*. This motley group of spatial and cultural transients – whatever they were called in local parlance – constituted a rapidly growing sector of the rural population in nineteenth-century Ecuador. In the emerging public sector, they often served as agents of the dictator; but many mestizos thrived from their mercantile activities as traders, muleteers, and labor contractors funneling Indian labor into labor-starved export economies of the coast.

From the perspective of white urban Ecuador, though, García Moreno's greatest (or, to the beleaguered Liberals, his most infamous) feat was to remake the Church into a powerful agent of cultural change. The potential was already there, because the Catholic Church had emerged almost unscathed from the chaos of the independence wars. It had escaped the sorry fate of clergies attacked by anticlerical movements in other parts of postindependence Latin America. The Catholic hierarchy never lost its political footing in the new republic. But until the regime of García Moreno, it had symbolized the hispanist past of colonial paternalism and the bastion of conservatism. García Moreno was a modern-day Erasmus: He wanted to cleanse the clergy of its corrupt ways and deploy the redeemed Church to educate and moralize the Indian peasantry in order to prepare them for their gradual entry into the lower ranks of "civilized" society. This modern spiritual conquest was the dictator's route to nationhood, and in 1863 he went to the Vatican for papal blessings. For the "salvation of the fatherland," the president charged the Church with Christianizing the heathen Indians and of creating political order out of civil discord. These momentous tasks were to be entrusted mainly to the Jesuit order, the only group endowed with the self-discipline, ambition, and militancy that García Moreno believed necessary for the job. Indeed he had in mind an imperialist venture of French Jesuits piercing Ecuador's "heart of darkness" to civilize the heathens through religion, education, and discipline (Fig 23.5). In 1861 the first battery of friars arrived from France to establish primary schools for poor boys. The education of girls was left to chance or to private charity.

According to observers of the day, the Churchmen had a herculean task before them. Even the more charitable commentators, who had nothing positive to say about Quito's polite society, heaped scorn on Indians for their filth, servility, superstition, drunkenness, and indolence. To religious and secular authorities, Indians were not only poor, de-

Figure 23.5. A Jesuit priest with his flock of Indian students, Pinchincha Province, ca. 1890. The Reverend Father Luis Calcagno poses with his students from the village of Zámbiza before the artificial backdrop of an elegant parlour. Source: Lucía Chiriboga and Silvana Caparrini, eds., *Identidades Desnudas. Ecuador, 1860–1920* (Quito Abya Yala, 1994), 66.

graded, and suffering laborers, but worse they were a fallen race without culture or reason. The frequency of their debauched fiestas seemed proof enough. While missionaries denounced Indian idolatries, hypocrisies, and licentiousness, secular authorities worried about rowdy, belligerent Indians converging on mestizo towns during week-long festivals. Political rhetoric was also somewhat colored by economistic concerns, which blamed Indian misery and poverty on the victims and pointed to their cultural deficiencies as the fundamental cause of the nation's economic backwardness.

A minor point of contention between Church and state was the issue of alcohol and who was to blame for the problem of chronic Indian drunkenness. Churchmen pointed to corrupt merchants, judges, and policemen who monopolized the sale of cane liquor and *chicha* (corn beer) in cities and towns that Indians frequented. Civil authorities denounced greedy priests who profited from Indian debauchery during religious festivals. At the local level such debates often reflected raw power struggles between religious and civil authorities over their privileged access to Indian labor and commerce. But at the national level, consensus gathered around the need for a harsher regime of moral and social discipline over unruly Indian infidels. Although they addressed the issues somewhat differently, both Church and state officials wanted to stamp out popular religious rituals and expressions.

If a strong authoritarian government was to keep order and a reformed Church was to advance the edge of Christendom and civilization, it was the Indian majority that was to serve the nation in its arduous journey toward economic progress. In this respect as in others, García Moreno grounded his modernizing project in the shallow sands of coercive colonial practices. This became increasingly clear in the 1860s, when he began to nationalize the use of conscript laborers, rounded up from Indian communities, to build the nation's infrastructure. Although the abolition of tribute in 1857 had demolished the legal basis for colonial forms of racial discrimination, an earlier decree still offered a mechanism for restoring compulsory Indian labor, now redirected to serve the nation's developmentalist goals. The old, Bolivarian law of universal "voluntary contributions" was revived in 1854. It decreed that every citizen owed the state 4 days of labor each year, or its monetary equivalent, to promote public works projects. Without a committed and strong state to enforce the tax levy fairly, it soon evolved into a discriminatory tax on Indians, which merely reinforced local customs of coercing Indians into providing unpaid services. By the 1860s the labor tax fell most heavily on Indian communities and smallholders, while estate-bound peons frequently found protection from their paternal landlords.

García Moreno constructed a modernized version of the colonial *mita* (the institution of compulsory rotating labor to which most tribute-paying Indian males were subject under Spanish rule) to realize his ambitious economic dreams. More than anything else he accomplished, he was remembered for his modern cart roads that scaled the cordilleras and finally brought Quito closer to the sea. Far more than a feat of modern engineering, it was a testimony to the coercive machinery he built and the sheer labor power that massive numbers of highland Indians were forced to invest. The dictator dispatched military men to round up Indian ditchdiggers, and in 1862 some 1,700 people began cutting the cart road through the cordillera, from mountainous Quito down to coastal Guayaquil. The sight of it was chilling even to García Moreno's admirers. In the early 1860s the North American diplomat, Friedrich Hassaurek, watched Indians building a section of the wagon road to Guayaquil.

> [I]t was a lamentable sight to see how it had to be carried on. Heavy excavations had to be made through the high hills on both sides of the old mule path. There were no instruments except crowbars and shovels. There were no spades and pickaxes to dig with, nor carts or wheelbarrows to haul away the earth. It had to be filled in sheepskins and ponchos, which the Indians carried on their backs, and with which they climbed the hills where they deposited their scanty contents . . . Paving stones, lime, and bricks for the construction of bridges . . . were carried in the same manner on human backs. Sometimes beasts of burden were used; but the simplest and cheapest beast of burden is the Indian.[30]

A few years later the villages of Otavalo and other northern regions were sent to dig hundreds of miles of mountainous roadway down to the northern port of Esmeraldas. They were also charged with repairing the treacherous northern roads to Colombia after heavy rains, staffing the inns, and carrying the mail. Through their state-building *corvée*, Indian gangs literally subsidized Ecuador's economic modernization, just as their ancestors had subsidized the development of colonial Ecuador's textile factories, cities, parishes, and grain estates. While Liberal reformists in the coffeehouses of Quito extolled the virtues of free enterprise, they watched Indian work parties lay the roads and rails of progress. For white city folks, gangs of laborers became fixtures in the real and imaginary landscape. That the Indian's station in life was to dig the roads and sink the telegraph poles seemed as inevitable and immutable as the earth and

[30] Friedrich Hassaurek, *Four Years among the Ecuadorians* [1867], 111. At another point in his travelog, this astute observer said that Indians were often referred to in slang as *bagajes menores* (small beasts of burdens): "that is to say, as a beast of burden, the Indian is considered below the horse and the mule, and on a level with the donkey" (105).

the sky. "The Indian does more work than all the other races together," observed Hassaurek, "but his position in the social scale is in an inverse proportion to his usefulness."[31]

Throughout the remaining years of the century, these official labor drafts and other duties hit the north-central Indian villages most heavily, wrenching people from their villages, fields, and families for long periods of time. Hassaurek made no pretense about the putative voluntarism behind "Indian contributions" to the nation: "The Indian does not work voluntarily, not even when paid for his labor, but is pressed into the service of the government . . . and is kept to his task by the whip of the overseer."[32] García Moreno had laid the institutional groundwork for this operation: a centralizing bureaucracy and military that penetrated to the local village and a judiciary that continued to criminalize Indian "laziness" and debt. More than any other institution, the debtors' prison symbolized the republic's continuing reliance on coerced Indian labor.[33]

It is hardly surprising, then, to learn that for most of the century Ecuador's Conservative modernizers eschewed Liberal ideals of free labor. García Moreno himself felt ambivalent toward the institution of indentured servitude. On the one hand, Indians in retainership on private estates were not easily mobilized for public works. On the other hand, his allies were conservative landowners unwilling to change their antiquarian ways. Indeed his very model of nation building embodied postcolonial contradictions of coercive and market forces. Although he worked hard to centralize state power, modernize the military and bureaucracy, build roads and rails, and establish rural schools, García Moreno was not inspired by liberal schemes of economic or genetic assimilation, as were his Colombian counterparts. His stance toward economic progress and the whitening solution was more equivocal. This was apparent in the official position on race and development, which surfaced in

[31] Ibid., 107. [32] Ibid., 111.

[33] My argument here is the importance of debt and forced labor as defining ideological components of imposed Indianness in mid- and late nineteenth-century Ecuador. However, this is not to say that debt servitude served as a blanket mechanism of Indian labor control in highland Ecuador. As I indicated earlier, highland landlords did not exercise unlimited power over Indian peons. Sharp regionalism, the postindependence period of peasant economic buoyancy, and rich local traditions of paternalism and resistance on estates all point toward an extremely variegated social landscape. In comparative perspective, however, Ecuador stands out for its strong colonial institutions of coerced labor and its relatively cohesive Catholic–Conservative aristocracy based in Quito (in the north) and Cuenca (in the south), which continued to promote compulsory Indian labor schemes.

Ecuador's first national textbook, *Catecismo de geografía de la República del Ecuador*, published in the early 1870s under García Moreno's second administration. While generally optimistic about Ecuador's economic future, the book characterized Indians as "unalterable and suffering laborers." The white race, in contrast, was cast as a people capable of carrying the republic into the company of civilized nations thanks to the conservation of their hispanic heritage. Whiteness was constructed around Conservative values and rooted in the colonial past (yet still inspired by Enlightenment ideals). The text characterized whites as "religious, honorable, generous, and lovers of independence and freedom."[34] Such, too, was the imagined national identity.

Remaking Ethnic Identities: Diverging Pathways to Cultural Change

This experiment in harnessing colonial forms of exploitation to modernist goals disrupted local rural societies throughout highland Ecuador. Southern regions surrounding the city of Cuenca had long traditions of *latifundismo* that shackled most Indians to their masters through varied forms of debt, dependence, and paternalism. But on the edges of those estates lived smallholding peasants, increasingly squeezed by the internal pressures of population and heavier labor quotas that they owed the state. Threatened by an increasingly precarious subsistence base, many Indian farmers passed into the ranks of the service tenantry on large estates. Others abandoned the highlands for wage work on the booming cacao plantations along the coast. The opening of the transcordillera highway in the 1870s only increased this migratory stream.

But economic and cultural change came more abruptly to the Indian regions of the north. For it was the northern Indian villages that suffered most from the dictator's draconian work projects. The network of white and mestizo towns tended to prosper on the growth of petty officialdom, a booming pack industry, and interregional commerce and trade in textiles and other goods. For Indian farmers and herders, the modernizing regime laid siege to their lands and labors but removed the legal and customary means of communal defense and redress. It threatened to recolonize shrunken and flattened Indian communities, now directly subordinate to agents of the state and Church. And it left little discursive

[34] Ibarra, "La identidad devaluada de los 'Modern Indians'," 319.

room for collective maneuver, by denying Indians the chance to use their colonial or customary past as a title to recover their lost lands or advance their democratic claims.

By all rights this transformation of ex-tributary Indians (once endowed with certain alienable rights under an early ambivalent republic) to a seasonal slave labor force under a modernizing state must have been subject to subterranean tremors and occasional eruptions (as in Riobamba in 1871, and Chimborazo in 1894). Yet, curiously, Indian unrest in northern Ecuador remained small-scale, scattered, and contained. Certainly in the broader Andean perspective, there were few significant indigenous movements or Indian *caudillos* compared to those in southern Colombia, Peru, and Bolivia during the late nineteenth century. Peasants were mobilized on both sides of Ecuador's Liberal Revolution of 1895, although we still lack historical research on the roots, nature, or scale of indigenous involvement.[35]

Racist rhetoric inevitably fixed on the "innate obedience and servility" of the "Indian race." Or, if cast in a more charitable light, it explained Indian docility in terms of centuries of hopelessness and degradation. The more sensitive ethnographic eye saw beyond these racist stereotypes yet continued to be blinded by them. Hassaurek, for example, essentialized the Indian's "stupid and beastly nature [which] never revolts." But he went on at great length to depict the stubborn disinclination of Indians to comply with the favors or services asked of them by white people, unless under threat of force. Thinly veiled behind an etiquette of politeness and servility lurked a recalcitrant, untrustworthy Indian who had to be watched, in the view of this enlightened traveler. Indeed Hassaurek was onto something![36]

Ecuador's relatively quiescent rural landscape also had to do with

[35] For a reflective essay, and provocative case study, on the realization and nonrealization of insurgent Indian threats in Andean history, see, respectively, Steve J. Stern, "New approaches to the study of peasant rebellion and consciousness: Implications of the Andean experience," in Steve J. Stern (ed.), *Resistance, Rebellion, and Consciousness in the Andean Peasant World, 18th to 20th Centuries* (Madison, 1987), 3–29, and Stern, "The age of Andean insurrection, 1742–1782," in the same collection, 34–93.

[36] Hassaurek, *Four Years among the Ecuadorians* [1867], 70–73. Ever since the publication of Eugene Genovese's masterful cultural history of slave strategies of accommodation and resistance to the paternalism, brutalities, and humiliations of slavery in *Roll Jordan Roll: The World the Slaves Made* (New York, 1972), this theme has attracted historical and ethnographic attention. Two other inspiring studies include E. P. Thompson, "Patrician society, plebeian culture," *Journal of Social History* 7:4 (1974), 382–405, and James Scott, *Domination and the Arts of Resistance: Hidden Transcripts* (New Haven, 1990).

structural and regional conditions that inhibited the development of collective forms of insurgent action. First, mid-century reforms had taken an authoritarian turn for the worse – by tightening the colonial infrastructure. García Moreno's project relied on a network of villages, missions, outposts, estates, roadways, and colonial labor systems not only for material sustenance but for purposes of social control. And the Church conspired in this modernizing theocracy. Its corrupt curates continued to reinforce caste divisions in the countryside, while the new European missionaries launched a spiritual *reconquista*. Second, indigenous society itself remained riddled by ethnic divisions and tensions, land disputes, and jurisdictional confusions and conflicts. Social and cultural fragmentation among northern ethnic groups was certainly not peculiar to the nineteenth century. But a century of halting deterritorialization of Indians (because of the spread of the estate during the eighteenth century and later, due to the postindependence land reforms subdividing the remaining Indian lands), and the gradual erosion of hereditary *caciques* as cultural brokers, ethnic adversaries, and local intellectuals, worked against translocal ethnic movements even in moments of acute political tension. Third, strong regional traditions of landlord paternalism exercised a powerful centrifugal pull on potentially insurgent communities. Not only did estates impose their own forms of oppression and vigilance, but they heightened feelings of competition and rivalry among Indians of different estates during annual festivals of ritual warfare.

But if we are to understand the dynamics of rural society in late nineteenth-century northern Ecuador, we need also to consider everyday strategies of livelihood and resistance that may have circumvented Indian dependence on landlord paternalism, degraded wage labor, or debt, as well as deflating the potential for insurgent violence. In some areas Indian farming families retreated upland before the advance of valley mestizo towns. Highland villages clung to steep hillsides and scratched out meager existences, sometimes serving as small pools of casual labor for distant enterprises. But even they did not escape compulsory road work. An ever greater number of Quichua-speaking families moved into the orbit of Quito, following along the rutted tracks made by centuries of cityward migrants. Nineteenth-century travelers were invariably spellbound by the sight of so many Indians "of a hundred different villages in every variety of costume" surging through the noisy, crowded streets of the capital. Hawkers, pack drivers, farmers, adobe brick makers, tailors, furniture makers, stable boys, servants, saloon keepers, beggars, and day laborers –

all these Indians and *cholos* performed the labor and services that whites would not do. But the sight that provoked most commentary was that of Indian porters carrying heavy loads of stone, brick, sand, furniture, flour sacks, meat, or firewood on their backs secured by tumplines. Women's burdens invariably included a small child, whom they carried astride their bundles while spinning cotton threads in their spindles, often as they trotted along footpaths or roads. "Almost everything that moves in Quito rides on the backs of Indians," wrote one North American traveler.[37]

Without the familiarity and security of the kin group, community, or landlord, most Indians probably found urban life to be dangerous and degrading. And while some people managed to integrate themselves into paternal or kinship networks in the city, others began to embrace strategies and relationships drawn from the dominant society that could offer pathways out of poverty and Indianness. Quito was not the only escape valve for Indian social-climbers. It was better for socially mobile, enterprising natives to seek refuge in the buoyant textile-producing towns and cities of Riobamba and Otavalo, or along the thriving pack-train routes that operated out of northern villages like Atuntaqui toward Colombia. After 1870 the quickening pace of textile production and trade and the expansion of petty officialdom created a growing sector of *cholos* – people of Indian roots or parentage whose culture, demeanor, and lifeways took on a more mestizo cast. Many lived on the geographic and cultural edges of mestizo towns. These new migrants sought work in trade, industry, and petty bureaucracy in a fluid cultural setting, where almost everyone spoke Quichua laced with Spanish, or vice-versa. Economic survival usually depended on their ability to serve as go-betweens, brokering economic, political, and cultural exchanges between the rural Indian world and the urban mestizo one, because it was precisely their knowledge and manipulation of the symbolic lexicon of Quichua-speaking villages that gave the migrants advantages over white competitors in dealing with Indian clients. On the other hand, social advancement usually required migrants to change their ethnic markers (language, dress, diet, place of residence, family name, etc.) in pursuit of status and prosperity in the urban milieu. To build rural clientele, itinerant *cholos* donned ponchos, "dusted off" their Quichua, and carried small tokens to their Indian *compadres* (co-godparents). They served as crucial inter-

[37] Harry A. Franck, *Vagabonding Down the Andes*, 161.

mediaries, facilitating Indian access to mestizo officialdom, and they periodically renewed their village contacts by returning for local fiestas, births, and baptisms.

The most vivid example is the mestizo merchant and labor contractor – a roving figure who traveled the mule paths across the interior landscape. The least ethical ones preyed openly on the miseries and misfortunes of Indians – wielding the ubiquitous threat of debtors' prison before their Indian customers. For many of them, this was the pathway to prosperity, even if it entailed the certainty of social alienation. Yet it is also true that mestizos seeking to secure long-term trading partners among their "social inferiors" rarely conducted their affairs with the Simon Legree ruthlessness that educated whites imputed to them. Daily expressions of ethnic, class, and gender inequalities were more subtle. Throughout Ecuador and the rest of the Andes, regionally specific vernaculars and social practices captured the gendered, class, and local nuances and contingencies of racial and ethnic ascriptions among an increasingly amorphous mass of rural peasants and commoners. Local terminologies of ethnic identity and attributes created slippery, ambiguous, interstitial groupings (*cholos, castas, ladinos, mistis,* etc.) that bespoke the dynamics and vigor of transculturation processes at work in many regions.[38]

A lesser known but equally significant mestizo stereotype emerged in the interstices of the political machinery of modernization during the late nineteenth century. He was the back-country lawyer – typically a literate, bilingual mestizo who knew the bureaucratic ropes and could fill small spaces left by the suppression of indigenous leaders and the official Protector of Indians (abolished in 1854). Self-styled litigants for Indians appeared on the provincial scene throughout the Andean highlands, and already by mid-century, *tinterillos* (pen-pushers) were familiar figures in rural highland Ecuador. These shadowy souls occupied a strategic posi-

[38] Much interesting new work is focusing on discursive practices of ethnic identity as historically rooted cultural process. For a sweeping overview see Olivia Harris, "Ethnic identity and market relations: Indians and mestizos in the Andes," in Brooke Larson and Olivia Harris (eds.), *Ethnicity, Markets, and Migration in the Andes: At the Crossroads of Anthropology and History* (Durham, 1995), 351–390, as well as older but still salient essays in Fernando Fuenzalida et al., *El indio y el poder en el Perú* (Lima, 1970). On the engendering of *chola*–(Indian identity in dynamic local contexts, see the important articles by Linda Seligmann, "To be in-between: The cholas as market women," *Comparative Studies in Society and History* 31:4 (1989), 694–721; and Marisol de la Cadena, " 'Women are more Indian.' Ethnicity and gender in a community near Cuzco," in Brooke Larson and Olivia Harris (eds.), *Ethnicity, Markets and Migration in the Andes*, 329–350.

tion in rural society amidst extreme judicial and political flux. Many *tinterillos* practiced chicanery of all sorts. But some individuals served as indispensable brokers helping Indians negotiate the posttributary judicial system in the absence of their own traditional ethnic lords and separate legal code. As such, they proved to be a major nuisance to white society, tying up landlords in interminable lawsuits over land titles, debts, or labor, or whipping up Indian resentment over debt contracts. Not surprisingly their reputation quickly soured: They became archetypal "outside agitators" who preyed upon Indian illiteracy for their own scheming ends and, in the process, slowed the march of order and progress. Even the more optimistic textbook of 1874 found the Ecuadorian mestizo wanting: He stood closer to the unwashed Indian masses than to the civilized whites on the racial-evolutionary scale.

There was one striking anomaly in this bleak ideological landscape of docile, indolent Indians and parasitic mestizos: the Indians of Otavalo, who inhabited the fertile valleys and mountain slopes 2 days' journey by mule to the northeast of Quito. Since early colonial times the Otavalans had attracted European admiration and royal protection for their superb skills as weavers. "I never saw a race of finer looking people than an assembly of Otavalans on a Sunday," wrote an English traveler in 1825.[39] And in recent times the villages of Otavalo have drawn anthropologists seeking to understand the secrets of their success – how they have managed the "acculturation problem" (through centuries of coercion and adaptation) and flourished as ethnic enclaves in a hostile political world in spite of their longstanding participation in market economies.[40] Theirs is a long, contentious history of cultural coercion, change, recovery, and self-affirmation through successive periods of regional, colonial, and national integration.

For the Otavalans the nineteenth century was punctuated by a postindependence period of cultural reprieve and relative autonomy, only to be followed by the authoritarian phase of forced modernization in later decades. They had withstood the corrosive effects of land reform and managed to reintegrate themselves under de facto *caciques*, who controlled the process of tribute collection and continued to exercise their

[39] William Bennett Stevenson, *A Historical and Descriptive Narrative of Twenty Years' Residence in South America*, 2 vols. (London, 1825), 2:347; quoted in Frank Salomon, "Weavers of Otavalo," in Norman E. Whitten, Jr., *Cultural Transformations and Ethnicity in Modern Ecuador* (Urbana, 1981), 420–449; 420.

[40] This formulation of the paradoxes of Otavalan cultural resilience belongs to Frank Salomon, ibid.

colonial prerogatives as ethnic authorities and advocates. Like the *ayllus* of the southern Peru and Bolivia, the Otavalans wielded their everyday knowledges of history, mythology, genealogy, and colonial precedence preserved in written, oral, and ritual forms, to defend communal interests and press their claims on the new republic.

The abolition of tribute broke the implicit colonial precedent for *cacique* authority. It opened the way to ethnic fragmentation, incursions, and subordination to the emerging authoritarian regime. *Caciques* could no longer function as the interlocutors of an adversarial community or caste. Ethnic authority structures were leveled, jurisdictions fragmented, and power diffused among local, rotating Indian functionaries, who were called on to serve as agents of the religious and secular branches of the state. This was no small burden to bear under an extractive republican state. The business of the Indian *alcalde de justicia*, for example, was to procure Indian laborers or carriers for the public service whenever demanded. Beginning in the 1860s Otavalan headmen had to dispatch small armies of conscript laborers to build wagon roads to the coast, down dizzying mountain faces overgrown with rain forest. Such terrible tasks could be performed only if the *alcaldes* backed up their own despotic powers with threats of government force and imprisonment. Equally complicit was the Indian *alcalde de doctrina* (beadle or church constable), charged with keeping the chapels in good repair, procuring labor for the parish priests, and meting out punishment for moral transgressions. Friedrich Hassaurek happened upon a Sunday mass in Otavalo one day and bore witness to the moral policing of Indian women.

> Standing on the open square in front of the church, my attention was attracted by about two dozen Indians, most of them women, brought up by a few Indian *alcaldes*, who led them tied to one another with a long rope. Their offense consisted in having failed to attend religious service, especially the *doctrina* (lesson), for which they are compelled to meet twice a week. They were driven up and cuffed by the *alcaldes*, who for this purpose are entrusted with a little despotic authority.[41]

This "little despotic authority" undermined the fragile basis of ethnic authority and collapsed communal options of political negotiation and defense. It necessarily changed the way peasants did politics. The new logic forced peasants to bargain for individual truces, rights, or favors in

[41] Hassaurek, *Four Years among the Ecuadorians*, 174.

exchange for the fulfillment of their labor duties as "Indian citizens." Otavalan villagers developed the politics of petty paternalism to wrest small favors or retributions from outside, mestizo authorities. But the most bitter pill was the fact that the state had abolished most customary jurisdictions and rights associated with tribute at the same time it reimposed extractive relations. Not only did Otavalans face new incursions; they now had few legal or institutional means of redress. Cultural lifeways adjusted, too, as villages honed ideological traditions of localism. Incursions, racial animosity, class, and language barriers increased the social and political isolation of Otavalans at the same time they were plucked from their villages to dig the nation's highways. Otavalan villages evolved their own defensive practices and norms of endogamy, bound together through customs of intermarriage, communal work parties, and reciprocal relations, but each now stood more separate from other Otavalan villages because all no longer recognized a common ethnic lord.

What, then, sustained the basis of ethnic reorganization and identity in this alienating and hostile environment? How did the Otavalan peoples manage to survive the oppressive and atomizing conditions imposed upon them during the second half of the nineteenth century? These are open questions, because more is known about colonial and contemporary Otavalan society than its nineteenth-century history. But there are enough clues to intuit how everyday forms of popular religion and market culture may have counterbalanced the destructive forces of fragmentation and extraction.

One set of clues comes from the pen of Friedrich Hassaurek, who recorded his impressions of a religious festival in Otavalo during the winter solstice. As elsewhere in the Andes, the Otavalan peoples celebrated the feast of San Juan, as they did a host of local patron-saints. Hassaurek was astonished to see "dancing saints," "quaint mummeries," and other "mixtures of Catholicism and heathenism." And he was scandalized by the "live sacrifices of cocks" and other "barbarous customs."[42] During this week-long festival of dance, song, stories, drink, games, masquerades, and mummeries, Otavalans came together in a celebration of ethnic affirmation and identity and, like subaltern revelers everywhere, briefly to "turn the world upside down" through ritual dances that mocked and mimicked their social superiors. But it would be a mistake to dismiss this burst of expressive culture as a cathartic release of accu-

[42] Ibid., 158–159.

mulated class and ethnic hatreds, ultimately in the interest of the status quo. In the context of nineteenth-century, nation-building projects, particularly Ecuador's theocratic-authoritarian model, this display of popular Catholicism and communal solidarity itself mocked the very cultural values that dominant white society was supposedly inculcating in the Indians. Such open acts of "barbarity" advanced alternative cultural values, a symbolic counterassault on the repressive civilizing mission of the Church.

No less importantly the theater of communal festivities renewed a shared sense of bounded ethnic self. At the festival people hailing from different places identified their ethnic-regional affiliations by their dress, hats, music, and dances and by their position in stylized spacial arrangements during the festivities. Hassaurek noticed the Otavalan women who dressed in identical fashion, wrapped in rustic, red shawls and adorned in glass beads (Fig. 23.6). Otavalan men were distinguished by their long braids, blue woolen ponchos, and short white pants. These visual ethnic boundaries were maintained throughout the riotous color and chaos of the festival.

Festivals also served to reinforce ethnic identity, pride, and loyalty in the domain of the marketplace, and here we have another clue as to the cultural and material counterforces pushing against atomization. For centuries Otavalans had privileged their own collective identity as specialized, superior weavers under both Inka and Spaniard. Before the Spanish conquest the Otavalan people had already developed a strong regional pride, even chauvinism, about their standing as weavers and traders of cotton blankets and cloaks. Eventually the Quichua language supplanted Cara, and the Inka introduced wool-bearing camelids, but the Otavalans emerged with the skills and breadth of their textile trade stronger than ever. When the Spaniards overran the Andes, the Otavalans fared better than did most native peoples. They eventually became major suppliers of the colony's textiles, especially rustic shirt cloth, woolen blankets, and ponchos. The Spanish crown recognized these skilled workers and set aside the villages in a crown *encomienda*. Spanish-owned mills developed a parallel track of industry, concentrated mainly in the Riobamba region to the south of Otavalo. Several Otavalan mills sprang up, but they belonged to corporate communities or the crown. Neither private industries nor estates made many inroads into Otavalan territory until the late colonial era. Even then, when those communities were under growing pressure from creeping latifundism and relentless labor

Figure 23.6. Otavalan women. With their distinctively elaborate ceremonial and market-day dress, composed of their own weavings, large brimmed hats, and multiple strands of gold and red beads, Otavalan women (as well as their menfolk) have drawn the ethnographic eye of foreign travelers and Ecuadorian nationalists, alike, since the late nineteenth century. This portrait might well have served as a nineteenth-century *carte de visite* for Europeans interested in the "exotic cultures" and "racial types" of South America, but it was published in the 1933 ethnographic study of Ecuador by Mexican anthropologist, Moisés Sáenz: *Sobre el Indio Ecuatoriano y sus incorporación al medio nacional* (Mexico: Secretariat of Public Education, 1933).

drafts, the Otavalans were able to function as independent textile producers and traders of great repute. Their commodities found markets throughout the length of the Andes.[43]

Postindependence political transformations – the violence and high cost of the independence wars, abolition of *cacicazgos*, state incursions, loss of traditional colonial markets, and influx of British textiles – conspired against Otavalan autonomy. But by mid-century the villages had rebounded as important textile suppliers of regional, national, and even international markets. They continued to face competition from large mills, now more capitalized than before. But unlike many of those precocious capitalist ventures, which could suddenly fall on hard times, Otavalan's cottage industry had staying power. Although they could not undersell English factory-made clothing or even the products of old-style *obrajes*, they could often outlast them. Their secret lay in the flexibility and diversity of their peasant family economies, which combined craft and agricultural production and therefore boasted a considerable degree of self-sufficiency and adaptability as market and harvest conditions fluctuated over time. Second, it lay in their strong cultural traditions of selective innovation and initiative, which guided the choices people made about how they used their labor, capital, and cash. At the base of these choices were cultural values and memories that placed a premium on communal strength, territoriality, and independence. Time and again Otavalans adopted European tools, techniques, and consumer products for use within the bounds of their own cultural matrix: to reinforce subsistence security and cultural autonomy and to stave off the poverty, servility, and alienation that so many highland Indians suffered.

In short they evolved an alternative mercantile culture, which reinforced the ethnic boundaries and identities of the whole group. The Sunday market at Otavalo was a weekly renewal of ethnic associations, norms, and identities at the same time that it served to integrate Otavalans into larger cash economies as both commodity producers and consumers. Like their rituals of folk Catholicism that indicted the dominant norms of white Catholic society, then, the marketplace served as the symbolic terrain of an alternative culture of commodity exchange – one that was integrally related to Otavalan histories and memories of struggle. Gradually over the last years of the nineteenth century and the early years of the twentieth, new market and capital breakthroughs sustained

[43] Salomon, "Weavers of Otavalo," 440–441.

the prosperity of many Otavalan families and allowed them to purchase parcels of fertile bottom land in their quest for territorial autonomy.

This remarkable case of ethnic resilience and adaptation was mostly lost on white nation builders, unwilling or unable to see small miracles in a vast landscape of poverty and misery. Most of them were blinded by frozen, homogenized stereotypes of the "Indian race." Others, like Hassaurek, who took the trouble to explore the Indian hinterlands, dismissed the Otavalans as a more haughty version of the heathen Indian. But by the end of the century, the ascendance of Liberal reformism saw social critics of Conservative-hispanism casting about for new real and symbolic models of nation building. The quest for national identity and authenticity became urgent in the 1890s, as Ecuador prepared for her national debut at the 1892 Chicago World's Fair on the occasion of the four-hundredth anniversary of Columbus's arrival. Ecuador was to offer an exhibit at the American Historical Exposition to promote a favorable image abroad and cultivate diplomatic and trading relations with Spain. Ecuador's propagandists searched for an exhibit of their country's "exotic cultures" that might excite European interest. After much debate they settled on specimens of the "Otavalan race." Deemed safe, quaint, and picturesque, the Otavalans were thought to display an industriousness consonant with the nation's modernizing mission. Decorative weavers would be on hand at the fair to show off their artisan abilities and colorful costumes. So began the first official indigenist project: to stereotype and stylize Indians in the service of national image making. Otavalans were folklorized as the antithesis of the "common Indian," yet they remained as isolated as ever from the exclusive white nation.

As we step back from the historical canvas of highland Ecuador, it appears clear that the white nation builders stood at an ideological and institutional crossroad in the late nineteenth century. Like their northern counterparts in Colombia, they bore witness to the gradual erosion of caste and the advance of cultural *mestizaje* in many highland areas. Southern Indian migration to the coast, as well as the bustling mestizo towns of the northern highlands – those nodal points of state control and plebeian commerce – were all symptomatic of the end of the old order. And yet the Conservative ruling élite remained deeply ambivalent about the historic role of the Indian and mestizo in the republic's past and future. For most of the century they refused to adopt unifying myths of the mestizo as historic agents of race mixture and cultural assimilation.

The liberal Colombian project of whitening had little political resonance in nineteenth-century Ecuador.

On the contrary the Church-sponsored republican project of Ecuador reinforced caste. Ecuador abolished tribute, but reinstitutionalization coerced Indian labor. Extractive modes of labor control, in turn, rested on cultural foundations that posited the immutability of race. By the 1870s the white race had become synonymous with civilization and citizenship, the Indian race with poverty and cultural depravity. As the backward race, Indians were biologically predestined to serve the nation as its laborers, servants, soldiers, and beasts of burden. They would build the nation's new roads but be denied membership in the imagined national community. They would pay taxes and serve in the military but be subject to a modern inquisition designed to root out idolatry, superstition, and shamanism. They would be effaced from Ecuador's censuses and silenced in public discourse but subject to discriminatory practices for purposes of public works, taxes, military conscription, and criminal and moral discipline. Still, élites thought there needed to be Indians. The evaporation of Indians into white peasants or laborers through progressive *mestizaje* and European immigration apparently did not grip the political imagination of most Ecuadorian leaders before the Liberal Revolution of 1895. Too much was vested in colonial modes of exploitation. Even after the Liberal victory, amidst heated Liberal–Conservative polemics, debt servitude and prison, as well as the degraded Indian peon, would remain fixtures of rural Ecuador until well into the twentieth century (see Chap. 25).

PERU: NATIONAL SOVEREIGNTY AND THE "INDIAN PROBLEM"

The construction of a modern nation-state in Peru was more violent and flawed than almost anywhere else in Latin America, and many of the country's daunting postcolonial dilemmas remain unresolved to this day. For real and imagined reasons, the "Indian problem" seemed almost intractable to nineteenth-century Creole nation builders, and they failed to reach any consensus about how to overcome it until the end of the century. But in the early 1880s Peru's defeat in the War of the Pacific crystallized one alarming idea in the collective consciousness of the ruling cliques – that the Indian problem put at risk the very viability of Peru.

Peru's peasantry was suddenly needed in the war effort against the Chilean occupiers. But as the international conflict ebbed, and Peru became engulfed in its own civil wars and regional rebellions, Creole leaders focused once more on the dangers of civil strife and popular uprisings in the heart of the Peruvian sierra. These experiences were to recast Creole thinking about citizenship, civilization, and nationhood after the war. The stakes seemed clear: Peru's own precarious social peace was at risk no less than its political and territorial sovereignty. And the "Indian problem" was said to be at the core of the republic's wartime collapse. For out of the shattering experiences of imperial invasion, civil war, and political betrayal there arose an official mythology that laid the nation's humiliating defeat by Chile at the feet of its "depraved" Indian majority. It proved useful to an ascendant oligarchy anxious to rebuild the state machinery of revenue, coercion, and patronage toward the internal conquest of Peru's Indian masses – in the name of order and progress, as well as sovereignty.

But throughout the mountains and valleys of the sierra, Peruvian farmers and herders who were swept into the powerful currents of warfare fashioned their own understandings of the nation they were defending. And they advanced their own claims against the social injustices they had long experienced. As we shall see, wartime events, experiences, and consequences were extremely varied across highland Peru, with some regions (in the Southern Highlands) remaining fairly peaceful, others (in the Northern Highlands) forging alliances with the Chilean invaders, others (in the Mantaro Valley) emerging as the sites of popular resistance and national defense, and still others (in the Callejón de Huaylas) rising up in regional rebellion. These flashpoints of peasant mobilizations offer glimpses of popular expressions usually lost to view. Historians have seized on this extraordinary period of upheaval to track Indian leaders who rose to prominence during the war, forged their own political and military pacts, defined their own enemies, and asserted their own claims, amid the promises and betrayals of war. Some would even launch autonomist microrepublics on the edges of a repressive, war-weary nation.

To understand the magnitude of the putative Indian problem facing the nation builders around mid-century, it is necessary to glance briefly at the broader picture of demographic, class, and power imbalances in nineteenth-century Peru. First, to a greater degree than in Ecuador, demographic-ethnic balances favored the Indian majority throughout the century. There was no "natural process" of ethnic atrophy at work, as appeared to be happening in Colombia and Ecuador. In the most germane study, George Kubler adopted the tax collectors' definitions of *indios* and *castas* to compile aggregate population estimates and chart demographic trends between 1795 (following the last colonial census) and 1940 (the year of a national census). His major conclusion was striking: The nineteenth century stood out as the only era in Andean history that halted – even reversed – the half-millennial trend of Indian depopulation and assimilation (through cultural and demographic *mestizaje*). More precisely, Kubler argued that it was in the four or five decades following independence (between the 1830s and 1870s) that Indian population rapidly recovered before the onset of "modern *mestizaje*" (associated with migration, urbanization, market expansion, etc.) beginning in the late nineteenth century. According to his estimates, Indians comprised about 58 percent of the total population of viceregal Peru in 1795 and then increased to 59 percent in the period between 1826 and 1854. Thereafter Indians declined to 55 percent of Peru's total population, as counted in the national census of 1876, sliding to some 40 percent in 1940. Gootenberg's analysis of little known 1827 provincial census records reveals an even larger proportion of Peruvian Indians than Kubler's study had shown. Of Peru's 1.5 million people in 1827, some 62 percent were registered as "Indian." His study confirms Kubler's assumptions about Indian stability during the turbulent, war-torn decades between the 1790s and 1830s and beyond. Official records (which continued to register colonial-styled categories of race – Indian, *casta*, white, black) provide a picture of remarkable Indian stability throughout the nineteenth century. In the 1830s more than 60 percent of the total population was classed as "Indian." The national census of 1876 recorded Indians as composing some 55 percent of the nation's population.[44]

Second, the chaos of the independence wars disrupted regional economies and catalyzed social and cultural change, ushering in a protracted process of political and economic fragmentation, or even balkanization. But it did not destroy regional peasant-based production or trade, nor unleash *latifundismo* upon battered Indian communities. The postinde-

[44] George Kubler, *The Indian Caste of Peru, 1795–1940. A Population Study Based on Tax Records and Census Reports* (Washington, 1952). See the discussion in Nicolás Sánchez Albornoz, *The Population of Latin America: A History* (Berkeley, 1974), 109 ff.; and more recently in Paul Gootenberg, "Population and ethnicity in early Republican Peru: Some revisions," *Latin American Research Review* 26:3 (1991).

pendence period showed signs of peasant economic activity in interregional markets, annual trading fairs and pilgrimages, pack industry, craft production, certain mining camps, and even the wool trade. The liberal land reforms did intensify intra-Andean land disputes, but there is little evidence of widespread despoliation before the 1870s. Furthermore the ambiguities of republican tributary policy allowed some legal maneuvering for defense of colonial-derived rights. In short, Indians in much of the southern highlands still controlled significant tracts of land. Peru did not boast an entrenched landholding aristocracy the likes of Ecuador's. Market capitalism would eventually have to deploy draconian means of divestiture and run the risks of agrarian violence.

Third, Peru inherited historical traditions and memories of Andean insurgency, which had surfaced in successive peasant uprisings between the 1740s and the 1780s, culminating in the massive Andean civil wars of 1781 (see Chap. 22). Repressive measures followed, with the first concerted effort to abolish hereditary Andean lordships and root out the cultural expressions of neo-Inka nationalism in the late eighteenth century. But the two-decade long struggle (1810s–1820s) between royalists and patriots over the fate of the colony unleashed a new cycle of reforms, repression, and warfare in which native communities were deeply involved. The rollback of liberal reforms immediately after the war did not restore hereditary lords, but neither did the new republic attempt to integrate Indian communities tightly into a centralizing bureaucracy. Instead in many regions local power was vested in *varayuq*, who continued to symbolize and use communal resources to advance or defend local interests. (The title *varayuq*, 'staffholder', refers to annually rotating officers who held the silver-clad staffs of authority.) During times of agrarian compression or war, these local networks of ethnic authority could mobilize scattered communities in revolt, or oil the machinery of Indian litigation and protest against land despoliation and other injustices. At mid-century, Indian communities in much of Peru were not so fragmented, beleaguered, or atrophied as historians once thought. This fact alone would make the civilizing project (once it was finally constructed) far more contentious and difficult than in either Ecuador or Colombia.

Conquest, Civilization, or Patronage? Competing Paradigms of Indian Oppression

Around mid-century the Peruvian state cast its lot with its resurgent export industries, the world market, and eurocentric ideologies. A booming coastal guano export business encouraged the Lima-based oligarchy to dream of a prospering and orderly Peru, where the formal trappings of Indian caste (and other rural anachronisms) would fade into a landscape of bustling markets, commercial estates, teeming cities, iron rails, and billowing smokestacks. Although the Indian problem had not yet become an urgent national priority, it demanded attention from politicians eager for recolonization of the Indian highlands by agrarian capitalists, merchants, and agents of "civilization." The roadblocks of the colonial past had to be removed so market capitalism could travel from the europeanizing seacoast into the mountainous interior. In particular, Indian lands and labor needed to be channeled and regulated in accord with the republic's changing national needs.

The 1850s heralded the revival of liberalism, adapted from the earlier constitutional liberalism of the 1820s to fit the aspirations of mid-century Limeño oligarchs. Groping toward a national language of citizenship, the government enacted two sets of reforms that redefined the relations of Indians to the state. The first was the Civil Code of 1852, a mixed bag of liberal, Roman, and Napoleonic legal codes that strictly interpreted individual equality before the law. The second was the abolition of tribute, promulgated by President Ramón Castilla (the self-proclaimed "Liberator" of slaves and Indians) in 1854.

On paper they accomplished what the earlier liberators had failed to do. They set forth the terms by which Indians were defined and regulated as individuals, subject to the same rights and obligations as all others under the auspices of the nation-state. Indians were to become, in effect, the "last among equals" in a new institutional and moral setting. The flip side was that this status removed their traditional rights to collective existence – that is, to "community," as indigenous peoples themselves later put it. The symbolic and real implications of these reforms cannot be overemphasized: They marked the beginning of the republic's sustained assault on Indian communities. The most significant, colonial-derived rights that indigenous peoples had struggled to recover at the end of the independence era were now struck down in the republic's search for a new basis of political authority, justice, and morality. The new legal code took the moderate 1828 Land Reform Act further down the road toward market individualism, leaving no room for corporate landholding. All lands in the nation were declared alienable, including those held by illiterate Indians. And all Indians, literate or not, were subject to contract law, which often proved deadly to Indians holding dubious labor or debt contracts.

Of course a gap yawned between liberal policies promulgated on the coast and social realities of the sierra. Some historians argue that the abolition of tribute was not really followed up with any positive institutional or integrationist developments, and probably even loosened ties between the Lima bureaucracy and Indian society.[45] There was as yet no Peruvian counterpart to Ecuador's tightening bureaucratic network of provincial power and social control under García Moreno. This became apparent when the Peruvian reformer, Ramón Castilla, discovered that the "providential revenues" from guano were not sufficient to finance the provincial bureaucracies that had always depended on tribute revenue as their lifeblood. He could not afford to build a state apparatus, unless he reimposed a new form of tribute. Just 2 years after the much-heralded abolition of tribute, Castilla quietly tried (and failed) to reinstate it. A later regime temporarily restored tribute in 1866, only to rescind it again in 1867 after the bloody *altiplano* rebellion of Huancané. The Indian head tax made its national reappearance in 1879, this time as an emergency "war tax" at the beginning of the War of the Pacific. But none of these taxes signified the legal reinstatement of communal rights lost in the political and judicial flux of mid-century.

The new civil code of the 1850s, therefore, did little to dislodge provincial potentates who claimed privileged access to Indian labor and tribute. Castilla was only too aware that prefects, subprefects, governors, and priests made a practice of holding Indians in personal servitude in the name of public service. This issue of Indian servitude and forced labor became the Achilles heel of the Liberator. Not only did the persistence of Indian servitude and *corvée* labor mock the new laws, but they anchored needed workers in the sierra, just when the coastal plantations cried out for cheap migratory laborers. To target highland Indians as potential wage workers for the highland mines and coastal plantations was to run up against deeply ingrained colonial habits. There was not yet any centralized institution of *corvée* Indian labor, as Ecuador had established in the 1850s. But at the local level, civil and religious authorities depended on Indians to repair the roads; staff the inns, waystations, and monasteries; carry the mail; build the jails; and dig the cemeteries. Estate owners needed small reserve armies from nearby Indian communities to help bring in the crop. And as they expanded and commercialized their estates, they sought to colonize Indian lands and reroot Indian laborers.

[45] Paul Gootenberg, "Population and ethnicity in early Republican Peru," 150.

Indeed these early decades of Peruvian commercial recovery boosted commercial landlordism in diverse highland regions. Profit-seeking hacendados and the middle sectors who serviced them began to emerge as a strong political counterforce to the Lima-based oligarchy, climaxing in the Arequipa-based "Aristocratic Republic" following the War of the Pacific. But already by the 1860s – long before the ascendant highland oligarchy of Arequipa consolidated and projected its political power onto the whole nation – provincial powerholders tried to bend liberal policies and paternalist practices to their own ends. In the phrase of Jean Piel, Peru's market-oriented landlords (and their lackeys) wanted to "privatize" the Andean reserve by converting communal peasants into servile laborers, captive consumers, contract laborers, and debtors.[46]

To the degree they succeeded, they blocked oligarchic efforts to recruit sierran wage laborers for the modernizing mines and plantations. The most dramatic case of Indian labor scarcity occurred along the northern coast of Peru, where booming plantations imported thousands of indentured workers from China between 1850 and 1874, sooner than depend upon the erratic migration of highland Indians. When the state later outlawed the importation of Chinese workers, the plantations sent labor recruiters through the Northern and Central Sierra to "hook" (*enganchar*) Indians into a binding 7-year contract of sweat work in the cane fields of the northern coast. In the highlands of Cajamarca, where estates had long dominated rural life, those draconian measures reflected the regional hacendado's determination to hold onto their own peasant laborers, even as the demand for cheap salaried workers exploded along the north coast.[47]

Thus, although the posttributary republic stumbled toward an institutional language of citizenship, it never constructed a "civilizing mis-

[46] Jean Piel, "Las articulaciones de la reserva andina al Estado y al mercado desde 1820 hasta 1950," in J. P. Deler and Y. Saint-Geours, *Estados y Naciones en los Andes*, 2 vols. (Lima, 1986), 323–336.

[47] On the development of modern coastal plantations and their labor control problems, see Michael J. González, "Capitalist agriculture and labour contracting in northern Peru," *Journal of Latin American Studies* 12:2 (1980), 291–315, and Peter Klaren, "The social and economic consequences of modernization in the Peruvian sugar industry," in K. Duncan and I. Rutledge (eds.), *Land and Labour in Latin America* (Cambridge, 1977), 229–252. Apparently "spontaneous" peasant migration to coastal plantations was more prevalent in the southern regions than previously thought, although labor demands were probably not so enormous there. See Henri Favre, "The dynamics of Indian peasant society and migration to coastal plantations in central Peru," ibid., 253–268, on the adaptive migratory strategies of the Astos Indians from highland Huancavelica. In contrast Juan Martínez-Alier discusses social and cultural factors inhibiting many highland Indians from making seasonal treks down to the coast in his article, "Relations of production in Andean estates: Peru," ibid., 141–164.

sion" to unify factious coastal and sierra élites. Highland and coastal élites shared their antipathy to the Indian race, diagnosed by the experts as unfit to vote and "injurious to the nation's health." But they parted company on how to cope with the Indian problem. In contrast to the Colombian class project of liberalism (which began to falter in the late nineteenth century), Lima's guano oligarchs managed to establish a beachhead of liberalism on the desert coast. But the peculiar seaward-oriented nature of their extractive economy, and the fiscal autonomy it granted Lima, created little immediate need to integrate peasants or provincial élites into the state-building project in the 1840s and 1850s.[48] On the other hand, highland élites remained regionally insular, entangled in local patronage networks and preoccupied by petty labor and land disputes.

Neither, however, was there a strong foundation upon which to build a hegemonic landlord–Church alliance capable of imposing its conservative political will on the rest of the country, as Ecuador's aristocrats did. Peru had no cohesive landed aristocracy, and its landed élites failed to consolidate power soon after independence. Furthermore the republic had inherited an Indian population still largely distributed among free-holding villages. These villages managed to recover local lands, markets, and autonomies after independence. The fragmented seigneurial regime only began to recover in the 1860s and 1870s, and then the War of the Pacific slowed and skewed the process of estate growth until almost the turn of the twentieth century. As we shall see shortly, peasant resistance also sabotaged and slowed efforts to divest communal lands and induce flows of national labor.

Against this broken landscape of power stood a contentious, weak oligarchy unable to cope with its highland Indian heritage. During the transitional decades between abolition (1854) and the beginning of the war (1879), Peru radically altered, and often reversed, its Indian policies. The 1860s and 1870s stand out as a period of clashing political paradigms of republican aggression, hammered out as much in the course of conflict as in the quiet chambers of Congress. The successive regimes of Mariano Ignacio Prado (1866–1868), Manuel Pardo (1872–1876), and Nicolás de Piérola (1879–1881) serve to illustrate.

[48] Paul Gootenberg, "Population and ethnicity in early Republican Peru," 150. See also his book, *Imagining Development: Economic Ideas in Peru's 'Fictitious Prosperity' of Guano, 1840–1880* (Berkeley, 1993).

In 1866 Mariano Prado inherited the failed liberal experiment of Castilla. He immediately tried to reimpose the Indian head tax (without restoring communal rights or protections). The head tax was but another discriminatory Indian levy to be piled on top of the localized labor and tax demands that had multiplied in recent years. The new extraction bore down heavily, especially on the Indian herding communities of the south. They were already diminished by prolonged drought, frequent border disputes, and military marauding, and a growing number of merchants scouring the highlands for cheap wool. In this setting the new levy was another blow – but one dealt by the republic itself. *Altiplano* villages became the first ones to set the limits of communal accommodation.

In 1866 indigenous resentment burst into flames in Huancané, near the city of Puno. But more than the new tax burden, it was the deliberate brutality of the state's reprisal that shattered any lingering illusions about the posttributary state. As expected Prado quickly dispatched troops to crush the rebels. Congress took further steps, however, and engineered a campaign of state terror designed to exterminate entire Indian communities – much as Porfirio Díaz would do later, and on a larger scale, against the rebellious Yaqui Indians of the Mexican northwest. Fired up by the emergency "Law of Terror," the Peruvian army banded together with mercenaries and estate owners to massacre and imprison Indians. Insurgent villages of the *altiplano* were uprooted and sent into exile to the labor camps in the steamy jungles of Carabaya. The first major Andean uprising since the wars of independence, the rebellion of Huancané, unmasked a harsher, militarized republic that redefined Indians – all Indians – as tributaries without rights, and as potential enemies of the nation.[49]

[49] Thomas M. Davies, Jr., *Indian Integration in Peru: A Half Century of Experience, 1900–1948* (Lincoln, 1974), 30–31. In the tumult of 1866 and 1867, there emerged an anomalous figure, Juan Bustamante, a mestizo wool merchant, writer, and politician from Puno, who cast himself in the roles of defender of the oppressed Indians and conscience of a tiny enlightened Creole élite. His moral outrage came in part from witnessing the brutality of the army as it rampaged through the provinces of Puno and Cusco. But even before the repression, Bustamante had begun to catalog the outrages and humiliations that highland Indians suffered in their daily lives. In 1867 he enlisted the support of other politicians to campaign against the military atrocities and founded a group that called itself Friends of the Indians. That same year Bustamante published *Los indios del Perú*, a little-read essay that linked the future of the nation to the well-being of its Indian citizens. Only in the 1870s and thereafter would Bustamante's pro-Indian sentiments influence the writings and ruminations of the *civilista* intellectuals and politicians of Lima. But in the crucible of the "caste war" and legal terrorism on the *altiplano*, Bustamante's activism and alliance with the Indian insurgents was seen as sheer treachery. In 1867 he was taken prisoner by the army

Under Manuel Pardo's regime, the government restored some civility to its Indian policies. This new *civilista* coalition of coastal oligarchs, intellectuals, and politicians launched the first state-directed civilizing project. Inspired by liberal precepts, the integrationist goals of the new government were also tempered by Pardo's acute awareness that Peru's "fictitious prosperity" was evaporating as quickly as its guano piles were settling. Even so, Pardo staked the nation's remaining bird-dung collateral on the frenzied construction of trans-Andean railroads during the 1870s. It was part of Pardo's dream to bring the miracles of European technology (and its attendant values) to highland Peru. He was convinced that Peru's future depended upon it.

This project also envisioned far-reaching cultural reforms. If the highlands were to be colonized by entrepreneurs, Indians had to be released from their material and moral bondage (to feudal estates, subsistence communities, religious fiestas, and the like) and socialized to the work rhythms and demands of a modernizing Peru. Much like Colombia's free-wheeling liberals, Peru's new prophets of progress manufactured a national vision of Indian redemption and assimilation – to be accompanied, of course, by aggressive efforts at importing European immigrants. Although it borrowed the emancipatory and free-labor rhetoric of Colombian liberals, Pardo's program also called for strong state intervention to coerce or cajole Indians into the modern political economy, without immediately striking racial categories from the public record. The *civilista* government strove for the selective assimilation of Indians, but whereas Colombia and Ecuador effaced race from their official records in the 1870s, Peru registered its Indian population in its 1876 census. Oligarchs obviously had no intention of assimilating Indians quickly.

The long-term goal, however, was to remake Peruvian Indians to serve the changing labor needs of the modernizing nation (from the perspective of coastal-urban Peru). Specifically Pardo's "civilizing mission" called for Indian education under a state-run system of primary schools. Although he never amassed the support he needed for his educational project, Pardo made a start. He established one of Peru's first trade schools for Indians in the city of Ayacucho. There a select group of boys were trained to be carpenters, stone masons, and iron workers.[50] Tailor-made by the

and stoned to death. See Jorge Basadre, *La multitud, la ciudad, y el campo en las historia del Perú* (Lima, 1947), 243–244.

[50] Davies, *Indian Integration in Peru*, 31–32.

state, the "new Indians" were to be transformed into Peru's laboring class. To that end the state was to penetrate the interior of Quechua and Aymara communities, eradicating indigenous languages and customs in the name of national unity. In much the same way that the late eighteenth-century Bourbons called for the "extirpation of the Indian language," Pardo promoted the forced hispanization of indigenous peoples. But just as the "hispanist" reformers had encountered staunch opposition to their plan 100 years earlier, Pardo himself immediately ran up against the resistance of highland élites vested in colonial forms of discrimination. In fact well into the twentieth century, many provincial powerholders in both Peru and Bolivia saw Indian literacy and education as threats to the social order. It was commonplace for landlords to forbid their peons from learning their letters. Such harsh realities of highland Peru deflated Pardo's grandiose schemes of language regulation. His civilizing mission was reduced to mere tokenism: He ordered the state to print 1,000 copies of a Spanish–Quechua dictionary for distribution among Indians! This was to be no "integrative revolution," to be sure, but Pardo's cultural politics laid the discursive groundwork for early twentieth-century "civilizing" projects.

When Nicolás de Piérola took office in 1879, the momentous year that brought the War of the Pacific, the republic reinvented Indian policy yet again. This time it was forged under the gun, as part of Peru's larger effort to defend the homeland against the Chilean invaders. Piérola reasoned well that if Peru were to prevail, he would have to mobilize the highlands behind the war effort. Of course that was not to be, and before long the Central Sierra roiled amidst the thunder of war. But in 1879, while war loomed on coastal horizons, Piérola began to whip up the provincial bureaucracies to collect "war taxes" in cash and kind from Indian constituencies. Local authorities were to reactivate the tributary apparatus and to requisition money, supplies, and later soldiers from highland communities and estates. For the next several years, Indian communities throughout Peru virtually bankrolled the war effort.

Long before national and regional events spun out of control, Piérola made his pitch for Indian loyalty and obedience, not in the constitutional language of citizenship and patriotism, but in the older idiom of paternalist absolutism. As the nation's father figure, he appealed to "his Indians" to make sacrifices for the national war effort, in return for which he promised his personal protection. Invoking the ideals of Spanish patrimonialism, Piérola proclaimed himself the "Protector of the

Indian Race" against the tyranny of local government. He would serve as the ultimate arbiter of justice, with the right to intervene personally in situations brought to his attention by the groups of aggrieved Indians waiting patiently outside his palace chambers. This self-styled Indian Protector wasted no time, however, in dispatching military men to comb the highlands for men, mules, and money. A heinous example of political opportunism in a moment of national emergency? To be sure. But Piérola's belated experiment in coercive paternalism reveals how some members of the coastal oligarchy apparently understood the basis of its own legitimacy and authority in Indian society. Rather than appealing to Indians in patriotic or constitutionalist terms, Piérola reverted to the idiom of paternalism. It was empty rhetoric, of course, because it proclaimed no legal reforms restoring communal rights or privileges. That far Piérola was unwilling to go. As we shall see, one of the great ironies of this period is that it was Indian soldiers themselves who punctured the myth of Piérola's "Protectorate," revived the rhetoric of equality and citizenship, and thereby took political matters into their own rough hands. So much for the power of paternalism!

But we are getting ahead of the story. For in the period between tribute abolition (1854) and the beginning of the Pacific War (1879), Indian communities confronted a fickle republic. The clashing paradigms of official Indian policy – from the "conquest government" of Prado, and the civilizing missions of Pardo, to the patron-state of Piérola – bring to light the ambivalences and discontinuities that mired the posttributary Peruvian state. Fractious élites continually reformulated the government's official role in resolving the nation's Indian question. They brought neither unity nor balance to the dangerous enterprise of governing Indians in times of economic change. Racial orthodoxies of domination would only begin to bind together the disparate elements of regional élites in the postwar period. In the years preceding the Pacific War, the coastal and sierran élites continued to work at cross-purposes, as they dismantled the remains of the tributary apparatus and fumbled around with the real-life implications of individual rights. Yet slowly and haltingly they began to gather consensus, groping toward a vague understanding that the state had an important role to play in reshaping the normative order of rural Peru. Whether that meant state repression, protection, or cultural regeneration of the "Indian race" were issues of lesser importance. At base the posttributary state was beginning to formulate a new set of political and discursive guidelines that would severely restrict entry into the nation and civil society. The crisis of war and peasant revindication in the 1880s and 1890s was all that was needed to clinch this emerging "pact of discrimination" against the Indian majority around the end of the nineteenth century.

Everyday Forms of Extraction, Resistance, and Social Climbing

The shifting political speech of mid-century was important in the symbolic downgrading of rural Andean lifeways. But we can only begin to understand the different meanings and effects of those anti-Indian policies if we set them down into local rural life and bear witness to the tangible forms of violence they encouraged or condoned. In the 1860s and 1870s, the Andean highlands were shot through with violence – driven not as much by the injustices of liberal-positivist doctrines as by the mundane brutalities of extraction. But what mattered so deeply to indigenous communities is that they had to suffer new, arbitrary hardships and abuses under a republic suddenly turned indifferent to their local heritages, their histories of sacrifice, and lawfulness under the old tributary republic. Furthermore they saw too well that official indifference could turn on a dime in the wrong direction: The new contract laws were becoming weapons of the strong in their quest to privatize Indian lands and discipline labor.

In the South Andes the booming overseas wool trade gave local commerce a violent edge that it had not had in previous decades. As wool prices rocketed upward in the late 1860s and early 1870s, the lowly sheep and alpaca trade, the historic staple of southern Indian communities, turned into a hot prospect for wholesale exporters and their agents. The whole Southern Highlands, from the high plains of Titicaca to southern Cusco and down into the valleys of Arequipa, was turning into a giant extractive economy feeding wool to the factories of northern Europe. This gradual transition would climax much later, in the early twentieth century. But the export-driven wool trade already picked up speed during the 1860s and 1870s, when British merchant and finance capital moved briskly into the Arequipa region and began to elbow aside indigenous wool traders. The capitalized wool business drove deeper into Indian territory – right to the thickest herds tucked away in the high sierra and clustered along the green and yellow lake shores of Titicaca. The interior *altiplano* was opened up to new forms of colonization after iron rails reached Puno in 1874; from the north the tracks moved southward to the lakeshore town of Juliaca in 1876. This triumph of European technology dealt a lethal blow to the centuries-old pack trade and wool industry that had sustained Aymara and Quechua communities throughout the Southern Highlands. Indigenous trading activities, muleteers, and markets were disrupted and sometimes displaced, as the terms and conditions of overland trade shifted sharply against them. Throughout Peru, weekly retail markets continued to dictate the rhythms of local economic life and their "picturesque characters" attracted the eye of European travelers (Fig. 23.7 and Fig. 23.8). But in the southern wool zones, Vilque and other great market fairs and

shrines faded in importance. Instead mestizo-dominated trade depots sprang up along the railroad tracks, and towns like Sicuani (province of Canchis, in southern Cusco) turned into commercial outposts for British merchant houses located in the city of Arequipa. In the southern valley of Colca, for example, Indian llama drivers who had once traveled down the mountains to Arequipa to hawk their alpaca wool were dislocated by the arrival of the railroad and foreign export firms. They found themselves wheeling and dealing with commercial agents who rode the rails up into the highlands, looking to secure the best deals among Indian wool suppliers who now converged on the rail-side towns and markets. The Colca traders were not alone. All over the highlands a small group of commercial agents took over the management of the interior wool trade, often on behalf of Arequipa houses.[51]

Figure 23.7 (*opposite*). An Indian Water-carrier in the Market of Cajamarca, in northern Peru, ca. 1880. This engraving was but one of hundreds that appeared in the published accounts of Charles Wiener, who wrote one of the century's most detailed, insightful, and richly illustrated travel-discovery accounts of the Andes. In his *Pérou et Bolivie: Recit du Voyage suivi archeologiques et ethnographiques et de notes sur l'ecriture et les langues des population indiennes* (Paris: Libraire Hachetter, 1880), Wiener, who undertook the journey for the French Ministry of Public Education between 1875 and 1877, conjoined ethnographic and archaeological investigation to bring the rural Andean past and present into one field of inquiry. But like other contemporary European travelers in the Andes, Wiener used many of his engravings and the *cartes de visite* that he purchased in Peru and Bolivia to depict "popular types," such as market vendors, healers, charcoal sellers, water-carriers, porters, miners, agriculturalists, mule drivers, domestic servants, and bandits. (See Deborah Poole, *Vision, Race, and Modernity: A Visual Economy of the Andean Image World* [Princeton: Princeton University Press, 1997], 131–132.) This particular engraving of a water-carrier accompanied a lively description of market relations in the plaza of Cajamarca, in which water-carriers (usually domestic Indians from the city) walked slowly and gravely through the city streets hauling their great *olla* of water to the marketplace, where suddenly their spirits lifted, as they smiled and laughed, greeted familiar merchants and hawkers, and made their way happily through the market's aisles and alley ways. When, suddenly, they were reminded of their servile station in life, they bid farewell to the pretty vendor, reassumed their "air of ennui and unhappiness" and headed reluctantly towards the mansion of their master (*Pérou et Bolivie*, 127).

[51] Benjamin Orlove, *Alpacas, Sheep and Men: The Wool Export Economy and Regional Society in Southern Peru* (New York, 1977); Nelson Manrique, "Gamonalismo, lanas, y violencia en los

Figure 23.8. A married and rich market vendor of Puno, ca. 1880. Charles Wiener (in his *Pérou et Bolivia*, 385) was fascinated by the southern highland towns he toured, especially on market days when streams of indigenous men and women flowed into them from surrounding villages, haciendas, and estancias. Wiener described Quechua and Aymara Indians as distinguishable by their physical characteristics (Aymaras were "shorter and darker") and by the dress of their womenfolk. He was particularly struck by the dress of Aymara women, such as that worn by the "rich merchant woman" shown here, because of their adaptation of European dress, particularly the pointed headdress once worn, he noted, by the likes of Isabel de Bavière or Agnes Sorel of France. Adorning the head of such fashionable ladies, he hastened to point out, the coiffure was charming, but on the squat Aymara woman it only made a mockery of her stature. Nonetheless, he recognized that their black hats served a function by making this "excellent cadre" stand out among the dark-skinned mass of haggling humanity that crowded the marketplaces of Vilque and other towns across the high plateau of southern Peru.

The new itinerant wool merchants walked a fine line between coaxing and coercing Indian suppliers into surrendering their wool on buyers' terms. Traders eager to bargain down prices often bypassed traditional peasant markets to purchase wool directly from Indian communities. As early as the late 1850s, Arequipa firms began to send agents to tour the bandit-ridden Cusco province of Chumbivilcas to buy wool directly from Indians. That practice spread rapidly across the South Andes over the next two decades. Many wool traders managed to insinuate themselves into long-term relations with their Indian suppliers. Often they secured their wool supplies by advancing money to Indian herders. The sheep rancher would redeem the debt by delivering a certain quantity and quality of wool. The value of his herds and pastures would underwrite the whole transaction. Doing business in this way cost the merchant money and time – and perhaps much more, if he stalked sheep ranchers in dangerous provinces like Chumbivilcas. Even where rural trade was less treacherous, wandering wool buyers had to work through the rituals of community and kinship to establish client sheep-ranching communities. But after a certain point, as market conditions shifted sharply against the raw wool suppliers, middlemen grew impatient with these ritualized customs of trade. Professional wool merchants took advantage of conditions to entrap Indians into debt and eventually expropriate their flocks and lands.

Over the late nineteenth century, then, the southern Peruvian highlands experienced a dramatic shift in the balance of social forces. Beginning in the 1860s, the wool export trade forged a new commercial axis connecting Arequipa (the merchant and banking city) to Puno (its commercial outpost in the sheep-breeding highlands). The arrival of the railroad in the 1870s clinched the wholesale trade by linking Puno and Arequipa to the Pacific ports. It was the beginning of the south's "commercial revolution" – one consolidated around the turn of the twentieth century. While the wool trade tapered off during the War of the Pacific, the landed aristocracy of Peru's "new south" emerged from the war even stronger than before. Part of the reason for the rise of the south rests with the fortuitous events of the Pacific War, which spared the Southern Highlands from massive destruction and casualty. As we shall see, the

Andes," in H. Urbano (ed.), *Poder y Violencia en los Andes* (Cusco, 1989), 211–223; Nils Jacobsen, *Mirages of Transition. The Peruvian Altiplano Between Colonialism and the World Market* (Berkeley, 1993), chaps. 5 and 6.

Central Highlands bore the brunt of that war. But the tax burdens of war weighed heavily on Indian communities of southern Peru, and they suffered a wave of violent spoliations, enclosures, and evictions during and after the War of the Pacific.[52]

The wool boom that bore down on most Indian agricultural-pastoralist economies also opened molecular spaces for upwardly mobile rural entrepreneurs. Gradually commerce also created a thin layer of bureaucrats and professionals (schoolteachers, lawyers, policemen) staffing the towns across the Peruvian high plains. In the countryside a new breed of *misti* (mestizo) landowner cropped up. Poised on the interior "Indian frontier" of Peru's wool trade, these social-climbing sheep ranchers were the country-bumpkin counterparts of the exquisitely "civilized" merchant-aristocrats conducting the export wool trade out of the city of Arequipa. Both kinds of landowners – the white latifundists and the mestizo sheep farmers – owed their wealth and power to the booming wool export market and, ultimately, to their monopoly over Indian land and labor. But it was the self-made mestizo landowners who directly subjugated Indian clients and who, in their growing power and prosperity, seemed to violate all the standard ethnic and class markers that white urban aristocrats so carefully maintained. Much like the *tinterillo* who inhabited both sides of the ethnic-class divide, the sheep ranchers of the Peruvian *altiplano* retained or assimilated elements of Indian culture. As Nils Jacobsen writes, "the *gamonales* [new landowners] . . . constructed their own position in society both through intimacy with the peasant world, from whence many had come themselves, and through difference from that world."[53]

This emerging regional subculture created dissonant ethnic and class images. Travelers to the bleak backlands of Puno and Azángaro brought back jarring images of hispanizing Indian bosses growing wealthy by eliminating all rival buyers, or of white landowners who seemed to be "sinking" into Indian lifeways. It happened more than once that a European traveler, expecting to be greeted by a wealthy Creole hacendado at the gates of his sheep ranch, encountered instead a rustic man whose habits of life were almost indistinguishable from those of Indian peons who watched over his flocks and planted his potatoes. Anthropol-

[52] Nelson Manrique, *Yawar Mayu. Sociedades terratenientes serranas, 1879–1910* (Lima, 1988); Nils Jacobsen, *Mirages of Transition*, chap. 6; and Alberto Flores Galindo, *Arequipa y el sur andino, siglos XIII–XX* (Lima, 1977).

[53] *Mirages of Transition*, 333.

ogist François Bourricaud describes the experience of meeting one Señor López, a man of European descent and the proud owner of some 1,500 hectares of land in Azángaro. His rustic cultural style clashed with his ascribed racial identity. His lips stained green by coca, he spoke a country Spanish, laced with Quechua. He had an "Indian wife" and two small sons, wearing ponchos and barefooted. According to Bourricaud, he was a kind of *declassé* mestizo who had assimilated into Indian culture.[54]

This profile points to local transformations that broke down and rearranged rigid ethnic and class categories into something more fluid and complex in Peru's *altiplano*. Out of an amorphous group of *misti* landowners and merchants arose a new stereotype: the predatory *gamonal* landowner living off the miseries of Indian underlings. In racial terms this provincial élite crystallized into the archetypal highland mestizo. The social product of Peru's commercial wool revolution, which inflicted havoc on indigenous herding communities, the mestizo *gamonal* came to represent in nationalist discourses all that was backward and wrong with rural Peru. Rather than being the bearer of "civilization," the *gamonal* had refeudalized the countryside and, in the process, descended into barbaric (Indian) lifeways. By the early twentieth century, under the centralizing, paternalist regime of President Augusto Ongañía, nationalist rhetoric had constructed a convenient straw man in order to promote official *indigenismo*. (*Indigenismo*, a blanket term for movements claiming to speak for Amerindian interests, in this case refers to a program promoted by one regime.) In this version of rural reality, Indians became lost souls victimized by mestizos, entrapped in feudal estates, and in need of rescue by the Lima state.

There is a certain irony in the early twentieth-century *indigenista* view of the hapless and helpless Indian, because late nineteenth- and early twentieth-century Peru was in fact rocked by insurgent peasant threats of all kinds and intensities in both the Southern Highlands and the Central Sierra. Many southern wool zones erupted repeatedly in rebellion, reprisal, and counterreprisal along the cutting edge of the advancing estates. In 1895 Indian revolt spread across the high pastures of Chucuito, near the Bolivian border, while local newspapers blasted "race-war" alarms across their banner headlines. Further south, in the province of Azángaro, where estates steamrolled over common pastures, early twentieth-century

[54] François Bourricaud, *Cambios en Puno* (Mexico City, 1967); cited in Flores Galindo, *Arequipa y el sur andino*, 56.

reports of Indian agitation, uprisings, and massacres punctured the precarious social peace in 1911, 1912, and 1913. Multiple uprisings on estates in those years, from Cusco to Puno to Arequipa, climaxed in the massive peasant movement of 1915, led by the peripatetic visionary, Teodomiro Gutiérrez Cuevas, alias Rumi Maqui ('Stone Hand').

Equally important was the groundswell of subterranean, everyday forms of peasant resistance in both the center and periphery of Peru's wool districts after about 1870. Recent research lays bare the extreme vulnerability of local estates trying to colonize Indian peasant lands and labor in response to market incentives in the late nineteenth and early twentieth centuries. Much of this research has focused on those agrarian issues once shoved under the rubric of "the transition to capitalism" in rural Peru. Lately interest focuses more on peasant agency, popular culture, and consciousness.[55]

Even before the dynamic wool market stimulated capitalist transition in the domain of production, would-be hacendados were vexed by the endemic problem of "peasant resistance." Although there is no question but that the wool trade triggered a massive process of estate expansion on the Peruvian *altiplano*, it would be a mistake to assume the functioning of a mature land market at the end of the nineteenth century. As Nils Jacobsen writes: "A fully developed land market is intimately connected to the notion of private property, as defined by laws and sanctioned by the state's law enforcement and judicial agencies. Such a notion was not unequivocally accepted in the altiplano. Land invasions, vague land boundaries, and livestock rustling remained pandemic."[56] This state of affairs persisted well into the twentieth century.

Martínez-Alier's comment about the "basic conflict over the legitimacy of haciendas" applies as well to regions outside the southern wool districts in the late nineteenth century. The resilient traditions of communal land usage and peasant household economy in the Central Highlands, for example, served to block, and sometimes reverse, the rapid expansion of commercial estates. In the northern reaches of the Callejón de Huaylas, indigenous *estancias* ('ranches') still controlled most pastoral lands on the eve of the War of the Pacific. In the Mantaro Basin peasant

[55] Alberto Flores Galindo and Juan Martínez-Alier, for example, have studied the power of Indian shepherds (*huacchilleros*) to resist modernizing sheep hacendados wanting to rationalize their use of land and labor. See Martínez-Alier, *Los huacchilleros del Perú* (Lima, 1973), and Flores Galindo, *Arequipa y el sur andino*, 114–127. Also see Nils Jacobsen, *Mirages of Transition*, chap. 7.

[56] Ibid., 335.

communities had managed to keep Creole hacendados at arm's length at least until mid-century. Even during the commercial boom of the 1870s, the regional élite did not manage to "break through the barrier of peasant resistance."[57]

Historians have begun to document this state of affairs in microcosm. In the remote southwestern edge of the Mantaro Valley, for example, a raging war of drovers destroyed any illusions that legal entitlement (that is, possession by deed) meant control over land. By night, pastoralists often drove their sheep, oxen, and cattle onto "stolen" pastures. Outright occupation, not title deeds, defined the status of "effective possession." In practice the nominal landowner had to prove possession through the violent eviction of Indian herders and the impounding of their animals. This situation created private turf wars conducted on the edges of civil society. A title deed served not as a symbol of indisputable rights but as one of many weapons wielded in the struggle over land. Estate owners often armed their service tenants with clubs and rifles, or hired mestizo townspeople, to expel the encroachers and establish "effective possession" by driving their own herds onto the disputed lands and posting guards. Similar boundary wars raged across the Central Sierra after 1870.[58]

This ongoing contest over property claims, water rights, and grazing fees sabotaged and slowed the consolidation of commercial estates in the Central Sierra. Even by the late 1870s agrarian class balances remained more precarious and unstable in the Central Sierra than in either the Peruvian far north (where highland estates were more firmly entrenched) or the far south (where the commercial wool revolution was delivering Indian lands and herds to commercial middlemen). A fledgling landed oligarchy, diversifying holdings out of mining and guano and into cattle ranching, coveted the rich pastures. But most peasants were smallholding farmers and herders, living in rural communities and supplementing their home production with petty commerce, artisanry, and wage work. In the more commercially isolated and "Indian" region of Huaylas, provincial authorities continued to call upon highland estancias to send contingents of Indian workers to repair roads and buildings "for the republic." To the south, across the bustling Mantaro Basin, peasants also rendered unpaid labor services to local authorities. But they participated in the

57 Florencia Mallon, *The Defense of Community in Peru's Central Highlands: Peasant Struggle and Capitalist Transition, 1860–1940* (Princeton, 1983), 56.

58 Gavin Smith, *Livelihood and Resistance: Peasants and the Politics of Land in Peru* (Berkeley, 1989), 57.

buoyant regional marketing and mining networks that continued to thrive in the 1860s and 1870s.

Before the outbreak of war, then, there was no radical polarization between white aristocrats and dispossessed Indians in the Central Sierra. Here, the fledgling landed-ranching oligarchy remained vulnerable to the small arms fire of peasant resistance and sabotage. Furthermore, the distant Limeño élite proved too economically myopic, fickle, and weak to put muscle or mind behind anti-Indian laws and policies sanctioning private property as against community. Would-be estate magnates had to rely on their own retainers to carry out nocturnal land invasions and evictions.

The most important shift in agrarian class relations in the Central Highlands was more subtle. It flowed from the growing population of mestizo townspeople and landowners. A historic stronghold of cultural *mestizaje*, the region's peasantry became more economically stratified and culturally assimilated during the late nineteenth century. Regional commerce, mining, and bureaucracy opened new possibilities for bilingual *misti* social climbers who stitched together small-scale rural properties – usually on the outskirts of town and along river bottoms. They lived from localized trading, usury, or political and productive opportunities that arose from Peru's expanding market economy and successive coastal booms in guano and agriculture. Although this expansive regional economy attracted upwardly mobile peasants who could mediate capital, culture, and language, it ultimately reinforced ethnic and class differences. It widened the differences between town and country, valley and highland, jacket and poncho. As elsewhere *misti* fortunes in the Central Sierra often rode on the daily, grinding miseries of Indians. As a result local society remained tense and precarious in the Central Highlands in the antebellum period.[59]

[59] Historians tend to agree about the deleterious impact of rising *mestizaje* on the climate of ethnic and class relations in the antebellum years. Nelson Manrique, Florencia Mallon, and, more recently, Mark Thurner point to the acute tensions that gripped peasant communities on the eve of the Pacific War, as petty and powerful regional élites tried to control and channel peasant labor and land to their own ends. They underscore the explosion of rural conflicts over land, labor, and credit as the best barometer of deteriorating ethnic and class relations.

Manrique and Thurner also examine rural–town relations during traditional religious fiestas as political theater that revealed deepening tensions and disengagement between rural Indians and town mestizos. Both historians note the gradual change in the climate of religious–municipal fiestas. Rather than serving as socially cathartic moments in which Indians and mestizos collapsed the social distance between them, letting off steam and channeling hostility, religious fiestas became an arena of mutual hostility between the highland Indians and the valley–town-based

Patriots or Barbarians? Armed Peasants Advance Their Claims Against a Hostile Nation

When the War of the Pacific shattered this precarious peace in 1879, the nation's need to rely on an armed and mobilized peasantry – for the first time since the independence wars – radically altered power balances in the Central Sierra. The small-arms fire of agrarian conflict of the 1870s rapidly gave way to a far more dangerous military situation: the rise of autonomous peasant guerrilla bands in the midst of Chilean invasion, civil war, and the collapse of political authority across the entire Central Highlands from the northern reaches of Ancash to the southeastern corners of the Mantaro Valley near the border of Huancavelica. It was there – in the mountainous tucks and folds of the Ancash and Junín cordilleras – where the fate of the nation hung in the balance during 1881 and 1882. There the bloodiest dramas of war, repression, and revindication were played out.

If we are to understand the conflagration in the Central Highlands during the War of the Pacific (1879–1883), we need to set it briefly in broader historical context. The War of the Pacific pitted Peru and Bolivia against an imperialist Chile, bent upon annexing the guano- and nitrate-rich coastal territory of southern Peru and Bolivia. For the first time since the independence wars, Peru was invaded, occupied, and pillaged by a foreign army. Notwithstanding constant border disputes and territorial conquests during the nineteenth century, no other Andean republic experienced such a costly and humiliating defeat. Peru shared its ignominious defeat with Bolivia, which also incurred territorial loss (including its only corridor to the sea). But Bolivia escaped the ravages of military invasion, as Chile focused its attack on the larger, more powerful nation of Peru.

mestizos and *cholos*. The latter viewed the fiestas as menacing moments of invasion by the ponchoed Indians of the interior highlands. The saints' festivals allowed Indians to take over and remake the site and symbols of mestizo power in their own image (Mark Thurner, *From Two Nations to One Divided: The Contradictions of Nation-building in Andean Peru: The Case of Huaylas*, unpublished Ph.D. dissertation, University of Wisconsin, 1993, 393–394). This disussion was trimmed in the book version, *From Two Republics to One Divided* (Durham, North Carolina, 1995). Manrique in turn examines the efforts of the provincial council of Huancayo in 1880 to suppress the "baile de los Capitanes" and other dances, as well as bull runs and entire civil–religious festivals. These measures reveal the jittery nerves of Huancayo's political mestizo élite during the War of the Pacific. Mestizo and Creole townspeople increasingly saw saints' day as dangerous moments in the civil calendar, when the Indian barbarians came down into town (Manrique, *Yawar Mayu. Sociedades terratenientes serranas, 1879–1910*, 43–50).

A foreign army tore the nation apart, decimating entire regional economies and dividing the country among regional élites who ultimately failed to forge a common front against the enemy. They split over military and diplomatic strategies. The northern élites of Cajamarca pursued a policy of appeasement toward Chile, hoping to cut losses and consolidate their own powerbase. The main body of troops in the Central Sierra, however, stood fast against the invaders and increasingly looked upon their northern allies as little more than traitors. By 1883, then, the international conflict was rapidly devolving into a civil war between the northern army (under General Iglesias) and the motley "irregular troops" of General Andrés Cáceres, who controlled the Central Highlands. Ultimately Iglesias's victory drew Cáceres into a political pact and thus began the third phase of the war: political pacification, repression, and demobilization.

In short, the period of violent conflict and warfare evolved through several phases, extending well beyond the end of the so-called War of the Pacific: (1) Peru's defensive war against Chile's territorial invasion (1879–1883); (2) the implosion of Peruvian civil and regional warfare (1883–1884); and (3) the consolidation of allied military forces against the nation's "internal enemies" – armed and unruly peasants and plebeians, now branded as "bandits" and "barbarians" (1884–1890). Thus Chilean aggression provoked the unraveling of fragile paternalist and coercive bonds that had barely contained ethnic and class hatreds during the 1860s and 1870s. The war initially catalyzed masses of rural peoples, creating a series of ephemeral yet pivotal opportunities for peasant-soldiers to grab the political limelight, forge multiethnic alliances, and force alternative visions and power constellations onto the political landscape – until the republic turned irreversibly against them.

The War of the Pacific soon left the sea lanes to become a campaign of territorial conquest engulfing the Northern and Central Highlands of Peru. In June 1880, after Chile took the southern port of Arica and effectively annexed Peru's southern nitrate-rich province of Tarapacá, her ships sailed up the coast to begin battering Peruvian ports, cities, and plantations. By early 1881, as Lima lay smoldering, 22,000 Chilean soldiers crossed a Maginot Line drawn in the coastal sands. So began a 3-year-long military occupation. Although Chile had no imperialist designs beyond its southern territorial conquest, it needed to bring Peru to the negotiating table.

Blocking Chile's way was the military commander, General Andrés Cáceres. After Lima's fall in 1881, he had retreated to the Central Highlands to begin organizing a national "campaign of resistance." His retreat into the province of Junín made sense for two reasons. First, the Central Highlands continued to serve as the main inland route from Lima. Just as the foreign liberators had found in the 1820s, the Chilean invaders had to control this corridor if they were to bring down Peru. Second, Cáceres himself had deep family roots in the Central Sierra. He could call on an extensive clientele network to build and supply his regular armies.

The beginning of Cáceres' resistance campaign inevitably thrust the peasant communities of the greater Mantaro Valley into the middle of the war. Almost immediately, the general required that they provide monthly quotas of potatoes, corn, cattle, and other food to feed his ragtag armies. Meanwhile estate owners in the northern areas of Junín began organizing and arming their own peasant clienteles to defend the region and nation against the foreign enemy. Under Cáceres' leadership they were to fight a defensive guerrilla campaign, relying on their knowledge of the land and village support networks. Even so, the regular armies of Cáceres, which numbered no more than 1500, were unprepared for the brutal realities of Chilean invasion (Fig. 23.9). Between 1881 and 1882 thousands of Chilean soldiers moved into the Central Highlands in two separate invasion forces. The second one, carried out in early 1882, was particularly devastating. Some 3,000 enemy soldiers combed the countryside looking for provisions and booty, all the while threatening to burn down the city of Huancayo if the hacendados did not meet their demands. Cáceres's armies retreated to Ayacucho, leaving the Central Highlands wide open to Chilean pillage and terrorism.

This proved to be a pivotal moment in the war, because both regional élites and peasants started to take matters into their own hands. Throughout 1882 peasant villages began to organize guerrilla bands (*montoneras*) to fight the Chileans. Although poorly armed and vastly outnumbered, they managed to inflict casualties, capture weapons, and erode the confidence of the Chilean patrols. In fact, in their sporadic rear-guard actions, the guerrillas waged the famous "resistance campaign" in the absence of Cáceres and his regular army, which had retreated temporarily from the region. In the eyes of the region's landowning élite, however, the specter of armed guerrilla fighters was terrifying. Their sudden rise to power as resistance fighters – free to roam the countryside, invade estates and

Figure 23.9. A Peruvian foot-soldier, his *Rabona,* and a cavalryman on the eve of the War of the Pacific. In the text that accompanies this engraving, E. George Squier, in his magesterial travelogue (*Peru: Incidences of Travel and Exploration in the Land of the Incas* [New York: Harper and Brothers, 1877], 46–47), expressed the profound moral ambivalence that most "enlightened" foreigners and creole nationalists felt towards Peruvian Indians who apparently were "brave but stupid," "patriotic but apolitical" – suitable, in other words, for soldiery but not citizenship. He wrote, "The Peruvian soldiers are tractable, and, if well led, as brave as any in the world. The native Indian tenacity and stubbornness are excellent elements in the composition of the soldier. Almost every Peruvian foot-soldier is attended by his *rabona,* who may be, but is not generally, his wife. She marches with him, cooks and mends for him, often carries his knapsack, sometimes his musket, and always the little roll of matting which, when unfolded and supported on a couple of sticks, constitutes his tent. It is of little moment on which side the Indian fights. He knows nothing about the political squabbles of the country, and cares less" (46–47).

towns, control the highways, and demand provisions, ammunition, and booty from merchants and hacendados – seemed far more threatening than the presence of the Chilean army.

Many merchants and landowners soon began to conspire against the peasant-soldiers, hoping for an early peace agreement with Chile that would restore order to the countryside. In the meantime the soldiers saw the writing on the wall. Although there is some controversy among historians over the timing, patterns, and motivations of peasant invasions of rural properties, there is little doubt that by mid-1882 the guerrillas began to look upon regional élites as "Peruvian traitors." By then Cáceres had returned to command the military campaign against Chile, but now he continued to rely on the peasant-guerrillas to rout the Chileans and punish their Peruvian collaborators. It was during the winter months of 1882 that guerrilla activity became more violent and menacing toward collaborationist landlords, particularly in the southern Mantaro Valley. As nationalist resistance fighters, the peasant guerrillas empowered themselves to take reprisals against the "traitorous" landlords, who had forsaken the nationalist front to save their own skins and properties. It is not surprising to find that many of those properties in the southern Mantaro were high *puna* regions only recently (and dubiously) acquired through enclosure and legal chicanery.

Here, then, was an extraordinary political opportunity: to turn their patriotic struggle against their own immediate class enemies and, in the name of national defense, legitimately appropriate crops, cash, and livestock to feed their own armies and, in some cases, even reclaim stolen lands for their villages. It is in this moment of national and regional crisis, Florencia Mallon argues, "with class and national concerns intermingled and reverberating against each other, . . . [that] the various land invasions and other actions in the area must be viewed."[60]

The Central Highlands thus became the main theater of national resistance and class warfare between 1881 and 1883. But while peasant soldiers were fighting against the Chilean invaders and Peruvian collaborators, a new threat to the patriotic forces of Cáceres loomed on the northern horizon. In 1882 General Miguel Iglesias, a wealthy hacendado from Cajamarca, organized a "Free North Government" and began to negotiate the terms of surrender to Chile. Iglesias wanted to cut Peru's

[60] Florencia Mallon, *The Defense of Community in Peru's Central Highlands*, 98. See also her book, *Peasant and Nation. The Making of Postcolonial Mexico and Peru* (Berkeley, 1995), ch. 6.

losses, and Peru's wealthy bankers, planters, and politicians supported him. They found natural allies among the landed élites of the Central Sierra, who feared the onslaught of "guerrilla-bandits." For Cáceres and many others, however, the 1883 Treaty of Ancón mocked his military campaign and disgraced the nation. No less important to the ambitious Cáceres, it catapulted the Iglesias faction into the presidency in 1883. The general now turned his war efforts against this partisan enemy. International conflict rapidly turned into civil war.

The formal end to the Pacific War in October 1883, then, did not restore the social peace. It unleashed the second phase of warfare. As drought worsened conditions in late 1883 and 1884, the civil war between Iglesias and Cáceres raged across the Mantaro Valley. The *montoneras* continued invading estates and combing the land for arms, livestock, and other meager provisions. To make matters worse, crops failed, food prices spiraled, and hunger spread. Even where estates and villages were not burned or abandoned, there was nothing left to sustain the escalating civil war between Iglesias and Cáceres. Military commanders resorted to draconian measures, wrecking local economies for years to come.

In the meantime the shifting tides of partisan warfare during 1883–1884 dealt a lethal blow to the Mantaro guerrilla movements. Already by early 1884, Peru's faction-ridden élites were beginning to put aside their differences and close ranks against the growing threat of rural anarchy in the Central Highlands. In June 1884 Cáceres turned his back on his own peasant-soldiers to forge tactical alliances with Iglesias and other powerholders. The civil war was over. Cáceres could capitalize on his heroic resistance efforts, but only if he threw his weight behind coastal oligarchs and serrano landlords. He especially needed the landowners in his own province of Junín to support his bid for political power. And to win it he had to crush the guerrillas who had once defended the nation in his name. This he did in one brutal gesture. In July 1884, barely a month after Cáceres agreed to honor the infamous Treaty of Ancón, he captured, tried, and executed a guerrilla leader, Tomás Laimes, and his three aides in a plaza of Huancayo.

With the public massacre Cáceres launched a military and rhetorical campaign of repression. Later, as president, he turned the full force of his office against the *montoneras*. In May 1886 he joined a conspiracy of officials to discredit the guerrillas and expunge them from the official memory of war heroes. Stripped of their status as patriots and veterans, the guerrillas were transfigured into "savage hordes and common criminals" who preyed upon the peace-loving landlords and peons of the region. As we shall see shortly, this effort to barbarianize the *montoneras* was not simply a feeble attempt to legitimate state violence against the guerrillas. It was part of a deeper debate within Creole political and literary circles over the culprits and causes of Peru's humiliating defeat.

But however Cáceres himself tried to justify his military aggression against the guerrillas, he underestimated their capacity to survive. Postwar pacification became the most protracted phase of Peru's crisis. As late as 1888, guerrillas still occupied dozens of estates, stretching along the length of the Central Highlands – from Cerro de Pasco in the north to the southern edge of the Mantaro. One of the last strongholds of guerrilla resistance was the peasant confederation of Comas, located in the isolated eastern mountains beyond Jauja. But like any semi-autonomous "*republiqueta*" (self-governing area unofficially detached from the state) or large maroon community, its existence fundamentally threatened the basis of national sovereignty, particularly in a fragmented and war-torn land like Peru. Inevitably the Comas federation became the target of state violence and cooptation. In 1902, long after Cáceres was gone, Lima's strategy of combined negotiation and repression finally smashed it.

It is worth pausing for a moment to consider the political experiences and discourses of the Comas and Acobamba guerrillas during the 1880s. Having born the brunt of the war, they emerged as the most autonomous guerrilla movement throughout the Central Sierra. More than other armed peasants, they came to understand the changing significance of the international and civil wars for themselves and their own communities. In 1881 they bore witness to the atrocities committed by the Chileans against their lands and people, and they organized the first successful military strikes against them. Therein lay the wellspring of an incipient "peasant patriotism," which expressed itself in their words and deeds. But just as they assumed the gravest burdens of national defense, becoming the ragged vanguard of Cáceres's floundering resistance movement, they saw the regional élite begin to cave in to Chilean demands. In their eyes treasonous landlords not only compromised the nation's honor before the Chilean "bandits" but denied what was most precious to the guerrilla fighters: their hard-won dignity and legitimacy as patriotic "citizen-soldiers." In an extraordinary communication sent to a prominent hacendado in April 1882, the Acobamba guerrillas exploded the hypocrisy of traitors like him, who "are in this province communicating and giving explanations on how they can ruin the Peruvians, to those treacherous

Chilean bandit invaders." Meanwhile, they wrote, hacendados had the audacity to stigmatize the guerrilla patriots as "barbarians" just because "we with reason and justice unanimously rose up to defend our homelands." Their written words express barely controlled anger and disdain. Yet the peasant correspondents were careful to couch their outrage in reasoned, even defensive, language. The letter concluded by denying that they had committed barbarous acts: In wartime, they argued, "any hacendado should be able to tolerate us [peasant guerrillas] as patriotic soldiers."[61]

An eloquent cry for justice, this letter reveals the racial and class antagonisms that cut deeply into the national front against Chilean extortions and occupation in early 1882. But, as Mallon suggests, this letter also hints at the political hopes and moral expectations that newly empowered veterans harbored: to command the tolerance and respect that the nation owed them as veterans of the campaign of La Breña. They demanded entry into the nation as citizens, not just as territorial inhabitants, in return for having spilled their own blood to defend Peru. And in so doing they constituted themselves as political subjects engaging nationalist ideals of honor and self-sacrifice to press their own alternative, inclusive notions of citizenship. This collective sense of moral empowerment and self-confidence, and their ability to subvert the codes of political virtue to justify their rites of violence, were precisely what became intolerable to the regional and national élites.[62]

Only 200 miles to the north of the Mantaro Basin, another political drama of war, rebellion, and repression unfolded along the Callejón de Huaylas. The agrarian crisis of 1883–1884 had been devastating for the

[61] Quotations in Florencia Mallon, *The Defense of Community in Peru's Central Highlands*, 89–90.

[62] As the cockpit of peasant politics and insurgent discourse, the Mantaro guerrilla movements of the 1880s and 1890s have been the subject of a lively, ongoing historical debate. At base the debate engages theoretical notions of peasant mentalities and the historical conditions that gave rise to translocal political coalitions and consciousness. The Mantaro guerrillas hold particular interest precisely because, for a brief period, they used the crisis of the Peruvian state to forge multiethnic solidarities, subvert the authority of regional landlords, and capture the public forum to redefine the very notions of civic virtue and citizenship in opposition to the oligarchic state. On this point historians tend to agree.

Where consensus breaks down is around three questions: (1) the genuine "nationalist" content of the Mantaro guerrilla movement; (2) its regional exceptionalism; and (3) the ambiguous legacies of peasant insurgency and guerrilla warfare for the regions and villages involved and, more generally, for the nation in the postwar years. For a lively exchange, see Heraclio Bonilla, "The Indian peasantry and 'Peru' during the war with Chile," in Steve J. Stern, *Resistance, Rebellion, and Consciousness in the Andean Peasant World*, 219–231, and Florencia Mallon, "Nationalist and anti-state coalition in the War of the Pacific: Junín and Cajamarca, 1879–1902," ibid., 232–279. See also Florencia Mallon's *Peasant and Nation*, 230–242.

region. And just as the drought cracked open the fields, the heat of civil war cracked open a weak social modus vivendi. Towns and villages along the Callejón de Huaylas were subjected to successive military requistions and cash-raising campaigns. Amidst these hardships local Creole authorities suddenly decided to enforce the collection of the 1879 war-tax. This double "poll-tax" (a quasi-tributary tax that carried none of the customary rights or privileges associated with Indian tributary status) was to prove the flashpoint of rebellion. The town of Huaylas exploded in a mass of rural and urban uprisings that briefly turned the whole Callejón de Huaylas into a cauldron of insurgency and repression.

On the surface the political events of state violence and Indian rebellion in Huaylas appear to have all the hallmarks of a classic anticolonial rebellion: state violence against Indian villages (a double poll-tax, heaped on top of customary *corvée* labor obligations and military impressment); Indian petitions for tax relief, met by the imprisonment and torture of the petitioners' chief *vara* (traditional officer), known as Atusparia; and the explosion of ethnic revindication against local "bad government," culminating in popular defeat at the hands of army troops dispatched from Lima. Furthermore the main target of Indian violence – the prefectural archive – was a powerful symbol of Indian grievances against heavy taxes. In short, Indian insurgency in Huaylas would appear to be a defensive, conservative Indian rebellion – in contrast to the precocious peasant nationalists of the Mantaro region, who were plunged into the middle of the War of the Pacific.

To understand these regional contrasts, whether superficial or not, it is important to set this insurgent movement – the so-called Atusparia rebellion of 1885 – into the regional and cultural context of nineteenth-century Huaylas. How did preexisting local power relations and political-cultural traditions of struggle shape indigenous responses to war-related pressures and events? How did the particular contingency of national events, particularly during the civil war phase, bear upon the internal evolution of Huaylas political strategies, agendas, and horizons as they were thrust into the national arena of struggle after 1885? The Huaylas case is particularly interesting because it clarifies precisely how the rise of ethnic militancy necessarily implicated the morality of nation building as it affected indigenous citizens.

That this insurgent movement originally coalesced around indigenous leaders and concerns in part reflects the fact that preexisting power relations in Huaylas were still negotiated largely through ethnic intermediaries. Mark Thurner notes that most Indians in Huaylas were semi-independent smallholders, grouped in land-hungry *estancias*, administered by rotating Indian authorities directly subordinate to provincial officials.[63] These village headmen served a vital function in provisioning *corvée* laborers for local public works projects. On the other hand, many of those communities had recently lost their use rights to alpine pastures, woodlands, and glacial ice, under a new wave of land privatization and enclosure. These local power dynamics set the initial parameters of Indian negotiation and protest when the war came to Huaylas in early 1885.

All that was needed was a precipitant: one more assault on Indian integrity and self-respect. That came in early 1885. Under the leadership of Pedro Pablo Atusparia, recently elected to the highest office of his rural district Independencia, the *varayuq* ('staffholder') of Huaylas submitted a petition asking for a 50 percent reduction of the "double poll tax" and more time to deliver the updated tribute lists. Prefect Noriega choked off all discussion. He had Atusparia seized, imprisoned, tortured, and made to "confess" his guilt. And in a brutal gesture hailing from the colonial Inquisition, Atusparia's jailers cut off his braid (a symbol of chiefly rank and authority) to make a mule's cinch. After a second delegation of Indians confronted intransigent authorities, they resorted to direct actions. Thousands of Huaylas peasants converged on the mountain slopes surrounding the provincial capital of Huaraz in March 1885. Noriega's belated concessions could not contain peasant political violence.

As in the Mantaro Valley, the complex alchemy of war, betrayal, and partisan politics shoved Huaylas peasants into the center of national turmoil. But they experienced neither the empowerment nor the ultimate betrayal of Cáceres's resistance movement, which first emboldened and then embittered the Mantaro guerrillas. The Huaylas people came face to face with the war only through the coerced extortions of local authorities, long after the Chilean invaders had gone home. Huaylas peasants were targeted for tax hikes because they were "Indians." They were not called up to join a national resistance campaign as "citizens" or "patriots" fighting against Chilean bandits. And when faced with a double war-tax slapped on them during a terrible drought, they resorted to the time-worn rituals of Indian protest, carried over from colonial times, to mount

[63] Thurner, *From Two Republics to One Divided*, 91–92.

a collective defense against this new tyranny. Thus the Huaylas villages initially shaped their politics of protest in response to the real and symbolic violence they experienced at the hands of the provincial state, and by wielding the well-worn political and discursive weapons at their disposal.

Such vivid images of localized Indian protest soon fade into the background, however. What began as revindicatory violent actions by aggrieved Indians soon evolved into a transregional, multiethnic, multiclass movement that harnessed ethnic defensiveness, memories, and moral legitimacy to broader political goals and historical consciousness. Three aspects reveal the 1885 Atusparia rebellion as far more complex, dynamic, and significant than once thought: its fluid and heterogeneous social makeup; the submergence of political violence in broader indigenous strategies of legal petition and negotiation before the provincial and national state; and the volatile mixture of ethnic and constitutional idioms with which Indians articulated their political grievances, claims, and visions in an effort to reach rapprochement with the state after military defeat.

First, the notion of a discrete "Indian rebellion" ignores the fact that the Huaylas rebels were plunged into the larger theater of war raging between Iglesias and Cáceres in the early 1880s, and the fact that this civil war pulled dissident elements from all niches of the region's ethnic-class hierarchy. William Stein notes that the movement attracted peasants and plebeians, Indians from estancias and *misti* townspeople – hardly the undifferentiated *indiada* ('native mob') that Lima newspapers depicted in 1885.[64] The escalation of violence also spawned guerrilla fighters only tenuously connected to Atusparia.[65] The movement's heterogenous eth-

[64] William Stein, "Town and country in revolt: Fragments from the Province of Carhuaz on the Atusparia uprising of 1885 (Callejón de Huaylas), *Actes du XLIIe Congrés International des Américanistes* (Paris, 1976), 3:171–187.

In sheer geographic scope the uprising eventually came to encompass the entire interior of the department of Ancash. In the early months of 1885, it spread like wildfire through the river valley, from the department's capital of Huaraz, to the towns of Yungay, Carhuaz, and Caraz, and fanned out across the Cordillera Negra and the Pacific slopes. How many people participated in the movement is unknown. Alarmist reports from Lima inflated the rebels into some 20,000 or more, branding them all as "Indian hordes." However suspect those numbers, historians have documented the rebellion's expansive regional scope and heterogeneous makeup. (See Thurner, *From Two Republics to One Divided*, ch. 6)

[65] Although most historical accounts have affixed the name of Atusparia to this movement, local oral histories often remember "Uchcu Pedro" (or "Tunnel Pedro") as the more colorful and heroic leader. Not an Indian peasant, but a "tough-minded mine operator and trader" of some

nic and class composition could be seen in the faces and actions of its leaders. Upon seizing Huaraz, Atusparia rebuilt the provincial government. Among others, he appointed two prominent Creoles: Manuel Mosquera, a lawyer, and Luís Felipe Montestruque, a journalist, writer, and orator. Both men joined the movement partly out of partisan interest. The Indian rebels had assaulted the prefect, a diehard Iglesista, and thus stood on the side of Cáceres, who by 1885 was en route to the presidency. These alliances at the top were politically convenient to all parties for a brief period. Atusparia's delegation of authority to Indians and mestizos was a fascinating, albeit brief, moment of provincial reconstruction under the *vara*'s leadership. In any event this insurgent movement soon escalated into a broad regional movement caught up in the chaos of Peru's civil war.

Second, if we expand the temporal scope beyond the early months of 1885 when popular political violence reached its apex, we can see how those violent incidents were embedded in an ongoing, contentious history of political engagement by Huaylas peasants, and how the rituals of violence and justice were part of the same repertory of political struggle that Indians had improvised and deployed for generations. On this point Mark Thurner's recent study is enlightening. He shows that between 1886 and 1889, the *varayuq* of Huaylas waged a paper campaign – petitioning and litigating for various reformist and restorative measures. Conventional historical accounts that focus on the violent episodes of the Atusparia rebellion tend to overlook the crucial political war-of-words that Atusparia and other traditional officers waged in the mid-and late 1880s. Unlike the Mantaro rebels who broke rank with Cáceres once he betrayed them, the Huaylas insurgents continued to manipulate partisan and paternalist strategies to wrest small concessions from him. Just as

wealth, Uchcu Pedro emerged as the most fearsome guerrilla leader. He fought alongside Atusparia, taking one river valley town after another in March 1885. And after Atusparia was wounded and captured, Uchcu Pedro and his forces escaped into the highlands. Ensconced in the high sierras of the Cordillera Negra, he continued to raid and attack valley towns and estates even after government troops came to pacify the region. The guerrilla-miner called their bluff and soon became a legend in the local lore of Huaraz. Eventually he was coaxed down from the mountains, ambushed, and executed in September 1885.

In his monumental work on crowds in Peruvian history, Jorge Basadre described an epic figure standing tall before his executioners at the bitter end of the rebellion (Basadre, *La multitud, la ciudad, y el campo en la historia del Perú* [Lima, 1947], 248). The fate of Atusparia is shrouded in ambiguity, on the other hand. As he died neither in battle nor before the firing squad, but perhaps in disgrace and by his own hand, Atusparia did not cut such a defiant, honorable, or colorful figure as did Uchcu Pedro in the local lore. See William Stein, "Town and country in revolt: Fragments from the Province of Carhuaz on the Atusparia uprising of 1885," 177 and 180.

their ancestors had trekked over the mountains to the viceregal courts and palaces of Lima, the *varayuq* of Huaylas traveled down to the coast, seeking audiences with the supreme commander, "Tayta Cáceres" ('Father Cáceres' in Quechua). Among other things, their petitions defined the terms under which the Indians would deliver, or not, the poll-tax and *corvée* labor to the republic. In particular they demanded a reduction of the poll-tax that Cáceres had tried to reimpose in 1886. But as we shall see, this petition campaign raised issues that transcended localist concerns. In effect it bid the republican state to restore its authority over Indian peoples, as their protector and ultimate arbiter. Rather than turn inward to create an alternative, oppositional *republiqueta* as did the Comas peasants in the same period, the peasants of Huaylas continued to accommodate themselves as Indian subjects of the Peruvian state. Ultimately they sought a return to "good government." Toward that end they defined a covenant under which Cáceres would bestow republican rights including material and cultural conditions necessary for their villages to survive. In the end their threats and petitions scared off the republican tax collectors and other authorities until early in the twentieth century. Thurner writes that "for two decades after 1885 Indian peasants in Huaylas successfully resisted what they considered to be the illegitimate exactions of an unprotective state."[66]

Third, observing indigenous politics before and after the uprising widens our perspectives of Huaylas people's political aspirations and values. In particular peasant political thought can be gleaned from the petitions that they pressed upon provincial and central authorities during the mid-1880s. Although the petitions were drawn up and submitted by *misti* lawyers and signed with the thumb-stamps of dozens of *varayuq*, they show how the Huaylas leaders improvised political strategies and rhetoric to curry favor with the President-Protector Cáceres and, at the same time, map out the moral principles by which the republic could rightly ask Indians to pay taxes, give labor, and otherwise participate in the nation as Indian subjects and citizens. Their petitions went far beyond their request for tax relief, land rights, and good local government. They imply a dissenting vision of politics as social contract.

By 1886 and 1887, long after Atusparia had retired from the political scene, the *varas* mounted a scathing moral critique of the Peruvian republic. They argued that the republic had violated all the protective

[66] Thurner, *From Two Republics to One Divided*, 128–129.

laws and policies toward Indians since the time of independence, and that with the abolition of tribute, the government had become its own worst enemy. They had "watched with pain as [mestizos and Spaniards] began to place obstacles in the . . . exercise of [their] rights, pretending that the community of pastures, wooded ravines, and waters had disappeared." Why, they asked rhetorically in the 1887 petition, should they give tribute and labor when they received in return only misery, hunger, and hardship?[67] "Insurgent nostalgia," was of course only part of a rhetorical arsenal that indigenous mediators had used since the beginning of the republican era. But in the postwar period of Chilean invasion and national humiliation, racial hysteria, and ongoing regional guerrilla warfare, the Huaylas peasants' petition campaign crystallized a powerful historical critique of Peru's experiment in nineteenth-century nation making. Not only did these dignified peasants indict the hypocritical élites for not recognizing their patriotic contributions to the republic before and during the Pacific War, but they framed a dissident history of the republic to challenge the moral basis of the posttributary state. Already in the 1880s the politics of ethnicity were beginning to implicate the ethics of nationalism.

Banishing Indians from History and the Nation

The Mantaro and Huaylas peasant movements had repercussions far beyond the Central Highlands during the last two decades of the century. They forced the Lima élite to confront the full measure of their failure as nation builders. Not only had the country suffered defeat under the guns of Chile, but it had seen its own rural masses rise up and destroy the legitimacy of republican law and order at a moment of national crisis. In 1885 newspapers reported gruesome details of "race wars" raging in the highlands of Huaylas and Mantaro. The "Indian race" soon became a convenient and favorite scapegoat for the republic's debacle. By the late 1880s and 1890s, coffeehouse talk had hardened into official history: It became self-evident among Peruvian élites that the war was lost because Indians, by their nature, were unmoved by sentiments of patriotism or civic virtue. In a letter written to Cáceres immediately after the war, Ricardo Palma, a popular folklorist-belletrist, crystallized this sentiment:

[67] Ibid., 112–113.

> The principal cause of the great defeat is that the majority of Peru is composed of a wretched and degraded race that you once attempted to dignify and ennoble. The Indian lacks a patriotic sense; he is a born enemy of the white and of the man of the coast. It makes no difference to him whether he is a Chilean or a Turk. To educate the Indian and to inspire in him a feeling for patriotism will not be the task of our institutions, but of the ages.[68]

This position was more pessimistic perhaps than some. Certainly there were various diagnoses and debates about the quintessential Indian character and the problems it posed to the nation. But amidst postwar angst, those debates grew sharper and more intense. On the one hand, imported theories of biological determinism allowed scientists, writers, and politicians to exercise more authority over issues concerning the "Indian race." European immigration assumed more importance, even urgency. On the other hand, hard-line racial theorists found worthy rivals among a younger generation of liberals and radical dissidents, who pointed to deep-rooted social causes of Indian backwardness. Among them were a group of social scientists in Lima who proposed the assimilation of Peruvian Indians toward a homogenizing national community. Like the Civilistas of the early 1870s, they advocated massive state investment in rural education, communication, and industry in order to open up the sierran backlands and integrate Indians into the national fold. A leading politician made the case succinctly: "Through wise tutelage, we must make the Indian a laborer or a soldier to liberate him from his local traditions and from his depressing and drab setting."[69] Order and progress depended on these reforms, and so now, it seemed, did national sovereignty.

Manuel González Prada and Clorinda Matto de Turner stood out among the more militant social critics and reformers of this period. In their writings and speeches, they tried to prick the conscience of the oligarchy. Although they shared the prevailing belief that Peru had lost the war because Indians were devoid of patriotism, they put the blame on Peru's antiquated feudal oligarchy. It was the highland *gamonal* in particular who was responsible for the degradation of Indians. In her best-selling novel, *Aves sin nidos* ('*Birds Without Nests*'), Matto de Turner threw open a window on that remote feudal-colonial world, shaded by

[68] Quoted in Efraín Kristal, *The Andes Viewed from the City: Literary and Political Discourse on the Indian in Peru, 1848–1930* (New York, 1987), 97.

[69] Quoted in Frederick Pike, *The Modern History of Peru* (New York, 1967), 183.

her childhood memories, to expose the brutality and exploitation that Indians endured at the hands of landlords and their agents (corrupt judges, governors, and priests). On pragmatic grounds Matto de Turner and González Prada (and other neo-positivists) advocated a renovated and aggressive national state to bring in foreign capital, industry, and technology to break the back of Peru's landed oligarchy. They believed that emancipated Indians were capable of being educated and assimilated. In the short run, however, the enlightened white man's burden was to protect Indians from abusive treatment.

This strain of muckraking and reformism was to inspire later incarnations of *indigenismo* (particularly the writings of José Carlos Mariátegui), as well as the reforms undertaken by the second administration of Augusto Leguía in the 1920s. By then, too, Cuzco intellectuals were engaged in a project of regional self-discovery that lay claim to the nation's authentic cultural patrimony in contradistinction to Lima's centralizing europeanizing self-image. Invoking the region's Inka heritage, Cuzco's cultural vanguard projected a noble "Quechua race" of Indians onto the national imaginary (Fig. 23.10). This redemptive racial discourse flourished in the first decades of the twentieth century, a time when much of Latin America was forging national cultures rooted in their own interior (non-European) soul and soil and in the prehispanic past. In the immediate aftermath of the War of the Pacific, however, Peru's pro-Indian dissidents confronted the virulent racism and intransigence of the fractured oligarchy eager to rebuild its power base and legitimacy. Eventually (although under different circumstances) both González Prada and Matto de Turner grew more pessimistic about the prospects of the "Indian race" and the nation. González Prada left Peru for Paris in 1891 and returned in 1898, newly armed with revolutionary socialist ideas. Matto de Turner fell from grace in 1895 after Piérola returned to the presidency, and she went into a lonely exile until her death. But they left a legacy of social criticism that began to chart a way toward national regeneration.

One of the bitter ironies of postwar Peru is that Lima's élite – from the conservative to the iconoclastic – wrote Indians out of the national script as potential or proven political subjects. As the official story of Peru's defeat crystallized around the image of the ignorant, apathetic Indian, the "Indian race" became seen as unfit for citizenship. Silenced, suppressed, or forgotten were the voices of Andean peasants – from the rebels of Ancash to the guerrillas of Junín – who had inserted themselves into the middle of the nation's crisis and empowered themselves as

Figure 23.10. Portrait of a Quechua Man in Cuzco, ca. 1909. This photograph (photographer unknown) represents a subtle aesthetic variation from the standard form of late nineteenth-century *cartes de visite*. It places its emphasis not on the purported occupation or emotional disposition of the indigenous subject, but on the material artifacts that depict (in a disembodied, decontextualized way) the semblance of a *cultural* identity. Posing before the ornate colonial doors of a church or monastery, gazing with head held high at distant (utopian) horizons, dressed in rustic *bayeta* clothing, and surrounded by the accoutrements of country life, this man exudes a certain sense of nobility and dignity in his exoticism, indicative of the emerging bohemian and regionalist *indigenism* of Cuzco that began to flourish in the early twentieth century. (On this regionalist-indigenist aesthetic, see Poole, *Vision, Race, and Modernity*, ch. 7.) Reprinted with permission from the Peabody Museum of Archaeology and Ethnology, Harvard University.

patriotic soldiers, taxpayers, and laborers of the republic. The new orthodoxy widened the political, cultural, and biological distance between the highland Indians and the coastal (or urban) whites. Race differences came to be seen as immutable, and the Indian problem as intractable. In a country where most people were still considered to be Indian and therefore beyond the bounds of nation and civilization, in a republic that had just been brought to its knees by foreign invaders, how could Peru enter the company of modern nations? There, in brief, was the social dilemma that Peruvian intellectuals had created for themselves toward the end of the nineteenth century. Cultural *mestizaje* offered no obvious solution, because most reformers considered the social-climbing mestizo to be a pariah, barely a leap beyond the Indian on the evolutionary scale. Postwar racist discourses had no way of positioning the mestizo as the unifying, or healing, race to help in the project of national reconstruction and political reopening. Postwar recovery and reconstruction turned into a lost opportunity for reinventing Peru around more inclusive principles of nationhood. Like its neighbor to the south, Peru carried into the early twentieth century the dead weight of its violent, repressive, and exclusivist republican past. Yet out of the tortured experiences of nineteenth-century nation building there also sprang twentieth-century indigenous political movements capable of engaging and contesting the modernizing state (see Chap. 25).

BOLIVIA: DANGEROUS PACTS, INSURGENT INDIANS

Bolivia followed a perilous path toward order and progress between the 1860s and 1890s. Half-hearted experiments in nation building were imposed on a pluri-ethnic society still fundamentally organized around colonial-caste relationships. But as liberalizing Creoles pressed their agenda on Quechua- and Aymara-speaking communities, they set the republic onto a collision course that would culminate in civil war and Indian insurgency in the final years of the nineteenth century. Daily forms of agrarian violence and occasional uprisings intensified in the 1870s and 1880s. But it was the 1899 Federalist War, complicated by the massive uprising of Aymara peoples across the northern *altiplano*, that proved to be as cathartic a moment for Bolivia as was the War of the Pacific for Peru. This *fin-de-siècle* crisis catapulted the northern liberal oligarchy into power and unleashed powerful market forces throughout Northern Highland Bolivia. War and rebellion also polarized the nation as never before, dispossessing Indians of their territorial and communal heritages and making them social outcasts in their own land.

The roots of escalating violence between native Andean communities and the Bolivian state after 1860 lay deep in the subsoil of corporate Indian communities, which survived and even flourished under the early tributary republic. Demography was one root. Grieshaber has found an unexpected Indian population tendency in his study of the tribute registers compiled periodically between the 1830s and 1870s. In brief he found a remarkable revival of highland Indian communities in the regions of La Paz, Oruro, and Potosí (the homes of 80 percent of Bolivia's Indians) in spite of overall population decline. Between 1838 and 1877 the *comunero* population (that is, village or *ayllu*-based) grew by 24 percent – even after successive waves of epidemic. In contrast the population of tributaries languished on estates, declining by 4 percent over the same period. Overall, Indian tributaries increasingly adhered to freeholding communities, increasing from 68 percent of all tribute-paying Indians in 1838 to 75 percent in 1877.

At the end of the independence wars, Indian *ayllu*-communities deployed multiple tactics to restore or protect territorial and political jurisdictions granted by the colonial caste system. Many advocated the return to idealized "tributary-land pacts" of remote colonial Hapsburg times, albeit without full legal jurisdictions or hereditary native lordships. Early republican leaders bowed to indigenous protest (as well as to the general anti-liberal sentiment and immediate revenue needs of the government). Where Peru and Ecuador restored only half the "tributary pact" (by reimposing the Indian head tax without legalizing communal lands), Bolivia's de facto policy continued to respect corporate rights. President Ballivián's reformulation of Indians as long-term "usufructs" (*enfiteutas*) gave the state theoretical ownership of communal lands in 1842 but did little to threaten customary rights and jurisdictions. Prudent fiscal policy also dictated against it. By the 1840s tribute accounted for close to 40 percent of state revenues. Bolivia's strong protectionist policies continued to shelter Indian producers, traders, and pack drivers from foreign competition.[70] In the 1830s and 1840s, national census-takers and European

[70] The census, taken under the supervision of José María Dalence, registered some 1.4 million "Bolivians," with another 700,000 "unpacified" tribal peoples inhabiting the eastern tropical lowlands and savannahs. Using such cultural markers as language, customs, dress, place of habitation, and rural poverty, Dalence estimated that 80 percent of the population was indigenous and monolingual (or bilingually conversant in more than one indigenous language). Fewer than

travelers made inventories of Bolivia's diverse ecological zones, regions, and races that seemed impervious to outside modernizing forces. Among the latter, Alcides D'Orbigny was perhaps the most influential travel-writer to represent postcolonial Bolivia as a composite of linguistic, racial, and regional types (Fig. 23.11). Of the four Andean nations, the colonial past insinuated itself most deeply into the cultural and institutional life of this fledgling republic. Thus Bolivia entered the mid-nineteenth century without having established an institutional or ideological beachhead of liberalism from which to launch a fullscale assault on indigenous communities.

Late nineteenth-century political violence also grew out of the long-standing ambivalence of provincial Creole society toward their Indian subjects. Incipient bourgeois values would not easily displace colonial habits. Accustomed to living off servile Indian labor, Creoles were not particularly anxious to open the country to imported goods or investments until the 1860s and 1870s. This clash between colonialism and modernity reverberated through the republic, because nowhere else was the colonial past – in ideology and practice – so deeply entrenched. Bolivia was the last of the Andean republics to abolish tribute, in 1874. Caste continued to structure and legitimate everyday forms of exploitation until the mid–twentieth century. Provincial authorities – from the lowly parish priest to the prefect – wanted to maintain colonial customs of servility and subordination, and they continued to rely on *hilacatas* (traditional community officers, like Peruvian *varayuq*) and other Indian authorities to dispatch temporary laborers for public and private works. The republic's enduring dependence on ethnic mediation was apparent even after the formal abolition of tribute. Whole provincial bureaucracies in the north of Potosí and elsewhere continued to function on the basis of Indian tribute and *corvée* labor until well into the twentieth century. And when the state sought to regulate Indian *corvée* labor for road

20 percent of Bolivians spoke Spanish in the 1840s. Quechua remained the predominant language (and, in fact, increasingly became the rural *lingua franca* throughout the Bolivian highlands over the course of the nineteenth century). Aymara remained the second most important language, spoken predominantly by ethnic groups inhabiting the high plateau stretching across the western part of the departments of La Paz and Oruro. Dalence's census also revealed the preponderance of *ayllu*-communal Indians (some 620,000), compared to the smaller group of Indians attached to estates (between 375,000 and 400,000). The national census of 1900 reveals little change in these ethnic balances. See José María Dalence, *Bosquejo estadístico de Bolivia, 1846* (La Paz, 1975), and Herbert S. Klein, *Bolivia: The Evolution of a Multiethnic Society* (New York, 1982), 166.

See Grieshaber "Survival of Indian communities in nineteenth century Bolivia: A regional comparison," *Journal of Latin American Studies* 12:2 (1980), 223 and 236.

Figure 23.11. Indians and mestizos of the Quechua nation, of Chuquisaca and its environs" (ca. 1833). Among the first Europeans to explore the interior of South America after the Independence Wars, Alcides D'Orbigny commenced his journey in 1825 under the auspices of the Museum of Natural History in Paris "to investigate thoroughly the language and physiological characteristics of the South American peoples" (quoted in Poole, *Vision, Race, and Modernity,* 79). D'Orbigny's racial-tribal map of South America appeared in his two-volume report entitled *L'Homme américain* (1839). A few years later, D'Orbigny published his nine-volume journal of his travels and explorations in South America. It remains one of the finest post-Enlightenment products of ethnographic, geographic, and historical description of the early nineteenth century.

D'Orbigny's journey from the eastern tropical lowlands up to the highlands of Potosí and Oruro took him through the city of Chuquisaca in 1833. He described the great number of "cultured people" who inhabited the city of Chuquisaca, making it a "pleasant and civil" place to reside. He also remarked on the gulf separating the "people of breeding" from the "inferior ranks," including the mestizo (or *"cholo"*) artisans and, below them, the Indians. He was especially taken with what he considered to be the outlandish, yet sensual, appearance of the city's *chola's.* Full-breasted, coquetish, and adorned, the mestiza (pictured here on the far left) displayed a medley (*"mescolanza"*) of European and Indian styles, combining Spanish balloon sleeves and full pleated skirt trimmed in ribbons with a regional variation of the indigenous *lliqlla* (Quechua term for a rectangular piece of woven cloth used as a shawl). "When they promenade clutching their hankies, with their hair adorned in showy beads, and their feet clad in silk slippers, they might as well have just emerged from a ball" (Alcides D'Orbigny, *Viaje a la America Meridional . . . realizado de 1826 a 1833* [1844] [Buenos Aires: Ed. Futuro, 1945], 4: 1486]. Illustration, p. 1352).

building in 1889, it ran into trouble as soon as it tried to bypass traditional ethnic networks of mediation.

The persistence of an implicit tributary pact under an ambivalent republic proved a dangerous thing later in the nineteenth century. As in Peru, Bolivia's nation builders made a futile effort to build consensus around a master "civilizing" project. More important, the contested meanings of republicanism – whether it legitimized colonial-style ethnic rights or mandated anti-Indian reformism – played into the hands of strong ethnic groups long accustomed to negotiating and resisting state extractions. Persistent tributary relations, no matter how ambiguous or contested, maintained the basis of ethnic militancy throughout the nineteenth century. Long-simmering tributary tensions bubbled up over the question of communal land. As long as Indians still confronted the state over their customary-colonial rights to territoriality, they continued to root their struggle for land, autonomy, and identity in a moral historical past. Oral cultures, collective memories, genealogies, communal archives, and ritual celebrations, all combined into the shaping of native historical interpretations, which in turn reaffirmed ethnic identity and militancy.

Yet indigenous uses of the past did not constrict their ability to adapt or alter their political and rhetorical strategies as power balances and historical circumstances changed. Building or breaking multiethnic alliances, playing partisan politics, forging pacts of patronage, and weaving webs of solidarity around the village eminences still called *caciques*, all were part of the shared repertoires and conventions characterizing nineteenth-century indigenous politics. Once the old tributary pact began to crumble – once Indians could no longer work the cultural and semantic ambiguities of "*república*" to their own advantage – indigenous communities altered their tactics and realigned themselves along partisan lines or popular-communal coalitions. They also intensified their pursuit of colonial legitimacies. As will become evident, the rise of new political pacts and alliances between militant Aymara communities and the Liberal Party at the end of the century proved explosive.

Between Conquest and Reconquest: The Communal Land Question

The recovery of silver mining in the 1860s and 1870s stiffened the resolve of a small group of liberal reformers to begin overhauling Bolivia's political economy. A new breed of modernizing silver miners appeared on the political scene, advancing their free-trade ideas. Fired up by the feverish commercial activity in guano, nitrates, and silver, this tiny oligarchy touted the benefits of government deregulation of mining and minting, the end of protectionism, and the promotion of railroad building to give the mine owners cheaper access to the world market. The rising spirit of economic liberalism sparked a revival of Bolivarian ideals as well. And that put the "Indian problem" at dead center of élite political debates for the first time since the 1820s. By the early 1860s liberal reformers were gathering consensus among themselves that the juridical basis of Indian communities had to be destroyed once and for all. Their arguments were both philosophic (the ideological incompatibility between caste and citizenship, communalism and private property, etc.) and pragmatic (the need to shift the tax base from Indian tribute to universal property taxes, to raise immediate revenues from the sale of land titles, and to promote commercial agriculture on newly privatized lands, etc.). But, as we shall see shortly, the naive and reckless proposals for Indian land reform of the 1860s did not anticipate a violent backlash. By the early 1870s liberal reformers came face to face with the frightening reality of peasant insurgency – of living under a weak, coercive, and unstable government largely incapable of disciplining an increasingly refractory *indiada*. Bolivia as yet had no rural police or professional military; nor could it rely upon Indian rural schools, a modern juridical system, or government agents to assimilate the Indian masses into civilized life. The advent of tribute and land reforms therefore was pressed upon a resentful peasantry under extremely precarious political conditions. By the early 1870s liberal reformers were painfully aware of this fact. From that point on they argued interminably among themselves about the least dangerous way to proceed. Not surprisingly, reformers introduced a series of half-hearted, contradictory "reforms and counter-reforms" aimed at waging economic and cultural warfare on Indian lifeways, while trying to contain the threat of violent insurrection. Such efforts were to prove impracticable.

The decade of 1860 saw two failed major efforts at Indian land reform: the aborted decree of 1863 under President José María de Achá, and the fundamental land reforms of 1866 and 1868 implemented by President Mariano Melgarejo. Although they failed in different ways (the 1863 decree was stillborn, and Melgarejo decrees were eventually repealed), they are interesting for their competing utopic visions of rural Bolivia and the fate of its peasantry under a modernizing nation. The proposal of 1863 revisited Bolivarian ideals of Indian smallholding. As with the earlier land reforms in Ecuador and Peru, Achá advocated the subdivision of communal lands and their redistribution to Indian households. According to his plan Indians would buy or sell lands at will. Motivated by market incentives they would improve agricultural production and eventually become prosperous yeoman. In the meantime the state would compel them to adopt civilized ways of life: fining Indians 10 pesos, for example, if they did not build "comfortable, spacious and ventilated houses" on their lands within the year, or erect schoolhouses for their offspring. As with most earlier land reforms in neighboring countries, however, the state had a vested financial interest in selling off vast acreage of "vacant lands" to the highest bidders. To politicians the sale of vacant lands seemed an easy fix: It would put wastelands into production while raising immediate state revenues. Such proposals showed abysmal ignorance of Andean patterns of land rotation (high altitude crop land must lie fallow for years at a time), as well as little awareness of the lingering effects of the 1856 epidemic. In any event, while the 1863 decree was abrogated that same year, it crystallized the "peasantization" view of liberal reformers.[71] Those promoting the smallholder-yeoman solution, however, were hardly Jeffersonian democrats; they were hard-nosed pragmatists imbued with positivist notions of racial backwardness. Thus their proposals to redistribute lands to Indian families were embedded in a more ambitious project of cultural reform aimed at the compulsory "civilization" of Indians.

Foreshadowing the famous land reform act of 1874, these early liberal ambitions were immediately swept aside by the larger-than-life *caudillo*-president, General Mariano Melgarejo. He rode to power on the crest of the silver mining boom, determined to throw Bolivia open to international capital and markets and to bolster state power. After seizing power in late 1864, he initiated a package of reforms that dismantled the whole edifice of protective tariffs, modernized the currency system, sold off large chunks of Bolivian territory, and launched the first sustained attack on Indian communal property rights since the independence era. By the terms of the 1866 confiscation decrees, Melgarejo declared the state to be the owner of all communal properties. All Indians residing on state-owned lands were now required to purchase individual titles at sums between 2 and 100 pesos within a 60-day period. Titles would allow

[71] Erick Langer, "El liberalismo y la abolición de la comunidad indígena en el siglo XIX," *Historia y Cultura* 14 (La Paz, 1988).

Indians to hold the land for 5 years, after which time they would again have to repurchase titles. In effect Indians would be advancing ground rent for 5 years, while absolute ownership rights would still rest with the state. Those Indians unable to purchase titles under the stipulated terms would have their lands confiscated and auctioned to the highest bidder. The 1868 decree put salt in the wounds inflicted by the earlier law: It allowed whole communities to be auctioned off as land units and imposed a universal head tax, with Indians liable for double the standard tax rate.

Many features of Melgarejo's land reform paid lip service to the liberal goal of converting Indians into property owners, once they purchased land titles. But the notoriously harsh terms that he imposed set the stage for large-scale despoliation, especially because his 1868 edict legitimated the sale of entire communities to one landowner. Thus Melgarejo aligned himself with the pro-latifundist faction of the oligarchy. By the early 1860s the seigneurial viewpoint was articulated as the preferable, and most likely, long-term outcome of liberal land reforms. Traditional landowners, as well as merchants and mining entrepreneurs, began to argue that advancing *latifundismo* held the secret to Bolivia's deliverance from rural backwardness. Some advocated estate expansion on paternalist grounds: Private landlords would step into the role of Indian protector, recently shed by the modernizing state. At the same time, it was argued, landlords would improve agriculture and supply the growing urban markets with food. Others tinged their arguments with assimilationist ideals: Indian absorption into the private estate sector would bring them more into contact with industrious mestizos and whites, eventually leading to racial miscegenation. Here, then, was a Bolivian analog to Colombia's popular "whitening solution" to justify the pro-*latifundista* polemic, or what their critics called the "refeudalization" position of greedy landowners. Although Melgarejo never defined his position in those terms, his policies in effect endorsed the seigneurial stance.

Although historians disagree about the global and regional effects of Melgarejo's reforms on Indian land divestiture, most agree that the government fell far short of its fiscal goals. By the end of the Melgarejo era in 1870, over 1.25 million pesos of land had been sold to whites and mestizos. But because most land purchases were made with devalued government bonds, the government actually made very little money. Furthermore market conditions were only beginning to ripen, and Creole demand for Indian lands was still sluggish in many regions. Nonetheless

Melgarejo's decrees shattered the agrarian peace in the thickly populated Aymara provinces of Sicasica, Omasuyos, and Pacajes, where despoliation was concentrated. Overnights indigenous peoples unable to prove land possession through colonial titles or too impoverished to purchase entitlement watched their common fields and pastures pass into private hands at the bidding of rich speculators. The beneficiaries were political clients of Melgarejo, traditional landowners who expanded their frontiers into indigenous territory, medium-scale miners and merchants, and prosperous Indians (often of *cacique* lineage). Privileged Indians frequently privatized the former *cacique* lands, which had once covered communal ritual and tributary costs. Certainly in the *altiplano* provinces surrounding the city of La Paz, we see the outlines of a diversified regional oligarchy beginning to consolidate power in this transitional period. Their windfall properties were soon jeopardized, however, by the rising tide of Indian resistance and rebellion. Indigenous violence escalated over a 3-year period (1869–1871) – to a degree unprecedented since Túpac Catari's siege of La Paz almost 100 years earlier. Most of the violent opposition gathered fury in the Aymara communities of Pacajes and Omasuyos, but by January 1871 thousands of Indians allied with Melgarejo's political enemies to lay siege to La Paz and drive the *caudillo* into permanent exile.

On a more prosaic but no less threatening level, Aymara communities mounted everyday counterattacks against the land reforms. By day they challenged the legitimacy of tributary and land reform, as well as denounced the extortion of individuals involved in local notary offices, government chambers, and courts. By night they waged guerrilla warfare over contested boundaries and pastures: posting sentinels at ancient landmarks, driving llama herds and sheep onto disputed pastures, and squatting on potato fields stolen by the state or its private agents during Melgarejo's violent enclosure movement.

The lesson was not lost on Creole reformers, who learned that a frontal attack on communal land would be perceived as sheer treachery. Trying to placate the masses, the 1871 Constitutional Convention voided all laws passed during the Melgarejo era. But the land reform issue continued to vex and divide lawmakers. On the one hand, they condemned Melgarejo's annexation of communal lands, arguing that the early Bolivarian decrees had given individual property rights to Indians. On the other hand, many legislators believed in the estate solution, publicly stating that the interests of indigenous peoples would be better served by paternal landlords protecting them from predatory mestizo lawyers, officials, and priests.

Out of these debates (and a deep-seated fear of rural insurgency) came the 1874 *Ley de Exvinculación.* Although not implemented until the 1880s, it set the basic terms of Indian landholding rights from that moment until the mid–twentieth century. At base the 1874 law conceded the right of individual landownership to Indians, abolishing the community as a juridical, taxpaying, and landholding unit. In its rejection of Melgarejo's efforts at annexation, the law leaned toward the Indian smallholding solution. But it was every bit as radical a break with the recent past. In law, propertied communalism was gone; but so were customary ethnic jurisdictions and traditions that had survived, even flourished, under Bolivia's tributary republic. The law dismantled the tributary apparatus, establishing a universal property tax (*catastro*) to be paid in the new devalued currency of *bolivianos* (which effectively raised Indian taxes by some 20 percent). After the Conservatives' electoral victory in 1880, and under growing fiscal pressures (as the War of the Pacific escalated), the central government rationalized the land-tax structure. It dispatched tax commissioners to draw up the first blueprints of propertyholding patterns and to begin collecting taxes. Indian authorities were swept aside from their own traditional roles as ethnic mediators. From then on Indians would be juridical subjects of civil law, directly subject to the authority of white and mestizo agents and to the siege of the land market.

Yet again the rising tide of Indian unrest in the 1880s rapidly forced new concessions from the Conservative regime. Whether by design or confusion, the government created legal loopholes through which indigenous communities could evade or contest the new tax and land policies. In innumerable cases local reports of Indian unrest or noncompliance forced government authorities to suspend tax collection or land sales during the early 1880s. In October 1885, for instance, appointed Indian authorities (*indios apoderados*) from the departments of La Paz, Oruro, and Potosí petitioned the Bolivian senate to rescind the tax increases, annul Indian land sales, and call off government land surveys. The senate hedged, telling the leaders to address their grievances to the executive branch. Frustrated by government indifference, Aymara peoples began organizing night meetings throughout Omasuyos to plan for further action. Reports of Indian disturbances also came in from Sicasica. In both cases white authorities petitioned for troops to crush the insurgents, setting off a vicious cycle of indigenous legal protest followed by military massacre. That same year the Southern Highland villages of Macha, Pocoata, Aymaya, and Condo (all located in northern Potosí) forced the tax commissioners to suspend their operations by threatening to invade the silver mining town of Colquechaca. Three years later, a more militant movement erupted in the northern Potosí village of Sacaca, where Indians demanded the head of the land-tax commissioner, while preaching a neo-Inka social order in alliances with the local branch of the dissident Liberal Party based in the nearby mining town of Colquechaca.[72]

What these reported incidents of violence hide, however, is the massive paper campaign that Indians began to wage in the 1880s for the restitution of their communal rights. The whole confusing welter of legislation over land and tax reforms, together with officialdom's corruption and inefficiency, were perverse ways of encouraging (and tying up) legal challenges by aggrieved Indians. Under pressures of indigenous protest, the government watered down the 1874 law in two basic ways. First, in November 1883 the state agreed to exempt from government title inspections all communal lands entitled by the colonial documents. This legal concession (*la ley pro-indiviso*) flew in the face of the 1874 land reform by allowing Indian communities to legitimate their collective claims if they presented proper colonial titles. Second, the government created labyrinthine procedures whereby new landowners had to consolidate, or "ratify," their property titles. In effect the ratification process created some "cooling off" time for aggrieved Indians seeking a legal means of redress. Most Indians in fact used these procedures in the late nineteenth and early twentieth centuries to argue for the annulment of land sales on grounds of fraud.

With what success did Indians use these laws to slow or reverse the earlier land reform acts? Most contemporary observers had little respect for these protectionist measures. On the contrary several people wrote prolifically about the disastrous effects of land reforms on indigenous peoples. One of the most prominent writers around the turn of the century was Rigoberto Paredes. An intellectual, lawyer, and latifundist, he commented on the sorry state of *altiplano* communities in his book, *Tiahuanaco*:

[72] Tristan Platt, "The Andean experience of Bolivian Liberalism, 1825–1900," 307–309; Erwin Grieshaber, "Indian reactions to the acquisition of communal land: La Paz, 1881–1920," unpublished paper presented at the FLACSO Conference on "Las comunidades indígenas de los Andes en el siglo XIX," Quito, March 27–30, 1989.

The legal abolition of the communities has done serious damage to the *indio*. Being accustomed to the collective form of cultivation, he lived perfectly peacefully and kept out of reach of covetous land-grabbers. But as soon as he was transformed into a proprietor he became their victim. Illiterate, unaware of the value of his landed property, and without guarantees of any kind, he was stripped of his lands, usually by means of violent spoliation. And thus the great estates were formed and Indian was reduced to serfdom; [he] lives in hope of reclaiming his rightful ancestral heritage one day.[73]

Recent historical research has tried to measure the scope of Indian land divestiture in the late nineteenth and early twentieth centuries. Erwin Grieshaber, for example, estimates that among 7,616 land-sale contracts registered in the vast department of La Paz between 1881 and 1920, only about two dozen were annulled and Indian lands returned.[74] Looking back over a 40- or 50-year period of vigorous real estate sales, there can be no doubt about the massive alienation of indigenous lands throughout the country. Herbert Klein sums it up: "Still holding half the lands and about half the rural population in 1880, the communities were reduced to less than a third of both by 1930. The power of the free Indian communities was definitively broken."[75]

Not everywhere and not completely, however. La Paz was the turf of raging territorial wars. Latifundist frontiers advanced rapidly in those districts of Omasuyos and Pacajes that had easy access to the growing urban market of La Paz and the railroad network. Land values soared, as booming mines, rails, and markets opened up commercial opportunities for highland agriculture and livestock raising across the north. Latifundists tended to be absentee landlords and prominent members of the oligarchy, playing politics in Sucre or La Paz. In their shadow a new layer of commercial intermediaries articulated rural and urban exchanges. As petty provincial bureaucrats, lawyers, merchants, and money lenders, these rural "mestizo" middlemen arose in the institutional crevices opened by the collapse of Indian communities and their local authorities.[76]

So the experience of Indian enserfment was less than universal throughout rural Bolivia. The tug and pull of state and market pressures,

[73] Rigoberto Paredes, *Tiahuanaco y la Provincia de Ingavi* (La Paz, 1965), 31.

[74] Grieshaber, "Indian reactions to the acquisition of communal land," 18–26.

[75] Klein, *Bolivia. The Evolution of a Multiethnic Society*, 152.

[76] Silvia Rivera, "La expansión del latifundio en el Altiplano boliviano. Elementos para la caracterización de una oligarquía regional," *Avances* 2 (La Paz, 1978), 95–118.

as well as the forms, forces, and consequences of indigenous response, worked out differently from place to place and from region to region. Here we need only point to divergent peasant responses to liberal land reforms in the contiguous departments of Cochabamba and northern Potosí in the late nineteenth century. In the eastern maize valleys of Cochabamba, a region quilted by estates and peasant smallholds deeply integrated into regional product markets, the liberal land policies gave many peasants a chance to buy small parcels of estate land that they had once cultivated through sharecropping or leasehold arrangements. Many estates also pushed against the borders of nearby Indian communities. The historically weak, engulfed nature of communal landholding in the rich Lower Valley of Cochabamba, together with a strong peasant tradition of petty commodity production on the edges of valley towns and landed estates, created the regional context for accelerated "peasantization" – especially in the early twentieth century, as peasant household economies revolved more and more around the maize-*chicha* complex. This region also began to lose some of its "surplus" peasants – those unable to live off their shrunken parcels of land – to distant silver, nitrate, and tin mines.[77]

The northern part of Potosí lies across the mountains and valleys to the southwest of Cochabamba. There the historically resilient *ayllus* of Chayanta (a province in northern Potosí) had posed strong opposition to earlier cycles of liberal reform and continuously struggled over the republican period to restore ethnic authorities and jurisdictions at the moiety level – the axis of their extended, interecological kin networks and ritual cycles. Under the early tributary-protectionist republic of Bolivia, these *ayllus* seemed to negotiate kin and cash economies in ways that maintained a semblance of political and social equilibrium.

The collapse of protectionism dealt the first blow. Free-trade policies in the 1870s and 1880s dislodged the Chayanta *ayllus* from their privileged position as wheat suppliers in regional and urban markets by opening Bolivia to cheap Chilean and Peruvian wheat flour. The second blow

[77] Gustavo Rodríguez Ostría, "Entre reformas y contrareformas: las comunidades indígenas en el Valle Bajo cochabambino (1825–1900)," in Heraclio Bonilla (ed.), *Los Andes en la Encrucijada* (Quito, 1991), 277–335; Brooke Larson *Cochabamba, 1550–1900. Colonialism and Agrarian Transformation in Bolivia* (Durham, North Carolina, 1998), chaps. 9 and 10; and Robert H. Jackson, *Regional Markets and Agrarian Transformation in Bolivia, Cochabamba, 1539–1960* (Albuquerque, 1994).

came with the land reform acts in the 1880s, when the region became an enclave of *ayllu* protest and rebellion.

However, they operated in a very different regional field of force than did the besieged Aymara communities of the northern high plateau or the peasant-artisan smallholders of Cochabamba. Their growing economic isolation, the small proportion of lands held in estates, the vested interest of provincial bureaucrats in maintaining Indian tribute (as it continued to finance local government), and the historical legacy of indigenous struggle and insurrection in the area (a scene of massive Indian rebellion during 1780 and 1781; see Chap. 22), all conspired against the onslaught of applied liberalism and latifundism in northern Potosí. If anything, smallholding mestizos grabbed more lands and turned their political back on *ayllu* Indians. But Chayanta was one region where liberal land-tax policies met with repeated resistance, and Creole authorities eventually retreated. In fact Tristan Platt notes that "in spite of economic crisis and growing pressure from private property, the *ayllus* entered the twentieth century with a substantial increase in fiscal autonomy." They had managed to scare off the land-tax commissioners and restore Indian tax collectors, chosen from among the *comuneros*. These *curacas recaudadores* symbolized not only the reassertion of *ayllu* control over critical aspects of communal life but the renegotiation of an informal "tributary pact" with provincial authorities (in opposition to hegemonic liberal policies and discourses of the day).[78]

Such strong regional variations undercut earlier assumptions about the inexorable enserfment of communal Indians. There was no essential "Andean experience of liberalism" – whether it be construed as the "definitive destruction" of Indian communities, "ethnocide" under liberalism, or millenarian outbursts of revindication. Under particular regional and class conditions, Andean peasants pursued strategies of cultural *mestizaje*, migration, and social climbing, which fundamentally transformed local landscapes of power in the late nineteenth century. Even across the northern *altiplano*, new opportunities opened for bilingual, literate lawyers, merchants, labor contractors, and others who used their indigenous roots for accumulative ends. But there is no doubt that the booming export, land, and product markets came at the expense of social justice and peace for the vast majority of indigenous peasants.

[78] Tristan Platt, "The Andean experience of Bolivian Liberalism," 318.

Most highland Indians were reintegrated economically into the market under sharply more disadvantageous terms under the liberalizing regime. They were displaced from traditional market circuits, subjected to new commercial monopolies on top of their traditional *corvée* obligations, hit with heavier head or land taxes, and threatened by laws and practices of divestiture. Accompanying this economic transition were deep cultural incursions into the most intimate corners of communal life – violating intra-*ayllu* norms of political succession, the administration of local justice, the allocation of lands, taxes, and ritual responsibilities, and the coordination of the "ethnic calendar." In theory indigenous jurisdictions evaporated as Indians became subject to law and bureaucracy controlled by and for whites and mestizos, landlords and merchants.

Yet liberal incursions had a contradictory effect on highland indigenous communities. Although the reforms half-heartedly, at times timidly, tried to abolish indigenous communities as legal entities, the imperatives of communal defense and survival revitalized a sense of communal identity and ethnic memory among a spreading transregional network of Aymara people. This was a slow, uneven grassroots process that assumed national scope in the final years of the nineteenth century, as local indigenous struggles merged briefly with the oligarchic north–south conflict of 1899. Ethnic militancy reached its zenith during the "cycle of Aymara rebellions" between 1910 and 1930. It was only then – during the frenzied growth of estates, rails, and tin mining, the modernization of La Paz's bureaucratic and military apparatus, and the beginning of an aggressive "civilizing" crusade – that local rebel actions began to fuse and articulate into a broader, national ethnic movement.[79]

But there is no doubt that the seeds of ethnic militancy and rebellion were planted in the 1880s and 1890s, when Aymara communities began to wage local battles in the provincial courts by day and on their stolen fields and pastures by night. It was then that Indians began to hone their legal and rhetorical strategies in ongoing campaigns to defend or recover lost rights. As we have seen, legal ambiguity and flux (particularly the *pro-indiviso* law of 1883 and the ratification process) encouraged many communities to take encroaching landlords to task for fraudulent title sales. In many regions the internal community-estate frontier became a perpetual war zone – turning property titles into mere figments of the

[79] See Silvia Rivera Cusicanqui, *'Oprimidos pero no vencidos.' Luchas del campesinado aymara y quechwa, 1900–1980* (La Paz, 1986), ch. 2.

aspiring landlord's imagination. Juan Martínez-Alier's generalization about the "dubious legitimacy" of property titles in Peru underscores the dilemma of Bolivian landowners as well.

On the other hand, the liberal reforms triggered a massive search by Indians for colonial titles in the legal defense of their lands. It became commonplace for Indian authorities to travel to colonial archives in Sucre, Lima, and Buenos Aires, in quest of colonial documents legitimating their ancient claims. More fortunate communities had secret caches of colonial documents locked away in their strong boxes, which served as wellsprings of ethnic memory and communal defense well into the twentieth century. This search for ancient land titles revitalized oral histories and gave new meaning to their ongoing struggle over local jurisdictions and contested lands. It also sharpened popular uses of postcolonial discourses, invoking a mythic paternal pact only recently broken by the modernizing state. Indians deployed this rhetorical strategy to condemn the degeneracy and ineptitude of the posttributary state and to legitimize their own actions. No less important, the avalanche of legal protest thrust Indian authorities into the center of long-term campaigns of communal defense. At the same time that civil law sought to level and atomize Indian society, it created the basis for the rise of militant "appointed *caciques*" to lead the legal struggle for ethnic revindication in the early twentieth century.

Aymara Resurgence, the Rebellion of Zárate Willka, and Popular Liberalism

Living on the edge of violent despoliation and repression, Aymara communities thus began to reorganize themselves as communities in opposition in the 1880s and 1890s. Rhetorically ready for reconciliation with a redemptive, protectionist republic, yet poised for violent counterattack against aggressive land-grabbers, Aymara peoples began to fashion multiple modes of struggle, inside and outside the bounds of Creole law. As the jittery La Paz élite often warned, incipient Aymara movement could escalate at any moment, sending the "savage warriors" across the northern *altiplano* to the edge of the dusty bowl that shelters the city of La Paz. That finally happened in 1899 – ironically at the invitation of the Liberal Party.

Already by the late 1880s, political and social conditions encouraged some Liberals to enlist Indians in their crusade for power. In 1888, a presidential election year, there was a groundswell of indigenous protest against the tax and land reforms that the Conservative Party had been pushing for some 8 years. In Sacaca, Macha, and elsewhere in the Southern Highlands, armed peasants set fire to municipal buildings and drove off government authorities trying to inspect properties and collect land title fees. These areas proved to be fertile ground for strategic alliances between defensive, antigovernment *ayllus* and dissident, anti-Conservative Liberals. For the rebellious *ayllus* of Chayanta and Charcas, the silver mining town of Colquechaca became a hotbed of Liberalism in the late 1880s. Liberals campaigned openly for Indian support. Party propaganda and slogans circulated through intricate rural webs of communication among large numbers of transient Indians trekking between their *ayllus* and the mines, markets, and shrines of Colquechaca. These transitory alliances with Liberal mestizo townsmen probably emboldened Indians openly to oppose Conservative land reform policies. In any event, Indian and mestizo protests against the new land commissioners in the region escalated in the late 1880s and early 1890s, and Indians continued to petition sympathetic legislators with the help of dissident Liberal lawyers and agitators.[80]

By the mid-1890s the Conservative oligarchy began to see its political and economic fortunes dissolve. Collapsing silver prices on the world market eroded the economic base of the Conservatives. The tin mines of the center and north of Bolivia would soon catapult La Paz into position as Bolivia's economic and political center, in fact the country's rival capital city. But for the moment the Conservative Party tried to cling to its political monopoly against the opposition party operating out of La Paz. Partisan élite politics increasingly manifested regional and economic schisms (the economic and political rise of the north and fall of the south), but the parties differed little in their pro-modernization stances. And yet the Liberal Party would only begin to champion order and progress, capitalism and civilization, after they seized power in 1900. In the 1880s and 1890s they defined their goals in narrow political terms: to share power at the top and restructure the bureaucracy along federalist lines. Most of all they wanted clean elections. They were willing to forge unholy alliances and espouse pro-Indian causes (for example, the restitution of communal lands, repeal of land reforms, etc.) to mobilize Indians against their Conservative enemies. As we have seen, Liberals had already

[80] Platt, "The Andean experience of Bolivian Liberalism," 311–312.

established local enclaves of Indian clientelism in northern Potosí during the late 1880s. But in the election year of 1896, a new political opportunity arose for La Paz Liberals to broaden their indigenous base of support in the north by hooking into a vast preexisting web of insurgent Indian communities scattered throughout the rural districts of Oruro and La Paz.

The powerful new Liberal–Indian coalition was built by two men: Colonel José Manuel Pando and Pablo Zárate Willka. They became historic partners (and later enemies) in the Federalist Revolution of 1899, which finally broke the Conservatives' political monopoly. Both were supreme political and military leaders who forged their own constituencies and agendas into a fragile popular-partisan front. For Pando the enemy was simply the opposition party that had kept the Liberals out of power since the beginning of civilian oligarchic rule in 1880. For indigenous communities under siege for more than two decades, the enemy transcended narrow party politics and implicated the whole social and moral order. Their common ideological ground was shallow at best.

Still, the first signs of political coalition between Pando and Zárate Willka were hopeful. On the eve of the 1896 election, they approached each other in mutual need and respect. Zárate Willka had already established himself as a widely respected, well-traveled, literate Aymara leader, mediating land conflicts in different communities, petitioning politicians on behalf of aggrieved *comunarios*, and spinning kinship and political webs across the *altiplano* (Fig. 23.12). This figure was no accidental hero spawned by the circumstances of war. He was a powerful Indian *caudillo* who participated in national-level war and rebellion, and who brought to the political partnership a rural constituency of aggrieved Indians. Mobilized and harnessed to the Liberal cause, they could terrorize the Conservatives into submission – or so Pando believed.

By the 1890s Pablo Zárate Willka enjoyed widespread political influence.[81] In correspondence to Pando on the eve of the election in 1896,

[81] Little is known about Pablo Zárate Willka's formative years, and his persona remains shrouded in rival black and white legends. At his trial he stated his birthplace to be Sicasica, though he was probably born in the small village of Imilla-Imilla, located in the western mountains of the province of Sicasica, in the department of La Paz. Stretching across mountains and *altiplano*, the province was located midway between the cities of Oruro and La Paz. In 1899 it became a battleground between the northern and southern armies locked in civil war. But long before then Sicasica was legendary for its bellicose Indian communities: It was the cradle of Indian rebels and successive uprisings – in 1781, 1811, and most recently under Melgarejo in 1871. Zárate Willka's

Figure 23.12. General Willka Condori and his troops in Arque, 1899. According to Ramiro Condarco Morales, the standing figure in the center of the photograph is Feliciano Willka, the "Third Willka," in charge of indigenous troops throughout the highlands of Cochabamba. This photograph was taken during the early phases of the Federalist War while the indigenous forces were still allied to Pando's Liberal Revolution. (Photo reproduced courtesy of the Archivo de la Paz.)

Zárate Willka alluded to the broad peasant constituency that he already commanded. The letter, dated June 27, 1896, was written from the village of Taraco, poised on the edge of Lake Titicaca. Zárate Willka had been engaged in settling land disputes between local estate owners and community members to their mutual benefit (so he reports). The letter also told of his perambulations among other lake district villages and offered to take Pando's greetings to other *caciques.* One of his next destinations was the shrine of Copacabana, across the lake from Taraco, where he would beg the Virgin's blessings for Pando. Finally he asked Pando for a

political sensibilities were undoubtedly influenced by local oral traditions about Sicasica's insurgent past.

For the following discussion of Zárate Willka and the 1899 rebellion, I am indebted to Ramiro Condarco Morales, for his pioneering study, *Zárate, el 'Temible' Willka, Historia de una rebelión indígena de 1899,* 2nd ed. (La Paz, 1982). This interpretative synthesis is my own, however.

favor: to bring back news from Sucre about congressional deliberations over the petitions that he and other Indians had sent. The letter reveals the kind of reciprocal relations already obtaining between Zárate Willka and Pando, even before military action began.

Here, then, are glimpses of a literate, bilingual Aymara man who had cultivated political and kinship links in villages across the northern lake district, far from his own homeland. He had established himself as a political *caudillo* and interlocutor among Taraco villages, on the defensive against rampant latifundism. His travels, political connections, and diplomacy had laid the groundwork for the rise of a broad Indian political movement, which Zárate provisionally offered to deliver to the Liberal Party. And as the Liberal Party turned to military action (following another electoral defeat in 1896), it asked Zárate Willka to mobilize an Indian army to fight the Conservatives (now called the Constitutionalists). It was a political pact of convenience – inevitably precarious and dangerous.

From the beginning Pando never really brought the Indian leader under his own direct command. Although Zárate Willka's stature was enhanced by his long political connection to Creole Liberals, he was no mere client. His primary allegiances and powerbase were rooted in Aymara communities throughout the north, where he had spent long years of networking, mediation, and struggle on their behalf (Fig. 23.13). As politics became militarized in 1899, Zárate Willka was determined to enter the war as both ally and equal of Pando. He conferred upon himself the combined military title of "General of a Division in the Federal Army" and "Commander-in-Chief of the Indigenous Army." It reflected his double identity: as Pando's military ally of equal rank, and as supreme leader of indigenous soldiers (and, by extension, all Indian communities). Incipient ideals of social equality and cultural pluralism were embedded in these formal titles. Later Zárate Willka was to express them more openly through words and deeds.

But if Pando was unable to subordinate Zárate Willka to his own military command, the Indian leader himself had difficulty containing grassroots peasant violence amidst the chaos and brutality of civil war. As the Conservative-Constitutionalist and Liberal-Federalist armies swarmed over the villages of Sicasica and other provinces, committing all kinds of atrocities, partisan politics faded rapidly before the brutal logic of ethnic and class warfare and survival. The movement of troops victimized peasants no matter what their political allegiance: "Each march of an army

Figure 23.13. The high ministers of Zárate Willka's army and government, 1899. This formal portrait of the various "Willkas" who served as *ministros* to Pablo Zárate Willka vividly demonstrates the collective, indeed consciously 'federative,' nature of the high command. To the degree that historians have focused on Pablo Zárate's " "terrifying," "irrational" or "savage" persona, his illicit "caudillo-styled" authority, or even his naive political opportunism, they overlook the crucial political and territorial base of support and hierarchy that undergirded this extraordinary indigenous movement. The Willka mobilizations built upon the enduring Aymara traditions of local self-rule and indigenous authority networks, colonial and republican legacies of political and litigious struggle, the resurgence of communal land restitution campaigns, and the escalating militarization of Aymara communities since the Melgarejo era. And Zárate Willka, himself, consciously decentralized political and military power among a handful of other newly designated "Willkas" in the northern zones, including the crucial "Third Willka" of Tapacarí, Feliciano Condori (pictured here in the top hat). His other highly ranked authorities included at least two "presidents" of southern districts: Juan Lero of Peñas, and Mariano Gómez of Challoma. (Photo courtesy of the Archivo de La Paz.)

brings [peasants] the same damage and terror as the most furious earthquake would," commented one sympathetic journalist in 1895.[82]

Furthermore, as we saw happen among Peru's Mantaro guerrillas during the War of the Pacific, nationalist or partisan politics may serve to inspire and legitimate peasant violence against ancient class and ethnic enemies. In the towns and villages of Sicasica, Zárate Willka's peasant-soldiers hunted down *alonsistas* (supporters of the Constitutionalist government). This hunt was an opportunity for peasants to settle old scores among hacendados and townsfolk. Throughout the war-torn provinces the Liberal Revolution of 1899 set indigenous peasants against mestizo towns – the administrative sites where servile labor had to be rendered, taxes paid, commercial monopolies set, and Indian justice mocked. In a similar vein peasant irregulars who saw their own communities sacked and their women raped began to turn against the regular (white) armies of both camps, even as they shouted "*Viva Pando!*". After a certain point the civil war became submerged in an indigenous rebellion, the likes of which had not been seen in Bolivia for more than a century.

The turning point came in February 1899 in the town of Mohoza. A squadron of well-armed Federalist cavalrymen encountered a roadblock of hostile peasants, who took them hostage. Through that terrible night the white soldiers were taken to the parish courtyard and cemetery where they were executed one by one. Several townspeople on both sides of the partisan divide also met their death that night. The exact circumstances of this mass extermination were never cleared up and remain obscure to this day. But that this autonomous peasant action had shattered the pact was all too clear. On the eve of his murder, a terrified commanding officer whispered to the local priest, "we are lost, father. The peasants have risen. The war is not between factions, but between races. We cheered Pando and the Federation, and they answered '*viva* Willka!' "[83]

There is some controversy as to Zárate Willka's role in these events, although the tribunal later accused him of commanding the mass execution. Certainly in the weeks to follow, Zárate Willka continued to profess his loyalty to the Liberal cause and to carry out military operations in many places. But as the doomed cavalry officer realized, the events of Mohoza reflected the radical drift of peasant violence. It also seems clear

[82] *El Comercio* (La Paz, April 1, 1895), quoted in Andrew Pearse, *The Latin American Peasant* (London, 1975), 134.

[83] Quoted in Condarco Morales, *Zárate, el 'Temible' Willka*, 273.

that Zárate Willka, while never disavowing partisan loyalty, increasingly indicted the injustices of Bolivian society and summoned peasants to take direct action against their local oppressors.

Yet Zárate Willka never unleashed an all-out "race war." In fact he was caught on the barbs of his own past history and identity as an Indian leader in postcolonial society. On the one hand, Zárate Willka had achieved the stature of a military and political *caudillo* through his astute partisan politics and long service as a widely respected mediator of local ethnic and class disputes. On the other hand, he was a militant Aymara advocate and activist, deeply committed to the ideals of territorial autonomy and cultural pluralism under republican rule. No wonder his later military actions were full of ambiguities and contradictions that few contemporary observers cared to figure out. Thus he sent circulars to his Indian troops to exercise self-restraint toward "whites and *vecinos*" and to remember their common goal (the overthrow of Alonso and the "regeneration of Bolivia"). *Vecino* ('neighbor') at that time connoted 'town-dweller' and applied to people with racial and class advantages. But he also took radical actions to subvert the moral and symbolic order of ethnic oppression. Although he never openly declared war on the white citizens' world, he envisioned a new order of social equality and mutual respect that would give real social content to the empty rhetoric of the Liberals. "We Indians are of the same blood," he said, "and [we are] all children of Bolivia."

In his uniquely daring practice, more than ideology, Zárate Willka actually inverted the hierarchy of caste. For what better way to impose one's vision of social and cultural equality on this deeply divided society than to coerce the "Indianization" of whites? To reverse the onward march of "Creole civilization" and compel the cultural assimilation of non-Indians into native Andean society? Breaking all the cultural codes, he ordered all "whites and *vecinos*" in the western Cochabamba province of Tapacari to dress in rustic homespuns and sandals (*traje indígena*) as they prepared to meet the Constitutionalists in battle. During his trial, testimony described Zárate Willka holding "court" in Tambo de Iro, where "serfs and gentry paid their respects; where men with . . . golden beards and pale skin put their pride in their pockets . . . and came to pay homage . . . picturesquely dressed in sandals and *bayeta* homespuns in the native style."[84] No whimsical act, this was subversive political theater

[84] Testimony recorded during the Mohoza trial, quoted in ibid., 299.

aimed at putting into practice the deep ideals that he had stood for all his life. Nurtured by Sicasica's oral traditions of Aymara insurgency, Zárate Willka was probably aware of similar acts of cultural defiance that Indian rebels had carried out during the 1781 uprisings in Sicasica, Oruro, and La Paz. Even if he were not, however, his actions assume deep symbolic significance when read against the ideals projected in his other actions and writings. In his proclamations and circulars, he hints of an imagined nation-state that not only redeemed Liberal promises of land restitution but invited indigenous communities into a new political covenant. His agenda embraced a kind of "federalism" attuned to indigenous aspirations toward autonomy, equality, and cultural respect.

But that, of course, was not to be. The victorious Federalist Army (and Liberal Party) unleashed their fury against their indigenous allies – capturing, trying, and eventually executing Zárate Willka and 288 other "guilty" Indians. The famous trial (*el proceso Mohoza*) dragged on for several years in Mohoza, Inquisivi, Oruro, and La Paz. It became a roving public spectacle, through which Creole élites scrutinized and judged the native defendants and, through them, the "Indian race." The trial incubated multiple racist theories explaining the biological and social origins of Indian inferiority. Journalists passionately engaged these legal, scientific, and philosophical debates, and in turn propagated images of the savage or forsaken Aymara race. After the turn of the century, scientific teams were imported from France and later Belgium to conduct studies measuring the cranial capacity of Indians. Physical anthropology proclaimed the "Indian race" to be unfit for national life. In the meantime other intellectuals plunged into literary, geographic, and ethnographic studies of native attributes and anachronisms, turning a critical eye on the traditional oppressors of the "Indian race." Most borrowed shamelessly from Social Darwinism. From whatever angle there was no getting around the centrality of race to the nation's future. Just as Peru had to come to grips with the "Indian problem" and the question of national sovereignty following the War of the Pacific, so Bolivia had to deal with its internal enemy: the Indian "other." Out of the 1899 crisis there came a new national obsession with the "Indian race" and the determination to conquer it once and for all.[85]

[85] Marie-Daniéle Démelas, "Darwinismo al la criolla: el darwinismo social en Bolivia, 1880–1919," *Historia boliviana* 1:2 (Cochabamba, 1981), 55–82. Marta Irurozqui, *La Armonía de las desigualdades. Elites y conflictos de poder en Bolivia, 1880–1920* (Cuzco, 1994), ch. 4.

This, then, became the historic burden of the triumphant Liberal oligarchy. While they inherited the mantle of modernization from their Conservative rivals, and while they paved the way for unbridled capitalism in tin mining, rail-building, and land-grabbing after 1900, their main mission necessarily had to be the domestication of the "Indian race." In their eyes the 1899 rebellion proved this to be a fundamental precondition of sustained economic progress and stable civilian rule. Political alliance, or even coexistence, was no longer a viable political option. And starting with Pando himself, the Liberal Party expunged from official memory all earlier collaborators with Indian allies. Zárate Willka was barbarianized into the "fearsome Willka" as intellectuals and policymakers argued about the linked destinies of the Indian and the nation.

For now they were inevitably conjoined. Much like the postwar intellectuals of Lima, Bolivian writers found no easy exit from their national dilemma. They could not harbor much hope of racial assimilation, given the numerical preponderance of indigenous peoples. Extermination campaigns could be (and were) carried out against specific tribal groups in Bolivia's vast tropical frontier, but they were unfeasible in the highlands. Thus thwarted, writers and politicians looked into the national soul and saw "mestizo" but could not agree on the worthiness of the mestizo to carry forth the national mandate. Indeed, until deep into the twentieth century, cultural *mestizaje* did not become an ideological rallying point of national identity. On the contrary Alcides Arguedas and other prominent writers found the mestizo to be a contemptible race – indeed the main cause of Bolivia's barbarous republican history of *caudillaje* (leadership by charismatic armed men). The orthodoxies of Social Darwinism may have held out some hope that over time the superior white race would prevail. But in a nation where whites composed less than 20 percent of the population, how long would that process take?

This dilemma called for an intermediate solution to the Indian problem. If cultural *mestizaje* offered no way out, then the government had to design policies to exclude Indians from the political sphere, remove them from their lands now coveted by a new breed of La Paz–dwelling rural landlord, contain Indian unrest, and convert them into disciplined manual laborers in the countryside and cities. Intellectuals, lawyers, and policymakers tried to fashion an informal system of racial apartheid: Indians would be civilized and molded into a laboring class yet simultaneously separated, protected, and their political aspirations contained. An emerging visual language of race undergirded this inchoate project of turning highland Indians into subaltern laborers. In particular, photography provided a crucial medium for penetrating the physiognomic interior of the Indian psyche and soul (Fig. 23.14). Biologized race differences naturalized Indians as exotic, potentially dangerous, "others" in need of state-imposed tutelage, social control, and moral improvement. Notwithstanding their racist rhetoric and civilizing impulses, however, La Paz Liberals had no unifying program of reform and, in any event, market forces proved far more virulent than any such policy agenda during the twenty-year reign of Liberalism (1900–1920). As a result the rapid expansion of *latifundismo* across the lake district after 1900 created the de facto basis for the "seigneurial solution" to land reform. Many indigenous communities were swallowed whole by expanding estates, though not without long struggles. But the alleged immutability of racial difference, the deepening of racial tension after 1899, shut Indians out of the nation. Policymakers began to tailor the civilizing mission to keep Indians back – to socialize them to perform manual labor, to stay in the countryside, and to keep their own customs. Ideals of racial and cultural assimilation through education were deemed unrealistic, even dangerous. Indians were to be taught temperance, hygiene, and crafts but not literacy. They were to cultivate their crops but not on their own communal lands. And they were to render their usual labor services and pay property taxes, but they were to remain disenfranchised. Much like the other Andean republics, then, Bolivia entered the twentieth century more fragmented and divided than ever before.

NATION BUILDING AND THE BURDEN OF RACE

This chapter has grappled with the dynamic interactions among highland Quechua- and Aymara-speaking peasants, internally divided Creole élites, and emerging sectors of ambiguous ethnically and culturally mixed people swelling the interstices of modernizing rural Andean societies. It maps diverse national and regional landscapes of power, which became more textured, fluid, and differentiated over the course of the nineteenth century.

The chapter also explores the ideological correlates of postcolonial nation building in the Andes – an increasingly rigid conceptual landscape in which Creole nationalists tried to impose a postcolonial order of hierarchy and legitimacy in their conflict-ridden, ethnically divided societies. Basically the postcolonial inequalities mandated the redefinition of

Figure 23.14. Sample *Cartes-de-Visite* featuring Aymara "Indian Types," 1910. The *carte-de-visite* was a popular convention that circulated "exotic" or "artistic" images through society. Applying the same standards as those used in bourgeois portraiture, photographers in La Paz (and elsewhere) froze anonymous Indians in standardized posed, gaping out at the viewer, perhaps carrying a water or chicha jug (as in the two photographs here) or wearing leather straps used for hauling heavy sacks of flour, firewood, or other loads that burdened rural men (as we see in the photograph of the man), but removed from any humanizing cultural or social context and set against a blank backdrop of the indoor studio. These stark studies of racialized subjects give only the barest hint of their occupations (which interested Wiener, as in Fig. 23.7 or Fig. 23.8, for example)

or their cultural heritage (alluded to by the careful placement of certain "ethnic artifacts" in Fig. 23.10). Postcard portraits like these were collected by the hundreds and analyzed by scientists to construct "composite types" that might be useful for genetic theories of race, criminology, or creole debates over Indian legislation, education, and civilizing potential. For example, Arthur Chervin made use of *cartes-de-visit* (in conjunction with his anthropometric studies) to assess Bolivia's racial makeup so as to be able to prognosticate its future development! (See his *Antropologie Bolivienne* [Paris: Imp. Nacionale, 1908], 3 vols. Discussed in Poole, *Vision, Race, and Modernity,* 134–35.) (Photographs reproduced with permission form the Peabody Museum of Archaeology and Ethnology, Harvard University.)

Indians from a historic corporate group to an inferior biological race living at the margins of nation and civilization. This reformulation dealt a double blow. Formally Indians lost their colonial-derived legal rights to collective existence and protection, and they became individuals subject to universal contract law. Informally they assumed the biological attributes of an inferior racial group, whose very character rendered them unfit for civil society or citizenship. By 1900 Creoles had constructed postcolonial nations around rigid concepts of race that excluded the indigenous majorities from republican history and political participation, but which coerced them into national economies as subaltern laborers.

Although the dialectics of race and nation making are familiar to historians of nineteenth-century Latin America (and elsewhere), the specific historical struggles that surrounded and shaped the construction of postcolonial nations are not. In contrast to the positivist cant saturating public discourse, there was no steady march toward order and progress over the nineteenth century, nor any inevitable outcome. Rather the century unleashed a cacophony of clashing visions, voices, and interests that reverberated across these broken landscapes. Postcolonial passages toward nationhood were always fought with conflict, violence, and reversal. Nowhere was this more true than in the Andean republics. Conflicts over the moral and political relationship between the Indian majorities and the dominant élites rent the social fabric and raged for almost a century. It was not until the late nineteenth century that modernity and capitalism mustered enough force to pull together the contentious élites. Only then did Creole cliques begin to forge pacts of domination and to mount civilizing projects to discipline their refractory rural masses.

In this struggle highland Andean peasantries emerged as powerful protagonists continuously negotiating and contesting the institutional terms under which they would participate in the new republics. Armed with local folk-legal traditions, honed in the colonial courts under the *república de indios*, Indian authorities evolved political, cultural, and discursive strategies to protect or recover stolen lands and local autonomies under the new republics. Andean peoples did not blindly adhere to the colonial past, but after two decades of war, repression, and reform, they came to understand that the advent of modernity threatened their most significant colonial patrimonies.

Furthermore Andeans were acutely aware of themselves as political subjects in the new nations. They built the roads and laid the rails, paid the lion's share of taxes, carried the mail and dug the municipal cemeteries, and supplied the soldiers for partisan and *caudillo* wars. They had come to expect justice and respect in return for their labors and sacrifices.

For many Andean communities, then, the abolition of tribute in mid-century marked a crossroads in the evolution of Indian–state relations. The collapse of the *pax republicana* left rural society wide open to anarchy, violence, and disorder. The ex-tributary republics withdrew from the business of paternalistic control, yet they lacked the modern apparatus to impose discipline in the countryside. Political terror and predatory violence, as well as everyday incursions and resistance, became the order of the day. But it was also a moment of acute tension among élite factions, as colonialism and liberalism clashed head-on. This is starkly revealed in the republics' welter of contradictory reforms and counterreforms through the 1850s, 1860s, and 1870s. In Peru three successive regimes reversed and reinvented Indian policies alternately to conquer, assimilate, and paternalize Indians. In Ecuador tribute abolition coincided with the state's efforts to conscript Indians to build the nation's trans-Andean highways. In both Colombia and Bolivia (albeit under very different circumstances), late nineteenth-century liberal reforms ceded to paternalistic policies to quell rural unrest.

These intraélite battles subsided in the last years of the century, with the ascent of liberal-positivist doctrines among prospering export oligarchies. For the first time Creole nationals (of whatever partisan stripe) began to link the national question to the "Indian problem." In search of knowledge and authority, and groping toward the construction of national identities, Creole élites looked inward toward their own interior frontiers to discover the secrets of the "other." In each republic a new canon of scientific reportage, ethnography, regionalist novels, romantic poetry, photography, and muckraking essays created a new age of discovery – once again, the prelude to conquest and colonization. Modernity came to the Andes in the guise of the scientific and literary explorers penetrating the primitive world of the barbarian races. In this hegemonic discourse, diverse racial doctrines competed against each other, and the "Indian race" often became a rhetorical pawn in their partisan polemics.

But most writers did not hesitate to describe contemporary Indian peasants in ways that made them the scourge and shame of their nations. No one thought that Indians had anything to say worth listening to, or that they possessed the capacity for political participation, or that their history was anything but ancillary to the development of the Andean republics. The manufacture of racialist discourse implicitly, but powerfully, redefined nation building as an exclusivist and violent exercise in power. Abandoning the ideal of universal citizenship, oligarchies concentrated instead on civilizing projects that would remake Indians into a class of laboring poor.

For Andean peoples the transfiguration into biological subjects narrowed the compass of political possibility and moral acceptability. It shut them out of the nation at the very moment when they were catapulted into the middle of national and international wars and increasingly subjected to violent despoliation under liberalizing laws. At the local level, Indians continued to deploy folk-legal discourses to defend customary and colonial legitimacies, manipulate legal ambiguities, and forge transitory political pacts. In the process they rediscovered and revitalized their own ethnic pasts and traditions of struggle, laying the foundations for the rise of militant ethnic movements in the early twentieth century.

Even before the rebellious cycles of the early twentieth century, indigenous peasantries in Peru and Bolivia briefly burst onto the national scene and made themselves heard amidst the din of military invasion and warfare. These moments of crisis significantly altered the site and scope of struggle, as well as regional and national power balances. Equally important, they now afford us glimpses into the political imaginings of Andean peasant-soldiers, who redefined themselves as political subjects entitled to justice, respect, and protection within their own societies. Indigenous leaders like Atusparia, Laimes, and Zárate Willka did not map political blueprints for alternative forms of nationhood or subscribe rigidly to any political orthodoxy. But in their own diverse and contradictory ways, they did envision nations that would let Aymara and Quechua communities to flourish and prosper. Political issues of citizenship, equality, and cultural pluralism were all deeply embedded in these broader moral hopes. As such, Andean popular discourses in the late nineteenth century provided powerful insurgent counterforces to the new racialist canon, working hard to naturalize, demean, and silence the "Indian race."

BIBLIOGRAPHIC ESSAY

Traditionally nineteenth-century Andean historiography has been the province of political historians who chronicle the instability of republican governments, and of economic historians critical of export-driven economic growth and late nineteenth-century oligarchic regimes. Ethnohistorians and anthropologists, in contrast, have tended to focus most on contemporary Andean cultures or on the transition from Inka to Spanish rule. More recently a new generation of social and ethnohistorians has reexamined Andean insurgency during the late eighteenth century.

Traditional historiographic neglect, as well as the severe limitations imposed by thin, discontinuous, and opaque republican sources, have long discouraged social and anthropological histories of Andean peoples under republican rule. Over the past 15 or 20 years, however, a surge of historical and anthropological research has opened new perspectives on Andean highland societies in the transition from colony to nation. Many of these historical studies fold the nineteenth century into longer time frames, sometimes framing the "long nineteenth century" between 1780 and 1930, or between 1810 and 1930. In many ways the Bourbon beginning of state centralization and modest free-trade reforms in the late eighteenth century anticipated what was to come later, just as Andean–state tensions that simmered during much of the nineteenth century might be seen as a long prelude to ethnic resurgence in the early twentieth century. Most of these studies center on specific regions or ethnic communities, combining thick ethnographic descriptions of local-level processes with broader analyses of translocal transitions to modern capitalist economies and nations. Over the late 1980s and early 1990s, historians and anthropologists have blended archival research, oral testimonies, and ethnological perspectives in order to capture a sense of Andean activities, subjectivities, and historiographies.

There is still no overarching comparative study of the nineteenth-century Andean republics and their "Indian policies." Several recent collections, however, cut across the four republics and raise many crucial issues about Andean experiences and responses to republican policies and practices. The two-volume collection, J. P. Deler and Y. Saint-Geours (eds.), *Estados y naciones en los andes. Hacia una historia comparativa: Bolivia, Colombia, Ecuador, y Perú* (Lima, 1986), intersperses illuminating, comparative commentary among solid essays on regional societies and Andean adjustments to external pressures. A more focused collection on Indian–state relations, estate–communal conflicts, and other nineteenth-century issues is developed in H. Bonilla (ed.), *Los Andes en la encrucijada: indios, comunidades, y estado en el siglo XIX* (Quito, 1991). See also the suggestive introductory essay and relevant articles in Steve J. Stern (ed.), *Resistance, Rebellion, and Consciousness in the Andean Peasant*

World, 18th to 20th centuries (Madison, 1987), as well as the introductory and concluding essays in Brooke Larson and Olivia Harris with Enrique Tandeter (eds.), *Ethnicity, Markets and Migration in the Andes: At the Crossroads of History and Anthropology* (Durham, 1995).

In lieu of richly documented government sources or ethnographies on nineteenth-century Andean societies, the student may tap the rich vein of foreign travel literature and embryonic social sciences produced by Europeans, North Americans, and a few educated Creoles engaged in the exploration, discovery, and diagnosis of native inhabitants of the new nations. Scientific and literary excursions into the internal frontiers of the Andes served the cause of imperial and national "white civilizers" anxious to recolonize Andean territories and cultures. Mary Louise Pratt's *Imperial Eyes. Travel Writing and Transculturation* (New York, 1992) discusses the politics and genre of travel writing in the broader context of (mainly) English imperial expansion in Africa and Latin America. Travel books on the nineteenth-century Andes range from the scornful or patronizing (hopelessly marred by racism or romanticism) to sympathetic and insightful narratives rich in ethnographic detail. Of the latter, see the illustrated travel narrative by Alcides D'Orbigny, *Voyage dans l'Amérique Meridionale. (Le Brasil, Uruguay, L'Argentine, Chili, Bolivia, Pérou, etc.) executé pendant les années 1623 a 1826*, 9 vols. (Paris, 1835–1847), for especially vivid descriptions of highland Bolivia. A valuable source for the independence period is William Bennett Stevenson's sympathetic and ethnographically accurate account, *Historical and Descriptive Narrative of Twenty Years' Residence in South America*, 3 vols. (London, 1825). This journal is especially insightful about highland Ecuador. Friedrich Hassaurek, an Austrian-born diplomat who served as Abraham Lincoln's ambassador to Ecuador, wrote a fascinating travel memoir of highland Ecuador. Although flawed by racist remarks, his *Four Years Among the Ecuadorians* [1867] (Carbondale, 1967) sketches vivid scenes of many facets of rural life. Good travel reports on Colombia include A. Hettner, *Viajes por los andes colombianos, 1882–1884* [1888] (Bogota, 1976), and Robert Cross, *Report by Robert Cross on his Mission to South America in 1877–1878* (London, 1879), the latter concerning the natural and social conditions of the quinine trade. By far the most important exploratory field research on rural Colombia was carried out by the *Comisión corográfica*, under the leadership of the Italian soldier and cartographer, Agustín Codazzi. He was contracted in 1850 to lead interdisciplinary expeditions into Colombia's hinterlands to survey and categorize the republic's resources, inhabitants, topographies, and boundaries. The expedition led to a series of studies and illustrations, some of them later published. On the *Comisión corográfica* and the birth of Colombia's social sciences, see O. Restrepo, " 'La comisión corográfica' y las ciencias sociales," in J. Arocha and N. de Friedemann (eds.), *Un siglo de investigación social: antropología en Colombia* (Bogotá, 1984). Peru, once the homeland of the Inka, attracted much interest among nineteenth-century antiquarians, historians, geographers, and scientists. Historian William Hickling Prescott's interest in the Inka influenced his colleague, Ephraim George Squier, who set new standards of ethnological description in his work, *Peru: Incidents of Travel and Exploration in the Land of the Incas* [1877] (New York, 1973). Other important travel memoirs and descriptions of highland Peru include: Sir Clements Markham, *Cuzco: A Journey to the Ancient Capital of Peru . . . and Lima . . .* (London, 1856), with excerpts recently republished in Peter Blanchard (ed.), *Markham in Peru: The Travels of Clements R. Markham, 1852–1853* (Austin, 1991); the observations of Englishman, Edmond Temple, in his *Travels in Various Parts of Peru, including a Year's Residence in Potosí* (Bolivia), 2 vols. (Philadelphia, 1833); and the journal of the Swiss naturalist, J. J. von Tschudi, *Travels in Peru during the Years 1838–1842 . . .* (London, 1847).

Among the four Andean experiences of nineteenth-century nation making, Colombia and Ecuador are the least studied. On the policies, politics, and thought of nineteenth-century Colombian reformers, see the pathbreaking, synthetic studies of Frank Safford: "Race, integration and progress: Elite attitudes and the Indian in Colombia 1750–1870," *Hispanic American Historical Review* 71:1 (1991), 1–34, and "The emergence of economic liberalism in Colombia," in J. Love and N. Jacobsen (eds.), *Guiding the Invisible Hand: Economic Liberalism and the State in Latin American History* (New York, 1988), 32–62. On racial discourses among nation builders, see Leon Helguera, *Indigenismo in Colombia: A Facet of the National Identity Search, 1821–1973* (Buffalo, 1974), and Peter Wade, "The language of race, place, and nation in Colombia," *América negra* 1 (1991), 41–65. In his study of lowland native peoples and the rubber boom, Michael Taussig discusses the real and rhetorical violence of extractive capitalism and imperial-civilizing projects: *Shamanism, Colonialism, and the Wild Man: A Study in Terror and Healing* (Chicago, 1987).

Research on the nineteenth-century Chibchas of Colombia's northeastern highlands is still spotty. Much of it revolves around the conflict over *resguardo* lands under liberal regimes. A classic study is Juan Friede,

El indio en la lucha por la tierra. Historia de los resguardos del macizo central Colombiano (Bogotá, 1944). The student will find a quick overview in Orlando Fals Borda's article, "Indian *Congregaciones* in the new kingdom of Granada: Land tenure aspects, 1595–1850," *The Americas* 13 (1957), 331–351. For specifically nineteenth-century anti-*resguardo* policies and conflicts, see Glen Curry, "The disappearance of the *Resguardos Indígenas* of Cundinamarca, Colombia, 1800–1863," unpublished Ph.D. dissertation, Vanderbilt University, 1981. See also Sylvia Broadbent, *Los Chibchas, organización socio-política* (Bogotá, 1964). For broader historical studies of land tenure, peasant societies, and agrarian change in nineteenth-century Colombia, see Marcos Palacios, *Coffee in Colombia. An Economic, Social, and Political History* (Cambridge, 1980); Catherine Legrand, *Frontier Expansion and Peasant Protest in Colombia, 1850–1936* (Albuquerque, 1986); and Sylvia Broadbent, "The formation of peasant society in central Colombia," *Ethnohistory* 28:3 (1981), 258–277. *Minifundio-latifundio* dynamics at the microlevel are examined in Orlando Fals Borda's monograph, *Peasant Society in the Colombian Andes: A Sociological Study of Saucío* (Gainesville, 1955).

Some of the most innovative historical anthropology on Colombia in recent years has come from Joanne Rappaport's two case studies of the southern Páez and Pasto peoples: respectively, *The Politics of Memory, Native Historical Interpretation in the Colombian Andes* (Cambridge, 1990), and *Cumbe Reborn: An Andean Ethnography of History* (Chicago, 1994). In both works Rappaport explores the contours of native historical consciousness and ethnic politics in the struggle over territory, community, and identity. Her study of the Páez peoples, in particular, traces the social, economic, and cultural forces and counterforces of change under the pressures of republican land reform, white colonization, and extractive capitalism during the second half of the nineteenth century. More traditional but informative studies of the Páez may be found in Elías Sevilla-Casas, *Anthropological Studies of Tierradentro* (Cali, 1976), and M. T. Findji and J. M. Rojas, *Territorio, economía, y sociedad páez* (Cali, 1985).

In the last several years, Ecuadorian scholars have broken new ground in nineteenth-century social and cultural issues of Indians and nation making. Emerging historical interest in peasant politics and political consciousness was sparked by the 1990 Indian uprising in highland Ecuador, and nurtured by a growing international network of young Andeanists drawn to the FLACSO program in Andean History and Anthropology, based in Quito. Several important collections have begun to bring this new research to light; see especially I. Almeida et al. (eds.), *Indios. Una reflexión sobre el levantamiento indígena de 1990* (Quito, 1991), particularly the contribution by Hernán Ibarra, "La identidad devaluada de los 'Modern Indians,' " ibid., 319–349; H. Bonilla (ed.), *Los Andes en la encrucijada: indios, comunidades, y estado en el siglo XIX* (Quito 1991); and B. Muratorio (ed.), *Imágenes e imagineros: representaciones de los indígenas ecuatorianos. Siglos XIX y XX* (Quito, 1994).

An older historical literature on Ecuadorian Indians and the nation begins with the classic *indigenista* studies by the noted Mexican anthropologist and ambassador to Ecuador, Moisés Sáenz, *Sobre el indio ecuatoriano y su incorporación al medio nacional*, and by Pío Jaramillo Alvarado, *El indio ecuatoriano. Contribución al estudio de la sociología indoamericano* (Quito, 1936). The famous muckraking novel by Jorge Icaza, *Huasipungo* (Quito, 1934), also belongs to this foundational literature of early twentieth-century *indigenismo*. But until recently few Ecuadorian historians have studied Indian political movements, except as discrete and largely insignificant uprisings (see O. Albornoz, *Las luchas indígenas en el Ecuador* [Guayaquil, 1971]), or as subordinate factions of larger intraélite political struggles (see Victor A. Jaramillo, *Participación de Otavalo en la Guerra de Independencia* [Otavalo, 1933], and V. Goncharov, "Los indígenas en la revolución liberal de Eloy Alfaro," *Los pueblos autóctonos en América latina: pasado y presente*, 2 vols. [Moscow, 1984], 2:19–206). Recent studies cultivate fine-grained analyses of peasant politics, the problem of political authority, everyday forms of resistance, popular discourses, and discontentments. See especially the three Ecuadorian contributions in H. Bonilla (ed.), *Los Andes en la encrucijada*: Martha Moscoso, "La tierra: espacio de conflicto y relación entre el Estado y la comunidad en el siglo XIX," 367–390; Silvia Palomeque, "Estado y comunidad en el siglo XIX. Las autoridades indígenas y su relación con el Estado," 391–418; and Galo Ramón V., "Los indios y la constitución del estado nacional," 419–456. As part of his broader, forthcoming study of ethnic politics and nineteenth-century nation building in Ecuador, Andrés Guerrero published an important article on the clashes between folk-legal and republican concepts of land and authority in nineteenth-century Otavalo: "Curagas y tenientes políticos: la ley de la costumbre y la ley del estado (Otavalo, 1830–1875)," *Revista Andina* 7: 2 (1989), 321–365.

On the interaction of élite and peasant practices and discourses related to state policies toward Indians, see the crucial article by Mark J. Van Aken, "The lingering death of Indian tribute in Ecuador," *Hispanic American Historical Review* 61:3 (1981), 429–445, and the thin overview of nation-building rhetoric in Mary Crain, "The social construction of national identity in highland Ecuador," *Anthopological Quarterly* 63:1 (1990), 43–59. A penetrating analysis of liberal representations of the "Indian race" is Andrés Guerrero, "Una imagen ventrílocua: el Discurso Liberal a la 'Desgraciada Raza Indígena' a fines del siglo XIX," in B. Muratorio (ed.), *Imágenes e imagineros*, ibid, 197–252. A stunning collection of photos of nineteenth-century Ecuadorian Indians appears in Lucía Chiriboga and Silvana Caparrini, *Identidades desnudas, Ecuador, 1860–1920* (Quito, 1994). Older notions of peasant immobility under hacienda-styled feudalism and debt peonage have come under the scrutiny of social historians interested in the subtle dynamics of Indian–landlord paternalism on nineteenth-century haciendas. For an overview of recent studies, as well as a suggestive methodological discussion of peasant negotiations of paternal power on a highland Ecuadorian estate, see Mark Thurner, "Peasant politics and Andean haciendas in the transition to capitalism: An ethnographic history," *Latin American Research Review* 28:3 (1993), 41–82. On the symbolic world of landlord paternalism, see Andrés Guerrero, *La semántica de la dominación: el concertaje de indios* (Quito, 1991) and Galo Ramón Valarezo: *El poder y los norandinos* (Quito, 1990).

The Otavalan communities of farmers, weavers, and merchants have long attracted anthropological interest in their cultural strategies of social reproduction and selective adaptation. Among Ecuador's native highland peoples, the Otavalans stand out for their ethnic cohesion, pride, and prosperity. Two recent studies provide very useful historical and ethnological orientations to Otavalans: Frank Salomon, "Weavers of Otavalo," in Norman E. Whitten, Jr. (ed.), *Cultural Transformations and Ethnicity in Modern Ecuador* (Urbana, 1981), 420–449, and Joseph B. Casagrande, "Strategies for survival: The Indians of highland Ecuador," ibid., 260–277. The latter article studies six highland communities including the Otavalan town of Peguche. An early classic ethnography of the Otavaleños is by Elsie Clews Parsons, *Peguche, Cantón of Otavalo, Province of Imbabura, Ecuador: A Study of Andean Indians* (Chicago, 1945). More generally Whitten's volume (already cited) includes a rich variety of ethnohistorical and ethnographic studies of contemporary Ecuador, besides the two articles mentioned. See especially the provocative study of the rise of an assimilationist project of national integration in twentieth-century Ecuador: Ronald Stutzman, "El *mestizaje:* An all-inclusive ideology of exclusion," 45–94.

The ethnological, historical, and documentary resources on nineteenth-century Peru are far more extensive and layered than those related to the other Andean republics. Several streams of historiography, ethnohistory, and published documentary collections feed into the study of nineteenth-century Peruvian social history and, more recently, into ethnohistorical research on indigenous societies in the transition from colony to nation. To begin with, nineteenth-century Peruvian historiography rests on a solid foundation of research into Andean societies under Spanish rule. A core of regional-ethnic studies of Andean-colonial "Indians" provides deep historical perspective on cultural continuities, changes, and diversities in the plural Andean world. Furthermore long-term temporal frameworks often bridge the conventional political divide between the late colonial and republican periods. Some colonial-Andean histories discuss the implications of "colonial legacies" for nineteenth-and twentieth-century patterns of Indian cultural adaptation, resistance, and poverty (for example, Steve J. Stern, *Peru's Indian Peoples and the Challenge of Conquest: Huamanga to 1640* [Madison, 1982]); others trace long-term sociocultural trends and ideologies across colonial and postcolonial periods of time (such as, Bruce Mannheim, *The Language of the Inca since the European Invasion* [Austin, 1991], and Manuel Burga, *Nacimiento de una utopía. Muerte y resurrección de los incas* [Lima, 1988]).

Second, modern anthropological research on Peru's highland indigenous peoples has flourished since the World War II, branching off in the 1960s and 1970s into a host of subfields and dialogues (see Frank Salomon, "The historical development of Andean ethnology," *Mountain Research and Development* 5:1 [1985], 79–98, for a detailed overview). Peruvian ethnologist, Luís E. Valcárcel, and later the ethnographic and literary works of José María Arguedas, inspired an international group of ethnological researchers and activists to write and lobby against modernizing models of forced assimilation. These ethnological studies of contemporary Andean societies drew much of their inspiration from older ethnohistorians like John V. Murra, John Rowe, Franklin Pease, and R. Tom Zuidema, who documented the adaptability and diversity of Andean cultural traditions and social organization under Inka and early colonial rule. Until recently, however, ethnologists have concentrated on contemporary Andean societies while ethnohistorians have focused on

Inka and post-Inkaic periods, leaving the study of nineteenth-century rural Peru to others.

Until a decade ago, research on nineteenth-century Peru was virtually monopolized by socioeconomic and political historians, many of them grounded in Marxian concerns of political economy, dependency, and the transition to capitalism. A third research tradition, then, which sometimes diverted attention from highland rural society, Andean agency, and cultural themes, was the rise of a (mostly Peruvian-based) Marxian historiography of nineteenth-century Peru. In this view the logic of the world capitalist market (and its human agents), creating its own peculiar conflicts and contradictions in precapitalist societies, determined the forces of historical change, leaving the Peruvian peasantry almost passive and impervious to social change (see Jean Piel, "The place of the peasantry in nineteenth century Peru," *Past and Present* 46 [1970], 108–133, for an extreme example of this position.) But out of this historiography also came a clarifying synthesis of nineteenth-century Peru: Manuel Burga and Alberto Flores-Galindo, *Apogeo y crisis de la república aristocrática*, 3rd. ed. (Lima, 1984). It still stands as a classic interpretation of three related trends: the persistence of Andean-colonial forms of landed paternalism in the twentieth century; the power of mercantile capitalism to reorganize rural society in the Southern Highlands during the wool boom; and the rise of agrarian capitalism in the northern sugar zones, the site of militant unionism.

Still fundamentally untapped by sociocultural historians of nineteenth-century Peru is the monumental 17-volume work by Jorge Basadre, *Historia de la República del Perú*, 6th ed. (Lima, 1968–1969); his path-breaking work on the social history of the republic, *La multitud, la ciudad, y el campo en la historia del la República* (Lima, 1947); and his documentary collection, *Introducción a las bases documentales para la historia de la República del Perú con algunas reflexiones*, 2 vols. (Lima, 1971). Researchers interested in official demographic statistics on Peruvian Indians may also count on a preliminary documentary base. George Kubler first outlined Indian population trends in his Smithsonian-sponsored study, *The Indian Caste of Peru, 1795–1910: A Population Study based upon Tax Records and Census Reports* (Washington, D.C., 1952). His major finding – that Indians remained a statistical majority of the nation's population during the nineteenth century – was recently reinforced and modestly revised by Paul Gootenberg's enlightening sociodemographic analysis, "Population and ethnicity in early republican Peru: Some revisions," *Latin American Research Review* 26:3 (1991), 109–158.

Recent research on rural highland peasantries during and after Peruvian independence clusters around several major topics. Defining the new historiographical landscape is a group of historical-anthropological studies that situate the particularities of peasant or ethnic involvement in postcolonial nation making, regional change, and local cultural adaptation within larger frameworks of long-term regional change (usually organized around periods of upheaval and economic transition – such as the independence wars, the War of the Pacific, regional uprisings, the expansion of commercial capitalism, and territorial incursions). Although they differ in important ways, these studies embrace a range of interlocking themes and perspectives, emphasizing Andean peasant social experiences, understandings, and inroads into hegemonic relations of power and representation. These keystone works include: Alberto Flores-Galindo, *Arequipa y el sur andino. Siglos XIII–XX* (Lima, 1977); Florencia Mallon, *The Defense of Community in Peru's Central Highlands. Peasant Struggle and Capitalist Transition, 1860–1940* (Princeton, 1983); Nelson Manrique, *Yawar mayu: Sociedades terratenientes serranas, 1879–1910* (Lima, 1988); Gavin Smith, *Livelihood and Resistance. Peasants and the Politics of Land in Peru* (Berkeley, 1989); Nils Jacobsen, *Mirages of Transition. The Peruvian Altiplano, 1780–1930* (Berkeley, 1993); and Mark Thurner, "From two Republics to one divided. contradictions of Postcolonial Nationmaking in Andean Peru (Durham, North Carolina, 1997).

Peasant participation in the War of the Pacific has been the subject of ongoing debates over broader issues of peasant political consciousness and imagined national projects in predominantly precapitalist societies. Beyond the polemics (see the debate crystallized in articles by F. Mallon and H. Bonilla in Steve J. Stern [ed.], *Resistance, Rebellion, and Consciousness in the Rural Andean World, 18th to 20th centuries*), historians have begun to rewrite the history of Peru's national crisis in the 1880s from the "bottom up" and from a comparative regional perspective. Focusing more on regional particularities of preexisting relations of power, and on peasant experiences, visions, and voices captured in fragmented form during the crisis of war, these recent histories are opening windows on rural Andean worlds usually lost to view. See especially Florencia Mallon, *The Defense of Community*, ch. 3, and her recent comparative study,

Peasant and Nation. The Making of Postcolonial Mexico and Peru (Berkeley, 1995). See also Nelson Manrique, *Campesino y nación: las guerrillas indígenas en la guerra con Chile* (Lima, 1981), and his *Yawar mayu.* A second focal point of insurgent peasant politics and political aspirations revolves around the 1885 rebellion in the Huaylas region. See especially Mark Thurner, "From two nations to one," ch. 5, and William W. Stein, *El levantamiento de Atusparia* (Lima, 1988), and his essay, "Myth and ideology in a nineteenth century Peruvian uprising," *Ethnohistory* 2:4 (1982), 237–264.

Research on Andean participation in the wars between patriots and royalists during the 1810s and 1820s is thinner. Until recently many historians tended to focus on the Andean civil wars during the 1780s, dismissing the formal "independence wars" as intraélite civil wars between the invading armies of foreign patriots and local Peruvian royalists. Christine Hühnefeldt's pathbreaking study of the independence era was the first major work to shatter élite-centric perspectives by studying local peasant reactions to Spanish constitutionalism and later Bolíva-styled liberalism, simmering tax and land-based conflicts, and spin-off rebellions like the 1812 Indian uprising of Huánuco; see her *Lucha por la tierra y protesta indígena: las comunidades indígenas entre la colonia y república* (Bonn, 1982). On peasants, *caudillo* politics, and banditry during the independence wars, see Charles Walker, *Peasants, Caudillos, and the State in Peru: Cusco in the Transition from Colony to Republic, 1780–1840.* 2 vols. unpublished Ph.D. dissertation, University of Chicago, 1992, and several articles in Carlos Aguirre and Charles Walker (eds.), *Bandoleros, abigeos y montoneras: criminalidad y violencia en el perú. siglos XVIII–XX* (Lima, 1990). For innovative research on peasant royalists in the Ayacucho region, see Cecilia Méndez, "Los campesinos, la independencia y la iniciación de la república. El caso de los iquichanos realistas: Ayacucho, 1825–1828," in H. Urbano (ed.), *Poder y violencia en los Andes* (Cusco, 1991) 165–188.

Other studies are beginning to focus attention on the coercive and negotiating processes by which republican authorities tried to impose new tax, land, and other policies on Indian communities. For an early institutional study, see Thomas M. Davies, *Indian Integration in Peru. A Half Century of Experience, 1900–1948* (Lincoln, 1974), chs. 1 and 2 on nineteenth-century background. A spate of recent books and articles deal with Indian tributary policies and politics, including: Victor Peralta Ruíz, *En pos del tributo en el Cusco rural, 1826–1854* (Cusco, 1991); and Carlos

Contreras, "Estado republicano y tributo indígena en la sierra central en la post-independencia," *Histórica* 13:1 (1989), 9–44. For a brilliant synthetic study of Peruvian ideological and cultural projects vis-à-vis the Inka, see for Alberto Flores Galindo, *Buscando un Inca. indentidad y utopía eulos Audes* (Lima, 1988). For an overview of Creole writings on the Indians between the mid–nineteenth century and the heyday of *indigenismo*, see Efraín Kristal, *The Andes Viewed from the City. Literary and Political Discourse on the Indian in Peru, 1848–1930* (New York, 1987). Also relevant is L. E. Tord, *El indio en los ensayistas peruanos (1848–1948)* (Lima, 1978). For an insightful study of Lima's anti-Andean nationalism during the Peru-Bolivia confederation of the 1830s, see Cecilia Méndez, "República sin indios: la comunidad imaginada del Perú," in H. Urbano (ed.), *Tradición y Modernidad en los Andes* (Cusco, 1992), 15–41. On the rise of indigenism around the turn of the twentieth century, see José Deustua and José Luís Rénique, *Intelectuales, indigenismo, y descentralismo en el Perú, 1897–1931* (Cusco, 1984), and Angel Rama, "El area cultural andina (hispanismo, mesticismo, indigenismo)," *Cuadernos Americanos* (Mexico City) 33 (1974), 136–173. Deborah Poole's *Vision, Race, and Modernity-A Visual Economy of the Andean Image World* (Princeton, 1997) innovatively explores the impact of images, especially photography, on racial ideas.

Fine-grained socioeconomic and cultural research on Andean rural society, agrarian power relations, and the changing contours of class and ethnic identity are to be found in many of the studies already cited. One particular theme, however, has been reexamined in recent studies: the power, politics, and political culture of regional landowning power holders (*gamonales*). Studies by Flores Galindo (*Arequipa y el sur andino*), François Bourricaud, *Cambios en Puno* (Mexico City, 1967), and more recently, Nils Jacobsen (*Mirages of Transition*), have put sociological and historical content into flat stereotypes of *gamonalismo* (first characterized by José María Mariátegui). Some researchers, like Juan Martínez Alier (*Los huachilleros el Perú* [Lima, 1973]), have deemphasized landlords' monopoly of power over Indian sheepherders, who fashioned their own strategies of resistance to modern property relations and the efforts to modernize sheep ranching. In the last few years, a new group of anthropologists and historians have renewed interest in the idioms, routines, and rituals of power and violence in regional highland cultures. See the important collections by Henrique Urbano (ed.), *Poder y violencia en los Andes* (Cusco, 1991), and Deborah Poole (ed.), *Unruly Order. Violence,*

Power, and Cultural Identity in the High Provinces of Southern Peru (Boulder, 1994).

Research on Bolivia's nineteenth-century Indians has been growing at the intersection of history and anthropology for almost two decades. Several factors account for this: the simple fact that Bolivia's "Indian problem" was always central to republican state making, given the numerical predominance of communal-based indigenous peoples; the pioneering ethnohistorical work of Tristan Platt, which set new interdisciplinary standards of field-archival scholarship on Andean *ayllus* under republican rule; and the rise of activist historians and anthropologists in Bolivia, whose work has placed Aymara and Quechua interests, narratives, and memories at the center of their historical research. Among the latter the collective oral history projects of the Taller de Historia Oral Aymara (THOA), together with the activist anthropology of the Centro de Investigación y Promoción del Campesino (CIPCA), have produced important bodies of oral documentation, field studies, and indigenous histories written in Quechua, Aymara, and Spanish. In addition Bolivia has attracted a lively international group of ethnologists, whose work on contemporary *ayllus* provides rich background for gathering historical perspectives.

Although Bolivia has no equivalent to Peru's Jorge Basadre, Josep Barnadas's bibliographic guide is still very useful: *Introducción a los estudios bolivianos contemporáneos, 1960–1984* (Cusco, 1987). A basic primary source for early nineteenth-century Bolivia, with suggestive census data and descriptions of Indian societies, is José María Dalence's compendium, *Bosquejo estadístico de Bolivia* (Chuquisaca, 1851). Indian population records were compiled periodically for purposes of tribute collection. Working with these *padrones*, Erwin P. Grieshaber compiled an aggregate overview of official Indian population trends in his important article, "Survival of Indian communities in nineteenth century Bolivia: A regional comparison," *Journal of Latin American Studies* 12 (1980), 223–269. As did Kubler for Peru, Grieshaber found remarkable demographic stability among highland Indians over the nineteenth century; moreover the proportion of landholding *comunarios* increased during the postindependence decades. (Bolivia was the one republic to preserve the status of corporate Indian lands until the 1870s.) There is still very little research on Andean rural societies during the wars for independence in Alto Peru (later, Bolivia), although see the preliminary study by René Arze, *Participación popular en la independencia de Bolivia* (La Paz, 1979).

One of the richest veins of research on indigenous politics, culture, and thought has been pursued by the anthropologist Tristan Platt, since the publication of his study, *Estado boliviano y ayllu andino. Tierra y tributo en el Norte de Postosí* (Lima, 1982). In that book and in later articles, Platt posed the *ayllus* of northern Potosí as historical subjects, negotiating the terms of their own integration into the postcolonial (but still tribute-collecting) republic of Bolivia. He framed the issue in terms of Indians' moral evaluations of their "tributary pact" with the fledgling republican state, and their insurgent reactions when that pact broke down in the late nineteenth century. See his articles, "Liberalism and ethnocide in the Southern Andes," *History Workshop* 17 (1984), 3–18, and "The Andean experience of Bolivian Liberalism, 1825–1900: The roots of rebellion in nineteenth century Chayanta (Potosí)," in Steve J. Stern (ed.), *Resistance, Rebellion, and Consciousness in the Rural Andean World,*" 280–326. More recently Platt has explored popular Andean conceptions of nationalist symbols and ideas in his provocative essay, "Simón Bolívar, the Sun of Justice and the Amerindian virgin: Andean conceptions of the *Patria* in nineteenth-century Potosí," *Journal of Latin American Studies* 25 (1993), 159–185. Platt's ethnohistorical work on northern Potosí *ayllus* is complemented by the historically sensitive ethnologies by Olivia Harris (see her "Labour and produce in an ethnic economy; Northern Potosí, Bolivia," in David Lehmann [ed.], *Ecology and Exchange in the Andes* [Cambridge, 1982]) and by Ricardo Godoy (see his *Mining and Agriculture in Highland Bolivia: Ecology, History, and Commerce among the Jukumanis* [Tucson, 1990]).

Other ethnohistorical works on Bolivia, produced by both anthropologists and historians, offer local ethnic or regional perspectives on sweeping nineteenth-century changes. Roger Neil Rasnake's *Domination and Cultural Resistance. Authority and Power among an Andean People* (Durham, 1988) traces the transformation of hereditary chiefdoms into fragmented, rotating ethnic authorities and the changing contours of ritual life among the Yuras near the mining town of Potosí. A panoramic historical vision of the Urus, living on the margins of the *altiplano*, is offered by the ethnohistorian Nathan Wachtel in his *Le rétour des ancêtres. Les indiens urus de Bolivie, XXe–XVIe siècle. Essai d'histoire regressive* (Paris, 1990).

Social and ethnohistories of the Quechua-speaking communities in their regional contexts have focused on the eastern valleys of Chuquisaca and Cochabamba. Erick D. Langer's *Economic Change and Rural Resis-*

tance in Southern Bolivia, 1880–1930 (Stanford, 1989) examines the cultural and social diversity of rural society in Chuquisaca during the rise and decline of the region's hacienda–silver mining complex. Several studies explore the heterogeneous rural subcultures of ethnically mixed Cochabamba in the nineteenth century, including Brooke Larson, Cochabamba, 1550–1900, 2nd ed. (Durham, North Corolina, 1998), chs. 9 and 10; Gustavo Rodríguez Ostría and Humberto Solares Serrano, *Sociedad Oligárquica, chicha y cultura popular* (Cochabamba, 1990); Rodríguez, "Entre reformas and contra-reformas: las comunidades indígenas en el Valle Bajo cochabambino (1825–1900)," in H. Bonilla (ed.), *Los Andes en la encrucijada*, 277–335; Robert H. Jackson, *Regional Markets and Agrarian Transformation in Bolivia. Cochabamba, 1539–1960* (Albuquerque, 1994); and María L. Lagos, *Autonomy and Power. The Dynamics of Class and Culture in Rural Bolivia* (Philadelphia, 1994).

Recent studies of Aymara regions of Northern Highland Bolivia chart a landscape of violence, conflict, and mobilization during the late nineteenth and early twentieth centuries. See Tomás Huanca, "Los procesos de desestructuración en las comunidades andinas a fines del siglo XIX: el altiplano lacustre," *Coloquio Estado y Región en los Andes* (Cusco, 1987), 45–86; Silvia Rivera Cusicanqui, "La expansión del latifundio en el altiplano boliviano," *Avances* 2 (1978), 95–118; and Herbert S. Klein, *Haciendas and Ayllus. Rural Society in the Bolivian Andes in the Eighteenth and Nineteenth Centuries* (Stanford, 1993). Aymara political movements are of particular interest. See especially the seminal work by Silvia Rivera Cusicanqui, *'Oprimidos pero no vencidos.' Luchas del campesinado aymara y qechwa, 1900–1980* (La Paz, 1986); but also see Ramiro Condarco Morales, *Zárate, el 'temible' Willka. Historia de la rebelión indígena de 1899*, 2nd ed. (La Paz, 1982); Carlos Mamani Condori, *Taraqu. Masacre, guerra, y 'renovación' en la biografía de Eduardo L. Nina Qhispi* (La Paz, 1991); and Victor Hugo Cárdenas, "La lucha de un pueblo," in Xavier Albó (ed.), *Raíces de América. El mundo Aymara* (Madrid, 1988), 495–534.

An incipient ethnohistorical literature exists on the more elusive themes of Indians in mining towns and cities, Aymara- and Quechua-based trading-kinship circuits, and popular meanings and uses of ethnic identity in different social and political settings. But these themes beckon nineteenth-century ethnohistorians. On urbanized Indians, cultural forms of *mestizaje*, and ethnic boundaries, see Rossana Barragán, *Espacio urbano y dinámica étnica; La Paz en el siglo XIX* (La Paz, 1990); and her article, "Entre polleras, lliqllas y ñañacas. Los mestizos y la emergencia de la tercera república," in Silvia Arze et al. (ed.), *Etnicidad, Economía. y Simbolismo en los Andes* (La Paz, 1982), 85–128. On ethnic identities, market participation, and class relations, see Olivia Harris, "Ethnic identity and market relations: Indians and mestizos in the Andes," in B. Larson and O. Harris (eds.), *Ethnicity, Markets and Migration in the Andes,* 351–390; and Tristan Platt, "Ethnic calendars and market interventions among the Ayllus of Lipes during the nineteenth century," ibid., 259–296. Thomas Abercrombie, in his article, "To be Indian, to be Bolivian: 'Ethnic' and 'national' discourses of identity," in G. Urban and J. Sherzer (eds.), *Nation-states and Indians in Latin America* (Austin, 1991), 95–130, explores interethnic subjectivities, representations, and rituals in the mining city of Oruro.

Curiously we still lack a synthetic study of the political, institutional, and discursive relations between Andean peasants and the republican state in nineteenth-century Bolivia. This theme informs many local or regional studies but has not yet been examined from a comparative or national perspective. For narrower studies on nineteenth-century tribute policy, however, see Jorge Alejandro Ovando Sanz, *El tributo indígena en las finanzas bolivianas del siglo XIX* (La Paz, 1986); Nicolás Sánchez-Albornoz, *Indios y tributos en el Alto Perú* (Lima, 1978), ch. 5; and Tristan Platt, *Estado tributario y librecambio en Potosí (siglo XIX)* (La Paz, 1986). Erick D. Langer examines liberal land reform rhetoric and policy in his "Liberalismo y la abolición de la comunidad indígena en el siglo XIX," *Historia y Cultura* 14 (1988). Finally the racist strains of oligarchic liberalism are examined in Marie-Daniéle Démelas's important study, *Nationalisme sans nation? La Bolivie aux XIXe–XXe siecles* (Paris, 1980), and Marta Irurozqui, Démelas *La Armonía de las desigualdades, élites y conflict os de poder ey Bolivia, 1880–1920* (Cusco, 1994). On the rise of indigenist discourse, see Josefa Salmón, *El Espejo indígena. El discurso indigenista en Bolivia* (La Paz, 1997).

24

INDIGENOUS PEOPLES AND THE RISE OF INDEPENDENT NATION-STATES IN LOWLAND SOUTH AMERICA

JONATHAN D. HILL

This chapter provides a survey of relations between indigenous peoples and the successor states to the Spanish empire in lowland regions of Venezuela, Colombia, Ecuador, Peru, and Bolivia. Geographically the survey covers an enormous arc of territory from the Guiana Shield – lower Orinoco Basin of Venezuela and British Guiana – through the *llanos* of Venezuela and Colombia, and across the headwater regions of the Amazon River's main tributaries in Venezuela, Colombia, Ecuador, Peru, and Bolivia (see Map 24.1). Within this vast region there were, and still are, pockets of remotely situated territory where indigenous peoples live in relative isolation from the independent nation-states that emerged during the nineteenth century. However, it is essential from the outset to assert that indigenous peoples throughout the *llanos* and headwater forest areas of the Amazon Basin had all adapted, either directly or through the mediation of other indigenous peoples, to long processes of conquest, missionization, and other forms of colonial domination prior to the rise of independent nation-states.

The historical point of departure for this study is the period of waning colonial power during the late eighteenth century. After the expulsion of Jesuit missions in 1767, the Spanish intensified their efforts to develop economically prosperous mission settlements in Guiana, the *llanos*, and riverine forest areas bordering Portuguese Brazil. In areas such as the *llanos* and the lower Orinoco Basin, Franciscan missionaries were relatively successful at reviving the Jesuits' system of production based upon tributary payments by indigenous laborers and the continuation of indigenous subsistence agriculture on communal *resguardo* lands. However, the Franciscans were far less successful at developing stable, much less growing, mission settlements in riverine forest areas where indigenous populations offered stronger resistance or where Portuguese merchants

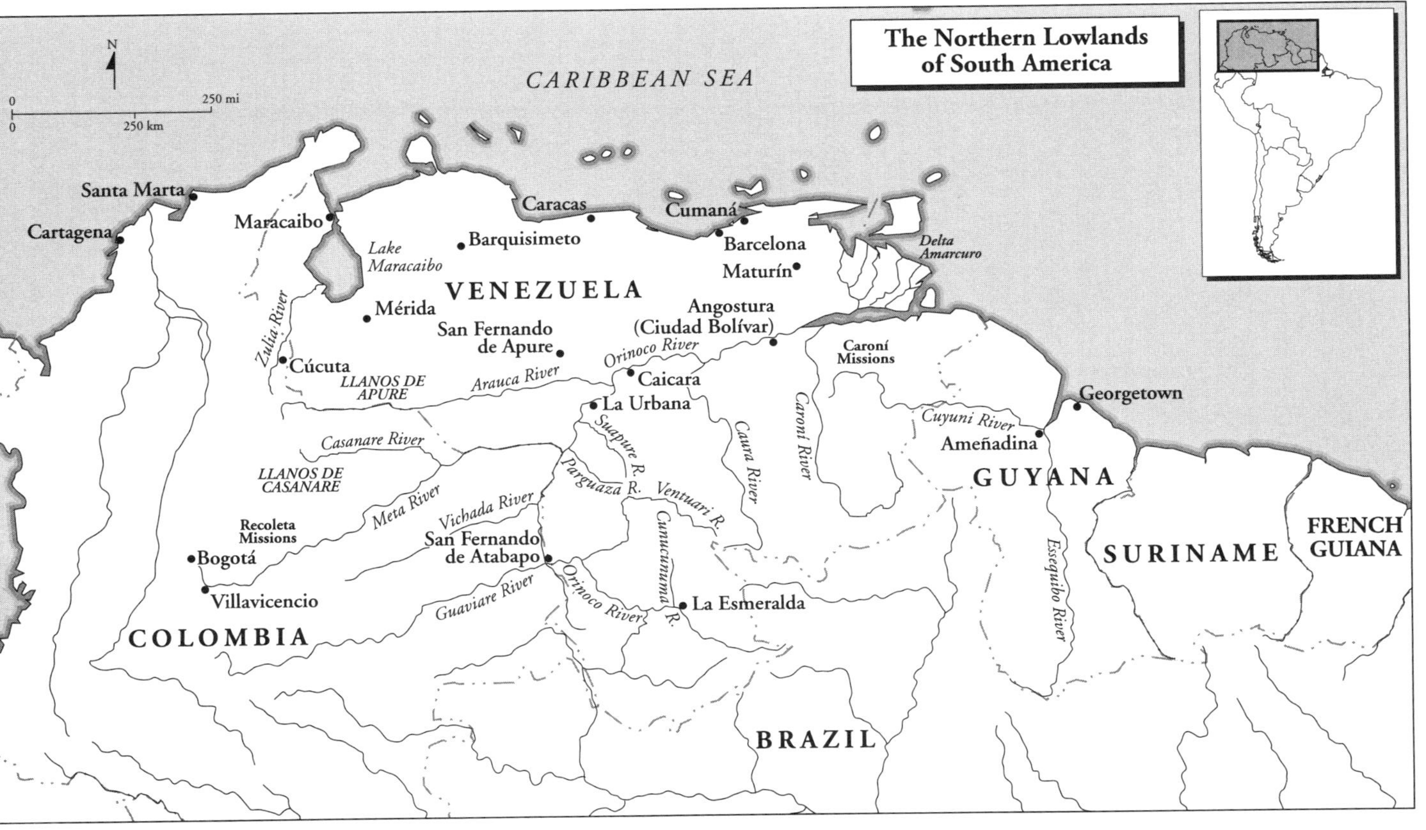
The Northern Lowlands of South America
CARIBBEAN SEA
N
0
250 mi
0
250 km
Santa Marta
Cartagena
Maracaibo
Lake Maracaibo
Barquisimeto
Caracas
Cumaná
Barcelona
Maturín
Delta Amarcuro
VENEZUELA
Mérida
San Fernando de Apure
Angostura (Ciudad Bolívar)
Orinoco River
Zulia River
Cúcuta
LLANOS DE APURE
Arauca River
Caicara
La Urbana
Caroní Missions
Caroní River
Caura River
Suapure R.
Parguaza R.
Ventuari R.
Cunucunuma R.
Casanare River
LLANOS DE CASANARE
Meta River
Vichada River
Recoleta Missions
Bogotá
Villavicencio
San Fernando de Atabapo
Guaviare River
Orinoco River
La Esmeralda
COLOMBIA
BRAZIL
Georgetown
Cuyuni River
Ameñadina
GUYANA
Essequibo River
SURINAME
FRENCH GUIANA

Map 24.1

had established long-term trading relations with indigenous peoples. This contrast between stronger mission settlements in northern areas of agricultural frontier expansion and much weaker ones in forested areas to the south foreshadowed major historical differences in the ways that indigenous peoples became enmeshed in the rise of independent nation-states in the nineteenth century.

REGIONAL DIFFERENCES

Indigenous peoples' experiences of the rise of independent nation-states were almost diametrically opposed between the riverine forests in southern lowlands and the *llanos* and Guiana Shield region to the north. The distinction between northern and southern areas became dramatically apparent from the outset of the wars of independence. For indigenous peoples living in the *llanos* and throughout the Guiana Shield region of the lower Orinoco and its tributaries, the wars brought forced conscriptions into both patriot and royalist armies and other forms of direct military action that resulted in major losses of population and communal *resquardo* lands. For peoples living in the northern portions of lowland South America, the wars of independence opened up a period in which the struggle for survival centered around the question of control over agricultural lands. Indigenous strategies in the northern lowlands varied widely according to diverse local conditions. Some groups sided with the royalists, whereas others either willingly joined or were forcefully conscripted into Simón Bolívar's patriot army. Many communities fled into remote forest areas away from the fighting or across the international border into British Guiana. The Guajibo, a large seminomadic group of the Colombian *llanos* who had remained largely outside the missionaries' process of settlement during colonial times, were perhaps the only group in the northern lowlands who did not suffer major losses and who were able to exploit the chaos of warfare to their own advantage by attacking patriots and royalists alike. Although the wars of independence did not directly affect indigenous peoples in remote headwater areas of the northern lowlands, the massive displacements of missionized indigenous people along the lower Orinoco and its tributaries resulted in major demographic and social changes in marginal areas, such as the Delta Amacuro and the interior forests of Guiana.

In contrast with the northern lowlands (Map 24.2), the forested areas along the Negro, Caquetá, Marañon, Ucayali, Madre de Dios, and other

The Southern Lowlands of South America
CARIBBEAN SEA
N
0
250 mi
0
250 km
PACIFIC OCEAN
VENEZUELA
COLOMBIA
ECUADOR
BRAZIL
PERU
BOLIVIA
Orinoco River
San Fernando de Atabapo
Orinoco River
Atabapo R.
Maroa
Guainía River
Casiquiare River
Solano
San Carlos de Río Negro
Vaupés River
Isana River
Rio Negro
Putumayo River
Caquetá River
Napo River
Puyo
Canelos
Bobonaza R.
Curaráy River
Pastaza River
Tigre River
Iquitos
Amazon River
Borja
Marañón R.
Yurimaguas
Ucayali River
Huallaga River
Madeira R.
Perené Colony
Perené R.
San Ramón
Tambo R.
Ene R.
Urubamba River
Manu River
Madre de Dios River

Map 24.2

tributaries at the headwaters of the Amazon Basin were not directly in the path of military action during the wars of independence. For the great majority of indigenous peoples inhabiting this vast expanse of rain forests, the early nineteenth century was a period of unintentionally benign neglect and recovery from massive losses of population during the colonial period. Colonial mission settlements were smaller and less stable in the southern lowlands than in the north, where agriculture and cattle raising provided a subsistence base for growing populations of indigenous laborers. In lowland Peru, the Asháninka (or Campa), Aguaruna, and other groups actively resisted the Franciscan missionaries' attempts to establish settlements, frequently killing missionaries during the early eighteenth century. In the 1740s to 1750s, an Asháninka uprising led by Juan Santos de Atahuallpa temporarily defeated Spanish military forces, and colonists abandoned settlements throughout the Peruvian lowlands in response to Indian attacks.

In the last quarter of the eighteenth century, the Spanish crown took a more active interest in the economic development of the Peruvian lowlands through a variety of official projects: road building, colonization, police protection, provisioning of land and tools, and exemption of colonists from sales tax. For the first of several times, the Peruvian *montaña* came to be perceived as a breadbasket of agricultural and silvicultural production for highland mining towns that were unable to support their own populations. This belated colonial push for economic development in the lowlands produced a diversity of results, ranging from relatively stable agricultural and mission settlements along the middle Huallaga Valley to the spawning of new interethnic conflicts between colonists and indigenous groups along the Madre de Dios River and its tributaries. Meanwhile indigenous uprisings during the same decade along the Madre de Dios River, perhaps in response to *cinchona* (quinine) and debt relations, resulted in the destruction of several whole towns along with the deaths of nearly all colonists inhabiting them.

Whereas the central and southern lowlands of Peru experienced a mixture of tenuous frontier expansion and staunch indigenous resistance during the late eighteenth century, the northeastern province of Mainas (the north central region of today's Peru) and adjacent areas along the Putumayo, Caquetá, Vaupés, and Negro rivers were zones of violent competition between Spanish and Portuguese military forces. In Peru the colonial government sent armed troops in response to Portuguese raids against missionaries and colonists along the Ucayali, Marañon, and Napo rivers, including one incursion that was intended to reach Popayán via the Putumayo and Caquetá rivers in 1776. Despite having to overcome greater geographic distances from its coastal population centers, Portuguese Brazil exerted far more political and economic control in the northern headwaters region of the Amazon Basin than the Spanish viceroyalties of Peru and Nueva Granada during the late eighteenth century. Alarmed by the presence of Portuguese merchants as far north as the middle Orinoco Basin, the Spanish sent military expeditions in the 1750s and 1760s to establish fortresses and mission settlements at San Carlos de Rio Negro, Solano, Maroa, and other strategic locations. Nevertheless Spanish efforts at colonizing the forested lowlands along southern and eastern borders with Brazil paled in comparison to Portuguese domination of these regions.

Portuguese slave trading and warfare against indigenous groups reached its zenith in the 1740s–1750s, when approximately 20,000 indigenous slaves were taken from the upper Rio Negro region. Peoples living in accessible downstream areas of the Caquetá (Japurá) and Negro rivers suffered total extinction, whereas those groups living in remote headwater areas remained numerous or expanded through the absorption of refugees from other societies. Although indigenous slavery was officially abolished at the time of the Jesuits' expulsion in 1767, the Portuguese government in Brazil implemented a system of forced relocations, called *descimentos* ('descents'), using military force to capture indigenous people and transport them downstream to Manaus. Indigenous peoples who resisted such enslavement or relocation were labeled as enemies and attacked in military raids called *guerras de rescate* ('rescue wars'). In the 1780s epidemics of flu, smallpox, measles, and other contagious diseases led to further depopulation so that by the end of the century entire rivers had been abandoned. Only the collapse of the colonial government at the end of the eighteenth century spared indigenous peoples of these headwater regions from total annihilation by giving them a few decades to recoup their losses in relative peace. The wars of independence and the subsequent period of instability in newly independent states of Venezuela, Colombia, Ecuador, and Peru sustained this period of recovery until the middle of the nineteenth century.

In the southern lowlands the wars of independence coincided with the cessation of open hostilities between competing Spanish and Portuguese colonial regimes, the end of enslavement and forced relocations in most areas, and recovery from traumatic losses of population and autonomy during the colonial period. In the northern *llanos* the wars of independence directly affected thousands of missionized indigenous peoples and resulted in sharp losses of population through the spread of disease, hunger, and violent interethnic relations.

In the mid- to late nineteenth century, indigenous peoples of the southern lowlands suffered further losses of population due to the demand for quinine, rubber, and other forest products. Unlike the struggles for control over agricultural lands in the *llanos* and Guiana Shield to the north, the Rubber Boom was essentially a struggle to control labor through artificially inflated debt in contexts of weak national sovereignty and disputed international borders. Renegade rubber barons, such as Tomás Funes in Venezuela, William Fitzcarraldo (Fitzgerald) in southern Peru, and the owners of the infamous Casa Araña along the northern Peru-Colombia border, amassed fortunes through enslaving and terrorizing entire indigenous societies. After Roger Casement's investigation brought these atrocities to international attention in 1910, the Peruvian government arrested seventy-five members of Casa Araña in 1911. Yet none of those arrested were ever brought to trial, much less sentenced, and the Peruvian government did not even issue a reprimand to the Peruvian Amazon Rubber Company (the British-owned corporation that nominally owned lands worked by Casa Araña along the Putumayo River), "because the abuses occurred in a disputed boundary area, and Peru needed a presence there to protect its sovereignty."[1] In the epistemological and political murkiness between weak national control and neo-colonial greed, some native peoples suffered total annihilation while others found ways to survive until the end of the Rubber Boom through resistance, accommodation, or migration to remote places of safety.

At the extreme southern end of the forested lowlands east of the Andes, the Llanos de Mojos of northern Bolivia was the setting for historical developments that combined aspects of both the northern and southern patterns just outlined. Like the *llanos* region of the northern lowlands in Venezuela and Colombia, the Llanos de Mojos provided conditions enabling the growth of relatively large mission settlements based upon cattle raising and agriculture. Jesuit missionaries built a network of twenty or so missions along major rivers in the Llanos de Mojos, with an estimated population of 30,000 indigenous people by

[1] David Werlich, "The conquest and settlement of the Peruvian montaña," Ph.D. thesis, University of Minnesota, 1968, 369.

1767. During the colonial period these Jesuit missions served as a buffer against Portuguese expansion up the Madeira River and across Mato Grosso. After the Jesuits' expulsion in 1767, the area was opened up for colonization, and many indigenous communities revolted or fled into forests to the north and east. Like the missionized indigenous communities of the northern *llanos* in Venezuela and Colombia, those of the Llanos de ooMojos were periodically ransacked for food, horses, and other valuables during the wars of independence. However, the northernmost portions of the Llanos de Mojos contain tropical forests forming the southwestern limit of the Amazon Basin, and these areas along the Madre de Dios and Madeira rivers became deeply enmeshed in the Rubber Boom during the late nineteenth century. Indigenous peoples of the Mojo region suffered sharp losses of population as a result of an influx of over 80,000 rubber gatherers who streamed into the northern forests from Santa Cruz. In the 1880s to 1890s, Brazil, Peru, and Bolivia struggled to control the Madre de Dios River, but no clear sovereignty emerged until Bolivia sold the state of Acre to Brazil in 1903, "after Bolivia had demonstrated its inability to control Brazilian rubber gatherers in the region."[2] By the end of the nineteenth century, an indigenous population that had reached possibly half a million in prehispanic times and that had remained at approximately 100,000 during the period of colonial missions was reduced to a mere 20,000. For indigenous peoples of the Llanos de Mojos the rise of independent nation-states brought the trauma of warfare and an expanding agricultural frontier together with the devastating effects of uncontrolled rubber extraction in conditions of disputed national sovereignty.

During the course of the nineteenth century, the Bolivian frontier pushed into forested lowlands in both northerly and southerly directions. In the southern Bolivian department of Chuquisaca, groups of fiercely independent Chiriguano expanded into missionized areas that had been weakened or abandoned during the wars of independence and their aftermath. "Until the 1860s, the Chiriguanos maintained the upper hand over the colonists."[3] However, by the 1870s a powerful array of missions, fortresses, and cattle ranches had engulfed the Chiriguano and destroyed their land base. Despite occasional acts of resistance in the late nineteenth century, the Chiriguano had become a conquered people whose lands

[2] Ibid., 392.

[3] Eric Langer, *Economic Change and Rural Resistance in Southern Bolivia* (Stanford, 1989), 126.

had been taken away by the 1890s. Like the situations of indigenous peoples in other areas of agricultural frontier expansion in lowland South America, the Chiriguano struggle to control lands necessary for their subsistence agriculture was directly opposed by land-hungry colonists in an expanding nation-state that offered little or no legal protection for its indigenous inhabitants.

The Rise of Liberal Independent States

The European concept of liberal nation-state placed indigenous peoples of lowland South America into contradictory social situations. On the one hand, the liberal state promised civil and legal equality to all citizens within its borders. On the other hand, the rationalist, assimilationist, individualist nature of this promised equality was extremely hostile to the older, royalist policy of granting collective rights to indigenous peoples as well as to the survival of indigenous modes of economic production and social organization. To the authors of the Constitution of the Province of Caracas in 1812, the two-sidedness of equality at the expense of diversity was not perceived as a contradiction but as the natural process of educating backward peoples, who would relinquish uncivilized ways of life when lifted out of their former ignorance. The Constitution of the Province of Caracas of 1812 endeavored

> by all possible means to attract the above-mentioned natural citizens to those houses of enlightenment and learning, to make them understand the intimate union that they have with all other citizens, the considerations that they, like those others, deserve from the Government, and the rights that they enjoy by the mere fact of being men who are equal to all members of their species, with the goal of succeeding by this means in removing them from the depression and rusticity in which the old state of things has maintained them, and that they no longer remain isolated and afraid to deal with other men.[4]

Thus, from their very inception during the wars of independence, liberal nation-states in Latin America perceived indigenous peoples, or "the natural citizens," as potential equals only if they could be educated and brought into more direct contact with other people.

The new nationalist rhetoric of equality masked older colonialist beliefs in the racial and cultural inferiority of indigenous and other non-

[4] Translated from Pedro Cunill Grau, *Geografia del poblamiento venezolano en el siglo xix*, 3 vols. (Caracas, 1987), I:66.

European peoples. For many thousands of indigenous people living in mission settlements and enjoying Spanish legal protection of communal *resguardo* lands, the new egalitarianism brought an end to such privileges through new laws that disbanded communal lands in favor of private ownership by individuals or individual families. The Constitution of 1812 left no doubt about the patriots' intentions of abolishing communal lands held by indigenous groups: "permiting them a share in the ownership of lands that they had been granted and over which they have possession, so that . . . these lands may be divided among and made accessible to the family-fathers in each community."[5] During the instability and chaos of the postwar years, the new republics passed a patchwork quilt of laws that tried to reverse the individualization of indigenous *resguardo* lands, but these belated attempts met with little or no success.

Paradoxically the Bolivarian project of unifying all of northern and western South America into the single nation-state of Gran Colombia had the opposite effect of strengthening the divisions among the countries that constituted it.[6] The tremendous social and ecological diversity encompassed within Gran Colombia did not readily lend itself to a uniform process of nation-state expansion through assimilation and integration. Also the historical legacy of centuries of Spanish colonialism and rigid social hierarchy persisted despite official rhetoric of equality in the new republics. The principal architect of Latin American democracy, Simón Bolívar, was aware of the sociocultural diversity within Gran Colombia, but ultimately the Great Liberator himself could not transcend the racist stereotyping of indigenous and African Americans.

> [These gentlemen] have not cast their vision over the Caribs of the Orinoco, over the pastoralists of Apure, over the sailors of Maracaibo, over the merchants of Magdalena, over the bandits of Patia, over the indomitable Pastusos, over the Guahibos of the Casanare and over all the savage hordes from Africa and America, who like male fallow deer, traverse the solitudes of Colombia.[7]

Throughout the nineteenth century, such racist ideologies and the political turmoil of the postwar period permeated the struggles among competing nation-states for control over remote border areas and their indigenous inhabitants.

[5] Ibid.

[6] Ibid., 114, cites General Carlos Soublette who in 1827 stated: "The name Colombian amongt us is devoid of meaning because we have remained so Venezuelan, New Granadan, and Quiteñan as we were before but perhaps with greater bitterness."

[7] Letter from Simón Bolívar to General Santander, June 13, 1821; in Grau, *Geografia*, I, 114.

So strongly rooted was the belief in the innate superiority of white European peoples that the new republics sought to attract, with varying degrees of success, European settlers to inhabit and develop the *llanos* of Colombia and the lowlands of eastern Peru. These plans for colonizing remote frontier regions in the northern and southern lowlands failed to achieve lasting results, because there were virtually no infrastructures for transportation, communication, and other basic services. Also European colonists preferred to settle in a more temperate climate as long as lands were available to them there. Nevertheless these feeble attempts at colonization in the *llanos* and tropical lowlands indicated a return to late colonial economic policies that had construed interior regions as potential breadbaskets for highland and coastal populations. Moreover the new efforts at colonizing frontier regions with European immigrants underscored the emerging national societies' belief that *mestizos* were less capable than Europeans when it came to developing productive frontier economies.

It was the economic necessity of international debt and the threat of bankruptcy after the wars of independence, however, that generated the search for new ways of transforming frontier regions into sources of surplus foods, forest products, and other material goods. During the reign of General Ramón Castilla in Peru (1844–1851, 1855–1862), the government distributed tools to indigenous peoples of Loreto Province in the eastern lowlands through Franciscan missionaries, who were given orders to put local peoples to work. Natural resources came to be regarded as ways for shaky national governments to purchase stability and relative prosperity in the short term without regard for the long-term management of resources and increasing indebtedness to North American and European moneylenders. During the so-called Guano Age (1840–1880) in Peru, the Castilla government gave large concessions allowing European corporations to extract over 600 million tons of guano. Guano exports paid for colonization projects in the Amazon lowlands, suppression of indigenous uprisings, and building railroads, but Peru's credit collapsed as soon as the guano deposits had been exhausted in the 1880s. The boom-and-bust economics of resource extraction, together with the concentration of rural landholdings into the possession of large landholders, fueled the expansion of agricultural frontiers into the forested lowlands, forcing indigenous peoples to retreat still further into remote areas.

As global demands for rubber began to accelerate in the mid- to late nineteenth century, the Latin American republics conceded control over large tracts of Amazonian forest lands to European corporations in return for relief from debts. British creditors formed the Peruvian Corporation in 1890 as part of a reorganization of the Peruvian government's debt, and the corporation founded a colony on 1,100,000 acres of land inhabited by Asháninka.[8] The largest of all land grants to creditors was the special decree of 1909 that gave 14,200,000 acres of forest lands along the Caquetá and Putumayo rivers to the British-owned Peruvian Amazon Rubber Company, Ltd. During this same period German import-export houses monopolized commercial activity in Santa Cruz and the lowlands of Bolivia.

By the end of the nineteenth century, the Amazon lowlands of Latin America had become sources of raw materials for export. Short-term economic gains and struggles among neighboring republics for political control over remote forest regions overrode any concern for the long-term social effects on indigenous inhabitants. All attempts at agricultural or other sustainable forms of development were abandoned in favor of an extractive, predatory economy based on debt relations and consumption of costly imported goods. In Iquitos, the capital of Peru's Loreto Province and commercial center of the rubber trade in upper Amazonia, colonists imported mostly tools and durable consumer goods in 1850. Twenty years later, when rubber exports had grown to over 58 metric tons per year, the colonists' main imports consisted of foods and luxury goods. In areas of the most intense rubber-gathering activity, merchants and their armed henchmen often forced indigenous people to accept "gifts" of food and tools in return for which they were obligated to collect rubber and prohibited from practicing subsistence agriculture or foraging.[9] In effect the creation of economic dependency and desperate attempts to pay off creditors had become a principle governing social relations at all levels, from international corporations to local interethnic relations between rubber merchants and indigenous rubber gatherers.

The Rubber Boom permanently transformed the cultural landscape of the southern lowlands in Peru, Ecuador, Colombia, and Venezuela. Economic pressures on these impoverished states to pay off international creditors were exacerbated by the growing, finally insupportable, competition from rubber produced on plantations in Dutch Java. By the end

[8] Michael Brown and Eduardo Fernández, *War of Shadows* (Berkeley, 1991), 56–57.

[9] Jon Landaburu and Roberto Pineda Camacho, *Tradiciones de la gente del Hacha: mitología de los indios Andoques del Amazonas* (Yerbabuena, 1984), 31–33.

of the nineteenth century, Latin America produced only a fraction of the world's supply of rubber. Many of the worst atrocities that rubber barons perpetrated against indigenous peoples took place during the first two decades of the twentieth century, a period when the declining commercial value of Amazonian latex was rapidly outpacing the rate at which rubber gatherers could produce, or be forced to produce, greater quantities.

In addition to the economic stranglehold of the late Rubber Boom period, indigenous peoples of the southern lowlands often found themselves caught in border disputes between nation-states or in areas where national sovereignty was extremely weak. The struggles among competing nation-states, like the earlier conflicts between Spanish and Portuguese imperial states during the late colonial period, embroiled indigenous peoples in local skirmishes and left them in increasingly vulnerable, marginalized political situations. The fragility of political control exercised by Latin American states over the Amazonian lowlands was dramatically illustrated by a separatist movement in eastern Peru during the height of the Rubber Boom. A former Peruvian military officer led the bloodless coup in May 1896 in Iquitos and was soon joined by rebels in other regional towns.[10] Although the rebellion failed due to lack of popular support, it demonstrated how little effective control Peru exerted over its eastern lowland territories. Brazilian authorities knew of the movement long before the news reached Lima, and the rebels had already abandoned Iquitos by the time government troops arrived in July 1896.

Political instability and economic desperation certainly go a long way toward explaining the atrocities committed against indigenous Amazonian peoples during the Rubber Boom. Nevertheless political and economic factors alone cannot account for the extent to which indigenous peoples were culturally stereotyped as "wild savages" whose labor could be exploited as if it were guano, rubber, or any other natural material. The wholesale torturing and execution of indigenous laborers living in the Caquetá-Putumayo region made little or no sense in terms of economic rationality, because it destroyed the very means of production that the rubber merchants sought to mobilize.

The new republics of nineteenth-century Latin America defined indig-

[10] "Word of the Loreto revolt did not reach Lima until sixteen days after it had begun, and this news came by means of a Rio de Janeiro newspaper which had been carried around Cape Horn by ship." Werlich, "The conquest," 380.

enous collectivities as marginalized, backward groups whose very existence threatened social order and progress. For example, the Law of July 30, 1824 ("Methods of Civilizing the Savage Indians") in the republic of Gran Colombia offered tools and land to indigenous groups who agreed to accept more sedentary settlement patterns, and those who agreed would be exempted from the military draft if they renounced their non-Christian customs. The nation-state pulled indigenous peoples of lowland South America in two conflicting directions. They could assimilate into the new national order, but only at the cost of renouncing their indigenous cultural practices and identities. If they chose to reject the new order of society, they were categorized as savage, wild, and subhuman.

The following sections provide a more detailed survey of historical processes of interethnic relations in lowland areas of Venezuela, Colombia, Ecuador, Peru, and Bolivia. The contrast between northern and southern lowlands, corresponding to differences between expanding agricultural frontiers and riverine forests that became objects of rubber extraction, serves as a basic principle for organizing the discussion of specific indigenous peoples in the two zones.

In one sense the contrast of northern versus southern lowlands can be understood in terms of relatively simple differences of ecology, demography, and political control. In the northern lowlands, indigenous peoples inhabited areas that were more suitable for large-scale agriculture and cattle raising, and colonists outnumbered indigenous peoples by such a large margin that the latter faced a choice between assimilation into the expanding frontier society or flight to remote forest locations. In the southern lowlands, indigenous peoples lived in densely forested environments that were far less propitious for plantation agriculture or cattle raising and that remained beyond the spheres of political and economic influence of the emergent nations of Venezuela, Colombia, Ecuador, and Peru in the nineteenth century. The invention of steamboat navigation and opening up of the Amazon River for international trade in the 1850s and 1860s exacerbated the centrifugal tendencies of the southern lowlands by strengthening Brazilian control over headwater regions of the Amazon Basin. Whereas the northern lowlands in the nineteenth century can be characterized as a zone of overwhelmed indigenous populations, the southern lowlands are more aptly understood as a zone of conflicting frontiers. In the lowlands of Bolivia, both historical patterns developed during the nineteenth century.

THE WARS OF INDEPENDENCE AND THE STRUGGLES OVER LANDS IN THE NORTHERN LOWLANDS

Interethnic Relations During the Waning Years of Colonial Rule

In the late eighteenth to early nineteenth centuries, Franciscan and Capuchin missionaries flourished in the *llanos* of Casanare after the Jesuits' expulsion. Whereas the seminomadic Guahibo fiercely resisted missionization and attacked the *Recoleto* missions on numerous occasions, more sedentary peoples such as the Saliba became engulfed in the mission frontier as it expanded eastward along the Arauca and Meta rivers. Areas to the south of the Meta remained largely uncolonized until the nineteenth century, when a road was built to connect Bogotá with Villavicencio and the southern *llanos*. The expansion of the *Recoleto* missions in Casanare was based primarily on the missionaries' success at cattle raising, which grew from 44,000 head of cattle in 1767 to over 100,000 head in 1800. Although illegal trade with Dutch and French Guiana continued patterns that had been established in earlier periods, the *llanos* of Casanare came increasingly under the influence of Colombian merchants in Cartagena and Santa Marta, who blocked plans to develop roads connecting the *llanos* to the Orinoco River.

The unique demographic and economic history of the *llanos* of Casanare in the late eighteenth century predisposed it to become a stronghold of insurgency during the wars of independence. Despite the economic growth of *Recoleto* missions, indigenous groups living in relative autonomy still remained numerous, and the small mestizo population of free laborers mixed with indigenous peoples and adopted indigenous cultural practices, including nomadism. These Colombian *llaneros* formed a ready-made army for the war against Spain. Church officials attempted to arrest this mixing together of indigenous and mestizo peoples by banning the latter from entering indigenous *resguardo* lands. However, the Spanish government had not fortified the *llanos* of Casanare with strong military garrisons as it had in the lower Orinoco Basin, so the missionaries were relatively helpless in the face of Guahibo attacks and cattle raiding. By 1800 the *llanos* of Casanare were in a state of perpetual warfare, which began in earnest when a Dominican priest led 1,070 indigenous men from Tame against Spanish garrisons in 1803.

The relative strength of indigenous populations in the *llanos* of Casanare was a unique situation in the northern lowlands of the late eighteenth century. Indigenous people still accounted for 72 percent of the population in Casanare in 1778, whereas the composite figure for indigenous peoples in all provinces of New Granada stood at only 19.5 percent. The total indigenous population in 1800 for all areas of what was soon to become the republic of Venezuela had fallen to a mere 258,000, a number that posed no real political threat to the predominantly European, African, and Creole majority. In the Venezuelan *llanos* north of the Apure and Orinoco rivers, the late eighteenth century was a period of rapid growth in cattle ranching due to the easier access from coastal and highland areas. Indigenous peoples who had survived the diseases, wars, and slave trading of earlier times became "hispanicized Indians," and they intermarried with a growing population of escaped African slaves coming from coastal areas and the Antilles. In 1789 a force of some 24,000 of these "hispanicized Indians" and African runaways moved through the Venezuelan *llanos*, stealing cattle and burning towns as they went along. Creole landowners and ranchers tried to force these marauding bands of *zambos* (mixed African and indigenous peoples) to live in settled towns. Unlike the "Indianized mestizos" of the Colombian *llanos*, the Afro-indigenous *llaneros* of Venezuela sided for the most part with royalist forces during the wars of independence.

Despite the great importance that the middle Orinoco Basin had as the hub of indigenous trade relations in prehispanic and early colonial times, the area had become peripheral to the economic boom of cattle ranching in the *llanos* and the growth of prosperous mission settlements in the lower Orinoco Basin during the late eighteenth century. The annual harvesting of turtle eggs for their oil still brought together a thousand or so indigenous people from nearby missions of La Urbana, Atures, and Carichana. During late March and early April, Otomaco and Guamo families from these missions and Carib-speakers from downstream locations set up temporary shelters on the exposed beaches and exchanged turtle oil, live forest animals, pigments and resins for cloth, axes, fishhooks, and other manufactured items. Franciscan missionaries and white merchants from Angostura [Ciudad Bolivar] on the lower Orinoco controlled production and trade of turtle oil. At the time of Humboldt's observation of the turtle harvesting in the 1790s, the harvest yielded only about 5,000 bottles of oil, which was used in Europe for culinary and medicinal purposes. He remarked:

> The products of the Orinoco have been bought at a vile price from the Indians who live as dependents of the missionaries, and it is precisely these same Indians who purchase from the missionaries, albeit it at very high prices, their instruments for fishing and horticulture.[11]

Prior to 1767 Jesuit missionaries had regulated the exploitation of turtle eggs in order to maintain a stable population, but their Franciscan successors allowed all beach areas to be harvested, resulting in a permanent decline in production.

Aside from the annual harvesting of turtle oil, the missionized indigenous population of the middle Orinoco region had fallen into a state of almost complete abandonment during the late eighteenth century. The mission at Atures, for example, had grown to several hundred people and 30,000 head of cattle under the Jesuits; by 1800 only 47 people (mostly Guahibo) lived at Atures, and there were no cattle at all. Likewise the mission at Maipures, located beside the powerful rapids of the same name, had declined from a population of 600 indigenous people in 1765 to less than 60 in 1800. The rapids at Atures and Maipures are impossible to ascend in any form of watercraft, even at the height of the April–August wet season, and areas above the rapids remained largely inaccessible to large-scale penetration by missionaries and the expanding agro-pastoral frontier of the late eighteenth century. The upper Orinoco and its tributaries remained a refuge for indigenous peoples, with only a handful of tiny mission settlements dotting an enormous expanse of riverine tropical forests.

The Spanish recognized the importance of the upper Orinoco Basin as a buffer against Portuguese incursions from the south and established settlements at La Esmeralda, Solano, Maroa, San Carlos de Rio Negro, and other strategic locations. After a brief initial period of cooperation in which the Spanish lavished goods on the Yekuana, a Carib-speaking people of the Ventuari and Cunucunuma rivers, relations between the Spanish and their indigenous hosts turned sour during the 1760s and 1770s.

> By 1767 the Spanish had embarked on a more aggressive policy of colonization of the Upper Orinoco. In an attempt to secure the entire region, an expeditionary force was sent out to build a road and 19 small forts connecting Angostura

[11] Alexander von Humboldt, *Personal Narrative of Travels to the Equinoctial Regions of the New Continent during the Years 1799–1804* (Helen Maria Williams, trans.), 7 vols. (London, 1819), 3: 291.

with La Esmeralda. This ambitious plan, which to this day has never been accomplished, was to cut directly through the homeland of the Yekuana. Refusing to cooperate, the Yekuana were forcibly relocated and set to work on chain gangs. This also marked their first exposure to Christianity, as Capuchin missionaries were dispatched to actively convert them. Amazed by this sudden change in behavior, the Yekuana decided that this was not Iaranavi, but rather a different species altogether. Fañuru, as they called him, was a creation of Odosha. Along with their allies, the Fadre (Padres, priests), they had come from Caracas to overrun their friend Iaranavi in Angostura.[12]

Conflicts between the Yekuana and the Spanish reached a climax in 1776, when a Yekuana-led coalition of indigenous groups rebelled and destroyed all nineteen forts, driving the Spanish out of their territory for the next 150 years.

What is remarkable about the story of Yekuana resistance to Spanish colonialism is that they were unusually successful at repulsing Spanish military forces from their territory. Whereas other sedentary, horticultural peoples of the *llanos* and tropical forests were simply overpowered and engulfed by missionization and frontier expansion, the Yekuana constructed a social barrier that halted Spanish expansion just as effectively as the natural obstacle of the Atures and Maipures rapids along the middle Orinoco. Had it not been for the successful Yekuana uprising, many other indigenous peoples of the Venezuelan Amazon would almost certainly have suffered the same fate as the Maipure, Achagua, and other missionized peoples living in accessible areas.

Today the Yekuana remember these historical events in a highly poeticized set of mythic and historical stories that form a continuation of their cycle of creation myths, the *Watunna*. In one of these stories, the Spaniards (*Fañuru*) came from Caracas (*Karakaña*) and overwhelmed the good white people of Angostura through sheer numbers.[13]

They [the Fañuru] came to the shore of the Uriñaku (Orinoco) in front of Ankosturaña. The river was very wide. . . . They didn't have canoes. They just got in the water and started swimming. . . . When the Ankosturañankomo saw them in the river, they thought: "They've come to fight. Let's fight." They shot at them with *arakusa* [arquebusses]. They had lots of *arakusa*. They killed lots of them. As they killed them, the bodies fell in the river; first one, then another and another and another, lots of them. They lined up like a bridge. Now, from the north shore, the Fañuru all began walking across the bridge. They all crossed.

[12] David Guss, "Keeping it oral: A Yekuana ethnology," *American Ethnologist* 13:3 (1986), 413–429.

[13] Marc de Civrieux, *Watunna: An Orinoco Creation Cycle* (David Guss, trans.) (San Francisco, 1980). The following excerpts are from pp. 155–180.

. . . Many Fañuru died as they came across. They killed them with *arakusa*. They had nothing but clubs. But they were many, that's why they won. They killed the men. They raped the women. They mixed the races again. That's how the Iaranavi were destroyed. It put an end to the good people in Ankosturaña.

The Spaniards believed that they were the rightful owners of everything on earth.

After destroying the Iaranavi of Angostura, the Spaniards and their priests (*Fadre*) ascended the Orinoco and its tributaries, attacking Wanadi's people (the Yekuana) from Angostura to the northeast and from Marakuhaña (San Fernando de Atabapo) to the west.

Some of them went to Marakuhaña [San Fernando de Atabapo]. That's where their fathers had come from. Others went to Meraraña [La Esmeralda]. They left soldiers there with cannons and gunpowder. They went up the Ventuari and Kunukunuma, up our rivers. They made the men and women prisoners. They forced the men to work. They didn't pay them. They raped the women. The old ones couldn't live anymore because of them. . . . The Fañuru came in canoes. . . . They were looking for people to kill and eat.

In this situation of genocidal enslavement and fanatical missionization, the Yekuana organized a multiethnic coalition of indigenous groups who succeeded in driving the Spaniards out of their territory.

Yekuana storytellers compress this complex act of resistance into the supernaturally powerful figure of Mahaiwadi, a great shaman capable of transforming into a mythic jaguar.

Mahaiwadi lived on the banks of the Arahame. He was very wise. . . . No one saw him. He hid in the jungle, playing maraca, singing, smoking. . . . He called the *mawadi* [anaconda spirit]. Then he went to the Kashishare [Casiquiare]. He threw his maraca in and hid in the forest. He just stayed there singing and smoking. The Fañuru's canoes turned over and the *mawadi* ate them. Some of them left their canoes and ran into the jungle. Mahaiwadi lay down in his hammock. He left his body there as a trick. He went out in a new body, like a jaguar. He sent the jaguar into the forest to eat the Fañuru. Mahaiwadi was sleeping, dreaming. His jaguar ran after the Fañuru. It ate one, then another and another and another. Mahaiwadi just lay there in his hammock as if he were dead. . . . Mahaiwadi's jaguar ran to tell the people. He screamed: "The Fañuru are in my stomach. You can come out of your caves now." Mahaiwadi woke up. He turned into a bird and took off singing: "Free, free, I'm free." That's how he sang.

In the end Mahaiwadi not only drove the Spaniards out of Yekuana territory but left Wanadi's people with powerful medicines to cure the sick.

Wanadi, the mythic creator, was preparing to leave this world of ceaseless bloodshed in the hands of Odosha's Spaniards, promising to return from heaven when Odosha died. However, Wanadi did not want to leave his people without any defenses, so he created a heavenly city called *Amenadiña*, the Dutch trading center at the mouth of the Essequibo River.

Wanadi went to the edge of the Earth, to the shore of the sea, to find Hurunko [the Dutch] and his village, Amenadiña. Hurunko was wise and powerful. He was a good man. Odosha hadn't come to his village. . . . "Good," Wanadi answered. "You're good. You did what I asked. You told the truth. The 'Doer,' that's what they'll call you now. Now I'll pay you." . . . Wanadi went to his house in the Sky, in the North, on the other side of the sea. He got shotguns, hooks, machetes, knives, shirts. He brought it all back and gave it to Hurunko. Then he started walking again. He made more houses. He made the other tribes. He made the Piaroa, the Maku, the Yabarana, the Warekena, the Haniwa, the Makushi. He made them all. He made lots of people to fight Odosha and his Fañuru. Then he said: "Okay. I'm going to leave the Earth now. I'm going to go back to Heaven. I'm going to say goodbye to my people."

Wanadi's final act of mythic protection, the creation of Saliban, Arawakan, and other indigenous peoples to help fight Odosha and the Spaniards, offers a poetic vision of a profound historical truth. The Yekuana-led uprising of 1776 created a social barrier that gave indigenous peoples of the upper Orinoco and Negro rivers a chance to survive Spanish colonialism in the late eighteenth century.

The Watunna creation cycle concludes with the story of the Waite, a group of Yekuana chiefs who led the people eastward into Makushi territory in search of Amenadiña, the heavenly source of iron trade goods.

When our grandfathers came to Traenida, they didn't have *sahadidi* [iron] or *arakusa* or machetes. They hadn't started trading yet. Then one day Eneiadi came to Maraca. He was one of the Ë'ti [Makushi] people. . . . That Ë'ti came to Maraca Island from where the sun rises. Our grandfathers looked at him. Right away, they became happy. Eneiadi was carrying a gun and a machete and some hooks. That iron was really bright. The *so'to* [Yekuana] looked at it and touched it. They remembered Iaranavi's iron from Ankosturaña.

The Yekuana agreed to give up their new settlements and gardens in the east in order to obtain iron trade goods from the Makushi.

The *so'to* moved away and started talking again. They thought about it, talking like that with each other. They didn't want Eneiadi to leave with the iron. . . . Okay. The people have decided. We're going to leave Traenida. We'll give you the house, the *conucos* [gardens], the whole island. We're going to go back up river to where our fathers came from. We'll go back west. Eneiadi was happy with the house. Our grandfathers kept the *arakusa*, the machete, the hooks. They shined and sparkled. They were glad to have them.

After safely returning to their ancestral territory at the remote headwaters of the Erebato and Ventuari rivers, the Waite chiefs sent a small group of men secretly to follow the powerful Matiuhana (Kariña) people to find the source of iron tools and firearms.

Now Iahena said: "Let's follow them. Don't make any noise." They got back in their canoe and followed them down the Ruhunini. They paddled north for days . . . until finally, they came to the end of the Earth. They came to Dama, the Sea. Now they saw a village there called Amenadiña. It wasn't a *so'to* village, but a spirit village. The chief of Amenadiña was Hurunko. He was Wanadi's friend. He went to Heaven with all his people to visit Wanadi. . . . Wanadi has huge stores in Heaven. . . . Hurunko held a huge feast. He got drunk with the Waite. Then he told them: "We're only in charge of giving the things from Heaven away. They're not ours. They're Wanadi's. We just give them to good people, to Wanadi's people. . . . Now we'll give them to you since you're Wanadi's people. You can take *arakusa* back to your people so they can defend themselves against Fañuru and the Shirishana [Yanomami]."

These Yekuana stories offer a rare instance of how an indigenous people of the northern lowlands interpreted the events of early European contact in terms of a mythic polarization between Wanadi and Odosha, or creative and destructive spiritual powers. Like other indigenous peoples of the late eighteenth century, the Yekuana were caught between their admiration for the material possessions and military strength of the Spanish and their contempt for the coercive and cruel behaviors that revealed the Spanish to be destroyers of life and autonomy.

Along the lower Orinoco and its southern tributary, the Caroní River, the Spanish had erected a network of heavily fortified Capuchin mission settlements to protect the southeastern borders with Dutch- and French-controlled Guiana. As in other regions the success of Spanish missionization relied upon a strategy of setting converted populations against groups inhabiting unconquered forest areas and using converts as evangelists.

By the end of the century, new divisions between "Spanish Caribs" and "Dutch Caribs" (later to become "English Caribs") had replaced the earlier colonial division between "Spanish Arawaks" and "Dutch Caribs." The practice of capturing Dutch Caribs across the border in Dutch

Essequibo and forcing them to settle in Spanish missions foreshadowed the forced conscription of Caribs from British Guiana into the patriots' army during the wars of independence.

Between 1800 and 1816 the mission settlements of the lower Orinoco-Caroní region remained relatively free of the warfare being waged in coastal and *llanos* areas, and indigenous populations in the twenty-eight missions increased from 15,908 to 19,540. The southern missions boasted herds of cattle and wild horses larger than 100,000 head in 1810, and many towns produced surpluses of cotton cloth, tobacco, and coffee for export. Work regulations in the Capuchin settlements provided missionized indigenous families with sufficient time for their own subsistence economy; each month consisted of 15 days' work in plantations or industry and 15 days for subsistence farming. Although most of these missionized peoples were classified simply as "Caribs," the missionaries' use of this term as a political coverall masked a diversity of linguistic and sociocultural identities.[14] Nevertheless mission records from the first decade of the nineteenth century leave no doubt that there were numerous different groups living within the Carib majority. In addition to Aruaca (Lokota), the records list Guayuno, Pariagoto, Paracayo, Arinogoto, Warao, Saliba, and "Guaica" (a derogatory term for yanomani) peoples. Some of these missionized peoples carried on active trading relations with free populations living in remote forest areas unsuited to ranching or plantation agriculture. Several hundred missionized Warao, for example, received regular visits from Warao who inhabited the labyrinth of canals, rivers, and islands making up the Delta Amacuro at the mouth of the Orinoco River.

Across the border from Spanish Guiana, Carib- and Arawak-speaking peoples of the Dutch colonies of Essequibo and Demerara occupied a precarious social niche as policemen who captured runaway African slaves for coastal plantation owners. These peoples, including Macusi, Arecuna, Waiwai, Wapishana, and Aruaca, suffered major losses of population during the wars between British, Dutch, and French armies in the eighteenth century. The strategic importance of these indigenous groups as a buffer against African slave rebellions and escape into the interior forests was underscored by a tremendous demographic imbalance in coastal plantation society: Slaves numbered 69,368 out of a total of 78,734

[14] Neil Whitehead, "Carib ethnic soldiering in Venezuela, the Guianas, and the Antilles, 1492–1820," *Ethnohistory* 37:4 (1990), 357–385.

in the 1829 census of British Guiana. In the late eighteenth century, Dutch policy relied on generous trade relations with indigenous peoples of the inland forests, and British authorities largely continued Dutch policies after taking over the Essequibo and Demerara territories in 1803. As the Caribs and other groups became less significant in military and economic terms, their status with the Europeans declined. Indigenous peoples who had become accustomed to privileged treatment under Dutch rule were reluctant to accept their lowered status in British Guiana, and Carib chiefs marched into Georgetown in 1810 to threaten war against the British if they did not receive more gifts of trade goods. This unsuccessful demand was to be the last gasp of the centuries-long tradition of Carib ethnic soldiering for competing colonial powers in the northern lowlands of South America. With the wars of independence already brewing in New Granada and the abolition of African slavery only a few years away in British and Dutch Guiana, the precarious autonomy of Carib militia was rapidly drawing to a close.

The Wars of Independence

By the time of the signing of the Constitution of Caracas in 1812, indigenous groups of the northern lowlands had nearly all succumbed to the colonial compromise of paying tribute to the Church in return for a limited freedom to continue subsistence farming on communally owned *resguardo* lands. In coastal and highland areas of Venezuela, small indigenous populations living on pockets of Church-protected land dotted a landscape that was otherwise dominated by an expanding, land-hungry mestizo and white population. In the years prior to the wars of independence, mestizo colonists moving westward from the Andean cordillera at Merida clashed with Motilón (Barí) and Guajiro peoples living along the southern and western shores of Lake Maracaibo. Capuchin missionaries, who had only initiated relations with the Motilóns in the 1780s and 1790s, tried with little success to protect indigenous lands against the expanding frontier. In consonance with the Constitution of Caracas and the prevailing sentiment that Church-protected indigenous lands were to be broken up in the new republic, the public treasurer of the province of Maracaibo authorized the redistribution in 1812 of mission lands along the Zulia River to a multitude of bidders. In September 1813 the court of Spain issued a decree ordering that all missionaries immediately give up their administration of indigenous lands. In Maracaibo and other provinces of New Granada, the new laws gave large landowners an opportunity to take private possession of formerly communal lands.

Throughout coastal, highland, and *llanos* areas of Venezuela, the wars of independence devastated small communities of indigenous farmers and herdsmen living on communal lands. Although most of these displaced indigenous groups fled to remote areas to escape direct conflict with the insurgents, some groups sided with the royalist army. The nomadic Guajiro, for example, served as guerilla warriors for the Spanish and effectively blocked the patriots' military communications between the provinces of Maracaibo and Hacha. In the arid coastal zone surrounding Barquisimeto, the Ayamane, Gayone, and Jirajira peoples who subsisted through goat-herding and maize cultivation were recruited into the royalist army "as auxiliary troops of indigenous bowmen, who struggled furiously against the patriot troops."[15] In other areas indigenous communities suffered severe losses of population during the early years of the wars, and survivors fled to remote forest areas away from the fighting. In the valleys extending inland from the coastal cities of Barcelona and Cumaná, a population of approximately 15,000 Chaima, 2,000 Guayqueríe, and smaller numbers of Pariagoto, Cuacua, Aruaca, Carib, and Warao was almost totally destroyed by fighting in 1815–1816 that left the region's towns and cities burned to the ground. With the exception of the relatively large group of Chaima from Santa Barbara de Tapirín, who came back to restore a successful industry in indigenous handicrafts after the wars, none of the missionized indigenous communities of the region recovered.

Indigenous participation in the wars of independence was a decisive military factor in the Wars' outcome in two key areas of the northern lowlands: the *llanos* of Casanare and the lower Orinoco Basin. Gaining control over these two regions, as well as the passage from Guiana to the *llanos* via the middle Orinoco River, enabled the patriot army to achieve a crushing defeat of the royalists at Boyacá on August 7, 1819. If Spanish defenses in the Llanos de Casanare had not remained weak during the late eighteenth century, it is unlikely that the patriot army would have succeeded in gaining such a decisive victory at Boyacá, which allowed them to take Santa Fe (Bogotá) and to expel the last Spanish viceroy. The mestizo population of the Llanos de Casanare, who had absorbed many features of the nomadic lifestyle of the Guahibo and other indige-

[15] Grau, *Geografía*, 278.

nous groups of the region, were among the first to join the patriot army. The majority of Catholic missionaries in Casanare also favored the cause of independence, even though the fighting resulted in a nearly total decimation of the cattle herds that they had slowly built up during the previous three decades. The most significant of all resources in Casanare were its missionized indigenous peoples.

The majority of new recruits in General Santander's 1818 reorganization of the patriot army were indigenous people from Tame and other mission settlements of the *llanos* and adjacent highland areas. Santander won the loyalty of these new indigenous recruits by promising that they would be allowed to return to their homes after the wars. Those indigenous people who were not conscripted into the patriot army were ordered to labor in the fields to produce badly needed food supplies. Despite these emergency measures, food production in Casanare was insufficient to supply the troops, and General Santander was forced to import supplies from Guiana.

In the lower Orinoco, or Guiana region, the relatively prosperous network of Capuchin mission settlements became a primary source of food, horses, and indigenous conscripts after the arrival of General Simón Bolívar's patriot army in 1817. Leaders of the patriot army saw the Guiana region as both an offensive staging area for their later movements into the *llanos* and as a defensive refuge into which they could retreat in the event of a major defeat. General Manuel Piar, writing in November 1816, described Guiana as

> the key to the *Llanos*, it is the fortress of Venezuela. . . . Guiana is, finally, the only region of Venezuela that escaped the calamities of the earlier warfare and offers us resources to provision ourselves with necessities, and the only point of defense that we can choose, whether it be to furnish our supplies or to have a safe asylum if fate reduces us to the ultimate extreme. The occupation of Guiana must be, therefore, with priority, the object of our efforts.[16]

Simón Bolívar agreed with General Piar's assessment, and in February 1817 Bolívar's forces took Angostura and the surrounding network of Capuchin missions along the Caroní and lower Orinoco rivers.

Upon their arrival in the Caroní missions, the patriot army's leaders ordered the execution of missionaries and gave speeches to the indigenous population assuring them of equality, justice, and freedom from the

[16] Grau, *Geografia*, 851.

missionaries' oppression. The rhetoric of equality and freedom cast a thin veneer of "liberation" upon what could more appropriately be characterized as genocide. By 1818 approximately 25 percent of the missionized indigenous population had died of malaria and other diseases introduced by Bolívar's army, and thousands more died of hunger brought on by the rapid decimation of cattle and other food supplies. "In 1816, the indigenous population concentrated in these settlements was estimated at 19,154 inhabitants, this population having diminished 47.45% in 1817, a year when only 10,065 indigenous people were counted. This process accelerated in following months."[17] Large herds of cattle and horses estimated at over 100,000 head in 1816 were reduced to less than 10,000 by 1818. In addition to disease and hunger, large numbers of indigenous men were forced to serve in the patriot army. Between February and November of 1817, approximately 2,000 men between 14 and 40 years of age were transported to Angostura and from there to San Fernando de Apure. As in other regions patriot commissioners promised indigenous conscripts that they would be returned to their homes after the war, but none returned. Many of these forced indigenous conscripts deserted at the first opportunity, and the provisional commissioner of the missions reacted with a more massive campaign of recruitment in late 1817 and early 1818.

By this time many missionized indigenous people had fled to remote forest areas in the Roraima Mountains, which formed the southern limit of the Caroní Basin, while others sought safety across the border into the Essequibo and Demerara territories of British Guiana. Remnants of the colonial "Spanish Arawaks" fled from Venezuela after the 1817 massacre of Capuchin missionaries and settled along the Moluka River, where they enjoyed British protection. After most of the missionized Caribs of Venezuela had fled into British Guiana in 1817, the provisional commissioner passed rules that forbade all unauthorized movements outside of or between settlements. In 1818 and 1819 the new government hired Carib mercenaries from the *llanos* north of the Orinoco to track down fugitive indigenous men and to kill those who resisted recruitment into the patriot army. These raiding parties frequently entered British Guiana and "were still a cause of bitterness between Spanish and English Carib communities at the end of the nineteenth century."[18]

Within 2 years the lucrative Capuchin missions of Venezuelan Guiana

[17] Grau, *Geografía*, 921. [18] Whitehead, "Ethnic soldiering," 370.

had been decimated by ransacking, raping, and banditry that were beyond the control of even the most highly ranked officials. As early as late 1817, Simón Bolívar had advised his officers to allow indigenous people more time for their own labors so that they might feed themselves and produce surplus foods for the army and for export. Despite these appeals groups of bandits roamed the countryside for the next several years, capturing and raping indigenous women who had remained in mission settlements. Deaths due to venereal diseases introduced by patriot troops were another source of increased mortality. The situation had degenerated into such a complete state of anarchy that even the local mestizo and white populations, estimated at 2,000 in 1816, fled to British Guiana or the British Antilles. In September 1819 the entire region was rented to a British colonel named James Hamilton, who siphoned off the meager resources left after the devastation of 1817–1818. The government agreed to this arrangement in order to cancel the interest on its huge war debts to the British.

During the later years of the wars, mission settlements at Caicara, La Encamarada, La Urbana, and Carichana along the middle Orinoco River served as strategic points of linkage between the Guiana region to the east and the *llanos* of Casanare and Apure to the west. These mission towns, which had steadily declined in population and significance after the Jesuits' expulsion in 1767, had been burned to the ground and abandoned in the early years of the wars to prevent the royalist troops from using them as bases against the patriot army. During the period 1817–1819 the patriot army used these sites as naval bases to control the middle Orinoco and lower Meta and Apure rivers, ensuring that the vital supplies of food, horses, and forced conscripts could reach battlefields in *llanos* areas upstream. As in other areas directly embroiled in the wars, indigenous people were either forced to serve in the patriot army or managed to flee into remote forest areas south of the Orinoco River.

An exception to this general pattern of forced conscription or flight were the Carib-speaking Mapoyo living along the eastern tributaries of the middle Orinoco between the Parguaza and Suapure rivers. This area of flooded forests, streams, and rocky hillsides became the focus of a battle in which the patriot army sought to dislodge royalist troops from the Cerro de Parguaza. According to Mapoyo oral testimony related by Pascual Meijas in the 1970s, General José Antonio Páez asked Mapoyo leaders to help him find an alternate way of reaching the Cerro de Parguaza so that patriot troops could ascend it without being detected by the royalist garrison at the top. A Mapoyo headman, Alejo Sandoval, is said to have shown General Páez how to reach the rear of the cerro via a small stream, which allowed the patriot army to launch a successful surprise attack on the royalists.

> And it was in this manner that General Páez ascended with all his troops up the hill, assisted by the indigenous Mapoyo and freeing the patriots from the battle, which took the name of the battle for la Boca del Cerro de Parguaza. General Bolivar asked Alejo Sandoval, headman of the village that existed then on Caño Villacoa, "What would you like to have in exchange for the favor that you have done?" . . . Paulino [Sandoval, the most senior headman of the Mapoyo] answered him: ". . . what we want is land to work and, as we have families, that they may later raise cattle. . . . " Bolivar asked Paulino Sandoval what area was encompassed in this zone. Answering him, the headman said: "from the banks of the mouth of the Suapure River to the mouth of the Parguaza River."[19]

At the end of the story, Bolívar promises Paulino Sandoval that his people's lands will be guaranteed by written documents that will remain in Caracas "so that no official can abuse you." When Alberto Valdez collected this oral testimony in 1976, the Mapoyo were living on a small parcel of land only one-tenth the size of the area that Simón Bolívar, according to the legend, had promised to give them during the wars.[20] Working through the National Agrarian Institute, Valdez and other Venezuelan anthropologists succeeded in obtaining a land title giving the Mapoyo collective control over an area of 45,000 hectares in 1977.

The Mapoyo oral testimony related above demonstrates how one small indigenous group has kept the memory of its historical role in the wars of independence alive through the story of Paulino Sandoval and Simón Bolívar. The story no doubt increased in value over time as a way for Mapoyo residents of the middle Orinoco to try to retain what little lands were left to them after the encroachments of nineteenth- and twentieth-century settlers. Whatever interpretive slant on the story one might favor, the issue of control over land for agriculture and cattle raising is clearly central to the narrator's intentions.

Whether or not the events recounted in the Mapoyo story actually took place, the fact that Mapoyo storytellers have chosen to remember the wars of independence primarily in terms of the new government's

[19] Alberto Valdez, "Los Mapoyo del Cano Caripo," in A. Valdez (ed.), *Autogestión Indígena* (Caracas, 1982), 151–152.

[20] Ibid. A search of historical archives has failed to produce any written evidence pertaining to the Mapoyo land claims (Silvia Vidal, personal communication, 1991).

unfulfilled promise to award their indigenous allies with a collective title to their lands is a highly appropriate metaphor for the losses of population, land, and autonomy that indigenous peoples experienced throughout the northern lowlands. At the congress of Cúcuta, the new government made clear its intention to abolish the missionaries' system of indigenous tribute and to "reintegrate" Church-protected *resguardo* lands in the decree of May 20, 1820.

However, as the situation in Guiana and other regions had shown beyond any doubt, the leaders of the wars of independence lacked any clear plan or vision for creating new political spaces that would allow indigenous peoples to retain collective land ownership in the absence of missionaries. Faced with the reality of indigenous flight from areas of conflict and increased mestizo presence, the new government on at least one occasion was prepared to consider allowing indigenous people a measure of autonomy over local political affairs. In the first article of the Regulations for Governing the Missions, written in July 1817, "it was reiterated to the Commissioners that they must treat indigenous people very well, making them understand that upon the completion of the war against Guiana, they would remain in charge of governing themselves without any constraint other than that of the supreme authority of the Republic."[21] Unfortunately this call for indigenous self-rule at local and regional levels within the overarching authority of the nation-state was completely drowned out in the chaos of warfare and the power vacuum of the postwar years. The congressional decree for reintegration of indigenous *resguardo* lands in 1820 was in fact the culmination of a process of disintegration in which communal ownership became individualized.

The new government's failure to articulate an adequate plan for protecting indigenous lands was overshadowed by its inability to raise sufficient revenues to carry on the costly war in Peru. Ironically the privatization of indigenous lands led to a loss of revenue from indigenous tribute, and a new tax levy of 10 percent on land and capital did little to compensate. Despite the agreement to rent the entire Guiana region to British owners in 1819 and the raising of a 20-million-pound loan in London in 1824, the new republic lingered on the verge of bankruptcy. The government was unable to compensate its war veterans in cash, so it promised instead to divide up royalist and national lands as the spoils of war. However, there were not enough of these lands available to compen-

[21] Grau, *Geografía*, 921.

sate all the veterans at the rate that Simón Bolívar had promised at the congress of Angostura, and the result was the granting of enormous estates to Páez, Urdanete, and other generals. The concentration of large properties into the possession of a few generals, who had almost all been large landowners before the wars, accelerated the process of concentration that was to continue throughout the nineteenth century.

The wars of independence presented indigenous peoples of the northern lowlands with the most serious threats to their physical and social survival since the arrival of European peoples and diseases in the early sixteenth century. The destruction of colonial missions created a void in which most indigenous peoples faced a choice between assimilation into the majority mestizo population as "hispanicized Indians" or migration into remote forest areas. Relatively large, nomadic peoples such as the Guahibo of the *llanos* and the Guajiro of the western shores of Lake Maracaibo were among the few groups who were able to exploit the chaos of warfare to their own advantage. For the vast majority of indigenous peoples, with the possible exception of the Mapoyo and other allies of the patriots, the wars of independence brought increasing marginalization, forced relocation, or even genocide.

The wars of independence also brought about changes in remote areas into which remnant groups fled from warfare in mission settlements. Along the lower Orinoco hundreds of missionized Warao living in settlements that dated from the early eighteenth century migrated into remote areas of the Delta Amacuro to escape mistreatment at the hands of mestizo landowners who had moved into the lower Orinoco region after the war.

> The mistreatment of these indigenous people and the eradication of their small farms rapidly caused the exhaustion of the short cycle of bonanza in these agricultural settlements, initiating in 1825 their decline, when a large number of indigenous Warao peons deserted and fled to the most isolated landscapes of the delta's streams.

These displacements required nonmissionized Warao to absorb large numbers of refugees into an existing territory that was already shrinking due to the expanding frontiers of the *llanos* to the west and along the Orinoco to the south. Fleeing from sugar plantations along the main channel of the Orinoco, large numbers of displaced Warao entered into the inaccessible forests of the delta, straining the region's fragile resources. There is no clear evidence on how this intensification of Warao settlements in remote areas of the delta changed social and economic relations among nonmissionized Warao. Nevertheless one can conclude that the wars of independence indirectly affected even the most remotely situated, nonmissionized Warao by increasing population densities in remote areas in direct proportion to the depopulation of mission settlements and sugar cane plantations along the Orinoco and its main channels through the delta.

The Struggle for Lands in the Northern Lowlands

The prolonged period of political instability after the wars of independence completed processes of dislocation, marginalization, and *mestizaje* of indigenous peoples living in the northern lowlands of South America. In the *llanos* of Casanare, the colonial system of mission settlements continued to decline and essentially vanished forever. Aside from the nomadic Guahibo, who continued to resist pressures to assimilate, indigenous peoples of the *llanos* were reduced to peons working for the owners of large haciendas. In the *llanos* of Apure, the expansion of latifundia for extensive cattle ranching continued throughout the nineteenth century at the expense of agricultural production, including the subsistence farming of indigenous peoples. In other areas the large-scale cultivation of coffee, sugar, cacao, and other export crops transformed indigenous peasant farmers into a landless rural proletariat. In the Guiana region, most of which remained under British ownership until 1832, mission settlements were almost totally abandoned by their former indigenous inhabitants despite official attempts to regain their loyalty through economic incentives.

The disappearance of mission settlements during the wars did not result in an immediate removal of indigenous groups from their communally owned *resguardo* lands. Despite the generally anticlerical tendencies of the postwar period, the legal status of indigenous *resguardo* lands was supported by a number of official laws and decrees. The law of April 9, 1832, for example, "exempted both indigenous *resguardos* and the ejidos of indigenous parishes from the sales of untilled land."[22] In February 1836 the Venezuelan Senate passed an identical law, and various other laws protecting indigenous lands were issued in 1837, 1840, 1848, 1850, 1859, and 1865. However, another set of laws, beginning with the law of

[22] Grau, *Geografia*, 1045.

April 2, 1836, ordered the redistribution of communally owned indigenous lands along the same lines as the earlier law that had been passed at the congress of Cúcuta in 1821. Like the latter the law of April 2, 1836 authorized the parceling out of different amounts of land to indigenous families, depending upon the number of adult individuals in each family. Predictably, the effects of the new law were "to weaken communal ties and to open up a portion of the *resguardo* lands to criollo renters and buyers."[23]

Thus, despite the effects of protective legislation designed to exempt indigenous lands from private ownership, the laws ordering redistribution and privatization of indigenous lands acted as a wedge that gave the majority mestizo population a legal mechanism for breaking down collective indigenous resistance to land invasions. The sale or rental of small plots of *resguardo* land to mestizo farmers often foresaged the complete eradication of indigenous lands by powerful officials and large landowners. In a well-documented case from Maracaibo, the state's governor in 1832 granted *resguardo* lands at El Placer as a military asset to a high-ranking officer. In turn this official immediately sold the lands to a cattle rancher who owned a large area adjacent to the *resguardo*. The rancher and his workers used violent force to prohibit indigenous families from cultivating the lands. Despite the state government's 1840 ruling that these lands be restored to indigenous farmers, there is no evidence that this decision was ever implemented. All traces of the indigenous community and *resguardo* lands at El Placer had vanished by the 1873 census.

The eradication of indigenous *resguardo* lands at El Placer demonstrates in microcosm the broader processes of marginalization and *mestizaje* that took place in areas of frontier expansion. Along the fertile river valleys south of Lake Maracaibo, a wave of spontaneous colonization by mestizo farmers overwhelmed the remaining Motilón (Barí) communities. An area that had consisted of a small mestizo minority centered in San Carlos del Zulia and surrounded by an indigenous majority living on *resguardo* lands prior to the wars transformed during the 1820s and 1830s into a small indigenous minority working on redistributed lands that were owned or rented by mestizo farmers. By 1836 only four of these Motilón *resguardos* contained any indigenous inhabitants, and the provincial government of Maracaibo ordered the remaining *resguardo* lands divided up in accordance with the law of April 2, 1836. By mid-century

[23] Grau, *Geografia*, 1,047.

the Motilón peoples of the area south of Lake Maracaibo had lost all their communal lands and had become assimilated into the regional mestizo population.

The law of April 2, 1836, had a similar effect of accelerating spontaneous mestizo colonization of indigenous lands in the eastern lowlands surrounding Cumaná and Maturín. Between 1836 and 1840 Chaima and other indigenous peoples lost all but one of their *resguardo* lands to mestizo landowners. The largest and wealthiest of these estates arose in areas of the densest indigenous populations, who served as laborers in large-scale production of coffee, cacao, sugar, and tobacco. Processes of *mestizaje* and assimilation brought an end to most of the region's indigenous population by the middle of the century. In the fertile coastal plains of Carupano and Rio Caribe, latifundistas had purchased or rented nearly all indigenous *resguardo* lands in 1829, and the law of April 2, 1836, opened the way for the sale of the few remaining *resguardo* lands to mestizo owners of large cacao plantations.

Indigenous peoples living in the *llanos* of Apure suffered similar, though less devastating, losses of land in the aftermath of the 1836 law. The large expanse of grasslands between the Arauca and Meta rivers served as a refuge area for Yaruro, Otomaco, Guama, and Guahibo peoples throughout the nineteenth century. An 1839 census estimated the indigenous population of the region at 5,295, and the census of 1873 registered 5,315 indigenous people. Although many of the more sedentary peoples had become assimilated into the region's *llanero* culture of extensive cattle ranching by the late nineteenth century, others persisted as indigenous communities based on a diversified subsistence economy of horticulture, fishing, hunting, and gathering supplemented by trading of hammocks and other handicrafts.

Along the lower Orinoco and its tributaries, the population of missionized Caribs and other indigenous groups continued to decline throughout the nineteenth century. A frontier based mainly on extensive cattle ranching spread southward from Ciudad Bolívar (formerly Angostura) into the region of mission settlements that had been devastated during the wars and further decimated under temporary British ownership. The new republic promoted foreign immigration and land grants to the sparse mestizo and indigenous population, including an 1841 project that offered land, tools, seed, and livestock to indigenous families who were willing to settle in mission towns. However, by offering the same incentives to mestizo and foreign settlers to establish small farms within indigenous communities, the 1841 law "unleashed a continuous process of expropriating indigenous homesteads and lands in these mixed communities. In effect, in the most consolidated mixed settlements and the adjoining communal lands, a spatial marginalization of indigenous people took place."[24] Unlike coastal and *llanos* areas where spontaneous immigration of mestizo colonists resulted in the assimilation of indigenous peoples into the rural society, the Guiana settlements attracted only small numbers of mestizo colonists, whose very survival depended upon cooperation with their indigenous neighbors. Despite this demographic situation, mestizo colonists in Guiana imitated the practices of other, more populous regions and exploited indigenous people as a source of cheap labor. Perhaps the gravest miscalculation was an attempt by the governor of Guiana in 1845 to apply a rule of mandatory peonage to all indigenous people who had resettled in accord with the law of 1841. By the end of the 1840s, indigenous people who had been lured into settling within the expanding frontier region had nearly all migrated into remote forest areas to the south or east, including the Essequibo region of British Guiana.

Throughout the first half of the nineteenth century, British Guiana continued to provide a safe haven for indigenous peoples fleeing oppressive situations in Venezuela and Brazilian slave traders emanating from the Rio Branco to the south. Anglican mission settlements attracted Warao and Arawakan converts into the strip of coastal lands running eastward from the Orinoco delta. Protestant missionaries also became the main agents of colonial contact with the Macusi, Akawaio, Waiwai, Wapisiana, and other indigenous peoples of the remote forested interior. Brazilian slave traders continued to exert pressures on southern border areas until the mid–nineteenth century. Under strong protest from British missionaries, the Brazilians raided settlements at Pirara and Curua, removing indigenous inhabitants to sites on the Rio Branco and forcing them to perform agricultural and other labor. In the 1840s a large group of Makusi and other Carib peoples followed Anglican missionaries into Georgetown to protest these Brazilian encroachments, and the governor dispatched a military expedition to restore order in Pirara.[25]

By the mid–nineteenth century the indigenous population of British

[24] Grau, *Geografia*, 2,099.

[25] Mary Noel Menezes, *British Policy Towards the Amerindians in British Guiana, 1803–1873* (Oxford, 1977), 157–158.

Guiana had become increasingly marginalized within the colony. An 1837 law had authorized British militia rather than indigenous mercenaries to rule over fugitive African-American slaves in the interior, and only a small number of black freedmen chose to enter the interior after the official abolition of slavery in 1838. This context of historical marginalization gave rise to messianic movements among the Akawaio and other Carib peoples in the 1840s. Later in the century these movements became institutionalized into a pan-Carib cult called "Hallelujah" that spread across the border into Venezuela. The Essequibo region remained under dispute between Venezuela and British Guiana, and open conflicts developed in the 1870s and 1880s when gold was discovered along the upper Cuyuni River. British Guiana passed a law granting land to miners in 1880, and Venezuelan authorities retaliated by arresting several British miners and protesting British incursions into its territory. In 1897 both countries agreed to settle the dispute through arbitration, leading to an 1899 decision weighted heavily in Great Britain's favor and granting it possession of nearly the entire Essequibo region.

Assimilation Versus Flight

In the northern lowlands of South America, the wars of independence and subsequent rise of independent liberal states created a power vacuum in which large landowners and mestizo colonists expanded into indigenous territories that the Church had formerly protected and developed. At the center of this power vacuum, there was a wide-open discrepancy between the assertion of equal rights for all citizens, including indigenous peoples, and the creation of new interethnic hierarchies that left indigenous groups landless, indebted, and powerless. Beginning with the Constitution of Caracas in 1812 and the forced conscription of indigenous men into the patriot army during the wars, the expansion of nation-states into the northern lowlands overwhelmed and assimilated indigenous peoples in coastal and *llanos* areas or forced them to seek refuge in inaccessible forests or across international borders.

By the end of the century, all indigenous territories were concentrated in remote areas at the borders between nation-states. By far the largest refuge for indigenous peoples were the *llanos* south of the Meta and the forests south and east of the Orinoco. In intermediate areas of the *llanos* between the Apure and Meta rivers and the former mission settlements of the Venezuelan Guiana region, the presence of indigenous groups interspersed with a relatively sparse mestizo population remained strong throughout the century. North of the Orinoco and Apure rivers, mestizo colonization and latifundia had largely if not absolutely overpowered and assimilated indigenous peoples who had survived the wars of independence. Two north–south axes of relatively autonomous indigenous territories cut through these three east–west bands of southward state expansion. One axis formed the border region between Venezuela and Colombia, an area where Guajiro, Barí, and other smaller groups have continued to predominate even in the late twentieth century. The other axis consisted of the disputed border along the Essequibo Basin in Venezuela and British Guiana, where displaced Warao, Carib, and Arawakan peoples remained numerous through the end of the nineteenth century.

RESISTANCE, REVITALIZATION, AND THE RUBBER BOOM: NATION-STATE EXPANSION IN THE SOUTHERN LOWLANDS

The great arc of forested lowlands stretching across the headwater regions of the Amazon River's major tributaries remained a stronghold for indigenous peoples in the Spanish viceroyalties of Nueva Granada and Peru during the late eighteenth century. Spanish mission settlements in the upper Orinoco region, the Peruvian province of Mainas, and the southeast Peruvian *montaña* never achieved the size and stability of mission settlements in the *llanos* and the Guiana region to the north. Indigenous uprisings, such as the famous Asháninka (Campa) rebellion led by Juan Santos de Atahualpa in the 1740s and 1750s, drew upon the nonmissionized majority to force missionaries to abandon or relocate their settlements.

Contrasting with the relative autonomy of indigenous peoples living in remote headwater regions of the Amazon Basin, there was the brutal domination of indigenous peoples in Portuguese Brazil during the late colonial period. In Brazil indigenous slavery, forced relocations (*descimentos*) to downstream locations, and diseases led to the annihilation or assimilation of entire societies. Conflicts between Spanish and Portuguese armies embroiled indigenous peoples of the headwater regions in warfare, but these local skirmishes never reached the proportions of Carib and Arawakan ethnic soldiering in the Guiana region, where fighting among Spanish, Dutch, French, and British forces resulted in major losses of indigenous population throughout the eighteenth century.

Up to a point geopolitical forces favored the survival of indigenous peoples in the southern lowlands. But the region's inhabitants were not spared from the ravages of Western diseases, such as smallpox and measles, transmitted by even sporadic contacts. Mission settlements were especially prone to become centers for major epidemics, because they concentrated indigenous populations into reduced areas of heightened interethnic contact. Among the Asháninka of lowland Peru, the "Indian population of the Eneno mission, for instance, fell from 800 to 220 as the result of a major epidemic in 1722–1723, though it is unclear how much of this rapid decline is attributable to defections rather than disease-related deaths."[26] Survivors of such epidemics carried the infections into remote, uncontacted areas, resulting in major losses of population even in areas where no Westerners were present. Although it is impossible to determine the exact amount of depopulation due to epidemics, infectious diseases were responsible for an overall decline of an estimated 55 percent of the indigenous population in the southern lowlands during the seventeenth and eighteenth centuries. These losses of population were partially offset by the absorption of remnant groups from downstream areas.

The same early nineteenth-century conflicts that ravaged populations of the northern lowlands provided indigenous groups of the southern lowlands with a period of relative autonomy and recovery from losses due to disease, warfare, and slave trading. In the Peruvian *montaña*, the wars of independence abruptly halted both missionization and colonization projects of the late colonial period. Franciscan missionaries, who had taken over administration of the province of Mainas after the Jesuits' expulsion in 1767, withdrew from all missions in eastern Peru in 1821 in response to the patriots' victory. The Peruvian government, facing bankruptcy during the wars of independence and the decades of the 1820s and 1830s, could no longer afford to provide economic incentives and support for its colonization projects along the Huallaga River. In this context of greatly reduced governmental and Church authority, indigenous peoples were free to raid settlements and isolated dwellings. White or mestizo colonists abandoned some of their formerly secure territories.

The most militant indigenous groups in the lowlands were the Aguaruna and other Jivaroan-speaking peoples who, outstandingly successful in resisting the early colonial Spanish invasions, remained in large part fully autonomous. In February and March 1830 their forces "attacked

[26] Brown and Fernandez, *War of Shadows*, 28–29.

Santiago de las Montañas, . . . and repeated their raids in the middle of the following year."[27] Aguaruna attacks continued against mission settlements on the upper Marañón (Amazon) for over a decade, culminating in the defeat of the regional administrative center at Borja in 1841, sending its inhabitants to seek safety downstream in the new capital of Loreto at Iquitos. South of the Marañón along the rivers that form the headwaters of the Ucayali River, Asháninka warriors raided colonists' settlements and fought against anyone traveling through their territory. In other areas of eastern Peru, indigenous groups recaptured downstream territories that they had lost during the colonial period. The Panoan-speaking Shipibo and Conibo, for example, expanded down into the middle Ucayali Valley into areas that had formerly been inhabited by the Setebo and Tupí-speaking Cocama.

The early nineteenth century was also a period of recovery and ethnogenesis for indigenous peoples of lowland Ecuador. Missionary influence spread primarily from the settlements at Puyo and Canelos in the province of Quijos down the Pastaza and Bobonaza rivers to Andoas, which was administered from Borja in Peruvian territory. The Bobonaza-Pastaza drainage area became a refuge for indigenous Jivaroan and Zaparoan peoples fleeing the slave trade and forced labor campaigns in other areas. Quichua-speakers who had migrated into the region to escape the colonial regime of *encomiendas* along the Napo River brought with them trade connections among the Quijos and Andean highland peoples. By the mid–nineteenth century, when Canelos had become a canton of Ecuador under the authority of the governor of Quijos, Quichua had emerged as the dominant language of the Bobonaza-Pastaza Valley, and a new multiethnic coalition of Záparo, Canelos, Achuar, and Quichua peoples had come to recognize themselves as one people, or *runa*, the Canelos-Quichua.

Similar processes of recovery and ethnogenesis developed in other upstream areas, such as the upper Rio Negro region of Colombia, Venezuela, and Brazil. Along the Isana and Aiarí rivers in northwestern Brazil, indigenous Arawak-speaking peoples returned from headwater areas in Venezuela and Colombia in order to reconstitute their social order of ranked phratries in the aftermath of colonial depopulation. During the early nineteenth century, these Arawakan phratries began to develop relations of trade and intermarriage with eastern Tukano-speaking peo-

[27] Werlich, "The conquest," 294.

ples of the Vaupés Basin to the south and west. The Cubeo, a large Tukano-speaking group living in the intermediate zone between Arawakan and Tukanoan territories, came into being as a result of this new pattern of interethnic relations.

During the wars of independence and the subsequent period of political instability that lasted until the middle of the nineteenth century, colonization and missionization of the southern lowlands receded or came to a halt. The newly independent republics were economically crippled by the wars and too politically unstable within their coastal and highland population centers to be very much concerned about the peripheral forested lowlands along their borders with Brazil. In the upper Orinoco region, over fifty mission settlements were abandoned between 1830 and 1850. In eastern Peru, despite the reinstatement of a Franciscan mission school at Ocopa in 1838, the line of colonization receded in the face of overwhelming indigenous resistance during the 1830s and 1840s. As indigenous populations expanded and moved in new directions, they entered into new relations of trade and intermarriage that brought into being new sociocultural identities, such as the Canelos-Quichua and the Cubeo. However, events in the 1850s, and especially the discovery that the southern lowlands contained valuable supplies of rubber for export, abruptly transformed the relative autonomy of indigenous peoples into a new era of enslavement, forced relocations, and even genocide.

Mid–Nineteenth-Century Developments

In the mid–nineteenth century the newly independent states of Latin America began to turn their attention to the southern lowlands as a potential source of land, food, and raw materials for export. The Brazilian government had initiated a new administrative program, called the "directorate," which gave greater authority to local officials in the Upper Amazon. The directorate created a strong Brazilian presence along its borders with other nations and foreshadowed the horrible abuses of indigenous laborers during the Rubber Boom. Under the rubric of "public service labor," indigenous peoples of the Brazilian Amazon were forced into relations of debt peonage to traveling merchants, and those who resisted were hunted down by the Brazilian military in a manner reminiscent of the "rescue wars" that had been waged in the late colonial period. Brazilian merchants engaged in a practice of indigenous slave trading that extended far beyond the international boundary into lowland Peru and Colombia. Along the Caquetá and Putumayo rivers in Peru, a region that was under dispute between Peru and Colombia throughout the nineteenth and early twentieth centuries, Brazilian merchants traded steel tools, firearms, and other manufactured items to Andoque headmen, who canceled their debts by furnishing indigenous men, women, and children from neighboring groups. Except for the greater emphasis on firearms, the terms of exchange were very similar to the payments that the Dutch slave traders had offered to Carib mercenaries in the *llanos* and Guiana during the early colonial period. "An infant costs the value of an American knife; a six-year-old girl is valued at one saber and sometimes an axe; an adult man and woman reached the price of one rifle."[28] Thus, despite laws prohibiting indigenous slavery in the new republics, the practice continued in remote forested areas.

The Peruvian government became increasingly aware that its eastern borders were weakly defined and feared the loss of territory to Brazil, Colombia, and Ecuador. Under the regime of General Ramón Castilla, Peru initiated military campaigns and new agricultural development projects in the eastern lowlands to secure lines of communication and protect settlers from Asháninka raids. A fort built at the junction of the Chanchamayo and Tulumayo rivers in 1847, named San Ramón after Peru's new leader, forced Asháninka to move eastward into the Perené and Ene valleys, where they continued to fight against travelers and colonists entering their territory. Although Asháninka warriors repelled a group of colonists from the highlands moving eastward from San Ramón in 1866, indigenous resistance was ultimately insufficient to halt the expanding frontier and the large-scale forces that propelled it eastward. In 1876 the Peruvian government dispatched soldiers to found a new fort at La Merced and granted small parcels of land to Italian and French immigrants. When lack of roads and continued Asháninka raids led to the failure of these European colonies in the 1880s, large landowners moved into the Chanchamayo Valley to found coffee plantations. Finally, as part of the reorganization of Peru's debt to Great Britain in 1890, the government awarded 1,100,000 acres of land along the Perené River, deep within Asháninka territory, to an English enterprise called the Peruvian Corporation, Ltd. Although the Perené Colony and other pro-

[28] Landaburu and Pineda Camacho, *Tradiciones*, 27.

jects attracted small numbers of land-hungry settlers from highland Peru, most of the settlers came from England, France, Germany, Italy, China, and Japan.

Peru's expansion into the eastern lowlands during the "Guano Age" (c. 1840–1875) also reflected a new interest in developing the region's economic potential as a source of export commodities. To accomplish this goal the government sent troops in the 1850s to suppress the Aguaruna and to rebuild Borja and other towns along the Marañón, Huallaga, and other major rivers. In 1851 Peru and Brazil signed a Treaty of Commerce and Navigation, and by 1864 the town of Iquitos boasted a fleet of steamships making regular runs between Yurimaguas on the Huallaga River and Loreto on the Brazilian border. Major export products included tobacco, saltfish, straw hats, sarsparilla, and rubber. Total foreign trade in the Peruvian northeast grew an exponential fifteenfold between 1854 and 1876. Rubber exports increased from 1,166 pounds to 58 metric tons during this period and made up 18 percent of the region's total exports by 1870. Indigenous peoples living in and around Iquitos withdrew to more inaccessible sites after the arrival of the steamships.

The expansion of Peru into eastern lowlands during the Guano Age brought into play new economic forces that had not existed in the colonial past of the region. "Conquest of the jungle was no longer in the hands of missionaries supported in a desultory fashion by detachments of poorly trained soldiers. Now it was driven by powerful economic interests, backed by a state scouring the region for exportable goods and pledged to territorial control."[29] These new political and economic forces provided the material grounding for ideologies of progress and increasingly dehumanized objectifications of indigenous peoples as animal-like beings whose destiny was to be assimilation, relocation, or death. By the beginning of the Rubber Boom, indigenous peoples were harvested like other natural resources, and gangs even raided the missions in search of workers. The missionaries, who had in colonial times seen themselves as agents of civilization and protection for indigenous peoples, also adopted the harsh rhetoric of progress and forced assimilation. Father Gabriel Sala stated:

> And what will we do with beings such as this? What is done the world over: supposing that they don't want to live as men, but instead as animals, one treats

[29] Brown and Fernandez, *War of Shadows*, 55.

them like animals and puts a bullet in them when they unjustly oppose the lives and well-being of the rest of us.[30]

The revitalization movement of 1858 led by Venancio Camico, a Baniwa man from the Guainía (Negro) River in Venezuela and Colombia, attempted to counteract the progressive impoverishment and powerlessness of indigenous peoples whose lands were in the path of nation-state expansion. By mid-century the river towns of Maroa and San Carlos de Rio Negro had become centers for boat building, collection of palm fibers used for making ropes, and regional trade. Indigenous workers who formed the backbone of this trade and industry became increasingly indebted to white and mestizo merchants. In addition to debt peonage, indigenous townspeople regularly endured food shortages due to over-exploitation of the region's nutrient-poor, blackwater environment. Conditions were ripe for rebellion, as Richard Spruce learned during his visit to San Carlos de Rio Negro in the early 1850s when the Arawakan Baré rebelled and threatened to kill all white and mestizo residents. Venancio Camico, like messianic leaders in many other regions of the world, was a bilingual, bicultural individual whose life experiences embodied the collective hardships and contradictions of indigenous peoples who had become inextricably part of emergent systems of exploitative interethnic relations. Venancio was both an indigenous shaman trained in the arts of interpreting and healing illnesses and a student of Catholicism. In June 1858 Venancio traveled among the Arawakan Wakuénai phratries of the Cuyarí and Isana rivers along the Colombian-Brazilian border, preaching that the white's domination of the world would end in a fiery conflagration on Saint John's Day. Using a synthesis of Christian and indigenous Arawakan symbols of ritual power, Venancio and his followers called for a complete break in political and economic relations with white and mestizo traders of the upper Rio Negro region.

What was at stake in this movement was the kind of transformation that the Wakuénai were to follow: whether to become totally subservient to the whiteman's system of debt peonage or to seize the historical moment and carve out a ritual time-space in which a degree of spiritual and political freedom was possible.[31]

[30] Brown and Fernandez, *War of Shadows*, 67.

[31] Jonathan D. Hill and Robin Wright, "Time, narrative, and ritual: Historical interpretations from an Amazonian society," in Jonathan Hill (ed.), *Rethinking History and Myth: Indigenous South American Perspectives on the Past* (Urbana, 1988), 78–106.

In a strictly military sense, Venancio Camico's movement had little or no effect in changing, much less halting, the progressive stranglehold of debt peonage into which Arawakan peoples of the region had become ensnared. Brazilian missionaries and military authorities captured Venancio and his disciples, who were then turned over to Venezuelan officials in San Carlos de Rio Negro. However, Venancio managed to escape from captivity while being sent to the territorial capital at San Fernando de Atabapo, and he lived among his followers at a remote village on the Cano Acqui until his death in 1903. Evaluation of the long-term effects of Venancio Camico's movement cannot be reduced to political and material factors alone but must also take into consideration the shaman-Christ's significance as a symbol of indigenous resistance to political domination and economic exploitation in the new republics of Venezuela and Colombia. Venancio's movement assimilated Christian symbols of ritual power into deeply rooted Arawakan beliefs in the historical opening up of material and political relations among diverse peoples during the time of powerful mythic ancestors. In addition to Venancio's historical significance as a symbol of indigenous powers to resist the whites' and mestizos' oppression, he embodied the mythic character of the trickster-creator, who could always escape from the lethal machinations of his enemies. This fusion of historical and mythical meanings reoriented indigenous Arawakan understandings of the dominant national society at a transitional historical moment, the dawn of the Rubber Boom. By the end of the nineteenth century, Venancio's teachings had become part of the ritual advice given to male and female initiants by their elders, and "the refusal to cooperate with the external, dominating order of the whiteman became elevated to the status of a sacred cosmological postulate."[32]

The Rubber Boom: A Native American Holocaust

In the late nineteenth century, rubber gathering quickly became the main economic activity throughout the southern lowlands of Peru, Ecuador, Colombia, and Venezuela. The leaders of national governments were eager to demonstrate their political presence in remote forest areas and to receive a share of the profits to be made from exporting raw latex to industrializing nations of the Northern Hemisphere. Mired in debt to foreign creditors and steeped in contemporary ideologies of material

[32] Ibid., 84.

progress at any cost, these nations took few if any steps to protect indigenous peoples of the southern lowlands from the voracious search for laborers to gather rubber for export. Throughout the southern lowlands, political and economic conditions degenerated into a frenzy of mercantile greed and coercion that reduced entire societies to a handful of ragged survivors. In the violent quest for laborers, rubber barons played upon preexisting divisions among indigenous peoples, factionalism within indigenous groups, and individual rivalries. The Rubber Boom brought an extremist ideology of cultural domination in which indigenous people were stereotyped as wild, cannibalistic savages even as they suffered from the most brutal forms of physical coercion, torture, and genocide.

The wildness and savagery attributed to indigenous peoples of the southern lowlands more accurately describes the manner in which rubber barons and their private armies made use of debt servitude and force to recruit indigenous laborers. In eastern Peru, an Irish-Peruvian fugitive, who had been accused of spying for Chile during the War of the Pacific and had fled to the remote headwater region of the Madre de Dios and Ucayali rivers in 1879, rose to become the leader of an army of indigenous and white warriors in the 1880s. Carlos F. Fitzcarrald (Fitzgerald) commanded thousands of Cashibo, Asháninka, Piro, and nonindigenous henchmen who scoured the forests of the Ucayali, Urubamba, Tambo, and Manu rivers for rubber trails and indigenous tappers to work them. By 1890 Fitzcarrald was wealthy enough to build a large private estate and buy a steam-powered launch for transporting latex to Iquitos. Fitzcarrald's fortunes resulted in part from his ability to control an overland passage that connected Bolivian and Brazilian areas of rubber gathering along the upper Madre de Dios River to the Ucayali Basin in Peru, thereby providing direct access to the central market in Iquitos and eliminating the need for longer journeys down the Madeira River to Manaus. In the 1890s Fitzcarrald formed a joint corporation with Bolivian merchants, bought several more steam launches, and carried out his most celebrated feat: the hauling of a motor launch across the strip of land between the Urubamba and Manu rivers. "Moving the launch required the labor of as many as a thousand Piros and Asháninkas and nearly a hundred whites."[33] Fitzcarrrald drowned in 1897 when a new

[33] Fitzcarrald's accomplishment was the subject of Werner Herzog's 1982 film, which according to Brown and Fernandez, *War of Shadows*, 225, "takes great liberties with geographical and ethnographic reality."

launch capsized in the rapids of the Urubamba River, yet his associates continued to wage an aggressive campaign that left thousands of indigenous people enslaved or dead.

The rise of Fitzcarrald's "empire" depended upon a pyramidal structure of indigenous headmen and foreign traders, each of whom commanded a small army of white and indigenous warriors. In the region of the upper Ucayali River and its tributaries, a number of culturally and linguistically distinct peoples formed a complex mosaic of ethnopolitical relations, and Fitzcarrald's armies exploited these divisions among indigenous groups to the fullest advantage. Along the Manu River (a tributary of the Madre de Dios), a group known as the Mashco (or Amarakaeri) resisted the penetration of rubber gatherers into their territory, but the Indians could not withstand the 400 heavily armed whites and Indians that Fitzcarrald assembled to suppress the revolt. When the fighting was over, an entire indigenous people lay slaughtered in the wake of Fitzcarrald's war of extermination.

Fitzcarrald's and other rubber barons' manipulations of ethnic rivalries among indigenous peoples of eastern Peru set in motion a deadly serious game of survival versus extinction. Along with the formation of indigenous armies, the rubber barons introduced firearms to the region's indigenous population on an unprecedented scale. The Shipibo-Conibo, a large Panoan group who had expanded into the middle Ucayali Basin during the early nineteenth century, obtained shotguns and rifles from mestizo merchants and used them to raid Cashibo and Asháninka along the Urubamba and Tambo rivers. "The method was simple. Winchesters were delivered to the Conibo, to be paid off with Campa slaves, after which Winchesters were delivered to the Campa to be paid off with Conibo or Amuesha slaves."[34] The competition for rubber and indigenous labor escalated to genocidal proportions as indigenous peoples of the region became more heavily armed. The mixture of technology, unbridled greed, geopolitical competition, and ethnic divisions provided all the ingredients for a bloodbath. By the end of the Rubber Boom, even the most remote bands of nomadic Amahuaca and Cashibo hunter-gatherers had been badly battered, and larger, more sedentary peoples of the Ucayali River and its tributaries had become survivors of a major holocaust.

[34] Stephan Varese, *La sal de los Cerros*, 2nd ed. (Lima, 1973), 246, cited in Brown and Fernandez, *War of Shadows*, 60.

Although manipulation of interethnic tensions among indigenous peoples was a significant factor in the culture of terror that emerged during the Rubber Boom, raids also took place within tribes. The Shipibo-Conibo, Asháninka, Cashibo, and other groups of the Peruvian lowlands were not unified ethnic blocs with loyalties to a central leader or chief but dispersed groupings of local communities and regional trading networks with many internal divisions. Within a single cultural-linguistic group, only a small number of factions emerged as allies of the rubber barons, and these "sell-out" headmen and their followers engaged in military raids against members of their own cultural group in return for weapons, knives, and other trade goods. Among the Asháninka, for example, a headman named Venancio sent Asháninka warriors to capture other Asháninka living in the Gran Pajonál (a remote plain in the hills between the Perené and Ucayali rivers) to be sent as rubber gatherers in Fitzcarrald's territory along the Manu River. Thus internecine warfare, based in part upon differential access to firearms, created new military hierarchies within as well as among indigenous societies of eastern Peru.

In areas away from major rivers where rubber gathering had little direct impact or developed only in later decades, the sale of firearms created a sort of regional arms race. Throughout the late nineteenth century, indigenous people of the Caquetá-Putumayo region were being sold into slavery to Brazilian merchants by Andoque middlemen at the price of one rifle per adult male-female couple. Among the Aguaruna and other Jivaroan peoples of north-central Peru and southeastern Ecuador, North American and European traders paid indigenous warriors one rifle for each shrunken head (*tsantsa*), setting off "a deadly internecine arms race and virtually indiscriminate slaughter."[35] Jivaroan shrunken heads became a highly valued item in Europe and North America, and between 1860 and 1920 the trading of rifles for shrunken heads continued to expand until the local population had destroyed itself. "Thus the Jívaro became known as 'the most warlike'." One may note some irony in the possibility that our archetypal head hunter became such a specialist in his violence because a Western demand for exotica was capitalizing the killers.[36] The Jivaroan arms race furnishes a sadly appropriate metaphor for the effects of the Rubber Boom in the southern lowlands of

[35] R. Brian Ferguson, "Blood of the leviathan: Western contact and warfare in Amazonia," *American Ethnologist* 17:2 (1990), 237–257.

[36] Ibid.

South America, a period when the blood and bodies of indigenous peoples paid for the industrializing nations' thirst for raw latex and the indebtedness of Latin America's new republics.

In lowland Ecuador rubber merchants and their private armies attacked mission settlements and raided isolated forest villages to capture indigenous laborers. In 1888 rubber merchants took over the Dominican mission settlement of Andoas on the Pastaza River and forced its indigenous inhabitants to work in rubber camps along the Tigre and lower Ucayali rivers. Other missions along the Pastaza and Bobonaza rivers were abandoned or destroyed in the 1880s and 1890s, and their indigenous residents were forced to work in rubber camps along the Curaráy and Tigre rivers. Conflicts between rubber merchants and missionaries erupted when indigenous peoples sought the latters' protection against forced labor in the camps. In theory missionaries wielded greater power in lowland Ecuador than in any other nation during the Rubber Boom, because the conservative government of Gabriel Garcia Moreno (1859–1875) had permitted the return of the Jesuits in 1869 and empowered them as the official government representatives for the Napo-Pastaza province. The Jesuits of eastern Ecuador appointed political officers, established schools, restricted commerce, and applied legal sanctions and punishments on the region's inhabitants. Inevitably the social and political authority of the Jesuits conflicted with the economic interests of rubber merchants, and in 1892

> the Jesuits were again expelled from the Napo region. In this same year the Napo region suffered an epidemic of smallpox, producing an indigenous rebellion in Loreto that was supposedly instigated by the white residents of Archidona. The missions were abandoned and left in the hands of "venturers," rubber barons and international merchants.[37]

In the 1890s English, French, Italian, and Peruvian entrepreneurs carved up the Curaráy River into private territories, which were worked primarily by Záparo and Achuar peoples. After 1900 the Napo River eclipsed the Curaráy as a center for rubber gathering, and merchants from Peru and various European countries had established twenty-four private territories along the Napo by 1907.

The Rubber Boom marked the final and definitive incorporation of

[37] Mary Elizabeth Reeve, *Los Quichua del Curaray: El proceso de formación de la identidad* (Quito, 1988), 77.

indigenous peoples of lowland Ecuador into the political and economic life of the emerging nation-state. Despite a brief experiment at renewing the authority of Catholic missionaries, rubber merchants and their henchmen seized control over the lowlands and its indigenous inhabitants. Many indigenous societies that had existed prior to the Rubber Boom simply vanished before its end. As Reeve argues: "Although the ethnohistorical sources . . . mention distinct groups such as the Záparo, Gaye, Semigaye, Caninche, and Canelos, by the end of the Rubber Boom in Amazonas [around 1935] all reference to these groups as peoples endowed with distinct identities completely disappears."[38] Processes of intermarriage between different groups and the absorption of remnants from formerly distinct peoples contributed to the consolidation of the shared, pan-indigenous identity known as Canelos-Quichua throughout the Curaráy, Pastaza, and Bobonaza basins during the Rubber Boom and its aftermath.

By the beginning of the twentieth century, the search for rubber territories and indigenous laborers had begun to intensify into its ugliest manifestations. Rubber exports made up 23 percent of the total value of Peru's international sales in 1904–1906, and the government encouraged foreign investors to buy or rent rubber territories at attractive low rates. In 1907 the British-owned Peruvian Amazon Rubber Company, Ltd., purchased more than 14 million acres in the Peruvian Amazon, and the Peruvian rubber baron Julio Cesar Arana initiated a joint venture on 20,000 square miles of land along the Caquetá and Putumayo rivers, an area that was still under dispute with Colombia and heavily influenced by Brazilian slave merchants. The rubber-gathering activities of La Casa Araña came to be centered along the tributaries between the Putumayo and Caquetá rivers, an area inhabited by Witoto, Muinane, Mirana, Ocaina, Bora, Carijona, Yukuna, Andoque, and other indigenous peoples. Using methods that were similar to, but still more violent than, those that Fitzcarrald's armies had employed in the upper Ucayali region, La Casa Arana dominated the indigenous labor force by sending heavily armed "recruitment and vigilance commissions" to practice psychological and physical terror. The commission leaders assigned production quotas to indigenous families and individuals and supervised the meeting of these quotas. "Those indigenous persons who did not produce the required quantity of rubber were whipped, tortured, cruelly punished in

[38] Ibid., 75.

stocks, or simply murdered. Disobedience was punished with such measures as mutilation or failure to provide food."[39] The company's thugs routinely destroyed indigenous subsistence gardens, forcing people to survive on costly imported foods and become yet more indebted to the company.

Public denunciations of these atrocities by a North American engineer led to Roger Casement's investigation in 1910 and subsequent hearings in the British Parliament. These inquiries revealed a series of mass murders: 100 Bora killed as they slept; 30 Ocaina disemboweled with machetes; 30 Bora decapitated; 30 Ocaina tortured and burned alive; and so forth. Numbers of victims probably reached the thousands. In 1911 a Peruvian judicial commission arrested 75 Casa Arana employees, but none was ever brought to trial or sentenced because the crimes had taken place in a disputed region over which the Peruvian government was anxious to assert de facto sovereignty.

Accounts of Rubber Boom terror from regions as widely dispersed as the Madre de Dios River in southeastern Peru to the upper Rio Negro and Orinoco rivers in southern Venezuela offer a uniformly horrifying scenario of torture, enforced debt, and genocide. The atrocities suffered by indigenous peoples of the Putumayo-Caquetá region in northeastern Peru received wider public attention but were probably no different from those endured by other peoples. However, a temporal progression of increasing brutality and genocide did parallel the intensification of rubber extraction in the southern lowlands, especially during the decade of 1910–1920, a time when the production of rubber in Javanese and Malaysian plantations more than tripled the world's supply, and the Amazonian Rubber Boom turned into a bust.

In the Venezuelan Amazon a rubber merchant named Tomás Funes took over the territorial capital at San Fernando de Atabapo and ruled the territory as an independent fiefdom until his own soldiers mutinied and executed him in 1921.

> Not satisfied with the enslavement of the Yekuana male population for the gathering of rubber, Funes sent out expeditions to destroy their villages and to murder and torture the inhabitants. . . . [N]o fewer than 1,000 Yekuana along with their 20 villages were destroyed before Funes's reign of terror came to an end.[40]

[39] Landaburu and Pineda Camacho, *Tradiciones*, 31.

[40] Guss, "Keeping it oral," 415.

Funes's troops dominated areas as far south as San Carlos de Rio Negro and decimated entire indigenous societies almost overnight. "Wakuénai and Baniwa groups living along the lower Guainía [Negro] fled from the terrorism of the Funes regime up the Guainía and its tributaries. . . . Other Arawakan societies, including the Baré, Mandahuaca, and Yavitero, suffered almost total annihilation during this period."[41] In the absence of formal, written accounts of Funes's reign of terror, oral testimonies from indigenous peoples of the upper Rio Negro and Orinoco region recall a pattern of torture, assassination, and genocide that was virtually identical to the atrocities that Casa Araña had perpetrated a decade earlier among indigenous peoples of the Caquetá-Putumayo region in Peru.

Survivors of the Rubber Boom

The Rubber Boom (c. 1875–1920) was the most definitive period in the history of the southern lowlands of Venezuela, Colombia, Ecuador, Peru, and Bolivia. Scores of indigenous societies perished in rubber camps or in failed attempts to resist the rubber barons' private armies. Governments did little or nothing to prevent these acts of aggression and enslavement against indigenous peoples, because national interests in establishing political presence and extracting economic profit from remote forested areas overrode any humanitarian concerns for indigenous peoples. The culture of terror that emerged during the Rubber Boom was a massive induction of indigenous peoples into the economics of indebtedness and the politics of nation-state expansion.

Had it not been for the rapid decline of rubber gathering in lowland South America, it is doubtful that any indigenous peoples of the southern lowlands would have survived into the twentieth century. The survivors of the Rubber Boom faced problems of constructing viable cultural identities in the aftermath of demographic collapse. Perhaps the first necessity of such unfortunate peoples, or of marginalized subcultural groups within a nation-state, is that of constructing a shared understanding of the historical past that enables them to understand their present conditions as the result of their own ways of making history. Recapturing the historical past is not simply a matter of constructing collective repre-

[41] Hill and Wright, "Time, narrative, and ritual," 95.

sentations of history but also a process of collective identification in which the remembrance of traumatic historical events must be socialized into new forms of historical discourse that both are intelligible and morally acceptable to specific peoples.

Indigenous historical discourses about the Rubber Boom portray whites and mestizos as greedy, powerful, and profoundly asocial beings whose behaviors resulted from a lack of cultural knowledge and values. The Canelos-Quichua of lowland Ecuador, for example, give recognition to the overwhelming significance of the Rubber Boom in their history through a cycle of narratives about "rubber times" (*cauchu uras*), the period of transition between mythic times and the recent past.[42] While acknowledging the importance of "rubber times," Canelos-Quichua narrators socialize the historical events of the Rubber Boom by portraying rubber merchants as less than full human beings who have failed to understand cultural knowledge derived from powerful mythic ancestors.

> How much was that rubber worth in *callari uras* [early historical times]? How much were those balls of rubber worth? Remembering as if it were now, how much was it worth? For no good reason we Runa came into debt, we exchanged five or six balls of rubber for two lengths of cloth. Because we were in debt, they only paid us half and we remained in debt, the old debt was never paid off, they never cancelled it. Without provocation they stole from us. That was how we worked in *callari uras*. From the rubber they became wealthy.[43]

For the Canelos-Quichua, the atrocities of the Rubber Boom are remembered and interpreted through narrative and ritual interweavings of mythic power and human history.

Among the Arawakan Wakuénai of Venezuela and Colombia, the history of the Rubber Boom is represented in narratives that juxtapose the historical personages of Venancio Camico and Tomás Funes as symbolic vehicles in a mythic struggle between indigenous, shamanistic powers of returning from death to life and alien, coercive forces that seek to extinguish these indigenous powers through acts of violence. In one narrative Venancio Camico is captured by Funes's soldiers and taken to San Fernando de Atabapo, where Funes orders him to be nailed inside a coffin that is weighted down with a stone and thrown into the Orinoco

[42] Mary Elizabeth Reeve," *Cauchu Uras*: Lowland Quichua histories of the Amazon Rubber Boom, in J. Hill (ed.), *Rethinking History and Myth* (Urbana, 1988), 19–34.
[43] Ibid, 27–28.

River. Venancio escapes to his home on the Caño Acqui, only to be captured and put through the same ordeal two more times.

So they went to fetch Venancio and encountered him at his home on the Acqui River. Again they ordered him to enter a coffin that was waiting inside Funes's home in San Fernando. This time they tied the coffin shut with a rope instead of a mere cord and spaced the nails only three fingers' width apart. They weighted down the coffin with a stone and threw it into the same deep part of the river. Again it was empty when they brought it back to Funes' house, and again the soldiers explained that there were not enough nails used to shut the coffin and that the rope was too thin.

The third time, they put nails very closely together, only one finger's width apart, and tied the coffin shut with a very thick rope made of rawhide. After waiting the usual one hour, they raised up the coffin and untied the stone. This time they felt that the coffin weighed more than the other times and were certain that they had finished off Venancio. They told Funes so when they reached his house with the coffin, but they were all surprised when the coffin was opened and there was a huge anaconda (*umáwari*) inside. The anaconda chased Funes and his soldiers out of San Fernando de Atabapo. At that moment, Funes decided that Venancio was really a saint and that he could never kill him no matter how hard he tried.

Five months passed, and Funes sent his soldiers to fetch Venancio from his home on the Acqui River again, just for a friendly talk. Funes told Venancio when he arrived that he now believed that Venancio was truly a saint since he'd survived three times underwater. Then Venancio pronounced a punishment on Funes, saying that he'd be killed one day in a revolt by his followers. Funes felt guilty about what he'd done and offered Venancio money, but Venancio wouldn't accept. Funes was very vexed about his refusal of his offer and continued to feel guilty until his death.[44]

On the surface the story of Venancio Camico and Tomás Funes is a relatively simple matter of asserting the ability of Venancio and his Wakuénai and Baniwa followers to escape from Funes's culture of terror and return back to the center of indigenous power on the Caño Acqui. The same episode of Venancio Camico's forced removal and shamanistic return is repeated three times, and in each case Venancio's shamanistic power to travel between the living and the dead allows him to return to life among his followers. However, after the third escape from the coffin, Venancio leaves behind a giant anaconda, and this explosive indigenous power drives Funes and his soldiers out of San Fernando de Atabapo, foreshadowing the eventual downfall of Funes's reign of terror.

[44] My field notes, 1981.

The story is less concerned with recounting the actual events of Rubber Boom history than with socializing the memory of Funes's brutality into indigenous forms of historical and mythic consciousness. Venancio Camico and Tomás Funes were not really contemporaries. Brazilian and Venezuelan soldiers put down Venancio's millenarian movement in June 1858, just as the Rubber Boom was getting underway. And Venancio died in 1903 at his home in Makareo on the Caño Acqui, a decade prior to Tomás Funes's rise to power in the Venezuelan Amazon. Funes's own soldiers mutinied and executed him by firing squad on January 20, 1921, in San Fernando de Atabapo.

The story of Venancio Camico and Tomás Funes reverberates with a multitude of sacred myths through which the Wakuénai and neighboring Arawakan peoples understand the origins of animal nature and human society. Venancio's ability to escape death evokes both the trickster-creator of mythic beginning times and the primordial human being of mythic creation.

> Tell him that he cannot kill me with machetes, for my body is made of machetes. My body, it is machetes. Poison, too, is my body. My hair is poison. He cannot kill me with water, for my body is water, and I live in water. He cannot tie me up with vines, for my body is made of vines. Logs and sticks, I am they; they are my body. I am all things, my body is all things.[45]

Like this primordial human being, Venancio Camico is described in stories as a powerful being who cannot be killed by water, ropes, wood, or other materials. In Wakuénai sacred myths movements across (or under) the landscape and naming of places are not understood as mere descriptions of spatial locations but as the creation of a historically dynamic world of different peoples and places. Similarly Venancio Camico's travels between Caño Acqui and San Fernando de Atabapo in the story are not intelligible as an attempt to render a literal account of historical events but are better understood as metaphors for the opening up of a historical space-time characterized as a struggle between the rubber barons' use of military coercion and the indigenous power to resist domination through shamanistic return from death.

The most dramatic moment in the story comes when Funes's soldiers open up the coffin for the third time *inside* Funes's house, releasing a deadly indigenous power in the form of a giant anaconda. Like the coffin that had contained Venancio's body, the anaconda swallows its prey

[45] My field notes, 1981.

whole. And like Venancio's multiple entombments within and escapes from the coffin, the anaconda vomits its prey several times before finishing its meal. The coffin, increasingly thick ropes, and more narrowly spaced nails make appropriate metaphors for the political economy of death during the Rubber Boom, a period when Funes's regime increasingly constricted the Wakuénai and other indigenous peoples of the region. But the anaconda, too, kills by increasingly tightening its powerfully coiled body around its prey and drowning it at the river's bottom.

In the story of Venancio Camico and Tomás Funes, the anaconda signifies a profound transformation, a turning inside-out and upside-down of the world. In the first two attempts to drown Venancio in a coffin, life is on the *outside* of the coffin and at the *surface* of the river, while death is *inside* the coffin and at the *bottom* of the river. In the third attempt to drown Venancio, life (in the form of the anaconda) is *inside* the coffin and at the bottom of the river. Funes's soldiers raise this new form of indigenous life up from the *bottom* of the river and carry it *inside* Funes's house, where they release death to the world *outside* the coffin at the *surface* of the river *inside* the center of Funes's power. In this highly compressed manner, the story of Venancio Camico and Tomás Funes ends with a powerful historical metaphor for Funes's death by mutiny, or the autodestruction of Funes's military power structure.

Thus the story of Venancio Camico and Tomás Funes is actually far more complex than a casual reading would suggest. Symbolic transformation through turning the world inside-out and upside-down forms the central core of Wakuénai cosmology. In the mythic history of Venancio Camico and Tomás Funes, the Wakuénai use this transformative power to socialize an alien form of power (military force), vomiting it out of the center of indigenous power into the rubber baron's capital at San Fernando de Atabapo. Like Mahaiwadi the powerful Yekuana shaman recounted in the cycle of *Watunna* creation myths, Venancio symbolizes an indigenous power to reverse historical processes of domination and terror through shamanistic knowledge and practice.

CONCLUSION: INDIGENOUS PEOPLES AND THE RISE OF INDEPENDENT NATION-STATES IN LOWLAND SOUTH AMERICA

This survey has demonstrated a basic, underlying contrast between historical processes in northern and southern lowlands. In the northern lowlands (an area comprising the Colombian and Venezuelan *llanos*, the middle and lower Orinoco Basin, and the Guiana regions of Venezuela and British Guiana), the majority of indigenous peoples had become assimilated into expanding networks of Catholic mission settlements by the late eighteenth century. Aside from nomadic groups, such as the Guahibo and Guajiro, who had managed to resist missionary projects of conversion and sedentarization, indigenous peoples of the northern lowlands were caught up in the wars of independence as forced conscripts, agricultural laborers, or refugees. During the period of political instability after the wars of independence, indigenous peoples struggled to retain agricultural and residential *resguardo* lands in the face of an expanding frontier of large landowners and mestizo colonists. By the mid–nineteenth century the legal status of indigenous lands versus mestizo colonization had been firmly decided in the latter's favor, and large landowners bought up small holdings for extensive cattle ranching and large-scale production of coffee, sugar, and cacao that became the backbone of Venezuela's national economy in the late nineteenth century. By the end of the century, indigenous peoples had largely vanished from coastal and *llanos* areas and lived in refuge areas south of the Apure and Orinoco rivers or in border areas along the Essequibo River in the east and the Guajiro Peninsula in the west. South of the Meta River, the Guahibo remained undisputed masters of the *llanos* throughout the nineteenth and early twentieth centuries.

In the southern lowlands (the area extending from the upper Orinoco region of Venezuela, across the upland forests of Colombia, Ecuador, and Peru, and to the Llanos de Mojos in Bolivia), the wars of independence and resultant period of instability provided indigenous peoples with an opportunity for recovery of population that had been lost to diseases, warfare, and slavery during the colonial period. Spanish colonization and missionization in forested areas bordering Portuguese Brazil had never been as strong as in the northern lowlands, and the wars of independence weakened the fragile line of missions and colonial towns. Indigenous expansion and raiding during the 1820s through 1840s pushed the frontier still further back. In the mid–nineteenth century, however, a series of developments with ominous consequences for indigenous peoples of the southern lowlands began to unfold. In Peru the government created new military outposts, promoted foreign agricultural colonies, and subsidized the new export economy based on steam-powered navigation of rivers. Along the Colombian-Peruvian border, Brazilian merchants traded firearms in exchange for indigenous slaves. In Ecuador the trading of firearms for shrunken heads led to violent interethnic and internecine warfare despite the political-religious authority of Jesuit, Dominican, and Franciscan missionaries along major rivers. And along the upper Negro and Orinoco rivers in Venezuela, the departure of missionaries paved the way for oppressive conditions of debt peonage and military suppression of indigenous resistance. During the Rubber Boom indigenous peoples throughout the southern lowlands suffered great losses of population, land, and autonomy as rubber barons and their private armies forced entire peoples into debt servitude. Indigenous groups who resisted, such as the Mashco of Bolivia and Peru, were slaughtered or reduced to a handful of survivors.

In both northern and southern lowlands, indigenous peoples confronted expanding national societies that systematically dismantled any legal basis for indigenous peoples to retain control over lands and political relations at regional or local levels. Although the founders of Latin American nation-states occasionally mentioned the possibility of a limited autonomy for indigenous peoples within the overarching structure of national sovereignty, in actual practice the new republics provided no political or social plan for indigenous peoples other than forced assimilation as indebted laborers to mestizo colonists, large landholders, or rubber barons. In the northern lowlands the contradiction between equality for all citizens and increasing powerlessness for indigenous peoples was played out in the struggles for control over agricultural lands and reflected in vast discrepancies between laws that excluded indigenous *resguardo* lands from redistribution and other laws that ordered all indigenous lands to be privatized. In the southern lowlands the struggle for control over indigenous laborers returned to older patterns of forced relocation and enslavement but without even the limited mediation that the Catholic Church had provided during the colonial period. Stripped of its religious overtones, political and economic domination deprived indigenous peoples of any human characteristics and allowed them to be exploited like animals, guano, rubber, or any other natural resource.

Indigenous interpretations of the Rubber Boom and earlier historical periods provide valuable alternative perspectives on the nineteenth century in lowland South America. These counterdiscourses demonstrate how indigenous peoples experienced the political and economic contradictions in which they had become the objects of nationalist assimilation. Moreover, by struggling to reconcile historically remembered processes of colonial domination, forced relocations, epidemics, and even genocide with culturally specific processes of mythic empowerment, such indigenous counterdiscourses aim at recapturing and synthesizing cognitive, moral, and aesthetic sensibilities in the context of dominant national societies that practice a Hobbesian "war of all against all" and that consistently elevate the principles of economic gain and territorial sovereignty above the cultural practices and survival needs of indigenous peoples of lowland South America.

BIBLIOGRAPHIC ESSAY

Scholarly works on the history of relations between indigenous peoples and nation-states in lowland South America consist largely of middle and microlevel studies of specific regions and localities rather than more general, synthetic treatments of broader processes affecting a number of different regions over long periods of time. No single source, for example, covers the entire set of regions making up the northern and southern lowlands. However, several sources provide relatively broad, regional perspectives that can be integrated into a general overview of indigenous peoples and the rise of national states in the vast arc of territories extending from coastal Guiana and Venezuela in the north to the lowlands in the south.

The most comprehensive source for information on indigenous peoples of the northern lowlands during the nineteenth century is Pedro Cunill Grau's *Geografía del Poblamiento Venezolano en el siglo XIX*, 3 vols. (Caracas, 1987). Grau's work is exceptional insofar as it provides both richly detailed accounts of the war of independence and later periods in specific regions as well as general, comparative perspectives on indigenous peoples in all regions of the emerging republic of Venezuela. Other general works that cover broad regions and diverse periods of time in the northern lowlands include Jane Rausch's *A Tropical Plains Frontier: The Llanos of Colombia 1531–1831* (Albuquerque, 1984), and Robert and Nancy Morey's ethnohistory of the Colombian and Venezuelan *llanos* in *Relaciones Comerciales en el Pasado en los Llanos de Colombia y Venezuela* (Caracas, 1975). Mary Noel Menezes' *British Policy Towards the Amerindians in British Guiana 1803–1873* (Oxford, 1977) gives a general overview of the changing social and legal conditions affecting indigenous peoples of British Guiana in the nineteenth century. In addition, general accounts of the conditions of indigenous mission settlements during the late colonial period are available in Juan Rivero's *Historia de las Misiones de los Llanos de Casanare y los Rios Orinoco y Meta* (Bogotá, 1956 [1733]) and Padre Felipe Gilij's *Ensayo de Historia Americana*, 3 vols. (Caracas, 1965 [1782]).

The common historical pattern of rising extractivist economics during the Rubber Boom and the accompanying devastation of indigenous peoples living throughout the southern lowlands has yet to generate any single comparative studies comparing situations in Venezuela, Colombia, Ecuador, Peru, and Bolivia. The most general sources on the Rubber Boom and earlier periods of national state expansion in the Peruvian lowlands are David Werlich's The conquest and settlement of the Peruvian montaña (Ph.D. dissertation, University of Minnesota, 1968), and *Peru: A Short History* (Carbondale, IL, 1978); and Paul Gootenberg's *Between Silver and Guano: Commercial Policy and the State in Postindependence Peru* (Princeton, 1989). A useful guide to historical sources on the Colombian Amazon is Beatriz Alzate's *Viajeros y Cronistas en la Amazonia Colombiana* (Bogotá, 1987). Eric Langer's *Economic Change and Rural Resistance in Southern Bolivia: 1880–1930* (Stanford, 1987) provides a general overview of the Bolivian lowlands. A volume of essays on *Rethinking History and Myth: Indigenous South American Perspectives on the Past*, edited by Jonathan Hill (Urbana, 1988), includes case studies on the Rubber Boom and its interpretations within indigenous societies of the upper Rio Negro region in Venezuela and Colombia, the Cururay River of Ecuador, and the Ucayali Basin of Peru. The violent oppression of indigenous peoples of the southern lowlands during the Rubber Boom has stimulated important developments in the theorizing of relations between national states and indigenous peoples, such as R. Brian Ferguson's "Blood of the leviathan: Western contact and warfare in Amazonia" (*American Ethnologist* 17, 1990), and Michael Taussig's powerful *Shamanism, Colonialism, and the Wild Man* (Chicago, 1987). Earlier indigenous losses of population and other major changes in the central Amazon Basin during the colonial period are assessed in David Sweet's A rich realm of nature destroyed: The middle Amazon Valley, 1640–1750 (Ph.D. dissertation, University of Wisconsin, 1974). Richard Spruce's *Notes of a Botanist on the Amazon and Andes*, 2 vol. (London, 1960 [1908]), gives a first-hand account of indigenous societies in many regions of the southern lowlands during the decade immediately prior to the commencement of the Rubber Boom in the 1860s.

More specialized sources on specific regions and peoples within the northern and southern lowlands can be grouped according to geographic areas. Important early works on British Guiana include Reverend W. H. Brett's *The Indian Tribes of Guiana; Their Conditions and Habits* (London, 1868); Robert H. Schomburgk's *A Description of British Guiana: Geographical and Statistical* (London, 1970 [1840]); James Rodway's *Guiana: British, Dutch and French* (London, 1912); and William Curtis Farabee's *The Central Caribs* (Philadelphia, 1967 [1924]). More recent ethnographic sources on indigenous peoples of (formerly British) Guiana include Audrey B. Colson's writings on intertribal religious and economic networks in the region – "Inter-tribal trade in the Guiana highlands," *Antropológica* 34 (1973); and "Routes of knowledge: An aspect of regional integration in the circum-Roraima area of the Guiana highlands," *Antropológica* 63–64 (1985) – as well as Colin Henfrey's *Through Indians Eyes: A Journey Among the Indian Tribes of Guiana* (New York, 1965); Andrew Sanders' *The Powerless People: An Analysis of the Amerindians of the Corentyne River* (London, 1987); and Peter Riviere's *Individual and Society in Guiana: A Comparative Study of Amerindian Social Organization* (New York, 1984). In addition Neil Whitehead's *Lords of the Tiger Spirit: A History of the Caribs in Colonial Venezuela and Guyana 1498–1820* (Dordrecht, Holland, 1988), and "Carib ethnic soldiering in Venezuela, the Guianas, and the Antilles, 1492–1820" (*Ethnohistory* 37, 1990), provide excellent, detailed historical accounts of ethnic soldiering, missionization, and other major changes during the late colonial and early republican period in British Guiana and the adjacent lower Orinoco Basin of Venezuela.

For the lower and middle Orinoco region, Horacio Biord Castillo's "El Contexto Multilingue del Sistema de Interdependencia Regional del Orinoco" (*Antropológica* 63–64, 1985), and Filadelfo Morales Mendez and Nelly Arvelo-Jimenez's "Hacia un Modelo de Estructura Social Caribe" (*America Indígena* 41, 1981), give useful overviews of the prehispanic and colonial periods. Important ethnographic sources on indigenous peoples of the lower and middle Orinoco region include Marc de Civrieux's *Watunna: An Orinoco Creation Cycle* (San Francisco, 1980); David Guss's "Keeping it oral: A Yekuana ethnology," *American Ethnologist* 13 (1986); David Thomas's "The indigenous trade system of southeast Estado Bolivar, Venezuela," *Antropológica* 33 (1972); Alberto Valdez's "Los Mapoyo del Caño Caripo," in A. Valdez (ed.), *Autogestión Indígena* (Caracas, 1982); and Johannes Wilbert's *Survivors of Eldorado: Four Indian Cultures of South America* (New York, 1972).

For the forested regions of the southern lowlands in Venezuela and

Colombia, early works include Alexander von Humboldt's *Personal Narrative of Travels to the Equinoctial Regions of the New Continent During the Years 1799–1804*, 7 vols. (London, 1819); Martin Matos Arvelo's *Vida Indiana* (Barcelona, 1912); and the *Relaciones de los Vireyes del Nuevo Reino de Granada, Ahora Estados Unidos de Venezuela, Estados Unidos de Colombia y Ecuador*, edited by José Garcia (New York, 1869). Specific ethnographic sources on the southern lowlands of Colombia and Venezuela include Irving Goldman's *The Cubeo: Indians of the Northwest Amazon* (Urbana, 1963); Nicolas Journet's "Les Jardins de Paix: Etude de Estructures Sociales chez les Curripaco du haut Rio Negro (Colombia)" (Paris, These de Doctorat, Ecole des Hautes Etudes en Sciences Sociales, 1988); Jonathan Hill's *Keepers of the Sacred Chants* (Tucson, 1993); and Jon Landaburu and Roberto Piñeda Camacho's *Tradiciones de la gente del Hacha: mitologia de los indios andoques del Amazonas* (Yerbabuena, 1984). Robin Wright's "History and religion of the Baniwa peoples of the upper Rio Negro Valley," Ph.D. dissertation, Stanford University, 1981, contains important information about the Arawak-speaking peoples living in the adjacent area of Brazil along the Isana River and its tributaries. In addition Robin Wright and Jonathan Hill have written two collaborative essays on the ethnohistory of Arawakan peoples of the upper Rio Negro region: "History, ritual, and myth: Nineteenth-century millenarian movements in the northwest Amazon," *Ethnohistory* 33 (1) (1986); and "Time, narrative, and ritual: Historical interpretations from an Amazonian society," in Jonathan Hill (ed.), *Rethinking History and Myth: Indigenous South American Perspectives on the Past* (Urbana, 1988).

Elsewhere in the southern lowlands, Norman Whitten's *Sacha Runa* (Urbana, 1976), and Mary Elizabeth Reeve's *Los Quichua del Curaray: El Proceso de Formación de la Identidad* (Quito, 1988), contain useful ethnohistorical information on the formation of new ethnic identities in the eastern lowlands of Ecuador. Effects of the Rubber Boom in lowland Ecuador are explored in R. Brian Ferguson's "Tribal warfare" (*Scientific American* 266, 1992), and indigenous interpretations of these devastating effects are documented in Mary Elizabeth Reeve's "*Cauchu Uras*: Lowland Quichua histories of the Amazon Rubber Boom" in Jonathan Hill (ed.), *Rethinking History and Myth*, pp. 19–34 (Urbana, 1988). Farther south in the Peruvian lowlands, Michael Brown and Eduardo Ferndanez's *War of Shadows* (Berkeley, 1991), and Stefano Varese's *La Sal de los Cerros* (2nd ed., Lima, 1973) focus on the Asháninka (Campa) and neighboring groups at the headwaters of the Ucayali River. For Bolivia, William Denevan's *The Aboriginal Cultural Geography of the Llanos de Mojos of Bolivia* (Berkeley, 1966), and Lesley Gill's *Peasants, Entrepreneurs and Social Change: Frontier Development in Lowland Bolivia* (Boulder, 1987), give detailed coverage of indigenous histories and state expansion in the forested lowlands.

25

ANDEAN PEOPLE IN THE TWENTIETH CENTURY

XAVIER ALBÓ[1]

This chapter centers on the recent history of Andean indigenous people in Ecuador, Peru, and Bolivia. In these countries indigenous history and the history of the peasantry overlap broadly; the majority of the rural population is indigenous in origin and most rural dwellers still subsist as peasants. (Exceptions are found along the Pacific coast, in the Amazonian lowlands, and in a few highland enclaves.) During the second half of the twentieth century, however, urban influences have become more and more a part of indigenous history, mostly via migration. In this chapter I take into account both rural and urban versions of indigenous identity. The indigenous peoples of Colombia and Chile are also discussed here, although their situations are somewhat distinct. The Andean area of Argentina receives passing mention. Intensifying relations among diverse modern native communities across political and ecological frontiers demand some treatment of these five countries' other, non-Andean, indigenous groups, especially Amazonian networks, which interact in fundamental ways with each state's Andean peoples. This articulation in turn generates new overarching processes. Following contemporary practices in various locations, we use the terms "indigenous", "Indian" and "native peoples" interchangeably for all these peoples.[2]

[1] Translation from Spanish by Blenda Femenias.

[2] For assistance with preparing this article, I am particularly grateful for their time and help to the librarians of the Instituto Indigenista Interamericano in Mexico, the Colegio Andino (Centro Las Casas) in Cusco, and CIPCA in La Paz. I extend my thanks as well for their valuable assistance and suggestions to José Bengoa, Rolf Foerster, Diego Iturralde, Miriam Jimeno, José Matos Mar, Ruth Moya, my editors Frank Salomon and Stuart Schwartz, and the staffs of CREAR, TEA, and TER in northern Chile. All of them have helped me to understand better Andean indigenous history and issues outside Bolivia. But above all I thank all the indigenous leaders and peoples who have allowed me to share their experience in meetings and travels along the length of the Andes. Here I have tried to present their perspectives.

Published demographic statistics are unreliable where ethnic identity is concerned. Only in Peru and Bolivia do censuses even provide estimates on this topic, and they do so indirectly at best, via language. Such data tend to be imprecise because they fail to define the subject clearly and underestimate numbers. Many census respondents tend to hide information that could cause them problems, and census takers cover peripheral regions poorly. Although it is dated, and although some planners suspect overestimates while indigenous organizations allege the reverse, Mayer and Masferrer's 1979 synthesis remains the most reliable detailed overview. According to those authors, as of about 1978 the indigenous composition of the Andean countries was as shown in Table 25.1.

These figures should be considered minima. Where detailed Indian censuses have been carried out, the actual figures tend to be higher. For example, in Chile, where the 1992 census specifically asked about ethnic identity, the resulting figure was 928,000 excluding people under 14 years of age.

We have tried to make our perspective reflect that of Andean and indigenous peoples themselves, more than that of states and larger societies. For that reason this chapter does not include a history of the movement known as *indigenismo* (indigenism), so influential in literature, philosophy, and the arts. Although *indigenismo* was especially important in the first half of this century, it was mainly internal to white urbanites and mestizos.

Nevertheless broader national and transnational contexts are indispensable even at the risk of complicating the argument. Despite the common origins and problems of many Andean indigenous peoples, it is increasingly difficult to analyze their historic processes in any unified manner, given divergent histories of the would-be "national" states (see Chap. 23). Certainly some broad common tendencies carry over from one country to the next, but these common processes do not always coincide in time, and their intensities and tendencies often vary widely along with features unique to each political and economic situation.

The difficulty of coordinating historiography across national lines is compounded by the absence of unifying studies. For example, González Casanova (1978), in his important edited volume on the political history of the Latin American peasantry, opted to treat each country separately. Only Wankar (pseudonym of Ramiro Reynaga; 1989) includes a useful, detailed year-by-year account from the European invasion up to 1957,

Table 25.1. *Indian Population of Six Andean Nations*

Country	Total indigenous population (approx. in thousands)	Indigenous as percent of total population	Andean peasant	Andean urban	Lowland	Major indigenous ethnic groups	Approx. number of ethnic groups (b)
Colombia	542	2.2	126 (a)	—	421	Guajiro (c), Paez	87
Ecuador	2564	33.9	2235	230	97	Quichua	12
Peru	6025	36.8	4010	1807	206	Quechua, Aymara	58
Bolivia	3526	59.2	2544	793	187	Quechua, Aymara	40
Chile	616	5.7	516	100	—	Mapuche (d), Aymara	3
Argentina	398	1.5	261 (a)	83	54	Mapuche, Colla (e)	14

(a) May include some non-Andean groups.
(b) There is some variation depending on selection criteria and sources.
(c) Non-Andean.
(d) Includes subdivisions like Hullinche, Pehuenche, etc.
(e) Generic local name, which includes Quechua and Aymara.

which consistently presents the Indian perspective in pulling together data about the Andean nations that once formed Tawantinsuyu, the Inka empire. But Wankar's coverage is uneven and does not, of course, include recent research.

As far as possible, I periodize by emphasizing broad common tendencies across the Andes (see Map 25.1). Within each period I highlight the most significant particular tendencies of each country.

RESISTANCE TO EXPROPRIATION (1900–1930)

The Situation at the Turn of the Century

At the beginning of the twentieth century almost all Andean communities took part in a widespread resistance against the threat of fragmentation, suppression, and expropriation by the respective states and by the landholding groups who supported those states. This assault occurred because, in many countries, the availability of new revenues and taxes upon them (for example, mining and agricultural-livestock exports) made

PAEZ & GUAMBIANO
INGANO
COLOMBIA
Quito
ECUADOR
Putumayo River
Napo River
Tigre River
Iquitos
SHUAR, ACHUAR AGUARUNA
LAMAS
CHACHAPOYAS
CAÑARISO
CAJAMARCA
OTHER AMAZONIAN ETHNIC GROUPS
BRAZIL
Marañón R.
Huallaga River
Ucayali R.
Trujillo
PERU
SHIPIBO & ASHANINKA
Huaraz
Mamoré River
Urubamba R.
Huancayo
Lima
Ayacucho
Cusco
Abancay
BOLIVIA
Ica
MOXOS
Lake Titicaca
Arequipa
La Paz
Cochabamba
PACIFIC OCEAN
Moquegua
Oruro
AYMARA
Arica
Lake Poopó
Sucre
Potosí
Tarija
GUARANÍ
CHILE
CHACO ETHNIC GROUPS
Antofagasta
N
0
300 mi
0
300 km
ARGENTINA
Santiago del Estero
Quechua Areas
Southern Cusqueño
Yungay
Central
Chinchay Northern
Main Non-Quechua Ethnic Groups

Map 25.1

the remnants of the tribute system seem an obsolete way to extract community resources and channel them to the state. (Tribute did continue for specific local goals such as road construction.) With the waning of tributary structures, the communities that had paid collective tribute levies came to seem less viable in the eyes of officialdom. At the same time outsiders' greed for community lands grew (see Chap. 23).

In Bolivia official language already termed them only "ex-communities." They were to lose half of their lands in the 50 years between 1880 and 1930. In Colombia and Chile, where only small pockets of indigenous communities remained, legislators repeatedly spoke of the "division" of communities as a first step toward their "liquidation." In Ecuador the perceived problem centered on labor relations within the haciendas (estates), because these had already controlled the best lands since the colonial period.

Expropriating sectors justified their economic interests by proclaiming the political-economic dogma of private property as the highroad to civic equality. In addition they were influenced by social Darwinism, which gave a pseudo-scientific gloss to their longstanding belief in themselves as the superior race, the destined bearers of progress. This led to a paradox: In the name of the liberal ideas then in vogue, such as the equality of all citizens, new neo-feudal–style estates (latifundios) were created everywhere. As the decades passed these would become the very institutions that agrarian reforms would seek to sweep away as obsolete.

Indians who were subject to hacienda regimes, whether established in the colonial period or more recently, maintained a certain form of communal life. But they retained it in context of subordination to the owner (*patrón*), under a feudalistic system that forced them to perform a wide range of agricultural and domestic tasks in exchange for usufruct rights to plots of hacienda land on their "free" days. This system was known by different names in different places: *yanaconaje* in Peru, *pongueaje* in Bolivia, *huasipungo* in Ecuador, *terraje* in Colombia, and *inquilinaje* in Chile. It tended to generate in its victims an ambiguous attitude, filially submissive and at the same time rebellious. It has been described brilliantly in the abundant indigenist literature of those countries, often by authors who were themselves estate owners. With few exceptions scholars paid little attention to this subject. Only on the eve of the agrarian reforms did studies of the estate system's darker side emerge.

In the last two decades of the nineteenth century, the situation became especially violent in the Andean regions of Peru and Bolivia. Violence resulted from attempts by whites and *mistis* (mestizos) to snatch communal lands. The landgrab was one of many new commercial opportunities springing up in the wake of both countries' political restructuring after defeat by Chile in the War of the Pacific. On both sides of the border, recurring situations of expropriation, rebellion, and repression resulted from these developments. In southern Peru the main cause was the "wool boom," which generated a "golden age" for several urban centers. In those years, for example, the small Lake Titicaca port city of Puno published four newspapers although it had only 12,000 inhabitants. This growth occurred at the expense of the communities. Thus, in the Lampa-Ayaviri region on the Peruvian high plains, haciendas quadrupled between 1879 and 1915. As one congressional deputy and ex-latifundist from Azángaro put it: "These disorders and abuses will continue as long as there are communities or potential buyers."[3] In Bolivia the stimulus was silver miners' desire to invest earnings in land. In both cases the boom was accompanied by the extension of new railroads from the coast into the high plains, from Mollendo and Arequipa to Juliaca, Puno and Cusco in Peru; from Antofagasta, Chile, to Uyuni, Oruro and La Paz in Bolivia. As the rails advanced, so did the value of land near them including community lands. And their ancient owners, the Aymaras and Quechuas, protested as much against speculative manipulations as against the simpler procedure of demanding labor to build new tracks.

Nevertheless by around 1900 the situation had changed somewhat. Following the discovery of new silver deposits in California, the price of silver collapsed after 1895; before long silver, formerly the determinant of South-Andean economies, would no longer be a significant resource. New mining alternatives were developed: copper in Peru, and above all, tin in Bolivia. Wool, much more closely linked to hacienda expansion, continued to be an important commodity in the southern Peruvian Andean highlands although always subject to market fluctuations.

These changes evoked a partial mobilization of the communities or *ayllus* (localized hereditary landholding groups), especially in Bolivia. There the besieged communities, led by their ancestral authorities (known by local titles such as *jilaqatas, kurakas*), had become increasingly involved in a growing organized movement that extended from Potosí to La Paz. This movement found short-term support in the newly emerging tin bourgeoisie, whose origins were relatively *cholo* (that is, common and

[3] Quoted in Hazen (1975), pp. 131–133.

"half-breed"). Centered in La Paz and identified with the Liberal Party, this group challenged the government's location in Sucre, the seat of the old silver oligarchy, which was more aristocratic and tied to the Conservative Party. Thus in 1899, in the so-called Federal War or War of the Capitals, the liberals, ably supported by the communities, defeated the Conservatives and moved the capital to La Paz. One important incident in this war occurred when the communities organized the first massive roadblock, cutting off the Conservatives' retreat along the newly built rails.

Within this alliance, however, the communities waged their own war and had their own objectives. At Peñas, in the southern high province of Oruro, for a short time they established their own republic. They named Juan Lero, a traditional authority from a local *ayllu* as president. In Mohoza the community members executed a lost battalion of the Liberal army, their supposed ally, because they considered it just as white and just as much their enemy as were the old Conservative estate owners (see Chap. 23). But the honeymoon between community members and Liberals was over soon enough. Their triumphs had accelerated because Liberals and Conservatives had perceived the danger of unleashing a "race war" that would threaten the interests of both sides. And once in power the Liberal Pando quickly betrayed the communities. The main Aymara leader, Zárate Willka, who had been named a general in the army for his decisive support in various acts of war, was arrested and, while in custody en route to La Paz, executed. His lands were then devoured by Pando's personal hacienda. And the expropriation, rebellious, and subsequent army massacres advanced inexorably. The communities had been cheated once again. Willka's downfall, at the turn of the twentieth century, was not much different from those that the indigenous *montoneras* of the Peruvian central highlands had suffered at the hands of that nation's new rulers, despite the fact that only a few years before they had ardently supported them against the Chilean invasion.

Looking northward to the highlands of Ecuador, one sees a scene where indigenous communities (called *comunas*) had already long borne the burden of the haciendas. After militant resistance such as that led in 1870 by Fernando Daquilema, "the last Guaminga," Indians found themselves cornered in high-lying "regions of refuge." Statistics collected in the mid – twentieth century suggest that there was far more land and population in these communities than might be expected given the sources' silence; they may have housed between one-third and one-half of the total indigenous population. But the lack of data and studies about many such communities leaves the impression that they constituted an unknown "other Ecuador." In any case the indigenous history of this whole period has been written around those groups, *comuna* members or not, who were directly or indirectly tied to traditional haciendas. To understand this two local terms merit further discussion: *concertaje* and *huasipungo*.

The first term, *concertaje*, refers to a system of debt peonage in which Indian "conciertos" agreed, supposedly of their own free will, to work on a given hacienda. Their nominal choice was generally constrained by debts, either their own or those their ancestors had contracted. By this or other means, a large share of the indigenous population had been reduced to a condition close to serfdom. Indians worked without pay in the *patrón*'s fields and house, in exchange for usufruct rights to a piece of land on the estate. This system, which also existed in other countries, was known in Ecuador by the Quichua name *huasipungo* or *huasipungaje*. In spite of the disorder and exploitation that it brought with it, this system also permitted the survival or formation of a characteristic captive community organized within the bounds of the hacienda.

But the new century brought a ray of hope for Ecuadorian Indians stemming from the Liberal revolution of Eloy Alfaro, spokesman of the financial power arising from the coastal cacao boom. In their eagerness to dislodge the defeated Conservatives, the new rulers finally abolished the indigenous contribution and associated labor tax, in theory already abolished since 1857. But, as in other countries, this amounted to little more than a transient upturn, because the interests of the liberals, from an indigenous perspective, were almost indistinguishable from those of the conservatives. Until 1925 this Liberal period became increasingly synonymous with government by Guayaquil's cacao oligarchy.

In the two outer Andean nations, Colombia and Chile, the population still considered indigenous was peripheral to the national "boom" economies and very much in the minority. Colombia had its coffee boom. Chile began to implement its plan for developing the interior with an agricultural boom in the central region, and it continued to exploit copper and nitrate in the recently conquered north. These processes did not directly affect the respective indigenous populations. Nevertheless, indirectly, they generated economic possibilities for expansion that threatened the survival of those territorial pockets still in indigenous hands.

In Colombia a system of indigenous *resguardos* or reservations remained viable, with their own governing councils and civil-religious hierarchies having roots as old as the end of the sixteenth century. However, various legal rulings throughout the nineteenth century (1830, 1840, 1851, 1890) had undermined the stability of the *resguardos*, ostensibly to "liberate" them, and in fact to get their lands auctioned off. With this goal in mind, in 1904 the division of the *resguardos* began without Indian consent. Miguel Triana commented in 1922: "From that moment began the definitive disappearance of the indigenous race in the 'Lands of the Chibchas'."[4] All of this occurred in one of the most anti-Indian contexts of the whole Andean region: Terms applied to Indians included "mammals [*sic*] from Panan," "incompetent," "irrational," and so on.[5] Nevertheless, paradoxically, the last of these legal dispositions, Law 89 of 1890, originally intended to force the "savages to be reduced to civilized life," has now become with minor changes the main legal recourse to which indigenous communities appeal in defense of their identities. The boomerang effect of these legal dispositions is not unusual; although initially discriminatory, in the long run they often became weapons for the defense of Indian identity, territory, and autonomy.

For the rest of this period, Colombia is, according to Tulio Halperin, an almost textbook case of an oligarchic republic. Except for the Thousand Day War (between 1900 and 1903), in the first three decades of this century a stable conservative government held power, in part because it conceded a stably subordinate role to the Liberal Party. The main difference, compared to the other countries, is the important role that the conservative government continued to give the Catholic Church, as much to pacify (and at the same time exploit) the Andean reserves as to "civilize" the lowland jungle groups.

In Chile a modernizing and "Chileanizing" frame of mind proved somewhat more aggressive, propelled by recent victories in two wars of expansion: first, in the north, against Peru and Bolivia (1879–1880), and immediately after that, in the south, against the Mapuches (1881). In the north the ancient Aymara and Atacaman communities were completely

[4] Cited in Jaramillo (1954), p. 217.

[5] Cited in the Dirección General de Integración (1971: 4). This contempt is alive and well today. In December 1967 in Arauca several colonists were arrested for killing Indians, but in the court case (1972) they were acquitted. The accused said in his defense: "Here we consider Indians wild animals. . . . I thought killing them was like a joke. . . . All I did was to kill one little female Indian and two Indians. . . . When I was a little boy I noticed that everybody killed Indians: the police, the Security Service, and the Navy." (Cited in Friedemann 1975: 25; 1981: 64–65.)

unrecognized as such. They were reduced to a few small family properties, although their inhabitants continued to observe a round of communal celebrations and maintained kinship ties. Some of these were soon trapped by the nitrate boom in the Iquique plains, which drew laborers from near and far, even Quechuas from distant Cochabamba, Bolivia. But the indigenous people were not so much incorporated as workers, as used in seasonal positions, especially as llama- and mule-train drivers.

In the south the Mapuche defeat was clinched in 1881 and officially known by the euphemism "Pacification of Araucania." This served to open their vast territory to large new estates and to new colonization, both by locals and by foreigners dreaming of a "Chilean California." Five million hectares of Mapuche territory were reduced to a half a million in discontinuous patches. Having lost 90 percent of their territory, the Mapuche found themselves forcibly transformed from wealthy livestock owners, who enjoyed great freedom of movement, into poor peasants, tied to the previously unknown and thus humiliating work of farming. By means of a lengthy process of "settling" or "rooting" the Mapuche, which lasted from 1884 to 1929, about 83,170 Mapuche (of an estimated total between 110,000 and 200,000) were settled and dispersed on a total of 526,285 hectares apportioned among 2,961 *reducciones*, or villages with land grant titles (*títulos de merced*). Life in these villages imposed an unaccustomed lifestyle on these free, warring, and mobile peoples. Besides, these "titles" failed to take account of lineages, family groups, or traditional lines of authority, which led to endless internal lawsuits. The Mapuche demonstrated a tremendous capacity for adaptation to this new structure. Little by little the new community became the means by which they reproduced and defended their lifeways, within an increasingly traditionalist framework, more so than when they were free.

During roughly the same years, around 1885, on the Argentine side of the mountains, the Mapuche endured the onslaught of the so-called Desert Campaign. Its immediate results included more than 1,300 Indians killed, about 12,000 taken captive, and 1,000 resettled, which led to a process of rapid social disorganization and isolation. Around 1910 another such campaign was launched against the indigenous groups of the north. The Argentinian state found no room for any possibility of including "different" citizens.

In the extreme south, in Tierra del Fuego, the Selk'nam (Ona), Kawashkar or Halakwulup (Alakaluf) and Yámana were well on the way to extinction. There were less than 11,000 in the last quarter of the nineteenth century, and only 3,000 by 1900. A scant 150 descendants of the last two groups remain today.

Five thousand kilometers to the north, also on the eastern slopes of the Andes, in the Bolivian Chaco, lived another warlike and warring group that had remained unconquered by the Spanish: the Chiriguano-Guaraní. Among them, wounds were still fresh from an 1892 defeat in Kuruyuki at the hands of the Bolivian army, aided in advance by cattlemen and missionaries. After that defeat the prisoners were made into peons on livestock estates. Others, called *chahuancos*, searched out a new way of life on the sugar refineries of northern Argentina. Some 20,000 – scarcely one-tenth of their former numbers – hung on aimlessly in their own communities or in mission settlements.

Finally, in the vast region of Amazonia, from Bolivia to Colombia, many groups of people continued to live in a traditional manner on the margins of the new states to which, unbeknownst to them, they had been annexed in the previous century. Because ethnic patterns were not taken into account, many groups found themselves divided by these new international borders. Sooner or later conflicts were bound to arise, and in the twentieth century they did. For many groups the first contact had come about, as in the colonial period, through pioneer missionaries and adventurers. But autonomy was increasingly less common. The republican governments, eager to establish sovereignty or seek out resources, greatly increased the number of their frontier expeditions. The most notable of the subsequent impacts resulted from rubber extraction. This raw material, so fundamental for the fledgling automobile industry and other manufactures, became the second most important export from Bolivia and Peru in the early twentieth century. In Bolivia the Rubber Boom caused the "Acre war" during those same years, after which the country had to cede part of its Amazonian territory to Brazil. This boom brought people from every walk of life into the very heart of the jungle, causing grave disruptions for several Amazonian ethnic groups. In some cases harm occurred because they were forcibly recruited to work at collecting latex, in other cases because of a new and harmful type of contact with the intruders. The following testimony, recently collected by a surviving Andoke (Andoque) Indian, shanghaied in Colombia by the Arana company, is a good example: "They killed and killed and killed and killed everyone. . . . They shot them and our leaders died of hunger . . . they killed all the leaders" (*Unidad Indígena* III–1977). Labor conditions in rubber tapping were dramatically reported by the explorer Fawcett and by Roger Casement among others; such accounts even prompted debates in the British Parliament about whether a system of slavery existed in South America.

The Mapuche, Chiriguano, and the Amazonian rubber tappers are noteworthy examples of processes at work in all these countries, which were for various reasons discovering the potential of their peripheral territories. Governments organized expeditions, often with foreign support, to finish off what Spanish conquest and colonization never had achieved. In this way previously autonomous ethnic groups were entrapped. In the following pages we shall see again and again how events in peripheral areas would come to affect, in the long run, the entire tenor of indigenous movements.

We have seen that in the three first decades of the twentieth century Indian groups were the protagonists of many violent uprisings, especially in the Andean regions. The earliest and most widespread events occurred in Peru and Bolivia; later and more localized incidents took place in Ecuador, and a few in the Páez region of Colombia. Except in this last case, these movements were frequently connected with urban movements that supported them. Sometimes these were indigenist organizations, but especially after the Russian Revolution in 1917, political parties were involved as well. In Chile the Mapuche opted for more legal routes. The sections to come examine the situation of each country in more detail.

Indigenous Resistance and Indigenist Socialism in Peru

The case of Peru is by far the most studied, and, in certain respects, the most paradigmatic one. In addition to the structural factors already mentioned, in the first 30 years of the century we find an interplay among three new sociopolitical factors: the emergence of urban *indigenista* currents beginning in 1909, the influx of left parties after about 1920, and above all the period called the *Oncenio*, the 11-year regime of President Augusto Leguía, who took power in 1919. The interaction among these three factors extended more and more to other movements, both of peasants and Indians, which had distinctive internal dynamics as well. This was true both on the coast and in the highlands.

The backdrop for the three aforementioned factors is the awakening consciousness of highland Indians themselves as they recognized their situation to be not only deteriorating but increasingly untenable. Numerous Indian initiatives sought to remedy the situation. These actions formed part of the so-called "explosion of the Indian masses (*indiada*)," to use a pejorative term common at the time. The parallel rhythms of these outbursts in Peru and Bolivia seemed far more than coincidental. In Peru the movement picked up steam beginning in 1915, especially in the south. That area's products were launched into a rising wool market stimulated by World War I, and the Creole élites developed a parallel rising appetite for communal lands. Resistance advanced full force, in the highlands as well as on the more capitalist or agroindustrial haciendas of the north coast, until 1924. Sometimes nonindigenous leaders arose, such as the celebrated and even mythical Rumi Maki (Rumi Maqui) in 1915. Rumi Maki, a Quechua phrase meaning 'Stone Hand,' was the nom de guerre of Teodomiro Gutiérrez Cuevas, a soldier who 2 years before had been a governmental delegate in another rebellion, also in Puno. But outside command was not the norm in those years: there was external contact but little leadership.

The most important development was without a doubt the emergence of the urban ideological movement called *indigenismo* (indigenism). The respected Peruvian historian Jorge Basadre stated that "the most important phenomenon of Peruvian culture was an increasingly awakened consciousness of the Indian among writers, artists, scientists and politicians."[6] Although we cannot analyze this phenomenon in great detail here, nevertheless it certainly had some impact on the history of Indians themselves by making non-Indian Peruvians conscious of Indian history and presence.

For a long time before that, certain sectors of the oligarchy had displayed some interest in understanding the Andean roots of Peruvian identity. But at the same time, they exercised utmost caution to avoid relating those precolonial roots – observable in archaeological monuments – to the contemporary reality of the Indian who was the direct descendant of those great cultures. Those attitudes now began to undergo two major shifts – in Cusco and Lima.

In Cusco the change began with a university rebellion in 1909 and grew after the discovery of Machu Picchu in 1911. (Before this the gigantic Inka ruins of Sacsayhuaman, which overlook the city, had been used as a quarry!) The greatest exponent was Luis E. Valcárcel; in 1913 he wrote a thesis about "the agrarian question," which prompted "a

[6] Cited in Tamayo (1980), 15.

veritable explosion of university theses about the Indian." José Carlos Mariátegui, regarded as the founder of the Peruvian left, himself maintained personal contacts with Valcárcel and supported his socioeconomic analysis with data from Cusqueños like Francisco Ponce, who in 1917 wrote pioneering studies of local agricultural tenancy systems.[7]

A related process began in Lima in 1909, when Pedro Zulen, Dora Mayer, and others formed the Pro-Indigenous Association. From the beginning, this association adopted a decided posture of social protest, denouncing the pollution caused by the Cerro de Pasco mining company, massacres and Catholic intolerance in Puno, and so forth. It made its presence felt by backing several indigenous mobilizations in the South Andes, and it influenced Peruvian legislation – for example, Law 1183 of 1909, which banned authorities from requiring unpaid service from Indians. The Pro-Indigenous Association declined in importance after 1917, but in 1920 the vacuum it left was quickly filled by the new Comité (later, Sociedad) Pro-Derecho Indígena Tahuantinsuyo ('Tahuantinsuyo Committee for Indian Rights'), which was formed in Lima primarily by migrants from throughout the highlands. Its most famous and eloquent spokesperson was Ezequiel Urviola, "the first Indian socialist of Peru," who also founded in Puno the Liga de Defensa Indígena ('Indian Defense League'). Because of the fearsome tendency toward grass-roots activism, the Lima aristocracy rejected it. When their second Congress convened in 1921, statements made in the National Parliament attacked it as "an assembly of illiterates who aim to divide Peru by race."[8]

But the new society quickly learned to take advantage of two new factors: the beginning of the *Oncenio* of President Leguía (1919–1930) and the presence of new political parties on the left. The dictator Leguía combined a policy of urban capitalist development with an indigenist posture in the highlands relying on the collaboration (albeit not unconditional) of the Tawantinsuyo Society, which in its Sixth Congress even named him its honorary president. This populist focus of "false indigenism," as Thomas Davies calls it, did pave the way for certain legal and practical achievements. For example, the new Constitution of 1920, setting aside an entire century of opposing liberal discourse, at last recognized the legal existence of indigenous communities. This set into motion a lengthy legal process of mapping and registering "recognized commu-

[7] Tamayo (1980), 174–183, 213–224, 353. [8] Quoted in Kapsoli (1984), 230.

nities," which continues until this day. In 1922 a governmental Section of Indian Affairs was also created, initially directed by another prominent social indigenist, Hildebrando Castro Pozo (1936), who later went on to establish the first rural Indian schools. But the pronounced opportunism of Leguía's proposals was far too obvious in other areas, especially in his sponsoring a conservative and paternalist "Trusteeship of the Indian Race" (Patronato de la Raza Indígena), a corporation created in 1922 under the guidance of Monsignor Emilio Lisson with the probable aim of marginalizing the Tawantinsuyo Society and its unpredictably independent peasant activists. Similarly Law 4113, the Highway Construction Draft Law of 1920, was widely denounced by pro-Indian organizations because it required unpaid service to build highways and intrinsically favored the expansion of haciendas.

Several examples of indigenous mobilizations deserve special mention here. First is the interesting experiment of creating the new town of Wanchu Lima, adjacent to Huancané in the Titicaca high plain of Puno. Around 1923 several Aymara communities, led by the charismatic Carlos Condorena, tried to create their own "Lima" there in flagrant defiance of the mestizo town of Huancané. The new city would have the same layout as the capital. Huancané immediately reacted with talk of a great insurrection and the danger of invasion, and the experiment was quickly cut off. Half a century later, the first Aymara to become the top-ranking leader of a peasant organization (the Peasant Confederation of Peru) hailed from just those communities.

Leguía's aim was probably to separate this important and explosive sector, with its populist approach to the Indian world, from the newly emerging left. Fired up by the recent revolutionary triumphs in Mexico and Russia, the left was quickly becoming a force to reckon with, and it incorporated a strong current of indigenism. Of particular importance were the American Popular Revolutionary Alliance (APRA), the party founded by Victor Raúl Haya de la Torre, and above all the Communist Party in its first incarnation as initiated by José Carlos Mariátegui. The former, much the more radical in its early phases, had a greater impact on the coastal haciendas. Its appeal was more classist than Indian, and little by little it would become involved directly in power struggles with the state. Mariátegui, on the other hand, was much more directly connected with the indigenous history that concerns us here. Due to his physical limitations, Mariátegui himself was not personally familiar with the Indian Peru of which he spoke so often, but he maintained frequent contact with indigenists like Valcárcel and Urviola, who aided him in his search for a Marxism and a socialism with an Indian face.

Peru's bilingual literary giant, the (Quechua) poet and (Spanish) novelist José María Arguedas,[9] believed that the indigenism of Mariátegui and his followers had indeed discovered "Andeanness" – but only to emphasize the wretched, mistreated Indian. They had not yet envisioned Andean natives as the historic creators of a culture and a nation. This specifically ethnic theme would be developed further by other indigenist colleagues, such as Valcárcel, who during the same period published the influential and now-classic, *Tempest in the Andes* (1927), which contains the following prophecy: "One day the men of the Andes will descend like the hordes of Tamerlaine. The barbarians of this lower empire are on the other side of the mountains."[10]

The combination of the four factors we have analyzed so far – social movements in the highlands, intellectual *indigenismo*, the indigenist populism of Leguía, and the new left – explain the heavily "millenarian" tone that Wilfredo Kapsoli detects in many indigenous mobilizations of the 1920s, especially in the southern highlands. They looked toward an egalitarian society inspired by Tawantinsuyu, the Inka empire. In the Aymara case Daniel Hazen has discovered something similar: Adventism, which took root in the early years of the century in Platería, on the shores of Lake Titicaca, and which from there spread across the Bolivian *altiplano*, also shared in the millenarian vision, religious focus, and modernism of the times – for example, in its emphasis on rural education.

But at the same time, the emergence of new revolutionary ideas privileging social class, which gained wider currency after the Russian Revolution, were the prelude to a new period beginning in 1923 with the creation of the Regional Indian Workers Federation, which had anarcho-syndicalist origins and was soon persecuted by Leguía, and in 1924 with the formation of the General Federation of Yanaconas (servile workers), which was later incorporated into the General Confederation of Workers promoted by Mariátegui.

Indigenous history as it developed in Peru was partially paralleled by developments in other Andean nations, whose characteristics are detailed in the following section.

[9] 1975: XIV–XVI. [10] Cited in Tamayo (1980), 189–190.

Indians and the Cacique *Movement in Bolivia*

Bolivia is the country whose Andean history most closely resembles that of Peru. During the indigenist years, Bolivia was also home to an urban *indigenista* intelligentsia, less vigorous and more ambiguous than in Peru. Its major voices were Alcides Arguedas and Franz Tamayo. An intellectual bridge spanned the two countries in the person of the Puneño Gamaliel Churata, pseudonym of Arturo Peralta, a friend and collaborator of Mariátegui in Lima. He was greatly influenced by his long journeys in Bolivia, where he participated in the creation of the intellectual movement in Potosí that called itself "Gesta Bárbara" ('Barbaric Prowess', approximately).

Political change also showed certain parallels to Peru, but in a minor key. During the first two decades the government was controlled by the Liberal Party. The state, forgetting its disastrous interactions with Willka and his communities, proceeded full speed ahead with the violent expropriation of communities, propelled by earnings from tin mining and the advance of the railroad. The year 1920, however, brought a sharp dissent led by Bautista Saavedra, a lawyer who in his youth had defended the Indians of Mohoza and had published an essay about the *ayllu*. Saavedra sought support among the aggrieved communities and *ayllus* (and from the new labor unions), promising to resolve their complaints once he took power. His party came to be known as the "*Cacique* Party" in the countryside because it affirmed the claims of the traditional ethnic leaders. However, once he became president, he quickly reneged on his promises: In 1921 his army massacred Aymaras in Jesús de Machaqa, and 2 years later he achieved the dubious privilege of being the first to massacre miners, in Uncía. Saavedra's *indigenismo* was even more "pseudo" than that of Leguía. Also in parallel with Peru, the first Bolivian leftist political parties were imbued with a kind of social indigenism. Major figures included Tristán Marof (pseudonym of Gustavo Navarro), future founder of the important Trotskyist POR, or Workers' Revolutionary Party, and José Antonio Arze, future founder of PIR, the Revolutionary Party of the Left, who in those years translated Louis Baudin's *Socialist Empire of the Incas* from French to Spanish.

Within Indian history proper the Bolivian Quechuas and Aymaras in those decades played a stellar role, at least until the Chaco War (1932–1935). Here as well we see continual widespread unrest, due above all to communal resistance to aggression from the *latifundios* and the Creole authorities. A growing number of studies about this period show both that there were more mobilizations and that these were more interconnected than in any other Andean country. Among the many incidents three cases are especially noteworthy.

First, the movement in Pacajes, near La Paz. This began in 1914 with a journey by its principal leader, Martín Vásquez, to Lima in search of colonial titles. The movement involved leaders from several provinces and departments. The uprising and massacre of Jesús de Machaqa in 1921 can be considered an offshoot of the same movement, which was more localized and soon brutally repressed. According to some contemporary oral testimonies, there were links on both sides of the Peru-Bolivia border around Lake Titicaca, carried out by messengers who carried written communiqués sewn inside their ponchos.

Second, the general uprising of Chayanta, Potosí. In 1927 several provinces in the southern departments were mobilized. The events drew commentaries on the front page of the *New York Times*, alongside columns about the notorious Sacco and Vanzetti case.

Third, toward the end of this period in Bolivia, general mobilizations spread across the whole *altiplano* during the Chaco War (1932–1935, ending with Bolivia's humiliating defeat). These conflicts prompted historian René Arze to conclude that during the whole violent conflict with Paraguay, an undeclared parallel war was going on at home as communities took advantage of the repressive army's absence.

Were all these movements articulated? In Bolivia coordination was not carried out so much by non-Indian radical groups, as in Peru, but rather by means of a subtle and complex network of communal authorities, known to historians today as the "*cacique* movement." This network represents an almost direct continuation of the one formed at the end of the nineteenth century. The new leadership included figures such as Santos Marka T'ula and Eduardo Leandro Nina Qhispi. For two long decades these and other leaders as grassroots activists traversed the countryside of several departments; they bargained with the government, seeking justice for their communal territories and aid for the Indian schools. The movement combined distinct cultural elements – such as rituals for the colonial documents – with legal struggles, political machinations, and insurrections, depending on the needs of the moment. Nina Qhispi, who began as a teacher, was even named President of the Republic of Collasuyo in the era of the Chaco War, a title that landed him in prison for "usurping the functions" of the chief of state. But he was no Quixote. As the Aymara historian Carlos Mamani perceptively observed, Nina Qhispi's claims to revise the communal boundaries appealed to the same kind of documentation that Bolivia was using against Paraguay – namely, colonial land titles.

Perhaps the only positive state response to all these demands was the creation of the first rural schools. In the *altiplano* there were already several nonstate schools, known as "pittance schools," because the community members themselves paid the teachers, as well as several mission schools, above all those run by Adventists who had come from the Peruvian side of Lake Titicaca. The first government efforts led to establishment of several schools on the frontier zone with Peru and Chile (located so as to defend Bolivian sovereignty), as well as two more widely publicized initiatives: the Indian schools of Caquiaviri and above all the *ayllu*-school of Warisat'a. The last, founded in 1931, was based on the organizational model of the Andean *ayllu*.

In light of all these facts, it becomes difficult to accept an idea that has become common currency among historians, political scientists, and sociologists – namely, that the events of this period belong to a period of "prepolitical" struggle. It is more accurate to speak, as does Silvia Rivera (1984), of another way – and perhaps a more genuine one – to practice indigenous politics.

The Burden of the Early Hacienda in Ecuador

Reflecting, perhaps, a certain amnesia, the available histories of Ecuador register next to no significant indigenous events from the end of the nineteenth to the third decade of the twentieth century. After Eloy Alfaro's turn-of-the-century revolution, the Liberal government moved ahead with consolidating the hacienda, bolstering it after 1908 with the Law of Disentailment of Lands, which once again called for the privatization of communities and their occupation by large landowners. The same regime greatly reduced the Church's power as a landholder.

What occurred, if anything, was a rhetorical modernization of Indian exploitation. In addition to *concertaje* and *huasipungo*, described previously, several other types of temporary labor relations based on sharecropping or tenancy persisted, to the benefit of nonindigenous peoples and at the cost of Quichua-speaking Ecuadorians whether they were *comuneros* (members of corporate communities), smallholders, or *huasipungueros*. In

1918 the government, which represented the capitalist interests of the coastal bankers, updated this essentially archaic system with a law that (once again) attempted to abolish the nominally free but actually coerced labor of *concertaje*, abolished juridical racial categories, suppressed *priostazgos* (costly festival sponsorships incumbent on Indians), and put an end to debt imprisonment. With the threat of imprisonment lifted, many Indians ran away from haciendas and plantations to which they owed insoluble debts. In many ways this law proved an empty gesture because it went against the interests of many landlords. In the parliamentary debate about the new law, one of them argued cynically: "The Indian day laborer earns a salary greater than his needs, cultivates in perpetuity lands that the hacendados assign him, has his own animals, collects his own firewood and charcoal, and enjoys a standard of living higher than that of many who live in more civilized society".[11] But in the early 1920s, all this began to change. Two tightly intertwined factors were influential in this case: economics and politics. The first has to do with a crisis in the cacao business, which until then represented two-thirds of exports and sustained Guayaquil banking and its Liberal Party; the second, more political factor, is that as a result of that crisis the Socialist Party gained a foothold, beginning as an offshoot of the Liberal Party. As in the other countries, the new party gained headway, pushed by revolutionary winds from Mexico and Russia, and supported uprisings and organizations. But what Ecuador lacked – except for the solitary, and therefore all the more admirable, figure of Pío Jaramillo Alvarado – was any complementary stimulus from an indigenist intelligentsia, as in Peru, or an organic indigenous movement, as in Bolivia. For this reason, and because of the economic structure of Ecuadorian agriculture itself, the struggle was concentrated mostly against individual rural estate-owners. In this smaller arena it achieved greater success than the other countries would witness until the following decade.

The first signs of change took place in 1920, when uprisings broke out in the provinces of Azuay, León, Chimborazo, and sporadically in Imbabura. Shortly thereafter, in 1922, a mobilized agrarian worker class was born, fired up by excessive exploitation brought on by the cacao crisis and by a massacre on November 15 in Guayaquil, which left thousands dead. The bankrupt plantations found themselves in the power of the banks and over the years were acquired by international companies. In

[11] Cited in Jaramillo (1954), 81.

the following months indigenous uprisings broke out against landlords and local governments in several highland locations: Sinincay, Jaday, Pichinchuela, Urcuquí, and Licto. Finally in 1925 came the "July Revolution," which ended 30 years of Liberal-banker government and introduced a military government with a "false socialist discourse." This opened a long period of political instability that was to last until 1944.

Because of the strength of the hacienda system, in 1925, after the July Revolution, Ecuador entered the next period of indigenous history, much earlier than the other Andean nations. It did so, however, without having gone through a phase of coordinated militant community-based resistance to expropriation in this century (although such events had occurred in the previous century).

The "Quintinada" in Colombia

The indigenous history of Colombia in this period revolves largely around one name and one region: the legendary and charismatic Manuel Quintín Lame, a rebel in the country's mountainous southwest corner, reputed to be its most "Indian" region. During the first 30 years of the century, scarcely any indigenous actions had disturbed the calm imposed by Conservative government. State dominion was such that even the Indian reservations supported and did not challenge the situation, much as they supported that strong right arm of the Conservatives the Catholic Church. The Church, indeed, was the main beneficiary of the various tributes: "obligation" or communal work for public works some 15 to 20 days a year; tithes auctioned off to merchants; and the "commissions" (processions) to the Virgin Mary in order to collect alms.

After 1914, however, in the Cauca region, an exception to this trend began. It followed the same contours as in the other countries: the defense of communal territory, in this case land of the *resguardos*. The person who disturbed the "Pax Conservadora" was the Páez Manuel Quintín Lame (1883–1967), "the Indian who came down from the mountain to the valley of civilization" (as he styled himself) to defend the rights of his people. He was a *terrajero* (that is, a peasant who earned use of a plot by serving estate lands) and a veteran of the Thousand Day War at the beginning of the century. In the past he had refused to perform services or to work building a new chapel. Now he began to call himself "the standard-bearer and defender of the Indian councils of Cauca," referring to the *cabildos* or community councils of colonial origin, and launched his first mobilization against San Isidro hacienda. He was immediately persecuted by Liberals, Conservatives, and clergy alike, and in 1915 he was captured for the first time.

This was the birth of the "Quintinada," in which other leaders were united as well. Some were from the Páez ethnic group, such as José Gonzalo Sánchez and Rosalino Yajimbo, and others were Guambianos, such as Marcelino Ulé and Julio Yaquimba. In 1920 Quintín Lame founded on his Páez reserve the "Supreme Council of the Indies of Natagaima," bringing together people from the Cauca and Tolima provinces "to protect, shield and defend everywhere the rights and territorial properties of the Indian tribes in all the territory of the nation." Two years later, pursued by the local powers, he retreated to Tolima, where he founded a similar institution – San José de Indias – in Ortega and Chaparral. He remained there until 1931, when the landlords' army attacked the site, provoking a massacre from which he escaped uninjured.

By 1939 he claimed to have been in jail 108 times, but his struggle was increasingly concentrated on legal means, writing memoranda that he would later judge "a waste of time and paper." He died in Ortega in 1967 at age 83, and even then the priest refused him a religious burial. This solitary hero is admired as well for his numerous, posthumously published writings, powerful and enlivened by a complex metaphoric imagery. In them Lame describes himself as "the *bola* that spun and passed through the center of the wild herd . . . and broke the mental tank of poison of the Supreme Court." (*Bola* refers to a hunting weapon thrown to tangle the legs of the prey.) He is also depicted as early as 1927 as one of the pioneers in the massive mobilization of indigenous women, from whose "wombs will be born flowers of intelligence who will make the entire civilization of exploiters take notice."

In the 1930s–1940s, after Quintín Lame retreated to Tolima, the Communist Party entered Páez territory, where it organized agrarian leagues with Lame's support and that of José González Sánchez. In Colombia as elsewhere the party's interests during its early years overlapped significantly with indigenous issues. In this case the relationship presaged events to come – in the time of the guerrillas.

Changing Mapuche Strategies in Chile

The case of the Mapuche in Chile in these three decades proceeded along two axes: on the structural level, pauperization, and agricultural sedentarization resulting from the defeat of a four-century armed resistance; and, on the political level, by a new kind of resistance that arose within the framework of an accepted Chilean state, with all the contradictions that integration into dominant society and simultaneous defense of territory and lifeways brought.

Pauperization has been tellingly described by Bengoa.[12]

> The society of the nineteenth century was rich in livestock and this wealth expressed itself in the silverwork that men and women wore ostentatiously. The first decades of the century saw the despoiling of Araucanian silver; the women sold their jewels in order to eat and the usurers were left with jewelry pieces, riding gear, and all kinds of valuable goods, in exchange for seeds and tools.

According to Bengoa, during "peasantization" the Mapuche established new patrilineal and patrilocal systems of inheritance of lands, adopted surnames, became endogamous, and retreated into a more ritualized and conservative vision of their culture.

In politics the awakening from the amnesia caused by defeat seems to have come about only after 1910. It was expressed above all in numerous lawsuits and violent acts all over their territory. One statistic of the Appellate Court in Temuco in 1929 mentions 3,707 Indian cases. There were 1,219 lawsuits for recovery of lands, originating in almost a third of the *reducciones*. In these cases it was no longer possible, as in other countries, to refer to the colonial titles; the only documents recognized were the grants (*títulos de merced*) issued in those same years. Nevertheless around 1929, the year in which the program of "rooting" or "settling" the Mapuche was completed, an estimated one-fifth of even the small amount of territory recognized as Mapuche in the "pacification" of 1881 had already been usurped. A review of the local press between 1910 and 1930, cited by Bengoa,[13] found thirty-two cases in which the conflicts involved bloodshed. Some included "branding Indians" by cutting their ears and even burning with firebrands, as if they were cattle.

A lengthy debate began – one that continues until today, as much among the Mapuches as among the "Huinca" or Euro-Chileans – about whether it was more useful to maintain those communal titles or to divide the lands into *hijuelas* or family parcels. In these early decades progressive sectors supported division, which they saw as the quickest route to integration into Chilean society. But little by little over the

[12] 1985, p. 367. [13] 1985, pp. 372–382.

years, a new ethnic consciousness viewed the maintenance of communal titles as a better way to defend Mapuche identity.

These power struggles and debates were expressed in practical terms through the various Mapuche "societies" that were established beginning in 1910. In one respect we can interpret their importance as the result of "pacification" policy: Many *lonko* (traditional chiefs) were required to hand over one son as a proof of peace; these boys were educated in the Chilean system, sometimes with military officers as their godfathers. When they returned they brought new proposals, ideas that combined older Mapuche pride with integration into Chilean society. This meant that during this period several types of leaders were recognized: *lonko* (a chief with a long lineage), *ulmen* (rich in land and relatives), and those called *hueupin* (grand tribune). Some leaders had considerable urban experience and sought links with state power, symbolized in the office of the president irrespective of party affiliation. The first of the young men to return were teachers, but little by little prosperous merchants got the upper hand.

The first society was founded in 1910: the Caupolicán Society in Defense of Araucania, led by two teachers, Manuel Neculmán and Manuel Manquilef; the latter withdrew in 1925 to become a Liberal *diputado* (congressman). It straddled the line between ancestral roots and an ideology of progress. It would lead the defense against abuses, and it proposed education for Indians. It held its main celebrations in hotels in Temuco, wearing Western formal dress, with impressive bilingual menus. Its stance in the debate over lands was clearly on the side of division into parcels. In 1916 the Mapuche Society for Mutual Protection was established in Loncoche, headed by the charismatic hereditary chief Manuel Aburto Panguilef, amidst a fierce local struggle for territory. It became more active after 1919, and in 1922 it was renamed the Araucanian Federation. This society was much more concerned with cultural identity and tradition. In frank defiance of Christian practice, it advocated indigenous-style marriages (which include polygamy). Its mass meetings, rallying as many as 15,000 people, always included ancestral ritual. In terms of the territory issue, it vigorously defended the communal character of the "reductions" or reserves, managing to destabilize even the pro-division stance of the Sociedad Caupolicán. Politically it was aligned with FOCH, the Federation of Chilean Workers.

In the South Andes we see much the same tendency toward an indigenist Marxism as we saw in Peru, Bolivia, and Ecuador during the same period. A third society arose in opposition to it. Reacting especially to the more radical position of Panguilef – who was repeatedly accused of being an Anarchist, Communist, and pagan – the Araucanian Union formed under the motto of "God, Country, Progress" in 1926. This society was the brainchild of the Capuchin bishop Guido Beck de Ramberga and was led by the Chihualaf brothers. Although it was sensitive to the abuses committed against the Mapuche, the society stood firmly against their traditions, especially religious ones, and in favor of the "whitening" of Mapuche culture as a whole. Although it pioneered in advocating women's rights, at the same time it opposed women serving as *machi* (traditional priestesses sometimes called shamans). It also consistently advocated the division of land into parcels.

The three societies were involved in a very Mapuche game of alliances with different parties and governments, in which the terminology of left and right blocs had little real meaning. The important thing for them rather was to achieve greater influence in the upper echelons of power in order to achieve their own goals. These efforts saw their first fruits as early as 1915, when they managed to abolish fiscal taxes, and especially after 1920, when the first signs of crisis in the nitrate industry led to a more populist platform defined by the Liberal Arturo Alessandri. Alessandri eliminated Indian tribute in 1921. In 1925 – under pressure from the Araucanian Federation and the first Mapuche diputado, the Democrat Francisco Melivilu – he suspended the auctioning of state lands. In 1927 General Carlos Ibáñez took power and imposed Law 4169, which called for mandatory division of lands. Parcelization was to be triggered if even one community member requested it. The Mapuche societies reacted in different ways. The Araucanian Union fully supported the law, and its leader Antonio Chihualaf was elected a member of the Land Division Tribunal. The Caupolicán Society was more indecisive; it gave partial support insofar as the process would permit the recuperation of some lands. On the other hand, the Araucanian Federation opposed the law. Its president, Panguilef, was prosecuted and imprisoned. But this new legal situation also galvanized an awakening Mapuche consciousness. Resistance to the division sprang up in several Mapuche sectors and forced future legal dispositions to soft-pedal the demands of the law. At the same time, this situation created a crisis in leadership in the organizations that had supported the law. In 1930 the Chihualaf brothers decided to break with Capuchin influence and dissolve the Araucanian Union, although the bishop managed to keep it alive under a new leadership. In 1931 the Caupolicán Society passed into the hands of the young merchant Venancio Coñuepán – a descendant of a hereditary chief who had supported "pacification" – and changed its former pro-division position.

UNIONS AND AGRARIAN REFORMS (1930–1973)

Overview

In almost all of the Andean countries, structural changes in the state arose around 1930, stimulating new ideas and demands about government relations with indigenous peoples. But compared to the previous period with its parallelisms, the various countries diverged in the ways these newer changes were played out.

The year 1930 marks the beginning of a new period largely because of the Great Depression of 1929–1930, which shook the world and which, within the Andean region, prompted changes in almost all export economies. On the heels of the initial crisis, the depression quickly stimulated political attempts at modernization. These tendencies became financially real several years later in the economic boom stimulated by World War II and then the Korean War, which temporarily improved local export opportunities – especially of strategic products – and even those for internal development. The impact varied according to the country. It was felt more in Peru and Chile, both of which exported minerals and had the potential for increased agroindustrial development. Ecuador, on the other hand, had to wait for a conjuncture favorable to banana production in order to pull out of its cacao crisis. Bolivia, unlike its neighbors, could not take full advantage of international export opportunities – in this case, tin. First, it suffered a calamitous setback from its defeat in the Chaco War; in addition the interplay among pro-Allied and pro-Axis forces eventuated in tin sales to the Allies at prices so low that the friends of the Allies later proved unable to distance themselves from the blame as more nationalist forces again took hold. In Colombia, where there was only a routine changing of the guard in 1930, serious internal conflicts – and soon the onset of chronic partisan bloodshed, *la violencia* – began in the 1940s and effectively put the brakes on any possibility of further development. In any case, in the 1950s international economic advantages began to disappear, and everywhere new crises and social unrest broke loose.

Major demographic changes characterized the Depression-through-wartime era and its sequels, both because of quickening general population growth and because of the major cities' increasing weight as they received swelling waves of migrants. All of these factors led to the consolidation of social movements and urban labor organizations. It was during this period that protective legislation for workers was demanded and approved, and popular parties emerged or were consolidated, such as APRA in Peru, Bolivia's MNR or Nationalist Revolutionary Movement, and numerous variants of socialism and communism in all the countries.

These large-scale processes had several distinct effects on the indigenous peoples. On one hand, their tenuous economic situation disposed Indians to migrate to the cities, with everything that implied in the way of sociocultural transformations. Migrants in turn influenced their places of origin. On the other hand, economic modernization processes themselves, as well as the accelerating departure of the labor force to the cities, stimulated drastic changes in traditional relations of production on some haciendas. Changes occurred more readily in those sectors that promised better entrepreneurial chances, such as wool in Peru, dairy in Ecuador, and a small wine grape complex in Bolivia – and even then only as the result of new pressures both from above and below. But these processes did not stimulate a specifically indigenous response to the situation. Modernization implied, even for the left, economic changes or agrarian reforms and not a reorganization of relations among peoples. Class was imposed onto ethnicity, and unions or cooperatives were imposed as new organizations onto the longstanding institutions of community. Except in the Mapuche part of Chile, the terms "Indian" (*indio*) and "indigenous" (*indígena*) came to sound passé and discriminatory and were replaced in all would-be progressive discourse by "peasant" (*campesino*).

Nevertheless this "classist" tendency obscures two countertendencies: one in the urban cultural-artistic sphere, and the other in "official indigenism." In the cultural sphere the Indian world continued to receive close scrutiny. The 1940s saw the emergence of writers such as Jorge Icaza in Ecuador, José María Arguedas in Peru, and somewhat later Jesús Lara in Bolivia. Indians were central characters in films since their earliest production in Bolivia and Peru, and they became the standard subjects for painters like Oswaldo Guayasamín in Ecuador, the sculptor Mérida in Peru, and Marina Núñez del Prado in Bolivia. Rural music inspired musicians in all those countries. Each of these authors still spoke of "the Indian" without being Indian, in quest of their own identities. Another novel feature of this era was that some intellectuals devoted their energies to compiling and analyzing popular cultural expressions in folklore, music, textiles, and so forth. Living Indians were no longer just the objects of pity and curiosity; they also evoked admiration. There was a serious lacuna, however: Indians themselves by and large could not present themselves and achieve full status as citizens in these circles without mediation by culturally privileged intellectuals. One standout exception was the brilliantly gifted photographer Martín Chambi, whose pictures from 1920 to 1950 provide a social as well as archaeological panorama of Cusco.

"Official indigenism" began with the Mexican Revolution. After the First Inter-American Indigenist Congress held in Pátzcuaro in 1940, an inter-American headquarters was established in Mexico City (sponsored by the Organization of American States), and branches were established in many other countries: 1941, Mexico; 1942, Ecuador; 1943, Colombia; 1945, Bolivia; and 1946, Peru (on a legal foundation set in 1943). In 1968 Chile acquired a branch, the last in Latin America, some 14 years behind the next-most reluctant countries, Argentina and Brazil. These efforts and others in rural education relied from the start on major funding from the United States.

After 1950 in the three central Andean nations, there arose a new version of official indigenism, in the form of the Andean Mission (*Misión Andina*), which, connecting with the United Nations' vastly expanding bureaucracy, created numerous specialized subagencies and programs in all three countries, especially in Ecuador. All this action was a prelude for what would come in the 1960s, the "development decade": a series of programmatic platforms like community development, colonization, integrated rural development, and so forth. In harmony with all modernization policies during this period, "official indigenism," still predicated on the concept of the "Indian problem," tended toward a policy of assimilating indigenous peoples into the dominant society.

But the great central theme, which increasingly came to dominate the entire period, was agrarian reform. The motto of the Mexican agrarian reform – "the land to those who work it" – had already been heard loud and clear in all the Andean lands since the 1930s; in the 1960s it became politically forceful. The movement was more concerned with the peasantry (whether indigenous or not) than with ethnic groups as such. The reforms took different paths depending on factors of time and place and, intentions to the contrary notwithstanding, culture. The process breaks down into three broad phases.

The first phase still concentrated on improving labor relations in the hacienda system, without questioning the system itself. This phase evolved over three different decades in the three central countries: beginning in 1925 in Ecuador, where it aborted and lay dormant until the mild reforms of the 1960s; beginning in 1935 in Bolivia, following the crisis caused by the Chaco War, and maturing with growing dynamism into the revolutionary processes that the 1952 political crisis would unleash; and beginning in 1945 in Peru, where it soon stalled, only to reacquire explosive force after 1956. In the other two peripheral countries, Chile and Colombia, this phase had less effect on the indigenous minorities, who were less concentrated on estates.

The second phase was the breakup of the old hacienda system itself. In the Andean region the path-breaking events occurred in Bolivia in 1953, as earlier grassroots processes came to fruition. The remaining countries had to await not only the outcome of the Bolivian example but also an extremely important outside event: the Cuban Revolution of 1959. Both events stimulated popular mobilizations. The United States government under Presidents Eisenhower and Kennedy, alarmed by the unrest in several countries and especially the socialist experiment taking place in its own backyard, convened the presidential summit of Punta del Este, launched the Alliance for Progress, and began to pressure the region's nations to carry out agrarian reforms of a nonrevolutionary sort.

These late processes defined a third phase. With it came reforms that were strictly gradualist in Ecuador (1964 and 1973), and an initially mild one in Peru (1964) followed by the later, more controversial, measures of the military nationalist government in 1969. Chile and Colombia also undertook late agrarian reforms, which involved for the most part non-Indian peasant sectors. In Chile over the years, the reform reached deeper, affected the Mapuche as well, and took on its own communal dynamic until it was abruptly truncated by General Augusto Pinochet's military coup. Colombia experienced the weakest, or most "decaffeinated," reform of the whole area; various state institutes were created to deal with the indigenous question, but the interested parties also sought more effective solutions on their own terms.

Above all in the 1960s, reform came packaged together with a new wave of "developmentism," with offers of credit, technical innovation, cooperatives, and so forth, expected to speed up the entry of small producers into the capitalist market. It also arrived together with "community development" – style support and self-help programs, which offered government aid in exchange for the depoliticization of agriculture. Except in Chile the proposals went hand-in-glove with colonization programs intending to push the agricultural and ranching frontier eastward into the Amazonian jungle. As a result forest-dwelling indigenous peoples, who had long lived in what governments mislabeled "empty" lands, became increasingly involved on disadvantageous terms.

The changes were accompanied by popular mobilizations. In Bolivia the reforms were preceded by numerous rebellions and land invasions, and mobilization continued in full force although, once the lands were obtained, reform was often plagued by internal factionalism. In Peru mobilization came later but once it took hold, it was both more intense and longer-lived than anywhere else. Nonetheless the final Peruvian result was an agrarian reform imposed from above by the state. Ecuador was perhaps the country where the mobilizations were most moderate. In Chile and Colombia the process was spearheaded by nonindigenous peasant sectors, but as these took root in indigenous areas, they had the unforeseen effect of revitalizing ethnic consciousness. It is noteworthy that in all cases popular agitation and mobilization concentrated on land invasions, not personal attacks, and in only a few cases did the uprisings lead to violent deaths. The killings that did occur were more often due to guerrilla outbreaks initiated by nonindigenous groups, as in Peru and Colombia, or to repression on the part of the army, the police, or the landlords themselves, or, in the case of Bolivia, to factional fighting within initially victorious mobilizations.

All these reforms significantly altered the rural scene in the three central Andean nations, where old servile relations of production disappeared or were diluted. Those who had for so long used tiny plots of hacienda land, in exchange for labor given to the hacienda, gained ownership of those plots and freed themselves at last from onerous feudalistic obligations. But in general they did not manage to increase their landholdings or get enough technical support and credit to improve their yield and market position. For that reason these reforms came to seem, over the long run, more a palliative to lower the voltage of social tensions, than a fundamental solution for peasant poverty. In the long run most local implementations of reform were to create chronic frustrations underlying peasant and indigenous struggles toward the end of the twentieth century.

During the era of agrarian reforms, it looked like the concept of "Indian" identity had been retired to the museums, outdistanced and replaced by more modern concepts like "peasant." But the actual outcome was very different. Having established the broader context for an unforeseen "re-Indianization" of political discussion, I turn now to the particular characteristics of each country.

Bolivia Turns Around Twice

In Bolivia the transition from community resistance to rejection of the whole agrarian old order occurred because of the severe national crisis that followed defeat in the Chaco War (1932–1935). From the perspective of Indian peoples, the impact of this war had several special features. The theater of war was the territory of the Chiriguano-Guaraní and other native peoples of the Chaco. The alien conflict brutally disrupted their way of life. The Chiriguano were well aware that they belonged to the Bolivian state; a few years before, several traditional authorities had traveled on foot to La Paz in search of the president to ratify their territorial rights. There they came in contact with the "*cacique* movement" of Nina Qhispi. But during the war their Guaranían language made them seem closer to the Paraguayans – Guaraní being the vernacular tongue of rural Paraguayans regardless of "race." Both sides therefore suspected them of being potential spies and traitors. Casiano Barrientos, the great *mburuvichá* (leader) of the Isoso, one of those who walked to La Paz, died shot by a Bolivian officer. His people dispersed for several years while the officer established his own cattle station on their land.

In addition, however, the Chaco campaign stimulated major changes in the political consciousness of Andean people. As mentioned previously, an internal parallel war broke out in Andean communities defending their lands. Many peasants were drafted, usually by force, to the battlefront, where they were soon made into cannon fodder while the officers lived comfortably in the rear guard. This new experience of discrimination, together with experiences of combat, of the discovery of other forms of organization, and of rubbing shoulders with people from all over the country, proved catalysts for a new postwar consciousness in which the entire country would be reborn.

On a national level the unique conjuncture of "mobilization in defeat" underlay the rapid emergence first of "military socialism" (associated with Presidents Toro and Busch), and then of new political parties, almost all of them flaunting an "R" for "Revolutionary" in their names (POR, PIR, and MNR, new rivals to the FSB or Bolivian Socialist Phalange, a rightist "socialist" party).[14] These events took place amidst an agitated period of coups and countercoups while popular movements – urban, mine-based, and rural – continued to grow. In the end it was the MNR, less ideologized than the rest but more popular and pragmatic, that would prove able to catalyze all this unrest and then attempt to satisfy it following its triumph in the 1952 Revolution.

In agriculture the older concept of the agrarian struggle – as that of communities and their *cacique* movement – was eclipsed by a reconceptualization of the struggle as an attack on the haciendas. Although many major estates had arisen in the prior 50 years amid a rhetoric of liberal progress, they now came to be labeled "feudal throwbacks" because of their labor relations, which were anything but liberal. At a historical moment when people sought a new national identity and structure, ancient forms of resistance (whether in communities or haciendas) counted less than the creation of something new, unprecedented, and modern, inspired by the winds blowing in from abroad.

The main center of this new rural unrest was the Cochabamba valleys, a region where all social classes knew Quechua, but the stigma of Indianness attached to peasants. There, since early colonial times, the *ayllus* and native communities had been shoved aside by the hacienda. The estate sector itself, however, was now in a chronic state of decrepitude because of demographic pressure and the shrinking of its traditional mining markets. In 1936, a group of Quechua farm laborers who had recently returned from the Chaco front now decided they could no longer tolerate their servile status on the Santa Clara convent's hacienda – the largest and one of the most backward in the area. With the support of various teachers and lawyers (soon allied to the new PIR), they organized the first successful peasant union in the country, managed to break free of the hacienda, and obtained the first rural school in the area. They

[14] The first two parties mentioned were Marxist, and their founders included Tristán Marof and José Antonio Arze, mentioned for the previous period, who drifted gradually away from their initial indigenism. The MNR (together with its ally the military arm RADEPA, 'Reason of the Fatherland') combined a leftist focus with an extremely Creole version of the German nationalism then in style. The FSB was the local version of Spanish Francoism.

were supported in these endeavors by the military socialist government then in power, and by the *ayllu*-school of Warisat'a, La Paz, founded with state support just before the war. They developed a network of twenty-four unions in the upper valley, and a long, well-publicized confrontation began with the local landed élite and the Catholic Church.

Several future leaders of the agrarian reform earned their stripes in these years and in these unions. The best known was José Rojas. Landlords expelled him and his parents from the area while he was still young. He went to work in Argentina and returned as the handyman of the school established thanks to the union's campaigning. After that he became a local union leader and over the years eventually became Minister of Peasant Affairs, the first Indian in Bolivian history to become a minister of state.

Other areas of Cochabamba, and also the hacienda regions of La Paz, Oruro, Potosí, and Chuquisaca, witnessed a new form of struggle: the sit-down strike (*huelga de brazos caídos*). These struggles, supported by the new parties and miners' and worker-anarchist organizations, demanded mainly the abolition of *pongueaje, colonato*, and other forms of compulsory service. The demand for agrarian reform as such was not yet part of their agenda, although the topic arose from time to time in more political circles. But after 1945, when the relatively radical Colonel Villarroel (of the RADEPA party) and his allies in the MNR seized the government, strikes took a new turn. In the hope of broadening his government's political base, in 1945 Villarroel organized the Indigenous Congress at La Paz, convening delegates from all of the Andean departments of the country – haciendas and native communities alike. Among those present were people who had already distinguished themselves (or would do so) by their contributions to the Indian cause. Among them figure the traditional Kallawaya (Callahuaya, etc.) folk-physician Antonio Alvarez Mamani, who over the years was to travel across the *altiplano* of Oruro organizing unions; Hilarión Grájeda of Cochabamba, who soon would lead a large rebellion in Ayopaya; and the pioneering Indianist ideologue Fausto Reinaga.

Nothing like it had ever been seen before. The president, himself from Cochabamba, led off with a speech in Quechua, and the congress concluded with the reading of four famous decrees that denounced servile labor *(pongueaje)* and demanded the creation of schools on all haciendas. But it continued to sidestep the issue of agrarian reform. It did not even attack the other major form of servitude: *colonato*, or unpaid labor in exchange for use rights to a piece of land. Plainly the government's goal was to gain control of the Indian-peasant movement (as it had recently done with the miners) and restrict it to the state's own objectives, which were less radical than those of some rural leaders.

Despite these limitations Villarroel became the "father" of the Indians and the MNR became their party. The oligarchy would not tolerate those new developments. In an implausible alliance with the PIR (which thus signed its own political death warrant), they instigated a riot in which Villarroel was overthrown and hung from a lightpost.

The next year, 1947, was one of general uprisings in many parts of the countryside. There could be no going back to the previous state of affairs. Some rebels, like the Aymaras of Ayqachi and Pucarani, were supported by anarchist worker organizations; the rest, by the temporarily overthrown MNR. The best known case was the great Quechua rebellion of Ayopaya in Cochabamba, which left many estates in ashes. Severe repression followed, and the main leaders were banished to rugged tropical exiles. But that episode sealed the fate of the hacienda and the traditional agrarian structure. Talk of agrarian reform (and revolution) gripped the nation, and the MNR saw itself more and more as the chosen agency that would transform the country.

The new conjuncture arrived in 1952. The main leader of the MNR, Víctor Paz Estenssoro, won the 1951 elections. When a military junta prevented him from taking office as president, supporters took to the streets. Demonstrations turned into a general popular revolution, which brought the MNR to power on April 9, 1952. The new government was most urgently concerned with nationalizing the mines, which were the main source of hard currency, but from the beginning it also showed interest in securing a broad rural base without losing control over it. The state declared Villarroel's decrees in effect, supported the unionization of agriculture, created a new Ministry of Peasant Affairs (the word "indígenas" was still banned) and even established universal suffrage, including women and those who could not read, for the first time ever in South America.

No clear agenda for an agrarian reform was yet forthcoming, although the issue was debated more and more. Then Quechua peasants of the upper valley of Cochabamba, who had led the struggle in previous years, took up the initiative begun by José Rojas and managed to displace the more moderate leaders backed by the government. In 1952 they took matters into their own hands and seized several haciendas in the valley.

By doing so they finally forced the government to establish an agrarian reform commission.

After some initial doubts, the government understood and decided that land redistribution was the only route to securing peasant support. On the first anniversary of the revolution, the government legalized land invasions by peasants of Ucureña, the hottest focus of the movement, and, a few months later, on August 2, 1953, in Ucureña itself the historic Agrarian Reform Decree was signed. This was the green light for a true agrarian revolution, only partially controlled by the government. Estate peasants in all Andean regions of the country began to take over the lands. The majority of the landlords, terrified, escaped leaving the way open for even more massive takeovers. Legal transfers came several years later, but in fact the peasants had already gained control of the land. In parts of Cochabamba, they did so even before the Ucureña decree; in other more central regions, a few months after it; and in distant places, only at the end of the decade.

The political linchpins of these massive changes were the MNR's local commands frequently in the hands of the peasant leaders. *Sindicatos campesinos* (agrarian unions) were formed around them. Their organization mimicked that of the miners' unions. Indeed in La Paz and Potosí, many veteran mine-union leaders set about organizing peasant unions, sometimes turning into peasant leaders themselves. The unions at first had a more clearly recovery-oriented position: to oppose the *patrón* and to win back their lands. Later the term *sindicato* became a new provisional name for the old communal organization, not only on the ex-haciendas but also in many of the free-standing traditional native communities. What was new in this arrangement was that, thanks to the union, this communal organization now would become part of an official network, expanded throughout almost the whole country, ensuring a permanent relationship among the government, political parties, and peasantry. This enabled communities to receive, via clientelistic relationships, benefits such as food aid, schools, and legally validated land titles.

During this rapid process, in some places what came to be called "peasant super-states" sprang up. Especially in Ucureña (Cochabamba), Achacachi (La Paz), San Pedro de Buenavista (Norte de Potosí), and to a lesser degree in several other places, a few peasant leaders managed to achieve enough power practically to push aside judges, subprefects, and other government authorities. This sometimes created conflicts with the MNR itself to which, in one way or another, everyone claimed to belong.

In Achacachi, for example, the Aymara leaders Toribio Salas and Paulino Quispe (nicknamed Wilasaco) were able to corner an ex-hacendado and minister of peasant affairs, who died in an ambush.

Once these first years passed, some of these places developed chronic conflicts related to factionalism within the MNR. Such conflicts often degenerated into deadly vendettas among leaders. The best known case is that of the *ch'ampa guerra* ('sod-brick war') of Cliza and Ucureña in Cochabamba, so-called because fighters built barricades from that rustic material. The struggle for leadership among José Rojas (linked more to the MNR of Paz Estenssoro) and José Veizaga (linked more to the dissident MNRA of Guevara Arze) cost hundreds of lives and in the end helped the military take power away from the Paz Estenssoro group. Also noteworthy was the struggle between the Layme and Jukumani *ayllus*, adjoining the mining district of the Norte de Potosí, exacerbated at one point by a conflict between government and miners in the same area.

At first the reform process was more radical and popular. But it became more moderate and later inwardly focused, especially from the 1960s on, as a result of the complications created by a serious internal economic crisis. Rightist factions also acquired much more power in the government, and dependence on the United States grew. For its part the United States after initial doubts decided to support the Bolivian government to prevent it falling into Communist hands. The United States applied pressure to break up the unions and related organizations; in exchange it promoted more strictly economic mechanisms such as so-called community development and cooperatives. Finally, in 1964, the government was taken over by the pro-U.S. military faction headed by General René Barrientos, whose claim to fame included the recent pacification of Cliza and Ucureña. Barrientos furthered the process of titling agrarian lands and managed the cooptation of peasant participants in the government. The "Military-Peasant Pact" promised public works in the countryside in exchange for political support to the generals. The pact also provided the major impetus for colonization programs that expanded the agricultural frontier into the eastern tropics, as the Andean Mission had proposed in the previous decade.

At this exact moment, in 1967, Ché Guevara began his guerrilla activities in Ñankaguasu, Bolivia. This initiative, which stirred worldwide attention, did not attain much local success (except in the distant mines and in some urban sectors) for various reasons, two of which relate directly to our story. In the first place, the agrarian reform and the government-peasantry rapprochement had only just begun and still had some political muscle. The government set up a theater of operations using the "René Barrientos" peasant regiment against the guerrillas. In the second place, the area that "Ché" chose, which was within Chiriguano-Guaraní territory, turned out to be too isolated and foreign to the anti-imperialist campaign espoused by the guerrillas. Although the episode took place in indigenous territory, it failed to become truly part of indigenous history.

In sum the process that began in 1935 and ended in 1953 had already come full circle by the 1960s. Along the way the government managed to coopt some Indians, now effectively categorized as peasants, who without realizing it supported administrations that were fully identified with the status quo.

Ecuador, an Aborted Process

As we have seen, the process of crisis and modernization took precocious form in Ecuador as a result of the collapse of the cacao-based economy. This in turn prompted the "July Revolution" of 1925 and then a long period of political instability, which witnessed twenty changes of government by 1944.

Almost simultaneously, indigenous insurrections, which had been breaking out frequently on estates since the beginning of the decade, took on a much more organized profile in several highland provinces. For two decades the main actions were carried out by Quichua workers on the haciendas in Cayambe, Pichincha Province, which formed the endowment of the state's Social Assistance program. In 1926 an agrarian union named after Juan Montalvo was born there, the first in the country and the embryo of the future FEI (Ecuadorian Federation of Indians). The movement quickly spread to other parts of Pichincha Province and stimulated the formation of the first peasant unions on the Pacific coast in 1928. These Quichua Indian estate peons' unions demanded more than better work conditions. They appealed as well to their own history, as distinct from Creole history, and by 1930 also demanded education in the Quichua language.

Farther south, in Chimborazo Province, the zone that housed Ecuador's biggest Quichua population, the year 1929 saw other serious disturbances. The communities of Colta and Columbe, Chimborazo, which had suffered encroachments by estate owners, flared up in revolt, but because this episode has not been studied we do not know if their fight was directly related to the movement in the north. The army repressed the movement and is reported to have left some 3,000 dead; if verified this figure would represent the worst massacre in twentieth-century Andean indigenous history. In the following decade there were other uprisings by the Chimborazo communities. As in other countries some uprisings were linked to land speculation caused by road and railroad construction.

The Socialist and Communist parties, founded in 1931, were present in the Indian organizations of the northern haciendas, following the Marxist-indigenist line promoted by Mariátegui in Peru. But the framework of all of this action was static; in a society that constantly changed governments without changing structures, agrarian structures remained "fossilized." Thus in 1936 a new Labor Code was written, but it still allowed *huasipungo* and sharecropping as a form of partial wages. A 1937 military coup supported by the left brought the only legal advance of the period, the Law and Statute of Communities, which remained in force until the 1990s. Under this law the state supported the transformation of communities into production cooperatives, to be administered under the same year's Law of Cooperatives. Thus the state sought an alternative not only to the community, which it viewed as antiquated, but also to unionism, which it viewed as dangerous. This modernization scheme generated internal conflicts between members and nonmembers of cooperatives, and it unleashed processes of class differentiation within peasant groups. But, on the other hand, it did initiate the legal registry of community lands, and this guaranteed at least some measure of continuity. Between 1937 and 1941, 1,080 communities were registered with a total of 503,000 inhabitants, many of them still tied to owners by rental and sharecrop contracts. At that time community members made up 27.6 percent of the total indigenous population, estimated at 1,824,000 (57 percent of the whole country).

The alliance between indigenous organizations on haciendas and the Communist Party lasted through the 1930s and 1940s. In 1945, following a congress at Cayambe, the FEI (Ecuadorian Federation of Indians) was legalized as part of the newly founded CTE (Central Organization of Ecuadorian Workers), a Communist-led general labor federation. Its program included an agrarian reform to eliminate *huasipungo*, the suppression of onerous religious services and female domestic service, improvements in access to credit, and use of the peasants' own language in education. But in practice it never tackled these bold tasks, and as time passed it became bogged down in legal disputes, especially in the hacienda sector, and lost the popular thrust of previous decades.

One of the chief leaders of this whole period was the Indian Dolores Cacuango. She organized strikes, unions, and many other actions in her home area of rural Cayambe. In retaliation her house was burned by the army and she was expelled from her lands. In the popular revolution of May 1944 – which brought the perennial populist José María Velasco Ibarra to power for a second time – she participated in a takeover of army headquarters at Cayambe. In 1946 she became president of the FEI. Until this day stories about her still circulate, some of them compiled in a volume of testimony edited by José Yáñez (1986). These testimonies defy translation because, unlike other chroniclers of the peasantry, Yáñez reproduces the stigmatized Quichua-influenced Spanish his witnesses actually spoke.

> "Mama Dulu Cacuango from San Pablo Hill, beat up as she was, used to talk about socialism – in favor of peasants, that is." Her attitude used to bring out fear in others: "Look at that Indian bandit. Don't get involved with socialists, don't get involved. They're devils, they're heretics. They're no good for you. The boss'll send you to jail."

At about this time, along the Amazonian foothills of the Andes, a military and diplomatic event took place whose repercussions among indigenous lowland people are still felt today. In 1941 Peru invaded Ecuador across a long-disputed border and defeated its army. The following year, under the agreement called the Río Protocol, Ecuador had to cede a large part of its Amazonian territory. As a result various indigenous groups, mostly belonging to the large Shuar linguistic family (known in literature by the stigmatizing word Jívaro), found themselves split across both sides of the new, contested border. At the same time, Ecuador's military defeat stimulated greater political and economic interest in the remaining part of Amazonia. Its development – for example, oil prospecting and military control – would in the long run stimulate lowland indigenous reorganization and participation in "national" political life.

In the Peruvian-Ecuadorian Amazon, as in the Bolivian-Paraguayan Chaco a few years earlier and in the Peruvian-Chilean-Bolivian *altiplano* in 1879, the native inhabitants of the territory, with their ancestral need to move freely about, turned out to be invisible. Officials in power passed laws, selected development sites, and even drew international borders without a glance at the inhabitants. Concepts like "equality among citizens," so much in vogue among politicians of the era, did not reach much beyond downtown districts.

Paradoxically the formation of the CTE and the FEI, which could be considered important advances in organization, coincided with the onset of an era of social demobilization caused by a new political-economic situation. Beginning with the election of the estate-owner Galo Plaza as president in 1948, the banana boom of 1948–1957 brought on the agricultural modernization described ably by Guerrero. It was a time of political stability, economic growth, and little social mobilization, but it brought appreciable updating of productive systems, especially on state-owned haciendas and a few private latifundios of dairy cattle. Such estates cut back the area assigned to "precarious" tenures – that is, *huasipungo*, sharecrop plots, and the like – and increased use of salaried and specialized labor. This conjuncture allowed for a certain degree of expansion in the peasant smallholder sector, whether by renting parts of state haciendas or by buying up lands formerly rented.

No really new developments took place until 1957, when the banana export economy, like cacao three decades earlier, fell into crisis. As when cacao went bust, an era of political instability followed; but, to quote Tulio Halperin, superficial instability masked "the unbearable stability of the basic facts" – that is, the persisting seigneurial landlord regime of the mountains and the plantation regime of the coast. The shortage of work provoked serious disturbances and massacres in Guayaquil. Cashiered banana workers went back to their highland homes. Thus the collapse of labor migration added to the pressure on land and the subsequent deterioration of living conditions. Meanwhile the archaic highland estates became ever less capable of meeting market demand without incurring losses, damaging the landlord classes' repute among urban élites. Neither could most estates meet the standard for improved work conditions, which those few haciendas well placed in the vanished boom market had unintentionally set. Rural workers were in line for disappointment and anger.

Beginning in 1960, in Ecuador as elsewhere, the Cuban revolution and U.S. reaction to it added to these pressures. An agrarian reform that would modernize the most archaic patronal structures became harder to resist. Increasing agitation was combined with improved organization in the countryside. Between 1960 and 1963 the largest plantations of the United Fruit Company, which quit the country because of the crisis, were violently occupied by peasants organized into cooperatives with the support of the Communist Party. In the mountains the FEI, also associated with the party, led mobilizations. Thus in February 1961 more than 2,000 *comuneros* of Columbe rose up and attacked the police force, which was in collusion with the landlords and was poised to repress them. The sixty prisoners were quickly released on the president's orders. At the end of the same year, Quito witnessed an unprecedentedly massive peaceful demonstration of 15,000 *huasipungueros* and community members. The mere fact that the government tolerated these mobilizations shows how the balance of forces was shifting.

The Ecuadorian agrarian reform was carried out under several laws, but the most developed of them was linked to a military government. In his fourth term as president (1960–1961), Velasco Ibarra named the first national commission for agrarian reform, but, overthrown by his successor Carlos Julio Arosemena, it went no further. In 1963 the military in turn overthrew Arosemena amid violent anti-Castro rhetoric, and in 1964 it promoted the first agrarian reform laws, establishing the Ecuadorian Institute of Agrarian Reform and Colonization (IERAC) to negotiate between landlords and angry *huasipungueros*. What was at stake in this limited reform, of course, was not the existence of the haciendas but only minimal portions of their land. Up to 1966 the law had benefited just 18,160 families with an average of 4.7 hectares per family,[15] and by 1969 the average distributed per family already had been reduced to 3.5 hectares, probably representing the same acreage to which peasants had already had usufruct rights in the past.[16] Nevertheless this limited redistribution was enough to increase internal differences among the peasantry.

The titling of *huasipungo* lands was just a small part of a larger project. In tune with the fashion of the times, more emphasis was placed on the colonization of what remained of the Ecuadorian Amazon than on redistribution. From 1960 on, the building of new roads speeded penetration of the tropical forest. In 1964 Law 2171 was passed, regulating "empty lands" (the term ignored the swidden cultivators already present) and colonization by ranchers, along with a process of allotment, transfer of population, and concessions to businesses. These processes mattered much more than the agrarian reform proper. During the 10 years ending in 1975, 76 percent of the total number of families who were granted

[15] Ibarra (1987), 65. [16] Santana (1988), 294.

lands received them for purposes of colonization, and this tendency became even more pronounced in later years.[17] It is no coincidence that the Shuar Federation emerged in 1960, the same year that the highway cut into the jungle. I return to this theme later in the chapter.

As in the other countries, the dominant discourse of the time was "peasantist," in both the government and the political parties. Trying to create a Catholic alternative to the Communist FEI, the Ecuadorian Confederation of Catholic Workers (CEDOC) began campaigning in the countryside, creating a rural branch that after 1968 was called FENOC (National Federation of Peasant Organizations). It was a sign of the times that before long the last letters of CEDOC would be reglossed to mean "of Classist Workers."

The limitations of the agrarian reform in the Quichua-speaking highlands stood in painful contrast to the hopes of its prospective beneficiaries. In 1965 some began new land invasions, takeovers of facilities and livestock, demonstrations, and other means of pressure. The most active were cultivators who were not actually *huasipungueros* but who had only precarious access to land and remained completely neglected by the 1964 law. This sector was markedly Indian, and its mobilizations took on an increasingly ethnic coloration, even though the government and its various leftist adversaries tacitly agreed to ignore the fact. The phenomenon of de facto, and then purposefully ethnic, Indian mobilization would grow in importance in the next period.

The government, which responded to all these mobilizations with a combination of legal maneuvers and repression, fell in 1966. The governments that followed initiated hardly any agrarian measures, but in 1973 the new military regime of Guillermo Rodríguez Lara, drafted a second and more significant agrarian reform law. The economic context had changed. After 1972 the discovery and exploitation of oil created a boom to replace bananas and cacao. In agriculture, credit and technification made possible a surge of agricultural exports and a rise in the power of modern – that is, agroindustrial-minded – landlords. But it also made possible better service to small farmers in terms of basic services, credit, infrastructure, and payment for expropriations. Oil posed a new threat to lowland ethnic groups, because along with oil exploration came merchants, logging firms, and agroindustrial concerns. These ethnic groups reacted, following the Shuar example, by organizing to fight for their

[17] Ibarra (1987), 67, 219.

territory and resources. Under these circumstances the second agrarian reform of 1973, taking warning from the land invasions of earlier years, prohibited all violation of property rights. At the same time, it took productive efficiency as its criterion, steering oil resources toward agroindustrial development and, to a lesser extent, to small producers.

In truth the law of 1973 was not so much an agrarian reform as a funeral for the philosophy of agrarian reform. It opened the way to a program of capitalist agricultural and livestock development that would simply cease to treat inequalities of tenure as problematic. One statistic from 1974 demonstrates this succinctly: 48 percent of land was in the hands of just 2 percent of the owners of farms of 500 or more hectares, and another 6.8 percent of land jammed 70 percent of owners into small parcels of 0 to 5 hectares.

Peru: A Gamut of Proposals and Invasions

Peru, which had led the indigenous Andean debate and mobilization in the first decades of the century, lost its leading role after 1930. Of course the debates of earlier years left their mark. In the constitutional congress of 1931–1932, the status of indigenous communities as juridical persons was recognized, although not their traditional form of organization. The Communist Party itself in its 1931 program cited the right of Indians to create their own culture, be educated in their own language, and organize themselves into independent governments – Quechua and Aymara republics – in strict alliance with workers. Also in 1931, on a more practical level, the first bilingual education projects began in Huanta, Ayacucho, followed in 1933 in Juliaca by the opening of "Rijchary" ('awakening') centers under the teaching guidance of Manuel Núñez Butrón.

The dominant image, however, is still that of loss of interest in Indian affairs. One direct cause was Leguía's fall from power in 1930. The same year saw the premature deaths of Mariátegui and the indigenista Urviola. More symptomatic, the voice and action of the Indians themselves was heard less than in the past. Another style took its place, as in the other countries: one tied less to the past and more to new forms of political action originating in the capital and in capitalism. The change can be explained in more structural terms by the fact that Peru first felt the effects of the Great Depression more pronouncedly than Ecuador or Bolivia, and it then was able to take better advantage of the possibilities for rebounding exports provided by World War II and the postwar period. Above all after 1939, with Manuel Prado's presidency, capitalism made strides that were consolidated under Manuel Odría's military regime starting in 1948. Their policies, supported by the export-business bourgeoisie, give impetus to suddenly expanding migration from the highlands to the cities and the agroindustrial enterprises of the coast.

Lima saw for the first time the formation of a shantytown by "invasion" in 1946. Before long, festivals of highland music filled Lima stadiums. A massive transformation of the country was beginning, one whose later stage José Matos Mar would call "the people in overflow" (*desborde popular*). The 1940 census registered a national growth up to 5.8 million, as against 1.9 million in 1900; 51 percent were registered as Indians, and only 16 percent as whites. In 1940 the highlands still accounted for 75 percent of the national population, and Lima only had 645,000 inhabitants. But within 20 years the coastal population would grow from 25 percent to 39 percent of the total population.

In the highland countryside there were 3,200 registered indigenous communities. The advance of capitalism was reflected not so much in new encroachments upon them as in modernizing efforts on numerous haciendas, especially the wool estates of the Sierra. In Puno, for example, 1932 to 1952 constituted a period that Tamayo characterized as one "of false peace and technological modernization of highland livestock."[18] Wool modernization required the elimination of old servile forms of labor (which, among other inconveniences, entailed paternalistic bonds to workers) and of those highland herders called *huacchilleros*, who tended *waqchu*, or "orphan" livestock lacking a clear owner. One motive for mechanical modernization was to counteract the loss of cheap labor that resulted from migration to the coast. But these changes also reflected the greater pressure that workers on other haciendas were exerting to improve their work conditions. The election and presidency of the populist José Luis Bustamante (1945–1948), coinciding with an economic slump and political unrest, opened a brief period during which these demands were more openly expressed and even led to the first recoveries of lands previously lost by communities. A contributing force was the Confederation of Peruvian Workers (CTP), founded in 1944 under the control of the now more centrist APRA party. It supported several of these reformist mobilizations and also campaigned for massive recognition of worker and peasant unions on a national level.

[18] (1982) pp. 102–110.

This uninnovative period – modernizing in economic terms, pro-development politically, union-oriented in popular organization, indigenist only in certain cultural circles – was to last until 1956. But 1956 opened another period of more than 10 extremely agitated years.

The dominant form of action from 1956 on was the massive land invasion, by native communities or by hacienda workers, often allied with unions supported by leftist parties.[19] This method, stimulated by the Bolivian agrarian revolution, began on the coast and quickly spread through the highlands, covering a much larger geographic area than had past actions and often reviving longstanding local conflicts. Relations with unions and parties favored an initial leadership originating in the cities (especially in state struggles). Other leaders arose from intermediate rural strata now attuned to the cities, the sort of people whom Quijano, putting a pejorative term for nonwhites to a new use, called "emerging *cholos.*"

But in most of the Andean highlands, the incipient expansion was above all the initiative of the native communities themselves. In them an underlying ethnic identity remained very much alive irrespective of ideological currents among the leaders. One of the many examples compiled by Kapsoli is illustrative. In 1964 the police repressed an uprising in Shumpillán, Ancash, causing several deaths. According to the police report, the rebellious community members, besides cheering "Long live Communism!", spoke of going as far as distant Cusco, and used an expression popular during the eighteenth-century uprising of Tupac Amaru II as well as the nineteenth-century rebellion of Atusparia: to drink *chicha* (corn beer) from the enemy's skull.

The two major theaters of action in this period were the valley of La Convención, in the eastern subtropical area of the department of Cusco, and the central highlands east of Lima, where there were haciendas owned by the U.S. mining company Cerro de Pasco. In La Convención the steep hilly lands of the tenant farmers, formerly considered marginal lands, had recently become more profitable than the low-lying lands owned by the estate lords because of new technologies and the rising price of coffee. This bolstered tenants' resolve to consolidate tenure and win control of their own working time. In 1958, following a strike by

[19] The FENCAP and the CCP stand out. FENCAP (of the APRA party), active on the coast, and the new CCP (Peasant Confederation of Peru, supported by the Communist Party) would both play an important role in the decades to follow.

hacienda serfs, the Peasant Confederation of La Convención and Lares was established. This confederation, under the leadership of the legendary Trotskyist Hugo Blanco, with its motto "land or death," won its stripes in the general strike of 1962 and became the nucleus for the creation of the Peasant Federation of Cusco in 1961. These developments were harshly repressed – for example, in Chaullay, where peasants were machine-gunned while they crossed a bridge.

The actions in the Sierra Central began in 1959 when some 1,200 *comuneros* retook the Paria hacienda, which had been appropiated by the mining concern in 1914. (This incident was to inspire Manuel Scorza's novel *Redoble por Rancas.*) Despite police repression the movement quickly spread to other haciendas in the area and into the neighboring department of Junín. In 1962 and 1963 alone, some 200 haciendas were invaded, with 500 to 3,000 peasants participating in each assault and affecting a total of more than 50,000 hectares.[20] This volatile state of affairs brought down more than ordinary police repression. The tenor of the times became clear in 1962, when the APRA leader Haya de la Torre won the presidental election. Although General Pérez Godoy's military coup stopped him from taking power, he felt obligated immediately to write a first agrarian reform law, which was limited to the parcelization of disputed lands in the Sierra Central and La Convención. In 1963 Fernando Belaúnde won the presidental election with a platform of agrarian reform and even using touches of a rhetoric appealing to Inka themes, which was especially effective in Cusco. Upon taking power he promoted the "Popular Cooperation" program (resembling that of "community development" in Bolivia), but resident workers on haciendas responded with a new, massive wave of land seizures in the Sierra Central and Cusco, which spread into neighboring departments. Belaúnde had no choice but to pass Law 15037, an agrarian reform law, this time of national scope. But at the same time, he ordered severe repression, producing several massacres and the arrest of the main leaders. In any event the new law, far from calming the situation, radicalized it.

Also in 1964 Luis de La Puente Uceda broke away from APRA to form the new Revolutionary Left Movement (MIR) and published what was then a novel prognosis: "The revolution is moving through the countryside . . . [because it is] the weakest aspect of the system . . . [and the peasantry] the most numerous and exploited class."[21] He was refer-

[20] Quijano (1979), 87. [21] Cited in Kapsoli (1987), 104.

ring to guerrillas, who began actions on three fronts in June 1965: in Mesa Pelada (La Convención, Cusco), under his own direction and with the support of Hugo Blanco and his followers; in Concepción and Jauja (Junín) with Guillermo Lobatón and Máximo Velando, also of the MIR; and in La Mar Province (Ayacucho) with Hector Béjar of the National Liberation Army (ELN). This initiative was led by urban people whose contact with the local community members was remote. "Language was always the barrier that separated the insurgents from the natives," Béjar recognized.[22] They were defeated by Belaúnde's army, but Belaúnde had already lost all credibility as a leader able to solve the increasingly explosive agrarian problem.

This was the situation, then, when General Juan Velasco Alvarado took power. He was a military man who offered Peru an unprecedented revolution. Key to it was an agrarian reform of a new sort, put into motion in 1969 with Decree-Law 17716. Its central point, inspired in part by the Yugoslavian model, was the transformation of the haciendas into various types of self-sustaining collective businesses known as SAIS (Agricultural Societies in the Social Interest), CAPS (Agrarian Cooperatives for Social Production), and others. This initiative, together with rigid control by the military state, was intended to maintain a high level of production on the ex-estates and at the same time transfer capital and professionals to coastal industrialization, which would itself be the object of other self-management reforms. These plans were quite different from the mere parcelization that occurred in other countries and also from the routinized nationalization of businesses in socialist countries. At first they created heady expectations in Peru and abroad. Nevertheless before long the community members and peasants developed an ambiguous attitude to the new reform.

The Velasco government's far-reaching reform went much deeper and was more popular than any earlier undertaking in Peru. It really did shake the old power structure of the sierra to its foundations in the hegemony of *gamonales* (abusive rural bosses), so much so that in 1974 the National Agrarian Society, a lobby of landlords and estate-owners, was officially dissolved (DL 19400). And it really did stimulate peasant political participation, supporting a new national organization, the CNA (National Agrarian Confederation), with several leaders of solidly Andean heritage and great popular wisdom, such as the Quechua Saturnino

[22] (1973), p. 143.

Huillca. It even seemed to take traditional culture into account, enacting in 1970 a Statute of Peasant Communities, Supreme Decree 37-70-A, and in 1974 a law for the native communities of the jungle and eastern Andean areas (DL 20653). In 1975 it marked a first for the whole continent by making Quechua an official language (DL 21156; this was later to be included in the Constitution of 1979). Quechua supplements immediately appeared in two Lima newspapers.

Despite all this the reforms did not quite take hold, mostly because the start-up costs were too high, and because they were opposed by the powerful. In the end Velasco was replaced by the more complaisant General Morales Bermúdez, who stood close to the old status quo. But the downfall of the reform was also due in part to its rejection by the indigenous peasant sector itself, for multiple reasons: the excessive size of the proposed enterprises, the exclusion of the free-standing (non-estate) communities, and the state-imposed, top–down organization through which the reform was carried out.

The disproportionate size of the new ex-estates – some occupied more than 30,000 hectares – made it difficult to manage them efficiently and made a mockery of self-management for the intended beneficiaries. They perceived the reform as a mere change of owner, as well they might when they observed that old overseers could stay in their jobs, now as administrators of the hacienda-cum-SAIS, or when they saw state functionaries and agronomists imposed on small cooperatives that neither wanted nor could afford extra staff. Even more troubling, the free-standing native communities – even more land-starved than the formerly enserfed communities – felt excluded from the process, so that the proposal actually increased polarization in agriculture. The top–down manner in which reform was implemented made the state seem merely a new boss, more powerful and omnipresent than the old ones. The statute of communities, for example, demanded, with little input from the concerned parties, the community institutions of several centuries' standing transform themselves into cooperative-type structures. The main sign of the state's omnipresence was SINAMOS (National System of Social Aid and Mobilization, a punning acronym that could also be read 'without bosses'). SINAMOS was conceived in 1972 as a mass organization to help promote changes, but in practice it turned into a feared instrument of rural control.

The result was another decade of peasant turmoil, especially in free-standing communities and other sectors marginalized by the reform. They now began to fight to recover lands from their giant neighbors, the reformed enterprises. In 1973 this began with a wave of land takeovers in the far northern regions of Piura and Cajamarca, populated by hispanicized Indians. In July and August 1974, a new front opened in Andahuaylas where 20,000 peasants took over several public offices and projects, took charge of sixty properties not affected by the agrarian reform, and created their own, traditional-style reform: division into family parcels with certain stipulated communal activities. The leader Lino Quintanilla remembers that "the first sowing was allotted to the *aypu* (sharing-out). . . . This first collective work was not wage labor . . . instead the whole yield was finally distributed equitably," not neglecting the elderly and orphans.[23] In this context organizations that earlier had found only local followings took on national dimensions. Events in Andahuaylas polarized peasants into the camps of two organizations: the CNA (National Agrarian Confederation), which was state-sponsored, and the left-opposition CCP, or Peruvian Peasant Confederation. The failure of Velasco's bold reform became the preamble to a new period, which would prove equally conflictive and polarized, but one in which the communities would again play leading roles.

Colombia: A Decaffeinated Reform and Its Counterreform

In Colombia the democratic-oligarchic regime lasted until the 1940s, with only two interruptions. In 1930 the Liberal Party assumed power because of a split in the Conservative Party. Then after 1942 a possible alternative appeared on the scene in the person of Jorge Eliécer Gaitán. It was quickly aborted by his assassination in the so-called "Bogotá Hit" (*Bogotazo*) of 1948. Political unrest, until now centered in the cities, immediately spread to the countryside, where it became chronic and entered history simply as "La Violencia" ('the violence'). Political conflict began as a Liberal reaction to the ultra-Conservative Laureano Gómez's efforts to keep his party eternally in power, and it soon divided the countryside into irreconcilable bands of Liberals and Conservatives. Over the years violent conflict took diverging forms, social protest and banditry. In 1965 Eric Hobsbawm characterized this phenomenon as "the

[23] Cited in García-Sayán (1982), 90.

greatest armed mobilization of peasants (guerrillas, bandits and self-defense groups) in the recent history of the western hemisphere," save for some periods of the Mexican Revolution.

This then was the picture in 1953 when Gustavo Rojas Pinilla's military coup momentarily upset the oligarchic system of democracy, but the old order returned with renewed vigor in 1958 under the new "national pact," which assured a long-term alternation in power between Liberals and Conservatives. This situation had repercussions in the indigenous Andean region of the south, especially Tolima, where Quintín Lame remained active and where, even before La Violencia took hold, systematic violence by estate-owners against communities was widespread.

At the state level the only new development was the creation of the Indigenist Institute of Colombia in 1943. The institute took its inspiration from the continent-wide agreements made at the Pátzcuaro Congress, where several justly renowned Colombian academics represented their country, including Gregorio Hernández de Alba, Gerardo Reichel-Dolmatoff, Alicia Reichel-Dolmatoff, Antonio García, and Juan Friede. The institute played some part in the struggle against the division of those Indian reserves that were already "civilized." Not until Law 81 was passed in 1958 did the practice of dividing up reserves without consent cease. Three years later, in 1961, an agrarian reform law was passed (Law 135), one that generally took hold although it was hindered by the cautionary recommendations of the Alliance for Progress, which the oligarchy used its considerable power to enforce. The law created INCORA, the Colombian Institute of Agrarian Reform, whose goals and practices were limited to smoothing over the effects of La Violencia by creating infrastructural adjustments, relocating people to areas of colonization, and, in agreement with landlords, the redistribution of some uncultivated lands to peasants. In regard to indigenous peoples, INCORA was in charge of the redistribution of reserves as well as other basic services to the peasantry, such as assigning additional lands, extending credit, organizing cooperatives, and so on. In 1962, after 10 years of negotiating with the government, the Summer Institute of Linguistics (a U.S.-based Protestant mission active in linguistic research) began to operate in the lowland regions, which by now were being colonized.

Despite its modest goals and bureaucratic lethargy, this reform provoked a strong reaction by landlords, who began to expel tenant farmers and sharecroppers, which led in turn to defensive actions on the part of peasants. These actions also mobilized Indians, especially those more connected to estates. The land takeovers and other actions that began in 1964 were harshly repressed. In the face of this situation, the new president Carlos Lleras Restrepo put into play in 1966 a reform program that placed more emphasis on development for small producers, and sought greater popular participation through organizations established and controlled by the government. The major one was the ANUC, National Organization of Peasant Land Tenants, initiated on the local level together with a Communal Action program (similar to community development programs in other countries), and finally consolidated as a national organization in 1970. Through ANUC the state meant to stem the radicalization of peasant struggles by giving certain concessions, and to increase the government's popularity in the countryside. In the specific case of Indians, the idea of distinguishing between "jungle" and "acculturated" groups remained in force. "Acculturated" groups were those of the Andean region, the Sibundoy Valley, and the Guajira Peninsula. For "jungle" groups the reserves were to remain in effect, but for "acculturated" groups the state proposed "a new type of land tenure that would protect them and at the same time expand production."[24]

The major accomplishments, however, were those initiated from below – in the indigenous sector. One 1967 case stands out in the department of Huila, where Indians recovered lands that had been held by Monseñor Vallejo, the local bishop. In the same period in the Cauca Valley, the estate-dependant peasants of Chimán and Credo began a similar struggle. ANUC developed an agenda of its own. It planned and after February 1971 carried out a national wave of land invasions on haciendas: In that month alone there were 316 cases in thirteen departments with the participation of 16,000 families; in 1971 this figure reached 654 cases. In August of the following year, ANUC organized a massive march in which peasants from all corners of the country would converge on the capital. The march began simultaneously in many places, but the army promptly repressed it.[25]

Andean Indians, who were of course peasants too, were massively involved in the invasions as well as the march. In that same crucial month of February 1971, an important meeting of 2,000 Páez and Guambiano Indians in Toribío created the CRIC (Regional Indigenous Council of Cauca). Although CRIC was born as part of ANUC, its mere existence added an ethnic dimension to the class issues then in vogue. In

[24] Dirección General de Integración (1971), 22, 41–44. [25] Rivera (1987), 96–97, 121, 141–142.

effect, from its birth CRIC combined agrarian demands, such as exemption from labor obligations and recovery of usurped *resguardo* lands, with culturally informed platform points such as the strengthening of their *cabildos* (traditional councils), the defense of language and culture, and the modification of the still-standing Law 89 of 1890, which classified indigenous people as legal minors (CRIC, 1988: 9–13). The organization grew so vigorously that in its few first years of existence it managed to recover more than 5,000 hectares. CRIC would continue to make its mark on Colombian indigenous history in the decades to follow.

The main power blocs in the National Front, which now frowned on Lleras's innovations, reacted severely against the growing rural mobilization. As a result the 1970s witnessed a harsh backlash, beginning with the controversial election of Misael Pastrana in 1970. Reaction increased even more after an informal agreement made between government and the landowning sector in Chicoral in January 1972. After this there were drastic changes in INCORA to "reform the reform," and a period of repression led to a rupture between the government and ANUC. Finally, Laws 4 and 5 of 1973 rang the death knell for Lleras's reformist attempts and opened the way for large-scale mechanized capitalist agriculture. Amidst these changes ANUC divided into two opposed branches, one named after the city of Armenia, which supported the state and did little, and the other named after Sinalejo, which won CRIC support and acted in opposition.

The Singular Case of the Mapuche in Chile

Events in the Mapuche area of southern Chile (see Map 25.2) are well worth analyzing in greater detail, because they form an interesting counterpoint to the other Andean nations. The focal point was the controversial Law 4169 promoted by President Ibáñez in 1927, which mandated the division of Mapuche communal lands, very much in keeping with modernizing and homogenizing tendencies all over the continent. This law evoked a reaction from the Mapuche societies opposed to breakup. Against such pressure, in 1930–1931 Ibáñez himself promoted Laws 4802 and 4111, which softened the previous stance, stipulating that division must be requested by at least a third of the *comuneros*. This was still not much of a concession. The historian Alejandro Lipschutz remarked it was "as if a third of investors could dissolve a corporation!"[26] But this

[26] (1956), p. 156–163.

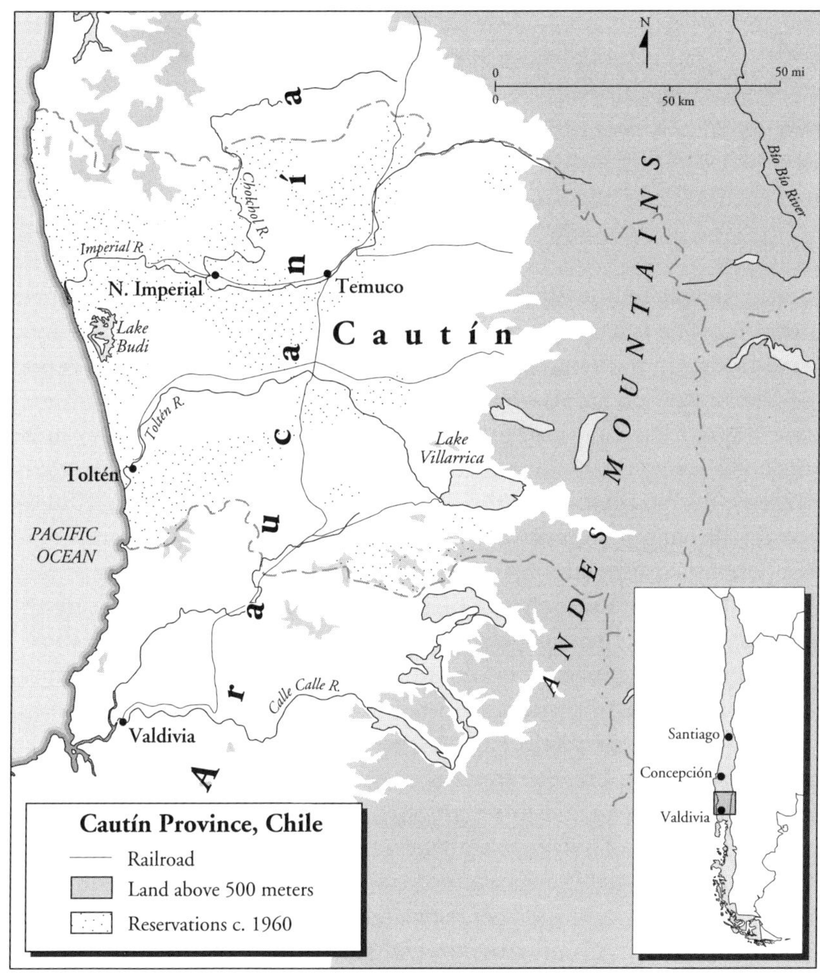

Map 25.2

small victory showed the Mapuche that they could modify and influence the decisions of the state.

This debate strengthened the position of those who opposed division, stimulated the defense of ethnic identity, and facilitated a rapprochement between the two most important organizations. One, the Araucanian Federation, had always defended communal land titling as a guarantee of indigenous identity. Its leader still was Manuel Aburto Panguilef. In its Eleventh Congress in 1931, the federation proposed "the constitution of an Indigenous Republic . . . in which the Araucanian People would govern itself and in which its progress and culture would be self-created."[27] Years later in its Eighteenth Congress in 1938, the priority given to strengthening cultural values remained clear:

> The morning is dedicated "to paying homage to the Allmighty and his Holy Ministry, as well as to all the caciques of Araucania, to their virtues and to the official flag, at 5 A.M. . . . homage that will consist of 28 leaps in unison shouting 'ya!' and with arms raised with flags and lances." They also exhorted the Mapuches "not to continue baptizing their children in the Catholic Church".[28]

But it was in the rival Caupolicán Society that the major changes occurred. The old guard, mainly pro-division, was replaced in 1931 by a new group led by Venancio Coñuepán, a rich 25-year-old merchant and descendant of the *lonkos* who had supported the Euro-Chileans, or *huincas*. He soon distinguished himself as the preeminent figure of the entire period. Relying on his personal experience and that of other merchant leaders, he proposed that the Mapuche win equality within Chilean society through economic success. He rose quickly and won tremendous support by creating an efficient Indigenous Credit Association operated by the Mapuche themselves. On this platform, and that of halting the division of family plots, several attempts at unification began in late 1930. They finally came to fruition in 1938 with the formation of the Araucanian Corporation, in which the traditional mystique of Panguilef combined with the entrepreneurial spirit of Coñuepán. The Mapuche would no longer aspire just to Westernize themselves but also to legitimize themselves as *lonkos* and to be educated in ancestral wisdom. At first the traditional logic of this independence-minded people prevailed. The societies meant to ally themselves only for specific purposes, and the component groups would not lose their autonomy. But after 1952 almost all action was catalyzed under the unifying auspices of the Araucanian Corporation, led by Coñuepán. It came to be, in Foerster's phrase, "a sort of Mapuche party," while the elder leader Panguilef fell into eclipse as he became increasingly absorbed in mystic visions of a utopian indigenous republic.

The corporation maintained a permanent, flexible relationship with the state and with the political groups that fought to control it. This was scarcely a new direction; as early as 1924–1925 the Mapuche had managed to elect congressmen. But the Mapuche presence in the state now became more pronounced. Chile, after having weathered the nitrate and copper

[27] Foerster-Montecino (1988), 49–50. [28] Foerster-Montecino (1988), 146–148.

crises during the Depression, was entering a period of heavy industrialization and still sought to develop its south. This could occur by means of the division and sale of "merced" (recently titled) lands, but those who aspired to govern there had to depend on a Mapuche constituency, drawn from a population of between 100,000 and 200,000 people. The Mapuche, in turn, needed more influence in the government to carry out their proposals. This explains in part the contradictions between the far-reaching modernizing proposals and certain local concessions to the Mapuche.

From 1930 to 1960 the political scene was still dominated, despite a few fluctuations, by people like Arturo Alessandri and his old minister of war, General Ibáñez. These men took positions farther to the right than in previous decades, but they continued to enjoy the pragmatic support of the main Mapuche leaders, who were convinced that they could only achieve their objectives by maintaining good relations with the government. Coñuepán consistently backed Ibáñez. After other failed attempts, in 1945 he finally won a seat as congressional deputy, an office that he would later leave only to assume important cabinet posts, including that of minister of Land and Colonization, vital to Mapuche interests. In 1953 his Araucanian Corporation gained two more congressional seats and twelve municipal council seats. This period witnessed the high tide of Mapuche participation in political power. Once installed in these positions, the main Mapuche leaders did more than docilely follow the orders of the parties that had helped them to ascend. They showed considerable independence in formulating an indigenous project.

Their determination paid off on several fronts. The main one was, of course, the defense of territory. Between 1941 and 1946 the government was working on a legal project that read in part (Art. 15): "The Tribunals for Indians will liquidate the Indian lands with land grant titles [*títulos de merced*], definitively relocating their community members on the lands that they were occupying."[29] In fact, according to data from 1949, the process of division had created 793 "reductions" totaling 126,749 hectares – that is, one-fourth of the total, and the parallel process of land alienation is estimated to have affected another 100,000 hectares.[30] Nevertheless in the teeth of this momentum, the new Mapuche movement commanded by Coñuepán in 1947 forced a new rule, Law 8736, to restrict at last the division and sale of Mapuche lands.

Encouraged by this triumph, the Araucanian Corporation launched a

[29] Lipschutz (1956), 162–163. [30] Babarovic et al. (1987), 46.

new and bolder program, a first on the whole continent: a "Mapuche law," proposed by the Mapuche themselves. In addition to prohibiting the division of land, among other points, it also included the creation of a Corporation of Indigenous Affairs and an Indigenist Institute, and the complete reform of Law 4111 of 1931, subject to review by a commission of Indians. Several months later the new Ministry of Land and Colonization presented a draft law that addressed several of these ideas. All these demands were supported by mobilizations of thousands of Mapuche.

In 1952 Ibáñez returned to the presidency, now espousing more populist attitudes at least in relation to the Mapuche. They supported him with tremendous marches in which ancestral rites were in no short supply. Coñuepán called him the defender of "the race," comparing him to Franklin Roosevelt and Mexico's Lázaro Cárdenas. All this praise helped them to realize other political dreams: the creation of an Indigenous Affairs Bureau with Mapuche participation, placement of their people in the most controversial Indian courts, freedom from taxes, and creation of a credit fund for indigenous projects channeled especially through 300 organized groups.

It was too much. The Corporación Araucana came under attack especially from the local oligarchy. Non-Mapuches complained in Parliament that "a state within the state" was being created, a "political machine . . . among people of fairly low culture . . . who have the very special peculiarity of speaking a language different from the one spoken by ordinary Chileans," and which might foment "a minoritarian feeling that never before existed." Similar complaints emerged in the press:

> All vernacular languages have words that damn the white man and the mestizo, and in their pagan rites exorcisms against the civilizing inspiration abound. . . . What would the United States have been if that great country had permitted the criterion of red skin to predominate over the mission of progress? . . . Don Alonso [de Ercilla] and his absurd poem [*La Araucana*, a national classic] cause more and more damage. Among us, tolerance for the Indian hovers on the brink of lunacy. This is no longer romantic sensitivity but foolishness.[31]

The campaign had a crushing effect. In the 1957 elections the Corporación Araucana lost all its congressmen, despite having backed the victor Alessandri. The division of communities began anew, the Indian courts were lost, and the corporation was split.

In this context Mapuche history passed its baton to a new type of

[31] Cited in Foerster-Montecino (1988), 235–240.

society, more concerned with the economic struggle than with Mapuche cultural identity or *lonko* ancestral lineage, and much more consistently tied to the leftist parties that were growing rapidly throughout the country. At the end of 1953, the National Association of Indians was born, directed by the veteran Mapuche laborer and fighter Martín Painemal. This association was tied above all to coal-miner unions and to the Popular Socialist Party of the future president Salvador Allende.[32] Its motto was "the unity of the Mapuches and the poor Chileans," and its platform included cultural issues, but these were subordinated to a socialist focus. Thus in its first congress it called for instruction in the mother tongue and rejected the subdivision of communities, espousing instead their transformation into cooperatives. Martín Painemal said of Coñuepan: "They were racists, pure indigenous race. They said that we were serving the white Chileans. We said that there was no reason to be divided, that we had to unite in brotherhood with the working class."[33] In Mapuche Chile, then, we see once again the same processes that dominated the scene in other Andean nations starting in Mariátegui's distant era, the 1920s and 1930s.

Despite low electoral support the new style of Mapuche leftist politics won the upper hand, especially given the rising concern for agrarian reform in Chile as in the entire continent. A potently symbolic event came in 1964 with the historic compromise between the presidential candidate Allende and the Mapuche leftist organizations on the Cerro Ñielol, the very hill that had been the last bastion of Araucanian resistance in 1881. The act of compromise began by promising respect for religion, whether traditional, Catholic, or Protestant, and went on to reiterate demands similar to those of 1953, now within the broader context of a future agrarian reform.

However, it was not Allende who won the election, but Frei. The

[32] Mapuche workers branded Coñuepán and his followers "lackeys of the government and unconditional servants of Yankee imperialism." On the other hand, the indigenista and Communist *diputado* Lipschutz understood and supported in Parliament Coñuepán's juggler stance. The critics, it must be said, were not completely wrong. After his fall Coñuepán continued to hold positions of power, such as in the Banco del Estado, but he showed an increasingly opportunistic attitude. Thus in 1961, in order to stay in the government, he did not oppose Law 14511, which put back in force the *juzgados de indios* and division of lands, which he had attacked before. Even more significant, in 1965 Coñuepán was a Diputado, now of the United Conservative party, but in his campaign he no longer referred to his Indian roots but only to his various public offices. He was to die 2 years later and was eulogized by the Mapuche, despite his rightist stance (Foerster y Montecino 1988:238–240, 294, 351–354).

[33] Foerster-Montecino (1988), 250–263.

latter, with his Christian Democratic party, sought a middle path between the old-guard Conservatives and an increasingly dynamic left. In 1967 the new government drafted Law 16640, an agrarian reform with substantial support from the peasantry. It was hoped that this law would be thoroughly applied in the Mapuche area where, according to one contemporary study, some 61 percent of families had access to less than 10 hectares, and 67 percent did not even own a yoke of oxen. Nevertheless only a few estates were expropriated there, and scarcely 1,443 hectares were restored to communities – a pitiful figure compared to the 3.7 million hectares expropriated in the whole country.

For this reason the number of leftist Mapuche organizations increased, and the Indian grassroots groups became more radical. In 1965 in Temuco the Indigenous Movement of Chile was formed, with Juan Huichalaf and Melillán Painemal as leaders. In 1966 in the same area, indigenous university organizations arose, associated with Vicente Mariqueo. In 1969 the veteran leader of coal-mining unionism, Rosendo Huanumán, founded the Luis Emilio Recabarren Federation, also a leftist group. Spontaneous land takeovers began in 1967, the same year as the agrarian reform, and proliferated at the end of the Frei period, in contrast to the slow pace of expropriations. Thus began what has been called the "Mapuche explosion."[34]

In 1970 Salvador Allende won the presidency, and the socialist regime of Popular Unity took hold. It was time to make good on the promises sealed 6 years before on Ñielol hill. The newly launched Confederation of Mapuche Societies took charge of reminding Allende about those promises and of advancing the "Mapuche explosion." At the end of 1970, the lands taken over measured more than 100,000 hectares. In December 1970, when the confederation had grown stronger, it convoked a great Second Mapuche Congress in which the major organizations, old and new, participated. The invited guests were President Allende and the ministers of Agriculture and of Land and Colonization. The Mapuche question was so important that the Minister of Agriculture, Jacques Chonchol, moved his base of operations to Temuco for 2 months. Results were not long in coming. In 1971 the government had already returned some 68,381 hectares of usurped lands to the Mapuches. Although this represented only half of the territory usurped since the

[34] Bavarovic et al. (1987), 55, 60.

"pacification," it was far more than the 1,441 hectares of the previous period.

The logical complement to these measures was institutional reform and improved legislation for the Mapuche. In the Second Congress of 1970 Law 14511, which was still in force as the base of all legislation and of land division, was roundly criticized. As a counterproposal Martín Alonqueo, leader of the Confederation of Mapuche Societies, presented a detailed Preliminary Draft Law on the Corporation of Mapuche Development. This group clearly recalled many actions of the Araucanian Corporation between 1930 and 1956. But these events now took shape in a more explicitly leftist context, with more emphasis on economics than on ethnicity. Financing was not sought directly from the state but from civil society through municipal taxes. In 1972 the government took up the challenge and approved the Indian Law (Ley de Indígenas, no. 17729), the fruit of lengthy consultations with the Mapuche people, begun in 1964 and greatly intensified in the early 1970s.[35] Among other points the new law recognized as Indians those who were indigenous by language and culture even if they did not have lands granted *de merced.* Communal property was declared inalienable to outsiders. If a community member left, he was to be indemnified for his labor, but his land would remain in the community. Communal land was to be indivisible; if the majority requested it, use rights could be parceled to families, but the family parcels would still be communal property. To speed up the processes of return, restitution, and expropriation, the Institute of Indigenous Development was created and charged with coordinating these actions with the Agrarian Reform Council.

But all these changes were cut off in 1973 with Augusto Pinochet's brutal military coup, which steered the country and the Mapuche people onto another course. Although Chile's reform had been more radical, it too ended in counterreform.

THE RETURN OF THE INDIAN (1973–1990s)

Overview

Between 1970 and 1990 virtually the entire region witnessed the return, with unexpected vigor and almost in simultaneity, of specifically indige-

[35] I was privileged to converse at length about this subject with the leader Melillán Paine-mal, who died in 1991, and who played a fundamental role in this whole process.

nous issues that had seemingly been put to rest once and for all in the 1950s. This came as a surprise to sociologists and political scientists. I now describe the most significant aspects of resurgent ethnicity on the heels of several decades of modernizing and "peasantizing" ideology.

In all of the countries, new organizations more directly based on ethnic identity emerged. The Mapuche had long since had their own organizations in various political colors. Aside from them the first significant organization formed in this new period was the Shuar Federation, which coalesced in the Ecuadorian jungle as early as 1961. The beginning of the following decade saw the almost simultaneous birth of the CRIC, leading the Páez and Guambianos in the Colombian Andes, and two other large federations serving the Quechua and Aymara highland majorities: ECUARUNARI among the Quichua-speakers of Ecuador, and, most far-reachingly, the Katarista movement among the Bolivian Aymara. These initiatives came to fruition in the 1980s as still more inclusive institutions were created on the national level: ONIC in Colombia, CONAIE in Ecuador, and Bolivia's CSUTCB and CIDOB.

Only in the Peruvian highlands did this new organizational development fail to take hold. In the 1970s the new agrarian reform of Velasco Alvarado had only recently gotten underway. After that the upheaval created by reform failure, and convulsive violence of both guerrillas and armed forces, together with a chronic economic and structural crisis, impeded the emergence of new initiatives. Amid the terrifying Peruvian social landscape of the 1980s, almost all rural efforts were geared to simple survival. Following these beginnings, in Bolivia and Chile the dictatorships of Bánzer (1971–1978) and Pinochet (1973–1990), respectively, prevented a more rapid development. But as these regimes weakened, the developments of the early 1970s gained new force and caught up with other countries within and beyond the Andean orbit.

All of these countries, especially Ecuador in the 1970s, had produced at first rather Manichean debates between "classist" and "indigenist" organizations, but the two opposed positions had been converging toward a more synthetic common vision. Something similar occurred in Colombia. Although the peasant organization ANUC split and lost its momentum, the example of CRIC took hold among other Colombian indigenous peoples, and in a few years this would lead to the formation of the Organization of Colombian Indigenous Nationalities (ONIC), which united practically all of Colombia's numerous Amerindian peoples. In Colombia the ethnnic–class debate was far from theoretical; rather it was forced by a practical necessity in the form of leftist guerrillas present in several indigenous Andean areas.

In the Andean regions of Bolivia, and later Peru, the inadequacies of state-led reforms and of the organizational alternatives they proposed led to a reevaluation of the community, as a basic cell of all higher-level social organization. Peru did not advance past this point, but in Bolivia the rethinking went much further than in other countries. Bolivian activists were concerned first with the recuperation and defense of Quechua and Aymara identity itself; then with the formation of parties with strong ethnic representation, above all among the Aymaras; and finally with a complete reformulation of the nature of the Bolivian state, which they redefined as plurinational. In the CSUTCB, the major advocacy group for the peasantry, the class issue always had been closely tied to the ethnic one, as two dimensions to be analyzed jointly. It is interesting that it was precisely this trade-unionist organization of "peasants," the stars of so many campaigns for economic justice, that also promoted the establishment of an "assembly of nationalities" in a new "plurinational" state.

The lowland peoples of those two countries followed the general contours seen in Ecuador and Colombia, leading to the formation of the interethnic coordinating group AIDESEP in Peru, which inspired in turn the CIDOB in Bolivia. But in these two countries there was still no organic articulation between these lowland umbrella groups and those of the highland peoples.

Chile joined this pan-Andean movement after the restoration of democracy in 1990 and the creation of an Indian Law, which once more led the various Mapuche organizations to join up in a more or less temporary coordinating group. But the main innovation in Chile took place in the far north. There the Aymara community had fallen into a century of inactivity after the Chilean victory annexed their (previously Peruvian and Bolivian) territory, but even this deeply submerged group saw the emergence of explicitly Aymara organizations.

Another unique aspect of many of these organizations is the role that urban Indians played, including some who had spent long periods in the major capitalist countries. All Andean countries saw a tremendous increase in rural–urban migration from 1950 on. Lima went from having less than 700,000 inhabitants in 1940 to some 7 million in 1990, and it became an open secret that the heart of coastal Creole culture now had a distinctly "highland" flavor. (But change did not go so far as to wash the stigma from "Indian" identity.) Quito and La Paz, besides being national capitals, more and more became the natural poles for ethnic mobilization, because so many Andean people were already installed right inside them. The more overtly political expressions of this new Indian awakening were born and nourished principally among those new urban Indians, who no longer lived by working the soil but who, finding themselves rebuffed in their urban social ascent, transformed contempt into a cause and their culture, now more idealized than lived, into an ideology. In the city the most radically Indianist parties were born under slogans like "as Indians they exploited us, as Indians we liberate ourselves."

Finally these organizational efforts included attempts to transcend state boundaries, which had historically dismembered indigenous population blocs. Bolivian Katarismo extended to the Aymara region of southern Peru and had an undeniable influence in the awakening of the Aymaras of northern Chile, although the times did not ripen for multistate unity of the Aymara "nation." Meetings among Indians from various countries were held in Cusco (Peru), Tiwanaku (Bolivia), Quito (Ecuador), and other places. A first attempt to join together all those indigenous groups in a single South American entity called CISA (Coordination of Indians of South America) did not jell, in part because of excessively top–down and personalistic leadership. A more stable maximum-scale effort was the coordinating group COICA, which joined the lowland indigenous confederations of all countries that have Amazonian territory.

Various international indigenous organizations exist at higher levels and even worldwide, among which a few individuals of Andean origin have played important roles. But within these, formal articulation with major local organizations either does not exist or is still untested. A detailed treatment of this topic is beyond the scope of this chapter. The Columbian quincentennial year of 1992, evoking dissonant thoughts about a half-millenium of European "discovery," "invasion," "coverup," or, as one satirist put it, "tourism," occasioned a growing number of indigenous gatherings across the continent. As of this writing (May 1995), they have not yet yielded solid, stable organizations. It was one of those meetings, the Quito reunion of 1990, that produced the motto which all represented peoples decided to adopt: "500 years of resistance."

The ideology of many of the organizations just mentioned is more multifaceted than that of their precursors, centered as those were in peasant class issues. Economic issues continue to be the most important, beginning with the most basic one of reclaiming lands, and followed by others of more recent significance like credit, fair prices for products, technical assistance, and provision of basic services. But many more themes have been added. It is significant, for example, that even in Andean farming communities, doubtless influenced by those of Amazonia, the old slogan of the Mexican agrarian reform "the land to those who work it" – has given way to others like "our own territory." This new concept implies much more: the right to all the natural resources of the territory and a certain leeway to develop lifeways and forms of government autonomously. It also goes together with demands for education in American langages and dignified recognition of folk-religious traditions.

This wider vision also helps one understand why throughout all the Andean nations, concepts like "class" and "union," which so recently dominated the discourse, now seem painfully inadequate. Renewed importance is accorded to other terms, like "community," "indigenous," "native" (*originario*), and even, increasingly, "nationality" and "nation." The new terminology emphasizes that the identity of each people is something of their own making, not merely a synonym for affiliation to a state. But a standout difference from European nationalist movements is that here these groups do not demand transformation into separate states, except in the highly theoretical discourse of a few intellectuals.

One significant feature of this indigenous renaissance is the vigor with which new symbols have been developed to mark the differentiated identities of these groups. As was the case several decades ago when Africa decolonized, many groups are readopting and publicizing self-given names and rejecting colonial denominations. Today, for example, there are no longer Jívaros or Colorados in Ecuador, but Shuar and Tsáchila (also written Tsátchila), while the Peruvians formerly called Campa have successfully publicized their own name, Asháninka. At the same time that words like "Indian" and "indigenous" are taking on a positive connotation, these peoples also prefer to call themselves "nations," rejecting the state's monopoly on this term; in Bolivia they have also coined the term "first peoples" (*pueblos originarios*), dodging the pejorative overtones of the usual Spanish ethnonyms. Another class of symbols, traditional dress, has acquired value almost as formal wear in certain marches and public demonstrations. The rainbow-colored *wiphala* flag (an invented tradition representing the Qullasuyu kingdom, or the Tawantinsuyu Inka empire, or the indigenous-as-such, as the case may be) has claimed a prominent place in the streets of Andean cities and villages and appears on buttons, posters, caps, and movies. The *wiphala* flew in the largest indigenous demonstrations, like those of Ecuador and Bolivia in 1990 and in many others held in reaction to the 1992 quincentennary. One group creating an Andean theology has for many years distributed its own calendar-poster *Mara Wata* ('year' in Aymara and Quechua). Instead of the Catholic saint for each day, it suggests Aymara and Quechua names, noted daily on several radio stations. On these stations the use of indigenous languages and music, whether Quechua, Aymara, Shuar, or other local cultures, has proliferated. Indigenous languages are beginning to appear on several television channels and in a few print publications. The "American" continent has been rebaptized by indigenous organizations with the name Abya Yala, which in the language of the Kuna of Panama means "fertile virgin land."

The response of the states to ethnic resurgence has been lukewarm, and – in contrast to the agrarian reform issue of the 1960s and 1970s – none has has taken any proactive posture to meet it. But neither would it be accurate to say that everything has been accomplished solely by the struggle of indigenous peoples against an unbendingly resistant system. Some external circumstances also have favored their proposals. On the one hand, since the 1960s the presence of NGOs (nongovernmental organizations) has become increasingly important. Although their wide spectrum of concerns and alliances makes them almost incommensurable, many NGOs are much closer to local problems and more sensitive to indigenous peoples' issues and proposals than are most governments. In addition, following Vatican II reforms and the influence of Latin American liberation theology, churches have demonstrated more solidarity with indigenous peoples. Some bishops, such as Leónidas Proaño in Riobamba (Ecuador), Samuel Ruiz in Chiapas (México), and Pedro Casaldáliga in the Brazilian Amazon, have become symbols of the sympathy of a sizable sector of the Catholic Church with indigenous peoples. Indeed a new school of thought labeled "Andean theology" has emerged; it reclaims ancestral values and rites, and is led by Aymara and Quechua speakers within the Methodist, Lutheran, and Catholic churches.

On the other hand, the arguments put forth by these peoples have scored points in higher circles for other reasons, such as the emergence of the green parties and the rising priorities of sustainable development and ecological conservation. The much-publicized issue of Amazonia as the ecosphere's "green lung" has made Amazonian indigenous politics media-visible worldwide. For these reasons, more than because of their rights as owners of the territory, jungle-dwelling groups have been taken into account even in projects run by international institutions, including specialized arms of the United Nations or the World Bank. Another new situation arose within the left, as statist and vanguardist dogmas, once considered unquestionable, eroded in the 1990s amid the sequels of Soviet collapse. In search of alternatives, several parties have begun to take the proposals of indigenous organizations more seriously and also those of a few formerly marginalized pro-indigenous intellectuals. Indeed it now seems that whatever does not include an ethnic theme looks less than up-to-date.

To conclude this overview of the period we live in, we must mention two less positive situations that in recent years have greatly affected the lifeways of communities and ethnic groups in three of the countries under consideration. These are, first, the spread of violence, and second, the expansion of the parallel economy based on coca and cocaine.

The violence born of guerrilla actions and army counterinsurgency has led to tremendous bloodshed in many areas of Colombia and most of Peru. In this type of internal war, indigenous communities have often found themselves trapped between two alien fronts, becoming the chief victims, and often the most anonymous ones. In Colombia hundreds of Páez and Guambiano Indian leaders have died, accused by the government of collaborating with the guerrillas, and some accused by the guerrillas of the reverse. Such accusations are often mere excuses for landholders and local power blocs to get rid of leaders in struggles to recover usurped territories. In Peru the situation became even more serious, and the violence spread to almost the entire sierra and parts of Amazonia. The war involved two communist guerrilla organizations, ultra-right paramilitary armed units, a repressive army, and local oligarchic power groups. All of them showed inflexible attitudes: One was either with them, or one ran the risk of death, especially when attempts were made to organize for self-defense. In a decade of terror, the result was over 20,000 dead and disappeared, mostly indigenous peasants. Many indigenous communities have stood semiabandoned as peasants fled to urban refuges.

Regarding the parallel economy built on coca and cocaine, the situation demands a more thorough analysis. Peru is the world's leading producer of coca and more recently also a major producer of "base" (semiprocessed cocaine paste, or sulfate of cocaine). Bolivia follows Peru closely in both commodities. Colombia is the major refiner and distributor of the final export product, chlorhydrate of cocaine, but in Colombia the indigenous population is much less involved. Since prehispanic times coca, cultivated in subtropical valleys, or *yunka* (*yunca, yunga*) has been a fundamental element of Andean culture and, since its use became more widespread in colonial times, also of the economy of the modern countries of Peru and Bolivia. The recent expansion of coca cultivation to satisfy the demand for illegal cocaine in the wealthy northern countries cannot easily be separated from that tradition. For local small producers the cocaine boom offered one of the very few profitable cash-crop alternatives available amid the severe economic crisis of Latin America's "lost decade" of development, the 1980s. For this reason the coca-producing zones became and still are a major destination for seasonal and permanent migrants, and their organizations are among the ones that have experienced the greatest growth, especially in Bolivia. In Peru the situation grew more complex because guerrilla groups also operate in the coca zones. They function there as a sort of brokerage among producers, buyer-smugglers, and the army, thwarting army repression in exchange for protection and economic advantage from the other two sectors. No producer can rely on a safe line separating simple legal production from illegal drug trafficking.

Let us now turn to the specific situation in each country.

Ecuador, a Tree of Nations

The Shuar Federation, founded in 1961 in Amazonia, and ECUARUNARI, founded in 1972 in the highlands, were the two sources of a movement that culminated in 1982 with the birth of CONAIE, the spectacularly successful Confederation of Indigenous Nationalities of Ecuador (see Map 25.3).

The Shuar, part of a major Amazonian linguistic family, today live divided between Peru and Ecuador. Unconquered by Spanish and Republican states, they were missionized intensively by Salesians from the late nineteenth century onward. Salesians established boarding schools that indoctrinated students in the most orthodox version of the "civiliz-

Map 25.3

ing mission." But, as often happens, the results were not exactly what the tutors had planned. One group of boarding alumni, cooperating with missionaries of a less traditional mentality, in 1961 formed the Local Association of Jívaro Centers. Three years later it was legalized as the Federation of Shuar Centers. Their effort was part of the broader Shuar effort to consolidate territory in the face of the imminent threat posed by highway construction. The new road was sure to bring an endless flood of highland immigrants. Deviating from previous "civilizing" schemes, the nontraditional clergy put a higher priority on the maintenance of Shuar identity, adapting it to the new challenges created by an increasingly active and unavoidable state presence, and also on the primary role of the Shuar themselves in their own defense. By 1987 this defiant proposal had already managed to establish 240 centers affiliating some 40,000 inhabitants. There were more than a few difficulties due to an economy too unreliable to underwrite consistently sustainable development. Nevertheless the Shuar Federation became an example of what ethnic development and consolidation of territory could achieve within the narrow confines of what laws permitted. The Shuar stimulus was fundamental to the organization of other Amazonian groups, especially after 1972, when the oil boom began. Oil drilling would bring with it a vast expansion of colonization and development of eastern Ecuador. This in turn generated new threats to the peoples who had long inhabited this area, threats sometimes veiled with the old Chilean euphemism, "pacification." In 1980 under Shuar leadership, the threatened groups created a center called CONFENIAE, the Confederation of Indigenous Nationalities of the Ecuadorian Amazon.

In the sierra, where a stronger tradition of organizing dated to the 1920s, ECUARUNARI initiated a new focus. Its acronym stood for the Quichua phrase *Ecuador runacunapac riccharimui* ('the awakening of the Indians of Ecuador'). It was founded in 1972 in the community of Tepeyac, with the initial support of several progressive priests, especially in Chimborazo Province, where Bishop Leónidas Proaño was a strong supporter of indigenous rights. Proaño was famous for breaking the traditional alliance of the Church with the estate owners, and for promoting a service-oriented as well as ritual-oriented pastoral practice. Following in the footsteps of Dolores Cacuango, Blanca Chancoso held the position of general secretary. In her own testimony, she remembers ECUARUNARI's impact on unions and politics:

> Before, on the level of the unions or parties, Indians were never even mentioned. When there were events, they would speak for us, but it was out of the question for an Indian to be in the leadership. Today, since our Indian leaders have been present at various events to make their own speeches, only now have these groups begun to show off the few Indians members they had. . . . They wanted to represent the Indians, depriving us of our legitimacy, but at least now they

acknowledged the Indians who were already in their midst. Today in their speeches they too talk of nationalities, and some sectors are even beginning to recognize the self-determination of Indian peoples.[36]

From the start, ECUARUNARI suffered an internal struggle between a more classist line and a more ethnic one. The latter had the upper hand until 1977; after that, because of the entry of the Pichincha delegation, more closely linked to the old organizations of Cayambe and to the classist workers' ambit, it regained a classist focus but without forgetting the ethnic one. From its foundation ECUARUNARI pressed for the creation of branches, called *huahua riccharimui* ('baby awakenings' in Quechua), and these began to proliferate all over the highlands. It has maintained a tense dialogue with classist organizations, like FEI and FENOC, mostly because of the shared need to defend themselves against the 1979 Law of Agricultural Development and Support, which was turning into a dead end for agrarian reform aspirations.

Despite all of these limitations, the combined processes of agrarian reform and colonization did multiply and diversify the smallholding farm sector. Smallholders increased from 252,000 in 1954 to 470,000 in 1968 and 650,000 in 1978.[37] The majority of estates and plantations, in their classical form, disappeared, but others, more technologized, took their place, dislodging peasants from land where they had become supernumeraries and driving them into seasonal migration. According to statistics of the Ecuadorian Institute of Agrarian Reform and Colonization, the combined processes of agrarian reform and colonization up to 1984 had legally assigned 2.3 million hectares to 50,122 families. The majority (21,307 families with 12 millions hectares) got lands in Amazonia, another 14,480 on the coast, and only 13,778 in the sierra. These last were mostly indigenous, as were 7,337 families in Amazonia.

In 1979 the military government fell, and democracy was restored. The new president, Jaime Roldós, emphasized indigenous issues in his 1979 inaugural speech, symbolically speaking in Quichua, much to the surprise of traditionalist Quiteños. Shortly afterward, in 1980, a huge National Indian March protested the agricultural development law passed the year before. The new government agreed to name an Indian representative to run the national office of bilingual education, and it recognized the "pluriethnic" and "pluricultural" nature of the country but stopped

[36] ALAI (1987), 9. [37] Iturralde (1988a), 48, 52.

short of using the term "plurinational," which protesting organizations preferred.

With this preamble the eighties marked the consolidation and unification of the Ecuadorian Indian movement. The Confederation of Indigenous Nationalities of the Ecuadorian Amazon (CONFENIAE) joined with ECUARUNARI in October 1980 at Sucúa to mount the first substantive effort at unifaction among the various "nationalities" of the three major regions of the country. The joint organization was at first called CONACNIE (Coordinating Council of Indigenous Nationalities of Ecuador) and after 1986 CONAIE (Confederation of Indigenous Nationalities of Ecuador). The insistent "N" for "Nationalities" in these terms mounted an explicit challenge to the Ecuadorian state and reflects a lengthy debate between class-centered and indigenist organizations. Although it has not achieved full articulation with the organizations that followed more of a class line, CONAIE has been since then the state's main interlocutor.

In June 1990 CONAIE effectively led a simultaneous mobilization of many thousands of indigenous people throughout the country, coast, highlands, and jungle. Demonstrators took over the much-revered Santo Domingo Church in Quito's colonial hub and lodged in it, while rural sympathizers blocked the roads bearing the capital's food supply. Urban spokespersons publicized a list of demands, ranging from settlement of a long list of land disputes to Ministry of Health recognition of shamanic medicine. It was more than a *coup de theatre*; it was for the urban public an epochal shock. One published comment bore as its title "The Ethnic Earthquake," but the event has entered the ledgers of history under the simple rubric of "The Uprising" (*levantamiento*). Nothing of this magnitude had occurred since the days of the rebel Fernando Daquilema some 100 years before. In the face of all of this, the rulers continued to sidestep the movement's demands. IERAC processed the land disputes at a snail's pace throughout the years of the Columbian quincentennial. In 1994 a government more rightist than its predecessors attempted to pass, without Indian participation, an agricultural development law favoring landlords at the expense of communities. Indian reaction was immediate. In June a second uprising took place, paralyzing the country for 10 days and forcing the government to sit down and talk with a commission, presided over by the Saraguro Indian Luis Macas and the Indian lawyer Nina Pacari (probably the most famous woman leader of the movement). They met in the banquet hall of the presidential palace, a symbolic concession insofar as the state had never before extended pomp and circumstance to indigenous persons. Against the neo-liberal tide of the times, under a presidency that (now for Conservative rather than Marxist reasons) wished to muffle ethnic issues in economic ones, CONAIE succeeded in maintaining its bridgehead in public discourse. While abstaining from party commitments, it has advanced proposals for "multinational" constitutional reforms, and it commands a stronghold within the Ministry of Education via the bilingual education establishment. It continues to espouse land claims in process. Although its long-term stability has been questioned, no one questions that CONAIE has changed the whole footing of interethnic discourse in what was, not long ago, arguably the most retrograde Andean state.

Ecuador is not the only Andean country from which indigenous emigrants have set out to cities like New York, Amsterdam, and Madrid, but it is the one whose indigenous diaspora plays the most conspicuous part in national affairs. The indigenous middle class, which especially since the 1980s has prospered from the tourist and textile industries of Imbabura Province, did not rally with anything like unanimity to the "uprising," although it did generate some outstanding intellectual and political leaders such as the feminist-ethnic leader Nina Pacari. Rather, this class has made itself felt in large measure by economic leadership: Textile-exporting indigenous entrepreneurs, many of whom themselves travel abroad to sell, have bought up a good third of the urban real estate in their region's capital, Otavalo, and a few have built spectacular high-rise buildings. Andean musicians playing and recording abroad have become two-way bearers of cultural innovation. Some families have developed a "transnational" way of life, with households both in indigenous places (urban or rural) and abroad, sometimes contributing important remittances to households or communities. The cultural self-confidence that grows around these successes increasingly emboldens Quechua-speaking university students to retain their indigenous dress and, to a still-uncertain degree, their language. Other Andean diasporas, though less obvious to the onlooker (such as the settlements of Colca Valley Peruvians in Washington, D.C., or of Huarochirí Peruvians in Texas) mark the emergence of a "deterritorialized" and markedly cosmopolitan Andean way of life.

Colombia: From CRIC to ONIC

The Regional Indigenous Council of the Cauca (CRIC) originated in 1971, in part because many Páez and Guambianos suspected that the ANUC as well as the National Indigenous Secretariat "sought to peasantize the Indians." This sentiment quickly extended to other groups, so that the same year other alternative organizations were born in the Chocó (UNDICH) and Vaupés (CRIVA); in 1974 in Arhuaco territory (COIA); and in 1975 in Tolima (CRIT). All of these groups (see Map 25.4) primarily demanded the recognition and recuperation of their territories or reserves. Toward the end of 1981, according to data from the Colombian Institute of Agrarian Reform, some 10 percent of the indigenous population had legalized their claims – that is, eighty-two reserves with 8,780 families and 5,694,180 hectares. The new organizations also managed to expel the Summer Institute of Linguistics from several regions.

One of the main problems that these organizations faced, especially in the Andean regions of Cauca and Tolima, was to maintain a distinctive position of independence in the face of increasing polarization between the official two-party system and the leftist forces, who, believing themselves excluded, resorted to guerrilla tactics. One early expression of this conflict was the split between the indigenous organizations and the peasant organization ANUC/Sincelejo, to which they had initially been linked. The reason was the Fourth Congress in 1976 at Tomala, called "the Tomala trap" by the Indians, because they refused a proposal to merge in a party, the ORP, or People's Revolutionary Organization. Tension intensified the following year when President César Turbay Ayala, using the excuse that the M-19 guerrilla organization had stolen arms from a military base, loosed a new wave of state repression against the Indians. By the end of 1978, more than thirty CRIC officials were murdered, and hundreds more were jailed. Compounding this physical violence were legal means, as the government attempted to impose new Indian laws, which "tended to disintegrate the communities, turning the *cabildos* into neighborhood associations and abolishing the collective property of the reserves."[38]

The contradictions increased further in the 1980s, as the "total war" waged by the government against the guerrillas turned into a "dirty war." The Indians were left, as usual, between a rock and a hard place, suffering

[38] Pineda ed. (1987), 25; UI VIII 1985.

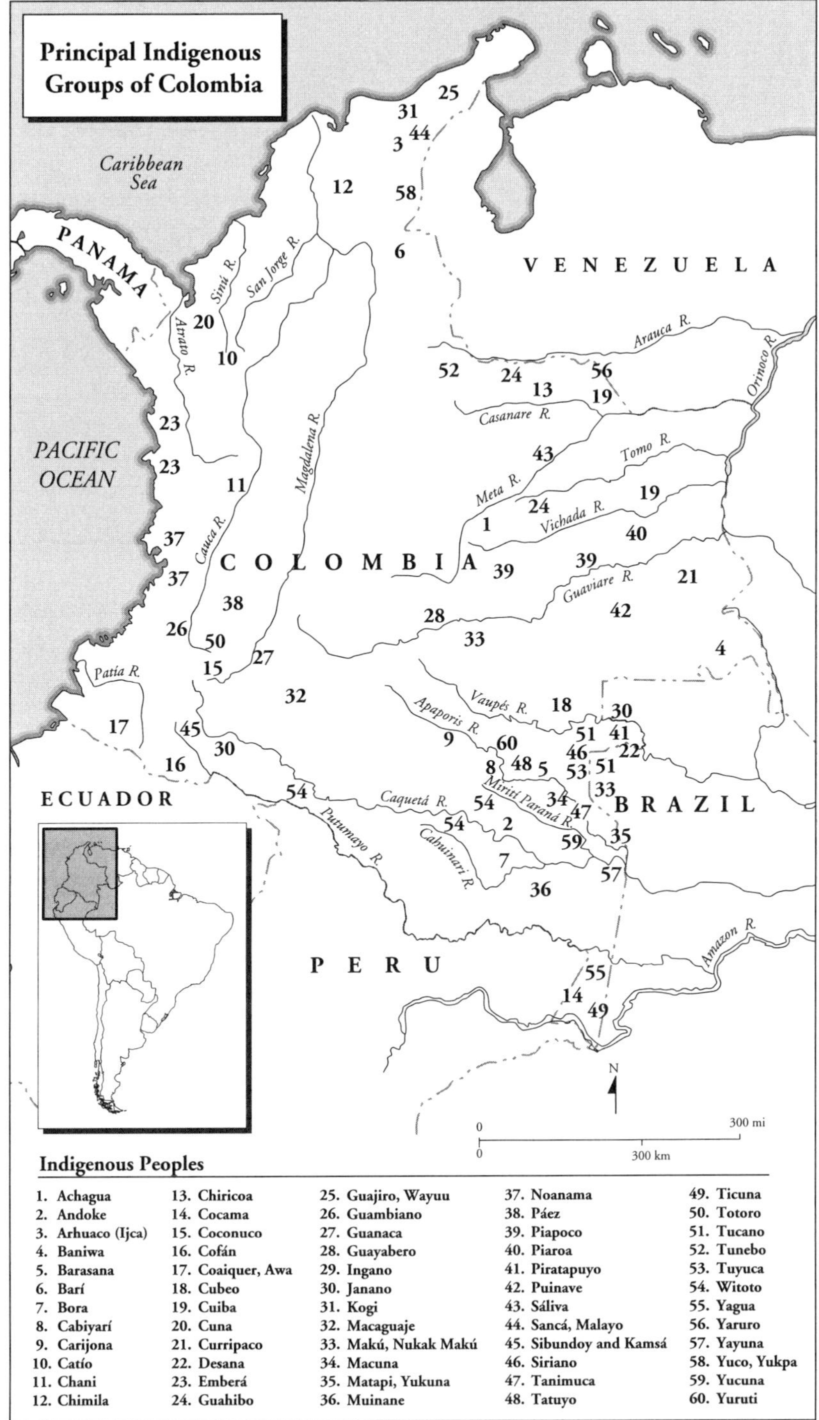

Principal Indigenous Groups of Colombia
Caribbean Sea
PANAMA
PACIFIC OCEAN
VENEZUELA
COLOMBIA
ECUADOR
BRAZIL
PERU
Sinú R.
San Jorge R.
Atrato R.
Magdalena R.
Cauca R.
Patía R.
Arauca R.
Casanare R.
Orinoco R.
Meta R.
Tomo R.
Vichada R.
Guaviare R.
Vaupés R.
Apaporis R.
Caquetá R.
Mirití Paraná R.
Putumayo R.
Cahuinarí R.
Amazon R.
N
0
300 mi
0
300 km
Indigenous Peoples
1. Achagua
2. Andoke
3. Arhuaco (Ijca)
4. Baniwa
5. Barasana
6. Barí
7. Bora
8. Cabiyarí
9. Carijona
10. Catío
11. Chani
12. Chimila
13. Chiricoa
14. Cocama
15. Coconuco
16. Cofán
17. Coaiquer, Awa
18. Cubeo
19. Cuiba
20. Cuna
21. Curripaco
22. Desana
23. Emberá
24. Guahibo
25. Guajiro, Wayuu
26. Guambiano
27. Guanaca
28. Guayabero
29. Ingano
30. Janano
31. Kogi
32. Macaguaje
33. Makú, Nukak Makú
34. Macuna
35. Matapi, Yukuna
36. Muinane
37. Noanama
38. Páez
39. Piapoco
40. Piaroa
41. Piratapuyo
42. Puinave
43. Sáliva
44. Sancá, Malayo
45. Sibundoy and Kamsá
46. Siriano
47. Tanimuca
48. Tatuyo
49. Ticuna
50. Totoro
51. Tucano
52. Tunebo
53. Tuyuca
54. Witoto
55. Yagua
56. Yaruro
57. Yayuna
58. Yuco, Yukpa
59. Yucuna
60. Yuruti

Map 25.4

repression from the leftist guerrilla armies FARC and M-19,[39] as well as from the army, the police, and landlords' mercenaries called *pájaros* ('birds'). Especially in Cauca and Tolima, news of arrests, torching of homes, evictions, kidnappings, injuries, and murders became daily routine. By 1994 more than 400 indigenous leaders had been murdered, especially in Cauca. This tension also created internal divisions among one Páez group that formed its own regional guerrilla force, named after Quintín Lame, as well as among those opposed to armed struggle.

In Colombia the relationship between these new organizations and various sectors of the Church was more conflictive than in Ecuador. The fledgling organizations repeatedly complained against the colonialist stance of some priests, clergymen, and bishops. Takeovers of Church lands even occurred. There was one notable exception: Father Alvaro Ulcué, locally known as "Nasa Pal," a Lazarist priest of Páez origin who, besides promoting Páez language and culture, openly supported CRIC and its struggle for land. His family was threatened; when he was finally killed by two policemen, he become a symbol of CRIC and its struggle. An article in *Unidad Indígena* ('Indigenous Unity', IX-1985) said of him:

> He surely is a true brother because he works with us, he eats with us. We never saw other priests do this. He got muddy, he sweated, he got wet for our Indian cause and for other poor people. Thanks to Mother Nature. . . . She has recovered this spilled blood through the rainbow.

Despite these difficulties CRIC did not disband; in fact it grew. In 1982 the first National Indian Congress took place in a locale of the Claretian fathers in Bosa, with 2,000 participants. There the National Indigenous Organization of Colombia (ONIC) was created. Since that time ONIC has maintained an active presence, with congresses, newspapers, and as of 1991 a total of thirty-six affiliated organizations. To its traditional concerns, summarized in its motto "unity, land, organization, autonomy," others have been added. These include defense of indigenous women's interests and a focus on communal economic enterprises. This last plank implies revising the cooperativist ideas of the agrarian reform.[40]

Not everything is rosy. Some organizations participate only nominally in ONIC, and there are internal conflicts among the leadership. In addition in 1990 a Guambiano sector whose conflicts with CRIC dated

[39] Revolutionary Armed Forces of Colombia and 19th of April Movement.

[40] I am grateful for the talks that Gabriel Muyuy shared with me. He is a speaker of Colombian Quechua or Ingano, ONIC official, and one of the few indigenous senators in Colombia.

to the late 1970s became a parallel organization called AICO (Indigenous Authorities of Colombia), ostensibly a national-level organization but actually stronger in Tolima and Nariño. The 1991 elections stimulated the formation of a third dissident group, ASI (Indigenous Social Alliance), which also reaches out to blacks and to urban popular sectors whether they are Indian or not.

The most significant achievement of recent years is that important indigenous demands were dealt with in the new Constitution of 1991. Three Indians, as members of the constitutional congress, helped to draft it. The first section, concerning the fundamental principles of the state, now includes the phrase "the State recognizes and protects the ethnic and cultural diversity of the Colombian Nation" (art. 7). It also recognizes the "official" character of the "languages and dialects of the ethnic groups" within their "territories," along with Spanish, thus providing a state basis for "bilingual education" (art. 10). It also recognizes the so-called indigenous territorial entities, including the *resguardos* or historic reserves, endowing them with the right to choose their own authorities and institutions according to their "habits and customs" (art. 329–330). It stipulates the autonomous appointment of two Indians to the Senate (art. 171). Compared to the older, protective Law 89 dating to the previous century, the new charter embodies a leap to constitutional recognition of difference on a jural level not yet achieved in the other Andean nations.

Although other more sensitive issues, like the assignment of resources to the reserves, were postponed, practical results are already evident. These include the presence of three Indians in the Senate (including one elected directly, in addition to those earmarked in the Constitution). Two others have sat in the House of Representatives since the 1991 elections. Paradoxically the division of organizations on the national level has facilitated the growth of Amerindian representation in Congress.

Bolivia: Hope for a Plurinational State

In Bolivia the rediscovery of native identity came somewhat later than in Ecuador and Colombia, precisely because the agrarian reform, with its uniformizing "peasantist" rhetoric, had shown such vigor there. But once the process was underway, it took hold much more forcefully than in any other country. One probable explanation is that here the change in orientation came from deep within extant peasant organization, which itself had strengthened greatly since the agrarian reform. Peasant institutional strength also helped the Bolivian countryside forestall chronic violence of the sort that has plagued Peru and Colombia.

State hegemony over peasantry began to wane in the late 1960s. The first signs of this change came when General Barrientos tried to levy a tax on the lands titled by the agrarian reform. This proposal led to a crisis that ended the honeymoon between the military and the peasants, especially in the Aymara high plains. There an economy based on self-sufficiency made the tax more onerous, and Barrientos could not appeal so readily to the magic of his Quechua origin. Thus the first opposition peasant organization was born, the Independent Peasant Bloc, formed by left-leaning officials who were marginalized from the state-affiliated organization. After Barrientos's death in 1969, a leftist military biennium sought to erase the "guilty conscience" lingering from the defeat of Ché Guevara in 1967. Although this regime was more oriented toward urban sectors and workers than toward peasants, it did create a space for greater peasant participation and, even more importantly for our story, an opening for the emergence of the Aymara political movement called Katarismo (see Map 25.5).

As Silvia Rivera has stressed, Katarismo is the recovery of a "long-term memory" obscured by the "short-term memory" of the agrarian reform and the peasant union struggle.[41] In the face of the partial failure of the uniformizing classist project, the Aymara once again remembered their ethnic and cultural roots, defended of old in lengthy anticolonial struggles. Long memory infused new symbolic life into the image of the eighteenth-century rebel hero, Tupaj Katari, who was born in the same Ayo Ayo region where modern Katarismo now sprang up. It took as its slogan the phrase that oral tradition recalls as Tupaj Katari's last words before being drawn and quartered in Peñas in 1781: "I will return as millions."

In the August 1971 peasant congress in Potosí, Katarismo topped off its dizzying ascent by placing its leader Jenaro Flores in the highest position in the National Confederation of Peasant Unions of Bolivia (CNTCB). Katarismo had economic objectives, such as the liquidation of those few haciendas spared by the agrarian reform, and it was fully supported by the union organization that expanded after the agrarian reform. This last factor largely explains the larger following that it at-

[41] (1984), pp. 163–171.

The Aymara World of Today
Town
Area of the Aymara language
Salt flats
Puno
BOLIVIA
Beni
Pelechuco
Charazani
Huancané
Wanqu
Mocomoco
Awqapata
Mapiri
Ayata
Caranavi
Puno
Lake Titicaca
Chucuito
La Paz
La Paz
PERU
ANDES MOUNTAINS
Desaguadero R.
Inquisivi
Independencia
Mohoza
Colquiri
Altamachi
Cochabamba
Ayopaya
Kami
Tapacari
Tarata
Leque
Challa
Tacna
Paria
Oruro
Sajama
Carangas
Sacaca
Coacarí
Choro
Poopó
Catavi
S. Pedro
Oruro
Valladas
Panacachi
CHILE
Lake Poopó
Oropeza
Pocoata
Pojpo
Atawallpa
Macha
Chuquisaca
Chipaya
Volcano Isluga
Pukina
Quillacas
Salar Coipasa
Condo
Chayanta
Llica
Urmiri
Salar Uyuni
Potosí
Chuquisaca
Yonza
Colcha
N
0
100 mi
0
100 km

Map 25.5

tracted, compared to other movements of the period. But the great innovation was that the Kataristas promoted a new ethnic ideology. They expressed this not only in their name and heroes but also in their own flag (the *wiphala*), the renewed value placed on traditional village authorities, their Aymara language radio programs, and many other details. Although the rise of the Kataristas cannot be understood apart from the structural changes that 1953 agrarian reform put into play, their style showed a thorough rejection of the homogenizing purposes of that project. Kataristas expressed it in an oft-repeated phrase: "We are not the peasants of 1952 any more."

This opening was interrupted by Hugo Bánzer's right wing military coup and the repression that followed, only a few days after Flores took office as leader of the peasant union. In rural areas the new regime, especially tied to the Oriente (eastern lowlands), began to devour jungle lands. General Bánzer and, a few years later, General Luis García Meza assigned 32 million hectares to a handful of people, so that after 30 years of agrarian reform 7 percent of rural landowners once again controlled over 90 percent of the land, and generally kept it out of production. In this period the state also extended many loans to agroindustry in Santa Cruz, but not always with the intended results. Funds were often channeled to other, more lucrative and illegal, activities, including the first drug-trafficking boom.

Bánzer, who neither spoke Quechua nor had the popular charisma of Barrientos, was unable to adhere to the letter or the spirit of the Military-Peasant Pact. A landmark incident signaling the breakdown of the pact came in January 1974 in the Cochabamba valleys, where loyalist Quechua peasants blockaded all highways in the futile hope that the "supreme leader" would alter his economic policies. The blockade ended with the massacre of a hundred Quechua activists. This act triggered new processes of independent peasant organization. It is significant that these efforts were led not by the Quechuas of Cochabamba but by the Aymara Kataristas, who had developed an alternative platform and who maintained a subtle but permanent presence throughout the territory by broadcasting cultural radio programs in Aymara. This restructuring, carried out on the quiet from community to community through almost the entire Aymara *altiplano*, culminated at the end of 1977 with the rejection of state-supporting leadership and the formal appearance of the Túpaj Katari Peasant Confederation, announced in a clandestine press conference.

At this time General Bánzer came under pressure from U.S. President

Jimmy Carter to address human rights issues and move toward a democratic process. This pressure intensified after a massive hunger strike, which the Kataristas also supported. But the transition to democracy would prove a wrestling match comparable to that of Haiti in future years. Between 1978 and 1982 there were three national elections, six military coups, and a total of thirteen presidents. In the midst of all these ups and downs, Katarista leaders gained control of the new Central Union Confederation of Bolivian Peasant Workers (CSUTCB), which dissolved the Military-Peasant Pact. After 1979 it became the primary organization representing virtually the entire peasantry. The CSUTB also won an important position within the general labor union, the COB. Despite its name, the result of compromise unifying various organizations, the CSUTCB from the beginning stressed the necessity to analyze with "two eyes": as peasants, together with other exploited classes, and as Aymaras, Quechuas, and others, together with the other oppressed nations of the country.

Katarismo's first electoral efforts in 1978 created Katarista parties, largely to express a lack of confidence in the traditional parties of both right and left, whose focus Kataristas considered too urban and colonialist. From the beginning there were two trends: the first, expressed in the MRTK (Túpaj Katari Revolutionary Movement), emphasized the idea of looking with "two eyes," more evident in the CSUTCB. The other, expressed in the MITKA (Túpaj Katari Indian Movement), was strong on urban Aymara militancy and more one-sidedly Indianist, following the platforms put forth by Fausto Reinaga and later revised by his son Ramiro. Economic and organizational problems, along with struggles over leadership and alliances, prevented them from solidifying into truly Indian parties. The two parties continued to subdivide while others arose as well, with none really representative or solid in its following. Nevertheless, thanks to those parties and the CSUTCB, Katarista proposals did gain a recognized space in national politics.

At the end of 1982, after 12 years of authoritarian military rule, the long-overdue return to democracy unleashed an avalanche of demands; everyone wanted their needs seen to at once. The peasantry, now led by the Kataristas, was also caught up in the euphoria. In the early days there were huge numbers of mobilizations, including massive roadblocks, takeovers of offices and projects, especially those run by the state, and other forms of protest. But now, instead of repression or rejection, these actions easily extracted decrees and concessions that promised what peasants asked for. The problem was that they were never implemented. This occurred in part because the ongoing economic crisis left little margin for action, and in part because the new government was weak and its policies ill-defined. Nonperformance nullified three seeming victories: the nationalization of 32 million hectares that had been illegally obtained in private title, the coverage of salaried farm workers under general labor law, and the institution of mandatory bilingual education. People began to talk of "decrees on wet paper," meaning they were not worth the paper they were printed on, and since victories proved empty, demonstrations decreased. From that point the Katarista leadership within the CSUTCB also weakened. The new currents that emerged were more related to various left parties. Although the CSUTCB did not break up, it lost force. This was true especially after the 1985 elections, which ushered in a period of ever-strengthening state control based on a neoliberal economic model, beginning with the presidency of Victor Paz and continuing under Jaime Paz, both allied with the ex-dictator Bánzer. The principal leaders of the CSUTCB were still Aymaras, and they upheld the platform demands of Katarismo without actually being Kataristas.

In truth the most successful mobilizations of recent years took place in other areas, especially in the tropical Chapare region of Cochabamba. There the coca question was creating a new and powerful battle flag to follow. As improving penetration of the insatiable U.S. market generated an international cocaine boom in the 1970s, this leading coca region attracted the majority of rural migration from the whole country. Migration leads to tremendous fluctuations in population, but at one point the whole population including both permanent dwellers and "floaters" was estimated at about 300,000 people. Most of them are Quechua, but there is a great variety, including many urban workers and miners thrown out of their jobs under new economic policies. In fact the best known pro-coca leader, Evo Morales, is an Aymara from a native community in Oruro. In contrast to Peru and Colombia, coca producers in Bolivia have managed to establish solid, recognized organizations, tied to the CSUTCB or to the Confederation of Colonists. Faced with U.S.-financed coca eradication campaigns and other dangers, they have staged important meetings, blockades, and marches. In one of them, in 1994, marchers reached La Paz traveling along little-known paths, making a mockery of the government whose helicopters dropped gas on them in an effort to look "in control." They have suffered various massacres and persecutions. But their voice, clearly distinguishable from that of the drug traffickers, has been heard. They have appealed even to the Andean cultural roots of the "sacred coca leaf." But their main argument is that to produce coca is not in itself a crime but simply a matter of taking advantage of almost the only opportunity to survive amidst an economic system that expels and marginalizes them. To blame them, they suggest, would be like blaming grape growers for alcoholism or uranium miners for nuclear war.

With CSUTCB and COB backing, these coca growers periodically make deals with the government, but they are never implemented because basically the two groups have opposed interests. On the one hand, growers are concerned above all with subsistence, although when the price of coca leaf goes down, some of them also participate in the risky business of primary refining from leaves into paste. On the other hand, neither is the government always exempt from involvement with drug traffickers, and it implements economic policies that fail to offer far-reaching strategies to create alternatives for small farmers. In addition the antidrug policy is strongly influenced by the U.S. government, on which Bolivia depends also in many other ways. This pressure led the state to quickly push through Law 1008 in 1988, which treats coca and cocaine as the same and creates a presumption of guilt. In the following years, the state increasingly accepted the presence of the army and even of the U.S. military in the coca-producing area under the dubious logic of the "war on drugs." Over and over in their congresses and speeches, coca producers together with other peasants and working-class sectors lacking economic alternatives call for the overturn of Law 1008 and protest militarization and foreign meddling.

In recent years strides have been made in other areas as well. For example, CSUTCB-sponsored mobilizations managed to postpone the application, and ultimately achieve the revocation, of a previously approved law of peasant taxation. CSUTCB also brought about the abandonment of various projects called for by the Agricultural Development Law. This law, similar to the Ecuadorian one, promoted an entrepreneurial model of capitalist development that endangered Indian communities. But its major achievement in recent years has been the greater coherence and acceptance, even outside the rural and Indian sphere, of its ideological proposals.

An initial landmark in this development was CSUTCB involvement in drafting part of the New Basic Agrarian Law in 1983–1984. The initiative had a wider scope than projects elsewhere in South America, except perhaps among the Mapuche in Chile. Its many meetings and drafts culminated in an extraordinary national congress. Shortly thereafter, the project – wrapped in Aymara ritual weavings – was delivered to President Siles amidst a huge demonstration celebrating CSUTCB's fifth birthday. Although this agrarian law was repeatedly voted down in Parliament, and several CSUTCB demands were deleted from it, the law was to become a central symbolic reference point in the organization's struggle. What it called for went much further than simply land redistribution, and it already contained the embryo of a new state. Beginning with the basic premise that actual work on the land is the root of ownership, and that communities have "native" (*originiario*) rights because they predate the Bolivian state, CSUTCB proposed a new state–community relationship. The CSUTCB posture oscillated between distrust and participation. On the one hand, they sought ample autonomy for the community, with its customary rights, and suggested a national corporation of communities, to be called CORACA; on the other, following an old proposal from the miners, it also asked for majority standing in co-administration of the state agencies that most concerned its constituents – for example, in all matters concerning agriculture and education.[42]

Two other key points of the ideological proposal, the plurinational state and autonomous territories, have developed along other paths. As early as 1979 the political position papers of the CSUTCB had addressed the necessity to reformulate Bolivian identity as "plurinational." After that the theme was repeated and developed with the proposal for an Assembly of Nationalities and the growing demand for a new constitution that would allow room for plural nationality. In a chain of events related to events in Eastern Europe, both planks were later supported by several parties. Finally in 1994 CSUTCB achieved limited success when Article 1 of the constitution was revised; it now begins: "Bolivia, free, independent, sovereign, multiethnic and pluricultural." But as in other countries of the region, the state continued to resist any change in its monopoly on the word "nation."

The concept of "territory," as applied to these oppressed nations, has achieved new currency mostly through the efforts of lowland indigenous peoples. As discussed previously, their organizational work concentrated

[42] Only the proposal of CORACA – an acronym that purposefully evokes *kuraka*, traditional community authority – was partly put into practice. CORACA should be autonomously run by peasant organizations, drawing on state funds and other sources, in a comparable manner to that of the Araucanian Corporation under Coñuepán in Chile in the 1940s. Unfortunately administrative problems and attention to too many diverse issues curtailed this initiative.

on two fronts. First, the CIDOB (now called the Confederation of Peoples and Indigenous Communities of Eastern Bolivia) came into being as a top–down coordinating organization, and since 1982 it stimulated the organization of the main lowland nationalities. Local initiatives have provided another route, one through which more solid organizations have emerged because they are more closely tied to grass roots. An example is the Assembly of the Guaraní People. Since 1987 it has managed to bring together 60,000 Guaraní-Chiriguano people in three departments and stimulated the organization of neighboring peoples in the Chaco, as well as the even more spectacular resurgence of indigenous peoples in the Beni, the same territory where the Jesuits' colonial Moxos mission villages once dominated the land. This began around 1986 with the strengthening of a few local councils or *cabildos*, and soon the "coordinating council of *cabildos*" was born. Their example caught on among other ethnic groups that did not have *cabildos*, like the Sirionó and the Yuracaré. From the beginning the main stimulus around which all these groups organized was the defense of their territories against the threat of ranching and logging concerns. In 1988 they put an unheard-of proposal before the government, asking that the state recognize two large territories shared by the various ethnic groups concerned. By August 1990 all these peoples had banded together in the CPIB (Coordination of the Indigenous Peoples of the Beni).

In that month, faced with government delays, they began the so-called "march for territory and dignity" in which 800 men, women, and children from twelve ethnic groups marched to La Paz. For 34 days the country's attention was riveted on them, and finally the people of La Paz gave them a hero's welcome. This action provided the leverage to obtain several government decrees that gave legal recognition to five indigenous or interethnic territories covering some 1.5 million hectares. On the crest of the Andean Cordillera, the marchers were received by Aymaras amidst a sea of waving *wiphala* flags. The two sides sealed a pact of blood by sacrificing a llama. In the following years another five territories were recognized. Still the reformed constitution, which had conceded juridical personhood to native communities along with other rights, resisted using the conflictive term "indigenous territories."

As is so often the case, newly formed organizations were not well received by the older ones, such as COB, CSUTCB, and even CIDOB. Nevertheless, as of this writing (May 1995), the net effect has been to broaden the range of interests of all those groups. For example, in 1991–

1993, as a result of the aforementioned march, highland and lowland peoples joined together to draft a proposal for a new law, which the lowland people preferred to call "indigenous" and the highlanders "of the native peoples." Although the law was never passed, it had the effect of mutual consciousness raising.

The final milestone was the election of an Aymara, the tenacious Katarista leader Victor Hugo Cárdenas, as vice-president of Bolivia in 1993. Although the Indian parties were dissolved, divided, or never advanced beyond a symbolic presence, little by little they overcame the resistance of the traditional larger parties and began to incorporate ethnic issues into platforms and slates. Especially noteworthy is the emergence of CONDEPA ('Conscience of the Fatherland'), led by the folklorist and media personality "compadre Palenque" and his female counterparts "comadre Monica" and "cholita Remedios," who won several successive elections in La Paz and its satellite El Alto. Their platform, although more populist than Indian, does explicitly recognize the importance of the ethnic dimension, especially the culture of the urban *cholo* sector. With their triumph, "cholita Remedios," who headed CONDEPA's slate of deputies, became the first parliamentarist "woman in *polleras*." (The *pollera*, or full skirt, is the traditional dress of highland *cholas*, or non-white women.) These advances can be explained in part by openings and concessions in other larger parties, culminating in the MNR's nomination and the subsequent victory of the Aymara vice-presidential candidate, Cárdenas. Indeed Cárdenas did not appear on the MNR slate but ran as a candidate for the MRTKL (Tupaj Katari Revolutionary Liberation Movement). This bold, surprising alliance between Aymaras and neo-liberals generated its share of conflicts with other left and Indian sectors, who had thought to put Cárdenas on their own slates.

Two years into this government, as of May 1995, the major achievements have occurred in the area of creating a new pluriethnic image of the country. Its ingredients include the aforementioned changes in the constitution, the building of a widespread intercultural and bilingual education system, the creation of new government agencies to serve the nonhispanic sector, and, on a more homely level, a novel public imagery linking previously stigmatized but comforting and realistic scenes of indigenous domesticity with civic legitimacy. For example, during one of his intervals as acting president, Cárdenas had an elderly Aymara woman sit in the presidential seat, while during another the television camera glimpsed his wife Lidia Katari wearing polleras, and seated on a stool next to other Aymara women amidst pots and pans for serving *wallaqi* (traditional fish soup). The occasion was a community meal honoring villagers and travelers who had accompanied the Indian president on his visit to his native community near Lake Titicaca. This was a totally new kind of first lady!

It is still too soon to know if all this will turn out to be empty symbols or "paper decrees." But what is certain is that today in Bolivia, too, indigenous actors are questioning and redefining the future structure of the Bolivian state.

Chile Joins the Crowd at Last

For the Mapuche the outcome of the Pinochet coup in September 1973, and its aftermath of neo-liberalism combined with brutal dictatorship, was a new assault on communal properties. The reversal culminated in Decree-Law 2568 of 1979, which put Mapuche lands within the common law jurisdiction and accelerated, more than ever, what was officially called the "liquidation of communities." After initial disorder the so-called "Mapuche Cultural Centers" and ADMAPU were able to reorganize, more or less, with support from the Catholic Church. In practice, however, this did little to stop the dictatorship's inexorable advance. In 3 years it divided up 40 percent of the undivided communities, and by 1986 the figure reached 60 percent, involving 56 percent of total Mapuche land.

Given this systematic program of destruction, it is difficult to understand why the Mapuche voted in favor of Pinochet, in the 1988 plebiscite, which marked the beginning of the end of his regime. According to Bengoa there were immediate practical reasons, such as government provision of roads, agricultural subsidies, and pensions for the elderly. Besides, the campaign for a "no" vote did little campaigning in rural areas but concentrated more on the cities. Bengoa also notes, though, that a more structural reason was the long tradition of pragmatic acceptance of the government in power.[43] In any case this vote did not represent a serious choice but a conditional acquiescence, as other events were to show. As the dictatorship waned the classic Mapuche tendency to form organizations reasserted itself. And again, as in the past, in June 1987 in Temuco, the seven major associations then in existence sought to unite, without actually achieving fusion. This time they did so by means

[43] The Aymaras also voted to support Pinochet, which seems to be the result of the "authoritarian assistentialism" of the military government (Van Kessel, en *Nütram* 6.3).

of a coordinating group that for the first time gave itself a Mapudungun name: *Futa Trawun Kiñewan Pu Mapuche* (Mapuche Unitary Coordination). In the proclamation of its charter, it called not only for the defense of land grant titles but also for "constitutional recognition of the Mapuche people and all the ethnic groups of the country." It asked that the laws applying to them be written "with the active participation of the various organizations representing aboriginal ethnic groups" (*El Araucano*, May–June 1987).

But the most striking innovation occurred in the far north, with the awakening of Aymara consciousness beginning in the late 1980s. One reason was certainly the influence of Bolivian Katarismo, spread by radio and by Aymara immigrants from Bolivia. The change of mood was demonstrated above all in urban Aymara organizations like *Pacha Aru* in Arica and *Aymar Marka* in Iquique. In 1989 Chilean Aymaras were the ones who, inspired by recent Bolivian events, decided to form the first Indian party, the Land and Identity Party. It had little success in the elections, perhaps because of poor funding and a certain ambiguity in its platform, but its audacity and innovativeness made it noteworthy.

In January 1990 the indigenous awakening led in Chile, as it had in other countries, to an interethnic agreement, carried out in Niagua, among twenty-seven indigenous organizations: sixteen Mapuche and three of the related Huillinches; six Aymaras and one representative of their neighbors, the historically indigenous Atacama; and even one Rapa Nui, from Chile's distant dependency Easter Island. When democracy was reestablished in 1990, the new Constitutional President Patricio Aylwin created the Special Commission of Indigenous Peoples (decree 30), to write a new Indian law that would become, in 1993, Law 19253. The commission had legal help from his own son. It was headed by a historian of Mapuche society, José Bengoa, and included both Mapuche and Aymara representatives. A great symbolic achievement was the 1992 expropriation and return of Quinquén, a vast sacred forest, to the Mapuche of Pehuenches.

The text of the law begins with a solemn preamble about the value of these peoples and culture, "as an essential part of the roots of the Chilean Nation," and it took up once again the main themes of the period before the dictatorship. For the first time it included indigenous issues concerning the Aymaras, Atacama natives, Rapa Nui, and other smaller southern groups, as well as the Mapuche. It also explicitly considered urban Indians and other migrants who no longer lived on the titled lands, and it recognized the right of all of these groups to form and participate in their own "indigenous associations" (art. 36, 76). In Chile as in the rest of the Andes, indigenous issues have been reevaluated, and even officially recognized, in ongoing dialectic with a more homogenizing ideology of development.

Peru: Overflow and Marginalization

Peruvian Indian history in the last quarter of the twentieth century diverged from other Andean histories because of many unresolved problems that the country faced. The underlying cause is the economic crisis, as in other countries, but in Peru it became even more serious, in part because of the greater complexity of its own difficult makeup as a country, and in part because of international "punishments" against previous governments for their attempts to implement new policies. Rather than stray too far afield to the international aspects of this problem, we limit ourselves here to noting the most salient factors figuring in our story: first, demographic developments that fortified the country's urban and coastal-centered structure; second, the failure of the military government's reforms; and third, the growth albeit uneven and largely spontaneous, of two movements, an Andean path and an Amazonian, which barely managed to intersect. Indigenous ventures generally aborted as they came into collision with a much more widespread wave of intolerable popular frustration, and soon with a grave situation of polarized violence in the 1980s.

The demographic flipflop that turned Peru from a mostly rural and highland country to a mostly coastal and urban one happened with amazing speed. Between 1940 and 1979 the urban population increased from 27 percent to 65 percent, and by the early 1990s Lima would shelter some 7 of the country's 23 million total inhabitants. Migration changed qualitatively, as well as speeding up; in the 1980s as opposed to the 1960s, migration occurred not so much in response to urban opportunity (opportunity was scarce indeed) but because highland peoples simply had to escape their most pressing problems: impoverishment verging on pauperization, and political terror. In 2,800 *barriadas* ('shantytowns') on the outskirts of Lima and other cities, there dwell some 11 million urban Indians. That is, self-built settlements of refugees and would-be urban workers house about twice as many Andean Peruvians as the 4,885 recognized communities. Thus Andean Indian history is now becoming urban history. Nevertheless the "highlandization" of Lima and several other coastal cities is both more conflictive and better camouflaged than that of La Paz or even Quito, which when all is said and done were already natural Andean capitals located in the heart of the Indian world. To move to Lima meant establishing oneself in alien territory. For this reason the "invisible Indians who go sowing frustrations" (in the late Flores Galindo's words) have been likened to the Trojan horse,[44] bringing, if not gifts, bargains of cheap labor, but also bringing doom to the Creole élites' once-tranquil urban hegemony. These "Indians," as Flores calls them, are in some ways "invisible" to themselves, because in the city they do not want to recognize any such identity. But, unlike in previous decades, today many of them are quite willing to display their *serrano* or "highland" loyalties; perhaps this is the first step toward fully coming to terms with their own roots and with themselves.

In the rural sector the first major change was the failure and dismantling of the military-nationalist agrarian model put into play by General Velasco Alvarado. The 1975 overthrow of one military man by another presaged the downfall of the reform, although many structural features were left in place. When democracy returned in 1980 under the same Fernando Belaúnde Terry who had led the country in the mid-1960s, the last vestiges of military-nationalist revolutionism were finished. But the old feudal highland estate complex was also wounded unto death. In 1984 the net effect of 15 years of reform was the legalization of 9 million hectares, mostly assigned to large pseudo-collective agrarian enterprises: 60 SAIS received 2.8 million; 598 cooperatives, 2 million; and a scant 483 communities (with 122,000 families), only 0.9 million. The communities, where 50 percent of the rural population was concentrated, were therefore the losers.[45]

As was reviewed previously, the main popular response to the collapse of the old order was land takeovers and the alternative organizations that they generated – first in the far north, and by August 1974 in Andahuaylas. Because of these events the CCP (Peruvian Peasant Confederation), the main opposition peasant organization, continued to grow and acquired a national role, enjoying the support of the Revolutionary Vanguard party. As the years passed, land invasions occurred less frequently on traditional haciendas, because there were now far fewer of them, and more on the SAIS and CAPS themselves, as well as other collective enterprises formed during the reform.

[44] Golte and Adams (1987). [45] Kapsoli (1987), 129–131.

Another major style of grassroots reorganization took the form of peasant patrols (*rondas campesinas*), again with far northern highlanders in the lead. This involved not land invasions, on either haciendas or SAIS and CAPS, but rather a change of the intracommunal dynamic itself as communities ceased waiting for help from an ever more ineffectual state structure and concentrated on learning to defend their own interests with self-disciplined force. The patrols were born in 1971 and spread like wildfire through the provinces of Cajamarca Department. Within 10 years the same thing happened in six more departments of northern and central Peru. Modern *rondas* are composed mainly of armed security patrols appointed by the communities themselves and charged especially with self-defense against robbery and rustling. In general they were democratically governed, which assured the active participation of every able-bodied man between 17 and 60. Each took his turn walking the night watch along roads and around fields and homes. In practice their function has expanded far beyond deterring rustling; it has come to include, as we shall see shortly, defense against groups with infinitely superior firepower and few scruples in using it. Self-defense had the effect of restructuring a system of communal government that might otherwise have continued fading away in the more hispanicized northern regions. Despite vigorous state opposition, first from the Morales Bermúdez administration and then from Belaúnde, the *rondas* were finally officially recognized by Law 24571 in 1986. By that time the government desperately needed their support.

Since 1983, when the First Unitary National Agrarian Congress (CUNA) took place, the venerable state-approved peasant organization CNA, the opposition CCP, and other smaller groups began closing gaps to create a more unified entity. But, unlike in other countries, Peruvian Andean groups have taken few strides toward affirming their ethnic identity. Despite the fact that Peru was the pioneer of South American indigenism and later the first republic to make an indigenous language an official language, all the organizations just mentioned maintained their peasant-oriented focus into the 1990s. Debate on the ethnic question took place only in small urban circles, mostly disconnected from grassroots organizations. "Indianness" in Peru today has remained a matter of personal experience – an experience still deeply clouded by stigma and the weight of racism – rather than being transformed into a collective revindication.

In Peruvian Amazonia the first influential indigenous organization was the Amuesha Congress, founded back in 1968. On its heels came the

Aguaruna and Huambisa Council (that is, an organ of the Shuar on the Peruvian side of the disputed boundary with Ecuador) and the Front for the Defense of Native Communities (Shipibo). Around 1980, capping off a process initiated in 1977, these three groups formed AIDESEP (Interethnic Association for the Development of the Peruvian Jungle). It became the principal advocacy for some 1,000 communities with an estimated 200,000 inhabitants spread over the vast eastern departments. Since that time AIDESEP, under the direction of the Aguaruna leader Evaristo Nugkuag, has continued to represent Peruvian Amazonian groups and has carried out various local development projects, handling functions that used to fall only to nonindigenous actors. Nugkuag also became president of COICA, the Indigenous Coordinator of the Amazonian Basin, which brought together indigenous organizations from five Amazonian countries.

Within Peru AIDESEP was later weakened because of two facts that stand out in contrast to the unifying steps achieved in other countries. One is the persistently poor articulation between organizations in Peruvian Amazonia and the Andes, as if they belonged to two different countries. The other was AIDESEP's difficulties in incorporating new organizations that arose autonomously or, at times, in competition with it. In 1987 some of them, supported by some aid institutions, organized a parallel umbrella group called CONAP. The split was widened further by the pressure of different political tendencies influencing the two coordinating organizations and, at times, even by parallel organizations within the same ethnic group. In 1990 AIDESEP represented twenty local federations, and CONAP twelve. Several ethnic groups had split over belonging to one group or the other. Three were in both. Only at the end of the 1980s was a better understanding reached, without actually achieving a union, and even then only under the pressing need to join forces against the common threat of armed violence spreading eastward from the highlands.

Ronda patrols and Amazonian federations alike became life-or-death necessities as region after region came face to face with the most dramatic and destructive crisis in all of modern Andean history. The point from which Peru's still-deadly political violence emanated is the movement named "Shining Path" (*Sendero Luminoso*) and more officially self-baptised as the "Communist Party of Peru on the Shining Path of Mariátegui." It originated as a splinter group dissenting with sectarian rage from all of Peru's various Communist movements, which it branded revisionist. Basically Stalinist and Maoist, and friendlier to the "ultras" of the socialist bloc such as Albania and North Korea than to Cuba, it was formed by a group of professors and students at the University of Huamanga, in Ayacucho, one of the most depressed and forgotten Andean regions. Ayacucho had seen short-lived model programs, many defunded by 1980, but little effective rural organizing. Only one of the main Shining Path leaders, the physician Julio César Mezzich, had previous combat experience in the land invasions of Andahuaylas. Among Sendero's first recruits were many rural schoolteachers and students who had migrated from the provincial towns to the city but found their social mobility blocked by prejudice and economic stagnation. Carlos Iván Degregori has characterized them as "the last children of the Enlightenment" because they embraced scholastically rigid Marxism as the occult science of modernity. The ideology of Sendero Luminoso had little Andean content, and its later actions evidence dogma and authoritarianism rather than respect for Andean structures and realities. Little but the party's name reflected Mariátegui's Andean approach. Party discourse came, and still comes, from a peculiar reading of Mao. Sendero's leader, "President Gonzalo" (Abimael Guzmán), considered himself Mao's fated successor, the rising sun of a worldwide true Communism, and encouraged an intensely personalistic hero worship throughout the party's ranks.

After an initial phase in which it restricted itself to symbolic actions and attacks on property, such as hanging dogs and blowing up electrical towers, in May 1981 Sendero Luminoso launched its first military action in the community of Chuschi, Ayachucho, quickly followed by many more throughout the region. In this early phase it garnered some support from Quechua communities because its actions stressed popular justice and moral behavior. It killed mercilessly, but for the time being its victims were mainly unpopular people like landlords, policemen, and other local exploiters. The police were too weak to confront Sendero Luminoso, and the revolutionaries soon became major players within the local sphere of action, much more so than the state. They achieved some measure of success in recruiting among the youth of the communities, especially students. But as early as 1982 communities began distancing themselves from Sendero's authoritarian style. Sendero's contempt for villagers' ancient self-governing institutions was especially resented. In December 1982 the army violently entered the scene, and the communities involved more and more found themselves caught in the crossfire. If they did not comply with all the army's demands, they were accused of being *terrucos* ('terrorists') and often done away with in terrible massacres. If they did yield, or simply did not submit to Sendero, they were accused of being *soplones* ('stool pigeons') and ran the risk of retaliation from the other side. This situation was especially brutal in the period up to 1985: In just 2 years some 5,567 people were killed, 96 percent of them civilians, as were most of those who "disappeared." Only among the military could the wounded be counted.

By 1985 the army progressed from mere carnage to partially effective warfare, using a more selective style of repression. The first Shining Path offensive seemed to be in retreat, shielded by the new presidency of Alán García, of APRA. Nevertheless that same year Sendero showed its ability to attract a large new following, and its flexibility in changing styles and arenas of action, by launching a new offensive. They expanded their action to such unforeseen fronts as the city of Lima, the department of Junín, which was much more tied into a market economy than was Ayacucho, and Puno, which already had relatively solid peasant organizations. In the early 1990s *senderista* infiltrators entered many of Lima's peripheral shantytowns, swollen with the tide of refugees, and formed clandestine networks that concentrated above all on picking off, mostly by assassination, the rising generation of non-*sendero* popular leadership. Many of these highland-born urbanites who found themselves in the guerrillas' gunsights were engaged in self-help responses to immiseration and the gross failures of both market and state. One signal change born of the crisis was the emergence of dynamic female leadership among those whom Lima scorned as provincials or *cholos*, most memorably the flamboyant Afro-Peruvian mayor of the vast neighborhood Villa El Salvador, María Elena Moyano, who was murdered by Shining Path in 1992 during the high tide of its power. In 10 short years, what began as a microscopic political sect had become a clandestine army well on its way to encircling the capital. Assaults on trucks supplying the city; thunderous car-bombings of television stations, barracks, and banks; "armed strikes" that kept workers away from their jobs on pain of death; and the incessant dynamiting of power lines, all made very real to Lima dwellers the fragility of the near-bankrupt state.

There was almost no part of the country that did not witness at least some symbolic action by Sendero Luminoso, often carried out by very young boys and girls. Their presence became felt in the Huallaga Valley, the core area of coca and cocaine production. There Sendero and another guerrilla group, the MRTA (Túpac Amaru Revolutionary Movement, closer in ideology to the tradition of Ché Guevara), became locked in combat over local hegemony. Each acquired financing and arms through a peculiar three-way brokerage among the army, cocaine dealers, and coca producers. They brought with them unheard-of levels of violence, taking many innocent victims among various ethnic groups of the region. Although the specifics fluctuated, the situation became a chronic state of dirty war, whose growing polarization resulted, as of 1992, in more than 22,000 dead and disappeared, mostly noncombatant community members who never were *terrucos* nor *soplones.*

This was the tragic national context through which Andean communities have had to find a way in recent years. The election of Alan García and his APRA party in 1985 seemed to offer the possibility of hope for a new direction in the countryside. In 1986 the new president proposed the so-called *rimanakuy* ('dialogue', in Quechua) consisting of direct meetings with community members. In 1987 a new law was passed, the Law of Communities (24656 and 24657), which this time included significant participation by peasant organizations. With the resources saved by nonpayment of the foreign debt, a special fund was also formed, with which communities were to carry out their own projects, often on lands taken back from the SAIS or CAPS and this time without intervention by the state bureaucracy. Thus various "communal enterprises" were born, especially in the southern sierra. But all of these positive fresh starts tumbled like a house of cards when the chronic economic crisis worsened, reducing currency to a hyperinflated ghost of its value, and when the equally chronic state of guerrilla violence made rural construction physically impossible. It was to be the community patrols, not initiatives from Lima, that brought communities through the crisis.

In 1990 the dark horse Alberto Fujimori (who was supported by an obscure minor party, and who, being of Japanese descent, stood outside the charmed circle of Lima power) upset the expected winner Mario Vargas Llosa. An almost unthinkable novelty – the presidency in non-white hands – dramatized popular hunger for change and an opening for marginalized sectors. In 1992 Fujimori's government at last captured Abimael Guzmán and then several of his subcommanders. Since then Shining Path actions have waned, persisting mostly in the coca zones and to some degree in the old Ayacucho strongholds. As state agencies reenter zones of high tundra and neglected backlands, where Shining Path had established a stranglehold on power, reports demonstrate that ruthlessness had not yielded real social control, because in scorning the traditional authorities and in trying to stamp out the ritual reproduction of village society, the cadres had reduced themselves to pillaging outsiders in the eyes of Andean peasants.

Although the Fujimori regime executed severe World Bank–style adjustment policies and in most respects conformed to the neo-liberal wave, it also had in some respects a populist streak. Bit by bit, overtures to the peasantry, such as widespread subsidies to village infrastructures, were put into the limelight. Fujimori and his slate took the 1995 elections by a more than ample margin. But in contrast to its Andean neighbors, this administration showed no sensitivity to the ethnic question. It put an end, for example, to the bilingual education projects that had been in place for several years in Puno.

As we conclude our story, the situation in Peru still seems somber. But beyond what is visible on the surface, perhaps something else is hidden, something similar to that which came to pass in the other Andean countries. As José Matos Mar remarks:

> The terms of interaction between Official Peru and the "other society" that is emerging, are becoming modified to the advantage of the latter group and its representatives. Grudgingly, gradually and almost surreptitiously, the State . . . finds itself obliged to accept the existence of ever-expanding spheres of self-government . . . The ongoing process corrodes and dissolves the old creole illusion of national identity and puts the institutional structures of the nation-state on trial. For the first time these two problems, buried since the Conquest in the basements of the national consciousness, can be set aside no longer.[46]

EPILOGUE

Our very closeness to recent events blocks a fuller understanding of the reasons why, after an apparently permanent fadeout during the era of the agrarian reforms, "the Indian" and "Indianness" now have returned, and with great force. Two counterpoised factors recurring in the various countries help us to understand this development.

In the first place, the phenomenon must be framed dialectically in its broadest context, which means acknowledging the increasing homogenization and penetration of the dominant society. However important it may be, the Indian renaissance is no more than a significant countertendency to, and a reaction against, other more predictable processes – those

[46] (1988), 106–108.

that in the long run undermine possibilities of survival for these self-designated native nations. The dominant model of development in the whole region continues, rather, to promote a growing homogenization within the nation-state. If the Indian renaissance does finally succeed, it will not be the result of any initiative by the dominant system, but because the indigenous protagonists show tirelessness in rowing upstream.

On the other hand, the dominant model also generates serious crises on the local level. Each ostensible remedy through "structural adjustments" in turn causes another crisis. One effect of this formula is to marginalize important sectors of the population, including the majority of indigenous people. The more they are marginalized from the system, the more readily they look to their own traditions in search of alternative ways to survive. This is the "boomerang effect" of homogenizing development schemes. Insofar as such proposals marginalize indigenous sectors and therefore fail, they fuel the fire, giving these sectors more reason to pursue their struggle on their own terms. We have seen how agrarian reforms ended up strengthening the very form of community that they sought to "liquidate" as obsolete, and we see it again in relation to the contradictory results of the neo-liberal economic model.

We are faced therefore with a dialectical situation. On one hand, the homogenizing tendency of society proceeds apace; according to this assimilationist ideology, each Indian must stop being one to gain entrée and advance in "national" society. But, on the other hand, Indian citizens have no desire to lose their special way of life, and the contradictions built into the system provide good reason to affirm the advantages of their distinctive views. Is there no room for a third approach – a more pluralist one, which includes those who are different by respecting them?

While this chapter was under review in early 1995, the ancient border conflict between Peru and Ecuador resurfaced once again and was fought out in the midst of Shuar native territory. Both sides seized every opportunity to use the ancestral owners of the territory in their causes, and every indigenous sector also seized on the situation to scramble for political space within its respective state. Shuar youths on both sides volunteered for national armies. But perhaps the most important outcome was a joint pronouncement issued by the two largest indigenous organizations of both countries – CONAIE in Ecuador and AIDESEP in Peru – exhorting their respective governments to rise above exaggerated nationalisms and to seek new ways to get along together.

The many different processes that we have analyzed in our story show that, not long after having celebrated 500 years of indigenous anticolonial resistance, and on the threshhold of the United Nations' Decade of Indigenous Peoples, these peoples and native nations have taken the offensive. They propose to society as a whole a new style of plurinational state, and of relations among states, such that no one will have to feel like a stranger in his or her own land. They give an invigorating breath of fresh air, and they contrast vividly with the fundamentalist intolerance of other, more "civilized" continents, including old Europe.

BIBLIOGRAPHIC ESSAY

No single work deals with all the periods and countries covered in this chapter. For the most recent era – that is, the period since the late 1960s – the reader may consult my essay on the same five countries addressed here: Xavier Albó, "El retorno del indio," *Revista Andina* (Cusco) 9:2 (1991), 299–366, published with comments by various authors. The edited volume by Pablo González Casanova, *Historia política de los campesinos latinoamericanos*, 3 vols. (Mexico, 1985), offers a skillfully rendered broader context for this century, but in it the indigenous theme proper emerges only obliquely. Although it lacks a bibliographic treatment, *Tawantinsuyu. Cinco siglos de lucha kheswaymara contra España* (La Paz, 1978), by the Indianist Wankar (pseudonym of Ramiro Reynaga), provides a stimulating chronological survey of these five centuries. There are also several later editions, the newest being titled *1492–1992. Palabra India* (Barcelona, 1989). Two recent volumes, the first edited by Salomon and Moreno, the other by Stern, offer an ample historic vision of the Andean countries since the colonial period, and the chapters on contemporary issues contain important materials about our theme, although most of them refer to Bolivia. These works are: Segundo Moreno and Frank Salomon (eds.), *Reproducción y transformación de las sociedades andinas, siglos XVI al XX* (Quito, 1991), and Steve J. Stern (ed.), *Resistance, Rebellion and Consciousness in the Andean Peasant World: 18th to 20th Centuries* (Madison, 1987). Several relevant essays that discuss more recent times are included in *Indianidad, etnocidio e indigenismo en América Latina*, by Claude Bataillon et al. (México, 1988; French original Paris, 1982); *Entre la ley y la costumbre. El derecho consuetudinario indígena en América Latina*, Rodolfo Stavenhagen and Diego Iturralde (eds.) (México, 1990);

and *Indigenous peoples and democracy in Latin America*, Donna Lee Van Cott (ed.) (New York, 1994).

The various agrarian reforms of the 1950s–1970s have been the subject of numerous bibliographies compiled by the Land Tenure Center of the University of Wisconsin–Madison. Despite its age, the most precise demographic reference on South American indigenous populations remains that of Enrique Mayer and Elio Masferrer, "La población indígena de América en 1978," *América Indígena* (México) 38 (1978): 211–337. However, some studies included in the most recent works compiled by the Centro Latinoamericano de Demografía (CELADE), *Estudios sociodemográficos de pueblos indígenas* (Santiago de Chile, 1994), remind us how seriously underestimated are the population figures given in much census data.

Because the major works concentrate on specific places and times, I have organized this essay by countries, moving from more general to more specific works within each. I do not include here references to the abundant anthropological and linguistic studies about each of the peoples involved in the history of each country, but only those that take into account the political processes by which indigenous peoples have claimed a place in the wider society. Neither do I include references to indigenist novels, nor to products of indigenism without indigenous participation. I begin with the three central Andean countries – Peru, Bolivia, and Ecuador – in which the indigenous presence is a substantial part of the social fabric; from there I move on to Colombia and Chile, where the indigenous condition is more peripheral and defines a minority.

Peru

Wilfredo Kapsoli is one author who has opened the field of highland Indian history. See his three books, *El pensamiento de la Asociación Pro Indígena* (Cusco, 1980); *Ayllus del sol. Anarquismo y utopía andina* (Lima, 1984); and *Los movimientos campesinos en el Perú* (Lima, 1987). In a much more abbreviated form, Quijano and Valderrama also put forward various syntheses and chronologies of movements of Indians, cholos, and peasants in the whole century. See Aníbal Quijano, *Problema agrario y movimientos campesinos* (Lima, 1979), and Mariano Valderrama, "Historia política del movimiento campesino peruano en el siglo XX," in Pablo González Casanova (ed.), *Historia política de los campesinos latinoameri-*

canos (Mexico, 1985). There is apparently no comparable work for the jungle region.

Concerning the rebellions that occurred from the late nineteenth century to about 1930, one may consult the unpublished anthropology doctoral dissertation by Rosalyn Gow, *Yawar mayu: Revolution in the Southern Andes 1860–1980* (University of Wisconsin–Madison, 1981); it presents data from both Peru and Bolivia. Indigenist currents of the early decades have been the subject of analyses by Lynch, Kapsoli, and Tamayo. Specific works include Nicolás Lynch, *El pensamiento social sobre la comunidad indígena a principios del siglo XX* (Cusco, 1979); Kapsoli, *El pensamiento . . .* (cited previously); and two books by José Tamayo Herrera, *Historia del indigenismo cuzqueño, siglos XVI-XX* (Lima, 1980), and *Historia social del Cuzco republicano* (Lima, 1981, 1st ed., 1978). In these two books, as well as a third one, *Historia social e indigenismo en el Altiplano* (Lima, 1982), this last author has also studied the social and indigenous history of Cusco and Puno. In his doctoral dissertation Dan C. Hazen complements this last focus, putting more emphasis on the Indian aspect: *The Awakening of Puno: Government Policy and the Indian Problem in Southern Peru, 1900–1955* (New Haven, Yale University, Department of History, 1974). José Deustua and José Luis Rénique, in *Intelectuales, indigenismo y descentralismo en el Peru, 1897–1931* (Cusco, 1984), take up this theme and place it within its broader national context. Thomas M. Davies, Jr., covers the evolution of legislation until 1948, in *Indian Integration in Peru. A Half Century of Experience, 1900–1948* (Lincoln, Nebraska, 1974). *Martin Chambi. Photographs 1920–1950* (Washington, 1993) offers a handsomely printed selection of images.

From mid-century onward Peruvian studies, following the general trend, emphasize ethnicity less and concentrate more on peasant politics. But the subjects of these studies nevertheless continued to be Indians. One theme that has received substantial attention is that of the guerrilla movements of the 1960s, about which Leon G. Campbell has compiled an extensive bibliography, "The historiography of the Peruvian guerrilla movement," *Latin American Research Review* 8:1 (1973), 45–70. There are several studies about the case of La Convención, the most widespread movement and the most widely publicized one. Eduardo Fioravanti's *Latifundio y sindicalismo agrario en el Perú: El caso de los valles de La Convención y Lares (1958–1964)* (Lima, 1974), presents a structural analysis. Another is the short interpretative essay by Eric Hobsbawm, "A case of neo-feudalism: La Convención, Peru," *Journal of Latin American Studies*

1:1 (1969), 31–50. The testimonies of the leaders Hugo Blanco and Héctor Béjar are also important: Hugo Blanco, *Tierra o muerte. Las luchas campesinas en Perú*, (México, 1972), and Héctor Béjar, *Las guerrillas de 1965: Balance y perspectiva* (Lima, 1973). The agrarian reform of Velasco Alvarado has also been the subject of many studies, and among those, for their synthetic treatment, I recommend the works of José María Caballero, *Economía agraria de la Sierra peruana* (Lima, 1981), and of C. Amat y León, J. M. Caballero, et al., *Realidad del campo peruano después de la reforma agraria. 10 ensayos críticos* (Lima, 1980). On popular mobilizations related to these reforms, there are several outstanding works. One chronological compilation is important: Diego García-Sayán, *Tomas de tierras en el Perú* (Lima, 1982). For Andahuaylas, birthplace of the CCP, Rodrigo E. Sánchez, *Toma de tierras y conciencia política campesina* (Lima, 1981), is essential. Direct testimonies are also available, such as those of the Indian leader Saturnino Huillca, who collaborated in the Velasco Alvarado reforms (see Hugo Neira, ed. *Huillca. Habla un campesino peruano*, Buenos Aires, 1975), and Lino Quintanilla (1981), a community member of Andahuayllas, who opposed them: Lino Quintanilla, *Andahuaylas: La lucha por la tierra* (Lima, 1981).

On the urban migrations of Indians, see Jürgen Golte y Norma Adams, *Los caballos de Troya de los invasores: Estrategias campesinas en la conquista de la gran Lima* (Lima, 1987), and José Matos Mar, *Desborde popular y crisis del estado. El nuevo rostro del Peru en la década de 1980* (Lima, 1988).

The literature about Sendero Luminoso is vast, as is shown by the already outdated bibliography by Everette E. Larson, "Sendero Luminoso: A bibliography," *Hispanic Focus* (Washington, D.C., Library of Congress) 3 (1985). Recent findings are collected in English in Steve J. Stern (ed.), *Shining and Other Paths* (Durham, North Carolina, 1998). For a brief survey, see Simon Strong's "Shining Path: A case study in ideological terrorism" (London, 1993), which appeared as no. 260 of the Conflict Studies published by the Research Institute for the Study of Conflict and Terrorism. Other English-language studies include those edited by David Scott Palmer in *The Shining Path of Peru* (New York, 1992), and Deborah Poole and Gerardo Rénique's *Peru, Time of Fear* (New York, 1992). Because of rapid change still developing in this area, one must keep date and viewpoint closely in mind. For this chapter I have relied in particular on three works: Alberto Flores Galindo and Nelson Manrique, *Violencia y campesinado* (Lima, 1985); C. Valqui et al.,

Perú: una luz en el sendero (México, 1988); and Nelson Manrique, "Sendero luminoso," *Cuarto Intermedio* (La Paz) 13 (1989), 3–79 (with Bolivian commentary, 80–109; also published in *Márgenes/Sur* [Lima] 1990 (with Peruvian commentary). A still-valuable early analysis is Carlos Iván Degregori, "How difficult it is to be God. Ideology and political violence in Sendero Luminoso," *Critique of Anthropology* 11:3 (1991), 233–250. One recent account that relies on internal Sendero documents is that of Gustavo Gorriti, *Sendero. Historia de la guerra milenaria en el Perú* (Lima, 1990), vol. I (two other volumes in press).

Bolivia

The broadest chronological synthesis, beginning in precolonial times, is a popular treatment by Xavier Albó and Josep M. Barnadas, *La cara india y campesina de nuestra historia* (La Paz, 1990, third expanded ed.; 1st ed., 1984). Studies that are limited to the Andean region include an unpublished sociology thesis on the ayllu, from the Universidad de San Marcos, by the Aymara Tomás Huanca, *La desestructuración de los espacios socio-económicos andinos en el altiplano lacustre: Agresión colonial o resistencia comunitaria* (La Paz, 1984), and Silvia Rivera Cusicanqui's *Oprimidos pero no vencidos. Luchas del campesino aymara-qheshwa, 1900–1980* (La Paz, 1984; also published in Geneva, 1986), which is confined to the twentieth century. The edited volume by Fernando Calderón and Jorge Dandler (ed.), *Bolivia: la fuerza histórica del campesinado* (La Paz, 1984; also published in Geneva, 1986), includes important works from the colonial Tupaj Katari rebellion to the present.

In Bolivia as nowhere else, the most significant indigenous historical events in the first decades of this century have been rescued from oblivion by bilingual historians of indigenous origin. A productive Aymara group is the Taller de Historia Oral Andina (THOA, Andean Oral History Workshop), which untangles the skein of the "*cacique* movement." Specific studies include, for example, two works by Roberto Choque Canqui, "De la defensa del ayllu a la creación de la República del Qollasuyu: Historia del movimiento indígena de Bolivia (1912–1935)," in *III Encuentro de Estudios Bolivianos. Historia y evolución del movimiento popular* (Cochabamba, 1986), and *La subrevación y masacre de Jesus de Machaca* (La Paz, 1996; new expanded edition, with testimonies compiled by Esteban Ticona). Other resources include Carlos Mamani's *Taraqu 1866–*

1935. Masacre, guerra y renovación en la biografía de Eduardo Nina Qhispi. Agresión colonial y resistencia indígena (La Paz, 1991), and the testimony of the scribe Leandro Condori, *El escribano de los caciques apoderados. Kasikinakan purirarunakan qillqiripa. Testimonios* (La Paz, 1992; compiled and edited by Esteban Ticona). Also useful are the collective works by THOA such as *El indio Santos Marka T'ula: cacique principal de los ayllus de Callapa y apoderado general de las comunidades originarias de la República* (La Paz, 1988), and those of THOA's Silvia Rivera, like "Pedimos la revisión general de límites: Un episodio de incomunicación de castas en el movimiento de caciques-apoderados de los Andes bolivianos, 1919–1921," in Segundo Moreno and Frank Salomon (eds.), *Reproducción y transformación de las sociedades andinas . . .* , op cit. In addition the excellent monograph by Ramiro Condarco, *Zárate, el "temible" Willka Historia de la rebelión indígena de 1899 en la república de Bolivia* (La Paz, 1983, 2nd expanded ed.; 1st ed., La Paz, 1966), gives a global view of rural conflict at the turn of the century. René Arze, in *Guerra y conflictos sociales. El caso rural boliviano durante el conflicto del Chaco* (La Paz, 1988), provides a vivid account of the "parallel war" of Andean Indians against the hacendados during the Chaco War.

For the mid-century, Bolivia is the most heavily studied country because of widespread interest in the early agrarian reform starting in 1952. As in Peru, in these studies the ethnic dimension is almost completely flattened. On the peasant movements of this era, the works of Jorge Dandler stand out. An extensive English-language literature of this sort was published under the political science rubric; it can be sampled in *Beyond the Revolution: Bolivia Since 1952* by James Malloy (Pittsburgh, 1971).

Many of the best studies concentrate on the Quechua-speaking area of Cochabamba, which took the lead in the rural revolution. These include Dandler's *El sindicalismo campesino en Bolivia: Los cambios estructurales en Ucureña* (Mexico, 1969; 2nd ed. Cochabamba, 1983) and several articles in the volume edited by Calderón and Dandler, *Bolivia: la fuerza histórica . . .* , op cit. These articles include two by Dandler himself: "Campesinado y reforma agraria en Cochabamba (1952–1953): Dinámica de un movimiento campesino en Bolivia" (a summary of his 1971 doctoral dissertation from the University of Wisconsin, originally published in La Paz, 1975); and "La 'ch'ampa guerra' de Cochabamba: Un proceso de disgregación política"; as well as another coauthored by Juan Torrico,

"El Congreso Nacional Indigena de 1945 y la rebelión campesina de Ayopaya (1947)." The last is also published in English in *Resistance, Rebellion, and Consciousness . . .* , Steve J. Stern (ed.), op cit.

For other parts of the country there is an immense edited volume by Luis Antezana E. and Hugo Romero B., *Origen, desarrollo y situación actual del sindicalismo campesino en Bolivia. I, Bosquejo histórico del movimiento sindical en Bolivia* (La Paz, 1968; see also the condensed version, *La revolución campesina en Bolivia*, by Luis Antezana (La Paz, 1982). The Aymara mobilizations of Achacachi have been studied by Xavier Albó in *Achacachi, medio siglo de lucha campesina* (La Paz, 1979), and those of the Norte de Potosí by Olivia Harris and Xavier Albó, *Monteras y guardatojos. Campesinos y mineros en el Norte de Potosí* (La Paz, 1986; originally published 1974; republished and expanded). The resulting changes in the agrarian structure have been synthesized by Xavier Albó in *¿Bodas de plata? O requiem por una reforma agraria* (La Paz, 1979; 2nd ed., 1983), and by Miguel Urioste, *Segunda reforma agraria: campesinos, tierra y educación popular* (La Paz, 1987).

The indigenous resurgence since the end of the 1960s has been the subject of numerous works. The writer-politician Fausto Reinaga pioneered in reviving the lost ethnic dimension, especially in *La revolución india* (La Paz, 1969). Javier Hurtado's thesis, *El katarismo* (La Paz, 1986), is the most complete monograph on the origins of Katarismo, and the double essay by Xavier Albó, "De MNRistas a Kataristas: Campesinado, estado y partidos, 1953, 1953–1980," appeared in *Historia Boliviana* (Cochabamba) 5 (1985), 87–128; see also the revised English version published in *Resistance, Rebellion and Consciousness*, Steve J. Stern (ed.), op cit.; as well as . . . *Y de kataristas a MNRistas. La sorprendente y audaz alianza entre aymaras y neoliberales* (La Paz, 1994; condensed English version in *Indigenous People and Democracy*, Donna Van Cott (ed.), op cit. Taken together these texts cover the movement's evolution up to the present. They are complemented from a more Indianist perspective by Diego Pacheco's work, *El indianismo y los indios contemporáneos en Bolivia* (La Paz, 1992).

The CSUTCB 1984 proposal for a Basic Agrarian Law was the subject of a special edition of *Historia Boliviana* (Cochabamba), "Encuesta a los partidos políticos sobre el proyecto de Ley Agraria Fundamental," 5:1–2 (1985), 29–44. (This issue has other articles related to the rural sector.) *CSUTCB: Debate sobre documentos políticos y asamblea de comunidades*, by Ricardo Calla, José E. Pinelo, and Miguel Urioste (eds.) (La Paz,

1989), and *La revuelta de las nacionalidades*, by Diego Cuadros (ed.) (La Paz, 1991), are rich sources for the most recent documents and testimonies from the grassroots organizations. The historic 1990 march of the eastern Bolivian peoples was examined by Alex Contreras in *Etapa de una larga marcha* (La Paz, 1991). Among the many works about coca and cocaine, the one that comes closest to taking the perspective of the small producers is Centro de Documentación e Investigación Bolivia, "La absurda guerra de la coca," in *Violencias encubiertas en Bolivia*, vol. II, edited by Xavier Albó and Raúl Barrios (La Paz, 1993).

Ecuador

The Indian history of this Andean nation has been studied primarily in works related to the colonial period and the rebellions of the first Republican era, up to the great uprising of Daquilema in 1870. But the first half of the twentieth century shows a deafening silence on the part of scholars, as if nonwhite Ecuador no longer existed. The main exception was the pioneering work of Pío Jaramillo Alvarado, *El indio ecuatoriano* (Quito, 1954, 4th ed.; 1st ed., 1922), which is not a history but does insist on the historic presence of the neglected majority. The *Misión Andina* mounted by various United Nation agencies helped break the silence; see two works of the indigenist Gonzalo Rubio Orbe, *Aspectos indígenas* (Quito, 1965), and *Los indios ecuatorianos. Evolución histórica y políticas indigenistas* (Quito, 1987).

In the last few decades, beginning with the vigorous reemergence of the Indian question, interest in indigenous history has flourished once more. Oswaldo Albornoz was one of the first scholars to pick up this theme in *Las luchas indígenas en el Ecuador* (Guayaquil, 1974). The broadest synthesis of indigenous history in this century is provided by two extensive articles by Diego Iturralde, "Notas para una historia política del campesinado ecuatoriano (1900–1980)," in Lauris McKee and Silvia Argüello (eds.), *Nuevas investigaciones antropológicas ecuatorianas* (Quito, 1988); and "Nacionalidades indígenas y estado nacional en el Ecuador," in *Nueva historia del Ecuador*, vol. XIII (Quito, 1988). The prolific and incisive historian Andrés Guerrero has explored many moments and dimensions in his monographs and articles – for example, *Haciendas, capital y lucha de clases andina* (Quito, 1984), and *La semántica de la dominación: el concertaje de indios* (Quito, 1991). The 1990 uprising also provoked many widespread reflections on longer historical processes, above all the works of Andrés Guerrero and León Zamosc in the anthology, *Sismo étnico en el Ecuador* (Quito, 1993). We have also consulted an unpublished manuscript by Ruth Moya, *Derechos culturales y pueblos indígenas: El caso del Ecuador*, presented to the División des Droits de l'Homme et de la Paix, UNESCO (Paris, 1987). CONAIE itself has compiled exhaustive histories of each indigenous organization, available in *Las nacionalidades indígenas en el Ecuador. Nuestro proceso organizativo* (Quito, 1989). This volume covers the decades of the 1960s to 1980s and also includes a useful chronology of achievements related to that history.

The early Cayambe uprisings, which led to the formation of the FEI in 1945, have inspired, among others, the beautiful anthology of Indian testimonies prepared by José Yánez del Pozo, *Yo declaro con franqueza. Cashnami causashcanchic. Memoria oral de Pesillo, Cayambe* (Quito, 1986). The period of the agrarian reforms, which in Ecuador was more explicitly founded on "classist" than "peasantist" lines, has been the subject of various works: Fernando Velasco, *Reforma agraria y movimiento campesino indígena en la Sierra* (Quito, 1983); Osvaldo Barsky, *La reforma agraria ecuatoriana* (Quito, 1984); CEDOC–CEDEP, *Las luchas campesinas, 1950–1983. Movilización campesina e historia de la FENOC* (Quito, 1984), which deals with FENOC, the principal classist organization; and Manuel Chiriboga, *El problema agrario en el Ecuador* (Quito, 1988). ECUARUNARI, which has been at the heart of the ethnicity versus class debates, has been studied from the "classist" perspective by Alicia Ibarra in *Los indígenas y el estado en el Ecuador. La práctica neoindigenista* (Quito, 1987).

It is the ethnic resurgence that has drawn the most attention by writers in the last few years. Roberto Santana, who realized the importance of ECUARUNARI before most others, has made several contributions: "En la sierra del Ecuador: reivindicaciones étnicas y agrarias. El caso de un movimiento indígena," in *Indianidad, etnocidio e indigenismo*, Claude Bataillon et al., op cit., and *Ciudadanos en la etnicidad. Los indios en la política o la política de los indios* (Quito, 1995). His *Les Indiens d'Equateur, citoyens dans l'ethnicité* (Paris, 1992) synthesizes a candid and astute viewpoint. For a broad overview, see the special edition of *Cuadernos de Nueva,* "La cuestión indígena en el Ecuador" (Número 7, monographic, edited by Manuel Chiriboga, 1983), Lourdes Conterón and Rosa de Viteri, *Organizaciones indígenas del Ecuador* (Quito, 1984), and above all the thorough compilation published by CONAIE itself, *Las nacionalidades indígenas*, cited previously.

The 1990 Indian uprising already has stimulated a substantial literature. Leon Zamosc has contributed a valuable English overview in "Agrarian protest and the Indian movement in the Ecuadorian highlands," *Latin American Research Review* 29:3 (1994), 37–68. For post-1992 developments an expert eyewitness account exists in English, Lynn A. Meisch's " 'We will not dance on the tomb of our grandparents': 500 years of resistance in Ecuador," *Latin American Anthropology Review* 4:2 (1994), 55–74. Recommended are Jorge León, *De campesinos a ciudadanos diferentes* (Quito, 1994; includes commentary by other authors); the collective works *Indios*, prepared by ILDIS (Instituto Latinoamericano de Investigaciones Sociales; 1992); and *Sismo étnico en el Ecuador*, prepared by CEDIME (Centro de Documentación e Información de los Movimientos Sociales del Ecuador, 1993). Especially interesting is *Kipu*'s *Informe especial sobre el levantamiento indígena en la prensa ecuatoriana* (nos. 14 and 15, 1990, and nos. 22 and 23, 1994). Abya Yala is the main publisher on indigenous peoples, cultures, and movements, not only in Ecuador but for all of South America.

Colombia

I do not know of any systematic history of all the numerous indigenous groups in this nation. Above all, the excellent work of Joanne Rappaport, *The Politics of Memory. Native Historical Interpretation in the Colombian Andes* (Cambridge, 1990), stands out in its treatment of the historic vision of the chief native Andean people of Colombia, the Páez, since mythic times. Other general ethnological works about Colombian Indians, such as that of Roberto Pineda (ed.), *Introducción a la Colombia indígena* (Bogotá, 1987), include some historical elements.

Considering the early period in which they were written, the brief but juicy texts of Juan Friede merit special mention: *El indio en lucha por la tierra. Historia de los resguardos del macizo central colombiano* (Bogotá, 1972; 1st ed., 1944). Above all it is essential to read the direct testimony of the indigenous Páez fighter and writer Quintín Lame, *En defensa de mi raza* (Bogotá, 1939/1971), and *Las luchas del indio que bajó de la montaña al valle de la "civilización"* (Bogotá, 1973). Lame can be read in English in *Liberation Theology from Below*, by Gonzalo Castillo Cárdenas (Maryknoll, N.Y., 1987). Chapter seven of Rappaport's *Politics of Memory* (op cit.) includes as well a detailed analysis of Victor Daniel Bonilla's interviews with the oral historian Julio Niquinás, who was Lame's secretary.

For long periods we have only been able to piece together the slight data about Indians in works dedicated to the peasantry, such as Jesús Antonio Bejarano, "Campesinado, luchas agrarias e historia social en Colombia: Notas para un balance historiográfico," in Pablo González Casanova (ed.), *Historia política de los campesinos latinoamericanos*, op cit.; León Zamosc, *La cuestión agraria y el movimiento campesino en Colombia. Luchas de la Asociación Nacional de Usuarios Campesinos (ANUC), 1967–1981* (Geneva, 1987); and the most specific one, by Silvia Rivera, *Política e ideología en el movimiento campesino colombiano. El caso de la ANUC (Asociación Nacional de Usuarios Campesinos)* (Geneva, 1987). For the period of *La Violencia* – which provoked so many studies – see Russell W. Ramsey, "Critical bibliography of La Violencia in Colombia," *Latin American Research Review* 8:1 (1973), 3–44; Germán Guzmán et al., *La violencia en Colombia*, 3 vols. (Bogotá, 1964); Russell Ramsey, *Guerrilleros y soldados* (Bogotá, 1981); and the brief essay by Eric J. Hobsbawm, "The revolutionary situation in Colombia," *World Today* (June 1963), 248–258. Nina S. de Friedemann, Juan Friede, and Darío Fajardo, *Indigenismo y aniquilamiento de indígenas en Colombia* (Bogotá, 1981, 2nd ed. expanded; 1st ed., 1975), is one of the few explicitly indigenist texts for all these periods.

For the years since the 1970s, I have relied on the history prepared by CRIC (Consejo Regional Indígena del Cauca), *Diez años de lucha. Historia y documentos* (Bogotá, 1981), and the useful day-by-day chronicle provided since 1975 by the newspaper *Unidad Indígena. UI* was the main organ of CRIC and later spoke also for ONIC (Organización Nacional Indígena de Colombia). It includes occasional historical accounts of earlier periods. Francisco Beltrán and Lucila Mejía have published a biography of the Páez martyr, Alvaro Ulcué: *La utopía mueve montañas* (Bogotá, 1989). The indigenous resurgence expressed in the new Political Constitution of 1991 has been collected by Avirama and Márquez in "The indigenous movement in Colombia," a contribution to Donna Lee Van Cott (ed.), *Indigenous Peoples and Democracy in Latin America* (New York, 1994), 83–106. This includes the English translation of several constitutional articles most relevant to the indigenous topic.

Chile

In the far south of the Andean chain, the most abundant information refers to the Mapuche, who are by far the most significant indigenous people. The outstanding work is the contribution of José Bengoa, *Historia del pueblo mapuche* (Santiago de Chile, 1985), above all regarding the era up to the end of the nineteenth century. For the period since 1900, that of Rolf Foerster and Sonia Montecino, *Organizaciones, líderes y contiendas mapuches (1900–1970)* (Santiago, 1988), has been the principal source used here. Louis C. Faron's *The Mapuche Indians of Chile* (New York, 1968) and *Mapuche Social Structure* (Urbana, Illinois, 1961) are familiar English references.

For other ethnic groups, Juan Van Kessel has provided additional data about the Aymara of the north in *Holocausto al progreso. Los aymaras de Tarapacá* (Amsterdam, 1980), and "Los aymaras contemporáneos de Chile (1879–1985); su historia social" (Iquique, 1988). Anne Chapman's *Drama and power in a hunting society. The Selk'nam of Tierra de Fuego* (Cambridge, 1982; Spanish version, Buenos Aires, 1986), and Angel Cabeza's "El etnocidio de los onas de Tierra del Fuego," *Nütram* (Santiago) 3:3 (1987): 49–67, complement the picture by concentrating on the minority groups of the far south. We have not discussed the natives of the Atacama desert oases, historically called Atacameños and already hispanicized. Their specific ethnic identity is reemerging only under the Nueva Ley Indígena of 1993. Also outside the main scope are the indigenous people of Easter Island, called Rapa Nui, who are only tenuously linked to Chilean history.

For more recent periods I have found especially useful the work of Ivo Bavarovic, Pilar Campaña, and Cecilia Díaz y Esteban Durán, *Campesinado mapuche y procesos socio-culturales regionales* (Santiago, 1987), which includes statistical data about the Mapuche world; Héctor González and Hans Gundermann, *Campesinos y aymaras en el norte de Chile* (Arica, 1989) for the Aymaras; and the bulletin *Nütram* (since 1985), at first concentrated on the Mapuche case but later treating the entire Indian question.

26

LOWLAND PEOPLES OF THE TWENTIETH CENTURY

DAVID MAYBURY-LEWIS

The indigenous peoples of lowland South America have until recently been marginal to the history of the continent.[1] The Spanish focused on the rich highland regions taken over from the Aztecs and the Inka and regarded the lowlands as frontier areas, difficult of access and lacking the large settled populations that could be put to work to enrich their overlords. The lowlands were therefore largely left to missionaries and those settlers who had failed to make their fortunes elsewhere. These were regions little involved in the major events of the Spanish empire or in the turbulent nineteenth-century histories of the republics that succeeded it in South America. It is true that the lowland peoples of the upper Amazon did give the Spanish authorities a serious fright in 1742, when they rebelled against Spanish rule under their leader, Juan Santos Atahuallpa whom they considered the new Inka. But the rebellion faded out, and the lowland peoples returned to their marginal obscurity until they were brutally dragged into the limelight during the Rubber Boom 150 years later.

In Portuguese America there were no great highland empires to be conquered. The lowland peoples *were* the native population, and the Portuguese systematically enslaved them. In fact the Portuguese slavers

[1] Because this chapter deals with so many countries, I am fortunate to have been able to rely on the help of a number of specialists. I particularly wish to thank Nelly Arvelo-Jiménez and David Guss for their advice on Venezuela, Jean Jackson and Maria Clemencia Ramirez de Jara (Colombia), Ted Macdonald Jr. (Ecuador), Bartholomew Dean (Peru), Bret Gustafson (Bolivia), and Richard Reed (Paraguay). I am also most grateful to Nicole Thornton Burnett, Denis McDonough, and Lena Mortensen for their invaluable research assistance. Finally I want to express my thanks to the Tinker Foundation, The Woodrow Wilson Center, and the John Simon Guggenheim Foundation for fellowships that enabled me to begin my comparative work on the indigenous peoples of the Americas, and to the United States Institute for Peace for a fellowship that enabled me to complete this manuscript.

became so ruthlessly efficient that they succeeded in eliminating the indigenous populations of large areas of the hinterland and driving the surviving native peoples into the least accessible parts of the continent. As the availability of forced indigenous labor dwindled in their Brazilian colony, the Portuguese took to importing black slaves from west Africa. By the end of the eighteenth century, Brazil had become a place where a white élite ruled over a large, servile black population, and the Indians were both socially and economically marginal.

This chapter deals with the lowland peoples of northern South America who inhabit the countries surrounding the Amazon Basin (see Map 26.1). These populations are scattered throughout Venezuela, Colombia, Ecuador, Peru, Bolivia, Paraguay, and Brazil, so it will be necessary to say something about the policies and particular circumstances of all of these countries. The approximate numbers of lowland Indians living in each of these nations are given in Table 26.1. Such numbers can be no more than rough estimates for a number of reasons. There is no precise definition of the lowlands and therefore no way to establish the geographical boundaries of such a region. The question of who consider themselves (or are considered) to be indigenous is also a highly ideological one. Official census figures often minimize the numbers of indigenous people in order to show that people once considered "Indians" have now abandoned their Indianness and passed into the mainstream. Individuals who might otherwise have been considered Indians may in certain times and places reject that designation for the same reason. Alternatively, people who were once reticent about being considered "Indian" may nowadays accept or insist on that designation, as a result of the growing influence of the indigenous rights movement. The numbers of Indians in any area thus fluctuate according to people's feelings about Indianness. In fact governments throughout the Americas have frequently sought to abolish Indianness (and therefore Indians) by a stroke of the pen. Simón Bolívar himself tried to abolish the status (and with it the derogatory term) of *indio* in Gran Colombia, and many others have sought to follow his lead by simply insisting that Indians are henceforward to be known and treated as *campesinos* – as, for example, after the Bolivian revolution of 1952 and under General Velasco's reformist regime that took power in Peru in 1968. Finally, accurate censuses of the native peoples of lowland South America have never been taken, precisely because they have always been so marginal and relatively inaccessible.

In this chapter I deal first with the indigenous peoples of the three major

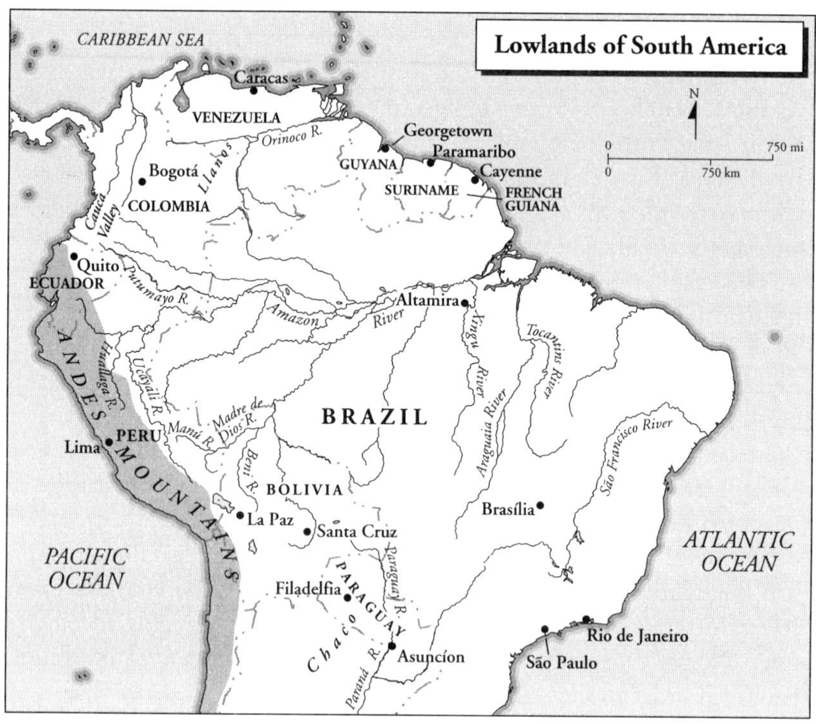

Map 26.1

lowland nations of Amazonian South America (Venezuela, Brazil, and Paraguay) and then with the lowland peoples of the Andean nations (Colombia, Ecuador, Peru, and Bolivia). Venezuela contains the northernmost spur of the Andes and is sometimes considered an Andean nation (e.g., in the Cambridge History of Latin America). I treat it here as a lowland country because its indigenous population is essentially a lowland one.

VENEZUELAN INDIANS IN THE TWENTIETH CENTURY

The captaincy general of Venezuela was Spain's most successful agricultural colony in the eighteenth century, exporting the finest cacao to Mexico and Europe. It was grown in plantations worked by slave labor – there were some 45,000 black slaves in a total population of about 900,000 around 1830. Coffee came to rival cacao in importance soon after independence, but it was cultivated by sharecroppers and free labor-

Table 26.1. *Estimates of Lowland and Total Indian Populations.* In the table below are estimations of Indian populations. The lowest, highest, and average populations are given by country. In cases where only one estimation was found, it alone is listed.

Country	Lowland peoples	Total Indian population	Average total Indian population as % of total population
Bolivia	low: 80,000 high: 187,000 average: 133,500	low: 2,514,851 high: 4,900,000 average: 3,755,228	63%
Brazil	low: 200,000 high: 300,000 average: 248,333	low: 200,000 high: 300,000 average: 248,333	.2%
Colombia	81,000	low: 300,000 high: 600,000 average: 441,356	1.8%
Ecuador	low: 70,000 high: 97,857 average: 83,928	low: 2,070,000 high: 4,100,000 average: 2,941,549	38%
Paraguay	low:67,000 high: 100,000 average: 79,000	low: 67,000 high: 100,000 average: 79,000	2.7%
Peru	low: 206,240 high: 242,000 average: 242,120	low: 3,367,140 high: 9,300,000 average: 6,230,750	38%
Venezuela	low: 105,000 high: 400,000 average: 235,889	low: 105,000 high: 400,000 average: 235,889	1.7%

Sources:

Burger, Julian. 1987. *Report from the Frontier: The State of the World's Indigenous Peoples.* Cambridge, MA: Cultural Survival, p. 89.

CELADE (Latin American Demographic Center). 1992. Demographic Bulletin 25(50). Santiago.

Gnerre, M. 1990. "Indigenous Peoples in Latin America." Working Paper #30, International Fund for Agricultural Development. Rome.

Mayer, Enrique, and Elio Masferrer. 1979. "La población Indígena de América en 1978." *América Indígena,* vol. XXXIX, no. 2: 211–337.

ers. Black slavery was soon abolished, and Indian labor had not been vital to the economy for some time. In fact Venezuela took early and firm steps to try to abolish Indians as a category altogether.

The nation's first constitution in 1821 followed the Bolivarian idea of denying legal existence to indigenous groups and only recognizing the rights of Indians as individuals. Throughout the nineteenth century, successive regimes followed this path, issuing further legislation to divide Indian lands and deprive indigenous peoples of group rights in 1836, 1838, and 1885. The trend was continued into the twentieth century with the passage of additional laws in the same vein in 1904 and 1936. No wonder that Francisco Hernández, writing from a lawyer's viewpoint, was constrained to remark that

> We can in fact distinguish two intimately related characteristics of [our] Indian Law, the one following from the other, namely its profusion of laws and decrees and their heterogeneity. It is an extraordinary legislative profusion, resulting from an excessive abundance of solutions given, without any legal innovation.[2]

The laws upon laws that Venezuela passed were all intended to abolish the *resguardos*, or reserves that the Spanish crown had established for indigenous communities, and to ensure the closing of every possible loophole that would allow indigenous peoples to maintain a corporate existence. They were successful. This process of what Arvelo-Jiménez has called "legalized theft" of indigenous lands[3] caused the virtual disappearance of all the indigenous groups north of the Orinoco River, with the sole exception of the Kariña in the far northeast.

The Indians to the south of the Orinoco were specifically exempted from these laws because they were considered savage forest dwellers, living far away from the heart of Venezuela in distant frontier regions. Under the dictatorship of Juan Vicente Gómez (1908–1935), these remote Indians were formally placed under the tutelage of the Catholic Church. The Mission Law (1915) signed by President Gómez and the Vatican declared that the areas occupied by Indians in the south were *tierras baldías*, or vacant lands, hence belonging to the nation. In a series of agreements signed subsequently, different Catholic orders were awarded areas of territory on condition that they devote themselves to the "reduction and attraction to national citizenry of the tribes and Indian groups which still exist in different regions of the Republic."[4] Because there were

[2] Hernández, Francisco, "Las Comunidades Indígenas en Venezuela y el Problema de la Tenencia de la Tierra," in Jiménez and Perezo (eds.), *Esperando a Kuyujani* (Caracas: GAIA-IVIC, 1994), 45–68. My translation from the original Spanish.

[3] Arvelo-Jiménez, Nelly, "The politics of cultural survival in Venezuela: Beyond indigenismo," In Marianne Schmink and Charles Wood (eds.), *Frontier Expansion in Amazonia* (Gainesville, FL: University of Florida Press, 1984): 106, fn4.

[4] Ibid., 107.

no pressing strategic or economic reasons for the development of the south, the state was content to leave its indigenous inhabitants in missionary hands until fairly recently. This meant that there really was no Venezuelan *indigenismo* in the sense of any special policy for the nation's Indians. On the contrary, from the earliest days of the republic, Venezuela's official policy had been to do away with Indian groups and incorporate their members as individuals into the mainstream of the nation. The missions in the south were seen as presiding over the first stage of this process.

It was not until 1945 that this policy was challenged. The period from 1945–1948 was a time of change in Venezuela. The death of Vicente Gómez brought his long dictatorship to an end in 1936, and in 1945 the military was removed from office. Rómulo Betancourt became president in an administration formed by the AD (Democratic Action) party. In the same year the Congress of Pátzcuaro, held in Mexico, focused for the first time on indigenous peoples and indigenous affairs throughout the hemisphere. Venezuelan *indigenistas* took the opportunity to press the government to form a special agency to deal with indigenous affairs. Such an agency – OCAI (The Central Office of Indigenous Affairs) – was created in the Ministry of the Interior, but whatever influence it might have had was limited by the military regime of Pérez Jiménez, which established a new dictatorship from 1948–1958. Authority over the Indians of the south and especially the control of their education were left in the hands of the missions. OCAI was forced to work outside the mission territories and focused almost exclusively on the protection of the Kariña, who were seriously threatened by oil drilling in the northeast.

Nor did the agrarian reform law, passed in 1960 after Betancourt and the AD returned to power, promise much for the Indians. It was intended mainly for the landless in the areas north of the Orinoco. The indigenous areas to the south were still treated as *tierras baldías*. Within them indigenous populations had no guarantees. On the contrary, their use of their lands was explicitly seen as temporary, and the new constitution adopted in 1961 called once again for the protection of indigenous communities *and their integration into national life*.

The decade of the 1960s, however, brought the frontier regions of Venezuela's far south into the forefront of the national consciousness. President Pérez Jiménez had misspent the growing oil revenues of the country and left it in bad financial shape. The Cuban revolution encouraged revolutionaries throughout Latin America and likewise mobilized counterrevolutionaries. There were armed uprisings in Veneuela, too. In 1964 there were sixteen separate guerilla groups operating in the field, but by the end of the decade this number had been reduced to three by the effective response of the Venezuelan army at a time when the gross national product was rising dramatically. Meanwhile there was growing national interest in the development of the remote regions of the country, leading the government to set up an agency (CODESUR) to coordinate activities involved in the "Conquest of the South," as the program was called.

CODESUR mobilized in the early seventies, when Venezuela was benefiting from the boom in oil prices. It instigated the building of roads and airports to link the Amazon region to the rest of the country; it set up a radio station that broadcast in Indian languages to the local populations; and it sponsored technical studies of the natural resources of the region. Its Indian policies continued however to be assimilationist. It relied on the agrarian reform law to expropriate indigenous territories. Through its special office for the donation of land to indigenous communities, it parceled out lands, but only to indigenous communities that set up as "peasant enterprises." This forced peoples who had often been seminomadic and in any case were accustomed to living off a richly variegated environment to settle on smaller plots and engage in agricultural production for the market. The results were predictable. The Indians ended up suffering from undernourishment and ill health.

It was also in the early seventies that the Indians began to form their own federations in the south. In 1972 indigenous federations were established in each southern state and territory, and in 1973 they came together in the Confederation of Venezuelan Indians. At the same time, there was influential opposition to this assertion of indigenous rights. The social democratic administration that took office under president Carlos Andrés Pérez in 1974 treated the Conquest of the South as a matter of national security. Under the previous administration Indian affairs had been handled nationally by OCAI, which dealt with the National Agrarian Institute (IAN) and CODESUR, whose indigenous policies were at least public and contestable. The new administration transformed OCAI into OMAFI, the Ministerial Office for Frontier and Indigenous Affairs, thus subordinating indigenous policy to the national security issues of the frontier. This was made quite explicit with the passage of the Organic Law for Security and Defense in 1976.

The late sixties and early seventies were a period when national security became an ideological doctrine and blueprint for policy in many South

American countries, such as Brazil, Argentina, and Chile. In Venezuela the doctrine did not involve a military takeover of the state, but it seems to have led to the adoption of policies in the south that were similar to and probably intended to counterbalance those of the Brazilian military on the other side of the frontier. A new Ministry of the Environment and Renewable Natural Resources was created with the authority to designate areas of the south as ABRAE (Areas under a Regime of Special Administration). This meant that, in the name of protecting and supervising the exploitation of the natural resources of the country, the government could take control of regions and expropriate their indigenous inhabitants.

The tenor of these policies is clearly shown by the sharp reaction to a proposal to create a biospheric reserve that would protect the Yanomami Indians and their environment. The Foreign Ministry, where an influential group of security and development advocates were located, castigated the proposed reserve as an undemocratic conspiracy against the nation, and it prevented its creation. Meanwhile the Yanomami have suffered horribly in the name of development, both on the Venezuelan and the Brazilian sides of the frontier.

Venezuela's policy toward its indigenous peoples has thus been one of total assimilation or, in remoter areas, missionary tutelage to prepare for assimilation. In recent years the development and national security aspects of the Conquest of the South have come to take precedence over missionary tutelage. This picture is somewhat confused by the entry of the Summer Institute of Linguistics (SIL) onto the scene. This Protestant group claims to be solely engaged in translating the Bible into all the native languages of the world and educating the native speakers to read it. It nevertheless engages in considerable missionary work alongside of its translating and educational efforts (Stoll, 1982), as indicated by its alternative designation – the New Tribes Mission. The SIL entered Venezuela without legal authorization, coming from Colombia, from which it had been expelled in 1946. Venezuela's Ministry of Justice granted it a permit to work in the Federal Territory of the Amazon in 1953. By the late 1960s the presence and activities of these American evangelists were being questioned both inside and outside of congress. The campaign against them gathered strength in the 1970s. They were accused in the Venezuelan Congress and the press of prospecting for precious resources, of espionage, of working for North American intelligence agencies, and implausibly also (or alternatively) having some connection with the Cubans. The accusations were investigated, but no action was taken other than to issue a formal condemnation of their educational methods. The reasons for this concern are not obscure. Indians had traditionally been entrusted to the care of missions in Venezuela, but this mission was different. It was well financed, with an infrastructure of planes and communications equipment such as the traditional missions did not possess. It was American, had entered the country illegally, worked only in the areas of national security, and reported back to its headquarters in the United States.

Meanwhile Indians and pro-indigenous sympathizers also mounted a campaign against the SIL for its disregard of and determination to destroy traditional Indian cultures. In 1978 a short documentary film "Yo hablo a Caracas" ("I speak to Caracas") was shown in the capital. In the course of it, an old Ye'kuana (YeKuana) shaman spoke as follows:

> I speak, I speak to Caracas
> to its people, to its men
> Wanadi has been my source
> Osedum, Osedum Wanadi
> The creation of people exists
> because I know it was that way
> The memory of my beginning is always here
> Because all that we have was created here
> The source of our food like Marawaka
> and the branch of the guayteyama that
> still exists and will always exist here . . .
> in our lands, those lands that speak in my tongue
> my land is this one, where my people live
>
> It's mine because my community's here
> because my source, Wanadi, lived here
> in this land which I love
> just as you love the land of Caracas
> Wanadi made good people with white dirt
> but he also made bad people
> Those were the Spanish, the French
> All those people came to the land of Caracas to do evil
> The whole population was swept up by them
> They were the same race as us
> They didn't have the strength to stop the white people
> After the people of Caracas were done with
> the bad people came to where we lived
> to where we still live today
> They're the bad white people
> They're the foreign missionaries we call Juruncu

Wanadi gave them the iron to make machines with
That's what my father told me

We, the Ye'kuana, we don't have any of that, so those
people exploit us because they think they own everything

I say: I don't accept
I don't accept the Catholic belief . . . the Evangelicals,
because those beliefs go against our life . . . our way of being

They want us to forget them
They tell us: "Don't make *ademi,* don't sing."
They say to us: "Don't drink *yarake.*"
They say: "That's not the truth."
That's the reason . . . that's why I don't accept

I never wanted to become an Evangelical or a Catholic
because
I always wanted to maintain my own tradition, my own
customs
Wanadi, no one knows how he began or who made him
All I know is that he existed
that he still exists

I ask for security and protection
I'm not claiming anyone else's lands
just those that belong to us:
the headwaters of the Cunucunuma, the Ventuari, the
Padamo and the Cuntinami . . . all those that speak in
my tongue

I say that we are friends
We live in the same land
but we must respect each other to be able to live
in harmony with our tribes
I know that all this is very difficult to understand
since we're all contradicting each other right now
We're guilty for the presence of bad whites
in our community

Yes, that's what I think

(by Barne Yavari, Ye'kuana shaman, Venezuela;
translated by David Guss)[5]

[5] Reprinted from the *Cultural Survival Quarterly* 4(1) (1980), 5.

This moving testimony caused a considerable stir in Caracas. The film won national and international awards and raised the consciousness of Venezuelans about their nation's Indian question. A Committee for National Identity was formed, supported by film producers, academics, poets, writers, and others who showed films, organized exhibitions, and published articles about indigenous issues. In 1979 the committee gathered eighty representatives from different Indian groups, who voted unanimously to demand the expulsion of the New Tribes Mission from Venezuela. In 1980 the committee organized protest marches in Caracas that drew upward of 3,000 to 4,000 marchers to reiterate this demand.

The mission was not expelled, but these events show how Venezuelan nationalism and the country's incipient indigenist movement came together in the 1970s. It was not the nationalism of the indigenists that carried the day eventually, but that of the national security advocates. The Venezuelan indigenous federation, although supported by the Venezuelan Peasant Federation, has not been strong enough or found enough backing in Venezuelan society to win many battles for indigenous rights. On the contrary, Venezuela has succeeded in going from a neocolonial policy of assimilation to a modern developmentalist policy of assimilation without ever admitting that indigenous groups have a right to maintain their own existence within the nation.

BRAZILIAN INDIANS IN THE TWENTIETH CENTURY

Brazil was explored early and settled late. Slavers and adventurers penetrated into the remote recesses of the hinterland as early as in the seventeenth century, yet the bulk of the nation's population still hugged the coast 200 years later. At the time when the United States was following its "manifest destiny" to the Pacific Ocean and Argentina and Chile were extending their national territories to the tip of the South American continent, there was no comparable push to settle the interior of Brazil.

Indigenous people were not therefore as hard pressed in nineteenth-century Brazil as they were elsewhere in the Americas. Nor were the effects of the Rubber Boom as devastating to them as they were in other Amazonian regions. Some Indian peoples managed to gather rubber without being sucked into slavery to do so. Others retreated out of reach of the rubber companies or traded with them rather than working for them. The bulk of the workforce that entered the virtual slavery of debt peonage[6] to gather rubber was eventually made up of poor migrants from Brazil's northeast, rather then of Amazonian Indians. It is true that Indians were usually and routinely mistreated whenever they came in contact with outsiders, but these contacts were not as intense as in other countries, where systematic efforts were made to eliminate indigenous cultures and often to exterminate the Indians as well. Independent Brazil, by contrast, was a settled agrarian society, governed by its own emperor, descended from the royal house of Portugal. It was a huge archipelago of poorly connected regions that largely communicated with each other by sea or by means of one or two of Brazil's innumerable river systems. It had long since stopped trying to force Indians to do the work of the nation, except in remote Amazonian regions, and had turned instead to slaves imported from Africa. At independence in 1822, less than a third of the population of about 2.5 million were considered white. The remainder were blacks or mixtures of black and white, with only about 5 percent considered Indian. As the nineteenth century wore on, Brazil was preoccupied with the future of its imperial house and the issue of black slavery, rather than with territorial expansion and what to do about the indigenous peoples who might stand in the way. It was in fact so slow to abolish slavery that some southerners from the United States emigrated to Brazil after the civil war in order to go on living as slave-holding plantation owners. This era came to an end with the abolition of slavery in 1888. The abdication of the emperor and the proclamation of the republic both followed swiftly in 1889.

Meanwhile the Indians were marginal to the life of the nation. They were exotic peoples at or beyond the effective frontiers, a nuisance to be dealt with by frontiersmen and an occasional topic for sentimental elegies by intellectuals. José de Alencar, who was venerated as the father of Brazilian literature during his lifetime (1829–1877), wrote his famous novels *O Guaraní* and *Iracema*, celebrating the loves of Indian men for white women and white men for Indian women and thus contributed to the Brazilian myth of amicable miscegenation. Karl von Martius, the famous German explorer-ethnographer wrote a prize-winning essay in

[6] This system, known as *aviamento* in Brazil, was one in which rubber tappers were advanced the bare necessities of life and the tools of their trade on credit by their overseers. The tapper was obliged to repay the overseer by bringing in latex. The overseer calculated the value of the latex and subtracted it from the tapper's debt but always found that the value of the rubber did not equal the value of the goods advanced. Tappers were therefore perpetually in debt. If they tried to escape this bondage by fleeing downriver, they would be intercepted by the rubber company or by the police and sent back to their masters for punishment and to work off their debt.

1844, suggesting that Brazilian history should be written as a tribute to the almalgamation of the Indian, white, and black races. The role of the Indians was critical to the self image of white Brazilians, because they were considered to be more acceptable ancestors than blacks who made up the lowest strata of Brazilian society. But the Indians, unlike the blacks or the whites, were expected to vanish. Their passing might be lamented, but it was felt to be inevitable. In fact a century later Gilberto Freyre, who was actually trained in anthropology by Franz Boas at Columbia University, wrote in *The Masters and the Slaves* of the formation of Brazil, its culture, and character. Like von Martius he considered that Brazil was a product of Indian, black, and white traditions, but he treated the Indians as if they were now only a memory, surviving in the customs, songs, games, and recipes that they had bequeathed to Brazilian culture.

Yet Brazil's Indians had not and still have not vanished. Freyre's neglect of his indigenous contemporaries is remarkable considering the fact that they became a national issue in the early twentieth century, when their cause was championed by a young army officer, Cândido Mariano da Silva Rondon. Rondon, who took pride in being part Bororo Indian, established a reputation as an explorer with a talent for befriending the Indians. He was therefore appointed by the president to lead a difficult expedition through the Indian country of northwestern Brazil to lay a telegraph line linking the nation's major cities in the southeast with the remote northwestern extremity of the country. His expedition was a resounding success, largely thanks to the policy that he enforced among his men, which was summed up in his motto: "Die if need be, but never kill." Rondon's men did not kill, and they did not die either; they succeeded in traveling for thousands of miles through "Indian country" while keeping on good terms with the peoples they met along the way. So Rondon returned to a hero's welcome in Rio de Janeiro in 1910, at a time when the killing of Indians in another part of Brazil was earning the country a bad press internationally. German immigrants, clearing land in the southern state of Santa Catarina, hired Indian hunters to get rid of Indians who were defending their forests and attacking the settlers. The atrocities committed against these Indians were denounced at an international congress held in Vienna in 1908 and embarrassed the Brazilian government, which was trying to encourage European immigration at the time. The settlers were defended, however, by Professor Hermann von Ihering, the German-born director of the Museum of the State of

São Paulo, one of Brazil's prestigious research institutions. Professor von Ihering argued that the Indians were bound to disappear anyway, to make way for civilization, and that in the meantime the settlers had a right to defend themselves.

Predictably Rondon opposed this view and was supported by scientists from the National Museum in Rio de Janeiro. The polemic thus pitted two major research institutions, drawn from Brazil's two major and rival cities, against each other. Public opinion sided with Rondon, whose policy of befriending the Indians was held to be in the best tradition of Brazil's own Christian values, as opposed to the imperialist and racist views of German immigrants and German-born scholars. There are ironies in these views. Rondon himself was not an orthodox Christian, but a devout positivist. The people killing Indians in Santa Catarina were themselves Brazilians, doing what Brazilians had been doing to Indians at the frontiers since the conquest. Nevertheless Rondon's standing in the country was so high that his views carried the day. In 1910 President Nilo Peçanha signed legislation to establish a department of the federal government to deal with indigenous affairs. In 1911 this department, known as the Service for the Protection of Indians and National Workers, came into being with Rondon as its president.

The legislation that brought the new Indian Service into being was extraordinarily liberal. At a time when von Ihering's views represented the conventional wisdom among educated people, the Brazilian congress approved laws that guaranteed to indigenous peoples not only the lands they occupied but also a series of other rights, including the right to maintain their own traditions. It was to be the duty of the Indian Service to see that these guarantees were enforced. The paradox of a conservative congress, dominated by rural oligarchs, passing such liberal laws regarding Indians is understandable if we consider that the laws did not affect the immediate interests of the oligarchs, who controlled the national and state legislatures and the settled agrarian society that was Brazil at that time. The new legislation was therefore a beautiful gesture that did not inconvenience the oligarchs. On the contrary, it had the practical effect of setting up an agency with federal funds to deal with remote indigenous peoples who might in the future interfere with settlers (the national workers) and otherwise create headaches for the states.

The agency soon came to be known as the SPI, because it early on lost that part of its title that made it responsible for settling national workers. This did at least clarify its mission. Settlers were usually the enemies of the Indians, and the mission of the SPI was to protect the latter, if necessary, against the former. It was a difficult task, which would have required a big budget and a large number of dedicated employees if it were to be carried out effectively in a country as large as Brazil. But the SPI was always underfunded, and its support, financial and otherwise, dwindled after Getúlio Vargas seized power in the revolution of 1930. Rondon had not supported Vargas, and his agency suffered corresponding neglect as a result.

In 1934 the SPI was made part of a new Special Inspectorate of Frontiers, reporting to the Ministry of War, which was anxious to secure Brazil's borders and to turn the Indians who lived near them into patriotic citizens. Meanwhile Vargas sponsored the Push to the West to open up the interior of the country, but he entrusted it to his newly created Central Brazil Foundation and gave the SPI no special role in it. At this time the SPI was perfecting the technique used in its "pacifications." It sent out its most experienced people to establish friendly contact with tribes that still had none with Brazilian society. These expeditionaries lived by Rondon's motto, now the motto of their own agency, that they should die if need be but never kill. Instead they went into remote areas and courted uncontacted tribes, leaving presents on the trails they were seen to use and waiting for weeks or even months until some of their members nervously appeared for a meeting. The technique worked and provided good publicity for the SPI, but its employees soon began to worry about the morality of attracting indigenous peoples to a civilization that would move in on their lands and overwhelm them as soon as they presented no threat. The parallel with earlier Jesuit policies of "bringing in" Indians who were then at the mercy of slavers and others was not lost on the more dedicated employees of the SPI.

The SPI never had the resources or the political influence necessary to carry out effectively its mandate of protecting the Indians. It did the best it could and succeeded in protecting some indigenous lives and lands over the years; but its inadequacies were scandalously exposed in the late 1960s. Getulio Vargas's push to the west in the 1930s soon ran out of steam, but in 1960 President Kubitschek inaugurated the new capital of Brasília deep inland with the express purpose of opening up the interior. At this time Brazil was preoccupied with the festering poverty of its rural areas, especially in the northeast of the country. Peasant leagues were forming and growing in influence, and the rise of populist leaders threatened the status quo and the power of the traditional oligarchies. There was real fear in Rio de Janeiro and in Washington that Brazil might be "the next Cuba," so in 1964 the military took over the government and repressed all clamor for reform. Instead it stepped up the penetration and development of the interior. The intention was to defuse protest and alleviate poverty by developing the riches of the hitherto neglected hinterland. It was also hoped to avoid agrarian reform by promoting settlement of the interior and bringing the "people without land to the land without people," as President Médici put it in 1968. The officially sponsored enthusiasm for developing the interior unleashed a process of landgrabbing and settlement that was bound to hurt indigenous peoples, who had hitherto been sheltered largely by their remoteness. In fact the killing and dispossession of Indians that ran rampant in the late 1960s caused Brazil to be accused in the world's press of committing genocide. There is no evidence that the government had a policy of exterminating Indians, but it did encourage development at all costs and took no measures to protect indigenous peoples from the predictable effects of its policies. As for the SPI, it too was caught up in the frontier frenzy. Many of its employees were accused of selling out the Indians that they were pledged to protect, and some were believed to have assisted the ranchers and frontiersmen who killed Indians without compunction. When this became an international scandal, the government resorted to damage control. It launched a publicity campaign to deny that genocide had occurred, disbanded the SPI, and sponsored an inconclusive inquiry into its activities that punished no one.

The SPI was replaced by the National Indigenous Foundation (FUNAI) in 1967, but FUNAI faced the same dilemma as its predecessor. It was an agency supposed to protect indigenous peoples, but it served an authoritarian government that wanted development at all costs and was quite prepared to deal severely with those who were thought to get in the way. As Brazil's "economic miracle" of the late 1960s gave way to the economic crisis of the late 1970s, the military regime talked more and more of development. Its ministers made statements to the effect that the development of the nation could not be held up by a handful of Indians, that the country could not tolerate ethnic cysts within itself, and that the Indians should be emancipated and absorbed into the mainstream of the nation as soon as possible.

The Minister of the Interior presented emancipation as a progressive measure and compared it to the abolition of slavery, which emancipated the blacks in 1888; but as Indians and others were quick to point out, this was a false analogy. Indians were not slaves and therefore could not be released from their servile status. The government's proposal to "emancipate" them aimed instead to release them from their Indianness and from any special protections that Indians enjoyed under Brazilian law. It was a bid to undo the legacy of Rondon, to abolish Indians (and therefore the government's responsibility for them) by a stroke of the pen, and to let the erstwhile Indians take their chances, as individual Brazilians, when they sought to protect themselves and their resources.

Mario Juruna, who was later elected to the Brazilian parliament as the first Indian to become a federal deputy in the history of Brazil, summed up the Indian objections graphically in his response to the Minister of the Interior. He said:

> I do not accept what Minister Rangel Reis says, that I am asking to be emancipated. Indians can live their own lives. All we need is that our lands are guaranteed – we know how to do all the rest. Now, the way they are talking, we shall all disappear. We shall cease to be Indians the moment FUNAI wishes it. We shall become mere backwoodsmen, without any guaranteed rights just like other backwoodsmen. I am against emancipation.[7]

Emancipation never became official policy, but FUNAI made strenuous attempts to implement it unofficially. It put pressure on individual Indians to declare themselves emancipated. It tried to prevent Indians who earned diplomas and other qualifications outside their tribal areas from receiving them, unless they were willing to sign that they were emancipated and thus no longer Indian. The agency hoped in this way to ensure that educated Indians were cut off from the rest and could not become indigenous leaders. It also strove to prevent the emergence of indigenous organizations, claiming that because FUNAI was the legal guardian of Brazil's indigenous peoples, no indigenous meeting could be held without its permission.

Daniel Mantenho Cabixi was one of those "trouble-making" Indians whom FUNAI was most anxious either to muzzle or emancipate. The agency denied him a passport and prevented him from attending a meeting of Latin American bishops in Puebla (Mexico). Had he been allowed to go, the bishops would have heard an extremely thoughtful

[7] Commissão Pró-Indio, *A Questão da Emancipação*: 42, Editora Global, São Paulo, 1979. (My translation from the Portuguese.)

analysis of the situation of Brazil's Indians, as these excerpts from Daniel Cabixi's speech go to show:

The ranchers have a disgusting outlook that Indians are dangerous vagabonds. They claim that the Indian does not work and, therefore, does not need land, and they ask: "Why does the Indian want so much land?" But we were born on the land, and are children of the land. So our rights are older than theirs. Just as they are human beings, we too are human beings. In fact I have found that we are even more human because we place human dignity first, rather than economic interest and concern for profit-making which can lead to human destruction.

The smallholders' problem is identical to that of the Indians. Indeed, we have some advantages, and we are better protected in some ways. I do not understand these matters entirely, but I have found that the smallholders are extremely downtrodden, and the only solution for them would be a very strong organization to defend their interests.

The big investors mask their role and incite the smallholders by saying: "The Indians do not produce. The Indians do not work. The land should belong to you." This is how conflicts begin. Areas are cleared by killings and the big ranchers take over.

Our people are at a disadvantage because the white man's world is different from ours in terms of technological development. They have modern weapons. In addition, our numbers are small. In order to destroy a village, all it takes is for twenty soldiers to come with machine guns and to shoot everyone. That is the end.

* * *

The FUNAI is supposed to be a government agency which specializes in Indian affairs. According to the impressive new statute concerning Indians, (Indian Emancipation Decree), the laws which define our rights and duties, as well as the commitments which White society has adopted toward the Indians and the commitments which the Indians have adopted toward White society, people are led to believe the government seeks emancipation of the Indian and wants White society to respect the customs, tradition and culture of the Indian. In reality, however, the statute concerning the Indian is a very attractively written document, but really is something else. It is destruction which is taking place. The Indian lives in a very difficult situation, with little support, especially where his land is concerned.

The FUNAI compares us to a reed which bends with the wind, but history demonstrates that Indians are becoming bolder and more aware of the struggle to free our people from the yoke of Western civilization. We are now passing through a critical period between true emancipation and the paper emancipation which has been decreed by the government and which we reject. On the one hand, there are Indians fighting for freedom, on the other hand, there is the

FUNAI, an official government agency which plays a policing role, preventing us from holding meetings and discussing our own problems, even though we are the only ones who have a deep understanding of those problems.

* * *

In the Church's new outlook concerning native groups, we are seen to possess true Christian values and are therefore bearers of the words of Christ. However, for the Church to institutionalize this new outlook, it must give up many of its prior concepts and values. More specifically, the Church must realize that the previous methods for imposing its cultural and material values, along with its ignorance of the values which we possess, was and still is a way of destroying the culture of many Brazilian Indian groups. That is why we still encounter priests and bishops who are only interested in saving the soul of the Indian, while they put respect for the dignity and culture of the Indian on a lower plane.

Recently the Church, through CIMI, has aided us through support and encouragement for meetings of chiefs, and CIMI has produced the most thorough analyses and discussions of our situation.

* * *

As Indians, we do not want emancipation to be a weapon which is used against all of the Indians living in Brazil. Our emancipation cannot come through a ministry, or through a government, or through anyone else. Our emancipation must be our own achievement.

The Indians have to adopt responsibility, and they have to be conscious of their own rights and duties. It must be understood that, for people to be independent, they must exercise self-determination and acquire economic independence. We are very far from these goals, but, perhaps, our people can attain them gradually. In the path toward self-determination, we need to reshape our consciousness. At present, the Indians suffer because they no longer possess tribal organization, as a cultural standard for themselves. Many remain half-Indian and half-civilized, without clearly knowing who they are and without attributing much value to the tribal form of organization which had previously existed. The tribes who live closest to the coast, in the more developed part of the country, are the ones who are most oppressed. Thus, one of the first things which is necessary is a method for organizing these groups, so that they can appreciate the value of Indian culture.

Today, the Indians in Brazil live in a state of oppression and manipulation. We must always struggle to combat the physical and cultural oppression which affects Indian communities. There is no Indian confederation in Brazil at the present time. There are only tribes, villages and chiefs.[8]

[8] Taken from *Brazil*, Cultural Survival Special Report #1: 11–13, 1979.

FUNAI's policy of emancipating educated or acculturated Indians and exercising tutelary control over all the rest could not be sustained. In 1971 a group of scholars and activists met in Barbados under the auspices of the World Council of Churches and issued the Declaration of Barbados, calling attention to the injustices routinely visited on the indigenous peoples of South America. In 1972 the Catholic Church in Brazil formed an organization known as the Missionary Indian Council (CIMI) specifically to assist indigenous peoples. CIMI, to which Daniel Cabixi alluded, helped indigenous leaders to meet and launch their own organizations in the face of daunting logistical difficulties. Other pro-Indian organizations were formed throughout the country largely by anthropologists and other professionals, though Friends of the Indian associations were also formed both locally and nationally, and international support for Brazilian Indians was soon forthcoming. It is probably fair to say that support for the rights of indigenous peoples was not deep in Brazil, but their issues were at least being discussed more widely than ever before. During the long drawn out period of political opening in the early 1980s, when the military regime was negotiating the transfer of power to a civilian government, the plight of the Indians came to be considered symbolic of the plight of the rural poor under the "Brazilian model of development." Soon, however, the Indians themselves were fighting back and taking the lead in their own struggle to defend themselves.

At first it was the Xavante who gained notoriety, because their outspoken leaders came to Brasília to demand their rights. It was then that Mário Juruna, whose caustic comments on "emancipation" have already been reported, was elected as a federal deputy in the Brazilian congress. He was the beneficiary of a protest vote that elected him in the state of Rio de Janeiro, where there are virtually no Indians, but his very presence in the parliament gave indigenous peoples a visibility that they had not previously enjoyed. After the end of the military regime in 1985, when the civilian government called a special assembly to draft a new constitution for the country (1987–1988), it was the Kaiapó who sat day after day in the antechambers of the parliament, wearing their full-feathered regalia and indicating by their presence that the new constitution should guarantee indigenous rights. It was also the Kaiapó who took the lead in organizing a meeting at Altamira in the Amazon in 1989 to protest the construction of a hydroelectric dam. The rally was well attended by Indians from all over the country, but they were almost outnumbered by journalists and other international observers drawn to the event, for the Kaiapó successfully linked their cause with international ecological concerns, especially regarding the use (or misuse) of the resources of the vast Amazon Basin.

The ability of the Xavante and the Kaiapó to fight back and of indigenous people in Brazil to get a hearing at long last has to be weighed against the pressures that they continue to suffer. The indigenous movement has provoked both public backlash and official anti-Indian policies. The backlash was most clearly seen at the time of the constitutional convention, when Brazil's leading newspaper, the *Estado de São Paulo*, ran front-page articles for a full week (August 9–15, 1988) detailing what it called the "conspiracy against Brazil." The alleged conspirators were the Indians who divided the nation and impeded its progress. They were accused, together with their allies, of doing the work of international mining interests (who are supposedly benefited by the inability of Brazilian companies to exploit resources that are located in indigenous territory) while pretending only to have the interests of the Indians at heart.

The constitutional convention voted down the provision that would have declared Brazil a multiethnic society. It did not legislate absolute protection for indigenous lands, but it did stipulate that they could be mined only under special circumstances and with specific government authorization. It also voted down the policy of emancipation. This partial victory for the Indians in law is offset by what continues to happen to them in fact. Mining companies and agribusinesses encroach on their lands and bring them disease, death, and expropriation, as most recently to the Yanomami close to the Venezuelan frontier. The government officially deplores such events but semiofficially encourages them.

Indigenous affairs in Brazil have been militarized under the civilian regime. The demarcation of Indian lands, always slow, has been brought to a virtual halt by the requirement that demarcations be approved by a council dominated by the military. Furthermore the Calha Norte (Northern Drainage) project for the Amazon Basin, elaborated and put into practice secretly by the military with no objection from the presidency, once more stresses the need for national security and national development to take precedence over indigenous rights. The project documents state that the development of the Amazon region depends on mining but that much of its mineral wealth lies in territory occupied by Indians. It proposes therefore that both the definition of Indian territory and the laws controlling mining on it be changed to allow development to proceed. Meanwhile it allocates substantial funds for the infrastructure of FUNAI but pays little attention otherwise to the needs of the indigenous populations that FUNAI is expected to serve, other than making it clear that they should be "civilized" and helped to disappear into the Brazilian mainstream as soon as possible.

What this meant for individual Indian peoples is devastatingly illustrated by the fate of the Yanomami. These are a people living on both sides of the border between Brazil and Venezuela and speaking Yanomami, Yanomam, Yanam, and Sanuma, languages that are more or less mutually intelligible. It is estimated that there were about 10,000 Yanomami at the beginning of the 1980s, making them perhaps the largest, relatively isolated group still living according to their traditional ways in the Amazonian rain forest. The comparative isolation of the Brazilian Yanomami came to an end in the 1970s when the military government sponsored a road-building program to open up the interior of the country. Together with the Transamazon Highway, which ran south of the Amazon River, they started building another highway known as the Northern Perimeter, which passed right through the territory of the Yanomami. This highway was left incomplete for lack of funds or perhaps lack of interest, but the penetration of Yanomami territory and the colonization project that went with it brought disease, starvation, and death to the Indians of the region.

Worse was to come. Gold miners started coming to the region in the mid-seventies, and by 1980 there was a full-fledged gold rush in progress. At this time the federal government was still making gestures to protect the Indians. FUNAI was supposed to give them health care, which it did not have the resources to do. The federal police were occasionally called in to try to expel the miners from Yanomami territory. On one occasion they had to come to the rescue of a FUNAI post that was being besieged by a uniformed contingent of gunmen in the pay of the miners.

Friends of the Yanomami, led by the CCPY (Commission for the Creation of a Yanomami Park) were by this time lobbying hard for the creation, demarcation, and protection of a continuous tract of territory that would be a Yanomami reserve. The idea was opposed by a combination of powerful forces – the miners, the state of Roraima, which had no interest in seeing a large tract of its territory cordoned off for indigenous peoples, and above all by the military. These interests consistently supported a counterproposal, the so-called archipelago plan, that would establish a rash of small Yanomami reserves in this remote region. Anthropologists critical of this plan argued that it would mean the extinction of the Yanomami.

A turning point in the Yanomami situation was reached in 1986, when the military dramatically enlarged a small airstrip that had previously been used by FUNAI and local missionaries. The new airstrip, which came to be known by the Yanomami name for the site – Paapiu – was part of the military's Calha Norte (Northern Drainage) Project, which had been kept secret up until that time. The immediate effect of the new airstrip was to intensify the gold rush into Yanomami country. Gold miners poured in. Planes were arriving and taking off from Paapiu all through the daylight hours. The roar of their engines hovered over Paapiu like a pall, while the surrounding jungles reverberated with the racket of mining machinery. The authorities knew very well what effect this would have on the Yanomami, because the military declared the region to be an area of national security. The missionaries who had been giving medical assistance to the Yanomami were told to leave. So were anthropologists and other researchers. Access was restricted to miners, the military, and FUNAI, which was now working under orders from the military. The agency's task had become that of ensuring that the Indians did not interfere with the gold mining and that pro-Indian witnesses were not allowed access to the region.

It was nearly 2 years before journalists managed to get into Paapiu, and what they saw horrified them. One-quarter of the Yanomami in the region were already dead. The majority of the rest were desperately sick, and many were starving and emaciated. They were particularly moved by the plight of starving and orphaned Yanomami children. Their reports provoked an international outcry, and the government hastily set up an emergency medical program for the Yanomami, but government policy remained essentially unchanged. The president now claimed that it was physically impossible to expel the miners from Yanomami territory. After all there were tens of thousands of them there, all armed to the teeth. The federal police were not strong enough to evict them. The state and its authorities were squarely on the side of the miners, and the army was unwilling to do such a messy and controversial job. In any case President José Sarney soon showed where his sympathies lay. In his lame duck period, before the next president was sworn in, he issued a decree for the demarcation of three reserves in Yanomami territory, not for the Indians (those were still being debated) but for the goldminers!

His successor, President Fernando Collor de Mello, now bore the brunt of international criticism concerning the treatment of the Yanomami and also the runaway pollution of land and water taking place as a result of the uncontrolled mining operations. Collor won praise for ordering the mining operations to cease and having the airstrips (there were now many of them) dynamited. Few newspapers outside of Brazil noted, however, that the airstrips were soon repaired and the miners back at work again. It is true that Collor was less responsive to the military than Sarney had been, and more anxious to improve Brazil's international image, especially on the eve of the world ecological conference, to be held in Rio de Janeiro in 1992, but he faced the same dilemma as his predecessor. A gold rush is as hard to stop as a herd of stampeding buffalo. The miners were many, well armed, and well connected, both politically and with the very drug traffickers who were the supposed targets of military vigilance in the north. When their airstrips were destroyed, they quietly repaired them. They were openly supported by the state authorities and tacitly supported by the army. The Yanomami were few and dying out rapidly. Their support came from pro-Indian activists and segments of public opinion in Brazil, backed up by international organizations, all of whom were horrified by the ongoing genocide.

The unequal contest still continues. There have been some successes. In 1991, for example, President Collor at long last signed a decree setting aside a contiguous tract of territory as a Yanomami reserve, albeit a much smaller one than originally requested. But the reserve is neither demarcated nor protected, and the miners still ride roughshod over the Yanomami. In fact 2 years after the reserve had been formally decreed, a group of Brazilian miners carried out a horrifying massacre of sixteen Yanomami in a village just across the border with Venezuela. The killings were carried out with the utmost brutality. The victims, mostly children, were stabbed and beheaded, and the killers were never brought to justice in spite of the outcry that the massacre produced.

Against the background of such events, it is easy to understand the passion that is all too evident in the speeches of indigenous leaders. Ailton Krenak is the founder of UNI (The Union of Indigenous Nations), an organization that has been trying for years to bring together leaders of the indigenous peoples, scattered throughout a vast country, so that they may find strength in their union. In 1990 he addressed a Brazilian audience at an exhibition of films, videos, and photographs about Indian life, in the following terms:

> My name is Ailton. I am of those people who survived in the region of the Rio Doce valley. We used be called Botocudo, but were later referred to as Krenak.

Our population has been greatly reduced, especially in this century. Our people came into contact with the advancing frontier of colonization in about 1910. Many of our areas were not colonized until 1920 but, once they were, our population was reduced from about two thousand people to 140. At that time we were in a situation very similar to the one that the Yanomami are facing today in Roraima. Then there were still two thousand of us. Now we are only 140. At that time there were only 26 million Brazilians. When we numbered two thousand, the Brazilians numbered 26 million. Now Brazil has 130 million people and we have 140. I think that perhaps by the time you reach 300 million people our population will be zero, because the count goes forward for you and backwards for us. This is a situation that is constantly repeated, in the Rio Doce valley, in the Xingu river basin, along the Rio Negro, in the valley of the Rio Javari. It is a situation so monotonously repeated that one gets the impression that Brazil is built on the cemeteries of Indians. I do not think that a nation built over cemeteries can sleep well at night. Brazil is being built over a cemetery – the cemetery of the Guaraní, the cemeteries of the Yanomami, the Tikuna, the Karaja, the Krenak, the Terena, the Kadiweu. A country, a nation that builds its history this way can undermine itself, can destroy that which should be its foundation and its strength, that which is essential for a people to become civilized and respected.

All government planning, all government action presumes that we shall disappear. The political plans of the government, the daily actions of government agencies are based on a very comfortable assumption, that all Brazil has to do is wait a little and the last Indian lands in Brazil can be taken over, because it is only a matter of time before the Indians all die out. That is the way the Ministry of the Interior thinks. That is the way the Ministry of the Interior works. That is the way the National Indian Foundation thinks. That is the way the National Indian Foundation works. Unfortunately the most important efforts made so far to create a different way of thinking in Brazil have not worked. They were not enough to get the Brazilian people involved, the Brazilian authorities involved.

* * *

All sorts of methods have been used to get the Indians off their lands. They are intimidated. They are gathered into colonization projects like hired hands, like peons, like cheap labor, like settlers. The ultimate recourse has also been used, and that is massacre. These extreme measures, these massacres have met with enormous complicity on the part of the government and of the authorities, to such an extent that in the recent history of Brazil there is no single instance of the decimation of a tribe or a massacre of Indians resulting in the prosecution or conviction of anybody. So hunting Indians is still a profession in Brazil.[9]

Given these kinds of continuing pressures on the indigenous peoples of Brazil, it is easy to understand the international outcry over their

[9] Eda Tassara and Maureen Bisilliat (eds.), *O Indio/Ontem, Hoje, Amanhã* (University of São Paulo Press, São Paulo, 1991), 20–22. (My translation from the Portuguese.)

treatment but difficult to see why they should be the objects of anti-Indian outbursts like the one in the *Estado de São Paulo* or to understand why indigenous affairs have come to be seen as the special preserve of the military. There is an apparent paradox here. Brazil is a country whose indigenous population is small in absolute numbers and virtually the smallest in the hemisphere as a percentage of the nation's population. Why then do its indigenous peoples receive so much attention, both nationally and internationally? Why have they gone from being treated in Brazil as savages, marginal to the national life, to being considered a matter of national security?

The answer lies partly in the concerns of the Brazilian military, and the theory of national security that underlies them, and partly in the general perceptions that Brazilians hold about themselves and their society. The military extenuation of the authoritarian regime that they imposed from 1964 to 1985 is that it saved Brazil from subversion and enabled the country to proceed with its economic development. In fact under dictatorship the two notions were telescoped, so that people who opposed the Brazilian "model of development" with its uneven distribution of gain and pain were often considered subversives. Such people might well engage in armed struggle against the regime. There were guerilla movements that took up arms against the government in the early years of the dictatorship, but they were crushed. Nevertheless the military continues to be alert to the possibility of further revolutionary action. The documents expounding the rationale for the Calha Norte project dwell on the unstable politics of Surinam and Guyana and the possibility of leftist revolution infiltrating Brazil from that quarter. Furthermore guerilla groups, often financed through the drug trade, are operating in neighboring Colombia and Peru. Because Brazil is currently awash with drugs, and the inequalities that prompt people to revolt have been exacerbated in recent years, the military is intent on preventing a similar linkage in the Amazon.

Meanwhile the international ecological concern over the Amazon, which has occasionally helped indigenous peoples in their struggle, is also much resented by the Brazilian population at large, which feels that it is hypocritical (especially when expressed by people from nations that have grown rich in the past by ignoring ecological constraints) and impertinent, because the use of the Brazilian Amazon is essentially a matter for Brazilians to decide. Finally, the idea that Indians want the right to maintain their own cultures without being relegated to second-class citizenship in Brazil runs counter to the perception, both public and official, that Brazil is a melting pot that blends different races and ethnicities together, but only on condition that they are willing and able to enter the mainstream.

All of these sensitivities implicate the Indians, especially those in the Amazonian region, at a time of national soul searching in Brazil. Many of them live near the nation's frontiers or in areas where guerillas or the drug trade could flourish. Alternatively they impede access to mineral and other resources and thus are said to "stand in the way of development." Worst of all, their plight has been compared to that of the rural poor and used as an object lesson to show the severe costs of authoritarian development. Finally, international attention to their situation gives Brazil a bad press because international attitudes have changed since the nineteenth century, when it was considered normal and acceptable for indigenous "savages" to be eliminated by the forces of civilization at the frontiers of settlement. This is no longer true. Massacres still happen all too frequently at such frontiers, but now they are internationally condemned and are embarrassing to the governments of the countries where they take place, who normally deny that they ever happened.

PARAGUAYAN INDIANS IN THE TWENTIETH CENTURY

In colonial times the area that is now Paraguay was a relatively isolated outpost of the Spanish empire, which attracted only those settlers who had neither the connections nor the opportunity to prosper in richer regions. Its isolation was enhanced by Spanish insistence that trade between Spain and Paraguay should be routed by sea to the isthmus of Panama; from there by mule train to the Pacific; by sea again to a port in Peru; from there overland through the highlands of what is now Bolivia and on to Buenos Aires; then finally up the Paraguay River to Asunción. The return journey was supposed to be made by traveling the same route in reverse! This remoteness enabled the Jesuits to establish their famous *reducciones*, or colonies, in Paraguay. In the early eighteenth century, these became virtually a state unto themselves, with the Jesuits administering the lives of perhaps as many as 100,000 Indians – an extraordinarily large population for that time and in that sparsely populated region. At the same time, there were higher than usual rates of intermarriage and concubinage between Spaniards and Indians in this backwater of the empire, which produced a mestizo population, relatively undivided by class distinctions, all of whom spoke Guaraní, often as their first or only language. After independence in 1811 José Rodrígues de Francia, Paraguay's populist dictator, virtually eliminated what remained of the small Spanish élite. He even decreed that men of Spanish descent could only marry indigenous, black, or mulatto women as he fashioned an egalitarian nation of small farmers.

Paraguay is divided into a verdant eastern region to the east of the Paraguay River, and the dry semidesert Chaco to the west of the Paraguay River. In colonial times and indeed through much of the nineteenth century, the Chaco was "Indian country" beyond the frontier of settlement. By the late nineteenth century, the indigenous peoples of Paraguay consisted of those Guaraní speakers in eastern Paraguay who had not been assimilated into the mestizo mainstream and the Indians of the Chaco, who were still beyond the frontier. The relative isolation that had protected them all since independence was brought to an end by the War of the Triple Alliance (1864–1869), during which Paraguay was invaded and crushingly defeated by the combined forces of Brazil, Uruguay, and Argentina. After the war Paraguay was both devastated and bankrupt. The government tried without much success to borrow money in London and then in desperation declared that all lands without registered private owners should be considered *tierras fiscales*, or state-owned. It then sold off huge tracts of these to foreign corporations and land speculators, most of them of Argentine, Anglo-Argentine, or English origin. At the turn of the century, Paraguay was therefore the scene of intensive land speculation in connection with logging, cattle ranching, and the production of tannin and *yerba mate*, the leaf that produces the caffeine-rich tea whose cultivation has been the mainstay of the Paraguayan economy since earliest times.

After years of fierce isolationism, Paraguay was now subject to commercial penetration on a large scale. The tracts of territory sold off in the Chaco were truly vast. In 1910 the Casado family of Argentina owned more than 3 million hectares. It had once owned 5 million but had sold off part of its holdings. Meanwhile there were twenty-nine properties of more than 100,000 hectares held by foreigners in the Chaco. Cattle ranches and factories to extract tannin from *quebracho* logs sprang up along the Paraguay River, and they provoked immediate clashes with the indigenous peoples of the region. Indian hostility appeared for a time to be a serious obstacle to economic activities in the Chaco, but it was overcome peacefully by the remarkable efforts of an English missionary, W. Barbrooke Grubb. Grubb's Anglican mission was so successful in attracting Indian converts that the Paraguayan government made him their legal representative in the Chaco for 18 years and bestowed on him the title "Pacifier of the Indians." Grubb's mission started out as a place that attracted independent and potentially hostile Indians, but once the "pacification" and commercial penetration of the Chaco were in full swing, the same mission became a place of refuge for Indians rendered destitute by the new economic order.

The commercial penetration of the Chaco disrupted the Indians' migration and land-use patterns, making it increasingly difficult for them to survive in that harsh environment. Some Indians tried to solve this problem by working for the newcomers, but they soon discovered that there was not enough work to go around and that such work as there was might vanish if their employers experienced an economic downturn or even a change of mind.

The Chaco War (1932–1935) with Bolivia made matters worse. It was fought over the very lands where the Indians were trying to eke out their existence. Many of them were forced to flee from their homes. Others were conscripted to work for the army or to act as scouts and footsoldiers. The Guaraní-speaking peoples had an especially difficult time, because their Bolivian enemies mistrusted them, along with Guaraní speakers who lived in Bolivia, and treated them especially severely if they could. The war in effect completed the dislocation of indigenous life in the Chaco that had begun at the turn of the century.

The Indians therefore began to move in increasing numbers to seek work in the Mennonite settlements in the central Chaco. The Mennonites had come from Canada and Europe to Paraguay in three waves, during the 1920s, the early thirties, and the mid-forties. They immediately began hiring Indians as agricultural laborers in the Chaco, but they did not have a major impact until the 1950s and 1960s. That was when their settlements grew prosperous, thanks to their development of an agricultural technology that overcame the difficult conditions of the Chaco and also to large infusions of outside money. As a result Indians flocked to the Mennonites around Filadelfia, and this created problems. Those (such as the Nivaklé) who had traditionally lived off herds of sheep and goats were strongly encouraged to get rid of their animals, who were a potential threat to Mennonite fields. They eventually did but then reacted indignantly when a drought in the early sixties caused the Mennonites to lay off workers. The Indians reminded the Mennonites that when the latter had first arrived in the Chaco, it was the Indians who had helped them and worked for them on the understanding that this exchange of work for food was to be a kind of covenant between their peoples. For all their problems, the Mennonite colonies of the central Chaco have been the best available option for the Indians of the region whose traditional lands and livelihood have been taken away from them. Very few of them have been settled in agricultural colonies with their lands guaranteed. The rest eke out a marginal existence on the fringes of the economy of the Chaco.

Paradoxically the Indians of eastern Paraguay, in what has always been considered the more accessible half of the country, enjoyed a longer period relatively free from outside interference than did their kin in the Chaco. This was because the large extractive industries in that half of the country specialized in logging or the production of *yerba mate*; so they used their lands extensively and left vast areas of them untouched at any given moment. They exploited the manual labor of the Indians but otherwise left them alone, so that indigenous communities survived intact within the *latifundia*. For example, the holdings of a firm by the name of La Industrial Paraguaya covered 13 percent of the entire surface of eastern Paraguay, and it was noted in 1976 that the map of their lands virtually coincided with the areas of greatest contemporary Guaraní population, almost as if the entire property had ended up as a kind of indigenous reserve.

This breathing space came to an end in the 1960s when General Alfredo Stroessner permitted a limited "liberalization" of his dictatorial regime. Opposition parties were tolerated within strict limits, and the government initiated a period of land reform. This involved resettling peasants on public lands, which were often occupied by Indians. This policy was soon abandoned with even worse consequences for Indians, because now large tracts of land were sold off to army officers and leaders of Stroessner's own Colorado Party, who resold them at a profit to land-hungry Brazilian colonists or to multinational agribusinesses. The pressures on indigenous land intensified, and reports began to circulate internationally that the Guaraní-speaking Aché, who still survived in the forests of eastern Paraguay, were being hunted down and massacred. These reports were fortunately an exaggeration, but clearly the Aché and the Indians of eastern Paraguay in general were under increasing threat.

In an effort to help them defend themselves, an anthropologist by the name of Chase Sardi started Proyecto Marandú (Project Information) in 1972. His aim was to assist in the formation of a confederation of all the indigenous peoples of Paraguay. Later the same year he was briefly imprisoned, together with other leaders of the project, but it transpired that the government acted to put a stop to a perceived danger of rural unrest, rather than specifically to impede the development of an indigenous confederation. Such a confederation was eventually formed in 1976 under the name of API (Association of Indigenous Peoples), with a directorate of indigenous leaders from both the Chaco and eastern Paraguay. It obtained substantial funding from overseas and sponsored a number of local projects, most notoriously projects to buy land and thus guarantee the land rights of indigenous peoples settled on it. This had the practical advantage of cutting through the political and bureaucratic obstacles that normally prevent indigenous peoples from acquiring title to land, but it established a dangerous precedent, because if some indigenous peoples could buy land, why should not all indigenous peoples be required to do so? If such a view gained acceptance, it would undercut all those who argue that indigenous peoples throughout the Americas have a right to land and who fight to see that this right is respected. Unfortunately API was riven with dissension, virtually from the start, much of it arising out of mutual accusations of misappropriation of the lavish funds that the organization controlled in its early days. It still exists but is both diminished and discredited and without much influence.

The paradoxical result of API's decline is that Paraguay's Indians, who were among the earliest to try to organize a national federation to protect their interests, now have no active federation in an era when indigenous federations are proliferating both nationally and internationally. Yet this is understandable. General Stroessner did not look kindly on national organizations that were not sponsored by himself or by the Colorado Party. API's decline thus reinforced the tendency for indigenous peoples to do what they have always done in Paraguay – namely, to look either to religious agencies or to the armed forces for protection.

The government's official agency for indigenous affairs was originally the Patronato Militar del Indígena, established in the ministry of defense in 1936 at the end of the Chaco War. This was revived as the DAI (Department of Indigenous Affairs) in 1959, which was in turn replaced by INDI (The National Indian Institute) in 1976, agencies that were likewise headed by military officers and located in the defense ministry. The government's own agency traditionally functioned as just one of a number of patrons who have worked on behalf of Paraguay's Indians.

The others were principally religious organizations. In addition to the Anglicans, whose work in the Chaco has already been mentioned, there have been numerous Catholic missions and, since the 1970s, missions run by the evangelical New Tribes organization. Likewise the Mennonites, who did not come to Paraguay to convert the Indians, are also a religious organization that has played an important role in their lives.

There is one possible exception to this rule that Paraguayan Indians, if they are helped at all, are helped by patrons on whom they remain dependent. This is the case of the Guaraní-speaking Pãi Indians of eastern Paraguay, who were assisted by the Indigenist Association of Paraguay (AIP) and a foreign aid mission to develop their own local organization through which they have succeeded in gaining title to their lands and improving their standard of living. Currently three other indigenous groups – the Chamacoco and the Nivaklé in the Chaco, and the Avá-Guaraní in the east – are emulating the Pãi. It seems that the Indians of Paraguay have, for historic reasons, been better able to organize themselves locally than regionally or nationally. Now that General Stroessner's dictatorship has been replaced by a democratic regime, and a new constitution has been adopted that at least recognizes indigenous groups as distinct and legitimate entities, it is just possible that Paraguay's local indigenous organizations will have more success in defending the rights of the groups they represent.

LOWLAND PEOPLES OF THE ANDEAN NATIONS

The lowland regions of the Spanish empire in South America were from the beginning the scene of intense missionary activity. The most famous, though by no means the only one of the missionary orders that set out to convert the jungle peoples, was that of the Jesuits. From what is now Paraguay in the south to the upper Amazon regions that they reached from Quito in the north, and over to the Casanare region of the Colombian grasslands, the Jesuits sought in the sixteenth and seventeenth centuries to establish indigenous communities of Christian converts. Their activities brought them into conflict with lay colonists, who saw the Jesuits as depriving them of a source of labor. They also attracted the sinister attentions of Portuguese slavers who saw the Jesuit communities as tempting targets, where large numbers of peaceable Indians could be seized and carried off into servitude. The Jesuits were finally expelled from the Spanish empire in 1767, and the indigenous peoples of the remote regions where they had worked were left once more to themselves.

The isolation of many of these lowland peoples, who were apparently only contacted by the outside world at the beginning of this century, is thus a relative matter. There were certainly precolumbian contacts between the Inkaic world and the peoples of the lowlands. The Quechua language of the Inka empire became a *lingua franca* of the jungles, so that Francisco de Orellana was able to speak to the local people in it as he started his famous voyage down the Amazon in 1541. Inkaic contacts were followed by centuries of missionary activity and then, most brutally, by the Rubber Boom in the late nineteenth and early twentieth centuries.

At that time the Amazon Basin was the only source of supply for rubber, which was made by processing the sap from trees that grow wild in the jungle. In the early years of the Rubber Boom, tappers in Brazil could live off the land and, in return for arduous toil, actually make a little money. Soon, however, the world demand for rubber increased dramatically. There were fortunes to be made in the trade, and methods of collection became correspondingly more ferocious. Rubber barons controlled the rivers and coerced the local Indians into becoming gatherers for them. Sometimes the control was justified in terms of debt-bondage, on the grounds that the Indians should, after all, repay their overseers for the goods that had been advanced to them. At other times even this fraudulent fiction was dispensed with. Indians were forced to bring in rubber because their families were held hostage, and any or all of them would suffer fearful reprisals if they did not.

The indigenous populations in the forests of northern Beni and Pandó in Bolivia were virtually wiped out by the rubber frenzy, but the worst atrocities were committed in Peru, where the notorious Julio Arana enslaved whole communities of Indians along the Putumayo River. The sheer sadism shown by Arana and his henchmen toward their Indian subjects, whom they tortured and murdered at will, became known to the outside world in 1907–1908, when eyewitness accounts of them were published in Iquitos and in Brazil. Arana represented the Peruvian Amazon Company, largely financed with British capital, and counted nearly 200 British subjects from Barbados among his overseers. When the scandal broke, the company sent a commission of enquiry up the Amazon to investigate. One of its members was Roger Casement, the British consul in Rio de Janeiro, who was famous for his investigation of atrocities in the Belgian Congo, in the course of which he had becomc friendly with Joseph Conrad. Casement's reports prompted a parliamentary committee to look into the matter in London, and the Peruvian government followed suit with an enquiry of its own, but no one was ever punished. The Amazonian Rubber Boom collapsed in the early 1920s, not because of any curbs on the excesses of the rubber barons but because of the notorious exploit of Henry Wickham, an Englishman who smuggled the seedlings of rubber trees out of the Brazilian Amazon. These were replanted in Southeast Asia, whose rubber plantations eventually put Amazonian rubber gatherers out of business.

Colombia

In the aftermath of independence, the Republic of Gran Colombia instituted the office of Protector de Indios and adopted laws to protect the rights of indigenous peoples. Yet from the very beginning, the lands of indigenous peoples were under attack, and measures were implemented to take away the *resguardos*, or reserves, that had been previously guaranteed to them. As early as 1834 an article in legislation pertaining to Indians states that "in no court or tribunal shall complaints be heard whose sole and specific object is to ask that *resguardos* not be divided up."[10] The battle over indigenous *resguardos* has continued ever since, with Indians fighting to hold on to their dwindling lands and occasionally rising in rebellion to protect their reserves. This was more than an economic issue for indigenous peoples. For them it was a struggle for survival. This issue has dominated the relations between Indians and others in the Colombian highlands and particularly in the bitterly contested regions of the Cauca Valley but has only slightly affected the lowland peoples. The state was interested in alienating the lands of highland Indians and turning them into a landless, rural proletariat. The lowland Indians, on the other hand, were considered savages who still had to be tamed and brought to civilization.

This task was entrusted to the Catholic Church. When, in the endless civil wars that marked the early history of the Colombian republic, the Conservatives triumphed over the Liberals[11] at the end of the nineteenth

[10] Juan Friede, *El indio en lucha por la tierra: Historia de los resguardos del macizo central colombiano* (Bogotá: Instituto Indigenista de Colombia, 1944), 111.

[11] Throughout this chapter I use the convention whereby Conservative and Liberal are spelled with initial capitals when they refer to political parties and without capitals when they do not.

century, they adopted a new constitution, and it was this conservative constitution of 1886 that set the institutional framework for modern Colombia. Immediately afterward (in 1887) they signed an agreement with the Vatican that established guidelines for missionary control of the more distant regions of the country. The special status, both of the missions and their wards, was formally recognized in 1890 when it was decided that the general legislation of the republic should not apply to "savages" who were being reduced to civilized life through the missions. At the turn of the century, then, Colombia was denying special status to settled indigenous peoples in order to deprive them of their lands. At the same time, it was insisting that indigenous peoples who were not settled were savages who had to be civilized. Clearly the civilizing process was intended to deprive native peoples of their Indianness, as well as their lands, though it did not deprive them of the stigma of being considered Indian.

The Indians of Colombia's remotest regions – the Amazon, bordering on Peru, and the eastern plains, or *llanos*, bordering on Venezuela – fell victim to border disputes and the whims of local strongmen who could set themselves up as a law unto themselves. Julio Arana could set up his ghastly Amazonian rubber-gathering empire, not simply because he was far from the centers of state control but also because he served the interests of Peru by battling Colombians and chasing them away from the ill-defined frontier between the two countries. Similarly Tomás Funes and his men succeeded in defeating and killing the Venezuelan general Roberto Pulido, who was making inroads into the Colombian *llanos*. This enabled Funes to set himself up as the local strongman and establish his own reign of terror in the east, which lasted from 1913 until he was defeated and executed in 1921.

Meanwhile missionary control over the lowlands was constantly reinforced. By the 1920s the missions had full civil control over the indigenous people who were their wards. They were in charge of their education, and it was a crime to assist Indian children who escaped from the mission schools. The missions were also entrusted with the task of watching over the nation's frontiers, and they were given the power of veto over civil appointments in the areas of their jurisdiction, which contained about a million Indians at mid-century.

In the more densely populated areas of the country, the 1920s were years of all-out attack on indigenous reserves. The Indian rebellions in the Cauca Valley, led by the charismatic Quintín Lame, had been put down. Measures were then taken to break up the reserves once and for all. Legislation was even introduced, making it a crime for Indians to defend themselves against legislation to divide up their lands! By the end of the decade, indigenous peoples were fighting side by side with the rest of the rural population in the struggle for land reform.

The struggle for land has been the dominant theme of recent Colombian history, which is an irony in a country where vast areas were still considered public lands in the second half of the nineteenth century. The availability of public lands for settlers and smallholders ran counter to the interests of the coffee growers and the large landowners, both of whom required labor that they were unlikely to get if their workers could acquire land and set up on their own. Wealthy agrarian entrepreneurs therefore acquired public lands and even lands already occupied by settlers and turned them, both legally and illegally, into private fiefs in order to create a landless proletariat. The peasantry fought back, and this generalized conflict throughout rural Colombia is generally thought to have been a major contributory cause of the period known in Colombian history simply as La Violencia ('The Violence'), which covered two decades from 1946–1966.

The Violencia devastated the rural areas of Colombia and could not help but affect even the remotest regions, where the nation's lowland Indians lived. These regions became areas where political or bandit chieftains (it was sometimes hard to tell the difference) could establish their bases of operations. At the same time, many people who were uninvolved in the fighting and wished to remain that way fled from the areas of violence and took refuge at the margins, thus putting new pressure on the indigenous inhabitants of those regions, who had been relatively protected by their comparative isolation.

The Violencia finally began to wind down when the Liberals and Conservatives agreed in 1958 to form a National Front, under the terms of which the two parties would alternate in the presidency and share political power at all levels. The government now began to talk seriously about land reform, which was intended to modernize agriculture, but this entailed a further attack on indigenous lands. Law 81 of 1958 stipulated once again that indigenous *resguardos* should be broken up in the interests of development and to put an end to the "millennial backwardness" of the Indians. Every department in the country was now required to set up a section to deal with indigenous business, and these sections reported to the Ministry of Agriculture and Animal Husbandry. These sections were soon superseded (in 1960) by a department of indigenous affairs in the Ministry of the Interior, which was supposed to work closely with INCORA, the agency overseeing agrarian reform (launched in 1961), to break up indigenous landholdings.

Indigenous resistance to these measures was fierce and had two results. The government (and INCORA) changed course. They decided to authorize *reservas indigenas*, which would not have the same legal status or the same presumption of perpetuity enjoyed by the *resguardos*. These new reserves were compromises that would enable indigenous peoples to enjoy theoretically unchallenged use of their common lands until such time as they were advanced enough to be able to break up their holdings into individual plots. The other important result of the indigenous fight for land was the emergence, starting in the early 1970s, of the indigenous organizations that led, and still lead, the struggle.

CRIC, the organization representing Indians of the department of Cauca, was predictably the earliest and most active of these, but it was soon followed by others, including CRIVA (which has now changed its name to OPIAC, the organization of the Indigenous Peoples of the Colombian Amazon), representing peoples of the Vaupés region, and UNUMA, representing peoples of the *llanos*. At first CRIC worked closely with ANUC, the officially established national peasant organization, but they soon parted company, because CRIC had indigenist goals, above and beyond the struggle for land, that were not shared by ANUC. In the 1970s CRIC led the struggle for land in the Cauca Valley. The landlords, who had illegally seized *resguardo* lands, accused the Indians of being subversives, guerillas, and drug runners, which brought the army in on their side. The region was militarized, and leaders of CRIC were systematically tortured and killed.

Meanwhile the government was rethinking its own policies. It decided to take back indigenous education from the Catholic missions to whom it had traditionally been entrusted and to support bilingual education instead. Much of this was to be done, especially in remoter areas, by the Summer Institute of Linguistics. The American Protestant evangelists were dedicated and well funded, so that they could supply infrastructure as well as instruction, all at their own expense. Best of all, they were unconcerned with ideas about social justice, which had recently made many Catholic clergy less than staunch defenders of the status quo. The SIL believed that their converts should focus on spiritual salvation and obey the authorities that God had provided for this earth, a doctrine that was enthusiastically welcomed by repressive regimes.

By the end of the 1970s, the government was ready to take a hard line with the Indians. It issued a new Indigenous Statute in 1979 that was intended to reestablish its control over indigenous peoples. According to its terms the government would now decide how and when indigenous communities could come into formal existence, how they could incorporate, and when their legal status could be suspended or canceled. The statute backfired, because it galvanized the indigenous organizations into united opposition.

Organizations representing indigenous peoples from all parts of the country began to hold frequent meetings, which led to the creation of ONIC, the national indigenous organization of Colombia. ONIC not only coordinated the indigenous struggle for their rights; it also started to publish its own analyses of the situation of Colombia's Indians. The following excerpt gives us a rare glimpse of how indigenous women viewed their situation.

THE INDIGENOUS WOMEN OF COLOMBIA

A long time ago there was a large number of peoples in these lands, peoples who all had a different view of the world and different beliefs about life, man, woman and nature. We lived together according to our own rules and our own dynamics. In general, there was great respect for the land, for motherhood and for life itself. Every one of our cultures had its own way of looking at women. Some saw us as the representation of Mother Earth, others as Nature itself, others as the Moon, Water, Rain, the great lagoons, but in general they saw us as *Givers of Life, as the Beginners, as Knowledge and Wisdom.* In our own history there are many legends where we represent these origins, these strengths that made us unshakeable.

However, suddenly everything began to change. Violent strangers, who had no respect for anybody or anything, began to encroach on our lands. Together with our kin and our children we had to abandon our lands and our customs, to flee to remote places for refuge and to confront the invaders in order to defend our rights.

Yet in doing so we were enslaved, sold, mercilessly put to work, and gradually we saw our husbands, our children and many of us die along with our culture. Some of us took up the struggle; women, like Gaitana, Tumbichuquia, Bartolina Sisa, and Gregoria Apaza but the mighty invaders could not be stopped. Our fighting, our tears did not help. They used us as servants and forced us to feed their children and abandon our own. We were deceived and exploited by the conquistadors who wanted to expand their influence, we were forced to blend our blood with that of the invaders. Gradually these areas became populated with mestizos who were also regarded as inferiors.

The so-called missionaries began to arrive to impart their beliefs, their education and their morals. They began to say that we represented sin. As if life was a sin! And they began to promote the idea that as women we were inferior, that we were not as intelligent, that studies and knowledge were for men – we were banished. After having been givers of life, many of us had to bear children in order to expand manpower for the benefit of others, or to satisfy the imposed machismo that was gaining stronghold in our families and husbands.

However, we have never stopped fighting for the recovery of our land, for the education of our sons and daughters and for the right to maintain our own culture because we firmly believe that we have our own rights given to us through our history as women and as indigenous, rights which we share with all our people which we must defend and protect until we can regain our true identity. Our never ending resistance will let us win and, together with our men and families, recover our history and mutual respect.[12]

Colombia's congress soon became aware of the fact that the country's indigenous peoples were reaching a new level of self-concious involvement in the nation's politics, and that they were fiercely opposed to the Indigenous Statute. They therefore refused to approve it. The government therefore changed course once again. It instructed INCORA to cease giving temporary land-use rights to indigenous peoples by granting them *reservas* and instead to give them permanent rights in *resguardos*. Moreover it set up a new National Indigenous Council, which recognized the errors of past policy toward the Indians and was instructed to proceed in future with *ethnodevelopment* in indigenous areas, or, in other words, to include Indians in decision making about themselves and to sponsor development programs that respected their traditions.

These changes must be understood in the special context of the 1980s. Colombia had just passed through yet another turbulent decade. Countless armed revolutionary groups were operating throughout the countryside, their emergence facilitated by the tradition of political banditry established during the Violencia. They became a potent force during the Liberal regime of president Alfonso López Michelson (1974–1978). This was the first administration after the official end of the National Front, and it aroused much popular opposition by carrying out neo-liberal economic policies while failing to follow through with the expected agrarian reforms. The next president, Turbay Ayala (1978–1982), also a Liberal, tried to crush the guerillas by means of military repression, but he succeeded only in strengthening them as they garnered popular support. Both López Michelson and Turbay reaped the benefits of high

[12] Originally published in Spanish by ONIC. Reprinted in English in the *Newsletter of the International Work Group for Indigenous Affairs #59*, December 1958 (Copenhagen).

growth rates in agriculture, which boomed throughout the 1970s through sugar, coffee (after the Brazilian frost), marijuana and, most significantly, cocaine; yet Colombia at the beginning of the 1980s was a country fragmented by insurrection and destabilized by the drug trade. It fell to President Belisario Betancur (1982–1986) and his successor, Virgilio Barco Vargas (1986–1990), to try to restore peace and harmony.

This is the context in which not only indigenous policy but the administration of the entire country is being rethought. President Barco launched a policy of reconciliation in the hope of putting an end to the violence that has become endemic in Colombian society. To this end he entered into a dialog not only with those who had taken up arms against the state but also with other categories of people within the state, including peasants, blacks, and Indians. He also took steps to decentralize the government and to begin a devolution of administrative authority right down to local levels. This project was formalized in the new constitution introduced by President César Gaviria and approved in 1991.

The new constitution postulates that Colombia is a multiethnic nation. It also sets out a blueprint for administrative decentralization and local autonomy, which is intended to reverse the élitist and oligarchical way in which the country has been governed since 1876 and to make for greater popular participation. The nation is to be divided into territorial entities that elect their own local authorities and administer their own affairs. The constitution also provides for indigenous territorial entities within the system. These will be run by their indigenous inhabitants, and non-Indians resident in them will have to obey the indigenous territorial authorities. The language of the constitution is of necessity imprecise in many areas, and it is not clear exactly how it will be implemented. What is clear, as far as the indigenous peoples are concerned, is that they are supposed to be able to control their own affairs locally, and some of them are expected to exercise administrative control over indigenous territorial entities. In fact, because some of the indigenous territorial entities are in the remote and thinly populated areas of the country in the Amazon Basin and the eastern plains, it seems that the constitution gives huge areas of Colombia over to indigenous local control.

Why has the government of Colombia, after nearly two centuries of repressing the indigenous peoples of the nation, suddenly adopted such totally different policies toward them? It is probably due to the weakness of the Colombian state, which is still plagued by violence and corrupted by the drug trade. Under these circumstances it makes sense to encourage citizens – in this case, Indians – to patrol their own lands on behalf of the state, rather than to throw in their lot with the revolutionaries. It might also make sense to grant local control over resources in indigenous territorial entities to the Indians themselves, because the government is currently in no position to exploit those resources.[13] Such control could presumably be renegotiated at a later time and under different circumstances. In fact the very concept of "indigenous control" at the local level is fraught with ambiguities and might very well be a more benevolent and finally effective way of coopting indigenous peoples and merging them into the Colombian mainstream, something that they have resisted since the conquest.

Ecuador

Since colonial times Quito has been a jumping-off point for the penetration of the upper Amazon regions. It was out of Quito that the Jesuits established their missions in Mainas, which are credited by some historians with maintaining Spanish, rather than Portuguese, control over the upper Amazon. Down to the present day, Ecuador insists on its Amazonian aspect, as in the official motto that "Ecuador has been, is, and will be the Amazonian country." Yet the *oriente*, as all territory east of the Andes is called, was until quite recently a remote and marginal part of the nation.

In the nineteenth century, Ecuador proper – the Pacific coastal region and the Andean highlands – was extremely conservative. President García Moreno ruled over a state where the Church and its prerogatives were so firmly entrenched that it was virtually theocratic. Under this regime the highland Indians suffered extremes of injustice. They worked under *concertaje*[14] agreements in a system of virtual slavery. It is significant that

[13] A similar point was made by Whitten, in explaining why President Velasco Ibarra of Ecuador granted a large tract of land in the Amazon to the indigenous peoples of the area soon after World War II. Whitten noted that this enabled the president to establish "a native 'holding' action through which national officials could block foreign intrusions for a while" (in Norman E. Whitten Jr., *Sacha Runa: Ethnicity and Adaptation of Ecuadorian Jungle Quichua* (Urbana, IL: University of Illinois Press, 1976), 237.

[14] The system of *concertaje*, or "arrangement," was one in which an employer made an arrangement with an Indian – henceforward his *concierto* – to work for him under certain terms. The terms, enforceable in law, reduced the *concierto* to a kind of serfdom from which there was no escape. Most Indians were forced to accept such an arrangement, which was often called the *enganche*, or

when the nation formally abolished slavery in 1857, it tightened the rules for *concertaje* in the same year. Freed slaves were now Ecuadorian citizens, but Indians (the majority of the population) were not. Unsurprisingly there were frequent Indian rebellions.

The indigenous peoples of the lowlands were not involved in these processes. They were protected by their relative inaccessibility and also by the reputation of some of them, particularly the Jivaroan peoples, for being great warriors and headhunters. Even these warriors could not match the ferocity and firepower of the rubber gatherers at the turn of the century, but fortunately for them the area most savagely exploited during the boom lay somewhat to the east of their territory. As the rubber gatherers moved westward, seeking to capture new communities of tappers, and setting off movements of Indian refugees before them and Indian allies with them, the boom petered out.

In the 1920s the relationship between the *oriente* and the rest of the country began to change when Royal Dutch Shell began drilling for oil in the Amazon. The serious prospect of Amazonian oil strikes certainly had something to do with Ecuador's dispute with Peru over the precise location of their mutual frontier in the Amazon. Peru occupied the disputed territory in 1940, and the two countries fought over it until the issue was supposedly resolved by the Rio de Janeiro protocol of 1942. Ecuadorians immediately repudiated the agreement, which they felt had been signed under duress. President Arroyo del Rio resigned, and the main participants in the military, and diplomatic events that led up to the loss of so much Ecuadorian territory, were put on trial. The territory is still in dispute and still occupied by Peru, with the result that the traditional patterns of movement and trade of some of the indigenous peoples of the *oriente* have had to be reoriented to take account of the new frontier.

The next great change to affect the region was the agrarian reform law, passed by President Rodríguez Lara in 1964. The law created IERAC (The Ecuadorian Institute for Agrarian Reform and Colonization) to carry out land reform in the highlands, combined with colonization of the Amazonian lowlands to relieve the pressure elsewhere. In the highlands the *huasipungo* system of servitude was abolished, but rural workers, now freed from the obligation to perform unpaid labor, also lost access

"hook." In Ecuador the system was called *huasipungo*, and the individual in this form of serfdom was known as a *huasipunguero*.

to *hacienda* lands and were, if anything, worse off than before. They were encouraged by IERAC to migrate to the *oriente*, where they would be granted title to land once they had cleared and planted it, but this pitted highlanders against lowlanders, who usually considered the cleared lands to be part of their traditional domains.

This conflict resulted in the formation of a lowland indigenous organization that was to become enormously influential by example – namely, the Shuar Federation. It was founded with the help of the Salesian mission in order to defend the Shuar against the colonists. The Salesians feared that otherwise the Shuar would be annihilated or that they would retreat into the forests. Either way they would be lost to the mission. The federation was formally recognized in 1964 as an organization to promote the welfare of the Shuar and to coordinate colonization projects instigated by the government. It was the first of the indigenous federations that have since proliferated throughout the lowlands of South America and has served as an example and inspiration to all the others.

In the 1970s there was increased pressure on the *oriente*, which was now seen by the government as a prime area for development. This was to come about through colonization, cash crop production, and exploitation of the resources of the region, particularly oil. In 1972 President Lara flew to Puyo and delivered a speech, stressing these themes. When a bishop mentioned that the region to be developed was already inhabited by 50,000 Indians, the president dismissed the objection by stating that there was no more Indian problem because there were essentially no more Indians. "We all become white men when we accept the goals of the national culture," he added.[15] Shortly afterward he issued a new "law of national culture," and in 1972–1973 his administration gave considerable publicity to the idea of using military institutions to inculcate this national culture.

In response to this developmental and assimilationist threat, the indigenous peoples of the *oriente* started to follow the Shuar lead and create federations to defend their interests. Various federations were formed, representing the peoples of Pastaza, of Napo, and other groups, which worked tirelessly to persuade IERAC to title and guarantee their lands. IERAC was, however, notoriously slow in granting title to Amazonian peoples. Meanwhile the Ministry of Agriculture's forestry division and

[15] Quoted in Norman Whitten, *Sacha Runa: Ethnicity and Adaptation of Ecuadorian Jungle Quichua* (Urbana, IL: University of Illinois Press, 1976), 268.

the national parks service began to impose restrictions on forest use, which were perceived as further impediments to Amazonian land titling. In the face of this increased threat, the lowland foundations came together in 1980 to form CONFENIAE, the Confederation of Indigenous Nationalities of the Ecuadorian Amazon.

CONFENIAE immediately joined forces with ECUARUNARI, the organization representing the indigenous peoples of the highlands, and this led to the formation of a third organization, COICE, representing the Indians of coastal Ecuador, so that all three could come together in CONAIE, the National Confederation of the Indians of Ecuador. The emergence of this national indigenous organization is all the more remarkable because of the divisions that traditionally existed between Indian groups. Lowland peoples who had traditionally been each others' enemies put aside their differences and formed CONFENIAE. The lowland organization was fighting explicitly to defend Indian lands and Indian cultures, whereas the highland Indians had often supported Ecuadorian peasant movements, whose aims were economic rather than ethnic.

The Roldós-Hurtado administration[16] (1979–1984) marked a return to civilian government after a period of military rule in Ecuador, but it promised more than a return to the status quo ante. Jaime Roldós set out to be the president of all the people, which included the Indians who were now permitted to vote thanks to recent constitutional reforms. He made a symbolic gesture at his inauguration by giving part of his acceptance speech in Quichua and took other measures to demonstrate his recognition of indigenous cultural as well as economic requirements. His administration promoted bilingual education and sponsored an agreement between the Ministry of Education and the Catholic University that trained Indians from the elementary to the university levels.[17] Many of Ecuador's present indigenous leaders received their training in those years. Furthermore President Roldós established a National Office of Indigenous Affairs in his Ministry of Social Welfare, indicating that Indians' concerns were not simply agrarian issues that could be handled,

[16] President Roldós was killed in a plane crash, and his term was served out by his vice-president, Oswaldo Hurtado.

[17] At first the government, ignoring the views of the Indians and over opposition from the universities, decided to entrust education in the *oriente* to the Summer Institute of Linguistics. In a spirit of nationalism, after border clashes with Peru in 1981, it reversed itself and gave the SIL 1 year's notice to leave Ecuador.

as before, by the office dealing with peasant affairs in the Ministry of Agriculture.

The progress made by President Roldós in changing the way the Ecuadorian state had treated the indigenous peoples of the country since independence was abruptly reversed by his successor President Febres Cordero (1984–1988). Agrarian reform was suspended and violent repression unleashed against those who fought for it. President Febres also tried to split the indigenous movement by creating a government-sponsored indigenous organization – *Jatun Ayllu* ('Big Family') – to compete with the Indians' own organizations. These continued to gather strength under his regime, however, and they hoped that things would improve under his successor, President Rodrigo Borja Cevallos.

President Borja came into office as the leader of the Party of the Democratic Left, bringing with him the hopes not only of the Indians but of much of the population for a social transformation of Ecuador. President Borja did indeed recognize CONAIE as the official mouthpiece of Ecuador's Indians, and he conducted talks with its representatives in the national palace. He also appointed his cousin to run a Commission on Indigenous Affairs and to report directly to him. Yet, as Ecuadorian newspapers pointed out at the time of the Indian uprising that took place halfway through his administration, neither the president nor his party really understood what the indigenous peoples wanted. They spoke of indigenous rights and of state action to guarantee them but continued with the same old measures that had proved ineffective before. They spoke of agrarian reform but left it to IERAC, whose dilatoriness had become legendary (it could take as much as 8 years for indigenous groups to receive land titles) and whose measures, honed during the developmentalist years, often favored large landowners. Their rural development programs were ineffective, and their provision of social services was underfunded. The generalized disappointment felt by indigenous people throughout Ecuador resulted in the historic Indian uprising of 1990.

Ecuadorian newspapers quickly pointed out that this uprising was unlike any previous one in the history of the country. There have been plenty of indigenous revolts since independence, all local and all suppressed. This one was different. Planned and coordinated on a national scale, it brought the country to a halt for about a week. It began when Indians occupied a church and said that they would not come out until indigenous demands had been met. In the following days Indians from the *oriente* to the coast took concerted action. They marched in demonstrations, blocked roads, and mobilized scores of people to prevent the roadblocks from being removed. They took over churches and *haciendas*. They demanded in effect to be heard and to have their grievances attended to.

The public reaction to this mass mobilization was surprisingly mild. Landowners and cattle ranchers predictably demanded repression of such disorder and insurgency, but much press coverage sympathized with the Indians, pointing out that they had been mistreated and ignored for five centuries and that it was only natural that they should demand acknowledgment of their presence and their rights. Groups of nonindigenous sympathizers staged brief sit-ins in churches and government buildings to show their support for the Indians. Most important of all, the president succeeded in restraining the army, and the Indians themselves acted with sufficient restraint so that there were few acts of violence, considering the emotional nature and the nationwide extent of the uprising. President Borja insisted that his administration had done a great deal for the Indians and that the uprising was instigated by agitators, a view that was roundly criticized in the press for implying once again that the Indians could not be the principal actors in their own lives. He did negotiate with CONAIE, however, rather than attempt to repress the uprising, and shortly afterward the government guaranteed extensive tracts of land in the *oriente* to the Quichua peoples of Pastaza Province and to a small group of Huaorani.[18]

The uprising made clear that the indigenous peoples of Ecuador were now political players on the national scene and, as such, were a force to be reckoned with. The sympathy this elicited from some segments of the public was not universal. The traditional and virulent racism of élitist Ecuadorian attitudes toward Indians was unlikely to disappear overnight, and there were still people at local and provincial levels of government who would tell foreign researchers in 1993 that Ecuador was a poor country because it had so many Indians.[19] Yet the Indians showed in 1990 that they could articulate a vision of reform in Ecuador and do

[18] The Huaorani became internationally famous when representatives of the Summer Institute of Linguistics attempted to contact them in 1956. The Huaorani killed those who sought the first contact but later accepted missionaries from the SIL, including the widow of one of those previously killed. The story of this "martyr" and his heroic widow has been much used by the SIL in its literature ever since.

[19] Melina Selverston, "The politics of culture: Indigenous peoples and the state in Ecuador," in Donna Lee Von Cott (ed.), *Indigenous Peoples and Democracy in Latin America* (New York: St Martin's Press in association with The InterAmerican Dialogue, 1994).

battle for it, at a time when the country as a whole had similar preoccupations.

The uprising was a success in that it changed the political scene and the terms of political dialog in Ecuador, not because it enabled the Indians to get what they wanted. On the contrary, their call for a revision of the constitution to declare Ecuador a plurinational state has not been accepted. This is opposed by the present administration of President Sixto Durán Ballén and resisted by much of public opinion, which feels, with the élites, that this would "divide the nation." Meanwhile Durán has sought to counterbalance CONAIE by appointing an Indian, unelected by his peers, to head the president's Office of Indigenous Affairs. Under his administration IERAC remains mired in bureaucracy, and agrarian violence against indigenous peoples goes largely unchecked and unpunished.

The recent history of Ecuador is remarkable for the strength, sophistication, and coordination of its indigenous federations, as well as for the fact that the lowland peoples have come into the center of national politics as a result of their federative flair and their insistence on indigenous ethnicity. But the struggle continues between an assimilationist view of the country, in which development as defined by the government takes priority and "all Ecuadorians can become white men" (or at least mestizos) if they accept the goals and burdens of such a program, and a pluralist alternative, which is currently also associated with social reform.

Peru

Peru, like Ecuador, is a country divided into three regions – the coastal strip, the Andean highlands, and the Amazonian lowlands. As in Ecuador, the lowlands have historically been remote from the life of the nation as a whole. As in Ecuador, conservative oligarchies dominated the country and oppressed the indigenous peasantry of the highlands throughout the nineteenth century, but here the parallels cease because Peru's recent history has been much more turbulent than that of its neighbor to the north.

At the end of the nineteenth century, the nation was in turmoil. Defeated by Chile in the War of the Pacific (1879–1883), it was in dire financial straits, with its administration in a shambles, its élites quarreling and humiliated, and the lower strata of its population smoldering with resentment and revolt. During this crisis the government started to grant huge tracts of Amazonian territory as concessions to private companies. Such concessions were considered empty lands to be colonized; indeed the concessionaires technically could have lost their rights in the land if they had not colonized it after 9 years. The Indians inhabiting the concessions were considered obstacles to progress, although they were much sought after during the years of the Rubber Boom, when they provided the labor on which the rubber fortunes were built. The barbarities inflicted on those Indians who were forced to gather rubber in the region of the Putumayo River (now Peru's northern border with Colombia) have been described in previous sections, but it was not only they who were affected by the rubber frenzy. Rubber was being gathered in the central Amazon and as far south as the Manu River, which flows into the Madre de Dios on its way through Bolivia northeastward into the Amazon proper. In all these regions the peoples who lived close to the rivers were severely affected. They lived in a state of constant terror, their insecurities stemming not only from the danger posed by rubber barons and their private armies but also from other Indian tribes who were often armed by the rubber collectors to go off and hunt for tappers among their neighbors.

During this period of national turmoil, influential Peruvians began to call for the reorganization and modernization of Peruvian society. In the 1880s González Prada advocated land reform and the creation of a new Peru, based on its Inkaic heritage, which would at last incorporate the indigenous population into the nation. In 1889 Clorinda Matto de Turner published *Aves sin Nido (Birds without Nests)*, a book whose description of the sufferings of the Indians had an effect in Peru similar to that produced by Harriet Beecher Stowe's *Uncle Tom's Cabin* in the United States. This vague and somewhat sentimental indigenism was transformed into a theoretical basis for political action by the two most famous protagonists of the Peruvian left. José Carlos Mariátegui insisted in *Peruanicemos el Peru (Let's Peruvianize Peru)* that without the Indian, Peruvianness was not possible. In *Seven Essays on Peruvian Reality*, he argued like González Prada for the revitalization of Peru through the incorporation of the Indians into its national life and a return to Inkaic socialism. Victor Haya de la Torre, who founded the leftist APRA party, went even further, prophesying an Indian revolution not just in Peru but throughout the Americas.

Meanwhile there were indigenous revolts throughout the highlands in the early years of the twentieth century, and the government concluded that all this talk of indigenous revolution was unacceptably radical. It therefore repressed Haya de la Torre's APRA party, as well as the communists and others who drew their inspiration from Mariátegui, and set out to control the indigenous situation in its own way. As part of his program to modernize the country in the 1920s, President Leguía created an official organization, the Patronato de la Raza Indígena ('Patronage for the Indigenous Race'), with himself at the head of it. At the same time, he outlawed the organization that the Indians themselves had recently formed, on the grounds that it was no longer necessary because the Indians now enjoyed the offical patronage of the president himself. The supreme patron did not, however, put an end to the abuses that continued to be visited on indigenous peoples, including the obligation to perform forced labor on the roads in Peru's difficult terrain.

The modernization of Peru was extremely difficult to accomplish, however. The oligarchy made up of coastal planters and financiers, and highland landowners and merchants, all backed by foreign investors, clung to power and kept the majority Indian and mestizo population marginalized. These alienated sectors of society organized to defend themselves during Leguía's presidency, but the inconclusive struggle between reform and repression continued for the next three decades. An armed uprising by APRA in the city of Trujillo was savagely put down in 1932, and APRA was a target of repression until the mid-1940s. As Basadre put it in his history of Peru, the decade of the 1920s was a time when the country became deeply aware of the Indian, but this was followed by a conservative backlash in the 1930s, during which the oligarchy reemphasized hispanicism as the defining characteristic of Peru (albeit of a minority of Peruvians).

While the nature and future of Peru was being debated and fought over, comparatively little attention was paid to the lowlands. Once the Rubber Boom had evaporated, the Amazonian region attracted colonists who cleared the land for coffee and cattle, expropriating and often detribalizing indigenous peoples in the process. Meanwhile the relations of dominance and dependency between patrons and Indians that grew up in the days of the boom were maintained as official policy long after the boom was over. Decrees were promulgated to prevent the indigenous labor force from dispersing, to force Indians to do military service or work on roads and trails. Patrons who had Indians working for them were given police powers to keep them at it and in their debt. Later the border war that erupted with Ecuador in 1941 affected more than 300 indigenous communities. Nevertheless the lowlands did not move to the center of national thinking and planning until the 1960s.

The idea that some fabulous El Dorado lies hidden in the Amazon jungles is as old as the conquest of the Americas. In Peru it was given a new twist in the nineteenth century by presidents Nicolas de Piérola and Ramón Castilla, who urged their countrymen to seek out the wealth of the Amazon, but the major push for the development of Peru's eastern lowlands came during the first term of President Fernando Belaúnde Terry (1963–1968). Belaúnde's Popular Action Party was now a major populist competitor of Haya de la Torre's APRA, and Belaúnde won election in a three-way contest against APRA and the conservatives. He himself was an architect by profession, a planner by training, and a visionary by vocation. The Amazonian hinterland captured his imagination, and in 1959 he published a book about it entitled, significantly, *la Conquista de Peru por los Peruanos.* When he assumed office he had plans for land reform in the heartland of the country and for development in the Amazon. His promise of land reform was overtaken by events, however. At the coast and in the highlands, peasants and agrarian workers were taking over the lands of agribusinesses and *haciendas* without waiting for the government to authorize them. So Belaúnde turned to the Amazon, with consequences that were predictably harsh for those indigenous peoples who might get in the way of development. The Matse Indians, for example, attempted to defend themselves by fighting back against the invading colonists. They were immediately attacked by a punitive expedition of the Peruvian army, backed up by local vigilantes, jet aircraft, helicopters, and other modern weaponry. They were driven out of their villages and forced to hide in the jungle for years, too terrified to rebuild their communities. Belaúnde's ambitious road-building and colonization projects were disastrous for Peru as well as for the lowland Indians. They cost money that the country did not have, forcing a devaluation of the currency and dramatic price increases that led to strikes which the government repressed. When his negotiations with the American-owned International Petroleum Company resulted in what most Peruvians considered a sellout, Belaúnde was deposed by a military coup.

The military regime imposed by General Juan Velasco Alvarado in 1968 was led by officers who had firsthand experience of the social problems of their country and were determined to impose solutions for them. The leadership and planning necessary for these solutions was to come from the idealistic cadres of a specially created agency known as SINAMOS (The National Movement for Social Mobilization). The acronym was also a pun because it could be read as *sin amos*, or 'without masters' in Spanish. Once more SINAMOS tried to implement land reform, and a young anthropologist, Stéfano Varese, was put in charge of developing a national policy for the Indians of the Amazonian lowlands. For the first time in the history of Peru, the policy aimed at protecting the cultures of, and granting corporate land title to, the peoples of that region. The first peoples to receive this recognition were those closest to the colonist frontier – the Campa, Aguaruna, Machiguenga, Amuesha, and others. The whole process ran counter to and hoped to reverse the secular trend that emphasized development and dispossession of the Indians. It was itself soon reversed, when General Velasco was removed from office. Enthusiasm for his reforms waned because even the potential beneficiaries of them wearied of the élitism and authoritarianism of the SINAMOS cadres. Peru's relations with the United States cooled because the Velasco regime was perceived as "leftist," and this in turn affected the country's prospects for borrowing money abroad. Meanwhile Peru failed to make the rich oil strikes it had hoped for, its fishmeal industry was devastated by changes in the Pacific currents, and the country was badly hit by a fall in the world price of copper. The ensuing financial crisis undermined both Velasco's reforms and his administration, and he was replaced by a more conservative general.

The fall of Velasco effectively brought to an end a half-century of attempted reforms. While successive administrations went to and fro on the issues, other forces were coming into play that would make any kind of democratic modernization of the country much more difficult. Armed revolutionary movements gathered strength in the 1970s, and during the same decade the coca trade established itself as a significant though illegitimate part of the nation's economy. These developments were to give the lowlands a significance in the nation's life that they had never enjoyed before, because the lowlands are where coca is grown and where guerillas have more freedom to operate.

The Marginal Highway, which was the centerpiece of President Belaúnde's plan for the development of the Amazon, is now the main artery for the transport of the coca leaves and chemicals that currently play such a large part in the Peruvian economy. In 1992 Peru produced 65 percent of the world's coca for cocaine, and coca generated about half of the nation's foreign exchange, all this in an impoverished country in the throes of the worst economic crisis in its history. Understandably, then, the valley of the Huallaga River, the main coca growing area of the country, has been much contested by the military in its "dirty war" against both the Sendero Luminoso and the Tupac Amaru guerilla movements. This is, however, an area that was long ago taken over by colonists. The indigenous peoples of the lowlands (as opposed to those of the highlands, who have been caught between the army and the revolutionaries) have not been much involved in the corruption, violence, and hostilities that have destabilized the rest of Peru. There are some exceptions, of course. The Asháninka, for example, were caught up in an early series of battles between the military and the Túpac Amaru in 1965. They are still much affected and deeply split by the drug wars and revolutionary hostilities. The majority of the indigenous peoples in the Amazon, however, have been engaged in following the example of the Ecuadorians and forming their own federations for self-defense. This process was started with SINAMOS's help in the Velasco years and has been going on ever since. The federations have also come together in an association (AIDESEP, or the Interethnic Association of the Peruvian Jungles) that claims to represent all the indigenous peoples of the lowlands. In spite of disputes between individuals and federations, which tend to undermine this claim, AIDESEP and the federative process in the Amazonian lowlands have succeeded in giving the indigenous peoples of the area a voice of their own. The quality of that voice is evident in the new indigenous publications put out by the associations starting in the 1980s. An editorial from the first issue of the new journal *Pueblo Indio* sums up the situation of Peru's Indians as follows.

> We exist, here we are, pale but calm after this punishing history to which Europe has subjected us throughout these 489 years of horror and human misery; they have not been able to make us disappear and we know . . . what type of people came in during the colonizing invasion. We know that their reason for being is not to work hard for everybody's good, but just for the privileged (who get fewer and fewer); that their modes of production (slavery, feudalism, capitalism) are pursued primarily through the extraction of the product of another's labor for individual, private and absolute accumulation. Due to this, they should be considered instead as modes of exploitation because that is their fundamental characteristic. Even though the form changes, the extraction of another's energy is the same.

Our peoples and nations are dismantled, plundered, dispersed, we must organize ourselves in peace with all the patience and serenity that has guided us through the hard passive resistance throughout these long years, dark and somber but sure for our children. Only our patience has saved us from extermination, but even the patience of the Indian has its limit. . . .

Many people hiding their real intentions and fears say jokingly, "But you want to return to the past." But we know that nobody who goes back home after an extended journey is "returning to the past." Nobody who has destroyed someone else's home can justly reproach the heirs of the disaster with being "regressive" for wanting to rebuild what is theirs, let alone when they still persist in destroying us and denying us. Gentlemen: the technology of our social organization is unique and without equal in the whole history of mankind. We want and we are building the future, but our future, not that of foreigners. . . . Our civilization is humanizing and it is different in that we have no private property; we give it, we hand it out freely, but none of the individualistic conquerors want to receive it for they deny us. In America it is the only thing that cannot be expropriated, it is the flame of our civilization, our spirit. . . . In the communities one learns from infancy about the form of family organization and about the form of organization for work. . . . If any revolution in the West (including in socialist countries) is to have value it should be through the "fusion of family and society" which returns to being one single entity.[20]

The new voice of the Indians of the *oriente* speaks out in defense of their cultures as well as their lands, and above all against the developmentalism that has traditionally dominated Peruvian policy for the lowlands. Their opportunity to defend their own interests during the pervasive crisis of contemporary Peru represents perhaps the first time that their relative marginalization within Peruvian society has been an advantage to them.

Bolivia

Bolivia is geographically an Amazonian country but historically, socially, and politically an Andean one. After losing its access to the ocean as a result of its defeat by Chile in the War of the Pacific, the country comprises two major zones. Its Andean highlands are 30 percent of its territory but are the traditional heart of the nation, where the bulk of its indigenous population lives and where its history and politics have been played out. Its eastern lowlands, or *oriente*, make up 70 percent of its

[20] Originally published in Spanish in *Pueblo Indio* and reprinted in English in the *Newsletter of the International Work Group on Indigenous Affairs* (IWGIA) 31–32 (June–October 1982), 53–54, Copenhagen.

territory but have traditionally been considered a wild, frontier region by governments located in the highlands and largely concerned with highland issues.

Highland issues have been principally Indian issues because Bolivia has the highest percentage of Indians in its population of any nation in the hemisphere. It was the highland Indians who bore the brunt of the tyrant Melgarejo's decree in 1866, depriving them of their traditional lands unless they could buy them from the state. It was the highland Indians who were in constant revolt in the latter half of the nineteenth century, helping to overthrow Melgarejo and giving decisive military support to the Liberals as they defeated the Conservatives in the civil war that closed out the century.

The lowland Indians were not involved in these national dramas. Instead they attracted missionaries and people on the lookout for sweated labor. The Jesuits gathered them into mission communities in colonial times, but it was the Rubber Boom that had the most dire and dramatic effect on them. The extractive frenzy was concentrated in the forests of northern Beni and Pando, whose indigenous inhabitants were essentially annihilated by the process. So workers were brought from the mission areas further south, leading to massive depopulation there, too. The Guaraní-speaking Chiriguano resisted and defended their independence by force of arms against the Spanish and later the Bolivians. Their final rebellion in 1892 was brutally suppressed. Six thousand Guaraní men were killed, and Guaraní women and children were distributed as slaves to military households in Sucre and Santa Cruz. It was not until the Chaco War (1932–1935) that the history of the lowlands became central to the history of Bolivia.

Bolivia and Paraguay had been expanding their areas of control in the arid and inhospitable Chaco region that separated them. When these frontiers of sparse settlement eventually met, they inspired nationalist rhetoric in both countries about their respective rights and territorial claims, with the result that they stumbled into a war that neither side particularly wanted over land that turned out to be not particularly valuable. The Bolivians fielded a much larger army, but it consisted mainly of highland Indian conscripts, rounded up and sent to fight in the blazing desert of the Chaco, for a cause that they neither understood nor cared about.

Lowland Indians were also conscripted, and some of them actually fought at the front, but the majority of them were assigned to road construction and agricultural work to supply the front lines. In fact the lowlanders were not considered real Bolivians. They were not thought of as defending their country but rather as a useful labor force that could be pressed into service by the army. While they were doing this, and even if they were captured and held prisoner by the Paraguayans, their cattle were stolen or slaughtered and even their lands seized by their own countrymen. The Guaraní-speaking Chiriguano were those worst affected because Guaraní is spoken by the majority of Paraguayans. The Bolivians, their own countrymen, considered them potential traitors, and the Paraguayans considered them potential spies.

The lowlanders in general suffered the worst, not only because of their marginal status in Bolivian society but also because the war was fought in lands that were theirs or close to theirs. Highlanders, too, were badly affected. They returned from the fighting to find that they were being forced off their lands. Even those who volunteered for the army, believing that this would ensure that their land rights were respected, found out too late that they were wrong. The Bolivians suffered a series of defeats and were driven back until the Paraguayans controlled most of the disputed territory. The negotiation that brought an end to the war required the Paraguayans to withdraw from some of the territory they had taken, but they kept control of most of it.

The defeat produced much soul searching in Bolivia. The ineptitude of the high command and the Bolivian officer corps had been cruelly exposed. The army was mutinous. The backwardness and disunity of the country was glaringly apparent. The country's élites began to search desperately for remedies that would encourage modernization. The military high command had to face the fact that Indians from the highlands made poor soldiers. Meanwhile those same Indians were less and less inclined to put up with the traditional discrimination and harsh working conditions to which they were subjected both in agriculture and in the tin mines, which were the mainstay of the Bolivian economy. The tin mines themselves were soon facing hard times. After the end of World War II, the guaranteed demand for Bolivian tin disappeared, and the country was forced to diversify its economy and to seek other sources of income. Social unrest and economic necessity led to a reordering of Bolivian society, ushered in by the revolution of 1952.

The revolution, which brought Victor Paz Estenssoro to power at the head of the MNR (The National Revolutionary Movement), sought at last to dignify the indigenous peoples of the nation by abolishing the term *Indio* altogether, and insisting that they be referred to henceforward as *campesinos*. It also introduced sweeping reforms intended to integrate the indigenous masses with the rest of the country. These included the breakup of large landholdings, the commercialization of agriculture, and the integration of the *oriente* into the nation. All of these measures had a profound effect on the lowland Indians.

The land reform was largely designed for the highlands and never widely applied in the lowlands. There, on the contrary, indigenous communities were rarely recognized as landholding corporations, and employers were reluctant to make formal agreements with individual Indians for fear that the latter might thereby acquire some rights under the agrarian reform laws. Because the lowlands were intended to be an area of development, based on commercial agriculture, they became the scene of land speculation and landgrabbing, with all the graft and violence that usually accompany them, while the production of cattle, cotton, sugar, oil, and gas all boomed. When coca for cocaine also became an important crop in the 1970s, the role of the lowlands as the economic engine of Bolivia was firmly established. As a result the lands of the lowland Indians have been under constant pressure from colonists and agribusinesses since the 1950s.

It would probably be more accurate to say that not only the lands but also the persons of the lowland peoples have been under threat for as long as anybody can remember. These are peoples who have suffered from slavers, rubber barons, military expeditions, and the attacks of any group seeking forced laborers in the wilderness. Some of them have been entirely obliterated, like the Guarasug'we, from whom the following account of their impending extinction was elicited by Jürgen Riester.[21]

OUR END HAS COME

It shall soon be the end of us, and therefore I want to tell you the last part. This part is sad and not as entertaining as the stories you already know. It goes like this:

Before there were many kinfolks that also called themselves Guarasug'we like we do.

Some lived near the River Paraguá, others lived on the other side of the River Iténez.

Long before that we all lived together on the banks of the River Pauserna.

[21] Taken from Jürgen Riester *Los Guarasug'we – Crónica de sus Ultimos Dias* Los Amigos del Libro. (Publicación del Museo Nacional de Etnografía y Folklore, La Paz, 1977). Reprinted in the *IWGIA Newsletter* 20–27 (1978), 44–49, Copenhagen.

There, there were big villages and we lived happily. There, there were no white men like today.

The whites call us "pauserna." We don't like that name because we are not savages. We got the name Guarasug'we from our ancestors. The name "pauserna" was given to us by the whites. My father and the elders say that they call us "pauserna" for the following reason: In the villages of the past, we used to plant big trunks of hard wood. These trunks were there in the memory of the ancestors. The trunks stood either in the village itself or outside. With the trunks, it was as if a person who had died or been absent for a long time were present.

Later on, the Brazilians came to the villages of the River Pauserna. They brought with them the terrible flu and the fever, diseases we had not known before. People left the villages of the River Pauserna. They say there were ten big villages, each of them with its own captain (capitán) and two assistants.

We left the villages of the River Pauserna. Some went to the River Iténez, others to the River Paraguá, others still went as far as beyond Suviuhu, the big pampa, to a lagoon that is to be found there. It was a great mass of people that left the River Pauserna. Many wept, many died, and many others did not know what would happen now. There, by the River Pauserna, we had lived in happiness. Yes, before we were happy, but today our end has come. But our story has not ended yet.

My friends and I we went to the River Paraguá. There I was born. It was while I still was a small child that the men looking for rubber came. These men made us suffer a great deal. The elders say that we were a big tribe when we left the River Pauserna and moved to the River Iténez. We came to the place where the Bella Vista River runs out into the lagoon. There, many of us died of the fever. They simply fell dead: while fetching water, talking with friends. . . . They tell that my mother's sister got up one morning, went out for water and never came back. The Guarasug'we went out to look for her and found the poor woman near the waterhole. Blood came out of her mouth. She had fever and you could hardly hear what she was saying: "The fever comes from the whites. We shall all die if we don't get away soon." Thus many of us died. Yes, before we had many kinfolks.

I am the son of Kunumis. My mother's name is Pesu. Savui is my brother and Hapik'wa, my sister. In those days my father was captain. Today the captain is Tarecuve, his son and our elder brother.

The captain of our kinfolks on the other side of the River Iténez was called Ovoptye. The whites called him by his other name, Fortunato.

While we were still living on the banks of the River Pauserna, there was no war between us, but afterwards when part of the tribe was living by the River Iténez and another by the River Paraguá, then the war between us started. The Guarasug'we from the River Iténez were very bad; we are nicer than they are. We suffered a great deal because of them. Those from the River Iténez were very aggressive, but we can also fight and we can also be brave. Those from the River Iténez fought with us on account of our women. They used to come over to steal our women but we would attack them and make them flee. My father told me that those of the River Iténez suffered a lot from the flu. He said that they suffered more they we did and when Fortunato died, there were only a few kinfolks left by the River Iténez. My wife Yeruv'sa is from the River Iténez. Tariku also. All the kinfolks from the River Iténez came over to us when Fortunato died. Now we all live together, as we did before by the River Pauserna. The only difference is that now there are less kinfolks, now we are only a few. My mother Pesu told me that the ancestors had not always lived on the River Pauserna but had come from the place where the great Barraca of San Ignacio is found. The ancestors travelled a lot, not as today when the Guarasug'we no longer want to walk. They have become lazy and tired. They walk a little and stop to rest, walk a little more and finally stay in one place. Before, the Guarasug'we were good and brave travellers: they did not stay in one place, but moved a great deal. Long before that, the Guarasug'we, guided by their *Karai* [shaman] came to the district of Barraca of San Ignacio. This happened a long time ago as it was told by my mother's ancestors and they should know. . . .

When my father Kunumis still was not very old, the white men came. They came to the village and all the Guarasug'we fled up into the hills. There they stayed for awhile without getting out. The whites went to the Big House and there they left axes, knives, and iron machetes, dresses made of cloth, combs and many other things. After that they left. Then the Guarasug'we came down from the hills and went to the Big House. What joy, my father told, when they saw all the things in the Big House! Now my kinfolks had iron tools, and now also they were lost.

Some days later, the whites came back. This time the Guarasug'we did not flee to the hills, except for a few women, children and some men. Most of the Guarasug'we stayed in the village. Once more the whites left beautiful things in the Big House and my people went inside. When almost all the Guarasug'we had gone into the house, the whites surrounded it and and shot at those who tried to escape. Many were deadly wounded. Afterwards the whites left with all those who had been in the Big House, men, women and children. The Guarasug'we who had not been in the Big House, stayed in the hills until the whites had gone.

The whites let my people walk all the way to Santa Cruz de la Sierra, which, they say, is further away than the Barraca of San Ignacio. In Santa Cruz the whites sold the Guarasug'we. They say that almost all of the young boys and girls died on the way to Santa Cruz. The whites raped the women and the young girls still virgins. The whites do not respect women, they were very cruel to us.

A few kinfolks have returned from Santa Cruz and told what happened. They told us about the city and the road to it. Those who managed to come back say that there are many things in that big city. They came back by way of the Guarayo territory. The Guarayo speak almost the same language as we. . . . In their country, there were also white men who sold our kinfolks, as you sell rubber. Those who were able to escape from the Guarayo territory say that the whites took our kinfolks to the Beni River.

For all of these reasons, the Guarasug'we of today do not like the whites because they are bad and treacherous. Look for instance at Sr . . . who lives with his own daughter and each year kills the child he begets with his daughter.

Yaneramai [The almightiest god of the Guarasug'we] does not want us to live with the whites. . . . When the end of the world comes, we do not want our souls to die. Yes, the end of the world will soon come, more or less in 2 × 13 years [to be understood as in the very near future]. Then it is really going to be terrible for the people of the Earth. In a short time the Earth will be completely destroyed. That will be our end too. You can see yourself how small our tribe is now, and that our end is near. It will only last another 2 × 13 years. But before that, we have to leave and go to live far away from the whites.

The Guarasug'we lived in the Bolivian forests near the Brazilian border in the 1960s. In the late 1960s they were raided by the Bolivian army, which was trying to recruit soldiers from their reduced population of some fifty people. Their chief was killed by neighboring Bolivians, and the remnants of the tribe, some twenty-five people in all, fled into Brazil and have never been heard of since.

The pressures that destroyed the Guarasug'we were the traditional ones. The booming development of the *oriente* has now brought modern pressures as well. It was in all probability because of his perception that the lowlanders were under intolerable pressure that Ché Guevara selected the Bolivian lowlands as the site for his famous attempt to spread revolution of the Cuban kind to other parts of the Americas. It was in some ways a logical choice. Bolivia in 1967, when Ché arrived there to ignite a revolution, was a classic case of rising expectations that had not been fullfilled. The revolution of 1952 seemed, like the Mexican revolution to which it was so often compared, to have made a decisive break with the past. In fact the rigid hierarchical structures of the past were undermined and partially dismantled, and the underprivileged, whether Indian or *cholo*, peasant, miner, or rural laborer, began to feel that they had rights and that they had above all the right to organize to defend their own interests. But the backlash in the decades following the revolution, as successive administrations tried to roll back the gains of 1952, created a general atmosphere of confusion and frustration. This was the situation that Ché Guevara hoped to exploit. He would start in the lowlands, which were not only neglected but were suffering all the injustices of a booming frontier. He made his base in the lands of the Chiriguano, which was a mistake. There is no reason to believe that they would have sympathized with his revolutionary aims and even less that Ché, as an orthodox Marxist, would have cared much about their centuries-old struggle for cultural survival. They were in any case too remote from the heartland of Bolivia to serve as a good jumping-off point for a revolution. Ché's betrayal and his killing by the Bolivian army are now a mere footnote in Bolivian history, though they have become legendary in Latin America.

The development of the *oriente* affected Bolivia in two major ways. The growing economic power of the lowland élites ensured that the nation would no longer be so exclusively focused on the Andes and La Paz. It also brought drug money and drug politics to Bolivia. These processes soon led the indigenous peoples of the lowlands to emulate the lowlanders in other Andean countries and form their own organizations. A number of them were launched in the 1980s, including CPIB, representing the people of the Beni, and APG, the Assembly of the Guarani People. These groups soon came together in CIDOB, the Indigenous Confederation of the Bolivian Oriente.

CIDOB came to prominence at a propitious time. Not only was the indigenous movement gaining international recognition, but ethnic issues were finally coming to the fore in Bolivia itself. After the revolution of 1952, the highland Indians received land guarantees and considerable local autonomy in what came to be known as "peasant superstates." For this they gratefully supported the MNR and the military, even as these moved rightward in their national policies. It was not until the regimes of Generals Banzer (1971–1978) and Garcia Mesa (1980–1981), the latter virtually a representative of the drug interests in the country, that the military–peasant alliance broke down as a result of the repression and killing of peasants. It was at this time that the Katarista movement among the Aymara began to gain strength and to assert its independence of the government. As the Katarista and the MNR moved toward their unexpected and historic alliance, which brought the current Bolivian government democratically to power, ethnic discourse became an acceptable way of describing the situation of Bolivia and prescribing for it.

Accordingly, when the peoples of the *oriente* organized a March for Territory and Dignity in 1991, it was not opposed by the authorities. Instead hundreds of representatives from twelve ethnic groups marched 700 kilometers up from the lowlands into La Paz, where they were met by thousands of Aymara in traditional dress, who gave them a festive and ceremonial welcome. The whole event served to bring the lowland Indians to national attention. The following year mass mobilizations were held in most cities of Bolivia to mark the "500 years of resistance" since 1492. The indigenous peoples, now wishing to be called the *pueblos originários* or *naciones originárias*, thus made their claim to be recognized as an integral but distinctive part of Bolivian society.

This alliance between highland and lowland Indians is of itself remarkable, given their separate histories and different, even competing, interests. Highland Indians are, for example, among the colonists flocking into the lowlands, particularly to grow coca, and thus putting pressure on land in the *oriente*. Remarkable, too, is the Bolivian government's new commitment to ethnic pluralism. The nation's vice-president and leading Katarista, Victor Hugo Cárdenas, has repeatedly described Bolivia as a multiethnic and plurinational country, but his Katarista Party is very much the weaker partner in the ruling coalition, and the more powerful MNR has a long history of insisting that Indians be merged into the mainstream. It is true that the government's *Plan de Todos* ('Plan for Everyone'), released in 1993, formally recognizes cultural pluralism and even the need for bilingual education in some areas of Bolivia, but it avoids speaking of the *naciones originárias*, which would be too much of a reversal for staunch MNRistas. It is not clear how or if this plan will be put into effect, or whether Bolivia's newfound pluralism will pass from rhetoric to reality.

CONCLUSION

The history, or rather the histories of the lowland peoples of South America, depend on the national agendas of the various states in which they find themselves. The most important variable in these agendas is whether the lowland Indians are the only Indians in the nation or whether they are the remote tribal peoples, seen as contrasting with the large mass of highland Indians.

This contrast is seen very clearly if we compare Peruvian *indigenismo* with Brazilian *indigenismo*. Peruvian *indigenismo* was part of the national soul searching that took place after the War of the Pacific. As influential Peruvians thought about ways to modernize their nation, they also began to reflect on the marginalization of the Indian majority of the Peruvian population and to consider ways to bringing these people into the national fold. When José Carlos Mariátegui and Haya de la Torre made these sentiments the basis for possible political action, Peruvian governments were panicked by the thought of socialist or communist revolution. Indeed the notion of granting Indians the rights of other citizens of Peru would have entailed, in the early years of this century, a social revolution, socialist or otherwise, and it could be argued that it would do so even today. The *indigenismo* of Cândido Rondon in Brazil was by contrast a frontier affair. Brazilians would woo savage Indians with kindness and in that way help them to blend into the Brazilian melting pot, but this would hardly affect the nation as a whole.

In the lowland countries – Venezuela, Brazil, and Paraguay – Indian issues have been marginal to national life because the Indians were marginal to the nation, both physically and socially. They could be left in charge of missionaries or other patrons, which were usually the military or other agencies of the state. This is clearly seen in Paraguay, where the government's agency for Indian affairs is a branch of the military, which does not attempt to act on behalf of all the nation's Indians but only as a patron to some of them, leaving the others to seek help largely from the missions. Even in Brazil, where the government, inspired by Rondon, once had a broader vision of its indigenist role, the SPI came to act largely as a patron of Indian communities and was seen as the competition by missions working with the same groups.

There are obvious advantages to governments of entrusting distant indigenous affairs to the missions, because the missions do the work of the state at their own expense. They represent a kind of holding action, maintaining a presence and "civilizing the Indians" until such time as the state may be ready to develop remote areas of the country. This accounts for the perennial ambivalence that Latin American countries have shown toward the Summer Institute of Linguistics/New Tribes Mission. This is a well-funded mission that can provide infrastructure in remote areas and has always been willing to put its travel and other facilities at the service of government representatives. It is a mission that takes care to keep on good terms with governments and teaches that all governments are divinely authorized. It is in fact a mission that legitimates the status quo, just as the Catholic Church traditionally used to in Latin America, but underwrites it with American money and technology. It is understandable, then, that governments besieged with demands for reform from their citizenry and from Catholic clergy speaking out on behalf of the poor, governments that may actually be facing armed insurrections, would look with favor on the SIL. On the other hand, the North American missionaries of the SIL inspire nationalist antagonism in country after country, precisely because of the quasi-official role often granted by governments to distant missions. In Colombia and Venezuela the missions that were entrusted with the tutelage of distant Indians were also given formal civil authority by the state in the regions under their jurisdiction, just as Barbrooke Grubb and the Anglicans were for a time the formal representatives of the Paraguayan state vis-à-vis the Indians of the Paraguayan Chaco.

These missionary holding actions came to an end in the 1960s. Missions continued to work in the field, but they became minor players in the new dramas of colonization, development, and counterrevolution. The success of the Cuban revolution posed a stark question for Latin American governments at that time. Were their own countries ripe for revolution? If so, how could it be avoided or defeated? The Alliance for Progress was a hemispheric effort to promote the reforms that might head off revolutions. Land reform was much discussed as a means of alleviating rural poverty and defusing social unrest.

The Brazilian military chose an alternative strategy. They avoided land reform, which would have entailed a head-on collision with the oligarchies of the northeast, who were ardent supporters of their regime. Instead they launched a massive effort to develop the interior of the country, hoping in this way to resettle the rural poor, to defuse the pressure for revolutionary solutions, and to establish the authority of the state in remote regions that might otherwise harbor revolutionaries. Their strategy did not resolve the social problems of the country, but it was, in the short run, immensely successful economically. Brazil posted very high growth rates in the decade that began in the late 1960s, which did not go unnoticed in the Andean countries. The Brazilian model was very much in President Belaúnde's mind as he persevered with his grandiose plans for the development of Peru's eastern regions. Ecuador, too, pushed for the development of its *oriente*, and so did Bolivia. In each case there was a definite hope that the newly created wealth of the lowland regions would help to solve the social problems of the country as a whole. Venezuela's Conquest of the South was different. It came later, when the country had snuffed out its insurgencies and was enjoying the benefits of its oil boom. Only Colombia and Paraguay, of the nations discussed in this chapter, have not launched national efforts to develop their remote lowlands. Colombia remained in the throes of the *Violencia* until the mid-sixties and has been struggling with drugs and insurgents ever since, but its lowlands have nevertheless been affected by considerable migrations of people fleeing from the violence elsewhere. Paraguay is also a special case. The whole country might be considered as a kind of economic frontier, depending on large enterprises to develop the Chaco, on

Brazilian agribusinesses to do the same in the east, and on massive projects like the dams built in collaboration with Argentina and Brazil. Paraguay registered even higher growth rates than Brazil in the 1970s, but the boom ended with the completion of the Itaipú dam, and the country plunged into recession in the 1980s.

All of these developmental efforts have had adverse effects on the lowland peoples, especially where they were further complicated by the drug trade or the emergence of armed revolutionary movements. It is largely in response to these pressures that lowland Indians have been so assiduously forming their own organizations for self-defense. Yet the battle for indigenous rights has so far had least success in the nations where lowland Indians are the only Indians. Brazil has systematically insisted that Indians *as Indians* have no place in the nation. They should be civilized or "emancipated" or in some other way obliged to disappear as communities. Meanwhile the country has moved to restrict the lands and the rights of those Indian groups that still exist and who therefore "stand in the way of development." It is true that the Indians have fought back and received considerable support both nationally and internationally as they demanded recognition and protection of their rights. In this way the Indian question did, at the time of the constitutional convention, become part of the nation's thinking about itself at a crucial moment of introspection. The result, however, was a rejection of the idea that Brazil should be a multiethnic nation, or that indigenous groups, maintaining their own distinctive cultures, should have a rightful place in it.

Venezuela, like Brazil, continues to insist that the rights of Indians are only temporary, until they disappear into the national mainstream, and that in the meantime these rights must be subordinated to considerations of development and national security. This amounts to a rejection of the ideas put forward by those Venezuelans who formed the Committee for National Identity, because they were seeking a way to include indigenous people as Indians in that identity.

It is the Andean countries that are currently more amenable to the idea of accepting indigenous ethnic identity (identities) as a legitimate part of the national identity. It is true that Peru has officially fought this idea ever since it was put forward by Mariátegui and Haya de la Torre, and that it put the self-definition of the nation on hold while the government dealt with insurgencies and their attendant economic and political crises; but it is also true that the latest Peruvian constitution stipulates that the state recognizes and protects the ethnic and cultural plurality of the nation, and that it recognizes Quechua, Aymara, "and other native languages" as official languages, in addition to Spanish. Likewise it is true that the new vision of the nation's future, and the Indians' role in it that was launched after the indigenous uprising in Ecuador is currently being sharply contested by the present government. In Ecuador, however, a debate has been going on about the nature of the national culture at least since President Lara floated the idea that it was essentially a culture of development and that the Ecuadorian military should inculcate it in the populace. The indigenous federations have altered the terms of this debate, which still continues. Meanwhile both Colombia and Bolivia have accepted the legitimacy of indigenous groups' existence within the state and have formally announced that they are multiethnic nations.

It may seem paradoxical that it is the Andean countries which are considering ethnic pluralism, because it is precisely these countries, with their large indigenous populations, that have traditionally opposed any special recognition of indigenous ethnicity, and that have branded as subversive all those who proposed it. Yet it is also these countries that are currently undergoing crises of national confidence and national identity. They seem willing to do an historic "about-face" and to consider reorganizing themselves as multiethnic nations, although these momentous changes are by no means firmly established and are still being strongly contested. These developments are paradoxical in another sense – namely, that the demand for ethnic autonomy has everywhere been most clearly articulated by the lowland peoples. Yet it is being more sympathetically received in those countries whose indigenous populations are largely highlanders, while it has been categorically rejected in countries like Venezuela and Brazil, whose populations are composed entirely of lowland Indians.

This underlines once more the importance of considering national contexts and national agendas when studying the history of indigenous peoples. The lowland peoples of the Andean countries have succeeded in gaining recognition of their desire for rights to land and local autonomy in order to enable them to maintain their own cultures. This is partly due to the federations they formed, which have been able to represent them politically at the regional, national, and even international levels, and partly due to the fact that their demands resonated with ideas already being discussed about rethinking and reorganizing the Andean nations.

By contrast, in countries like Brazil and Venezuela, containing only lowland Indians, who make up a small percentage of the national population, the formation of indigenous federations has been much more difficult, and national policy continues to insist that indigenous peoples should disappear into the melting pot.

Clearly the indigenous federations are the heroes of the story that I have tried to tell in this chapter. The first (Shuar) federation in Ecuador was launched with the help of a Salesian mission. Catholic agencies such as missions or CIMI in Brazil were those most active in helping indigenous peoples form their own organizations in the 1960s. These were soon joined by national and international nongovernmental organizations who provided financial and technical assistance to indigenous peoples trying to organize to defend their own rights.

In the Andean countries these indigenous federations soon began to play a role in politics and to be heard at the national level. This was much harder for indigenous organizations in the lowland countries. In Brazil the immense distances that separated indigenous groups, and the expense involved for their leaders to meet with each other, made the logistics of indigenous organization especially difficult, and the hostility of the government and of FUNAI exacerbated the problems they had to face. Note that it was in Brazil and Venezuela that sectors of the government branded indigenous demands and pro-indigenous activism as subversive. In Paraguay, under General Stroessner, all forms of organization not sponsored by the state were considered subversive. Nevertheless a vocal indigenous movement, supported by indigenous organizations and national and international sympathizers, did emerge in Brazil. This was partly due to international concern over the destruction of the Amazon rain forests, which highlighted the problems of the inhabitants of those rain forests and the ruthless treatment they were receiving in the name of "development."

Moreover a coordinating federation (COICA) has also been formed, representing all the indigenous peoples of the Amazon Basin, and COICA has put the case for the lowland peoples internationally at places like the United Nations. These federations sometimes ally themselves with peasant organizations, or with organizations of highland Indians who pursue an essentially peasant agenda, but the lowlanders differ from both of these in that they have always stressed the ethnic and cultural dimensions of their struggle.

The fortunes of these federations depend on a number of factors.

They require charismatic leaders to get going, and they have found them in abundance. They need outside assistance to get established and to weather the first political and financial crises that affect them, and they have also been fortunate in receiving that. They need to be able to moderate their own internal differences, both personal and political, so that these do not disrupt their organizations. This has proved much more difficult. Above all they need to find or create some receptivity to their demands at the national level. International attention and assistance can be very helpful here, but such helpers are also fickle, and their assistance can also provoke a political backlash in the national context. They do have one thing going for them, however. They speak out unambiguously for the rights of indigenous groups to be recognized as corporate entities and to maintain their own cultures, in effect for the recognition of ethnic pluralism. This is an issue that will not go away, because it is now very much on the world's agenda.

BIBLIOGRAPHIC ESSAY

There are no general works on the lowland peoples of South America for reasons that are made clear in this chapter. The lowlanders have always been marginal, first to the imperial regimes established by European conquerors, and later to the independent states of the continent. Their situation has therefore to be studied piecemeal in terms of varying colonial and national agendas and of differing historical and economic circumstances.

The best source of general information to help us contextualize the circumstances of the lowlanders is to be found in the various national entries in *The Cambridge History of Latin America*, edited by Leslie Bethell. The present circumstances of the lowland peoples themselves are discussed in *Frontier Expansion in Amazonia* (eds. Marianne Schmink and Charles Wood, University of Florida Press, 1984), in *Nation-States and Indians in Latin America* (eds. Greg Urban and Joel Scherzer, University of Texas Press 1991), and in *Indigenous Peoples and Democracy in Latin America* (ed. Donna Lee Van Cott, New York, St. Martin's Press, 1994).

The revolt of the lowland peoples that gave their Spanish overlords such a fright in the mid–eighteenth century is discussed in André Marcel d'Ans *L'Amazonie Péruvienne Indigène* (Paris: Payot, 1982); Jay Lehnertz

"Juan Santos: Primitive rebel on the Campa frontier (1742–1752)" *XXXIV Congreso Internacional de Americanistas*, vol. IV (Lima, 1972), 111–125, and in Steven Stern (ed.), *Resistance, Rebellion and Consciousness in the Andean Peasant World: Eighteenth to Twentieth Centuries* (The University of Wisconsin Press, 1987).

The Rubber Boom that devastated many of the lowland peoples at the turn of the century was originally denounced by Roger Casement in "Correspondence respecting the treatment of British colonial subjects and native Indians employed in the collection of rubber in the Putumayo district," presented to both Houses of the Parliament by command of His Majesty, London, and by Walter Hardenburg in *The Putumayo, the Devil's Paradise: Travels in the Peruvian Amazon Region and an Account of the Atrocities Committed Upon the Indians Therein* (London: T. F. Unwin, 1912). It is more accessibly described in John Hemming's *Amazon Frontier: The Defeat of the Brazilian Indians* (Harvard University Press, 1987) and is powerfully analyzed by Michael Taussig in *Shamanism, Colonialism and the Wild Man* (University of Chicago Press, 1987).

There is comparatively little written on the contemporary problems of Venezuela's Indians (as opposed to ethnographies dedicated to describing their lives). Two standard sources are Cesáreo de Armellada *Fuero Indígena Venezolano* (Caracas, Instituto de Investigaciones Históricas, Universidad Católica Andres Bello, 1977), and Esteban Mosonyi, *Identidad Nacional y Culturas Populares* (Caracas: La Enseñanza Viva, 1982). Much of the literature focuses on the New Tribes Mission (or Wycliffe Bible Translators) and the polemics concerning whether they should or should not be allowed to work among Venezuelan Indians. Mosonyi edited an important volume on this issue entitled *El Caso Nuevas Tribus* (Caracas: Ateneo de Caracas, 1981). The standard general reference work on the activities of this mission is David Stoll, *Fishers of Men or Founders of Empire? The Wycliffe Bible Translators in Latin America* (London: Zed Press/Cultural Survival, 1982). Another hotly debated issue in Venezuela concerns the possible colonialist designs of foreign enterprises on the Amazonian regions of the south. This is discussed at length by Alexander Luzardo in *Amazonas, el Negocio de este Mundo: Investigación Indigenista* (Caracas: Ediciones Centauro, 1988). More recent analyses of the indigenous situation can be found in Simeón Jiménez and Abel Perozo (eds.), *Esperando a Kuyujani* (San Pedro de los Altos: Asociación Otro Futuro Gaia/IVIC, 1994), and especially in an unpublished report by Nelly

Arvelo-Jiménez entitled *Se Acta pero no se Cumple: La Legislación y su Incumplimiento en la Tenecia de la Tierra Indigena* (report presented to the International Fund for Agricultural Development, 1995).

There is, by contrast, a surprisingly extensive literature on the recent history of the indigenous peoples of Brazil, considering that they make up such a small proportion of the population of that country. Most of it is highly specific and in Portuguese. The best sources in English for a general overview are Susanna Hecht and Alexander Coburn, *The Fate of the Forest: Developers, Destroyers and Defenders of the Amazon* (London: Penguin, 1990), and John Hemming, op. cit. Gilberto Freyre's famous book *The Masters and the Slaves* shows how even an anthropologist apparently sympathetic to the Indian cause could assume in the 1930s that Brazil's indigenous peoples must inevitably die out. Arguments to the contrary and analyses of the contemporary struggles of Brazilian Indians can be found in the columns of the *Cultural Survival Quarterly* over the last two decades. See also David Maybury-Lewis's "Becoming Indian in lowland South America," in Urban and Scherzer, op. cit., and "From savages to security risks: The Indian question in Brazil," in Oliver Mendelsohn and Upendra Baxi (eds.), *The Rights of Subordinated Peoples* (Oxford University Press, 1994). Probably no single issue has epitomized the plight of the forest-dwelling Indians of Brazil more than the sufferings of the Yanomami near the Brazilian-Venezuelan border. The CCPY (Comissão para a Creação do Parque Yanomami) publishes *Urihi*, a journal that provides regular bulletins in English about the Yanomami. Meanwhile the recent appearance in an English translation of Alcida Ramos's book, *Sanumá Memories: Yanomami Ethnography in Times of Crisis* (University of Wisconsin Press, 1995), has made an up-to-date analysis of the plight of the Yanomami available to those who do not read Portuguese.

The best general sources in Portuguese for current information about the situation of Brazilian Indians are the publications of CEDI (the Centro Ecumênico de Documentação e Informação) in São Paulo. Excellent analyses of indigenous issues are also to be found in the publications of the Comissão Pró-Indio of São Paulo and of the Comissão Pró-Indio of Rio de Janeiro. Luiz Beltrão gives a general account of Brazil's indigenist policies in *O Indio, Um Mito Brasileiro* (Petrópolis: Editora Vozes, 1977), and Danton Jobim discusses the issue of genocide in response to the first time that accusation was leveled against Brazil in the late 1960s (see *O Problema do Indio e a Acusação de Genocídio*,

Bulletin 2 of the Conselho de Defesa dos Direitos da Pessoa Humana, Rio de Janeiro, Ministry of Justice, 1970).

Roberto Cardoso de Oliveira is the dean of contemporary writers on indigenous questions and his *A Sociologia do Brasil Indígena* (Rio de Janeiro: Tempo Brasileiro, 1978), and especially his more recent *A Crise do Indigenismo* (Campinas: Editora Unicamp, 1988), provide valuable insights into the unfolding of Brazil's policies toward its Indians. Excellent analyses of the situation of indigenous lands and the militarization of Brazil's indigenous policies are found in João Pacheco de Oliveira (ed.), *Os Poderes e as Terras dos Indios* (Rio de Janeiro: Programa de Pós-Graduação em Antropologia Social, 1989), and João Pacheco de Oliveira (ed.), *Projeto Calha Norte: Militares, Indios e Fronteiras* (Rio de Janeiro: Editora UFRJ, 1990). Finally, a volume edited by Aracy Lopes da Silva, *A Questõ Indígena na Sala de Aula* (São Paulo: Editora Brasiliense, 1987), shows how indigenous peoples are presented in Brazilian schoolbooks.

The sources on indigenous peoples and policies in Paraguay are much more scarce, which makes it even more important to consult the general studies on Paraguayan history and the formation of Paraguayan society. There is a large literature on the Jesuit missions in what later became Paraguay, but this is not discussed here because it antedates the period of this chapter by some centuries. A useful summary of those events can be found in Elman Service, *Spanish–Guarani Relations in Early Colonial Paraguay* (Michigan Anthropological Papers #9, University of Michigan Press, 1954). Good general treatments of the development of Paraguayan society can be found in Richard White, *Paraguay's Autonomous Revolution 1810–1840* (University of New Mexico Press, 1978), and Domingo Laino, *Paraguay: De la Independencia a la Dependencia* (Asunción: Editorial Cerro Cora, 1976). For more recent treatments of the situation of the indigenous peoples of Paraguay, see Bartolomé Meliá, Georg Grünberg, and Friedl Grünberg, *Los Pãi Tavyterã: Etnografía Guaraní del Paraguay Contemporáneo* (Asunción: Centro de Estudios Antropologicos, 1976); Miguel Chase-Sardi, *La Situación Actual de los Indigenas del Paraguay* (Asunción: Centro de Estudios Antropológicos de la Universidad Católica, 1972); David Maybury-Lewis and James Howe, *The Indian Peoples of Paraguay: Their Plight and their Prospects* (Cambridge, Mass.: Cultural Survival, 1980); Richard Reed, *Prophets of Agroforestry: Guarani Communities and Commercial Gathering* (University of Texas Press, 1995); and Esther Prieto, "Indigenous peoples in Paraguay," in Donna Van Cott (1994) op. cit.

There are certain major issues in the history of twentieth-century Colombia that need to be understood by anyone who is interested in the lowland indigenous peoples of that country. They are (in chronological order) the indigenous uprising led by the charismatic Quintín Lame, the *Violencia*, the guerilla wars carried out by opponents of the state, and the emergence of Colombia as a major drug exporter. Useful works on Quintín Lame are Diego Castrillón Arboleda, *El Indio Quintín Lame* (Bogotá: Tercer Mundo, 1973), and Gonzalo Castillo-Cárdenas, *Liberation Theology from Below* (Maryknoll, NY: Orbis Books, 1987). There is a vast literature on the *Violencia* and on Colombia's guerilla movements, but two authoritative works that give an overview of the issues are Orlando Fals-Borda, *Subversion and Social Change in Colombia* (Columbia University Press, 1969), and Charles Bergquist, Ricardo Peñaranda, and Gonzalo Sánchez (eds.), *Violence in Colombia: The Contemporary Crisis in Historical Perspective* (Wilmington, Del.: Scholarly Resources, 1992). For the narcotics trade, see Deborah Pacini and Christine Franquemont (eds.), *Coca and Cocaine: Effects on People and Policy in Latin America* (Cambridge, Mass.: Cultural Survival, 1986), and Jaime Jaramillo, Leónidas Mora, and Fernando Cubides (eds.), *Colonización, Coca y Guerilla* (Bogotá: Universidad Nacional de Colombia, 1986).

A centrally important work in Colombian *indigenismo* is Juan Friede's *El Indio en Lucha por la Tierra: Historia de los Resguardos del Macizo Central Colombiano* (Bogotá: Instituto Indigenista de Colombia, 1944). Friede also co-edited another important work with Nina de Friedemann and Dario Fajardo under the title *Indigenismo y Aniquilamiento de Indígenas en Colombia* (Bogotá: Universidad Nacional de Colombia, 1975). Camilo Dominguez discusses the prospects for Colombia's Amazon regions and their inhabitants in *Amazonía Colombiana* (Bogotá: Biblioteca Banco Popular, 1985). More recently Colombia's indigenous and pro-indigenous organizations, such as CRIC, ONIC, FUNCOL, and CINEP, have been publishing up-to-date analyses of indigenous issues in journals such as *Unidad Indígena, Colombia Amerindia*, and *Controversia*. A major contributor to these analyses is Adolfo Triana Antorveza, the director of FUNCOL (the Fundación para las Comunidades Colombianas). Together with Myriam Jimeno he co-edited an important volume entitled *Estado y Minorías Etnicas en Colombia* (Bogotá: FUNCOL y Cuadernos del Jaguar, 1985). He is also author of *La Autodeterminación de los Países y la Autonomía de los Grupos Etnicos* (Bogotá: Cuadernos del Jaguar, 1984), and FUNCOL has put out another important collection entitled *Grupos Etnicos, Derecho y Cultura* (Bogotá: Cuadernos del Jaguar, 1987). Meanwhile the most up-to-date published work on indigenous issues in Colombia is Christian Gros's study entitled *Colombia Indígena: Identidad Cultural y Cambio Social* (Bogotá: CEREC, 1991). In this chapter I have also relied on two unpublished works, analyzing the prospective impact of Colombia's new constitution on the indigenous peoples of the lowlands – namely, Jean Jackson's paper, "The impact of recent legislation in the Vaupés region of Colombia" and Maria Clemencia Ramírez de Jara's article "La cuestión indígena en Colombia (Siglos XVI hasta el presente)."

An essential reference work for the history of Ecuadorian Indians is Oswaldo Albornoz, *Las Luchas Indígenas en el Ecuador* (Guayaquil: Claridad, 1974). A useful general discussion, albeit one that is firmly focused on the highlands, is Alicia lbarra's *Los Indígenas y el Estado en el Ecuador* (Quito: Abya-Yala, 1987). The point of departure for understanding the situation of the Indians of Ecuador's eastern lowlands is Norman Whitten Jr.'s study, *Sacha Runa: Ethnicity and Adaptation of Ecuadorian Jungle Quichua* (University of Illinois Press, 1976). Whitten also edited an important collection of papers that appeared as *Cultural Transformations and Ethnicity in Modern Ecuador* (Cambridge, Mass.: Cultural Survival, 1981) and later in a Spanish edition, *Amazonía Ecuatoriana: La Otra Cara del Progreso* (Quito: Mundo Shuar, 1981).

The most significant development in the Ecuadorian *oriente* in recent years has been the emergence of indigenous federations among the lowlanders. Jaime Galarza Zavalo in *Los Campesinos de Loja y Zamora* (Quito: Editorial Universitaria, 1973), and particularly Ernesto Salazar in *An Indian Federation in Lowland Ecuador* (Copenhagen: IWGIA, 1976), describe how the first federation among the Shuar was established. A later, comprehensive volume, published by the national indigenous organization CONAIE describes the process of indigenous organization nationwide: *Las Nacionalidades Indígenas del Ecuador: Nuestro Proceso Organizativo* (Quito: Ediciones Tinkui, 1988). It was the Salesian order that helped the original Shuar federation to get started, and the Salesians have made their Abya-Yala press the major source of serious publications on indigenous issues. A good recent summary of the situation in the *oriente* is William Vickers's paper on "Indian policy in Amazonian Ecuador" in Schmink and Wood, op. cit. (1984). Two more recent publications consider the implications of the national indigenous uprising of 1990. They are Melina Selverston's paper on "The politics of culture:

Indigenous peoples and the state in Ecuador" in Donna Lee Van Cott, op. cit. (1994), and particularly the important collection put out by CEDIME (the Centro de Investigación de los Movimientos Sociales) entitled *Sismo Etnico en el Ecuador* (Quito: Abya-Yala, 1993).

Peru has historically been one of the most conservative countries in South America, yet it has had a long tradition of *indigenismo*, dating back to Florinda Mattos de Turner's book, *Aves sin Nido* (1889), which did for Peruvian Indians what Harriet Beecher Stowe's *Uncle Tom's Cabin* did for American blacks. The idea that the indigenous peoples had an important part to play in Peru and indeed in the Americas was later taken up by José Carlos Mariátegui in *Seven Interpretive Essays on Peruvian Reality* (University of Texas Press, 1971, originally published in 1928) and especially in *Peruanicemos al Perú* (a series of articles published in *Mundial* in Lima between September 11, 1925, and May 19, 1929, which have been published in book form by Editora Amauta, Lima, 1970); see also Jesús Chavarria, *José Carlos Mariátegui and the Rise of Modern Peru* (University of New Mexico Press, 1979). Victor Raul Haya de la Torre, Peru's leading opposition politician in the first half of this century, also flirted with this idea (see *Construyendo el Aprismo,* Buenos Aires, Claridad, 1934). A valuable recent discussion of the history and development of Peruvian *indigenismo* is contained in Carlos Ivan Degregori et al., *Indigenismo, Clases Sociales y Problema Nacional* (Lima: CELATS, 1979). Peruvian plans (or dreams as some people might call them) for the eastern lowlands are outlined in the book written by President Belaúnde entitled *La Conquista del Perú por los Peruanos* (Lima: Editorial Minerva, 1994).

Under General Velasco's administration serious studies of the situation of the lowland Indians of Peru began to appear because of the work of SINAMOS. Stéfano Varese published his important book, *La Sal de los Cerros* (Lima: UPCT, 1968), and later *The Forest Indians in the Present Political Situation of Peru* (Copenhagen: IWGIA, 1972). His collaborator, Alberto Chirif, together with Carlos Mora, put out the valuable *Atlas de Comunidades Nativas* (Lima: SINAMOS, 1977). In 1982 Varese published "Restoring multiplicity: Indianities and the civilizing project in Latin America," *Latin American Perspectives* 33(9), 29–41, and Chirif followed up in 1985 with "The present policy of developing Peruvian Amazonia and its social and ecological impact" in John Hemming (ed.), *The Frontier after a Decade of Colonization* (Manchester University Press). Anthony Stocks published a useful summary of the situation in the *oriente* entitled "Indian policy in Eastern Peru" (in Schmink and Wood 1984, op. cit.), and Richard Chase Smith wrote an important analysis of the problems faced by the lowland federations and their leaders – see "A search for unity within diversity: Peasant unions, ethnic federations and Andean republics" in Theodore Macdonald Jr (ed.), *Native Peoples and Economic Development: Six Case Studies from Latin America* (Cambridge, MA, Cultural Survival Paper #16, 1985). He also published a critique of Peruvian development plans for the Amazon region entitled *The Dialectics of Domination in Peru: Native Communities and the Myth of the Vast Amazonian Emptyness* (Cambridge, Mass., Cultural Survival Paper #8, 1982). Another critique of Peru's hopes for developing the Amazon is found in Frederica Barclay Rey de Castro (ed.), *Amazonía 1940–1990: El Extravío de una Ilusión* (Lima: Terra Nuova/CISEPA/PICP, 1991).

For general background on the current crisis in Peru and its effects on indigenous peoples, two useful sources are Deborah Poole and Gerardo Renique, *Peru: Time of Fear* (London: Latin American Bureau, 1992), and David Scott Palmer (ed.), *Shining Path of Peru* (New York: St Martin's Press, 1992). More recent general works on the Peruvian lowlands are Alberto Chirif, *El Indígena y su Territorio* (Lima: OXFAM and COICA, 1991), and Marc Dourojeanni *Amazonía: ¿Que Hacer?* (Iquitos: CETA, 1990). Finally two recent ethnographies also contain much information on the current situation of the lowland Indians. They are Peter Gow, *Of Mixed Blood: Kinship and History in Peruvian Amazonia* (Oxford: The Clarendon Press, 1991), and Kenneth Kensinger, *How Real People Ought to Live: The Cashinaua of Eastern Peru* (Prospect Heights, Ill.: The Waveland Press, 1995). The best and most consistent publication to consult for information on the lowlands is *Amazonía Peruana*, published by the Centro Amazónico de Antropología e Aplicación Práctica.

Most of the literature from Bolivia deals with the indigenous peoples of the Andean higlands, so that those interested in the lowland peoples have had, until recently, to glean what information they could by reading more general studies. For instance, Ramiro Condarco Morales' book, *Zarate, el "Temible" Willka: Historia de la Rebelión Indígena de 1899 en la República de Bolivia* (La Paz: Renovación, 1982), provides an excellent survey of the situation of Bolivia's Indians in the late nineteenth century. Similarly Xavier Albó and Joseph Barnadas' book, *La Cara Campesina de Nuestra Historia* (La Paz: Unitas, 1985), is informative about the lowlands almost by exclusion. Xavier Albó is the dean of Bolivian *indigenismo*, and his writings, even when they focus largely on the highlands, are essential reading for those who would understand the context in which the lowlanders operate. See his *Para Comprender las Culturas Rurales en Bolivia* (La Paz: MEC/CIPCA/UNICEF, 1990), and his important recent paper "And from Kataristas to MNRistas? The surprising and bold alliance between Aymaras and neoliberals in Bolivia" (in Donna Van Cott, ed., 1994, op. cit.)

The lowland peoples are more directly dealt with in studies of the Chaco War against Paraguay. See, for example, René Arze Aguirre, *Guerra y Conflictos Sociales: El Caso Rural Boliviano durante la Campaña del Chaco* (La Paz: CERES, 1987), Claudia Ranaboldo, *El Camino Perdido: Biografía del Lider Campesino Kallawaya Antonio Alvárez Mamani* (La Paz: SEMTA, 1987), and two papers by Barbara Schuchard "La conquista de tierra: Relatos Guaraníes de Bolivia acerca de experiencias guerreras y pacíficas recientes," in *Suplemento Antropológico* (Asunción) vol. XXI (2), 1986, 67–98; and "The Chaco War: An account from a Bolivian Guarani" in *Latin American Indian Literatures*, vol. V (2), 1981, 47–58. Similarly the book by José Luis Alcazar and José Valdivia, *Ñancahuazú: La Guerilla del Ché en Bolivia* (Mexico City: Era, 1969), is informative about Ché Guevara's attempt to foment an indigenous uprising in the lowlands and why it failed.

It is with the work of Jürgen Riester that the Bolivian lowlands finally come into their own; see his *Indians of Eastern Bolivia: Aspects of their Present Situation* (Copenhagen: IWGIA, 1975), and also his study entitled *En Busca de la Loma Santa* (Lima: Los Amigos del Libro, 1976). James Jones has also published a number of useful papers on the Bolivian *oriente*. See his "Native peoples of Lowland Bolivia," in Schmink and Wood, 1984, op. cit., and his "Economics, political power and ethnic conflict on a changing frontier: Notes from the Beni department, Eastern Bolivia" (Binghamton, NY, Institute for Development Anthropology Working Paper #58, 1991). James Jones has also published one of the rare analyses in English of the March for Dignity, when lowland peoples marched on La Paz and met there ceremonially and symbolically with highland indigenous representatives. See his "The March for Dignity: Rationale and response for a native movement in Eastern Bolivia," in *Bulletin of the Institute for Development Anthropology*, vol. 8 (2), 1992.

Finally, in Bolivia as elsewhere in the lowlands of South America, indigenous organizations are forming and publishing. Two recent publications by them are of special interest: one from APCOB entitled *La Población Indígena de las Tierras Bajas de Bolivia* (Santa Cruz: APCOB, 1994), and another from CPIB/CIDDEBENI entitled *Hacia una Propuesta Indígena de Descentralización del Estado* (La Paz: PROADE/ILDIS, 1995).

INDEX